The Writings of

WILLIAM JAMES

The Writings

WILLIAM JAMES
A Comprehensive Edition

EDITED, WITH AN INTRODUCTION
AND NEW PREFACE, BY
John J. McDermott

INCLUDING AN *Annotated Bibliography*
UPDATED THROUGH 1977

THE UNIVERSITY OF CHICAGO PRESS
Chicago and London

Virginia

For whom words and ideas do neither
dictate nor dilute the joys and sorrows
of experience

The University of Chicago Press, Chicago 60637
The University of Chicago Press, Ltd., London

Selections from the works of William James are reprinted
with the kind permission of Alexander R. James.
ISBN: 0–226–39188–4
LCN: 77–89625

Contents

Contents

"Let me repeat once more that a man's vision is the great fact about him."

—*A Pluralistic Universe*

Preface to the Phoenix Edition

The personality and thought of William James have consistently received public attention since his death on August 26, 1910. As with most criticism of great thinkers, however, there has been an ebb and flow in the quality of the response to James's work. I began this comprehensive edition of *The Writings of William James* in 1965, and it was published in 1967. At that time, most of James's publications were either out of print or reissued without editorial apparatus sufficient to provide the reader with a historical or interpretive context. Further, these editions usually duplicated each other, so that several publications of *Pragmatism* and of *The Varieties of Religious Experience* were available but none of *Essays in Radical Empiricism* or of *A Pluralistic Universe*. In short, the popular and often misunderstood aspect of James's thought was brought to the fore, whereas the more technical philosophical underpinnings of his work were neglected.

The original publication of this comprehensive edition was intended to correct that imbalance and to encourage new readers of William James's writings to approach his thought in terms of a much wider range of his published work. Given that intention, the present edition is still the most viable and comprehensive collection of James's writings. The reader will find in this volume a meshing of James's popular and technical philosophy. This is made possible by the inclusion of representative selections from virtually all of James's major works, as well as the complete text of *Pragmatism,* and of the 1943 edition of *Essays in Radical Empiricism,* and *A Pluralistic Universe*. Within the limitations of space I have made additions to the Annotated Bibliography, updating it through 1977. The Bibliography, originally the work of Ralph Barton Perry, is now the standard reference for James's writings. In the intervening decade, some new entries have been uncovered by Ignas Skrupskelis of the University of South Carolina. Although they are not major items, most being only a page or so, they do help to clarify some of James's interests. It was not possible to insert them in the present edition and, as Professor Skrupskelis is still at work on the bibliography, arrangements will be made to publish them in the future under separate cover.

It is gratifying to note that the last ten years have witnessed a renascence of interest in the thought of William James and an accompanying increase in the availability of both primary and secondary sources. The most auspicious aspect of this development is the ongoing publication of the critical edition of *The Works of William James,* sponsored by the American Council of Learned Societies and supported by the National Endowment for the Humanities. Projected to be sixteen volumes, this edition will contain all of James's published work and his unpublished papers.

With regard to recent commentaries on the philosophy of James, three developments are notable. First, his radical empiricism has been taken more seriously, viewed now as an indispensable dimension of his thought. In their writings on William James, A. J. Ayer, Richard J. Bernstein, Edward Madden, John E. Smith, and H. S. Thayer, each in his own way, widen the focus to include the important relationship between radical empiricism and pragmatism in his work. A second development is the increased philosophical attention paid to James's *Principles of Psychology.* Of note here is the work of James Edie, Craig Eisendrath, Gerald Myers, and Bruce Wilshire. Finally, James's thought is now being more explicitly integrated into the history of classical American philosophy, and his significance for the work of John Dewey, C. S. Peirce, and Josiah Royce is under renewed scrutiny. I have appended to this Preface a list of some of the important contributions to the secondary literature, published since 1967, on the philosophy of James.

In response to the helpful suggestions of readers and reviewers with regard to the material selected for this book, I offer that had I slightly more space at my disposal, two further selections would have been included. The first is an essay of 1878, "Remarks on 'Spencer's Definition of Mind as Correspondence,'" in which James first sets out his position that mind is essentially interest oriented. In addition, I would have included some further material from *The Varieties of Religious Experience.* The essay of 1884, "On Some Omissions of Introspective Psychology," is crucial for a historical understanding of James's doctrine of relations, but it is largely restated in the essay included below, "The Stream of Thought." Actually, given the economic difficulties besetting publishing, I am grateful to Random House and now to the University of Chicago Press, for providing such an extensive collection of James's writings within the convenience of a single volume.

While preparing material for this new edition of the present volume, I have had occasion to reread the Introduction. I retain confidence in its fundamental accuracy. As to scope, were I writing it at this time, I would consider one further theme, namely, James's response to the ethical, political, and social causes of his time. Over against the often hagiographic interpretations of Ralph Barton Perry and Gay Wilson Allen, some scholars, such as Edward Madden, are beginning to criticize James's sensitivity to social problems. Although historical anachronism is always a danger in a revisionist approach, it does seem that James often was insufficiently aware of the importance of liberating social movements contemporary with his public life. In this vein, I do not believe that James took an aggressively reactionary position with regard to movements of social amelioration, such as civil liberties, women's rights, and radical economic reform. Rather, the very strength and imagination of James's position invoked a weaker side. Few thinkers have had James's confidence in the capacity of individuals to transform their world by tapping the energy of a voluntaristic ethic. This fundamental attitude of James is especially convincing given the power of his prose and, above all, our knowledge that at the deepest recesses of his own complex personal life, this confidence was transforming and liberating. Nonetheless, as the generations of thinkers subsequent to James knew all too well, the individual is a social category, contexted over and over again by the swirling factors of institutional and communal history.

In technical terms, James knew that the self was irreducibly social, yet he did not take that contention into sufficient account in his own social philosophy. He was fundamentally right in his epistemological critique of Hegel, Bradley, and Royce, but he missed the crucial significance of Hegel's thought, namely, the historical and social conditioning of all inquiry. Texts abound in James in which the very originality and strength of purpose cloak some dire implications if placed in other hands. I refer here to only one such instance. In *The Varieties of Religious Experience* (p. 368), James resuscitates "the ancient idealization of poverty." He asks of the English-speaking peoples that they again sing the "praise of poverty" and proceeds to write that: "There are thousands of conjectures in which a wealth-bound man must be a slave, whilst a man for whom poverty has no terrors becomes a freeman."

Now there is an aspect of this text and its surrounding discussion which is wise and incisive, for it is true indeed that we are often trapped by our accomplishments and by our possessions. James had an extraordinary ability to diagnose the obstacles to a creative personal life and an equal capacity so to stimulate us as to break the fetters of the obvious and the assumed. Long before the term was common, he had a deep insight to the perils of self-deception, especially our tendency to accept our situation as *necessarily* ours, thereby closing off the possibilities which emerge only as a result of personal risk and the quest for novelty.

What James does not see, however, is that certain social conditions are self-perpetuating and self-enforcing. Poverty, for example, is not merely the absence of "material attachments" or the absence of the burdens of acquisition. Rather, it is the presence of a social conditioning which often wrecks the capacity to exercise the very "energies" and "powers" which James so brilliantly extols. It is true that here our criticism of James is from hindsight. Whatever the disagreements between Marx and Dewey, they have both taught us that social institutions are not mere external containers in which we live out our personal lives. To the contrary, they penetrate our consciousness and condition all of our expectations, valuations, and sensibilities. The creative possibilities of individual life are inseparable from the transformation of social institutions.

Admittedly, the advent of much of twentieth-century social thought provides a dimension to the analysis of human life which is missing in the philosophy of William James. The question before us is whether this severely curtails the importance of James, rendering him simply a reflection of nineteenth-century culture or merely a forerunner of the existentialists. I take issue with these judgments and offer that the contribution of James yields to neither approach. Further, I would hold that James is an indispensable thinker for our time, especially with regard to social philosophy.

Given the above criticism of James, this may seem a paradoxical remark, yet upon reflection, it makes good sense. A social philosophy is worth no more than its ability to sustain and encourage the widest range of human possibilities, realized, as they must be, in the lives of individuals. Plurality of style, belief, and attitude, as well as the often idiosyncratic experiences of personal life, cannot be accounted for adequately by overarching social structures, much less social theories. To use a contemporary term, James is a master phenomenologist of the original and novel qualities of personal life. His perceptions, evaluations, skepticism, and sense for the unusual, should be integrated into any subsequent social philosophy. James makes it clear that he was not a pollyanna optimist, yet he had a refreshing tendency to seek out the positive, the possible, in human activity. In *Memories and Studies* (p. 322) he writes: "Real culture lives by sympathies and admirations, not by dislikes and disdains; under all misleading wrappings it pounces unerringly upon the human core."

The task before us is to build a society in which our institutions make possible the realization of our capacity for growth so tellingly detailed in the writings of William James. The readers of this volume will not find James a dated thinker. Rather, they will come upon a sustained vision which will cast light on the human situation and especially on those often neglected recesses of the human life where we are most distinctively ourselves. No matter how complex our society or our world, the philosophy of William James aids us in our experiencing them at dead reckoning, and teaches us to be always alert to the complications and surprises which inevitably attend even the most ordinary aspects of our lives.

John J. McDermott
New York, 1977

Selected Secondary Sources

(These materials have been published since the original 1967 edition of *The Writings of William James*.)

Allen, Gay Wilson. *William James: A Biography*. New York: The Viking Press, 1967.

Ayer, A. J. *The Origins of Pragmatism: Studies in the Philosophy of Charles Sanders Peirce and William James*. San Francisco: Freeman, Cooper and Co., 1968.

Corti, W. Robert, ed. *The Philosophy of William James*. Winthertur: Archiv für genetische Philosophie, 1976.

Dilworth, D. "The Initial Formations of 'Pure Experience' in Nishida Kitaro and William James." *Monumenta Nipponica* 24 (1969): 93–111.

Edie, James M. "The Genesis of a Phenomenological Theory of the Experience of Personal Identity: William James on Consciousness and the Self." *Man and World* 6 (September, 1973): 322–38.

Eisendrath, Craig R. *The Unifying Moment: The Psychological Philosophy of William James and Alfred North Whitehead*. Cambridge: Harvard University Press, 1971.

Lentricchia, Frank. "The Romanticism of William James." *Salmagundi* 25 (Winter, 1974): 81–108.

Madden, Edward H. and Chakrabarti, Chandana. "James' 'Pure Experience' versus Ayer's 'Weak Phenomenalism.' " *Transactions of the Charles S. Peirce Society* 12 (Winter, 1976): 3–17.

McDermott, John J. *The Culture of Experience: Philosophical Essays in the American Grain*. New York: New York University Press, 1976. (See "To Be Human Is to Humanize: A Radically Empirical Aesthetic," pp. 21–62, and "Life Is in the Transitions: Radical Empiricism and Contemporary Concerns," pp. 99–117.)

Myers, Gerald E. "William James's Theory of Emotion." *Transactions of the Charles S. Peirce Society* 2 (Spring, 1969): 67–89.

Roth, John K. *Freedom and the Moral Life: The Ethics of William James*. Philadelphia: Westminster Press, 1969.

Stevens, Richard. *James and Husserl: The Foundations of Meaning*. The Hague: Martinus Nijhoff, 1974.

Thayer, H. S. *Meaning and Action: A Critical History of Pragmatism*. Indianapolis: Bobbs-Merrill Co., 1968.

Wild, John. *The Radical Empiricism of William James*. Garden City, N. Y.: Doubleday and Co., 1969.

Wilshire, Bruce. *William James and Phenomenology: A Study of "The Principles of Psychology."* Bloomington: Indiana University Press, 1968.

The ongoing edition of *The Works of William James* (1975–1) contains extensive "introductions" to each volume. A partial listing is found at the end of the Annotated Bibliography of this volume.

Preface

William James was involved polemically with most of the major figures and crucial issues of his time. When read as a whole, however, his work is remarkably free from being dated. Even when tied to specific data and problems no longer relevant, James's version of reality has a subtlety and direction that is still profoundly important. His uncanny sense for living issues should not be thought to be overshadowed by his affection for discrete events and idiomatic expression. Those thinkers of our time who contend that James is meaningful for contemporary thought because he anticipates certain specific philosophical concerns or analyses of experience, actually sell him short. His relevance lies in his ability to offer philosophical insight of the kind which refuses to be localized by any strictly circumscribed method or doctrine. James was neither a phenomenologist nor an existentialist. And, as will be discussed at greater length in the Introduction, to speak of James as a pragmatist is also inadequate. He was a genius of his own kind, who gave to philosophy, largely by virtue of his personal qualities, a perspective and a context wholly novel in implication.

With James, the philosophical enterprise begins anew, for if one is imbued with his viewpoint, nothing is seen in quite the same way again. He once said that "there can *be* no difference anywhere that doesn't *make* a difference elsewhere" (Pragm., 49–50). The most signal instance of this truth is the reading of James himself, who helps us to restructure our very context of apprehension. In the most basic sense, James is a seminal thinker. It is, therefore, extremely important that the public mind, for whom he primarily wrote, more fully realize his originality and relevance. Not only in his inspirational essays, but in his technical thought as well, James had everyday experience in view, and he devoted a long series of lectures and articles to the articulation of psychological and philosophical truths, for the purpose of enhancing the immediate situation. He was, in fact, a meliorist and saw philosophy itself as "the habit of always seeing an alternative" (L.W.J., I, 190).

Unfortunately, James has been approached, in the main, from primarily two vantage points: his doctrine of the "Will to Believe" and his "Pragmatism." While both of these concerns in James are intriguing and carry important philosophical implications, they are subject to grave distortions if seen apart from his insight into the meaning of relations as formulated in his psychology and metaphysics. This, too, will be discussed in the Introduction.

In the Introduction, I have attempted to refocus the main lines of James's thought, to effect a continuity between his personalized philosophical vision and the complexity of his radical empiricism. By no means complete, this Introduction is not meant to be a technical exposition of his thought but, rather, an effort to urge the reading of James afresh. The recent study of William James by Edward C. Moore will provide the reader with a helpful over-all introduction to his philosophy.

The present volume is an attempt to present the full range of James's thought. The serious students of James will want to avail themselves of the collection of his works, including the still unpublished papers, in the Houghton Library at Harvard University. I have gathered here a group of essays that is comprehensive in scope: in addition to representative and complete selections from the *Principles of Psychology, The Will to Believe* and *The Varieties of Religious Experience,* I have reprinted the complete 1943 edition of the *Essays in Radical Empiricism* and *A Pluralistic Universe.* Also included is the original 1907 edition of *Pragmatism,* as well as classic selections from all of James's other major volumes. Of particular significance for James scholarship is the presence of a corrected and supplemented version of the *Annotated Bibliography of the Writings of William James* by Ralph Barton Perry.

In some instances, the arrangements of James's essays have been altered from the original editing provided by Ralph Barton Perry. This is not to be taken as a criticism of Perry's editions, without which students of James would be at a severe loss. Instead, the rearrangement is a function of a more comprehensive volume than has represented James in the past. James's punctuation and spelling, however unusual, are retained throughout.

It is to be hoped that in this new format, the breadth as well as the incisiveness of the vision of William James will be recognized and celebrated anew.

J. J. McD.

Huntington Village
New York, 1966

Acknowledgments

For early encouragement in the preparation of this volume, I am grateful to Joseph E. Cunneen, Managing Editor of *Cross Currents,* R. W. Sleeper of Queens College, Herman Shapiro of San Jose State College, and Morris Philipson, formerly editor of Modern Library. For access to the Jameses' papers, I should like to thank the staff of Houghton Library at Harvard University. In this regard, I appreciate also the kindness of William Alfred of Harvard University and Marion Cummings. Mr. John S. R. James and Gay Wilson Allen graciously gave me permission to cite material from the "Unpublished Papers."

Mrs. Robert Stern of Paul R. Reynolds, Inc. and Mr. Roy Sadow of Random House were helpful in facilitating the complex permissions' arrangements. In the preparation of the "Bibliography," I am grateful for help from Bernard B. Perry and above all, to Ralph Barton Perry III, who generously allowed me to use his corrected version of the original edition. I am thankful for the prompt and excellent translation of "La Notion de Conscience" by Salvatore Saladino of Queens College.

Editorial assistance in the preparation of the manuscript was provided by Robert A. McDermott of Manhattanville College and Eugene Fontinell of Queens College, both of whom offered incisive suggestions as to its improvement. Mr. McDermott and F. J. Fontinell were particularly helpful during the period of proofreading. The manuscript was brought to publication by the scrupulous care of Miss Berenice Hoffman, editor for Random House. Several last-minute difficulties were resolved by the kindness of Mrs. Leona Beck, secretary to the Department of Philosophy at Queens College. Mr. Joseph Bernstein offered professional proofreading service and concern for the manuscript of an extraordinary kind. The completion of the volume would have been impossible without the creative assistance, first to last, of my wife Virginia. She was responsible for all of the secretarial work as well as for the resolution of many of the countless problems which accrue in a manuscript of this scope.

A concluding word of gratitude for Robert C. Pollock, who has opened three generations of Fordham University graduate students to the richness of the thought of James. His insights to the world of process, contemporary humanism and to the lasting drama of Western culture, are legendary among those who have heard him lecture. Robert Pollock stands out in our time as one who embodies the majestic vision of William James.

Introduction

_____

PERSON, PROCESS AND THE
RISK OF BELIEF

In his poem "Our Country," Thoreau wrote the lines that well suggest the philosophical vision of William James.

> All things invite this earth's inhabitants
> To rear their lives to an unheard of height
> And meet the expectation of the land: . . .[1]

James himself had said in his essay on "The Sentiment of Rationality" that "the inmost nature of the reality is congenial to powers which you possess" (W.B. 86). In many ways, it was the attempt to structure the powers or "energies of men" which most occupied him. This concern found its most explicit statement in the essays collected in his _Will to Believe._ Further supporting evidence of the promethean

[1] _Collected Poems of Henry Thoreau,_ ed. Carl Bode (Baltimore, The Johns Hopkins Press, 1964), p. 135.

quality of his thought is found throughout the *Pragmatism*. At one place he tells us that:

> In our cognitive as well as in our active life we are creative. We add, both to the subject and to the predicate part of reality. The world stands really malleable, waiting to receive its final touches at our hand. Like the kingdom of heaven, it suffers violence willingly. Man engenders truths upon it. [Pragm. 256–257.]

As rich as is this direction of James's thought, it is unfortunate that the pragmatic attitude, so readily identified as Jamesian, often overshadows two other major aspects of his total work. First, James spent a good part of his life rationalizing his decision not to commit suicide. As late as 1896, in a letter to Benjamin Paul Blood, he wrote: "I take it that no man is educated who has never dallied with the thought of suicide" (L.W.J., II, 39). Second, he believed in the empirical reality of "conjunctive relations," which enabled him to develop a version of the world that was capable of supporting the pragmatic attitude. John Dewey, still the most incisive commentator on the thought of James, saw this more expansive view, when he wrote

> Long after "pragmatism" in any sense save as an application of his *Weltanschauung** shall have passed into a not unhappy oblivion, the fundamental idea of an open universe in which uncertainty, choice, hypotheses, novelties and possibilities are naturalized will remain associated with the name of James; the more he is studied in his historic setting the more original and daring will the idea appear.[2]

And Ralph Barton Perry offers of James that "It was a metaphysics of vision and insight, rather than either activism or positivism that sprung from the ancient roots of his thought" (T.C., II, 582).

Although James's views are disparate and primarily found in volumes of loosely connected essays (with the exception of the *Principles of Psychology*), he returns again and again to several major themes. His work can best be approached in terms of his personal confrontation with nihilism; his belief in a continuous, intelligible, but unfinished universe; and his attempt to develop a method of inquiry which does justice to the processive quality of both nature and man while providing for the fruitful realization of human "interest." James's preoccupation with individualized energies, psychic states, religious experience, extrasensory perception and the problem of truth, should be viewed as a function of these larger concerns.

In addition to these philosophical problems, James has to be set

---

* Vision of the world.

[2] John Dewey, *Characters and Events* (New York, Henry Holt and Co., 1929), II, p. 440.

within the complex and turbulent life of his family. Relevant also is his relationship to the revolutionary intellectual forces at work in the late nineteenth century, particularly in their American setting. In an incisive text, Robert C. Pollock evaluates the historical context in which James matured.

As the point of convergence of a potentially infinite number of perspectives, the human mind's interest in itself was enormously intensified, with the result that experience in its widest range assumed a commanding position. . . . With the maturation of the historical sense and the genetic point of view ushered in by evolutionary theories, a respect for the temporal and becoming aspect of things took a firm hold of men's minds. And it became imperative to examine the problem of knowledge afresh, once human experience was viewed in the more all-inclusive relationships of history, and on the developmental plane.[3]

In writing of James, Gardner Murphy gives us a more specific historical setting. "Of all the nineteenth century currents most fundamentally congenial to him, because so closely related to such [personal] needs, the most important was evolutionism; an evolutionism which meant creativeness through struggle, the primacy of the immediate task to be done over any abstraction which is removed from life." [4]

With the exception of *The Thought and Character of William James,* the massive intellectual biography by R. B. Perry, deservedly famed for its wealth of detail, clarity and philosophical acumen, the literature about James has been disappointing. Perhaps Perry's work has been too successful, reducing much of the rest of the James scholarship to pale imitations characterized by the repetition of what are by now clichés about James's nobility, openness to experience, Americanism, and philosophical profundity *malgré lui.* As with all clichés, they have considerable truth at their core. But they have also obscured the technical and unfinished side of James's thought. They have led us into reading his popular works without benefit of the complex reasoning process that enabled him to offer such imaginative and relevant philosophical hints. Writers on James have constantly to avoid the temptation simply to join together a series of brilliant asides and avoid commenting at all. We should pay special heed to the warning

[3] Robert C. Pollock, "James: Pragmatism," *The Great Books,* ed. Harold C. Gardiner (New York, The Devin-Adair Co., 1953), pp. 187, 188.
[4] Gardner Murphy, *Historical Introduction to Modern Psychology* (New York, Harcourt, Brace and World, 1949), p. 194. The relationship of the thought of William James to the developing contemporary theories of evolution, is set out in careful detail by Philip P. Wiener, *Evolution and the Founders of Pragmatism* (Cambridge, Harvard University Press, 1949).

of Julius Bixler: "the isolated reference from James is always unreliable." [5] Much of the problem in assessing James, stems from his predilection for publishing, as such, what originally were public lectures. He was unhappy about this "popular lecture style" and wanted to do something more technically rigorous, in the German manner, more *strengwissenschaftlich* (T.C. II, 583). Yet the combined factors of his generosity, his superb skill in the presentation of ideas, and his deep sense of responsibility to the immediate community, forced James again and again into the lecture hall. In these lectures, his lucidity, charm and ever-present philosophical commonsense pervade what is often the most difficult of undertakings. The richly metaphorical style of the lectures as published have often been the recipient of heady praise. Such encomiums, however, have rendered James more beloved than analyzed. This situation is to be lamented, for in our time the viability of philosophical vision depends largely on the ability to sustain a dialectic between the increased understanding of man's inner life and the ever-widening cosmological setting in which we find ourselves. Such a dialectic was an integral aspect of James's philosophical insight.

James does not belong to a single generation or to a specific philosophical movement, although his qualities and cast of mind are unintelligible if he is not seen in his historical and sociological context. We should take seriously the seemingly extravagant claim of Whitehead, that the four great philosophical "assemblers" are Plato, Aristotle, Leibniz and William James. His choice of James was based on the judgment that James "had discovered intuitively the great truth with which modern logic is now wrestling," namely, "that every finite set of premises must indicate notions which are excluded from its direct purview." [6] Whitehead arrives at this judgment because he reads James, as we should, with an eye to the implications and as yet unrealized dimensions of his foresightful and trenchant viewpoint. Indeed, we should follow the advice of James himself, who warns a student that, in analyzing another's thought, the stringing out of texts leads nowhere "unless you have first grasped his centre of vision, by an act of imagination" (L.W.J. II, 355).

In addition to Whitehead, other formulators of major contemporary philosophical traditions have expressed a similar debt to the originating qualities of James. Thinkers as diverse as Unamuno,[7] Witt-

[5] Julius Seelye Bixler, *Religion in the Philosophy of William James* (Boston, Marshall Jones Co., 1926), p. XI.

[6] Alfred North Whitehead, *Modes of Thought* (New York, Capricorn Books, 1958), pp. 2–4.

[7] Cf. Pelayo Hipolito Fernandez, *Miguel de Unamuno y William James—Un Paralelo Pragmatico* (Salamanca, Libreria Cervantes, 1961).

genstein[8] and Husserl,[9] highly original thinkers in their own right, trace decisive insights to the work of James. And while Edward Moore, in his recent work on James, tends to deny to James any necessarily historical influence, he does comment that "the turn of the wheel is almost complete, so that the student of William James seems to feel that in reading many contemporary philosophers he is rereading William James." [10]

And of course we can but mention here the critical influence of James on the American philosophical tradition. Certainly the "Golden Age" of American philosophy, which gave us the work of Royce, Santayana, Peirce, Dewey and Mead, is inconceivable without James as an originating force. In a remarkable address, given less than a year after the death of James, Josiah Royce sees him as the third representative American philosopher. James, like Jonathan Edwards and Emerson before him, has "thought for himself, fruitfully, with true independence, and with successful inventiveness. And he has given utterance to ideas which are characteristic of a stage and an aspect of the spiritual life of this people." [11] As Royce indicates, the realization of national self-consciousness was not a planned effort of James. In the words of one commentator, M. Le Breton, *"Il a pu passer en Amérique pour le plus cosmopolite et en Europe pour le plus américain des philosophes"** (T.C. I, 383). But by the nature of his genius and the press of his situation, he had also realized inadvertently or no, what Emerson in his essay on "Nature" had seen as our need for "an original relation to the universe." [12] If James's originality constituted a stage of the national self-consciousness in his time, his vision now replies to the needs of man today, who confronts an endless but increasingly controllable cosmos. An analysis of the life history and thought of William James involves us in the three great mooring points of human experience: self-consciousness, national culture and cosmic setting. By virtue of his spirit, his concerns, and even the direction of his unfinished technical thought, William James places us at a vantage

[8] Cf. e.g. John Passmore, *A Hundred Years of Philosophy* (London, The Macmillan Co., 1962), p. 482, n. 2.

[9] Cf. Herbert Spiegelberg, *The Phenomenological Movement* (The Hague, Martinus Nijhoff, 1960), I, pp. 66–69, 111–117. Cf. also Marvin Farber, *The Foundations of Phenomenology* (Cambridge, Harvard University Press, 1943), p. 277.

[10] Edward Carter Moore, *William James* (New York, Washington Square Press, 1965), p. 162.

[11] Josiah Royce, *William James and Other Essays on the Philosophy of Life* (New York, The Macmillan Co., 1911), p. 7.

* In America he could pass for the most cosmopolitan of philosophers, and in Europe for the most American.

[12] R. W. Emerson, *The Complete Works* (Boston, Houghton, Mifflin and Co., 1903), I, p. 3.

point, from which we can attempt to reconstitute the human endeavor in a way that is creative and honest.

II

Few families have been more thoroughgoingly analyzed than the James family. In addition to the intellectual biography of William James by R. B. Perry, we have a study of the family by F. O. Matthiessen[13] and *The Three Jameses* by C. Harley Grattan.[14] The father, Henry James, Sr., has been the subject of a careful and rich intellectual biography by Frederic Young.[15] The life of William's brother Henry has been recounted in his own *Autobiography*[16] and in the ongoing, justly praised biography by Leon Edel.[17] The relationship between William and his brother Henry has been evaluated from many perspectives, one of the most prominent being their often variant interpretations of European and American culture. Several volumes of Henry's letters have appeared.[18] And just recently we have had the advantage of a new edition of *The Diary of Alice James*[19] and the publication of *The Letters of William James and Theodore Flournoy.*[20]

Further, publication of a forthcoming full-length biography of William James, by Gay Wilson Allen, has been announced. This work is to be based on official access to most of the extensive family papers at Houghton Library of Harvard University, and should round out

[13] F. O. Matthiessen, *The James Family* (New York, Alfred A. Knopf, 1947).

[14] C. Harley Grattan, *The Three Jameses* (New York, New York University Press, 1962).

[15] Frederic Harold Young, *The Philosophy of Henry James Sr.* (New York, Bookman Associates, 1951). Cf. also, the older study by Austin Warren, *The Elder Henry James* (New York, The Macmillan Co., 1934).

[16] Henry James, *Autobiography,* ed. Frederick W. Dupee (New York, Criterion Books, 1956).

[17] Thus far, the volumes written by Leon Edel are *Henry James: The Untried Years, 1843–1870* (New York, J. B. Lippincott Company, 1953); *Henry James: The Conquest of London, 1870–1881* (1962); *Henry James: The Middle Years, 1882–1895* (1962).

[18] Percy Lubbock, ed., *The Letters of Henry James*, 2 vols. (New York, Charles Scribners Sons, 1920), and Leon Edel, ed., *The Selected Letters of Henry James* (New York, Farrar, Straus and Cudahy, 1955).

[19] Leon Edel, ed., *The Diary of Alice James* (New York, Dodd, Mead and Co., 1964). This version is complete and replaces the excised edition of Anna Robeson Burr, *Alice James: Her Brothers—Her Journal* (New York, Dodd, Mead and Co., 1934). The latter, however, features an eighty-page introductory essay, devoted primarily to Garth Wilkinson and Robertson James.

[20] Robert C. Le Clair, *The Letters of William James and Theodore Flournoy* (Madison, University of Wisconsin Press, 1966).

the unanalyzed family relationships as presented in the Perry biography. Of particular importance will be Allen's consideration of Alice Howe Gibbens James, William's wife.

All of the above works stand beside the voluminous literary output of Henry James, the philosophical writings of William and inimitable social theology of the father. There are also countless volumes of commentary and marginalia, particularly as devoted to the two brothers, William and Henry.

Despite this avalanche of material, the James family still retains its fascination and even its mystery. We need to know more about the two younger brothers, Garth Wilkinson and Robertson, whose lives, from any perspective, were a series of crippling frustrations. Some of this can be traced to their participation in the Civil War, but much of it comes from sibling pressures and invidious comparisons with their spoiled but successful older brothers. And we must think more of Alice, who rejoiced at the discovery of her cancer, as it was a real disease at last and promised to take her from the neurasthenia and hypochondria that so dominated her life and that ran through the family as a whole. No doubt the person of William James also has to be rethought. Though he was lionized by everyone for his generosity and charm, a close reading of his life tells us that he rarely was trapped in an unwanted situation and that his drive for self-understanding often buried lesser persons in its wake.

For many reasons, however, the family figure most significant for understanding the life and work of William James is his father. The inner spirit of the James family can be traced in the main to this highly original and profoundly religious man. Gardner Murphy catches some of his quality in this passage.

> He created in the home atmosphere an exhilarating sense of the worth-whileness of pursuing problems of cosmic dimensions, of asking for-ever one more question as to the place of man in this world and as to the real basis for ethics and religion; everybody in the family was apparently always ready for a debate which wound up with humor and with agreement to live and let live. [P.R., 4.]

Quite aside from this overpowering personal influence, day by day, and the bequeathing of a restless and literally transatlantic passion for new scenes and situations, the father's ultimate influence on William James, was to be found in his persistent encouragement of a genuine religious sensitivity and concern. The father's major insight could be phrased as a restating of the medieval "image" doctrine, in which man took his meaning from his participation in the experiential richness of the godhead. For Henry James the Elder, however, human social experience was the telling one, so that the relationship was reversed, and

God, himself, imaged man's striving for perfection. Speaking of the elder James, Matthiessen comments that "he found his own enlargement in the doctrine of 'our glorified natural humanity,' the three terms of which blended for him into an organic whole." [21] Saturated with the doctrines of Swedenborg and Fourier, he could write a work on *Society—The Redeemed Form of Man* and an "Oration" devoted to the *Social Significance of Our Institutions*. Matthiessen wisely states that even more than William James, "Henry Senior 'believed in believing,' and the 'one great truth' in his ontology was God's alienation for the sake of an ultimate and blissful reunion. He dwelt, mainly, not on the fall, but on the promise of the rise of the common man." [22]

From Brazil in 1865, William James wrote, "I think Father is the *wisest* of all men whom I know" (L.W.J., I, 60). And he later said of his father: "He was a religious prophet and genius, if ever prophet and genius there were. He published an intensely positive, radical, and fresh conception of God, and an intensely vital view of our connection with him" (L.R.H.J., 12). William James was not, however, at this point sympathetic with much of his father's teaching, even opposing its basic drift while editing *The Literary Remains of Henry James,* in 1885. As his own horizon widened and his search into the vagaries of self-consciousness increased, William became increasingly more sympathetic with his father's outlook. He acknowledges this in a letter to his sister Alice, in 1891:

> These inhibitions, these split-up selves, all these new facts that are gradually coming to light about our organization, these enlargements of the self in trance, etc., are bringing me to turn for light in the direction of all sorts of despised spiritualistic and unscientific ideas. Father would find in me today a much more receptive listener—all *that* philosophy has got to be brought in. [L.W.J., I, 310.]

Whatever may be the ultimate assessment of his father's work, William continued the "religious persuasion" in his own thought. It is true that this attitude was undoubtedly characterized by a deep reluctance to effect any personal commitment to specific doctrine. Both attitudes are expressed in the following remark to Henry W. Rankin in 1897: "You see that, although religion is the great interest of my life, I am rather hopelessly non-evangelical, and take the whole thing too impersonally" (L.W.J., II, 58). But Oliver Wendell Holmes, Jr., a close friend of the young James, and one who knew the father, said of the *Pragmatism,* "I now see, as I have seen in his other books that I have read, that the aim and end of the whole business is religious." [23] John

---

[21] Matthiessen, *op. cit.,* p. 8.
[22] *Ibid.,* p. 11.
[23] Oliver Wendell Holmes, Jr., *Holmes-Pollock Letters,* ed., Mark De Wolfe Howe (Cambridge, Harvard University Press, 1941), I, p. 140.

Jay Chapman also speaks of "The great religious impulse at the back of all his work . . . which controlled his whole life and mind, and accomplished a great work in the world." [24] More than even William James would care to admit, that impulse was the continuing spirit of his father.

We cannot present here a detailed analysis of the multiple relationships of this family—as close to a microcosm of the human situation as a family can bring us. We must, however, examine James's recovery from his neurasthenic crisis of 1869–1870. After a period of severe depression, James rejected the real possibility of suicide. This event marked a decisive break in his attitude toward death and signalized his new belief in the creative dimensions of personal existence. While it cannot be said that the resolution of this crisis ended the pervasiveness of what Perry calls his "morbid traits," it did symbolize for James a new set of possibilities. More important, the decision reached at that time remained the most influential single factor on *all* of his subsequent work. Chapman writes, "the intellectual part of him was enfeebled by the agnosticism of 1870. And yet what difference did it make? Some sort of light shone out of his cloud as he took his way across the sands, and men followed him." [25]

Having rejected suicide in favor of the possibility of a creative life unsupported by certitude, James developed a doctrine to sustain such a belief. His personal needs at this point ultimately generated not only the essays on "The Sentiment of Rationality," "The Dilemma of Determinism," and "The Will to Believe," but also helped to formulate his aggressive view of the "self" in the *Principles of Psychology* and his lifelong attempt at structuring a personalized cosmology. If it can be said that James assented to "The Will to Believe" until the end, we must caution that it was a belief always shot through with irresolution and doubt. Behind the consistent cadences of a rich and future-oriented prose, there lurked a well-controlled but omnipresent sense of despair. James was neither an optimist nor a cynic; he was a man of moral courage, who knew, all too well, the ambiguity and precariousness of the human condition.

As Perry is careful to note, the crisis of 1870 is not to be confused with the hallucinatory experience of William James as recorded anonymously in the *Varieties of Religious Experience*. There are, however, several reasons for reflecting on this account in the *Varieties*. First the description of this event gives to us a highly vivid version of one side

[24] John Jay Chapman, "William James," *The Selected Writings of John Jay Chapman,* ed. Jacques Barzun (New York, Farrar, Straus and Cudahy, 1957), p. 206.

[25] John Jay Chapman, *Memories and Milestones* (New York, Moffat, Yard and Co., 1915), p. 160.

of James's many-faceted temperament. Second, although the date has not been precisely fixed, both Perry and James's son, Henry James the third, put the experience in the same period as that of the crisis texts, namely 1869–1870. Third, as William James indicates, his hallucination had a remarkable affinity to one undergone earlier by his father. (See below, Section I, for these Crisis texts.)

The difference, of course, between James's experience as told in the *Varieties* and the crisis account as found in his "Diary" is to be seen in the source of sustenance. In the former, James seeks nurture in the scriptural tradition as sustenance before the terrors of existence. In the "Diary" account, however, for perhaps the first time in his life, he avoids what had been for him a derivative and escapist solution. The direction he takes can be seen as an attempt to confront the actualities of his situation, and despite all of its uncertainty, to proceed from that point. Like Albert Camus of *The Rebel,* James does not resolve his fundamental problem, but he no longer allows it to crush future options. The first breakthrough for James is recorded in an entry in his "Diary" on February 1, 1870.

> Today I about touched/bottom, and perceive plainly that I must face the choice with open/eyes: shall I frankly throw the moral business overboard, as one unsuited to my innate aptitudes, or shall I follow it, and it alone, making everything else merely stuff for it: I will give the latter alternative a fair trial. Who knows but the moral interest may become developed. [T.C., I, 322.]

Then on April 30, 1870, after affirming the work of Renouvier and asserting the belief in free will, James concludes his entry with an entirely new understanding of the meaning and direction of his own life.

> Not in maxims, not in *Anschauungen,** but in accumulated *acts* of thought lies salvation. *Passer outre.*** Hitherto, when I have felt like taking a free initiative, like daring to act originally, without carefully waiting for contemplation of the external world to determine all for me, suicide seemed the most manly form to put my daring into; now, I will go a step further with my will, not only act with it, but believe as well; believe in my individual reality and creative power. My belief, to be sure, *can't* be optimistic—but I will posit life (the real, the good) in the self-governing *resistance* of the ego to the world. Life shall [be built in]*** doing and suffering and creating. [L.W.J., I, 148.]

It is important to realize that although this "belief in belief" gave

* Contemplations.
** Let us go beyond—that is, beyond these maxims, let us make a fresh start and not be bound by abstract rules.
*** Ms. doubtful.

to James the necessary impetus to rebuild his life, it did not exhaust the commitment he made. Despite the refusal of most commentators to acknowledge this, James was profoundly aware of the need to affirm a kind of world texture which would support a "Will to Believe" doctrine. Such is the implication of the following statement, written in 1879, and published in the later version of "The Sentiment of Rationality":

> If we survey the field of history and ask what feature all great periods of revival, of expansion of the human mind, display in common, we shall find, I think, simply this: that each and all of them have said to the human being, "The inmost nature of the reality is congenial to powers which you possess." [W.B., 86.]

The active relationship between "congeniality" as a character of the real, and the "powers" of men, is a central insight in the thought of James. Congeniality, in James's context, points to the realm of possibility as against a sheer nihilism. James assumes the presence of meaning but remains pessimistic about the attainment of clarity, and above all, certitude. This generalized position of James helps us to understand why his view of the self, while understood as supremely active and intensely personal, is never cut off from the needs and obligations at work in the stream of consciousness. And although he sees truth as a function of "interest," this position does not encourage predatory action, for the dialectic between man's "powers" and the "congeniality" of nature is always framed out within the demanding context of empirically given relationships. Further, this interaction leads James, who was a champion of rugged individualism and a proponent of the importance of "Great Men" in their environment, constantly to set all human activity into the wider process of "seeing and feeling the total push and pressure of the cosmos" (Pragm., 4). In effect, for James, the more promethean he sees man, the more expansive is the total universe of experience as the context for human activity.

The crisis of 1870 and the ensuing development of the philosophy of the "Will to Believe" is unquestionably of critical importance to any understanding of the thought of James. These events cannot, however, be isolated from other equally profound concerns in James's work. Though chary of totality of any kind and hostile to the rigors of logical systems, James was no subjectivist. In a passage from a "Notebook," devoted to "radical empiricism," James wrote "surely, Nature itself and subjective construction are radically opposed, one's higher indignations are nourished by the opposition" (U.P., L.N., II). For those critics who see James primarily in terms of his formulation of "The Will to Believe," it would be well always to recall the purpose and content of his belief. He expresses this aspect of his thought with equal religious fervor in an extraordinary text from the *Pragmatism.*

> Woe to him whose beliefs
> play fast and loose with
> the order which realities
> follow in his experience;
> they will lead him nowhere
> or else make false connexions. [Pragm., 205.]

Belief for James is a wedge into the tissue of experience, for the purpose of liberating dimensions otherwise closed to the agnostic standpoint. James does not ask that belief perpetuate itself beyond its ability to generate supporting data, nor does he ask for total verification. In this way, his view is profoundly different from the Pascalian wager. In a real sense he anticipates the present discussion of the difference between "believing that" and "believing in." James's view is of the latter kind; and in this connection it is significant that in a commentary on Wittgenstein's *Tractatus,* R. W. Sleeper can remark that "to use religious language rightly is to move beyond language to what is manifest in life itself." [26] This is the essence of James's position.

The line of development from the crisis texts of 1869–1870, through "The Will to Believe" and on to the *Pragmatism* and *Pluralistic Universe,* has two major links in it. James wrought a novel doctrine of selfhood in the *Principles,* and a novel doctrine of the constituency of reality as experienced, in his *Essays on Radical Empiricism.* Both of these efforts were directed toward enhancing human participation in the world while simultaneously acknowledging the irreducibility and stubborness of facts. (L.W.J., I, 225.) Indeed, John Smith says of the "radical empiricism," that it "is a radically new account of how the self penetrates and is penetrated by the world." [27] The continuity from the "belief in belief" to the *Pragmatism* is thus forged by James's psychological and metaphysical understanding of the human situation. This development becomes more intelligible when one refuses the temptation to see the crisis of 1870 as an existentialist type of experience, primarily characterized by alienation. We hold that it is better viewed within the context of a classical Stoic setting, with the bond to nature accepted but the resignation and the impossibility of novelty rejected.

James as a young man had been a careful reader of Marcus Aurelius. In many ways his vision shared the Aurelian contention that

[26] Ralph W. Sleeper, "Linguistic Philosophy and Religious Belief," *Cross Currents,* XIV (Summer, 1964), p. 357. The reference to the *Tractatus* is 6.521 and 6.522.

[27] John E. Smith, "The Course of American Philosophy," *Review of Metaphysics,* XI (Dec., 1957), p. 291.

"all things are implicated with one another, and the bond is holy; and there is hardly anything unconnected with any other thing." [28] In his *Varieties,* James had favorably cited Aurelius. "Everything harmonizes with me, which is harmonious to thee, O Universe." [29] On closer analysis, however, we find this doctrine of harmony held by the Stoics to be an inadequate response to the problems generated by the struggle to achieve personal identity. In such an outlook, the human situation takes its meaning from the inexorable cycle of Nature; dignity and worth are always qualities derived from Nature. In preparing for his Gifford Lectures on *The Varieties of Religious Experience,* James sensed this difficulty in the Stoic position. He left an entry in a "Notebook" that referred to the "curious paradox" found in Aurelius, namely, that all life equaled the present but the present was too short to have significance. Aurelius, concluded James, doesn't seem to make too much of life either way. (U.P., L.J.) The underlying crisis of the Stoic view is not so much one of alienation as one proceeding from an absorption in sameness. This attitude is powerfully expressed by Aurelius in Book II of the *Meditations.* "And, to say all in a word, everything which belongs to the body is a stream, and what belongs to the soul is a dream and vapour, and life is a warfare and a stranger's sojourn, and after-fame is oblivion." [30] James no doubt felt this way at one time, but his later view of life, influenced by evolutionary theory and by his affection for an open universe, is striking in its contrast with that of Marcus Aurelius. In speaking of "classic *Weltanschauungen,*" James affirms that they "violate the character with which life concretely comes and the expression which it bears of being, or at least of involving, a muddle and struggle, with an 'ever not quite' to all our formulas, and novelty and possibility forever leaking in." (T.C., II, 700.)

James, no more than Emerson or Whitman, could reject our inextricable binding to nature. And like his predecessors, he attempted, within the limits of that binding, to affirm and structure a doctrine of novelty. The central difficulty is incisively put by Whitman.

> The press of my foot to the earth springs a hundred
> affections;
> They scorn the best I can do to relate them.[31]

For James, it is precisely the ability of man to enter into the relational fabric of the world, in a participative and liberating way,

[28] Marcus Aurelius, *Meditations* (Chicago, Henry Regnery Co., 1956), VII, No. 9, p. 79.

[29] *Ibid.,* IV, No. 23, p. 36.

[30] *Ibid.,* II, No. 17, pp. 18–19.

[31] Walt Whitman, "Leaves of Grass" *The Portable Walt Whitman,* ed. Mark Van Doren (New York, Viking Press, 1959), No. 14, p. 75.

which enables him to become human. His doctrine of nature is open-ended and does not offer ready-made meanings but rather the possibilities for meaning. Intelligibility becomes then a function of the interaction between the self and the world; it will not yield to any privileged *a priori* conceptual scheme. Thus, James can say in the *Pragmatism* that "our experience meanwhile is all shot through with regularities. One bit of it can warn us to get ready for another bit, can 'intend' or be 'significant of' that remoter object" (Pragm., 205). Given a world of this kind, the "belief in belief" is not a vacuous affirmation but rather a bold, yet grounded methodology for human inquiry. The presence of regularity and novelty, synechistically conjoined, increasingly came to occupy a central role in James's philosophy. As late as 1909, in a letter to James Ward, he writes: "I think the centre of my whole *Anschauung,* since years ago I read Renouvier, has been the belief that something is doing in the universe, and that *novelty* is real" (T.C., II, 656). Such a belief can lead James to say, as he does in the *Psychology—Briefer Course,* that "the more *active-feeling* states of consciousness are thus the more central portions of the spiritual Me" (P.B.C., 194). Confidence without arrogance, intelligibility without certitude, direction without totality; such is the rhythm of James's view of our participation in the stream of life.

James's philosophy does not appeal to systematic justification or even to simple rational explication. This is not to be taken as so crippling to James's philosophical worth as some may hold; for, despite claims to the contrary, it is a moot question whether any philosophical position can ultimately and totally justify itself. In any event, whatever may be its personal or temperamental origins, James's understanding of the human situation must be evaluated on its ability to locate each of us in an informing way within our own experience. James would be the last to deny the personal origins of his doctrine. He would, however, affirm with great conviction, the wider legitimacy and seminality of his thought. No doubt he held on to his early judgment that "no one sees farther into a generalization than his own knowledge of details extends" (L.W.J., II, 2). Further, in connection with his work on psychical research, he was "sure that the more we can steer clear of theories at first, the better," and urged that *"Facts* are what are wanted" (L.W.J., I, 250). Above all, he would point to his psychology and to his radical empiricism as important contributions to an understanding of the empirical context for the human situation. He said at the end that his thought was "too much like an arch built only on one side" (S.P.P., VIII). That side, as well as its unfinished companion, is well worth our concern and examination.

III

Students of James tend to agree that the *Principles of Psychology* is his masterpiece. Perhaps more revealing is the fact that those commentators for whom James's philosophy is seriously inadequate, will nonetheless acknowledge the genius of the *Principles*. Praise for the work was immediate and unstinting, both by psychologists and critics in general. Gardner Murphy writes that "the *Principles* burst upon the world like a volcanic eruption." [32] Whatever may be its continued relevance for psychology,[33] the *Principles* still teems with implications for philosophy.[34] Indeed, some contemporary critics read it as a masterful prototype of phenomenological analysis,[35] although others of this persuasion lament the direction taken in the subsequent work of James.[36] No such split in the thought of James is honored here. The "psychology," "will to believe," "radical empiricism," and "pragmatism" are of a piece in his philosophy. To separate these doctrines may well result in a more sympathetic and incisive treatment of aspects of James's thought but on the other hand, such an approach can prevent us from taking seriously the full range of human obligations which, according to James, had to be met if we were to develop a legitimate philosophical viewpoint. Actually, except for his lack of concern with James's notion of marginal psychic states (particularly of a religious nature), the only thinker to assume the full thrust of James's philosophy is John Dewey.

Quite aside from the various philosophical perspectives taken, the *Principles* remains essential to any understanding of James. Although

[32] Murphy, *Modern Psychology,* p. 195.

[33] Indications are that such relevance is considerable. Cf. e.g., Margaret Knight, *William James* (Baltimore, Penguin Books, 1954), pp. 8, 43–44, 67, and Henry E. Garrett, *General Psychology* (New York, American Book Co., 1955), p. 341. Cf. also Ernest Becker, *The Revolution in Psychiatry* (Glencoe, Free Press, 1964).

[34] The most promising revaluation of the *Principles,* for purposes of elucidating contemporary philosophical themes, is found in James Edie "Notes on the Philosophical Anthropology of William James," *An Invitation to Phenomenology* (Chicago, Quadrangle Books, 1965), pp. 110–132. Cf. also Hermann Schmidt, *Der Begriff der Erfahrungskontinuität bei William James und seine Bedeutung für den amerikanischen Pragmatismus* (Heidelberg, Carl Winter, 1959).

[35] Cf. Johannes Linschoten, *Auf dem Weg zu Einer Phänomenologischen Psychologie: Die Psychologie von William James* (Berlin, Walter de Gruyter and Co., 1961).

[36] Cf. Aron Gurwitsch, *The Field of Consciousness* (Pittsburgh, Duquesne University Press, 1964), p. 6. Gurwitsch does go on to give a penetrating analysis of one aspect of James's later thought: his radical empiricism.

he early decided to forgo painting as his life's work, his sensitivity for vivid portrayal and his concern for the slightest nuance within the concrete, remained with him. James's *Principles* is actually a running commentary on the total human experience as well as a rich expression of much of its untold psychic activity. To this day, the chapter on "Habit" is the classic statement on that aspect of human life. No detail is too slight to be given a full and complete hearing in the melange of sensations which is open to James's analysis. He tells us that he wishes to "press on the attention," the "reinstatement of the vague to its proper place in our mental life" (Principles, I, 254). His struggle toward such a goal, while utilizing nearly all available literature, resulted in a massive work; one which can only be treated here in a limited way.

James's approach in the *Principles* proceeded from the physiology in which he was technically trained.[37] He held a medical degree and had begun his teaching career in 1873 by offering a course in "Comparative Anatomy and Physiology." Making careful and extensive use of the latest psychological research, James was particularly dependent on the work of nineteenth-century German experimental psychology.

When James comes to analyze consciousness, or what he calls the phenomenon that "thinking of some sort goes on" (Principles, I, 224), he is forced to break with the reigning psychological and, implicitly, philosophical hypotheses. By "naming our thought by its own objects, we almost all of us assume that as the objects are, so the thought must be" (Principles, I, 195). James sees no introspective support for such an approach and warns of the "paradoxes and contradictions" which it engenders:

> The continuous flow of the mental stream is sacrificed, and in its place an atomism, a brickbat plan of construction is preached . . . These words are meant to impeach the entire English psychology derived from Locke and Hume, and the entire German psychology derived from Herbart, so far as they both treat "ideas" as separate subjective entities that come and go. [Principles I, 196.]

Such a negative judgment forces James to structure a novel doctrine of consciousness. This new direction, in turn, begets several corollaries of crucial importance to his subsequent theory of relations and pragmatic theory of truth. Whitehead speaks of the importance of this effort in the *Principles,* especially when seen in relation to James's later essay of 1904, "Does 'Consciousness' Exist?". "The sci-

[37] Antony Flew says of the *Principles,* that "it was this book more than anything else which· gave to psychology its present physiological orientation." Cf. Flew, *Body, Mind, and Death* (New York, The Macmillan Company, 1965), p. 299.

entific materialism and the Cartesian ego were both challenged at the
same moment, one by science and the other by philosophy, as represented by William James and his psychological antecedents; and the
double challenge marks the end of a period which lasted for about two
hundred and fifty years." [38]

There is no doubt that James wished to oppose the traditional
tendency to treat consciousness as a sort of container, through which
unchanging, simple ideas pass. He had no confidence in the view that
complex ideas were formed simply by means of association. For James
"a permanently existing idea or Vorstellung *which makes its appearance before the footlights of consciousness at periodical intervals, is
as mythological an entity as the Jack of Spades"* (Principles, I, 236).
What then does he mean by consciousness and how does he view the
"process"[39] of thinking?

In the *Principles,* James, for the most part, holds to the long-
standing dualistic relationship between mind and body. He does, however, take the first step toward ending this dualism, by means of his
sense of consciousness as a stream or flow. In an essay on "The Development of American Pragmatism," Dewey sees this new direction
as one of two major contentions in the *Principles;* the other being
James's view of consciousness as natively selective. Dewey holds that
we are given "a re-interpretation of introspective psychology in which
James denies that sensations, images and ideas are discrete and in
which he replaces them by a continuous stream which he calls the
'stream of consciousness.' This conception necessitates a consideration of relations as an immediate part of the field of consciousness,
having the same status as qualities." [40]

If we dovetail the treatment of consciousness in the *Principles* with
that in the *Briefer Course,* we find that James points to five major
characteristics. First, consciousness is personal and has changing and
sensibly continuous states; second, consciousness has a fringe as well as
a focus and thus is able to grasp a sliding stream of impressions at the
periphery of attention; third, consciousness includes the apprehension
of relations as well as of elements, of "transitive" as well as of "substantive" states; fourth, the activity of consciousness is selective, that
is, consciousness welcomes, rejects and chooses from among the objects presented; fifth, in that human thought appears to deal with

[38] Alfred North Whitehead, *Science and the Modern World* (New York,
Mentor Books, 1953), p. 143.

[39] William James is credited with being among the first, if not the first, to use
the important term "process" in relation to conscious life. Cf. Edwin G. Boring,
The Physical Dimensions of Consciousness (New York, The Century Co.,
1933), p. 216.

[40] John Dewey, "The Development of American Pragmatism," *Philosophy
and Civilization* (New York, Capricorn Books, 1963), p. 28.

objects independent of itself, it is cognitive.[41] In turn, the doctrines of
"relations" and "sensible continuity" are the forerunners of his radical
empiricism. The emphasis on the "fringe" of consciousness gives empirical structure to his fealty to extrasensory perception and also provides a context for the doctrine of connections in *A Pluralistic
Universe.* And the notion of consciousness as selective is obviously a
beginning principle for the *Pragmatism.* Finally, for James, the entire
activity of consciousness assumes the existence of a world that has
extra-mental reality.

Two of the distinguishing qualities of consciousness, namely, those
pertaining to relations and selectivity, are particularly important.
James states unequivocally that there exists a corresponding feeling
for each of the relations at work in the flow of the stream of consciousness through the various substantive states. He contends "if there be
such things as feelings at all, *then so surely as relations between objects exist* in rerum naturâ,* *so surely, and more surely, do feelings
exist to which these relations are known"* (Principles I, 245). So that
no misunderstanding of his meaning remain, James affirms his position by contending that "we ought to say a feeling of *and,* a feeling of
if, a feeling of *by,* quite as readily as we say a feeling of *blue* or a feeling of *cold"* (Principles I, 245–246). Consciousness does not leap
from one "substantive" state to another, but rather is always in "felt"
continuity by virtue of the experiencing of "transitive" relationships.
This insight will ultimately force James to hold a different view of the
source of intelligibility and will render the role of logical relations as
external and derivative. Much of the psychology, the radical empiricism and the theory of truth; indeed, given its generalized implications,
the whole of James leans on the legitimacy of this specific contention
about relations as experienced.

As a description of what is actually given in our experience,
James's viewpoint can be sustained only by a corroboration in one's
own situation. James admits that the analyses of introspective psychology are unequal to the task of verifying this claim about relations.
Even within the framework of a dualism, as maintained in the *Principles,* James sees the hopelessness of making explicit the tumultuous
range of relationships. "If we speak objectively, it is the real relations

---

[41] It is at this point that phenomenologically oriented thinkers, as James
Edie, see a nascent doctrine of "intentionality" in James's thought. Cf. Edie,
art. cit., p. 117. Although often overlooked, such implicit awareness of "intentionality" abounds elsewhere in James's writings, as for example, *Pragmatism,*
his essay on "The Function of Cognition" in *The Meaning of Truth* and especially his extract from a "World of Pure Experience," significantly entitled
"The Relation Between Knower and Known," as included in *The Meaning of
Truth.*

* In the nature of things.

that appear revealed; if we speak subjectively, it is the stream of consciousness that matches each of them by an inward coloring of its own. In either case the relations are numberless, and no existing language is capable of doing justice to all their shades" (Principles I, 245). This inability does not, however, deter James from his conviction of the reality of his description. In short, the grounding for this position is found in the intuitive genius of James and, following good pragmatic style, in its salutary results for subsequent philosophical thought. John Dewey, for one, can say "long ago I learned from William James that there are immediate experiences of the connections linguistically expressed by conjunctions and prepositions. My doctrinal position is but a generalization of what is involved in this fact." [42] Victor Lowe, writing of Whitehead, states that if we deny "transitions" are felt "after reading James's psychology and radical empiricism, it is probably useless to take *Process and Reality* in hand." [43] And Bradley, for whom "Immediate Experience is presentational and without relations," [44] rejects the contention of experienced relations at a primary level but sees such a view as central to all of James's thought. Perhaps Henri Bergson sees the implication of this stand of James's best of all.

> Most philosophies, therefore, restrict our experience on the side of feeling and will as at the same time they indefinitely prolong it on the side of thought. What James asks of us is not to add too much to experience through hypothetical considerations, and also not to mutilate it in its solid elements. We are absolutely sure only of what experience gives us; but we should accept experience wholly, and our feelings are a part of it by the same right as our perceptions, consequently, by the same right as "things." In the eyes of William James, the whole man counts.[45]

We now turn to the other major characteristic of James's view of consciousness, that of selectivity. James had said, in the very first chapter of the *Principles,* that "the pursuance of future ends and the choice of means for their attainment are thus the mark and criterion of the presence of mentality in a phenomenon" (Principles, I, 8). Beginning "at the bottom," he asks "what are our very senses themselves

[42] John Dewey, "Experience, Knowledge and Value—A Rejoinder," *The Philosophy of John Dewey,* ed. Paul Arthur Schilpp (New York, Tudor Publishing Co., 1951), p. 533, n. 16.

[43] Victor Lowe, "William James and Whitehead's Doctrine of Prehensions," *Understanding Whitehead* (Baltimore, The Johns Hopkins Press, 1962), p. 357.

[44] Richard Wollheim, *F. H. Bradley* (Baltimore, Penguin Books, 1959), p. 132. This criticism is answered by James in S.P.P., pp. 92–95.

[45] Henri Bergson, "On the Pragmatism of William James—Truth and Reality," *The Creative Mind* (New York, Philosophical Library, 1946), pp. 211–212.

but organs of selection" (Principles, I, 284). This is primarily by virtue of their negative activity. Though literally inundated by stimuli, they tend to avoid or even ignore all that does not pertain to the immediate field of the sense organ in question.

James holds that "out of what is in itself an undistinguishable, swarming *continuum,* devoid of distinction or emphasis, our senses make for us, by attending to this motion and ignoring that, a world full of contrasts, of sharp accents, of abrupt changes, of picturesque light and shade" (Principles, I, 284–285). The question remains as to why we choose to recognize some sensations rather than others? James is very clear on this matter. It is not because such sensations point to things, as Helmholtz had maintained, for things are "but special groups of sensible qualities, which happen practically or aesthetically to interest us, to which we therefore give substantive names and which we exalt to this exclusive status of independence and dignity" (Principles, I, 285). Interest, then, is the determining factor in our response to the welter of sensations, which make up our general field of primary experience. Even then, the notice given to such sensations would be short-lived except for habits of attention.

In his chapter on "Attention," James shows the interrelationship between interest, selectivity and personalizing activity at a primitive level, the field of our experience. "Millions of items of the outward order are present to my senses which never properly enter into my experience. Why? Because they have no *interest* for me. *My experience is what I agree to attend to.* Only those items which I *notice* shape my mind—without selective interest, experience is an utter chaos" (Principles, I, 402).

Attention varies in intensity, proportionate to the scope and intention of the individual interests in question. Furthermore, attention provides the continuity which is necessary to sustain the often accompanying activity of reflection. The work of attention, however, is not so obsessive as to feature a constant preoccupation with a single object. Unless there be considerable change within the experienced context of the object under question, particularly with regard to its relationship with other proximate aspects of one's experience, the attention will flag and be carried away by other more powerful impressions. In this way, only those objects or events of "interest" are "attended to" by the activity of consciousness, and then only so long as they are able to point to new dimensions of their own structure or on to wholly new aspects of the stream of experience. The field of experience, sensibly undergone, is related throughout. In his later thought, James gives this a metaphysical and cosmological dimension by referring to the concatenated type of unity, in which certain relationships of a disjunctive type, hang loose, but are nonetheless experienced and carry us along the flow, giving meaning all the while. It is important to realize that even in James's early, psychological version of the field of experience, the possibility of novelty does not conflict with the presence of sensible continuity. More, novelty can be seen as a function of continuity, for the meaning of novelty refers not only to totally new experiences, but also to prior experiences, when had from a different conceptual context. Novelty in this last sense is sustained by James's assertion that *"there is no property* ABSOLUTELY *essential to any one thing"* (Principles, II, 333). Each way of conceiving, to the extent that it involves a different property of the "thing" as the focal point, will thus provide for a different objective question and correspondingly a different experience. So basic in his thought is this allowance for novelty, that James urges us to *"make this ability to deal with* NOVEL data the technical differentia of reasoning" (Principles, II, 330).

What then becomes of the classical doctrine of essence? James, on empirical psychological grounds, answers directly: *"the only meaning of essence is teleological, and that classification and conception are purely teleological weapons of the mind.* The essence of a thing is that one of its properties which is so *important for my interests* that in comparison with it I may neglect the rest" (Principles, II, 335). The role of "interest" in the developing thought of James is crucial, for it ties together his early moral philosophy with his later psychology and of course with his pragmatism. As early as 1877 James had said that "the human mind always has and always will be able to interpret facts in accordance with its moral interests" (T.C. II, 27). In 1881, in an essay entitled "Reflex Action and Theism," James wrote that "perception and thinking are only there for behavior's sake" (W. B., 114). In the *Principles,* this concern is phrased in a text very symptomatic of James's basic attitude. Stressing our finite and practical nature, James affirms: "my thinking is first and last and always for the sake of my doing, and I can only do one thing at a time" (Principles, II, 333).

Much later, in 1907, when James was under severe attack by critics of his *Pragmatism,* he wrote a letter to Dickinson S. Miller, modifying somewhat the role given to interest. "All that Schiller and I contend for is that there is *no* 'truth' without *some* interest, and that non-intellectual interests play a part as well as intellectual ones" (L.W.J., II, 296). At no time, however, does he exclude the role of interest as a basic determinant for understanding man and the way in which he formulates the nature of his environment. This is, after all, a basic quality of our living situation and unlike most philosophers, James faces up to it with integrity. The notion of consciousness as selective and the notion of essence as teleological are thereby co-

respondents in human experience. The die is cast for the future of
James's thought and for more directions of contemporary philosophy
than commentators seem willing to admit. What Perry says of James
as a whole can be read as a specific summation of his *Principles of
Psychology.* "His object is man the organism, saving himself and asserting his interests within the natural environment." [46]

One of the ways in which James attempted to account for the relationship of human interests to the natural environment, was through
his development of the pragmatic method. Although it is true that
James saw this approach as but a "method of conducting discussions"
(T.C., II, 502), the publication of the *Pragmatism* involved him in
the most controversial period of his career.[47] While James, in his later
work on the *Meaning of Truth,* responded vigorously to his critics,
much of the difficulty could be traced to the infelicity of his own presentation in the *Pragmatism.* Furthermore, he indulged a tendency to
see this work as more closely related to the companion efforts of
Charles Sanders Peirce, John Dewey, and F. C. S. Schiller,[48] rather
than to the broader dimensions of his own thought. When put in context, pragmatism is for James a specifically epistemological statement
of the sprawling implications of the *Principles.* This is particularly
true of his emphasis on selective interest and the role of conflict in the
attainment of a fruitful relationship with our environment. In his chapter on "Common Sense," James writes:

> Ought not the existence of the various types of thinking which we
> have reviewed, each so splendid for certain purposes, yet all conflict-
> ing still, and neither one of them able to support a claim of absolute
> veracity, to awaken a presumption favorable to the pragmatistic view
> that all our theories are *instrumental,* are mental modes of *adaptation*
> to reality, rather than revelations or gnostic answers to some divinely
> instituted world-enigma? . . . Certainly the restlessness of the actual
> theoretic situation, the value for some purposes of each thought-level,

[46] Ralph Barton Perry, *Present Philosophical Tendencies* (New York, George
Braziller and Co., 1955), p. 350.

[47] The literature about James's pragmatism is more extensive than the combined literature about all the other aspects of his thought. This is a misleading
and unfortunate emphasis on the part of his critics. The most trenchant criticism of James's pragmatism is found in Arthur O. Lovejoy, *The Thirteen Prag-
matisms and Other Essays* (Baltimore, The Johns Hopkins Press, 1963).

[48] For the historical development of pragmatism cf. Perry, II, pp. 441–553
and Herbert Schneider, *A History of American Philosophy* (New York, Columbia University Press, 1963), pp. 433–459. An analysis of the fundamental
aspects of pragmatism, particularly with regard to the question of truth, is given
in Edward C. Moore, *American Pragmatism: Peirce, James and Dewey* (New
York, Columbia University Press, 1961). Pragmatism in its cultural setting is
discussed by C. Wright Mills, *Sociology and Pragmatism,* ed. Irving Louis Horo-
witz (New York, Paine-Whitman Publishers, 1964).

and the inability of either to expel the others decisively, suggest this pragmatistic view. [Pragm., 193–194.]

The "restlessness of the actual theoretic situation" is a corollary to James's long-standing commitment to the "stream of consciousness" metaphor as a description of how man actually is aware in his environment. From the perspective of psychology, "restlessness" and "selectivity" describes man's reaching out to the world. From the perspective of metaphysics, process rather than substance or essence is the crucial term in our analysis of reality. The central problem of pragmatism is to account for mediation between an interest-oriented self and a processive pluralistic world. To consider the claims of pragmatism apart from this dialectic, that is, to consider it simply as another type of theory about truth, is to be wide of the mark.[49] Indeed, nothing less than a full grasp of James's view of relations, in its psychological origins as well as the later statement in his *Essays on Radical Empiricism,* can give an adequate framework to the understanding of his pragmatism. James says as much when he states that:

> Primarily, and on the common-sense level, the truth of a state of mind means this function of *a leading that is worth while.* When a moment in our experience, of any kind whatever, inspires us with a thought that is true, that means that sooner or later we dip by that thought's guidance into the particulars of experience again and make advantageous connexion with them. [Pragm., 205.]

James then adds, significantly, that "this is a vague enough statement, but I beg you to retain it, for it is essential" (Pragm., 205). He considers it essential because it is a telescoped statement of his central insight, namely, that "knowing" is a process which takes place inside the relational field of concrete experience. Radical Empiricism was James's effort to describe this process in detail and deal with the vagueness of the earlier statements.

IV

On October 7, 1900, in a letter to Shadworth Hodgson, James wrote that "I am myself trying to get a non-dualistic formulation of the can-

[49] Instances of such narrow criticism of James's pragmatism are many. Cf., e.g., the essay written in 1908 by G. E. Moore, "William James 'Pragmatism' " *Philosophical Studies* (London, Routledge and Kegan Paul, 1958). A more sympathetic treatment of the logic of James's position is found in Morton White, *Toward Reunion in Philosophy* (New York, Atheneum, 1963), pp. 268–278. Both original statements and contemporary assessments of the controversy about pragmatism can be found in an excellent anthology, edited by Amelie Rorty, *Pragmatic Philosophy* (New York, Doubleday and Co., 1966).

vass of experience, and like all such people, can't take a book objectively, but for what it brings to my own mill, and I find your radical
dualism provoking, or at least disappointing" (T.C., I, 649). He had,
by this time, become fully aware of the impossibility of sustaining any
longer the explicit dualism as found in the *Principles*. Although he
struggled mightily with this difficulty in the extensive and important
final chapter of the *Principles,* devoted to "Necessary Truths and the
Effects of Experience," even there he accepted the existence of inner
and outer realities. Perry contends that James adopted the dualistic
position in his *Principles* as a convenience, but by the time of his
Presidential address to the American Psychological Association in
1894, under the title of "The Knowing of Things Together," he had
begun to abandon the method of dualism. (T.C., II, 364–365.) The
"Notebooks" devoted to the Psychological Seminary of 1895–1896
are filled with early statements of his radical empiricism.

The historical development and formulation of his radical empiricism is a very complex affair. Only the unabridged version of
Perry's *Thought and Character of William James* does it justice.[50]
James, himself, is not always clear as to the place of his radical empiricism in the over-all scheme of his thought. The reason for this
may be that despite its variant formulations, radical empiricism stands
for his entire philosophical position. One thing is obvious: to under-
play the importance of radical empiricism in any understanding of
James, is to risk missing him altogether.

James does say in one place that there is no "logical connection"
between pragmatism and radical empiricism (Pragm. IX), while elsewhere he sees pragmatism as an important step in "making radical
empiricism prevail" (M.T., XII). Taking radical empiricism as a
"general metaphysics," Perry sees pragmatism as providing a "metaphysics of truth which is consistent with that general metaphysics
which James advocates, through bringing the entire process of cognition within the field of possible experience" (T.C., II, 585). Perhaps
James's most explicit statement on the importance of his radical empiricism appears in a letter which he wrote to François Pillon, in 1904.
In that context, he isolates radical empiricism, pluralism, and theism
as the basic elements of his thought. To these he adds tychism, a notion taken from the thought of Charles Sanders Peirce which affirmed
the role of chance and spontaneity in the origin and activity of experience.

> My philosophy is what I call a radical empiricism, a pluralism, a
> "tychism," which represents order as being gradually won and always
> in the making. It is theistic, but not *essentially* so. It rejects all doc-

[50] A summary of Perry's version is found in his book: *In the Spirit of William James* (Bloomington, Indiana University Press, 1958), pp. 44–123.

trines of the Absolute. It is finitist; but it does not attribute to the question of the Infinite the great methodological importance which you and Renouvier attribute to it. I fear that you may find my system too *bottomless* and romantic. I am sure that, be it in the end judged true or false, it is essential to the evolution of clearness in philosophic thought that *someone* should defend a pluralistic empiricism radically. [L.W.J., II, 203–204.]

As can be readily seen from the texts included in the present volume, James states the essentials of radical empiricism in several different ways. For expository purposes, we isolate two persistent elements of his doctrine: first, his claim that matter and mind are but functional distinctions; and second, his metaphysical version of the position previously taken in the *Principles,* in which he held we have feelings of the relations which exist between objects of our experience. Quite aside from their critical function in his radical empiricism, a careful reading of James's unpublished papers will show these considerations, under diverse terminology, to be the central preoccupations of his entire speculative life.

James viewed his major problem as having to account for the relationship existing between the world of objects and the world of consciousness, without recourse to positing a dualism of subject and object. He approaches the problem in two controversial steps. First, in reply to the rhetorical question "Does Consciousness Exist?" James answers "No." Then he cautions:

> To deny plumply that 'consciousness' exists seems so absurd on the face of it—for undeniably 'thoughts' do exist—that I fear some readers will follow me no farther. Let me then immediately explain that I mean only to deny that the word stands for an entity, but to insist most emphatically that it does stand for a function. [E.R.E., 3.]

What James wishes to avoid is the view of consciousness as an "aboriginal stuff or quality of being," that is, as a metaphysical reality. He holds that "the attributes 'subject' and 'object,' 'represented and representative,' 'thing and thought' mean, then, a practical distinction which is of a FUNCTIONAL order only, and not at all ontological as understood by classical dualism" (E.R.E., 235).

By way of supporting this claim of a simply functional differentiation between thought and thing, James introduces his notion of "pure experience." This is the name he gives "to the immediate flux of life which furnishes the material to our later reflection with its conceptual categories" (E.R.E., 93). As a descriptive category, "pure experience" is more expansive than the realities of thought and thing, and cannot be reduced to any other single substance.

There is little question that this doctrine of James's remains somewhat ambiguous in meaning as well as in the various ways in which James chooses to develop it. Although he came to it comparatively late, James stresses the importance of working out his meaning of pure experience.[51] He writes to Theodore Flournoy, in 1903: "What I want to get at, and let no interruptions interfere, is (at last) my *system of tychistic and pluralistic philosophy of pure experience*" (L.W.J., II, 187). Acknowledging its ambiguity, Perry can still say James's "notion of pure experience was his deepest insight, his most constructive idea, and his favorite solvent of traditional philosophical difficulties" (T.C., II, 388).

Despite interpretations to the contrary, James did not see the meaning of "pure experience" as a monistic type of catch-all which could account for all other versions of reality. The blame for these misinterpretations clearly falls on James and his use of the word "stuff." Bertrand Russell, who borrowed the term from James, later lamented its use and the neutral monism which he thought it implied.[52] The difficulty in James's use of the term arises in his essay on "Does 'Consciousness' Exist?" in which he refers to "pure experience" as a "stuff" (E.R.E., 4). Within that same essay, however, James corrects this version and explicitly holds "there is no *general* stuff of which experience at large is made" (E.R.E., 26).[53] James then wavered between a totally pluralistic and ad-hoc statement about the meaning of "pure experience," and the parallel attempt to account for the general features of experience as we have it. By way of illustration, he first states that "there are as many stuffs as there are 'natures' in the things experienced" (E.R.E., 26). He then goes on to say "experience is only a collective name for all these sensible natures, and save for time and space (and if you like, for 'being') there appears no universal element of which all things are made" (E.R.E., 27). In effect, James appeals to direct experience but seems reluctant to let go of some of the large organizing categories, which in other philosophical contexts are seen as *a priori*. In a perceptive essay on James's radical empiricism, John Smith contends that James never resolved this problem in his own

[51] Cf. Perry, T.C., I, 588, where he states that Ernst Mach's work in 1897, *The Analysis of Sensations* (New York, Dover Publications, Inc., 1959), should be considered as a precursor to James's doctrine of pure experience.

[52] Cf. W. T. Stace, "Russell's Neutral Monism," *The Philosophy of Bertrand Russell*, ed. Paul Arthur Schilpp (Evanston, Tudor Publishing Co., 1946), pp. 353–355, and in the same volume, Russell's "Reply to Criticisms," pp. 698, 706–710. The complexity of James's view of consciousness is examined by Charles Sanders Peirce, *Collected Papers*, Vol. VIII, ed., Arthur W. Burks (Cambridge, Harvard University Press, 1958), par. 270–305; pp. 195–208.

[53] Few commentators have caught this shift in James's language and the only one to probe its implications is Arthur F. Bentley in his brilliant but chaotic essay, "The Jamesian Datum," *Inquiry Into Inquiries*, ed. Sidney Ratner (Boston, The Beacon Press, 1954), pp. 230–267.

thought.[54] The still open question is whether it can be resolved as an extension of James's radically empirical point of view.

It is unfortunate that James did not stay with the language he utilized in preparing for his Psychological Seminary of 1895–1896. At that time, he resorted to the metaphor of "fields" in order to account descriptively for the primal activity of the process of experience. James wished to show that in the most fundamental sense, the question which asks "what" is a misleading one, when addressed to the nature of experience. Smith correctly assesses James, when he writes "pure experience has no general nature of its own. It is a pure *that,* a virtual somewhat, to be sure, but unknown as this specific *what* until it is 'taken,' talked about, analyzed, identified, classified and categorized." [55] In other language, this is precisely what James was getting at in his "Notebook" preparations of 1895–1896. At that time, James saw the "final content" to be "a plurality of fields more or less ejective to each other, but still continuous in various ways" (T.C., II, 365). From this point of view, he hoped to avoid the reduction of experience to either "pure ego" or "material substance." James admitted that "field," as a vague and necessarily complex metaphor involving a plurality of interacting aspects, would not give "stability." Indeed, he adds that such an approach results in an "almost maddening restlessness." James insists, however, that by moving in this direction we gain "concreteness" (T.C., II, 365). He never adequately developed this language of "fields" and "ejects" relative to his doctrine of "pure experience." This is a real loss, for it should not be overlooked that in contemporary thought, "field" is a highly valuable metaphor in all the major disciplines, precisely because of its ability to convey process and concretion.

As an overview, perhaps we should say of his notion of "pure experience" what James himself said in answer to the question, how do finite beings come to be? "Who knows? The question of Being is the darkest in all Philosophy. All of us are beggars here" (S.P.P., 46). Is not the notion of "pure experience," James's way of formulating what Parmenides, Schelling and Heidegger look upon as the first, if not perhaps the only question. Why is there something rather than nothing? While James does not phrase his thought that way, of one thing we can be sure: he does not utilize the notion of "pure experience" to close off the analysis of the real but to give it new impetus and send it away from traditional but narrow categories. Perhaps he meant it as a heuristic device, as a sort of waiting game. After all, the phenomena of extrasensory perception, as well as the reach of cosmological experi-

---

[54] John E. Smith, "Radical Empiricism," *Proceedings of the Aristotelian Society,* LXV (March, 1965), pp. 205–218.
[55] *Ibid.,* p. 209.

ence had convinced James that to appropriate the meaning of the world in an ultimate and final way, simply by virtue of the categories of western epistemology, was pretense of a high order. Holding, then, to the doctrine of "pure experience" enables James to say that "the world is in so far forth a pluralism of which the unity is not fully experienced as yet" (E.R.E., 89).

The second element to be discussed in this brief analysis of James's radical empiricism is his doctrine of relations. In contrast to the notion of "pure experience," James is far more explicit and consistent when he discusses relations. A major reason for this better formulation is the longevity of James's concern with this problem. The meaning of relations occupied him from the very beginning of his thought. In his essay on "The Psychology of William James in Relation to Philosophy," George S. Brett comments on the importance of James by virtue of his doctrine of relations. Having gone beyond Locke and Hume, Brett sees James as aware that "the status of relations is always a crucial question. To ignore them is to leave reality disconnected and to make the connecting parts of speech superfluous." [56]

James was always bothered about the dangers in a disconnected or atomistic view of the universe. What he feared most in that regard was the introduction of trans-empirical constructs, used to leap over the separateness created when relations were ignored. This concern accounted for his long-standing hostility to what he called the "block-universe" of the absolute idealists, and generated his polemical exchanges with Bradley, [57] Royce and the Hegelian school. In opposition to those thinkers, like Bradley, who would heal a disconnected universe by an appeal to "a higher Reality which at once transcends, and yet re-includes, the sphere of mere feeling," [58] James singles out the relationship of continuous transition as immediately felt.

Continuous transition is one sort of a conjunctive relation; and to be a radical empiricist means to hold fast to this conjunctive relation

[56] George S. Brett, "The Psychology of William James in Relation to Philosophy," *In Commemoration of William James—1842–1910,* ed. Horace M. Kallen (New York, Columbia University Press, 1942), p. 83.

[57] Despite his unswerving and thorough disagreement with James on the matter of relations as immediately felt, Bradley can say, "I can imagine no task more interesting to, and more incumbent on, the disciples of Professor James, than to make an attempt in earnest to explain and to develop his doctrine of Radical Empiricism," *Essays on Truth and Reality* (Oxford, Oxford University Press, 1962), pp. 157–158. The Bradley-James analysis of this problem has been recently clarified with the publication of *Ten Unpublished Letters from William James, 1842–1910, to Francis Herbert Bradley, 1846–1924,* with Introduction and Notes by J. C. Kenna. *Mind,* Vol. xxxv, No. 299 (July, 1966), 309–331.

[58] *Ibid.,* p. 157.

of all others, for this is the strategic point, the position through which, if a hole be made, all the corruptions of dialectics and all the metaphysical fictions pour into our philosophy. [E.R.E., 48.]

James insists that this experience of continuity is "felt" and not just posited or "talked about" as a logical connector. The principle of unity is thereby not imposed from without but is rather found as an ongoing and intrinsic activity of the flow of experience. Holding to the "fact of coalescence of next with next in concrete experience," James deftly moves between the Scylla of a disjointed, atomistic world-view and the Charybdis of a world totally unified by a "purely intellectual principle" (P.U., 326). Also rejecting pan-psychism, James refuses to give any single perspective a privileged place from which to deal with the problem of how the world is continuous. He sees no alternative but to admit that "life is in the transitions as much as in the terms connected" (E.R.E., 87). Given the multiplicity of our experiences we still have a "universe," for "these relations of continuous transition experienced are what make our experiences cognitive. In the simplest and completest cases the experiences are cognitive of one another" (E.R.E., 87–88). Again, as in the *Principles* and the *Pragmatism,* we have intelligibility without a principle of total meaning, and the experience of continuity without the knowledge of finality.

In awarding this informing dimension to experience, James becomes subjected to those series of charges which come under the generic name of anti-intellectualism. But this attitude also gives him the option to entertain events and leads systematically rejected by more closed versions of the real. By assuming the presence of an extra-cognitive source of informing, James anticipates the existentialist, psychoanalytical, and modern aesthetic versions of human knowing. As early as the *Principles,* James held the "relation of knowing" to be "the most mysterious thing in the world" (Principles, I, 216). Leaving no stone unturned, he opens himself to a variety of experiences not usually found within the ken of philosophical analysis.[59] Some of these experiences have been regarded as beyond the reach of philosophy, as for example, the mystical experiences; while others have often been viewed as the "underworld of philosophy," as instance the

[59] Given the high seriousness of much of contemporary philosophy, it might be well to note here the remark of Gilbert Ryle that James "restored to philosophy, what had been missing since Hume, that sense of the ridiculous which saves one from taking seriously everything that is said solemnly." "Introduction," *The Revolution in Philosophy,* eds. A. J. Ayer, *et alii* (New York, St. Martin's Press, 1957), p. 9. It is also worth noting, in this context, that students of linguistic philosophy would better serve their own purpose if they were to analyze the wealth of detail in the complete *Principles,* rather than mounting critical attacks on the *Pragmatism.* Wittgenstein, for one, was well aware of the importance of the *Principles,* especially for its insight to the problems of meaning and language.

instinctual, the habitual, and, above all, the entire range of phenomena grouped under the heading of extrasensory perception. The latter area of concern, which James called a "wild-beast of the philosophic desert" (P.U., 330), did not endear him to his philosophical colleagues. Yet no matter the origins, James took experiences at dead-reckoning and kept to a minimum the multiplication of concepts stemming from a single experiential root.

James contended it was better to be prodigal in a descriptive sense, following all the relationships offered, than to effect "insulating cuts" as "artificial products of the conceptualizing faculty," bent on unifying experience (P.U., 326). In this connection, he warns further against "vicious intellectualism," by which he means "the treating of a name as excluding from the fact named what the name's definition fails positively to include" (P.U., 60). Utilizing this stricture, James cuts into one of the central and most pervasive sophistries of philosophy, namely, the generating of an elaborate network of concepts, begetting and begotten, one by the other, yet totally uprooted from the concrete. He would hold that it is not increased conceptual activity which forces us to reconsider our views, but rather new experience, in its "ways of *boiling over* and making us correct our present formulas" (Pragm., 222). For those who seek intelligent control and insight to our actual situation, it should be remembered that the real drama of cognition is found in the network of relations, which web our experience of objects and events. The viability and relevance of our concepts is thereby directly related to James's contention that "knowledge of sensible realities thus comes to life inside the tissue of experience. It is *made;* and made by relations that unroll themselves in time" (E.R.E., 57).

The later import of radical empiricism is found in its significance for James's cosmology. Although *A Pluralistic Universe* is concerned with these questions in theme, much of the work is devoted to "the present situation in philosophy." James wanted very much to show that he could incisively analyze the philosophical positions then extant. The joy of his rhetoric, notwithstanding, he never quite manages this objective. His interpretations of the German philosophical tradition are particularly wide of the mark. Nevertheless, the leads furnished in *A Pluralistic Universe,* and later developed somewhat in the unfinished *Some Problems of Philosophy,* give us real possibilities for effecting a contemporary cosmology.

Significantly, James faces up to the paradox bequeathed to man by the Copernican revolution. Post-Copernican man, no longer the center of the universe by virtue of his planetary setting, has had to affirm his centrality and dignity by the humanizing of all entities and events, including the cosmos itself. It is this last concern which particularly occupies contemporary man. We can learn here from James, who knew from the first, that if human life were to maintain itself in its most significant and creative aspects, it would have to build itself into the apparently limitless and awesome dimensions of space. The same tentative and free-wheeling character of his thought which provided such a scandal to traditional philosophy should appear to us, bereft of an adequate cosmology, as a plausible and fruitful point of departure.

From James's perspective, the framing of a viable cosmology is not to be accomplished by a capitulation to the majesty of cosmic life. In *The Varieties of Religious Experience,* James urges "so long as we deal with the cosmic and the general, we deal only with the symbols of reality, but *as soon as we deal with private and personal phenomena as such, we deal with realities in the completest sense of the term*" (V.R.E., 498). And he never relents in his fidelity to a highly personalized view of conscious life. The universe may be pluralistic and unfinished for James, but he sees this as liberating with regard to the human situation. "In a word, the believer is continuous to his own consciousness, at any rate, with a wider self from which saving experiences flow in" (P.U., 307).

Taking radical empiricism seriously, then, involves an acceptance of a far wider range of continuous and experienced relationships than that usually associated with the normal confines of the self. It means building novelty and chance into the very fabric of our understanding of the universe. And a commitment to a radically empirical world suggests "that our natural experience, our strictly moralistic and prudential experience, may be only a fragment of real human experience" (P.U., 306). James would agree that philosophy cannot avoid confronting a "sheer datum at some point." Yet he also argues for the "ultimate origins of things" as being "both plural and spontaneous" (T.C., II, 374). And so far as a systematic philosophical interpretation is concerned, James's viewpoint denies that any single perspective or single theoretical formulation can do justice to what is a processive type of unity, held together loosely, literally "after the pattern of our daily experience" (P.U., 76). Because of the on-going and informative quality of continuous transitions, the attainment of deep insight to our "inner life" leads us to participate in no less than the very rhythm of the world at large.

> In principle, then, as I said, intellectualism's edge is broken; it can only approximate to reality, and its logic is inapplicable to our inner life, which spurns its vetoes and mocks at its impossibilities. Every bit of us at every moment is part and parcel of a wider self, it quivers along various radii like the wind-rose on a compass, and the actual in it is continuously one with possibles not yet in our present sight. [P.U., 289.]

V

The philosophy of William James calls for a never-ending series of descriptions and analyses, each from a specific vantage point but no one of them burdened with having to account for everything. It is a world far better expressed by poets such as Gerard M. Hopkins and Dylan Thomas, and painters such as Hans Hofmann and Jackson Pollock, than by anything we can say here. It is a world-view corroborated daily by descriptions in other disciplines, especially morphological analyses, various "models" of human behavior and contemporary art forms, particularly the extraordinary reconstruction by modern sculpture, of the supposedly fixed character of natural materials. The very hybridization of disciplines and of aesthetic realities points to the soundness of James's critique of the "block universe," in which all could be viewed from one principle of explanation. Sound also is his critique of the overextension of formal logic as applied to on-going realities.

If it is true that James's radically empirical philosophy and particularly his notions of "pure experience" and a "pluralistic universe" leave many questions unanswered and even unformulated, it is also true that his thought wedges us into areas in which genuine problems exist. His treatment of these problems may or may not be adequate, but there is seldom a concern in James's work which does not portend some grave and seminal aspect of the human situation.

Admittedly, we have touched only bare bones in this treatment of the rich legacy of James's writing. It is to be hoped that the themes which occupied him will be seen in their full contemporaneity. On the basis of increasing evidence in our own time, the judgments of William James about the constituency of the human personality, the network of relations which are our binding in the world of experience, and his assessment of the quality and importance of religious and psychic experience, seem to have been extraordinarily prescient.

CHRONOLOGY

1906	Acting Professor for half-term at Stanford University. (Interrupted by San Francisco earthquake.)
1906	Lowell Institute lectures, subsequently published as *Pragmatism*.
1907	Resigned all active duties at Harvard.
1908	Hibbert lectures at Manchester College, Oxford; subsequently published as *A Pluralistic Universe*.
1910	August 26. Died at Chocorua, N.H.

William James was the eldest of five children. His brothers and sister, with their dates, were: Henry, 1843–1916; Garth Wilkinson, 1845–1883; Robertson, 1846–1910; Alice, 1848–1892. He and his wife had five children: Henry, William, Hermann, Margaret Mary and Alexander Robertson.

BIBLIOGRAPHIC ABBREVIATIONS
AND EDITOR'S NOTES ON THE TEXT

The following abbreviations have been used in the "Introduction" and for purpose of identifying the sources of the selected essays. The original publication dates of James's books are given in parentheses. The "Annotated Bibliography" will give the full context for James's publications.

I—WORKS OF WILLIAM JAMES

Principles—*The Principles of Psychology* (New York, Henry Holt and Co., 1927) (1890)

P.B.C.—*Psychology. Briefer Course.* (New York, Henry Holt and Co., 1923) (1892)

W.B.—*The Will to Believe and Others Essays in Popular Philosophy* (New York, Henry Holt and Co., 1912) (1897)

T.T.—*Talks to Teachers on Psychology: and to Students on Some of Life's Ideals* (New York, Henry Holt and Company, 1912) (1899)

V.R.E.—*The Varieties of Religious Experience* (New York, Longman's Green and Co., 1928) (1902)

Pragm.—*Pragmatism: A New Name for Some Old Ways of Thinking,* (New York, Longman's Green and Co., 1947) (1907)

M.T.—*The Meaning of Truth* (New York, Longman's, Green and Co., 1932) (1909)

P.U.—*A Pluralistic Universe* (New York, Longman's Green and Co., 1947) (1909)

S.P.P.—*Some Problems of Philosophy* (New York, Longman's Green and Co., 1948 (1911). Posthumous, ed. by Henry James, Jr.

M.S.—*Memories and Studies* (Longman's Green and Co., 1911) (1911) Posthumous, ed. by Henry James, Jr.

ERE.—*Essays in Radical Empiricism* (New York, Longman's Green and Co., 1938, 1947) (1912). Posthumous, ed. by R. B. Perry.

C.E.R.—*Collected Essays and Reviews* (Longman's Green and Co., 1920) (1920). Posthumous, ed. by R. B. Perry.

P.R.—*William James on Psychical Research* (New York, The Viking Press, 1960). Posthumous, ed. by Gardner Murphy and Robert O. Ballou.

U.P.—"Unpublished Papers," Houghton Library, Harvard University. References given are to alphabetized boxes of "Loose Notes."

II—OTHER WORKS PERTAINING TO JAMES

L.R.H.J.—*The Literary Remains of the Late Henry James,* ed. with an introduction by William James (Boston, James R. Osgood and Co., 1885).

L.W.J.—*The Letters of William James,* ed. by Henry James, Jr. 2 vols. (Boston, Atlantic Monthly Press, 1920).

T.C.—Ralph Barton Perry, *The Thought and Character of William James,* 2 vols. (Boston, Little, Brown and Co., 1935)

III—EDITORIAL NOTES

Aside from the excerpts from the *Letters,* the introductory material on "Personal Depression and Recovery" and the two brief statements on radical empiricism in Section III, all the material in this volume represents complete essays. Information on the original sources of these selections as well as James's footnotes have been retained. In the essays themselves, unless otherwise noted, the reference to "ed.," is to Ralph Barton Perry who edited many of these pieces after James's death. There are several small instances of repetition. We have not excised these passages in deference to the integrity of the essay in question. Further, such material is an indication of what James considered still viable in later formulations of his position. Actually, the only editorial change in the essays themselves occurs in the deletion of some awkward cross-referencing and of several transition remarks at the beginning or end of each essay. With the shifting of these essays into a different context, these transitional phrases no longer serve their original purpose.

The Writings of

WILLIAM JAMES

$$\sim i \sim$$

Personal Depression
and Recovery

The following texts are excerpts from materials by Henry James, Sr., and William James, recording their hallucinatory experiences. Added also are the "Crisis" texts from William James's diary of 1870.

HENRY JAMES, SENIOR*

One day, however, towards the close of May, having eaten a comfortable dinner, I remained sitting at the table after the family had dispersed, idly gazing at the embers in the grate, thinking of nothing, and feeling only the exhilaration incident to a good digestion, when suddenly—in a lightning-flash as it were—"fear came upon me, and trembling, which made all my bones to shake." To all appearance it was a perfectly insane and abject terror, without ostensible cause, and only to be accounted for, to my perplexed imagination, by some damnèd shape squatting invisible to me within the precincts of the room, and raying out from his fetid personality influences fatal to life. The thing had not lasted ten seconds before I felt myself a wreck, that is, reduced from a state of firm, vigorous, joyful manhood to one of almost helpless infancy. The only self-control I was capable of exerting was to keep my seat. I felt the greatest desire to run incontinently to the foot of the stairs and shout for help to my wife,—to run to the roadside even, and appeal to the public to protect me; but by an immense effort I controlled these frenzied impulses, and determined not to budge from my chair till I had recovered my lost self-possession.

* From: *Society the Redeemed Form of Man* (Cambridge, 1879), 44–49.

This purpose I held to for a good long hour, as I reckoned time, beat upon meanwhile by an ever-growing tempest of doubt, anxiety, and despair, with absolutely no relief from any truth I had ever encountered save a most pale and distant glimmer of the Divine existence,— when I resolved to abandon the vain struggle, and communicate without more ado what seemed my sudden burden of inmost, implacable unrest to my wife.

Now, to make a long story short, this ghastly condition of mind continued with me, with gradually lengthening intervals of relief, for two years, and even longer. I consulted eminent physicians, who told me that I had doubtless overworked my brain, an evil for which no remedy existed in medicine, but only in time, and patience, and growth into improved physical conditions. They all recommended by way of hygiene a resort to the water-cure treatment, a life in the open air, cheerful company, and so forth, and thus quietly and skilfully dismissed me to my own spiritual medication. At first, when I began to feel a half-hour's respite from acute mental anguish, the bottomless mystery of my disease completely fascinated me. The more, however, I worried myself with speculations about the cause of it, the more the mystery deepened, and the deeper also grew my instinct of resentment at what seemed so needless an interference with my personal liberty. I went to a famous water-cure, which did nothing towards curing my malady but enrich my memory with a few morbid specimens of English insularity and prejudice, but it did much to alleviate it by familiarizing my senses with the exquisite and endless charm of English landscape, and giving me my first full rational relish of what may be called England's pastoral beauty. To be sure I had spent a few days in Devonshire when I was young, but my delight then was simple enthusiasm, was helpless æsthetic intoxication in fact. The "cure" was situated in a much less lovely but still beautiful country, on the borders of a famous park, to both of which, moreover, it gave you unlimited right of possession and enjoyment. At least this was the way it always struck my imagination. The thoroughly disinterested way the English have of looking at their own hills and vales,—the indifferent, contemptuous, and as it were *disowning* mood they habitually put on towards the most ravishing pastoral loveliness man's sun anywhere shines upon,—gave me always the sense of being a discoverer of these things, and of a consequent right to enter upon their undisputed possession. At all events the rich light and shade of English landscape, the gorgeous cloud-pictures that forever dimple and diversify her fragrant and palpitating bosom, have awakened a tenderer chord in me than I have ever felt at home almost; and time and again while living at this dismal water-cure, and listening to its endless "strife of tongues" about diet, and regimen, and disease, and politics, and parties, and persons, I have said to myself: *The curse of mankind, that which keeps our manhood so little and so depraved, is its sense of selfhood, and the absurd abominable opinionativeness it engenders. How sweet it would be to find oneself no longer man, but one of those innocent and ignorant sheep pasturing upon that placid hillside, and drinking in eternal dew and freshness from nature's lavish bosom!*

But let me hasten to the proper upshot of this incident. My stay at the water-cure, unpromising as it was in point of physical results, made me conscious erelong of a most important change operating in the sphere of my will and understanding. It struck me as very odd, soon after my breakdown, that I should feel no longing to resume the work which had been interrupted by it; and from that day to this—nearly thirty-five years—I have never once cast a retrospective glance, even of curiosity, at the immense piles of manuscript which had erewhile so absorbed me. I suppose if any one had designated me previous to that event as an earnest seeker after truth, I should myself have seen nothing unbecoming in the appellation. But now—within two or three months of my catastrophe—I felt sure I had never caught a glimpse of truth. My present consciousness was exactly that of an utter and plenary destitution of truth. Indeed an ugly suspicion had more than once forced itself upon me, that I had never really wished the truth, but only to ventilate my own ability in discovering it. I was getting sick to death in fact with a sense of my downright intellectual poverty and dishonesty. My studious mental activity had served manifestly to base a mere "castle in the air," and the castle had vanished in a brief bitter moment of time, leaving not a wrack behind. I never felt again the most passing impulse, even, to look where it stood, having done with it forever. Truth indeed! How should a beggar like me be expected to discover it? How should any man of woman born pretend to such ability? Truth must *reveal itself* if it would be known, and even then how imperfectly known at best! For truth is God, the omniscient and omnipotent God, and who shall pretend to comprehend that great and adorable perfection? And yet who that aspires to the name of man, would not cheerfully barter all he knows of life for a bare glimpse of the hem of its garment?

WILLIAM JAMES *

"Whilst in this state of philosophic pessimism and general depression of spirits about my prospects, I went one evening into a dressing-room in the twilight to procure some article that was there; when suddenly there fell upon me without any warning, just as if it came out of the darkness, a horrible fear of my own existence. Simultaneously there arose in my mind the image of an epileptic patient whom I had seen in the asylum, a black-haired youth with greenish skin, entirely idiotic, who used to sit all day on one of the benches, or rather shelves against the wall, with his knees drawn up against his chin, and the coarse gray undershirt, which was his only garment, drawn over them inclosing his entire figure. He sat there like a sort of sculptured Egyptian cat or Peruvian mummy, moving nothing but his black eyes and looking absolutely non-human. This image and my fear entered into a species of combination with each other. *That shape am I,* I felt, potentially. Nothing that I possess can defend me against that fate, if the hour for it should strike for me as it struck for him. There was such a horror of him, and such a perception of my own merely momentary discrepancy from him, that it was as if something hitherto solid within my breast gave way entirely, and I became a mass of quivering fear. After this the universe was changed for me altogether. I awoke morning after morning with a horrible dread at the pit of my stomach, and with a sense of the insecurity of life that I never knew before, and that I have never felt since.[1] It was like a revelation; and although the immediate feelings passed away, the experience has made me sympathetic with the morbid feelings of others ever since. It gradually faded, but for months I was unable to go out into the dark alone.

"In general I dreaded to be left alone. I remember wondering how other people could live, how I myself had ever lived, so unconscious of that pit of insecurity beneath the surface of life. My mother in particular, a very cheerful person, seemed to me a perfect paradox in

---

* From: V.R.E., 160–161.

[1] Compare Bunyan: "There was I struck into a very great trembling, insomuch that at some times I could, for days together, feel my very body, as well as my mind, to shake and totter under the sense of the dreadful judgment of God, that should fall on those that have sinned that most fearful and unpardonable sin. I felt also such clogging and heat at my stomach, by reason of this my terror, that I was, especially at some times, as if my breast-bone would have split asunder. . . . Thus did I wind, and twine, and shrink, under the burden that was upon me; which burden also did so oppress me that I could neither stand, nor go, nor lie, either at rest or quiet."

her unconsciousness of danger, which you may well believe I was very careful not to disturb by revelations of my own state of mind. I have always thought that this experience of melancholia of mine had a religious bearing." "I mean that the fear was so invasive and powerful that if I had not clung to scripture-texts like 'The eternal God is my refuge,' etc., 'Come unto me, all ye that labor and are heavy-laden,' etc., 'I am the resurrection and the life,' etc., I think I should have grown really insane."

WILLIAM JAMES

Feb. 1, 1870 *

. . . "Today I about touched bottom, and perceive plainly that I must face the choice with open eyes: shall I frankly throw the moral business overboard, as one unsuited to my innate aptitudes, or shall I follow it, and it alone, making everything else merely stuff for it? I will give the latter alternative a fair trial. Who knows but the moral interest may become developed . . . Hitherto I have tried to fire myself with the moral interest, as an aid in the accomplishing of certain utilitarian ends."

WILLIAM JAMES

April 30, 1870 †

"I think that yesterday was a crisis in my life. I finished the first part of Renouvier's second "Essais" and see no reason why his definition of Free Will—"the sustaining of a thought *because I choose to* when I might have other thoughts"—need be the definition of an illusion. At any rate, I will assume for the present—until next year—that it is no illusion. My first act of free will shall be to believe in free will. For the remainder of the year, I will abstain from the mere speculation and contemplative *Grüblei* in which my nature takes most delight, and

* From: "Diary," T.C. I, 322.
† From: "Diary," L.W.J., I, 147–148.

voluntarily cultivate the feeling of moral freedom, by reading books favorable to it, as well as by acting. After the first of January, my callow skin being somewhat fledged, I may perhaps return to metaphysical study and skepticism without danger to my powers of action. For the present then remember: care little for speculation; much for the *form* of my action; recollect that only when habits of order are formed can we advance to really interesting fields of action—and consequently accumulate grain on grain of willful choice like a very miser; never forgetting how one link dropped undoes an indefinite number. *Principiis obsta*—Today has furnished the exceptionally passionate initiative which Bain posits as needful for the acquisition of habits. I will see to the sequel. Not in maxims, not in *Anschauungen,* but in accumulated *acts* of thought lies salvation. *Passer outre.* Hitherto, when I have felt like taking a free initiative, like daring to act originally, without carefully waiting for contemplation of the external world to determine all for me, suicide seemed the most manly form to put my daring into; now, I will go a step further with my will, not only act with it, but believe as well; believe in my individual reality and creative power. My belief, to be sure, *can't* be optimistic—but I will posit life (the real, the good) in the self-governing *resistance* of the ego to the world. Life shall [be built in] * doing and suffering and creating."

* Ms. doubtful.

~ ii ~

Psychological Foundations

The material in this section represents basic elements in James's psychology and provides the background for an understanding of his philosophical development.

HABIT*

ITS IMPORTANCE FOR PSYCHOLOGY

There remains a condition of general neural activity so important as to deserve a chapter by itself—I refer to the aptitude of the nerve-centres, especially of the hemispheres, for acquiring habits. *An acquired habit, from the physiological point of view, is nothing but a new pathway of discharge formed in the brain, by which certain incoming currents ever after tend to escape.* That is the thesis of this chapter; and we shall see in the later and more psychological chapters that such functions as the association of ideas, perception, memory, reasoning, the education of the will, etc., etc., can best be understood as results of the formation *de novo* of just such pathways of discharge.

Habit has a physical basis. The moment one tries to define what habit is, one is led to the fundamental properties of matter. The laws of Nature are nothing but the immutable habits which the different elementary sorts of matter follow in their actions and reactions upon each other. In the organic world, however, the habits are more variable than this. Even instincts vary from one individual to another of a kind; and are modified in the same individual, as we shall later see, to

* From: P.B.C., 134–150.

suit the exigencies of the case. On the principles of the atomistic phi-losophy the habits of an elementary particle of matter cannot change, because the particle is itself an unchangeable thing; but those of a com-pound mass of matter can change, because they are in the last instance due to the structure of the compound, and either outward forces or inward tensions can, from one hour to another, turn that structure into something different from what it was. That is, they can do so if the body be plastic enough to maintain its integrity, and be not dis-rupted when its structure yields. The change of structure here spoken of need not involve the outward shape; it may be invisible and molec-ular, as when a bar of iron becomes magnetic or crystalline through the action of certain outward causes, or india-rubber becomes friable, or plaster "sets." All these changes are rather slow; the material in question opposes a certain resistance to the modifying cause, which it takes time to overcome, but the gradual yielding whereof often saves the material from being disintegrated altogether. When the structure has yielded, the same inertia becomes a condition of its comparative permanence in the new form, and of the new habits the body then manifests. *Plasticity,* then, in the wide sense of the word, means the possession of a structure weak enough to yield to an influence, but strong enough not to yield all at once. Each relatively stable phase of equilibrium in such a structure is marked by what we may call a new set of habits. Organic matter, especially nervous tissue, seems en-dowed with a very extraordinary degree of plasticity of this sort; so that we may without hesitation lay down as our first proposition the following: that *the phenomena of habit in living beings are due to the plasticity of the organic materials of which their bodies are composed.*

The philosophy of habit is thus, in the first instance, a chapter in physics rather than physiology or psychology. That it is at bottom a physical principle, is admitted by all good recent writers on the sub-ject. They call attention to analogues of acquired habits exhibited by dead matter. Thus, M. Léon Dumont writes:

> Every one knows how a garment, after having been worn a certain time, clings to the shape of the body better than when it was new; there has been a change in the tissue, and this change is a new habit of cohesion. A lock works better after being used some time; at the outset more force was required to overcome certain roughness in the mechanism. The overcoming of their resistance is a phenomenon of habituation. It costs less trouble to fold a paper when it has been folded already; . . . and just so in the nervous system the impressions of outer objects fashion for themselves more and more appropriate paths, and these vital phenomena recur under similar excitements from with-out, when they have been interrupted a certain time.

Not in the nervous system alone. A scar anywhere is a *locus mi-noris resistentiæ,* more liable to be abraded, inflamed, to suffer pain and cold, than are the neighboring parts. A sprained ankle, a dislocated arm, are in danger of being sprained or dislocated again; joints that have once been attacked by rheumatism or gout, mucous membranes that have been the seat of catarrh, are with each fresh recurrence more prone to a relapse, until often the morbid state chronically substitutes itself for the sound one. And in the nervous system itself it is well known how many so-called functional diseases seem to keep themselves going simply because they happen to have once begun; and how the forcible cutting short by medicine of a few attacks is often sufficient to enable the physiological forces to get possession of the field again, and to bring the organs back to functions of health. Epilepsies, neuralgias, convulsive affections of various sorts, insomnias, are so many cases in point. And, to take what are more obviously habits, the success with which a "weaning" treatment can often be applied to the victims of unhealthy indulgence of passion, or of mere complaining or irascible disposition, shows us how much the morbid manifestations themselves were due to the mere inertia of the nervous organs, when once launched on a false career.

Habits are due to pathways through the nerve-centres. If habits are due to the plasticity of materials to outward agents, we can immediately see to what outward influences, if to any, the brain-matter is plastic. Not to mechanical pressures, not to thermal changes, not to any of the forces to which all the other organs of our body are exposed; for, as we [previously] saw, Nature has so blanketed and wrapped the brain about that the only impressions that can be made upon it are through the blood, on the one hand, and the sensory nerve-roots, on the other; and it is to the infinitely attenuated currents that pour in through these latter channels that the hemispherical cortex shows itself to be so peculiarly susceptible. The currents, once in, must find a way out. In getting out they leave their traces in the paths which they take. The only thing they *can* do, in short, is to deepen old paths or to make new ones; and the whole plasticity on the brain sums itself up in two words when we call it an organ in which currents pouring in from the sense-organs make with extreme facility paths which do not easily disappear. For, of course, a simple habit, like every other nervous event—the habit of snuffling, for example, or of putting one's hands into one's pockets, or of biting one's nails—is, mechanically, nothing but a reflex discharge; and its anatomical substratum must be a path in the system. The most complex habits, as we shall presently see more fully, are, from the same point of view, nothing but *concatenated* discharges in the nerve-centres, due to the presence there of systems of reflex paths, so organized as to wake each other up successively—the impression produced by one muscular contraction serving as a stimulus to provoke the next, until a final impression inhibits the process and closes the chain.

It must be noticed that the growth of structural modification in living matter may be more rapid than in any lifeless mass, because the incessant nutritive renovation of which the living matter is the seat tends often to corroborate and fix the impressed modification, rather than to counteract it by renewing the original constitution of the tissue that has been impressed. Thus, we notice after exercising our muscles or our brain in a new way, that we can do so no longer at that time; but after a day or two of rest, when we resume the discipline, our increase in skill not seldom surprises us. I have often noticed this in learning a tune; and it has led a German author to say that we learn to swim during the winter, and to skate during the summer.

PRACTICAL EFFECTS OF HABIT

First, habit simplifies our movements, makes them accurate, and diminishes fatigue.

Man is born with a tendency to do more things than he has ready-made arrangements for in his nerve-centres. Most of the performances of other animals are automatic. But in him the number of them is so enormous that most of them must be the fruit of painful study. If practice did not make perfect, nor habit economize the expense of nervous and muscular energy, he would be in a sorry plight. As Dr. Maudsley says:[1]

> If an act became no easier after being done several times, if the careful direction of consciousness were necessary to its accomplishment on each occasion, it is evident that the whole activity of a lifetime might be confined to one or two deeds—that no progress could take place in development. A man might be occupied all day in dressing and undressing himself; the attitude of his body would absorb all his attention and energy; the washing of his hands or the fastening of a button would be as difficult to him on each occasion as to the child on its first trial; and he would, furthermore, be completely exhausted by his exertions. Think of the pains necessary to teach a child to stand, of the many efforts which it must make, and of the ease with which it at last stands, unconscious of any effort. For while secondarily-automatic acts are accomplished with comparatively little weariness—in this regard approaching the organic movements, or the original reflex movements—the conscious effort of the will soon produces exhaustion. A spinal cord without . . . memory would simply be an idiotic spinal cord. . . . It is impossible for an individual to realize how much he owes to its automatic agency until disease has impaired its functions.

Secondly, *habit diminishes the conscious attention with which our acts are performed.*

[1] *The Physiology of Mind,* p. 155.

One may state this abstractly thus: If an act require for its execution a chain, *A, B, C, D, E, F, G,* etc., of successive nervous events, then in the first performances of the action the conscious will must choose each of these events from a number of wrong alternatives that tend to present themselves; but habit soon brings it about that each event calls up its own appropriate successor without any alternative offering itself, and without any reference to the conscious will, until at last the whole chain, *A, B, C, D, E, F, G,* rattles itself off as soon as *A* occurs, just as if *A* and the rest of the chain were fused into a continuous stream. Whilst we are learning to walk, to ride, to swim, skate, fence, write, play, or sing, we interrupt ourselves at every step by unnecessary movements and false notes. When we are proficients, on the contrary, the results follow not only with the very minimum of muscular action requisite to bring them forth, but they follow from a single instantaneous "cue." The marksman sees the bird, and, before he knows it, he has aimed and shot. A gleam in his adversary's eye, a momentary pressure from his rapier, and the fencer finds that he has instantly made the right parry and return. A glance at the musical hieroglyphics, and the pianist's fingers have rippled through a shower of notes. And not only is it the right thing at the right time that we thus involuntarily do, but the wrong thing also, if it be an habitual thing. Who is there that has never wound up his watch on taking off his waistcoat in the daytime, or taken his latch-key out on arriving at the doorstep of a friend? Persons in going to their bedroom to dress for dinner have been known to take off one garment after another and finally to get into bed, merely because that was the habitual issue of the first few movements when performed at a later hour. We all have a definite routine manner of performing certain daily offices connected with the toilet, with the opening and shutting of familiar cupboards, and the like. But our higher thought-centres know hardly anything about the matter. Few men can tell off-hand which sock, shoe, or trousers-leg they put on first. They must first mentally rehearse the act; and even that is often insufficient—the act must be *performed*. So of the questions, Which valve of the shutters opens first? Which way does my door swing? etc. I cannot *tell* the answer; yet my *hand* never makes a mistake. No one can *describe* the order in which he brushes his hair or teeth; yet it is likely that the order is a pretty fixed one in all of us.

These results may be expressed as follows:

In action grown habitual, what instigates each new muscular contraction to take place in its appointed order is not a thought or a perception, but the *sensation occasioned by the muscular contraction just finished.* A strictly voluntary act has to be guided by idea, perception, and volition, throughout its whole course. In habitual action, mere sensation is a sufficient guide, and the upper regions of brain and mind are set comparatively free. A diagram will make the matter clear:

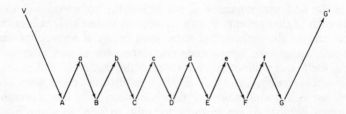

Let *A, B, C, D, E, F, G* represent an habitual chain of muscular contractions, and let *a, b, c, d, e, f* stand for the several sensations which these contractions excite in us when they are successively performed. Such sensations will usually be in the parts moved, but they may also be effects of the movement upon the eye or the ear. Through them, and through them alone, we are made aware whether or not the contraction has occurred. When the series, *A, B, C, D, E, F, G*, is being learned, each of these sensations becomes the object of a separate act of attention by the mind. We test each movement intellectually, to see if it have been rightly performed, before advancing to the next. We hesitate, compare, choose, revoke, reject, etc.; and the order by which the next movement is discharged is an express order from the ideational centres after this deliberation has been gone through.

In habitual action, on the contrary, the only impulse which the intellectual centres need send down is that which carries the command to *start*. This is represented in the diagram by *V;* it may be a thought of the first movement or of the last result, or a mere perception of some of the habitual conditions of the chain, the presence, e.g., of the keyboard near the hand. In the present example, no sooner has this conscious thought or volition instigated movement *A*, than *A*, through the sensation *a* of its own occurrence, awakens *B* reflexly; *B* then excites *C* through *b*, and so on till the chain is ended, when the intellect generally takes cognizance of the final result. The intellectual perception at the end is indicated in the diagram by the sensible effect of the movement *G* being represented at *G'*, in the ideational centres above the merely sensational line. The sensational impressions, *a, b, c, d, e, f*, are all supposed to have their seat below the ideational level.

Habits depend on sensations not attended to. We have called *a, b, c, d, e, f*, by the name of "sensations." If sensations, they are sensations to which we are usually inattentive; but that they are more than unconscious nerve-currents seems certain, for they catch our attention if they go wrong. Schneider's account of these sensations deserves to be quoted. In the act of walking, he says, "even when our attention is entirely absorbed elsewhere, it is doubtful whether we could preserve equilibrium if no sensation of our body's attitude were there, and doubtful whether we should advance our leg if we had no sensation of its movement as executed, and not even a minimal feeling of impulse to set it down. Knitting appears altogether mechanical, and the knitter keeps up her knitting even while she reads or is engaged in lively talk. But if we ask her how this is possible, she will hardly reply that the knitting goes on of itself. She will rather say that she has a feeling of it, that she feels in her hands that she knits and how she must knit, and that therefore the movements of knitting are called forth and regulated by the sensations associated therewithal, even when the attention is called away. . . ." Again: "When a pupil begins to play on the violin, to keep him from raising his right elbow in playing a book is placed under his right armpit, which he is ordered to hold fast by keeping the upper arm tight against his body. The muscular feelings, and feelings of contact connected with the book, provoke an impulse to press it tight. But often it happens that the beginner, whose attention gets absorbed in the production of the notes, lets drop the book. Later, however, this never happens; the faintest sensations of contact suffice to awaken the impulse to keep it in its place, and the attention may be wholly absorbed by the notes and the fingering with the left hand. *The simultaneous combination of movements is thus in the first instance conditioned by the facility with which in us, alongside of intellectual processes, processes of inattentive feeling may still go on.*"

ETHICAL AND PEDAGOGICAL IMPORTANCE OF THE PRINCIPLE OF HABIT

"Habit a second nature! Habit is ten times nature," the Duke of Wellington is said to have exclaimed; and the degree to which this is true no one probably can appreciate as well as one who is a veteran soldier himself. The daily drill and the years of discipline end by fashioning a man completely over again, as to most of the possibilities of his conduct.

"There is a story," says Prof. Huxley, "which is credible enough, though it may not be true, of a practical joker who, seeing a discharged veteran carrying home his dinner, suddenly called out, 'Attention!' whereupon the man instantly brought his hands down, and lost his mutton and potatoes in the gutter. The drill had been thorough, and its effects had become embodied in the man's nervous structure."

Riderless cavalry-horses, at many a battle, have been seen to come together and go through their customary evolutions at the sound of the bugle-call. Most domestic beasts seem machines almost pure and simple, undoubtingly, unhesitatingly doing from minute to minute the duties they have been taught, and giving no sign that the possibility of an alternative ever suggests itself to their mind. Men grown old in prison have asked to be readmitted after being once set free. In a railroad accident a menagerie-tiger, whose cage had broken open, is said to have emerged, but presently crept back again, as if too much bewildered by his new responsibilities, so that he was without difficulty secured.

Habit is thus the enormous fly-wheel of society, its most precious conservative agent. It alone is what keeps us all within the bounds of ordinance, and saves the children of fortune from the envious uprisings of the poor. It alone prevents the hardest and most repulsive walks of life from being deserted by those brought up to tread therein. It keeps the fisherman and the deck-hand at sea through the winter; it holds the miner in his darkness, and nails the countryman to his log-cabin and his lonely farm through all the months of snow; it protects us from invasion by the natives of the desert and the frozen zone. It dooms us all to fight out the battle of life upon the lines of our nurture or our early choice, and to make the best of a pursuit that disagrees, because there is no other for which we are fitted, and it is too late to begin again. It keeps different social strata from mixing. Already at the age of twenty-five you see the professional mannerism settling down on the young commercial traveller, on the young doctor, on the young minister, on the young counsellor-at-law. You see the little lines of cleavage running through the character, the tricks of thought, the prejudices, the ways of the "shop," in a word, from which the man can by-and-by no more escape than his coat-sleeve can suddenly fall into a new set of folds. On the whole, it is best he should not escape. It is well for the world that in most of us, by the age of thirty, the character has set like plaster, and will never soften again.

If the period between twenty and thirty is the critical one in the formation of intellectual and professional habits, the period below twenty is more important still for the fixing of *personal* habits, properly so called, such as vocalization and pronunciation, gesture, motion, and address. Hardly ever is a language learned after twenty spoken without a foreign accent; hardly ever can a youth transferred to the society of his betters unlearn the nasality and other vices of speech bred in him by the associations of his growing years. Hardly ever, indeed, no matter how much money there be in his pocket, can he even learn to *dress* like a gentleman-born. The merchants offer their wares as eagerly to him as to the veriest "swell," but he simply *cannot* buy the right things. An invisible law, as strong as gravitation, keeps him within his orbit, arrayed this year as he was the last; and how his better-clad acquaintances contrive to get the things they wear will be for him a mystery till his dying day.

The great thing, then, in all education, is to *make our nervous system our ally instead of our enemy*. It is to fund and capitalize our acquisitions, and live at ease upon the interest of the fund. *For this we must make automatic and habitual, as early as possible, as many useful actions as we can,* and guard against the growing into ways that are likely to be disadvantageous to us, as we should guard against the plague. The more of the details of our daily life we can hand over to the effortless custody of automatism, the more our higher powers of mind will be set free for their own proper work. There is no more miserable human being than one in whom nothing is habitual but indecision, and for whom the lighting of every cigar, the drinking of every cup, the time of rising and going to bed every day, and the beginning of every bit of work, are subjects of express volitional deliberation. Full half the time of such a man goes to the deciding, or regretting, of matters which ought to be so ingrained in him as practically not to exist for his consciousness at all. If there be such daily duties not yet ingrained in any one of my readers, let him begin this very hour to set the matter right.

In Professor Bain's chapter on "The Moral Habits" there are some admirable practical remarks laid down. Two great maxims emerge from his treatment. The first is that in the acquisition of a new habit, or the leaving off of an old one, we must take care to *launch ourselves with as strong and decided an initiative as possible*. Accumulate all the possible circumstances which shall re-enforce the right motives; put yourself assiduously in conditions that encourage the new way; make engagements incompatible with the old; take a public pledge, if the case allows; in short, envelop your resolution with every aid you know. This will give your new beginning such a momentum that the temptation to break down will not occur as soon as it otherwise might; and every day during which a break-down is postponed adds to the chances of its not occurring at all.

The second maxim is: *Never suffer an exception to occur till the new habit is securely rooted in your life.* Each lapse is like the letting fall of a ball of string which one is carefully winding up; a single slip undoes more than a great many turns will wind again. *Continuity* of training is the great means of making the nervous system act infallibly right. As Professor Bain says:

> The peculiarity of the moral habits, contradistinguishing them from the intellectual acquisitions, is the presence of two hostile powers, one to be gradually raised into the ascendant over the other. It is necessary, above all things, in such a situation, never to lose a battle. Every

gain on the wrong side undoes the effect of many conquests on the right. The essential precaution, therefore, is so to regulate the two opposing powers that the one may have a series of uninterrupted successes, until repetition has fortified it to such a degree as to enable it to cope with the opposition, under any circumstances. This is the theoretically best career of mental progress.

The need of securing success at the *outset* is imperative. Failure at first is apt to damp the energy of all future attempts, whereas past experiences of success nerve one to future vigor. Goethe says to a man who consulted him about an enterprise but mistrusted his own powers: "Ach! you need only blow on your hands!" And the remark illustrates the effect on Goethe's spirits of his own habitually successful career.

The question of "tapering-off," in abandoning such habits as drink and opium-indulgence comes in here, and is a question about which experts differ within certain limits, and in regard to what may be best for an individual case. In the main, however, all expert opinion would agree that abrupt acquisition of the new habit is the best way, *if there be a real possibility of carrying it out.* We must be careful not to give the will so stiff a task as to insure its defeat at the very outset; but, *provided one can stand it,* a sharp period of suffering, and then a free time, is the best thing to aim at, whether in giving up a habit like that of opium, or in simply changing one's hours of rising or of work. It is surprising how soon a desire will die of inanition if it be *never* fed.

> One must first learn, unmoved, looking neither to the right nor left, to walk firmly on the strait and narrow path, before one can begin "to make one's self over again." He who every day makes a fresh resolve is like one who, arriving at the edge of the ditch he is to leap, forever stops and returns for a fresh run. Without *unbroken* advance there is no such thing as *accumulation* of the ethical forces possible, and to make this possible, and to exercise us and habituate us in it, is the sovereign blessing of regular work.[2]

A third maxim may be added to the preceding pair: *Seize the very first possible opportunity to act on every resolution you make, and on every emotional prompting you may experience in the direction of the habits you aspire to gain.* It is not in the moment of their forming, but in the moment of their producing *motor effects,* that resolves and aspirations communicate the new "set" to the brain. As the author last quoted remarks:

"The actual presence of the practical opportunity alone furnishes the fulcrum upon which the lever can rest, by means of which the moral will may multiply its strength, and raise itself aloft. He who has

---

[2] J. Bahnsen: *Beiträge zu Charakterologie* (1867), vol. I. p. 209.

no solid ground to press against will never get beyond the stage of empty gesture-making."

No matter how full a reservoir of *maxims* one may possess, and no matter how good one's *sentiments* may be, if one have not taken advantage of every concrete opportunity to *act,* one's character may remain entirely unaffected for the better. With mere good intentions, hell is proverbially paved. And this is an obvious consequence of the principles we have laid down. A "character," as J. S. Mill says, "is a completely fashioned will"; and a will, in the sense in which he means it, is an aggregate of tendencies to act in a firm and prompt and definite way upon all the principal emergencies of life. A tendency to act only becomes effectively ingrained in us in proportion to the uninterrupted frequency with which the actions actually occur, and the brain "grows" to their use. When a resolve or a fine glow of feeling is allowed to evaporate without bearing practical fruit it is worse than a chance lost; it works so as positively to hinder future resolutions and emotions from taking the normal path of discharge. There is no more contemptible type of human character than that of the nerveless sentimentalist and dreamer, who spends his life in a weltering sea of sensibility and emotion, but who never does a manly concrete deed. Rousseau, inflaming all the mothers of France, by his eloquence, to follow Nature and nurse their babies themselves, while he sends his own children to the foundling hospital, is the classical example of what I mean. But every one of us in his measure, whenever, after glowing for an abstractly formulated Good, he practically ignores some actual case, among the squalid "other particulars" of which that same Good lurks disguised, treads straight on Rousseau's path. All Goods are disguised by the vulgarity of their concomitants, in this work-a-day world; but woe to him who can only recognize them when he thinks them in their pure and abstract form! The habit of excessive novel-reading and theatre-going will produce true monsters in this line. The weeping of the Russian lady over the fictitious personages in the play, while her coachman is freezing to death on his seat outside, is the sort of thing that everywhere happens on a less glaring scale. Even the habit of excessive indulgence in music, for those who are neither performers themselves nor musically gifted enough to take it in a purely intellectual way, has probably a relaxing effect upon character. One becomes filled with emotions which habitually pass without prompting to any deed, and so the inertly sentimental condition is kept up. The remedy would be, never to suffer one's self to have an emotion at a concert, without expressing it afterward in *some* active way. Let the expression be the least thing in the world—speaking genially to one's grandmother, or giving up one's seat in horse-car, if nothing more heroic offers—but let it not fail to take place.

These latter cases make us aware that it is not simply *particular lines* of discharge, but also *general forms* of discharge, that seem to be grooved out by habit in the brain. Just as, if we let our emotions evaporate, they get into a way of evaporating; so there is reason to suppose that if we often flinch from making an effort, before we know it the effort-making capacity will be gone; and that, if we suffer the wandering of our attention, presently it will wander all the time. Attention and effort are, as we shall see later, but two names for the same psychic fact. To what brain-processes they correspond we do not know. The strongest reason for believing that they do depend on brain-processes at all, and are not pure acts of the spirit, is just this fact, that they seem in some degrees subject to the law of habit, which is a material law. As a final practical maxim, relative to these habits of the will, we may, then, offer something like this: *Keep the faculty of effort alive in you by a little gratuitous exercise every day*. That is, be systematically ascetic or heroic in little unnecessary points, do every day or two something for no other reason than that you would rather not do it, so that when the hour of dire need draws nigh, it may find you not unnerved and untrained to stand the test. Asceticism of this sort is like the insurance which a man pays on his house and goods. The tax does him no good at the time, and possibly may never bring him a return. But if the fire *does* come, his having paid it will be his salvation from ruin. So with the man who has daily inured himself to habits of concentrated attention, energetic volition, and self-denial in unnecessary things. He will stand like a tower when everything rocks around him, and when his softer fellow-mortals are winnowed like chaff in the blast.

The physiological study of mental conditions is thus the most powerful ally of hortatory ethics. The hell to be endured hereafter, of which theology tells, is no worse than the hell we make for ourselves in this world by habitually fashioning our characters in the wrong way. Could the young but realize how soon they will become mere walking bundles of habits, they would give more heed to their conduct while in the plastic state. We are spinning our own fates, good or evil, and never to be undone. Every smallest stroke of virtue or of vice leaves its never so little scar. The drunken Rip Van Winkle, in Jefferson's* play, excuses himself for every fresh dereliction by saying, "I won't count this time!" Well! he may not count it, and a kind Heaven may not count it; but it is being counted none the less. Down among his nerve-cells and fibres the molecules are counting it, registering and storing it up to be used against him when the next temptation comes. Nothing we ever do is, in strict scientific literalness, wiped out. Of

* Dion Boucicault and Joseph Jefferson wrote *Rip Van Winkle;* the actor Jefferson made it his most famous role.

course this has its good side as well as its bad one. As we become permanent drunkards by so many separate drinks, so we become saints in the moral, and authorities and experts in the practical and scientific spheres, by so many separate acts and hours of work. Let no youth have any anxiety about the upshot of his education, whatever the line of it may be. If he keep faithfully busy each hour of the working day, he may safely leave the final result to itself. He can with perfect certainty count on waking up some fine morning, to find himself one of the competent ones of his generation, in whatever pursuit he may have singled out. Silently, between all the details of his business, the *power of judging* in all that class of matter will have built itself up within him as a possession that will never pass away. Young people should know this truth in advance. The ignorance of it has probably engendered more discouragement and faint-heartedness in youths embarking on arduous careers than all other causes put together.

THE STREAM OF THOUGHT*

We[3] now begin our study of the mind from within. Most books start with sensations, as the simplest mental facts, and proceed synthetically, constructing each higher stage from those below it. But this is abandoning the empirical method of investigation. No one ever had a simple sensation by itself. Consciousness, from our natal day, is of a teeming multiplicity of objects and relations, and what we call simple sensations are results of discriminative attention, pushed often to a very high degree. It is astonishing what havoc is wrought in psychology by admitting at the outset apparently innocent suppositions, that nevertheless contain a flaw. The bad consequences develop themselves later on, and are irremediable, being woven through the whole texture of the work. The notion that sensations, being the simplest things, are the first things to take up in psychology is one of these suppositions. The only thing which psychology has a right to postulate at the outset is the fact of thinking itself, and that must first be taken up and analyzed. If sensations then prove to be amongst the elements of the thinking, we shall be no worse off as respects them than if we had taken them for granted at the start.

* From: *Principles*, I, 224–290.

[3] A good deal of this chapter is reprinted from an article "On some Omissions of Introspective Psychology" which appeared in *Mind* for January 1884.

The first fact for us, then, as psychologists, is that thinking of some sort goes on. I use the word thinking, in accordance with what was [earlier] said, for every form of consciousness indiscriminately. If we could say in English 'it thinks,' as we say 'it rains' or 'it blows,' we should be stating the fact most simply and with the minimum of assumption. As we cannot, we must simply say that *thought goes on.*

FIVE CHARACTERS IN THOUGHT

How does it go on? We notice immediately five important characters in the process, of which it shall be the duty of the present chapter to treat in a general way:

1) Every thought tends to be part of a personal consciousness.

2) Within each personal consciousness thought is always changing.

3) Within each personal consciousness thought is sensibly continuous.

4) It always appears to deal with objects independent of itself.

5) It is interested in some parts of these objects to the exclusion of others, and welcomes or rejects—*chooses* from among them, in a word—all the while.

In considering these five points successively, we shall have to plunge *in medias res* as regards our vocabulary, and use psychological terms which can only be adequately defined in later chapters of the book. But every one knows what the terms mean in a rough way; and it is only in a rough way that we are now to take them. This chapter is like a painter's first charcoal sketch upon his canvas, in which no niceties appear.

1) Thought tends to Personal Form

When I say *every thought is part of a personal consciousness,* 'personal consciousness' is one of the terms in question. Its meaning we know so long as no one asks us to define it, but to give an accurate account of it is the most difficult of philosophic tasks. This task we must confront in the next chapter; here a preliminary word will suffice.

In this room—this lecture-room, say—there are a multitude of thoughts, yours and mine, some of which cohere mutually, and some not. They are as little each-for-itself and reciprocally independent as they are all-belonging-together. They are neither: no one of them is separate, but each belongs with certain others and with none beside. My thought belongs with my other thoughts, and your thought with your other thoughts. Whether anywhere in the room there be a mere thought, which is nobody's thought, we have no means of ascertaining, for we have no experience of its like. The only states of consciousness that we naturally deal with are found in personal consciousnesses, minds, selves, concrete particular I's and you's.

Each of these minds keeps its own thoughts to itself. There is no giving or bartering between them. No thought even comes into direct *sight* of a thought in another personal consciousness than its own. Absolute insulation, irreducible pluralism, is the law. It seems as if the elementary psychic fact were not *thought* or *this thought* or *that thought,* but *my thought,* every thought being *owned.* Neither contemporaneity, nor proximity in space, nor similarity of quality and content are able to fuse thoughts together which are sundered by this barrier of belonging to different personal minds. The breaches between such thoughts are the most absolute breaches in nature. Everyone will recognize this to be true, so long as the existence of *something* corresponding to the term 'personal mind' is all that is insisted on, without any particular view of its nature being implied. On these terms the personal self rather than the thought might be treated as the immediate datum in psychology. The universal conscious fact is not 'feelings and thoughts exist,' but 'I think' and 'I feel.' [4] No psychology, at any rate, can question the *existence* of personal selves. The worst a psychology can do is so to interpret the nature of these selves as to rob them of their worth. A French writer, speaking of our ideas, says somewhere in a fit of anti-spiritualistic excitement that, misled by certain peculiarities which they display, we 'end by personifying' the procession which they make,—such personification being regarded by him as a great philosophic blunder on our part. It could only be a blunder if the notion of personality meant something essentially different from anything to be found in the mental procession. But if that procession be itself the very 'original' of the notion of personality, to personify it cannot possibly be wrong. It is already personified. There are no marks of personality to be gathered *aliunde,* and then found lacking in the train of thought. It has them all already; so that to whatever farther analysis we may subject that form of personal selfhood under which thoughts appear, it is, and must remain, true that the thoughts which psychology studies do continually tend to appear as parts of personal selves.

I say 'tend to appear' rather than 'appear,' on account of those facts of subconscious personality, automatic writing, etc., of which we studied a few in the last chapter. The buried feelings and thoughts proved now to exist in hysterical anæsthetics, in recipients of post-hypnotic suggestion, etc., themselves are parts of *secondary personal*

[4] B. P. Bowne: *Metaphysics,* p. 362.

selves. These selves are for the most part very stupid and contracted, and are cut off at ordinary times from communication with the regular and normal self of the individual; but still they form conscious unities, have continuous memories, speak, write, invent distinct names for themselves, or adopt names that are suggested; and, in short, are entirely worthy of that title of secondary personalities which is now commonly given them. According to M. Janet these secondary personalities are always abnormal, and result from the splitting of what ought to be a single complete self into two parts, of which one lurks in the background whilst the other appears on the surface as the only self the man or woman has. For our present purpose it is unimportant whether this account of the origin of secondary selves is applicable to all possible cases of them or not, for it certainly is true of a large number of them. Now although the *size* of a secondary self thus formed will depend on the number of thoughts that are thus split-off from the main consciousness, the *form* of it tends to personality, and the later thoughts pertaining to it remember the earlier ones and adopt them as their own. M. Janet caught the actual moment of inspissation (so to speak) of one of these secondary personalities in his anæsthetic somnambulist Lucie. He found that when this young woman's attention was absorbed in conversation with a third party, her anæsthetic hand would write simple answers to questions whispered to her by himself. "Do you hear?" he asked. *"No,"* was the unconsciously written reply. "But to answer you must hear." *"Yes, quite so."* "Then how do you manage?" *"I don't know."* "There must be some one who hears me." *"Yes."* "Who?" *"Someone other than Lucie."* "Ah! another person. Shall we give her a name?" *"No."* "Yes, it will be more convenient." *"Well, Adrienne, then."* "Once baptized, the subconscious personage," M. Janet continues, "grows more definitely outlined and displays better her psychological characters. In particular she shows us that she is conscious of the feelings excluded from the consciousness of the primary or normal personage. She it is who tells us that I am pinching the arm or touching the little finger in which Lucie for so long has had no tactile sensations." [5]

In other cases the adoption of the name by the secondary self is more spontaneous. I have seen a number of incipient automatic writers and mediums as yet imperfectly 'developed,' who immediately and of their own accord write and speak in the name of departed spirits. These may be public characters, as Mozart, Faraday, or real persons formerly known to the subject, or altogether imaginary beings. Without prejudicing the question of real 'spirit-control' in the more developed sorts of trance-utterance, I incline to think that these (often deplorably unintelligent) rudimentary utterances are the work of an

[5] *L'Automatisme Psychologique*, p. 318.

inferior fraction of the subject's own natural mind, set free from control by the rest, and working after a set pattern fixed by the prejudices of the social environment. In a spiritualistic community we get optimistic messages, whilst in an ignorant Catholic village the secondary personage calls itself by the name of a demon, and proffers blasphemies and obscenities, instead of telling us how happy it is in the summer-land.[6]

Beneath these tracts of thought, which, however rudimentary, are still organized selves with a memory, habits, and sense of their own identity, M. Janet thinks that the facts of catalepsy in hysteric patients drive us to suppose that there are thoughts quite unorganized and impersonal. A patient in cataleptic trance (which can be produced artificially in certain hypnotized subjects) is without memory on waking, and seems insensible and unconscious as long as the cataleptic condition lasts. If, however, one raises the arm of such a subject it stays in that position, and the whole body can thus be moulded like wax under the hands of the operator, retaining for a considerable time whatever attitude he communicates to it. In hysterics whose arm, for example, is anæsthetic, the same thing may happen. The anæsthetic arm may remain passively in positions which it is made to assume; or if the hand be taken and made to hold a pencil and trace a certain letter, it will continue tracing that letter indefinitely on the paper. These acts, until recently, were supposed to be accompanied by no consciousness at all: they were physiological reflexes. M. Janet considers with much more plausibility that feeling escorts them. The feeling is probably merely that of the position or movement of the limb, and it produces no more than its natural effects when it discharges into the motor centres which keep the position maintained, or the movement incessantly renewed.[7] Such thoughts as these, says M. Janet, "are known by *no one,* for disaggregated sensations reduced to a state of mental dust are not synthetized in any personality."[8] He admits, however, that these very same unutterably stupid thoughts tend to develop memory,—the cataleptic ere long moves her arm at a bare hint; so that they form no important exception to the law that all thought tends to assume the form of personal consciousness.

2) Thought is in Constant Change

I do not mean necessarily that no one state of mind has any duration—even if true, that would be hard to establish. The change which

[6] Cf. A. Constans: *Relation sur une Epidémie d'hystéro-démonopathie en 1861.* 2me ed. Paris, 1863.—Chiap e Franzolini: *L'Epidemia d'isterodemonopatie in Verzegnis.* Reggio, 1879.—See also J. Kerner's little work: *Nachricht von dem Vorkommen des Besessenseins.* 1836.

[7] For the Physiology of this compare the chapter on the Will.

[8] *Loc. cit.* p. 316.

I have more particularly in view is that which takes place in sensible intervals of time; and the result on which I wish to lay stress is this, that *no state once gone can recur and be identical with what it was before.* Let us begin with Mr. Shadworth Hodgson's description:

> I go straight to the facts, without saying I go to perception, or sensation, or thought, or any special mode at all. What I find when I look at my consciousness at all is that what I cannot divest myself of, or not have in consciousness, if I have any consciousness at all, is a sequence of different feelings. I may shut my eyes and keep perfectly still, and try not to contribute anything of my own will; but whether I think or do not think, whether I perceive external things or not, I always have a succession of different feelings. Anything else that I may have also, of a more special character, comes in as parts of this succession. Not to have the succession of different feelings is not to be conscious at all. . . . The chain of consciousness is a sequence of *differents.*[9]

Such a description as this can awaken no possible protest from any one. We all recognize as different great classes of our conscious states. Now we are seeing, now hearing; now reasoning, now willing; now recollecting, now expecting; now loving, now hating; and in a hundred other ways we know our minds to be alternately engaged. But all these are complex states. The aim of science is always to reduce complexity to simplicity; and in psychological science we have the celebrated 'theory of *ideas*' which, admitting the great difference among each other of what may be called concrete conditions of mind, seeks to show how this is all the resultant effect of variations in the *combination* of certain simple elements of consciousness that always remain the same. These mental atoms or molecules are what Locke called 'simple ideas.' Some of Locke's successors made out that the only simple ideas were the sensations strictly so called. Which ideas the simple ones may be does not, however, now concern us. It is enough that certain philosophers have thought they could see under the dissolving-view-appearance of the mind elementary facts of *any* sort that remained unchanged amid the flow.

And the view of these philosophers has been called little into question, for our common experience seems at first sight to corroborate it entirely. Are not the sensations we get from the same object, for example, always the same? Does not the same piano-key, struck with the same force, make us hear in the same way? Does not the same grass give us the same feeling of green, the same sky the same feeling of blue, and do we not get the same olfactory sensation no matter how many times we put our nose to the same flask of cologne? It seems a piece of metaphysical sophistry to suggest that we do not; and yet a

[9] *The Philosophy of Reflection,* I. 248, 290.

close attention to the matter shows that *there is no proof that the same bodily sensation is ever got by us twice.*

What is got twice is the same OBJECT. We hear the same *note* over and over again; we see the same *quality* of green, or smell the same objective perfume, or experience the same *species* of pain. The realities, concrete and abstract, physical and ideal, whose permanent existence we believe in, seem to be constantly coming up again before our thought, and lead us, in our carelessness, to suppose that our 'ideas' of them are the same ideas. When we come, some time later, to the chapter on Perception, we shall see how inveterate is our habit of not attending to sensations as subjective facts, but of simply using them as stepping-stones to pass over to the recognition of the realities whose presence they reveal. The grass out of the window now looks to me of the same green in the sun as in the shade, and yet a painter would have to paint one part of it dark brown, another part bright yellow, to give its real sensational effect. We take no heed, as a rule, of the different way in which the same things look and sound and smell at different distances and under different circumstances. The sameness of the *things* is what we are concerned to ascertain; and any sensations that assure us of that will probably be considered in a rough way to be the same with each other. This is what makes off-hand testimony about the subjective identity of different sensations well-nigh worthless as a proof of the fact. The entire history of Sensation is a commentary on our inability to tell whether two sensations received apart are exactly alike. What appeals to our attention far more than the absolute quality or quantity of a given sensation is its *ratio* to whatever other sensations we may have at the same time. When everything is dark a somewhat less dark sensation makes us see an object white. Helmholtz calculates that the white marble painted in a picture representing an architectural view by moonlight is, when seen by daylight, from ten to twenty thousand times brighter than the real moonlit marble would be.[10]

Such a difference as this could never have been *sensibly* learned; it had to be inferred from a series of indirect considerations. There are facts which make us believe that our sensibility is altering all the time, so that the same object cannot easily give us the same sensation over again. The eye's sensibility to light is at its maximum when the eye is first exposed, and blunts itself with surprising rapidity. A long night's sleep will make it see things twice as brightly on wakening, as simple rest by closure will make it see them later in the day.[11] We feel things differently according as we are sleepy or awake, hungry or full, fresh or tired; differently at night and in the morning, differently in summer

---

[10] *Populäre Wissenschaftliche Vorträge,* Drittes Heft (1876), p. 72.
[11] Fick, in L. Hermann's *Handb. d. Physiol.,* Bd. III. Th. I. p. 225.

and in winter, and above all things differently in childhood, manhood, and old age. Yet we never doubt that our feelings reveal the same world, with the same sensible qualities and the same sensible things occupying it. The difference of the sensibility is shown best by the difference of our emotion about the things from one age to another, or when we are in different organic moods. What was bright and exciting becomes weary, flat, and unprofitable. The bird's song is tedious, the breeze is mournful, the sky is sad.

To these indirect presumptions that our sensations, following the mutations of our capacity for feeling, are always undergoing an essential change, must be added another presumption, based on what must happen in the brain. Every sensation corresponds to some cerebral action. For an identical sensation to recur it would have to occur the second time *in an unmodified brain*. But as this, strictly speaking, is a physiological impossibility, so is an unmodified feeling an impossibility; for to every brain-modification, however small, must correspond a change of equal amount in the feeling which the brain subserves.

All this would be true if even sensations came to us pure and single and not combined into 'things.' Even then we should have to confess that, however we might in ordinary conversation speak of getting the same sensation again, we never in strict theoretic accuracy could do so; and that whatever was true of the river of life, of the river of elementary feeling, it would certainly be true to say, like Heraclitus, that we never descend twice into the same stream.

But if the assumption of 'simple ideas of sensation' recurring in immutable shape is so easily shown to be baseless, how much more baseless is the assumption of immutability in the larger masses of our thought!

For there it is obvious and palpable that our state of mind is never precisely the same. Every thought we have of a given fact is, strictly speaking, unique, and only bears a resemblance of kind with our other thoughts of the same fact. When the identical fact recurs, we *must* think of it in a fresh manner, see it under a somewhat different angle, apprehend it in different relations from those in which it last appeared. And the thought by which we cognize it is the thought of it-in-those-relations, a thought suffused with the consciousness of all that dim context. Often we are ourselves struck at the strange differences in our successive views of the same thing. We wonder how we ever could have opined as we did last month about a certain matter. We have outgrown the possibility of that state of mind, we know not how. From one year to another we see things in new lights. What was unreal has grown real, and what was exciting is insipid. The friends we used to care the world for are shrunken to shadows; the women, once so divine, the stars, the woods, and the waters, how now so dull and common; the young girls that brought an aura of infinity, at present hardly distinguishable existences; the pictures so empty; and as for the books, what *was* there to find so mysteriously significant in Goethe, or in John Mill so full of weight? Instead of all this, more zestful than ever is the work, the work; and fuller and deeper the import of common duties and of common goods.

But what here strikes us so forcibly on the flagrant scale exists on every scale, down to the imperceptible transition from one hour's outlook to that of the next. Experience is remoulding us every moment, and our mental reaction on every given thing is really a resultant of our experience of the whole world up to that date. The analogies of brain-physiology must again be appealed to to corroborate our view.

Our earlier chapters have taught us to believe that, whilst we think, our brain changes, and that, like the aurora borealis, its whole internal equilibrium shifts with every pulse of change. The precise nature of the shifting at a given moment is a product of many factors. The accidental state of local nutrition or blood-supply may be among them. But just as one of them certainly is the influence of outward objects on the sense-organs during the moment, so is another certainly the very special susceptibility in which the organ has been left at that moment by all it has gone through in the past. Every brain-state is partly determined by the nature of this entire past succession. Alter the latter in any part, and the brain-state must be somewhat different. Each present brain-state is a record in which the eye of Omniscience might read all the foregone history of its owner. It is out of the question, then, that any total brain-state should identically recur. Something like it may recur; but to suppose *it* to recur would be equivalent to the absurd admission that all the states that had intervened between its two appearances had been pure nonentities, and that the organ after their passage was exactly as it was before. And (to consider shorter periods) just as, in the senses, an impression feels very differently according to what has preceded it; as one color succeeding another is modified by the contrast, silence sounds delicious after noise, and a note, when the scale is sung up, sounds unlike itself when the scale is sung down; as the presence of certain lines in a figure changes the apparent form of the other lines, and as in music the whole æsthetic effect comes from the manner in which one set of sounds alters our feeling of another; so, in thought, we must admit that those portions of the brain that have just been maximally excited retain a kind of soreness which is a condition of our present consciousness, a codeterminant of how and what we now shall feel.[12]

[12] It need of course not follow, because a total brain-state does not recur, that no *point* of the brain can ever be twice in the same condition. That would be as improbable a consequence as that in the sea a wave-crest should never

Ever some tracts are waning in tension, some waxing, whilst others actively discharge. The states of tension have as positive an influence as any in determining the total condition, and in deciding what the *psychosis* shall be. All we know of submaximal nerve-irritations, and of the summation of apparently ineffective stimuli, tends to show that *no* changes in the brain are physiologically ineffective, and that presumably none are bare of psychological result. But as the brain-tension shifts from one relative state of equilibrium to another, like the gyrations of a kaleidoscope, now rapid and now slow, is it likely that its faithful psychic concomitant is heavier-footed than itself, and that it cannot match each one of the organ's irradiations by a shifting inward iridescence of its own? But if it can do this, its inward iridescences must be infinite, for the brain-redistributions are in infinite variety. If so coarse a thing as a telephone-plate can be made to thrill for years and never reduplicate its inward condition, how much more must this be the case with the infinitely delicate brain?

I am sure that this concrete and total manner of regarding the mind's changes is the only true manner, difficult as it may be to carry it out in detail. If anything seems obscure about it, it will grow clearer as we advance. Meanwhile, if it be true, it is certainly also true that no two 'ideas' are ever exactly the same, which is the proposition we started to prove. The proposition is more important theoretically than it at first sight seems. For it makes it already impossible for us to follow obediently in the footprints of either the Lockian or the Herbartian school, schools which have had almost unlimited influence in Germany and among ourselves. No doubt it is often *convenient* to formulate the mental facts in an atomistic sort of way, and to treat the higher states of consciousness as if they were all built out of unchanging simple ideas. It is convenient often to treat curves as if they were composed of small straight lines, and electricity and nerve-force as if they were fluids. But in the one case as in the other we must never forget that we are talking symbolically, and that there is nothing in nature to answer to our words. *A permanently existing 'idea' or 'Vorstellung' which makes its appearance before the footlights of consciousness at periodical intervals, is as mythological an entity as the Jack of Spades.*

What makes it convenient to use the mythological formulas is the whole organization of speech, which, as was remarked a while ago, was not made by psychologists, but by men who were as a rule only interested in the facts their mental states revealed. They only spoke of

---

come twice at the same point of space. What can hardly come twice is an identical *combination* of wave-forms all with their crests and hollows reoccupying identical places. For such a total combination as this is the analogue of the brain-state to which our actual consciousness at any moment is due.

their states as *ideas of this or of that thing*. What wonder, then, that the thought is most easily conceived under the law of the thing whose name it bears! If the thing is composed of parts, then we suppose that the thought of the thing must be composed of the thoughts of the parts. If one part of the thing have appeared in the same thing or in other things on former occasions, why then we must be having even now the very same 'idea' of that part which was there on those occasions. If the thing is simple, its thought is simple. If it is multitudinous, it must require a multitude of thoughts to think it. If a succession, only a succession of thoughts can know it. If permanent, its thought is permanent. And so on *ad libitum*. What after all is so natural as to assume that one object, called by one name, should be known by one affection of the mind? But, if language must thus influence us, the agglutinative languages, and even Greek and Latin with their declensions, would be the better guides. Names did not appear in them inalterable, but changed their shape to suit the context in which they lay. It must have been easier then than now to conceive of the same object as being thought of at different times in non-identical conscious states.

This, too, will grow clearer as we proceed. Meanwhile a necessary consequence of the belief in permanent self-identical psychic facts that absent themselves and recur periodically is the Humian doctrine that our thought is composed of separate independent parts and is not a sensibly continuous stream. That this doctrine entirely misrepresents the natural appearances is what I next shall try to show.

3) Within Each Personal Consciousness, Thought is Sensibly Continuous

I can only define 'continuous' as that which is without breach, crack, or division. I have already said that the breach from one mind to another is perhaps the greatest breach in nature. The only breaches that can well be conceived to occur within the limits of a single mind would either be *interruptions, time*-gaps during which the consciousness went out altogether to come into existence again at a later moment; or they would be breaks in the *quality*, or content, of the thought, so abrupt that the segment that followed had no connection whatever with the one that went before. The proposition that within each personal consciousness thought feels continuous, means two things:

1. That even where there is a time-gap the consciousness after it feels as if it belonged together with the consciousness before it, as another part of the same self;

2. That the changes from one moment to another in the quality of the consciousness are never absolutely abrupt.

The case of the time-gaps, as the simplest, shall be taken first. And first of all, a word about time-gaps of which the consciousness may not be itself aware.

[In an earlier chapter] we saw that such time-gaps existed, and that they might be more numerous than is usually supposed. If the consciousness is not aware of them, it cannot feel them as interruptions. In the unconsciousness produced by nitrous oxide and other anæsthetics, in that of epilepsy and fainting, the broken edges of the sentient life may meet and merge over the gap, much as the feelings of space of the opposite margins of the 'blind spot' meet and merge over that objective interruption to the sensitiveness of the eye. Such consciousness as this, whatever it be for the onlooking psychologist, is for itself unbroken. It *feels* unbroken; a waking day of it is sensibly a unit as long as that day lasts, in the sense in which the hours themselves are units, as having all their parts next each other, with no intrusive alien substance between. To expect the consciousness to feel the interruptions of its objective continuity as gaps, would be like expecting the eye to feel a gap of silence because it does not hear, or the ear to feel a gap of darkness because it does not see. So much for the gaps that are unfelt.

With the felt gaps the case is different. On waking from sleep, we usually know that we have been unconscious, and we often have an accurate judgment of how long. The judgment here is certainly an inference from sensible signs, and its ease is due to long practice in the particular field.[13] The result of it, however, is that the consciousness is, *for itself,* not what it was in the former case, but interrupted and continuous, in the mere time-sense of the words. But in the other sense of continuity, the sense of the parts being inwardly connected and belonging together because they are parts of a common whole, the consciousness remains sensibly continuous and one. What now is the common whole? The natural name for it is *myself, I,* or *me.*

When Paul and Peter wake up in the same bed, and recognize that they have been asleep, each one of them mentally reaches back and makes connection with but *one* of the two streams of thought which were broken by the sleeping hours. As the current of an electrode buried in the ground unerringly finds its way to its own similarly buried mate, across no matter how much intervening earth; so Peter's present instantly finds out Peter's past, and never by mistake knits itself on to that of Paul. Paul's thought in turn is as little liable to go astray. The past thought of Peter is appropriated by the present Peter alone. He may have a *knowledge,* and a correct one too, of what

[13] The accurate registration of the 'how long' is still a little mysterious.

Paul's last drowsy states of mind were as he sank into sleep, but it is an entirely different sort of knowledge from that which he has of his own last states. He *remembers* his own states, whilst he only *conceives* Paul's. Remembrance is like direct feeling; its object is suffused with a warmth and intimacy to which no object of mere conception ever attains. This quality of warmth and intimacy and immediacy is what Peter's *present* thought also possesses for itself. So sure as this present is me, is mine, it says, so sure is anything else that comes with the same warmth and intimacy and immediacy, me and mine. What the qualities called warmth and intimacy may in themselves be will have to be matter for future consideration. But whatever past feelings appear with those qualities must be admitted to receive the greeting of the present mental state, to be owned by it, and accepted as belonging together with it in a common self. This community of self is what the time-gap cannot break in twain, and is why a present thought, although not ignorant of the time-gap, can still regard itself as continuous with certain chosen portions of the past.

Consciousness, then, does not appear to itself chopped up in bits. Such words as 'chain' or 'train' do not describe it fitly as it presents itself in the first instance. It is nothing jointed; it flows. A 'river' or a 'stream' are the metaphors by which it is most naturally described. *In talking of it hereafter, let us call it the stream of thought, of consciousness, or of subjective life.*

But now there appears, even within the limits of the same self, and between thoughts all of which alike have this same sense of belonging together, a kind of jointing and separateness among the parts, of which this statement seems to take no account. I refer to the breaks that are produced by sudden *contrasts in the quality* of the successive segments of the stream of thought. If the words 'chain' and 'train' had no natural fitness in them, how came such words to be used at all? Does not a loud explosion rend the consciousness upon which it abruptly breaks, in twain? Does not every sudden shock, appearance of a new object, or change in a sensation, create a real interruption, sensibly felt as such, which cuts the conscious stream across at the moment at which it appears? Do not such interruptions smite us every hour of our lives, and have we the right, in their presence, still to call our consciousness a continuous stream?

This objection is based partly on a confusion and partly on a superficial introspective view.

The confusion is between the thoughts themselves, taken as subjective facts, and the things of which they are aware. It is natural to make this confusion, but easy to avoid it when once put on one's guard. The things are discrete and discontinuous; they do pass before

us in a train or chain, making often explosive appearances and rend-
ing each other in twain. But their comings and goings and contrasts no
more break the flow of the thought that thinks them than they break
the time and the space in which they lie. A silence may be broken by a
thunder-clap, and we may be so stunned and confused for a moment
by the shock as to give no instant account to ourselves of what has
happened. But that very confusion is a mental state, and a state that
passes us straight over from the silence to the sound. The transition
between the thought of one object and the thought of another is no
more a break in the *thought* than a joint in a bamboo is a break in the
wood. It is a part of the *consciousness* as much as the joint is a part of
the *bamboo*.

The superficial introspective view is the overlooking, even when
the things are contrasted with each other most violently, of the large
amount of affinity that may still remain between the thoughts by
whose means they are cognized. Into the awareness of the thunder
itself the awareness of the previous silence creeps and continues; for
what we hear when the thunder crashes is not thunder *pure,* but thun-
der-breaking-upon-silence-and-contrasting-with-it.[14] Our feeling of the
same objective thunder, coming in this way, is quite different from
what it would be were the thunder a continuation of previous thunder.
The thunder itself we believe to abolish and exclude the silence; but
the *feeling* of the thunder is also a feeling of the silence as just gone;
and it would be difficult to find in the actual concrete consciousness of
man a feeling so limited to the present as not to have an inkling of
anything that went before. Here, again, language works against our
perception of the truth. We name our thoughts simply, each after its
thing, as if each knew its own thing and nothing else. What each really
knows is clearly the thing it is named for, with dimly perhaps a thousand other things. It ought to be named after all of them, but it never
is. Some of them are always things known a moment ago more clearly;
others are things to be known more clearly a moment hence.[15] Our
own bodily position, attitude, condition, is one of the things of which

[14] Cf. Brentano; *Psychologie,* vol. I. pp. 219–20. Altogether this chapter of
Brentano's on the Unity of Consciousness is as good as anything with which I
am acquainted.

[15] Honor to whom honor is due! The most explicit acknowledgment I have
anywhere found of all this is in a buried and forgotten paper by the Rev. Jas.
Wills, on 'Accidental Association,' in the *Transactions of the Royal Irish Academy,* vol. XXI. part I (1846). Mr. Wills writes:

"At every instant of conscious thought there is a certain sum of perceptions,
or reflections, or both together, present, and together constituting one whole
state of apprehension. Of this some definite portion may be far more distinct
than all the rest; and the rest be in consequence proportionably vague, even to
the limit of obliteration. But still, within this limit, the most dim shade of perception enters into, and in some infinitesimal degree modifies, the whole existing

some awareness, however inattentive, invariably accompanies the knowledge of whatever else we know. We think; and as we think we feel our bodily selves as the seat of the thinking. If the thinking be *our* thinking, it must be suffused through all its parts with that peculiar warmth and intimacy that make it come as ours. Whether the warmth and intimacy be anything more than the feeling of the same old body always there, is a matter for the next chapter to decide. *Whatever* the content of the ego may be, it is habitually felt *with* everything else by us humans, and must form a *liaison* between all the things of which we become successively aware.[16]

On this gradualness in the changes of our mental content the principles of nerve-action can throw some more light. When studying, in Chapter III, the summation of nervous activities, we saw that no state of the brain can be supposed instantly to die away. If a new state comes, the inertia of the old state will still be there and modify the result accordingly. Of course we cannot tell, in our ignorance, what in each instance the modifications ought to be. The commonest modifications in sense-perception are known as the phenomena of contrast. In æsthetics they are the feelings of delight or displeasure which certain particular orders in a series of impressions give. In thought, strictly and narrowly so called, they are unquestionably that consciousness of the *whence* and the *whither* that always accompanies its flows. If recently the brain-tract *a* was vividly excited, and then *b,* and now vividly *c,* the total present consciousness is not produced simply by *c*'s excitement, but also by the dying vibrations of *a* and *b* as well. If we want to represent the brain-process we must write it thus: *c—*

$$\begin{matrix} & c— \\ & b \\ & a \end{matrix}$$

---

state. This state will thus be in some way modified by any sensation or emotion, or act of distinct attention, that may give prominence to any part of it; so that the actual result is capable of the utmost variation, according to the person or the occasion. . . . To any portion of the entire scope here described there may be a special direction of the attention, and this special direction is recognized as strictly what is *recognized* as the idea present to the mind. This idea is evidently not commensurate with the entire state of apprehension, and much perplexity has arisen from not observing this fact. However deeply we may suppose the attention to be engaged by any thought, any considerable alteration of the surrounding phenomena would still be perceived; the most abstruse demonstration in this room would not prevent a listener, however absorbed, from noticing the sudden extinction of the lights. Our mental states have always an *essential unity,* such that each state of apprehension, however variously compounded, is a single whole, of which every component is, therefore, strictly apprehended (so far as it is apprehended) as a part. Such is the elementary basis from which all our intellectual operations commence."

[16] Compare the charming passage in Taine *On Intelligence* (N. Y. ed.), I. 83–4.

three different processes coexisting, and correlated with them a thought which is no one of the three thoughts which they would have produced had each of them occurred alone. But whatever this fourth thought may exactly be, it seems impossible that it should not be something *like* each of the three other thoughts whose tracts are concerned in its production, though in a fast-waning phase.

It all goes back to what we said in another connection only a few pages ago (above, p. 28). As the total neurosis changes, so does the total psychosis change. But as the changes of neurosis are never absolutely discontinuous, so must the successive psychoses shade gradually into each other, although their *rate* of change may be much faster at one moment than at the next.

This difference in the rate of change lies at the basis of a difference of subjective states of which we ought immediately to speak. When the rate is slow we are aware of the object of our thought in a comparatively restful and stable way. When rapid, we are aware of a passage, a relation, a transition *from* it, or *between* it and something else. As we take, in fact, a general view of the wonderful stream of our consciousness, what strikes us first is this different pace of its parts. Like a bird's life, it seems to be made of an alternation of flights and perchings. The rhythm of language expresses this, where every thought is expressed in a sentence, and every sentence closed by a period. The resting-places are usually occupied by sensorial imaginations of some sort, whose peculiarity is that they can be held before the mind for an indefinite time, and contemplated without changing; the places of flight are filled with thoughts of relations, static or dynamic, that for the most part obtain between the matters contemplated in the periods of comparative rest.

Let us call the resting-places the 'substantive parts,' and the places of flight the 'transitive parts,' of the stream of thought. It then appears that the main end of our thinking is at all times the attainment of some other substantive part than the one from which we have just been dislodged. And we may say that the main use of the transitive parts is to lead us from one substantive conclusion to another.

Now it is very difficult, introspectively, to see the transitive parts for what they really are. If they are but flights to a conclusion, stopping them to look at them before the conclusion is reached is really annihilating them. Whilst if we wait till the conclusion *be* reached, it so exceeds them in vigor and stability that it quite eclipses and swallows them up in its glare. Let anyone try to cut a thought across in the middle and get a look at its section, and he will see how difficult the introspective observation of the transitive tracts is. The rush of the thought is so headlong that it almost always brings us up at the conclusion before we can arrest it. Or if our purpose is nimble enough and we do arrest it, it ceases forthwith to be itself. As a snowflake crystal caught in the warm hand is no longer a crystal but a drop, so, instead of catching the feeling of relation moving to its term, we find we have caught some substantive thing, usually the last word we were pronouncing, statically taken, and with its function, tendency, and particular meaning in the sentence quite evaporated. The attempt at introspective analysis in these cases is in fact like seizing a spinning top to catch its motion, or trying to turn up the gas quickly enough to see how the darkness looks. And the challenge to *produce* these psychoses, which is sure to be thrown by doubting psychologists at anyone who contends for their existence, is as unfair as Zeno's treatment of the advocates of motion, when, asking them to point out in what place an arrow *is* when it moves, he argues the falsity of their thesis from their inability to make to so preposterous a question an immediate reply.

The results of this introspective difficulty are baleful. If to hold fast and observe the transitive parts of thought's stream be so hard, then the great blunder to which all schools are liable must be the failure to register them, and the undue emphasizing of the more substantive parts of the stream. Were we not ourselves a moment since in danger of ignoring any feeling transitive between the silence and the thunder, and of treating their boundary as a sort of break in the mind? Now such ignoring as this has historically worked in two ways. One set of thinkers have been led by it to *Sensationalism*. Unable to lay their hands on any coarse feelings corresponding to the innumerable relations and forms of connection between the facts of the world; finding no *named* subjective modifications mirroring such relations, they have for the most part denied that feelings of relation exist, and many of them, like Hume, have gone so far as to deny the reality of most relations *out* of the mind as well as in it. Substantive psychoses, sensations and their copies and derivatives, juxtaposed like dominoes in a game, but really separate, everything else verbal illusion,—such is the upshot of this view.[17] The *Intellectualists,* on the other hand, unable to give up the reality of relations *extra mentem,* but equally unable to point to any distinct substantive feelings in which they were known, have made the same admission that the feelings do not exist. But they have drawn an opposite conclusion. The relations must be known, they say, in something that is no feeling, no mental modification continuous and consubstantial with the subjective tissue out of which sen-

[17] E.g.: "The stream of thought is not a continuous current, but a series of distinct ideas, more or less rapid in their succession; the rapidity being measurable by the number that pass through the mind in a given time." (Bain: *E. and W.*, p. 29.)

sations and other substantive states are made. They are known, these relations, by something that lies on an entirely different plane, by an *actus purus* of Thought, Intellect, or Reason, all written with capitals and considered to mean something unutterably superior to any fact of sensibility whatever.

But from our point of view both Intellectualists and Sensationalists are wrong. If there be such things as feelings at all, *then so surely as relations between objects exist in rerum naturâ, so surely, and more surely, do feelings exist to which these relations are known.* There is not a conjunction or a preposition, and hardly an adverbial phrase, syntactic form, or inflection of voice, in human speech, that does not express some shading or other of relation which we at some moment actually feel to exist between the larger objects of our thought. If we speak objectively, it is the real relations that appear revealed; if we speak subjectively, it is the stream of consciousness that matches each of them by an inward coloring of its own. In either case the relations are numberless, and no existing language is capable of doing justice to all their shades.

We ought to say a feeling of *and,* a feeling of *if,* a feeling of *but,* and a feeling of *by,* quite as readily as we say a feeling of *blue* or a feeling of *cold.* Yet we do not: so inveterate has our habit become of recognizing the existence of the substantive parts alone, that language almost refuses to lend itself to any other use. The Empiricists have always dwelt on its influence in making us suppose that where we have a separate name, a separate thing must needs be there to correspond with it; and they have rightly denied the existence of the mob of abstract entities, principles, and forces, in whose favor no other evidence than this could be brought up. But they have said nothing of that obverse error, of which we said a word in Chapter VII, of supposing that where there is *no* name no entity can exist. All *dumb* or anonymous psychic states have, owing to this error, been coolly suppressed; or, if recognized at all, have been named after the substantive perception they led to, as thoughts 'about' this object or 'about' that, the stolid word *about* engulfing all their delicate idiosyncrasies in its monotonous sound. Thus the greater and greater accentuation and isolation of the substantive parts have continually gone on.

Once more take a look at the brain. We believe the brain to be an organ whose internal equilibrium is always in a state of change,—the change affecting every part. The pulses of change are doubtless more violent in one place than in another, their rhythm more rapid at this time than at that. As in a kaleidoscope revolving at a uniform rate, although the figures are always rearranging themselves, there are instants during which the transformation seems minute and interstitial and almost absent, followed by others when it shoots with magical rapidity, relatively stable forms thus alternating with forms we should not distinguish if seen again; so in the brain the perpetual rearrangement must result in some forms of tension lingering relatively long, whilst others simply come and pass. But if consciousness corresponds to the fact of rearrangement itself, why, if the rearrangement stop not, should the consciousness ever cease? And if a lingering rearrangement brings with it one kind of consciousness, why should not a swift rearrangement bring another kind of consciousness as peculiar as the rearrangement itself? The lingering consciousnesses, if of simple objects, we call 'sensations' or 'images,' according as they are vivid or faint; if of complex objects, we call them 'percepts' when vivid, 'concepts' or 'thoughts' when faint. For the swift consciousnesses we have only those names of 'transitive states,' or 'feelings of relation,' which we have used.[18] As the brain-changes are continuous,

[18] Few writers have admitted that we cognize relations through feeling. The intellectualists have explicitly denied the possibility of such a thing—e.g., Prof. T. H. Green (*Mind,* vol. VII. p. 28): "No feeling, as such or as felt, is [of?] a relation. . . . Even a relation between feelings is not itself a feeling or felt." On the other hand, the sensationists have either smuggled in the cognition without giving any account of it, or have denied the relations to be cognized, or even to exist, at all. A few honorable exceptions, however, deserve to be named among the sensationists. Destutt de Tracy, Laromiguière, Cardaillac, Brown, and finally Spencer, have explicitly contended for feelings of relation, consubstantial with our feelings or thoughts of the terms 'between' which they obtain. Thus Destutt de Tracy says (*Éléments d'Idéologie,* T. Ier, chap. IV): "The faculty of judgment is itself a sort of sensibility, for it is the faculty of feeling the relations among our ideas; and to feel relations is to feel." Laromiguière writes (*Leçons de Philosophie,* IIme Partie, 3me Leçon):

"There is no one whose intelligence does not embrace simultaneously many ideas, more or less distinct, more or less confused. Now, when we have many ideas at once, a peculiar feeling arises in us: we feel, among these ideas, resemblances, differences, relations. Let us call this mode of feeling, common to us all, the feeling of relation, or relation-feeling (*sentiment-rapport*). One sees immediately that these relation-feelings, resulting from the propinquity of ideas, must be infinitely more numerous than the sensation-feelings (*sentiments-sensations*) or the feelings we have of the action of our faculties. The slightest knowledge of the mathematical theory of combinations will prove this. . . . *Ideas* of relation originate in feelings of relation. They are the effect of our comparing them and reasoning about them."

Similarly, de Cardaillac (*Études Élémentaires de Philosophie,* Section I. chap. VII):

"By a natural consequence, we are led to suppose that at the same time that we have several sensations or several ideas in the mind, we feel the relations which exist between these sensations, and the relations which exist between these ideas. . . . If the feeling of relations exists in us, . . . it is necessarily the most varied and the most fertile of all human feelings: 1° the most varied, because, relations being more numerous than beings, the feelings of relation must be in the same proportion more numerous than the sensations whose presence gives rise to their formation; 2°, the most fertile, for the relative ideas of which the feeling-of-relation is the source . . . are more important than absolute

so do all these consciousnesses melt into each other like dissolving views. Properly they are but one protracted consciousness, one unbroken stream.

---

ideas, if such exist. . . . If we interrogate common speech, we find the feeling of relation expressed there in a thousand different ways. If it is easy to seize a relation, we say that it is *sensible,* to distinguish it from one which, because its terms are too remote, cannot be as quickly perceived. A sensible difference, or resemblance. . . . What is taste in the arts, in intellectual productions? What but the feeling of those relations among the parts which constitutes their merit? . . . Did we not feel relations we should never attain to true knowledge, . . . for almost all our knowledge is of relations. . . . We never have an isolated sensation; . . . we are therefore never without the feeling of relation. . . . An *object* strikes our senses; we see in it only a sensation. . . . The relative is so near the absolute, the relation-feeling so near the sensation-feeling, the two are so intimately fused in the composition of the object, that the relation appears to us as part of the sensation itself. It is doubtless to this sort of fusion between sensations and feelings of relation that the silence of metaphysicians as to the latter is due; and it is for the same reason that they have obstinately persisted in asking from sensation alone those ideas of relation which it was powerless to give."

Dr. Thomas Brown writes (*Lectures,* XLV. *init.*): "There is an extensive order of our feelings which involve this notion of relation, and which consist indeed in the mere perception of a relation of some sort. . . . Whether the relation be of two or of many external objects, or of two or many affections of the mind, the feeling of this relation . . . is what I term a relative suggestion; that phrase being the simplest which it is possible to employ, for expressing, without any theory, the mere fact of the rise of certain feelings of relation, after certain other feelings which precede them; and therefore, as involving no particular theory, and simply expressive of an undoubted fact. . . . That the feelings of relation are states of the mind essentially different from our simple perceptions, or conceptions of the objects, . . . that they are not what Condillac terms *transformed sensations,* I proved in a former lecture, when I combated the excessive simplification of that ingenious but not very accurate philosopher. There is an original tendency or susceptibility of the mind, by which, on perceiving together different objects, we are instantly, without the intervention of any other mental process, sensible of their relation in certain respects, as truly as there is an original tendency or susceptibility by which, when external objects are present and have produced a certain affection of our sensorial organ, we are instantly affected with the primary elementary feelings of perception; and, I may add, that as our sensations or perceptions are of various species, so are there various species of relations;—the number of relations, indeed, even of external things, being almost infinite, while the number of perceptions is, necessarily, limited by that of the objects which have the power of producing some affection of our organs of sensation. . . . Without that susceptibility of the mind by which it has the feeling of relation, our consciousness would be as truly limited to a single point, as our body would become, were it possible to fetter it to a single atom."

Mr. Spencer is even more explicit. His philosophy is crude in that he seems to suppose that it is only in transitive states that outward relations are known; whereas in truth space-relations, relations of contrast, etc., are felt along with their terms, in substantive states as well as in transitive states, as we shall abundantly see. Nevertheless Mr. Spencer's passage is so clear that it also deserves to be quoted in full (*Principles of Psychology,* § 65):

FEELINGS OF TENDENCY

So much for the transitive states. But there are other unnamed states or qualities of states that are just as important and just as cognitive as they, and just as much unrecognized by the traditional sensationalist

---

"The proximate components of Mind are of two broadly-contrasted kinds—Feelings and the relations between feelings. Among the members of each group there exist multitudinous unlikenesses, many of which are extremely strong; but such unlikenesses are small compared with those which distinguish members of the one group from members of the other. Let us, in the first place, consider what are the characters which all Feelings have in common, and what are the characters which all Relations between feelings have in common.

"Each feeling, as we here define it, is any portion of consciousness which occupies a place sufficiently large to give it a perceivable individuality; which has its individuality marked off from adjacent portions of consciousness by qualitative contrasts; and which, when introspectively contemplated, appears to be homogeneous. These are the essentials. Obviously if, under introspection, a state of consciousness is decomposable into unlike parts that exist either simultaneously or successively, it is not one feeling but two or more. Obviously if it is indistinguishable from an adjacent portion of consciousness, it forms one with that portion—is not an individual feeling, but part of one. And obviously if it does not occupy in consciousness an appreciable area, or an appreciable duration, it cannot be known as a feeling.

"A Relation between feelings is, on the contrary, characterized by occupying no appreciable part of consciousness. Take away the terms it unites, and it disappears along with them; having no independent place, no individuality of its own. It is true that, under an ultimate analysis, what we call a relation proves to be itself a kind of feeling—the momentary feeling accompanying the transition from one conspicuous feeling to an adjacent conspicuous feeling. And it is true that, notwithstanding its extreme brevity, its qualitative character is appreciable; for relations are (as we shall hereafter see) distinguishable from one another only by the unlikenesses of the feelings which accompany the momentary transitions. Each relational feeling may, in fact, be regarded as one of those nervous shocks which we suspect to be the units of composition of feelings; and, though instantaneous, it is known as of greater or less strength, and as taking place with greater or less facility. But the contrast between these relational feelings and what we ordinarily call feelings is so strong that we must class them apart. Their extreme brevity, their small variety, and their dependence on the terms they unite, differentiate them in an unmistakable way.

"Perhaps it will be well to recognize more fully the truth that this distinction cannot be absolute. Besides admitting that, as an element of consciousness, a relation is a momentary feeling, we must also admit that just as a relation can have no existence apart from the feelings which form its terms, so a feeling can exist only by relations to other feelings which limit it in space or time or both. Strictly speaking, neither a feeling nor a relation is an independent element of consciousness: there is throughout a dependence such that the appreciable areas of consciousness occupied by feelings can no more possess individualities apart from the relations which link them, than these relations can possess individualities apart from the feelings they link. The essential distinction between the two,

and intellectualist philosophies of mind. The first fails to find them at all, the second finds their *cognitive function,* but denies that anything in the way of *feeling* has a share in bringing it about. Examples will make clear what these inarticulate psychoses, due to waxing and waning excitements of the brain, are like.[19]

Suppose three successive persons say to us: 'Wait!' 'Hark!' 'Look!' Our consciousness is thrown into three quite different attitudes of expectancy, although no definite object is before it in any one of the three cases. Leaving out different actual bodily attitudes, and leaving out the reverberating images of the three words, which are of course diverse, probably no one will deny the existence of a residual conscious affection, a sense of the direction from which an impression is about to come, although no positive impression is yet there. Meanwhile we have no names for the psychoses in question but the names hark, look, and wait.

Suppose we try to recall a forgotten name. The state of our consciousness is peculiar. There is a gap therein; but no mere gap. It is a gap that is intensely active. A sort of wraith of the name is in it, beckoning us in a given direction, making us at moments tingle with the sense of our closeness, and then letting us sink back without the longed-for term. If wrong names are proposed to us, this singularly definite gap acts immediately so as to negate them. They do not fit

---

then, appears to be that whereas a relational feeling is a portion of consciousness inseparable into parts, a feeling, ordinarily so called, is a portion of consciousness that admits imaginary division into like parts which are related to one another in sequence or coexistence. A feeling proper is either made up of like parts that occupy time, or it is made up of like parts that occupy space, or both. In any case, a feeling proper is an aggregate of related like parts, while a relational feeling is undecomposable. And this is exactly the contrast between the two which must result if, as we have inferred, feelings are composed of units of feelings, or shocks."

[19] M. Paulhan (*Revue Philosophique*, xx. 455–6), after speaking of the faint mental images of objects and emotions, says: "We find other vaguer states still, upon which attention seldom rests, except in persons who by nature or profession are addicted to internal observation. It is even difficult to name them precisely, for they are little known and not classed; but we may cite as an example of them that peculiar impression which we feel when, strongly preoccupied by a certain subject, we nevertheless are engaged with, and have our attention almost completely absorbed by, matters quite disconnected therewithal. We do not then exactly think of the object of our preoccupation; we do not represent it in a clear manner; and yet our mind is not as it would be without this preoccupation. Its object, absent from consciousness, is nevertheless represented there by a peculiar unmistakable impression, which often persists long and is a strong feeling, although so obscure for our intelligence." "A mental sign of the kind is the unfavorable disposition left in our mind towards an individual by painful incidents erewhile experienced and now perhaps forgotten. The sign remains, but is not understood; its definite meaning is lost." (P. 458.)

into its mould. And the gap of one word does not feel like the gap of another, all empty of content as both might seem necessary to be when described as gaps. When I vainly try to recall the name of Spalding, my consciousness is far removed from what it is when I vainly try to recall the name of Bowles. Here some ingenious persons will say: "How *can* the two consciousnesses be different when the terms which might make them different are not there? All that is there, so long as the effort to recall is vain, is the bare effort itself. How should that differ in the two cases? You are making it seem to differ by prematurely filling it out with the different names, although these, by the hypothesis, have not yet come. Stick to the two efforts as they are, without naming them after facts not yet existent, and you'll be quite unable to designate any point in which they differ." Designate, truly enough. We can only designate the difference by borrowing the names of objects not yet in the mind. Which is to say that our psychological vocabulary is wholly inadequate to name the differences that exist, even such strong differences as these. But namelessness is compatible with existence. There are innumerable consciousnesses of emptiness, no one of which taken in itself has a name, but all different from each other. The ordinary way is to assume that they are all emptinesses of consciousness, and so the same state. But the feeling of an absence is *toto cœlo* other than the absence of a feeling. It is an intense feeling. The rhythm of a lost word may be there without a sound to clothe it; or the evanescent sense of something which is the initial vowel or consonant may mock us fitfully, without growing more distinct. Every one must know the tantalizing effect of the blank rhythm of some forgotten verse, restlessly dancing in one's mind, striving to be filled out with words.

Again, what is the strange difference between an experience tasted for the first time and the same experience recognized as familiar, as having been enjoyed before, though we cannot name it or say where or when? A tune, an odor, a flavor sometimes carry this inarticulate feeling of their familiarity so deep into our consciousness that we are fairly shaken by its mysterious emotional power. But strong and characteristic as this psychosis is—it probably is due to the submaximal excitement of wide-spreading associational brain-tracts—the only name we have for all its shadings is 'sense of familiarity.'

When we read such phrases as 'naught but,' 'either one or the other,' '*a* is *b,* but,' 'although it is, nevertheless,' 'it is an excluded middle, there is no *tertium quid,*' and a host of other verbal skeletons of logical relation, is it true that there is nothing more in our minds than the words themselves as they pass? What then is the meaning of the words which we think we understand as we read? What makes that meaning different in one phrase from what it is in the other?

'Who?' 'When?' 'Where?' Is the difference of felt meaning in these interrogatives nothing more than their difference of sound? And is it not (just like the difference of sound itself) known and understood in an affection of consciousness correlative to it, though so impalpable to direct examination? Is not the same true of such negatives as 'no,' 'never,' 'not yet'?

The truth is that large tracts of human speech are nothing but *signs of direction* in thought, of which direction we nevertheless have an acutely discriminative sense, though no definite sensorial image plays any part in it whatsoever. Sensorial images are stable psychic facts; we can hold them still and look at them as long as we like. These bare images of logical movement, on the contrary, are psychic transitions, always on the wing, so to speak, and not to be glimpsed except in flight. Their function is to lead from one set of images to another. As they pass, we feel both the waxing and the waning images in a way altogether peculiar and a way quite different from the way of their full presence. If we try to hold fast the feeling of direction, the full presence comes and the feeling of direction is lost. The blank verbal scheme of the logical movement gives us the fleeting sense of the movement as we read it, quite as well as does a rational sentence awakening definite imaginations by its words.

What is that first instantaneous glimpse of some one's meaning which we have, when in vulgar phrase we say we 'twig' it? Surely an altogether specific affection of our mind. And has the reader never asked himself what kind of a mental fact is his *intention of saying a thing* before he has said it? It is an entirely definite intention, distinct from all other intentions, an absolutely distinct state of consciousness, therefore; and yet how much of it consists of definite sensorial images, either of words or of things? Hardly anything! Linger, and the words and things come into the mind; the anticipatory intention, the divination is there no more. But as the words that replace it arrive, it welcomes them successively and calls them right if they agree with it, it rejects them and calls them wrong if they do not. It has therefore a nature of its own of the most positive sort, and yet what can we say about it without using words that belong to the later mental facts that replace it? The intention *to-say-so-and-so* is the only name it can receive. One may admit that a good third of our psychic life consists in these rapid premonitory perspective views of schemes of thought not yet articulate. How comes it about that a man reading something aloud for the first time is able immediately to emphasize all his words aright, unless from the very first he have a sense of at least the form of the sentence yet to come, which sense is fused with his consciousness of the present word, and modifies its emphasis in his mind so as to make him give it the proper accent as he utters it? Emphasis of this kind is almost altogether a matter of grammatical construction. If we read 'no more' we expect presently to come upon a 'than'; if we read 'however' at the outset of a sentence it is a 'yet,' a 'still,' or a 'nevertheless,' that we expect. A noun in a certain position demands a verb in a certain mood and number, in another position it expects a relative pronoun. Adjectives call for nouns, verbs for adverbs, etc., etc. And this foreboding of the coming grammatical scheme combined with each successive uttered word is so practically accurate that a reader incapable of understanding four ideas of the book he is reading aloud, can nevertheless read it with the most delicately modulated expression of intelligence.

Some will interpret these facts by calling them all cases in which certain images, by laws of association, awaken others so very rapidly that we think afterwards we felt the very *tendencies* of the nascent images to arise, before they were actually there. For this school the only possible materials of consciousness are images of a perfectly definite nature. Tendencies exist, but they are facts for the outside psychologist rather than for the subject of the observation. The tendency is thus a *psychical* zero; only its *results* are felt.

Now what I contend for, and accumulate examples to show, is that 'tendencies' are not only descriptions from without, but that they are among the *objects* of the stream, which is thus aware of them from within, and must be described as in very large measure constituted of *feelings* of *tendency*, often so vague that we are unable to name them at all. It is, in short, the re-instatement of the vague to its proper place in our mental life which I am so anxious to press on the attention. Mr. Galton and Prof. Huxley have, as we shall see in Chapter XVIII, made one step in advance in exploding the ridiculous theory of Hume and Berkeley that we can have no images but of perfectly definite things. Another is made in the overthrow of the equally ridiculous notion that, whilst simple objective qualities are revealed to our knowledge in subjective feelings, relations are not. But these reforms are not half sweeping and radical enough. What must be admitted is that the definite images of traditional psychology form but the very smallest part of our minds as they actually live. The traditional psychology talks like one who should say a river consists of nothing but pailsful, spoonsful, quartpotsful, barrelsful, and other moulded forms of water. Even were the pails and the pots all actually standing in the stream, still between them the free water would continue to flow. It is just this free water of consciousness that psychologists resolutely overlook. Every definite image in the mind is steeped and dyed in the free water that flows round it. With it goes the sense of its relations, near and remote, the dying echo of whence it came to us, the dawning sense of whither it is to lead. The significance, the value, of the image is all in this halo or penumbra that surrounds and escorts it,—or rather that is fused into one with it and has become bone of its bone and flesh of its flesh; leaving it, it is true, an image of the same *thing* it was before, but making it an image of that thing newly taken and freshly understood.

What is that shadowy scheme of the 'form' of an opera, play, or book, which remains in our mind and on which we pass judgment when the actual thing is done? What is our notion of a scientific or philosophical system? Great thinkers have vast premonitory glimpses of schemes of relation between terms, which hardly even as verbal images enter the mind, so rapid is the whole process.[20] We all of us have this permanent consciousness of whither our thought is going. It is a feeling like any other, a feeling of what thoughts are next to arise, before they have arisen. This field of view of consciousness varies very much in extent, depending largely on the degree of mental freshness or fatigue. When very fresh, our minds carry an immense horizon with them. The present image shoots its perspective far before it, irradiating in advance the regions in which lie the thoughts as yet unborn. Under ordinary conditions the halo of felt relations is much more circumscribed. And in states of extreme brain-fag the horizon is narrowed almost to the passing word,—the associative machinery, however, providing for the next word turning up in orderly sequence, until at last the tired thinker is led to some kind of a conclusion. At certain moments he may find himself doubting whether his thoughts have not come to a full stop; but the vague sense of a *plus ultra* makes him ever struggle on towards a more definite expression of what it may be; whilst the slowness of his utterance shows how difficult, under such conditions, the labor of thinking must be.

The awareness that our *definite* thought has come to a stop is an entirely different thing from the awareness that our thought is definitively completed. The expression of the latter state of mind is the falling inflection which betokens that the sentence is ended, and silence. The expression of the former state is 'hemming and hawing,' or else such phrases as *'et cetera,'* or 'and so forth.' But notice that every part of the sentence to be left incomplete feels differently as it passes,

[20] Mozart describes thus his manner of composing: First bits and crumbs of the piece come and gradually join together in his mind; then the soul getting warmed to the work, the thing grows more and more, "and I spread it out broader and clearer, and at last its gets almost finished in my head, even when it is a long piece, so that I can see the whole of it at a single glance in my mind, as if it were a beautiful painting or a handsome human being; in which way I do not hear it in my imagination at all as a succession—the way it must come later—but all at once, as it were. It is a rare feast! All the inventing and making goes on in me as in a beautiful strong dream. But the best of all is the *hearing of it all at once*."

by reason of the premonition we have that we shall be unable to end it. The 'and so forth' casts its shadow back, and is as integral a part of the object of the thought as the distinctest of images would be.

Again, when we use a common noun, such as *man,* in a universal sense, as signifying all possible men, we are fully aware of this intention on our part, and distinguish it carefully from our intention when we mean a certain group of men, or a solitary individual before us. In the chapter on Conception we shall see how important this difference of intention is. It casts its influence over the whole of the sentence, both before and after the spot in which the word *man* is used.

Nothing is easier than to symbolize all these facts in terms of brain-action. Just as the echo of the *whence,* the sense of the starting point of our thought, is probably due to the dying excitement of processes but a moment since vividly aroused; so the sense of the *whither,* the foretaste of the terminus, must be due to the waxing excitement of tracts or processes which, a moment hence, will be the cerebral correlatives of some thing which a moment hence will be vividly present to the thought. Represented by a curve, the neurosis underlying consciousness must at any moment be like this:

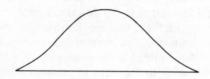

Each point of the horizontal line stands for some brain-tract or process. The height of the curve above the line stands for the intensity of the process. All the processes are *present,* in the intensities shown by the curve. But those before the latter's apex *were* more intense a moment ago; those after it *will be* more intense a moment hence. If I recite *a, b, c, d, e, f, g,* at the moment of uttering *d,* neither *a, b, c,* nor *e, f, g,* are out of my consciousness altogether, but both, after their respective fashions, 'mix their dim lights' with the stronger one of the *d,* because their neuroses are both awake in some degree.

There is a common class of mistakes which shows how brain-processes begin to be excited before the thoughts attached to them are *due*—due, that is, in substantive and vivid form. I mean those mistakes of speech or writing by which, in Dr. Carpenter's words, "we mispronounce or misspell a word, by introducing into it a letter or syllable of some other, whose turn is shortly to come; or, it may be, the whole of the anticipated word is substituted for the one which ought to have been expressed." [21] In these cases one of two things must have happened: either some local accident of nutrition *blocks* the process that is *due,* so that other processes discharge that ought as yet to be but nascently aroused; or some opposite local accident *furthers* the *latter processes* and makes them explode before their time. In the chapter on Association of Ideas, numerous instances will come before us of the actual effect on consciousness of neuroses not yet maximally aroused.

It is just like the 'overtones' in music. Different instruments give the 'same note,' but each in a different voice, because each gives more than that note, namely, various upper harmonics of it which differ from one instrument to another. They are not separately heard by the ear; they blend with the fundamental note, and suffuse it, and alter it; and even so do the waxing and waning brain-processes at every moment blend with and suffuse and alter the psychic effect of the processes which are at their culminating point.

Let us use the words *psychic overtone, suffusion,* or *fringe,* to designate the influence of a faint brain-process upon our thought, as it makes it aware of relations and objects but dimly perceived.[22]

If we then consider the *cognitive function* of different states of mind, we may feel assured that the difference between those that are mere 'acquaintance,' and those that are 'knowledges-*about*' is reducible almost entirely to the absence or presence of psychic fringes or overtones. Knowledge *about* a thing is knowledge of its relations. Acquaintance with it is limitation to the bare impression which it makes. Of most of its relations we are only aware in the penumbral nascent way of a 'fringe' of unarticulated affinities about it. And, before passing to the next topic in order, I must say a little of this sense of affinity, as itself one of the most interesting features of the subjective stream.

[21] *Mental Physiology,* § 236. Dr. Carpenter's explanation differs materially from that given in the text.

[22] Cf. also S. Stricker: *Vorlesungen über allg. u. exp. Pathologie* (1879), pp. 462–3, 501, 547; Romanes: *Origin of Human Faculty,* p. 82. It is so hard to make one's self clear that I may advert to a misunderstanding of my views by the late Prof. Thos. Maguire of Dublin (*Lectures on Philosophy,* 1885). This author considers that by the 'fringe' I mean some sort of psychic material by which sensations in themselves separate are made to cohere together, and wittily says that I ought to "see that uniting sensations by their 'fringes' is more vague than to construct the universe out of oysters by platting their beards" (p. 211). But the fringe, as I use the word, means nothing like this; it is part of the *object cognized,*—substantive *qualities* and *things* appearing to the mind in a *fringe of relations.* Some parts—the transitive parts—of our stream of thought cognize the relations rather than the things; but both the transitive and the substantive parts form one continuous stream, with no discrete 'sensations' in it such as Prof. Maguire supposes, and supposes me suppose, to be there.

In all our voluntary thinking there is some topic or subject about which all the members of the thought revolve. Half the time this topic is a problem, a gap we cannot yet fill with a definite picture, word, or phrase, but which, in the manner described some time back, influences us in an intensely active and determinate psychic way. Whatever may be the images and phrases that pass before us, we feel their relation to this aching gap. To fill it up is our thought's destiny. Some bring us nearer to that consummation. Some the gap negates as quite irrelevant. Each swims in a felt fringe of relations of which the aforesaid gap is the term. Or instead of a definite gap we may merely carry a mood of interest about with us. Then, however vague the mood, it will still act in the same way, throwing a mantle of felt affinity over such representations, entering the mind, as suit it, and tingeing with the feeling of tediousness or discord all those with which it has no concern.

Relation, then, to our topic or interest is constantly felt in the fringe, and particularly the relation of harmony and discord, of furtherance or hindrance of the topic. When the sense of furtherance is there, we are 'all right;' with the sense of hindrance we are dissatisfied and perplexed, and cast about us for other thoughts. Now *any* thought the quality of whose fringe lets us feel ourselves 'all right,' is an acceptable member of our thinking, whatever kind of thought it may otherwise be. Provided we only feel it to have a place in the scheme of relations in which the interesting topic also lies, that is quite sufficient to make of it a relevant and appropriate portion of our train of ideas.

For the important thing about a train of thought is its conclusion. That is the *meaning,* or, as we say, the topic of the thought. That is what abides when all its other members have faded from memory. Usually this conclusion is a word or phrase or particular image, or practical attitude or resolve, whether rising to answer a problem or fill a pre-existing gap that worried us, or whether accidentally stumbled on in revery. In either case it stands out from the other segments of the stream by reason of the peculiar interest attaching to it. This interest *arrests* it, makes a sort of crisis of it when it comes, induces attention upon it and makes us treat it in a substantive way.

The parts of the stream that precede these substantive conclusions are but the means of the latter's attainment. And, provided the same conclusion be reached, the means may be as mutable as we like, for the 'meaning' of the stream of thought will be the same. What difference does it make what the means are? *"Qu'importe le flacon, pourvu qu'on ait l'ivresse?"* The relative unimportance of the means appears from the fact that when the conclusion is there, we have always forgotten most of the steps preceding its attainment. When we have uttered a proposition, we are rarely able a moment afterwards to recall our exact words, though we can express it in different words easily enough. The practical upshot of a book we read remains with us, though we may not recall one of its sentences.

The only paradox would seem to lie in supposing that the fringe of felt affinity and discord can be the same in two heterogeneous sets of images. Take a train of words passing through the mind and leading to a certain conclusion on the one hand, and on the other hand an almost wordless set of tactile, visual and other fancies leading to the same conclusion. Can the halo, fringe, or scheme in which we feel the words to lie be the same as that in which we feel the images to lie? Does not the discrepancy of terms involve a discrepancy of felt relations among them?

If the terms be taken *quâ* mere sensations, it assuredly does. For instance, the words may rhyme with each other,—the visual images can have no such affinity as *that*. But *quâ* thoughts, *quâ* sensations *understood,* the words have contracted by long association fringes of mutual repugnance or affinity with each other and with the conclusion, which run exactly parallel with like fringes in the visual, tactile and other ideas. The most important element of these fringes is, I repeat, the mere feeling of harmony or discord, of a right or wrong direction in the thought. Dr. Campbell has, so far as I know, made the best analysis of this fact, and his words, often quoted, deserve to be quoted again. The chapter is entitled "What is the cause that nonsense so often escapes being detected, both by the writer and by the reader?" The author, in answering this question, makes (*inter alia*) the following remarks:[23]

> That connection [he says] or relation which comes gradually to subsist among the different words of a language, in the minds of those who speak it, . . . is merely consequent on this, that those words are employed as signs of connected or related things. It is an axiom in geometry that things equal to the same thing are equal to one another. It may, in like manner, be admitted as an axiom in psychology that ideas associated by the same idea will associate one another. Hence it will happen that if, from experiencing the connection of two things, there results, as infallibly there will result, an association between the ideas or notions annexed to them, as each idea will moreover be associated by its sign, there will likewise be an association between the ideas of the signs. Hence the sounds considered as signs will be conceived to have a connection analogous to that which subsisteth among the things signified; I say, the sounds considered as signs; for this way of considering them constantly attends us in speaking, writing, hearing, and reading. When we purposely abstract from it, and regard them merely as sounds, we are instantly sensible that they are quite unconnected, and have no other relation than what ariseth from simili-

[23] George Campbell: *Philosophy of Rhetoric,* book II. chap. VII.

tude of tone or accent. But to consider them in this manner commonly results from previous design, and requires a kind of effort which is not exerted in the ordinary use of speech. In ordinary use they are regarded solely as signs, or, rather, they are confounded with the things they signify; the consequence of which is that, in the manner just now explained, we come insensibly to conceive a connection among them of a very different sort from that of which sounds are naturally susceptible.

Now this conception, habit, or tendency of the mind, call it which you please, is considerably strengthened by the frequent use of language and by the structure of it. Language is the sole channel through which we communicate our knowledge and discoveries to others, and through which the knowledge and discoveries of others are communicated to us. By reiterated recourse to this medium, it necessarily happens that when things are related to each other, the words signifying those things are more commonly brought together in discourse. Hence the words and names by themselves, by customary vicinity, contract in the fancy a relation additional to that which they derive purely from being the symbols of related things. Farther, this tendency is strengthened by the structure of language. All languages whatever, even the most barbarous, as far as hath yet appeared, are of a regular and analogical make. The consequence is that similar relations in things will be expressed similarly; that is, by similar inflections, derivations, compositions, arrangement of words, or juxtaposition of particles, according to the genius or grammatical form of the particular tongue. Now as, by the habitual use of a language (even though it were quite irregular), the signs would insensibly become connected in the imagination wherever the things signified are connected in nature, so, by the regular structure of a language, this connection among the signs is conceived as analogous to that which subsisteth among their archetypes.

If we know English and French and begin a sentence in French, all the later words that come are French; we hardly ever drop into English. And this affinity of the French words for each other is not something merely operating mechanically as a brain-law, it is something we feel at the time. Our understanding of a French sentence heard never falls to so low an ebb that we are not aware that the words linguistically belong together. Our attention can hardly so wander that if an English word be suddenly introduced we shall not start at the change. Such a vague sense as this of the words belonging together is the very minimum of fringe that can accompany them, if 'thought' at all. Usually the vague perception that all the words we hear belong to the same language and to the same special vocabulary in that language, and that the grammatical sequence is familiar, is practically equivalent to an admission that what we hear is sense. But if an unusual foreign word be introduced, if the grammar trip, or if a term from an incongruous vocabulary suddenly appear, such as 'rattrap' or 'plumber's bill' in a philosophical discourse, the sentence detonates, as it were, we receive a shock from the incongruity, and the drowsy assent is gone. The feeling of rationality in these cases seems rather a negative than a positive thing, being the mere absence of shock, or sense of discord, between the terms of thought.

So delicate and incessant is this recognition by the mind of the mere fitness of words to be mentioned together that the slightest misreading, such as 'casualty' for 'causality,' or 'perpetual' for 'perceptual,' will be corrected by a listener whose attention is so relaxed that he gets no idea of the *meaning* of the sentence at all.

Conversely, if words do belong to the same vocabulary, and if the grammatical structure is correct, sentences with absolutely no meaning may be uttered in good faith and pass unchallenged.[24] Discourses at prayer-meetings, reshuffling the same collection of cant phrases, and the whole genus of penny-a-line-isms and newspaper-reporter's flourishes give illustrations of this. "The birds filled the tree-tops with their morning song, making the air moist, cool, and pleasant," is a sentence I remember reading once in a report of some athletic exercises in Jerome Park. It was probably written unconsciously by the hurried reporter, and read uncritically by many readers. An entire volume of 784 pages lately published in Boston[25] is composed of stuff like this passage picked out at random:

> The flow of the efferent fluids of all these vessels from their outlets at the terminal loop of each culminate link on the surface of the nuclear organism is continuous as their respective atmospheric fruitage up to the altitudinal limit of their expansibility, whence, when atmosphered by like but coalescing essences from higher altitudes,—those sensibly expressed as the essential qualities of external forms,—they descend, and become assimilated by the afferents of the nuclear organism.

There are every year works published whose contents show them to be by real lunatics. To the reader, the book quoted from seems pure

[24] M. G. Tarde, quoting (in Delbœuf, *Le Sommeil et les Rêves* [1885], p. 226) some nonsense-verses from a dream, says "they show how prosodic forms may subsist in a mind from which logical rules are effaced. . . . I was able, in dreaming, to preserve the faculty of finding two words which rhymed, to appreciate the rhyme, to fill up the verse as it first presented itself with other words which, added, gave the right number of syllables, and yet I was ignorant of the sense of the words. . . . Thus we have the extraordinary fact that the words called each other up, without calling up their sense. . . . Even when awake, it is more difficult to ascend to the meaning of a word than to pass from one word to another; or to put it otherwise, *it is harder to be a thinker than to be a rhetorician,* and on the whole nothing is commoner than trains of words not understood."

[25] *Substantialism or Philosophy of Knowledge,* by 'Jean Story' (1879).

nonsense from beginning to end. It is impossible to divine, in such a case, just what sort of feeling of rational relation between the words may have appeared to the author's mind. The border line between objective sense and nonsense is hard to draw; that between subjective sense and nonsense, impossible. Subjectively, any collocation of words may make sense—even the wildest words in a dream—if one only does not doubt their belonging together. Take the obscurer passages in Hegel: it is a fair question whether the rationality included in them be anything more than the fact that the words all belong to a common vocabulary, and are strung together on a scheme of predication and relation,—immediacy, self-relation, and what not,—which has habitually recurred. Yet there seems no reason to doubt that the subjective feeling of the rationality of these sentences was strong in the writer as he penned them, or even that some readers by straining may have reproduced it in themselves.

To sum up, certain kinds of verbal associate, certain grammatical expectations fulfilled, stand for a good part of our impression that a sentence has a meaning and is dominated by the Unity of one Thought. Nonsense in grammatical form sounds half rational; sense with grammatical sequence upset sounds nonsensical; e.g., "Elba the Napoleon English faith had banished broken to he Saint because Helena at." Finally, there is about each word the psychic 'overtone' of feeling that it brings us nearer to a forefelt conclusion. Suffuse all the words of a sentence, as they pass, with these three fringes or haloes of relation, let the conclusion seem worth arriving at, and all will admit the sentence to be an expression of thoroughly continuous, unified, and rational thought.[26]

Each word, in such a sentence, is felt, not only as a word, but as having a *meaning*. The 'meaning' of a word taken thus dynamically in a sentence may be quite different from its meaning when taken statically or without context. The dynamic meaning is usually reduced to the bare fringe we have described, of felt suitability or unfitness to the context and conclusion. The static meaning, when the word is con-

---

[26] We think it odd that young children should listen with such rapt attention to the reading of stories expressed in words half of which they do not understand, and of none of which they ask the meaning. But their thinking is in form just what ours is when it is rapid. Both of us make flying leaps over large portions of the sentences uttered and we give attention only to substantive starting points, turning points, and conclusions here and there. All the rest, 'substantive' and separately intelligible as it may *potentially* be, actually serves only as so much transitive material. It is *internodal* consciousness, giving us the sense of continuity, but having no significance apart from its mere gap-filling function. The children probably feel no gap when through a lot of unintelligible words they are swiftly carried to a familiar and intelligible terminus.

crete, as 'table,' 'Boston,' consists of sensory images awakened; when it is abstract, as 'criminal legislation,' 'fallacy,' the meaning consists of other words aroused, forming the so-called 'definition.'

Hegel's celebrated dictum that pure being is identical with pure nothing results from his taking the words statically, or without the fringe they wear in a context. Taken in isolation, they agree in the single point of awakening no sensorial images. But taken dynamically, or as significant,—as *thought,*—their fringes of relation, their affinities and repugnances, their function and meaning, are felt and understood to be absolutely opposed.

Such considerations as these remove all appearance of paradox from those cases of extremely deficient visual imagery of whose existence Mr. Galton has made us aware (see below). An exceptionally intelligent friend informs me that he can frame no image whatever of the appearance of his breakfast-table. When asked how he then remembers it at all, he says he simple *'knows'* that it seated four people, and was covered with a white cloth on which were a butter-dish, a coffee-pot, radishes, and so forth. The mind-stuff of which this 'knowing' is made seems to be verbal images exclusively. But if the words 'coffee,' 'bacon,' 'muffins,' and 'eggs' lead a man to speak to his cook, to pay his bills, and to take measures for the morrow's meal exactly as visual and gustatory memories would, why are they not, for all practical intents and purposes, as good a kind of material in which to think? In fact, we may suspect them to be for most purposes better than terms with a richer imaginative coloring. The scheme of relationship and the conclusion being the essential things in thinking, that kind of mind-stuff which is handiest will be the best for the purpose. Now words, uttered or unexpressed, are the handiest mental elements we have. Not only are they very *rapidly* revivable, but they are revivable as actual sensations more easily than any other items of our experience. Did they not possess some such advantage as this, it would hardly be the case that the older men are and the more effective as thinkers, the more, as a rule, they have lost their visualizing power and depend on words. This was ascertained by Mr. Galton to be the case with members of the Royal Society. The present writer observes it in his own person most distinctly.

On the other hand, a deaf and dumb man can weave his tactile and visual images into a system of thought quite as effective and rational as that of a word-user. *The question whether thought is possible without language* has been a favorite topic of discussion among philosophers. Some interesting reminiscences of his childhood by Mr. Ballard, a deaf-mute instructor in the National College at Washington, show it to be perfectly possible. A few paragraphs may be quoted here.

In consequence of the loss of my hearing in infancy, I was debarred from enjoying the advantages which children in the full possession of their senses derive from the exercises of the common primary school, from the every-day talk of their school-fellows and playmates, and from the conversation of their parents and other grown-up persons.

I could convey my thoughts and feelings to my parents and brothers by natural signs or pantomime, and I could understand what they said to me by the same medium; our intercourse being, however, confined to the daily routine of home affairs and hardly going beyond the circle of my own observation. . . .

My father adopted a course which he thought would, in some measure, compensate me for the loss of my hearing. It was that of taking me with him when business required him to ride abroad; and he took me more frequently than he did my brothers; giving, as the reason for his apparent partiality, that they could acquire information through the ear, while I depended solely upon my eye for acquaintance with affairs of the outside world. . . .

I have a vivid recollection of the delight I felt in watching the different scenes we passed through, observing the various phases of nature, both animate and inanimate; though we did not, owing to my infirmity, engage in conversation. It was during those delightful rides, some two or three years before my initiation into the rudiments of written language, that I began to ask myself the question: *How came the world into being?* When this question occurred to my mind, I set myself to thinking it over a long time. My curiosity was awakened as to what was the origin of human life in its first appearance upon the earth, and of vegetable life as well, and also the cause of the existence of the earth, sun, moon, and stars.

I remember at one time when my eye fell upon a very large old stump which we happened to pass in one of our rides, I asked myself, "Is it possible that the first man that ever came into the world rose out of that stump? But that stump is only a remnant of a once noble magnificent tree, and how came that tree? Why, it came only by beginning to grow out of the ground just like those little trees now coming up." And I dismissed from my mind, as an absurd idea, the connection between the origin of man and a decaying old stump. . . .

I have no recollection of what it was that first suggested to me the question as to the origin of things. I had before this time gained ideas of the descent from parent to child, of the propagation of animals, and of the production of plants from seeds. The question that occurred to my mind was: whence came the first man, the first animal, and the first plant, at the remotest distance of time, before which there was no man, no animal, no plant; since I knew they all had a beginning and an end.

It is impossible to state the exact order in which these different questions arose, i.e., about men, animals, plants, the earth, sun, moon, etc. The lower animals did not receive so much thought as was bestowed upon man and the earth; perhaps because I put man and beast in the same class, since I believed that man would be annihilated and there was no resurrection beyond the grave,—though I am told by my mother that, in answer to my question, in the case of a deceased uncle who looked to me like a person in sleep, she had tried to make me understand that he would be awake in the far future. It was my belief that man and beast derived their being from the same source, and were to be laid down in the dust in a state of annihilation. Considering the brute animal as of secondary importance, and allied to man on a lower level, man and the earth were the two things on which my mind dwelled most.

I think I was five years old, when I began to understand the descent from parent to child and the propagation of animals. I was nearly eleven years old, when I entered the Institution where I was educated; and I remember distinctly that it was at least two years before this time that I began to ask myself the question as to the origin of the universe. My age was then about eight, not over nine years.

Of the form of the earth, I had no idea in my childhood, except that, from a look at a map of the hemispheres, I inferred there were two immense disks of matter lying near each other. I also believed the sun and moon to be round, flat plates of illuminating matter; and for those luminaries I entertained a sort of reverence on account of their power of lighting and heating the earth. I thought from their coming up and going down, travelling across the sky in so regular a manner that there must be a certain something having power to govern their course. I believed the sun went into a hole at the west and came out of another at the east, travelling through a great tube in the earth, describing the same curve as it seemed to describe in the sky. The stars seemed to me to be tiny lights studded in the sky.

The source from which the universe came was the question about which my mind revolved in a vain struggle to grasp it, or rather to fight the way up to attain to a satisfactory answer. When I had occupied myself with this subject a considerable time, I perceived that it was a matter much greater than my mind could comprehend; and I remember well that I became so appalled at its mystery and so bewildered at my inability to grapple with it that I laid the subject aside and out of my mind, glad to escape being, as it were, drawn into a vortex of inextricable confusion. Though I felt relieved at this escape, yet I could not resist the desire to know the truth; and I returned to the subject; but as before, I left it, after thinking it over for some time. In this state of perplexity, I hoped all the time to get at the truth, still believing that the more I gave thought to the subject, the more my mind would penetrate the mystery. Thus I was tossed like a shuttlecock, returning to the subject and recoiling from it, till I came to school.

I remember that my mother once told me about a being up above, pointing her finger towards the sky and with a solemn look on her countenance. I do not recall the circumstance which led to this communication. When she mentioned the mysterious being up in the sky, I was eager to take hold of the subject, and plied her with questions concerning the form and appearance of this unknown being, asking if it was the sun, moon, or one of the stars. I knew she meant that there was a living one somewhere up in the sky; but when I realized that she could not answer my questions, I gave it up in despair, feeling sorrowful that I could not obtain a definite idea of the mysterious living one up in the sky.

One day, while we were haying in a field, there was a series of heavy thunder-claps. I asked one of my brothers where they came from. He pointed to the sky and made a zigzag motion with his finger, signifying lightning. I imagined there was a great man somewhere in the blue vault, who made a loud noise with his voice out of it; and each time I heard [27] a thunder-clap I was frightened, and looked up at the sky, fearing he was speaking a threatening word.[28]

Here we may pause. The reader sees by this time that it makes little or no difference in what sort of mind-stuff, in what quality of imagery, his thinking goes on. The only images *intrinsically* important are the halting-places, the substantive conclusions, provisional or final, of the thought. Throughout all the rest of the stream, the feelings of relation are everything, and the terms related almost naught. These feelings of relation, these psychic overtones, halos, suffusions, or fringes about the terms, may be the same in very different systems of imagery. A diagram may help to accentuate this indifference of the mental means where the end is the same. Let *A* be some experience from which a number of thinkers start. Let *Z* be the practical conclusion rationally inferrible from it. One gets to the conclusion by one line, another by another; one follows a course of English, another of German, verbal imagery. With one, visual images predominate; with another, tactile. Some trains are tinged with emotions, others not; some are very abridged, synthetic and rapid, others, hesitating and broken into many steps. But when the penultimate terms of all the trains, however differing *inter se,* finally shoot into the same conclusion, we say and rightly say, that all the thinkers have had substantially the same thought. It would probably astound each of them

---

[27] Not literally *heard,* of course. Deaf mutes are quick to perceive shocks and jars that can be felt, even when so slight as to be unnoticed by those who can hear.

[28] Quoted by Samuel Porter: '*Is Thought Possible without Language?*' in *Princeton Review,* 57th year, pp. 108–12 (Jan. 1881?). Cf. also W. W. Ireland: *The Blot upon the Brain* (1886), Paper X, part II; G. J. Romanes: *Mental Evolution in Man,* pp. 81–83, and references therein made. Prof. Max Müller gives a very complete history of this controversy in pp. 30–64 of his *Science of Thought* (1887). His own view is that Thought and Speech are inseparable; but under speech he includes any conceivable sort of symbolism or even mental imagery, and he makes no allowance for the wordless summary glimpses which we have of systems of relation and direction.

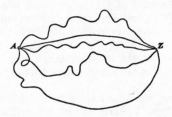

beyond measure to be let into his neighbor's mind and to find how different the scenery there was from that in his own.

Thought is in fact a kind of Algebra, as Berkeley long ago said, "in which, though a particular quantity be marked by each letter, yet to proceed right, it is not requisite that in every step each letter suggest to your thoughts that particular quantity it was appointed to stand for." Mr. Lewes has developed this algebra-analogy so well that I must quote his words:

> The leading characteristic of algebra is that of operation on relations. This also is the leading characteristic of Thought. Algebra cannot exist without values, nor Thought without Feelings. The operations are so many blank forms till the values are assigned. Words are vacant sounds, ideas are blank forms, unless they symbolize images and sensations which are their values. Nevertheless it is rigorously true, and of the greatest importance, that analysts carry on very extensive operations with blank forms, never pausing to supply the symbols with values until the calculation is completed; and ordinary men, no less than philosophers, carry on long trains of thought without pausing to translate their ideas (words) into images. . . . Suppose some one from a distance shouts "a lion!" At once the man starts in alarm. . . . To the man the word is not only an . . . expression of all that he has seen and heard of lions, capable of recalling various experiences, but is also capable of taking its place in a connected series of thoughts without recalling any of those experiences, without reviving an image, however faint, of the lion—simply as a sign of a certain relation included in the complex so named. Like an algebraic symbol it may be operated on without conveying other significance than an abstract relation: it is a sign of Danger, related to fear with all its motor sequences. Its logical position suffices. . . . Ideas are *substitutions* which require a secondary process when what is symbolized by them is translated into the images and experiences it replaces; and this secondary process is frequently not performed at all, generally only performed to a very small extent. Let anyone closely examine what has passed in his mind when he has constructed a chain of reasoning, and he will be surprised at the fewness and faintness of the images which have accompanied the ideas. Suppose you inform me

that "the blood rushed violently from the man's heart, quickening his pulse at the sight of his enemy." Of the many latent images in this phrase, how many were salient in your mind and in mine? Probably two—the man and his enemy—and these images were faint. Images of blood, heart, violent rushing, pulse, quickening, and sight, were either not revived at all, or were passing shadows. Had any such images arisen, they would have hampered thought, retarding the logical process of judgment by irrelevant connections. The symbols had substituted *relations* for these *values*. . . . There are no images of two things and three things, when I say "two and three equal five;" there are simply familiar symbols having precise relations. . . . The verbal symbol "horse," which stands for all our experiences of horses, serves all the purposes of Thought, without recalling one of the images clustered in the perception of horses, just as the sight of a horse's form serves all the purposes of *recognition* without recalling the sound of its neighing or its tramp, its qualities as an animal of draught, and so forth.[29]

It need only be added that as the Algebrist, though the sequence of his terms is fixed by their relations rather than by their several values, must give a real value to the *final* one he reaches; so the thinker in words must let his concluding word or phrase be translated into its full sensible-image-value, under penalty of the thought being left unrealized and pale.

This is all I have to say about the sensible continuity and unity of our thought as contrasted with the apparent discreteness of the words, images, and other means by which it seems to be carried on. Between all their substantive elements there is 'transitive' consciousness, and the words and images are 'fringed,' and not as discrete as to a careless view they seem. Let us advance now to the next head in our description of Thought's stream.

4) Human thought appears to deal with objects independent of itself; that is, it is cognitive, or possesses the function of knowing.

For Absolute Idealism, the infinite Thought and its objects are one. The Objects are, through being thought; the eternal Mind is, through thinking them. Were a human thought alone in the world there would be no reason for any other assumption regarding it. Whatever it might have before it would be its vision, would be there, in *its* 'there,' or then, in *its* 'then'; and the question would never arise whether an extramental duplicate of it existed or not. The reason why we all believe that the objects of our thoughts have a duplicate existence outside, is that there are *many* human thoughts, each with the *same* objects, as

[29] *Problems of Life and Mind,* 3d Series, Problem IV, chapter 5. Compare also Victor Egger: *La Parole Intérieure* (Paris, 1881), chap. VI.

we cannot help supposing. The judgment that *my* thought has the same object as *his* thought is what makes the psychologist call my thought cognitive of an outer reality. The judgment that my own past thought and my own present thought are of the same object is what makes *me* take the object out of either and project it by a sort of triangulation into an independent position, from which it may *appear* to both. *Sameness* in a multiplicity of objective appearances is thus the basis of our belief in realities outside of thought.[30] In Chapter XII we shall have to take up the judgment of sameness again.

To show that the question of reality being extra-mental or not is not likely to arise in the absence of repeated experiences of the *same*, take the example of an altogether unprecedented experience, such as a new taste in the throat. Is it a subjective quality of feeling, or an objective quality felt? You do not even ask the question at this point. It is simply *that taste*. But if a doctor hears you describe it, and says: "Ha! Now you know what *heartburn* is," then it becomes a quality already existent *extra mentem tuam*, which you in turn have come upon and learned. The first spaces, times, things, qualities, experienced by the child probably appear, like the first heartburn, in this absolute way, as simple *beings*, neither in nor out of thought. But later, by having other thoughts than this present one, and making repeated judgments of sameness among their objects, he corroborates in himself the notion of realities, past and distant as well as present, which realities no one single thought either possesses or engenders, but which all may contemplate and know. This, as was stated in the last chapter, is the *psychological* point of view, the relatively uncritical non-idealistic point of view of all natural science, beyond which this book cannot go. A mind which has become conscious of its own cognitive function, plays what we have called 'the psychologist' upon itself. It not only knows the things that appear before it; it knows that it knows them. This stage of reflective condition is, more or less explicitly, our habitual adult state of mind.

It cannot, however, be regarded as primitive. The consciousness of objects must come first. We seem to lapse into this primordial condition when consciousness is reduced to a minimum by the inhalation of anæsthetics or during a faint. Many persons testify that at a certain stage of the anæsthetic process objects are still cognized whilst the thought of self is lost. Professor Herzen says:[31]

> During the syncope there is absolute psychic annihilation, the absence of all consciousness; then at the beginning of coming to, one has at a certain moment a vague, limitless, infinite feeling—a sense of

[30] If but one person sees an apparition we consider it his private hallucination. If more than one, we begin to think it may be a real external presence.

[31] *Revue Philosophique*, vol. XXI. p. 671.

existence in general without the least trace of distinction between the me and the not-me.

Dr. Shoemaker of Philadelphia describes during the deepest conscious stage of ether-intoxication a vision of

> two endless parallel lines in swift longitudinal motion . . . on a uniform misty background . . . together with a constant sound or whirr, not loud but distinct . . . which seemed to be connected with the parallel lines. . . . These phenomena occupied the whole field. There were present no dreams or visions in any way connected with human affairs, no ideas or impressions akin to anything in past experience, no emotions, of course no idea of personality. There was no conception as to what being it was that was regarding the two lines, or that there existed any such thing as such a being; the lines and waves were all.[32]

Similarly a friend of Mr. Herbert Spencer, quoted by him in 'Mind' (vol. III. p. 556), speaks of "an undisturbed empty quiet everywhere except that a stupid presence lay like a heavy intrusion *somewhere*—a blotch on the calm." This sense of objectivity and lapse of subjectivity, even when the object is almost indefinable, is, it seems to me, a somewhat familiar phase in chloroformization, though in my own case it is too deep a phase or any articulate after-memory to remain. I only know that as it vanishes I seem to wake to a sense of my own existence as something additional to what had previously been there.[33]

Many philosophers, however, hold that the reflective consciousness of the self is essential to the cognitive function of thought. They hold that a thought, in order to know a thing at all, must expressly distinguish between the thing and its own self.[34] This is a perfectly wanton

[32] Quoted from the *Therapeutic Gazette,* by the N. Y. semi-weekly *Evening Post* for Nov. 2, 1886.

[33] In half-stunned states self-consciousness may lapse. A friend writes me: "We were driving back from —— in a wagonette. The door flew open and X., alias 'Baldy,' fell out on the road. We pulled up at once, and then he said, 'Did anybody fall out?' or 'Who fell out?'—I don't exactly remember the words. When told that Baldy fell out, he said, 'Did Baldy fall out? Poor Baldy!' "

[34] Kant originated this view. I subjoin a few English statements of it. J. Ferrier, "Institutes of Metaphysic," Proposition I: "Along with whatever any intelligence knows it must, as the ground or condition of its knowledge, have some knowledge of itself." Sir Wm. Hamilton, *Discussions,* p. 47: "We know, and we know that we know,—these propositions, logically distinct, are really identical; each implies the other. . . . So true is the scholastic brocard: *non sentimus nisi sentiamus nos sentire.*" H. L. Mansel, *Metaphysics,* p. 58: "Whatever variety of materials may exist within reach of my mind, I can become conscious of them only by recognizing them as mine. . . . Relation to the conscious self is thus the permanent and universal feature which every state of consciousness as such must exhibit." T. H. Green, *Introduction to Hume,* p. 12: "A consciousness by the man . . . of himself, in negative relation to the thing that is his object, and

assumption, and not the faintest shadow of reason exists for supposing it true. As well might I contend that I cannot dream without
dreaming that I dream, swear without swearing that I swear, deny
without denying that I deny, as maintain that I cannot know without
knowing that I know. I may have either acquaintance-with, or knowledge-about, an object O without thinking about myself at all. It
suffices for this that I think O, and that it exist. If, in addition to thinking O, I also think that I exist and that I know O, well and good; I
then know one more thing, a fact about O, of which I previously was
unmindful. That, however, does not prevent me from having already
known it a good deal. O *per se,* or O *plus* P, are as good objects of
knowledge as O *plus me* is. The philosophers in question simply
substitute one particular object for all others, and call it *the* object *par
excellence.* It is a case of the 'psychologist's fallacy'. *They* know the object to be one thing and the thought another; and they forthwith foist
their own knowledge into that of the thought of which they pretend to
give a true account. To conclude, then, *thought may, but need not, in
knowing, discriminate between its object and itself.*

We have been using the word Object. *Something must now be said
about the proper use of the term Object in Psychology.*

In popular parlance the word object is commonly taken without
reference to the act of knowledge, and treated as synonymous with
individual subject of existence. Thus if anyone ask what is the mind's
object when you say 'Columbus discovered America in 1492,' most
people will reply 'Columbus,' or 'America,' or, at most, 'the discovery
of America.' They will name a substantive kernel or nucleus of the
consciousness, and say the thought is 'about' that,—as indeed it is,—
and they will call that your thought's 'object.' Really that is usually
only the grammatical object, or more likely the grammatical subject,
of your sentence. It is at most your 'fractional object;' or you may call
it the 'topic' of your thought, or the 'subject of your discourse.' But
the *Object* of your thought is really its entire content or deliverance,
neither more nor less. It is a vicious use of speech to take out a substantive kernel from its content and call that its object; and it is an
equally vicious use of speech to add a substantive kernel not articulately included in its content, and to call that its object. Yet either one
of these two sins we commit, whenever we content ourselves with saying that a given thought is simply 'about' a certain topic, or that that
topic is its 'object.' The object of my thought in the previous sentence,
for example, is strictly speaking neither Columbus, nor America, nor
its discovery. It is nothing short of the entire sentence, 'Columbus-

---

this consciousness must be taken to go along with the perceptive act itself. Not
less than this indeed can be involved in any act that is to be the beginning of
knowledge at all. It is the minimum of possible thought or intelligence."

discovered-America-in-1492.' And if we wish to speak of it substantively, we must make a substantive of it by writing it out thus with hyphens between all its words. Nothing but this can possibly name its delicate idiosyncrasy. And if we wish to *feel* that idiosyncrasy we must reproduce the thought as it was uttered, with every word fringed and the whole sentence bathed in that original halo of obscure relations, which, like an horizon, then spread about its meaning.

Our psychological duty is to cling as closely as possible to the actual constitution of the thought we are studying. We may err as much by excess as by defect. If the kernel or 'topic,' Columbus, is in one way less than the thought's object, so in another way it may be more. That is, when named by the psychologist, it may mean much more than actually is present to the thought of which he is reporter. Thus, for example, suppose you should go on to think: 'He was a daring genius!' An ordinary psychologist would not hesitate to say that the object of your thought was still 'Columbus.' True, your thought is *about* Columbus. It 'terminates' in Columbus, leads from and to the direct idea of Columbus. But for the moment it is not fully and immediately Columbus, it is only 'he,' or rather 'he-was-a-daring-genius;' which, though it may be an unimportant difference for conversational purposes, is, for introspective psychology, as great a difference as there can be.

The object of every thought, then, is neither more nor less than all that the thought thinks, exactly as the thought thinks it, however complicated the matter, and however symbolic the manner of the thinking may be. It is needless to say that memory can seldom accurately reproduce such an object, when once it has passed from before the mind. It either makes too little or too much of it. Its best plan is to repeat the verbal sentence, if there was one, in which the object was expressed. But for inarticulate thoughts there is not even this resource, and introspection must confess that the task exceeds her powers. The mass of our thinking vanishes for ever, beyond hope of recovery, and psychology only gathers up a few of the crumbs that fall from the feast.

The next point to make clear is that, *however complex the object may be, the thought of it is one undivided state of consciousness.* As Thomas Brown says:[35]

> I have already spoken too often to require again to caution you against the mistake into which, I confess, that the terms which the poverty of our language obliges us to use might of themselves very naturally lead you; the mistake of supposing that the most complex

[35] *Lectures on the Philosophy of the Human Mind,* Lecture 45.

states of mind are not truly, in their very essence, as much one and indivisible as those which we term simple—the complexity and seeming coexistence which they involve being relative to our feeling[36] only, not to their own absolute nature. I trust I need not repeat to you that, in itself, every notion, however seemingly complex, is, and must be, truly simple—being one state or affection, of one simple substance, mind. Our conception of a whole army, for example, is as truly this one mind existing in this one state, as our conception of any of the individuals that compose an army. Our notion of the abstract numbers, eight, four, two, is as truly one feeling of the mind as our notion of simple unity.

The ordinary associationist-psychology supposes, in contrast with this, that whenever an object of thought contains many elements, the thought itself must be made up of just as many ideas, one idea for each element, and all fused together in appearance, but really separate.[37] The enemies of this psychology find (as we have already seen) little trouble in showing that such a bundle of separate ideas would never form one thought at all, and they contend that an Ego must be added to the bundle to give it unity, and bring the various ideas into relation with each other.[38] We will not discuss the ego just yet, but it is obvious that if things are to be thought in relation, they must be thought together, and in one *something,* be that something ego, psychosis, state of consciousness, or whatever you please. If not thought with each other, things are not thought in relation at all. Now most believers in the ego make the same mistake as the associationists and sensationists whom they oppose. Both agree that the elements of the subjective stream are discrete and separate and constitute what Kant calls a 'manifold.' But while the associationists think that a 'manifold' can form a single knowledge, the egoists deny this, and say that the knowledge comes only when the manifold is subjected to the synthetizing activity of an ego. Both make an identical initial hypothesis; but the egoist, finding it won't express the facts, adds another hypothesis to correct it. Now I do not wish just yet to 'commit myself' about the existence or nonexistence of the ego, but I do contend that we need not invoke it for this particular reason—namely, because the manifold of ideas has to be reduced to unity. *There is no manifold of coexisting ideas;* the notion of such a thing is a chimera. *Whatever things are*

[36] Instead of saying *to our feeling only,* he should have said, to the *object* only.

[37] "There can be no difficulty in admitting that association does form the ideas of an indefinite number of individuals into one complex idea; because it is an acknowledged fact. Have we not the idea of an army? And is not that precisely the ideas of an indefinite number of men formed into one idea?" (Jas. Mill's *Analysis of the Human Mind* [J. S. Mill's Edition], vol. I. p. 264.)

[38] For their arguments, see above, pp. 61–62.

thought in relation are thought from the outset in a unity, in a single pulse of subjectivity, a single psychosis, feeling, or state of mind.

The reason why this fact is so strangely garbled in the books seems to be what on an earlier page I called the psychologist's fallacy. We have the inveterate habit, whenever we try introspectively to describe one of our thoughts, of dropping the thought as it is in itself and talking of something else. We describe the things that appear to the thought, and we describe other thoughts *about* those things—as if these and the original thought were the same. If, for example, the thought be 'the pack of cards is on the table,' we say, "Well, isn't it a thought of the pack of cards? Isn't it of the cards as included in the pack? Isn't it of the table? And of the legs of the table as well? The table has legs— how can you think the table without virtually thinking its legs? Hasn't our thought then, all these parts—one part for the pack and another for the table? And within the pack-part a part for each card, as within the table-part a part for each leg? And isn't each of these parts an idea? And can our thought, then, be anything but an assemblage or pack of ideas, each answering to some element of what it knows?"

Now not one of these assumptions is true. The thought taken as an example is, in the first place, not of 'a pack of cards.' It is of 'the-pack-of-cards-is-on-the-table,' an entirely different subjective phe-nomenon, whose Object implies the pack, and every one of the cards in it, but whose conscious constitution bears very little resemblance to that of the thought of the pack *per se*. What a thought *is,* and what it may be developed into, or explained to stand for, and be equivalent to, are two things, not one.[39]

An analysis of what passes through the mind as we utter the phrase *the pack of cards is on the table* will, I hope, make this clear, and may at the same time condense into a concrete example a good deal of what has gone before.

It takes time to utter the phrase. Let the horizontal line in [the figure below] represent time. Every part of it will then stand for a fraction, every point for an instant, of the time. Of course the thought has *time-parts*. The part 2-3 of it, though continuous with 1-2, is yet a

---

[39] I know there are readers whom nothing can convince that the thought of a complex object has not as many parts as are discriminated in the object itself. Well, then, let the word parts pass. Only observe that these parts are not the separate 'ideas' of traditional psychology. No one of them can live out of that particular thought, any more than my head can live off of my particular shoul-ders. In a sense a soap-bubble has parts; it is a sum of juxtaposed spherical tri-angles. But these triangles are not separate realities; neither are the 'parts' of the thought separate realities. Touch the bubble and the triangles are no more. Dismiss the thought and out go its parts. You can no more make a new thought out of 'ideas' that have once served than you can make a new bubble out of old triangles. Each bubble, each thought, is a fresh organic unity, *sui generis*.

different part from 1-2. Now I say of these time-parts that we cannot take any one of them so short that it will not after some fashion or other be a thought of the whole object 'the pack of cards is on the table.' They melt into each other like dissolving views, and no two of them feel the object just alike, but each feels the total object in a unitary undivided way. This is what I mean by denying that in the thought any parts can be found corresponding to the object's parts. Time-parts are not such parts.

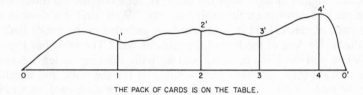

THE PACK OF CARDS IS ON THE TABLE.

The Stream of Consciousness

Now let the vertical dimensions of the figure stand for the objects or contents of the thoughts. A line vertical to any point of the horizontal, as 1–1′, will then symbolize the object in the mind at the instant 1; a space above the horizontal, as 1–1′–2′–2, will symbolize all that passes through the mind during the time 1–2 whose line it covers. The entire diagram from 0 to 0′ represents a finite length of thought's stream.

Can we now define the psychic constitution of each vertical section of this segment? We can, though in a very rough way. Immediately after 0, even before we have opened our mouths to speak, the entire thought is present to our mind in the form of an intention to utter that sentence. This intention, though it has no simple name, and though it is a transitive state immediately displaced by the first word, is yet a perfectly determinate phase of thought, unlike anything else [see p. 44]. Again, immediately before 0′, after the last word of the sentence is spoken, all will admit that we again think its entire content as we inwardly realize its completed deliverance. All vertical sections made through any other parts of the diagram will be respectively filled with other ways of feeling the sentence's meaning. Through 2, for example, the cards will be the part of the object most emphatically present to the mind; through 4, the table. The stream is made higher in the drawing at its end than at its beginning, because the final way of feeling the content is fuller and richer than the initial way. As Joubert says, "we only know just what we meant to say, after we have said it." And as M. V. Egger remarks, "before speaking, one barely knows what one intends to say, but afterwards one is filled with admiration and surprise at having said and thought it so well."

This latter author seems to me to have kept at much closer quarters with the facts than any other analyst of consciousness.[40] But even he does not quite hit the mark, for, as I understand him, he thinks that each word as it occupies the mind *displaces* the rest of the thought's content. He distinguishes the 'idea' (what I have called the total *object* or meaning) from the consciousness of the words, calling the former a very feeble state, and contrasting it with the liveliness of the words, even when these are only silently rehearsed. "The feeling," he says, "of the words makes ten or twenty times more noise in our consciousness than the sense of the phrase, which for consciousness is a very slight matter." [41] And having distinguished these two things, he goes on to separate them in time, saying that the idea may either precede or follow the words, but that it is a 'pure illusion' to suppose them simultaneous.[42] Now I believe that in all cases where the words are *understood,* the total idea may be and usually is present not only before and after the phrase has been spoken, but also whilst each separate word is uttered.[43] It is the overtone, halo, or fringe of the word, *as spoken in that sentence.* It is never absent; no word in an understood sentence comes to consciousness as a mere noise. We feel its meaning as it passes; and although our object differs from one moment to another as to its verbal kernel or nucleus, yet it is *similar* throughout the entire segment of the stream. The same object is known everywhere, now from the point of view, if we may so call it, of this word, now from the point of view of that. And in our feeling of each word there chimes an echo or foretaste of every other. The consciousness of the 'Idea' and that of the words are thus consubstantial. They are made of the same 'mind-stuff,' and form an unbroken

[40] In his work, *La Parole Intérieure* (Paris, 1881), especially chapters VI and VII.

[41] Page 301.

[42] Page 218. To prove this point, M. Egger appeals to the fact that we often hear some one speak whilst our mind is preoccupied, but do not understand him until some moments afterwards, when we suddenly 'realize' what he meant. Also to our digging out the meaning of a sentence in an unfamiliar tongue, where the words are present to us long before the idea is taken in. In these special cases the word does indeed precede the idea. The idea, on the contrary, precedes the word whenever we try to express ourselves with effort, as in a foreign tongue, or in an unusual field of intellectual invention. Both sets of cases, however, are exceptional, and M. Egger would probably admit, on reflection, that in the former class there is some sort of a verbal suffusion, however evanescent, of the idea, when it is grasped—we hear the echo of the words as we catch their meaning. And he would probably admit that in the second class of cases the idea persists after the words that came with so much effort are found. In normal cases the simultaneity, as he admits, is obviously there.

[43] A good way to get the words and the sense separately is to inwardly articulate word for word the discourse of another. One then finds that the meaning will often come to the mind in pulses, after clauses or sentences are finished.

stream. Annihilate a mind at any instant, cut its thought through whilst yet uncompleted, and examine the object present to the cross-section thus suddenly made; you will find, not the bald word in process of utterance, but that word suffused with the whole idea. The word may be so loud, as M. Egger would say, that we cannot *tell* just how its suffusion, as such, feels, or how it differs from the suffusion of the next word. But it does differ; and we may be sure that, could we see into the brain, we should find the same processes active through the entire sentence in different degrees, each one in turn becoming maximally excited and then yielding the momentary verbal 'kernel,' to the thought's content, at other times being only sub-excited, and then combining with the other sub-excited processes to give the overtone or fringe.[44]

THE PACK OF CARDS IS ON THE TABLE.

We may illustrate this by a farther development of the diagram on p. 66. Let the objective content of any vertical section through the stream be represented no longer by a line, but by a plane figure, high-

THE PACK OF CARDS IS ON THE TABLE.

est opposite whatever part of the object is most prominent in consciousness at the moment when the section is made. This part, in verbal thought, will usually be some word. A series of sections 1–1′, taken at the moments 1, 2, 3, would then look like this:

THE PACK OF CARDS IS ON THE TABLE.

[44] The nearest approach (with which I am acquainted) to the doctrine set forth here is in O. Liebmann's *Zur Analysis der Wirklichkeit,* pp. 427–438.

The horizontal breadth stands for the entire object in each of the figures; the height of the curve above each part of that object marks the relative prominence of that part in the thought. At the moment symbolized by the first figure *pack* is the prominent part; in the third figure it is *table,* etc.

We can easily add all these plane sections together to make a solid, one of whose solid dimensions will represent time, whilst a cut across this at right angles will give the thought's content at the moment when the cut is made.

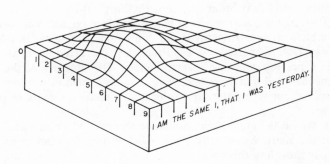

Let it be the thought, 'I am the same I that I was yesterday.' If at the fourth moment of time we annihilate the thinker and examine how the last pulsation of his consciousness was made, we find that it was an awareness of the whole content with *same* most prominent, and the other parts of the thing known relatively less distinct. With each prolongation of the scheme in the time-direction, the summit of the curve of section would come further towards the end of the sentence. If we make a solid wooden frame with the sentence written on its front, and the time-scale on one of its sides, if we spread flatly a sheet of India rubber over its top, on which rectangular co-ordinates are painted, and slide a smooth ball under the rubber in the direction from 0 to 'yesterday,' the bulging of the membrane along this diagonal at successive moments will symbolize the changing of the thought's content in a way plain enough, after what has been said, to call for no more explanation. Or to express it in cerebral terms, it will show the relative intensities, at successive moments, of the several nerve-processes to which the various parts of the thought-object correspond.

The last peculiarity of consciousness to which attention is to be drawn in this first rough description of its stream is that

5) It is always interested more in one part of its object than in another, and welcomes and rejects, or chooses, all the while it thinks.

The phenomena of selective attention and of deliberative will are of course patent examples of this choosing activity. But few of us are aware how incessantly it is at work in operations not ordinarily called by these names. Accentuation and Emphasis are present in every perception we have. We find it quite impossible to disperse our attention impartially over a number of impressions. A monotonous succession of sonorous strokes is broken up into rhythms, now of one sort, now of another, by the different accent which we place on different strokes. The simplest of these rhythms is the double one, tick-tóck, tick-tock, tick-tóck. Dots dispersed on a surface are perceived in rows and groups. Lines separate into diverse figures. The ubiquity of the distinctions, *this* and *that, here* and *there, now* and *then,* in our minds is the result of our laying the same selective emphasis on parts of place and time.

But we do far more than emphasize things, and unite some, and keep others apart. We actually *ignore* most of the things before us. Let me briefly show how this goes on.

To begin at the bottom, what are our very senses themselves but organs of selection? Out of the infinite chaos of movements, of which physics teaches us that the outer world consists, each sense-organ picks out those which fall within certain limits of velocity. To these it responds, but ignores the rest as completely as if they did not exist. It thus accentuates particular movements in a manner for which objectively there seems no valid ground; for, as Lange says, there is no reason whatever to think that the gap in Nature between the highest sound-waves and the lowest heat-waves is an abrupt break like that of our sensations; or that the difference between violet and ultra-violet rays has anything like the objective importance subjectively represented by that between light and darkness. Out of what is in itself an undistinguishable, swarming *continuum,* devoid of distinction or emphasis, our senses make for us, by attending to this motion and ignoring that, a world full of contrasts, of sharp accents, of abrupt changes, of picturesque light and shade.

If the sensations we receive from a given organ have their causes thus picked out for us by the conformation of the organ's termination, Attention, on the other hand, out of all the sensations yielded, picks out certain ones as worthy of its notice and suppresses all the rest. Helmholtz's work on Optics is little more than a study of those visual sensations of which common men never become aware—blind spots, *muscæ volitantes,* after-images, irradiation, chromatic fringes, mar-

ginal changes of color, double images, astigmatism, movements of accommodation and convergence, retinal rivalry, and more besides. We
do not even know without special training on which of our eyes an
image falls. So habitually ignorant are most men of this that one may
be blind for years of a single eye and never know the fact.

Helmholtz says that we notice only those sensations which are
signs to us of *things*. But what are things? Nothing, as we shall abundantly see, but special groups of sensible qualities, which happen
practically or æsthetically to interest us, to which we therefore give
substantive names, and which we exalt to this exclusive status of independence and dignity. But in itself, apart from my interest, a particular dust-wreath on a windy day is just as much of an individual thing,
and just as much or as little deserves an individual name, as my own
body does.

And then, among the sensations we get from each separate thing,
what happens? The mind selects again. It chooses certain of the sensations to represent the thing most *truly,* and considers the rest as its
appearances, modified by the conditions of the moment. Thus my
table-top is named *square,* after but one of an infinite number of retinal sensations which it yields, the rest of them being sensations of two
acute and two obtuse angles; but I call the latter *perspective* views,
and the four right angles the *true* form of the table, and erect the
attribute squareness into the table's essence, for æsthetic reasons of my
own. In like manner, the real form of the circle is deemed to be the
sensation it gives when the line of vision is perpendicular to its centre
—all its other sensations are signs of this sensation. The real sound of
the cannon is the sensation it makes when the ear is close by. The real
color of the brick is the sensation it gives when the eye looks squarely
at it from a near point, out of the sunshine and yet not in the gloom;
under other circumstances it gives us other color-sensations which are
but signs of this—we then see it looks pinker or blacker than it really
is. The reader knows no object which he does not represent to himself
by preference as in some typical attitude, of some normal size, at
some characteristic distance, of some standard tint, etc., etc. But all
these essential characteristics, which together form for us the genuine
objectivity of the thing and are contrasted with what we call the subjective sensations it may yield us at a given moment, are mere sensations like the latter. The mind chooses to suit itself, and decides what
particular sensation shall be held more real and valid than all the rest.

Thus perception involves a twofold choice. Out of all present sensations, we notice mainly such as are significant of absent ones; and
out of all the absent associates which these suggest, we again pick out
a very few to stand for the objective reality *par excellence.* We could
have no more exquisite example of selective industry.

That industry goes on to deal with the things thus given in perception. A man's empirical thought depends on the things he has experienced, but what these shall be is to a large extent determined by his habits of attention. A thing may be present to him a thousand times, but if he persistently fails to notice it, it cannot be said to enter into his experience. We are all seeing flies, moths, and beetles by the thousand, but to whom, save an entomologist, do they say anything distinct? On the other hand, a thing met only once in a lifetime may leave an indelible experience in the memory. Let four men make a tour in Europe. One will bring home only picturesque impressions—costumes and colors, parks and views and works of architecture, pictures and statues. To another all this will be non-existent; and distances and prices, populations and drainage-arrangements, door- and window-fastenings, and other useful statistics will take their place. A third will give a rich account of the theatres, restaurants, and public balls, and naught beside; whilst the fourth will perhaps have been so wrapped in his own subjective broodings as to tell little more than a few names of places through which he passed. Each has selected, out of the same mass of presented objects, those which suited his private interest and has made his experience thereby.

If, now, leaving the empirical combination of objects, we ask how the mind proceeds *rationally* to connect them, we find selection again to be omnipotent. In a future chapter we shall see that all Reasoning depends on the ability of the mind to break up the totality of the phenomenon reasoned about, into parts, and to pick out from among these the particular one which, in our given emergency, may lead to the proper conclusion. Another predicament will need another conclusion, and require another element to be picked out. The man of genius is he who will always stick in his bill at the right point, and bring it out with the right element—'reason' if the emergency be theoretical, 'means' if it be practical—transfixed upon it. I here confine myself to this brief statement, but it may suffice to show that Reasoning is but another form of the selective activity of the mind.

If now we pass to its æsthetic department, our law is still more obvious. The artist notoriously selects his items, rejecting all tones, colors, shapes, which do not harmonize with each other and with the main purpose of his work. That unity, harmony, 'convergence of characters,' as M. Taine calls it, which gives to works of art their superiority over works of nature, is wholly due to *elimination*. Any natural subject will do, if the artist has wit enough to pounce upon some one feature of it as characteristic, and suppress all merely accidental items which do not harmonize with this.

Ascending still higher, we reach the plane of Ethics, where choice reigns notoriously supreme. An act has no ethical quality whatever unless it be chosen out of several all equally possible. To sustain the arguments for the good course and keep them ever before us, to stifle our longing for more flowery ways, to keep the foot unflinchingly on the arduous path, these are characteristic ethical energies. But more than these; for these but deal with the means of compassing interests already felt by the man to be supreme. The ethical energy *par excellence* has to go farther and choose which *interest* out of several, equally coercive, shall become supreme. The issue here is of the utmost pregnancy, for it decides a man's entire career. When he debates, Shall I commit this crime? choose that profession? accept that office, or marry this fortune?—his choice really lies between one of several equally possible future Characters. What he shall *become* is fixed by the conduct of this moment. Schopenhauer, who enforces his determinism by the argument that with a given fixed character only one reaction is possible under given circumstances, forgets that, in these critical ethical moments, what consciously *seems* to be in question is the complexion of the character itself. The problem with the man is less what act he shall now choose to do, than what being he shall now resolve to become.

Looking back, then, over this review, we see that the mind is at every stage a theatre of simultaneous possibilities. Consciousness consists in the comparison of these with each other, the selection of some, and the suppression of the rest by the reinforcing and inhibiting agency of attention. The highest and most elaborated mental products are filtered from the data chosen by the faculty next beneath, out of the mass offered by the faculty below that, which mass in turn was sifted from a still larger amount of yet simpler material, and so on. The mind, in short, works on the data it receives very much as a sculptor works on his block of stone. In a sense the statue stood there from eternity. But there were a thousand different ones beside it, and the sculptor alone is to thank for having extricated this one from the rest. Just so the world of each of us, howsoever different our several views of it may be, all lay embedded in the primordial chaos of sensations, which gave the mere *matter* to the thought of all of us indifferently. We may, if we like, by our reasonings unwind things back to that black and jointless continuity of space and moving clouds of swarming atoms which science calls the only real world. But all the while the world *we* feel and live in will be that which our ancestors and we, by slowly cumulative strokes of choice, have extricated out of this, like sculptors, by simply rejecting certain portions of the given stuff. Other sculptors, other statues from the same stone! Other minds, other worlds from the same monotonous and inexpressive chaos! My world is but one in a million alike embedded, alike real to those who may abstract them. How different must be the worlds in the consciousness of ant, cuttle-fish, or crab!

But in my mind and your mind the rejected portions and the selected portions of the original world-stuff are to a great extent the same. The human race as a whole largely agrees as to what it shall notice and name, and what not. And among the noticed parts we select in much the same way for accentuation and preference or subordination and dislike. There is, however, one entirely extraordinary case in which no two men ever are known to choose alike. One great splitting of the whole universe into two halves is made by each of us; and for each of us almost all of the interest attaches to one of the halves; but we all draw the line of division between them in a different place. When I say that we all call the two halves by the same names, and that those names are *'me'* and *'not-me'* respectively, it will at once be seen what I mean. The altogether unique kind of interest which each human mind feels in those parts of creation which it can call *me* or *mine* may be a moral riddle, but it is a fundamental psychological fact. No mind can take the same interest in his neighbor's *me* as in his own. The neighbor's *me* falls together with all the rest of things in one foreign mass, against which his own *me* stands out in startling relief. Even the trodden worm, as Lotze somewhere says, contrasts his own suffering self with the whole remaining universe, though he have no clear conception either of himself or of what the universe may be. He is for me a mere part of the world; for him it is I who am the mere part. Each of us dichotomizes the Kosmos in a different place.

NECESSARY TRUTHS AND THE EFFECTS OF EXPERIENCE*

In this chapter I shall treat of what has sometimes been called *psychogenesis,* and try to ascertain just how far the connections of things in the outward environment can account for our tendency to think of, and to react upon, certain things in certain ways and in no others, even though personally we have had of the things in question no experience, or almost no experience, at all. It is a familiar truth that some propositions are *necessary.* We *must* attach the predicate 'equal' to the subject 'opposite sides of a parallelogram' if we think those terms together at all, whereas we need not in any such way attach the predicate 'rainy,' for example, to the subject 'to-morrow.' The dubious sort

* From: *Principles,* II, 617–688.

of coupling of terms is universally admitted to be due to 'experience'; the certain sort is ascribed to the 'organic structure' of the mind. This structure is in turn supposed by the so-called *apriorists* to be of transcendental origin, or at any rate not to be explicable by experience; whilst by evolutionary empiricists it is supposed to be also due to experience, only not to the experience of the individual, but to that of his ancestors as far back as one may please to go. Our emotional and instinctive tendencies, our irresistible impulses to couple certain movements with the perception or thought of certain things, are also features of our connate mental structure, and like the necessary judgments, are interpreted by the apriorists and the empiricists in the same warring ways.

I shall try in the course of the chapter to make plain three things:

1) That, taking the word experience as it is universally understood, the experience of the race can no more account for our necessary or *a priori* judgments than the experience of the individual can;

2) That there is no good evidence for the belief that our instinctive reactions are fruits of our ancestors' education in the midst of the same environment, transmitted to us at birth.

3) That the features of our organic mental structure cannot be explained at all by our conscious intercourse with the outer environment, but must rather be understood as congenital variations, 'accidental' [45] in the first instance, but then transmitted as fixed features of the race.

On the whole, then, the account which the apriorists give of the facts is that which I defend; although I should contend (as will hereafter appear) for a naturalistic view of their cause.

The first thing I have to say is that all schools (however they otherwise differ) must allow that the *elementary qualities* of cold, heat, pleasure, pain, red, blue, sound, silence, etc., are original, innate, or *a priori* properties of our subjective nature, even though they should require the touch of experience to waken them into actual consciousness, and should slumber, to all eternity, without it.

This is so on either of the two hypotheses we may make concerning the relation of the feelings to the realities at whose touch they become alive. For in the first place, if a feeling do *not* mirror the reality which wakens it and to which we say it corresponds, if it mirror no reality whatever outside of the mind, it of course is a purely mental product. By its very definition it can be nothing else. But in the second place, even if it *do* mirror the reality exactly, still it *is* not that reality itself, it is a duplication of it, the result of a mental reaction.

[45] 'Accidental' in the Darwinian sense, as belonging to a cycle of causation inaccessible to the present order of research.

And that the mind should have the power of reacting in just that duplicate way can only be stated as a *harmony* between its nature and the nature of the truth outside of it, a harmony whereby it follows that the qualities of both parties match.

The originality of these *elements* is not, then, a question for dispute. *The warfare of philosophers is exclusively relative to their* FORMS OF COMBINATION. The empiricist maintains that these forms can only follow the order of combination in which the elements were originally awakened by the impressions of the external world; the apriorists insist, on the contrary, that *some* modes of combination, at any rate, follow from the natures of the elements themselves, and that no amount of experience can modify this result.

WHAT IS MEANT BY EXPERIENCE?

The phrase 'organic mental structure' names the matter in dispute. Has the mind such a structure or not? Are its contents *arranged* from the start, or is the arrangement they may possess simply due to the shuffling of them by experience in an absolutely plastic bed? Now the first thing to make sure of is that when we talk of 'experience,' we attach a definite meaning to the word. *Experience means experience of something foreign supposed to impress us,* whether spontaneously or in consequence of our own exertions and acts. Impressions, as we well know, affect certain orders of sequence and coexistence, and the mind's habits copy the habits of the impressions, so that our images of things assume a time- and space-arrangement which resembles the time- and space-arrangements outside. To uniform outer coexistences and sequences correspond constant conjunctions of ideas, to fortuitous coexistences and sequences casual conjunctions of ideas. We are sure that fire will burn and water wet us, less sure that thunder will come after lightning, not at all sure whether a strange dog will bark at us or let us go by. In these ways experience moulds us every hour, and makes of our minds a mirror of the time- and space-connections between the things in the world. The principle of habit within us so *fixes* the copy at last that we find it difficult even to imagine how the outward order could possibly be different from what it is, and we continually divine from the present what the future is to be. These habits of transition, from one thought to another, are features of mental structure which were lacking in us at birth; we can see their growth under experience's moulding finger, and we can see how often experience undoes her own work, and for an earlier order substitutes a new one. '*The order of experience,*' in this matter of the time- and space-conjunctions of things, is thus an indisputably *vera causa* of our forms of thought. It is our educator, our sovereign helper and friend; and its name, standing for something with so real and definite a use, ought to be kept sacred and encumbered with no vaguer meaning.

If *all* the connections among ideas in the mind could be interpreted as so many combinations of sense-data wrought into fixity in this way from without, then experience in the common and legitimate sense of the word would be the sole fashioner of the mind.

The empirical school in psychology has in the main contended that they can be so interpreted. Before our generation, it was the experience of the individual only which was meant. But when one nowadays says that the human mind owes its present shape to experience, he means the experience of ancestors as well. Mr. Spencer's statement of this is the earliest emphatic one, and deserves quotation in full:[46]

> The supposition that the inner cohesions are adjusted to the outer persistences by *accumulated* experience of those outer persistences is in harmony with all our actual knowledge of mental phenomena. Though in so far as reflex actions and instincts are concerned, the experience-hypothesis seems insufficient; yet its seeming insufficiency occurs only where the evidence is beyond our reach. Nay, even here such few facts as we can get point to the conclusion that automatic psychical connections result from the registration of *experiences continued for numberless generations*.
>
> In brief, the case stands thus: It is agreed that all psychical relations, save the absolutely indissoluble, are determined by experiences. Their various strengths are admitted, other things equal, to be proportionate to the *multiplication of experiences*. It is an unavoidable corollary that an *infinity of experiences* will produce a psychical relation that is indissoluble. Though such infinity of experiences cannot be received by a single individual, yet it may be received by the succession of individuals forming a race. And if there is a transmission of induced tendencies in the nervous system, it is inferrible that *all psychical relations whatever,* from the necessary to the fortuitous, result from the experiences of the corresponding external relations; and are so brought into harmony with them.
>
> Thus, the experience-hypothesis furnishes an adequate solution. The genesis of instinct, the development of memory and reason out of it, and the consolidation of rational actions and inferences into instinctive ones, are alike explicable on the *single principle* that the cohesion between psychical states is proportionate to the *frequency* with which the relation between the answering external phenomena has been *repeated in experience*.

[46] The passage is in § 207 of the *Principles of Psychology,* at the end of the chapter entitled 'Reason.' I italicize certain words in order to show that the essence of this explanation is to demand *numerically frequent* experiences. The bearing of this remark will later appear. (Cf. pp. 94–95, below.)

The *universal law* that, other things equal, the cohesion of psychical states is proportionate to the *frequency* with which they have followed one another in experience, supplies an explanation of the so-called "forms of thought," as soon as it is supplemented by the law that *habitual* psychical successions entails some hereditary tendency to such successions, which, under persistent conditions, will become cumulative in generation after generation. We saw that the establishment of those compound reflex actions called instincts is comprehensible on the principle that inner relations are, by *perpetual repetition,* organized into correspondence with outer relations. We have now to observe that the establishment of those consolidated, those indissoluble, those instinctive mental relations constituting our ideas of Space and Time is comprehensible on the same principle. For if even to external relations that are *often* experienced during the life of a single organism, answering internal relations are established that become next to automatic—if such a combination of psychical changes as that which guides a savage in hitting a bird with an arrow becomes, by constant repetition, so organized as to be performed almost without thought of the processes of adjustment gone through—and if skill of this kind is so far transmissible that particular races of men become characterized by particular aptitudes, which are nothing else than partially-organized psychical connections; then, if there exist certain external relations which are experienced by all organisms at all instants of their waking lives—relations which are absolutely constant, absolutely universal— there will be established answering internal relations that are absolutely constant, absolutely universal. Such relations we have in those of Space and Time. The organization of subjective relations adjusted to these objective relations has been cumulative, not in each race of creatures only, but throughout successive races of creatures; and such subjective relations have, therefore, become more consolidated than all others. Being experienced in every perception and every action of each creature, these connections among outer existences must, for this reason too, be responded to by connections among inner feelings, that are, above all others, indissoluble. As the substrata of all other relations in the *non-ego*, they must be responded to by conceptions that are the substrata of all other relations in the *ego*. Being the *constant and infinitely-repeated* elements of thought, they must become the automatic elements of thought—the elements of thought which it is impossible to get rid of—the 'forms of intuition.'

Such, it seems to me, is the only possible reconciliation between the experience-hypothesis and the hypothesis of the transcendentalists; neither of which is tenable by itself. Insurmountable difficulties are presented by the Kantian doctrine (as we shall hereafter see); and the antagonist doctrine, taken alone, presents difficulties that are equally insurmountable. To rest with the unqualified assertion that, antecedent to experience, the mind is a blank, is to ignore the questions— whence comes the power of organizing experiences? whence arise the different degrees of that power possessed by different races of organisms, and different individuals of the same race? If, at birth, there exists nothing but a passive receptivity of impressions, why is not a horse as educable as a man? Should it be said that language makes the difference, then why do not the cat and the dog, reared in the same household, arrive at equal degrees and kinds of intelligence? Understood in its current form, the experience-hypothesis implies that the presence of a definitely-organized nervous system is a circumstance of no moment—a fact not needing to be taken into account! Yet it is the all-important fact—the fact to which, in one sense, the criticisms of Leibnitz and others pointed—the fact without which an assimilation of experiences is inexplicable. Throughout the animal kingdom in general, the actions are dependent on the nervous structure. The physiologist shows us that each reflex movement implies the agency of certain nerves and ganglia; that a development of complicated instincts is accompanied by complication of the nervous centres and their commissural connections; that the same creature in different stages, as larva and imago for example, changes its instincts as its nervous structure changes; and that as we advance to creatures of high intelligence, a vast increase in the size and in the complexity of the nervous system takes place. What is the obvious inference? It is that the ability to co-ordinate impressions and to perform the appropriate actions always implies the pre-existence of certain nerves arranged in a certain way. What is the meaning of the human brain? It is that the many *established* relations among its parts stand for so many *established* relations among the psychical changes. Each of the constant connections among the fibres of the cerebral masses answers to some *constant connection* of phenomena in the experiences of the race. Just as the organized arrangement subsisting between the sensory nerves of the nostrils and the motor nerves of the respiratory muscles not only makes possible a sneeze, but also, in the newly-born infant, implies sneezings to be hereafter performed; so, all the organized arrangements subsisting among the nerves of the infant's brain not only make possible certain combinations of impressions, but also imply that such combinations will hereafter be made—imply that there are answering combinations in the outer world—imply a preparedness to cognize these combinations —imply faculties of comprehending them. It is true that the resulting compound psychical changes do not take place with the same readiness and automatic precision as the simple reflex action instanced—it is true that some individual experiences seem required to establish them. But while this is partly due to the fact that these combinations are highly involved, extremely varied in their modes of occurrence, made up therefore of psychical relations less completely coherent, and hence need further repetitions to perfect them; it is in a much greater degree due to the fact that at birth the organization of the brain is incomplete, and does not cease its spontaneous progress for twenty or thirty years afterwards. Those who contend that knowledge results wholly from the experiences of the individual, ignoring as they do the mental evolution which accompanies the autogenous development of the nervous system, fall into an error as great as if they were to ascribe all bodily growth and structure to exercise, forgetting the innate tendency to assume the adult form. Were the infant born with a full-sized and completely-constructed brain, their position would be less untenable. But, as the case stands, the gradually-increasing intelligence displayed throughout childhood and youth is more attributable to the completion of the cerebral organization than to the individual experiences—a truth proved by the fact that in adult life there is sometimes displayed a high endowment of some faculty which, during education, was never brought into play. Doubtless, experiences received by the individual furnish the concrete materials for all thought. Doubtless, the organized and semi-organized arrangements existing among the cerebral nerves can give no knowledge until there has been a presentation of the external relations to which they correspond. And doubtless the child's daily observations and reasonings aid the formation of those involved nervous connections that are in process of spontaneous evolution; just as its daily gambols aid the development of its limbs. But saying this is quite a different thing from saying that its intelligence is wholly *produced* by its experiences. That is an utterly inadmissible doctrine—a doctrine which makes the presence of a brain meaningless —a doctrine which makes idiocy unaccountable.

In the sense, then, that there exist in the nervous system certain pre-established relations answering to relations in the environment, there is truth in the doctrine of 'forms of intuition'—not the truth which its defenders suppose, but a parallel truth. Corresponding to absolute external relations, there are established in the structure of the nervous system absolute internal relations—relations that are potentially present before birth in the shape of definite nervous connections; that are antecedent to, and independent of, individual experiences; and that are automatically disclosed along with the first cognitions. And, as here understood, it is not only these fundamental relations which are thus predetermined, but also hosts of other relations of a more or less constant kind, which are congenitally represented by more or less complete nervous connections. But these predetermined internal relations, though independent of the experiences of the individual, are not independent of experiences in general: they have been determined by the experiences of preceding organisms. The corollary here drawn from the general argument is that the human brain is an organized register of *infinitely-numerous* experiences received during the evolution of life, or rather during the evolution of that series of organisms through which the human organism has been reached. The effects of the most *uniform and frequent* of these experiences have been successively bequeathed, principal and interest; and have slowly amounted to that high intelligence which lies latent in the brain of the infant— which the infant in after-life exercises and perhaps strengthens or further complicates—and which, with minute additions, it bequeaths to future generations. And thus it happens that the European inherits from twenty to thirty cubic inches more brain that the Papuan. Thus it happens that faculties, as of music, which scarcely exist in some inferior human races, become congenital in superior ones. Thus it happens that out of savages unable to count up to the number of their fingers, and speaking a language containing only nouns and verbs, arise at length our Newtons and Shakspeares.

This is a brilliant and seductive statement, and it doubtless includes a good deal of truth. Unfortunately it fails to go into details; and when the details are scrutinized, as they soon must be by us, many of them will be seen to be inexplicable in this simple way, and the choice will then remain to us either of denying the experiential origin of certain of our judgments, or of enlarging the meaning of the word experience so as to include these cases among its effects.

TWO MODES OF ORIGIN OF BRAIN STRUCTURE

If we adopt the former course we meet with a controversial difficulty. The 'experience-philosophy' has from time immemorial been the opponent of theological modes of thought. The word experience has a halo of anti-supernaturalism about it; so that if anyone express dissatisfaction with any function claimed for it, he is liable to be treated as if he could only be animated by loyalty to the catechism, or in some way have the interests of obscurantism at heart. I am entirely certain that, on this ground alone, what I have erelong to say will make this a sealed chapter to many of my readers. "He denies experience!" they will exclaim, "denies science; believes the mind created by miracle; is a regular old partisan of innate ideas! That is enough! we'll listen to such antediluvian twaddle no more." Regrettable as is the loss of readers capable of such wholesale discipleship, I feel that a definite meaning for the word experience is even more important than their company. 'Experience' does not mean every natural, as opposed to every supernatural, cause. It means a particular sort of natural agency, alongside of which other more recondite natural agencies may perfectly well exist. With the scientific animus of anti-supernaturalism we ought to agree, but we ought to free ourselves from its verbal idols and bugbears.

Nature has many methods of producing the same effect. She may make a 'born' draughtsman or singer by tipping in a certain direction at an opportune moment the molecules of some human ovum; or she may bring forth a child ungifted and make him spend laborious but successful years at school. She may make our ears ring by the sound of a bell, or by a dose of quinine; make us see yellow by spreading a field of buttercups before our eyes, or by mixing a little santonine powder with our food; fill us with terror of certain surroundings by making them really dangerous, or by a blow which produces a pathological alteration of our brain. It is obvious that we need two words to designate these two modes of operating. *In the one case the natural agents produce perceptions which take cognizance of the agents themselves; in the other case, they produce perceptions which take cognizance of something else.* What is taught to the mind by the 'experience,' in the first case, is the *order of the experience itself*—the 'inner relation' (in Spencer's phrase) 'corresponds' to the 'outer relation' which produced it, by remembering and knowing the latter. But in the case of the *other* sort of natural agency, what is taught to the mind has nothing to do with the agency itself, but with some different outer relation altogether. A diagram will express the alternatives. B stands for our human brain in the midst of the world. All the little *o*'s with

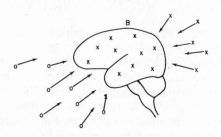

arrows proceeding from them are natural objects (like sunsets, etc.), which impress it through the senses, and in the strict sense of the word give it *experience,* teaching it by habit and association what is the order of their ways. All the little *x*'s inside the brain and all the little *x*'s outside of it are other natural objects and processes (in the ovum, in the blood, etc.), which equally modify the brain, but mould it to no cognition of *themselves*. The *tinnitus aurium* discloses no properties of the quinine; the musical endowment teaches no embryology; the morbid dread (of solitude, perhaps) no brain-pathology; but the way in which a dirty sunset and a rainy morrow hang together in the mind copies and teaches the sequences of sunsets and rainfall in the outer world.

In zoological evolution we have two modes in which an animal race may grow to be a better match for its environment.

First, the so-called way of 'adaptation,' in which the environment may itself modify its inhabitant by exercising, hardening, and habituating him to certain sequences, and these habits may, it is often maintained, become hereditary.

Second, the way of 'accidental variation,' as Mr. Darwin termed it, in which certain young are born with peculiarities that help them and their progeny to survive. That variations of *this* sort tend to become hereditary, no one doubts.

The first mode is called by Mr. Spencer direct, the second indirect, equilibration. Both equilibrations must of course be natural and physical processes, but they belong to entirely different physical spheres. The direct influences are obvious and accessible things. The causes of variation in the young are, on the other hand, molecular and hidden. The direct influences are the animal's 'experiences,' in the widest sense of the term. Where what is influenced by them is the *mental* organism, they are *conscious* experiences, and become the *objects* as well as the causes of their effects. That is, the effect consists in a tendency of the experience itself to be remembered, or to have its elements thereafter coupled in imagination just as they were coupled in the experience. In the diagram these experiences are represented by the *o*'s exclusively. The *x*'s, on the other hand, stand for the indirect causes of mental modification—causes of which we are not immediately conscious as such, and which are not the direct *objects* of the effects they produce. Some of them are molecular accidents before birth; some of them are collateral and remote combinations, unintended combinations, one might say, of more direct effects wrought in the unstable and intricate brain-tissue. Such a result is unquestionably the susceptibility to music, which some individuals possess at the present day. It has no zoological utility; it corresponds to no object in the natural environment; it is a pure *incident* of having a hearing organ, an incident depending on such instable and inessential conditions that one brother may have it and another brother not. Just so with the susceptibility to sea-sickness, which, so far from being engendered by long experience of its 'object' (if a heaving deck can be called its object) is erelong annulled thereby. Our higher æsthetic, moral, and intellectual life seems made up of affections of this collateral and incidental sort, which have entered the mind by the back stairs, as it were, or rather have not entered the mind at all, but got surreptitiously born in the house. No one can successfully treat of psychogenesis, or the factors of mental evolution, without distinguishing between these two ways in which the mind is assailed. The way of 'experience' proper is the front door, the door of the five senses. The agents which affect the brain in this way immediately become the mind's *objects*. The other agents do not. It would be simply silly to say of two men with perhaps equal effective skill in drawing, one an untaught natural genius, the other a mere obstinate plodder in the studio, that both alike owe their skill to their 'experience.' The reasons of their several skills lie in wholly disparate natural cycles of causation.[47]

[47] *Principles of Biology*, part III. chaps. XI, XII.—Goltz and Loeb have found that dogs become mild in character when their occipital, and fierce when their

I will then, with the reader's permission, *restrict the word 'experience' to processes which influence the mind by the front-door-way of simple habits and association.* What the back-door-effects may be will probably grow clearer as we proceed; so I will pass right on to a scrutiny of the actual mental structure which we find.

THE GENESIS OF THE ELEMENTARY MENTAL CATEGORIES

We find: 1. Elementary sorts of sensation, and feelings of personal activity.

2. Emotions; desires; instincts; ideas of worth; æsthetic ideas.

3. Ideas of time and space and number.

4. Ideas of difference and resemblance, and of their degrees.

5. Ideas of causal dependence among events; of end and means; of subject and attribute.

6. Judgments affirming, denying, doubting, supposing any of the above ideas.

7. Judgments that the former judgments logically involve, exclude, or are indifferent to, each other.

---

frontal, brain-lobes are cut off. "A dog which originally was cross in an extreme degree, never suffering himself to be touched, and even refusing, after two days' fasting, to take a piece of bread from my hand, became, after a bilateral operation on the occipital lobes, perfectly trustful and harmless. He underwent five operations on these parts. . . . Each one of them made him more good-natured; so that at last (just as Goltz observed of his dogs) he would let other dogs take away the very bones which he was gnawing" (Loeb, Pflüger's Archiv, xxxix. 300). A course of kind treatment and training might have had a similar effect. But how absurd to call two such different causes by the same name, and to say both times that the beast's 'experience of outer relations' is what educates him to good-nature. This, however, is virtually what all writers do who ignore the distinction between the 'front-door' and the 'back-door' manners of producing mental change.

One of the most striking of these back-door affections is *susceptibility to the charm of drunkenness.* This (taking drunkenness in the broadest sense, as teetotalers use the word) is one of the deepest functions of human nature. Half of both the poetry and the tragedy of human life would vanish if alcohol were taken away. As it is, the thirst for it is such that in the United States the cash-value of its sales amounts to that of the sales of meat and of bread put together. And yet what ancestral 'outer relation' is responsible for this peculiar reaction of ours? The only 'outer relation' could be the alcohol itself, which, comparatively speaking, came into the environment but yesterday, and which, so far from creating, is tending to eradicate, the love of itself from our mental structure, by letting only those families of men survive in whom it is not strong. The love of drunkenness is a purely accidental susceptibility of a brain, evolved for entirely different uses, and its causes are to be sought in the molecular realm, rather than in any possible order of 'outer relations.'

Now we may postulate at the outset that all these forms of thought have a *natural* origin, if we could only get at it. That assumption must be made at the outset of every scientific investigation, or there is no temptation to proceed. But the first account of their origin which we are likely to hit upon is a snare. All these mental affections are ways of knowing objects. Most psychologists nowadays believe that the objects first, in some natural way, engendered a brain from out of their midst, and then imprinted these various cognitive affections upon it. But how? The ordinary evolutionist answer to this question is exceedingly simple-minded. The idea of most speculators seems to be that, since it suffices *now* for us to become acquainted with a complex object, that it should be simply *present* to us often enough, so it must be fair to assume universally that, with time enough given, the *mere presence* of the various objects and relations to be known must end by bringing about the latter's cognition, and that in this way all mental structure was from first to last evolved. Any ordinary Spencerite will tell you that just as the experience of blue objects wrought into our mind the color blue, and hard objects got it to feel hardness, so the presence of large and small objects in the world gave it the notion of size, moving objects made it aware of motion, and objective successions taught it time. Similarly in a world with different impressing things, the mind had to acquire a sense of difference, whilst the like parts of the world as they fell upon it kindled in it the perception of similarity. Outward sequences which sometimes held good, and sometimes failed, naturally engendered in it doubtful and uncertain forms of expectation, and ultimately gave rise to the disjunctive forms of judgment; whilst the hypothetic form, 'if *a*, then *b*,' was sure to ensue from sequences that were invariable in the outer world. On this view, if the outer order suddenly were to change its elements and modes, we should have no faculties to cognize the new order by. At most we should feel a sort of frustration and confusion. But little by little the new presence would work on us as the old one did; and in course of time another set of psychic categories would arise, fitted to take cognizance of the altered world.

This notion of the outer world inevitably building up a sort of mental duplicate of itself if we only give it time, is so easy and natural in its vagueness that one hardly knows how to start to criticise it. One thing, however, is obvious, namely that *the manner in which we now become acquainted with complex objects need not in the least resemble the manner in which the original elements of our consciousness grew up.* Now, it is true, a new sort of animal need only be present to me, to impress its image permanently on my mind; but this is because I am already in possession of categories for knowing each and all of its several attributes, and of a memory for retracing the order of their conjunction. I now have preformed categories for all possible objects. The objects need only awaken these from their slumber. But it is a very different matter to account for the categories themselves. I think we must admit that the origin of the various elementary feelings is a recondite history, even after some sort of neural tissue is there for the outer world to begin its work on. The mere existence of things to be known is even now not, as a rule, sufficient to bring about a knowledge of them. Our abstract and general discoveries usually come to us as lucky fancies; and it is only *après coup* that we find that they correspond to some reality. What immediately produced them were previous thoughts, with which, and with the brain-processes of which, that reality had naught to do.

Why may it not have been so of the original elements of consciousness, sensation, time, space, resemblance, difference, and other relations? Why may they not have come into being by the back-door method, by such physical processes as lie more in the sphere of morphological accident, of inward summation of effects, than in that of the 'sensible presence' of objects? Why may they not, in short, be pure *idiosyncrasies,* spontaneous variations, fitted by good luck (those of them which have survived) to take cognizance of objects (that is, to steer us in our active dealings with them), without being in any intelligible sense immediate derivatives from them? I think we shall find this view gain more and more plausibility as we proceed.[48]

All these elements are subjective duplicates of outer objects. They *are* not the outer objects. The secondary qualities among them are not supposed by any educated person even to resemble the objects. Their *nature* depends more on the reacting brain than on the stimuli which touch it off. This is even more palpably true of the natures of pleasure and pain, effort, desire and aversion, and of such feelings as those of cause and substance, of denial and of doubt. Here then is a native wealth of inner forms whose origin is shrouded in mystery, and which

[48] Mr. Grant Allen, in a brilliant article entitled "Idiosyncrasy" (*Mind,* VIII. 493), seeks to show that accidental morphological changes in the brain cannot possibly be imagined to result in any mental change of a sort which would *fit the animal to its environment.* If spontaneous variation ever works on the brain, its product, says Mr. Allen, ought to be an idiot or a raving madman, not a minister and interpreter of Nature. Only the environment can change us in the direction of accommodation *to itself.* But I think we ought to know a little better just what the molecular changes in the brain are on which thought depends, before we talk so confidently about what the effect can be of their possible variations. Mr. Allen, it should be said, has made a laudable effort to conceive them distinctly. To me his conception remains too purely anatomical. Meanwhile this essay and another by the same author in the *Atlantic Monthly* are probably as serious attempts as any that have been made towards applying the Spencerian theory in a radical way to the facts of human history.

at any rate were not simply 'impressed' from without, in any intelligible sense of the verb 'to impress.'

Their *time- and space-relations,* however, *are* impressed from without—for two outer things at least the evolutionary psychologist must believe to resemble our thoughts of them, these are the time and space in which the objects lie. *The time- and space-relations between things do stamp copies of themselves within.* Things juxtaposed in space impress us, and continue to be thought, in the relation in which they exist there. Things sequent in time, ditto. And thus, through experience in the legitimate sense of the word, there can be truly explained an immense number of our mental habitudes, many of our abstract beliefs, and all our ideas of concrete things, and of their ways of behavior. Such truths as that fire burns and water wets, that glass refracts, heat melts snow, fishes live in water and die on land, and the like, form no small part of the most refined education, and are the all-in-all of education amongst the brutes and lowest men. Here the mind is passive and tributary, a servile copy, fatally and unresistingly fashioned from without. It is the merit of the associationist school to have seen the wide scope of these effects of neighborhood in time and space; and their exaggerated applications of the principle of mere neighborhood ought not to blind us to the excellent service it has done to Psychology in their hands. As far as a large part of our thinking goes, then, it can intelligibly be formulated as a mere lot of *habits* impressed upon us from without. The degree of cohesion of our inner relations, is, in this part of our thinking, proportionate, in Mr. Spencer's phrase, to the degree of cohesion of the outer relations; the causes and the objects of our thought are one; and we are, in so far forth, what the materialistic evolutionists would have us altogether, mere offshoots and creatures of our environment, and naught besides.[49]

But now the plot thickens, for the images impressed upon our memory by the outer stimuli are not restricted to the mere time- and space-relations, in which they originally came, but revive in various manners (dependent on the intricacy of the brain-paths and the instability of the tissue thereof), and form secondary combinations such as the *forms of judgment,* which, taken *per se,* are not congruent either with the forms in which reality exists or in those in which experiences befall us, but which may nevertheless be explained by the way in which experiences befall in a mind gifted with memory, expectation, and the possibility of feeling doubt, curiosity, belief, and denial. The conjunctions of experience befall more or less invariably, variably, or

[49] In my own previous chapters on habit, memory, association, and perception, justice has been done to all these facts.

never. The idea of one term will then engender a fixed, a wavering, or a negative expectation of another, giving affirmative, the hypothetical, disjunctive, interrogative, and negative judgments, and judgments of actuality and possibility about certain things. The separation of attribute from subject in all judgments (which violates the way in which nature exists) may be similarly explained by the piecemeal order in which our perceptions come to us, a vague nucleus growing gradually more detailed as we attend to it more and more. These particular secondary mental forms have had ample justice done them by associationists from Hume downwards.

Associationists have also sought to account for discrimination, abstraction, and generalization by the rates of frequency in which attributes come to us conjoined. With much less success, I think. In the chapter on Discrimination, I have, under the "law of dissociation by varying concomitants," sought to explain as much as possible by the passive order of experience. But the reader saw how much was left for active interest and unknown forces to do. In the chapter on Imagination I have similarly striven to do justice to the 'blended image' theory of generalization and abstraction. So I need say no more of these matters here.

THE GENESIS OF THE NATURAL SCIENCES

Our 'scientific' ways of thinking the outer reality are highly abstract ways. The essence of things for science is not to be what they seem, but to be atoms and molecules moving to and from each other according to strange laws. Nowhere does the account of inner relations produced by outer ones in proportion to the frequency with which the latter have been met, more egregiously break down than in the case of scientific conceptions. The order of scientific thought is quite incongruent either with the way in which reality exists or with the way in which it comes before us. Scientific thought goes by selection and emphasis exclusively. We break the solid plenitude of fact into separate essences, conceive generally what only exists particularly, and by our classifications leave nothing in its natural neighborhood, but separate the contiguous, and join what the poles divorce. The reality *exists* as a *plenum*. All its parts are contemporaneous, each is as real as any other, and each as essential for making the whole just what it is and nothing else. But we can neither experience nor think this *plenum*. What we experience, what *comes before us,* is a chaos of fragmentary impressions interrupting each other;[50] what we *think* is an abstract system of hypothetical data and laws.[51]

[50] "The order of nature, as perceived at a first glance, presents at every instant a chaos followed by another chaos. We must decompose each chaos into

This sort of scientific algebra, little as it immediately resembles the reality given to us, turns out (strangely enough) applicable to it. That is, it yields expressions which, at given places and times, can be

---

single facts. We must learn to see in the chaotic antecedent a multitude of distinct antecedents, in the chaotic consequent a multitude of distinct consequents. This, supposing it done, will not of itself tell us on which of the antecedents each consequent is invariably attendant. To determine that point, we must endeavor to effect a separation of the facts from one another, not in our minds only, but in nature. The mental analysis, however, must take place first. And every one knows that in the mode of performing it, one intellect differs immensely from another." (J. S. Mill, *Logic*, bk. iii. chap. vii. § 1.)

51 I quote from [my] address entitled "Reflex Action and Theism," published in the *Unitarian Review* for November 1881, and translated in the *Critique Philosophique* for January and February 1882. "The conceiving or theorizing faculty works exclusively for the sake of ends that do not exist at all in the world of the impressions received by way of our senses, but are set by our emotional and practical subjectivity. It is a transformer of the world of our impressions into a totally different world, the world of our conception; and the transformation is effected in the interests of our volitional nature, and for no other purpose whatsoever. Destroy the volitional nature, the definite subjective purposes, preferences, fondnesses for certain effects, forms, orders, and not the slightest motive would remain for the brute order of our experience to be remodelled at all. But, as we have the elaborate volitional constitution we do have, the remodelling must be effected, there is no escape. The world's contents are *given* to each of us in an order so foreign to our subjective interests that we can hardly by an effort of the imagination picture to ourselves what it is like. We have to break that order altogether, and by picking out from it the items that concern us, and connecting them with others far away, which we say 'belong' with them, we are able to make out definite threads of sequence and tendency, to foresee particular liabilities and get ready for them, to enjoy simplicity and harmony in the place of what was chaos. Is not the sum of your actual experience taken at this moment and impartially added together an utter chaos? The strains of my voice, the lights and shades inside the room and out, the murmur of the wind, the ticking of the clock, the various organic feelings you may happen individually to possess, do these make a whole at all? Is it not the only condition of your mental sanity in the midst of them that most of them should become nonexistent for you, and that a few others—the sounds, I hope, which I am uttering—should evoke from places in your memory, that have nothing to do with this scene, associates fitted to combine with them in what we call a rational train of thought? —rational because it leads to a conclusion we have some organ to appreciate. We have no organ or faculty to appreciate the simply given order. The real world as it is given at this moment is the sum total of all its beings and events now. But can we think of such a sum? Can we realize for an instant what a cross-section of all existence at a definite point of time would be? While I talk and the flies buzz, a sea gull catches a fish at the mouth of the Amazon, a tree falls in the Adirondack wilderness, a man sneezes in Germany, a horse dies in Tartary, and twins are born in France. What does that mean? Does the contemporaneity of these events with each other and with a million more as disjointed as they form a rational bond between them, and unite them into anything that means for us a world? Yet just such a collateral contemporaneity, and nothing else, is the *real* order of the world. It is an order with which we have nothing to do but to get away from it as fast as possible. As I said, we break it: we break it into histories, and we break it into arts, and we break it into sciences; and then

translated into real values, or interpreted as definite portions of the chaos that falls upon our sense. It becomes thus a practical guide to our expectations as well as a theoretic delight. But I do not see how any one with a sense for the facts can possibly call our systems immediate results of 'experience' in the ordinary sense. Every scientific conception is in the first instance a 'spontaneous variation' in some one's brain.[52] For one that proves useful and applicable there are a thousand that perish through their worthlessness. Their genesis is strictly akin to that of the flashes of poetry and sallies of wit to which the instable brain-paths equally give rise. But whereas the poetry and wit (like the science of the ancients) are their 'own excuse for being,' and have to run the gauntlet of no farther test, the 'scientific' conceptions must prove their worth by being 'verified.' This test, however, is the cause of their *preservation,* not that of their production; and one might as well account for the origin of Artemus Ward's jokes by the 'cohesion' of subjects with predicates in proportion to the 'persistence of the outer relations' to which they 'correspond' as to treat the genesis of scientific conceptions in the same ponderously unreal way.

The most persistent outer relations which science believes in are never matters of experience at all, but have to be disengaged from under experience by a process of elimination, that is, by ignoring conditions which are always present. The *elementary* laws of mechanics, physics, and chemistry are all of this sort. The principle of uniformity in nature is of this sort; it has to be *sought* under and in spite of the

---

we begin to feel at home. We make ten thousand separate serial orders of it. On any one of these, we may react as if the rest did not exist. We discover among its parts relations that were never given to sense at all,—mathematical relations, tangents, squares, and roots and logarithmic functions,—and out of an infinite number of these we call certain ones essential and lawgiving, and ignore the rest. Essential these relations are, but only *for our purpose,* the other relations being just as real and present as they; and our purpose is to *conceive simply* and to *foresee.* Are not simple conception and prevision subjective ends, pure and simple? They are the ends of what we call science; and the miracle of miracles, a miracle not yet exhaustively cleared up by any philosophy, is that the given order lends itself to the remodelling. It shows itself plastic to many of our scientific, to many of our æsthetic, to many of our practical purposes and ends." Cf. also Hodgson: *Philos. of Refl.,* ch. v; Lotze: *Logik,* §§ 342–351; Sigwart: *Logik,* §§ 60–63, 105.

[52] In an article entitled 'Great Men, Great Thoughts, and the Environment,' published in the *Atlantic Monthly* for October 1880, the reader will find some ampler illustrations of these remarks. I have there tried to show that both mental and social evolution are to be conceived after the Darwinian fashion, and that the function of the environment properly so called is much more that of *selecting* forms, produced by invisible forces, than *producing* of such forms,—producing being the only function thought of by the pre-Darwinian evolutionists, and the only one on which stress is laid by such contemporary ones as Mr. Spencer and Mr. Allen.

most rebellious appearances; and our conviction of its truth is far more like a religious faith than like assent to a demonstration. The only cohesions which experience in the literal sense of the word produces in our mind are, as we contended some time back, the proximate laws of nature, and habitudes of concrete things, that heat melts ice, that salt preserves meat, that fish die out of water, and the like.[53] Such 'empirical truths' as these we admitted to form an enormous part

[53] "It is perfectly true that our world of experience begins with such associations as lead us to expect that what has happened to us will happen again. These associations lead the babe to look for milk from its nurse and not from its father, the child to believe that the apple he sees will taste good; and whilst they make him wish for it, they make him fear the bottle which contains his bitter medicine. But whereas a part of these associations grows confirmed by frequent repetition, another part is destroyed by contradictory experiences; and the world becomes divided for us into two provinces, one in which we are at home and anticipate with confidence always the same sequences; another filled with alternating, variable, accidental occurrences.

". . . Accident is, in a wide sphere, such an every-day matter that we need not be surprised if it sometimes invades the territory where order is the rule. And one personification or another of the capricious power of chance easily helps us over the difficulties which further reflection might find in the exceptions. Yes, indeed, Exception has a peculiar fascination; it is a subject of astonishment, a $\theta a\widehat{v}\mu a$, and the credulity with which in this first stage of pure association we adopt our supposed rules is matched by the equal credulity with which we adopt the miracles that interfere with them.

"The whole history of popular beliefs about nature refutes the notion that the thought of an universal physical order can possibly have arisen through the purely passive reception and association of particular perceptions. Indubitable as it is that all men infer from known cases to unknown, it is equally certain that this procedure, if restricted to the phenomenal materials that spontaneously offer themselves, would never have led to the belief in a general uniformity, but only to the belief that law and lawlessness rule the world in motley alternation. From the point of view of strict empiricism nothing exists but the sum of particular perceptions with their coincidences on the one hand, their contradictions on the other.

"That there is more order in the world than appears at first sight is not discovered till the order is looked for. The first impulse to look for it proceeds from practical needs: where ends must be attained, we must know trustworthy means which infallibly possess a property or produce a result. But the practical need is only the first occasion for our reflection on the conditions of a true knowledge; even were there no such need, motives would still be present to carry us beyond the stage of mere association. For not with an equal interest, or rather with an equal lack of interest, does man contemplate those natural processes in which like is joined to like, and those in which like and unlike are joined; the former processes harmonize with the conditions of his thinking, the latter do not; in the former his concepts, judgments, inferences apply to realities, in the latter they have no such application. And thus the intellectual satisfaction which at first comes to him without reflection, at last excites in him the conscious wish to find realized throughout the entire phenomenal world those rational continuities, uniformities, and necessities which are the fundamental element and guiding principle of his own thought." (C. Sigwart: *Logik,* II. 380–2.)

of human wisdom. The 'scientific' truths have to harmonize with these truths, or be given up as useless; but they arise in the mind in no such passive associative way as that in which the simpler truths arise. Even those experiences which are used to prove a scientific truth are for the most part artificial experiences of the laboratory gained after the truth itself has been conjectured. Instead of experiences engendering the 'inner relations,' the inner relations are what engender the experiences here.

What happens in the brain after experience has done its utmost is what happens in every material mass which has been fashioned by an outward force,—in every pudding or mortar, for example, which I may make with my hands. The fashioning from without brings the elements into collocations which set new internal forces free to exert their effects in turn. And the random irradiations and resettlements of our ideas, which *supervene upon experience,* and constitute our free mental play, are due entirely to these secondary internal processes, which vary enormously from brain to brain, even though the brains be exposed to exactly the same 'outer relations.' The higher thought-processes owe their being to causes which correspond far more to the sourings and fermentations of dough, the setting of mortar, or the subsidence of sediments in mixtures, than to the manipulations by which these physical aggregates came to be compounded. Our study of similar association and reasoning taught us that the whole superiority of man depended on the facility with which in his brain the paths worn by the most frequent outer cohesions could be ruptured. The causes of the instability, the reasons why now this point and now that become in him the seat of rupture, we saw to be entirely obscure. The only clear thing about the peculiarity seems to be its interstitial character, and the certainty that no mere appeal to man's 'experience' suffices to explain it.

When we pass from scientific to æsthetic and ethical systems, every one readily admits that, although the elements are matters of experience, the peculiar forms of relation into which they are woven are incongruent with the order of passively received experience. The world of æsthetics and ethics is an ideal world, a Utopia, a world which the outer relations persist in contradicting, but which we as stubbornly persist in striving to make actual. Why do we thus invincibly crave to alter the given order of nature? Simply because other relations among things are far more interesting to us and more charming than the mere rates of frequency of their time- and space-conjunctions. These other relations are all secondary and brain-born, 'spontaneous variations' most of them, of our sensibility, whereby certain elements of experience, and certain arrangements in time and space, have acquired an agreeableness which otherwise would not have been felt. It is true that habitual arrangements may also become agreeable. But this agreeableness of the merely habitual is felt to be a mere ape and counterfeit of real inward fitness; and one sign of intelligence is never to mistake the one for the other.

There are then ideal and inward relations amongst the objects of our thought which can in no intelligible sense whatever be interpreted as reproductions of the order of outer experience. In the æsthetic and ethical realms they conflict with its order—the early Christian with his kingdom of heaven, and the contemporary anarchist with his abstract dream of justice, will tell you that the existing order must perish, root and branch, ere the true order can come. Now the peculiarity of those relations among the objects of our thought which are dubbed 'scientific' is this, that although they no more are inward *reproductions* of the outer order than the ethical and æsthetic relations are, yet they do not conflict with that order, but, once having sprung up by the play of the inward forces, are found—some of them at least, namely the only ones which have survived long enough to be matters of record—to be *congruent* with the time- and space-relations which our impressions affect.

In other words, though nature's materials lend themselves slowly and discouragingly to our translation of them into ethical forms, but more readily into æsthetic forms; to translation into scientific forms they lend themselves with relative ease and completeness. The translation, it is true, will probably never be ended. The perceptive order does not give way, nor the right conceptive substitute for it arise, at our bare word of command.[54] It is often a deadly fight; and many a man of science can say, like Johannes Müller, after an investigation, *'Es klebt Blut an der Arbeit.'* But victory after victory makes us sure that the essential doom of our enemy is defeat.[55]

[54] Cf. Hodgson: *Philosophy of Reflection,* book II, chap. v.

[55] The aspiration to be 'scientific' is such an idol of the tribe to the present generation, is so sucked in with his mother's milk by every one of us, that we find it hard to conceive of a creature who should not feel it, and harder still to treat it freely as the altogether peculiar and one-sided subjective interest which it is. But as a matter of fact, few even of the cultivated members of the race have shared it; it was invented but a generation or two ago. In the middle ages it meant only impious magic; and the way in which it even now strikes orientals is charmingly shown in the letter of a Turkish cadi to an English traveller asking him for statistical information, which Sir A. Layard prints at the end of his 'Nineveh and Babylon.' The document is too full of edification not to be given in full. It runs thus:

My Illustrious Friend, and Joy of my Liver!

The thing you ask of me is both difficult and useless. Although I have passed all my days in this place, I have neither counted the houses nor inquired into the number of the inhabitants; and as to what one person loads on his mules and the other stows away in the bottom of his ship, that is no

THE GENESIS OF THE PURE SCIENCES

I have now stated in general terms the relation of the natural sciences to experience strictly so called, and shall complete what I have to say by reverting to the subject on a later page. At present I will pass to the so-called *pure* or *a priori sciences* of Classification, Logic, and Mathematics. My thesis concerning these is that they are even less than the natural sciences effects of the order of the world as it comes to our experience. THE PURE SCIENCES EXPRESS RESULTS OF COMPARISON *exclusively; comparison is not a conceivable effect of the order in which outer impressions are experienced—it is one of the house-born* [p. 83] *portions of our mental structure; therefore the pure sciences form a body of propositions with whose genesis experience has nothing to do.*

First, consider the nature of comparison. *The relations of resemblance and difference among things have nothing to do with the time-*

---

business of mine. But, above all, as to the previous history of this city, God only knows the amount of dirt and confusion that the infidels may have eaten before the coming of the sword of Islam. It were unprofitable for us to inquire into it.

O my soul! O my lamb! seek not after the things which concern thee not. Thou camest unto us and we welcomed thee: go in peace.

Of a truth thou hast spoken many words; and there is no harm done, for the speaker is one and the listener is another. After the fashion of thy people thou hast wandered from one place to another, until thou art happy and content in none. We (praise be to God) were born here, and never desire to quit it. Is it possible, then, that the idea of a general intercourse between mankind should make any impression on our understandings? God forbid!

Listen, O my son! There is no wisdom equal unto the belief in God! He created the world, and shall we liken ourselves unto Him in seeking to penetrate into the mysteries of His creation? Shall we say, Behold this star spinneth round that star, and this other star with a tail goeth and cometh in so many years! Let it go! He from whose hand it came will guide and direct it.

But thou wilt say unto me, Stand aside, O man, for I am more learned than thou art, and have seen more things. If thou thinkest that thou art in this respect better than I am, thou art welcome. I praise God that I seek not that which I require not. Thou art learned in the things I care not for; and as for that which thou hast seen, I spit upon it. Will much knowledge create thee a double belly, or wilt thou seek Paradise with thine eyes?

O my friend! if thou wilt be happy, say, There is no God but God! Do no evil, and thus wilt thou fear neither man nor death; for surely thine hour will come!

The meek in spirit (El Fakir)

IMAUM ALI ZADI.

and space-order in which we may experience the latter. Suppose a hundred beings created by God and gifted with the faculties of memory and comparison. Suppose that upon each of them the same lot of sensations are imprinted, but in different orders. Let some of them have no single sensation more than once. Let some have this one and others that one repeated. Let every conceivable permutation prevail. And then let the magic-lantern show die out, and keep the creatures in a void eternity, with naught but their memories to muse upon. Inevitably in their long leisure they will begin to play with the items of their experience and rearrange them, make classificatory series of them, place gray between white and black, orange between red and yellow, and trace all other degrees of resemblance and difference. And this new construction will be absolutely identical in all the hundred creatures, the diversity of the sequence of the original experiences having no effect as regards this rearrangement. Any and every form of sequence will give the same result, because the result expresses the relation between the *inward natures* of the sensations; and to that the question of their outward succession is quite irrelevant. Black will differ from white just as much in a world in which they always come close together as in one in which they always come far apart; just as much in one in which they appear rarely as in one in which they appear all the time.

But the advocate of 'persistent outer relations' may still return to the charge: These *are* what make us so sure that white and black differ, he may say; for in a world where sometimes black resembled white and sometimes differed from it, we could never be so sure. It is because in this world black and white have *always* differed that the sense of their difference has become a necessary form of thought. The pair of colors on the one hand and the sense of difference on the other, inseparably experienced, not only by ourselves but by our ancestors, have become inseparably connected in the mind. Not through any essential structure of the mind, which made difference the only possible feeling which they could arouse; no, but because they simply *did* differ so often that at last they begat in us an impotency to imagine them doing anything else, and made us accept such a fabulous account as that just presented, of creatures to whom a single experience would suffice to make us feel the necessariness of this relation.

I know not whether Mr. Spencer would subscribe to this or not;— nor do I care, for there are mysteries which press more for solution than the meaning of this vague writer's words. But to me such an explanation of our difference-judgment is absolutely unintelligible. We now find black and white different, the explanation says, *because we always have so found them.* But why should we always have so found them? Why should difference have popped into our heads so invariably with the thought of them? There must have been either a subjective or an objective reason. The subjective reason can only be that our minds were so constructed that a sense of difference was the only sort of conscious transition possible between black and white; the objective reason can only be that difference was always there, with these colors, outside the mind as an objective fact. The subjective reason explains outer frequency by inward structure, not inward structure by outer frequency; and so surrenders the experience-theory. The objective reason simply says that if an outer difference is there the mind must needs know it—which is no explanation at all, but a mere appeal to the fact that somehow the mind does know what is there.

The only clear thing to do is to give up the sham of a pretended explanation, and to fall back on the fact that the sense of difference *has* arisen, in some natural manner doubtless, but in a manner which we do not understand. It was by the back-stairs way, at all events; and, from the very first, happened to be the only mode of reaction by which consciousness could feel the transition from one term to another of what (in *consequence* of this very reaction) we now call a contrasted pair.

In noticing the differences and resemblances of things, and their degrees, the mind feels its own activity, and has given the name of *comparison* thereto. It need not compare its materials, but if once roused to do so, it can compare them with but one result, and this a fixed consequence of the nature of the materials themselves. Difference and resemblance are thus relations between ideal objects, or conceptions as such. To learn whether black and white differ, I need not consult the world of experience at all; the mere ideas suffice. *What I mean* by black differs from *what I mean* by white, whether such colors exist *extra mentem meam* or not. If they ever do so exist, they *will* differ. White things may blacken, but the black of them will differ from the white of them, so long as I mean anything definite by these three words.[56]

I shall now in what follows call all propositions which express time- and space-relations empirical propositions, and I shall give the name

[56] "Though a man in a fever should from sugar have a bitter taste which at another time would produce a sweet one, yet the idea of bitter in that man's mind would be as clear and distinct from the idea of sweet as if he had tasted only gall. Nor does it make any more confusion between the two ideas of sweet and bitter that the same sort of body produces at one time one and at another time another idea by the taste, than it makes a confusion in two ideas of white and sweet, or white and round, that the same piece of sugar produces them both in the mind at the same time." Locke's *Essay*, bk. II. ch. XI. § 3.

of rational propositions to all propositions which express the results of a comparison. The latter denomination is in a sense arbitrary, for resemblance and difference are not usually held to be the only rational relations between things. I will next proceed to show, however, how many other rational relations commonly supposed distinct can be resolved into these, so that my definition of rational propositions will end, I trust, by proving less arbitrary than it now appears to be.

SERIES OF EVEN DIFFERENCE AND MEDIATE COMPARISON

In Chapter XII we saw that the mind can at successive moments *mean the same,* and that it gradually comes into possession of a stock of permanent and fixed meanings, ideal objects, or conceptions, some of which are universal qualities, like the black and white of our example, and some, individual things. We now see that not only are the objects permanent mental possessions, but the results of their comparison are permanent too. The objects and their differences together form an immutable system. *The same objects, compared in the same way, always give the same results;* if the result be not the same, then the objects are not those originally meant.

This last principle, which we may call the *axiom of constant result,* holds good throughout all our mental operations, not only when we compare, but when we add, divide, class, or infer a given matter in any conceivable way. Its most general expression would be *"the Same operated on in the same way gives the Same."* In mathematics it takes the form of "equals added to, or subtracted from, equals give equals," and the like. We shall meet with it again.

The next thing which we observe is that *the operation of comparing may be repeated on its own results;* in other words, that we can think of the various resemblances and differences which we find and compare them with each other, making differences and resemblances of a higher order. *The mind thus becomes aware of sets of similar differences, and forms series of terms with the same kind and amount of difference between them, terms which, as they succeed each other, maintain a constant direction of serial increase.* This sense of constant direction in a series of operations we saw in Chapter XIII to be a cardinal mental fact. "A differs from B differs from C differs from D, etc.," makes a *series* only when the differences are in the same direction. In any such difference-series all terms differ in just the same way from their predecessors. The numbers, 1, 2, 3, 4, 5, . . . the notes of the chromatic scale in music, are familiar examples. As soon as the mind grasps such a series as a whole, it perceives that *two terms taken far apart differ more than two terms taken near together,* and that any one term differs more from a remote than from a near successor, and this no matter what the terms may be, or what the sort of difference may be, provided it is always the same sort.

This PRINCIPLE OF MEDIATE COMPARISON might be briefly (though obscurely) expressed by the formula *"more than the more is more than the less"*—the words *more* and *less* standing simply for degrees of increase along a constant direction of differences. Such a formula would cover all possible cases, as, earlier than early is earlier than late, worse than bad is worse than good, east of east is east of west; etc., etc., *ad libitum.*[57] Symbolically, we might write it as $a < b < c < d$ . . . . and say that any number of intermediaries may be expunged without obliging us to alter anything in what remains written.

The principle of mediate comparison is only one form of a law which holds in many series of homogeneously related terms, the law that *skipping intermediary terms leaves relations the same.* This AXIOM OF SKIPPED INTERMEDIARIES or of TRANSFERRED RELATIONS occurs, as we soon shall see, in logic as the fundamental principle of inference, in arithmetic as the fundamental property of the number-series, in geometry as that of the straight line, the plane and the parallel. *It seems to be on the whole the broadest and deepest law of man's thought.*

In certain lists of terms the result of comparison may be to find no-difference, or equality in place of difference. Here also intermediaries may be skipped, and mediate comparison be carried on with the general result expressed by the *axiom of mediate equality,* "equals of equals are equal," which is the great principle of the mathematical sciences. This too as a result of the mind's mere acuteness, and in utter independence of the order in which experiences come associated together. Symbolically, again: $a = b = c = d$ . . . , with the same consequence as regards expunging terms which we saw before.

CLASSIFICATORY SERIES

Thus we have a rather intricate system of necessary and immutable *ideal truths of comparison,* a system applicable to terms *experienced* in any order of sequence or frequency, or even to terms never experienced or to be experienced, such as the mind's imaginary constructions would be. These truths of comparison result in *Classifications.* It is, for some unknown reason, a great æsthetic delight for the mind to break the order of experience, and class its materials in serial orders, proceeding from step to step of difference, and to contemplate untir-

[57] Cf. Bradley, *Logic,* p. 226.

ingly the crossings and inosculations of the series among themselves. The first steps in most of the sciences are purely classificatory. Where facts fall easily into rich and intricate series (as plants and animals and chemical compounds do), the mere sight of the series fills the mind with a satisfaction *sui generis;* and a world whose *real* materials naturally lend themselves to serial classification is *pro tanto* a more rational world, a world with which the mind will feel more intimate, than with a world in which they do not. By the pre-evolutionary naturalists, whose generation has hardly passed away, classifications were supposed to be ultimate insights into God's mind, filling us with adoration of his ways. The fact that Nature lets us make them was a proof of the presence of his Thought in her bosom. So far as the facts of experience can *not* be serially classified, therefore, so far experience fails to be rational in *one* of the ways, at least, which we crave.

THE LOGIC-SERIES

Closely akin to the function of comparison is that of *judging, predicating, or subsuming.* In fact, these elementary intellectual functions run into each other so, that it is often only a question of practical convenience whether we shall call a given mental operation by the name of one or of the other. Comparisons result in groups of like things; and presently (through discrimination and abstraction) in conceptions of the *respects* in which the likenesses obtain. The groups are *genera* or *classes,* the respects are *characters* or *attributes.* The attributes again may be compared, forming genera of higher orders, and their characters singled out; so that we have a new sort of series, *that of predication, or of kind including kind.* Thus horses are quadrupeds, quadrupeds animals, animals machines, machines liable to wear out, etc. In such a series as this the several couplings of terms may have been made out originally at widely different times and under different circumstances. But memory may bring them together afterwards; and whenever it does so, our faculty of apprehending serial increase makes us conscious of them as a single system of successive terms united by the same relation.[58]

Now whenever we become thus conscious, we may become aware of an additional relation which is of the highest intellectual importance, inasmuch as upon it the whole structure of logic is reared. *The*

[58] This apprehension of them as forming a single system is what Mr. Bradley means by the act of *construction* which underlies all reasoning. The awareness, which then supervenes, of the additional relation of which I speak in the next paragraph of my text, is what this author calls the act of *inspection.* Cf. *Principles of Logic,* bk. II. pt. I. chap. III.

principle of mediate predication or subsumption is only the axiom of skipped intermediaries applied to a series of successive predications. It expresses the fact that any earlier term in the series stands to any later term in the same relation in which it stands to any intermediate term; in other words, that *whatever has an attribute has all the attributes of that attribute;* or more briefly still, that *whatever is of a kind is of that kind's kind.* A little explanation of this statement will bring out all that it involves.

We learned in the chapter on Reasoning what our great motive is for abstracting attributes and predicating them. It is that our varying practical purposes require us to lay hold of different angles of the reality at different times. But for these we should be satisfied to 'see it whole,' and always alike. The purpose, however, makes one aspect essential; so, to avoid dispersion of the attention, we treat the reality as if for the time being it were nothing but that aspect, and we let its supernumerary determinations go. In short, we substitute the aspect for the whole real thing. *For our purpose* the aspect *can* be substituted for the whole, and the two treated as the same; and the word *is* (which couples the whole with its aspect or attribute in the categoric judgment) expresses (among other things) the identifying operation performed. The predication-series *a* is *b, b* is *c, c* is *d,* . . . closely resembles for certain practical purposes the equation-series $a = b,$ $b = c, c = d,$ etc.

But what is our purpose in predicating? Ultimately, it may be anything we please; but proximately and immediately, it is always the gratification of a certain curiosity as to whether the object in hand is or is not *of a kind* connected with that ultimate purpose. Usually the connection is not obvious, and we only find that the object S is of a kind connected with P, after first finding that it is of a kind M, which itself is connected with P. Thus, to fix our ideas by an example, we have a curiosity (our ultimate purpose being conquest over nature) as to how Sirius may move. It is not obvious whether Sirius is a kind of thing which moves in the line of sight or not. When, however, we find it to be a kind of thing in whose spectrum the hydrogen-line is shifted, and when we reflect that *that* kind of thing is a kind of thing which moves in the line of sight; we conclude that Sirius does so move. Whatever Sirius's attribute is, Sirius is; its adjective's adjective can supersede its own adjective in our thinking, and this with no loss to our knowledge, *so long as we stick to the definite purpose in view.*

Now please note that this elimination of intermediary kinds and transfer of *is*'s along the line, results from our insight into the very meaning of the word *is,* and into the constitution of any series of terms connected by that relation. It has naught to do with what any particular thing is or is not; but, *whatever* any given thing may be, we see that it also is whatever *that* is, indefinitely. To grasp in one view a succession of *is*'s is to apprehend this relation between the terms which they connect, just as to grasp a list of successive equals is to apprehend their *mutual* equality throughout. The principle of mediate subsumption thus expresses relations of ideal objects as such. It can be discovered by a mind left at leisure with any set of meanings (however originally obtained), of which some are predicable of others. The moment we string them in a serial line, that moment we see that we can drop intermediaries, use remote terms just like near ones, and put a genus in the place of a species. This shows that *the principle of mediate subsumption has nothing to do with the particular order of our experiences, or with the outer coexistences and sequences of terms*. Were it a mere outgrowth of habit and association, we should be forced to regard it as having no universal validity; for every hour of the day we meet things which we consider to be of this kind or of that, but later learn that they have none of the kind's properties, that they *do not* belong to the kind's kind. Instead, however, of correcting the principle by these cases, we correct the cases by the principle. We say that if the thing we named an M has not M's properties, then we were either mistaken in calling it an M, or mistaken about M's properties; or else that it is no longer M, but has changed. But we never say that it is an M without M's properties; for by conceiving a thing as of the kind M I mean that it *shall* have M's properties, be of M's kind, even though I should never be able to find in the real world anything which is an M. The principle emanates from my perception of what a lot of successive is's *mean*. This perception can no more be confirmed by one set, or weakened by another set, of outer facts, than the perception that black is not white can be confirmed by the fact that snow never blackens, or weakened by the fact that photographer's paper blackens as soon as you lay it in the sun.

The abstract scheme of successive predications, extended indefinitely, with all the possibilities of substitution which it involves, is thus an immutable system of truth which flows from the very structure and form of our thinking. *If* any real terms ever do fit into such a scheme, they will obey its laws; *whether* they do is a question as to nature's facts, the answer to which can only be empirically ascertained. *Formal logic* is the name of the Science which traces in skeleton form all the remote relations of terms connected by successive *is*'s with each other, and enumerates their possibilities of mutual substitution. To our principle of mediate subsumption she has given various formulations, of which the best is perhaps this broad expression, that *the same can be substituted for the same in any mental operation.*[59]

[59] Realities fall under this only so far as they prove to *be* the same. So far as

The ordinary logical series contains but three terms—"Socrates, man, mortal." But we also have 'Sorites'—Socrates, man, animal, machine, run down, mortal, etc.—and it violates psychology to represent these as syllogisms with terms suppressed. The ground of there being any logic at all is our power to grasp any series as a whole, and the more terms it holds the better. This synthetic consciousness of an uniform direction of advance through a multiplicity of terms is, apparently, what the brutes and lower men cannot accomplish, and what gives to us our extraordinary power of ratiocinative thought. The mind which can grasp a string of *is*'s as a whole—the objects linked by them may be ideal or real, physical, mental, or symbolic, indifferently—can also apply to it the principle of skipped intermediaries. *The logic-list is thus in its origin and essential nature just like those graded classificatory lists which we erewhile described.* The 'rational proposition' which lies at the basis of all reasoning, the *dictum de omni et nullo* in all the various forms in which it may be expressed, the fundamental law of thought, is thus *only the result of the function of comparison* in a mind which has come by some lucky variation to apprehend a series of more than two terms at once.[60] So far, then, *both Systematic Classification and Logic are seen to be incidental results of the mere capacity for discerning difference and likeness,* which capacity is a thing with which the *order of experience,* properly so styled, has absolutely nothing to do.

But how comes it (it may next be asked) when systematic classifications have so little ultimate theoretic importance—for the conceiving of things according to their mere degrees of resemblance always yields to other modes of conceiving when these can be obtained—that the logical relations among things should form such a mighty engine for dealing with the facts of life?

Chapter XXII already gave the reason. This world *might* be a world in which all things differed, and in which what properties there were were ultimate and had no farther predicates. In such a world there would be as many kinds as there were separate things. We could never subsume a new thing under an old kind; or if we could, no consequences would follow. Or, again, this might be a world in which innumerable things were of a kind, but in which no concrete thing

---

they cannot be substituted for each other, for the purpose in hand, so far they are not the same; though for other purposes and in other respects they might be substituted, and then be treated as the same. Apart from purpose, of course; no realities ever are absolutely and exactly the same.

[60] A mind, in other words, which has got *beyond* the merely *dichotomic* style of thought which Wundt alleges to be the essential form of human thinking (*Physiol. Psych.,* II. 312).

remained of the same kind long, but all objects were in a flux. Here again, though we could subsume and infer, our logic would be of no practical use to us, for the subjects of our propositions would have changed whilst we were talking. In such worlds, logical relations would obtain, and be known (doubtless) as they are now, but they would form a merely theoretic scheme and be of no use for the conduct of life. But our world is no such world. It is a very peculiar world, and plays right into logic's hands. *Some* of the things, at least, which it contains are of the same kind as other things; *some* of them remain always of the kind of which they once were; and some of the properties of them cohere indissolubly and are always found together. *Which* things these latter things are we learn by experience in the strict sense of the word, and the results of the experience are embodied in 'empirical propositions.' Whenever such a thing is met with by us now, our sagacity notes it to be of a certain kind; our learning immediately recalls that kind's kind, and then *that* kind's kind, and so on; so that a moment's thinking may make us aware that the thing is of a kind so remote that we could never have directly perceived the connection. The flight to this last kind *over the heads of the intermediaries* is the essential feature of the intellectual operation here. Evidently it is a pure outcome of our sense for apprehending serial increase; and, unlike the several propositions themselves which make up the series (and which may all be empirical), it has nothing to do with the time- and space-order in which the things have been experienced.

MATHEMATICAL RELATIONS

So much for the *a priori* necessities called systematic classification and logical inference. The other couplings of data which pass for *a priori* necessities of thought are the *mathematical* judgments, and certain metaphysical propositions. These latter we shall consider farther on. As regards the mathematical judgments, they are all 'rational propositions' in the sense defined on pp. 96–97, for they express results of comparison and nothing more. The mathematical sciences deal with similarities and equalities exclusively, and not with coexistences and sequences. Hence they have, in the first instance, no connection with the order of experience. The comparisons of mathematics are between numbers and extensive magnitudes, giving rise to arithmetic and geometry respectively.

Number seems to signify primarily the strokes of our attention in discriminating things. These strokes remain in the memory in groups, large or small, and the groups can be compared. The discrimination is, as we know, psychologically facilitated by the mobility of the thing as a total. But within each thing we discriminate parts; ·so that the number of things which any one given phenomenon may be depends in the last instance on our way of taking it. A globe is one, if undivided; two, if composed of hemispheres. A sand-heap is one thing, or twenty thousand things, as we may choose to count it. We amuse ourselves by the counting of *mere* strokes, to form rhythms, and these we compare and name. Little by little in our minds the number-series is formed. This, like all lists of terms in which there is a direction of serial increase, carries with it the sense of those mediate relations between its terms which we expressed by the axiom "the more than the more is more than the less." That axiom seems, in fact, only a way of stating that the terms do form an increasing series. But, in addition to this, we are aware of certain other relations among our strokes of counting. We may interrupt them where we like, and go on again. All the while we feel that the interruption does not alter the strokes themselves. We may count 12 straight through; or count 7 and pause, and then count 5, but still the strokes will be the same. We thus distinguish between our acts of counting and those of interrupting or grouping, as between an unchanged matter and an operation of mere shuffling performed on it. The matter is the original units or strokes; which all modes of grouping or combining simply give us back unchanged. In short, *combinations of numbers are combinations of their units,* which is the fundamental axiom of arithmetic,[61] leading to such consequences as that $7 + 5 = 8 + 4$ because both $= 12$. The general axiom of mediate equality, that equals of equals are equal, comes in here.[62] The principle of constancy in our meanings, when applied to strokes of counting, also gives rise to the axiom that the same number, operated on (interrupted, grouped) in the same way will always give the same result or be the same. How shouldn't it? Nothing is supposed changed.

Arithmetic and its fundamental principles are thus independent of our experiences or of the order of the world. The matter of arithmetic is *mental matter;* its principles flow from the fact that the matter forms a series, which can be cut into by us wherever we like without the matter changing. The empiricist school has strangely tried to interpret the truths of number as results of coexistences among outward things. John Mill calls number a physical property of things. 'One,' according to Mill, means one sort of passive sensation which we re-

[61] Said to be expressed by Grassman in the fundamental *Axiom of Arithmetic* $(a + b) + 1 = a + (b + 1)$.

[62] Compare Helmholtz's more technically expressed Essay 'Zählen u. Messen,' in the *Philosophische Aufsätze,* Ed. Zeller gewidmet (Leipzig, 1887), p. 17.

ceive, 'two' another, 'three' a third. The same things, however, can give us different number-sensations. Three things arranged thus, ○ ○ ○ , for example, impress us differently from three things arranged thus, ○○○ . But experience tells us that every real object-group which can be arranged in one of these ways can always be arranged in the other also, and that 2 + 1 and 3 are thus modes of numbering things which 'coexist' invariably with each other. The indefeasibility of our belief in their 'coexistence' (which is Mill's word for their equivalence) is due solely to the enormous amount of experience we have of it. For all things, whatever other sensations they may give us, give us at any rate number-sensations. Those number-sensations which the same thing may be successively made to arouse are the numbers which we deem equal to each other; those which the same thing refuses to arouse are those which we deem unequal.

This is as clear a restatement as I can make of Mill's doctrine.[63] And its failure is written upon its front. Woe to arithmetic, were such the only grounds for its validity! The same real things are countable in numberless ways, and pass from one numerical form, not only to its equivalent (as Mill implies), but to its other, as the sport of physical accidents or of our mode of attending may decide. How could our notion that one and one are eternally and necessarily two ever maintain itself in a world where every time we add one drop of water to another we get not two but one again? in a world where every time we add a drop to a crumb of quicklime we get a dozen or more?—had it no better warrant than such experiences? At most we could then say that one and one are *usually* two. Our arithmetical propositions would never have the confident tone which they now possess. That confident tone is due to the fact that they deal with abstract and ideal numbers exclusively. *What we mean* by one plus one *is* two; we *make* two out of it; and it would mean two still even in a world where *physically* (according to a conceit of Mill's) a third thing was engendered every time one thing came together with another. We are masters of our meanings, and discriminate between the things we mean and our ways of taking them, between our strokes of numeration themselves, and our bundlings and separatings thereof.

Mill ought not only to have said, "All things are numbered." He ought, in order to prove his point, to have shown that they are *un-equivocally* numbered, which they notoriously are not. Only the abstract numbers themselves are unequivocal, only those which we create mentally and hold fast to as ideal objects always the same. A concrete natural thing can always be numbered in a great variety of ways. "We need only conceive a thing divided into four equal parts

[63] For the original statements, cf. J. S. Mill's *Logic*, bk. II. chap. VI. §§ 2, 3; and bk. III. chap. XXIV. § 5.

(and all things may be conceived as so divided)," as Mill is himself compelled to say, to find the number four in it, and so on.

The relation of numbers to experience is just like that of 'kinds' in logic. So long as an experience will keep its kind we can handle it by logic. So long as it will keep its number we can deal with it by arithmetic. *Sensibly,* however, things are constantly changing their numbers, just as they are changing their kinds. They are forever breaking apart and fusing. Compounds and their elements are never numerically identical, for the elements are sensibly many and the compounds sensibly one. Unless our arithmetic is to remain without application to life, we must somehow *make* more numerical continuity than we spontaneously find. Accordingly Lavoisier discovers his weight-units which remain the same in compounds and elements, though volume-units and quality-units all have changed. A great discovery! And modern science outdoes it by denying that compounds exist at all. There is no such thing as 'water' for 'science;' that is only a handy name for H_2 and O when they have got into the position H-O-H, and then affect our senses in a novel way. The modern theories of atoms, of heat, and of gases are, in fact, only intensely artificial devices for gaining that constancy in the numbers of things which sensible experience will not show. "Sensible things are not the things for me," says Science, "because in their changes they will not keep their numbers the same. Sensible qualities are not the qualities for me, because they can with difficulty be numbered at all. These hypothetic atoms, however, are the things, these hypothetic masses and velocities are the qualities for me; they will stay numbered all the time."

By such elaborate inventions, and at such a cost to the imagination, do men succeed in making for themselves a world in which real things shall be coerced *per fas aut nefas* under arithmetical law.

The other branch of mathematics is *geometry*. Its objects are also ideal creations. Whether nature contain circles or not, I can know what I mean by a circle and can stick to my meaning; and when I mean two circles I mean two things of an identical kind. The axiom of constant results (see above, p. 97) holds in geometry. The same forms, treated in the same way (added, subtracted, or compared), give the same results—how shouldn't they? The axioms of mediate comparison (p. 98), of logic (p. 99), and of number (p. 104) all apply to the forms which we imagine in space, inasmuch as these resemble or differ from each other, form kinds, and are numerable things. But in addition to these general principles, which are true of space-forms only as they are of other mental conceptions, there are certain axioms relative to space-forms exclusively, which we must briefly consider.

Three of them give marks of identity among straight lines, planes, and parallels. Straight lines which have two points, planes which have three points, parallels to a given line which have one point, in common, coalesce throughout. Some say that the certainty of our belief in these axioms is due to repeated experiences of their truth; others that it is due to an intuitive acquaintance with the properties of space. It is neither. We experience lines enough which pass through two points only to separate again, only we won't call them straight. Similarly of planes and parallels. We have a definite idea of what we mean by each of these words; and when something different is offered us, we see the difference. Straight lines, planes, and parallels, as they figure in geometry, are mere inventions of our faculty for apprehending serial increase. The farther continuations of these forms, we say, *shall* bear the same relation to their last visible parts which these did to still earlier parts. It thus follows (from that axiom of skipped intermediaries which obtains in all regular series) that parts of these figures separated by other parts must agree in direction, just as contiguous parts do. This uniformity of direction throughout is, in fact, all that makes us care for these forms, gives them their beauty, and stamps them into fixed conceptions in our mind. But obviously if two lines, or two planes, with a common segment, were to part company beyond the segment, it could only be because the direction of at least one of them had changed. Parting company in lines and planes *means* changing direction, means assuming a new relation to the parts that preexist; and assuming a new relation means ceasing to be straight or plane. If we mean by a parallel a line that will never meet a second line; and if we have one such line drawn through a point, any third line drawn through that point which does not coalesce with the first must be inclined to it, and if inclined to it must approach the second, i.e., cease to be parallel with it. No properties of outlying space need come in here: only a definite conception of uniform direction, and constancy in sticking to one's point.

The other two axioms peculiar to geometry are that figures can be moved in space without change, and that no variation in the way of subdividing a given amount of space alters its total quantity.[64] This last axiom is similar to what we found to obtain in numbers. 'The whole is equal to its parts' is an abridged way of expressing it. A man is not the same biological whole if we cut him in two at the neck as if we divide him at the ankles; but geometrically he is the same whole, no matter in which place we cut him. The axiom about figures being

---

[64] The subdivision itself consumes none of the space. In all practical experience our subdivisions do consume space. They consume it in our geometrical figures. But for simplicity's sake, in geometry we postulate subdivisions which violate experience and consume none of it.

movable in space is rather a postulate than an axiom. *So far as they are* so movable, then certain fixed equalities and differences obtain between forms, *no matter where placed.* But if translation through space warped or magnified forms, then the relations of equality, etc., would always have to be expressed with a position-qualification added. A geometry as absolutely certain as ours could be invented on the supposition of such a space, if the laws of its warping and deformation were fixed. It would, however, be much more complicated than our geometry, which makes the simplest possible supposition; and finds, luckily enough, that it is a supposition with which the space of our experience seems to agree.

By means of these principles, all playing into each other's hands, the mutual equivalences of an immense number of forms can be traced, even of such as at first sight bear hardly any resemblance to each other. We move and turn them mentally, and find that parts of them will superpose. We add imaginary lines which subdivide or enlarge them, and find that the new figures resemble each other in ways which show us that the old ones are equivalent too. We thus end by expressing all sorts of forms in terms of other forms, enlarging our knowledge of the kinds of things which certain other kinds of things are, or to which they are equivalent.

The result is a new system of mental objects which can be treated as identical for certain purposes, a new series of *is*'s almost indefinitely prolonged, just like the series of equivalencies among numbers, part of which the multiplication-table expresses. And all this is in the first instance regardless of the coexistences and sequences of nature, and regardless of whether the figures we speak of have ever been outwardly experienced or not.

CONSCIOUSNESS OF SERIES IS THE BASIS OF RATIONALITY

Classification, logic, and mathematics all result, then, from the mere play of the mind comparing its conceptions, no matter whence the latter may have come. The essential condition for the formation of all these sciences is that we should have grown capable of apprehending series as such, and of distinguishing them as homogeneous or heterogeneous, and as possessing definite directions of what I have called 'increase.' This consciousness of series is a human perfection which has been gradually evolved, and which varies amazingly from one man to another. No accounting for it as a result of habitual associations among outward impressions, so we must simply ascribe it to the factors, whatever they be, of inward cerebral growth. Once this consciousness attained to, however, *mediate* thought becomes possible; with our very awareness of a series may go an awareness that dropping terms out of it will leave identical relations between the terms that remain; and thus arises a perception of relations between things so naturally separate that we should otherwise never have compared them together at all.

The axiom of skipped intermediaries applies, however, only to certain particular series, and among them to those which we have considered, in which the recurring relation is either of difference, of likeness, of kind, of numerical addition, or of prolongation in the same linear or plane direction. It is therefore not a purely formal law of thinking, but flows from the nature of the matters thought about. It will not do to say universally that in all series of homogeneously related terms the remote members are related to each other as the near ones are; for that will often be untrue. The series A is not B is not C is not D . . . does not permit the relation to be traced between remote terms. From two negations no inference can be drawn. Nor, to become more concrete, does the lover of a woman generally love her beloved, or the contradictor of a contradictor contradict whomever he contradicts. The slayer of a slayer does not slay the latter's victim; the acquaintances or enemies of a man need not be each other's acquaintances or enemies; nor are two things which are on top of a third thing necessarily on top of each other.

All skipping of intermediaries and transfer of relations occurs within homogeneous series. But not all homogeneous series allow of intermediaries being skipped and relations transferred. It depends on which series they are, on what relations they contain.[65] Let it not be said that it is a mere matter of verbal association, due to the fact that language sometimes permits us to transfer the *name* of a relation over skipped intermediaries, and sometimes does not; as where we call men 'progenitors' of their remote as well as of their immediate posterity, but refuse to call them 'fathers' thereof. There are relations which are *intrinsically* transferable, whilst others are not. The relation of *condition,* e.g., is intrinsically transferable. What conditions a condition conditions what it conditions—"cause of cause is cause of effect." The relations of negation and *frustration,* on the other hand, are not transferable: what frustrates a frustration does not frustrate what it frustrates. No changes of terminology would annul the intimate difference between these two cases.

Nothing but the clear sight of the ideas themselves shows whether the axiom of skipped intermediaries applies to them or not. Their connections, immediate and remote, flow from their inward natures. We

[65] Cf. A. de Morgan: *Syllabus of a Proposed System of Logic* (1860), pp. 46–56.

try to consider them in certain ways, to bring them into certain relations, and we find that sometimes we can and sometimes we cannot. *The question whether there are or are not inward and essential connections between conceived objects as such, really is the same thing as the question whether we can get any new perception from mentally coupling them together, or pass from one to another by a mental operation which gives a result.* In the case of some ideas and operations we get a result; but no result in the case of others. Where a result comes, it is due exclusively to the *nature* of the ideas and of the operation. Take blueness and yellowness, for example. We can operate on them in some ways, but not in other ways. We can compare them; but we cannot add one to or subtract it from the other. We can refer them to a common kind, color; but we cannot make one a kind of the other, or infer one from the other. This has nothing to do with experience. For we *can* add blue *pigment* to yellow *pigment,* and subtract it again, and get a result both times. Only we know perfectly that this is no addition or subtraction of the blue and yellow qualities or natures themselves.[66]

There is thus no denying the fact that *the mind is filled with necessary and eternal relations which it finds between certain of its ideal conceptions, and which form a determinate system, independent of the order of frequency in which experience may have associated the conception's originals in time and space.*

Shall we continue to call these sciences 'intuitive,' 'innate,' or '*a priori*' bodies of truth, or not? [67] Personally I should like to do so. But

[66] Cf. Locke's *Essay,* bk. II. chap. XVII. § 6.

[67] Some readers may expect me to plunge into the old debate as to whether the *a priori* truths are 'analytic' or 'synthetic.' It seems to me that the distinction is one of Kant's most unhappy legacies, for the reason that it is impossible to make it sharp. No one will say that such analytic judgments as "equidistant lines can nowhere meet" are *pure* tautologies. The predicate is a somewhat new way of conceiving as well as of naming the subject. There is *something* 'ampliative' in our greatest truisms, our state of mind is richer after than before we have uttered them. This being the case, the question "at what point does the new state of mind cease to be *implicit* in the old?" is too vague to be answered. The only sharp way of defining synthetic propositions would be to say that they express a relation between *two data* at least. But it is hard to find any proposition which cannot be construed as doing this. Even verbal definitions do it. Such painstaking attempts as that latest one by Mr. D. G. Thompson to prove all necessary judgments to be analytic (*System of Psychology,* II. pp. 232 ff.) seem accordingly but *nugæ difficiles,* and little better than wastes of ink and paper. All philosophic interest vanishes from the question, the moment one ceases to ascribe to *any a priori* truths (whether analytic or synthetic) that "legislative character for all possible experience" which Kant believed in. We ourselves have denied such legislative character, and contended that it was for experience itself to prove whether its data can or cannot be assimilated to those ideal terms between which *a priori* relations obtain. The analytic-synthetic debate is thus for

I hesitate to use the terms, on account of the odium which controversial history has made the whole of their connotation for many worthy persons. The most politic way not to alienate these readers is to flourish the name of the immortal Locke. For in truth I have done nothing more in the previous pages than to make a little more explicit the teachings of Locke's fourth book:

> The immutability of the same relations between the same immutable things is now the idea that shows him that if the three angles of a triangle were once equal to two right angles, they will always be equal to two right ones. And hence he comes to be certain that what was once true in the case is always true; what ideas once agreed will always agree . . . Upon this ground it is that particular demonstrations in mathematics afford general knowledge. If, then, the perception that the same ideas will eternally have the same habitudes and relations be not a sufficient ground of knowledge, there could be no knowledge of general propositions in mathematics. . . . All general knowledge lies only in our own thoughts, and consists barely in the contemplation of our abstract ideas. Wherever we perceive any agreement or disagreement amongst them, there we have general knowledge; and by putting the names of those ideas together accordingly in propositions, can with certainty pronounce general truths. . . . What is once known of such ideas will be perpetually and forever true. So that, as to all general knowledge, we must search and find it only in our own minds and it is only the examining of our own ideas that furnisheth us with that. Truths belonging to essences of things (that is, to abstract ideas) are eternal, and are to be found out only by the contemplation of those essences. . . . Knowledge is the consequence of the ideas (be they what they will) that are in our minds, producing there certain general propositions. . . . Such propositions are therefore called "eternal truths," . . . because, being once made about abstract ideas so as to be true, they will, whenever they can be supposed to be made again, at any time past or to come, by a mind having those ideas, always actually be true. For names being supposed to stand perpetually for the same ideas, and the same ideas having immutably the same habitudes one to another, propositions concerning any abstract ideas that are once true must needs be eternal verities.

But what are these eternal verities, these 'agreements,' which the mind discovers by barely considering its own fixed meanings, except what I have said?—relations of likeness and difference, immediate or mediate, between the terms of certain series. Classification is serial comparison, logic mediate subsumption, arithmetic mediate equality of different bundles of attention-strokes, geometry mediate equality of

---

us devoid of all significance. On the whole, the best recent treatment of the question known to me is in one of A. Spir's works, his *Denken und Wirklichkeit,* I think, but I cannot now find the page.

different ways of carving space. None of these eternal verities has anything to say about facts, about what is or is not in the world. Logic
does not say whether Socrates, men, mortals or immortals *exist;* arithmetic does not tell us where her 7's, 5's, and 12's are to be *found;*
geometry affirms not that circles and rectangles are *real.* All that these
sciences make us sure of is, that *if* these things are anywhere to be
found, the eternal verities will obtain of them. Locke accordingly
never tires of telling us that the

> universal propositions of whose truth or falsehood we can have cer-
> tain knowledge, concern not existence. . . . These universal and self-
> evident principles, being only our constant, clear, and distinct knowl-
> edge of our own ideas more general or comprehensive, can assure us
> of nothing that passes without the mind; their certainty is founded
> only upon the knowledge of each idea by itself, and of its distinction
> from others; about which we cannot be mistaken whilst they are in our
> minds. . . . The mathematician considers the truth and properties be-
> longing to a rectangle or circle only as they are in idea in his own
> mind. For it is possible he never found either of them existing mathe-
> matically, i.e., precisely true, in his life. But yet the knowledge he has
> of any truths or properties belonging to a circle, or any other mathe-
> matical figure, is nevertheless true and certain even of real things
> existing; because real things are no farther concerned nor intended to
> be meant by any such propositions, than as things really agree to those
> archetypes in his mind. Is it true of the idea of a triangle, that its
> three angles are equal to two right ones? It is true also of a triangle
> wherever it really exists. Whatever other figure exists that is not ex-
> actly answerable to that idea in his mind is not at all concerned in that
> proposition. And therefore he is certain all his knowledge concerning
> such ideas is real knowledge: because, intending things no farther than
> they agree with those his ideas, he is sure what he knows concerning
> those figures when they have barely an ideal existence in his mind will
> hold true of them also when they have a real existence in matter. [But]
> that any or what bodies do exist, that we are left to our senses to dis-
> cover to us as far as they can.[68]

Locke accordingly distinguishes between 'mental truth' and 'real
truth.'[69] The former is intuitively certain; the latter dependent on experience. Only *hypothetically* can we affirm intuitive truths of real
things—by *supposing,* namely, that real things exist which correspond
exactly with the ideal subjects of the intuitive propositions.

If our senses corroborate the supposition all goes well. But note
the strange descent in Locke's hands of the dignity of *a priori* propositions. By the ancients they were considered, without farther question,
to reveal the constitution of Reality. Archetypal things existed, it was

[68] Book IV. chaps. IX. § 1; VII. 14; IV. 6.
[69] Chap. V. §§ 6, 8.

assumed, in the relations in which we had to think them. The mind's necessities were a warrant for those of Being; and it was not till Descartes' time that scepticism had so advanced (in 'dogmatic' circles) that the warrant must itself be warranted, and the veracity of the Deity invoked as a reason for holding fast to our natural beliefs.

But the intuitive propositions of Locke leave us as regards outer reality none the better for their possession. We still have to "go to our senses" to find what the reality is. The vindication of the intuitionist position is thus a barren victory. The eternal verities which the very structure of our mind lays hold of do not necessarily themselves lay hold on extra-mental being, nor have they, as Kant pretended later,[70] a legislating character even for all possible experience. They are primarily interesting only as subjective facts. They stand waiting in the mind, forming a beautiful ideal network; and the most we can say is that we *hope* to discover realities over which the network may be flung so that ideal and real may coincide.

And this brings us back to 'science' from which we diverted our attention so long ago (see p. 93). Science thinks she has discovered the objective realities in question. Atoms and ether, with no properties but masses and velocities expressible by numbers, and paths expressible by analytic formulas, these at last are things over which the mathematico-logical network may be flung, and by supposing which instead of sensible phenomena science becomes yearly more able to manufacture for herself a world about which rational propositions may be framed. Sensible phenomena are pure delusions for the mechanical philosophy. The 'things' and qualities we instinctively believe in do not exist. The only realities are swarming solids in everlasting motion, undulatory or continued, whose expressionless and meaningless changes of position form the history of the world, and are deducible from initial collocations and habits of movement hypothetically assumed. Thousands of years ago men started to cast the chaos of nature's sequences and juxtapositions into a form that might seem intelligible. Many were their ideal prototypes of rational order: teleological and æsthetic ties between things, causal and substantial bonds,

[70] Kant, by the way, made a strange tactical blunder in his way of showing that the forms of our necessary thought are underived from experience. He insisted on thought-forms with which experience largely *agrees,* forgetting that the only forms which could not by any possibility be the results of experience would be such as experience *violated.* The first thing a Kantian ought to do is to discover forms of judgment to which *no* order in 'things' runs parallel. These would indeed be features native to the mind. I owe this remark to Herr A. Spir, in whose *Denken und Wirklichkeit* it is somewhere contained. I have myself already to some extent proceeded, and in the pages which follow shall proceed still farther, to show the originality of the mind's structure in this way.

as well as logical and mathematical relations. The most promising of these ideal systems at first were of course the richer ones, the sentimental ones. The baldest and least promising were the mathematical ones; but the history of the latter's application is a history of steadily advancing successes, whilst that of the sentimentally richer systems is one of relative sterility and failure.[71] Take those aspects of phenomena which interest you as a human being most, and class the phenomena as perfect and imperfect, as ends and means to ends, as high and low, beautiful and ugly, positive and negative, harmonious and discordant, fit and unfit, natural and unnatural, etc., and barren are all your results. In the ideal world the kind 'precious' has characteristic properties. What is precious should be preserved; unworthy things should be sacrificed for its sake; exceptions made on its account; its preciousness is a reason for other things' actions, and the like. But none of these things need happen to your 'precious' object in the real world. Call the things of nature as much as you like by sentimental, moral, and æsthetic names, no natural consequences follow from the naming. They may be of the kinds you allege, but they are not of *the kind's kind;* and the last great system-maker of this sort, Hegel, was obliged explicitly to repudiate logic in order to make any inferences at all from the names he called things by.

But when you give things mathematical and mechanical names and call them just so many solids in just such positions, describing just such paths with just such velocities, all is changed. Your sagacity finds its reward in the verification by nature of all the deductions which you may next proceed to make. Your 'things' realize all the *consequences* of the names by which you classed them. The modern mechanico-physical philosophy of which we are all so proud, because it includes the nebular cosmogony, the conservation of energy, the kinetic theory of heat and gases, etc., etc., begins by saying that the *only* facts are collocations and motions of primordial solids, and the only laws the changes of motion which changes in collocation bring. The ideal which this philosophy strives after is a mathematical world-formula, by which, if all the collocations and motions at a given mo-

[71] Yet even so late as Berkeley's time one could write: "As in reading other books a wise man will choose to fix his thoughts on the sense and apply it to use, rather than lay them out in grammatical remarks on the language: so in perusing the volume of nature methinks it is beneath the dignity of the mind to affect an exactness in reducing each particular phenomenon to general rules, or showing how it follows from them. We should propose to ourselves nobler views, namely, to recreate and exalt the mind with a prospect of the beauty, order, extent, and variety of natural things: hence, by proper inferences, to enlarge our notions of the grandeur, wisdom, and beneficence of the Creator," etc., etc., etc. (*Principles of Human Knowledge,* § 109.)

ment were known, it would be possible to reckon those of any wished-for future moment, by simply considering the necessary geometrical, arithmetical, and logical implications. Once we have the world in this bare shape, we can fling our net of *a priori* relations over all its terms, and pass from one of its phases to another by inward thought-necessity. Of course it is a world with a very minimum of rational *stuff*. The sentimental facts and relations are butchered at a blow. But the rationality yielded is so superbly complete in *form* that to many minds this atones for the loss, and reconciles the thinker to the notion of a purposeless universe, in which all the things and qualities men love, *dulcissima mundi nomina,* are but illusions of our fancy attached to accidental clouds of dust which the eternal cosmic weather will dissipate as carelessly as it has formed them.

The popular notion that 'Science' is forced on the mind *ab extra,* and that our interests have nothing to do with its constructions, is utterly absurd. The craving to believe that the things of the world belong to kinds which are related by inward rationality together, is the parent of Science as well as of sentimental philosophy; and the original investigator always preserves a healthy sense of how plastic the materials are in his hands.

"Once for all," says Helmholtz in beginning that little work of his which laid the foundations of the 'conservation of energy,' "it is the task of the physical sciences to seek for laws by which particular processes in nature may be referred to general rules, and deduced from such again. Such rules (for example the laws of reflection or re-fraction of light, or that of Mariotte and Gay-Lussac for gas-volumes) are evidently nothing but generic-concepts for embracing whole classes of phenomena. The search for them is the business of the experimental division of our Science. Its theoretic division, on the other hand, tries to discover the unknown causes of processes from their visible effects; tries to understand them by the law of causality. . . . The ultimate goal of theoretic physics is to find the last *unchanging* causes of the processes in Nature. Whether all processes be really ascribable to such causes, whether, in other words, *nature be completely intelligible,* or whether there be changes which would elude the law of a necessary causality, and fall into a realm of spontaneity or freedom, is not here the place to determine; but at any rate it is clear that the Science whose aim it is to make nature appear intelligible [*die Natur zu begreifen*] must start with the *assumption* of her intelligibility, and draw consequences in conformity with this assumption, until irrefutable facts show the limitations of this method. . . . The postulate that natural phenomena must be reduced to changeless ultimate causes next shapes itself so that *forces unchanged by time* must be found to be these causes. Now in Science we have already found portions of matter with changeless forces (indestructible qualities), and called them (chemical) elements. If, then, we imagine the world composed of elements with inalterable qualities, the only changes that can remain possible in such a world are spatial changes, i.e. movements, and the only outer relations which can modify the action of the forces are spatial too, or, in other words, the forces are motor forces dependent for their effect only on spatial relations. More exactly still: The phenomena of nature must be reduced to [*zurückgeführt*, conceived as, classed as] motions of material points with inalterable motor forces acting according to space-relations alone. . . . But points have no mutual space-relations except their distance, . . . and a motor force which they exert upon each other can cause nothing but a change of distance—i.e. be an attractive or a repulsive force. . . . And its intensity can only depend on distance. So that at last the task of Physics resolves itself into this, to refer phenomena to inalterable attractive and repulsive forces whose intensity varies with distance. The solution of this task would at the same time be the condition of Nature's complete intelligibility." [72]

The subjective interest leading to the assumption could not be more candidly expressed. What makes the assumption 'scientific' and not merely poetic, what makes a Helmholtz and his kin *discoverers,* is that the things of Nature turn out to act as if they *were* of the kind assumed. They behave as such mere drawing and driving atoms would behave; and so far as they have been distinctly enough translated into molecular terms to test the point, so far a certain fantastically ideal object, namely, the mathematical sum containing their mutual distances and velocities, is found to be constant throughout all their movements. This sum is called the total energy of the molecules considered. Its constancy or 'conservation' gives the name to the hypothesis of molecules and central forces from which it was logically deduced.

Take any other mathematico-mechanical theory and it is the same. They are all translations of sensible experiences into other forms, substitutions of items between which ideal relations of kind, number, form, equality, etc., obtain, for items between which no such relations obtain; coupled with declarations that the experienced form is false and the ideal form true, declarations which are justified by the appearance of new sensible experiences at just those times and places at which we logically infer that their ideal correlates ought to be. Wave-hypotheses thus make us predict rings of darkness and color, distortions, dispersions, changes of pitch in sonorous bodies moving from us, etc.; molecule-hypotheses lead to predictions of vapor-density, freezing point, etc.,—all which predictions fall true.

Thus the world grows more orderly and rational to the mind, which passes from one feature of it to another by deductive necessity, as soon as it conceives it as made up of so few and so simple phenom-

[72] *Die Erhaltung der Kraft* (1847), pp. 2–6.

ena as bodies with no properties but number and movement to and fro.

METAPHYSICAL AXIOMS

But alongside of these ideal relations between terms which the world verifies there are other ideal relations not as yet so verified. I refer to those propositions (no longer expressing mere results of comparison) which are formulated in such metaphysical and æsthetic axioms as "The Principle of things is one;" "The quantity of existence is unchanged;" "Nature is simple and invariable;" "Nature acts by the shortest ways;" *"Ex nihilo nihil fit;"* "Nothing can be evolved which was not involved;" "Whatever is in the effect must be in the cause;" "A thing can only work where it is;" "A thing can only affect another of its own kind;" *"Cessante causa, cessat et effectus;"* "Nature makes no leaps;" "Things belong to discrete and permanent kinds;" "Nothing is or happens without a reason;" "The world is throughout rationally intelligible;" etc., etc., etc. Such principles as these, which might be multiplied to satiety,[73] are properly to be called *postulates of rationality,* not propositions of fact, If nature *did* obey them, she *would* be *pro tanto* more intelligible; and we seek meanwhile so to conceive her phenomena as to show that she does obey them. To a certain extent we succeed. For example, instead of the 'quantity of existence' so vaguely postulated as unchanged, Nature allows us to suppose that curious sum of distances and velocities which for want of a better term we call 'energy.' For the effect being 'contained in the cause,' nature lets us substitute 'the effect *is* the cause,' so soon as she lets us conceive both effect and cause as the same molecules, in two successive positions.—But all around these incipient successes (as all around the molecular world, so soon as we add to it as its 'effects' those illusory 'things' of common-sense which we had to butcher for its sake), there still spreads a vast field of irrationalized fact whose items simply *are* together, and from one to another of which we can pass by no ideally 'rational' way.

It is not that these more metaphysical postulates of rationality are absolutely barren—though barren enough they were when used, as the scholastics used them, as immediate propositions of fact.[74] They have

[73] Perhaps the most influential of all these postulates is that the nature of the world must be such that sweeping statements may be made about it.

[74] Consider, e.g., the use of the axioms *'nemo potest supra seipsum,'* and *'nemo dat quod non habet,'* in this refutation of 'Darwinism,' which I take from the much-used scholastic compendium of *Logic and Metaphysics of Liberatore,* 3d ed. (Rome, 1880): "Hæc hypothesis . . . aperte contradicit principiis Me-

a fertility as ideals, and keep us uneasy and striving always to recast the world of sense until its lines become more congruent with theirs. Take for example the principle that 'nothing can happen without a cause.' We have no definite idea of what we mean by cause, or of what causality consists in. But the principle expresses a demand for *some* deeper sort of inward connection between phenomena than their merely habitual time-sequence seems to us to be. The word 'cause' is, in short, an altar to an unknown god; an empty pedestal still marking the place of a hoped-for statue. *Any* really inward belonging-together of the sequent terms, if discovered, would be accepted as what the word cause was meant to stand for. So we seek, and seek; and in the molecular systems we find a sort of inward belonging in the notion of identity of matter with change of collocation. Perhaps by still seeking we may find other sorts of inward belonging, even between the mole-cules and those 'secondary qualities,' etc., which they produce upon our minds.

It cannot be too often repeated that the triumphant application of any one of our ideal systems of rational relations to the real world justifies our hope that other systems may be found also applicable. Metaphysics should take heart from the example of physics, simply confessing that hers is the longer task. Nature *may* be remodelled, nay, certainly will be remodelled, far beyond the point at present reached. Just how far?—is a question which only the whole future history of Science and Philosophy can answer.[75] Our task being Psy-chology, we cannot even cross the threshold of that larger problem.

---

taphysicæ, quæ docent essentias rerum esse immutabiles, et effectum non posse superare causam. Et sane, quando, juxta Darwin, species inferior se evolvit in superiorem, unde trahit maiorem illam nobilitatem? Ex ejus carentia. At nihil dat quod non habet; et minus gignere nequit plus, aut negatio positionem. Præ-terea in transformatione quæ fingitur, natura prioris speciei, servatur aut de-struitur? Si primum, mutatio erit tantum accidentalis, qualem reapse videmus in diversis stirpibus animantium. Sin alterum asseritur, ut reapse fert hypothesis darwiniana, res tenderet ad seipsam destruendam; cum contra omnia naturaliter tendant ad sui conservationem, et nonnisi per actionem contrarii agentis cor-ruant." It is merely a question of fact whether these ideally proper relations do or do not obtain between animal and vegetable ancestors and descendants. If they do not, what happens? simply this, that we cannot continue to class animal and vegetal facts under the *kinds* between which those ideal relations obtain. Thus, we can no longer call animal breeds by the name of 'species'; cannot call generating a kind of 'giving,' or treat a descendant as an 'effect' of his ancestor. The ideal scheme of terms and relations can remain, if you like; but it must re-main purely mental, and without application to life, which 'gangs its ain gait' regardless of ideal schemes. Most of us, however, would prefer to doubt whether such abstract axioms as that 'a thing cannot tend to its own destruction' express ideal relations of an important sort at all.

[75] Compare A. Riehl: *Der Philosophische Kriticismus,* Bd. II. Thl. I. Abschn. I. Cap. III. § 6.

• • •

Besides the mental structure which results in such metaphysical principles as those just considered, there is a mental structure which expresses itself in

ÆSTHETIC AND MORAL PRINCIPLES

The æsthetic principles are at bottom such axioms as that a note sounds good with its third and fifth, or that potatoes need salt. We are once for all so made that when certain impressions come before our mind, one of them will seem to call for or repel the others as its companions. To a certain extent the principle of habit will explain these æsthetic connections. When a conjunction is repeatedly experienced, the cohesion of its terms grows grateful, or at least their disruption grows unpleasant. But to explain *all* æsthetic judgments in this way would be absurd; for it is notorious how seldom natural experiences come up to our æsthetic demands. Many of the so-called metaphysical principles are at bottom only expressions of æsthetic feeling. Nature is simple and invariable; makes no leaps, or makes nothing but leaps; is rationally intelligible; neither increases nor diminishes in quantity; flows from one principle, etc., etc.,—what do all such principles express save our sense of how pleasantly our intellect would feel if it had a Nature of that sort to deal with? The subjectivity of which feeling is of course quite compatible with Nature also turning out objectively to be of that sort, later on.

The *moral* principles which our mental structure engenders are quite as little explicable *in toto* by habitual experiences having bred inner cohesions. Rightness is not *mere* usualness, wrongness not *mere* oddity, however numerous the facts which might be invoked to prove such identity. Nor are the moral judgments those most invariably and emphatically impressed on us by public opinion. The most characteristically and peculiarly moral judgments that a man is ever called on to make are in unprecedented cases and lonely emergencies, where no popular rhetorical maxims can avail, and the hidden oracle alone can speak; and it speaks often in favor of conduct quite unusual, and suicidal as far as gaining popular approbation goes. The forces which conspire to this resultant are subtle harmonies and discords between the elementary ideas which form the data of the case. Some of these harmonies, no doubt, have to do with habit; but in respect to most of them our sensibility must assuredly be a phenomenon of supernumerary order, correlated with a brain-function quite as secondary as that which takes cognizance of the diverse excellence of elaborate musical compositions. No more than the higher musical sensibility can the higher moral sensibility be accounted for by the frequency with which outer relations have cohered.[76] Take judgments of justice or equity, for example. Instinctively, one judges everything differently, according as it pertains to one's self or to some one else. Empirically one notices that everybody else does the same. But little by little there dawns in one the judgment "nothing can be right for me which would not be right for another similarly placed;" or "the fulfilment of my desires is intrinsically no more imperative than that of anyone else's;" or "what it is reasonable that another should do for me, it is also reasonable that I should do for him;" [77] and forthwith the whole mass of the habitual gets overturned. It gets *seriously* overturned only in a few fanatical heads. But its overturning is due to a back-door and not to a front-door process. Some minds are preternaturally sensitive to logical consistency and inconsistency. When they have ranked a thing under a kind, they *must* treat it as of that kind's kind, or feel all out of tune. In many respects we do class ourselves with other men, and call them and ourselves by a common name. They agree with us in having the same Heavenly Father, in not being consulted about their birth, in not being themselves to thank or blame for their natural gifts, in having the same desires and pains and pleasures, in short in a host of fundamental relations. Hence, *if these things be our essence,* we should be substitutable for other men, and they for us, in any proposition in which either of us is involved. The more fundamental and common the essence chosen, and the more simple the reasoning,[78] the more wildly radical and unconditional will the justice be which is aspired to. Life is one long struggle between conclusions based on abstract ways of conceiving cases, and opposite conclusions prompted by our instinctive perception of them as individual facts. The logical

[76] As one example out of a thousand of exceptionally delicate idiosyncrasy in this regard, take this: "I must quit society. I would rather undergo twice the danger from beasts and ten times the danger from rocks. It is not pain, it is not death, that I dread,—it is the hatred of a man; there is something in it so shocking that I would rather submit to any injury than incur or increase the hatred of a man by revenging it. . . . . Another sufficient reason for suicide is that I was this morning out of temper with Mrs. Douglas (for no fault of hers). I did not betray myself in the least, but I reflected that to be exposed to the possibility of such an event once a year, was evil enough to render life intolerable. The disgrace of using an impatient word is to me overpowering." (Elton Hammond, quoted in Henry Crabb Robinson's *Diary,* vol. I. p. 424.)

[77] Compare H. Sidgwick, *Methods of Ethics,* bk. III. chap. XIII. § 3.

[78] A gentleman told me that he had a conclusive argument for opening the Harvard Medical School to women. It was this: "Are not women human?"—which major premise of course had to be granted. "Then are they not entitled to all the rights of humanity?" My friend said that he had never met anyone who could successfully meet this reasoning.

stickler for justice always seems pedantic and mechanical to the man who goes by tact and the particular instance, and who usually makes a poor show at argument. Sometimes the abstract conceiver's way is better, sometimes that of the man of instinct. But just as in our study of reasoning we found it impossible to lay down any mark whereby to distinguish *right* conception of a concrete case from *confusion*, so here we can give no general rule for deciding when it is morally useful to treat a concrete case as *sui generis*, and when to lump it with others in an abstract class.[79]

An adequate treatment of the way in which we come by our æsthetic and moral judgments would require a separate chapter, which I cannot conveniently include in this book. Suffice it that these judgments express inner harmonies and discords between objects of thought; and that whilst outer cohesions frequently repeated will often

[79] You reach the Mephistophelian point of view as well as the point of view of justice by treating cases as if they belonged rigorously to abstract classes. Pure rationalism, complete immunity from prejudice, consists in refusing to see that the case before one is absolutely unique. It is always possible to treat the country of one's nativity, the house of one's fathers, the bed in which one's mother died, nay, the mother herself if need be, on a naked equality with all other specimens of so many respective genera. It shows the world in a clear frosty light from which all fuliginous mists of affection, all swamp-lights of sentimentality, are absent. Straight and immediate action becomes easy then—witness a Napoleon's or a Frederick's career. But the question always remains, "Are not the mists and vapors *worth* retaining?" The illogical refusal to treat certain concretes by the mere law of their genus has made the drama of human history. The obstinate insisting that tweedledum is *not* tweedledee is the bone and marrow of life. Look at the Jews and the Scots, with their miserable factions and sectarian disputes, their loyalties and patriotisms and exclusions,—their annals now become a classic heritage, because men of genius took part and sang in them. A thing is important if any one *think* it important. The process of history consists in certain folks becoming possessed of the mania that certain special things are important infinitely, whilst other folks cannot agree in the belief. The Shah of Persia refused to be taken to the Derby Day, saying "It is already known to me that one horse can run faster than another." He made the question "*which* horse?" immaterial. Any question can be made immaterial by subsuming all its answers under a common head. Imagine what college ballgames and races would be if the teams were to forget the absolute distinctness of Harvard from Yale and think of both as One in the higher genus College. The sovereign road to indifference, whether to evils or to goods, lies in the thought of the higher genus. "When we have meat before us," says Marcus Aurelius, seeking indifference to *that* kind of good, "we must receive the impression that this is the dead body of a fish, and this is the dead body of a bird or of a pig; and again that this Falernian is only a little grape-juice, and this purple robe some sheep's wool dyed with the blood of a shell-fish. Such, then, are these impressions, and they reach the things themselves and penetrate them, and we see what kind of things they are. Just in the same way ought we to act through life, and where there are things which appear most worthy of our approbation, we ought to lay them bare and look at their worthlessness and strip them of all the words by which they are exalted." (Long's *Translation*, VI. 13.)

seem harmonious, all harmonies are not thus engendered, but our feeling of many of them is a secondary and incidental function of the mind. Where harmonies are asserted of the real world, they are obviously mere postulates of rationality, so far as they transcend experience. Such postulates are exemplified by the ethical propositions that the individual and universal good are one, and that happiness and goodness are bound to coalesce in the same subject.

SUMMARY OF WHAT PRECEDES

I will now sum up our progress so far by a short summary of the most important conclusions which we have reached.

The mind has a native structure in this sense, that certain of its objects, if considered together in certain ways, give definite results; and that no other ways of considering, and no other results, are possible if the same objects be taken.

The results are 'relations' which are all expressed by judgments of subsumption and of comparison.

The judgments of subsumption are themselves subsumed under the *laws of logic*.

Those of comparison are expressed in *classifications,* and in the *sciences of arithmetic and geometry*.

Mr. Spencer's opinion that our consciousness of classificatory, logical, and mathematical relations between ideas is due to the frequency with which the corresponding 'outer relations' have impressed our minds, is unintelligible.

Our consciousness of these relations, no doubt, has a natural genesis. But it is to be sought rather in the inner forces which have made the brain grow, than in any mere paths of 'frequent' association which outer stimuli may have ploughed in that organ.

But let our sense for these relations have arisen as it may, the relations themselves form a fixed system of lines of cleavage, so to speak, in the mind, by which we naturally pass from one object to another; and the objects connected by these lines of cleavage are often not connected by any regular time- and space-associations. We distinguish, therefore, between the empirical order of things, and this their rational order of comparison; and, so far as possible, we seek to translate the former into the latter, as being the more congenial of the two to our intellect.

Any classification of things into kinds (especially if the kinds form series, or if they successively involve each other) is a more rational way of conceiving the things than is that mere juxtaposition or separation of them as individuals in time and space which is the order of their crude perception. Any assimilation of things to terms between which such classificatory relations, with their remote and mediate transactions, obtain, is a way of bringing the things into a more rational scheme.

Solids in motion are such terms; and the mechanical philosophy is only a way of conceiving nature so as to arrange its items along some of the more natural lines of cleavage of our mental structure.

Other natural lines are the moral and æsthetic relations. Philosophy is still seeking to conceive things so that these relations also may seem to obtain between them.

As long as things have not successfully been so conceived, the moral and æsthetic relations obtain only between *entia rationis,* terms in the mind; and the moral and æsthetic principles remain but postulates, not propositions, with regard to the real world outside.

There is thus a large body of *a priori* or intuitively necessary truths. As a rule, these are truths of *comparison* only, and in the first instance they express relations between merely mental terms. Nature, however, acts as if some of her realities were identical with these mental terms. So far as she does this, we can make *a priori* propositions concerning natural fact. The aim of both science and philosophy is to make the identifiable terms more numerous. So far it has proved easier to identify nature's things with mental terms of the mechanical than with mental terms of the sentimental order.

The widest postulate of rationality is that the world *is* rationally intelligible throughout, after the pattern of *some* ideal system. The whole war of the philosophies is over that point of faith. Some say they can see their way already to the rationality; others that it is hopeless in any other but the mechanical way. To some the very fact that there is a world at all seems irrational. Nonentity would be a more natural thing than existence, for these minds. One philosopher at least says that the relatedness of things to each other is irrational anyhow, and that a world of relations can never be made intelligible.[80]

With this I may be assumed to have completed the programme which I announced at the beginning of the chapter, so far as the *theoretic* part of our organic mental structure goes. It can be due neither to our own nor to our ancestors' experience. I now pass to those practical parts of our organic mental structure. Things are a little different here; and our conclusion, though it lies in the same direction, can be by no means as confidently expressed.

[80] *"An sich, in seinem eignen Wesen, ist jedes reale Object mit sich selbst identisch und unbedingt"*—that is, the *"allgemeinste Einsicht a priori,"* and the *"allgemeinste aus Erfahrung"* is *"Alles erkennbare ist bedingt."* (A. Spir: *Denken und Wirklichkeit.* Compare also Herbart and Hegel.)

To be as short and simple as possible, I will take the case of instincts, and, supposing the reader to be familiar with Chapter XXIV, I will plunge *in medias res*.

THE ORIGIN OF INSTINCTS

Instincts must have been either
  1) Each specially created in complete form, or
  2) Gradually evolved.

As the first alternative is nowadays obsolete, I proceed directly to the second. The two most prominent suggestions as to the way in which instincts may have been evolved are associated with the names of Lamarck and Darwin.

Lamarck's statement is that animals have *wants,* and contract, to satisfy them, *habits* which transform themselves gradually into so many propensities which they can neither resist nor change. These *propensities,* once acquired, propagate themselves by way of transmission to the young, so that they come to exist in new individuals, anteriorly to all exercise. Thus are the same emotions, the same habits, the same *instincts,* perpetuated without variation from one generation to another, so long as the outward conditions of existence remain the same.[81] Mr. Lewes calls this the theory of 'lapsed intelligence.' Mr. Spencer's words are clearer than Lamarck's, so that I will quote from him:[82]

> Setting out with the unquestionable assumption, that every new form of emotion making its appearance in the individual or the race is a modification of some pre-existing emotion, or a compounding of several pre-existing emotions, we should be greatly aided by knowing what always are the pre-existing emotions. When, for example, we find that very few, if any, of the lower animals show any love of accumulation, and that this feeling is absent in infancy; when we see that an infant in arms exhibits anger, fear, wonder, while yet it manifests

[81] *Philosophie Zoölogique,* 3me partie, chap. v., 'de l'Instinct.'

[82] It should be said that Mr. Spencer's most formal utterance about instinct is in his *Principles of Psychology,* in the chapter under that name. Dr. Romanes has reformulated and criticised the doctrine of this chapter in his *Mental Evolution in Animals,* chapter XVII. I must confess my inability to state its vagueness in intelligible terms. It treats instincts as a further development of reflex actions, and as forerunners of intelligence,—which is probably true of many. But when it ascribes their formation to the mere 'multiplication of experiences,' which, at first simple, mould the nervous system to 'correspond to outer relations' by simple reflex actions, and, afterwards complex, make it 'correspond' by 'compound reflex actions,' it becomes too mysterious to follow without more of a key than is given. The whole thing becomes perfectly simple if we suppose the reflex actions to be accidental inborn idiosyncrasies preserved.

no desire of permanent possession; and that a brute which has no ac-
quisitive emotion can nevertheless feel attachment, jealousy, love of
approbation,—we may suspect that the feeling which property satisfies is compounded out of simpler and deeper feelings. We may conclude that as when a dog hides a bone there must exist in him a
prospective gratification of hunger, so there must similarly, at first, in
all cases where anything is secured or taken possession of, exist an
ideal excitement of the feeling which that thing will gratify. We may
further conclude that when the intelligence is such that a variety of
objects come to be utilized for different purposes; when, as among
savages, divers wants are satisfied through the articles appropriated
for weapons, shelter, clothing, ornament,—the act of appropriating
comes to be one constantly involving agreeable associations, and one
which is therefore pleasurable, irrespective of the end subserved. And
when, as in civilized life, the property acquired is of a kind not con-
ducing to one order of gratifications, but is capable of ministering to
all gratifications, the pleasure of acquiring property grows more distinct from each of the various pleasures subserved—is more completely differentiated into a separate emotion.[83] It is well known that
on newly-discovered islands not inhabited by man, birds are so devoid
of fear as to allow themselves to be knocked over with sticks, but that
in the course of generations they acquire such a dread of man as to
fly on his approach, and that this dread is manifested by young as well
as old. Now unless this change be ascribed to the killing off of the
least fearful, and the preservation and multiplication of the more fearful, which, considering the small number killed by man, is an inadequate cause, it must be ascribed to accumulated experiences, and each
experience must be held to have a share in producing it. We must conclude that in each bird that escapes with injuries inflicted by man, or
is alarmed by the outcries of other members of the flock, . . . there
is established an association of ideas between the human aspect and
the pains, direct and indirect, suffered from human agency. And we

[83] This account of acquisitiveness differs from our own. Without denying the
associationist account to be a true description of a great deal of our proprietary
feeling, we admitted in addition an entirely primitive form of desire. The reader
must decide as to the plausibilities of the case. Certainly appearances are in favor
of there being in us *some* cupidities quite disconnected with the ulterior uses of
the things appropriated. The source of their fascination lies in their appeal to
our æsthetic sense, and we wish thereupon simply to *own* them. Glittering, hard,
metallic, odd, pretty things; curious things especially; natural objects that look
as if they were artificial, or that mimic other objects;— these form a class of
things which human beings snatch at as magpies snatch rags. They simply fascinate us. What house does not contain some drawer or cupboard full of senseless odds and ends of this sort, with which nobody knows what to do, but which
a blind instinct saves from the ash-barrel? Witness people returning from a walk
on the sea-shore or in the woods, each carrying some *lusus naturæ* in the shape
of stone or shell, or strip of bark or odd-shaped fungus, which litter the house
and grow daily more unsightly, until at last reason triumphs over blind propensity and sweeps them away.

must further conclude that the state of consciousness which impels the bird to take flight is at first nothing more than an ideal reproduction of those painful impressions which before followed man's approach; that such ideal reproduction becomes more vivid and more massive as the painful experiences, direct or sympathetic, increase; and that thus the emotion, in its incipient state, is nothing else than an aggregation of the revived pains before experienced. As, in the course of generations, the young birds of this race begin to display a fear of man before they have been injured by him, it is an unavoidable inference that the nervous system of the race has been organically modified by these experiences; we have no choice but to conclude that when a young bird is thus led to fly, it is because the impression produced on its senses by the approaching man entails, through an incipiently reflex action, a partial excitement of all those nerves which, in its ancestors, had been excited under the like conditions; that this partial excitement has its accompanying painful consciousness; and that the vague painful consciousness thus arising constitutes emotion proper—*emotion undecomposable into specific experiences, and therefore seemingly homogeneous. If such be the explanation of the fact in this case, then it is in all cases. If the emotion is so generated here, then it is so generated throughout.* If so, we must perforce conclude that the emotional modifications displayed by different nations, and those higher emotions by which civilized are distinguished from savage, are to be accounted for on the same principle. And, concluding this, we are led strongly to suspect that the emotions in general have severally thus originated.[84]

Obviously the word 'emotion' here means instinct as well,—the actions we call instinctive are expressions or manifestations of the emotions whose genesis Mr. Spencer describes. Now if habit could thus bear fruit outside the individual life, and if the modifications so painfully acquired by the parents' nervous systems could be found readymade at birth in those of the young, it would be hard to overestimate the importance, both practical and theoretical, of such an extension of its sway. In principle, instincts would then be assimilated to 'secondarily-automatic' habits, and the origin of many of them out of tentative experiments made during ancestral lives, perfected by repetition, addition, and association through successive generations, would be a comparatively simple thing to understand.

Contemporary students of instinct have accordingly been alert to discover all the facts which would seem to establish the possibility of such an explanation. The list is not very long, considering what a burden of conclusions it has to bear. Let acquisitiveness and fear of man, as just argued for by Spencer, lead it off. Other cases of the

[84] Review of Bain in H. Spencer: *Illustrations of Universal Progress* (New York, 1864), pp. 311, 315.

latter sort are the increased shyness of the woodcock noticed to have occurred within sixty years' observation by Mr. T. A. Knight, and the greater shyness everywhere shown by large than by small birds, to which Darwin has called attention. Then we may add—

The propensities of 'pointing,' 'retrieving,' etc., in sporting dogs, which seem partly, at any rate, to be due to training, but which in well-bred stock are all but innate. It is in these breeds considered bad for a litter of young if its sire or dam have not been trained in the field.

Docility of domestic breeds of horses and cattle.

Tameness of young of tame rabbit—young wild rabbits being invincibly timid.

Young foxes are most wary in those places where they are most severely hunted.

Wild ducks, hatched out by tame ones, fly off. But if kept close for some generations, the young are said to become tame.[85]

Young savages at a certain age will revert to the woods.

English greyhounds taken to the high plateau of Mexico could not at first run well, on account of rarefied air. Their whelps entirely got over the difficulty.

Mr. Lewes somewhere[86] tells of a terrier pup whose parents had been taught to 'beg,' and who constantly threw himself spontaneously into the begging attitude. Darwin tells of a French orphan-child, brought up out of France, yet *shrugging* like his ancestors.[87]

Musical ability often increases from generation to generation in the families of musicians.

The hereditarily epileptic guinea-pigs of Brown-Séquard, whose parents had become epileptic through surgical operations on the spinal cord or sciatic nerve. The adults often lose some of their hind toes, and the young, in addition to being epileptic, are frequently born with the corresponding toes lacking. The offspring of guinea-pigs whose cervical sympathetic nerve has been cut on one side will have the ear larger, the eyeball smaller, etc., just like their parents after the operation. Puncture of the 'restiform body' of the medulla will, in the same animal, congest and enlarge one eye, and cause gangrene of one ear. In the young of such parents the same symptoms occur.

Physical refinement, delicate hands and feet, etc., appear in families well-bred and rich for several generations.

The 'nervous' temperament also develops in the descendants of sedentary brain-working people.

Inebriates produce offspring in various ways degenerate.

Nearsightedness is produced by indoor occupation for genera-

[85] Ribot: *De l'Hérédité*, 2me éd. p. 26.
[86] Quoted (without reference) in Spencer's *Biology*, vol. I. p. 247.
[87] *Expression of Emotions* (N. Y.), p. 387.

tions. It has been found in Europe much more frequent among schoolchildren in towns than among the children of the same age in the country.

These latter cases are of the inheritance of structural rather than of functional peculiarities. But as structure gives rise to function it may be said that the principle is the same. Amongst other inheritances of adaptive[88] structural change may be mentioned:

The 'Yankee' type.

Scrofula, rickets, and other diseases of bad conditions of life.

The udders and permanent milk of the domestic breeds of cow.

The 'fancy' rabbit's ears, drooping through lack of need to erect them. Dog's, ass's, etc., in some breeds ditto.

The obsolete eyes of mole and various cave-dwelling animals.

The diminished size of the wing-bones of domesticated ducks, due to ancestral disuse of flight.[89]

These are about all the facts which, by one author or another, have been invoked as evidence in favor of the 'lapsed intelligence' theory of the origin of instincts.

Mr. Darwin's theory is that of the natural selection of accidentally produced tendencies to action.

"It would," says he, "be the most serious error to suppose that the greater number of instincts have been acquired by habit in one generation, and then transmitted by inheritance in succeeding generations. It can clearly be shown that the most wonderful instincts with which we are acquainted, namely, those of the hive-bee and of many ants, could not possibly have been thus acquired.[90] It will be universally admitted that instincts are as important as corporeal structure for the welfare of each species, under its present conditions of life. Under changed conditions of life, it is at least possible that slight modifications of instinct might be profitable to a species; and if it can be shown that instincts do vary ever so little, then I can see no difficulty in natural selection preserving and continually accumulating variations of instinct to any extent that may be profitable. It is thus, as I believe, that

[88] 'Adaptive' changes are those produced by the direct effect of outward conditions on an organ or organism. Sunburned complexion, horny hands, muscular toughness, are illustrations.

[89] For these and other facts cf. Th. Ribot: *De l'Hérédité;* W. B. Carpenter: *Contemporary Review,* vol. 21, p. 295, 779, 867; H. Spencer: *Princ. of Biol.* pt. II. ch. V, VIII, IX, X; pt. III. ch. XI, XII; C. Darwin: *Animals and Plants under Domestication,* ch. XII, XIII, XIV; Sam'l Butler: *Life and Habit;* T. A. Knight: *Philos. Trans.* 1837; E. Dupuy: *Popular Science Monthly,* vol. XI. p. 332; F. Papillon: *Nature and Life,* p. 330; Crothers, in *Pop. Sci. M.,* Jan. (or Feb.) 1889.

[90] Because, being exhibited by neuter insects, the effects of mere practice cannot accumulate from one generation to another.

all the most complex and wonderful instincts have arisen. . . . I believe that the effects of habit are of quite subordinate importance to
the effects of the natural selection of what may be called accidental
variations of instincts;—that is, of variations produced by the same
unknown causes which produce slight deviations of bodily structure." [91]

The evidence for Mr. Darwin's view is too complex to be given in
this place. To my own mind it is quite convincing. If, with the Darwinian theory in mind, one re-reads the list of examples given in favor of
the Lamarckian theory, one finds that many of the cases are irrelevant, and that some make for one side as well as for the other. This is
so obvious in many of the cases that it is needless to point it out in
detail. The shrugging child and the begging pup, e.g., prove somewhat
too much. They are examples so unique as to suggest spontaneous
variation rather than inherited habit. In other cases the observations
much need corroboration, e.g., the effects of not training for a generation in sporting dogs and race-horses, the difference between young
wild rabbits born in captivity and young tame ones, the cumulative
effect of many generations of captivity on wild ducks, etc.

Similarly, the increased wariness of the large birds, of those on
islands frequented by men, of the woodcock, of the foxes, may be due
to the fact that the bolder families have been killed off, and left none
but the naturally timid behind, or simply to the individual experience
of older birds being imparted by example to the young so that a new
educational tradition has occurred.—The cases of physical refinement,
nervous temperament, Yankee type, etc., also need much more discriminating treatment than they have yet received from the Lamarck-
ians. There is no real evidence that physical refinement and nervosity
tend to accumulate from generation to generation in aristocratic or
intellectual families; nor is there any that the change in that direction
which Europeans transplanted to America undergo is not all completed in the first generation of children bred on our soil. To my mind,
the facts all point that way. Similarly the better breathing of the greyhounds born in Mexico was surely due to a post-natal adaptation of
the pups' thorax to the rarer air.

Distinct neurotic *degeneration* may undoubtedly accumulate from
parent to child, and as the parent usually in this case grows worse by
his own irregular habits of life, the temptation lies near to ascribe the
child's deterioration to this cause. This, again, is a hasty conclusion.
For neurotic degeneration is unquestionably a disease whose original
causes are unknown; and like other 'accidental variations' it is hereditary. But it ultimately ends in sterility; and it seems to me quite unfair
to draw any conclusions from its natural history in favor of the trans-

[91] *Origin of Species*, chap. VII.

mission of acquired peculiarities. Nor does the degeneration of the children of alcoholics prove anything in favor of their having inherited the shattered nervous system which the alcohol has induced in their parents: because the poison usually has a chance to directly affect their own bodies before birth, by acting on the germinal matter from which they are formed whilst it is still nourished by the alcoholized blood of the parent. In many cases, however, the parental alcoholics are themselves degenerates neurotically, and the drink-habit is only a symptom of their disease, which in some form or other they also propagate to their children.

There remain the inherited mutilations of the guinea-pig. But these are such startling exceptions to the ordinary rule with animals that they should hardly be used as examples of a typical process. The docility of domestic cattle is certainly in part due to man's selection, etc., etc. In a word, the proofs form rather a beggarly array.

Add to this that the writers who have tried to carry out the theory of transmitted habit with any detail are always obliged *somewhere* to admit inexplicable variation. Thus Spencer allows that

> Sociality can begin only where, through some slight variation, there is less tendency than usual for the individuals to disperse. . . . That slight variations of mental nature, sufficient to initiate this process, may be fairly assumed, all our domestic animals show us: differences in their characters and likings are conspicuous. Sociality having thus commenced, and survival of the fittest tending ever to maintain and increase it, it will be further strengthened by the inherited effects of habit.[92] Again, in writing of the pleasure of pity, Mr. Spencer says: "This feeling is not one that has arisen through the inherited effects of experiences, but belongs to a quite different group, traceable to the survival of the fittest simply—to the natural selection of incidental variations. In this group are included all the bodily appetites, together with those simpler instincts, sexual and parental, by which every race is maintained; and which must exist before the higher processes of mental evolution can commence." [93]

The inheritance of tricks of manner and trifling peculiarities, such as handwriting, certain odd gestures when pleased, peculiar movements during sleep, etc., have also been quoted in favor of the theory of transmission of acquired habits. Strangely enough; for of all things in the world these tricks seem most like idiosyncratic variations. They are usually defects or oddities which the education of the individual, the pressure of what is really *acquired* by him, would counteract, but which are too native to be repressed, and breaks through all artificial barriers, in his children as well as in himself.

[92] *Princ. of Psychol.,* II. 561.
[93] *Ibid.* p. 623.

. . .

I leave my text practically just as it was written in 1885. I proceeded at that time to draw a tentative conclusion to the effect that the origin of *most* of our instincts must certainly be deemed fruits of the back-door method of genesis, and not of ancestral experience in the proper meaning of the term. Whether acquired ancestral habits played any part at all in their production was still an open question in which it would be as rash to affirm as to deny. Already before that time, however, Professor Weismann of Freiburg had begun a very serious attack upon the Lamarckian theory,[94] and his polemic has at last excited such a widespread interest among naturalists that the whilom almost unhesitatingly accepted theory seems almost on the point of being abandoned.

I will therefore add some of Weismann's criticisms of the supposed evidence to my own. In the first place, he has a captivating theory of descent of his own,[95] which makes him think it *a priori* impossible that any peculiarity acquired during lifetime by the parent should be transmitted to the germ. Into the nature of that theory this is not the place to go. Suffice to say that it has made him a keener critic of Lamarck's and Spencer's theory than he otherwise might have been. The only way in which the germinal products can be influenced whilst in the body of the parent is, according to Weismann, by good or bad nutrition. Through this they may degenerate in various ways or lose vitality altogether. They may also be infected through the blood by small-pox, syphilis, or other virulent diseases, and otherwise be poisoned. But peculiarities of neural structure and habit in the parents *which the parents themselves were not born with,* they can never acquire unless perhaps accidentally through some coincidental variation of their own. *Accidental* variations develop of course into idiosyncrasies which tend to pass to later generations in virtue of the well-known law which no one doubts.

Referring to the often-heard assertion that the increase of talent found in certain families from one generation to another is due to the transmitted effects of *exercise* of the faculty concerned (the Bachs, the Bernoullis, Mozart, etc.), he sensibly remarks, that the talent being kept in exercise, it ought to have gone on growing for an indefinite number of generations. As a matter of fact, it quickly reaches a maximum, and then we hear no more of it, which is what happens always when an idiosyncrasy is exposed to the effects of miscellaneous intermarriage.

The hereditary epilepsy and other degenerations of the operated

---

[94] *Ueber die Vererbung* (Jena, 1883). Prof. Weismann's *Essays on Heredity* have recently (1889) been published in English in a collected form.
[95] Best expressed in the Essay on the *Continuität des Keimplasmas* (1885).

guinea-pigs are explained by Professor Weismann as results of *infection* of the young by the parent's blood. The latter he supposes to undergo a pathologic change in consequence of the original traumatic injury. The obsolescence of disused organs he explains very satisfactorily, without invoking any transmission of the direct effects of disuse, by his theory of *panmixy,* for which I must refer to his own writings. Finally, he criticises searchingly the stories we occasionally hear of inherited mutilations in animals (dogs' ears and tails, etc.), and cites a prolonged series of experiments of his own on mice, which he bred for many generations, cutting off both parental tails each time, without interfering in the least with the length of tail with which the young continued to be born.

The strongest argument, after all, in favor of the Lamarckian theory remains the *a priori* one urged by Spencer in his little work (much the solidest thing, by the way, which he has ever written) 'The Factors of Organic Evolution.' Since, says Mr. Spencer, the accidental variations of all parts of the body are independent of each other, if the entire organization of animals were due to such accidental variations alone, the amount of mutual adaptation and harmony that we now find there could hardly possibly have come about in any finite time. We must rather suppose that the divers varying parts *brought* the other parts into harmony with themselves by *exercising them ad hoc,* and that the effects of the exercise remained and were passed on to the young. This forms, of course, a great *presumption* against the all-sufficiency of the view of selection of accidental variations exclusively. But it must be admitted that in favor of the contrary view, that adaptive changes are inherited, we have as yet perhaps not one single unequivocal item of positive proof.

I must therefore end this chapter on the genesis of our mental structure by reaffirming my conviction that the so-called Experience-philosophy has failed to prove its point. No more if we take ancestral experiences into account than if we limit ourselves to those of the individual after birth, can we believe that the couplings of terms within the mind are simple copies of corresponding couplings impressed upon it by the environment. This indeed is true of a small part of our cognitions. But so far as logical and mathematical, ethical, æsthetical, and metaphysical propositions go, such an assertion is not only untrue but altogether unintelligible; for these propositions say nothing about the time and space-order of things, and it is hard to understand how such shallow and vague accounts of them as Mill's and Spencer's could ever have been given by thinking men.

The causes of our mental structure are doubtless natural, and connected, like all our other peculiarities, with those of our nervous structure. Our interests, our tendencies of attention, our motor impulses, the æsthetic, moral, and theoretic combinations we delight in, the extent of our power of apprehending schemes of relation, just like the elementary relations themselves, time, space, difference and similarity, and the elementary kinds of feeling, have all grown up in ways of which at present we can give no account. Even in the clearest parts of Psychology our insight is insignificant enough. And the more sincerely one seeks to trace the actual course of *psychogenesis,* the steps by which as a race we may have come by the peculiar mental attributes which we possess, the more clearly one perceives "the slowly gathering twilight close in utter night."

iii

Radical Empiricism

Radical empiricism is the name given by James to his entire philosophical endeavor. For purposes of clarification, we have excerpted the two statements wherein James isolates the central meaning of this position. This is followed by a series of essays, which present the metaphysical, epistemological and cosmological dimensions of radical empiricism.

RADICAL EMPIRICISM

1897 *

Were I obliged to give a short name to the attitude in question, I should call it that of *radical empiricism,* in spite of the fact that such brief nicknames are nowhere more misleading than in philosophy. I say 'empiricism,' because it is contented to regard its most assured conclusions concerning matters of fact as hypotheses liable to modification in the course of future experience; and I say 'radical,' because it treats the doctrine of monism itself as an hypothesis, and, unlike so much of the half-way empiricism that is current under the name of positivism or agnosticism or scientific naturalism, it does not dogmatically affirm monism as something with which all experience has got to square. The difference between monism and pluralism is perhaps the most pregnant of all the differences in philosophy. *Primâ facie* the world is a pluralism; as we find it, its unity seems to be that of any collection; and our higher thinking consists chiefly of an effort to redeem it from that first crude form. Postulating more unity than the

* From: W.B., VII–X.

first experiences yield, we also discover more. But absolute unity, in spite of brilliant dashes in its direction, still remains undiscovered, still remains a *Grenzbegriff*. "Ever not quite" must be the rationalistic philosopher's last confession concerning it. After all that reason can do has been done, there still remains the opacity of the finite facts as merely given, with most of their peculiarities mutually unmediated and unexplained. To the very last, there are the various 'points of view' which the philosopher must distinguish in discussing the world; and what is inwardly clear from one point remains a bare externality and datum to the other. The negative, the alogical, is never wholly banished. Something—"call it fate, chance, freedom, spontaneity, the devil, what you will"—is still wrong and other and outside and unincluded, from *your* point of view, even though you be the greatest of philosophers. Something is always mere fact and *givenness;* and there may be in the whole universe no one point of view extant from which this would not be found to be the case. "Reason," as a gifted writer says, "is but one item in the mystery; and behind the proudest consciousness that ever reigned, reason and wonder blushed face to face. The inevitable stales, while doubt and hope are sisters. Not unfortunately the universe is wild,—game-flavored as a hawk's wing. Nature is miracle all; the same returns not save to bring the different. The slow round of the engraver's lathe gains but the breadth of a hair, but the difference is distributed back over the whole curve, never an instant true,—ever not quite." [1]

This is pluralism, somewhat rhapsodically expressed. He who takes for his hypothesis the notion that it is the permanent form of the world is what I call a radical empiricist. For him the crudity of experience remains an eternal element thereof. There is no possible point of view from which the world can appear an absolutely single fact. Real possibilities, real indeterminations, real beginnings, real ends, real evil, real crises, catastrophes, and escapes, a real God, and a real moral life, just as common-sense conceives these things, may remain in empiricism as conceptions which that philosophy gives up the attempt either to 'overcome' or to reinterpret in monistic form.

Many of my professionally trained *confrères* will smile at the irrationalism of this view, and at the artlessness of my essays in point of technical form. But they should be taken as illustrations of the radically empiricist attitude rather than as argumentations for its validity. That admits meanwhile of being argued in as technical a shape as any one can desire, and possibly I may be spared to do later a share of that work. Meanwhile these essays seem to light up with a certain dramatic reality the attitude itself, and make it visible alongside of the

[1] B. P. Blood: *The Flaw in Supremacy:* Published by the Author, Amsterdam, N. Y., 1893.

higher and lower dogmatisms between which in the pages of philosophic history it has generally remained eclipsed from sight.

RADICAL EMPIRICISM

1909 *

Radical empiricism consists first of a postulate, next of a statement of fact, and finally of a generalized conclusion.

The postulate is that the only things that shall be debatable among philosophers shall be things definable in terms drawn from experience. [Things of an unexperienceable nature may exist ad libitum, but they form no part of the material for philosophic debate.]

The statement of fact is that the relations between things, conjunctive as well as disjunctive, are just as much matters of direct particular experience, neither more so nor less so, than the things themselves.

The generalized conclusion is that therefore the parts of experience hold together from next to next by relations that are themselves parts of experience. The directly apprehended universe needs, in short, no extraneous trans-empirical connective support, but possesses in its own right a concatenated or continuous structure.

THE FUNCTION OF COGNITION†²

The following inquiry is (to use a distinction familiar to readers of Mr. Shadworth Hodgson) not an inquiry into the 'how it comes,' but into the 'what it is' of cognition. What we call acts of cognition are evidently realized through what we call brains and their events, whether there be 'souls' dynamically connected with the brains or not. But with neither brains nor souls has this essay any business to transact. In it we shall simply assume that cognition *is* produced, somehow,

---

* From: M.T., xii–xiii.
† From: M.T., 1–41.
² Read before the Aristotelian Society, December 1, 1884, and first published in *Mind*, vol. x (1885).—This, and the following articles have received a very slight verbal revision, consisting mostly in the omission of redundancy.

and limit ourselves to asking what elements it contains, what factors it implies.

Cognition is a function of consciousness. The first factor it implies is therefore a state of consciousness wherein the cognition shall take place. Having elsewhere used the word 'feeling' to designate generically all states of consciousness considered subjectively, or without respect to their possible function, I shall then say that, whatever elements an act of cognition may imply besides, it at least implies the existence of a *feeling*. [If the reader share the current antipathy to the word 'feeling,' he may substitute for it, wherever I use it, the word 'idea,' taken in the old broad Lockian sense, or he may use the clumsy phrase 'state of consciousness,' or finally he may say 'thought' instead.]

Now it is to be observed that the common consent of mankind has agreed that some feelings are cognitive and some are simple facts having a subjective, or, what one might almost call a physical, existence, but no such self-transcendent function as would be implied in their being pieces of knowledge. Our task is again limited here. We are not to ask, 'How is self-transcendence possible?' We are only to ask, 'How comes it that common sense has assigned a number of cases in which it is assumed not only to be possible but actual? And what are the marks used by common sense to distinguish those cases from the rest?' In short, our inquiry is a chapter in descriptive psychology,—hardly anything more.

Condillac embarked on a quest similar to this by his famous hypothesis of a statue to which various feelings were successively imparted. Its first feeling was supposed to be one of fragrance. But to avoid all possible complication with the question of genesis, let us not attribute even to a statue the possession of our imaginary feeling. Let us rather suppose it attached to no matter, nor localized at any point in space, but left swinging *in vacuo,* as it were, by the direct creative *fiat* of a god. And let us also, to escape entanglement with difficulties about the physical or psychical nature of its 'object,' not call it a feeling of fragrance or of any other determinate sort, but limit ourselves to assuming that it is a feeling of q. What is true of it under this abstract name will be no less true of it in any more particular shape (such as fragrance, pain, hardness) which the reader may suppose.

Now, if this feeling of q be the only creation of the god, it will of course form the entire universe. And if, to escape the cavils of that large class of persons who believe that *semper idem sentire ac non sentire* are the same,[3] we allow the feeling to be of as short a duration

---

[3] 'The Relativity of Knowledge,' held in this sense, is, it may be observed in passing, one of the oddest of philosophic superstitions. Whatever facts may be cited in its favor are due to the properties of nerve-tissue, which may be ex-

as they like, that universe will only need to last an infinitesimal part of a second. The feeling in question will thus be reduced to its fighting weight, and all that befalls it in the way of a cognitive function must be held to befall in the brief instant of its quickly snuffed-out life,—a life, it will also be noticed, that has no other moment of consciousness either preceding or following it.

Well now, can our little feeling, thus left alone in the universe,— for the god and we psychological critics may be supposed left out of the account,—can the feeling, I say, be said to have any sort of a cognitive function? For it to *know,* there must be something to be known. What is there, on the present supposition? One may reply, 'the feeling's content *q.*' But does it not seem more proper to call this the feeling's *quality* than its content? Does not the word 'content' suggest that the feeling has already dirempted itself as an act from its content as an object? And would it be quite safe to assume so promptly that the quality *q* of a feeling is one and the same thing with a feeling of the quality *q?* The quality *q,* so far, is an entirely subjective fact which the feeling carries so to speak endogenously, or in its pocket. If any one pleases to dignify so simple a fact as this by the name of knowledge, of course nothing can prevent him. But let us keep closer to the path of common usage, and reserve the name knowledge for the cognition of 'realities,' meaning by realities things that exist independently of the feeling through which their cognition occurs. If the content of the feeling occur nowhere in the universe outside of the feeling itself, and perish with the feeling, common usage refuses to call it a reality, and brands it as a subjective feature of the feeling's constitution, or at the most as the feeling's *dream.*

For the feeling to be cognitive in the specific sense, then, it must be self-transcendent; and we must prevail upon the god to *create a reality outside of it* to correspond to its intrinsic quality *q.* Thus only can it be redeemed from the condition of being a solipsism. If now the new-created reality *resemble* the feeling's quality *q,* I say that the feeling may be held by us *to be cognizant of that reality.*

This first instalment of my thesis is sure to be attacked. But one word before defending it. 'Reality' has become our warrant for calling

---

hausted by too prolonged an excitement. Patients with neuralgias that last unremittingly for days can, however, assure us that the limits of this nerve-law are pretty widely drawn. But if we physically could get a feeling that should last eternally unchanged, what atom of logical or psychological argument is there to prove that it would not be felt as long as it lasted, and felt for just what it is, all that time? The reason for the opposite prejudice seems to be our reluctance to think that so *stupid* a thing as such a feeling would necessarily be, should be allowed to fill eternity with its presence. An interminable acquaintance, leading to no knowledge-*about,*—such would be its condition.

a feeling cognitive; but what becomes our warrant for calling anything reality? The only reply is—the faith of the present critic or inquirer. At every moment of his life he finds himself subject to a belief in *some* realities, even though his realities of this year should prove to be his illusions of the next. Whenever he finds that the feeling he is studying contemplates what he himself regards as a reality, he must of course admit the feeling itself to be truly cognitive. We are ourselves the critics here; and we shall find our burden much lightened by being allowed to take reality in this relative and provisional way. Every science must make some assumptions. *Erkenntnisstheoretiker* are but fallible mortals. When they study the function of cognition, they do it by means of the same function in themselves. And knowing that the fountain cannot go higher than its source, we should promptly confess that our results in this field are affected by our own liability to err. *The most we can claim is, that what we say about cognition may be counted as true as what we say about anything else.* If our hearers agree with us about what are to be held 'realities,' they will perhaps also agree to the reality of our doctrine of the way in which they are known. We cannot ask for more.

Our terminology shall follow the spirit of these remarks. We will deny the function of knowledge to any feeling whose quality or content we do not ourselves believe to exist outside of that feeling as well as in it. We may call such a feeling a dream if we like; we shall have to see later whether we can call it a fiction or an error.

To revert now to our thesis. Some persons will immediately cry out, 'How *can* a reality resemble a feeling?' Here we find how wise we were to name the quality of the feeling by an algebraic letter q. We flank the whole difficulty of resemblance between an inner state and an outward reality, by leaving it free to any one to postulate as the reality whatever sort of thing he thinks *can* resemble a feeling,—if not an outward thing, then another feeling like the first one,—the mere feeling q in the critic's mind for example. Evading thus this objection, we turn to another which is sure to be urged.

It will come from those philosophers to whom 'thought,' in the sense of a knowledge of relations, is the all in all of mental life; and who hold a merely feeling consciousness to be no better—one would sometimes say from their utterances, a good deal worse—than no consciousness at all. Such phrases as these, for example, are common to-day in the mouths of those who claim to walk in the footprints of Kant and Hegel rather than in the ancestral English paths: 'A perception detached from all others, "left out of the heap we call a mind," being out of all relation, has no qualities—is simply nothing. We can no more consider it than we can see vacancy.' 'It is simply in itself fleeting, momentary, unnameable (because while we name it it has become another), and for the very same reason unknowable, the very negation of knowability.' 'Exclude from what we have considered real all qualities constituted by relation, we find that none are left.'

Altho such citations as these from the writings of Professor Green might be multiplied almost indefinitely, they would hardly repay the pains of collection, so egregiously false is the doctrine they teach. Our little supposed feeling, whatever it may be, from the cognitive point of view, whether a bit of knowledge or a dream, is certainly no psychical zero. It is a most positively and definitely qualified inner fact, with a complexion all its own. Of course there are many mental facts which it is *not*. It knows *q*, if *q* be a reality, with a very minimum of knowledge. It neither dates nor locates it. It neither classes nor names it. And it neither knows itself as a feeling, nor contrasts itself with other feelings, nor estimates its own duration or intensity. It is, in short, if there is no more of it than this, a most dumb and helpless and useless kind of thing.

But if we must describe it by so many negations, and if it can say nothing *about* itself or *about* anything else, by what right do we deny that it is a psychical zero? And may not the 'relationists' be right after all?

In the innocent-looking word 'about' lies the solution of this riddle; and a simple enough solution it is when frankly looked at. A quotation from a too seldom quoted book, the *Exploratio Philosophica* of John Grote (London, 1865), p. 60, will form the best introduction to it.

'Our knowledge,' writes Grote, 'may be contemplated in either of two ways, or, to use other words, we may speak in a double manner of the "object" of knowledge. That is, we may either use language thus: we *know* a thing, a man, etc.; or we may use it thus: we know such and such things *about* the thing, the man, etc. Language in general, following its true logical instinct, distinguishes between these two applications of the notion of knowledge, the one being γνῶναι, *noscere, kennen, connaître,* the other being εἰδέναι, *scire, wissen, savoir.* In the origin, the former may be considered more what I have called phenomenal—it is the notion of knowledge as *acquaintance* or familiarity with what is known; which notion is perhaps more akin to the phenomenal bodily communication, and is less purely intellectual than the other; it is the kind of knowledge which we have of a thing by the presentation to the senses or the representation of it in picture or type, a *Vorstellung.* The other, which is what we express in judgments or propositions, what is embodied in *Begriffe* or concepts without any necessary imaginative representation, is in its origin the more intellectual notion of knowledge. There is no reason, however, why we should not express our knowledge, whatever its kind, in either manner, provided only we do not confusedly express it, in the same proposition or piece of reasoning, in both.'

Now obviously if our supposed feeling of q is (if knowledge at all) only knowledge of the mere acquaintance-type, it is milking a he-goat, as the ancients would have said, to try to extract from it any deliverance *about* anything under the sun, even about itself. And it is as unjust, after our failure, to turn upon it and call it a psychical nothing, as it would be, after our fruitless attack upon the billy-goat, to proclaim the non-lactiferous character of the whole goat-tribe. But the entire industry of the Hegelian school in trying to shove simple sensation out of the pale of philosophic recognition is founded on this false issue. It is always the 'speechlessness' of sensation, its inability to make any 'statement,' [4] that is held to make the very notion of it meaningless, and to justify the student of knowledge in scouting it out of existence. 'Significance,' in the sense of standing as the sign of other mental states, is taken to be the sole function of what mental states we have; and from the perception that our little primitive sensation has as yet no significance in this literal sense, it is an easy step to call it first meaningless, next senseless, then vacuous, and finally to brand it as absurd and inadmissible. But in this universal liquidation, this everlasting slip, slip, slip, of direct acquaintance into knowledge-*about,* until at last nothing is left about which the knowledge can be supposed to obtain, does not all 'significance' depart from the situation? And when our knowledge about things has reached its never so complicated perfection, must there not needs abide alongside of it and inextricably mixed in with it some acquaintance with *what* things all this knowledge is about?

Now, our supposed little feeling gives a *what;* and if other feelings should succeed which remember the first, its *what* may stand as subject or predicate of some piece of knowledge-about, of some judgment, perceiving relations between it and other *whats* which the other feelings may know. The hitherto dumb q will then receive a name and be no longer speechless. But every name, as students of logic know, has its 'denotation'; and the denotation always means some reality or content, relationless *ab extra* or with its internal relations unanalyzed, like the q which our primitive sensation is supposed to know. No relation-expressing proposition is possible except on the basis of a preliminary acquaintance with such 'facts,' with such contents, as this. Let the q be fragrance, let it be toothache, or let it be a more complex kind of feeling, like that of the full-moon swimming in her blue abyss, it must first come in that simple shape, and be held fast in that first intention, before any knowledge *about* it can be attained. The knowl-

[4] See, for example, Green's Introduction to Hume's *Treatise of Human Nature,* p. 36.

edge *about* it is *it* with a context added. Undo *it,* and what is added cannot be *context*.[5]

Let us say no more then about this objection, but enlarge our thesis, thus: If there be in the universe a *q* other than the *q* in the feeling, the latter may have acquaintance with an entity ejective to itself; an acquaintance moreover, which, as mere acquaintance, it would be hard to imagine susceptible either of improvement or increase, being in its way complete; and which would oblige us (so long as we refuse not to call acquaintance knowledge) to say not only that the feeling is cognitive, but that all qualities of feeling, *so long as there is anything outside of them which they resemble,* are feelings *of* qualities of existence, and perceptions of outward fact.

The point of this vindication of the cognitive function of the first feeling lies, it will be noticed, in the discovery that *q* does exist elsewhere than in it. In case this discovery were not made, we could not be sure the feeling was cognitive; and in case there were nothing outside to be discovered, we should have to call the feeling a dream. But the feeling itself cannot make the discovery. Its own *q* is the only *q* it grasps; and its own nature is not a particle altered by having the self-transcendent function of cognition either added to it or taken away. The function is accidental; synthetic, not analytic; and falls outside and not inside its being.[6]

A feeling feels as a gun shoots. If there be nothing to be felt or hit, they discharge themselves *ins blaue hinein.* If, however, something starts up opposite them, they no longer simply shoot or feel, they hit and know.

[5] If A enters and B exclaims, 'Didn't you see my brother on the stairs?' we all hold that A may answer, 'I saw him, but didn't know he was your brother'; ignorance of brotherhood not abolishing power to see. But those who, on account of the unrelatedness of the first facts with which we become acquainted, deny them to be 'known' to us, ought in consistency to maintain that if A did not perceive the relationship of the man on the stairs to B, it was impossible he should have noticed him at all.

[6] It seems odd to call so important a function accidental, but I do not see how we can mend the matter. Just as, if we start with the reality and ask how it may come to be known, we can only reply by invoking a feeling which shall *reconstruct* it in its own more private fashion; so, if we start with the feeling and ask how it may come to know, we can only reply by invoking a reality which shall *reconstruct* it in its own more public fashion. In either case, however, the datum we start with remains just what it was. One may easily get lost in verbal mysteries about the difference between quality of feeling and feeling of quality, between receiving and reconstructing the knowledge of a reality. But at the end we must confess that the notion of real cognition involves an unmediated dualism of the knower and the known. See Bowne's *Metaphysics,* New York, 1882, pp. 403–412, and various passages in Lotze, *e. g., Logic,* §308. ['Unmediated' is a bad word to have used.—1909. W.J.]

But with this arises a worse objection than any yet made. We the critics look on and see a real q and a feeling of q; and because the two resemble each other, we say the one knows the other. But what right have we to say this until we know that the feeling of q means to stand for or represent just that *same* other q? Suppose, instead of one q, a number of real q's in the field. If the gun shoots and hits, we can easily see which one of them it hits. But how can we distinguish which one the feeling knows? It knows the one it stands for. But which one *does* it stand for? It declares no intention in this respect. It merely resembles; it resembles all indifferently; and resembling, *per se,* is not necessarily representing or standing-for at all. Eggs resemble each other, but do not on that account represent, stand for, or know each other. And if you say this is because neither of them is a *feeling,* then imagine the world to consist of nothing but toothaches, which *are* feelings, feelings resembling each other exactly,—would they know each other the better for all that?

The case of q being a bare quality like that of toothache-pain is quite different from that of its being a concrete individual thing. There is practically no test for deciding whether the feeling of a bare quality means to represent it or not. It can *do* nothing to the quality beyond resembling it, simply because an abstract quality is a thing to which nothing can be done. Being without context or environment or *principium individuationis,* a quiddity with no hæcceity, a platonic idea, even duplicate editions of such a quality (were they possible), would be indiscernible, and no sign could be given, no result altered, whether the feeling meant to stand for this edition or for that, or whether it simply resembled the quality without meaning to stand for it at all.

If now we grant a genuine pluralism of editions to the quality q, by assigning to each a *context* which shall distinguish it from its mates, we may proceed to explain which edition of it the feeling knows, by extending our principle of resemblance to the context too, and saying the feeling knows the particular q whose context it most exactly duplicates. But here again the theoretic doubt recurs: duplication and coincidence, are they knowledge? The gun shows which q it points to and hits, by *breaking* it. Until the feeling can show us which q it points to and knows, by some equally flagrant token, why are we not free to deny that it either points to or knows any one of the *real* q's at all, and to affirm that the word 'resemblance' exhaustively describes its relation to the reality?

Well, as a matter of fact, every actual feeling *does* show us, quite as flagrantly as the gun, which q it points to; and practically in concrete cases the matter is decided by an element we have hitherto left out. Let us pass from abstractions to possible instances, and ask our obliging *deus ex machina* to frame for us a richer world. Let him send me, for example, a dream of the death of a certain man, and let him simultaneously cause the man to die. How would our practical instinct spontaneously decide whether this were a case of cognition of the reality, or only a sort of marvellous coincidence of a resembling reality with my dream? Just such puzzling cases as this are what the 'society for psychical research' is busily collecting and trying to interpret in the most reasonable way.

If my dream were the only one of the kind I ever had in my life, if the context of the death in the dream differed in many particulars from the real death's context, and if my dream led me to no action about the death, unquestionably we should all call it a strange coincidence, and naught besides. But if the death in the dream had a long context, agreeing point for point with every feature that attended the real death; if I were constantly having such dreams, all equally perfect, and if on awaking I had a habit of *acting* immediately as if they were true and so getting 'the start' of my more tardily instructed neighbors,—we should in all probability have to admit that I had some mysterious kind of clairvoyant power, that my dreams in an inscrutable way meant just those realities they figured, and that the word 'coincidence' failed to touch the root of the matter. And whatever doubts any one preserved would completely vanish, if it should appear that from the midst of my dream I had the power of *interfering* with the course of the reality, and making the events in it turn this way or that, according as I dreamed they should. Then at least it would be certain that my waking critics and my dreaming self were dealing with the *same*.

And thus do men invariably decide such a question. *The falling of the dream's practical consequences* into the real world, and the *extent* of the resemblance between the two worlds are the criteria they instinctively use.[7] All feeling is for the sake of action, all feeling results

---

[7] The thoroughgoing objector might, it is true, still return to the charge, and, granting a dream which should completely mirror the real universe, and all the actions dreamed in which should be instantly matched by duplicate actions in this universe, still insist that this is nothing more than harmony, and that it is as far as ever from being made clear whether the dream-world refers to that other world, all of whose details it so closely copies. This objection leads deep into metaphysics. I do not impugn its importance, and justice obliges me to say that but for the teachings of my colleague, Dr. Josiah Royce, I should neither have grasped its full force nor made my own practical and psychological point of view as clear to myself as it is. On this occasion I prefer to stick steadfastly to that point of view; but I hope that Dr. Royce's more fundamental criticism of the function of cognition may ere long see the light. [I referred in this note to Royce's *Religious Aspect of Philosophy*, then about to be published. This powerful book maintained that the notion of *referring* involved that of an inclusive mind that shall own both the real *q* and the mental *q*, and use the latter expressly as a representative symbol of the former. At the time I could not refute

in action,—to-day no argument is needed to prove these truths. But by a most singular disposition of nature which we may conceive to have been different, *my feelings act upon the realities within my critic's world.* Unless, then, my critic can prove that my feeling does not 'point to' those realities which it acts upon, how can he continue to doubt that he and I are alike cognizant of one and the same real world? If the action is performed in one world, that must be the world the feeling intends; if in another world, *that* is the world the feeling has in mind. If your feeling bear no fruits in my world, I call it utterly detached from my world; I call it a solipsism, and call its world a dream-world. If your toothache do not prompt you to *act* as if I had a toothache, nor even as if I had a separate existence; if you neither say to me, 'I know now how you must suffer!' nor tell me of a remedy, I deny that your feeling, however it may resemble mine, is really cognizant of mine. It gives no *sign* of being cognizant, and such a sign is absolutely necessary to my admission that it is.

Before I can think you to mean my world, you must affect my world; before I can think you to mean much of it, you must affect much of it; and before I can be sure you mean it *as I do,* you must affect it *just as I should* if I were in your place. Then I, your critic, will gladly believe that we are thinking, not only of the same reality, but that we are thinking it *alike,* and thinking of much of its extent.

Without the practical effects of our neighbor's feelings on our own world, we should never suspect the existence of our neighbor's feelings at all, and of course should never find ourselves playing the critic as we do in this article. The constitution of nature is very peculiar. In the world of each of us are certain objects called human bodies, which move about and act on all the other objects there, and the occasions of their action are in the main what the occasions of our action would be, were they our bodies. They use words and gestures, which, if we used them, would have thoughts behind them,—no mere thoughts *überhaupt,* however, but strictly determinate thoughts. I think you have the notion of fire in general, because I see you act towards this fire in my room just as I act towards it,—poke it and present your person towards it, and so forth. But that binds me to believe that if you feel 'fire' at all, *this* is the fire you feel. As a matter of fact, whenever we constitute ourselves into psychological critics, it is not by dint of discovering which reality a feeling 'resembles' that we find out which reality it means. We become first aware of which one it means,

this transcendentalist opinion. Later, largely through the influence of Professor D. S. Miller (see his essay 'The meaning of truth and error,' in the *Philosophical Review* for 1893, vol. 2, p. 403) I came to see that any definitely experienceable workings would serve as intermediaries quite as well as the absolute mind's intentions would.]

and then we suppose that to be the one it resembles. We see each
other looking at the same objects, pointing to them and turning them
over in various ways, and thereupon we hope and trust that all of our
several feelings resemble the reality and each other. But this is a thing
of which we are never theoretically sure. Still, it would practically be a
case of *grübelsucht,* if a ruffian were assaulting and drubbing my
body, to spend much time in subtle speculation either as to whether
his vision of my body resembled mine, or as to whether the body he
really *meant* to insult were not some body in his mind's eye, altogether
other from my own. The practical point of view brushes such metaphysical cobwebs away. If what he have in mind be not *my* body, why
call we it a body at all? His mind is inferred by me as a term, to whose
existence we trace the things that happen. The inference is quite void
if the term, once inferred, be separated from its connection with the
body that made me infer it, and connected with another that is not
mine at all. No matter for the metaphysical puzzle of how our two
minds, the ruffian's and mine, *can* mean the same body. Men who see
each other's bodies sharing the same space, treading the same earth,
splashing the same water, making the same air resonant, and pursuing
the same game and eating out of the same dish, will never practically
believe in a pluralism of solipsistic worlds.

Where, however, the actions of one mind seem to take no effect in
the world of the other, the case is different. This is what happens in
poetry and fiction. Every one knows *Ivanhoe,* for example; but so
long as we stick to the story pure and simple without regard to the
facts of its production, few would hesitate to admit that there are as
many different Ivanhoes as there are different minds cognizant of the
story.[8] The fact that all these Ivanhoes *resemble* each other does not

---

[8] That is, there is no *real* 'Ivanhoe,' not even the one in Sir Walter Scott's
mind as he was writing the story. That one is only the *first* one of the Ivanhoe-
solipsisms. It is quite true we can make it the real Ivanhoe if we like, and then
say that the other Ivanhoes know it or do not know it, according as they refer
to and resemble it or no. This is done by bringing in Sir Walter Scott himself as
the author of the real Ivanhoe, and so making a complex object of both. This
object, however, is not a story pure and simple. It has dynamic relations with
the world common to the experience of all the readers. Sir Walter Scott's Ivanhoe got itself printed in volumes which we all can handle, and to any one of
which we can refer to see which of our versions be the true one, *i. e.,* the original one of Scott himself. We can see the manuscript; in short we can get back
to the Ivanhoe in Scott's mind by many an avenue and channel of this real
world of our experience,—a thing we can by no means do with either the Ivanhoe or the Rebecca, either the Templar or the Isaac of York, of the story taken
simply as such, and detached from the conditions of its production. Everywhere,
then, we have the same test: can we pass continuously from two objects in two
minds to a third object which seems to be in *both* minds, because each mind
feels every modification imprinted on it by the other? If so, the first two objects
named are derivatives, to say the least, from the same third object, and may be
held, if they resemble each other, to refer to one and the same reality.

prove the contrary. But if an alteration invented by one man in his version were to reverberate immediately through all the other versions, and produce changes therein, we should then easily agree that all these thinkers were thinking the *same* Ivanhoe, and that, fiction or no fiction, it formed a little world common to them all.

Having reached this point, we may take up our thesis and improve it again. Still calling the reality by the name of *q* and letting the critic's feeling vouch for it, we can say that any other feeling will be held cognizant of *q*, provided it both resemble *q*, and refer to *q*, as shown by its either modifying *q* directly, or modifying some other reality, *p* or *r*, which the critic knows to be continuous with *q*. Or more shortly, thus: *The feeling of q knows whatever reality it resembles, and either directly or indirectly operates on.* If it resemble without operating, it is a dream; if it operate without resembling, it is an error.[9]

It is to be feared that the reader may consider this formula rather insignificant and obvious, and hardly worth the labor of so many pages, especially when he considers that the only cases to which it applies are *percepts,* and that the whole field of symbolic or conceptual thinking seems to elude its grasp. Where the reality is either a material thing or act, or a state of the critic's consciousness, I may both mirror it in my mind and operate upon it—in the latter case

[9] Among such errors are those cases in which our feeling operates on a reality which it does partially resemble, and yet does not intend: as for instance, when I take up your umbrella, meaning to take my own. I cannot be said here either to know your umbrella, or my own, which latter my feeling more completely resembles. I am mistaking them both, misrepresenting their context, etc.

We have spoken in the text as if the critic were necessarily one mind, and the feeling criticised another. But the criticised feeling and its critic may be earlier and later feelings of the same mind, and here it might seem that we could dispense with the notion of operating, to prove that critic and criticised are referring to and meaning to represent the *same.* We think we see our past feelings directly, and know what they refer to without appeal. At the worst, we can always fix the intention of our present feeling and *make* it refer to the same reality to which any one of our past feelings may have referred. So we need no 'operating' here, to make sure that the feeling and its critic mean the same real *q.* Well, all the better if this is so! We have covered the more complex and difficult case in our text, and we may let this easier one go. The main thing at present is to stick to practical psychology, and ignore metaphysical difficulties.

One more remark. Our formula contains, it will be observed, nothing to correspond to the great principle of cognition laid down by Professor Ferrier in his *Institutes of Metaphysic* and apparently adopted by all the followers of Fichte, the principle, namely, that for knowledge to be constituted there must be knowledge of the knowing mind along with whatever else is known: not *q,* as we have supposed, but *q plus myself,* must be the least I can know. It is certain that the common sense of mankind never dreams of using any such principle when it tries to discriminate between conscious states that are knowledge and conscious states that are not. So that Ferrier's principle, if it have any relevancy at all, must have relevancy to the metaphysical possibility of consciousness at large, and not to the practically recognized constitution of cognitive consciousness. We may therefore pass it by without further notice here.

indirectly, of course—as soon as I perceive it. But there are many cognitions, universally allowed to be such, which neither mirror nor operate on their realities.

In the whole field of symbolic thought we are universally held both to intend, to speak of, and to reach conclusions about—to know in short—particular realities, without having in our subjective consciousness any mind-stuff that resembles them even in a remote degree. We are instructed about them by language which awakens no consciousness beyond its sound; and we know *which* realities they are by the faintest and most fragmentary glimpse of some remote context they may have and by no direct imagination of themselves. As minds may differ here, let me speak in the first person. I am sure that my own current thinking has *words* for its almost exclusive subjective material, words which are made intelligible by being referred to some reality that lies beyond the horizon of direct consciousness, and of which I am only aware as of a terminal *more* existing in a certain direction, to which the words might lead but do not lead yet. The *subject,* or *topic,* of the words is usually something towards which I mentally seem to pitch them in a backward way, almost as I might jerk my thumb over my shoulder to point at something, without looking round, if I were only entirely sure that it was there. The *upshot,* or *conclusion,* of the words is something towards which I seem to incline my head forwards, as if giving assent to its existence, tho all my mind's eye catches sight of may be some tatter of an image connected with it, which tatter, however, if only endued with the feeling of familiarity and reality, makes me feel that the whole to which it belongs is rational and real, and fit to be let pass.

Here then is cognitive consciousness on a large scale, and yet what it knows, it hardly resembles in the least degree. The formula last laid down for our thesis must therefore be made more complete. We may now express it thus: *A percept knows whatever reality it directly or indirectly operates on and resembles; a conceptual feeling, or thought knows*[10] *a reality, whenever it actually or potentially terminates in a percept that operates on, or resembles that reality, or is otherwise connected with it or with its context.* The latter percept may be either sensation or sensorial idea; and when I say the thought must *terminate* in such a percept, I mean that it must ultimately be capable of leading up thereto,—by the way of practical experience, if the terminal feeling be a sensation; by the way of logical or habitual suggestion, if it be only an image in the mind.

Let an illustration make this plainer. I open the first book I take up, and read the first sentence that meets my eye: 'Newton saw the handiwork of God in the heavens as plainly as Paley in the animal kingdom.' I immediately look back and try to analyze the subjective

[10] Is an incomplete 'thought about' that reality, that reality is its 'topic,' etc.

state in which I rapidly apprehended this sentence as I read it. In the first place there was an obvious feeling that the sentence was intelligible and rational and related to the world of realities. There was also a sense of agreement or harmony between 'Newton,' 'Paley,' and 'God.' There was no apparent image connected with the words 'heavens,' or 'handiwork,' or 'God'; they were words merely. With 'animal kingdom' I think there was the faintest consciousness (it may possibly have been an image of the steps) of the Museum of Zoölogy in the town of Cambridge where I write. With 'Paley' there was an equally faint consciousness of a small dark leather book; and with 'Newton' a pretty distinct vision of the right-hand lower corner of a curling periwig. This is all the mind-stuff I can discover in my first consciousness of the meaning of this sentence, and I am afraid that even not all of this would have been present had I come upon the sentence in a genuine reading of the book, and not picked it out for an experiment. And yet my consciousness was truly cognitive. The sentence is 'about realities' which my psychological critic—for we must not forget him—acknowledges to be such, even as he acknowledges my distinct feeling that they *are* realities, and my acquiescence in the general rightness of what I read of them, to be true knowledge on my part.

Now what justifies my critic in being as lenient as this? This singularly inadequate consciousness of mine, made up of symbols that neither resemble nor affect the realities they stand for,—how can he be sure it is cognizant of the very realities he has himself in mind?

He is sure because in countless like cases he has seen such inadequate and symbolic thoughts, by developing themselves, terminate in percepts that practically modified and presumably resembled his own. By 'developing' themselves is meant obeying their tendencies, following up the suggestions nascently present in them, working in the direction in which they seem to point, clearing up the penumbra, making distinct the halo, unravelling the fringe, which is part of their composition, and in the midst of which their more substantive kernel of subjective content seems consciously to lie. Thus I may develop my thought in the Paley direction by procuring the brown leather volume and bringing the passages about the animal kingdom before the critic's eyes. I may satisfy him that the words mean for me just what they mean for him, by showing him *in concreto* the very animals and their arrangements, of which the pages treat. I may get Newton's works and portraits; or if I follow the line of suggestion of the wig, I may smother my critic in seventeeth-century matters pertaining to Newton's environment, to show that the word 'Newton' has the same *locus* and relations in both our minds. Finally I may, by act and word, persuade him that what I mean by God and the heavens and the analogy of the handiworks, is just what he means also.

My demonstration in the last resort is to his *senses*. My thought makes me act on his senses much as he might himself act on them, were he pursuing the consequences of a perception of his own. Practically then *my* thought terminates in *his* realities. He willingly supposes it, therefore, to be *of* them, and inwardly to *resemble* what his own thought would be, were it of the same symbolic sort as mine. And the pivot and fulcrum and support of his mental persuasion, is the sensible operation which my thought leads me, or may lead, to effect—the bringing of Paley's book, of Newton's portrait, etc., before his very eyes.

In the last analysis, then, we believe that we all know and think about and talk about the same world, because *we believe our PER-CEPTS are possessed by us in common.* And we believe this because the percepts of each one of us seem to be changed in consequence of changes in the percepts of some one else. What I am for you is in the first instance a percept of your own. Unexpectedly, however, I open and show you a book, uttering certain sounds the while. These acts are also your percepts, but they so resemble acts of yours with feelings prompting them, that you cannot doubt I had the feelings too, or that the book is one book felt in both our worlds. That it is felt in the same way, that my feelings of it resemble yours, is something of which we never can be sure, but which we assume as the simplest hypothesis that meets the case. As a matter of fact, we never *are* sure of it, and, as *erkenntnisstheoretiker,* we can only say that of feelings that should *not* resemble each other, both could not know the same thing at the same time in the same way.[11] If each holds to its own percept as the reality, it is bound to say of the other percept, that, though it may *intend* that reality, and prove this by working change upon it, yet, if it do not resemble it, it is all false and wrong.[12]

If this be so of percepts, how much more so of higher modes of thought! Even in the sphere of sensation individuals are probably different enough. Comparative study of the simplest conceptual elements seems to show a wider divergence still. And when it comes to general theories and emotional attitudes towards life, it is indeed time to say with Thackeray, 'My friend, two different universes walk about under your hat and under mine.'

What can save us at all and prevent us from flying asunder into a chaos of mutually repellent solipsisms? Through what can our several minds commune? Through nothing but the mutual resemblance of

[11] Though both might terminate in the same thing and be incomplete thoughts 'about' it.

[12] The difference between Idealism and Realism is immaterial here. What is said in the text is consistent with either theory. A law by which my percept shall change yours directly is no more mysterious than a law by which it shall first change a physical reality, and then the reality change yours. In either case you and I seem knit into a continuous world, and not to form a pair of solipsisms.

those of our perceptual feelings which have this power of modifying one another, *which are mere dumb knowledges-of-acquaintance,* and which must also resemble their realities or not know them aright at all. In such pieces of knowledge-of-acquaintance all our knowledge-about must end, and carry a sense of this possible termination as part of its content. These percepts, these *termini,* these sensible things, these mere matters-of-acquaintance, are the only realities we ever directly know and the whole history of our thought is the history of our substitution of one of them for another, and the reduction of the substitute to the status of a conceptual sign. Contemned though they be by some thinkers, these sensations are the mother-earth, the anchorage, the stable rock, the first and last limits, the *terminus a quo* and the *terminus ad quem* of the mind. To find such sensational *termini* should be our aim with all our higher thought. They end discussion; they destroy the false conceit of knowledge; and without them we are all at sea with each other's meaning. If two men act alike on a percept, they believe themselves to feel alike about it; if not, they may suspect they know it in differing ways. We can never be sure we understand each other till we are able to bring the matter to this test.[13] This is why metaphysical discussions are so much like fighting with the air; they have no practical issue of a sensational kind. 'Scientific' theories, on the other hand, always terminate in definite percepts. You can deduce a possible sensation from your theory and, taking me into your laboratory, prove that your theory is true of my world by giving me the sensation then and there. Beautiful is the flight of conceptual reason through the upper air of truth. No wonder philosophers are dazzled by it still, and no wonder they look with some disdain at the low earth of feeling from which the goddess launched herself aloft. But woe to her if she return not home to its acquaintance; *Nirgends haften dann die unsicheren Sohlen*—every crazy wind will take her, and, like a fire-balloon at night, she will go out among the stars.

NOTE.—The reader will easily see how much of the account of the truth-function developed later in *Pragmatism* was already explicit in this earlier article, and how much came to be defined later. In this earlier article we find distinctly asserted:—

1. The reality, external to the true idea;
2. The critic, reader, or epistemologist, with his own belief, as warrant for this reality's existence;

---

[13] 'There is no distinction of meaning so fine as to consist in anything but a possible difference of practice. . . . It appears, then, that the rule for attaining the [highest] grade of clearness of apprehension is as follows: Consider what effects, which might conceivably have practical bearings, we conceive the object of our conception to have. Then, our conception of these effects is the whole of our conception of the object.' Charles S. Peirce: 'How to make our Ideas clear,' in *Popular Science Monthly,* New York, January, 1878, p. 293.

3. The experienceable environment, as the vehicle or medium connecting knower with known, and yielding the cognitive *relation;*

4. The notion of *pointing,* through this medium, to the reality, as one condition of our being said to know it;

5. That of *resembling* it, and eventually *affecting* it, as determining the pointing to *it* and not to something else.

6. The elimination of the 'epistemological gulf,' so that the whole truth-relation falls inside of the continuities of concrete experience, and is constituted of particular processes, varying with every object and subject, and susceptible of being described in detail.

The defects in this earlier account are:—

1. The possibly undue prominence given to resembling, which altho a fundamental function in knowing truly, is so often dispensed with;

2. The undue emphasis laid upon operating on the object itself, which in many cases is indeed decisive of that being what we refer to, but which is often lacking, or replaced by operations on other things related to the object.

3. The imperfect development of the generalized notion of the *workability* of the feeling or idea as equivalent to that *satisfactory adaptation* to the particular reality, which constitutes the truth of the idea. It is this more generalized notion, as covering all such specifications as pointing, fitting, operating or resembling, that distinguishes the developed view of Dewey, Schiller, and myself.

4. The treatment, on page 151, of percepts as the only realm of reality. I now treat concepts as a co-ordinate realm.

THE KNOWING OF THINGS TOGETHER *

[1895] 14

I

The nature of the synthetic unity of consciousness is one of those great underlying problems that divide the psychological schools. We

* From: C.E.R., 371–400.

14 Read as the President's Address before the American Psychological Association at Princeton, December, 1894, and reprinted with some unimportant omissions, a few slight revisions, and the addition of some explanatory notes. [Reprinted from the *Psychological Review,* 1895, 2, 105–124. Pages 374–379, dealing with the distinction between representative and immediate knowledge, were reprinted in *The Meaning of Truth* (1909), pp. 43–50, under the title of "The Tigers in India." For a later elaboration of this topic, cf. also *Essays in Radical*

know, say, a dozen things singly through a dozen different mental states. But on another occasion we may know the same dozen things together through a single mental state. The problem is as to the relation of the previous many states to the later one state. In physical nature, it is universally agreed, a multitude of facts always remain the multitude they were and appear as one fact only when a mind comes upon the scene and so views them, as when H–O–H appear as "water" to a human spectator. But when, instead of extramental "things," the mind combines its own "contents" into a unity, what happens is much less plain.

The matters of fact that give the trouble are among our most familiar experiences. We know a lot of friends and can think of each one singly. But we can also think of them together, as composing a "party" at our house. We can see single stars appearing in succession between the clouds on a stormy night, but we can also see whole constellations of those stars at once when the wind has blown the clouds away. In a glass of lemonade we can taste both the lemon and the sugar at once. In a major chord our ear can single out the c, e, g, and c′, if it has once become acquainted with these notes apart. And so on through the whole field of our experience, whether conceptual or sensible. Neither common sense nor commonplace psychology finds anything special to explain in these facts. Common sense simply says the mind "brings the things together," and common psychology says the "ideas" of the various things "combine," and at most will admit that the occasions on which ideas combine may be made the subject of inquiry. But to formulate the phenomenon of knowing things together thus as a combining of ideas, is already to foist in a theory about the phenomenon simply. Not so should a question be approached. The phenomenon offers itself, in the first instance, as that of *knowing things together;* and it is in those terms that its solution must, in the first instance at least, be sought.

"Things," then; to "know" things; and to know the "same" things "together" which elsewhere we knew singly—here, indeed, are terms concerning each of which we must put the question, "What do we *mean* by it when we use it?"—that question that Shadworth Hodgson lays so much stress on, and that is so well taught to students, as the beginning of all sound method, by our colleague Fullerton. And in

Empiricism (1912), below, pp. 169–214. The remainder of the present article, dealing with the problem of the unity of consciousness, should be read in the light of the earlier view maintained in the *Principles* (1890), Vol. I., pp. 177, 278, and *passim*, and the later view adopted in *The Pluralistic Universe* (1909), below, pp. 549, 555–558. It was on this issue of "the compounding of consciousness" that James finally broke with "logic" and adopted Bergsonism (*ibid.*, 557, 558). Ed.]

exactly ascertaining what we do mean by such terms there might lie a
lifetime of occupation.

For we do mean something; and we mean something true. Our
terms, whatever confusion they may connote, denote at least a fundamental fact of our experience, whose existence no one here present
will deny.

II

What, then, do we mean by "things"? To this question I can only
make the answer of the idealistic philosophy.[15] For the philosophy
that began with Berkeley, and has led up in our tongue to Shadworth
Hodgson, things have no other nature than thoughts have, and we
know of no things that are not given to somebody's experience. When
I see the thing white paper before my eyes, the nature of the thing and
the nature of my sensations are one. Even if with science we supposed
a molecular achitecture beneath the smooth whiteness of the paper,
that architecture itself could only be defined as the stuff of a farther
possible experience, a vision, say, of certain vibrating particles with
which our acquaintance with the paper would terminate if it were prolonged by magnifying artifices not yet known. A thing may be my
phenomenon or some one else's; it may be frequently or infrequently
experienced; it may be shared by all of us; one of our copies of it may
be regarded as the original, and the other copies as representatives of
that original; it may appear very differently at different times; but
whatever it be, the stuff of which it is made is thought-stuff, and
whenever we speak of a thing that is out of our own mind, we either
mean nothing; or we mean a thing that was or will be in our own mind
on another occasion; or, finally, we mean a thing in the mind of some
other possible receiver of experiences like ours.

Such being "things," what do we mean by saying that we "know"
them?

There are two ways of knowing things, knowing them immediately
or intuitively, and knowing them conceptually or representatively. Although such things as the white paper before our eyes can be known
intuitively, most of the things we know, the tigers now in India, for
example, or the scholastic system of philosophy, are known only representatively or symbolically.

Suppose, to fix our ideas, that we take first a case of conceptual
knowledge; and let it be our knowledge of the tigers in India, as we sit

[15] [This view James later modifies. The "radical empiricism" which he later
formulates "has, in fact, more affinities with natural realism than with the views
of Berkeley or of Mill" (*Essays in Radical Empiricism,* see below p. 208). ED.]

here. Exactly what do we *mean* by saying that we here know the tigers? What is the precise fact that the cognition so confidently claimed is *known-as,* to use Shadworth Hodgson's inelegant but valuable form of words?

Most men would answer that what we mean by knowing the tigers is having them, however absent in body, become in some way present to our thought; or that our knowledge of them is known as presence of our thought to them. A great mystery is usually made of this peculiar presence in absence; and the scholastic philosophy, which is only common sense grown pedantic, would explain it as a peculiar kind of existence, called *intentional inexistence,* of the tigers in our mind. At the very least, people would say that what we mean by knowing the tigers is mentally *pointing* towards them as we sit here.

But now what do we mean by *pointing,* in such a case as this? What is the pointing known-as, here?

To this question I shall have to give a very prosaic answer—one that traverses the prepossessions not only of common sense and scholasticism, but also those of nearly all the epistemological writers whom I have ever read. The answer, made brief, is this: The pointing of our thought to the tigers is known simply and solely as a procession of mental associates and motor consequences that follow on the thought, and that would lead harmoniously, if followed out, into some ideal or real context, or even into the immediate presence, of the tigers. It is known as our rejection of a jaguar, if that beast were shown us as a tiger; as our assent to a genuine tiger if so shown. It is known as our ability to utter all sorts of propositions which don't contradict other propositions that are true of the real tigers. It is even known, if we take the tigers very seriously, as actions of ours which may terminate in directly intuited tigers, as they would if we took a voyage to India for the purpose of tiger-hunting and brought back a lot of skins of the striped rascals which we had laid low. In all this there is no self-transcendency in our mental images taken by themselves. They are one physical fact; the tigers are another; and their pointing to the tigers is a perfectly commonplace physical relation, if you once grant a connecting world to be there. In short, the ideas and the tigers are in themselves as loose and separate, to use Hume's language, as any two things can be; and pointing means here an operation as external and adventitious as any that nature yields.[16]

I hope you may agree with me now that in representative knowl-

---

[16] A stone in one field may "fit," we say, a hole in another field. But the relation of "fitting," so long as no one carries the stone to the hole and drops it in, is only one name for the fact that such an act may happen. Similarly with the knowing of the tigers here and now. It is only an anticipatory name for a further associative and terminative process that may occur.

edge there is no special inner mystery, but only an outer chain of physical or mental intermediaries connecting thought and thing. *To know an
object is here to lead to it through a context which the world supplies.*
All this was most instructively set forth by our colleague Miller, of
Bryn Mawr, at our meeting in New York last Christmas, and for re-
confirming my sometime wavering opinion, I owe him this acknowledgment.[17]

Let us next pass on to the case of immediate or intuitive acquaintance with an object, and let the object be the white paper before our
eyes. The thought-stuff and the thing-stuff are here indistinguishably
the same in nature, as we saw a moment since, and there is no context
of intermediaries or associates to stand between and separate the
thought and thing. There is no "presence in absence" here, and no
"pointing," but rather an all-round embracing of the paper by the
thought; and it is clear that the knowing cannot now be explained exactly as it was when the tigers were its object. Dotted all through our
experience are states of immediate acquaintance just like this. Somewhere our belief always does rest on ultimate data like the whiteness,
smoothness, or squareness of this paper. Whether such qualities be
truly ultimate aspects of being or only provisional suppositions of
ours, held-to till we get better informed, is quite immaterial for our
present inquiry. So long as it is believed in, we see our object face to
face. What now do we mean by "knowing" such a sort of object as
this? For this is also the way in which we should know the tiger if our
conceptual idea of him were to terminate by having led us to his lair.

This address must not become too long, so I must give my answer
in the fewest words. And let me first say this: So far as the white
paper or other ultimate datum of our experience is considered to enter
also into some one else's experience, and we, in knowing it, are held
to know it there as well as here; so far again as it is considered to be a
mere mask for hidden molecules that other now impossible experiences of our own might some day lay bare to view; so far it is a case of
tigers in India again—the things known being absent experiences, the
knowing can only consist in passing smoothly towards them through
the intermediary context that the world supplies. But if our own private vision of the paper be considered in abstraction from every other
event, as if it constituted by itself the universe (and it might perfectly
well do so, for aught we can understand to the contrary), then the
paper seen and the seeing of it are only two names for one indivisible
fact which, properly named, is *the datum, the phenomenon, or the
experience.* The paper is in the mind and the mind is around the paper,
because paper and mind are only two names that are given later to

[17] See also Dr. Miller's article on "Truth and Error," in the *Philosophical
Review,* July, 1893.

the one experience, when, taken in a larger world of which it forms a part, its connections are traced in different directions.[18] *To know*

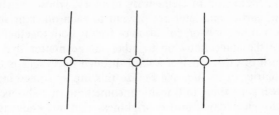

immediately, then, or intuitively, is for mental content and object to be identical. This is a very different definition from that which we gave of representative knowledge; but neither definition involves those mysterious notions of self-transcendency and presence in absence which are such essential parts of the ideas of knowledge, both of common men and of philosophers. Is there no experience that can justify these notions, and show us somewhere their original?

I think the mystery of presence in absence (though we fail to find it between one experience and another remote experience to which it points, or between the "content" and "object" of any one experience falsely rent asunder by the application to it of these two separate names) may yet be found, and found between the parts of a single experience. Let us look for it, accordingly, in its simplest possible form. What is the smallest experience in which the mystery remains? If we seek, we find that there is no datum so small as not to show the mystery. The smallest effective pulse of consciousness, whatever else it may be consciousness of, is also consciousness of passing time. The tiniest feeling that we can possibly have involves for future reflection two sub-feelings, one earlier and the other later, and a sense of their continuous procession. All this has been admirably set forth by Mr. Shadworth Hodgson,[19] who shows that there is literally no such datum

[18] What is meant by this is that "the experience" can be referred to either of two great associative systems, that of the experiencer's mental history, or that of the experienced facts of the world. Of both of these systems it forms part, and may be regarded, indeed, as one of their points of intersection. One might let a vertical line stand for the mental history; but the same object, O, appears also in the mental history of different persons, represented by the other vertical lines. It thus ceases to be the private property of one experience, and becomes, so to speak, a shared or public thing. We can track its outer history in this way, and represent it by the horizontal line. [It is also known representatively at other points of the vertical lines, or intuitively there again, so that the line of its outer history would have to be looped and wandering, but I make it straight for simplicity's sake.] In any case, however, it is the same *stuff* that figures in all the sets of lines.

[19] *Philosophy of Reflection*, Vol. I., p. 248 ff.

as that of the present moment, and no such content, and no such object, except as an unreal postulate of abstract thought. The *passing* moment is the only thing that ever concretely was or is or shall be; and in the phenomenon of elementary memory, whose function is to apprehend it, earlier and later are present to each other in an experience that feels either only on condition of feeling both together.

We have the same knowing together in the matter that fills the time. The rush of our thought forward through its fringes is the everlasting peculiarity of its life. We realize this life as something always off its balance, something in transition, something that shoots out of a darkness through a dawn into a brightness that we know to be the dawn fulfilled. In the very midst of the alteration our experience comes as one continuous fact. "Yes," we say at the moment of full brightness, *this* is what I meant. No, we feel at the moment of the dawning, this is not yet the meaning, there is more to come. In every crescendo of sensation, in every effort to recall, in every progress towards the satisfaction of desire, this succession of an emptiness and fulness that have reference to each other and are one flesh is the essence of the phenomenon. In every hindrance of desire the sense of ideal presence of what is absent in fact, of an absent, in a word, which the only function of the present is to *mean,* is even more notoriously there. And in the movement of thoughts not ordinarily classed as involving desire, we have the same phenomenon. When I say *Socrates is mortal,* the moment *Socrates* is incomplete; it falls forward through the *is* which is pure movement, into the *mortal,* which is indeed bare mortal on the tongue, but for the mind, is *that mortal,* the *mortal Socrates,* at last satisfactorily disposed of and told off.

Here, then, inside of the minimal pulse of experience which, taken as object, is change of feeling, and, taken as content, is feeling of change, is realized that absolute and essential self-transcendency which we swept away as an illusion when we sought it between a content taken as a whole and a supposed objective thing outside. *Here in the elementary datum of which both our physical and our mental worlds are built, we find included both the original of presence in absence and the prototype of that operation of knowing many things together which it is our business to discuss.*[20] For the fact that past and

[20] It seems to me that we have here something like what comes before us in the psychology of space and time. Our original intuition of space is the single field of view; our original intuition of time covers but a few seconds; yet by an ideal piecing together and construction we frame the notions of immensity and eternity, and suppose dated events and located things therein, of whose actual intervals we grasp no distinct idea. So in the case before us. The way in which the constituents of one undivided datum drag each other in and run into one, saying *this* is what *that* means, gives us our original intuition of what knowing is. That intuition we extend and constructively build up into the notion of a vast

future are already parts of the least experience that can really be, is just like what we find in any other case of an experience whose parts are many. Most of these experiences are of objects perceived to be simultaneous and not to be immediately successive as in the heretofore considered case. The field of view, the chord of music, the glass of lemonade are examples. But the gist of the matter is the same—it is always knowing-together. You cannot separate the consciousness of one part from that of all the rest. What is given is pooled and mutual; there is no dark spot, no point of ignorance; no one fraction is eclipsed from any other's point of view. Can we account for such a being-known-together of complex facts like these?

The general *nature* of it we can probably never account for, or tell how such a unity in manyness can be, for it seems to be the ultimate essence of all experience, and anything less than it apparently cannot be at all. But the particular *conditions* whereby we know particular things together might conceivably be traced, and to that humble task I beg leave to devote the time that remains.

III

Let me say forthwith that I have no pretension to give any positive solution. My sole ambition now is, by a little classification, to smooth the ground somewhat so that some of you, more able than I, may be helped to advance, before our next meeting perhaps, to results that I cannot obtain.

Now, the first thing that strikes us in these complex cases is that the condition by which one thing may come to be known together with other things is an *event*. It is often an event of the purely physical order. A man walks suddenly into my field of view, and forthwith becomes part of it. I put a drop of cologne-water on my tongue, and, holding my nostrils, get the taste of it alone, but when I open my nostrils I get the smell together with the taste in mutual suffusion.

---

tissue of knowledge, shed along from experience to experience until, dropping the intermediary data from our thought, we assume that terms the most remote still know each other, just after the fashion of the parts of the prototypal fact. Cognition here is only constructive, as we have already seen. But he who should say, arguing from its nature here, that it nowhere is direct, and seek to construct it without an originally given pattern, would be like those psychologists who profess to develop our idea of space out of the association of data that possess no original extensity. Grant the *sort* of thing that is meant by presence in absence, by self-transcendency, by reference to another, by pointing forward or back, by knowledge in short, somewhere in our experience, be it in ever so small a corner, and the construction of pseudo-cases elsewhere follows as a matter of course. But to get along without the real thing *anywhere* seems difficult indeed.

Here it would seem as if a sufficient condition of the knowing of (say) three things together were the fact that the three several physical conditions of the knowing of each of them were realized at once. But in many other cases we find on the contrary that the physical conditions are realized without the things being known together at all. When absorbed in experiments with the cologne-water, for example, the clock may strike, and I not know that it has struck. But again, some seconds after the striking has elapsed, I may, by a certain shifting of what we call my attention, hark back to it and resuscitate the sound, and even count the strokes in memory. The condition of knowing the clock's striking is here an event of the mental order which must be added to the physical event of the striking before I can know it and the cologne-water at once. Just so in the field of view I may entirely overlook and fail to notice even so important an object as a man, until the inward event of altering my attention makes me suddenly see him with the other objects there. In those curious phenomena of dissociation of consciousness with which recent studies of hypnotic, hysteric and trance states have made us familiar (phenomena which surely throw more new light on human nature than the work of all the psycho-physical laboratories put together), the event of hearing a "suggestion," or the event of passing into trance or out of it, is what decides whether a human figure shall appear in the field of view or disappear, and whether a whole set of memories shall come before the mind together, along with its other objects, or be excluded from their company. There is in fact no possible object, however completely fulfilled may be the outer condition of its perception, whose entrance into a given field of consciousness does not depend on the additional inner event called attention.

Now, it seems to me that this need of a final inner event, over and above the mere sensorial conditions, quite refutes and disposes of the associationist theory of the unity of consciousness. By associationist theory, I mean any theory that says, either implicitly or explicitly, that for a lot of objects to be known together, it suffices that a lot of conscious states, each with one of them as its content, should exist, as James Mill says, "synchronically." Synchronical existence of the ideas does not suffice, as the facts we now have abundantly show. Gurney's, Binet's, and Janet's proofs of several dissociated consciousnesses existing synchronically, and dividing the subject's field of knowledge between them, is the best possible refutation of any such view.

Union in consciousness must be *made* by something, must be brought about; and to have perceived this truth is the great merit of the anti-associationist psychologists.[21] The form of unity, they have

[21] In this rapid paper I content myself with arguing from the experimental fact that something *happens* over and above the realization of sensorial condi-

obstinately said, must be specially accounted for; and the form of unity the radical associationists have as obstinately shied away from and ignored, though their accounts of those preliminary conditions that supply the matters to be united have never been surpassed. As far as these go, we are all, I trust, associationists, and reverers of the names of Hartley, Mill, and Bain.

Let us now rapidly review the chief attempts of the anti-associationists to fill the gap they discern so well in the associationist tale.

1. *Attention.*—Attention, we say, by turning to an object, includes it with the rest; and the naming of this faculty in action has by some writers been considered a sufficient account of the decisive "event." [22] But it is plain that the act of Attention itself needs a farther account to be given, and such an account is what other theories of the event implicitly give.

We find four main types[23] of other theory of how particular things get known together, a physiological, a psychological, an animistic, and a transcendentalist type. Of the physiological or "psycho-physical" type many varieties are possible, but it must be observed that none of them pretends to assign anything more than an empirical law. A psycho-physical theory can couple certain antecedent conditions with their result; but an explanation, in the sense of an inner reason why the result should have the nature of one content with many parts instead of some entirely different nature, is what a psycho-physical theory cannot give.[24]

---

tions, wherever an object adds itself to others already "before the mind." I say nothing of the logical self-contradiction involved in the associationist doctrine that the two facts, "A is known," and "B is known," *are* the third fact, "A + B are known together." Those whom the criticisms already extant in print of this strange belief have failed to convince, would not be persuaded, even though one rose from the dead. The appeal to the actual facts of dissociation may make impression, however, even on such hardened hearts as theirs.

[22] It might seem natural to mention Wundt's doctrine of "Apperception" here. But I must confess my inability to say anything about it that would not resolve itself into a tedious comparison of texts. Being alternately described as intellection, will, feeling, synthesis, analysis, principle and result, it is too "protean" a function to lend itself to any simplified account at second hand.

[23] It is only for the sake of completeness that we need mention such notions of a sort of mechanical and chemical activity between the ideas as we find in Herbart, Steinthal, and others. These authors see clearly that mere synchronical existence is not combination, and attribute to the ideas of dynamic influences upon each other; pressures and resistances according to Herbart, and according to Steinthal "psychic attractions." But the philosophical foundations of such physical theories have been so slightly discussed by their authors that it is better to treat them only as rhetorical metaphors and pass on. Herbart, moreover, must also be mentioned later, along with the animistic writers.

[24] We find this impotence already when we seek the conditions of the passing pulse of consciousness, which, as we saw, always involves time and change. We

2. *Reminiscence.*—Now, empirically, we have learned that things must be known in succession and singly before they can be known together.[25] If A, B, and C, for example, were outer things that came for the first time and affected our senses all at once, we should get one content from the lot of them and make no discriminations. The content would symbolically point to the objects A, B, and C, and eventually terminate there, but would contain no parts that were immediately apprehended as standing for A, B, and C severally. Let A, B, and C stand for pigments, or for a tone and its overtones, and you will see what I mean when I say that the first result on consciousness of their falling together on the eye or ear would be a single new kind of feeling rather than a feeling with three kinds of inner part. Such a result has been ascribed to a "fusion" of the three feelings of A, B, and C; but there seems no ground for supposing that, under the conditions assumed, these distinct feelings have ever been aroused at all. I should call the phenomenon one of *indiscriminate knowing together,* for the most we can say under the circumstances is that the content resembles somewhat each of the objects A, B, and C, and knows them each potentially, knows them, that is, by possibly leading to each smoothly hereafter, as we know Indian tigers even whilst sitting in this room.

But if our memory possess stored-up images of former A-s, B-s, and C-s, experienced in isolation, we get an altogether different content, namely, one through which we know A, B, and C together, and yet know each of them in discrimination through one of the content's own parts. This has been called a "colligation" or *Verknüpfung* of the "ideas" of A, B, and C, to distinguish it from the aforesaid fusion. Whatever we may call it, we see that its physiological condition is more complex than in the previous case. In both cases the outer objects, A, B, and C, exert their effects on the sensorium. But in this case there is a co-operation of higher tracts of memory which in the former case was absent. *Discriminative knowing-together, in short, involves higher processes of reminiscence.* Do these give the element of manyness, whilst the lower sensorial processes that by themselves would result in mere "fusion," give the unity to the experience? The

---

account for the passing pulse, physiologically, by the overlapping of dying and dawning brain-processes; and at first sight the elements time and change, involved in both the brain-processes and their mental result, give a similarity that, we feel, might be the real reason for the psycho-physic coupling. But the moment we ask "metaphysical" questions—"Why not each brain-process felt apart?—Why just this amount of time, neither more nor less?" etc., etc.—we find ourselves falling back on the empirical view as the only safe one to defend.

[25] The latest empirical contribution to this subject, with which I am acquainted, is Dr. Herbert Nichols's excellent little monograph, *Our Notions of Number and Space*. Boston: Ginn & Co., 1894.

suggestion is one that might repay investigation, although it has against it two pretty solid objections: first, that in man the consciousness attached to infra-cortical centres is altogether subliminal, if it exist; and, second, that in the cortex itself we have not yet discriminated sensorial from ideational processes. Possibly the frontal lobes, in which Wundt has supposed an *Apperceptionsorgan,* might serve a turn here. In any case it is certain that, into our present rough notions of the cortical functions, the future will have to weave distinctions at present unknown.

3. *Synergy.*—The theory that, physiologically, the oneness precedes the manyness, may be contrasted with a theory that our colleagues Baldwin and Münsterberg are at present working out, and which places the condition of union of many data into one datum, in the fact that the many pour themselves into one motor discharge. The motor discharge being the last thing to happen, the condition of manyness would physiologically here precede and that of oneness follow. A printed word is apprehended as one object, at the same time that each letter in it is apprehended as one of its parts. Our secretary, Cattell, long ago discovered that we recognized words of four or five letters by the eye as quickly, or even more quickly, then we recognize single letters. Recognition means here the motor process of articulation; and the quickness comes from the fact that all the letters in the particular combination unhesitatingly co-operate in the one articulatory act. I suppose such facts as these to lie at the base of our colleagues' theories, which probably differ in detail, and which it would be manifestly unjust to discuss or guess about in advance of their completer publication. Let me only say that I hope the latter may not be long delayed.

These are the only types of physiological theory worthy of mention. I may next pass to what, for brevity's sake, may be called *psychological accounts* of the event that lets an object into consciousness, or, by not occurring, leaves it out. These accounts start from the fact that what figures as part of a larger object is often perceived to have relations to the other parts. Accordingly the event in question is described as an *act of relating thought.* It takes two forms.

4. *Relating to Self.*—Some authors say that nothing can enter consciousness except on condition that it be related to the self. Not *object,* but *object-plus-me,* is the minimum knowable.

5. *Relating to other Objects.*—Others think it enough if the incoming object be related to the other objects already there. To fail to appear related is to fail to be known at all. To appear related is to appear with other objects. If relations were correlates of special cerebral processes, the addition of these to the sensorial processes would be the wished-for event. But brain physiology as yet knows nothing of

such special processes, so I have called this explanation purely psychological. There seem to be fatal objections to it as a universal statement, for the reference to self, if it exist, must in a host of cases be altogether subconscious; and introspection assures us that in many half-waking and half-drunken states the relations between things that we perceive together may be of the dimmest and most indefinable kind.

6. *The Individual Soul.*—So we next proceed to *the animistic account.* By this term I mean to cover every sort of individualistic soul-theory. I will say nothing of older opinions; but in modern times we have two views of the way in which the union of a many by a soul occurs. For Herbart, for example, it occurs because the soul itself *is* unity, and all its *Selbsterhaltungen* are obliged to necessarily share this form. For our colleague Ladd, on the other hand, to take the best recent example, it occurs because the soul, which *is* a real unity indeed, furthermore performs a unifying *act* on the naturally separate data of sense—an act, moreover, for which no psycho-physical analogon can be found. It must be admitted that much of the reigning bias against the soul in so-called scientific circles is an unintelligent prejudice, traceable far more to a vague impression that it is a theological superstition than to exact logical grounds. The soul is an "entity," and, indeed, that worst sort of entity, a "scholastic entity"; and, moreover, it is something to be damned or saved; so let's have no more of it! I am free to confess that in my own case the antipathy to the soul with which I find myself burdened is an ancient hardness of heart of which I can frame no fully satisfactory account even to myself. I passively agree that if there were souls that we could use as principles of explanation, the *formal* settlement of the questions now before us could run far more smoothly towards its end. I admit that a soul is a medium of union, and that brain-processes and ideas, be they never so "synchronical," leave all mediating agency out. Yet, in spite of these concessions, I never find myself actively taking up the soul, so to speak, and making it to do work in my psychologizing. I speak of myself here because I am one amongst many, and probably few of us can give adequate reasons for our dislike. The more honor to our colleague from Yale, then, that he remains so unequivocally faithful to this unpopular principle! And let us hope that his forthcoming book may sweep what is blind in our hostility away.[26]

[26] I ought, perhaps, to apologize for not expunging from my printed text these references to Professor Ladd, which were based on the impression left on my mind by the termination of his *Physiological Psychology.* It would now appear from the paper read by him at the Princeton meeting, and his *Philosophy of Mind,* just published, that he disbelieves in the soul of old-fashioned ontology; and on looking again at the *P. P.,* I see that I may well have misinterpreted his deeper meaning there. I incline to suspect, however, that he had himself not fully disentangled it when that work was written; and that between now and

But all is not blind in our hostility. When, for example, you say that A, B, and C, which are distinct contents on other occasions, are now on this occasion joined into the compound content ABC by a unifying act of the soul, you say little more than that now they *are* united, unless you give some hint as to *how* the soul unites them. When, for example, the hysteric women which Pierre Janet has studied with such loving care, go to pieces mentally, and their souls are unable any longer to connect the data of their experience together, though these data remain severally conscious in dissociation, what is the condition on which this inability of the soul depends? Is it an impotence in the soul itself? or is it an impotence in the physiological conditions, which fail to stimulate the soul sufficiently to its synthetic task? The *how* supposes on the soul's part a constitution adequate to the act. An hypothesis, we are told in the logic books, ought to propose a being that has some other constitution and definition than that of barely performing the phenomenon it is evoked to explain. When physicists propose the "ether," for example, they propose it with a lot of incidental properties. But the soul proposed to us has no special properties or constitution of which we are informed. Nevertheless, since particular conditions do determine its activity, it must have a constitution of some sort. In either case, we ought to know the facts. But the soul-doctrine, as hitherto professed, not only doesn't answer such questions, it doesn't even ask them; and it must be radically rejuvenated if it expects to be greeted again as a useful principle in psychological philosophy. Here is work for our spiritualist colleagues, not only for the coming year, but for the rest of their lives.[27]

7. *The World-soul.*—The second spiritualist theory may be named as that of *transcendentalism*. I take it typically and not as set forth by

---

then his thought has been evolving somewhat, as Lotze's did, between his *Medical Psychology* and his *Metaphysic*. It is gratifying to note these converging tendencies in different philosophers; but I leave the text as I read it at Princeton, as a mark of what one could say not so very unnaturally at that date.

[27] The soul can be taken in three ways as a unifying principle. An already existing lot of animated sensations (or other psychic data) may be simply *woven* into one by it; in which case the form of unity is the soul's only contribution, and the original stuff of the Many remains in the One as its stuff also. Or, secondly, the resultant synthetic One may be regarded as an immanent *re-action* of the Soul on the preëxisting psychic Many; and in this case the Soul, in addition to creating the new form, reproduces in itself the old stuff of the Many, superseding it for our use, and making it for us become subliminal, but not suppressing its existence. Or, thirdly, the One may again be the Soul's immanent reaction on a physiological, not on a mental, Many. In this case preëxisting *sensations or ideas* would not be there at all, to be either woven together or superseded. The synthetic One would be a primal psychic datum with parts, either of which might know the same object that a possible sensation, realized under other physiological conditions, could also know.

any single author. Transcendentalism explains things by an over-soul of which all separate souls, sensations, thoughts, and data generally are parts. To be, as it would be known together with everything else in the world by this over-soul, is for transcendentalism the *true* condition of each single thing, and to pass into this condition is for things to fulfil their vocation. Such being known together, since it is the innermost reality of life, cannot on transcendentalist principles be explained or accounted for as a work wrought on a previous sort of reality. The monadic soul-theory starts with separate sensational data, and must show how they are *made* one. The transcendentalist theory has rather for its task to show how, being one, they can spuriously and illusorily be made to appear separate. The problem for the monadic soul, in short, is that of unification, and the problem for the over-soul is that of insulation. The removal of insulating obstructions would sufficiently account for things reverting to their natural place in the over-soul and being known together. The most natural insulating or individualizing principle to invoke is the bodily organism. As the pipes of an organ let the pressing mass of air escape only in single notes, so do our brains, the organ pipes of the infinite, keep back everything but the slender threads of truth to which they may be pervious. As they obstruct more, the insulation increases, as they obstruct less it disappears. Now transcendental philosophers have as a rule not done much dabbling in psychology. But one sees no abstract reason why they might not go into psychology as fully as any one, and erect a psychophysical science of the conditions of more separate and less separate cognition which would include all the facts that psycho-physicist in general might discover. And they would have the advantage over other psycho-physicists of not needing to explain the nature of the resultant knowing-together when it should occur, for they could say that they simply begged it as the ultimate nature of the world.

This is as broad a disjunction as I can make of the different ways in which men have considered the conditions of our knowing things together. You will agree with me that I have brought no new insight to the subject, and that I have only gossiped to while away this unlucky presidential hour to which the constellations doomed me at my birth. But since gossip we have had to have, let me make the hour more gossipy still by saying a final word about the position taken up in my own *Principles of Psychology* on the general question before us, a position which, as you doubtless remember, was so vigorously attacked by our colleague from the University of Pennsylvania at our meeting in New York a year ago.[28] That position consisted in this, that

---

[28] Printed as an article entitled "The Psychological Standpoint," in this [*Psychological*] *Review*, Vol. I., p. 113. (March, 1894.) [The author was G. S. Fullerton. For James's own earlier views, *cf.* the *Principles* (1890), especially Chaps. VI., IX. Ed.]

I proposed to simply eliminate from psychology "considered as a natural science" the whole business of ascertaining *how* we come to know things together or to know them at all. Such considerations, I said, should fall to metaphysics. That we do know things, sometimes singly and sometimes together, is a fact. That states of consciousness are the vehicle of the knowledge, and depend on brain states, are two other facts. And I thought that a natural science of psychology might legitimately confine itself to tracing the functional variations of these three sorts of fact, and ascertaining and tracing what determinate bodily states are the condition when the states of mind know determinate things and groups of things. Most states of mind can be designated only by naming what objects they are "thoughts-of," *i.e.,* what things they know.

Most of those which know compound things are utterly unique and solitary mental entities demonstrably different from any collection of simpler states to which the same objects might be singly known.[29] Treat them all as unique in entity, I said then; let their complexity reside in their plural cognitive function; and you have a psychology

[29] When they know conceptually they don't even remotely resemble the simpler states. When they know intuitively they resemble, sometimes closely, sometimes distantly, the simpler states. The sour and sweet in lemonade are extremely unlike the sour and sweet of lemon juice and sugar, singly taken, yet like enough for us to "recognize" these "objects" in the compound taste. The several objective "notes" recognized in the chord sound differently and peculiarly there. In a motley field of view successive and simultaneous contrast give to each several tint a different hue and luminosity from that of the "real" color into which it turns when viewed without its neighbors by a rested eye. The difference is sometimes so slight, however, that we overlook the "representative" character of each of the parts of a complex content, and speak as if the latter were a cluster of the original "intuitive" states of mind that, occurring singly, know the "object's" several parts in separation. Professor Meinong, for example, even after the true state of things had been admirably set forth by Herr H. Cornelius (in the *Vierteljahrschrift f. wiss. Phil.,* XVI., 404; XVII., 30), returns to the defence of the radical associationist view (in the *Zeitschrift f. Psychologie,* VI., 340, 417). According to him, the single sensations of the several notes lie unaltered in the chord-sensations; but his analysis of the phenomenon is vitiated by his non-recognition of the fact that the *same objects* (*i.e.,* the notes) *can be known* representatively through one compound state of mind, and directly in several simple ones, without the simple and the compound states having strictly anything in common with each other. In Meinong's earlier work, *Ueber Begriff und Eigenschaften der Empfindung* (*Vierteljahrschrift,* Vol. XII.), he seems to me to have hit the truth much better, when he says that the aspect *color, e.g.,* in a concrete sensation of *red,* is not an abstractable *part* of the sensation, but an *external relation of resemblance* between that sensation and other sensations to the whole lot of which we give the name of colors. Such, I should say, are the aspects of *c, e, g,* and *c′* in the chord. We may call them *parts* of the chord if we like, but they are not *bits* of it, identical with *c*'s, *e*'s, *g*'s, and *c*'s elsewhere. They simply resemble the *c*'s, *e*'s, *g*'s, and *c″*'s elsewhere, and know these contents or objects representatively.

which, if it doesn't ultimately explain the facts, also does not, in expressing them, make them self-contradictory (as the associationist psychology does when it calls them many ideas fused into one idea) or pretend to explain them (as the soul-theory so often does) by a barren verbal principle.

My intention was a good one, and a natural science infinitely more complete than the psychologies we now possess could be written without abandoning its terms. Like all authors, I have, therefore, been surprised that this child of my genius should not be more admired by others—should, in fact, have been generally either misunderstood or despised. But do not fear that on this occasion I am either going to defend or to re-explain the bantling. I am going to make things more harmonious by simply *giving it up*.[30] I have become convinced since publishing that book that no conventional restrictions *can* keep metaphysical and so-called epistemological inquiries out of the psychology books. I see, moreover, better now than then that my proposal to designate mental states merely by their cognitive function leads to a somewhat strained way of talking of dreams and reveries, and to quite an unnatural way of talking of some emotional states. I am willing, consequently, henceforward that mental contents should be called complex, just as their objects are, and this even in psychology. Not because their parts are separable, as the parts of objects are, not because they have an eternal or quasi-eternal individual existence, like the parts of objects; for the various "contents" of which they are parts are integers, existentially, and their parts only live as long as *they* live. Still, *in* them, we can call parts, parts.—But when, without circumlocution or disguise, I thus come over to your views, I insist that those of you who applaud me (if any such there be) should recognize the obligations which the new agreement imposes on yourselves. Not till you have dropped the old phrases, so absurd or so empty, of ideas "self-compounding" or "united by a spiritual principle"; not till you have in your turn succeeded in some such long inquiry into conditions as the one I have just failed in; not till you have laid bare more of the nature of that altogether unique kind of complexity in unity which mental states involve; not till then, I say, will psychology reach any real benefit from the conciliatory spirit of which I have done what I can to set an example.

[30] [But *cf. Pluralistic Universe* (1909), see below p. 549, note, where it appears that he does not abandon his earlier view unqualifiedly. ED.]

DOES "CONSCIOUSNESS" EXIST? * 31

'Thoughts' and 'things' are names for two sorts of object, which common sense will always find contrasted and will always practically oppose to each other. Philosophy, reflecting on the contrast, has varied in the past in her explanations of it, and may be expected to vary in the future. At first, 'spirit and matter,' 'soul and body,' stood for a pair of equipollent substances quite on a par in weight and interest. But one day Kant undermined the soul and brought in the transcendental ego, and ever since then the bipolar relation has been very much off its balance. The transcendental ego seems nowadays in rationalist quarters to stand for everything, in empiricist quarters for almost nothing. In the hands of such writers as Schuppe, Rehmke, Natorp, Münsterberg—at any rate in his earlier writings, Schubert-Soldern and others, the spiritual principle attenuates itself to a thoroughly ghostly condition, being only a name for the fact that the 'content' of experience *is known*. It loses personal form and activity—these passing over to the content—and becomes a bare *Bewusstheit* or *Bewusstsein überhaupt*, of which in its own right absolutely nothing can be said.

I believe that 'consciousness,' when once it has evaporated to this estate of pure diaphaneity, is on the point of disappearing altogether. It is the name of a nonentity, and has no right to a place among first principles. Those who still cling to it are clinging to a mere echo, the faint rumor left behind by the disappearing 'soul' upon the air of philosophy. During the past year, I have read a number of articles whose authors seemed just on the point of abandoning the notion of consciousness,[32] and substituting for it that of an absolute experience not due to two factors. But they were not quite radical enough, not quite daring enough in their negations. For twenty years past I have mistrusted 'consciousness' as an entity; for seven or eight years past I have suggested its non-existence to my students, and tried to give them its pragmatic equivalent in realities of experience. It seems to me that the hour is ripe for it to be openly and universally discarded.

To deny plumply that 'consciousness' exists seems so absurd on

* From: E.R.E., 1–38.

31 [Reprinted from the *Journal of Philosophy, Psychology and Scientific Methods,* vol. I, No. 18, September 1, 1904. For the relation between this essay and those which follow, cf. below, pp. 199–200. ED.]

32 Articles by Baldwin, Ward, Bawden, King, Alexander and others. Dr. Perry is frankly over the border.

the face of it—for undeniably 'thoughts' do exist—that I fear some readers will follow me no farther. Let me then immediately explain that I mean only to deny that the word stands for an entity, but to insist most emphatically that it does stand for a function. There is, I mean, no aboriginal stuff or quality of being,[33] contrasted with that of which material objects are made, out of which our thoughts of them are made; but there is a function in experience which thoughts perform, and for the performance of which this quality of being is invoked. That function is *knowing*. 'Consciousness' is supposed necessary to explain the fact that things not only are, but get reported, are known. Whoever blots out the notion of consciousness from his list of first principles must still provide in some way for that function's being carried on.

I

My thesis is that if we start with the supposition that there is only one primal stuff or material in the world, a stuff of which everything is composed, and if we call that stuff 'pure experience,' then knowing can easily be explained as a particular sort of relation towards one another into which portions of pure experience may enter. The relation itself is a part of pure experience; one of its 'terms' becomes the subject or bearer of the knowledge, the knower,[34] the other becomes the object known. This will need much explanation before it can be understood. The best way to get it understood is to contrast it with the alternative view; and for that we may take the recentest alternative, that in which the evaporation of the definite soul-substance has proceeded as far as it can go without being yet complete. If neo-Kantism has expelled earlier forms of dualism, we shall have expelled all forms if we are able to expel neo-Kantism in its turn.

For the thinkers I call neo-Kantian, the word consciousness today does no more than signalize the fact that experience is indefeasibly dualistic in structure. It means that not subject, not object, but object-plus-subject is the minimum that can actually be. The subject-object distinction meanwhile is entirely different from that between mind and matter, from that between body and soul. Souls were detachable, had separate destinies; things could happen to them. To consciousness as such nothing can happen, for, timeless itself, it is only a witness of happenings in time, in which it plays no part. It is, in

---

[33] [Similarly, there is no "activity of 'consciousness' as such." See below, pp. 283–284, note. ED.]

[34] In my *Psychology* I have tried to show that we need no knower other than the 'passing thought.' [*Principles of Psychology*, vol. I, pp. 338 ff.]

a word, but the logical correlative of 'content' in an Experience of which the peculiarity is that *fact comes to light* in it, that *awareness of content* takes place. Consciousness as such is entirely impersonal— 'self' and its activities belong to the content. To say that I am self-conscious, or conscious of putting forth volition, means only that certain contents, for which 'self' and 'effort of will' are the names, are not without witness as they occur.

Thus, for these belated drinkers at the Kantian spring, we should have to admit consciousness as an 'epistemological' necessity, even if we had no direct evidence of its being there.

But in addition to this, we are supposed by almost every one to have an immediate consciousness of consciousness itself. When the world of outer fact ceases to be materially present, and we merely recall it in memory, or fancy it, the consciousness is believed to stand out and to be felt as a kind of impalpable inner flowing, which, once known in this sort of experience, may equally be detected in presentations of the outer world. "The moment we try to fix our attention upon consciousness and to see *what,* distinctly, it is," says a recent writer, "it seems to vanish. It seems as if we had before us a mere emptiness. When we try to introspect the sensation of blue, all we can see is the blue; the other element is as if it were diaphanous. Yet it *can* be distinguished, if we look attentively enough, and know that there is something to look for." [34a] "Consciousness" (Bewusstheit), says another philosopher, "is inexplicable and hardly describable, yet all conscious experiences have this in common that what we call their content has this peculiar reference to a centre for which 'self' is the name, in virtue of which reference alone the content is subjectively given, or appears. . . . While in this way consciousness, or reference to a self, is the only thing which distinguishes a conscious content from any sort of being that might be there with no one conscious of it, yet this only ground of the distinction defies all closer explanations. The existence of consciousness, although it is the fundamental fact of psychology, can indeed be laid down as certain, can be brought out by analysis, but can neither be defined nor deduced from anything but itself." [35]

'Can be brought out by analysis,' this author says. This supposes that the consciousness is one element, moment, factor—call it what you like—of an experience of essentially dualistic inner constitution, from which, if you abstract the content, the consciousness will remain revealed to its own eye. Experience, at this rate, would be much like a paint of which the world pictures were made. Paint has a dual constitution, involving, as it does, a menstruum[36] (oil, size or what not) and

[34a] G. E. Moore: *Mind,* vol. XII, N. S., [1903], p .450.
[35] Paul Natorp: *Einleitung in die Psychologie,* 1888, pp. 14, 112.
[36] "Figuratively speaking, consciousness may be said to be the one universal

a mass of content in the form of pigment suspended therein. We can get the pure menstruum by letting the pigment settle, and the pure pigment by pouring off the size or oil. We operate here by physical subtraction; and the usual view is, that by mental subtraction we can separate the two factors of experience in an analogous way—not isolating them entirely, but distinguishing them enough to know that they are two.

II

Now my contention is exactly the reverse of this. *Experience, I believe, has no such inner duplicity; and the separation of it into consciousness and content comes, not by way of subtraction, but by way of addition*—the addition, to a given concrete piece of it, of other sets of experiences, in connection with which severally its use or function may be of two different kinds. The paint will also serve here as an illustration. In a pot in a paint-shop, along with other paints, it serves in its entirety as so much saleable matter. Spread on a canvas, with other paints around it, it represents, on the contrary, a feature in a picture and performs a spiritual function. Just so, I maintain, does a given undivided portion of experience, taken in one context of associates, play the part of a knower, of a state of mind, of 'consciousness'; while in a different context the same undivided bit of experience plays the part of a thing known, of an objective 'content.' In a word, in one group it figures as a thought, in another group as a thing. And, since it can figure in both groups simultaneously we have every right to speak of it as subjective and objective both at once. The dualism connoted by such double-barrelled terms as 'experience,' 'phenomenon,' 'datum,' '*Vorfindung*'—terms which, in philosophy at any rate, tend more and more to replace the single-barrelled terms of 'thought' and 'thing'—that dualism, I say, is still preserved in this account, but reinterpreted, so that, instead of being mysterious and elusive, it becomes verifiable and concrete. It is an affair of relations, it falls outside, not inside, the single experience considered, and can always be particularized and defined.

The entering wedge for this more concrete way of understanding the dualism was fashioned by Locke when he made the word 'idea' stand indifferently for thing and thought, and by Berkeley when he said that what common sense means by realities is exactly what the philosopher means by ideas. Neither Locke nor Berkeley thought his

solvent, or menstruum, in which the different concrete kinds of psychic acts and facts are contained, whether in concealed or in obvious form." G. T. Ladd: *Psychology, Descriptive and Explanatory*, 1894, p. 30.

truth out into perfect clearness, but it seems to me that the conception I am defending does little more than consistently carry out the 'pragmatic' method which they were the first to use.

If the reader will take his own experiences, he will see what I mean. Let him begin with a perceptual experience, the 'presentation,' so called, of a physical object, his actual field of vision, the room he sits in, with the book he is reading as its centre; and let him for the present treat this complex object in the common-sense way as being 'really' what it seems to be, namely, a collection of physical things cut out from an environing world of other physical things with which these physical things have actual or potential relations. Now at the same time it is just *those self-same things* which his mind, as we say, perceives; and the whole philosophy of perception from Democritus's time downwards has been just one long wrangle over the paradox that what is evidently one reality should be in two places at once, both in outer space and in a person's mind. 'Representative' theories of perception avoid the logical paradox, but on the other hand they violate the reader's sense of life, which knows no intervening mental image but seems to see the room and the book immediately just as they physically exist.

The puzzle of how the one identical room can be in two places is at bottom just the puzzle of how one identical point can be on two lines. It can, if it be situated at their intersection; and similarly, if the 'pure experience' of the room were a place of intersection of two processes, which connected it with different groups of associates respectively, it could be counted twice over, as belonging to either group, and spoken of loosely as existing in two places, although it would remain all the time a numerically single thing.

Well, the experience is a member of diverse processes that can be followed away from it along entirely different lines. The one self-identical thing has so many relations to the rest of experience that you can take it in disparate systems of association, and treat it as belonging with opposite contexts.[37] In one of these contexts it is your 'field of consciousness'; in another it is 'the room in which you sit,' and it enters both contexts in its wholeness, giving no pretext for being said to attach itself to consciousness by one of its parts or aspects, and to outer reality by another. What are the two processes, now, into which the room-experience simultaneously enters in this way?

One of them is the reader's personal biography, the other is the history of the house of which the room is part. The presentation, the experience, the *that* in short (for until we have decided *what* it is it must be a mere *that*) is the last term of a train of sensations, emo-

---

[37] [For a parallel statement of this view, cf. the author's *Meaning of Truth*, above, p. 157, note. Cf. also below, pp. 306–307. ED.]

tions, decisions, movements, classifications, expectations, etc., ending
in the present, and the first term of a series of similar 'inner' operations extending into the future, on the reader's part. On the other
hand, the very same *that* is the *terminus ad quem* of a lot of previous
physical operations, carpentering, papering, furnishing, warming, etc.,
and the *terminus a quo* of a lot of future ones, in which it will be
concerned when undergoing the destiny of a physical room. The physical and the mental operations form curiously incompatible groups.
As a room, the experience has occupied that spot and had that environment for thirty years. As your field of consciousness it may never
have existed until now. As a room, attention will go on to discover
endless new details in it. As your mental state merely, few new ones
will emerge under attention's eye. As a room, it will take an earthquake, or a gang of men, and in any case a certain amount of time, to
destroy it. As your subjective state, the closing of your eyes, or any
instantaneous play of your fancy will suffice. In the real world, fire
will consume it. In your mind, you can let fire play over it without
effect. As an outer object, you must pay so much a month to inhabit
it. As an inner content, you may occupy it for any length of time rent-
free. If, in short, you follow it in the mental direction, taking it along
with events of personal biography solely, all sorts of things are true of
it which are false, and false of it which are true if you treat it as a real
thing experienced, follow it in the physical direction, and relate it to
associates in the outer world.

III

So far, all seems plain sailing, but my thesis will probably grow less
plausible to the reader when I pass from percepts to concepts, or from
the case of things presented to that of things remote. I believe, nevertheless, that here also the same law holds good. If we take conceptual
manifolds, or memories, or fancies, they also are in their first intention mere bits of pure experience, and, as such, are single *thats* which
act in one context as objects, and in another context figure as mental
states. By taking them in their first intention, I mean ignoring their
relation to possible perceptual experiences with which they may be
connected, which they may lead to and terminate in, and which then
they may be supposed to 'represent.' Taking them in this way first, we
confine the problem to a world merely 'thought of' and not directly felt
or seen.[38] This world, just like the world of percepts, comes to us at

[38] [For the author's recognition of "concepts as a co-ordinate realm" of reality, cf. his *Meaning of Truth*, above, pp. 151–152; *A Pluralistic Universe*, below, pp. 570–572; *Some Problems of Philosophy*, below, pp. 234–237, 240–241;

first as a chaos of experiences, but lines of order soon get traced. We find that any bit of it which we may cut out as an example is connected with distinct groups of associates, just as our perceptual experiences are, that these associates link themselves with it by different relations,[39] and that one forms the inner history of a person, while the other acts as an impersonal 'objective' world, either spatial and temporal, or else merely logical or mathematical, or otherwise 'ideal.'

The first obstacle on the part of the reader to seeing that these non-perceptual experiences have objectivity as well as subjectivity will probably be due to the intrusion into his mind of *percepts,* that third group of associates with which the non-perceptual experiences have relations, and which, as a whole, they 'represent,' standing to them as thoughts to things. This important function of the non-perceptual experiences complicates the question and confuses it; for, so used are we to treat percepts as the sole genuine realities that, unless we keep them out of the discussion, we tend altogether to overlook the objectivity that lies in non-perceptual experiences by themselves. We treat them, 'knowing' percepts as they do, as through and through subjective, and say that they are wholly constituted of the stuff called consciousness, using this term now for a kind of entity, after the fashion which I am seeking to refute.[40]

Abstracting, then, from percepts altogether, what I maintain is, that any single non-perceptual experience tends to get counted twice over, just as a perceptual experience does, figuring in one context as an object or field of objects, in another as a state of mind: and all this without the least internal self-diremption on its own part into consciousness and content. It is all consciousness in one taking; and, in the other, all content.

I find this objectivity of non-perceptual experiences, this complete parallelism in point of reality between the presently felt and the remotely thought, so well set forth in a page of Münsterberg's *Grundzüge,* that I will quote it as it stands.

"I may only think of my objects," says Professor Münsterberg; "yet, in my living thought they stand before me exactly as perceived

---

and below, note 39. Giving this view the name 'logical realism,' he remarks elsewhere that his philosophy "may be regarded as somewhat eccentric in its attempt to combine logical realism with an otherwise empiricist mode of thought" (*Some Problems of Philosophy,* see below, p. 255). Ed.]

[39] Here as elsewhere the relations are of course *experienced* relations, members of the same originally chaotic manifold of non-perceptual experience of which the related terms themselves are parts. [Cf. below, p. 195.]

[40] Of the representative function of non-perceptual experience as a whole, I will say a word in a subsequent article: it leads too far into the general theory of knowledge for much to be said about it in a short paper like this. [Cf. below, pp. 199 ff.]

objects would do, no matter how different the two ways of apprehending them may be in their genesis. The book here lying on the table before me, and the book in the next room of which I think and which I mean to get, are both in the same sense given realities for me, realities which I acknowledge and of which I take account. If you agree that the perceptual object is not an idea within me, but that percept and thing, as indistinguishably one, are really experienced *there, outside,* you ought not to believe that the merely thought-of object is hid away inside of the thinking subject. The object of which I think, and of whose existence I take cognizance without letting it now work upon my senses, occupies its definite place in the outer world as much as does the object which I directly see."

"What is true of the here and the there, is also true of the now and the then. I know of the thing which is present and perceived, but I know also of the thing which yesterday was but is no more, and which I only remember. Both can determine my present conduct, both are parts of the reality of which I keep account. It is true that of much of the past I am uncertain, just as I am uncertain of much of what is present if it be but dimly perceived. But the interval of time does not in principle alter my relation to the object, does not transform it from an object known into a mental state. . . . The things in the room here which I survey, and those in my distant home of which I think, the things of this minute and those of my long-vanished boyhood, influence and decide me alike, with a reality which my experience of them directly feels. They both make up my real world, they make it directly, they do not have first to be introduced to me and mediated by ideas which now and here arise within me. . . . This not-me character of my recollections and expectations does not imply that the external objects of which I am aware in those experiences should necessarily be there also for others. The objects of dreamers and hallucinated persons are wholly without general validity. But even were they centaurs and golden mountains, they still would be 'off there,' in fairy land, and not 'inside' of ourselves." [41]

This certainly is the immediate, primary, naïf or practical way of taking our thought-of world. Were there no perceptual world to serve as its 'reductive,' in Taine's sense, by being 'stronger' and more genuinely 'outer' (so that the whole merely thought-of world seems weak and inner in comparison), our world of thought would be the only world, and would enjoy complete reality in our belief. This actually happens in our dreams, and in our day-dreams so long as percepts do not interrupt them.

And yet, just as the seen room (to go back to our late example) is *also* a field of consciousness, so the conceived or recollected room is

41 Münsterberg: *Grundzüge der Psychologie,* vol. I, p. 48.

also a state of mind; and the doubling-up of the experience has in both cases similar grounds.

The room thought-of, namely, has many thought-of couplings with many thought-of things. Some of these couplings are inconstant, others are stable. In the reader's personal history the room occupies a single date—he saw it only once perhaps, a year ago. Of the house's history, on the other hand, it forms a permanent ingredient. Some couplings have the curious stubbornness, to borrow Royce's term, of fact; others show the fluidity of fancy—we let them come and go as we please. Grouped with the rest of its house, with the name of its town, of its owner, builder, value, decorative plan, the room maintains a definite foothold, to which, if we try to loosen it, it tends to return, and to reassert itself with force.[42] With these associates, in a word, it coheres, while to other houses, other towns, other owners, etc., it shows no tendency to cohere at all. The two collections, first of its cohesive, and, second, of its loose associates, inevitably come to be contrasted. We call the first collection the system of external realities, in the midst of which the room, as 'real,' exists; the other we call the stream of our internal thinking, in which, as a 'mental image,' it for a moment floats.[43] The room thus again gets counted twice over. It plays two different rôles, being *Gedanke* and *Gedachtes,* the thought-of-an-object, and the object-thought-of, both in one; and all this without paradox or mystery, just as the same material thing may be both low and high, or small and great, or bad and good, because of its relations to opposite parts of an environing world.

As 'subjective' we say that the experience represents; as 'objective' it is represented. What represents and what is represented is here numerically the same; but we must remember that no dualism of being represented and representing resides in the experience *per se*. In its pure state, or when isolated, there is no self-splitting of it into consciousness and what the consciousness is 'of.' Its subjectivity and objectivity are functional attributes solely, realized only when the experience is 'taken,' *i.e.,* talked of, twice, considered along with its two differing contexts respectively, by a new retrospective experience, of which that whole past complication now forms the fresh content.

The instant field of the present is at all times what I call the 'pure' experience. It is only virtually or potentially either object or subject as yet. For the time being, it is plain, unqualified actuality, or existence,

---

[42] Cf. A. L. Hodder: *The Adversaries of the Sceptic,* pp. 94–99.

[43] For simplicity's sake I confine my exposition to 'external' reality. But there is also the system of ideal reality in which the room plays its part. Relations of comparison, of classification, serial order, value, also are stubborn, assign a definite place to the room, unlike the incoherence of its places in the mere rhapsody of our successive thoughts. [Cf. above, p. 175.]

a simple *that*. In this *naïf* immediacy it is of course *valid;* it is *there,* we *act* upon it; and the doubling of it in retrospection into a state of mind and a reality intended thereby, is just one of the acts. The 'state of mind,' first treated explicitly as such in retrospection, will stand corrected or confirmed, and the retrospective experience in its turn will get a similar treatment; but the immediate experience in its passing is always 'truth,' [44] practical truth, *something to act on,* at its own movement. If the world were then and there to go out like a candle, it would remain truth absolute and objective, for it would be 'the last word,' would have no critic, and no one would ever oppose the thought in it to the reality intended.[45]

I think I may now claim to have made my thesis clear. Consciousness connotes a kind of external relation, and does not denote a special stuff or way of being. *The peculiarity of our experiences, that they not only are, but are known, which their 'conscious' quality is invoked to explain, is better explained by their relations—these relations themselves being experiences—to one another.*

IV

Were I now to go on to treat of the knowing of perceptual by conceptual experiences, it would again prove to be an affair of external relations. One experience would be the knower, the other the reality known; and I could perfectly well define, without the notion of 'consciousness,' what the knowing actually and practically amounts to—leading-towards, namely, and terminating-in percepts, through a series of transitional experiences which the world supplies. But I will not treat of this, space being insufficient.[46] I will rather consider a few

[44] Note the ambiguity of this term, which is taken sometimes objectively and sometimes subjectively.

[45] In the *Psychological Review* for July [1904], Dr. R. B. Perry has published a view of Consciousness which comes nearer to mine than any other with which I am acquainted. At present, Dr. Perry thinks, every field of experience is so much 'fact.' It becomes 'opinion' or 'thought' only in retrospection, when a fresh experience, thinking the same object, alters and corrects it. But the corrective experience becomes itself in turn corrected, and thus experience as a whole is a process in which what is objective originally forever turns subjective, turns into our apprehension of the object. I strongly recommend Dr. Perry's admirable article to my readers.

[46] I have given a partial account of the matter in *Mind*, vol. x, p. 27, 1885 [reprinted above, pp. 136–152], and in the *Psychological Review,* vol. ii, p. 105, 1895. See also C. A. Strong's article in the *Journal of Philosophy, Psychology and Scientific Methods,* vol. i, p. 253, May 12, 1904. I hope myself very soon to recur to the matter. [See below, pp. 199 ff.]

objections that are sure to be urged against the entire theory as it stands.

V

First of all, this will be asked: "If experience has not 'conscious' existence, if it be not partly made of 'consciousness,' of what then is it made? Matter we know, and thought we know, and conscious content we know, but neutral and simple 'pure experience' is something we know not at all. Say *what* it consists of—for it must consist of something—or be willing to give it up!"

To this challenge the reply is easy. Although for fluency's sake I myself spoke early in this article of a stuff of pure experience, I have now to say that there is no *general* stuff of which experience at large is made. There are as many stuffs as there are 'natures' in the things experienced. If you ask what any one bit of pure experience is made of, the answer is always the same: "It is made of *that,* of just what appears, of space, of intensity, of flatness, brownness, heaviness, or what not." Shadworth Hodgson's analysis here leaves nothing to be desired.[47] Experience is only a collective name for all these sensible natures, and save for time and space (and, if you like, for 'being') there appears no universal element of which all things are made.

VI

The next objection is more formidable, in fact it sounds quite crushing when one hears it first.

"If it be the self-same piece of pure experience, taken twice over, that serves now as thought and now as thing"—so the objection runs—"how comes it that its attributes should differ so fundamentally in the two takings. As thing, the experience is extended; as thought, it occupies no space or place. As thing, it is red, hard, heavy; but who ever heard of a red, hard or heavy thought? Yet even now you said that an experience is made of just what appears, and what appears is just such adjectives. How can the one experience in its thing-function be made of them, consist of them, carry them as its own attributes, while in its thought-function it disowns them and attributes them elsewhere. There is a self-contradiction here from which the radical dualism of thought and thing is the only truth that can save us. Only if the thought is one kind of being can the adjectives exist in it 'intention-

[47] [Cf. Shadworth Hodgson: *The Metaphysic of Experience,* vol. I *passim; The Philosophy of Reflection,* bk. II, ch. IV, § 3. ED.]

ally' (to use the scholastic term); only if the thing is another kind, can they exist in it constitutively and energetically. No simple subject can take the same adjectives and at one time be qualified by it, and at another time be merely 'of' it, as of something only meant or known."

The solution insisted on by this objector, like many other common-sense solutions, grows the less satisfactory the more one turns it in one's mind. To begin with, *are* thought and thing as heterogeneous as is commonly said?

No one denies that they have some categories in common. Their relations to time are identical. Both, moreover, may have parts (for psychologists in general treat thoughts as having them); and both may be complex or simple. Both are of kinds, can be compared, added and subtracted and arranged in serial orders. All sorts of adjectives qualify our thoughts which appear incompatible with consciousness, being as such a bare diaphaneity. For instance, they are natural and easy, or laborious. They are beautiful, happy, intense, interesting, wise, idiotic, focal, marginal, insipid, confused, vague, precise, rational, casual, general, particular, and many things besides. Moreover, the chapters on 'Perception' in the psychology-books are full of facts that make for the essential homogeneity of thought with thing. How, if 'subject' and 'object' were separated 'by the whole diameter of being,' and had no attributes in common, could it be so hard to tell, in a presented and recognized material object, what part comes in through the sense-organs and what part comes 'out of one's own head'? Sensations and apperceptive ideas fuse here so intimately that you can no more tell where one begins and the other ends, than you can tell, in those cunning circular panoramas that have lately been exhibited, where the real foreground and the painted canvas join together.[48]

Descartes for the first time defined thought as the absolutely unextended, and later philosophers have accepted the description as correct. But what possible meaning has it to say that, when we think of a foot-rule or a square yard, extension is not attributable to our thought? Of every extended object the *adequate* mental picture must have all the extension of the object itself. The difference between objective and subjective extension is one of relation to a context solely. In the mind the various extents maintain no necessarily stubborn order relatively to each other, while in the physical world they bound each other stably, and, added together, make the great enveloping Unit

---

[48] Spencer's proof of his 'Transfigured Realism' (his doctrine that there is an absolutely non-mental reality) comes to mind as a splendid instance of the impossibility of establishing radical heterogeneity between thought and thing. All his painfully accumulated points of difference run gradually into their opposites, and are full of exceptions. [Cf. Spencer: *Principles of Psychology,* part VII, ch. XIX.]

which we believe in and call real Space. As 'outer,' they carry themselves adversely, so to speak, to one another, exclude one another and maintain their distances; while, as 'inner,' their order is loose, and they form a *durcheinander* in which unity is lost.[49] But to argue from this that inner experience is absolutely inextensive seems to me little short of absurd. The two worlds differ, not by the presence or absence of extension, but by the relations of the extensions which in both worlds exist.

Does not this case of extension now put us on the track of truth in the case of other qualities? It does; and I am surprised that the facts should not have been noticed long ago. Why, for example, do we call a fire hot, and water wet, and yet refuse to say that our mental state, when it is 'of' these objects, is either wet or hot? 'Intentionally,' at any rate, and when the mental state is a vivid image, hotness and wetness are in it just as much as they are in the physical experience. The reason is this, that, as the general chaos of all our experiences gets sifted, we find that there are some fires that will always burn sticks and always warm our bodies, and that there are some waters that will always put out fires; while there are other fires and waters that will not act at all. The general group of experiences that *act,* that do not only possess their natures intrinsically, but wear them adjectively and energetically, turning them against one another, comes inevitably to be contrasted with the group whose members, having identically the same natures, fail to manifest them in the 'energetic' way.[50] I make for myself now an experience of blazing fire; I place it near my body; but it does not warm me in the least. I lay a stick upon it, and the stick either burns or remains green, as I please. I call up water, and pour it on the fire, and absolutely no difference ensues. I account for all such facts by calling this whole train of experiences unreal, a mental train. Mental fire is what won't burn real sticks; mental water is what won't necessarily (though of course it may) put out even a mental fire. Mental knives may be sharp, but they won't cut real wood. Mental triangles are pointed, but their points won't wound. With 'real' objects, on the contrary, consequences always accrue; and thus the real experiences get sifted from the mental ones, the things from our thoughts of them, fanciful or true, and precipitated together as the stable part of the whole experience-chaos, under the name of the physical world. Of this our perceptual experiences are the nucleus, they being the originally *strong* experiences. We add a lot of conceptual experiences to

---

[49] I speak here of the complete inner life in which the mind plays freely with its materials. Of course the mind's free play is restricted when it seeks to copy real things in real space.

[50] [But there are also "mental activity trains," in which thoughts do "work on each other." Cf. below, p. 289, note. ED.]

them, making these strong also in imagination, and building out the remoter parts of the physical world by their means; and around this core of reality the world of laxly connected fancies and mere rhapsodical objects floats like a bank of clouds. In the clouds, all sorts of rules are violated which in the core are kept. Extensions there can be indefinitely located; motion there obeys no Newton's laws.

VII

There is a peculiar class of experiences to which, whether we take them as subjective or as objective, we *assign* their several natures as attributes, because in both contexts they affect their associates actively, though in neither quite as 'strongly' or as sharply as things affect one another by their physical energies. I refer here to *appreciations,* which form an ambiguous sphere of being, belonging with emotion on the one hand, and having objective 'value' on the other, yet seeming not quite inner nor quite outer, as if a diremption had begun but had not made itself complete.[51]

Experiences of painful objects, for example, are usually also painful experiences; perceptions of loveliness, of ugliness, tend to pass muster as lovely or as ugly perceptions; intuitions of the morally lofty are lofty intuitions. Sometimes the adjective wanders as if uncertain where to fix itself. Shall we speak of seductive visions or of visions of seductive things? Of wicked desires or of desires for wickedness? Of healthy thoughts or of thoughts of healthy objects? Of good impulses, or of impulses towards the good? Of feelings of anger, or of angry feelings? Both in the mind and in the thing, these natures modify their context, exclude certain associates and determine others, have their mates and incompatibles. Yet not as stubbornly as in the case of physical qualities, for beauty and ugliness, love and hatred, pleasant and painful can, in certain complex experiences, coexist.

If one were to make an evolutionary construction of how a lot of originally chaotic pure experiences became gradually differentiated into an orderly inner and outer world, the whole theory would turn upon one's success in explaining how or why the quality of an experience, once active, could become less so, and, from being an energetic attribute in some cases, elsewhere lapse into the status of an inert or merely internal 'nature.' This would be the 'evolution' of the psychical from the bosom of the physical, in which the esthetic, moral and otherwise emotional experiences would represent a halfway stage.

[51] [This topic is resumed below, pp. 271 ff. Ed.]

VIII

But a last cry of *non possumus* will probably go up from many readers. "All very pretty as a piece of ingenuity," they will say, "but our consciousness itself intuitively contradicts you. We, for our part, *know* that we are conscious. We *feel* our thought, flowing as a life within us, in absolute contrast with the objects which it so unremittingly escorts. We can not be faithless to this immediate intuition. The dualism is a fundamental *datum:* Let no man join what God has put asunder."

My reply to this is my last word, and I greatly grieve that to many it will sound materialistic. I can not help that, however, for I, too, have my intuitions and I must obey them. Let the case be what it may in others, I am as confident as I am of anything that, in myself, the stream of thinking (which I recognize emphatically as a phenomenon) is only a careless name for what, when scrutinized, reveals itself to consist chiefly of the stream of my breathing. The 'I think' which Kant said must be able to accompany all my objects, is the 'I breathe' which actually does accompany them. There are other internal facts besides breathing (intracephalic muscular adjustments, etc., of which I have said a word in my larger Psychology), and these increase the assets of 'consciousness,' so far as the latter is subject to immediate perception;[52] but breath, which was ever the original of 'spirit,' breath moving outwards, between the glottis and the nostrils, is, I am persuaded, the essence out of which philosophers have constructed the entity known to them as consciousness. *That entity is fictitious, while thoughts in the concrete are fully real. But thoughts in the concrete are made of the same stuff as things are.*

I wish I might believe myself to have made that plausible in this article. In another article I shall try to make the general notion of a world composed of pure experiences still more clear.

[52] [*Principles of Psychology*, vol. i, pp. 299–305. Cf. below, pp. 283–284, note.]

THE NOTION* OF CONSCIOUSNESS**

I should like to convey to you several doubts which have occurred to me on the subject of the notion of consciousness that holds sway in all our treatises on psychology.

Psychology is usually defined as the science of the facts, or the *phenomena* or, yet, the *states* of consciousness. Whether one admits consciousness to be fastened to personal egos, or believes it to be impersonal after the fashion of Kant's "transcendental ego," of the *Bewusstheit* or the *Bewusstsein überhaupt* of our German contemporaries, it is always considered as possessing a stuff or quality of being absolutely distinct from the stuff of material objects which, by a mysterious gift, it can represent and know. Taken in their materiality, material things are not *felt,* they are not objects of *experience,* nor are they *related* as such. In order that they may assume the form of the system in which we feel ourselves to be living, it is necessary that material things *appear;* and this fact of appearance, superadded to their raw existence, is called the consciousness which we have of them or, perhaps (according to the panpsychical hypothesis) which they have of themselves.

There we have an inveterate dualism which it seems impossible to dismiss from our view of the world. The world may well exist by itself, but we know nothing of this because for us it is exclusively an object of experience; and the indispensable condition for this experience is that the world be related to witnesses, that it be known by a mental subject or subjects. Object and subject, these are the two legs without which it seems philosophy could not take a step forward.

All the schools—Scholastic, Cartesian, Kantian, Neo-Kantian—are in agreement on this, all admit to a fundamental dualism. It is true that the positivism or agnosticism of our own day—which prides itself as coming under the physical sciences—freely assumes the name of monism. But it is a monism in name only. It posits an unknown reality, but then tells us that this reality always presents itself under two "aspects," on the one side consciousness and on the other matter; and

* This is the word James uses in "Does 'Consciousness' Exist?" p. 2. [Translator's note.]

** From: E.R.E., 206–233. [A communication made, in French, at the Fifth International Congress of Psychology, in Rome, April 30, 1905. The original was reprinted from the *Archives de Psychologie,* vol. v. No. 17, June, 1905. ED.] "This communication is a résumé, by necessity very condensed, which the author has developed in the course of these latter months by a series of articles, published in *The Journal of Philosophy, Psychology, and Scientific Methods,* 1904 and 1905"—W.J.

these two sides remain as irreducible as the fundamental attributes of Spinoza's God, extension and thought. Contemporary monism is, at bottom, pure Spinozism.

Now, how to portray this consciousness the existence of which we are all so disposed to admit? We are told that it is impossible to define it but that all of us have an immediate intuition of it: to begin with, consciousness is conscious of itself. Ask the first person you meet, man or woman, psychologist or layman, and he will tell you that he feels himself thinking, enjoying, suffering, willing, just as he feels himself breathing. That person perceives directly his mental life as a sort of interior current—active, light, fluid, delicate, diaphanous, so to speak—and absolutely different from whatever is material. In short, subjective existence seems to be not only a logically indispensable condition for the existence of an objective world which *appears,* it is also an element of experience itself which we feel directly, for the same reason we feel our own body.

How can we not recognize the dualism of Ideas and Things; how can we doubt the absolute heterogeneity of Feelings and Objects?

So-called scientific psychology admits this heterogeneity, as did the old spiritualist psychology. How not admit it? Each science arbitrarily carves out a field from the scheme of things in which to lodge itself and the content of which it describes and studies. Now, psychology takes precisely for its domain the field of the facts of consciousness. It postulates these facts without criticizing them, and opposes them to material facts; and, also without criticizing the notion of the latter, psychology relates them to consciousness by the mysterious bond of *knowing,* of *apperception,* which is for psychology a third kind of fundamental and ultimate fact. By following this approach contemporary psychology has enjoyed great triumphs. It has been able to fashion a sketch of the evolution of conscious life by conceiving the latter as adapting itself more and more completely to the environing physical world. It has been able to establish a parallelism within dualism, that of psychical facts and cerebral events. It has explained delusions, hallucinations, and, up to a certain point, mental illnesses. These are handsome achievements; but many problems yet remain. Above all, general philosophy—which has as its task the scrutiny of all postulates—finds paradoxes and obstacles precisely where science takes no notice; and only dilettantes of popular science are never perplexed. The more one probes into the bottom of things, the more enigmas one finds. And, for my part, I confess that, since I began to concern myself seriously with psychology, this old dualism of matter and thought, this heterogeneity of the two stuffs posited as an absolute, has always presented difficulties for me. I should like to engage you now with several of these difficulties.

To begin with, there is one which I am sure has struck you all. Let us take outer perception, the direct sensation which, for example, the walls of these rooms give us. Can we say that the psychical and the physical are absolutely heterogeneous? On the contrary, they are so little heterogeneous that if we adopt the common-sense point of view, if we disregard all explanatory inventions—molecules and ether waves, for example, which at bottom are metaphysical entities—if, in short, we take reality naïvely, as it is given, an immediate; then this sensible reality on which our vital interests rest and from which all our actions proceed, this sensible reality and the sensation which we have of it are absolutely identical one with the other at the time the sensation occurs. Reality is apperception itself. The words, "the walls of this room," have only one meaning, and that is the fresh and sonorous whiteness which surrounds us, divided as it is by these windows and bounded by these lines and angles. In this instance, the content of the physical is none other than the psychical. Subject and object confuse,[53] as it were.

It is Berkeley who first gave prestige to this truth. *Esse est percipi.* Our sensations are not small inner duplicates of things, they are the things themselves in so far as the things are presented to us. And whatever one may wish to believe of the absent, hidden, and, so to speak, private life of things; whatever may be the hypothetical constructions of this private life; it remains true that the public life of things, this present actuality with which things confront us, from which all our theoretical constructions are derived and to which they must all return and be linked under penalty of floating in the air and in the unreal; this actuality, I say, is homogeneous—nay, more than homogeneous, but numerically one—with a certain part of our inner life.

So much for outer perception. When one addresses oneself to imagination, to memory, or to faculties of abstract representation—although the facts in these instances are much more complicated—I believe that the same essential homogeneity is revealed. In order to simplify the problem, let us exclude at the outset all sensible reality. Let us take pure thought, such as it occurs in dreams or reveries, or in remembrance of the past. In this case as well, does not the stuff of experience perform a double duty; do not the physical and the psychical intermingle and con-fuse as one? If I dream of a golden mountain, surely it does not exist outside of the dream; but *in* the dream the mountain is of a perfectly physical nature or stuff, it is *as* physical that it appears to me. If at this moment I allow myself to recall my home in America and particulars of my recent embarkation for Italy, what is the pure phenomenon or the fact resulting thereby? The reply would be that it is my thought and its content. But, again, this content, what

[53] *Se confondent.* [Tr.]

is it? It bears the form of a part of the real world; a part, it is true, six thousand kilometers distant in space and six weeks in time; but a part of the real world bound to this room by a crowd of things, objects, and events homogeneous with this room on the one hand and with the object of my recollection on the other.

This content is not given to be at first a tiny inner fact which I would afterwards project into the distance; it presents itself at the first onset as the distant fact itself. And the act of thinking this content as well as the consciousness I have of it, what are they? Are they at bottom anything other than retrospective ways of naming the content itself at the time when one separates the content from all these physical intermediaries and reties it to a new group of associates which make it re-enter into my mental life—such associates as, for example, the emotions which it has awakened in me, the attention which I give to it, and my ideas of a few minutes ago which evoked it as a recollection? It is only in becoming related to these latter associates that the phenomenon becomes classed as *thought;* so long as it remains related to the former, that is, the physical intermediaries, it remains an *objective* phenomenon.

It is true that we usually oppose our inner representations to objects and that we consider them as little copies, as enfeebled tracings or counterparts of the latter. It is simply that a present object has a vivacity and clearness superior to those of the representation. The present object thus serves as a contrast to it and, to employ Taine's excellent term, as a *reductive* of it. When the two are present together, the object takes the foreground and the representation "recedes," it becomes an "absent" thing. But this present object, what is it in itself? Of what stuff is it made? Of the same stuff as the representation. It is made of *sensations;* it is a thing perceived. Its *esse* is *percipi,* and object and representation are generically homogeneous.

If at this moment I think of my hat which a while ago I left in the cloak-room, where is the dualism, the discontinuity between the hat of my thoughts and the real hat? My mind is thinking of a truly *absent hat.* I reckon with it practically as with a reality. If it were present on this table, the hat would occasion a movement of my hand: I would pick it up. In the same way, this hat as a concept, this idea-hat, will presently determine the direction of my steps. I will go retrieve it. The idea I have of it will last up to the sensible presence of the hat, and then will blend harmoniously with it.

I conclude, then, that—although there be a practical dualism—inasmuch as representations are distinguished from objects, stand in their stead and lead us to them, there is no reason to attribute to them an essential difference of nature. Thought and actuality are made of one and the same stuff, the stuff of experience in general.

The psychology of outer perception leads us to the same conclusion. When I perceive the object before me as a table of such and such a shape, at such a distance, I am told that this fact of perception is due to two factors: a sensible matter that penetrates into me by means of my eyes and which provides the element of real exteriority, and ideas which are awakened, which meet with this reality, classify and interpret it. But who can distinguish in the table concretely perceived between what is sensation and what is idea? The external and the internal, the extended and the not extended fuse and make an indissoluble marriage. This brings to mind those circular panoramas in which real objects—rocks, grass, broken carts, etc., placed in the foreground—are so cunningly joined to the canvas backdrop on which there is represented a battle-scene or a vast landscape, that one can no longer distinguish between objects and painted representations. Seams and joints are imperceptible.

Could this occur if object and idea were absolutely dissimilar in nature?

I am convinced that considerations similar to those I have just expressed will have already given rise to some doubts, in you as well, on the subject of so-called dualism.

Still other reasons for doubt arise. There is a whole sphere of adjectives and attributes which are neither exclusively objective nor subjective in nature and which we employ at times in one fashion and then in another, as if delighting in their ambiguity. I am speaking of qualities which we *appreciate* in things, so to speak: their esthetic or moral side, their value for us. For example, where does beauty reside? Is it in the statue, the sonata, or in our mind? George Santayana, my colleague at Harvard, has written a book[53a] on esthetics in which he calls beauty "pleasure objectified"; and, in truth, it is precisely in this case that one could speak of projection outward. We say indiscriminately, "an agreeable warmth," or "an agreeable sensation of warmth." The rarity and preciousness of a diamond appear to us to be qualities essential to it. We speak of a frightful storm, a hateful man, a mean action, and we think to be speaking objectively, although in a strict sense these terms express only relations to our own emotive sensibility. We speak even of an arduous road, a sullen sky, a superb sunset. All this animistic manner of looking at things, which appears to have been mankind's earliest manner of thinking, may well be explained (and Mr. Santayana, in another and very recent book,[53b] has in fact explained it thusly) by the practice of attributing to the object *all* which we feel in its presence. The distinction between subjective and objective as the act of a very advanced reflection is something which

53a *The Sense of Beauty*, pp. 44 ff.
53b *The Life of Reason* [vol. I, "Reason in Common Sense," p. 142].

we still prefer to put off in many places. Unless practical necessity forcefully pulls us away from it, it seems that we prefer to indulge in vagueness.

Even today, secondary qualities themselves—heat, sound, light—have but a vague place in the scheme of understanding. In the common-sense meaning and for practical purposes, they are absolutely objective, absolutely physical. For the physicist, they are subjective. For him, only form, mass, and movement have an outer reality. On the contrary, for the idealistic philosopher form and movement are as much subjective as light and heat, and only the unknown thing-in-itself, the "noumena," enjoys a complete and extra-mental reality.

Our intimate sensations still retain this ambiguity of place in the scheme of understanding. There are delusions of movement which prove that our first sensations of movement were generalized. It is the entire world which moved, with us. Now we discriminate between our own movement from that of the objects about us, and among these objects we discriminate those which are at rest. But, for example, there are states of dizziness in which even today we fall back into the earlier condition of indifferentiation.

You know, undoubtedly, of the theory which has made of the emotions the sum of visceral and muscular sensations. It has occasioned many controversies, and no one opinion has yet won unanimous support. You know, as well, of the controversies on the nature of mental activity. Some maintain that it is a purely spiritual force which we are in a condition immediately to perceive as such. Others claim that that which we call mental activity (for example, effort, attention) is only the felt reflex of certain effects of which our organism is the seat, such as: muscular tensions in the skull and in the throat, arrest or course of breathing, flow of blood, etc.

However these controversies may be resolved, their very existence proves one thing quite clearly: it is very difficult, or even absolutely impossible, to know solely by intimate examination whether certain phenomena are of a physical nature—occupying space, etc.—or whether they are of a purely psychical and inner nature. We must always find reasons to support our opinion; we must look for the most probable classification of the phenomenon; and in the final accounting it could well be that all our usual classifications may have derived their motives more from practical needs than from some faculty we possess of perceiving two ultimate and diverse stuffs which together are supposed to comprise the scheme of things. Our own individual body offers a practical and often violent contrast to all the rest of the environing world. All that happens inside this body is more intimate and important for us than that which happens elsewhere. It becomes identified with our ego; it is classed with it. Soul, life, breath—who can truly and exactly distinguish between these? Even our representations and our memories, which act upon the physical world only by means of our body, seem to belong to the body itself: we treat them as inner and put them in the same class as affective sentiments. In short, we must acknowledge that the problem of the dualism of thought and matter is quite far from a final resolution.

And thus I have completed the first part of my address. Ladies and Gentlemen, I have wanted to impress you with my doubts and of the reality of the problem, as well as of its importance.

As for me, after many years of hesitation I have ended by making my choice squarely. I believe that consciousness (as it is commonly represented, either as an entity, or as pure activity, but in any case as being fluid, inextended, diaphanous, devoid of self-content, but directly self-knowing—spiritual, in short), I believe, I say, that this sort of consciousness is pure fancy, and that the sum of concrete realities which the word consciousness should cover deserves quite a different description. Besides, this deserved description is one which a philosophy attentive to facts and capable of a little analysis should be henceforth capable of providing, or, rather, capable of beginning to provide. And these words lead me to the second part of my address. It will be shorter than the first part because, if I were to develop it on the same scale as the first, it would be far too long. As a consequence, it is necessary that I limit myself exclusively to indispensable indications.

Let us assume that consciousness—*Bewusstheit,* conceived of as stuff, entity, activity, as irreducible half of every experience—is suppressed, that the fundamental and, so to speak, ontological dualism is abolished, and that that which we suppose to exist is only that which until now has been called the *content,* the *Inhalt,* of consciousness. How can philosophy carry on with the sort of vague monism which results therefrom? I shall try to indicate to you several positive suggestions on this matter, although I fear that for the lack of necessary development my ideas will not shed a very great light. It may perhaps be enough for me to indicate the beginning of the road to follow.

At bottom, why do we cling so tenaciously to this idea of a consciousness superadded to the existence of the content of things? Why do we lay claim to it so strongly to the point that whoever would deny it would seem to us to be a sorry jester rather than a thinker? Is it not in order to preserve this undeniable fact: that the content of experience has not only an existence of its own, as immanent and intrinsic, but also that each part of this content fades, so to speak, into neighboring parts, gives an account of itself to others, in some fashion issues from itself in order to be known; and that thereby the entire field of experience is found to be transparent from part to part, or is constituted as a room filled with mirrors?

This bilaterality of the parts of experience—namely on the one hand, that they *are,* with qualities of their own; and, on the other hand, that they are related to other parts and are *known*—is affirmed by the prevailing opinion, which explains the bilaterality by a fundamentally dualistic inner constitution belonging to every bit of experience as such. One says, in this sheet of paper there is not only the content, whiteness, thinness, etc., there is also this second fact of the consciousness of this whiteness and this thinness. This function of being "reported," of being part of the entire scheme of a more comprehensive experience, is raised to an ontological fact, and this fact is lodged in the very interior of the paper by coupling it with the paper's whiteness and its thinness. What is supposed here is not an extrinsic relation but, rather, a half part of the phenomenon itself.

I believe that, in short, reality is currently represented as being constituted in the same fashion as are the "colors" we use in painting. We have, at first, the coloring materials, which correspond to the content; and there is a menstruum, oil or size, which holds them in suspension, and which corresponds to consciousness. This is a complete dualism in which, by employing certain procedures, one can separate every element from the other by means of subtraction. It is in this manner that we are assured that by making a great effort of introspective abstraction we can capture our consciousness life-like, as a pure spiritual activity, neglecting almost completely the materials which consciousness illuminates at any given moment.

Now I ask you, could we not overthrow quite entirely this manner of viewing the problem? In fact, let us suppose that primary reality is of a neutral nature, and let us call it by some name also ambiguous, such as *phenomenon, datum,* or *Vorfindung.* As for me, I would willingly use the plural, and I give it the name *pure experiences.* Call this a monism, if you will; but it is an altogether rudimentary monism and absolutely opposed to the so-called bilateral monism of scientific positivism or that of the Spinozists.

These pure experiences exist and succeed one another; they enter into infinitely varied relations; and these relations are themselves essential parts of the web of experiences. There is a "Consciousness" of these relations for the same reason that there is a "Consciousness" of their terms. As a result, fields of experiences are observable and distinguishable and, in the light of the great variety of its relations, one self-identical experience can play a role in several fields at the same time. It is thus that in a certain context of associates one experience would be classed as a physical phenomenon, while in another setting it would figure as a fact of consciousness, almost as one self-identical particle of ink can belong simultaneously to two lines—one vertical and the other horizontal—provided the particle is situated at their intersection.

In order to fix our ideas, let us take the experience which at this moment we have of the place where we are, the experience of these walls, this table, these chairs, this room. In this experience—full, concrete, undivided, such as it is, there, a *datum*—the objective physical world and the inner personal world of each one of us meet and fuse as do the lines at their intersection. As a physical thing this room is related to all the rest of the building, a building which we in this room do not know and shall not know. It owes its existence to a whole history of financiers, architects, and workmen. It weighs on the ground; it will last indefinitely in time; if a fire were to break out, the chairs and the table now in it would be quickly reduced to ashes.

But, as a personal experience, as something "reported," known, conscious, this room has quite different dimensions. Its antecedents are not the workmen; they are our thoughts respective to this instant. Soon it will figure only as a transitory fact in our biographies, associated with pleasant memories. As a psychical phenomenon this room has no weight whatever; its furniture is not combustible. It exerts no physical force except only on our brains, and much within us yet denies this influence; whereas the physical room is in a relation of physical influence with all the rest of the world.

And yet it is a question in both cases of absolutely the same room. So long as we do not engage in speculative physics, as long as we view the matter in a common-sense way, it is the room as seen and felt which is surely the physical room. Of what are we speaking, then, if not of *that*, of that same part of material nature which all our minds embrace at this moment, which enters such as it is into the actual and intimate experience of each one of us, and which our memory will consider always as an integral part of our history? It is absolutely the same stuff which, accordingly to the context in which one considers it, figures simultaneously as a material and physical fact or as a fact of intimate consciousness.

I believe, then, that one should not treat consciousness and matter as being of disparate stuff. One obtains neither one nor the other, neither consciousness nor matter, by subtraction, by neglecting each time the other half of an experience of double composition. On the contrary, experiences are originally of a rather simple nature. They *become* conscious in their entirety; they *become* physical in their entirety; and it is *by the way of addition* that this result comes about. Forasmuch as experiences extend in time, enter into relations of physical influence, reciprocally split, warm, illuminate, etc., each other, we make of them a field apart which we call the physical world. On the other hand, forasmuch as they are transitory, physically inert, with a succession which does not follow a determined order but seems rather to obey emotive fancies, we make of them another field which we call the psychical world. It is by its entry at present into a great number of these psychical groups that this room now becomes a conscious thing, a known and reported thing. In becoming henceforth a part of our respective biographies, this room will not be attended by that stupid and monotonous repetition of itself in time which characterizes its physical existence. Rather, it will be attended by other experiences which will be discontinuous with it, or which will have that very special kind of continuity which we call memory.

By tomorrow it will have acquired its place in the past of each one of us; but the various presents to which all these pasts will be tied tomorrow will be quite different from the present which this room will possess tomorrow as a physical entity.

The two kinds of fields (physical and psychical) are made up of experiences, but the relations of the experiences among themselves differ from one field to the other. It is, therefore, by the addition of other phenonema that a given phenomenon becomes conscious or known, and not by a halving of interior stuff. Knowledge of things *supervenes* them; it is not immanent in them. It is a fact neither of a transcendental ego nor of a *Bewusstheit* or act of consciousness which would animate each one of them. *They know each other,* or rather, there are some which know the others; and the relation which we call knowledge is in many cases but a series of intermediary experiences perfectly susceptible of being described in concrete terms. Knowledge is not at all a matter of the transcendental mystery in which so many philosophers have delighted.

But this problem would lead us too far off. I cannot enter here into all the recesses of the theory of knowledge or of what you Italians call gnosiology. I must remain satisfied with these abbreviated remarks or simple suggestions which are, I fear, still quite obscure for want of necessary development.

Allow me, then, to sum up my views—too summarily and in a somewhat dogmatic style—in the following six theses:

1. *Consciousness as it is ordinarily understood does not exist, any more than does that Matter to which Berkeley gave the coup de grâce;*
2. *What does exist and constitutes the portion of truth covered over by the word "Consciousness" is the susceptibility possessed by the parts of experience to be reported or known;*
3. *This susceptibility is explained by the fact that certain experiences can lead some to others by means of distinctly characterized intermediary experiences, in such a fashion that some play the role of known things, the others that of knowing subjects;*
4. *These two roles can be defined perfectly without departing from*

the flow of experience itself and without invoking anything
transcendental;

5. The attributes "subject" and "object," "represented" and "representative," "thing" and "thought" [54] mean, then, a practical
distinction of the utmost importance, but a distinction which is
of a FUNCTIONAL order only, and not at all ontological as
understood by classical dualism;

6. Finally, things and thought are not fundamentally heterogeneous; they are made of one and the same stuff, which as such
cannot be defined but only experienced; and which, if one
wishes, one can call the stuff of experience in general.

Translated by Salvatore Saladino

A WORLD OF PURE EXPERIENCE* [55]

It is difficult not to notice a curious unrest in the philosophic atmosphere of the time, a loosening of old landmarks, a softening of oppositions, a mutual borrowing from one another on the part of systems
anciently closed, and an interest in new suggestions, however vague,
as if the one thing sure were the inadequacy of the extant school-
solutions. The dissatisfaction with these seems due for the most part
to a feeling that they are too abstract and academic. Life is confused
and superabundant, and what the younger generation appears to crave
is more of the temperament of life in its philosophy, even though it
were at some cost of logical rigor and of formal purity. Transcendental idealism is inclining to let the world wag incomprehensibly, in spite
of its Absolute Subject and his unity of purpose. Berkeleyan idealism
is abandoning the principle of parsimony and dabbling in panpsychic
speculations. Empiricism flirts with teleology; and, strangest of all,
natural realism, so long decently buried, raises its head above the turf,
and finds glad hands outstretched from the most unlikely quarters to

[54] Quotes added. [Tr.]

* From: E.R.E., 39–91.

[55] [Reprinted from the Journal of Philosophy, Psychology, and Scientific
Methods, vol. I, 1904, No. 20, September 29, and No. 21, October 13. Pp. 199–
208 have also been reprinted, with some omissions, alterations and additions, in
The Meaning of Truth, pp. 102–120. The alterations have been adopted in the
present text. This essay is referred to in A Pluralistic Universe, below, p. 293,
note 191. ED.]

help it to its feet again. We are all biased by our personal feelings, I know, and I am personally discontented with extant solutions; so I seem to read the signs of a great unsettlement, as if the upheaval of more real conceptions and more fruitful methods were imminent, as if a true landscape might result, less clipped, straight-edged and artificial.

If philosophy be really on the eve of any considerable rearrangement, the time should be propitious for any one who has suggestions of his own to bring forward. For many years past my mind has been growing into a certain type of *Weltanschauung*. Rightly or wrongly, I have got to the point where I can hardly see things in any other pattern. I propose, therefore, to describe the pattern as clearly as I can consistently with great brevity, and to throw my description into the bubbling vat of publicity where, jostled by rivals and torn by critics, it will eventually either disappear from notice, or else, if better luck befall it, quietly subside to the profundities, and serve as a possible ferment of new growths or a nucleus of new crystallization.

I. RADICAL EMPIRICISM

I give the name of 'radical empiricism' to my *Weltanschauung*. Empiricism is known as the opposite of rationalism. Rationalism tends to emphasize universals and to make wholes prior to parts in the order of logic as well as that of being. Empiricism, on the contrary, lays the explanatory stress upon the part, the element, the individual, and treats the whole as a collection and the universal as an abstraction. My description of things, accordingly, starts with the parts and makes of the whole a being of the second order. It is essentially a mosaic philosophy, a philosophy of plural facts, like that of Hume and his descendants, who refer these facts neither to Substances in which they inhere nor to an Absolute Mind that creates them as its objects. But it differs from the Humian type of empiricism in one particular which makes me add the epithet radical.

To be radical, an empiricism must neither admit into its constructions any element that is not directly experienced, nor exclude from them any element that is directly experienced. For such a philosophy, *the relations that connect experiences must themselves be experienced relations, and any kind of relation experienced must be accounted as 'real' as anything else in the system.* Elements may indeed be redistributed, the original placing of things getting corrected, but a real place must be found for every kind of thing experienced, whether term or relation, in the final philosophic arrangement.

Now, ordinary empiricism, in spite of the fact that conjunctive and disjunctive relations present themselves as being fully co-ordinate parts of experience, has always shown a tendency to do away with the connections of things, and to insist most on the disjunctions. Berkeley's nominalism, Hume's statement that whatever things we distinguish are as 'loose and separate' as if they had 'no manner of connection,' James Mill's denial that similars have anything 'really' in common, the resolution of the causal tie into habitual sequence, John Mill's account of both physical things and selves as composed of discontinuous possibilities, and the general pulverization of all Experience by association and the mind-dust theory, are examples of what I mean.[56]

The natural result of such a world-picture has been the efforts of rationalism to correct its incoherencies by the addition of transexperiential agents of unification, substances, intellectual categories and powers, or Selves; whereas, if empiricism had only been radical and taken everything that comes without disfavor, conjunction as well as separation, each at its face value, the results would have called for no such artificial correction. *Radical empiricism,* as I understand it, *does full justice to conjunctive relations,* without, however, treating them as rationalism always tends to treat them, as being true in some supernal way, as if the unity of things and their variety belonged to different orders of truth and vitality altogether.

II. CONJUNCTIVE RELATIONS

Relations are of different degrees of intimacy. Merely to be 'with' one another in a universe of discourse is the most external relation that terms can have, and seems to involve nothing whatever as to farther consequences. Simultaneity and time-interval come next, and then space-adjacency and distance. After them, similarity and difference, carrying the possibility of many inferences. Then relations of activity, tying terms into series involving change, tendency, resistance, and the causal order generally. Finally, the relation experienced between terms that form states of mind, and are immediately conscious of continuing each other. The organization of the Self as a system of memories, purposes, strivings, fulfilments or disappointments, is incidental to this most intimate of all relations, the terms of which seem in many cases actually to compenetrate and suffuse each other's being.[57]

---

[56] [Cf. Berkeley: *Principles of Human Knowledge,* Introduction; Hume: *An Enquiry Concerning Human Understanding,* sect. VII, part II (Selby-Bigge's edition, p. 74); James Mill: *Analysis of the Phenomena of the Human Mind,* ch. VIII; J. S. Mill: *An Examination of Sir William Hamilton's Philosophy,* ch. XI, XII; W. K. Clifford: *Lectures and Essays,* pp. 274 ff.]

[57] [See "The Experience of Activity," below, pp. 277–291.]

Philosophy has always turned on grammatical particles. With, near, next, like, from, towards, against, because, for, through, my— these words designate types of conjunctive relation arranged in a roughly ascending order of intimacy and inclusiveness. *A priori,* we can imagine a universe of withness but no nextness; or one of nextness but no likeness, or of likeness with no activity, or of activity with no purpose, or of purpose with no ego. These would be universes, each with its own grade of unity. The universe of human experience is, by one or another of its parts, of each and all these grades. Whether or not it possibly enjoys some still more absolute grade of union does not appear upon the surface.

Taken as it does appear, our universe is to a large extent chaotic. No one single type of connection runs through all the experiences that compose it. If we take space-relations, they fail to connect minds into any regular system. Causes and purposes obtain only among special series of facts. The self-relation seems extremely limited and does not link two different selves together. *Prima facie,* if you should liken the universe of absolute idealism to an aquarium, a crystal globe in which goldfish are swimming, you would have to compare the empiricist universe to something more like one of those dried human heads with which the Dyaks of Borneo deck their lodges. The skull forms a solid nucleus; but innumerable feathers, leaves, strings, beads, and loose appendices of every description float and dangle from it, and, save that they terminate in it, seem to have nothing to do with one another. Even so my experiences and yours float and dangle, terminating, it is true, in a nucleus of common perception, but for the most part out of sight and irrelevant and unimaginable to one another. This imperfect intimacy, this bare relation of *withness* between some parts of the sum total of experience and other parts, is the fact that ordinary empiricism over-emphasizes against rationalism, the latter always tending to ignore it unduly. Radical empiricism, on the contrary, is fair to both the unity and the disconnection. It finds no reason for treating either as illusory. It allots to each its definite sphere of description, and agrees that there appear to be actual forces at work which tend, as time goes on, to make the unity greater.

The conjunctive relation that has given most trouble to philosophy is *the co-conscious transition,* so to call it, by which one experience passes into another when both belong to the same self. About the facts there is no question. My experiences and your experiences are 'with' each other in various external ways, but mine pass into mine, and yours pass into yours in a way in which yours and mine never pass into one another. Within each of our personal histories, subject, object, interest and purpose *are continuous or may be continuous.*[58] Per-

[58] The psychology books have of late described the facts here with approximate adequacy. I may refer to the chapters on 'The Stream of Thought' and on

sonal histories are processes of change in time, and *the change itself is one of the things immediately experienced*. 'Change' in this case means continuous as opposed to discontinuous transition. But continuous transition is one sort of a conjunctive relation; and to be a radical empiricist means to hold fast to this conjunctive relation of all others, for this is the strategic point, the position through which, if a hole be made, all the corruptions of dialectics and all the metaphysical fictions pour into our philosophy. The holding fast to this relation means taking it at its face value, neither less nor more; and to take it at its face value means first of all to take it just as we feel it, and not to confuse ourselves with abstract talk *about* it, involving words that drive us to invent secondary conceptions in order to neutralize their suggestions and to make our actual experience again seem rationally possible.

What I do feel simply when a later moment of my experience succeeds an earlier one is that though they are two moments, the transition from the one to the other is *continuous*. Continuity here is a definite sort of experience; just as definite as is the *discontinuity-experience* which I find it impossible to avoid when I seek to make the transition from an experience of my own to one of yours. In this latter case I have to get on and off again, to pass from a thing lived to another thing only conceived, and the break is positively experienced and noted. Though the functions exerted by my experience and by yours may be the same (*e.g.,* the same objects known and the same purposes followed), yet the sameness has in this case to be ascertained expressly (and often with difficulty and uncertainty) after the break has been felt; whereas in passing from one of my own moments to another the sameness of object and interest is unbroken, and both the earlier and the later experience are of things directly lived.

There is no other *nature,* no other whatness than this absence of break and this sense of continuity in that most intimate of all conjunctive relations, the passing of one experience into another when they belong to the same self. And this whatness is real empirical 'content,' just as the whatness of separation and discontinuity is real content in the contrasted case. Practically to experience one's personal continuum in this living way is to know the originals of the ideas of continuity and of sameness, to know what the words stand for concretely, to own all that they can ever mean. But all experiences have their conditions; and over-subtle intellects, thinking about the facts here, and asking how they are possible, have ended by substituting a lot of static objects of conception for the direct perceptual experiences.

---

the Self in my own *Principles of Psychology,* as well as to S. H. Hodgson's *Metaphysic of Experience,* vol. I, ch. VII and VIII.

"Sameness," they have said, "must be a stark numerical identity; it can't run on from next to next. Continuity can't mean mere absence of gap; for if you say two things are in immediate contact, *at* the contact how can they be two? If, on the other hand, you put a relation of transition between them, that itself is a third thing, and needs to be related or hitched to its terms. An infinite series is involved," and so on. The result is that from difficulty to difficulty, the plain conjunctive experience has been discredited by both schools, the empiricists leaving things permanently disjoined, and the rationalist remedying the looseness by their Absolutes or Substances, or whatever other fictitious agencies of union they may have employed.[59] From all which artificiality we can be saved by a couple of simple reflections: first, that conjunctions and separations are, at all events, co-ordinate phenomena which, if we take experiences at their face value, must be accounted equally real; and second, that if we insist on treating things as really separate when they are given as continuously joined, invoking, when union is required, transcendental principles to overcome the separateness we have assumed, then we ought to stand ready to perform the converse act. We ought to invoke higher principles of *dis*-union, also, to make our merely experienced *dis*junctions more truly real. Failing thus, we ought to let the originally given continuities stand on their own bottom. We have no right to be lopsided or to blow capriciously hot and cold.

III. THE COGNITIVE RELATION

The first great pitfall from which such a radical standing by experience will save us is an artificial conception of the *relations between knower and known*. Throughout the history of philosophy the subject and its object have been treated as absolutely discontinuous entities; and thereupon the presence of the latter to the former, or the 'apprehension' by the former of the latter, has assumed a paradoxical character which all sorts of theories had to be invented to overcome. Representative theories put a mental 'representation,' 'image,' or 'content' into the gap, as a sort of intermediary. Common-sense theories left the gap untouched, declaring our mind able to clear it by a self-transcending leap. Transcendentalist theories left it impossible to traverse by finite knowers, and brought an Absolute in to perform the saltatory act. All the while, in the very bosom of the finite experience, every conjunction required to make the relation intelligible is given in full. Either the knower and the known are:

(1) the self-same piece of experience taken twice over in different contexts; or they are

[59] [See "The Thing and its Relations," below, pp. 214–226.]

(2) two pieces of *actual* experience belonging to the same subject, with definite tracts of conjunctive transitional experience between them; or

(3) the known is a *possible* experience either of that subject or another, to which the said conjunctive transitions *would* lead, if sufficiently prolonged.

To discuss all the ways in which one experience may function as the knower of another, would be incompatible with the limits of this essay.[60] I have just treated of type 1, the kind of knowledge called perception.[61] This is the type of case in which the mind enjoys direct 'acquaintance' with a present object. In the other types the mind has 'knowledge-about' an object not immediately there. Of type 2, the simplest sort of conceptual knowledge, I have given some account in two [earlier] articles.[62] Type 3 can always formally and hypothetically be reduced to type 2, so that a brief description of that type will put the present reader sufficiently at my point of view, and make him see what the actual meanings of the mysterious cognitive relation may be.

Suppose me to be sitting here in my library at Cambridge, at ten minutes' walk from 'Memorial Hall,' and to be thinking truly of the latter object. My mind may have before it only the name, or it may have a clear image, or it may have a very dim image of the hall, but such intrinsic differences in the image make no difference in its cognitive function. Certain *extrinsic* phenomena, special experiences of conjunction, are what impart to the image, be it what it may, its knowing office.

For instance, if you ask me what hall I mean by my image, and I can tell you nothing; or if I fail to point or lead you towards the Harvard Delta; or if, being led by you, I am uncertain whether the

---

[60] For brevity's sake I altogether omit mention of the type constituted by knowledge of the truth of general propositions. This type has been thoroughly and, so far as I can see, satisfactorily, elucidated in Dewey's *Studies in Logical Theory*. Such propositions are reducible to the *S-is-P* form; and the 'terminus' that verifies and fulfils is the *SP* in combination. Of course percepts may be involved in the mediating experiences, or in the 'satisfactoriness' of the *P* in its new position.

[61] [See above, pp. 172–174.]

[62] ["On the Function of Cognition," *Mind*, vol. x, 1885, and "The Knowing of Things Together," *Psychological Review*, vol. II, 1895. [These articles are reprinted in full, above, pp. 136–152, and 152–168.—J. J. McD.] These articles and their doctrine, unnoticed apparently by any one else, have lately gained favorable comment from Professor Strong. ["A Naturalistic Theory of the Reference of Thought to Reality," *Journal of Philosophy, Psychology, and Scientific Methods*, vol. I, 1904.] Dr. Dickinson S. Miller has independently thought out the same results ["The Meaning of Truth and Error," *Philosophical Review*, vol. II, 1893; "The Confusion of Function and Content in Mental Analysis," *Psychological Review*, vol. II, 1895], which Strong accordingly dubs the James-Miller theory of cognition.

Hall I see be what I had in mind or not; you would rightly deny that I
had 'meant' that particular hall at all, even though my mental image
might to some degree have resembled it. The resemblance would
count in that case as coincidental merely, for all sorts of things of a
kind resemble one another in this world without being held for that
reason to take cognizance of one another.

On the other hand, if I can lead you to the hall, and tell you of its
history and present uses; if in its presence I feel my idea, however
imperfect it may have been, to have led hither and to be now *termi-.*
nated; if the associates of the image and of the felt hall run parallel, so
that each term of the one context corresponds serially, as I walk, with
an answering term of the others; why then my soul was prophetic, and
my idea must be, and by common consent would be, called cognizant
of reality. That percept was what I *meant,* for into it my idea has
passed by conjunctive experiences of sameness and fulfilled intention.
Nowhere is there jar, but every later moment continues and corroborates an earlier one.

In this continuing and corroborating, taken in no transcendental
sense, but denoting definitely felt transitions, *lies all that the knowing*
of a percept by an idea can possibly contain or signify. Wherever such
transitions are felt, the first experience *knows* the last one. Where they
do not, or where even as possibles they can not, intervene, there can
be no pretence of knowing. In this latter case the extremes will be
connected, if connected at all, by inferior relations—bare likeness or
succession, or by 'withness' alone. Knowledge of sensible realities
thus comes to life inside the tissue of experience. It is *made;* and made
by relations that unroll themselves in time. Whenever certain intermediaries are given, such that, as they develop towards their terminus,
there is experience from point to point of one direction followed, and
finally of one process fulfilled, the result is that *their starting-point*
thereby becomes a knower and their terminus an object meant or
known. That is all that knowing (in the simple case considered) can
be known-as, that is the whole of its nature, put into experiential
terms. Whenever such is the sequence of our experiences we may
freely say that we had the terminal object 'in mind' from the outset,
even although *at* the outset nothing was there in us but a flat piece of
substantive experience like any other, with no self-transcendency about
it, and no mystery save the mystery of coming into existence and of
being gradually followed by other pieces of substantive experience,
with conjunctively transitional experiences between. That is what we
mean here by the object's being 'in mind.' Of any deeper more real
way of being in mind we have no positive conception, and we have no
right to discredit our actual experience talking of such a way at all.

I know that many a reader will rebel at this. "Mere intermediaries," he will say, "even though they be feelings of continuously growing fulfilment, only *separate* the knower from the known, whereas what we have in knowledge is a kind of immediate touch of the one by the other, an 'apprehension' in the etymological sense of the word, a leaping of the chasm as by lightning, an act by which two terms are smitten into one, over the head of their distinctness. All these dead intermediaries of yours are out of each other, and outside of their termini still."

But do not such dialectic difficulties remind us of the dog dropping his bone and snapping at its image in the water? If we knew any more real kind of union *aliunde,* we might be entitled to brand all our empirical unions as a sham. But unions by continuous transition are the only ones we know of, whether in this matter of a knowledge-about that terminates in an acquaintance, whether in personal identity, in logical predication through the copula 'is,' or elsewhere. If anywhere there were more absolute unions realized, they could only reveal themselves to us by just such conjunctive results. These are what the unions are *worth,* these are all that *we can ever practically mean* by union, by continuity. Is it not time to repeat what Lotze said of substances, that to *act like* one is to *be* one? [63] Should we not say here that to be experienced as continuous is to be really continuous, in a world where experience and reality come to the same thing? In a picture gallery a painted hook will serve to hang a painted chain by, a painted cable will hold a painted ship. In a world where both the terms and their distinctions are affairs of experience, conjunctions that are experienced must be at least as real as anything else. They will be 'absolutely' real conjunctions, if we have no transphenomenal Absolute ready, to derealize the whole experienced world by, at a stroke. If, on the other hand, we had such an Absolute, not one of our opponents' theories of knowledge could remain standing any better than ours could; for the distinctions as well as the conjunctions of experience would impartially fall its prey. The whole question of how 'one' thing can know 'another' would cease to be a real one at all in a world where otherness itself was an illusion.[64]

So much for the essentials of the cognitive relation, where the knowledge is conceptual in type, or forms knowledge 'about' an object. It consists in intermediary experiences (possible, if not actual) of continuously developing progress, and, finally, of fulfilment, when the

---

[63] [Cf. H. Lotze: *Metaphysik,* §§ 37–39, 97, 98, 243.]

[64] Mr. Bradley, not professing to know his absolute *aliunde,* nevertheless derealizes Experience by alleging it to be everywhere infected with self-contradiction. His arguments seem almost purely verbal, but this is no place for arguing that point out. [Cf. F. H. Bradley; *Appearance and Reality, passim;* and below, pp. 220–226.]

sensible percept, which is the object, is reached. The percept here not only *verifies* the concept, proves its function of knowing that percept to be true, but the percept's existence as the terminus of the chain of intermediaries *creates* the function. Whatever terminates that chain was, because it now proves itself to be, what the concept 'had in mind.'

The towering importance for human life of this kind of knowing lies in the fact that an experience that knows another can figure as its *representative,* not in any quasi-miraculous 'epistemological' sense, but in the definite practical sense of being its *substitute* in various operations, sometimes physical and sometimes mental, which lead us to its associates and results. By experimenting on our ideas of reality, we may save ourselves the trouble of experimenting on the real experiences which they severally mean. The ideas form related systems, corresponding point for point to the systems which the realities form; and by letting an ideal term call up its associates systematically, we may be led to a terminus which the corresponding real term would have led to in case we had operated on the real world. And this brings us to the general question of substitution.

IV. SUBSTITUTION

In Taine's brilliant book on 'Intelligence,' substitution was for the first time named as a cardinal logical function, though of course the facts had always been familiar enough. What, exactly, in a system of experiences, does the 'substitution' of one of them for another mean?

According to my view, experience as a whole is a process in time, whereby innumerable particular terms lapse and are superseded by others that follow upon them by transitions which, whether disjunctive or conjunctive in content, are themselves experiences, and must in general be accounted at least as real as the terms which they relate. What the nature of the event called 'superseding' signifies, depends altogether on the kind of transition that obtains. Some experiences simply abolish their predecessors without continuing them in any way. Others are felt to increase or to enlarge their meaning, to carry out their purpose, or to bring us nearer to their goal. They 'represent' them, and may fulfil their function better than they fulfilled it themselves. But to 'fulfil a function' in a world of pure experience can be conceived and defined in only one possible way. In such a world transitions and arrivals (or terminations) are the only events that happen, though they happen by so many sorts of path. The only function that one experience can perform is to lead into another experience; and the only fulfilment we can speak of is the reaching of a certain experienced end. When one experience leads to (or can lead to) the same end as another, they agree in function. But the whole system of experiences as they are immediately given presents itself as a quasi-chaos through which one can pass out of an initial term in many directions and yet end in the same terminus, moving from next to next by a great many possible paths.

Either one of these paths might be a functional substitute for another, and to follow one rather than another might on occasion be an advantageous thing to do. As a matter of fact, and in a general way, the paths that run through conceptual experiences, that is, through 'thoughts' or 'ideas' that 'know' the things in which they terminate, are highly advantageous paths to follow. Not only do they yield inconceivably rapid transitions; but, owing to the 'universal' character[65] which they frequently possess, and to their capacity for association with one another in great systems, they outstrip the tardy consecutions of the things themselves, and sweep us on towards our ultimate termini in a far more labor-saving way than the following of trains of sensible perception ever could. Wonderful are the new cuts and the short-circuits which the thought-paths make. Most thought-paths, it is true, are substitutes for nothing actual; they end outside the real world altogether, in wayward fancies, utopias, fictions or mistakes. But where they do re-enter reality and terminate therein, we substitute them always; and with these substitutes we pass the greater number of our hours.

This is why I called our experiences, taken all together, a quasi-chaos. There is vastly more discontinuity in the sum total of experiences than we commonly suppose. The objective nucleus of every man's experience, his own body, is, it is true, a continuous percept; and equally continuous as a percept (though we may be inattentive to it) is the material environment of that body, changing by gradual transition when the body moves. But the distant parts of the physical world are at all times absent from us, and form conceptual objects merely, into the perceptual reality of which our life inserts itself at points discrete and relatively rare. Round their several objective nuclei, partly shared and common and partly discrete, of the real physical world, innumerable thinkers, pursuing their several lines of physically true cogitation, trace paths that intersect one another only at discontinuous perceptual points, and the rest of the time are quite incongruent; and around all the nuclei of shared 'reality,' as around

[65] Of which all that need be said in this essay is that it also can be conceived as functional, and defined in terms of transitions, or of the possibility of such. [Cf. *Principles of Psychology*, vol. I, pp. 473–480, vol. II, pp. 337–340; *Pragmatism*, below, p. 459; *Some Problems of Philosophy*, below, pp. 239–243; *Meaning of Truth*, pp. 246–247, etc. ED.]

the Dyak's head of my late metaphor, floats the vast cloud of experiences that are wholly subjective, that are non-substitutional, that find not even an eventual ending for themselves in the perceptual world—the mere day-dreams and joys and sufferings and wishes of the individual minds. These exist *with* one another, indeed, and with the objective nuclei, but out of them it is probable that to all eternity no interrelated system of any kind will ever be made.

This notion of the purely substitutional or conceptual physical world brings us to the most critical of all the steps in the development of a philosophy of pure experience. The paradox of self-transcendency in knowledge comes back upon us here, but I think that our notions of pure experience and of substitution, and our radically empirical view of conjunctive transitions, are *Denkmittel* that will carry us safely through the pass.

V. WHAT OBJECTIVE REFERENCE IS

Whosoever feels his experience to be something substitutional even while he has it, may be said to have an experience that reaches beyond itself. From inside of its own entity it says 'more,' and postulates reality existing elsewhere. For the transcendentalist, who holds knowing to consist in a *salto mortale* across an 'epistemological chasm,' such an idea presents no difficulty; but it seems at first sight as if it might be inconsistent with an empiricism like our own. Have we not explained that conceptual knowledge is made such wholly by the existence of things that fall outside of the knowing experience itself—by intermediary experiences and by a terminus that fulfils? Can the knowledge be there before these elements that constitute its being have come? And, if knowledge be not there, how can objective reference occur?

The key to this difficulty lies in the distinction between knowing as verified and completed, and the same knowing as in transit and on its way. To recur to the Memorial Hall example lately used, it is only when our idea of the Hall has actually terminated in the percept that we know 'for certain' that from the beginning it was truly cognitive of *that*. Until established by the end of the process, its quality of knowing that, or indeed of knowing anything, could still be doubted; and yet the knowing really was there, as the result now shows. We were *virtual* knowers of the Hall long before we were certified to have been its actual knowers, by the percept's retroactive validating power. Just so we are 'mortal' all the time, by reason of the virtuality of the inevitable event which will make us so when it shall have come.

Now the immensely greater part of all our knowing never gets beyond this virtual stage. It never is completed or nailed down. I speak not merely of our ideas of imperceptibles like ether-waves or dissociated 'ions,' or of 'ejects' like the contents of our neighbors' minds; I speak also of ideas which we might verify if we would take the trouble, but which we hold for true although unterminated perceptually, because nothing says 'no' to us, and there is no contradicting truth in sight. *To continue thinking unchallenged is, ninety-nine times out of a hundred, our practical substitute for knowing in the completed sense.* As each experience runs by cognitive transition into the next one, and we nowhere feel a collision with what we elsewhere count as truth or fact, we commit ourselves to the current as if the port were sure. We live, as it were, upon the front edge of an advancing wave-crest, and our sense of a determinate direction in falling forward is all we cover of the future of our path. It is as if a differential quotient should be conscious and treat itself as an adequate substitute for a traced-out curve. Our experience, *inter alia,* is of variations of rate and of direction, and lives in these transitions more than in the journey's end. The experiences of tendency are sufficient to act upon —what more could we have *done* at those moments even if the later verification comes complete?

This is what, as a radical empiricist, I say to the charge that the objective reference which is so flagrant a character of our experiences involves a chasm and a mortal leap. A positively conjunctive transition involves neither chasm nor leap. Being the very original of what we mean by continuity, it makes a continuum wherever it appears. I know full well that such brief words as these will leave the hardened transcendentalist unshaken. Conjunctive experiences *separate* their terms, he will still say: they are third things interposed, that have themselves to be conjoined by new links, and to invoke them makes our trouble infinitely worse. To 'feel' our motion forward is impossible. Motion implies terminus; and how can terminus be felt before we have arrived? The barest start and sally forwards, the barest tendency to leave the instant, involves the chasm and the leap. Conjunctive transitions are the most superficial of appearances, illusions of our sensibility which philosophical reflection pulverizes at a touch. Conception is our only trustworthy instrument, conception and the Absolute working hand in hand. Conception disintegrates experience utterly, but its disjunctions are easily overcome again when the Absolute takes up the task.

Such transcendentalists I must leave, provisionally at least, in full possession of their creed.[66] I have no space for polemics in this article, so I shall simply formulate the empiricist doctrine as my hypothesis, leaving it to work or not work as it may.

Objective reference, I say then, is an incident of the fact that so

66 [Cf. below, pp. 214 ff.]

much of our experience comes as an insufficient and consists of process and transition. Our fields of experience have no more definite boundaries than have our fields of view. Both are fringed forever by a *more* that continuously develops, and that continuously supersedes them as life proceeds. The relations, generally speaking, are as real here as the terms are, and the only complaint of the transcendentalist's with which I could at all sympathize would be his charge that, by first making knowledge to consist in external relations as I have done, and by then confessing that nine-tenths of the time these are not actually but only virtually there, I have knocked the solid bottom out of the whole business, and palmed off a substitute of knowledge for the genuine thing. Only the admission, such a critic might say, that our ideas are self-transcendent and 'true' already, in advance of the experiences that are to terminate them, can bring solidity back to knowledge in a world like this, in which transitions and terminations are only by exception fulfilled.

This seems to me an excellent place for applying the pragmatic method. When a dispute arises, that method consists in auguring what practical consequences would be different if one side rather than the other were true. If no difference can be thought of, the dispute is a quarrel over words. What then would the self-transcendency affirmed to exist in advance of all experiential mediation or termination, be *known-as?* What would it practically result in for *us,* were it true?

It could only result in our orientation, in the turning of our expectations and practical tendencies into the right path; and the right path here, so long as we and the object are not yet face to face (or can never get face to face, as in the case of ejects), would be the path that led us into the object's nearest neighborhood. Where direct acquaintance is lacking, 'knowledge about' is the next best thing, and an acquaintance with what actually lies about the object, and is most closely related to it, puts such knowledge within our grasp. Etherwaves and your anger, for example, are things in which my thoughts will never *perceptually* terminate, but my concepts of them lead me to their very brink, to the chromatic fringes and to the hurtful words and deeds which are their really next effects.

Even if our ideas did in themselves carry the postulated self-transcendency, it would still remain true that their putting us into possession of such effects *would be the sole cash-value of the self-transcendency for us.* And this cash-value, it is needless to say, is *verbatim et literatim* what our empiricist account pays in. On pragmatist principles therefore, a dispute over self-transcendency is a pure logomachy. Call our concepts of ejective things self-transcendent or the reverse, it makes no difference, so long as we don't differ about the nature of that exalted virtue's fruits—fruits for us, of course, humanistic fruits. If an Absolute were proved to exist for other reasons, it might well appear that *his* knowledge is terminated in innumerable cases where ours is still incomplete. That, however, would be a fact indifferent to our knowledge. The latter would grow neither worse nor better, whether we acknowledged such an Absolute or left him out.

So the notion of a knowledge still *in transitu* and on its way joins hands here with that notion of a 'pure experience' which I tried to explain in my [essay] entitled 'Does Consciousness Exist?' The instant field of the present is always experience in its 'pure' state, plain unqualified actuality, a simple *that,* as yet undifferentiated into thing and thought, and only virtually classifiable as objective fact or as some one's opinion about fact. This is as true when the field is conceptual as when it is perceptual. 'Memorial Hall' is 'there' in my idea as much as when I stand before it. I proceed to act on its account in either case. Only in the later experience that supersedes the present one is this *naïf* immediacy retrospectively split into two parts, a 'consciousness' and its 'content,' and the content corrected or confirmed. While still pure, or present, any experience—mine, for example, of what I write about in these very lines—passes for 'truth.' The morrow may reduce it to 'opinion.' The transcendentalist in all his particular knowledges is as liable to this reduction as I am: his Absolute does not save him. Why, then, need he quarrel with an account of knowing that merely leaves it liable to this inevitable condition? Why insist that knowing is a static relation out of time when it practically seems so much a function of our active life? For a thing to be valid, says Lotze, is the same as to make itself valid. When the whole universe seems only to be making itself valid and to be still incomplete (else why its ceaseless changing?) why, of all things, should knowing be exempt? Why should it not be making itself valid like everything else? That some parts of it may be already valid or verified beyond dispute, the empirical philosopher, of course, like any one else, may always hope.

VI. THE CONTERMINOUSNESS OF DIFFERENT MINDS [67]

With transition and prospect thus enthroned in pure experience, it is impossible to subscribe to the idealism of the English school. Radical empiricism has, in fact, more affinities with natural realism than with the views of Berkeley or of Mill, and this can be easily shown.

For the Berkeleyan school, ideas (the verbal equivalent of what I term experiences) are discontinuous. The content of each is wholly

[67] [Cf. "How Two Minds Can Know One Thing," below, pp. 227–232.]

immanent, and there are no transitions with which they are consubstantial and through which their beings may unite. Your Memorial Hall and mine, even when both are percepts, are wholly out of connection with each other. Our lives are a congeries of solipsisms, out of which in strict logic only a God could compose a universe even of discourse. No dynamic currents run between my objects and your objects. Never can our minds meet in the *same*.

The incredibility of such a philosophy is flagrant. It is 'cold, strained, and unnatural' in a supreme degree; and it may be doubted whether even Berkeley himself, who took it so religiously, really believed, when walking through the streets of London, that his spirit and the spirits of his fellow wayfarers had absolutely different towns in view.

To me the decisive reason in favor of our minds meeting in *some* common objects at least is that, unless I make that supposition, I have no motive for assuming that your mind exists at all. Why do I postulate your mind? Because I see your body acting in a certain way. Its gestures, facial movements, words and conduct generally, are 'expressive,' so I deem it actuated as my own is, by an inner life like mine. This argument from analogy is my *reason,* whether an instinctive belief runs before it or not. But what is 'your body' here but a percept in *my* field? It is only as animating *that* object, *my* object, that I have any occasion to think of you at all. If the body that you actuate be not the very body that I see there, but some duplicate body of your own with which that has nothing to do, we belong to different universes, you and I, and for me to speak of you is folly. Myriads of such universes even now may coexist, irrelevant to one another; my concern is solely with the universe with which my own life is connected.

In that perceptual part of *my* universe which I call *your* body, your mind and my mind meet and may be called conterminous. Your mind actuates that body and mine sees it; my thoughts pass into it as into their harmonious cognitive fulfilment; your emotions and volitions pass into it as causes into their effects.

But that percept hangs together with all our other physical percepts. They are of one stuff with it; and if it be our common possession, they must be so likewise. For instance, your hand lays hold of one end of a rope and my hand lays hold of the other end. We pull against each other. Can our two hands be mutual objects in this experience, and the rope not be mutual also? What is true of the rope is true of any other percept. Your objects are over and over again the same as mine. If I ask you *where* some object of yours is, our old Memorial Hall, for example, you point to *my* Memorial Hall with *your* hand which *I* see. If you alter an object in your world, put out a candle, for example, when I am present, *my* candle *ipso facto* goes out. It is only as altering my objects that I guess you to exist. If your objects do not coalesce with my objects, if they be not identically where mine are, they must be proved to be positively somewhere else. But no other location can be assigned for them, so their place must be what it seems to be, the same.[68]

Practically, then, our minds meet in a world of objects which they share in common, which would still be there, if one or several of the minds were destroyed. I can see no formal objection to this supposition's being literally true. On the principles which I am defending, a 'mind' or 'personal consciousness' is the name for a series of experiences run together by certain definite transitions, and an objective reality is a series of similar experiences knit by different transitions. If one and the same experience can figure twice, once in a mental and once in a physical context (as I have tried, in my article on 'Consciousness,' to show that it can), one does not see why it might not figure thrice, or four times, or any number of times, by running into as many different mental contexts, just as the same point, lying at their intersection, can be continued into many different lines. Abolishing any number of contexts would not destroy the experience itself or its other contexts, any more than abolishing some of the point's linear continuations would destroy the others, or destroy the point itself.

I well know the subtle dialectic which insists that a term taken in another relation must needs be an intrinsically different term. The crux is always the old Greek one, that the same man can't be tall in relation to one neighbor, and short in relation to another, for that would make him tall and short at once. In this essay I can not stop to refute this dialectic, so I pass on, leaving my flank for the time exposed.[69] But if my reader will only allow that the same *'now'* both ends his past and begins his future; or that, when he buys an acre of land from his neighbor, it is the same acre that successively figures in the two estates; or that when I pay him a dollar, the same dollar goes into his pocket that came out of mine; he will also in consistency have to allow that the same object may conceivably play a part in, as being related to the rest of, any number of otherwise entirely different minds. This is enough for my present point: the common-sense notion of minds sharing the same object offers no special logical or epistemological difficulties of its own; it stands or falls with the general possibility of things being in conjunctive relation with other things at all.

In principle, then, let natural realism pass for possible. Your mind and mine *may* terminate in the same percept, not merely against it, as if it were a third external thing; but by inserting themselves into it and

[68] The notion that our objects are inside of our respective heads is not seriously defensible, so I pass it by.

[69] [The argument is resumed below, pp. 218 ff. Ed.]

coalescing with it, for such is the sort of conjunctive union that appears to be experienced when a perceptual terminus 'fulfils.' Even so, two hawsers may embrace the same pile, and yet neither one of them touch any other part except that pile, of what the other hawser is attached to.

It is therefore not a formal question, but a question of empirical fact solely, whether, when you and I are said to know the 'same' Memorial Hall, our minds do terminate at or in a numerically identical percept. Obviously, as a plain matter of fact, they do *not*. Apart from color-blindness and such possibilities, we see the Hall in different perspectives. You may be on one side of it and I on another. The percept of each of us, as he sees the surface of the Hall, is moreover only his provisional terminus. The next thing beyond my percept is not your mind, but more percepts of my own into which my first percept develops, the interior of the Hall, for instance, or the inner structure of its bricks and mortar. If our minds were in a literal sense *con*terminous, neither could get beyond the percept which they had in common, it would be an ultimate barrier between them—unless indeed they flowed over it and became 'co-conscious' over a still larger part of their content, which (thought-transference apart) is not supposed to be the case. In point of fact the ultimate common barrier can always be pushed, by both minds, farther than any actual percept of either, until at last it resolves itself into the mere notion of imperceptibles like atoms or ether, so that, where we do terminate in percepts, our knowledge is only speciously completed, being, in theoretic strictness, only a virtual knowledge of those remoter objects which conception carries out.

Is natural realism, permissible in logic, refuted then by empirical fact? Do our minds have no object in common after all?

Yes, they certainly have *Space* in common. On pragmatic principles we are obliged to predicate sameness wherever we can predicate no assignable point of difference. If two named things have every quality and function indiscernible, and are at the same time in the same place, they must be written down as numerically one thing under two different names. But there is no test discoverable, so far as I know, by which it can be shown that the place occupied by your percept of Memorial Hall differs from the place occupied by mine. The percepts themselves may be shown to differ; but if each of us be asked to point out where his percept is, we point to an identical spot. All the relations, whether geometrical or causal, of the Hall originate or terminate in that spot wherein our hands meet, and where each of us begins to work if he wishes to make the Hall change before the other's eyes. Just so it is with our bodies. That body of yours which you actuate and feel from within must be in the same spot as the body of yours which I see or touch from without. 'There' for me means where I place my finger. If you do not feel my finger's contact to be 'there' in *my* sense, when I place it on your body, where then do you feel it? Your inner actuations of your body meet my finger *there:* it is *there* that you resist its push, or shrink back, or sweep the finger aside with your hand. Whatever farther knowledge either of us may acquire of the real constitution of the body which we thus feel, you from within and I from without, it is in that same place that the newly conceived or perceived constituents have to be located, and it is *through* that space that your and my mental intercourse with each other has always to be carried on, by the mediation of impressions which I convey thither, and of the reactions thence which those impressions may provoke from you.

In general terms, then, whatever differing contents our minds may eventually fill a place with, the place itself is a numerically identical content of the two minds, a piece of common property in which, through which, and over which they join. The receptacle of certain of our experiences being thus common, the experiences themselves might some day become common also. If that day ever did come, our thoughts would terminate in a complete empirical identity, there would be an end, so far as *those* experiences went, to our discussions about truth. No points of difference appearing, they would have to count as the same.

VII. CONCLUSION

With this we have the outlines of a philosophy of pure experience before us. At the outset of my essay, I called it a mosaic philosophy. In actual mosaics the pieces are held together by their bedding, for which bedding the Substances, transcendental Egos, or Absolutes of other philosophies may be taken to stand. In radical empiricism there is no bedding; it is as if the pieces clung together by their edges, the transitions experienced between them forming their cement. Of course such a metaphor is misleading, for in actual experience the more substantive and the more transitive parts run into each other continuously, there is in general no separateness needing to be overcome by an external cement; and whatever separateness is actually experienced is not overcome, it stays and counts as separateness to the end. But the metaphor serves to symbolize the fact that Experience itself, taken at large, can grow by its edges. That one moment of it proliferates into the next by transitions which, whether conjunctive or disjunctive, continue the experiential tissue, can not, I contend, be denied. Life is in the transitions as much as in the terms connected; often, indeed, it seems to be there more emphatically, as if our spurts and sallies forward were the real firing-line of the battle, were like the thin line of flame advancing across the dry autumnal field which the farmer proceeds to burn. In this line we live prospectively as well as retrospectively. It is 'of' the past, inasmuch as it comes expressly as the past's continuation; it is 'of' the future in so far as the future, when it comes, will have continued *it*.

These relations of continuous transition experienced are what make our experiences cognitive. In the simplest and completest cases the experiences are cognitive of one another. When one of them terminates a previous series of them with a sense of fulfilment, it, we say, is what those other experiences 'had in view.' The knowledge, in such a case, is verified; the truth is 'salted down.' Mainly, however, we live on speculative investments, or on our prospects only. But living on things *in posse* is as good as living in the actual, so long as our credit remains good. It is evident that for the most part it is good, and that the universe seldom protests our drafts.

In this sense we at every moment can continue to believe in an existing *beyond*. It is only in special cases that our confident rush forward gets rebuked. The beyond must, of course, always in our philosophy be itself of an experiential nature. If not a future experience of our own or a present one of our neighbor, it must be a thing in itself in Dr. Prince's and Professor Strong's sense of the term—that is, it must be an experience *for* itself whose relation to other things we translate into the action of molecules, ether-waves, or whatever else the physical symbols may be.[70] This opens the chapter of the relations of radical empiricism to panpsychism, into which I can not enter now.[71]

The beyond can in any case exist simultaneously—for it can be experienced *to have existed* simultaneously—with the experience that practically postulates it by looking in its direction, or by turning or changing in the direction of which it is the goal. Pending that actuality of union, in the virtuality of which the 'truth,' even now, of the postulation consists, the beyond and its knower are entities split off from each other. The world is in so far forth a pluralism of which the unity is not fully experienced as yet. But, as fast as verifications come, trains of experience, once separate, run into one another; and that is why I said, earlier in my article, that the unity of the world is on the

[70] Our minds and these ejective realities would still have space (or pseudo-space, as I believe Professor Strong calls the medium of interaction between 'things-in-themselves') in common. These would exist *where*, and begin to act *where*, we locate the molecules, etc., and *where* we perceive the sensible phenomena explained thereby. [Cf. Morton Prince: *The Nature of Mind, and Human Automatism*, part I, ch. III, IV; C. A. Strong: *Why the Mind Has a Body*, ch. XII.]

[71] [Cf. below, p. 291; pp. 529–581.]

whole undergoing increase. The universe continually grows in quantity by new experiences that graft themselves upon the older mass; but these very new experiences often help the mass to a more consolidated form.

These are the main features of a philosophy of pure experience. It has innumerable other aspects and arouses innumerable questions, but the points I have touched on seem enough to make an entering wedge. In my own mind such a philosophy harmonizes best with a radical pluralism, with novelty and indeterminism, moralism and theism, and with the 'humanism' lately sprung upon us by the Oxford and the Chicago schools.[72] I can not, however, be sure that all these doctrines are its necessary and indispensable allies. It presents so many points of difference, both from the common sense and from the idealism that have made our philosophic language, that it is almost as difficult to state it as it is to think it out clearly, and if it is ever to grow into a respectable system, it will have to be built up by the contributions of many co-operating minds. It seems to me, as I said at the outset of this essay, that many minds are, in point of fact, now turning in a direction that points towards radical empiricism. If they are carried farther by my words, and if then they add their stronger voices to my feebler one, the publication of this essay will have been worth while.

THE THING AND ITS RELATIONS*[73]

Experience in its immediacy seems perfectly fluent. The active sense of living which we all enjoy, before reflection shatters our instinctive world for us, is self-luminous and suggests no paradoxes. Its difficulties are disappointments and uncertainties. They are not intellectual contradictions.

When the reflective intellect gets at work, however, it discovers incomprehensibilities in the flowing process. Distinguishing its ele-

---

[72] I have said something of this latter alliance in an article entitled 'Humanism and Truth,' in *Mind,* October, 1904. [Reprinted in *The Meaning of Truth,* pp. 51–101.]

* From: E.R.E., 92–122.

[73] [Reprinted from *The Journal of Philosophy, Psychology, and Scientific Methods,* vol. II, No. 2, January 19, 1905. Reprinted also as Appendix A in *A Pluralistic Universe,* pp. 347–369. The author's corrections have been adopted in the present text. ED.]

ments and parts, it gives them separate names, and what it thus disjoins it can not easily put together. Pyrrhonism accepts the irrationality and revels in its dialectic elaboration. Other philosophies try, some by ignoring, some by resisting, and some by turning the dialectic procedure against itself, negating its first negations, to restore the fluent sense of life again, and let redemption take the place of innocence. The perfection with which any philosophy may do this is the measure of its human success and of its importance in philosophic history. In [the last essay], 'A World of Pure Experience,' I tried my own hand sketchily at the problem, resisting certain first steps of dialectics by insisting in a general way that the immediately experienced conjunctive relations are as real as anything else. If my sketch is not to appear too *naïf,* I must come closer to details, and in the present essay I propose to do so.

1

'Pure experience' is the name which I gave to the immediate flux of life which furnishes the material to our later reflection with its conceptual categories. Only new-born babes, or men in semi-coma from sleep, drugs, illnesses, or blows, may be assumed to have an experience pure in the literal sense of a *that* which is not yet any definite *what,* tho' ready to be all sorts of whats; full both of oneness and of manyness, but in respects that don't appear; changing throughout, yet so confusedly that its phases interpenetrate and no points, either of distinction or of identity, can be caught. Pure experience in this state is but another name for feeling or sensation. But the flux of it no sooner comes than it tends to fill itself with emphases, and these salient parts become identified and fixed and abstracted; so that experience now flows as if shot through with adjectives and nouns and prepositions and conjunctions. Its purity is only a relative term, meaning the proportional amount of unverbalized sensation which it still embodies.

Far back as we go, the flux, both as a whole and in its parts, is that of things conjunct and separated. The great continua of time, space, and the self envelope everything, betwixt them, and flow together without interfering. The things that they envelope come as separate in some ways and as continuous in others. Some sensations coalesce with some ideas, and others are irreconcilable. Qualities compenetrate one space, or exclude each other from it. They cling together persistently in groups that move as units, or else they separate. Their changes are abrupt or discontinuous; and their kinds resemble or differ; and, as they do so, they fall into either even or irregular series.

In all this the continuities and the discontinuities are absolutely co-ordinate matters of immediate feeling. The conjunctions are as primordial elements of 'fact' as are the distinctions and disjunctions. In the same act by which I feel that this passing minute is a new pulse of my life, I feel that the old life continues into it, and the feeling of continuance in no wise jars upon the simultaneous feeling of a novelty. They, too, compenetrate harmoniously. Prepositions, copulas, and conjunctions, 'is,' 'is n't,' 'then,' 'before,' 'in,' 'on,' 'beside,' 'between,' 'next,' 'like,' 'unlike,' 'as,' 'but,' flower out of the stream of pure experience, the stream of concretes or the sensational stream, as naturally as nouns and adjectives do, and they melt into it again as fluidly when we apply them to a new portion of the stream.

II

If now we ask why we must thus translate experience from a more concrete or pure into a more intellectualized form, filling it with ever more abounding conceptual distinctions, rationalism and naturalism give different replies.

The rationalistic answer is that the theoretic life is absolute and its interests imperative; that to understand is simply the duty of man; and that who questions this need not be argued with, for by the fact of arguing he gives away his case.

The naturalist answer is that the environment kills as well as sustains us, and that the tendency of raw experience to extinguish the experient himself is lessened just in the degree in which the elements in it that have a practical bearing upon life are analyzed out of the continuum and verbally fixed and coupled together, so that we may know what is in the wind for us and get ready to react in time. Had pure experience, the naturalist says, been always perfectly healthy, there would never have arisen the necessity of isolating or verbalizing any of its terms. We should just have experienced inarticulately and unintellectually enjoyed. This leaning on 'reaction' in the naturalist account implies that, whenever we intellectualize a relatively pure experience, we ought to do so for the sake of redescending to the purer or more concrete level again; and that if an intellect stays aloft among its abstract terms and generalized relations, and does not reinsert itself with its conclusions into some particular point of the immediate stream of life, it fails to finish out its function and leaves its normal race unrun.

Most rationalists nowadays will agree that naturalism gives a true enough account of the way in which our intellect arose at first, but they will deny these latter implications. The case, they will say, resembles that of sexual love. Originating in the animal need of getting another generation born, this passion has developed secondarily such imperious spiritual needs that, if you ask why another generation ought to be born at all, the answer is: 'Chiefly that love may go on.' Just so with our intellect: it originated as a practical means of serving life; but it has developed incidentally the function of understanding absolute truth; and life itself now seems to be given chiefly as a means by which that function may be prosecuted. But truth and the understanding of it lie among the abstracts and universals, so the intellect now carries on its higher business wholly in this region, without any need of redescending into pure experience again.

If the contrasted tendencies which I thus designate as naturalistic and rationalistic are not recognized by the reader, perhaps an example will make them more concrete. Mr. Bradley, for instance, is an ultra-rationalist. He admits that our intellect is primarily practical, but says that, for philosophers, the practical need is simply Truth. Truth, moreover, must be assumed 'consistent.' Immediate experience has to be broken into subjects and qualities, terms and relations, to be understood as truth at all. Yet when so broken it is less consistent than ever. Taken raw, it is all undistinguished. Intellectualized, it is all distinction without oneness. 'Such an arrangement may *work,* but the theoretic problem is not solved.' The question is *'how* the diversity can exist in harmony with the oneness.' To go back to pure experience is unavailing. 'Mere feeling gives no answer to our riddle.' Even if your intuition is a fact, it is not an *understanding.* 'It is a mere experience, and furnishes no consistent view.' The experience offered as facts or truths 'I find that my intellect rejects because they contradict themselves. They offer a complex of diversities conjoined in a way which it feels is not its way and which it can not repeat as its own. . . . For to be satisfied, my intellect must understand, and it can not understand by taking a congeries in the lump.' [74] So Mr. Bradley, in the sole interests of 'understanding' (as he conceives that function), turns his back on finite experience forever. Truth must lie in the opposite direction, the direction of the Absolute; and this kind of rationalism and naturalism, or (as I will now call it) pragmatism, walk thenceforward upon opposite paths. For the one, those intellectual products are most true which, turning their face towards the Absolute, come nearest to symbolizing its ways of uniting the many and the one. For the other, those are most true which most successfully dip back into the finite stream of feeling and grow most easily confluent with some particular wave or wavelet. Such confluence not only proves the intellectual operation to have been true (as an addition may 'prove' that a subtraction is

[74] [F. H. Bradley: *Appearance and Reality,* second edition, pp. 152–153, 23, 118, 104, 108–109, 570.]

already rightly performed), but it constitutes, according to pragmatism, all that we mean by calling it true. Only in so far as they lead us, successfully or unsuccessfully, back into sensible experience again, are our abstracts and universals true or false at all.[75]

III

In Section VI of "A World of Pure Experience," I adopted in a general way the common-sense belief that one and the same world is cognized by our different minds; but I left undiscussed the dialectical arguments which maintain that this is logically absurd. The usual reason given for its being absurd is that it assumes one object (to wit, the world) to stand in two relations at once; to my mind, namely, and again to yours; whereas a term taken in a second relation can not logically be the same term which it was at first.

I have heard this reason urged so often in discussing with absolutists, and it would destroy my radical empiricism so utterly, if it were valid, that I am bound to give it an attentive ear, and seriously to search its strength.

For instance, let the matter in dispute be term M, asserted to be on the one hand related to L, and on the other to N; and let the two cases of relation be symbolized by L—M and M—N respectively. When, now, I assume that the experience may immediately come and be given in the shape L—M—N, with no trace of doubling or internal fission in the M, I am told that this is all a popular delusion; that L—M—N logically means two different experiences, L—M and M—N, namely; and that although the Absolute may, and indeed must, from its superior point of view, read its own kind of unity into M's two editions, yet as elements in finite experience the two M's lie irretrievably asunder, and the world between them is broken and unbridged.

In arguing this dialectic thesis, one must avoid slipping from the logical into the physical point of view. It would be easy, in taking a concrete example to fix one's ideas by, to choose one in which the letter M should stand for a collective noun of some sort, which noun, being related to L by one of its parts and to N by another, would inwardly be two things when it stood outwardly in both relations. Thus, one might say: 'David Hume, who weighed so many stone by his body, influences posterity by his doctrine.' The body and the doctrine are two things, between which our finite minds can discover no real sameness, though the same name covers both of them. And then,

---

[75] Compare Professor MacLennan's admirable *Auseinandersetzung* with Mr. Bradley, in *The Journal of Philosophy, Psychology, and Scientific Methods*, vol. I, [1904], pp. 403 ff., especially pp. 405–407.

one might continue: 'Only an Absolute is capable of uniting such a non-identity.' We must, I say, avoid this sort of example, for the dialectic insight, if true at all, must apply to terms and relations universally. It must be true of abstract units as well as of nouns collective; and if we prove it by concrete examples we must take the simplest, so as to avoid irrelevant material suggestions.

Taken thus in all its generality, the absolutist contention seems to use as its major premise Hume's notion 'that all our distinct perceptions are distinct existences, and that the mind never perceives any real connexion among distinct existences.'[76] Undoubtedly, since we use two phrases in talking first about 'M's relation to L' and then about 'M's relation to N,' we must be having, or must have had, two distinct perceptions;—and the rest would then seem to follow duly. But the starting-point of the reasoning here seems to be the fact of the two *phrases;* and this suggests that the argument may be merely verbal. Can it be that the whole dialectic consists in attributing to the experience talked-about a constitution similar to that of the language in which we describe it? Must we assert the objective doubleness of the M merely because we have to name it twice over when we name its two relations?

Candidly, I can think of no other reason than this for the dialectic conclusion;[77] for, if we think, not of our words, but of any simple concrete matter which they may be held to signify, the experience itself belies the paradox asserted. We use indeed two separate concepts in analyzing our object, but we know them all the while to be but substitutional, and that the M in L—M and the M in M—N *mean* (*i.e.,* are capable of leading to and terminating in) one self-same piece, M, of sensible experience. This persistent identity of certain units (or emphases, or points, or objects, or members—call them what you will) of the experience-continuum, is just one of those conjunctive features of it, on which I am obliged to insist so emphatically.[78] For samenesses are parts of experience's indefeasible structure. When I hear a bell-stroke and, as life flows on, its after image dies away, I still hark back to it as 'that same bell-stroke.' When I see a thing M, with L to the left of it and N to the right of it, I see it *as* one M; and if you tell me I have had to 'take' it twice, I reply that if I 'took' it a thousand times I should still *see* it as a unit.[79] Its unity is

---

[76] [Hume: *Treatise of Human Nature,* Appendix, Selby-Bigge's edition, p. 636.]

[77] Technically, it seems classable as a 'fallacy of composition.' A duality, predicable of the two wholes, L—M and M—N, is forthwith predicated of one of their parts, M.

[78] See above, pp. 195 ff.

[79] I may perhaps refer here to my *Principles of Psychology*, vol. I, pp. 459 ff. It really seems 'weird' to have to argue (as I am forced now to do) for the notion that it is one sheet of paper (with its two surfaces and all that lies between)

aboriginal, just as the multiplicity of my successive takings is aboriginal. It comes unbroken as *that M*, as a singular which I encounter; they come broken, as *those* takings, as my plurality of operations. The unity and the separateness are strictly co-ordinate. I do not easily fathom why my opponents should find the separateness so much more easily understandable that they must needs infect the whole of finite experience with it, and relegate the unity (now taken as a bare postulate and no longer as a thing positively perceivable) to the region of the Absolute's mysteries. I do not easily fathom this, I say, for the said opponents are above mere verbal quibbling; yet all that I can catch in their talk is the substitution of what is true of certain words for what is true of what they signify. They stay with the words,—not returning to the stream of life whence all the meaning of them came, and which is always ready to reabsorb them.

IV

For aught this argument proves, then, we may continue to believe that one thing can be known by many knowers. But the denial of one thing in many relations is but one application of a still profounder dialectic difficulty. Man can't be good, said the sophists, for man is *man* and *good* is good; and Hegel [80] and Herbart in their day, more recently A. Spir,[81] and most recently and elaborately of all, Mr. Bradley, informs us that a term can logically only be a punctiform unit, and that not one of the conjunctive relations between things, which experience seems to yield, is rationally possible.

Of course, if true, this cuts off radical empiricism without even a shilling. Radical empiricism takes conjunctive relations at their face value, holding them to be as real as the terms united by them.[82] The world it represents as a collection, some parts of which are conjunctively and others disjunctively related. Two parts, themselves disjoined, may nevertheless hang together by intermediaries with which they are severally connected, and the whole world eventually may hang together similarly, inasmuch as *some* path of conjunctive transition by which to pass from one of its parts to another may always be discernible. Such determinately various hanging-together may be

---

which is both under my pen and on the table while I write—the 'claim' that it is two sheets seems so brazen. Yet I sometimes suspect the absolutists of sincerity!

[80] [For the author's criticism of Hegel's view of relations, cf. *Will to Believe*, pp. 278–279. Ed.]

[81] [Cf. A. Spir: *Denken und Wirklichkeit*, part I, bk. III, ch. IV (containing also account of Herbart). Ed.]

[82] [See above, pp. 195, 198.]

called *concatenated* union, to distinguish it from the 'through-and-through' type of union, 'each in all and all in each' (union of *total conflux,* as one might call it), which monistic systems hold to obtain when things are taken in their absolute reality. In a concatenated world a partial conflux often is experienced. Our concepts and our sensations are confluent; successive states of the same ego, and feelings of the same body are confluent. Where the experience is not of conflux, it may be of conterminousness (things with but one thing between); or of contiguousness (nothing between); or of likeness; or of nearness; or of simultaneousness; or of in-ness; or of on-ness; or of for-ness; or of simple with-ness; or even of mere and-ness; which last relation would make of however disjointed a world otherwise, at any rate for that occasion a universe 'of discourse.' Now Mr. Bradley tells us that none of these relations, as we actually experience them, can possibly be real.[83] My next duty, accordingly, must be to rescue radical empiricism from Mr. Bradley. Fortunately, as it seems to me, his general contention, that the very notion of relation is unthinkable clearly, has been successfully met by many critics.[84]

It is a burden to the flesh, and an injustice both to readers and to the previous writers, to repeat good arguments already printed. So, in noticing Mr. Bradley, I will confine myself to the interests of radical empiricism solely.

V

The first duty of radical empiricism, taking given conjunctions at their face-value, is to class some of them as more intimate and some as more external. When two terms are *similar,* their very natures enter into the relation. Being *what* they are, no matter where or when, the

[83] Here again the reader must beware of slipping from logical into phenomenal considerations. It may well be that we *attribute* a certain relation falsely, because the circumstances of the case, being complex, have deceived us. At a railway station we may take our own train, and not the one that fills our window, to be moving. We here put motion in the wrong place in the world, but in its original place the motion is a part of reality. What Mr. Bradley means is nothing like this, but rather that such things as motion are nowhere real, and that, even in their aboriginal and empirically incorrigible seats, relations are impossible of comprehension.

[84] Particularly so by Andrew Seth Pringle-Pattison, in his *Man and the Cosmos;* by L. T. Hobhouse, in chapter XII ("The Validity of Judgment") of his *Theory of Knowledge;* and by F. C. S. Schiller, in his *Humanism,* essay XI. Other fatal reviews (in my opinion) are Hodder's, in the *Psychological Review,* vol. I, [1894], p. 307; Stout's in the *Proceedings of the Aristotelian Society,* 1901–1902, p. 1; and MacLennan's in [*The Journal of Philosophy, Psychology, and Scientific Methods,* vol. I, 1904, p. 403].

likeness never can be denied, if asserted. It continues predicable as long as the terms continue. Other relations, the *where* and the *when,* for example, seem adventitious. The sheet of paper may be 'off' or 'on' the table, for example; and in either case the relation involves only the outside of its terms. Having an outside, both of them, they contribute by it to the relation. It is external: the term's inner nature is irrelevant to it. Any book, any table, may fall into the relation, which is created *pro hac vice,* not by their existence, but by their casual situation. It is just because so many of the conjunctions of experience seem so external that a philosophy of pure experience must tend to pluralism in its ontology. So far as things have space-relations, for example, we are free to imagine them with different origins even. If they could get to *be,* and get into space at all, then they may have done so separately. Once there, however, they are *additives* to one another, and, with no prejudice to their natures, all sorts of space-relations may supervene between them. The question of how things could come to be anyhow, is wholly different from the question what their relations, once the being accomplished, may consist in.

Mr. Bradley now affirms that such external relations as the space-relations which we here talk of must hold of entirely different subjects from those of which the absence of such relations might a moment previously have been plausibly asserted. Not only is the *situation* different when the book is on the table, but the *book itself* is different as a book, from what it was when it was off the table.[85] He admits that "such external relations seem possible and even existing. . . . That you do not alter what you compare or rearrange in space seems to common sense quite obvious, and that on the other side there are as obvious difficulties does not occur to common sense at all. And I will begin by pointing out these difficulties. . . . There is a relation in the result, and this relation, we hear, is to make no difference in its terms. But, if so, to what does it make a difference? [*Does n't it make a difference to us onlookers, at least?*] and what is the meaning and sense of qualifying the terms by it? [*Surely the meaning is to tell the truth about their relative position.*[86]] If, in short, it is external to the

[85] Once more, don't slip from logical into physical situations. Of course, if the table be wet, it will moisten the book, or if it be slight enough and the book heavy enough, the book will break it down. But such collateral phenomena are not the point at issue. The point is whether the successive relations 'on' and 'not-on' can rationally (not physically) hold of the same constant terms, abstractly taken. Professor A. E. Taylor drops from logical into material considerations when he instances color-contrast as a proof that *A,* 'as contra-distinguished from *B,* is not the same thing as mere *A* not in any way affected' (*Elements of Metaphysics,* p. 145). Note the substitution, for 'related' of the word 'affected,' which begs the whole question.

[86] But "is there any sense," asks Mr. Bradley, peevishly, on p. 579, "and if so, what sense in truth that is only outside and 'about' things?" Surely such a question may be left unanswered.

terms, how can it possibly be true *of* them? [*Is it the 'intimacy' suggested by the little word 'of,' here, which I have underscored, that is the root of Mr. Bradley's trouble?*] . . . If the terms from their inner nature do not enter into the relation, then, so far as they are concerned, they seem related for no reason at all. . . . Things are spatially related, first in one way, and then become related in another way, and yet in no way themselves are altered; for the relations, it is said, are but external. But I reply that, if so, I can not *understand* the leaving by the terms of one set of relations and their adoption of another fresh set. The process and its result to the terms, if they contribute nothing to it [*Surely they contribute to it all there is 'of' it!*] seem irrational throughout. [*If 'irrational' here means simply 'non-rational,' or non-deducible from the essence of either term singly, it is no reproach; if it means 'contradicting' such essence, Mr. Bradley should show wherein and how.*] But, if they contribute anything, they must surely be affected internally. [*Why so, if they contribute only their surface? In such relations as 'on,' 'a foot away,' 'between,' 'next,' etc., only surfaces are in question.*] . . . If the terms contribute anything whatever, then the terms are affected [*inwardly altered?*] by the arrangement. . . . That for working purposes we treat, and do well to treat, some relations as external merely I do not deny, and that of course is not the question at issue here. That question is . . . whether in the end and in principle a mere external relation [*i.e., a relation which can change without forcing its terms to change their nature simultaneously*] is possible and forced on us by the facts." [87]

Mr. Bradley next reverts to the antinomies of space, which, according to him, prove it to be unreal, although it appears as so prolific a medium of external relations; and he then concludes that "Irrationality and externality can not be the last truth about things. Somewhere there must be a reason why this and that appear together. And this reason and reality must reside in the whole from which terms and relations are abstractions, a whole in which their internal connection must lie, and out of which from the background appear those fresh results which never could have come from the premises." And he adds that "Where the whole is different, the terms that qualify and contribute to it must so far be different. . . . They are altered so far only [*How far? farther than externally, yet not through and through?*] but still they are altered. . . . I must insist that in each case the terms are qualified by their whole [*Qualified how?—Do their external relations, situations, dates, etc., changed as these are in the new whole, fail to qualify them 'far' enough?*], and that in the second case there is a whole which differs both logically and psychologically from the first whole; and I urge that in contributing to the change the terms so far are altered."

[87] *Appearance and Reality*, second edition, pp. 575–576.

Not merely the relations, then, but the terms are altered: *und zwar* 'so far.' But just *how* far is the whole problem; and 'through-and-through' would seem (in spite of Mr. Bradley's somewhat undecided utterances[88]) to be the full Bradleyan answer. The 'whole' which he here treats as primary and determinative of each part's manner of 'contributing,' simply *must,* when it alters, alter in its entirety. There *must* be total conflux of its parts, each into and through each other. The 'must' appears here as a *Machtspruch,* as an *ipse dixit* of Mr. Bradley's absolutistically tempered 'understanding,' for he candidly confesses that how the parts *do* differ as they contribute to different wholes, is unknown to him.[89]

Although I have every wish to comprehend the authority by which Mr. Bradley's understanding speaks, his words leave me wholly unconverted. 'External relations' stand with their withers all unwrung, and remain, for aught he proves to the contrary, not only practically workable, but also perfectly intelligible factors of reality.

VI

Mr. Bradley's understanding shows the most extraordinary power of perceiving separations and the most extraordinary impotence in comprehending conjunctions. One would naturally say 'neither or both,' but not so Mr. Bradley. When a common man analyzes certain *whats* from out the stream of experience, he understands their distinctness *as thus isolated.* But this does not prevent him from equally well understanding their combination with each other *as originally experienced*

---

[88] I say 'undecided,' because, apart from the 'so far,' which sounds terribly half-hearted, there are passages in these very pages in which Mr. Bradley admits the pluralistic thesis. Read, for example, what he says, on p. 578, of a billiard ball keeping its 'character' unchanged, though, in its change of place, its 'existence' gets altered; or what he says, on p. 579, of the possibility that an abstract quality A, B, or C, in a thing, 'may throughout remain unchanged' although the thing be altered; or his admission that in red-hairedness, both as analyzed out of a man and when given with the rest of him, there may be 'no change' (p. 580). Why does he immediately add that for the pluralist to plead the non-mutation of such abstractions would be an *ignoratio elenchi?* It is impossible to admit it to be such. The entire *elenchus* and inquest is just as to whether parts which you can abstract from existing wholes can also contribute to other wholes without changing their inner nature. If they can thus mould various wholes into new *gestaltqualitäten,* then it follows that the same elements are logically able to exist in different wholes [whether physically able would depend on additional hypotheses]; that partial changes are thinkable, and through-and-through change not a dialectic necessity; that monism is only an hypothesis; and that an additively constituted universe is a rationally respectable hypothesis also. All the theses of radical empiricism, in short, follow.

[89] *Op. cit.,* pp. 577–579.

in the concrete, or their confluence with new sensible experiences in which they recur as 'the same.' Returning into the stream of sensible presentation, nouns and adjectives, and *thats* and abstract *whats,* grow confluent again, and the word 'is' names all these experiences of conjunction. Mr. Bradley understands the isolation of the abstracts, but to understand the combination is to him impossible.[90] "To understand a complex *AB,*" he says, "I must begin with *A* or *B.* And beginning, say with *A,* if I then merely find *B,* I have either lost *A,* or I have got beside A, [*the word 'beside' seems here vital, as meaning a conjunction 'external' and therefore unintelligible*] something else, and in neither case have I understood.[91] For my intellect can not simply unite a diversity, nor has it in itself any form or way of togetherness, and you gain nothing if, beside *A* and *B,* you offer me their conjunction in fact. For to my intellect that is no more than another external element. And 'facts,' once for all, are for my intellect not true unless they satisfy it. . . . The intellect has in its nature no principle of mere togetherness."[92]

Of course Mr. Bradley has a right to define 'intellect' as the power by which we perceive separations but not unions—provided he give due notice to the reader. But why then claim that such a maimed and amputated power must reign supreme in philosophy, and accuse on its behoof the whole empirical world of irrationality? It is true that he elsewhere attributes to the intellect a *proprius motus* of transition, but says that when he looks for *these* transitions in the detail of living experience, he 'is unable to verify such a solution.'[93]

Yet he never explains what the intellectual transitions would be like in case we had them. He only defines them negatively—they are not spatial, temporal, predicative, or causal; or qualitatively or otherwise serial; or in any way relational as we naïvely trace relations, for relations *separate* terms, and need themselves to be hooked on *ad*

---

[90] So far as I catch his state of mind, it is somewhat like this: 'Book,' 'table,' 'on'—how does the existence of these three abstract elements result in *this* book being livingly on *this* table. Why is n't the table on the book? Or why does n't the 'on' connect itself with another book, or something that is not a table? Must n't something *in* each of the three elements already determine the two others to *it,* so that they do not settle elsewhere or float vaguely? Must n't the *whole fact be prefigured in each part,* and exist *de jure* before it can exist *de facto?* But, if so, in what can the jural existence consist, if not in a spiritual miniature of the whole fact's constitution actuating every partial factor as its purpose? But is this anything but the old metaphysical fallacy of looking behind a fact *in esse* for the ground of the fact, and finding it in the shape of the very same fact *in posse?* Somewhere we must leave off with a *constitution* behind which there is nothing.

[91] Apply this to the case of 'book-on-table'! W.J.

[92] *Op. cit.,* pp. 570, 572.

[93] *Op. cit.,* pp. 568, 569.

infinitum. The nearest approach he makes to describing a truly intellectual transition is where he speaks of *A* and *B* as being 'united, each from its own nature, in a whole which is the nature of both alike.'[94] But this (which, *pace* Mr. Bradley, seems exquisitely analogous to 'taking' a congeries in a 'lump,' if not to 'swamping') suggests nothing but that *conflux* which pure experience so abundantly offers, as when 'space,' 'white' and 'sweet' are confluent in a 'lump of sugar,' or kinesthetic, dermal, and optical sensations confluent in 'my hand.'[95] All that I can verify in the transitions which Mr. Bradley's intellect desiderates as its *proprius motus* is a reminiscence of these and other sensible conjunctions (especially space-conjunctions), but a reminiscence so vague that its originals are not recognized. Bradley in short repeats the fable of the dog, the bone, and its image in the water. With a world of particulars, given in loveliest union, in conjunction definitely various, and variously definite, the 'how' of which you 'understand' as soon as you see the fact of them,[96] for there is no 'how' except the constitution of the fact as given; with all this given him, I say, in pure experience, he asks for some ineffable union in the abstract instead, which, if he gained it, would only be a duplicate of what he has already in his full possession. Surely he abuses the privilege which society grants to all us philosophers, of being puzzle-headed.

Polemic writing like this is odious; but with absolutism in possession in so many quarters, omission to defend my radical empiricism against its best known champion would count as either superficiality or inability. I have to conclude that its dialectic has not invalidated in the least degree the usual conjunctions by which the world, as experienced, hangs so variously together. In particular it leaves an empirical theory of knowledge[97] intact, and lets us continue to believe with common sense that one object *may* be known, if we have any ground for thinking that it *is* known, to many knowers.

In the next essay I shall return to this last supposition, which seems to me to offer other difficulties much harder for a philosophy of pure experience to deal with than any of absolutism's dialectic objections.

[94] *Op. cit.,* p. 570.

[95] How meaningless is the contention that in such wholes (or in 'book-on-table,' 'watch-in-pocket,' etc.) the relation is an additional entity *between* the terms, needing itself to be related again to each! Both Bradley (*op. cit.,* pp. 32–33) and Royce (*The World and the Individual,* vol. I, p. 128) lovingly repeat this piece of profundity.

[96] The 'why' and the 'whence' are entirely other questions, not under discussion, as I understand Mr. Bradley. Not how experience gets itself born, but how it can be what it is after it is born, is the puzzle.

[97] Above, p. 199.

HOW TWO MINDS CAN
KNOW ONE THING* [98]

In the essay entitled 'Does Consciousness Exist?' I have tried to show that when we call an experience 'conscious,' that does not mean that it is suffused throughout with a peculiar modality of being ('psychic' being) as stained glass may be suffused with light, but rather that it stands in certain determinate relations to other portions of experience extraneous to itself. These form one peculiar 'context' for it; while, taken in another context of experiences, we class it as a fact in the physical world. This 'pen,' for example, is, in the first instance, a bald *that,* a datum, fact, phenomenon, content, or whatever other neutral or ambiguous name you may prefer to apply. I called it in that article a 'pure experience.' To get classed either as a physical pen or as some one's percept of a pen, it must assume a *function,* and that can only happen in a more complicated world. So far as in that world it is a stable feature, holds ink, marks paper and obeys the guidance of a hand, it is a physical pen. That is what we mean by being 'physical,' in a pen. So far as it is instable, on the contrary, coming and going with the movements of my eyes, altering with what I call my fancy, continuous with subsequent experiences of its 'having been' (in the past tense), it is the percept of a pen in my mind. Those peculiarities are what we mean by being 'conscious,' in a pen.

In Section VI of another [essay] [99] I tried to show that the same *that,* the same numerically identical pen of pure experience, can enter simultaneously into many conscious contexts, or, in other words, be an object for many different minds. I admitted that I had not space to treat of certain possible objections in that article; but in [the last essay] I took some of the objections up. At the end of that [essay] I said that still more formidable-sounding objections remained; so, to leave my pure-experience theory in as strong a state as possible, I propose to consider those objections now.

* From: E.R.E., 123–136.

[98] [Reprinted from *The Journal of Philosophy, Psychology, and Scientific Methods,* vol. II, No. 7, March 30, 1905.]

[99] "A World of Pure Experience," above, pp. 194–214.

1

The objections I previously tried to dispose of were purely logical or dialectical. No one identical term, whether physical or psychical, it had been said, could be the subject of two relations at once. This thesis I sought to prove unfounded. The objections that now confront us arise from the nature supposed to inhere in psychic facts specifically. Whatever may be the case with physical objects, a fact of consciousness, it is alleged (and indeed very plausibly), can not, without self-contradiction, be treated as a portion of two different minds, and for the following reasons.

In the physical world we make with impunity the assumption that one and the same material object can figure in an indefinitely large number of different processes at once. When, for instance, a sheet of rubber is pulled at its four corners, a unit of rubber in the middle of the sheet is affected by all four of the pulls. It *transmits* them each, as if it pulled in four different ways at once itself. So, an air-particle or an ether-particle 'compounds' the different directions of movement imprinted on it without obliterating their several individualities. It delivers them distinct, on the contrary, at as many several 'receivers' (ear, eye or what not) as may be 'tuned' to that effect. The apparent paradox of a distinctness like this surviving in the midst of compounding is a thing which, I fancy, the analyses made by physicists have by this time sufficiently cleared up.

But if, on the strength of these analogies, one should ask: "Why, if two or more lines can run through one and the same geometrical point, or if two or more distinct processes of activity can run through one and the same physical thing so that it simultaneously plays a rôle in each and every process, might not two or more streams of personal consciousness include one and the same unit of experience so that it would simultaneously be a part of the experience of all the different minds?" one would be checked by thinking of a certain peculiarity by which phenomena of consciousness differ from physical things.

While physical things, namely, are supposed to be permanent and to have their 'states,' a fact of consciousness exists but once and *is* a state. Its *esse* is *sentiri;* it is only so far as it is felt; and it is unambiguously and unequivocally exactly *what* is felt. The hypothesis under consideration would, however, oblige it to be felt equivocally, felt now as part of my mind and again at the same time *not* as a part of my mind, but of yours (for my mind is *not* yours), and this would seem impossible without doubling it into two distinct things, or, in other words, without reverting to the ordinary dualistic philosophy of insulated minds each knowing its object representatively as a third thing, —and that would be to give up the pure-experience scheme altogether.

Can we see, then, any way in which a unit of pure experience might enter into and figure in two diverse streams of consciousness without turning itself into the two units which, on our hypothesis, it must not be?

II

There is a way; and the first step towards it is to see more precisely how the unit enters into either one of the streams of consciousness alone. Just what, from being 'pure,' does its becoming 'conscious' *once* mean?

It means, first, that new experiences have supervened; and, second, that they have borne a certain assignable relation to the unit supposed. Continue, if you please, to speak of the pure unit as 'the pen.' So far as the pen's successors do but repeat the pen or, being different from it, are 'energetically' [100] related to it, it and they will form a group of stably existing physical things. So far, however, as its successors differ from it in another well-determined way, the pen will figure in their context, not as a physical, but as a mental fact. It will become a passing 'percept,' *my* percept of that pen. What now is that decisive well-determined way?

In the chapter on 'The Self,' in my *Principles of Psychology*, I explained the continuous identity of each personal consciousness as a name for the practical fact that new experiences[101] come which look back on the old ones, find them 'warm,' and greet and appropriate them as 'mine.' These operations mean, when analyzed empirically, several tolerably definite things, viz.:

1. That the new experience has past time for its 'content,' and in that time a pen that 'was';

2. That 'warmth' was also about the pen, in the sense of a group of feelings ('interest' aroused, 'attention' turned, 'eyes' employed, etc.) that were closely connected with it and that now recur and evermore recur with unbroken vividness, though from the pen of now, which may be only an image, all such vividness may have gone;

3. That these feelings are the nucleus of 'me';

4. That whatever once was associated wtih them was, at least for that one moment, 'mine'—my implement if associated with hand-

[100] [For an explanation of this expression, see above, p. 181.]

[101] I call them 'passing thoughts' in the book—the passage in point goes from pages 330 to 342 of vol. I.

feelings, my 'percept' only, if only eye-feelings and attention-feelings were involved.

The pen, realized in this retrospective way as my percept, thus figures as a fact of 'conscious' life. But it does so only so far as 'appropriation' has occurred; and appropriation is *part of the content of a later experience* wholly additional to the originally 'pure' pen. *That* pen, virtually both objective and subjective, is at its own moment actually and intrinsically neither. It has to be looked back upon and *used,* in order to be classed in either distinctive way. But its use, so called, is in the hands of the other experience, while *it* stands, throughout the operation, passive and unchanged.

If this pass muster as an intelligible account of how an experience originally pure can enter into one consciousness, the next question is as to how it might conceivably enter into two.

III

Obviously no new kind of condition would have to be supplied. All that we should have to postulate would be a second subsequent experience, collateral and contemporary with the first subsequent one, in which a similar act of appropriation should occur. The two acts would interfere neither with one another nor with the originally pure pen. It would sleep undisturbed in its own past, no matter how many such successors went through their several appropriative acts. Each would know it as 'my' percept, each would class it as a 'conscious' fact.

Nor need their so classing it interfere in the least with their classing it at the same time as a physical pen. Since the classing in both cases depends upon the taking of it in one group or another of associates, if the superseding experience were of wide enough 'span' it could think the pen in both groups simultaneously, and yet distinguish the two groups. It would then see the whole situation conformably to what we call 'the representative theory of cognition,' and that is what we all spontaneously do. As a man philosophizing 'popularly,' I believe that what I see myself writing with is double—I think it in its relations to physical nature, and also in its relations to my personal life; I see that it is in my mind, but that it also is a physical pen.

The paradox of the same experience figuring in two consciousnesses seems thus no paradox at all. To be 'conscious' means not simply to be, but to be reported, known, to have awareness of one's being added to that being; and this is just what happens when the appropriative experience supervenes. The pen-experience in its original immediacy is not aware of itself, it simply *is,* and the second experience is required for what we call awareness of it to occur.[102] The difficulty of understanding what happens here is, therefore, not a logical difficulty: there is no contradiction involved. It is an ontological difficulty rather. Experiences come on an enormous scale, and if we take them all together, they come in a chaos of incommensurable relations that we can not straighten out. We have to abstract different groups of them, and handle these separately if we are to talk of them at all. But how the experiences ever *get themselves made,* or *why* their characters and relations are just such as appear, we can not begin to understand. Granting, however, that, by hook or crook, they *can* get themselves made, and can appear in the successions that I have so schematically described, then we have to confess that even although (as I began by quoting from the adversary) 'a feeling only is as it is felt,' there is still nothing absurd in the notion of its being felt in two different ways at once, as yours, namely, and as mine. It is, indeed, 'mine' only as it is felt as mine, and 'yours' only as it is felt as yours. But it is felt as neither *by itself,* but only when 'owned' by our two several remembering experiences, just as one undivided estate is owned by several heirs.

IV

One word, now, before I close, about the corollaries of the views set forth. Since the acquisition of conscious quality on the part of an experience depends upon a context coming to it, it follows that the sum total of all experiences, having no context, can not strictly be called conscious at all. It is a *that,* an Absolute, a 'pure' experience on an enormous scale, undifferentiated and undifferentiable into thought and thing. This the post-Kantian idealists have always practically acknowledged by calling their doctrine an *Identitätsphilosophie.* The question of the *Beseelung* of the All of things ought not, then, even to be asked. No more ought the question of its *truth* to be asked, for truth is a relation inside of the sum total, obtaining between thoughts and something else, and thoughts, as we have seen, can only be contextual things. In these respects the pure experiences of our philosophy are, in themselves considered, so many little absolutes, the

---

[102] Shadworth Hodgson has laid great stress on the fact that the minimum of consciousness demands two subfeelings, of which the second retrospects the first. (Cf. the section 'Analysis of Minima' in his *Philosophy of Reflection,* vol. I, p. 248; also the chapter entitled 'The Moment of Experience' in his *Metaphysic of Experience,* vol. I, p. 34.) 'We live forward, but we understand backward' is a phrase of Kierkegaard's which Höffding quotes. [H. Höffding: "A Philosophical Confession," *Journal of Philosophy, Psychology and Scientific Methods,* vol. II, 1905, p. 86.]

philosophy of pure experience being only a more comminuted *Identitätsphilosophie*.[103]

Meanwhile, a pure experience can be postulated with any amount whatever of span or field. If it exert the retrospective and appropriative function on any other piece of experience, the latter thereby enters into its own conscious stream. And in this operation time intervals make no essential difference. After sleeping, my retrospection is as perfect as it is between two successive waking moments of my time. Accordingly if, millions of years later, a similarly retrospective experience should anyhow come to birth, my present thought would form a genuine portion of its long-span conscious life. 'Form a portion,' I say, but not in the sense that the two things could be entitatively or substantively one—they cannot, for they are numerically discrete facts—but only in the sense that the *functions* of my present thought, its knowledge, its purpose, its content and 'consciousness,' in short, being inherited, would be continued practically unchanged. Speculations like Fechner's, of an Earth-soul, of wider spans of consciousness enveloping narrower ones throughout the cosmos, are, therefore, philosophically quite in order, provided they distinguish the functional from the entitative point of view, and do not treat the minor consciousness under discussion as a kind of standing material of which the wider ones *consist*.[104]

PERCEPT AND CONCEPT—
THE IMPORT OF CONCEPTS*

The problem convenient to take up next in order will be that of the difference between thoughts and things. 'Things' are known to us by our senses, and are called 'presentations' by some authors, to distinguish them from the ideas or 'representations' which we may have when our senses are closed. I myself have grown accustomed to the words 'percept' and 'concept' in treating of the contrast, but concepts flow out of percepts and into them again, they are so interlaced, and our life rests on them so interchangeably and undiscriminatingly, that it is often difficult to impart quickly to beginners a clear notion of the difference meant. Sensation and thought in man are mingled, but they

[103] [Cf. below, pp. 307, 309.]

[104] [Cf. *A Pluralistic Universe*, below, pp. 529–545, 'Concerning Fechner,' and pp. 546–561, 'The Compounding of Consciousness.']

* From: S.P.P., 47–74.

vary independently. In our quadrupedal relatives thought proper is at a minimum, but we have no reason to suppose that their immediate life of feeling is either less or more copious than ours. Feeling must have been originally self-sufficing; and thought appears as a super-added function, adapting us to a wider environment than that of which brutes take account. Some parts of the stream of feeling must be more intense, emphatic, and exciting than others in animals as well as in ourselves; but whereas lower animals simply react upon these more salient sensations by appropriate movements, higher animals remember them, and men react on them intellectually, by using nouns, adjectives, and verbs to identify them when they meet them elsewhere.

The great difference between percepts and concepts[105] is that percepts are continuous and concepts are discrete. Not discrete in their *being,* for conception as an *act* is part of the flux of feeling, but discrete from each other in their several *meanings.* Each concept means just what it singly means, and nothing else; and if the conceiver does not know whether he means this or means that, it shows that his concept is imperfectly formed. The perceptual flux as such, on the contrary, *means* nothing, and is but what it immediately is. No matter how small a tract of it be taken, it is always a much-at-once, and contains innumerable aspects and characters which conception can pick out, isolate, and thereafter always intend. It shows duration, intensity, complexity or simplicity, interestingness, excitingness, pleasantness or their opposites. Data from all our senses enter into it, merged in a general extensiveness of which each occupies a big or little share. Yet all these parts leave its unity unbroken. Its boundaries are no more distinct than are those of the field of vision. Boundaries are things that intervene; but here nothing intervenes save parts of the perceptual flux itself, and these are overflowed by what they separate, so that whatever we distinguish and isolate conceptually is found perceptually to telescope and compenetrate and diffuse into its neighbors. The cuts we make are purely ideal. If my reader can succeed in abstracting from all conceptual interpretation and lapse back into his immediate sensible life at this very moment, he will find it to be what someone has called a big blooming buzzing confusion, as free from contradiction in its 'much-at-onceness' as it is all alive and evidently there.[106]

[105] In what follows I shall freely use synonyms for these two terms. 'Idea,' 'thought,' and 'intellection' are synonymous with 'concept.' Instead of 'percept' I shall often speak of 'sensation,' 'feeling,' 'intuition,' and sometimes of 'sensible experience' or of the 'immediate flow' of conscious life. Since Hegel's time what is simply perceived has been called the 'immediate,' while the 'mediated' is synonymous with what is conceived.

[106] Compare W. James: *A Pluralistic Universe,* below, pp. 294–296. Also *Psychology, Briefer Course,* pp. 157–166.

Out of this aboriginal sensible muchness attention carves out objects, which conception then names and identifies forever—in the sky 'constellations,' on the earth 'beach,' 'sea,' 'cliff,' 'bushes,' 'grass.' Out of time we cut 'days' and 'nights,' 'summers' and 'winters.' We say *what* each part of the sensible continuum is, and all these abstracted *whats* are concepts.[107]

The intellectual life of man consists almost wholly in his substitution of a conceptual order for the perceptual order in which his experience originally comes. But before tracing the consequences of the substitution, I must say something about the conceptual order itself.[108]

Trains of concepts unmixed with percepts grow frequent in the adult mind; and parts of these conceptual trains arrest our attention just as parts of the perceptual flow did, giving rise to concepts of a higher order of abstractness. So subtle is the discernment of man, and so great the power of some men to single out the most fugitive elements of what passes before them, that these new formations have no limit. Aspect within aspect, quality after quality, relation upon relation, absences and negations as well as present features, end by being noted and their names added to the store of nouns, verbs, adjectives, conjunctions, and prepositions by which the human mind interprets life. Every new book verbalizes some new concept, which becomes important in proportion to the use that can be made of it. Different universes of thought thus arise, with specific sorts of relation among their ingredients. The world of common-sense 'things'; the world of material tasks to be done; the mathematical world of pure forms; the

---

[107] On the function of conception consult: Sir William Hamilton's *Lectures on Logic*, 9, 10; H. L. Mansel, *Prolegomena Logica*, chap. i; A. Schopenhauer, *The World as Will*, etc., Supplements 6, 7 to book ii; W. James, *Principles of Psychology*, chap. xii; *Briefer Course*, chap. xiv. Also J. G. Romanes: *Mental Evolution in Man*, chaps. iii, iv; Th. Ribot: *l'Evolution des Idées Générales*, chap. vi; Th. Ruyssen, *Essai sur l'Evolution psychologique du Jugement*, chap. vii; Laromiguière, *Leçons de Philosophie*, part 2, lesson 12. The account I give directly contradicts that which Kant gave which has prevailed since Kant's time. Kant always speaks of the aboriginal sensible flux as a 'manifold' of which he considers the essential character to be its disconnectedness. To get any togetherness at all into it requires, he thinks, the agency of the 'transcendental ego of apperception,' and to get any definite connections requires the agency of the understanding, with its synthetizing concepts or 'categories.' 'Die Verbindung (conjunctio) eines Mannigfaltigen kann überhaupt niemals durch Sinne in uns kommen, und kann also auch nicht in der reinen Form der sinnlichen Anschauung zugleich mit enthalten sein; denn sie ist ein Actus der Spontaneität der Einbildungskraft, und, da man diese, zum Unterschiede von der Sinnlichkeit, Verstand nennen muss, so ist alle Verbindung . . . eine Verstandeshandlung.' K. d. r. V., 2te, Aufg., pp. 129–130. The reader must decide which account agrees best with his own actual experience.

[108] The substitution was first described in these terms by S. H. Hodgson in his *Philosophy of Reflection*, i, 288–310.

world of ethical propositions; the worlds of logic, of music, etc., all abstracted and generalized from long forgotten perceptual instances, from which they have as it were flowered out, return and merge themselves again in the particulars of our present and future perception. By those *whats* we apperceive all our *thises*. Percepts and concepts interpenetrate and melt together, impregnate and fertilize each other. Neither, taken alone, knows reality in its completeness. We need them both, as we need both our legs to walk with.

From Aristotle downwards philosophers have frankly admitted the indispensability, for complete knowledge of fact, of both the sensational and the intellectual contribution.[109] For complete knowledge of fact, I say; but facts are particulars and connect themselves with practical necessities and the arts; and Greek philosophers soon formed the notion that a knowledge of so-called 'universals,' consisting of concepts of abstract forms, qualities, numbers, and relations was the only knowledge worthy of the truly philosophic mind. Particular facts decay and our perceptions of them vary. A concept never varies; and between such unvarying terms the relations must be constant and express eternal verities. Hence there arose a tendency, which has lasted all through philosophy, to contrast the knowledge of universals and intelligibles, as god-like, dignified, and honorable to the knower, with that of particulars and sensibles as something relatively base which more allies us with the beasts.[110]

[109] See, for example, book i, chap. ii, of Aristotle's *Metaphysics.*

[110] Plato in numerous places, but chiefly in books 6 and 7 of the *Republic,* contrasts perceptual knowledge as 'opinion' with real knowledge, to the latter's glory. For an excellent historic sketch of this platonistic view see the first part of E. Laas's *Idealismus und Positivismus,* 1879. For expressions of the ultra-intellectualistic view, read the passage from *Plotinus on the Intellect* in C. M. Bakewell's *Source-book in Ancient Philosophy,* N. Y. 1907, pp. 353 f.; Bossuet, *Traité de la Connaissance de Dieu,* chap. iv, §§ v, vi; R. Cudworth, *A Treatise concerning eternal and immutable Morality,* books iii, iv.—'Plato,' writes Prof. Santayana, 'thought that all the truth and meaning of earthly things was the reference they contained to a heavenly original. This heavenly original we remember to recognize even among the distortions, disappearances, and multiplications of its ephemeral copies. . . . The impressions themselves have no permanence, no intelligible essence, but are always either arising or ceasing to be. There must be, he tells us, an eternal and clearly definable object of which the visible appearances to us are the multiform semblance; now by one trait, now by another, the phantom before us reminds us of that half-forgotten celestial reality and makes us utter its name. . . . We and the whole universe exist only in the attempt to return to our perfection, to lose ourselves again in God. That ineffable good is our natural possession; and all we honor in this life is but a partial recovery of our birthright; every delightful thing is like a rift in the clouds, through which we catch a glimpse of our native heaven. And if that heaven seems so far away, and the idea of it so dim and unreal, it is because we are so far from perfect, so immersed in what is alien and destructive to the soul.'

For rationalistic writers conceptual knowledge was not only the more noble knowledge, but it originated independently of all perceptual particulars. Such concepts as God, perfection, eternity, infinity, immutability, identity, absolute beauty, truth, justice, necessity, freedom, duty, worth, etc., and the part they play in our mind, are, it was supposed, impossible to explain as results of practical experience. The empiricist view, and probably the true view, is that they do result from practical experience.[111] But a more important question than that as to the origin of our concepts is that as to their functional use and value; —is *that* tied down to perceptual experience, or out of all relation to it? Is conceptual knowledge self-sufficing and a revelation all by itself, quite apart from its uses in helping to a better understanding of the world of sense?

Rationalists say, Yes. For, as we shall see in later places (page 241), the various conceptual universes referred to on page 234 can be considered in complete abstraction from perceptual reality, and when they are so considered, all sorts of fixed relations can be discovered among their parts. From these the *a priori* sciences of logic, mathematics, ethics, and æsthetics (so far as the last two can be called sciences at all) result. Conceptual knowledge must thus be called a self-sufficing revelation; and by rationalistic writers it has always been treated as admitting us to a diviner world, the world of universal rather than that of perishing facts, of essential qualities, immutable relations, eternal principles of truth and right. Emerson writes: 'Generalization is always a new influx of divinity into the mind: hence the thrill that attends it.' And a disciple of Hegel, after exalting the knowledge of 'the General, Unchangeable, and alone Valuable' above that of 'the Particular, Sensible and Transient,' adds that if you reproach philosophy with being unable to make a single grass-blade grow, or even to know how it does grow, the reply is that since such a

---

('Platonic Love in some Italian Poets,' in *Interpretations of Poetry and Religion*, 1896.)

This is the interpretation of Plato which has been current since Aristotle. It should be said that its profundity has been challenged by Prof. A. J. Stewart. (Plato's *Doctrine of Ideas*, Oxford, 1909.)

Aristotle found great fault with Plato's treatment of ideas as heavenly originals, but he agreed with him fully as to the superior excellence of the conceptual or theoretic life. In chapters vii and viii of book x of the *Nicomachean Ethics* he extols contemplation of universal relations as alone yielding pure happiness. 'The life of God, in all its exceeding blessedness, will consist in the exercise of philosophic thought; and of all human activities, that will be the happiest which is most akin to the divine.'

[111] John Locke, in his *Essay concerning Human Understanding*, books i, ii, was the great popularizer of this doctrine. Condillac's *Traité des Sensations*, Helvetius's work, *De l'Homme*, and James Mill's *Analysis of the Human Mind*, were more radical successors of Locke's great book.

particular 'how' stands not above but below knowledge, strictly so-called, such an ignorance argues no defect.[112]

To this ultra-rationalistic opinion the empiricist contention that *the significance of concepts consists always in their relation to perceptual particulars* has been opposed. Made of percepts, or distilled from parts of percepts, their essential office, it has been said, is to coalesce with percepts again, bringing the mind back into the perceptual world with a better command of the situation there. Certainly whenever we *can* do this with our concepts, we do *more* with them than when we leave them flocking with their abstract and motionless companions. It is possible therefore, to join the rationalists in allowing conceptual knowledge to be self-sufficing, while at the same time one joins the empiricists in maintaining that the full *value* of such knowledge is got only by combining it with perceptual reality again. This mediating attitude is that which this book must adopt. But to understand the nature of concepts better we must now go on to distinguish their *function* from their *content*.

The concept 'man,' to take an example, is three things: 1, the word itself; 2, a vague picture of the human form which has its own value in the way of beauty or not; and 3, an instrument for symbolizing certain objects from which we may expect human treatment when occasion arrives. Similarly of 'triangle,' 'cosine,'—they have their substantive value both as words and as images suggested, but they also have a functional value whenever they lead us elsewhere in discourse.

There are concepts, however, the image-part of which is so faint that their whole value seems to be functional. 'God,' 'cause,' 'number,' 'substance,' 'soul,' for example, suggest no definite picture; and their significance seems to consist entirely in their *tendency,* in the further turn which they may give to our action or our thought.[113] We cannot rest in the contemplation of their form, as we can in that of a 'circle' or a 'man'; we must pass beyond.

Now however beautiful or otherwise worthy of stationary contemplation the substantive part of a concept may be, the more important part of its significance may naturally be held to be the consequences to which it leads. These may lie either in the way of making us think, or in the way of making us act. Whoever has a clear idea of these knows effectively what the concept practically signifies, whether its substantive content be interesting in its own right or not.

[112] Michelet, Hegel's *Werke*, vii, 15, quoted by A. Gratry, *De la Connaissance de l'Âme*, i, 231. Compare the similar claim for philosophy in W. Wallace's *Prolegomena to Hegel*, 2d ed., 1894, pp. 28–29, and the long and radical statement of the same view in book iv of Ralph Cudworth's *Treatise on Eternal and Immutable Morality*.

[113] On this functional tendency compare H. Taine, *On Intelligence*, book i, chap. ii (1870).

This consideration has led to a method of interpreting concepts to which I shall give the name of *the Pragmatic Rule*.[114]

The pragmatic rule is that the meaning of a concept may always be found, if not in some sensible particular which it directly designates, then in some particular difference in the course of human experience which its being true will make. Test every concept by the question 'What sensible difference to anybody will its truth make?' and you are in the best possible position for understanding what it means and for discussing its importance. If, questioning whether a certain concept be true or false, you can think of absolutely nothing that would practically differ in the two cases, you may assume that the alternative is meaningless and that your concept is no distinct idea. If two concepts lead you to infer the same particular consequence, then you may assume that they embody the same meaning under different names.

This rule applies to concepts of every order of complexity, from simple terms to propositions uniting many terms.

So many disputes in philosophy hinge upon ill-defined words and ideas, each side claiming its own word or idea to be true, that any accepted method of making meanings clear must be of great utility. No method can be handier of application than our pragmatic rule. If you claim that any idea is true, assign at the same time some difference that its being true will make in some possible person's history, and we shall know not only just what you are really claiming but also how important an issue it is, and how to go to work to verify the claim. In obeying this rule we neglect the substantive content of the concept, and follow its function only. This neglect might seem at first sight to need excuse, for the content often has a value of its own which might conceivably add lustre to reality, if it existed, apart from any modification wrought by it in the other parts of reality. Thus it is often supposed that 'Idealism' is a theory precious in itself, even though no definite change in the details of our experience can be deduced from it. Later discussion will show that this is a superficial view, and that particular consequences are the only criterion of a concept's meaning, and the only test of its truth.

Instances are hardly called for, they are so obvious. That A and B are 'equal,' for example, means either that 'you will find no difference' when you pass from one to the other, or that in substituting one for the other in certain operations 'you will get the same result both times.' 'Substance' means that 'a definite group of sensations will recur.' 'Incommensurable' means that 'you are always confronted with a remainder.' 'Infinite' means either that, or that 'you can count

114 Compare W. James, *Pragmatism*, below, pp. 376–390 and *passim;* also Baldwin's *Dictionary of Philosophy*, article 'Pragmatism,' by C. S. Peirce.

as many units in a part as you can in the whole.' 'More' and 'less' mean certain sensations, varying according to the matter. 'Freedom' means 'no feeling of sensible restraint.' 'Necessity' means that 'your way is blocked in all directions save one.' 'God' means that 'you can dismiss certain kinds of fear,' 'cause' that 'you may expect certain sequences,' etc. etc. We shall find plenty of examples in the rest of this book; so I go back now to the more general question of whether the whole import of the world of concepts lies in its relation to perceptual experience, or whether it be also an independent revelation of reality. Great ambiguity is possible in answering this question, so we must mind our Ps and Qs.

The first thing to notice is that in the earliest stages of human intelligence, so far as we can guess at them, thought proper must have had an exclusively practical use. Men classed their sensations, substituting concepts for them, in order to 'work them for what they were worth,' and to prepare for what might lie ahead. Class-names suggest consequences that have attached themselves on other occasions to other members of the class—consequences which the present percept will also probably or certainly show.[115] The present percept in its immediacy may thus often sink to the status of a bare sign of the consequences which the substituted concept suggests.

The substitution of concepts and their connections, of a whole conceptual order, in short, for the immediate perceptual flow, thus widens enormously our mental panorama. Had we no concepts we should live simply 'getting' each successive moment of experience, as the sessile sea-anemone on its rock receives whatever nourishment the wash of the waves may bring. With concepts we go in quest of the absent, meet the remote, actively turn this way or that, bend our experience, and make it tell us whither it is bound. We change its order, run it backwards, bring far bits together and separate near bits, jump about over its surface instead of plowing through its continuity, string its items on as many ideal diagrams as our mind can frame. All these are ways of *handling* the perceptual flux and *meeting* distant parts of it; and as far as this primary function of conception goes, we can only conclude it to be what I began by calling it, a faculty superadded to our barely perceptual consciousness for its use in practically adapting us to a larger environment than that of which brutes take account.[116] We *harness* perceptual reality in concepts in order to drive it better to our ends.

[115] For practical uses of conception compare W. James, *Principles of Psychology*, chap. xxii; J. E. Miller, *The Psychology of Thinking*, 1909, *passim*, but especially chaps. xv, xvi, xvii.

[116] Herbert Spencer in his *Psychology*, parts iii and iv, has at great length tried to show that such adaptation is the sole meaning of our intellect.

Does our conceptual translation of the perceptual flux enable us also to understand the latter better? What do we mean by making us 'understand'? Applying our pragmatic rule to the interpretation of the word, we see that the better we understand anything the more we are able to *tell about it*. Judged by this test, concepts do make us understand our percepts better: knowing *what* these are, we can tell all sorts of farther truths about them, based on the relation of those whats to other whats. The whole system of relations, spatial, temporal, and logical, of our fact, gets plotted out. An ancient philosophical opinion, inherited from Aristotle, is that we do not understand a thing until we know it by its causes. When the maidservant says that 'the cat' broke the tea-cup, she would have us conceive the fracture in a causally explanatory way. No otherwise when Clerk-Maxwell asks us to conceive of gas-electricity as due to molecular bombardment. An imaginary agent out of sight becomes in each case a part of the cosmic context in which we now place the percept to be explained; and the explanation is valid in so far as the new causal *that* is itself conceived in a context that makes its existence probable, and with a nature agreeable to the effects it is imagined to produce. All our scientific explanations would seem to conform to this simple type of the 'necessary cat.' The conceived order of nature built round the perceived order and explaining it theoretically, as we say, is only a system of hypothetically imagined *thats,* the *whats* of which harmoniously connect themselves with the *what* of any *that* which we immediately perceive.

The system is essentially a topographic system, a system of the distribution of things. It tells us what's what, and where's where. In so far forth it merely prolongs that opening up of the perspective of practical consequences which we found to be the primordial utility of the conceiving faculty: it adapts us to an immense environment. Working by the causes of things we gain advantages which we never should have compassed had we worked by the things alone.

But in order to reach such results the concepts in the explanatory system must, I said, 'harmoniously connect.' What does that mean? Is this also only a practical advantage, or is it something more? It seems something more, for it points to the fact that when concepts of various sorts are once abstracted or constructed, new relations are then found between them, connecting them in peculiarly intimate, 'rational,' and unchangeable ways. In another book[117] I have tried to show that these rational relations are all products of our faculty of comparison and of our sense of 'more.'

The sciences which exhibit these relations are the so-called *a pri-*

---

[117] *Principles of Psychology*, 1890, above, pp. 74–133.

ori sciences of mathematics and logic.[118] But these sciences express relations of comparison and identification exclusively. Geometry and algebra, for example, first define certain conceptual objects, and then establish equations between them, substituting equals for equals. Logic has been defined as the 'substitution of similars'; and in general one may say that the perception of likeness and unlikeness generates the whole of 'rational' or 'necessary' truth. Nothing *happens* in the worlds of logic, mathematics or moral and æsthetic preference. The static nature of the relations in these worlds is what gives to the propositions that express them their 'eternal' character: The binomial theorem, e.g., expresses the value of any power of any sum of two terms, to the end of time.

These vast unmoving systems of universal terms form the new worlds of thought of which I spoke on page 236. The terms are elements (or are framed of elements) abstracted from the perceptual flux; but in their abstract shape we note relations between them (and again between these relations) which enable us to set up various schemes of fixed serial orders or of 'more and more.' The terms are indeed man-made, but the order, being established solely by comparison, is fixed by the nature of the terms on the one hand and by our power of perceiving relations on the other. Thus two abstract twos are always the same as an abstract four; what contains the container contains the contained of whatever material either be made; equals added to equals always give equal results, in the world in which abstract equality is the only property the terms are supposed to possess; the more than the more is more than the less, no matter in what direction of moreness we advance; if you dot off a term in one series every time you dot one off in another, the two series will either never end, or will come to an end together, or one will be exhausted first, etc. etc.; the result being those skeletons of 'rational' or 'necessary' truth in which our logic- and mathematics-books (sometimes our philosophy-books) arrange their universal terms.

The 'rationalization' of any mass of perceptual fact consists in assimilating its concrete terms, one by one, to so many terms of the conceptual series, and then in assuming that the relations intuitively found among the latter are what connect the former too. Thus we rationalize gas-pressure by identifying it with the blows of hypothetic molecules; then we see that the more closely the molecules are crowded the more frequent the blows upon the containing walls will become; then we discern the exact proportionality of the crowding with the number of blows; so that finally Mariotte's empirical law gets

[118] The 'necessary' character of the abstract truths which these sciences exhibit is well explained by G. H. Lewes: *Problems of Life and Mind,* Problem 1, chapters iv, xiii, especially p. 405 f. of the English edition (1874).

rationally explained. All our transformations of the sense-order into a more rational equivalent are similar to this one. We interrogate the beautiful apparition, as Emerson calls it, which our senses ceaselessly raise upon our path, and the items there refer us to their interpretants in the shape of ideal constructions in some static arrangement which our mind has already made out of its concepts alone. The interpretants are then substituted for the sensations, which thus get rationally conceived. To 'explain' means to coördinate, one to one, the *thises* of the perceptual flow with the *whats* of the ideal manifold, whichever it be.[119]

We may well call this a theoretic conquest over the order in which nature orginally comes. The conceptual order into which we translate our experience seems not only a means of practical adaptation, but the revelation of a deeper level of reality in things. Being more constant, it is *truer*, less illusory than the perceptual order, and ought to command our attention more.

There is still another reason why conception appears such an exalted function. Concepts not only guide us over the map of life, but we *revalue* life by their use. Their relation to percepts is like that of sight to touch. Sight indeed helps us by preparing us for contacts while they are yet far off, but it endows us in addition with a new world of optical splendor, interesting enough all by itself to occupy a busy life. Just so do concepts bring their proper splendor. The mere possession of such vast and simple pictures is an inspiring good: they arouse new feelings of sublimity, power, and admiration, new interests and motivations.

Ideality often clings to things only when they are taken thus abstractly. "Causes, as anti-slavery, democracy, etc., dwindle when realized in their sordid particulars. Abstractions will touch us when we are callous to the concrete instances in which they lie embodied. Loyal in our measure to particular ideals, we soon set up abstract loyalty as something of a superior order, to be infinitely loyal to; and truth at large becomes a 'momentous issue' compared with which truths in detail are 'poor scraps, mere crumbling successes.' "[120] So

[119] Compare W. Ostwald: *Vorlesungen über Naturphilosophie, Sechste Vorlesung.*

[120] J. Royce: *The Philosophy of Loyalty,* 1908, particularly Lecture vii, § 5.
Emerson writes: 'Each man sees over his own experience a certain stain of error, whilst that of other men looks fair and ideal. Let any man go back to those delicious relations which make the beauty of his life, which have given him sincerest instruction and nourishment, he will shrink and moan. Alas! I know not why, but infinite compunctions embitter in mature life the remembrances of budding joy, and cover every beloved name. Everything is beautiful seen from the point of view of the intellect, or as truth, but all is sour, if seen as experience. Details are melancholy; the plan is seemly and noble. In the actual world—the painful kingdom of time and place—dwell care, and canker, and fear. With thought, with the ideal, is immortal hilarity, the rose of Joy.

strongly do objects that come as universal and eternal arouse our sensibilities, so greatly do life's values deepen when we translate percepts into ideas! The translation appears as far more than the original's equivalent.

Concepts thus play three distinct parts in human life.

1. They steer us practically every day, and provide an immense map of relations among the elements of things, which, though not now, yet on some possible future occasion, may help to steer us practically;

2. They bring new values into our perceptual life, they reanimate our wills, and make our action turn upon new points of emphasis;

3. The map which the mind frames out of them is an object which possesses, when once it has been framed, an independent existence. It suffices all by itself for purposes of study. The 'eternal' truths it contains would have to be acknowledged even were the world of sense annihilated.

We thus see clearly what is gained and what is lost when percepts are translated into concepts. Perception is solely of the here and now; conception is of the like and unlike, of the future, of the past, and of the far away. But this map of what surrounds the present, like all maps, is only a surface; its features are but abstract signs and symbols of things that in themselves are concrete bits of sensible experience. We have but to weigh extent against content, thickness against spread, and we see that for some purposes the one, for other purposes the other, has the higher value. Who can decide offhand which is absolutely better to live or to understand life? We must do both alternately, and a man can no more limit himself to either than a pair of scissors can cut with a single one of its blades.

PERCEPT AND CONCEPT—
THE ABUSE OF CONCEPTS* [121]

In spite of this obvious need of holding our percepts fast if our conceptual powers are to mean anything distinct, there has always been a

---

Round it all the muses sing. But grief clings to names and persons, and the partial interests of to-day and yesterday.' (*Essay on Love*.)

* From: S.P.P., 75–97.

[121] [This chapter and the following chapter do not appear as separate chapters in the manuscript. ED.] [See below, p. 852, Annotated Bibliography, 1911, #1. J. J. McD.]

tendency among philosophers to treat conception as the more essential thing in knowledge.[122] The Platonizing persuasion has ever been that the intelligible order ought to supersede the senses rather than interpret them. The senses, according to this opinion, are organs of wavering illusion that stand in the way of 'knowledge,' in the unalterable sense of that term. They are an unfortunate complication on which philosophers may safely turn their backs.

'Your sensational modalities,' writes one of these, 'are but darkness, remember that. Mount higher, up to reason, and you will see light. Impose silence on your senses, your imagination, and your passions, and you will then hear the pure voice of interior truth, the clear and evident replies of our common mistress [reason]. Never confound that evidence which results from the comparison of ideas with the vivacity of those feelings which move and touch you. . . . We must follow reason despite the caresses, the threats and the insults of the body to which we are conjoined, despite the action of the objects that surround us. . . . I exhort you to recognize the difference there is between knowing and feeling, between our clear ideas, and our sensations always obscure and confused.' [123]

This is the traditional intellectualist creed. When Plato, its originator, first thought of concepts as forming an entirely separate world and treated this as the only object fit for the study of immortal minds, he lit up an entirely new sort of enthusiasm in the human breast. These objects were precious objects, concrete things were dross. Introduced by Dion, who had studied at Athens, to the corrupt and worldly court of the tyrant of Syracuse, Plato, as Plutarch tells us, 'was received with wonderful kindness and respect. . . . The citizens began to entertain marvellous hopes of a speedy reformation when they observed the modesty which now ruled the banquets, and the general decorum which reigned in all the court, their tyrant also behaving himself with gentleness and humanity. . . . There was a general passion for reasoning and philosophy, so much so that the very palace, it is reported, was filled with dust by the concourse of the students in mathematics who were working their problems there' in the sand. Some 'professed to be indignant that the Athenians, who formerly had come to Syracuse with a great fleet and numerous army, and perished miserably without being able to take the city, should now, by means of one sophister, overturn the sovereignty of Dionysius; inveigling him to cashier his guard of 10,000 lances, dismiss a

---

[122] The traditional rationalist view would have it that to understand life, without entering its turmoil, is the absolutely better part. Philosophy's 'special work,' writes William Wallace, 'is to comprehend the world, not try to make it better.' (*Prolegomena to the Study of Hegel's Philosophy,* 2d edition, Oxford, 1894, p. 29).

[123] Malebranche: *Entretiens sur la Métaphysique,* 3me. Entretien, viii, 9.

navy of 400 galleys, disband an army of 10,000 horse and many times over that number of foot, and go seek in the schools an unknown and imaginary bliss, and learn by the mathematics how to be happy.'

Having now set forth the merits of the conceptual translation, I must proceed to show its shortcomings. We extend our view when we insert our percepts into our conceptual map. We learn *about* them, and of some of them we transfigure the value; but the map remains superficial through the abstractness, and false through the discreteness of its elements; and the whole operation, so far from making things appear more rational, becomes the source of quite gratuitous unintelligibilities. Conceptual knowledge is forever inadequate to the fulness of the reality to be known. Reality consists of existential particulars as well as of essences and universals and class-names, and of existential particulars we become aware only in the perceptual flux. The flux can never be superseded. We must carry it with us to the bitter end of our cognitive business, keeping it in the midst of the translation even when the latter proves illuminating, and falling back on it alone when the translation gives out. 'The insuperability of sensation' would be a short expression of my thesis.

To prove it, I must show: 1. That concepts are secondary formations, inadequate, and only ministerial; and 2. That they falsify as well as omit, and make the flux impossible to understand.

1. Conception is a secondary process, not indispensable to life. It presupposes perception, which is self-sufficing, as all lower creatures, in whom conscious life goes on by reflex adaptations, show.

To understand a concept you must know what it *means*. It means always some *this*, or some abstract portion of a *this,* with which we first made acquaintance in the perceptual world, or else some grouping of such abstract portions. All conceptual content is borrowed: to know what the concept 'color' means you must have *seen* red or blue, or green. To know what 'resistance' means, you must have made some effort; to know what 'motion' means, you must have had some experience, active or passive, thereof. This applies as much to concepts of the most rarified order as to qualities like 'bright' and 'loud.' To know what the word 'illation' means one must once have sweated through some particular argument. To know what a 'proportion' means one must have compared ratios in some sensible case. You can create new concepts out of old elements, but the elements must have been perceptually given; and the famous world of universals would disappear like a soap-bubble if the definite contents of feeling, the *thises* and *thats,* which its terms severally denote, could be at once withdrawn. Whether our concepts live by returning to the perceptual world or not, they live by having come from it. It is the nourishing ground from which their sap is drawn.

2. Conceptual treatment of perceptual reality makes it seem para-

doxical and incomprehensible; and when radically and consistently carried out, it leads to the opinion that perceptual experience is not reality at all, but an appearance or illusion.

Briefly, this is a consequence of two facts: First, that when we substitute concepts for percepts, we substitute their relations also. But since the relations of concepts are of static comparison only, it is impossible to substitute them for the dynamic relations with which the perceptual flux is filled. Secondly, the conceptual scheme, consisting as it does of discontinuous terms, can only cover the perceptual flux in spots and incompletely. The one is no full measure of the other, essential features of the flux escaping whenever we put concepts in its place.

This needs considerable explanation, for we have concepts not only of qualities and relations, but of happenings and actions; and it might seem as if these could make the conceptual order active.[124] But this would be a false interpretation. The concepts themselves are fixed, even though they designate parts that move in the flux; they do not act, even though they designate activities; and when we substitute them and their order, we substitute a scheme the intrinsically stationary nature of which is not altered by the fact that some of its terms symbolize changing originals. The concept of 'change,' for example, is always that fixed concept. If it changed, its original self would have to stay to mark what it had changed from; and even then the change would be a perceived continuous process, of which the translation into concepts could only consist in the judgment that later and earlier parts of it *differed*—such 'differences' being conceived as absolutely static relations.

[124] Prof. Hibben, in an article in the *Philosophic Review*, vol. xix, pp. 125 ff. (1910), seeks to defend the conceptual order against attacks similar to those in the text, which, he thinks, come from misapprehensions of the true function of logic. 'The peculiar function of thought is to represent the continuous,' he says, and he proves it by the example of the calculus. I reply that the calculus, in substituting for certain perceptual continuities its peculiar symbols, lets us follow changes point by point, and is thus their *practical,* but not their *sensible* equivalent. It cannot *reveal* any change to one who never felt it, but it can lead him to where the change would lead him. It may practically replace the change, but it cannot *reproduce* it. What I am contending for is that the non-reproducible part of reality is an essential part of the content of philosophy, whilst Hibben and the logicists seem to believe that conception, if only adequately attained to, might be all-sufficient. 'It is the peculiar duty and privilege of philosophy,' Mr. Hibben writes, 'to exalt the prerogatives of intellect.' He claims that universals are able to deal adequately with particulars, and that concepts do not so exclude each other, as my text has accused them of doing. Of course 'synthetic' concepts abound, with subconcepts included in them, and the *a priori* world is full of them. But they are all designative; and I think that no careful reader of my text will accuse me of identifying 'knowledge' with either perception or conception absolutely or exclusively. Perception gives 'intension,' conception gives 'extension' to our knowledge.

Whenever we conceive a thing we *define* it; and if we still don't understand, we define our definition. Thus I define a certain percept by saying 'this is motion,' or 'I am moving'; and then I define motion by calling it the 'being in new positions at new moments of time.' This habit of telling what everything is becomes inveterate. The farther we push it, the more we learn *about* our subject of discourse, and we end by thinking that knowing the latter always consists in getting farther and farther away from the perceptual type of experience. This uncriticized habit, added to the intrinsic charm of the conceptual form, is the source of 'intellectualism' in philosophy.

But intellectualism quickly breaks down. When we try to exhaust motion by conceiving it as a summation of parts, *ad infinitum,* we find only insufficiency. Although, when you have a continuum given, you can make cuts and dots in it, *ad libitum,* enumerating the dots and cuts will not give you your continuum back. The rationalist mind admits this; but instead of seeing that the fault is with the concepts, it blames the perceptual flux. This, Kant contends, has no reality in itself, being a mere apparitional birth-place for concepts, to be substituted indefinitely. When these themselves are seen never to attain to a completed sum, reality is sought by such thinkers outside both of the perceptual flow and of the conceptual scheme. Kant lodges it before the flow, in the shape of so-called 'things in themselves';[125] others place it beyond perception, as an Absolute (Bradley), or represent it as a Mind whose ways of thinking transcend ours (Green, the Cairds, Royce). In either case, both our percepts and our concepts are held by such philosophers to falsify reality; but the concepts less than the percepts, for they are static, and by all rationalist authors the ultimate reality is supposed to be static also, while perceptual life fairly boils over with activity and change.

If we take a few examples, we can see how many of the troubles of philosophy come from assuming that to be understood (or 'known' in the only worthy sense of the word) our flowing life must be cut into discrete bits and pinned upon a fixed relational scheme.

Example 1. *Activity and causation are incomprehensible,* for the conceptual scheme yields nothing like them. Nothing happens therein: concepts are 'timeless,' and can only be juxtaposed and compared. The concept 'dog' does not bite; the concept 'cock' does not crow. So Hume and Kant translate the fact of causation into the crude juxtaposition of two phenomena. Later authors, wishing to mitigate the crudeness, resolve the adjacency, whenever they can, into identity: cause and effect must be the same reality in disguise, and our perception of difference in these successions thus becomes an illusion. Lotze

---

[125] 'We must suppose Noumena,' says Kant, 'in order to set bounds to the objective validity of sense-knowledge' (*Krit. d. reinen Vernunft,* 2d ed., p. 310). The old moral need of somehow rebuking 'Sinnlichkeit'!

elaborately establishes that the 'influencing' of one thing by another is inconceivable. 'Influence' is a concept, and, as such, a distinct third thing, to be identified neither with the agent nor the patient. What becomes of it on its way from the former to the latter? And when it finds the latter, how does it act upon it? By a second influence which it puts forth in turn?—But then again how? and so forth, and so forth till our whole intuition of activity gets branded as illusory because you cannot possibly reproduce its flowing substance by juxtaposing the discrete. Intellectualism draws the dynamic continuity out of nature as you draw the thread out of a string of beads.

Example 2. *Knowledge is impossible;* for knower is one concept, and known is another. Discrete, separated by a chasm, they are mutually 'transcendent' things, so that how an object can ever get into a subject, or a subject ever get at an object, has become the most unanswerable of philosophic riddles. An insincere riddle, too, for the most hardened 'epistemologist' never really doubts that knowledge somehow does come off.

Example 3. *Personal identity is conceptually impossible.* 'Ideas' and 'states of mind' are discrete concepts, and a series of them in time means a plurality of disconnected terms. To such an atomistic plurality the associationists reduce our mental life. Shocked at the discontinuous character of their scheme, the spiritualists assume a 'soul' or 'ego' to melt the separate ideas into one collective consciousness. But this ego itself is but another discrete concept; and the only way not to pile up more puzzles is to endow it with an incomprehensible power of producing that very character of manyness-in-oneness of which rationalists refuse the gift when offered in its immediate perceptual form.

Example 4. *Motion and change are impossible.* Perception changes pulsewise, but the pulses continue each other and melt their bounds. In conceptual translation, however, a continuum can only stand for elements with other elements between them *ad infinitum,* all separately conceived; and such an infinite series can never be exhausted by successive addition. From the time of Zeno the Eleatic, this intrinsic contradictoriness of continuous change has been one of the worst skulls at intellectualism's banquet.

Example 5. *Resemblance, in the way in which we naïvely perceive it, is an illusion.* Resemblance must be *defined;* and when defined it reduces to a mixture of identity with otherness. To know a likeness understandingly we must be able to abstract the identical point distinctly. If we fail of this, we remain in our perceptual limbo of 'confusion.'

Example 6. *Our immediate life is full of the sense of direction, but no concept of the direction of a process is possible until the process is completed.* Defined as it is by a beginning and an ending, a direction can never be prospectively but only retrospectively known. Our perceptual discernment beforehand of the way we are going, and all our dim foretastes of the future, have therefore to be treated as inexplicable or illusory features of experience.

Example 7. *No real thing can be in two relations at once;* the same moon, for example, cannot be seen both by you and by me. For the concept 'seen by you' is not the concept 'seen by me'; and if, taking the moon as a grammatical subject and, predicating one of these concepts of it, you then predicate the other also, you become guilty of the logical sin of saying that a thing can both be A and not-A at once. Learned trifling again; for clear though the conceptual contradictions be, nobody sincerely disbelieves that two men see the same thing.

Example 8. *No relation can be comprehended or held to be real in the form in which we innocently assume it.* A relation is a distinct concept; and when you try to make two other concepts continuous by putting a relation between them, you only increase the discontinuity. You have now conceived three things instead of two, and have two gaps instead of one to bridge over. Continuity is impossible in the conceptual world.

Example 9. *The very relation of subject to predicate in our judgments, the backbone of conceptual thinking itself, is unintelligible and self-contradictory.* Predicates are ready-made universal ideas by which we qualify perceptual singulars or other ideas. Sugar, for example, we say 'is' sweet. But if the sugar was *already* sweet, you have made no step in knowledge; whilst if not so already, you are identifying it with a concept, with which, in its universality, the particular sugar cannot be identical. Thus neither the sugar as described, nor your description, is comprehensible.[126]

These profundities of inconceivability, and many others like them, arise from the vain attempt to reconvert the manifold into which our conception has resolved things, back into the continuum out of which it came. The concept 'many' is not the concept 'one'; therefore the

[126] I have cited in the text only such conceptual puzzles as have become classic in philosophy, but the concepts current in physical science have also developed mutual oppugnancies which (although not yet classic commonplaces in philosophy) are beginning to make physicists doubt whether such notions develop unconditional 'truth.' Many physicists now think that the concepts of 'matter,' 'mass,' 'atom,' 'ether,' 'inertia,' 'force,' etc. are not so much duplicates of hidden realities in nature as mental instruments to handle nature by after-substitution of their scheme. They are considered, like the kilogram or the imperial yard, 'artefacts,' not revelations. The literature here is copious: J. B. Stallo's *Concepts and Theories of Modern Physics* (1882); pp. 136–140 especially, are fundamental. Mach, Ostwald, Pearson, Duhem, Milhaud, LeRoy, Wilbois, H. Poincaré, are other critics of a similar sort.

manyness-in-oneness which perception offers is impossible to construe intellectually. Youthful readers will find such difficulties too whimsical to be taken seriously; but since the days of the Greek sophists these dialectic puzzles have lain beneath the surface of all our thinking like the shoals and snags in the Mississippi river; and the more intellectually conscientious the thinkers have been, the less they have allowed themselves to disregard them. But most philosophers have noticed this or that puzzle only, and ignored the others. The pyrrhonian Sceptics first, then Hegel,[127] then in our day Bradley and Bergson, are the only writers I know who have faced them collectively, and proposed a solution applicable to them all.

The sceptics gave up the whole notion of truth light-heartedly, and advised their pupils not to care about it.[128] Hegel wrote so abominably that I cannot understand him, and will say nothing about him here.[129] Bradley and Bergson write with beautiful clearness and their arguments continue all that I have said.

Mr. Bradley agrees that immediate feeling possesses a native wholeness which conceptual treatment analyzes into a many, but cannot unite again. In every 'this' as merely felt, Bradley says, we 'encounter' reality, but we encounter it only as a fragment, see it, as it were, only 'through a hole.' [130] Our sole practicable way of extending and completing this fragment is by using our intellect with its universal ideas. But with ideas, that harmonious compenetration of manyness-in-oneness which feeling originally gave is no longer possible. Concepts indeed extend our *this,* but lose the inner secret of its wholeness; when ideal 'truth' is substituted for 'reality' the very nature of 'reality' disappears.

The fault being due entirely to the conceptual form in which we have to think things, one might naturally expect that one who recognizes its inferiority to the perceptual form as clearly as Mr. Bradley does, would try to save both forms for philosophy, delimiting their scopes, and showing how, as our experience works, they supplement each other. This is M. Bergson's procedure; but Bradley, though a traitor to orthodox intellectualism in holding fast to feeling as a revealer of the inner oneness of reality, has yet remained orthodox

---

[127] I omit Herbart, perhaps wrongly.

[128] See any history of philosophy, *sub voce* 'Pyrrho.'

[129] Hegel connects immediate perception with ideal truth by a ladder of intermediary concepts—at least, I suppose they are concepts. The best opinion among his interpreters seems to be that ideal truth does not abolish immediate perception, but preserves it as an indispensable 'moment.' Compare, e. g., H. W. Dresser: *The Philosophy of the Spirit,* 1908; Supplementary Essay: 'On the Element of Irrationality in the Hegelian Dialectic.' In other words Hegel does not pull up the ladder after him when he gets to the top, and may therefore be counted as a non-intellectualist, in spite of his desperately intellectualist *tone.*

[130] F. H. Bradley: *The Principles of Logic,* book i, chap. ii, pp. 29–32.

enough to refuse to admit immediate feeling into 'philosophy' at all. 'For worse or for better,' he writes, 'the man who stays on particular feeling must remain outside philosophy.' The philosopher's business, according to Mr. Bradley, is to qualify the real 'ideally' (i. e. by concepts), and never to look back. The 'ideas' meanwhile yield nothing but a patchwork, and show no unity like that which the living perception gave. What shall one do in these perplexing circumstances? Unwilling to go back, Bradley only goes more desperately forward. He makes a flying leap ahead, and assumes, beyond the vanishing point of the whole conceptual perspective, an 'absolute' reality, in which the coherency of feeling and the completeness of the intellectual ideal shall unite in some indescribable way. Such an absolute totality-in unity *can* be, it *must* be, it *shall* be, it *is* he says. Upon this incomprehensible metaphysical object the Bradleyan metaphysic establishes its domain.[131]

The sincerity of Bradley's criticisms has cleared the air of metaphysics and made havoc with old party lines. But, critical as he is, Mr. Bradley preserves one prejudice uncriticized. Perception 'untransmuted,' he believes, must not, cannot, shall not, enter into final 'truth.'

Such loyalty to a blank direction in thought, no matter where it leads you, is pathetic: concepts disintegrate—no matter, their way must be pursued; percepts are integral—no matter, they must be left behind. When anti-sensationalism has become an obstinacy like this, one feels that it draws near its end.

Since it is only the conceptual form which forces the dialectic contradictions upon the innocent sensible reality, the remedy would seem to be simple. Use concepts when they help, and drop them when they hinder understanding; and take reality bodily and integrally up into philosophy in exactly the perceptual shape in which it comes. The aboriginal flow of feeling sins only by a quantitative defect. There is always much-at-once of it, but there is never enough, and we desiderate the rest. The only way to get the rest without wading through all future time in the person of numberless perceivers, is to substitute our various conceptual systems which, monstrous abridgments though they be, are nevertheless each an equivalent, for some partial aspect of the full perceptual reality which we can never grasp.

This, essentially, is Bergson's view of the matter, and with it I think that we should rest content.[132]

I will now sum up compendiously the result of what precedes. If

[131] Mr. Bradley has expressed himself most pregnantly in an article in volume xviii, N. S. of *Mind*, p. 489. See also his *Appearance and Reality, passim*, especially the Appendix to the second edition.

[132] Bergson's most compendious statement of his doctrine is in the 'Introduction à la Métaphysique,' in the *Revue de Métaphysique et de Morale*, 1903, p. i. For a brief comparison between him and Bradley, see an essay by W. James, in the *Journal of Philosophy*, vol. vii, no. 2.

the aim of philosophy were the taking full possession of all reality by the mind, then nothing short of the whole of immediate perceptual experience could be the subject-matter of philosophy, for only in such experience is reality intimately and concretely found. But the philosopher, although he is unable as a finite being to compass more than a few passing moments of such experience, is yet able to extend his knowledge beyond such moments by the ideal symbol of the other moments.[133] He thus commands vicariously innumerable perceptions that are out of range. But the concepts by which he does this, being thin extracts from perception, are always insufficient representatives thereof; and, although they yield wider information, must never be treated after the rationalistic fashion, as if they gave a deeper quality of truth. The deeper features of reality are found only in perceptual experience. Here alone do we acquaint ourselves with continuity, or the immersion of one thing in another, here alone with self, with substance, with qualities, with activity in its various modes, with time, with cause, with change, with novelty, with tendency, and with freedom. Against all such features of reality the method of conceptual translation, when candidly and critically followed out, can only raise its *non possumus,* and brand them as unreal or absurd.

PERCEPT AND CONCEPT—
SOME COROLLARIES*

The first corollary of the conclusions of the foregoing chapter is that *the tendency known in philosophy as empiricism, becomes confirmed.* Empiricism proceeds from parts to wholes, treating the parts as fundamental both in the order of being and in the order of our knowledge.[134] In human experience the parts are percepts, built out into wholes by our conceptual additions. The percepts are singulars that

[133] It would seem that in 'mystical' ways, he may extend his vision to an even wider perceptual panorama than that usually open to the scientific mind. I understand Bergson to favor some such idea as this. See W. James: 'A Suggestion about Mysticism,' *Journal of Philosophy,* vii, 4. The subject of mystical knowledge, as yet very imperfectly understood, has been neglected both by philosophers and scientific men.

* From: S.P.P., 98–112.

[134] Naturally this applies in the present place only to the greater whole which philosophy considers; the universe namely, and its parts, for there are plenty of minor wholes (animal and social organisms, for example) in which both the being of the parts and our understanding of the parts are founded.

change incessantly and never return exactly as they were before. This brings an element of concrete novelty into our experience. This novelty finds no representation in the conceptual method, for concepts are abstracted from experiences already seen or given, and he who uses them to divine the new can never do so but in ready-made and ancient terms. Whatever actual novelty the future may contain (and the singularity and individuality of each moment makes it novel) escapes conceptual treatment altogether. Properly speaking, concepts are postmortem preparations, sufficient only for retrospective understanding; and when we use them to define the universe prospectively we ought to realize that they can give only a bare abstract outline or approximate sketch, in the filling out of which perception must be invoked.

Rationalistic philosophy has always aspired to a rounded-in view of the whole of things, a closed system of kinds, from which the notion of essential novelty being possible is ruled out in advance. For empiricism, on the other hand, reality cannot be thus confined by a conceptual ring-fence. It overflows, exceeds, and alters. It may turn into novelties, and can be known adequately only by following its singularities from moment to moment as our experience grows. Empiricist philosophy thus renounces the pretension to an all-inclusive vision. It ekes out the narrowness of personal experience by concepts which it finds useful but not sovereign; but it stays inside the flux of life expectantly, recording facts, not formulating laws, and never pretending that man's relation to the totality of things as a philosopher is essentially different from his relation to the parts of things as a daily patient or agent in the practical current of events. Philosophy, like life, must keep the doors and windows open.

In the remainder of this book we shall hold fast to this empiricist view. We shall insist that, as reality is created temporally day by day, concepts, although a magnificent sketch-map for showing us our bearings, can never fitly supersede perception, and that the 'eternal' systems which they form should least of all be regarded as realms of being to know which is a kind of knowing that casts the knowledge of particulars altogether into the shade. That rationalist assumption is quite beside the mark. Thus does philosophy prove again that essential identity with science which we argued for in our first chapter.[135]

The last paragraph does not mean that concepts and the relations between them are not just as 'real' in their 'eternal' way as percepts are in their temporal way. What is it to be 'real'? The best definition I know is that which the pragmatist rule gives: 'anything is real of

[135] One way of stating the empiricist contention is to say that the 'alogical' enters into philosophy on an equal footing with the 'logical.' Mr. Belfort Bax, in his book, *The Roots of Reality* (1907), formulates his empiricism (such as it is) in this way. (See particularly chap. iii.) Compare also E. D. Fawcett: *The Individual and Reality, passim,* but especially part ii, chaps. iv and v.

which we find ourselves obliged to take account in any way.' [136] Concepts are thus as real as percepts, for we cannot live a moment without taking account of them. But the 'eternal' kind of being which they enjoy is inferior to the temporal kind, because it is so static and schematic and lacks so many characters which temporal reality possesses. Philosophy must thus recognize many realms of reality which mutually interpenetrate. The conceptual systems of mathematics, logic, æsthetics, ethics, are such realms, each strung upon some peculiar form of relation, and each differing from perceptual reality in that in no one of them is history or happening displayed. Perceptual reality involves and contains all these ideal systems, and vastly more besides.

A concept, it was said above, means always the same thing: Change means always change, white always white, a circle always a circle. On this self-sameness of conceptual objects the static and 'eternal' character of our systems of ideal truth is based; for a relation, once perceived to obtain, must obtain always, between terms that do not alter. But many persons find difficulty in admitting that a concept used in different contexts can be intrinsically the same. When we call both snow and paper 'white' it is supposed by these thinkers that there must be two predicates in the field. As James Mill says: [137] 'Every colour is an individual colour, every size is an individual size, every shape is an individual shape. But things have no individual colour in common, no individual shape in common; no individual size in common; that is to say, they have neither shape, colour, nor size in common. What, then, is it which they have in common which the mind can take into view? Those who affirmed that it was something, could by no means tell. They substituted words for things; using vague and mystical phrases, which, when examined, meant nothing.' The truth, according to this nominalist author, is that the only thing that can be possessed in common by two objects is the same *name*. Black in the coat and black in the shoe are the same in so far forth as both shoe and coat are called black—the fact that on this view the name can never twice be the 'same' being quite overlooked. What now does the concept 'same' signify? Applying, as usual, the pragmatic rule, we find that when we call two objects the same we mean either (a) that no difference can be found between them when compared, or (b) that we can substitute the one for the other in certain operations without changing the result. If we are to discuss sameness profitably we must bear these pragmatic meanings in mind.

Do then the snow and the paper show no difference in color? And can we use them indifferently in operations? They may certainly re-

---

[136] Prof. A. E. Taylor gives this pragmatist definition in his *Elements of Metaphysics* (1903), p. 51. On the nature of logical reality, cf. B. Russell: *Principles of Mathematics*.

[137] *Analysis of the Human Mind* (1869), i, 249.

place each other for reflecting light, or be used indifferently as backgrounds to set off anything dark, or serve as equally good samples of what the word 'white' signifies. But the snow may be dirty, and the paper pinkish or yellowish without ceasing to be called 'white'; or both snow and paper in one light may differ from their own selves in another and still be 'white,'—so the no-difference criterion seems to be at fault. This physical difficulty (which all house painters know) of matching two tints so exactly as to show no difference seems to be the sort of fact that nominalists have in mind when they say that our ideal meanings are never twice the same. Must we therefore admit that such a concept as 'white' can never keep exactly the same meaning?

It would be absurd to say so, for we know that under all the modifications wrought by changing light, dirt, impurity in pigment, etc., there is an element of color-quality, different from other color-qualities, which we mean that our word *shall* inalterably signify. The impossibility of isolating and fixing this quality physically is irrelevant, so long as we can isolate and fix it mentally, and decide that whenever we say 'white,' that identical quality, whether applied rightly or wrongly, is what we shall be held to mean. Our meanings can be the same as often as we intend to have them so, quite irrespective of whether what is meant be a physical possibility or not. Half the ideas we make use of are of impossible or problematic things,—zeros, infinites, fourth dimensions, limits of ideal perfection, forces, relations sundered from their terms, or terms defined only conceptually, by their relations to other terms which may be equally fictitious. 'White' means a color quality of which the mind appoints the standard, and which it can decree to be there under all physical disguises. *That* white is always the same white. What sense can there be in insisting that although we ourselves have fixed it as the same, it cannot be the same twice over? It works perfectly for us on the supposition that it is there self-identically; so the nominalist doctrine is false of things of that conceptual sort, and true only of things in the perceptual flux.

What I am affirming here is the platonic doctrine that concepts are singulars, that concept-stuff is inalterable, and that physical realities are constituted by the various concept-stuffs of which they 'partake.' It is known as 'logical realism' in the history of philosophy; and has usually been favored by rationalistic than by empiricist minds. For rationalism, concept-stuff is primordial and perceptual things are secondary in nature. The present book, which treats concrete percepts as primordial and concepts as of secondary origin, may be regarded as somewhat eccentric in its attempt to combine logical realism with an otherwise empiricist mode of thought.[138]

[138] For additional remarks in favor of the sameness of conceptual objects, see W. James in *Mind*, vol. iv, 1879, pp. 331–335; F. H. Bradley: *Ethical Studies* (1876), pp. 151–154, and *Principles of Logic* (1883), pp. 260 ff., 282 ff. The

I mean by this that they are made of the same kind of stuff, and melt into each other when we handle them together. How could it be otherwise when the concepts are like evaporations out of the bosom of perception, into which they condense again whenever practical service summons them? No one can tell, of the things he now holds in his hand and reads, how much comes in through his eyes and fingers, and how much, from his apperceiving intellect, unites with that and makes of it this particular 'book'? The universal and the particular parts of the experience are literally immersed in each other, and both are indispensable. Conception is not like a painted hook, on which no real chain can be hung; for we hang concepts upon percepts, and percepts upon concepts interchangeably and indefinitely; and the relation of the two is much more like what we find in those cylindrical 'panoramas' in which a painted background continues a real foreground so cunningly that one fails to detect the joint. The world we practically live in is one in which it is impossible, except by theoretic retrospection, to disentangle the contributions of intellect from those of sense. They are wrapt and rolled together as a gunshot in the mountains is wrapt and rolled in fold on fold of echo and reverberative clamor. Even so do intellectual reverberations enlarge and prolong the perceptual experience which they envelop, associating it with remoter parts of existence. And the ideas of these in turn work like those resonators that pick out partial tones in complex sounds. They help us to decompose our percept into parts and to abstract and isolate its elements.

The two mental functions thus play into each other's hands. Perception prompts our thought, and thought in turn enriches our perception. The more we see, the more we think; while the more we think, the more we see in our immediate experiences, and the greater grows the detail and the more significant the articulateness of our perception.[139] Later, when we come to treat of causal activity, we shall see how practically momentous is this enlargement of the span of our knowledge through the wrapping of our percepts in ideas. It is the whole coil and compound of both by which effects are determined, and they may then be different effects from those to which the perceptual nucleus would by itself give rise. But the point is a difficult one

---

nominalist view is presented by James Mill, as above, and by John Stuart Mill in his *System of Logic,* 8th ed. i, 77.

[139] Cf. F. C. S. Schiller: 'Thought and Immediacy,' in the *Journal of Philosophy,* etc., iii, 234. The interpretation goes so deep that we may even act as if experience consisted of nothing but the different kinds of concept-stuff into which we analyze it. Such concept-stuff may often be treated, for purposes of action and even of discussion, as if it were a full equivalent for reality. But it is needless to repeat, after what precedes, that no amount of it can ever be a *full* equivalent, and that in point of genesis it remains a secondary formation.

and at the present stage of our argument this brief mention of it must suffice.

Readers who by this time agree that our conceptual systems are secondary and on the whole imperfect and ministerial forms of being, will now feel able to return and embrace the flux of their hourly experience with a hearty feeling that, however little of it at a time be given, what is given is absolutely real. Rationalistic thought, with its exclusives interest in the unchanging and the general, has always de-realized the passing pulses of our life. It is no small service on empiricism's part to have exorcised rationalism's veto, and reflectively justified our instinctive feeling about immediate experience. 'Other world?' says Emerson, 'there is no other world,'—than this one, namely, in which our several biographies are founded.

> Natur hat weder Kern noch Schale;
> Alles ist sie mit einem male.
> Dich prüfe du nur allermeist,
> Ob du Kern oder Schale seist.

The belief in the genuineness of each particular moment in which we feel the squeeze of this world's life, as we actually do work here, or work is done upon us, is an Eden from which rationalists seek in vain to expel us, now that we have criticized their state of mind.

But they still make one last attempt, and charge us with self-stultification.

'Your belief in the particular moments,' they insist, 'so far as it is based on reflective argument (and is not a mere omission to doubt, like that of cows and horses) is grounded in abstraction and conception. Only by using concepts have you established percepts in reality. The concepts are the vital things, then, and the percepts are dependent on them for the character of "reality" with which your reasoning endows them. You stand self-contradicted: concepts appear as the sole triumphant instruments of truth, for you have to employ their proper authority, even when seeking to install perception in authority above them.'

The objection is specious; but it disappears the moment one recollects that in the last resort a concept can only be *designative;* and that the concept 'reality,' which we restore to immediate perception, is no new conceptual creation, but only a kind of practical relation to our Will, *perceptively experienced,*[140] which reasoning had temporarily interfered with, but which, when the reasoning was neutralized by still further reasoning, reverted to its original seat as if nothing had happened. That concepts can neutralize other concepts is one of their

[140] Compare W. James: *Principles of Psychology*, chap. xxi, 'The Perception of Reality.'

great practical functions. This answers also the charge that it is self-contradictory to use concepts to undermine the credit of conception in general. The best way to show that a knife will not cut is to try to cut with it. Rationalism itself it is that has so fatally undermined conception, by finding that, when worked beyond a certain point, it only piles up dialectic contradictions.[141]

THE ONE AND THE MANY*

The full nature, as distinguished from the full amount, of reality, we now believe to be given only in the perceptual flux. But, though the flux is continuous from next to next, nonadjacent portions of it are separated by parts that intervene, and such separation seems in a variety of cases to work a positive disconnection. The latter part, e.g., may contain no element surviving from the earlier part, may be unlike it, may forget it, may be shut off from it by physical barriers, or what-not. Thus when we use our intellect for cutting up the flux and individualizing its members, we have (provisionally and practically at any rate) to treat an enormous number of these as if they were unrelated or related only remotely, to one another. We handle them piecemeal or distributively, and look at the entire flux as if it were their sum or collection. This encourages the empiricist notion, that the parts are distinct and that the whole is a resultant.

This doctrine rationalism opposes, contending that the whole is fundamental, that the parts derive from it and all belong with one-another, that the separations we uncritically accept are illusory, and that the entire universe, instead of being a sum, is the only genuine unit in existence, constituting (in the words often quoted from d'Alembert) 'un seul fait et une grande vérité.'

The alternative here is known as that between pluralism and monism. It is the most pregnant of all the dilemmas of philosophy, although it is only in our time that it has been articulated distinctly. Does reality exist distributively? or collectively?—in the shape of *eaches, everys, anys, eithers?* or only in the shape of an *all* or *whole?* An identical content is compatible with either form obtaining, the Latin *omnes,* or *cuncti,* or the German *alle* or *sämmtliche* expressing

---

[141] Compare further, as to this objection, a note in W. James: *A Pluralistic Universe,* below, pp. 570–571.

* From: S.P.P., 113–134.

the alternatives familiarly. Pluralism stands for the distributive, monism for the collective form of being.

Please note that pluralism need not be supposed at the outset to stand for any particular kind or amount of disconnection between the many things which it assumes. It only has the negative significance of contradicting monism's thesis that there is absolutely *no* disconnection. The irreducible outness of *any*thing, however infinitesimal, from *any*thing else, in *any* respect, would be enough, if it were solidly established, to ruin the monistic doctrine.

I hope that the reader begins to be pained here by the extreme vagueness of the terms I am using. To say that there is 'no disconnection,' is on the face of it simply silly, for we find practical disconnections without number. My pocket is disconnected with Mr. Morgan's bank-account, and King Edward VII's mind is disconnected with this book. Monism must mean that all such apparent disconnections are bridged over by some deeper absolute union in which it believes, and this union must in some way be more real than the practical separations that appear upon the surface.

In point of historical fact monism has generally kept itself vague and mystical as regards the ultimate principle of unity. To be One is more wonderful than to be many, so the principle of things must be One, but of that One no exact account is given. Plotinus simply calls it the One. 'The One is all things and yet no one of them. . . . For the very reason that none of them was in the One, are all derived from it. Furthermore, in order that they may be real existences, the One is not an existence, but the father of existences. And the generation of existence is as it were the first act of generation. Being perfect by reason of neither seeking nor possessing nor needing anything, the One overflows, as it were, and what overflows forms another hypostasis. . . . How should the most perfect and primal good stay shut up in itself as if it were envious or impotent? . . . Necessarily then something comes from it.' [142]

This is like the Hindoo doctrine of the Brahman, or of the Âtman. In the Bhagavat-gita the holy Krishna speaking for the One, says: 'I am the immolation. I am the sacrificial rite. I am the libation offered to ancestors. I am the drug. I am the incantation. I am the sacrificial butter also. I am the fire. I am the incense. I am the father, the mother, the sustainer, the grandfather of the universe—the mystic doctrine, the purification, the syllable "Om" . . . the path, the supporter, the master, the witness, the habitation, the refuge, the friend,

---

[142] Compare the passages in C. M. Bakewell's *Source-Book in Ancient Philosophy*, pp. 363–370, or the first four books of the Vth Ennead generally, in F. Bouillier's translation.

the origin, the dissolution, the place, the receptacle, the inexhaustible seed. I heat (the world) I withhold and pour out the rain. I am ambrosia and death, the existing and the non-existing. . . . I am the same to all beings. I have neither foe nor friend. . . . Place thy heart on me, worshipping me, sacrificing to me, saluting me.' [143]

I call this sort of monism mystical, for it not only revels in formulas that defy understanding,[144] but it accredits itself by appealing to states of illumination not vouchsafed to common men. Thus Porphyry, in his life of Plotinus, after saying that he himself once had such an insight, when 68 years old, adds that whilst he lived with Plotinus, the latter four times had the happiness of approaching the supreme God and consciously uniting with him in a real and ineffable act.

The regular mystical way of attaining the vision of the One is by ascetic training, fundamentally the same in all religious systems. But this ineffable kind of Oneness is not strictly philosophical, for philosophy is essentially talkative and explicit, so I must pass it by.

The usual philosophic way of reaching deeper oneness has been by the conception of substance. First used by the Greeks, this notion was elaborated with great care during the Middle Ages. Defined as any being that exists *per se,* so that it needs no further subject in which to inhere (*Ens ita per se existens, ut non indigeat alio tamquam subjecto, cui inhaereat, ad existendum*) a 'substance' was first distinguished from all 'accidents' (which do require such a subject of inhesion—*cujus esse est inesse*). It was then identified with the 'principle of individuality' in things, and with their 'essence,' and divided into various types, for example into first and second, simple and compound, complete and incomplete, specific and individual, material and spiritual substances. God, on this view, is a substance, for he exists *per se,* as well as *a se;* but of secondary beings, he is the creator, not the substance, for once created, they also exist *per se* though not *a se.* Thus, for scholasticism, the notion of substance is only a partial uni-

---

[143] J. C. Thomson's translation, chap. iv.

[144] Al-Ghazzali, the Mohammedan philosopher and mystic, gives a more theistic version of essentially the same idea: 'Allah is the guider aright and the leader astray; he does what he wills and decides what he wishes; there is no opposer of his decision and no repeller of his decree. He created the Garden, and created for it a people, then used them in obedience. And he created the Fire, and create for it a people, then used them in rebellion. . . . Then he said, as has been handed down from the Prophet: "These are in the Garden, and I care not; and these are in the Fire, and I care not." So he is Allah, the Most High, the King, the Reality. He is not asked concerning what he does; but they are asked.' (D. B. MacDonald's translation, in *Hartford Seminary Record,* January, 1910.) Compare for other quotations, W. James: *The Varieties of Religious Experience,* pp. 415–422.

fier, and in its totality, the universe forms a pluralism from the substance-point-of-view.[145]

Spinoza broke away from the scholastic doctrine. He began his 'Ethics' by demonstrating that only one substance is possible, and that that substance can only be the infinite and necessary God.[146] This heresy brought reprobation on Spinoza, but it has been favored by philosophers and poets ever since. The pantheistic spinozistic unity was too sublime a prospect not to captivate the mind. It was not till Locke, Berkeley, and Hume began to put in their 'critical' work that the suspicion began to gain currency that the notion of substance might be only a word masquerading in the shape of an idea.[147]

Locke believed in substances, yet confessed that 'we have no such

[145] Consult the word 'substance' in the index of any scholastic manual, such as J. Rickaby: *General Metaphysics;* A. Stöckl: *Lehrbuch d. Phil.;* or P. M. Liberatore: *Compendium Logicæ et Metaphysicæ.*

[146] Spinoza has expressed his doctrine briefly in part i of the Appendix to his *Ethics:* 'I have now explained,' he says, 'the nature of God, and his properties; such as that he exists necessarily; that he is unique; that what he is and does flows from the sole necessity of his nature; that he is the free cause of all things whatever; that all things are in God and depend on him in such wise that they can neither be nor be conceived without him; and finally, that all things have been predetermined by God, not indeed by the freedom of his will, or according to his good pleasure, but in virtue of his absolute nature or his infinite potentiality.'—Spinoza goes on to refute the vulgar notion of *final causes.* God pursues no ends—if he did he would lack something. He acts out of the logical necessity of the fulness of his nature.—I find another good monistic statement in a book of the spinozistic type:—'. . . The existence of every compound object in manifestation does not lie in the object itself, but lies in the universal existence which is an absolute unit, containing in itself all that is manifested. All the particularized beings, therefore, . . . are incessantly changing one into the other, coming and going, forming and dissolving through the one universal cause of the *potential universe,* which is the absolute unit of universal existence, depending on the one general law, the one mathematical bond, which is the absolute being, and it changes not in all eternity. Thus, . . . it is the universe as a whole, *in its potential being,* from which the physical universe is individualized; and its being is a mathematical inference from a mathematical or an intellectual universe which was and ever is previously formed by an intellect standing and existing by itself. This mathematical or intellectual universe I call Absolute Intellectuality, the God of the Universe.'
(Solomon J. Silberstein: *The Disclosures of the Universal Mysteries,* New York, 1906, pp. 12–13.)

[147] No one believes that such words as 'winter,' 'army,' 'house,' denote substances. They designate collective facts, of which the parts are held together by means that can be experimentally traced. Even when we can't define what groups the effects together, as in 'poison,' 'sickness,' 'strength,' we don't assume a substance, but are willing that the word should designate some phenomenal agency yet to be found out. Nominalists treat all substances after this analogy, and consider 'matter,' 'gold,' 'soul,' as but the names of so many grouped properties, of which the bond of union must be, not some unknowable substance corresponding to the name, but rather some hidden portion of the whole phenomenal fact.

clear idea at all, but only an uncertain supposition of we know not what, which we take to be the substratum, or support of those ideas we do not know.' [148] He criticized the notion of personal substance as the principles of self-sameness in our different minds. *Experientially,* our personal identity consists, he said, in nothing more than the functional and perceptible fact that our later states of mind continue and remember our earlier ones.[149]

Berkeley applied the same sort of criticism to the notion of bodily substance. 'When I consider,' he says, 'the two parts ("being" in general, and "supporting accidents") which make the signification of the words "material substance," I am convinced there is no distinct meaning annexed to them. . . . Suppose an intelligence without the help of external bodies to be affected with the same train of sensations that you are, imprinted in the same order, and with like vividness in his mind. I ask whether that intelligence hath not all the reason to believe the existence of corporeal substances, represented by his ideas, and exciting them in his mind, that you can possibly have for believing the same thing.' [150] Certain *grouped sensations,* in short, are all that corporeal substances are *known-as,* therefore the only meaning which the word 'matter' can claim is that it denotes such sensations and their groupings. They are the only verifiable aspect of the word.

The reader will recognize that in these criticisms our own pragmatic rule is used. What difference in practical experience is it supposed to make that we have each a personal substantial principle? This difference, that we can remember and appropriate our past, calling it 'mine.' What difference that in this book there is a substantial principle? This, that certain optical and tactile sensations cling permanently together in a cluster. The fact that certain perceptual experiences do seem to *belong together* is thus all that the word substance means. Hume carries the criticism to the last degree of clearness. 'We have no idea of substance,' he says, 'distinct from that of a collection of particular qualities, nor have we any other meaning when we either talk or reason concerning it. The idea of a substance . . . is nothing but a collection of simple ideas that are united by the imagination and have a particular name assigned them by which we are able to recall that collection.' [151] Kant's treatment of substance agrees with Hume's in denying all positive content to the notion. It differs in insisting that, by attaching shifting percepts to the permanent name, the category of substance unites them *necessarily* together, and thus makes nature in-

[148] *Essay concerning Human Understanding,* book i, chap. iv, § 18.
[149] *Ibid.,* book ii, chap. xxvii, §§ 9–27.
[150] *Principles of Human Knowledge,* part i, §§ 17, 20.
[151] *Treatise on Human Nature,* part 1, § 6.

telligible.[152] It is impossible to assent to this. The grouping of qualities becomes no more intelligible when you call substance a 'category' than when you call it a bare word.

Let us now turn our backs upon ineffable or unintelligible ways of accounting for the world's oneness, and inquire whether, instead of being a principle, the 'oneness' affirmed may not merely be a name like 'substance,' descriptive of the fact that certain *specific and verifiable connections* are found among the parts of the experiential flux. This brings us back to our pragmatic rule: Suppose there is a oneness in things, what may it be known-as? What differences to you and me will it make?

Our question thus turns upside down, and sets us on a much more promising inquiry. We can easily conceive of things that shall have no connection whatever with each other. We may assume them to inhabit different times and spaces, as the dreams of different persons do even now. They may be so unlike and incommensurable, and so inert towards one another, as never to jostle or interfere. Even now there may actually be whole universes so disparate from ours that we who know ours have no means of perceiving that they exist. We conceive their diversity, however; and by that fact the whole lot of them form what is known in logic as one 'universe of discourse.' To form a universe of discourse argues, as this example shows, no further kind of connection. The importance attached by certain monistic writers to the fact that any chaos may become a universe by being merely named, is to me incomprehensible. We must seek something better in the way of oneness than this susceptibility of being mentally considered together, and named by a collective noun.

What connections may be perceived concretely or in point of fact, among the parts of the collection abstractly designated as our 'world'?

There are innumerable modes of union among its parts, some obtaining on a larger, some on a smaller scale. Not all the parts of our world are united *mechanically,* for some can move without the others moving. They all seem united by *gravitation,* however, so far as they are material things. Some again of these are united *chemically,* while others are not; and the like is true of thermic, optical, electrical, and other *physical* connections. These connections are specifications of what we mean by the word oneness when we apply it to our world. We should not call it one unless its parts were connected in these and other ways. But then it is clear that by the same logic we ought to call

[152] *Critique of Pure Reason:* First Analogy of Experience. For further criticism of the substance-concept see J. S. Mill: *A System of Logic,* book i, chap. iii, §§ 6–9; B. P. Bowne: *Metaphysics,* part 1, chap. i. Bowne uses the words being and substance as synonymous.

it 'many' so far as its parts are disconnected in these same ways, chemically inert towards one another or non-conductors to electricity, light and heat. In all these modes of union, some parts of the world prove to be conjoined with other parts, so that if you choose your line of influence and your items rightly, you may travel from pole to pole without an interruption. If, however, you choose them wrongly, you meet with obstacles and non-conductors from the outset, and cannot travel at all. There is thus neither absolute oneness nor absolute manyness from the physical point of view, but a mixture of well-definable modes of both. Moreover, neither the oneness nor the manyness seems the more essential attribute, they are co-ordinate features of the natural world.

There are plenty of other practical differences meant by calling a thing One. Our world, being strung along in time and space, has *temporal and spatial unity*. But time and space relate things by determinately sundering them, so it is hard to say whether the world ought more to be called 'one' or 'many' in this spatial or temporal regard.

The like is true of the *generic oneness* which comes from so many of the world's parts being similar. When two things are similar you can make inferences from the one which will hold good of the other, so that this kind of union among things, so far as it obtains, is inexpressibly precious from the logical point of view. But an infinite heterogeneity among things exists alongside of whatever likeness of kind we discover; and our world appears no more distinctly or essentially as a One than as a Many, from this generic point of view.

We have touched on the noetic unity predicable of the world in consequence of our being able to mean the whole of it at once. Widely different from unification by an abstract designation, would be the concrete noetic union wrought by an all-knower of perceptual type who should be acquainted at one stroke with every part of what exists. In such an absolute all-knower idealists believe. Kant, they say, virtually replaced the notion of Substance, by the more intelligible notion of Subject. The 'I am conscious of it,' which on some witness's part must accompany every possible experience, means in the last resort, we are told, one individual witness of the total frame of things, world without end, amen. You may call his undivided act of omniscience instantaneous or eternal, whichever you like, for time is its object just as everything else is, and itself is not in time.

We shall find reasons later for treating noetic monism as an unverified hypothesis. Over against it there stands the noetic pluralism which we verify every moment when we seek information from our friends. According to this, everything in the world might be known by somebody, yet not everything by the same knower, or in one single cognitive act,—much as all mankind is knit in one network of acquaintance, A knowing B, B knowing C,—Y knowing Z, and Z possibly knowing A again, without the possibility of anyone knowing everybody at once. This 'concatenated' knowing, going from next to next, is altogether different from the 'consolidated' knowing supposed to be exercised by the absolute mind. It makes a coherent type of universe in which the widest knower that exists may yet remain ignorant of much that is known to others.

There are other systems of concatenation besides the noetic concatenation. We ourselves are constantly adding to the connections of things, organizing labor-unions, establishing postal, consular, mercantile, railroad, telegraph, colonial, and other systems that bind us and things together in ever wider reticulations. Some of these systems involve others, some do not. You cannot have a telephone system without air and copper connections, but you can have air and copper connections without telephones. You cannot have love without acquaintance, but you can have acquaintance without love, etc. The same thing, moreover, can belong to many systems, as when a man is connected with other objects by heat, by gravitation, by love, and by knowledge.

From the point of view of these partial systems, the world hangs together from next to next in a variety of ways, so that when you are off of one thing you can always be on to something else, without ever dropping out of your world. Gravitation is the only positively known sort of connection among things that reminds us of the consolidated or monistic form of union. If a 'mass' should change anywhere, the mutual gravitation of all things would instantaneously alter.

Teleological and æsthetic unions are other forms of systematic union. The world is full of partial purposes, of partial stories. That they all form chapters of one supreme purpose and inclusive story is the monistic conjecture. They *seem,* meanwhile, simply to run alongside of each other—either irrelevantly, or, where they interfere, leading to mutual frustrations,—so the appearance of things is invincibly pluralistic from this purposive point of view.

It is a common belief that all particular beings have one origin and source, either in God, or in atoms all equally old. There is no real novelty, it is believed, in the universe, the new things that appear having either been eternally prefigured in the absolute, or being results of the same *primordia rerum,* atoms, or monads, getting into new mixtures. But the question of being is so obscure anyhow, that whether realities have burst into existence all at once, by a single 'bang,' as it were; or whether they came piecemeal, and have different ages (so that real novelties may be leaking into our universe all the time), may here be left an open question, though it is undoubtedly intellectually economical to suppose that all things are equally old, and that no novelties leak in.

These results are what the Oneness of the Universe is *known-as.*

They *are* the oneness, pragmatically considered. A world coherent in any of these ways would be no chaos, but a universe of such or such a grade. (The grades might differ, however. The parts, e.g., might have space-relations, but nothing more; or they might also gravitate; or exchange heat; or know, or love one another, etc.)

Such is the cash-value of the world's unity, empirically realized. Its total unity is the sum of all the partial unities. It consists of them and follows upon them. Such an idea, however, outrages rationalistic minds, which habitually despise all this practical small-change. Such minds insist on a deeper, more through-and-through union of all things in the absolute, 'each in all and all in each,' as the prior condition of these empirically ascertained connections. But this may be only a case of the usual worship of abstractions, like calling 'bad weather' the cause of to-day's rain, etc., or accounting for a man's features by his 'face,' when really the rain *is* the bad weather, is what you *mean* by 'bad weather,' just as the features are what you mean by the face.

To sum up, the world is 'one' in some respects, and 'many' in others. But the respects must be distinctly specified, if either statement is to be more than the emptiest abstraction. Once we are committed to this soberer view, the question of the One or the Many may well cease to appear important. The amount either of unity or of plurality is in short only a matter for observation to ascertain and write down, in statements which will have to be complicated, in spite of every effort to be concise.

THE ONE AND THE MANY (*continued*)— VALUES AND DEFECTS* [153]

We might dismiss the subject with the preceding chapter[154] were it not for the fact that further consequences follow from the rival hypotheses, and make of the alternative of monism or pluralism what I called it on page 258, the most 'pregnant' of all the dilemmas of metaphysics.

* From: S.P.P., 135–146.

[153] [This chapter was not indicated as a separate chapter in the manuscript. ED.]

[154] For an amplification of what precedes, the lecture on 'The One and the Many' in W. James: *Pragmatism* (1907), may be referred to. [Cf. below, pp. 405–417.]

To begin with, the attribute 'one' seems for many persons to confer a value, an ineffable illustriousness and dignity upon the world, with which the conception of it as an irreducible 'many' is believed to clash.

Secondly, a through-and-through noetic connection of everything with absolutely everything else is in some quarters held to be indispensable to the world's rationality. Only then might we believe that all things really do *belong* together, instead of being connected by the bare conjunctions 'with' or 'and.' The notion that this latter pluralistic arrangement may obtain is deemed 'irrational'; and of course it does make the world partly alogical or non-rational from a purely intellectual point of view.

Monism thus holds the oneness to be the more vital and essential element. The entire cosmos must be a consolidated unit, within which each member is determined by the whole to be just that, and from which the slightest incipiency of independence anywhere is ruled out. With Spinoza, monism likes to believe that all things follow from the essence of God as necessarily as from the nature of a triangle it follows that the angles are equal to two right angles. The whole is what yields the parts, not the parts the whole. The universe is *tight,* monism claims, not loose; and you must take the irreducible whole of it just as it is offered, or have no part or lot in it at all. The only alternative allowed by monistic writers is to confess the world's non-rationality— and no philosopher can permit himself to do that. The form of monism regnant at the present day in philosophic circles is *absolute idealism.* For this way of thinking, the world exists no otherwise than as the object of one infinitely knowing mind. The analogy that suggests the hypothesis here is that of our own finite fields of consciousness, which at every moment envisage a much-at-once composed of parts related variously, and in which both the conjunctions and the disjunctions that appear are there only in so far as we are there as their witnesses, so that they are both 'noetically' and monistically based.

We may well admit the sublimity of this noetic monism and of its vague vision of an underlying connection among all phenomena without exception.[155] It shows itself also able to confer religious stability and peace, and it invokes the authority of mysticism in its favor. Yet, on the other hand, like many another concept unconditionally carried out, it introduces into philosophy puzzles peculiar to itself, as follows:—

1. It does not account for our finite consciousness. If nothing exists but as the Absolute Mind knows it, how can anything exist otherwise than as that Mind knows it? That Mind knows each thing in one

---

[155] In its essential features, Spinoza was its first prophet, Fichte and Hegel were its middle exponents, and Josiah Royce is its best contemporary representative.

act of knowledge, along with every other thing. Finite minds know things without other things, and this ignorance is the source of most of their woes. We are thus not simply objects to an all-knowing subject: we are subjects on our own account and know differently from its knowing.

2. It creates a problem of evil. Evil, for pluralism, presents only the practical problem of how to get rid of it. For monism the puzzle is theoretical: How—if Perfection be the source, should there be Imperfection? If the world as known to the Absolute be perfect, why should it be known otherwise, in myriads of inferior finite editions also? The perfect edition surely was enough. How do the breakage and dispersion and ignorance get in?

3. It contradicts the character of reality as perceptually experienced. Of our world, change seems an essential ingredient. There is history. There are novelties, struggles, losses, gains. But the world of the Absolute is represented as unchanging, eternal, or 'out of time,' and is foreign to our powers either of apprehension or of appreciation. Monism usually treats the sense-world as a mirage or illusion.

4. It is fatalistic. Possibility, as distinguished from necessity on the one hand and from impossibility on the other, is an essential category of human thinking. For monism, it is a pure illusion; for whatever is is necessary, and aught else is impossible, if the world be such a unit of fact as monists pretend.

Our sense of 'freedom' supposes that some things at least are decided here and now, that the passing moment may contain some novelty, be an original starting-point of events, and not merely transmit a push from elsewhere. We imagine that in some respects at least the future may not be co-implicated with the past, but may be really addable to it, and indeed addable in one shape or another, so that the next turn in events can at any given moment genuinely be ambiguous, i.e., possibly this, but also possibly that.

Monism rules out this whole conception of possibles, so native to our common-sense. The future and the past are linked, she is obliged to say; there can be no genuine novelty anywhere, for to suppose that the universe has a constitution simply additive, with nothing to link things together save what the words 'plus,' 'with,' or 'and' stand for, is repugnant to our reason.

Pluralism, on the other hand, taking perceptual experience at its face-value, is free from all these difficulties. It protests against working our ideas in a vacuum made of conceptual abstractions. Some parts of our world, it admits, cannot exist out of their wholes; but others, it says, can. To some extent the world *seems* genuinely additive: it may really be so. We cannot explain conceptually *how* genuine novelties can come; but if one did come we could experience *that* it came. We do, in fact, experience perceptual novelties all the while. Our perceptual experience overlaps our conceptual reason: the *that* transcends the *why*. So the common-sense view of life, as something really dramatic, with work done, and things decided here and now, is acceptable to pluralism. 'Free will' means nothing but real novelty; so pluralism accepts the notion of free will.

But pluralism, accepting a universe unfinished, with doors and windows open to possibilities uncontrollable in advance, gives us less religious certainty than monism, with its absolutely closed-in world. It is true that monism's religious certainty is not rationally based, but is only a faith that 'sees the All-Good in the All-Real.' In point of fact, however, monism is usually willing to exert this optimistic faith: its world is certain to be saved, yes, is saved already, unconditionally and from eternity, in spite of all the phenomenal appearances of risk.[156]

A world working out an uncertain destiny, as the phenomenal world appears to be doing, is an intolerable idea to the rationalistic mind.

Pluralism, on the other hand, is neither optimistic nor pessimistic, but melioristic, rather. The world, it thinks, may be saved, on condition that its parts shall do their best. But shipwreck in detail, or even on the whole, is among the open possibilities.

There is thus a practical lack of balance about pluralism, which contrasts with monism's peace of mind. The one is a more moral, the other a more religious view; and different men usually let this sort of consideration determine their belief.[157]

So far I have sought only to show the respective implications of the rival doctrines without dogmatically deciding which is the more true. It is obvious that pluralism has three great advantages:—

1. It is more 'scientific,' in that it insists that when oneness is predicated, it shall mean definitely ascertainable conjunctive forms. With these the disjunctions ascertainable among things are exactly on a par. The two are co-ordinate aspects of reality. To make the conjunctions more vital and primordial than the separations, monism has to abandon verifiable experience and proclaim a unity that is indescribable.

2. It agrees more with the moral and dramatic expressiveness of life.

3. It is not obliged to stand for any particular amount of plurality, for it triumphs over monism if the smallest morsel of disconnect-

[156] For an eloquent expression of the monistic position, from the religious point of view, read J. Royce: *The World and the Individual,* vol. ii, lectures 8, 9, 10.

[157] See, as to this religious difference, the closing lecture in W. James's *Pragmatism.* [Cf. below, pp. 461–472.]

edness is once found undeniably to exist. 'Ever not quite' is all it says to monism; while monism is obliged to prove that what pluralism asserts can in no amount whatever possibly be true—an infinitely harder task.

The advantages of monism, in turn, are its natural affinity with a certain kind of religious faith, and the peculiar emotional value of the conception that the world is a unitary fact.

So far has our use of the pragmatic rule brought us towards understanding this dilemma. The reader will by this time feel for himself the essential practical difference which it involves. The word 'absence' seems to indicate it. The monistic principle implies that nothing that is can in any way whatever be absent from anything else that is. The pluralistic principle, on the other hand, is quite compatible with some things being absent from operations in which other things find themselves singly or collectively engaged. *Which* things are absent from which other things, and *when,*—these of course are questions which a pluralistic philosophy can settle only by an exact study of details. The past, the present, and the future in perception, for example, are absent from one another, while in imagination they are present or absent as the case may be. If the time-content of the world be not one monistic block of being, if some part, at least, of the future, is added to the past without being virtually one therewith, or implicitly contained therein, then it is absent really as well as phenomenally and may be called an absolute novelty in the world's history in so far forth.

Towards this issue, of the reality or unreality of the novelty that appears, the pragmatic difference between monism and pluralism seems to converge. That we ourselves may be authors of genuine novelty is the thesis of the doctrine of free-will. That genuine novelties can occur means that from the point of view of what is already given, what comes may have to be treated as a matter of *chance*. We are led thus to ask the question: In what manner does new being come? Is it through and through the consequence of older being or is it matter of chance so far as older being goes?—which is the same thing as asking: Is it original, in the strict sense of the word?

We connect again here with what was said at the end of Chapter III.* We there agreed that being is a datum or gift and has to be begged by the philosopher; but we left the question open as to whether he must beg it all at once or beg it bit by bit or in instalments. The latter is the more consistently empiricist view.

* [See S.P.P., p. 46.]

THE PLACE OF AFFECTIONAL FACTS IN A WORLD OF PURE EXPERIENCE* [158]

Common sense and popular philosophy are as dualistic as it is possible to be. Thoughts, we all naturally think, are made of one kind of substance, and things of another. Consciousness, flowing inside of us in the forms of conception or judgment, or concentrating itself in the shape of passion or emotion, can be directly felt as the spiritual activity which it is, and known in contrast with the space-filling objective 'content' which it envelopes and accompanies. In opposition to this dualistic philosophy, I tried, in "Does 'Consciousness' Exist?" to show that thoughts and things are absolutely homogeneous as to their material, and that their opposition is only one of relation and of function. There is no thought-stuff different from thing-stuff, I said; but the same identical piece of 'pure experience' (which was the name I gave to the *materia prima* of everything) can stand alternately for a 'fact of consciousness' or for a physical reality, according as it is taken in one context or in another. For the right understanding of what follows, I shall have to presuppose that the reader will have read that [essay].[159]

The commonest objection which the doctrine there laid down runs up against is drawn from the existence of our 'affections.' In our pleasures and pains, our loves and fears and angers, in the beauty, comicality, importance or preciousness of certain objects and situations, we have, I am told by many critics, a great realm of experience intuitively recognized as spiritual, made, and felt to be made, of consciousness exclusively, and different in nature from the space-filling kind of being which is enjoyed by physical objects. In Section VII of "Does 'Consciousness' Exist?" I treated of this class of experiences very inadequately, because I had to be so brief. I now return to the subject, because I believe that, so far from invalidating my general thesis, these phenomena, when properly analyzed, afford it powerful support.

The central point of the pure-experience theory is that 'outer' and 'inner' are names for two groups into which we sort experiences ac-

* From: E.R.E., 137–154.

158 [Reprinted from *The Journal of Philosophy, Psychology, and Scientific Methods*, vol. II, No. 11, May 25, 1905.]

159 It will be still better if he shall have also read the essay entitled 'A World of Pure Experience,' which develops its ideas still farther. [See above, pp. 169–183 and pp. 194–214.]

cording to the way in which they act upon their neighbors. Any one 'content,' such as *hard,* let us say, can be assigned to either group. In the outer group it is 'strong,' it acts 'energetically' and aggressively. Here whatever is hard interferes with the space its neighbors occupy. It dents them; is impenetrable by them; and we call the hardness then a physical hardness. In the mind, on the contrary, the hard thing is nowhere in particular, it dents nothing, it suffuses through its mental neighbors, as it were, and interpenetrates them. Taken in this group we call both it and them 'ideas' or 'sensations'; and the basis of the two groups respectively is the different type of interrelation, the mutual impenetrability, on the one hand, and the lack of physical interference and interaction, on the other.

That what in itself is one and the same entity should be able to function thus differently in different contexts is a natural consequence of the extremely complex reticulations in which our experiences come. To her offspring a tigress is tender, but cruel to every other living thing—both cruel and tender, therefore, at once. A mass in movement resists every force that operates contrariwise to its own direction, but to forces that pursue the same direction, or come in at right angles, it is absolutely inert. It is thus both energetic and inert; and the same is true (if you vary the associates properly) of every other piece of experience. It is only towards certain specific groups of associates that the physical energies, as we call them, of a content are put forth. In another group it may be quite inert.

It is possible to imagine a universe of experiences in which the only alternative between neighbors would be either physical interaction or complete inertness. In such a world the mental or the physical *status* of any piece of experience would be unequivocal. When active, it would figure in the physical, and when inactive, in the mental group.

But the universe we live in is more chaotic than this, and there is room in it for the hybrid or ambiguous group of our affectional experiences, of our emotions and appreciative perceptions. In the paragraphs that follow I shall try to show:

(1) That the popular notion that these experiences are intuitively given as purely inner facts is hasty and erroneous; and

(2) That their ambiguity illustrates beautifully my central thesis that subjectivity and objectivity are affairs not of what an experience is aboriginally made of, but of its classification. Classifications depend on our temporary purposes. For certain purposes it is convenient to take things in one set of relations, for other purposes in another set. In the two cases their contexts are apt to be different. In the case of our affectional experiences we have no permanent and steadfast purpose that obliges us to be consistent, so we find it easy to let them float ambiguously, sometimes classing them with our feelings, sometimes

with more physical realities, according to caprice or to the convenience of the moment. Thus would these experiences, so far from being an obstacle to the pure experience philosophy, serve as an excellent corroboration of its truth.

First of all, then, it is a mistake to say, with the objectors whom I began by citing, that anger, love and fear are affections purely of the mind. That, to a great extent at any rate, they are simultaneously affections of the body is proved by the whole literature of the James-Lange theory of emotion.[160] All our pains, moreover, are local, and we are always free to speak of them in objective as well as in subjective terms. We can say that we are aware of a painful place, filling a certain bigness in our organism, or we can say that we are inwardly in a 'state' of pain. All our adjectives of worth are similarly ambiguous—I instanced some of the ambiguities in "Does 'Consciousness' Exist?" Is the preciousness of a diamond a quality of the gem? or is it a feeling in our mind? Practically we treat it as both or as either, according to the temporary direction of our thought. 'Beauty,' says Professor Santayana, 'is pleasure objectified'; and in Sections 10 and 11 of his work, *The Sense of Beauty,* he treats in a masterly way of this equivocal realm. The various pleasures we receive from an object may count as 'feelings' when we take them singly, but when they combine in a total richness, we call the result the 'beauty' of the object, and treat it as an outer attribute which our mind perceives. We discover beauty just as we discover the physical properties of things. Training is needed to make us expert in either line. Single sensations also may be ambiguous. Shall we say an 'agreeable degree of heat,' or an 'agreeable feeling' occasioned by the degree of heat? Either will do; and language would lose most of its esthetic and rhetorical value were we forbidden to project words primarily connoting our affections upon the objects by which the affections are aroused. The man is really hateful; the action really mean; the situation really tragic—all in themselves and quite apart from our opinion. We even go so far as to talk of a weary road, a giddy height, a jocund morning or a sullen sky; and the term 'indefinite' while usually applied only to our apprehensions, functions as a fundamental physical qualification of things in Spencer's 'law of evolution,' and doubtless passes with most readers for all right.

Psychologists, studying our perceptions of movement, have unearthed experiences in which movement is felt in general but not ascribed correctly to the body that really moves. Thus in optical vertigo, caused by unconscious movements of our eyes, both we and the external universe appear to be in a whirl. When clouds float by the

---

[160] [Cf. *The Principles of Psychology,* vol. ii, ch. xxv; and "The Physical Basis of Emotion," *Psychological Review,* vol. i, 1894, p. 516.]

moon, it is as if both clouds and moon and we ourselves shared in the motion. In the extraordinary case of amnesia of the Rev. Mr. Hanna, published by Sidis and Goodhart in their important work on *Multiple Personality,* we read that when the patient first recovered consciousness and "noticed an attendant walk across the room, he identified the movement with that of his own. He did not yet discriminate between his own movements and those outside himself." [161] Such experiences point to a primitive stage of perception in which discriminations afterwards needful have not yet been made. A piece of experience of a determinate sort is there, but there at first as a 'pure' fact. Motion originally simply *is;* only later is it confined to this thing or to that. Something like this is true of every experience, however complex, at the moment of its actual presence. Let the reader arrest himself in the act of reading this article now. *Now* this is a pure experience, a phenomenon, or datum, a mere *that* or content of fact. *'Reading'* simply *is, is there;* and whether there for some one's consciousness, or there for physical nature, is a question not yet put. At the moment, it is there for neither; later we shall probably judge it to have been there for both.

With the affectional experiences which we are considering, the relatively 'pure' condition lasts. In practical life no urgent need has yet arisen for deciding whether to treat them as rigorously mental or as rigorously physical facts. So they remain equivocal; and, as the world goes, their equivocality is one of their great conveniences.

The shifting place of 'secondary qualities' in the history of philosophy[162] is another excellent proof of the fact that 'inner' and 'outer' are not coefficients with which experiences come to us aboriginally stamped, but are rather results of a later classification performed by us for particular needs. The common-sense stage of thought is a perfectly definite practical halting-place, the place where we ourselves can proceed to act unhesitatingly. On this stage of thought things act on each other as well as on us by means of their secondary qualities. Sound, as such, goes through the air and can be intercepted. The heat of the fire passes over, as such, into the water which it sets a-boiling. It is the very light of the arc-lamp which displaces the darkness of the midnight street, etc. By engendering and translocating just these qualities, actively efficacious as they seem to be, we ourselves succeed in altering nature so as to suit us; and until more purely intellectual, as distinguished from practical, needs had arisen, no one ever thought of calling these qualities subjective. When, however, Galileo, Descartes, and others found it best for philosophic purposes to class sound, heat,

[161] Page 102.
[162] [Cf. Janet and Séailles: *History of the Problems of Philosophy,* trans. by Monahan, part I, ch. III.]

and light along with pain and pleasure as purely mental phenomena, they could do so with impunity.[163]

Even the primary qualities are undergoing the same fate. Hardness and softness are effects on us of atomic interactions, and the atoms themselves are neither hard nor soft, nor solid nor liquid. Size and shape are deemed subjective by Kantians; time itself is subjective according to many philosophers;[164] and even the activity and causal efficacy which lingered in physics long after secondary qualities were banished are now treated as illusory projections outwards of phenomena of our own consciousness. There are no activities or effects in nature, for the most intellectual contemporary school of physical speculation. Nature exhibits only *changes,* which habitually coincide with one another so that their habits are describable in simple 'laws.' [165]

There is no original spirituality or materiality of being, intuitively discerned, then; but only a translocation of experiences from one world to another; a grouping of them with one set or another of associates for definitely practical or intellectual ends.

I will say nothing here of the persistent ambiguity of *relations.* They are undeniable parts of pure experience; yet, while common sense and what I call radical empiricism stand for their being objective, both rationalism and the usual empiricism claim that they are exclusively the 'work of the mind'—the finite mind or the absolute mind, as the case may be.

Turn now to those affective phenomena which more directly concern us.

We soon learn to separate the ways in which things appeal to our interests and emotions from the ways in which they act upon one another. It does not *work* to assume that physical objects are going to act outwardly by their sympathetic or antipathetic qualities. The beauty of a thing or its value is no force that can be plotted in a polygon of compositions, nor does its 'use' or 'significance' affect in the minutest degree its vicissitudes or destiny at the hands of physical nature. Chemical 'affinities' are a purely verbal metaphor; and, as I just said, even such things as forces, tensions, and activities can at a pinch be regarded as anthropomorphic projections. So far, then, as the physical world means the collection of contents that determine in each other certain regular changes, the whole collection of our appreciative attributes has to be treated as falling outside of it. If we mean by

---

[163] [Cf. Descartes: *Meditation* II; *Principles of Philosophy,* part I, XLVIII.]
[164] [Cf. A. E. Taylor: *Elements of Metaphysics,* bk. III, ch. IV.]
[165] [Cf. K. Pearson: *Grammar of Science,* ch. III.]

physical nature whatever lies beyond the surface of our bodies, these attributes are inert throughout the whole extent of physical nature.

Why then do men leave them as ambiguous as they do and not class them decisively as purely spiritual?

The reason would seem to be that, although they are inert as regards the rest of physical nature, they are not inert as regards that part of physical nature which our own skin covers. It is those very appreciative attributes of things, their dangerousness, beauty, rarity, utility, etc., that primarily appeal to our attention. In our commerce with nature these attributes are what give *emphasis* to objects; and for an object to be emphatic, whatever spiritual fact it may mean, means also that it produces immediate bodily effects upon us, alterations of tone and tension, of heart-beat and breathing, of vascular and visceral action. The 'interesting' aspects of things are thus not wholly inert physically, though they be active only in these small corners of physical nature which our bodies occupy. That, however, is enough to save them from being classed as absolutely non-objective.

The attempt, if any one should make it, to sort experiences into two absolutely discrete groups, with nothing but inertness in one of them and nothing but activities in the other, would thus receive one check. It would receive another as soon as we examined the more distinctively mental group; for though in that group it be true that things do not act on one another by their physical properties, do not dent each other or set fire to each other, they yet act on each other in the most energetic way by those very characters which are so inert extracorporeally. It is by the interest and importance that experiences have for us, by the emotions they excite, and the purposes they subserve, by their affective values, in short, that their consecution in our several conscious streams, as 'thoughts' of ours, is mainly ruled. Desire introduces them; interest holds them; fitness fixes their order and connection. I need only refer for this aspect of our mental life, to Wundt's article 'Ueber psychische Causalität,' which begins Volume X of his *Philosophische Studien*.[166]

It thus appears that the ambiguous or amphibious *status* which we find our epithets of value occupying is the most natural thing in the world. It would, however, be an unnatural status if the popular opinion which I cited at the outset were correct. If 'physical' and 'mental' meant two different kinds of intrinsic nature, immediately, intuitively, and infallibly discernible, and each fixed forever in whatever bit of experience it qualified, one does not see how there could ever have arisen any room for doubt or ambiguity. But if, on the contrary, these

---

[166] It is enough for my present purpose if the appreciative characters but *seem* to act thus. Believers in an activity *an sich,* other than our mental experiences of activity, will find some farther reflections on the subject in my address on 'The Experience of Activity.' [Cf. below, pp. 277–291.]

words are words of sorting, ambiguity is natural. For then, as soon as the relations of a thing are sufficiently various it can be sorted variously. Take a mass of carrion, for example, and the 'disgustingness' which for us is part of the experience. The sun caresses it, and the zephyr wooes it as if it were a bed of roses. So the disgustingness fails to *operate* within the realm of suns and breezes,—it does not function as a physical quality. But the carrion 'turns our stomach' by what seems a direct operation—it *does* function physically, therefore, in that limited part of physics. We can treat it as physical or as non-physical according as we take it in the narrower or in the wider context, and conversely, of course, we must treat it as non-mental or as mental.

Our body itself is the palmary instance of the ambiguous. Sometimes I treat my body purely as a part of outer nature. Sometimes, again, I think of it as 'mine,' I sort it with the 'me,' and then certain local changes and determinations in it pass for spiritual happenings. Its breathing is my 'thinking,' its sensorial adjustments are my 'attention,' its kinesthetic alterations are my 'efforts,' its visceral perturbations are my 'emotions.' The obstinate controversies that have arisen over such statements as these (which sound so paradoxical, and which can yet be made so seriously) prove how hard it is to decide by bare introspection what it is in experiences that shall make them either spiritual or material. It surely can be nothing intrinsic in the individual experience. It is their way of behaving towards each other, their system of relations, their function; and all these things vary with the context in which we find it opportune to consider them.

I think I may conclude, then (and I hope that my readers are now ready to conclude with me), that the pretended spirituality of our emotions and of our attributes of value, so far from proving an objection to the philosophy of pure experience, does, when rightly discussed and accounted for, serve as one of its best corroborations.

THE EXPERIENCE OF ACTIVITY* [167]

BRETHREN OF THE
PSYCHOLOGICAL ASSOCIATION

In casting about me for a subject for your President this year to talk about it has seemed to me that our experiences of activity would form

* From: E.R.E., 155–189.

[167] President's Address before the American Psychological Association, Philadelphia Meeting, December, 1904. [Reprinted from the *Psychological Review*,

a good one; not only because the topic is so naturally interesting, and because it has lately led to a good deal of rather inconclusive discussion, but because I myself am growing more and more interested in a certain systematic way of handling questions, and want to get others interested also, and this question strikes me as one in which, although I am painfully aware of my inability to communicate new discoveries or to reach definitive conclusions, I yet can show, in a rather definite manner, how the method works.

The way of handling things I speak of, is, as you already will have suspected, that known sometimes as the pragmatic method, sometimes humanism, sometimes as Deweyism, and in France, by some of the disciples of Bergson, as the Philosophie nouvelle. Professor Woodbridge's *Journal of Philosophy*[168] seems unintentionally to have become a sort of meeting place for those who follow these tendencies in America. There is only a dim identity among them; and the most that can be said at present is that some sort of gestation seems to be in the atmosphere, and that almost any day a man with a genius for finding the right word for things may hit upon some unifying and conciliating formula that will make so much vaguely similar aspiration crystallize into more definite form.

I myself have given the name of 'radical empiricism' to that version of the tendency in question which I prefer; and I propose, if you will now let me, to illustrate what I mean by radical empiricism, by applying it to activity as an example, hoping at the same time incidentally to leave the general problem of activity in a slightly—I fear very slightly—more manageable shape than before.

Mr. Bradley calls the question of activity a scandal to philosophy, and if one turns to the current literature of the subject—his own writings included—one easily gathers what he means. The opponents cannot even understand one another. Mr. Bradley says to Mr. Ward: "I do not care what your oracle is, and your preposterous psychology may here be gospel if you please; . . . but if the revelation does contain a meaning, I will commit myself to this: either the oracle is so confused that its signification is not discoverable, or, upon the other hand, if it can be pinned down to any definite statement, then that statement will be false."[169] Mr. Ward in turn says of Mr. Bradley: "I

---

vol. XII, No. 1, Jan., 1905. Also reprinted, with some omissions, as Appendix B, *A Pluralistic Universe*, pp. 370–394. Pp. 166–167 have also been reprinted in *Some Problems of Philosophy*, p. 212. The present essay is referred to in *ibid.*, p. 219, note. The author's corrections have been adopted for the present text. ED.]

[168] [*The Journal of Philosophy, Psychology, and Scientific Methods.*]

[169] *Appearance and Reality*, second edition, pp. 116–117.—Obviously written *at* Ward, though Ward's name is not mentioned.

cannot even imagine the state of mind to which his description applies. . . . [It] reads like an unintentional travesty of Herbartian psychology by one who has tried to improve upon it without being at the pains to master it." [170] Münsterberg excludes a view opposed to his own by saying that with any one who holds it a *Verständigung* with him is *"grundsätzlich ausgeschlossen";* and Royce, in a review of Stout,[171] hauls him over the coals at great length for defending 'efficacy' in a way which I, for one, never gathered from reading him, and which I have heard Stout himself say was quite foreign to the intention of his text.

In these discussions distinct questions are habitually jumbled and different points of view are talked of *durcheinander*.

(1) There is a psychological question: "Have we perceptions of activity? and if so, what are they like, and when and where do we have them?"

(2) There is a metaphysical question: "Is there a *fact* of activity? and if so, what idea must we frame of it? What is it like? and what does it do, if it does anything?" And finally there is a logical question:

(3) "Whence do we *know* activity? By our own feelings of it solely? or by some other source of information?" Throughout page after page of the literature one knows not which of these questions is before one; and mere description of the surface-show of experience is proferred as if it implicitly answered every one of them. No one of the disputants, moreover, tries to show what pragmatic consequences his own view would carry, or what assignable particular differences in any one's experience it would make if his adversary's were triumphant.

It seems to me that if radical empiricism be good for anything, it ought, with its pragmatic method and its principle of pure experience, to be able to avoid such tangles, or at least to simplify them somewhat. The pragmatic method starts from the postulate that there is no difference of truth that does n't make a difference of fact somewhere; and it seeks to determine the meaning of all differences of opinion by making the discussion hinge as soon as possible upon some practical or particular issue. The principle of pure experience is also a methodical postulate. Nothing shall be admitted as fact, it says, except what can be experienced at some definite time by some experient; and for every feature of fact ever so experienced, a definite place must be found somewhere in the final system of reality. In other words: Everything real must be experienceable somewhere, and every kind of thing experienced must somewhere be real.

Armed with these rules of method let us see what face the problems of activity present to us.

[170] [*Mind,* vol. xii, 1887, pp. 573–574.]

[171] *Mind,* N. S., vol. vi, [1897], p. 379.

By the principle of pure experience, either the word 'activity' must have no meaning at all, or else the original type and model of what it means must lie in some concrete kind of experience that can be definitely pointed out. Whatever ulterior judgments we may eventually come to make regarding activity, *that sort* of thing will be what the judgments are about. The first step to take, then, is to ask where in the stream of experience we seem to find what we speak of as activity. What we are to think of the activity thus found will be a later question.

Now it is obvious that we are tempted to affirm activity wherever we find anything *going on.* Taken in the broadest sense, any apprehension of something *doing,* is an experience of activity. Were our world describable only by the words 'nothing happening,' 'nothing changing,' 'nothing doing,' we should unquestionably call it an 'inactive' world. Bare activity then, as we may call it, means the bare fact of event or change. 'Change taking place' is a unique content of experience, one of those 'conjunctive' objects which radical empiricism seeks so earnestly to rehabilitate and preserve. The sense of activity is thus in the broadest and vaguest way synonymous with the sense of 'life.' We should feel our own subjective life at least, even in noticing and proclaiming an otherwise inactive world. Our own reaction on its monotony would be the one thing experienced there in the form of something coming to pass.

This seems to be what certain writers have in mind when they insist that for an experient to be at all is to be active. It seems to justify, or at any rate to explain, Mr. Ward's expression that we *are* only as we are active,[172] for we *are* only as experients; and it rules out Mr. Bradley's contention that "there is no original experience of anything like activity." [173] What we ought to say about activities thus elementary, whose they are, what they effect, or whether indeed they effect anything at all—these are later questions, to be answered only when the field of experience is enlarged.

Bare activity would thus be predicable, though there were no definite direction, no actor, and no aim. Mere restless zigzag movement, or a wild *Ideenflucht,* or *Rhapsodie der Wahrnehmungen,* as Kant would say,[174] would constitute an active as distinguished from an inactive world.

[172] *Naturalism and Agnosticism,* vol. ii, p. 245. One thinks naturally of the peripatetic *actus primus* and *actus secundus* here. ["Actus autem est *duplex: primus* et *secundus.* Actus quidem primus est forma, et integritas sei. Actus autem secundus est operatio." Thomas Aquinas: *Summa Theologica,* edition of Leo XIII, (1894), vol. i, p. 391. Cf. also Blanc: *Dictionnaire de Philosophie,* under 'acte.' Ed.]

[173] [*Appearance and Reality,* second edition, p. 116.]

[174] [*Kritik der reinen Vernunft, Werke,* (1905), vol. iv, p. 110 (trans. by Max Müller, second edition, p. 128).]

But in this actual world of ours, as it is given, a part at least of the activity comes with definite direction; it comes with desire and sense of goal; it comes complicated with resistances which it overcomes or succumbs to, and with the efforts which the feeling of resistance so often provokes; and it is in complex experiences like these that the notions of distinct agents, and of passivity as opposed to activity arise. Here also the notion of causal efficacy comes to birth. Perhaps the most elaborate work ever done in descriptive psychology has been the analysis by various recent writers of the more complex activity-situations.[175] In their descriptions, exquisitely subtle some of them,[176] the activity appears as the *gestaltqualität* or the *fundirte inhalt* (or as whatever else you may please to call the conjunctive form) which the content falls into when we experience it in the ways which the describers set forth. Those factors in those relations are what we mean by activity-situations; and to the possible enumeration and accumulation of their circumstances and ingredients there would seem to be no natural bound. Every hour of human life could contribute to the picture gallery; and this is the only fault that one can find with such descriptive industry—where is it going to stop? Ought we to listen forever to verbal pictures of what we have already in concrete form in our own breasts? [177] They never take us off the superficial plane. We knew the facts already—less spread out and separated, to be sure— but we knew them still. We always felt our own activity, for example, as 'the expansion of an idea with which our Self is identified, against an obstacle';[178] and the following out of such a definition through a multitude of cases elaborates the obvious so as to be little more than an exercise in synonymic speech.

All the descriptions have to trace familiar outlines, and to use familiar terms. The activity is, for example, attributed either to a physical or to a mental agent, and is either aimless or directed. If

---

[175] I refer to such descriptive work as Ladd's (*Psychology, Descriptive and Explanatory*, part I, chap. V, part II, chap. XI, part III, chaps. XXV and XXVI); as Sully's (*The Human Mind*, part V); as Stout's (*Analytic Psychology*, book I, chap. VI, and book II, chaps. I, II, and III); as Bradley's (in his long series of analytic articles on Psychology in *Mind*); as Titchener's (*Outline of Psychology*, part I, chap. VI); as Shand's (*Mind*, N. S., III, 449; IV, 450; VI, 289); as Ward's (*Mind*, XII, 67; 564); as Loveday's (*Mind*, N. S., X, 455); as Lipps's (Vom Fühlen, Wollen und Denken, 1902, chaps. II, IV, VI); and as Bergson's (*Revue Philosophique*, LIII, 1)—to mention only a few writings which I immediately recall.

[176] Their existence forms a curious commentary on Prof. Münsterberg's dogma that will-attitudes are not describable. He himself has contributed in a superior way to their description, both in his *Willenshandlung*, and in his *Grundzüge [der Psychologie]*, part II, chap. IX, § 7.

[177] I ought myself to cry *peccavi*, having been a voluminous sinner in my own chapter on the will. [*Principles of Psychology*, vol. II, chap. XXVI.]

[178] [Cf. F. H. Bradley, *Appearance and Reality*, second edition, pp. 96–97.]

directed it shows tendency. The tendency may or may not be resisted. If not, we call the activity immanent, as when a body moves in empty space by its momentum, or our thoughts wander at their own sweet will. If resistance is met, *its* agent complicates the situation. If now, in spite of resistance, the original tendency continues, effort makes its appearance, and along with effort, strain or squeeze. Will, in the narrower sense of the word, then comes upon the scene, whenever, along with the tendency, the strain and squeeze are sustained. But the resistance may be great enough to check the tendency, or even to reverse its path. In that case, we (if 'we' were the original agents or subjects of the tendency) are overpowered. The phenomenon turns into one of tension simply, or of necessity succumbed-to, according as the opposing power is only equal, or is superior to ourselves.

Whosoever describes an experience in such terms as these describes an experience *of* activity. If the word have any meaning, it must denote what there is found. *There* is complete activity in its original and first intention. What it is 'known-as' is what there appears. The experiencer of such a situation possesses all that the idea contains. He feels the tendency, the obstacle, the will, the strain, the triumph, or the passive giving up, just as he feels the time, the space, the swiftness or intensity, the movement, the weight and color, the pain and pleasure, the complexity, or whatever remaining characters the situation may involve. He goes through all that ever can be imagined where activity is supposed. If we suppose activities to go on outside of our experience, it is in forms like these that we must suppose them, or else give them some other name; for the word 'activity' has no imaginable content whatever save these experiences of process, obstruction, striving, strain, or release, ultimate *qualia* as they are of the life given us to be known.

Were this the end of the matter, one might think that whenever we had successfully lived through an activity-situation we should have to be permitted, without provoking contradiction, to say that we had been really active, that we had met real resistance and had really prevailed. Lotze somewhere says that to be an entity all that is necessary is to *gelten* as an entity, to operate, or to be felt, experienced, recognized, or in any way realized, as such.[179] In our activity-experiences the activity assuredly fulfils Lotze's demand. It makes itself *gelten*. It is witnessed at its work. No matter what activities there may really be in this extraordinary universe of ours, it is impossible for us to conceive of any one of them being either lived through or authentically known otherwise than in this dramatic shape of something sustaining a felt purpose against felt obstacles and overcoming or being overcome. What 'sustaining' means here is clear to anyone who has lived through

179 [Cf. above, p. 202, note.]

the experience, but to no one else; just as 'loud,' 'red,' 'sweet,' mean something only to beings with ears, eyes, and tongues. The *percipi* in these originals of experience is the *esse;* the curtain is the picture. If there is anything hiding in the background, it ought not to be called activity, but should get itself another name.

This seems so obviously true that one might well experience astonishment at finding so many of the ablest writers on the subject flatly denying that the activity we live through in these situations is real. Merely to feel active is not to be active, in their sight. The agents that appear in the experience are not real agents, the resistances do not really resist, the effects that appear are not really effects at all.[180] It is

---

[180] *Verborum gratiâ:* "The feeling of activity is not able, *quâ* feeling, to tell us anything about activity" (Loveday: *Mind,* N. S., vol. x, [1901], p. 463); "A sensation or feeling or sense *of* activity . . . is not, looked at in another way, an experience *of* activity at all. It is a mere sensation shut up within which you could by no reflection get the idea of activity. . . . Whether this experience is or is not later on a character essential to our perception and our idea of activity, it, as it comes first, is not in itself an experience of activity at all. It, as it comes first, is only so for extraneous reasons and only so for an outside observer" (Bradley, *Appearance and Reality,* second edition, p. 605); "In dem Tätigkeitsgefühle liegt an sich nicht der geringste Beweis für das Vorhandensein einer psychischen Tätigkeit" (Münsterberg: *Grundzüge der Psychologie*). I could multiply similar quotations and would have introduced some of them into my text to make it more concrete, save that the mingling of different points of view in most of these author's discussions (not in Münsterberg's) make it impossible to disentangle exactly what they mean. I am sure in any case, to be accused of misrepresenting them totally, even in this note, by omission of the context, so the less I name names and the more I stick to abstract characterization of a merely possible style of opinion, the safer it will be. And apropos of misunderstandings, I may add to this note a complaint on my own account. Professor Stout, in the excellent chapter on 'Mental Activity,' in vol. I of his *Analytic Psychology,* takes me to task for identifying spiritual activity with certain muscular feelings and gives quotations to bear him out. They are from certain paragraphs on 'the Self,' in which my attempt was to show what the central nucleus of the activities that we call 'ours' is. [*Principles of Psychology,* vol. I, pp. 299–305.] I found it in certain intracephalic movements which we habitually oppose, as 'subjective,' to the activities of the transcorporeal world. I sought to show that there is no direct evidence that we feel the activity of an inner spiritual agent as such (I should now say the activity of 'consciousness' as such, see above, pp. 169–183, 'Does Consciousness Exist?'). There are, in fact, three distinguishable 'activities' in the field of discussion: the elementary activity involved in the mere *that* of experience, in the fact that *something* is going on, and the farther specification of this *something* into two *whats,* an activity felt as 'ours,' and an activity ascribed to objects. Stout, as I apprehend him, identifies 'our' activity with that of the total experience-process, and when I circumscribe it as a part thereof, accuses me of treating it as a sort of external appendage to itself (Stout: *op. cit.,* vol. I, pp. 162–163), as if I 'separated the activity from the process which is active.' But all the processes in question are active, and their activity is inseparable from their being. My book raised only the question of *which* activity deserved the name of 'ours.' So far as we are 'persons,' and con-

evident from this that mere descriptive analysis of any one of our activity-experiences is not the whole story that there is something still to tell *about* them that has led such able writers to conceive of a *Simon-pure* activity, of an activity *an sich,* that does, and does n't merely appear to us to do, and compared with whose real doing all this phenomenal activity is but a specious sham.

The metaphysical question opens here; and I think that the state of mind of one possessed by it is often something like this: "It is all very well," we may imagine him saying, "to talk about certain experience-series taking on the form of feelings of activity, just as they might take on musical or geometric forms. Suppose that they do so; suppose we feel a will to stand a strain. Does our feeling do more than *record* the fact that the strain is sustained? The *real* activity, meanwhile, is the *doing* of the fact; and what is the doing made of before the record is made. What in the will *enables* it to act thus? And these trains of experience themselves, in which activities appear, what makes them *go* at all? Does the activity in one bit of experience bring the next bit into being? As an empiricist you cannot say so, for you

---

trasted and opposed to an 'environment,' movements in our body figure as our activities; and I am unable to find any other activities that are ours in this strictly personal sense. There is a wider sense in which the whole 'choir of heaven and furniture of the earth,' and their activities, are ours, for they are our 'objects.' But 'we' are here only another name for the total process of experience, another name for all that is, in fact; and I was dealing with the personal and individualized self exclusively in the passages with which Professor Stout finds fault.

The individualized self, which I believe to be the only thing properly called self, is a part of the content of the world experienced. The world experienced (otherwise called the 'field of consciousness') comes at all times with our body as its centre, centre of vision, centre of action, centre of interest. Where the body is is 'here'; when the body acts is 'now'; what the body touches is 'this'; all other things are 'there' and 'then' and 'that.' These words of emphasized position imply a systematization of things with reference to a focus of action and interest which lies in the body; and the systematization is now so instinctive (was it ever not so?) that no developed or active experience exists for us at all except in that ordered form. So far as 'thoughts' and 'feelings' can be active, their activity terminates in the activity of the body, and only through first arousing its activities can they begin to change those of the rest of the world. [Cf. also *A Pluralistic Universe,* below, p. 297, note.] The body is the storm centre, the origin of co-ordinates, the constant place of stress in all that experience-train. Everything circles round it, and is felt from its point of view. The word 'I,' then, is primarily a noun of position, just like 'this' and 'here.' Activities attached to 'this' position have prerogative emphasis and, if activities have feelings, must be felt in a peculiar way. The word 'my' designates the kind of emphasis. I see no inconsistency whatever in defending, on the one hand, 'my' activities as unique and opposed to those of outer nature, and, on the other hand, in affirming, after introspection, that they consist in movements in the head. The 'my' of them is the emphasis, the feeling of perspective-interest in which they are dyed.

have just declared activity to be only a kind of synthetic object, or conjunctive relation experienced between bits of experience already made. But what made them at all? What propels experience *über-haupt* into being? *There* is the activity that *operates;* the activity *felt* is only its superficial sign."

To the metaphysical question, popped upon us in this way, I must pay serious attention ere I end my remarks; but, before doing so, let me show that without leaving the immediate reticulations of experience, or asking what makes activity itself act, we still find the distinction between less real and more real activities forced upon us, and are driven to much soul-searching on the purely phenomenal plane.

We must not forget, namely, in talking of the ultimate character of our activity-experiences, that each of them is but a portion of a wider world, one link in the vast chain of processes of experience out of which history is made. Each partial process, to him who lives through it, defines itself by its origin and its goal; but to an observer with a wider mind-span who should live outside of it, that goal would appear but as a provisional halting-place, and the subjectively felt activity would be seen to continue into objective activities that led far beyond. We thus acquire a habit, in discussing activity-experiences, of defining them by their relation to something more. If an experience be one of narrow span, it will be mistaken as to what activity it is and whose. You think that *you* are acting while you are only obeying someone's push. You think you are doing *this,* but you are doing something of which you do not dream. For instance, you think you are but drinking this glass; but you are really creating the liver-cirrhosis that will end your days. You think you are just driving this bargain, but, as Stevenson says somewhere, you are laying down a link in the policy of mankind.

Generally speaking, the onlooker, with his wider field of vision, regards the *ultimate outcome* of an activity as what it is more really doing; and *the most previous agent* ascertainable, being the first source of action, he regards as the most real agent in the field. The others but transmit that agent's impulse; on him we put responsibility; we name him when one asks us 'Who's to blame?'

But the most previous agents ascertainable, instead of being of longer span, are often of much shorter span than the activity in view. Brain-cells are our best example. My brain-cells are believed to excite each other from next to next (by contiguous transmission of katabolic alteration, let us say) and to have been doing so long before this present stretch of lecturing-activity on my part began. If any one cell-group stops its activity, the lecturing will cease or show disorder of form. *Cessante causa, cessat et effectus*—does not this look as if the short-span brain activities were the more real activities, and the lecturing activities on my part only their effects? Moreover, as Hume so clearly pointed out,[181] in my mental activity-situation the words physically to be uttered are represented as the activity's immediate goal. These words, however, cannot be uttered without intermediate physical processes in the bulb and vagi nerves, which processes nevertheless fail to figure in the mental activity-series at all. That series, therefore, since it leaves out vitally real steps of action, cannot represent the real activities. It is something purely subjective; the *facts* of activity are elsewhere. They are something far more interstitial, so to speak, than what my feelings record.

The *real* facts of activity that have in point of fact been systematically pleaded for by philosophers have, so far as my information goes, been of three principal types.

The first type takes a consciousness of wider time-span than ours to be the vehicle of the more real activity. Its will is the agent, and its purpose is the action done.

The second type assumes that 'ideas' struggling with one another are the agents, and that the prevalence of one set of them is the action.

The third type believe that nerve-cells are the agents, and that resultant motor discharges are the acts achieved.

Now if we must de-realize our immediately felt activity-situations for the benefit of either of these types of substitute, we ought to know what the substitution practically involves. *What practical difference ought it to make if,* instead of saying naïvely that 'I' am active now in delivering this address, I say that *a wider thinker is active,* or that *certain ideas are active,* or that *certain nerve-cells are active,* in producing the result?

This would be the pragmatic meaning of the three hypotheses. Let us take them in succession in seeking a reply.

If we assume a wider thinker, it is evident that his purposes envelope mine. I am really lecturing *for* him; and although I cannot surely know to what end, yet if I take him religiously, I can trust it to be a good end, and willingly connive. I can be happy in thinking that my activity transmits his impulse, and that his ends prolong my own. So long as I take him religiously, in short, he does not de-realize my activities. He tends rather to corroborate the reality of them, so long as I believe both them and him to be good.

When now we turn to ideas, the case is different, inasmuch as ideas are supposed by the association psychology to influence each other only from next to next. The 'span' of an idea or pair of ideas, is assumed to be much smaller instead of being larger than that of my total conscious field. The same results may get worked out in both

[181] [*Enquiry Concerning Human Understanding,* sect. VII, part I, Selby-Bigge's edition, pp. 65 ff.]

cases, for this address is being given anyhow. But the ideas supposed to 'really' work it out had no prevision of the whole of it; and if I was lecturing for an absolute thinker in the former case, so, by similar reasoning, are my ideas now lecturing for me, that is, accomplishing unwittingly a result which I approve and adopt. But, when this passing lecture is over, there is nothing in the bare notion that ideas have been its agents that would seem to guarantee that my present purposes in lecturing will be prolonged. *I* may have ulterior developments in view; but there is no certainty that my ideas as such will wish to, or be able to, work them out.

The like is true if nerve-cells be the agents. The activity of a nerve-cell must be conceived of as a tendency of exceedingly short reach, an 'impulse' barely spanning the way to the next cell—for surely that amount of actual 'process' must be 'experienced' by the cells if what happens between them is to deserve the name of activity at all. But here again the gross resultant, as *I* perceive it, is indifferent to the agents, and neither wished or willed or foreseen. Their being agents now congruous with my will gives me no guarantee that like results will recur again from their activity. In point of fact, all sorts of other results do occur. My mistakes, impotencies, perversions, mental obstructions, and frustrations generally, are also results of the activity of cells. Although these are letting me lecture now, on other occasions they make me do things that I would willingly not do.

The question *Whose is the real activity?* is thus tantamount to the question *What will be the actual results?* Its interest is dramatic; how will things work out? If the agents are of one sort, one way; if of another sort, they may work out very differently. The pragmatic meaning of the various alternatives, in short, is great. It makes no merely verbal difference which opinion we take up.

You see it is the old dispute come back! Materialism and teleology; elementary short-span actions summing themselves 'blindly,' or far foreseen ideals coming with effort into act.

Naïvely we believe, and humanly and dramatically we like to believe, that activities both of wider and of narrower span are at work in life together, that both are real, and that the long-span tendencies yoke the others in their service, encouraging them in the right direction, and damping them when they tend in other ways. But how to represent clearly the *modus operandi* of such steering of small tendencies by large ones is a problem which metaphysical thinkers will have to ruminate upon for many years to come. Even if such control should eventually grow clearly picturable, the question how far it is successfully exerted in this actual world can be answered only by investigating the details of fact. No philosophic knowledge of the general nature and constitution of tendencies, or of the relation of larger to smaller ones, can help us to predict which of all the various competing tendencies that interest us in this universe are likeliest to prevail. We know as an empirical fact that far-seeing tendencies often carry out their purpose, but we know also that they are often defeated by the failure of some contemptibly small process on which success depends. A little thrombus in a statesman's meningeal artery will throw an empire out of gear. I can therefore not even hint at any solution of the pragmatic issue. I have only wished to show you that that issue is what gives the real interest to all inquiries into what kinds of activity may be real. Are the forces that really act in the world more foreseeing or more blind? As between 'our' activities as 'we' experience them, and those of our ideas, or of our brain-cells, the issue is well-defined.

I said a while back[182] that I should return to the 'metaphysical' question before ending; so, with a few words about that, I will now close my remarks.

In whatever form we hear this question propounded, I think that it always arises from two things, a belief that *causality* must be exerted in activity, and a wonder as to how causality is made. If we take an activity-situation at its face-value, it seems as if we caught *in flagrante delicto* the very power that makes facts come and be. I now am eagerly striving, for example, to get this truth which I seem half to perceive, into words which shall make it show more clearly. If the words come, it will seem as if the striving itself had drawn or pulled them into actuality out from the state of merely possible being in which they were. How is this feat performed? How does the pulling *pull?* How do I get my hold on words not yet existent, and when they come by what means have I *made* them come? Really it is the problem of creation; for in the end the question is: How do I make them *be?* Real activities are those that really make things be, without which the things are not, and with which they are there. Activity, so far as we merely feel it, on the other hand, is only an impression of ours, it may be maintained; and an impression is, for all this way of thinking, only a shadow of another fact.

Arrived at this point, I can do little more than indicate the principles on which, as it seems to me, a radically empirical philosophy is obliged to rely in handling such a dispute.

If there *be* real creative activities in being, radical empiricism must say, somewhere they must be immediately lived. Somewhere the *that* of efficacious causing and the *what* of it must be experienced in one, just as the what and the that of 'cold' are experienced in one whenever a man has the sensation of cold here and now. It boots not to say that our sensations are fallible. They are indeed; but to see the thermometer contradict us when we say 'it is cold' does not abolish

[182] Page 284, above.

cold as a specific nature from the universe. Cold is in the arctic circle if not here. Even so, to feel that our train is moving when the train beside our window moves, to see the moon through a telescope come twice as near, or to see two pictures as one solid when we look through a stereoscope at them, leaves motion, nearness, and solidity still in being—if not here, yet each in its proper seat elsewhere. And wherever the seat of real causality *is,* as ultimately known 'for true' (in nerve-processes, if you will, that cause our feelings of activity as well as the movements which these seem to prompt), a philosophy of pure experience can consider the real causation as no other *nature* of thing than that which even in our most erroneous experiences appears to be at work. Exactly what appears there is what we *mean* by working, though we may later come to learn that working was not exactly *there.* Sustaining, persevering, striving, paying with effort as we go, hanging on, and finally achieving our intention—this *is* action, this *is* effectuation in the only shape in which, by a pure experience-philosophy, the whereabouts of it anywhere can be discussed. Here is creation in its first intention, here is causality at work.[183] To treat this offhand as the bare illusory surface of a world whose real causality is an unimaginable ontological principle hidden in the cubic deeps, is, for the more empirical way of thinking, only animism in another shape. You explain your given fact by your 'principle,' but the principle itself, when you look clearly at it, turns out to be nothing but a previous little spiritual copy of the fact. Away from that one and only kind of fact your mind, considering causality, can never get.[184]

[183] Let me not be told that this contradicts 'Does Consciousness Exist?' in which it was said that while 'thoughts' and 'things' have the same natures, the natures work 'energetically' on each other in the things (fire burns, water wets, etc.) but not in the thoughts. Mental activity-trains are composed of thoughts, yet their members do work on each other, they check, sustain, and introduce. They do so when the activity is merely associational as well as when effort is there. But, and this is my reply, they do so by other parts of their nature than those that energize physically. One thought in every developed activity-series is a desire or thought of purpose, and all the other thoughts acquire a feeling tone from their relation of harmony or oppugnancy to this. The interplay of these secondary tones (among which 'interest,' 'difficulty,' and 'effort' figure) runs the drama in the mental series. In what we term the physical drama these qualities play absolutely no part. The subject needs careful working out; but I can see no inconsistency.

[184] I have found myself more than once accused in print of being the assertor of a metaphysical principle of activity. Since literary misunderstandings retard the settlement of problems, I should like to say that such an interpretation of the pages I have published on Effort and on Will is absolutely foreign to what I meant to express. [*Principles of Psychology,* vol. II, ch. XXVI.] I owe all my doctrines on this subject to Renouvier; and Renouvier, as I understand him, is (or at any rate then was) an out and out phenomenist, a denier of 'forces' in the most strenuous sense. [Cf. Ch. Renouvier: *Esquisse d'une Classification Systématique*

I conclude, then, that real effectual causation as an ultimate nature, as a 'category,' if you like, of reality, is *just what we feel it to be,* just that kind of conjunction which our own activity-series reveal. We have the whole butt and being of it in our hands; and the healthy thing for philosophy is to leave off grubbing underground for what effects effectuation, or what makes action act, and to try to solve the concrete questions of where effectuation in this world is located, of which things are the true causal agents there, and of what the more remote effects consist.

From this point of view the greater sublimity traditionally attributed to the metaphysical inquiry, the grubbing inquiry, entirely disappears. If we could know what causation really and transcendentally is in itself, the only *use* of the knowledge would be to help us to recognize an actual cause when we had one, and so to track the future course of operations more intelligently out. The mere abstract inquiry into causation's hidden nature is not more sublime than any other inquiry equally abstract. Causation inhabits no more sublime level than anything else. It lives, apparently, in the dirt of the world as well as in the absolute, or in man's unconquerable mind. The worth and interest of the world consists not in its elements, be these elements things, or be they the conjunctions of things; it exists rather in the dramatic outcome in the whole process, and in the meaning of the succession stages which the elements work out.

My colleague and master, Josiah Royce, in a page of his review of Stout's *Analytic Psychology*[185] has some fine words on this point with which I cordially agree. I cannot agree with his separating the notion

---

des Doctrines Philosophiques (1885), vol. II, pp. 390–392; *Essais de Critique Générale* (1859), vol. II, §§ ix, xiii. For an acknowledgment of the author's general indebtedness to Renouvier, cf. *Some Problems of Philosophy*, p. 165, note. ED.] Single clauses in my writing, or sentences read out of their connection, may possibly have been compatible with a transphenomenal principle of energy; but I defy anyone to show a single sentence which, taken with its context, should be naturally held to advocate that view. The misinterpretation probably arose at first from my defending (after Renouvier) the indeterminism of our efforts. 'Free will' was supposed by my critics to involve a supernatural agent. As a matter of plain history the only 'free will' I have ever thought of defending is the character of novelty in fresh activity-situations. If an activity-process is the form of a whole 'field of consciousness,' and if each field of consciousness is not only in its totality unique (as is now commonly admitted) but has its elements unique (since in that situation they are all dyed in the total) then novelty is perpetually entering the world and what happens there is not pure *repetition*, as the dogma of the literal uniformity of nature requires. Activity-situations come, in short, each with an original touch. A 'principle' of free will if there were one, would doubtless manifest itself in such phenomena, but I never saw, nor do I now see, what the principle could do except rehearse the phenomenon beforehand, or why it ever should be invoked.

[185] *Mind*, N. S., vol. VI, 1897; cf. pp. 392–393.

of efficacy from that of activity altogether (this I understand to be one contention of his) for activities are efficacious whenever they are real activities at all. But the inner nature both of efficacy and of activity are superficial problems, I understand Royce to say; and the only point for us in solving them would be their possible use in helping us to solve the far deeper problem of the course and meaning of the world of life. Life, says our colleague, is full of significance, of meaning, of success and of defeat, of hoping and of striving, of longing, of desire, and of inner value. It is a total presence that embodies worth. To live our own lives better in this presence is the true reason why we wish to know the elements of things; so even we psychologists must end on this pragmatic note.

The urgent problems of activity are thus more concrete. They are all problems of the true relation of longer-span to shorter-span activities. When, for example, a number of 'ideas' (to use the name traditional in psychology) grow confluent in a larger field of consciousness, do the smaller activities still co-exist with the wider activities then experienced by the conscious subject? And, if so, do the wide activities accompany the narrow ones inertly, or do they exert control? Or do they perhaps utterly supplant and replace them and short-circuit their effects? Again, when a mental activity-process and a brain-cell series of activities both terminate in the same muscular movement, does the mental process steer the neural processes or not? Or, on the other hand, does it independently short-circuit their effects? Such are the questions that we must begin with. But so far am I from suggesting any definitive answer to such questions, that I hardly yet can put them clearly. They lead, however, into that region of pan-psychic and ontologic speculation of which Professors Bergson and Strong have lately enlarged the literature in so able and interesting a way.[186] The results of these authors seem in many respects dissimilar, and I understand them as yet but imperfectly; but I cannot help suspecting that the direction of their work is very promising, and that they have the hunter's instinct for the fruitful trails.

186 [Cf. *A Pluralistic Universe,* below, pp. 561–581 (on Bergson); H. Bergson: *Creative Evolution,* trans. by A. Mitchell; C. A. Strong: *Why the Mind has a Body,* ch. XII. ED.]

THE CONTINUITY OF EXPERIENCE*

I fear that few of you will have been able to obey Bergson's call upon you to look towards the sensational life for the fuller knowledge of reality, or to sympathize with his attempt to limit the divine right of concepts to rule our mind absolutely. It is too much like looking downward and not up. Philosophy, you will say, doesn't lie flat on its belly in the middle of experience, in the very thick of its sand and gravel, as this Bergsonism does, never getting a peep at anything from above. Philosophy is essentially the vision of things from above. It doesn't simply feel the detail of things, it comprehends their intelligible plan, sees their forms and principles, their categories and rules, their order and necessity. It takes the superior point of view of the architect. Is it conceivable that it should ever forsake that point of view and abandon itself to a slovenly life of immediate feeling? To say nothing of your traditional Oxford devotion to Aristotle and Plato, the leaven of T. H. Green probably works still too strongly here for his anti-sensationalism to be outgrown quickly. Green more than any one realized that knowledge *about* things was knowledge of their relations; but nothing could persuade him that our sensational life could contain any relational element. He followed the strict intellectualist method with sensations. What they were not expressly defined as including, they must exclude. Sensations are not defined as relations, so in the end Green thought that they could get related together only by the action on them from above of a 'self-distinguishing' absolute and eterna mind, present to that which is related, but not related itself. 'A relation,' he said, 'is not contingent with the contingency of feeling. It is permanent with the permanence of the combining and comparing thought which alone constitutes it.' [187] In other words, relations are purely conceptual objects, and the sensational life as such cannot relate itself together. Sensation in itself, Green wrote, is fleeting, momentary, unnameable (because, while we name it, it has become another), and for the same reason unknowable, the very negation of knowability. Were there no permanent objects of conception for our sensations to be 'referred to,' there would be no significant names, but only noises, and a consistent sensationalism must be speechless.[188] Green's intellectualism was so earnest that it produced a natural and an inevitable effect. But the atomistic and unrelated sensations which

* From: P. U., 277–300.
[187] *Introduction to Hume*, 1874, p. 151.
[188] *Ibid.*, pp. 16, 21, 36, *et passim.*

he had in mind were purely fictitious products of his rationalist fancy. The psychology of our own day disavows them utterly,[189] and Green's laborious belaboring of poor old Locke for not having first seen that his ideas of sensation were just that impracticable sort of thing, and then fled to transcendental idealism as a remedy,—his belaboring of poor old Locke for this, I say, is pathetic. Every examiner of the sensible life *in concreto* must see that relations of every sort, of time, space, difference, likeness, change, rate, cause, or what not, are just as integral members of the sensational flux as terms are, and that conjunctive relations are just as true members of the flux as disjunctive relations are.[190] This is what in some recent writings of mine I have called the 'radically empiricist' doctrine (in distinction from the doctrine of mental atoms which the name empiricism so often suggests). Intellectualistic critics of sensation insist that sensations are *dis*joined only. Radical empiricism insists that conjunctions between them are just as immediately given as disjunctions are, and that relations, whether disjunctive or conjunctive, are in their original sensible givenness just as fleeting and momentary (in Green's words), and just as 'particular,' as terms are. Later, both terms and relations get universalized by being conceptualized and named.[191] But all the thickness, concreteness, and individuality of experience exists in the immediate and relatively unnamed stages of it, to the richness of which, and to the standing inadequacy of our conceptions to match it, Professor Bergson so emphatically calls our attention.

And now I am happy to say that we can begin to gather together some of the separate threads of our argument, and see a little better the general kind of conclusion toward which we are tending. [In my essay on "The Compounding of Consciousness" (below, pp. 546–561) I spoke] about the difficulty of seeing how states of consciousness can compound themselves. The difficulty seemed to be the same, you [see], whether we took it in psychology as the composition of finite states of mind out of simpler finite states, or in metaphysics as the composition of the absolute mind out of finite minds in general. It is the general conceptualist difficulty of any one thing being the same with many things, either at once or in succession, for the abstract

[189] See, *inter alia*, the chapter on the 'Stream of Thought' in my own Psychologies; H. Cornelius, *Psychologie*, 1897, chaps. i and iii; G. H. Luquet, *Idées Générales de Psychologie*, 1906, *passim*.

[190] Compare, as to all this, an article by the present writer, entitled 'A world of pure experience,' in the *Journal of Philosophy*, New York, vol. i, pp. 533, 561 (1905). [See above, pp. 194–214.]

[191] Green's attempt to discredit sensations by reminding us of their 'dumbness,' in that they do not come already *named*, as concepts may be said to do, only shows how intellectualism is dominated by verbality. The unnamed appears in Green as synonymous with the unreal.

concepts of oneness and manyness must needs exclude each other. In the particular instance that we have dwelt on so long, the one thing is the all-form of experience, the many things are the each-forms of experience in you and me. To call them the same we must treat them as if each were simultaneously its own other, a feat on conceptualist principles impossible of performance.

On the principle of going behind the conceptual function altogether, however, and looking to the more primitive flux of the sensational life for reality's true shape, a way is open to us, as I tried in my last lecture to show. Not only the absolute is its own other, but the simplest bits of immediate experience are their own others, if that hegelian phrase be once for all allowed. The concrete pulses of experience appear pent in by no such definite limits as our conceptual substitutes for them are confined by. They run into one another continuously and seem to interpenetrate. What in them is relation and what is matter related is hard to discern. You feel no one of them as inwardly simple, and no two as wholly without confluence where they touch. There is no datum so small as not to show this mystery, if mystery it be. The tiniest feeling that we can possibly have comes with an earlier and a later part and with a sense of their continuous procession. Mr. Shadworth Hodgson showed long ago that there is literally no such object as the present moment except as an unreal postulate of abstract thought.[192] The 'passing' moment is, as I already have reminded you, the minimal fact, with the 'apparition of difference' inside of it as well as outside. If we do not feel both past and present in one field of feeling, we feel them not at all. We have the same many-in-one in the matter that fills the passing time. The rush of our thought forward through its fringes is the everlasting peculiarity of its life. We realize this life as something always off its balance, something in transition, something that shoots out of a darkness through a dawn into a brightness that we feel to be the dawn fulfilled. In the very midst of the continuity our experience comes as an alteration. 'Yes,' we say at the full brightness, '*this* is what I just meant.' 'No,' we feel at the dawning, 'this is not yet the full meaning, there is more to come.' In every crescendo of sensation, in every effort to recall, in every progress towards the satisfaction of desire, this succession of an emptiness and fulness that have reference to each other and are one flesh is the essence of the phenomenon. In every hindrance of desire the sense of an ideal presence which is absent in fact, of an absent, in a word, which the only function of the present is to *mean,* is even more notoriously there. And in the movement of pure thought we have the same phenomenon. When I say *Socrates is mortal,* the moment *Socrates* is incomplete; it falls forward through the *is* which is pure movement,

192 *Philosophy of Reflection,* i, 248 ff.

into the *mortal* which is indeed bare mortal on the tongue, but for the mind is *that mortal,* the *mortal Socrates,* at last satisfactorily disposed of and told off.[193]

Here, then, inside of the minimal pulses of experience, is realized that very inner complexity which the transcendentalists say only the absolute can genuinely possess. The gist of the matter is always the same—something ever goes indissolubly with something else. You cannot separate the same from its other, except by abandoning the real altogether and taking to the conceptual system. What is immediately given in the single and particular instance is always something pooled and mutual, something with no dark spot, no point of ignorance. No one elementary bit of reality is eclipsed from the next bit's point of view, if only we take reality sensibly and in small enough pulses—and by us it has to be taken pulse-wise, for our span of consciousness is too short to grasp the larger collectivity of things except nominally and abstractly. No more of reality collected together at once is extant anywhere, perhaps, than in my experience of reading this page, or in yours of listening; yet within those bits of experience as they come to pass we get a fulness of content that no conceptual description can equal. Sensational experiences *are* their 'own others,' then, both internally and externally. Inwardly they are one with their parts, and outwardly they pass continuously into their next neighbors, so that events separated by years of time in a man's life hang together unbrokenly by the intermediary events. Their *names,* to be sure, cut them into separate conceptual entities, but no cuts existed in the continuum in which they originally came.

If, with all this in our mind, we turn to our own particular predicament, we see that our old objection to the self-compounding of states of consciousness, our accusation that it was impossible for purely logical reasons, is unfounded in principle. Every smallest state of consciousness, concretely taken, overflows its own definition. Only concepts are self-identical; only 'reason' deals with closed equations; nature is but a name for excess; every point in her opens out and runs into the more; and the only question, with reference to any point we may be considering, is how far into the rest of nature we may have to go in order to get entirely beyond its overflow. In the pulse of inner life immediately present now in each of us is a little past, a little future, a little awareness of our own body, of each other's persons, of these sublimities we are trying to talk about, of the earth's geography and the direction of history, of truth and error, of good and bad, and

[193] Most of this paragraph is extracted from an address of mine before the American Psychological Association, printed in the *Psychological Review*, vol. ii, p. 105. I take pleasure in the fact that already in 1895 I was so far advanced towards my present bergsonian position.

of who knows how much more? Feeling, however dimly and subconsciously, all these things, your pulse of inner life is continuous with them, belongs to them and they to it. You can't identify it with either one of them rather than with the others, for if you let it develop into no matter which of those directions, what it develops into will look back on it and say, 'That was the original germ of me.'

In *principle,* then, the real units of our immediately-felt life are unlike the units that intellectualist logic holds to and makes its calculations with. They are not separate from their own others, and you have to take them at widely separated dates to find any two of them that seem unblent. Then indeed they do appear separate even as their concepts are separate; a chasm yawns between them; but the chasm itself is but an intellectualist fiction, got by abstracting from the continuous sheet of experiences with which the intermediary time was filled. It is like the log carried first by William and Henry, then by William, Henry, and John, then by Henry and John, then by John and Peter, and so on. All real units of experience *overlap.* Let a row of equidistant dots on a sheet of paper symbolize the concepts by which we intellectualize the world. Let a ruler long enough to cover at least three dots stand for our sensible experience. Then the conceived changes of the sensible experience can be symbolized by sliding the ruler along the line of dots. One concept after another will apply to it, one after another drop away, but it will always cover at least two of them, and no dots less than three will ever adequately cover *it.* You falsify it if you treat it conceptually, or by the law of dots.

What is true here of successive states must also be true of simultaneous characters. They also overlap each other with their being. My present field of consciousness is a centre surrounded by a fringe that shades insensibly into a subconscious more. I use three separate terms here to describe this fact; but I might as well use three hundred, for the fact is all shades and no boundaries. Which part of it properly is in my consciousness, which out? If I name what is out, it already has come in. The centre works in one way while the margins work in another, and presently overpower the centre and are central themselves. What we conceptually identify ourselves with and say we are thinking of at any time is the centre; but our *full* self is the whole field, with all those indefinitely radiating subconscious possibilities of increase that we can only feel without conceiving, and can hardly begin to analyze. The collective and the distributive ways of being coexist here, for each part functions distinctly, makes connexion with its own peculiar region in the still wider rest of experience and tends to draw us into that line, and yet the whole is somehow felt as one pulse of our life,—not conceived so, but felt so.

In principle, then, as I said, intellectualism's edge is broken; it can only approximate to reality, and its logic is inapplicable to our inner life, which spurns its vetoes and mocks at its impossibilities. Every bit of us at every moment is part and parcel of a wider self, it quivers along various radii like the wind-rose on a compass, and the actual in it is continuously one with possibles not yet in our present sight.[194] And just as we are co-conscious with our own momentary margin, may not we ourselves form the margin of some more really central self in things which is co-conscious with the whole of us? May not you and I be confluent in a higher consciousness, and confluently active there, tho we now know it not?

I am tiring myself and you, I know, by vainly seeking to describe by concepts and words what I say at the same time exceeds either conceptualization or verbalization. As long as one continues *talking,* intellectualism remains in undisturbed possession of the field. The return to life can't come about by talking. It is an *act;* to make you return to life, I must set an example for your imitation, I must deafen you to talk, or to the importance of talk, by showing you, as Bergson does, that the concepts we talk with are made for purposes of *practice* and not for purposes of insight. Or I must *point,* point to the mere *that* of life, and you by inner sympathy must fill out the *what* for yourselves. The minds of some of you, I know, will absolutely refuse to do so, refuse to think in non-conceptualized terms. I myself absolutely refused to do so for years together, even after I knew that the denial of manyness-in-oneness by intellectualism must be false, for the same reality does perform the most various functions at once. But I hoped ever for a revised intellectualist way round the difficulty, and it was only after reading Bergson that I saw that to continue using the intellectualist method was itself the fault. I saw that philosophy had been on a false scent ever since the days of Socrates and Plato, that an *intellectual* answer to the intellectualist's difficulties will never come, and that the real way out of them, far from consisting in the discovery of such an answer, consists in simply closing one's ears to the question. When conceptualism summons life to justify itself in conceptual terms, it is like a challenge addressed in a foreign language to some one who is absorbed in his own business; it is irrelevant to him alto-

[194] The conscious self of the moment, the central self, is probably determined to this privileged position by its functional connexion with the body's imminent or present acts. It is the present *acting* self. Tho the more that surrounds it may be 'subconscious' to us, yet if in its 'collective capacity' it also exerts an active function, it may be conscious in a wider way, conscious, as it were, over our heads.

On the relations of consciousness to action see Bergson's *Matière et Mémoire, passim,* especially chap. i. Compare also the hints in Münsterberg's *Grundzüge der Psychologie,* chap. xv; those in my own *Principles of Psychology,* vol. ii, pp. 581–592; and those in W. McDougall's *Physiological Psychology,* chap. vii.

gether—he may let it lie unnoticed. I went thus through the 'inner catastrophe' of which I spoke in the last lecture; I had literally come to the end of my conceptual stock-in-trade, I was bankrupt intellectualistically, and had to change my base. No words of mine will probably convert you, for words can be the names only of concepts. But if any of you try sincerely and pertinaciously on your own separate accounts to intellectualize reality, you may be similarly driven to a change of front. I say no more: I must leave life to teach the lesson.

We have now reached a point of view from which the self-compounding of mind in its smaller and more accessible portions seems a certain fact, and in which the speculative assumption of a similar but wider compounding in remoter regions must be reckoned with as a legitimate hypothesis. The absolute is not the impossible being I once thought it. Mental facts do function both singly and together, at once, and we finite minds may simultaneously be co-conscious with one another in a superhuman intelligence. It is only the extravagant claims of coercive necessity on the absolute's part that have to be denied by *a priori* logic. As an hypothesis trying to make itself probable on analogical and inductive grounds, the absolute is entitled to a patient hearing. Which is as much as to say that our serious business from now onward lies with Fechner and his method, rather than with Hegel, Royce, or Bradley. Fechner treats the superhuman consciousness he so fervently believes in as an hypothesis only, which he then recommends by all the resources of induction and persuasion.

It is true that Fechner himself is an absolutist in his books, not actively but passively, if I may say so. He talks not only of the earth-soul and of the star-souls, but of an integrated soul of all things in the cosmos without exception, and this he calls God just as others call it the absolute. Nevertheless he *thinks* only of the subordinate superhuman souls, and content with having made his obeisance once for all to the august total soul of the cosmos, he leaves it in its lonely sublimity with no attempt to define its nature. Like the absolute, it is 'out of range,' and not an object for distincter vision. Psychologically, it seems to me that Fechner's God is a lazy postulate of his, rather than a part of his system positively thought out. As we envelop our sight and hearing, so the earth-soul envelops us, and the star-soul and the earth-soul, until—what? Envelopment can't go on forever; it must have an *abschluss,* a total envelope must terminate the series, so God is the name that Fechner gives to this last all-enveloper. But if nothing escapes this all-enveloper, he is responsible for everything, including evil, and all the paradoxes and difficulties which I found in the absolute at the end of our third lecture recur undiminished. Fechner tries sincerely to grapple with the problem of evil, but he always solves it in the leibnitzian fashion by making his God non-absolute, placing him under conditions of 'metaphysical necessity' which even his omnipotence cannot violate. His will has to struggle with conditions not imposed on that will by itself. He tolerates provisionally what he has not created, and then with endless patience tries to overcome it and live it down. He has, in short, a history. Whenever Fechner tries to represent him clearly, his God becomes the ordinary God of theism, and ceases to be the absolutely totalized all-enveloper.[195] In this shape, he represents the ideal element in things solely, and is our champion and our helper and we his helpers, against the bad parts of the universe.

Fechner was in fact too little of a metaphysician to care for perfect formal consistency in these abstract regions. He believed in God in the pluralistic manner, but partly from convention and partly from what I should call intellectual laziness, if laziness of any kind could be imputed to a Fechner, he let the usual monistic talk about him pass unchallenged. I propose to you that we should discuss the question of God without entangling ourselves in advance in the monistic assumption. Is it probable that there is any superhuman consciousness at all, in the first place? When that is settled, the further question whether its form be monistic or pluralistic is in order.

Before advancing to either question, however, and I shall have to deal with both but very briefly after what has been said already, let me finish our retrospective survey by one more remark about the curious logical situation of the absolutists. For what have they invoked the absolute except as a being the peculiar inner form of which shall enable it to overcome the contradictions with which intellectualism has found the finite many as such to be infected? The many-in-one character that, as we have seen, every smallest tract of finite experience offers, is considered by intellectualism to be fatal to the reality of finite experience. What can be distinguished, it tells us, is separate; and what is separate is unrelated, for a relation, being a 'between,' would bring only a twofold separation. Hegel, Royce, Bradley, and the Oxford absolutists in general seem to agree about this logical absurdity of manyness-in-oneness in the only places where it is empirically found. But see the curious tactics! Is the absurdity *reduced* in the absolute being whom they call in to relieve it? Quite otherwise, for that being shows it on an infinitely greater scale, and flaunts it in its very definition. The fact of its not being related to any outward environment, the fact that all relations are inside of itself, doesn't save it, for Mr. Bradley's great argument against the finite is that *in* any given bit of it (a bit of sugar, for instance) the presence of a plurality of characters (whiteness and sweetness, for example) is self-contradictory; so that in the final end all that the absolute's name appears to stand

[195] Compare *Zend-Avesta*, 2d edition, vol. i, pp. 165 ff., 181, 206, 244 ff., etc.; *Die Tagesansicht*, etc., chap. v, § 6; and chap. xv.

for is the persistent claim of outraged human nature that reality *shall* not be called absurd. *Somewhere* there must be an aspect of it guiltless of self-contradiction. All we can see of the absolute, meanwhile, is guilty in the same way in which the finite is. Intellectualism sees what it calls the guilt, when comminuted in the finite object; but is too near-sighted to see it in the more enormous object. Yet the absolute's constitution, if imagined at all, has to be imagined after the analogy of some bit of finite experience. Take any *real* bit, suppress its environment and then magnify it to monstrosity, and you get identically the type of structure of the absolute. It is obvious that all your difficulties here remain and go with you. If the relative experience was inwardly absurd, the absolute experience is infinitely more so. Intellectualism, in short, strains off the gnat, but swallows the whole camel. But this polemic against the absolute is as odious to me as it is to you, so I will say no more about that being. It is only one of those wills of the wisp, those lights that do mislead the morn, that have so often impeded the clear progress of philosophy, so I will turn to the more general positive question of whether superhuman unities of consciousness should be considered as more probable or more improbable.

In [another] lecture I went over some of the fechnerian reasons for their plausibility, or reasons that at least replied to our more obvious grounds of doubt concerning them. The numerous facts of divided or split human personality which the genius of certain medical men, as Janet, Freud, Prince, Sidis, and others, have unearthed were unknown in Fechner's time, and neither the phenomena of automatic writing and speech, nor of mediumship and 'possession' generally, had been recognized or studied as we now study them, so Fechner's stock of analogies is scant compared with our present one. He did the best with what he had, however. For my own part I find in some of these abnormal or supernormal facts the strongest suggestions in favor of a superior co-consciousness being possible. I doubt whether we shall ever understand some of them without using the very letter of Fechner's conception of a great reservoir in which the memories of earth's inhabitants are pooled and preserved, and from which, when the threshold lowers or the valve opens, information ordinarily shut out leaks into the mind of exceptional individuals among us. But those regions of inquiry are perhaps too spook-haunted to interest an academic audience, and the only evidence I feel it now decorous to bring to the support of Fechner is drawn from ordinary religious experience. I think it may be asserted that there *are* religious experiences of a specific nature, not deducible by analogy or psychological reasoning from our other sorts of experience. I think that they point with reasonable probability to the continuity of our consciousness with a wider spiritual environment from which the ordinary prudential man (who is the only man that scientific psychology, so called, takes cognizance of) is shut off.

ON THE NOTION OF
REALITY AS CHANGING*

In my *Principles of Psychology* (above, p. 98) I gave the name of the 'axiom of skipped intermediaries and transferred relations' to a serial principle of which the foundation of logic, the *dictum de omni et nullo* (or, as I expressed it, the rule that what is of a kind is of that kind's kind), is the most familiar instance. More than the more is more than the less, equals of equals are equal, sames of the same are the same, the cause of a cause is the cause of its effects, are other examples of this serial law. Altho it applies infallibly and without restriction throughout certain abstract series, where the 'sames,' 'causes,' etc., spoken of, are 'pure,' and have no properties save their sameness, causality, etc., it cannot be applied offhand to concrete objects with numerous properties and relations, for it is hard to trace a straight line of sameness, causation, or whatever it may be, through a series of such objects without swerving into some 'respect' where the relation, as pursued originally, no longer holds: the objects have so many 'aspects' that we are constantly deflected from our original direction, and find, we know not why, that we are following something different from what we started with. Thus a cat is in a sense the same as a mouse-trap, and a mouse-trap the same as a bird-cage; but in no valuable or easily intelligible sense is a cat the same as a bird-cage. Commodore Perry was in a sense the cause of the new régime in Japan, and the new régime was the cause of the russian Douma; but it would hardly profit us to insist on holding to Perry as the cause of the Douma: the terms have grown too remote to have any real or practical relation to each other. In every series of real terms, not only do the terms themselves and their associates and environments change, but we change, and their *meaning* for us changes, so that new kinds of sameness and types of causation continually come into view and appeal to our interest. Our earlier lines, having grown irrelevant, are then dropped. The old terms can no longer be substituted nor the relations 'transferred,' because of so many new dimensions into which experi-

* From: P.U., 347–352.

ence has opened. Instead of a straight line, it now follows a zigzag; and
to keep it straight, one must do violence to its spontaneous development. Not that one might not possibly, by careful seeking (tho I doubt
it), *find* some line in nature along which terms literally the same, or
causes causal in the same way, might be serially strung without limit,
if one's interest lay in such finding. Within such lines our axioms
might hold, causes might cause their effect's effects, etc.; but such
lines themselves would, if found, only be partial members of a vast
natural network, within the other lines of which you could not say, in
any sense that a wise man or a sane man would ever think of, in any
sense that would not be concretely *silly,* that the principle of skipt
intermediaries still held good. In the *practical* world, the world whose
significances we follow, sames of the same are certainly not sames of
one another; and things constantly cause other things without being
held responsible for everything of which those other things are causes.

Professor Bergson, believing as he does in a heraclitean 'devenir
réel,' ought, if I rightly understand him, positively to deny that in the
actual world the logical axioms hold good without qualification. Not
only, according to him, do terms change, so that after a certain time
the very elements of things are no longer what they were, but relations
also change, so as no longer to obtain in the same identical way between the new things that have succeeded upon the old ones. If this
were really so, then however indefinitely sames might still be substituted for sames in the logical world of nothing but pure sameness, in
the world of real operations every line of sameness actually started
and followed up would eventually give out, and cease to be traceable
any farther. Sames of the same, in such a world, will not always (or
rather, in a strict sense will never) be the same as one another, for in
such a world there *is* no literal or ideal sameness among numerical
differents. Nor in such a world will it be true that the cause of the
cause is unreservedly the cause of the effect; for if we follow lines of
real causation, instead of contenting ourselves with Hume's and
Kant's eviscerated schematism, we find that remoter effects are seldom aimed at by causal intentions,[196] that no one kind of causal activity continues indefinitely, and that the principle of skipt intermediaries
can be talked of only *in abstracto.*[197]

Volumes i, ii, and iii of the *Monist* (1890–1893) contain a number of articles by Mr. Charles S. Peirce, articles the originality of
which has apparently prevented their making an immediate impression, but which, if I mistake not, will prove a gold-mine of ideas for
thinkers of the coming generation. Mr. Peirce's views, tho reached so

[196] Compare the Douma with what Perry aimed at.

[197] Compare above, [*Principles*], Vol. I, Essay VI, as to what I mean here by
'real' causal activity.

differently, are altogether congruous with Bergson's. Both philosophers believe that the appearance of novelty in things is genuine. To an observer standing outside of its generating causes, novelty can appear only as so much 'chance'; to one who stands inside it is the expression of 'free creative activity.' Peirce's 'tychism' is thus practically synonymous with Bergson's 'devenir réel.' The common objection to admitting novelties is that by jumping abruptly in, *ex nihilo,* they shatter the world's rational continuity. Peirce meets this objection by combining his tychism with an express doctrine of 'synechism' or continuity, the two doctrines merging into the higher synthesis on which he bestows the name of 'agapasticism' (*loc. cit.,* iii, 188), which means exactly the same thing as Bergson's 'évolution créatrice.' Novelty, as empirically found, doesn't arrive by jumps and jolts, it leaks in insensibly, for adjacents in experience are always interfused, the smallest real datum being both a coming and a going, and even numerical distinctness being realized effectively only after a concrete interval has passed. The intervals also deflect us from the original paths of direction, and all the old identities at last give out, for the fatally continuous infiltration of otherness warps things out of every original rut. Just so, in a curve, the same direction is *never* followed, and the conception of it as a myriad-sided polygon falsifies it by supposing it to do so for however short a time. Peirce speaks of an 'infinitesimal' tendency to diversification. The mathematical notion of an infinitesimal contains, in truth, the whole paradox of the same and yet the nascent other, of an identity that won't *keep* except so far as it keeps *failing,* that won't *transfer,* any more than the serial relations in question transfer, when you apply them to reality instead of applying them to concepts alone.

A friend of mine has an idea, which illustrates on such a magnified scale the impossibility of tracing the same line through reality, that I will mention it here. He thinks that nothing more is needed to make history 'scientific' than to get the content of any two epochs (say the end of the thirteenth and the end of the nineteenth century) accurately defined, then accurately to define the direction of the change that led from the one epoch into the other, and finally to prolong the line of that direction into the future. So prolonging the line, he thinks, we ought to be able to define the actual state of things at any future date we please. We all feel the essential unreality of such a conception of 'history' as this; but if such a synechistic pluralism as Peirce, Bergson, and I believe in, be what really exists, every phenomenon of development, even the simplest, would prove equally rebellious to our science should the latter pretend to give us literally accurate instead of approximate, or statistically generalized, pictures of the development of reality.

I can give no further account of Mr. Peirce's ideas in this note, but

I earnestly advise all students of Bergson to compare them with those of the french philosopher.

THE ESSENCE OF HUMANISM* [198]

Humanism is a ferment that has 'come to stay.' [199] It is not a single hypothesis or theorem, and it dwells on no new facts. It is rather a slow shifting in the philosophic perspective, making things appear as from a new centre of interest or point of sight. Some writers are strongly conscious of the shifting, others half unconscious, even though their own vision may have undergone much change. The result is no small confusion in debate, the half-conscious humanists often taking part against the radical ones, as if they wished to count upon the other side. [200]

If humanism really be the name for such a shifting of perspective, it is obvious that the whole scene of the philosophic stage will change in some degree if humanism prevails. The emphasis of things, their foreground and background distribution, their sizes and values, will not keep just the same. [201] If such pervasive consequences be involved

---

* From: E.R.E., 190–205.

[198] [Reprinted from the *Journal of Philosophy, Psychology, and Scientific Methods*, vol. II, No. 5, March 2, 1905. Also reprinted, with slight changes in *The Meaning of Truth*, pp. 121–135. The author's corrections have been adopted for the present text. Ed.]

[199] [Written *apropos* of the appearance of three articles in *Mind*, N.S., vol. XIV, No. 53, January, 1905: " 'Absolute' and 'Relative' Truth," H. H. Joachim; "Professor James on 'Humanism and Truth,'" H. W. B. Joseph; "Applied Axioms," A. Sidgwick. Of these articles the second and third "continue the humanistic (or pragmatistic) controversy," the first "deeply connects with it." Ed.]

[200] Professor Baldwin, for example. His address 'On Selective Thinking' (*Psychological Review*, [vol. v], 1898, reprinted in his volume, *Development and Evolution*) seems to me an unusually well-written pragmatic manifesto. Nevertheless in 'The Limits of Pragmatism' (*ibid.*, [vol. XI], 1904), he (much less clearly) joins in the attack.

[201] The ethical changes, it seems to me, are beautifully made evident in Professor Dewey's series of articles, which will never get the attention they deserve till they are printed in a book. I mean: 'The Significance of Emotions,' *Psychological Review*, vol. II, [1895], p. 13; 'The Reflex Arc Concept in Psychology,' *ibid.*, vol. III, [1896], p. 357; 'Psychology and Social Practice,' *ibid.*, vol. VII, [1900], p. 105; 'Interpretation of Savage Mind,' *ibid.*, vol. IX, [1902], p. 217; 'Green's Theory of the Moral Motive,' *Philosophical Review*, vol. I, [1892], p. 593; 'Self-realization as the Moral Ideal,' *ibid.*, vol. II, [1893], p. 652;

in humanism, it is clear that no pains which philosophers may take, first in defining it, and then in furthering, checking, or steering its progress, will be thrown away.

It suffers badly at present from incomplete definition. Its most systematic advocates, Schiller and Dewey, have published fragmentary programs only; and its bearing on many vital philosophic problems has not been traced except by adversaries who, scenting heresies in advance, have showered blows on doctrines—subjectivism and scepticism, for example—that no good humanist finds it necessary to entertain. By their still greater reticences, the anti-humanists have, in turn, perplexed the humanists. Much of the controversy has involved the word 'truth.' It is always good in debate to know your adversary's point of view authentically. But the critics of humanism never define exactly what the word 'truth' signifies when they use it themselves. The humanists have to guess at their view; and the result has doubtless been much beating of the air. Add to all this, great individual differences in both camps, and it becomes clear that nothing is so urgently needed, at the stage which things have reached at present, as a sharper definition by each side of its central point of view.

Whoever will contribute any touch of sharpness will help us to make sure of what's what and who is who. Anyone can contribute such a definition, and, without it, no one knows exactly where he stands. If I offer my own provisional definition of humanism[202] now and here, others may improve it, some adversary may be led to define his own creed more sharply by the contrast, and a certain quickening of the crystallization of general opinion may result.

1

The essential service of humanism, as I conceive the situation, is to have seen that *though one part of our experience may lean upon another part to make it what it is in any one of several aspects in which it may be considered, experience as a whole is self-containing and leans on nothing.*

Since this formula also expresses the main contention of transcen-

---

'The Psychology of Effort,' *ibid.,* vol. VI, [1897], p. 43; 'The Evolutionary Method as Applied to Morality,' *ibid.,* vol. XI, [1902], pp. 107, 353; 'Evolution and Ethics,' *Monist,* vol. VIII, [1898], p. 321; to mention only a few.

202 [The author employs the term 'humanism' either as a synonym for 'radical empiricism' (cf. *e.g.,* above, p. 278; or as that general philosophy of life of which 'radical empiricism' is the theoretical ground (cf. below, p. 306). For other discussions of 'humanism,' cf. below, pp. 449–461, and *The Meaning of Truth,* essay III. ED.]

dental idealism, it needs abundant explication to make it unambiguous. It seems, at first sight, to confine itself to denying theism and pantheism. But, in fact, it need not deny either; everything would depend on the exegesis; and if the formula ever became canonical, it would certainly develop both right-wing and left-wing interpreters. I myself read humanism theistically and pluralistically. If there be a God, he is no absolute all-experiencer, but simply the experiencer of widest actual conscious span. Read thus, humanism is for me a religion susceptible of reasoned defence, though I am well aware how many minds there are to whom it can appeal religiously only when it has been monistically translated. Ethically the pluralistic form of it takes for me a stronger hold on reality than any other philosophy I know of—it being essentially a *social* philosophy, a philosophy of *'co,'* in which conjunctions do the work. But my primary reason for advocating it is its matchless intellectual economy. It gets rid, not only of the standing 'problems' that monism engenders ('problem of evil' 'problem of freedom,' and the like), but of other metaphysical mysteries and paradoxes as well.

It gets rid, for example, of the whole agnostic controversy, by refusing to entertain the hypothesis of trans-empirical reality at all. It gets rid of any need for an absolute of the Bradleyan type (avowedly sterile for intellectual purposes) by insisting that the conjunctive relations found within experience are faultlessly real. It gets rid of the need of an absolute of the Roycean type (similarly sterile) by its pragmatic treatment of the problem of knowledge [a treatment of which I have already give a version in two very inadequate articles].[203] As the views of knowledge, reality and truth imputed to humanism have been those so far most fiercely attacked, it is in regard to these ideas that a sharpening of focus seems most urgently required. I proceed therefore to bring the views which *I* impute to humanism in these respects into focus as briefly as I can.

II

If the central humanistic thesis, printed above in italics, be accepted, it will follow that, if there be any such thing at all as knowing, the knower and the object known must both be portions of experience. One part of experience must, therefore, either

   (1) Know another part of experience—in other words, parts

[203] [Omitted from reprint in *Meaning of Truth*. The articles referred to are 'Does Consciousness Exist?' and 'A World of Pure Experience,' reprinted above, pp. 169–183 and pp. 194–214.]

must, as Professor Woodbridge says,[204] represent *one another* instead of representing realities outside of 'consciousness'—this case is that of conceptual knowledge; or else

(2) They must simply exist as so many ultimate *thats* or facts of being, in the first instance; and then, as a secondary complication, and without doubling up its entitative singleness, any one and the same *that* must figure alternately as a thing known and as a knowledge of the thing, by reason of two divergent kinds of context into which, in the general course of experience, it gets woven.[205]

This second case is that of sense-perception. There is a stage of thought that goes beyond common sense, and of it I shall say more presently; but the common-sense stage is a perfectly definite halting-place of thought, primarily for purposes of action; and, so long as we remain on the common-sense stage of thought, object and subject *fuse* in the fact of 'presentation' or sense-perception—the pen and hand which I now *see* writing, for example, *are* the physical realities which those words designate. In this case there is no self-transcendency implied in the knowing. Humanism, here, is only a more comminuted *Identitätsphilosophie*.[206]

In case (1), on the contrary, the representative experience does transcend itself in knowing the other experience that is its object. No one can talk of the knowledge of the one by the other without seeing them as numerically distinct entities, of which the one lies beyond the other and away from it, along some direction and with some interval, that can be definitely named. But, if the talker be a humanist, he must also see this distance-interval concretely and pragmatically, and confess it to consist of other intervening experiences—of possible ones, at all events, if not of actual. To call my present idea of my dog, for example, cognitive of the real dog means that, as the actual tissue of experience is constituted, the idea is capable of leading into a chain of other experiences on my part that go from next to next and terminate at last in vivid sense-perceptions of a jumping, barking, hairy body. Those *are* the real dog, the dog's full presence, for my common sense. If the supposed talker is a profound philosopher, although they may not *be* the real dog for him, they *mean* the real dog, are practical substitutes for the real dog, as the representation was a practical substitute for them, that real dog being a lot of atoms, say, or of mind-stuff, that lie *where* the sense-perceptions lie in his experience as well as in my own.

---

204 In *Science*, November 4, 1904, p. 599.

205 This statement is probably excessively obscure to any one who has not read my two articles, 'Does Consciousness Exist?' and 'A World of Pure Experience.'

206 [Cf. above, p. 231; and below, p. 309.]

III

The philosopher here stands for the stage of thought that goes beyond
the stage of common sense; and the difference is simply that he 'interpolates' and 'extrapolates,' where common sense does not. For common sense, two men see the same identical real dog. Philosophy, noting actual differences in their perceptions, points out the duality of
these latter, and interpolates something between them as a more real
terminus—first, organs, viscera, etc.; next, cells; then, ultimate atoms;
lastly, mind-stuff perhaps. The original sense-termini of the two men,
instead of coalescing with each other and with the real dog-object, as
at first supposed, are thus held by philosophers to be separated by
invisible realities with which, at most, they are conterminous.

Abolish, now, one of the percipients, and the interpolation
changes into 'extrapolation.' The sense-terminus of the remaining per-
cipient is regarded by the philosopher as not quite reaching reality. He
has only carried the procession of experiences, the philosopher thinks,
to a definite, because practical, halting-place somewhere on the way
towards an absolute truth that lies beyond.

The humanist sees all the time, however, that there is no absolute
transcendency even about the more absolute realities thus conjectured
or believed in. The viscera and cells are only possible percepts following upon that of the outer body. The atoms again, though we may
never attain to human means of perceiving them, are still defined perceptually. The mind-stuff itself is conceived as a kind of experience;
and it is possible to frame the hypothesis (such hypotheses can by no
logic be excluded from philosophy) of two knowers of a piece of mind-
stuff and the mind-stuff itself becoming 'confluent' at the moment at
which our imperfect knowing might pass into knowing of a completed
type. Even so do you and I habitually represent our two perceptions
and the real dog as confluent, though only provisionally, and for the
common-sense stage of thought. If my pen be inwardly made of mind-
stuff, there is no confluence *now* between that mind-stuff and my visual perception of the pen. But conceivably there might come to be
such confluence; for, in the case of my hand, the visual sensations and
the inward feelings of the hand, its mind-stuff, so to speak, are even
now as confluent as any two things can be.

There is, thus, no breach in humanistic epistemology. Whether
knowledge be taken as ideally perfected, or only as true enough to
pass muster for practice, it is hung on one continuous scheme. Reality, howsoever remote, is always defined as a terminus within the general possibilities of experience; and what knows it is defined as an

experience *that 'represents' it, in the sense of being substitutable for it in our thinking* because it leads to the same associates, *or in the sense of 'pointing to it'* through a chain of other experiences that either intervene or may intervene.

Absolute reality here bears the same relation to sensation as sensation bears to conception or imagination. Both are provisional or final termini, sensation being only the terminus at which the practical man habitually stops, while the philosopher projects a 'beyond' in the shape of more absolute reality. These termini, for the practical and the philosophical stages of thought respectively, are self-supporting. They are not 'true' of anything else, they simply *are,* are *real.* They 'lean on nothing,' as my italicized formula said. Rather does the whole fabric of experience lean on them, just as the whole fabric of the solar system, including many relative positions, leans, for its absolute position in space, on any one of its constituent stars. Here, again, one gets a new *Identitätsphilosophie* in pluralistic form.[207]

IV

If I have succeeded in making this at all clear (though I fear that brevity and abstractness between them may have made me fail), the reader will see that the 'truth' of our mental operations must always be an intra-experiential affair. A conception is reckoned true by common sense when it can be made to lead to a sensation. The sensation, which for common sense is not so much 'true' as 'real,' is held to be *provisionally* true by the philosopher just in so far as it *covers* (abuts at, or occupies the place of) a still more absolutely real experience, in the possibility of which to some remoter experient the philosopher finds reason to believe.

Meanwhile what actually *does* count for true to any individual trower, whether he be philosopher or common man, is always a result of his *apperceptions.* If a novel experience, conceptual or sensible, contradict too emphatically our pre-existent system of beliefs, in ninety-nine cases out of a hundred it is treated as false. Only when the older and the newer experiences are congruous enough to mutually apperceive and modify each other, does what we treat as an advance in truth result. [Having written of this point in an article in reply to Mr. Joseph's criticism of my humanism, I will say no more about truth here, but refer the reader to that review.]* In no case, however, need truth consist in a relation between our experiences and something archetypal or trans-experiential. Should we ever reach absolutely ter-

[207] [Cf. above, pp. 231, 307.]
* [Cf. below, p. 844, 1905–5].

minal experiences, experiences in which we all agreed, which were superseded by no revised continuations, these would not be *true*, they would be *real*, they would simply *be*, and be indeed the angles, corners, and linchpins of all reality, on which the truth of everything else would be stayed. Only such *other* things as led to these by satisfactory conjunctions would be 'true.' Satisfactory connection of some sort with such termini is all that the word 'truth' means. On the commonsense stage of thought sense-presentations serve as such termini. Our ideas and concepts and scientific theories pass for true only so far as they harmoniously lead back to the world of sense.

I hope that many humanists will endorse this attempt of mine to trace the more essential features of that way of viewing things. I feel almost certain that Messrs. Dewey and Schiller will do so. If the attackers will also take some slight account of it, it may be that discussion will be a little less wide of the mark than it has hitherto been.

~ iv ~

The Pragmatic
Method

The essays in this section trace the development of pragmatism in the thought of James. Represented are the early pragmatic attitude, the controversial lectures of 1907, and his response to hostile critics. James saw his *Pragmatism* as "something quite like the protestant reformation." (L.W.J., II, 279)

[PRAGMATISM AND RADICAL EMPIRICISM*]

The pivotal part of my book named *Pragmatism* is its account of the relation called 'truth' which may obtain between an idea (opinion, belief, statement, or what not) and its object. 'Truth,' I there say, 'is a property of certain of our ideas. It means their agreement, as falsity means their disagreement, with reality. Pragmatists and intellectualists both accept this definition as a matter of course.

'Where our ideas [do] not copy definitely their object, what does agreement with that object mean? . . . Pragmatism asks its usual question. "Grant an idea or belief to be true," it says, "what concrete difference will its being true make in any one's actual life? What experiences [may] be different from those which would obtain if the belief were false? How will the truth be realized? What, in short, is the truth's cash-value in experiential terms?" The moment pragmatism asks this question, it sees the answer: *True ideas are those that we can assimilate, validate, corroborate, and verify. False ideas are those that we cannot.* That is the practical difference it makes to us to have true

* From: M.T., v–xx.

ideas; that therefore is the meaning of truth, for it is all that truth is known as.

'The truth of an idea is not a stagnant property inherent in it. Truth *happens* to an idea. It *becomes* true, is *made* true by events. Its verity *is* in fact an event, a process, the process namely of its verifying itself, its veri*fication*. Its validity is the process of its valida*tion*.[1]

'To agree in the widest sense with a reality can only mean to be guided either straight up to it or into its surroundings, or to be put into such working touch with it as to handle either it or something connected with it better than if we disagreed. Better either intellectually or practically. . . . Any idea that helps us to deal, whether practically or intellectually, with either the reality or its belongings, that does n't entangle our progress in frustrations, that *fits,* in fact, and adapts our life to the reality's whole setting, will agree sufficiently to meet the requirement. It will be true of that reality.

'*The true,* to put it very briefly, *is only the expedient in the way of our thinking, just as the right is only the expedient in the way of our behaving.* Expedient in almost any fashion, and expedient in the long run and on the whole, of course; for what meets expediently all the experience in sight won't necessarily meet all farther experiences equally satisfactorily. Experience, as we know, has ways of *boiling over,* and making us correct our present formulas.'

This account of truth, following upon the similar ones given by Messrs. Dewey and Schiller, has occasioned the liveliest discussion. Few critics have defended it, most of them have scouted it. It seems evident that the subject is a hard one to understand, under its apparent simplicity; and evident also, I think, that the definitive settlement of it will mark a turning point in the history of epistemology, and consequently in that of general philosophy. In order to make my own thought more accessible to those who hereafter may have to study the question, I have collected in the volume that follows all the work of my pen that bears directly on the truth-question. My first statement was in 1884, in the article that begins the present volume.*

One of the accusations which I oftenest have had to meet is that of making the truth of our religious beliefs consist in their 'feeling good' to us, and in nothing else. I regret to have given some excuse for this charge, by the unguarded language in which, in the book *Prag-*

---

[1] But *'verifiability,'* I add, 'is as good as verification. For one truth-process completed, there are a million in our lives that function in [the] state of nascency. They lead us towards direct verification; lead us into the surroundings of the object they envisage; and then, if everything runs on harmoniously, we are so sure that verification is possible that we omit it, and are usually justified by all that happens.'

* See above, "The Function of Cognition," pp. 136–152.

matism, I spoke of the truth of the belief of certain philosophers in the absolute. Explaining why I do not believe in the absolute myself (below, 389), yet finding that it may secure 'moral holidays' to those who need them, and is true in so far forth (if to gain moral holidays be a good),[2] I offered this as a conciliatory olive-branch to my enemies. But they, as is only too common with such offerings, trampled the gift under foot and turned and rent the giver. I had counted too much on their good will—oh for the rarity of christian charity under the sun! Oh for the rarity of ordinary secular intelligence also! I had supposed it to be matter of common observation that, of two competing views of the universe which in all other respects are equal, but of which the first denies some vital human need while the second satisfies it, the second will be favored by sane men for the simple reason that it makes the world seem more rational. To choose the first view under such circumstances would be an ascetic act, an act of philosophic self-denial of which no normal human being would be guilty. Using the pragmatic test of the meaning of concepts, I had shown the concept of the absolute to *mean* nothing but the holiday giver, the banisher of cosmic fear. One's objective deliverance, when one says 'the absolute exists,' amounted, on my showing, just to this, that 'some justification of a feeling of security in presence of the universe,' exists, and that systematically to refuse to cultivate a feeling of security would be to do violence to a tendency in one's emotional life which might well be respected as prophetic.

Apparently my absolutist critics fail to see the workings of their own minds in any such picture, so all that I can do is to apologize, and take my offering back. The absolute is true in *no* way then, and least of all, by the verdict of the critics, in the way which I assigned!

My treatment of 'God,' 'freedom,' and 'design' was similar. Reducing, by the pragmatic test, the meaning of each of these concepts to its positive experienceable operation, I showed them all to mean the same thing, viz., the presence of 'promise' in the world. 'God or no God?' means 'promise or no promise?' It seems to me that the alternative is objective enough, being a question as to whether the cosmos has one character or another, even though our own provisional answer be made on subjective grounds. Nevertheless christian and non-christian critics alike accuse me of summoning people to say 'God exists,' *even when he does n't exist,* because forsooth in my philosophy the 'truth' of the saying does n't really mean that he exists in any shape whatever, but only that to say so feels good.

Most of the pragmatist and anti-pragmatist warfare is over what the word 'truth' shall be held to signify, and not over any of the facts embodied in truth-situations; for both pragmatists and anti-pragma-

2 [Cf. below, p. 388.]

tists believe in existent objects, just as they believe in our ideas of them. The difference is that when the pragmatists speak of truth, they mean exclusively something about the ideas, namely their workableness; whereas when anti-pragmatists speak of truth they seem most often to mean something about the objects. Since the pragmatist, if he agrees that an idea is 'really' true, also agrees to whatever it says about its object; and since most anti-pragmatists have already come round to agreeing that, if the object exists, the idea that it does so is workable; there would seem so little left to fight about that I might well be asked why instead of reprinting my share in so much verbal wrangling, I do not show my sense of 'values' by burning it all up.

I understand the question and I will give my answer. I am interested in another doctrine in philosophy to which I give the name of radical empiricism, and it seems to me that the establishment of the pragmatist theory of truth is a step of first-rate importance in making radical empiricism prevail. Radical empiricism consists first of a postulate, next of a statement of fact, and finally of a generalized conclusion.

The postulate is that the only things that shall be debatable among philosophers shall be things definable in terms drawn from experience. [Things of an unexperienceable nature may exist ad libitum, but they form no part of the material for philosophic debate.]

The statement of fact is that the relations between things, conjunctive as well as disjunctive, are just as much matters of direct particular experience, neither more so nor less so, than the things themselves.

The generalized conclusion is that therefore the parts of experience hold together from next to next by relations that are themselves parts of experience. The directly apprehended universe needs, in short, no extraneous trans-empirical connective support, but possesses in its own right a concatenated or continuous structure.

The great obstacle to radical empiricism in the contemporary mind is the rooted rationalist belief that experience as immediately given is all disjunction and no conjunction, and that to make one world out of this separateness, a higher unifying agency must be there. In the prevalent idealism this agency is represented as the absolute all-witness which 'relates' things together by throwing 'categories' over them like a net. The most peculiar and unique, perhaps, of all these categories is supposed to be the truth-relation, which connects parts of reality in pairs, making of one of them a knower, and of the other a thing known, yet which is itself contentless experientially, neither describable, explicable, nor reduceable to lower terms, and denotable only by uttering the name 'truth.'

The pragmatist view, on the contrary, of the truth-relation is that it has a definite content, and that everything in it is experienceable. Its whole nature can be told in positive terms. The 'workableness' which ideas must have, in order to be true, means particular workings, physical or intellectual, actual or possible, which they may set up from next to next inside of concrete experience. Were this pragmatic contention admitted, one great point in the victory of radical empiricism would also be scored, for the relation between an object and the idea that truly knows it, is held by rationalists to be nothing of this describable sort, but to stand outside of all possible temporal experience; and on the relation, so interpreted, rationalism is wonted to make its last most obdurate rally.

Now the anti-pragmatist contentions which I try to meet in this volume can be so easily used by rationalists as weapons of resistance, not only to pragmatism but to radical empiricism also (for if the truth-relation were transcendent, others might be so too), that I feel strongly the strategical importance of having them definitely met and got out of the way. What our critics most persistently keep saying is that though workings go with truth, yet they do not constitute it. It is numerically additional to them, prior to them, explanatory *of* them, and in no wise to be explained *by* them, we are incessantly told. The first point for our enemies to establish, therefore, is that *something* numerically additional and prior to the workings is involved in the truth of an idea. Since the *object* is additional, and usually prior, most rationalists plead *it,* and boldly accuse us of denying it. This leaves on the bystanders the impression—since we cannot reasonably deny the existence of the object—that our account of truth breaks down, and that our critics have driven us from the field. Altho in various places in this volume I try to refute the slanderous charge that we deny real existence, I will say here again, for the sake of emphasis, that the existence of the object, whenever the idea asserts it 'truly,' is the only reason, in innumerable cases, why the idea does work successfully, if it work at all; and that it seems an abuse of language, to say the least, to transfer the word 'truth' from the idea to the object's existence, when the falsehood of ideas that won't work is explained by that existence as well as the truth of those that will.

I find this abuse prevailing among my most accomplished adversaries. But once establish the proper verbal custom, let the word 'truth' represent a property of the idea, cease to make it something mysteriously connected with the object known, and the path opens fair and wide, as I believe, to the discussion of radical empiricism on its merits. The truth of an idea will then mean only its workings, or that in it which by ordinary psychological laws sets up those workings; it will mean neither the idea's object, nor anything 'saltatory' inside the idea, that terms drawn from experience cannot describe.

One word more, ere I end this preface. A distinction is sometimes made between Dewey, Schiller and myself, as if I, in supposing the object's existence, made a concession to popular prejudice which they, as more radical pragmatists, refuse to make. As I myself understand these authors, we all three absolutely agree in admitting the transcendency of the object (provided it be an experienceable object) to the subject, in the truth-relation. Dewey in particular has insisted almost ad nauseam that the whole meaning of our cognitive states and processes lies in the way they intervene in the control and revaluation of independent existences or facts. His account of knowledge is not only absurd, but meaningless, unless independent existences be there of which our ideas take account, and for the transformation of which they work. But because he and Schiller refuse to discuss objects and relations 'transcendent' in the sense of being *altogether trans-experiential,* their critics pounce on sentences in their writings to that effect to show that they deny the existence *within the realm of experience* of objects external to the ideas that declare their presence there.[3] It seems incredible that educated and apparently sincere critics should so fail to catch their adversary's point of view.

What misleads so many of them is possibly also the fact that the universes of discourse of Schiller, Dewey, and myself are panoramas of different extent, and that what the one postulates explicitly the other provisionally leaves only in a state of implication, while the reader thereupon considers it to be denied. Schiller's universe is the smallest, being essentially a psychological one. He starts with but one sort of thing, truth-claims, but is led ultimately to the independent objective facts which they assert, inasmuch as the most successfully validated of all claims is that such facts are there. My universe is more essentially epistemological. I start with two things, the objective facts and the claims, and indicate which claims, the facts being there, will work successfully as the latter's substitutes and which will not. I call the former claims true. Dewey's panorama, if I understand this colleague, is the widest of the three, but I refrain from giving my own account of its complexity. Suffice it that he holds as firmly as I do to objects independent of our judgments. If I am wrong in saying this, he

---

[3] It gives me pleasure to welcome Professor Carveth Read into the pragmatistic church, so far as his epistemology goes. See his vigorous book, *The Metaphysics of Nature,* 2d Edition, Appendix A. (London, Black, 1908.) The work *What is Reality?* by Francis Howe Johnson (Boston, 1891), of which I make the acquaintance only while correcting these proofs, contains some striking anticipations of the later pragmatist view. *The Psychology of Thinking,* by Irving E. Miller (New York, Macmillan Co., 1909), which has just appeared, is one of the most convincing pragmatist documents yet published, tho it does not use the word 'pragmatism' at all. While I am making references, I cannot refrain from inserting one to the extraordinarily acute article by H. V. Knox in the *Quarterly Review* for April, 1909.

must correct me. I decline in this matter to be corrected at second hand.

I have not pretended in the following pages to consider all the critics of my account of truth, such as Messrs. Taylor, Lovejoy, Gardiner, Bakewell, Creighton, Hibben, Parodi, Salter, Carus, Lalande, Mentré, McTaggart, G. E. Moore, Ladd and others, especially not Professor Schinz, who has published under the title of *Anti-pragmatisme* an amusing sociological romance. Some of these critics seem to me to labor under an inability almost pathetic, to understand the thesis which they seek to refute. I imagine that most of their difficulties have been answered by anticipation elsewhere in this volume, and I am sure that my readers will thank me for not adding more repetition to the fearful amount that is already there.

    95 IRVING ST., CAMBRIDGE (MASS.),
        August, 1909.

THE SENTIMENT OF RATIONALITY* [4]

I

What is the task which philosophers set themselves to perform; and why do they philosophize at all? Almost every one will immediately reply: They desire to attain a conception of the frame of things which shall on the whole be more rational than that somewhat chaotic view which every one by nature carries about with him under his hat. But suppose this rational conception attained, how is the philosopher to recognize it for what it is, and not let it slip through ignorance? The only answer can be that he will recognize its rationality as he recognizes everything else, by certain subjective marks with which it affects him. When he gets the marks, he may know that he has got the rationality.

What, then, are the marks? A strong feeling of ease, peace, rest, is one of them. The transition from a state of puzzle and perplexity to rational comprehension is full of lively relief and pleasure.

But this relief seems to be a negative rather than a positive charac-

---

* From: W.B., 63–110.

[4] This essay as far as page 324 consists of extracts from an article printed in *Mind* for July, 1879. Thereafter it is a reprint of an address to the Harvard Philosophical Club, delivered in 1880, and published in the *Princeton Review*, July, 1882.

ter. Shall we then say that the feeling of rationality is constituted merely by the absence of any feeling of irrationality? I think there are very good grounds for upholding such a view. All feeling whatever, in the light of certain recent psychological speculations, seems to depend for its physical condition not on simple discharge of nerve-currents, but on their discharge under arrest, impediment, or resistance. Just as we feel no particular pleasure when we breathe freely, but a very intense feeling of distress when the respiratory motions are prevented, —so any unobstructed tendency to action discharges itself without the production of much cogitative accompaniment, and any perfectly fluent course of thought awakens but little feeling; but when the movement is inhibited, or when the thought meets with difficulties, we experience distress. It is only when the distress is upon us that we can be said to strive, to crave, or to aspire. When enjoying plenary freedom either in the way of motion or of thought, we are in a sort of anæsthetic state in which we might say with Walt Whitman, if we cared to say anything about ourselves at such times, "I am sufficient as I am." This feeling of the sufficiency of the present moment, of its absoluteness,—this absence of all need to explain it, account for it, or justify it,—is what I call the Sentiment of Rationality. As soon, in short, as we are enabled from any cause whatever to think with perfect fluency, the thing we think of seems to us *pro tanto* rational.

Whatever modes of conceiving the cosmos facilitate this fluency, produce the sentiment of rationality. Conceived in such modes, being vouches for itself and needs no further philosophic formulation. But this fluency may be obtained in various ways; and first I will take up the theoretic way.

The facts of the world in their sensible diversity are always before us, but our theoretic need is that they should be conceived in a way that reduces their manifoldness to simplicity. Our pleasure at finding that a chaos of facts is the expression of a single underlying fact is like the relief of the musician at resolving a confused mass of sound into melodic or harmonic order. The simplified result is handled with far less mental effort than the original data; and a philosophic conception of nature is thus in no metaphorical sense a labor-saving contrivance. The passion for parsimony, for economy of means in thought, is the philosophic passion *par excellence;* and any character or aspect of the world's phenomena which gathers up their diversity into monotony will gratify that passion, and in the philosopher's mind stand for that essence of things compared with which all their other determinations may by him be overlooked.

More universality or extensiveness is, then, one mark which the philosopher's conceptions must possess. Unless they apply to an enormous number of cases they will not bring him relief. The knowledge of things by their causes, which is often given as a definition of rational knowledge, is useless to him unless the causes converge to a minimum number, while still producing the maximum number of effects. The more multiple then are the instances, the more flowingly does his mind rove from fact to fact. The phenomenal transitions are no real transitions; each item is the same old friend with a slightly altered dress.

Who does not feel the charm of thinking that the moon and the apple are, as far as their relation to the earth goes, identical; of knowing respiration and combustion to be one; of understanding that the balloon rises by the same law whereby the stone sinks; of feeling that the warmth in one's palm when one rubs one's sleeve is identical with the motion which the friction checks; of recognizing the difference between beast and fish to be only a higher degree of that between human father and son; of believing our strength when we climb the mountain or fell the tree to be no other than the strength of the sun's rays which made the corn grow out of which we got our morning meal?

But alongside of this passion for simplification there exists a sister passion, which in some minds—though they perhaps form the minority—is its rival. This is the passion for distinguishing; it is the impulse to be *acquainted* with the parts rather than to comprehend the whole. Loyalty to clearness and integrity of perception, dislike of blurred outlines, of vague identifications, are its characteristics. It loves to recognize particulars in their full completeness, and the more of these it can carry the happier it is. It prefers any amount of incoherence, abruptness, and fragmentariness (so long as the literal details of the separate facts are saved) to an abstract way of conceiving things that, while it simplifies them, dissolves away at the same time their concrete fulness. Clearness and simplicity thus set up rival claims, and make a real dilemma for the thinker.

A man's philosophic attitude is determined by the balance in him of these two cravings. No system of philosophy can hope to be universally accepted among men which grossly violates either need, or entirely subordinates the one to the other. The fate of Spinoza, with his barren union of all things in one substance, on the one hand; that of Hume, with his equally barren 'looseness and separateness' of everything, on the other,—neither philosopher owning any strict and systematic disciples to-day, each being to posterity a warning as well as a stimulus,—show us that the only possible philosophy must be a compromise between an abstract monotony and a concrete heterogeneity. But the only way to mediate between diversity and unity is to class the diverse items as cases of a common essence which you discover in them. Classification of things into extensive 'kinds' is thus the first step; and classification of their relations and conduct into extensive 'laws' is the last step, in their philosophic unification. A completed theoretic philosophy can thus never be anything more than a completed classification of the world's ingredients; and its results must always be abstract, since the basis of every classification is the abstract essence embedded in the living fact,—the rest of the living fact being for the time ignored by the classifier. This means that none of our explanations are complete. They subsume things under heads wider or more familiar; but the last heads, whether of things or of their connections, are mere abstract genera, data which we just find in things and write down.

When, for example, we think that we have rationally explained the connection of the facts A and B by classing both under their common attribute x, it is obvious that we have really explained only so much of these items as *is* x. To explain the connection of choke-damp and suffocation by the lack of oxygen is to leave untouched all the other peculiarities both of choke-damp and of suffocation,—such as convulsions and agony on the one hand, density and explosibility on the other. In a word, so far as A and B contain $l, m, n,$ and $o, p, q,$ respectively, in addition to x, they are not explained by x. Each additional particularity makes its distinct appeal. A single explanation of a fact only explains it from a single point of view. The entire fact is not accounted for until each and all of its characters have been classed with their likes elsewhere. To apply this now to the case of the universe, we see that the explanation of the world by molecular movements explains it only so far as it actually *is* such movements. To invoke the 'Unknowable' explains only so much as is unknowable, 'Thought' only so much as is thought, 'God' only so much as is God. *Which* thought? *Which* God?—are questions that have to be answered by bringing in again the residual data from which the general term was abstracted. All those data that cannot be analytically identified with the attribute invoked as universal principle, remain as independent kinds or natures, associated empirically with the said attribute but devoid of rational kinship with it.

Hence the unsatisfactoriness of all our speculations. On the one hand, so far as they retain any multiplicity in their terms, they fail to get us out of the empirical sand-heap world; on the other, so far as they eliminate multiplicity the practical man despises their empty barrenness. The most they can say is that the elements of the world are such and such, and that each is identical with itself wherever found; but the question Where is it found? the practical man is left to answer by his own wit. Which, of all the essences, shall here and now be held the essence of this concrete thing, the fundamental philosophy never attempts to decide. We are thus led to the conclusion that the simple classification of things is, on the one hand, the best possible theoretic philosophy, but is, on the other, a most miserable and inadequate substitute for the fulness of the truth. It is a monstrous abridgment of life, which, like all abridgments is got by the absolute loss and casting out of real matter. This is why so few human beings truly care for philosophy. The particular determinations which she ignores are the real matter exciting needs, quite as potent and authoritative as hers. What does the moral enthusiast care for philosophical ethics? Why does the *Æsthetik* of every German philosopher appear to the artist an abomination of desolation?

> Grau, theurer Freund, ist alle Theorie
> Und grün des Lebens goldner Baum.

The entire man, who feels all needs by turns, will take nothing as an equivalent for life but the fulness of living itself. Since the essences of things are as a matter of fact disseminated through the whole extent of time and space, it is in their spread-outness and alternation that he will enjoy them. When weary of the concrete clash and dust and pettiness, he will refresh himself by a bath in the eternal springs, or fortify himself by a look at the immutable natures. But he will only be a visitor, not a dweller in the region; he will never carry the philosophic yoke upon his shoulders, and when tired of the gray monotony of her problems and insipid spaciousness of her results, will always escape gleefully into the teeming and dramatic richness of the concrete world.

So our study turns back here to its beginning. Every way of classifying a thing is but a way of handling it for some particular purpose. Conceptions, 'kinds,' are teleological instruments. No abstract concept can be a valid substitute for a concrete reality except with reference to a particular interest in the conceiver. The interest of theoretic rationality, the relief of identification, is but one of a thousand human purposes. When others rear their heads, it must pack up its little bundle and retire till its turn recurs. The exaggerated dignity and value that philosophers have claimed for their solutions is thus greatly reduced. The only virtue their theoretic conception need have is simplicity, and a simple conception is an equivalent for the world only so far as the world is simple,—the world meanwhile, whatever simplicity it may harbor, being also a mightily complex affair. Enough simplicity remains, however, and enough urgency in our craving to reach it, to make the theoretic function one of the most invincible of human impulses. The quest of the fewest elements of things is an ideal that some will follow, as long as there are men to think at all.

But suppose the goal attained. Suppose that at last we have a system unified in the sense that has been explained. Our world can now be conceived simply, and our mind enjoys the relief. Our universal concept has made the concrete chaos rational. But now I ask, Can that which is the ground of rationality in all else be itself properly called rational? It would seem at first sight that it might. One is tempted at any rate to say that, since the craving for rationality is appeased by the identification of one thing with another, a datum which left nothing else outstanding might quench that craving definitively, or be rational *in se*. No otherness being left to annoy us, we should sit down at peace. In other words, as the theoretic tranquillity of the boor results from his spinning no further considerations about his chaotic universe, so any datum whatever (provided it were simple, clear, and ultimate) ought to banish puzzle from the universe of the philosopher and confer peace, inasmuch as there would then be for him absolutely no further considerations to spin.

This in fact is what some persons think. Professor Bain says,—

> A difficulty is solved, a mystery unriddled, when it can be shown to resemble something else; to be an example of a fact already known. Mystery is isolation, exception, or it may be apparent contradiction: the resolution of the mystery is found in assimilation, identity, fraternity. When all things are assimilated, so far as assimilation can go, so far as likeness holds, there is an end to explanation; there is an end to what the mind can do, or can intelligently desire. . . . The path of science as exhibited in modern ages is toward generality, wider and wider, until we reach the highest, the widest laws of every department of things; there explanation is finished, mystery ends, perfect vision is gained.

But, unfortunately, this first answer will not hold. Our mind is so wedded to the process of seeing an *other* beside every item of its experience, that when the notion of an absolute datum is presented to it, it goes through its usual procedure and remains pointing at the void beyond, as if in that lay further matter for contemplation. In short, it spins for itself the further positive consideration of a nonentity enveloping the being of its datum; and as that leads nowhere, back recoils the thought toward its datum again. But there is no natural bridge between nonentity and this particular datum, and the thought stands oscillating to and fro, wondering "Why was there anything but nonentity; why just this universal datum and not another?" and finds no end, in wandering mazes lost. Indeed, Bain's words are so untrue that in reflecting men it is just when the attempt to fuse the manifold into a single totality has been most successful, when the conception of the universe as a unique fact is nearest its perfection, that the craving for further explanation, the ontological wonder-sickness, arises in its extremest form. As Schopenhauer says, "The uneasiness which keeps the never-resting clock of metaphysics in motion, is the consciousness that the non-existence of this world is just as possible as its existence."

The notion of nonentity may thus be called the parent of the philosophic craving in its subtilest and profoundest sense. Absolute existence is absolute mystery, for its relations with the nothing remain unmediated to our understanding. One philosopher only has pretended to throw a logical bridge over this chasm. Hegel, by trying to show that nonentity and concrete being are linked together by a series of identities of a synthetic kind, binds everything conceivable into a unity, with no outlying notion to disturb the free rotary circulation of the mind within its bounds. Since such unchecked movement gives the feeling of rationality, he must be held, if he has succeeded, to have eternally and absolutely quenched all rational demands.

But for those who deem Hegel's heroic effort to have failed, nought remains but to confess that when all things have been unified to the supreme degree, the notion of a possible other than the actual may still haunt our imagination and prey upon our system. The bottom of being is left logically opaque to us, as something which we simply come upon and find, and about which (if we wish to act) we should pause and wonder as little as possible. The philosopher's logical tranquillity is thus in essence no other than the boor's. They differ only as to the point at which each refuses to let further considerations upset the absoluteness of the data he assumes. The boor does so immediately, and is liable at any moment to the ravages of many kinds of doubt. The philosopher does not do so till unity has been reached, and is warranted against the inroads of those considerations, but only practically, not essentially, secure from the blighting breath of the ultimate Why? If he cannot exorcise this question, he must ignore or blink it, and, assuming the data of his system as something given, and the gift as ultimate, simply proceed to a life of contemplation or of action based on it. There is no doubt that this acting on an opaque necessity is accompanied by a certain pleasure. See the reverence of Carlyle for brute fact: "There is an infinite significance in fact." "Necessity," says Dühring, and he means not rational but given necessity, "is the last and highest point that we can reach. . . . It is not only the interest of ultimate and definitive knowledge, but also that of the feelings, to find a last repose and an ideal equilibrium in an uttermost datum which can simply not be other than it is."

Such is the attitude of ordinary men in their theism, God's fiat being in physics and morals such an uttermost datum. Such also is the attitude of all hard-minded analysts and *Verstandesmenschen*. Lotze, Renouvier, and Hodgson promptly say that of experience as a whole no account can be given, but neither seek to soften the abruptness of the confession nor to reconcile us with our impotence.

• • •

But mediating attempts may be made by more mystical minds. The peace of rationality may be sought through ecstasy when logic fails. To religious persons of every shade of doctrine moments come when the world, as it is, seems so divinely orderly, and the acceptance of it by the heart so rapturously complete, that intellectual questions vanish; nay, the intellect itself is hushed to sleep,—as Wordsworth says, "thought is not; in enjoyment it expires." Ontological emotion so fills the soul that ontological speculation can no longer overlap it and put her girdle of interrogation-marks round existence. Even the least religious of men must have felt with Walt Whitman, when loafing on the grass on some transparent summer morning, that "swiftly arose and spread round him the peace and knowledge that pass all the argument of the earth." At such moments of energetic living we feel as if there were something diseased and contemptible, yea vile, in theoretic grubbing and brooding. In the eye of healthy sense the philosopher is at best a learned fool.

Since the heart can thus wall out the ultimate irrationality which the head ascertains, the erection of its procedure into a systematized method would be a philosophic achievement of first-rate importance. But as used by mystics hitherto it has lacked universality, being available for few persons and at few times, and even in these being apt to be followed by fits of reaction and dryness; and if men should agree that the mystical method is a subterfuge without logical pertinency, a plaster but no cure, and that the idea of nonentity can never be exorcised, empiricism will be the ultimate philosophy. Existence then will be a brute fact to which as a whole the emotion of ontologic wonder shall rightfully cleave, but remain eternally unsatisfied. Then wonderfulness or mysteriousness will be an essential attribute of the nature of things, and the exhibition and emphasizing of it will continue to be an ingredient in the philosophic industry of the race. Every generation will produce its Job, its Hamlet, its Faust, or its Sartor Resartus.

With this we seem to have considered the possibilities of purely theoretic rationality. But we saw at the outset that rationality meant only unimpeded mental function. Impediments that arise in the theoretic sphere might perhaps be avoided if the stream of mental action should leave that sphere betimes and pass into the practical. Let us therefore inquire what constitutes the feeling of rationality in its *practical* aspect. If thought is not to stand forever pointing at the universe in wonder, if its movement is to be diverted from the issueless channel of purely theoretic contemplation, let us ask what conception of the universe will awaken active impulses capable of effecting this diversion. A definition of the world which will give back to the mind the free motion which has been blocked in the purely contemplative path may so far make the world seem rational again.

Well, of two conceptions equally fit to satisfy the logical demand, that one which awakens the active impulses, or satisfies other æsthetic demands better than the other, will be accounted the more rational conception, and will deservedly prevail.

There is nothing improbable in the supposition that an analysis of the world may yield a number of formulæ, all consistent with the facts. In physical science different formulæ may explain the phenomena equally well,—the one-fluid and the two-fluid theories of electricity, for example. Why may it not be so with the world? Why may there not be different points of view for surveying it, within each of which all data harmonize, and which the observer may therefore either choose between, or simply cumulate one upon another? A Beethoven string-quartet is truly, as some one has said, a scraping of horses' tails on cats' bowels, and may be exhaustively described in such terms; but the application of this description in no way precludes the simultaneous applicability of an entirely different description. Just so a thoroughgoing interpretation of the world in terms of mechanical sequence is compatible with its being interpreted teleologically, for the mechanism itself may be designed.

If, then, there were several systems excogitated, equally satisfying to our purely logical needs, they would still have to be passed in review, and approved or rejected by our æsthetic and practical nature. Can we define the tests of rationality which these parts of our nature would use?

Philosophers long ago observed the remarkable fact that mere familiarity with things is able to produce a feeling of their rationality. The empiricist school has been so much struck by this circumstance as to have laid it down that the feeling of rationality and the feeling of familiarity are one and the same thing, and that no other kind of rationality than this exists. The daily contemplation of phenomena juxtaposed in a certain order begets an acceptance of their connection, as absolute as the repose engendered by theoretic insight into their coherence. To explain a thing is to pass easily back to its antecedents; to know it is easily to foresee its consequents. Custom, which lets us do both, is thus the source of whatever rationality the thing may gain in our thought.

In the broad sense in which rationality was defined at the outset of this essay, it is perfectly apparent that custom must be one of its factors. We said that any perfectly fluent and easy thought was devoid of the sentiment of irrationality. Inasmuch then as custom acquaints us with all the relations of a thing, it teaches us to pass fluently from that thing to others, and *pro tanto* tinges it with the rational character.

Now, there is one particular relation of greater practical importance than all the rest,—I mean the relation of a thing to its future consequences. So long as an object is unusual, our expectations are baffled; they are fully determined as soon as it becomes familiar. I therefore propose this as the first practical requisite which a philosophic conception must satisfy: *It must, in a general way at least, banish uncertainty from the future.* The permanent presence of the sense of futurity in the mind has been strangely ignored by most writers, but the fact is that our consciousness at a given moment is never free from the ingredient of expectancy. Every one knows how when a painful thing has to be undergone in the near future, the vague feeling that it is impending penetrates all our thought with uneasiness and subtly vitiates our mood even when it does not control our attention; it keeps us from being at rest, at home in the given present. The same is true when a great happiness awaits us. But when the future is neutral and perfectly certain, 'we do not mind it,' as we say, but give an undisturbed attention to the actual. Let now this haunting sense of futurity be thrown off its bearings or left without an object, and immediately uneasiness takes possession of the mind. But in every novel or unclassified experience this is just what occurs; we do not know what will come next; and novelty *per se* becomes a mental irritant, while custom *per se* is a mental sedative, merely because the one baffles while the other settles our expectations.

Every reader must feel the truth of this. What is meant by coming 'to feel at home' in a new place, or with new people? It is simply that, at first, when we take up our quarters in a new room, we do not know what draughts may blow in upon our back, what doors may open, what forms may enter, what interesting objects may be found in cupboards and corners. When after a few days we have learned the range of all these possibilities, the feeling of strangeness disappears. And so it does with people, when we have got past the point of expecting any essentially new manifestations from their character.

The utility of this emotional effect of expectation is perfectly obvious; 'natural selection,' in fact, was bound to bring it about sooner or later. It is of the utmost practical importance to an animal that he should have prevision of the qualities of the objects that surround him, and especially that he should not come to rest in presence of circumstances that might be fraught either with peril or advantage,— go to sleep, for example, on the brink of precipices, in the dens of enemies, or view with indifference some new-appearing object that might, if chased, prove an important addition to the larder. Novelty *ought* to irritate him. All curiosity has thus a practical genesis. We need only look at the physiognomy of a dog or a horse when a new object comes into his view, his mingled fascination and fear, to see that the element of conscious insecurity or perplexed expectation lies at the root of his emotion. A dog's curiosity about the movements of his master or a strange object only extends as far as the point of deciding what is going to happen next. That settled, curiosity is quenched. The dog quoted by Darwin, whose behavior in presence of a newspaper moved by the wind seemed to testify to a sense 'of the supernatural,' was merely exhibiting the irritation of an uncertain future. A newspaper which could move spontaneously was in itself so unexpected that the poor brute could not tell what new wonders the next moment might bring forth.

To turn back now to philosophy. An ultimate datum, even though it be logically unrationalized, will, if its quality is such as to define expectancy, be peacefully accepted by the mind; while if it leave the least opportunity for ambiguity in the future, it will to that extent cause mental uneasiness if not distress. Now, in the ultimate explanations of the universe which the craving for rationality has elicited from the human mind, the demands of expectancy to be satisfied have always played a fundamental part. The term set up by philosophers as primordial has been one which banishes the incalculable. 'Substance,' for example, means, as Kant says, *das Beharrliche,* which will be as it has been, because its being is essential and eternal. And although we may not be able to prophesy in detail the future phenomena to which the substance shall give rise, we may set our minds at rest in a general way, when we have called the substance God, Perfection, Love, or Reason, by the reflection that whatever is in store for us can never at bottom be inconsistent with the character of this term; so that our attitude even toward the unexpected is in a general sense defined. Take again the notion of immortality, which for common people seems to be the touchstone of every philosophic or religious creed: what is this but a way of saying that the determination of expectancy is the essential factor of rationality? The wrath of science against miracles, of certain philosophers against the doctrine of free-will, has precisely the same root,—dislike to admit any ultimate factor in things which may rout our prevision or upset the stability of our outlook.

Anti-substantialist writers strangely overlook this function in the doctrine of substance: "If there be such a *substratum,*" says Mill, "suppose it at this instant miraculously annihilated, and let the sensations continue to occur in the same order, and how would the *substratum* be missed? By what signs should we be able to discover that its existence had terminated? Should we not have as much reason to believe that it still existed as we now have? And if we should not then be warranted in believing it, how can we be so now?" Truly enough, if we have already securely bagged our facts in a certain order, we can dispense with any further warrant for that order. But with regard to the facts yet to come the case is far different. It does not follow that if substance may be dropped from our conception of the irrecoverably past, it need be an equally empty complication to our notions of the future. Even if it were true that, for aught we know to the contrary, the substance might develop at any moment a wholly new set of attributes, the mere logical form of referring things to a substance would still (whether rightly or wrongly) remain accompanied by a feeling of rest and future confidence. In spite of the acutest nihilistic criticism, men will therefore always have a liking for any philosophy which explains things *per substantiam*.

A very natural reaction against the theosophizing conceit and hidebound confidence in the upshot of things, which vulgarly optimistic minds display, has formed one factor of the scepticism of empiricists, who never cease to remind us of the reservoir of possibilities alien to our habitual experience which the cosmos may contain, and which, for any warrant we have to the contrary, may turn it inside out tomorrow. Agnostic substantialism like that of Mr. Spencer, whose Unknowable is not merely the unfathomable but the absolute-irrational, on which, if consistently represented in thought, it is of course impossible to count, performs the same function of rebuking a certain stagnancy and smugness in the manner in which the ordinary philistine feels his security. But considered as anything else than as reactions against an opposite excess, these philosophies of uncertainty cannot be acceptable; the general mind will fail to come to rest in their presence, and will seek for solutions of a more reassuring kind.

We may then, I think, with perfect confidence lay down as a first point gained in our inquiry, that a prime factor in the philosophic craving is the desire to have expectancy defined; and that no philosophy will definitively triumph which in an emphatic manner denies the possibility of gratifying this need.

We pass with this to the next great division of our topic. It is not sufficient for our satisfaction merely to know the future as determined, for it may be determined in either of many ways, agreeable or disagreeable. For a philosophy to succeed on a universal scale it must define the future *congruously with our spontaneous powers*. A philosophy may be unimpeachable in other respects, but either of two defects will be fatal to its universal acceptance. First, its ultimate principle must not be one that essentially baffles and disappoints our dearest desires and most cherished powers. A pessimistic principle like Schopenhauer's incurably vicious Will-substance, or Hartmann's wicked jack-of-all-trades the Unconscious, will perpetually call forth essays at other philosophies. Incompatibility of the future with their desires and

active tendencies is, in fact, to most men a source of more fixed dis-
quietude than uncertainty itself. Witness the attempts to overcome the
'problem of evil,' the 'mystery of pain.' There is no 'problem of good.'

But a second and worse defect in a philosophy than that of contradicting our active propensities is to give them no object whatever to
press against. A philosophy whose principle is so incommensurate
with our most intimate powers as to deny them all relevancy in universal affairs, as to annihilate their motives at one blow, will be even
more unpopular than pessimism. Better face the enemy than the eternal Void! This is why materialism will always fail of universal adoption, however well it may fuse things into an atomistic unity, however
clearly it may prophesy the future eternity. For materialism denies
reality to the objects of almost all the impulses which we most cherish.
The real *meaning* of the impulses, it says, is something which has no
emotional interest for us whatever. Now, what is called 'extradition' is
quite as characteristic of our emotions as of our senses: both point to
an object as the cause of the present feeling. What an intensely objective reference lies in fear! In like manner an enraptured man and a
dreary-feeling man are not simply aware of their subjective states; if
they were, the force of their feelings would all evaporate. Both believe
there is outward cause why they should feel as they do: either, "It is a
glad world! how good life is!" or, "What a loathsome tedium is existence!" Any philosophy which annihilates the validity of the reference
by explaining away its objects or translating them into terms of no
emotional pertinency, leaves the mind with little to care or act for.
This is the opposite condition from that of nightmare, but when
acutely brought home to consciousness it produces a kindred horror.
In nightmare we have motives to act, but no power; here we have
powers, but no motives. A nameless *unheimlichkeit* comes over us at
the thought of there being nothing eternal in our final purposes, in the
objects of those loves and aspirations which are our deepest energies.
The monstrously lopsided equation of the universe and its knower,
which we postulate as the ideal of cognition, is perfectly paralleled by
the no less lopsided equation of the universe and the *doer*. We demand in it a character for which our emotions and active propensities
shall be a match. Small as we are, minute as is the point by which the
cosmos impinges upon each one of us, each one desires to feel that his
reaction at that point is congruous with the demands of the vast
whole,—that he balances the latter, so to speak, and is able to do
what it expects of him. But as his abilities to do lie wholly in the line
of his natural propensities; as he enjoys reacting with such emotions
as fortitude, hope, rapture, admiration, earnestness, and the like; and
as he very unwillingly reacts with fear, disgust, despair, or doubt,—a
philosophy which should only legitimate emotions of the latter sort

would be sure to leave the mind a prey to discontent and craving.

It is far too little recognized how entirely the intellect is built up of practical interests. The theory of evolution is beginning to do very good service by its reduction of all mentality to the type of reflex action. Cognition, in this view, is but a fleeting moment, a cross-section at a certain point, of what in its totality is a motor phenomenon. In the lower forms of life no one will pretend that cognition is anything more than a guide to appropriate action. The germinal question concerning things brought for the first time before consciousness is not the theoretic 'What is that?' but the practical 'Who goes there?' or rather, as Horwicz has admirably put it, 'What is to be done?'— 'Was fang' ich an?' In all our discussions about the intelligence of lower animals, the only test we use is that of their *acting* as if for a purpose. Cognition, in short, is incomplete until discharged in act; and although it is true that the later mental development, which attains its maximum through the hypertrophied cerebrum of man, gives birth to a vast amount of theoretic activity over and above that which is immediately ministerial to practice, yet the earlier claim is only postponed, not effaced, and the active nature asserts its rights to the end.

When the cosmos in its totality is the object offered to consciousness, the relation is in no whit altered. React on it we must in some congenial way. It was a deep instinct in Schopenhauer which led him to reinforce his pessimistic argumentation by a running volley of invective against the practical man and his requirements. No hope for pessimism unless he is slain!

Helmholtz's immortal works on the eye and ear are to a great extent little more than a commentary on the law that practical utility wholly determines which parts of our sensations we shall be aware of, and which parts we shall ignore. We notice or discriminate an ingredient of sense only so far as we depend upon it to modify our actions. We *comprehend* a thing when we synthetize it by identity with another thing. But the other great department of our understanding, *acquaintance* (the two departments being recognized in all languages by the antithesis of such words as *wissen* and *kennen; scire* and *noscere*, etc.), what is that also but a synthesis,—a synthesis of a passive perception with a certain tendency to reaction? We are acquainted with a thing as soon as we have learned how to behave towards it, or how to meet the behavior which we expect from it. Up to that point it is still 'strange' to us.

If there be anything at all in this view, it follows that however vaguely a philosopher may define the ultimate universal datum, he cannot be said to leave it unknown to us so long as he in the slightest degree pretends that our emotional or active attitude toward it should be of one sort rather than another. He who says "life is real, life is earnest," however much he may speak of the fundamental mysteriousness of things, gives a distinct definition to that mysteriousness by ascribing to it the right to claim from us the particular mood called seriousness,—which means the willingness to live with energy, though energy bring pain. The same is true of him who says that all is vanity. For indefinable as the predicate 'vanity' may be *in se,* it is clearly something that permits anæsthesia, mere escape from suffering, to be our rule of life. There can be no greater incongruity than for a disciple of Spencer to proclaim with one breath that the substance of things is unknowable, and with the next that the thought of it should inspire us with awe, reverence, and a willingness to add our co-operative push in the direction toward which its manifestations seem to be drifting. The unknowable may be unfathomed, but if it make such distinct demands upon our activity we surely are not ignorant of its essential quality.

If we survey the field of history and ask what feature all great periods of revival, of expansion of the human mind, display in common, we shall find, I think, simply this: that each and all of them have said to the human being, "The inmost nature of the reality is congenial to *powers* which you possess." In what did the emancipating message of primitive Christianity consist but in the announcement that God recognizes those weak and tender impulses which paganism had so rudely overlooked? Take repentance: the man who can do nothing rightly can at least repent of his failures. But for paganism this faculty of repentance was a pure supernumerary, a straggler too late for the fair. Christianity took it, and made it the one power within us which appealed straight to the heart of God. And after the night of the middle ages had so long branded with obloquy even the generous impulses of the flesh, and defined the reality to be such that only slavish natures could commune with it, in what did the *sursum corda* of the platonizing renaissance lie but in the proclamation that the archetype of verity in things laid claim on the widest activity of our whole æsthetic being? What were Luther's mission and Wesley's but appeals to powers which even the meanest of men might carry with them,—faith and self-despair,—but which were personal, requiring no priestly intermediation, and which brought their owner face to face with God? What caused the wildfire influence of Rousseau but the assurance he gave that man's nature was in harmony with the nature of things, if only the paralyzing corruptions of custom would stand from between? How did Kant and Fichte, Goethe and Schiller, inspire their time with cheer, except by saying, "Use all your powers; that is the only obedience the universe exacts"? And Carlyle with his gospel of work, of fact, of veracity, how does he move us except by saying that the universe imposes no tasks upon us but such as the most humble can perform? Emerson's creed that everything that ever was or will be is here in the enveloping now; that man has but to obey himself,—"He who will rest in what he *is*, is a part of destiny,"—is in like manner nothing but an exorcism of all scepticism as to the pertinency of one's natural faculties.

In a word, "Son of Man, *stand upon thy feet* and I will speak unto thee!" is the only revelation of truth to which the solving epochs have helped the disciple. But that has been enough to satisfy the greater part of his rational need. *In se* and *per se* the universal essence has hardly been more defined by any of these formulas than by the agnostic x; but the mere assurance that my powers, such as they are, are not irrelevant to it, but pertinent; that it speaks to them and will in some way recognize their reply; that I can be a match for it if I will, and not a footless waif,—suffices to make it rational to my feeling in the sense given above. Nothing could be more absurd than to hope for the definitive triumph of any philosophy which should refuse to legitimate, and to legitimate in an emphatic manner, the more powerful of our emotional and practical tendencies. Fatalism, whose solving word in all crises of behavior is "all striving is vain," will never reign supreme, for the impulse to take life strivingly is indestructible in the race. Moral creeds which speak to that impulse will be widely successful in spite of inconsistency, vagueness, and shadowy determination of expectancy. Man needs a rule for his will, and will invent one if one be not given him.

But now observe a most important consequence. Men's active impulses are so differently mixed that a philosophy fit in this respect for Bismarck will almost certainly be unfit for a valetudinarian poet. In other words, although one can lay down in advance the rule that a philosophy which utterly denies all fundamental ground for seriousness, for effort, for hope, which says the nature of things is radically alien to human nature, can never succeed,—one cannot in advance say what particular dose of hope, or of gnosticism of the nature of things, the definitely successful philosophy shall contain. In short, it is almost certain that personal temperament will here make itself felt, and that although all men will insist on being spoken to by the universe in some way, few will insist on being spoken to in just the same way. We have here, in short, the sphere of what Matthew Arnold likes to call *Aberglaube*, legitimate, inexpugnable, yet doomed to eternal variations and disputes.

Take idealism and materialism as examples of what I mean, and suppose for a moment that both give a conception of equal theoretic clearness and consistency, and that both determine our expectations equally well. Idealism will be chosen by a man of one emotional constitution, materialism by another. At this very day all sentimental natures, fond of conciliation and intimacy, tend to an idealistic faith. Why? Because idealism gives to the nature of things such kinship with our personal selves. Our own thoughts are what we are most at home with, what we are least afraid of. To say then that the universe essentially is thought, is to say that I myself, potentially at least, am all. There is no radically alien corner, but an all-pervading *intimacy*. Now, in certain sensitively egotistic minds this conception of reality is sure to put on a narrow, close, sick-room air. Everything sentimental and priggish will be consecrated by it. That element in reality which every strong man of common-sense willingly feels there because it calls forth powers that he owns—the rough, harsh, sea-wave, northwind element, the denier of persons, the democratizer—is banished because it jars too much on the desire for communion. Now, it is the very enjoyment of this element that throws many men upon the materialistic or agnostic hypothesis, as a polemic reaction against the contrary extreme. They sicken at a life wholly constituted of intimacy. There is an overpowering desire at moments to escape personality, to revel in the action of forces that have no respect for our ego, to let the tides flow, even though they flow over us. The strife of these two kinds of mental temper will, I think, always be seen in philosophy. Some men will keep insisting on the reason, the atonement, that lies in the heart of things, and that we can act *with;* others, on the opacity of brute fact that we must react *against*.

Now, there is one element of our active nature which the Christian religion has emphatically recognized, but which philosophers as a rule have with great insincerity tried to huddle out of sight in their pretension to found systems of absolute certainty. I mean the element of faith. Faith means belief in something concerning which doubt is still theoretically possible; and as the test of belief is willingness to act, one may say that faith is the readiness to act in a cause the prosperous issue of which is not certified to us in advance. It is in fact the same moral quality which we call courage in practical affairs; and there will be a very widespread tendency in men of vigorous nature to enjoy a certain amount of uncertainty in their philosophic creed, just as risk lends a zest to worldly activity. Absolutely certified philosophies seeking the *inconcussum* are fruits of mental natures in which the passion for identity (which we saw to be but one factor of the rational appetite) plays an abnormally exclusive part. In the average man, on the contrary, the power to trust, to risk a little beyond the literal evidence, is an essential function. Any mode of conceiving the universe which makes an appeal to this generous power, and makes the man seem as if he were individually helping to create the actuality of the truth whose metaphysical reality he is willing to assume, will be sure to be responded to by large numbers.

The necessity of faith as an ingredient in our mental attitude is strongly insisted on by the scientific philosophers of the present day; but by a singularly arbitrary caprice they say that it is only legitimate when used in the interests of one particular proposition,—the proposition, namely, that the course of nature is uniform. That nature will follow to-morrow the same laws that she follows to-day is, they all admit, a truth which no man can *know;* but in the interests of cognition as well as of action we must postulate or assume it. As Helmholtz says: "Hier gilt nur der eine Rath: vertraue und handle!" And Professor Bain urges: "Our only error is in proposing to give any reason or justification of the postulate, or to treat it as otherwise than begged at the very outset."

With regard to all other possible truths, however, a number of our most influential contemporaries think that an attitude of faith is not only illogical but shameful. Faith in a religious dogma for which there is no outward proof, but which we are tempted to postulate for our emotional interests, just as we postulate the uniformity of nature for our intellectual interests, is branded by Professor Huxley as "the lowest depth of immorality." Citations of this kind from leaders of the modern *Aufklärung* might be multiplied almost indefinitely. Take Professor Clifford's article on the 'Ethics of Belief.' He calls it 'guilt' and 'sin' to believe even the truth without 'scientific evidence.' But what is the use of being a genius, unless *with the same scientific evidence* as other men, one can reach more truth than they? Why does Clifford fearlessly proclaim his belief in the conscious-automaton theory, although the 'proofs' before him are the same which make Mr. Lewes reject it? Why does he believe in primordial units of 'mind-stuff' on evidence which would seem quite worthless to Professor Bain? Simply because, like every human being of the slightest mental originality, he is peculiarly sensitive to evidence that bears in some one direction. It is utterly hopeless to try to exorcise such sensitiveness by calling it the disturbing subjective factor, and branding it as the root of all evil. 'Subjective' be it called! and 'disturbing' to those whom it foils! But if it helps those who, as Cicero says, "vim naturæ magis sentiunt," it is good and not evil. Pretend what we may, the whole man within us is at work when we form our philosophical opinions. Intellect, will, taste, and passion co-operate just as they do in practical affairs; and lucky it is if the passion be not something as petty as a love of personal conquest over the philosopher across the way. The absurd abstraction of an intellect verbally formulating all its evidence and carefully estimating the probability thereof by a vulgar fraction by the size of whose denominator and numerator alone it is swayed, is ideally as inept as it is actually impossible. It is almost incredible that men who are themselves working philosophers should pretend that any philosophy can be, or ever has been, constructed without the help of personal preference, belief, or divination. How have they succeeded in so stultifying their sense for the living facts of human nature as not to perceive that every philosopher, or man of science either, whose initiative counts for anything in the evolution of thought, has taken his stand on a sort of dumb conviction that the truth must lie in one direction rather than another, and a sort of preliminary assurance that his notion can be made to work; and has borne his best fruit in trying to make it work? These mental instincts in different men are the spontaneous variations upon which the intellectual struggle for existence is based. The fittest conceptions survive, and with them the names of their champions shining to all futurity.

The coil is about us, struggle as we may. The only escape from faith is mental nullity. What we enjoy most in a Huxley or a Clifford is not the professor with his learning, but the human personality ready to go in for what it feels to be right, in spite of all appearances. The concrete man has but one interest,—to be right. That for him is the art of all arts, and all means are fair which help him to it. Naked he is flung into the world, and between him and nature there are no rules of civilized warfare. The rules of the scientific game, burdens of proof, presumptions, *experimenta crucis,* complete inductions, and the like, are only binding on those who enter that game. As a matter of fact we all more or less do enter it, because it helps us to our end. But if the means presume to frustrate the end and call us cheats for being right in advance of their slow aid, by guesswork or by hook or crook, what shall we say of them? Were all of Clifford's works, except the Ethics of Belief, forgotten, he might well figure in future treatises on psychology in place of the somewhat threadbare instance of the miser who has been led by the association of ideas to prefer his gold to all the goods he might buy therewith.

In short, if I am born with such a superior general reaction to evidence that I can guess right and act accordingly, and gain all that comes of right action, while my less gifted neighbor (paralyzed by his scruples and waiting for more evidence which he dares not anticipate, much as he longs to) still stands shivering on the brink, by what law shall I be forbidden to reap the advantages of my superior native sensitiveness? Of course I yield to my belief in such a case as this or distrust it, alike at my peril, just as I do in any of the great practical decisions of life. If my inborn faculties are good, I am a prophet; if poor, I am a failure: nature spews me out of her mouth, and there is an end of me. In the total game of life we stake our persons all the while; and if in its theoretic part our persons will help us to a conclusion, surely we should also stake them there, however inarticulate they may be.[5]

But in being myself so very articulate in proving what to all readers with a sense for reality will seem a platitude, am I not wasting words? We cannot live or think at all without some degree of faith. Faith is synonymous with working hypothesis. The only difference is that while some hypotheses can be refuted in five minutes, others may defy ages. A chemist who conjectures that a certain wall-paper contains arsenic, and has faith enough to lead him to take the trouble to put some of it into a hydrogen bottle, finds out by the results of his action whether he was right or wrong. But theories like that of Darwin, or that of the kinetic constitution of matter, may exhaust the labors of generations in their corroboration, each tester of their truth proceeding in this simple way,—that he acts as if it were true, and expects the result to disappoint him if his assumption is false. The longer disappointment is delayed, the stronger grows his faith in his theory.

Now, in such questions as God, immortality, absolute morality, and free-will, no non-papal believer at the present day pretends his faith to be of an essentially different complexion; he can always doubt his creed. But his intimate persuasion is that the odds in its favor are strong enough to warrant him in acting all along on the assumption of its truth. His corroboration or repudiation by the nature of things may be deferred until the day of judgment. The uttermost he now means is something like this: "I *expect* then to triumph with tenfold glory; but if it should turn out, as indeed it may, that I have spent my days in a fool's paradise, why, better have been the dupe of *such* a dreamland than the cunning reader of a world like that which then beyond all doubt unmasks itself to view" In short, we *go in* against materialism very much as we should *go in,* had we a chance, against the second

[5] At most, the command laid upon us by science to believe nothing not yet verified by the senses is a prudential rule intended to maximize our right thinking and minimize our errors *in the long run*. In the particular instance we must frequently lose truth by obeying it; but on the whole we are safer if we follow it consistently, for we are sure to cover our losses with our gains. It is like those gambling and insurance rules based on probability, in which we secure ourselves against losses in detail by hedging on the total run. But this hedging philosophy requires that long run should be there; and this makes it inapplicable to the question of religious faith as the latter comes home to the individual man. He plays the game of life not to escape losses, for he brings nothing with him to lose; he plays it for gains; and it is now or never with him, for the long run which exists indeed for humanity, is not there for him. Let him doubt, believe, or deny, he runs his risk, and has the natural right to choose which one it shall be.

French empire or the Church of Rome, or any other system of things toward which our repugnance is vast enough to determine energetic action, but too vague to issue in distinct argumentation. Our reasons are ludicrously incommensurate with the volume of our feeling, yet on the latter we unhesitatingly act.

Now, I wish to show what to my knowledge has never been clearly pointed out, that belief (as measured by action) not only does and must continually outstrip scientific evidence, but that there is a certain class of truths of whose reality belief is a factor as well as a confessor; and that as regards this class of truths faith is not only licit and pertinent, but essential and indispensable. The truths cannot become true till our faith has made them so.

Suppose, for example, that I am climbing in the Alps, and have had the ill-luck to work myself into a position from which the only escape is by a terrible leap. Being without similar experience, I have no evidence of my ability to perform it successfully; but hope and confidence in myself make me sure I shall not miss my aim, and nerve my feet to execute what without those subjective emotions would perhaps have been impossible. But suppose that, on the contrary, the emotions of fear and mistrust preponderate; or suppose that, having just read the Ethics of Belief, I feel it would be sinful to act upon an assumption unverified by previous experience,—why, then I shall hesitate so long that at last, exhausted and trembling, and launching myself in a moment of despair, I miss my foothold and roll into the abyss. In this case (and it is one of an immense class) the part of wisdom clearly is to believe what one desires; for the belief is one of the indispensable preliminary conditions of the realization of its object. *There are then cases where faith creates its own verification.* Believe, and you shall be right, for you shall save yourself; doubt, and you shall again be right, for you shall perish. The only difference is that to believe is greatly to your advantage.

The future movements of the stars or the facts of past history are determined now once for all, whether I like them or not. They are given irrespective of my wishes, and in all that concerns truths like these subjective preference should have no part; it can only obscure the judgment. But in every fact into which there enters an element of personal contribution on my part, as soon as this personal contribution demands a certain degree of subjective energy which, in its turn, calls for a certain amount of faith in the result,—so that, after all, the future fact is conditioned by my present faith in it,—how trebly asinine would it be for me to deny myself the use of the subjective method, the method of belief based on desire!

In every proposition whose bearing is universal (and such are all the propositions of philosophy), the acts of the subject and their consequences throughout eternity should be included in the formula. If M represent the entire world *minus* the reaction of the thinker upon it, and if $M + x$ represent the absolutely total matter of philosophic propositions (x standing for the thinker's reaction and its results),—what would be a universal truth if the term x were of one complexion, might become egregious error if x altered its character. Let it not be said that x is too infinitesimal a component to change the character of the immense whole in which it lies imbedded. Everything depends on the point of view of the philosophic proposition in question. If we have to define the universe from the point of view of sensibility, the critical material for our judgment lies in the animal kingdom, insignificant as that is, quantitatively considered. The moral definition of the world may depend on phenomena more restricted still in range. In short, many a long phrase may have its sense reversed by the addition of three letters, *n-o-t;* many a monstrous mass have its unstable equilibrium discharged one way or the other by a feather weight that falls.

Let us make this clear by a few examples. The philosophy of evolution offers us to-day a new criterion to serve as an ethical test between right and wrong. Previous criteria, it says, being subjective, have left us still floundering in variations of opinion and the *status belli.* Here is a criterion which is objective and fixed: *That is to be called good which is destined to prevail or survive.* But we immediately see that this standard can only remain objective by leaving myself and my conduct out. If what prevails and survives does so by my help, and cannot do so without that help; if something else will prevail in case I alter my conduct,—how can I possibly now, conscious of alternative courses of action open before me, either of which I may suppose capable of altering the path of events, decide which course to take by asking what path events will follow? If they follow my direction, evidently my direction cannot wait on them. The only possible manner in which an evolutionist can use his standard is the obsequious method of forecasting the course society would take *but for him,* and then putting an extinguisher on all personal idiosyncrasies of desire and interest, and with bated breath and tiptoe tread following as straight as may be at the tail, and bringing up the rear of everything. Some pious creatures may find a pleasure in this; but not only does it violate our general wish to lead and not to follow (a wish which is surely not immoral if we but lead aright), but if it be treated as every ethical principle must be treated,—namely, as a rule good for all men alike,—its general observance would lead to its practical refutation by bringing about a general deadlock. Each good man hanging back and waiting for orders from the rest, absolute stagnation would ensue. Happy, then, if a few unrighteous ones contribute an initiative which sets things moving again!

All this is no caricature. That the course of destiny may be altered by individuals no wise evolutionist ought to doubt. Everything for him has small beginnings, has a bud which may be 'nipped,' and nipped by a feeble force. Human races and tendencies follow the law, and have also small beginnings. The best, according to evolution, is that which has the biggest endings. Now, if a present race of men, enlightened in the evolutionary philosophy, and able to forecast the future, were able to discern in a tribe arising near them the potentiality of future supremacy; were able to see that their own race would eventually be wiped out of existence by the new-comers if the expansion of these were left unmolested,—these present sages would have two courses open to them, either perfectly in harmony with the evolutionary test: Strangle the new race *now,* and ours survives; help the new race, and *it* survives. In both cases the action is right as measured by the evolutionary standard,—it is action for the winning side.

Thus the evolutionist foundation of ethics is purely objective only to the herd of nullities whose votes count for zero in the march of events. But for others, leaders of opinion or potentates, and in general those to whose actions position or genius gives a far-reaching import, and to the rest of us, each in his measure,—whenever we espouse a cause we contribute to the determination of the evolutionary standard of right. The truly wise disciple of this school will then admit faith as an ultimate ethical factor. Any philosophy which makes such questions as, What is the ideal type of humanity? What shall be reckoned virtues? What conduct is good? depend on the question, What is going to succeed?—must needs fall back on personal belief as one of the ultimate conditions of the truth. For again and again success depends on energy of act; energy again depends on faith that we shall not fail; and that faith in turn on the faith that we are right,—which faith thus verifies itself.

Take as an example the question of optimism or pessimism, which makes so much noise just now in Germany. Every human being must sometime decide for himself whether life is worth living. Suppose that in looking at the world and seeing how full it is of misery, of old age, of wickedness and pain, and how unsafe is his own future, he yields to the pessimistic conclusion, cultivates disgust and dread, ceases striving, and finally commits suicide. He thus adds to the mass M of mundane phenomena, independent of his subjectivity, the subjective complement $x,$ which makes of the whole an utterly black picture illumined by no gleam of good. Pessimism completed, verified by his moral reaction and the deed in which this ends, is true beyond a doubt. $M + x$ expresses a state of things totally bad. The man's belief supplied all that was lacking to make it so, and now that it is made so the belief was right.

But now suppose that with the same evil facts M, the man's reaction x is exactly reversed; suppose that instead of giving way to the evil he braves it, and finds a sterner, more wonderful joy than any passive pleasure can yield in triumphing over pain and defying fear; suppose he does this successfully, and however thickly evils crowd upon him proves his dauntless subjectivity to be more than their match,—will not every one confess that the bad character of the M is here the *conditio sine qua non* of the good character of the x? Will not every one instantly declare a world fitted only for fair-weather human beings susceptible of every passive enjoyment, but without independence, courage, or fortitude, to be from a moral point of view incommensurably inferior to a world framed to elicit from the man every form of triumphant endurance and conquering moral energy? As James Hinton says,—

> Little inconveniences, exertions, pains,—these are the only things in which we rightly feel our life at all. If these be not there, existence becomes worthless, or worse; success in putting them all away is fatal. So it is men engage in athletic sports, spend their holidays in climbing up mountains, find nothing so enjoyable as that which taxes their endurance and their energy. This is the way we are made, I say. It may or may not be a mystery or a paradox; it is a fact. Now, this enjoyment in endurance is just according to the intensity of life: the more physical vigor and balance, the more endurance can be made an element of satisfaction. A sick man cannot stand it. The line of enjoyable suffering is not a fixed one; it fluctuates with the perfectness of the life. That our pains are, as they are, unendurable, awful, overwhelming, crushing, not to be borne save in misery and dumb impatience, which utter exhaustion alone makes patient,—that our pains are thus unendurable, means not that they are too great, but that *we are sick*. We have not got our proper life. So you perceive pain is no more necessarily an evil, but an essential element of the highest good.[6]

But the highest good can be achieved only by our getting our proper life; and that can come about only by help of a moral energy born of the faith that in some way or other we shall succeed in getting it if we try pertinaciously enough. This world *is* good, we must say, since it is what we make it,—and we shall make it good. How can we exclude from the cognition of a truth a faith which is involved in the creation of the truth? M has its character indeterminate, susceptible of forming part of a thoroughgoing pessimism on the one hand, or of a meliorism, a moral (as distinguished from a sensual) optimism on the other. All depends on the character of the personal contribution x.

---

[6] *Life of James Hinton*, pp. 172, 173. See also the excellent chapter on "Faith and Sight" in the *Mystery of Matter*, by J. Allanson Picton. Hinton's *Mystery of Pain* will undoubtedly always remain the classical utterance on this subject.

Wherever the facts to be formulated contain such a contribution, we may logically, legitimately, and inexpugnably believe what we desire. The belief creates its verification. The thought becomes literally father to the fact, as the wish was father to the thought.[7]

Let us now turn to the radical question of life,—the question whether this be at bottom a moral or an unmoral universe,—and see whether the method of faith may legitimately have a place there. It is really the question of materialism. Is the world a simple brute actuality, an existence *de facto* about which the deepest thing that can be said is that it happens so to be; or is the judgment of *better* or *worse*, of *ought*, as intimately pertinent to phenomena as the simple judgment *is* or *is not?* The materialistic theorists say that judgments of worth are themselves mere matters of fact; that the words 'good' and 'bad' have no sense apart from subjective passions and interests which we may, if we please, play fast and loose with at will, so far as any duty of ours to the non-human universe is concerned. Thus, when a materialist says it is better for him to suffer great inconvenience than to break a promise, he only means that his social interests have become so knit up with keeping faith that, those interests once being granted, it *is* better for him to keep the promise in spite of everything. But the interests themselves are neither right nor wrong, except possibly with reference to some ulterior order of interests which themselves again are mere subjective data without character, either good or bad.

For the absolute moralists, on the contrary, the interests are not there merely to be felt,—they are to be believed in and obeyed. Not only is it best for my social interests to keep my promise, but best for me to have those interests, and best for the cosmos to have this me. Like the old woman in the story who described the world as resting on a rock, and then explained that rock to be supported by another rock, and finally when pushed with questions said it was rocks all the way down,—he who believes this to be a radically moral universe must hold the moral order to rest either on an absolute and ultimate *should,* or on a series of *shoulds* all the way down.[8]

The practical difference between this objective sort of moralist

---

[7] Observe that in all this not a word has been said of free-will. It all applies as well to a predetermined as to an indeterminate universe. If $M + x$ is fixed in advance, the belief which leads to x and the desire which prompts the belief are also fixed. But fixed or not, these subjective states form a phenomenal condition necessarily preceding the facts; necessarily constitutive, therefore, of the truth $M + x$ which we seek. If, however, free acts be possible, a faith in their possibility, by augmenting the moral energy which gives them birth, will increase their frequency in a given individual.

[8] In either case, as a later essay explains (see p. 616), the *should* which the moralist regards as binding upon *him* must be rooted in the feeling of some other thinkers, or collection of thinkers, to whose demands he individually bows.

and the other one is enormous. The subjectivist in morals, when his moral feelings are at war with the facts about him, is always free to seek harmony by toning down the sensitiveness of the feelings. Being mere data, neither good nor evil in themselves, he may pervert them or lull them to sleep by any means at his command. Truckling, compromise, time-serving, capitulations of conscience, are conventionally opprobrious names for what, if successfully carried out, would be on his principles by far the easiest and most praiseworthy mode of bringing about that harmony between inner and outer relations which is all that he means by good. The absolute moralist, on the other hand, when his interests clash with the world, is not free to gain harmony by sacrificing the ideal interests. According to him, these latter should be as they are and not otherwise. Resistance then, poverty, martyrdom if need be, tragedy in a word,—such are the solemn feasts of his inward faith. Not that the contradiction between the two men occurs every day; in commonplace matters all moral schools agree. It is only in the lonely emergencies of life that our creed is tested: then routine maxims fail, and we fall back on our gods. It cannot then be said that the question, Is this a moral world? is a meaningless and unverifiable question because it deals with something non-phenomenal. Any question is full of meaning to which, as here, contrary answers lead to contrary behavior. And it seems as if in answering such a question as this we might proceed exactly as does the physical philosopher in testing an hypothesis. He deduces from the hypothesis an experimental action, x; this he adds to the facts M already existing. It fits them if the hypothesis be true; if not, there is discord. The results of the action corroborate or refute the idea from which it flowed. So here: the verification of the theory which you may hold as to the objectively moral character of the world can consist only in this,—that if you proceed to act upon your theory it will be reversed by nothing that later turns up as your action's fruit; it will harmonize so well with the entire drift of experience that the latter will, as it were, adopt it, or at most give it an ampler interpretation, without obliging you in any way to change the essence of its formulation. If this be an objectively moral universe, all acts that I make on that assumption, all expectations that I ground on it, will tend more and more completely to interdigitate with the phenomena already existing. $M + x$ will be in accord; and the more I live, and the more the fruits of my activity come to light, the more satisfactory the consensus will grow. While if it be not such a moral universe, and I mistakenly assume that it is, the course of experience will throw ever new impediments in the way of my belief, and become more and more difficult to express in its language. Epicycle upon epicycle of subsidiary hypothesis will have to be invoked to give to the discrepant terms a temporary appearance of squaring with each other; but at last even this resource will fail.

If, on the other hand, I rightly assume the universe to be not moral, in what does my verification consist? It is that by letting moral interests sit lightly, by disbelieving that there is any duty about *them* (since duty obtains only as *between* them and other phenomena), and so throwing them over if I find it hard to get them satisfied,—it is that by refusing to take up a tragic attitude, I deal in the long-run most satisfactorily with the facts of life. "All is vanity" is here the last word of wisdom. Even though in certain limited series there may be a great appearance of seriousness, he who in the main treats things with a degree of good-natured scepticism and radical levity will find that the practical fruits of his epicurean hypothesis verify it more and more, and not only save him from pain but do honor to his sagacity. While, on the other hand, he who contrary to reality stiffens himself in the notion that certain things absolutely should be, and rejects the truth that at bottom it makes no difference what is, will find himself ever-more thwarted and perplexed and bemuddled by the facts of the world, and his tragic disappointment will, as experience accumulates, seem to drift farther and farther away from that final atonement or reconciliation which certain partial tragedies often get.

Anæsthesia is the watchword of the moral sceptic brought to bay and put to his trumps. *Energy* is that of the moralist. Act on my creed, cries the latter, and the results of your action will prove the creed true, and that the nature of things is earnest infinitely. Act on mine, says the epicurean, and the results will prove that seriousness is but a superficial glaze upon a world of fundamentally trivial import. You and your acts and the nature of things will be alike enveloped in a single formula, a universal *vanitas vanitatum*.

For the sake of simplicity I have written as if the verification might occur in the life of a single philosopher,—which is manifestly untrue, since the theories still face each other, and the facts of the world give countenance to both. Rather should we expect, that, in a question of this scope, the experience of the entire human race must make the verification, and that all the evidence will not be 'in' till the final integration of things, when the last man has had his say and contributed his share to the still unfinished x. Then the proof will be complete; then it will appear without doubt whether the moralistic x has filled up the gap which alone kept the M of the world from forming an even and harmonious unity, or whether the non-moralistic x has given the finishing touches which were alone needed to make the M appear outwardly as vain as it inwardly was.

But if this be so, is it not clear that the facts M, taken *per se*, are inadequate to justify a conclusion either way in advance of my action? My action is the complement which, by proving congruous or not, reveals the latent nature of the mass to which it is applied. The world may in fact be likened unto a lock, whose inward nature, moral or unmoral, will never reveal itself to our simply expectant gaze. The positivists, forbidding us to make any assumptions regarding it, condemn us to eternal ignorance, for the 'evidence' which they wait for can never come so long as we are passive. But nature has put into our hands two keys, by which we may test the lock. If we try the moral key *and it fits,* it is a moral lock. If we try the unmoral key and *it* fits, it is an unmoral lock. I cannot possibly conceive of any other sort of 'evidence' or 'proof' than this. It is quite true that the co-operation of generations is needed to educe it. But in these matters the solidarity (so called) of the human race is a patent fact. The essential thing to notice is that our active preference is a legitimate part of the game,—that it is our plain business as men to try one of the keys, and the one in which we most confide. If then the proof exist not till I have acted, and I must needs in acting run the risk of being wrong, how can the popular science professors be right in objurgating in me as infamous a 'credulity' which the strict logic of the situation requires? If this really be a moral universe; if by my acts I be a factor of its destinies; if to believe where I may doubt be itself a moral act analogous to voting for a side not yet sure to win,—by what right shall they close in upon me and steadily negate the deepest conceivable function of my being by their preposterous command that I shall stir neither hand nor foot, but remain balancing myself in eternal and insoluble doubt? Why, doubt itself is a decision of the widest practical reach, if only because we may miss by doubting what goods we might be gaining by espousing the winning side. But more than that! it is often practically impossible to distinguish doubt from dogmatic negation. If I refuse to stop a murder because I am in doubt whether it be not justifiable homicide, I am virtually abetting the crime. If I refuse to bale out a boat because I am in doubt whether my efforts will keep her afloat, I am really helping to sink her. If in the mountain precipice I doubt my right to risk a leap, I actively connive at my destruction. He who commands himself not to be credulous of God, of duty, of freedom, of immortality, may again and again be indistinguishable from him who dogmatically denies them. Scepticism in moral matters is an active ally of immorality. Who is not for is against. The universe will have no neutrals in these questions. In theory as in practice, dodge or hedge, or talk as we like about a wise scepticism, we are really doing volunteer military service for one side or the other.

Yet obvious as this necessity practically is, thousands of innocent magazine readers lie paralyzed and terrified in the network of shallow negations which the leaders of opinion have thrown over their souls. All they need to be free and hearty again in the exercise of their birthright is that these fastidious vetoes should be swept away. All that the human heart wants is its chance. It will willingly forego certainty in universal matters if only it can be allowed to feel that in them it has that same inalienable right to run risks, which no one dreams of refusing to it in the pettiest practical affairs. And if I, in these last pages, like the mouse in the fable, have gnawed a few of the strings of the sophistical net that has been binding down its lion-strength, I shall be more than rewarded for my pains.

To sum up: No philosophy will permanently be deemed rational by all men which (in addition to meeting logical demands) does not to some degree pretend to determine expectancy, and in a still greater degree make a direct appeal to all those powers of our nature which we hold in highest esteem. Faith, being one of these powers, will always remain a factor not to be banished from philosophic constructions, the more so since in many ways it brings forth its own verification. In these points, then, it is hopeless to look for literal agreement among mankind.

The ultimate philosophy, we may therefore conclude, must not be too strait-laced in form, must not in all its parts divide heresy from orthodoxy by too sharp a line. There must be left over and above the propositions to be subscribed, *ubique, semper, et ab omnibus,* another realm into which the stifled soul may escape from pedantic scruples and indulge its own faith at its own risks; and all that can here be done will be to mark out distinctly the questions which fall within faith's sphere.

PHILOSOPHICAL CONCEPTIONS
AND PRACTICAL RESULTS *

[1898] [9]

An occasion like the present would seem to call for an absolutely untechnical discourse. I ought to speak of something connected with life

* From: C.E.R., 406–437.

[9] [Reprinted from *The University Chronicle* (Berkeley, California) September, 1898. An address delivered before the Philosophical Union of the University of California on August 26, 1898. It was reprinted with slight verbal revision, and with omission of first three pages, and concluding paragraph, in *Journal of Philosophy, Psychology, and Scientific Methods,* 1904, *1,* 673–687, under the title of "The Pragmatic Method." Afterwards most of pages 347–348, below, was used in the *Varieties of Religious Experience* (1902, p. 444); and

rather than with logic. I ought to give a message with a practical
outcome and an emotional musical accompaniment, so to speak, fitted
to interest men as men, and yet also not altogether to disappoint philosophers—since philosophers, let them be as queer as they will, still
are men in the secret recesses of their hearts, even here at Berkeley. I
ought, I say, to produce something simple enough to catch and inspire
the rest of you, and yet with just enough of ingenuity and oddity about
it to keep the members of the Philosophical Union from yawning and
letting their attention wander away.

I confess that I have something of this kind in my mind, a perfectly ideal discourse for the present occasion. Were I to set it down
on paper, I verily believe it would be regarded by everyone as the final
word of philosophy. It would bring theory down to a single point, at
which every human being's practical life would begin. It would solve
all the antinomies and contradictions, it would let loose all the right
impulses and emotions; and everyone, on hearing it, would say,
"Why, that *is* the truth!—*that* is what I have been believing, that is
what I have really been living on all this time, but I never could find
the words for it before. All that eludes, all that flickers and twinkles,
all that invites and vanishes even whilst inviting, is here made a solidity and a possession. Here is the end of unsatisfactoriness, here the
beginning of unimpeded clearness, joy, and power." Yes, my friends, I
have such a discourse within me! But, do not judge me harshly, I
cannot produce it on the present occasion. I humbly apologize; I have
come across the continent to this wondrous Pacific Coast—to this
Eden, not of the mythical antiquity, but of the solid future of mankind
—I ought to give you something worthy of your hospitality, and not
altogether unworthy of your great destiny, to help cement our rugged
East and your wondrous West together in a spiritual bond,—and yet,
and yet, and yet, I simply cannot. I have tried to articulate it, but it
will not come. Philosophers are after all like poets. They are pathfind-
ers. What every one can feel, what every one can know in the bone
and marrow of him, they sometimes can find words for and express.
The words and thoughts of the philosophers are not exactly the words
and thoughts of the poets—worse luck. But both alike have the same

---

pp. 350–355, below were reprinted with further slight revision in *Pragmatism*
(1907), see below, pp. 395–399. This article marks the beginning of the pragmatist movement. Nine years later, speaking of the pragmatist principle which
he attributed to Charles Peirce, James wrote: "It lay entirely unnoticed by any
one for twenty years, until I, in an address before Professor Howison's philosophical union at the University of California, brought it forward again and
made a special application of it to religion. By that date (1898) the times
seemed ripe for its reception. The word 'pragmatism' spread, and at present it
fairly spots the pages of the philosophical journals" (*Pragmatism*, 1907, p. 378,
below.) ED.]

function. They are, if I may use a simile, so many spots, or blazes,—blazes made by the axe of the human intellect on the trees of the otherwise trackless forest of human experience. They give you somewhere to go from. They give you a direction and a place to reach. They do not give you the integral forest with all its sunlit glories and its moonlit witcheries and wonders. Ferny dells, and mossy waterfalls, and secret magic nooks escape you, owned only by the wild things to whom the region is a home. Happy they without the need of blazes! But to us the blazes give a sort of ownership. We can now use the forest, wend across it with companions, and enjoy its quality. It is no longer a place merely to get lost in and never return. The poet's words and the philosopher's phrases thus are helps of the most genuine sort, giving to all of us hereafter the freedom of the trails they made. Though they create nothing, yet for this marking and fixing function of theirs we bless their names and keep them on our lips, even whilst the thin and spotty and half-casual character of their operations is evident to our eyes.

No one like the pathfinder himself feels the immensity of the forest, or knows the accidentality of his own trails. Columbus, dreaming of the ancient East, is stopped by poor pristine simple America, and gets no farther on that day; and the poets and philosophers themselves know as no one else knows that what their formulas express leaves unexpressed almost everything that they organically divine and feel. So I feel that there is a centre in truth's forest where I have never been: to track it out and get there is the secret spring of all my poor life's philosophic efforts; at moments I almost strike into the final valley, there is a gleam of the end, a sense of certainty, but always there comes still another ridge, so my blazes merely circle towards the true direction; and although now, if ever, would be the fit occasion, yet I cannot take you to the wondrous hidden spot to-day. To-morrow it must be, or to-morrow, or to-morrow, and pretty surely death will overtake me ere the promise is fulfilled.

Of such postponed achievements do the lives of all philosophers consist. Truth's fulness is elusive; ever not quite, not quite! So we fall back on the preliminary blazes—a few formulas, a few technical conceptions, a few verbal pointers—which at least define the initial direction of the trail. And that, to my sorrow, is all that I can do here at Berkeley to-day. Inconclusive I must be, and merely suggestive, though I will try to be as little technical as I can.

I will seek to define with you merely what seems to be the most likely direction in which to start upon the trail of truth. Years ago this direction was given to me by an American philosopher whose home is in the East, and whose published works, few as they are and scattered in periodicals, are no fit expression of his powers. I refer to Mr.

Charles S. Peirce, with whose very existence as a philosopher I dare say many of you are unacquainted. He is one of the most original of contemporary thinkers; and the principle of practicalism—or pragmatism, as he called it, when I first heard him enunciate it at Cambridge in the early '70's—is the clue or compass by following which I find myself more and more confirmed in believing we may keep our feet upon the proper trail.

Peirce's principle, as we may call it, may be expressed in a variety of ways, all of them very simple. In the *Popular Science Monthly* for January, 1878, he introduces it as follows: The soul and meaning of thought, he says, can never be made to direct itself towards anything but the production of belief, belief being the demicadence which closes a musical phrase in the symphony of our intellectual life. Thought in movement has thus for its only possible motive the attainment of thought at rest. But when our thought about an object has found its rest in belief, then our action on the subject can firmly and safely begin. Beliefs, in short, are really rules for action; and the whole function of thinking is but one step in the production of habits of action. If there were any part of a thought that made no difference in the thought's practical consequences, then that part would be no proper element of the thought's significance. Thus the same thought may be clad in different words; but if the different words suggest no different conduct, they are mere outer accretions, and have no part in the thought's meaning. If, however, they determine conduct differently, they are essential elements of the significance. "Please open the door," and, *"Veuillez ouvrir la porte,"* in French, mean just the same thing; but "D—n you, open the door," although in English, *means* something very different. Thus to develop a thought's meaning we need only determine what conduct it is fitted to produce; that conduct is for us its sole significance. And the tangible fact at the root of all our thought-distinctions, however subtle, is that there is no one of them so fine as to consist in anything but a possible difference of practice. To attain perfect clearness in our thoughts of an object, then, we need only consider what effects of a conceivably practical kind the object may involve—what sensations we are to expect from it, and what reactions we must prepare. Our conception of these effects, then, is for us the whole of our conception of the object, so far as that conception has positive significance at all.

This is the principle of Peirce, the principle of pragmatism. I think myself that it should be expressed more broadly than Mr. Peirce expresses it. The ultimate test for us of what a truth means is indeed the conduct it dictates or inspires. But it inspires that conduct because it first foretells some particular turn to our experience which shall call for just that conduct from us. And I should prefer for our purposes this evening to express Peirce's principle by saying that the effective meaning of any philosophic proposition can always be brought down to some particular consequence, in our future practical experience, whether active or passive; the point lying rather in the fact that the experience must be particular, than in the fact that it must be active.

To take in the importance of this principle, one must get accustomed to applying it to concrete cases. Such use as I am able to make of it convinces me that to be mindful of it in philosophical disputations tends wonderfully to smooth out misunderstandings and to bring in peace. If it did nothing else, then, it would yield a sovereignly valuable rule of method for discussion. So I shall devote the rest of this precious hour with you to its elucidation, because I sincerely think that if you once grasp it, it will shut your steps out from many an old false opening, and head you in the true direction for the trail.

One of its first consequences is this. Suppose there are two different philosophical definitions, or propositions, or maxims, or what not, which seem to contradict each other, and about which men dispute. If, by supposing the truth of the one, you can foresee no conceivable practical consequence to anybody at any time or place, which is different from what you would foresee if you supposed the truth of the other, why then the difference between the two propositions is no difference,—it is only a specious and verbal difference, unworthy of further contention. Both formulas mean radically the same thing, although they may say it in such different words. It is astonishing to see how many philosophical disputes collapse into insignificance the moment you subject them to this simple test. There can be no difference which doesn't make a difference—no difference in abstract truth which does not express itself in a difference of concrete fact, and of conduct consequent upon the fact, imposed on somebody, somehow, somewhere, and somewhen. It is true that a certain shrinkage of values often seems to occur in our general formulas when we measure their meaning in this prosaic and practical way. They diminish. But the vastness that is merely based on vagueness is a false appearance of importance, and not a vastness worth retaining. The x's, y's, and z's always do shrivel, as I have heard a learned friend say, whenever at the end of your algebraic computation they change into so many a's, b's, and c's; but the whole function of algebra is, after all, to get them into that more definite shape; and the whole function of philosophy ought to be to find out what definite difference it will make to you and me, at definite instants of our life, if this world-formula or that world-formula be the one which is true.

If we start off with an impossible case, we shall perhaps all the more clearly see the use and scope of our principle. Let us, therefore, put ourselves, in imagination, in a position from which no forecasts of consequence, no dictates of conduct, can possibly be made, so that the principle of pragmatism finds no field of application. Let us, I mean, assume that the present moment is the absolutely last moment of the world, with bare nonentity beyond it, and no hereafter for either experience or conduct.

Now I say that in that case there would be no sense whatever in some of our most urgent and envenomed philosophical and religious debates. The question is, "Is matter the producer of all things, or is a God there too?" would, for example, offer a perfectly idle and insignificant alternative if the world were finished and no more of it to come. Many of us, most of us, I think, now feel as if a terrible coldness and deadness would come over the world were we forced to believe that no informing spirit or purpose had to do with it, but it merely accidentally had come. The actually experienced details of fact might be the same on either hypothesis, some sad, some joyous; some rational, some odd and grotesque; but without a God behind them, we think they would have something ghastly, they would tell no genuine story, there would be no speculation in those eyes that they do glare with. With the God, on the other hand, they would grow solid, warm, and altogether full of real significance.

But I say that such an alternation of feelings, reasonable enough in a consciousness that is prospective, as ours now is, and whose world is partly yet to come, would be absolutely senseless and irrational in a purely retrospective consciousness summing up a world already past. For such a consciousness, no emotional interest could attach to the alternative. The problem would be purely intellectual; and if unaided matter could, with any scientific plausibility, be shown to cipher out the actual facts, then not the faintest shadow ought to cloud the mind, of regret for the God that by the same ciphering would prove needless and disappear from our belief.

For just consider the case sincerely, and say what would be the *worth* of such a God if he *were* there, with his work accomplished and his world run down.[10] He would be worth no more than just that world was worth. To that amount of result, with its mixed merits and defects, his creative power could attain, but go no farther. And since there is to be no future; since the whole value and meaning of the world has been already paid in and actualized in the feelings that went with it in the passing, and now go with it in the ending; since it draws

[10] [Of this and the following passage James later wrote: "I had no sooner given the address than I perceived a flaw in that part of it; but I have left the passage unaltered ever since, because the flaw did not spoil its illustrative value. . . . Even if matter could do every outward thing that God does, the idea of it would not work as satisfactorily, because the chief call for a God on modern men's part is for a being who will inwardly recognize them and judge them sympathetically" (*The Meaning of Truth,* 1909, pp. 189–190, note). ED.]

no supplemental significance (such as our real world draws) from its function of preparing something yet to come; why then, by it we take God's measure, as it were. He is the Being who could once for all do *that;* and for that much we are thankful to him, but for nothing more. But now, on the contrary hypothesis, namely, that the bits of matter following their "laws" could make that world and do no less, should we not be just as thankful to them? Wherein should we suffer loss, then, if we dropped God as an hypothesis and made the matter alone responsible? Where would the special deadness, "crassness," and ghastliness come in? And how, experience being what it is once for all, would God's presence in it make it any more "living," any richer in our sight?

Candidly, it is impossible to give any answer to this question. The actually experienced world is supposed to be the same in its details on either hypothesis, "the same, for our praise or blame," as Browning says. It stands there indefeasibly; a gift which can't be taken back. Calling matter the cause of it retracts no single one of the items that have made it up, nor does calling God the cause augment them. They are the God or the atoms, respectively, of just that and no other world. The God, if there, has been doing just what atoms could do— appearing in the character of atoms, so to speak—and earning such gratitude as is due to atoms, and no more. If his presence lends no different turn or issue to the performance, it surely can lend it no increase of dignity. Nor would indignity come to it were he absent, and did the atoms remain the only actors on the stage. When a play is once over, and the curtain down, you really make it no better by claiming an illustrious genius for its author, just as you make it no worse by calling him a common hack.

Thus if no future detail of experience or conduct is to be deducted from our hypothesis, the debate between materialism and theism becomes quite idle and insignificant. Matter and God in that event mean exactly the same thing—the power, namely, neither more nor less, that can make just this mixed, imperfect, yet completed world—and the wise man is he who in such a case would turn his back on such a supererogatory discussion. Accordingly most men instinctively—and a large class of men, the so-called positivists or scientists, deliberately —do turn their backs on philosophical disputes from which nothing in the line of definite future consequences can be seen to follow. The verbal and empty character of our studies is surely a reproach with which you of the Philosophical Union are but too sadly familiar. An escaped Berkeley student said to me at Harvard the other day,—he had never been in the philosophical department here,—"Words, words, words, are all that you philosophers care for." We philosophers think it all unjust; and yet, if the principle of pragmatism be true, it is a perfectly sound reproach unless the metaphysical alternatives under investigation can be shown to have alternative practical outcomes, however delicate and distant these may be. The common man and the scientist can discover no such outcomes. And if the metaphysician can discern none either, the common man and scientist certainly are in the sight of it, as against him. His science is then but pompous trifling; and the endowment of a professorship for such a being would be something really absurd.

Accordingly, in every genuine metaphysical debate some practical issue, however remote, is really involved. To realize this, revert with me to the question of materialism or theism; and place yourselves this time in the real world we live in, the world that has a future, that is yet uncompleted whilst we speak. In this unfinished world the alternative of "materialism or theism?" is intensely practical; and it is worth while for us to spend some minutes of our hour in seeing how truly this is the case.

How, indeed, does the programme differ for us, according as we consider that the facts of experience up to date are purposeless configurations of atoms moving according to eternal elementary laws, or that on the other hand they are due to the providence of God? As far as the past facts go, indeed there is no difference. These facts are in, are bagged, are captured; and the good that's in them is gained, be the atoms or be the God their cause. There are accordingly many materialists about us to-day who, ignoring altogether the future and practical aspects of the question, seek to eliminate the odium attaching to the word materialism, and even to eliminate the word itself, by showing that, if matter could give birth to all these gains, why then matter, functionally considered, is just as divine an entity as God, in fact coalesces with God, is what you mean by God. Cease, these persons advise us, to use either of these terms, with their outgrown opposition. Use terms free of the clerical connotations on the one hand; of the suggestion of grossness, coarseness, ignobility, on the other. Talk of the primal mystery, of the unknowable energy, of the one and only power, instead of saying either God or matter. This is the course to which Mr. Spencer urges us at the end of the first volume of his *Psychology*. In some well-written pages he there shows us that a "matter" so infinitely subtile, and performing motions as inconceivably quick and fine as modern science postulates in her explanations, has no trace of grossness left. He shows that the conception of spirit, as we mortals hitherto have framed it, is itself too gross to cover the exquisite complexity of Nature's facts. Both terms, he says, are but symbols, pointing to that one unknowable reality in which their oppositions cease.

Throughout these remarks of Mr. Spencer, eloquent, and even

noble in a certain sense, as they are, he seems to think that the dislike of the ordinary man to materialism comes from a purely æsthetic disdain of matter, as something gross in itself, and vile and despicable. Undoubtedly such an æsthetic disdain of matter has played a part in philosophic history. But it forms no part whatever of an intelligent modern man's dislikes. Give him a matter bound forever by its laws to lead our world nearer and nearer to perfection, and any rational man will worship that matter as readily as Mr. Spencer worships his own so-called unknowable power. It not only has made for righteousness up to date, but it will make for righteousness forever; and that is all we need. Doing practically all that a God can do, it is equivalent to God, its function is a God's function, and in a world in which a God would be superfluous; from such a world a God could never lawfully be missed.

But *is* the matter by which Mr. Spencer's process of cosmic evolution is carried on any such principle of never-ending perfection as this? Indeed it is not, for the future end of every cosmically evolved thing or system of things is tragedy; and Mr. Spencer, in confining himself to the æsthetic and ignoring the practical side of the controversy, has really contributed nothing serious to its relief. But apply now our principle of practical results, and see what a vital significance the question of materialism or theism immediately acquires.

Theism and materialism, so indifferent when taken retrospectively, point when we take them prospectively to wholly different practical consequences, to opposite outlooks of experience. For, according to the theory of mechanical evolution, the laws of redistribution of matter and motion, though they are certainly to thank for all the good hours which our organisms have ever yielded us and for all the ideals which our minds now frame, are yet fatally certain to undo their work again, and to redissolve everything that they have once evolved. You all know the picture of the last foreseeable state of the dead universe, as evolutionary science gives it forth. I cannot state it better than in Mr. Balfour's words: "The energies of our system will decay, the glory of the sun will be dimmed, and the earth, tideless and inert, will no longer tolerate the race which has for a moment disturbed its solitude. Man will go down into the pit, and all his thoughts will perish. The uneasy consciousness which in this obscure corner has for a brief space broken the contented silence of the universe, will be at rest. Matter will know itself no longer. 'Imperishable monuments' and 'immortal deeds,' death itself, and love stronger than death, will be as if they had not been. Nor will anything that is, be better or worse for all that the labor, genius, devotion, and suffering of man have striven through countless ages to effect." [11]

11 *The Foundations of Belief,* p. 30.

That is the sting of it, that in the vast driftings of the cosmic weather, though many a jewelled shore appears, and many an enchanted cloud-bank floats away, long lingering ere it be dissolved—even as our world now lingers, for our joy—yet when these transient products are gone, nothing, absolutely *nothing* remains, to represent those particular qualities, those elements of preciousness which they may have enshrined. Dead and gone are they, gone utterly from the very sphere and room of being. Without an echo; without a memory; without an influence on aught that may come after, to make it care for similar ideals. This utter final wreck and tragedy is of the essence of scientific materialism as at present understood. The lower and not the higher forces are the eternal forces, or the last surviving forces within the only cycle of evolution which we can definitely see. Mr. Spencer believes this as much as any one; so why should he argue with us as if we were making silly æsthetic objections to the "grossness" of "matter and motion,"—the principles of his philosophy,—when what really dismays us in it is the disconsolateness of its ulterior practical results?

No, the true objection to materialism is not positive but negative. It would be farcical at this day to make complaint of it for what it *is*, for "grossness." Grossness is what grossness *does*—we now know *that*. We make complaint of it, on the contrary, for what it is *not*—not a permanent warrant for our more ideal interests, not a fulfiller of our remotest hopes.

The notion of God, on the other hand, however inferior it may be in clearness to those mathematical notions so current in mechanical philosophy, has at least this practical superiority over them, that it guarantees an ideal order that shall be permanently preserved. A world with a God in it to say the last word, may indeed burn up or freeze, but we then think of Him as still mindful of the old ideals and sure to bring them elsewhere to fruition; so that, where He is, tragedy is only provisional and partial, and shipwreck and dissolution not the absolutely final things. This need of an eternal moral order is one of the deepest needs of our breast. And those poets, like Dante and Wordsworth, who live on the conviction of such an order, owe to that fact the extraordinary tonic and consoling power of their verse. Here then, in these different emotional and practical appeals, in these adjustments of our concrete attitudes of hope and expectation, and all the delicate consequences which their differences entail, lie the real meanings of materialism and theism—not in hair-splitting abstractions about matter's inner essence, or about the metaphysical attributes of God. Materialism means simply the denial that the moral order is eternal, and the cutting off of ultimate hopes; theism means the affirmation of an eternal moral order and the letting loose of hope. Surely here is an issue genuine enough, for any one who feels it; and, as long as men are men, it will yield matter for serious philosophic debate. Concerning this question, at any rate, the positivists and pooh-pooh-ers of metaphysics are in the wrong.

But possibly some of you may still rally to their defence. Even whilst admitting that theism and materialism make different prophecies of the world's future, you may yourselves pooh-pooh the difference as something so infinitely remote as to mean nothing for a sane mind. The essence of a sane mind, you may say, is to take shorter views, and to feel no concern about such chimæras as the latter end of the world. Well, I can only say that if you say this, you do injustice to human nature. Religious melancholy is not disposed of by a simple flourish of the word "insanity." The absolute things, the last things, the overlapping things, are the truly philosophic concern; all superior minds feel seriously about them, and the mind with the shortest views is simply the mind of the more shallow man.

However, I am willing to pass over these very distant outlooks on the ultimate, if any of you so insist. The theistic controversy can still serve to illustrate the principle of pragmatism for us well enough, without driving us so far afield. If there be a God, it is not likely that he is confined solely to making differences in the world's latter end; he probably makes differences all along its course. Now the principle of practicalism says that the very meaning of the conception of God lies in those differences which must be made in our experience if the conception be true. God's famous inventory of perfections, as elaborated by dogmatic theology, either means nothing, says our principle, or it implies certain definite things that we can feel and do at particular moments of our lives, things which we could not feel and should not do were no God present and were the business of the universe carried on by material atoms instead. So far as our conceptions of the Deity involve no such experiences, so far they are meaningless and verbal, —scholastic entities and abstractions, as the positivists say, and fit objects for their scorn. But so far as they do involve such definite experiences, God means something for us, and may be real.

Now if we look at the definitions of God made by dogmatic theology, we see immediately that some stand and some fall when treated by this test. God, for example, as any orthodox text-book will tell us, is a being existing not only *per se,* or by himself, as created beings exist, but *a se,* or from himself; and out of this "aseity" flow most of his perfections. He is, for example, necessary; absolute; infinite in all respects; and single. He is simple, not compounded of essence and existence, substance and accident, actuality and potentiality, or subject and attributes, as are other things. He belongs to no genus; he is inwardly and outwardly unalterable; he knows and wills all things, and first of all his own infinite self, in one indivisible eternal act. And he is absolutely self-sufficing, and infinitely happy. Now in which one of us practical Americans here assembled does this conglomeration of attributes awaken any sense of reality? And if in no one, then why not? Surely because such attributes awaken no responsive active feelings and call for no particular conduct of our own. How does God's "aseity" come home to *you?* What specific thing can I do to adapt myself to his "simplicity"? Or how determine our behavior henceforward if his "felicity" is anyhow absolutely complete? In the '50's and '60's Captain Mayne Reid was the great writer of boys' books of out-of-door adventure. He was forever extolling the hunters and field-observers of living animals' habits, and keeping up a fire of invective against the "closet-naturalists," as he called them, the collectors and classifiers, and handlers of skeletons and skins. When I was a boy I used to think that a closet-naturalist must be the vilest type of wretch under the sun. But surely the systematic theologians are the closet-naturalists of the Deity, even in Captain Mayne Reid's sense. Their orthodox deduction of God's attributes is nothing but a shuffling and matching of pedantic dictionary-adjectives, aloof from morals, aloof from human needs, something that might be worked out from the mere word "God" by a logical machine of wood and brass as well as by a man of flesh and blood. The attributes which I have quoted have absolutely nothing to do with religion, for religion is a living practical affair. Other parts, indeed, of God's traditional description do have practical connection with life, and have owed all their historic importance to that fact. His omniscience, for example, and his justice. With the one he sees us in the dark, with the other he rewards and punishes what he sees. So do his ubiquity and eternity and unalterability appeal to our confidence, and his goodness banish our fears. Even attributes of less meaning to this present audience have in past times so appealed. One of the chief attributes of God, according to the orthodox theology, is his infinite love of himself, proved by asking the question, "By what but an infinite object can an infinite affection be appeased?" An immediate consequence of this primary self-love of God is the orthodox dogma that the manifestation of his own glory is God's primal purpose in creation; and that dogma has certainly made very efficient practical connection with life. It is true that we ourselves are tending to outgrow this old monarchical conception of a Deity with his "court" and pomp—"his state is kingly, thousands at his bidding speed," etc.—but there is no denying the enormous influence it has had over ecclesiastical history, nor, by repercussion, over the history of European states. And yet even these more real and significant attributes have the trail of the serpent over them as the books on theology have actually worked them out. One feels that, in the theologians' hands, they are only a set of dictionary-adjectives, mechanically deduced; logic has stepped into the place of vision, professionalism into that of life. Instead of bread we get a stone; instead of a fish a serpent. Did such a conglomeration of abstract general terms give really the gist of our knowledge of the Deity, divinity-schools might indeed continue to flourish, but religion, vital religion, would have taken its flight from this world. What keeps religion going is something else than abstract definitions and systems of logically concatenated adjectives, and something different from faculties of theology and their professors. All these things are after-effects, secondary accretions upon a mass of concrete religious experiences, connecting themselves with feeling and conduct that renew themselves in *sæcula sæculorum* in the lives of humble private men. If you ask what these experiences are, they are conversations with the unseen, voices and visions, responses to prayer, changes of heart, deliverances from fear, inflowings of help, assurances of support, whenever certain persons set their own internal attitude in certain appropriate ways. The power comes and goes and is lost, and can be found only in a certain definite direction, just as if it were a concrete material thing. These direct experiences of a wider spiritual life with which our superficial consciousness is continuous, and with which it keeps up an intense commerce, form the primary mass of direct religious experience on which all hearsay religion rests, and which furnishes that notion of an ever-present God, out of which systematic theology thereupon proceeds to make capital in its own unreal pedantic way. What the word "God" means is just those passive and active experiences of your life. Now, my friends, it is quite immaterial to my purpose whether you yourselves enjoy and venerate these experiences, or whether you stand aloof and, viewing them in others, suspect them of being illusory and vain. Like all other human experiences, they too certainly share in the general liability to illusion and mistake. They need not be infallible. But they are certainly the originals of the God-idea, and theology is the translation; and you remember that I am now using the God-idea merely as an example, not to discuss as to its truth or error, but only to show how well the principle of pragmatism works. That the God of systematic theology should exist or not exist is a matter of small practical moment. At most it means that you may continue uttering certain abstract words and that you must stop using others. But if the God of these particular experiences be false, it is an awful thing for you, if you are one of those whose lives are stayed on such experiences. The theistic controversy, trivial enough if we take it merely academically and theologically, is of tremendous significance if we test it by its results for actual life.

I can best continue to recommend the principle of practicalism to you by keeping in the neighborhood of this theological idea. I reminded you a few minutes ago that the old monarchical notion of the Deity as a sort of Louis the Fourteenth of the Heavens is losing nowadays much of its ancient prestige. Religious philosophy, like all philosophy, is growing more and more idealistic. And in the philosophy of the Absolute, so called, that post-Kantian form of idealism which is carrying so many of our higher minds before it, we have the triumph of what in old times was summarily disposed of as the pantheistic heresy,—I mean the conception of God, not as the extraneous creator, but as the indwelling spirit and substance of the world. I know not where one can find a more candid, more clear, or, on the whole, more persuasive statement of this theology of Absolute Idealism than in the addresses made before this very Union three years ago by your own great Californian philosopher (whose colleague at Harvard I am proud to be), Josiah Royce. His contributions to the resulting volume, *The Conception of God,* form a very masterpiece of popularization. Now you will remember, many of you, that in the discussion that followed Professor Royce's first address, the debate turned largely on the ideas of unity and plurality, and on the question whether, if God be One in All and All in All, "One with the unity of a single instant," as Royce calls it, "forming in His wholeness one luminously transparent moment," any room is left for real morality or freedom. Professor Howison, in particular, was earnest in urging that morality and freedom are relations between a manifold of selves, and that under the régime of Royce's monistic Absolute Thought "no true manifold of selves is or can be provided for." I will not go into any of the details of that particular discussion, but just ask you to consider for a moment whether, in general, any discussion about monism or pluralism, any argument over the unity of the universe, would not necessarily be brought into a shape where it tends to straighten itself out, by bringing our principle of practical results to bear.

The question whether the world is at bottom One or Many is a typical metaphysical question. Long has it raged! In its crudest form it is an exquisite example of the *loggerheads* of metaphysics. "I say it is one great fact," Parmenides and Spinoza exclaim. "I say it is many little facts," reply the atomists and associationists. "I say it is both one and many, many in one," say the Hegelians; and in the ordinary popular discussions we rarely get beyond this barren reiteration by the disputants of their pet adjectives of number. But is it not first of all clear that when we take such an adjective as "One" absolutely and abstractly, its meaning is so vague and empty that it makes no difference whether we affirm or deny it? Certainly this universe is not the mere number One; and yet you can number it "one," if you like, in talking about it as contrasted with other possible worlds numbered "two" and "three" for the occasion. What exact thing do you *practi-*

cally mean by "One," when you call the universe One, is the first question you must ask. In what ways does the oneness come home to your own personal life? By what difference does it express itself in your experience? How can you act differently towards a universe which is one? Inquired into in this way, the unity might grow clear and be affirmed in some ways and denied in others, and so cleared up, even though a certain vague and worshipful portentousness might disappear from the notion of it in the process.

For instance, one practical result that follows when we have one thing to handle, is that we can pass from one part of it to another without letting go of the thing. In this sense oneness must be partly denied and partly affirmed of our universe. Physically we can pass continuously in various manners from one part of it to another part. But logically and psychically the passage seems less easy, for there is no obvious transition from one mind to another, or from minds to physical things. You have to step off and get on again; so that in these ways the world is not one, as measured by that practical test.

Another practical meaning of oneness is susceptibility of collection. A collection is one, though the things that compose it be many. Now, can we practically "collect" the universe? Physically, of course we cannot. And mentally we cannot, if we take it concretely in its details. But if we take it summarily and abstractly, then we collect it mentally whenever we refer to it, even as I do now when I fling the term "universe" at it, and so seem to leave a mental ring around it. It is plain, however, that such abstract noetic unity (as one might call it) is practically an extremely insignificant thing.

Again, oneness may mean generic sameness, so that you can treat all parts of the collection by one rule and get the same results. It is evident that in this sense the oneness of our world is incomplete, for in spite of much generic sameness in its elements and items, they still remain of many irreducible kinds. You can't pass by mere logic all over the field of it.

Its elements have, however, an affinity or commensurability with each other, are not wholly irrelevant, but can be compared, and fit together after certain fashions. This again might practically mean that they were one *in origin,* and that, tracing them backwards, we should find them arising in a single primal causal fact. Such unity of origin would have definite practical consequences, would have them for our scientific life at least.

I can give only these hasty superficial indications of what I mean when I say that it tends to clear up the quarrel between monism and pluralism to subject the notion of unity to such practical tests. On the other hand, it does but perpetuate strife and misunderstanding to continue talking of it in an absolute and mystical way. I have little doubt myself that this old quarrel might be completely smoothed out to the satisfaction of all claimants, if only the maxim of Peirce were methodically followed here. The current monism on the whole still keeps talking in too abstract a way. It says the world must be either pure disconnectedness, no universe at all, or absolute unity. It insists that there is no stopping-place half way. Any connection whatever, says this monism, is only possible if there be still more connection, until at last we are driven to admit the absolutely total connection required. But this absolutely total connection either means nothing, is the mere word "one" spelt long; or else it means the sum of all the partial connections that can possibly be conceived. I believe that when we thus attack the question, and set ourselves to search for these possible connections, and conceive each in a definite practical way, the dispute is already in a fair way to be settled beyond the chance of misunderstanding, by a compromise in which the Many and the One both get their lawful rights.

But I am in danger of becoming technical; so I must stop right here, and let you go.

I am happy to say that it is the English-speaking philosophers who first introduced the custom of interpreting the meaning of conceptions by asking what difference they make for life. Mr. Peirce has only expressed in the form of an explicit maxim what their sense for reality led them all instinctively to do. The great English way of investigating a conception is to ask yourself right off, "What is it *known as?* In what facts does it result? What is its *cash-value,* in terms of particular experience? and what special difference would come into the world according as it were true or false?" Thus does Locke treat the conception of personal identity. What you mean by it is just your chain of memories, says he. That is the only concretely verifiable part of its significance. All further ideas about it, such as the oneness or manyness of the spiritual substance on which it is based, are therefore void of intelligible meaning; and propositions touching such ideas may be indifferently affirmed or denied. So Berkeley with his "matter." The cash-value of matter is our physical sensations. That is what it is known as, all that we concretely verify of its conception. That therefore is the whole meaning of the word "matter"—any other pretended meaning is mere wind of words. Hume does the same thing with causation. It is known as habitual antecedence, and tendency on our part to look for something definite to come. Apart from this practical meaning it has no significance whatever, and books about it may be committed to the flames, says Hume. Stewart and Brown, James Mill, John Mill, and Bain, have followed more or less consistently the same method; and Shadworth Hodgson has used it almost as explicitly as Mr. Peirce. These writers have many of them no doubt been too sweeping in their negations; Hume, in particular, and James Mill, and Bain. But when all is said and done, it was they, not Kant, who introduced "the critical method" into philosophy, the one method fitted to make philosophy a study worthy of serious men. For what seriousness can possibly remain in debating philosophic propositions that will never make an appreciable difference to us in action? And what matters it, when all propositions are practically meaningless, which of them be called true or false?

The shortcomings and the negations and baldnesses of the English philosophers in question come, not from their eye to merely practical results, but solely from their failure to track the practical results completely enough to see how far they extend. Hume can be corrected and built out, and his beliefs enriched, by using Humian principles exclusively, and without making any use of the circuitous and ponderous artificialities of Kant. It is indeed a somewhat pathetic matter, as it seems to me, that this is not the course which the actual history of philosophy has followed. Hume had no English successors of adequate ability to complete him and correct his negations; so it happened, as a matter of fact, that the building out of critical philosophy has mainly been left to thinkers who were under the influence of Kant. Even in England and this country it is with Kantian catch-words and categories that the fuller view of life is pursued, and in our universities it is the courses in transcendentalism that kindle the enthusiasm of the more ardent students, whilst the courses in English philosophy are committed to a secondary place. I cannot think that this is exactly as it should be. And I say this not out of national jingoism, for jingoism has no place in philosophy; or out of excitement over the great Anglo-American alliance against the world, of which we nowadays hear so much—though heaven knows that to that alliance I wish a God-speed. I say it because I sincerely believe that the English spirit in philosophy is intellectually, as well as practically and morally, on the saner, sounder, and truer path. Kant's mind is the rarest and most intricate of all possible antique bric-à-brac museums, and connoisseurs and dilettanti will always wish to visit it and see the wondrous and racy contents. The temper of the dear old man about his work is perfectly delectable. And yet he is really—although I shrink with some terror from saying such a thing before some of you here present—at bottom a mere curio, a "specimen." I mean by this a perfectly definite thing: I believe that Kant bequeaths to us not one single conception which is both indispensable to philosophy and which philosophy either did not possess before him, or was not destined inevitably to acquire after him through the growth of men's reflection upon the hypotheses by which science interprets nature. The true line of philosophic progress lies, in short, it seems to me, not so much *through* Kant as *round* him to the point where now we stand. Philosophy can perfectly well outflank him, and build herself up into adequate fulness by prolonging more directly the older English lines.

May I hope, as I now conclude, and release your attention from the strain to which you have so kindly put it on my behalf, that on this wonderful Pacific Coast, of which our race is taking possession, the principle of practicalism, in which I have tried so hard to interest you, and with it the whole English tradition in philosophy, will come to its rights, and in your hands help the rest of us in our struggle towards the light.

THE PRESENT DILEMMA IN PHILOSOPHY*

In the preface to that admirable collection of essays of his called 'Heretics,' Mr. Chesterton writes these words: "There are some people—and I am one of them—who think that the most practical and important thing about a man is still his view of the universe. We think that for a landlady considering a lodger it is important to know his income, but still more important to know his philosophy. We think that for a general about to fight an enemy it is important to know the enemy's numbers, but still more important to know the enemy's philosophy. We think the question is not whether the theory of the cosmos affects matters, but whether in the long run anything else affects them."

I think with Mr. Chesterton in this matter. I know that you, ladies and gentlemen, have a philosophy, each and all of you, and that the most interesting and important thing about you is the way in which it determines the perspective in your several worlds. You know the same of me. And yet I confess to a certain tremor at the audacity of the enterprise which I am about to begin. For the philosophy which is so important in each of us is not a technical matter; it is our more or less dumb sense of what life honestly and deeply means. It is only partly got from books; it is our individual way of just seeing and feeling the total push and pressure of the cosmos. I have no right to assume that many of you are students of the cosmos in the classroom sense, yet here I stand desirous of interesting you in a philosophy which to no small extent has to be technically treated. I wish to fill you with sympathy with a contemporaneous tendency in which I profoundly believe, and yet I have to talk like a professor to you who are not stu-

* From: Pragm., 3–40.

dents. Whatever universe a professor believes in must at any rate be a universe that lends itself to lengthy discourse. A universe definable in two sentences is something for which the professorial intellect has no use. No faith in anything of that cheap kind! I have heard friends and colleagues try to popularize philosophy in this very hall, but they soon grew dry, and then technical, and the results were only partially encouraging. So my enterprise is a bold one. The founder of pragmatism himself recently gave a course of lectures at the Lowell Institute with that very word in its title,—flashes of brilliant light relieved against Cimmerian darkness! None of us, I fancy, understood *all* that he said —yet here I stand, making a very similar venture.

I risk it because the very lectures I speak of *drew*—they brought good audiences. There is, it must be confessed, a curious fascination in hearing deep things talked about, even though neither we nor the disputants understand them. We get the problematic thrill, we feel the presence of the vastness. Let a controversy begin in a smoking-room anywhere, about free-will or God's omniscience, or good and evil, and see how every one in the place pricks up his ears. Philosophy's results concern us all most vitally, and philosophy's queerest arguments tickle agreeably our sense of subtlety and ingenuity.

Believing in philosophy myself devoutly, and believing also that a kind of new dawn is breaking upon us philosophers, I feel impelled, *per fas aut nefas,* to try to impart to you some news of the situation.

Philosophy is at once the most sublime and the most trivial of human pursuits. It works in the minutest crannies and it opens out the widest vistas. It 'bakes no bread,' as has been said, but it can inspire our souls with courage; and repugnant as its manners, its doubting and challenging, its quibbling and dialectics, often are to common people, no one of us can get along without the far-flashing beams of light it sends over the world's perspectives. These illuminations at least, and the contrast-effects of darkness and mystery that accompany them, give to what it says an interest that is much more than professional.

The history of philosophy is to a great extent that of a certain clash of human temperaments. Undignified as such a treatment may seem to some of my colleagues, I shall have to take account of this clash and explain a good many of the divergencies of philosophers by it. Of whatever temperament a professional philosopher is, he tries, when philosophizing, to sink the fact of his temperament. Temperament is no conventionally recognized reason, so he urges impersonal reasons only for his conclusions. Yet his temperament really gives him a stronger bias than any of his more strictly objective premises. It loads the evidence for him one way or the other, making for a more sentimental or a more hard-hearted view of the universe, just as this fact or that principle would. He *trusts* his temperament. Wanting a universe that suits it, he believes in any representation of the universe that does suit it. He feels men of opposite temper to be out of key with the world's character, and in his heart considers them incompetent and 'not in it,' in the philosophic business, even though they may far excel him in dialectical ability.

Yet in the forum he can make no claim, on the bare ground of his temperament, to superior discernment or authority. There arises thus a certain insincerity in our philosophic discussions: the potentest of all our premises is never mentioned. I am sure it would contribute to clearness if in these lectures we should break this rule and mention it, and I accordingly feel free to do so.

Of course I am talking here of very positively marked men, men of radical idiosyncracy, who have set their stamp and likeness on philosophy and figure in its history. Plato, Locke, Hegel, Spencer, are such temperamental thinkers. Most of us have, of course, no very definite intellectual temperament, we are a mixture of opposite ingredients, each one present very moderately. We hardly know our own preferences in abstract matters; some of us are easily talked out of them, and end by following the fashion or taking up with the beliefs of the most impressive philosopher in our neighborhood, whoever he may be. But the one thing that has *counted* so far in philosophy is that a man should *see* things, see them straight in his own peculiar way, and be dissatisfied with any opposite way of seeing them. There is no reason to suppose that this strong temperamental vision is from now onward to count no longer in the history of man's beliefs.

Now the particular difference of temperament that I have in mind in making these remarks is one that has counted in literature, art, government, and manners as well as in philosophy. In manners we find formalists and free-and-easy persons. In government, authoritarians and anarchists. In literature, purists or academicals, and realists. In art, classics and romantics. You recognize these contrasts as familiar; well, in philosophy we have a very similar contrast expressed in the pair of terms 'rationalist' and 'empiricist,' 'empiricist' meaning your lover of facts in all their crude variety, 'rationalist' meaning your devotee to abstract and eternal principles. No one can live an hour without both facts and principles, so it is a difference rather of emphasis; yet it breeds antipathies of the most pungent character between those who lay the emphasis differently; and we shall find it extraordinarily convenient to express a certain contrast in men's ways of taking their universe, by talking of the 'empiricist' and of the 'rationalist' temper. These terms make the contrast simple and massive.

More simple and massive than are usually the men of whom the terms are predicated. For every sort of permutation and combination is possible in human nature; and if I now proceed to define more fully what I have in mind when I speak of rationalists and empiricists, by adding to each of those titles some secondary qualifying characteristics, I beg you to regard my conduct as to a certain extent arbitrary. I select types of combination that nature offers very frequently, but by no means uniformly, and I select them solely for their convenience in helping me to my ulterior purpose of characterizing pragmatism. Historically we find the terms 'intellectualism' and 'sensationalism' used as synonyms of 'rationalism' and 'empiricism.' Well, nature seems to combine most frequently with intellectualism an idealistic and optimistic tendency. Empiricists on the other hand are not uncommonly materialistic, and their optimism is apt to be decidedly conditional and tremulous. Rationalism is always monistic. It starts from wholes and universals, and makes much of the unity of things. Empiricism starts from the parts, and makes of the whole a collection—is not averse therefore to calling itself pluralistic. Rationalism usually considers itself more religious than empiricism, but there is much to say about this claim, so I merely mention it. It is a true claim when the individual rationalist is what is called a man of feeling, and when the individual empiricist prides himself on being hard-headed. In that case the rationalist will usually also be in favor of what is called free-will, and the empiricist will be a fatalist—I use the term most popularly current. The rationalists finally will be of dogmatic temper in his affirmations, while the empiricist may be more sceptical and open to discussion.

I will write these traits down in two columns. I think you will practically recognize the two types of mental make-up that I mean if I head the columns by the titles 'tender-minded' and 'tough-minded' respectively.

THE TENDER-MINDED.	THE TOUGH-MINDED.
Rationalistic (going by 'principles'),	Empiricist (going by 'facts'),
Intellectualistic,	Sensationalistic,
Idealistic,	Materialistic,
Optimistic,	Pessimistic,
Religious,	Irreligious,
Free-willist,	Fatalistic,
Monistic,	Pluralistic,
Dogmatical.	Sceptical.

Pray postpone for a moment the question whether the two contrasted mixtures which I have written down are each inwardly coherent and self-consistent or not—I shall very soon have a good deal to say on that point. It suffices for our immediate purpose that tender-minded and tough-minded people, characterized as I have written them down, do both exist. Each of you probably knows some well-marked example of each type, and you know what each example thinks of the example on the other side of the line. They have a low opinion of each other. Their antagonism, whenever as individuals their temperaments have been intense, has formed in all ages a part of the philosophic atmosphere of the time. It forms a part of the philosophic atmosphere to-day. The tough think of the tender as sentimentalists and soft-heads. The tender feel the tough to be unrefined, callous, or brutal. Their mutual reaction is very much like that that takes place when Bostonian tourists mingle with a population like that of Cripple Creek. Each type believes the other to be inferior to itself; but disdain in the one case is mingled with amusement, in the other it has a dash of fear.

Now, as I have already insisted, few of us are tender-foot Bostonians pure and simple, and few are typical Rocky Mountain toughs, in philosophy. Most of us have a hankering for the good things on both sides of the line. Facts are good, of course—give us lots of facts. Principles are good—give us plenty of principles. The world is indubitably one if you look at in one way, but as indubitably is it many, if you look at it in another. It is both one and many—let us adopt a sort of pluralistic monism. Everything of course is necessarily determined, and yet of course our wills are free: a sort of free-will determinism is the true philosophy. The evil of the parts is undeniable, but the whole can't be evil: so practical pessimism may be combined with metaphysical optimism. And so forth—your ordinary philosophic layman never being a radical, never straightening out his system, but living vaguely in one plausible compartment of it or another to suit the temptations of successive hours.

But some of us are more than mere laymen in philosophy. We are worthy of the name of amateur athletes, and are vexed by too much inconsistency and vacillation in our creed. We cannot preserve a good intellectual conscience so long as we keep mixing incompatibles from opposite sides of the line.

And now I come to the first positively important point which I wish to make. Never were as many men of a decidedly empiricist proclivity in existence as there are at the present day. Our children, one may say, are almost born scientific. But our esteem for facts has not neutralized in us all religiousness. It is itself almost religious. Our scientific temper is devout. Now take a man of this type, and let him be also a philosophic amateur, unwilling to mix a hodge-podge system after the fashion of a common layman, and what does he find his situation to be, in this blessed year of our Lord 1906? He wants facts; he wants science; but he also wants a religion. And being an amateur and not an independent originator in philosophy he naturally looks for guidance to the experts and professionals whom he finds already in the field. A very large number of you here present, possibly a majority of you, are amateurs of just this sort.

Now what kinds of philosophy do you find actually offered to meet your need? You find an empirical philosophy that is not religious enough, and a religious philosophy that is not empirical enough for your purpose. If you look to the quarter where facts are most considered you find the whole tough-minded program in operation, and the 'conflict between science and religion' in full blast. Either it is that Rocky Mountain tough of a Haeckel with his materialistic monism, his ether-god and his jest at your God as a 'gaseous vertebrate'; or it is Spencer treating the world's history as a redistribution of matter and motion solely, and bowing religion politely out at the front door:— she may indeed continue to exist, but she must never show her face inside the temple.

For a hundred and fifty years past the progress of science has seemed to mean the enlargement of the material universe and the diminution of man's importance. The result is what one may call the growth of naturalistic or positivistic feeling. Man is no lawgiver to nature, he is an absorber. She it is who stands firm; he it is who must accommodate himself. Let him record truth, inhuman though it be, and submit to it! The romantic spontaneity and courage are gone, the vision is materialistic and depressing. Ideals appear as inert by-products of physiology; what is higher is explained by what is lower and treated forever as a case of 'nothing but'—nothing but something else of a quite inferior sort. You get, in short, a materialistic universe, in which only the tough-minded find themselves congenially at home.

If now, on the other hand, you turn to the religious quarter for consolation, and take counsel of the tender-minded philosophies, what do you find?

Religious philosophy in our day and generation is, among us English-reading people, of two main types. One of these is more radical and aggressive, the other has more the air of fighting a slow retreat. By the more radical wing of religious philosophy I mean the so-called transcendental idealism of the Anglo-Hegelian school, the philosophy of such men as Green, the Cairds, Bosanquet, and Royce. This philosophy has greatly influenced the more studious members of our protestant ministry. It is pantheistic, and undoubtedly it has already blunted the edge of the traditional theism in protestantism at large.

That theism remains, however. It is the lineal descendant, through one stage of concession after another, of the dogmatic scholastic theism still taught rigorously in the seminaries of the catholic church. For a long time it used to be called among us the philosophy of the Scottish school. It is what I meant by the philosophy that has the air of fighting a slow retreat. Between the encroachments of the hegelians and other philosophers of the 'Absolute,' on the one hand, and those of the scientific evolutionists and agnostics, on the other, the men that give us this kind of a philosophy, James Martineau, Professor Bowne, Professor Ladd and others, must feel themselves rather tightly squeezed. Fair-minded and candid as you like, this philosophy is not radical in temper. It is eclectic, a thing of compromises, that seeks a *modus vivendi* above all things. It accepts the facts of Darwinism, the facts of cerebral physiology, but it does nothing active or enthusiastic with them. It lacks the victorious and aggressive note. It lacks *prestige* in consequence; whereas absolutism has a certain *prestige* due to the more radical style of it.

These two systems are what you have to choose between if you turn to the tender-minded school. And if you are the lovers of facts I have supposed you to be, you find the trail of the serpent of rationalism, of intellectualism, over everything that lies on that side of the line. You escape indeed the materialism that goes with the reigning empiricism; but you pay for your escape by losing contact with the concrete parts of life. The more absolutistic philosophers dwell on so high a level of abstraction that they never even try to come down. The absolute mind which they offer us, the mind that makes our universe by thinking it, might, for aught they show us to the contrary, have made any one of a million other universes just as well as this. You can deduce no single actual particular from the notion of it. It is compatible with any state of things whatever being true here below. And the theistic God is almost as sterile a principle. You have to go to the world which he has created to get any inkling of his actual character: he is the kind of god that has once for all made that kind of a world. The God of the theistic writers lives on as purely abstract heights as does the Absolute. Absolutism has a certain sweep and dash about it, while the usual theism is more insipid, but both are equally remote and vacuous. What *you* want is a philosophy that will not only exercise your powers of intellectual abstraction, but that will make some positive connexion with this actual world of finite human lives.

You want a system that will combine both things, the scientific loyalty to facts and willingness to take account of them, the spirit of adaptation and accommodation, in short, but also the old confidence in human values and the resultant spontaneity, whether of the religious or of the romantic type. And this is then your dilemma: you find the two parts of your *quaesitum* hopelessly separated. You find empiricism with inhumanism and irreligion; or else you find a rationalistic philosophy that indeed may call itself religious, but that keeps out of all definite touch with concrete facts and joys and sorrows.

I am not sure how many of you live close enough to philosophy to realize fully what I mean by this last reproach, so I will dwell a little longer on that unreality in all rationalistic systems by which your serious believer in facts is so apt to feel repelled.

I wish that I had saved the first couple of pages of a thesis which a student handed me a year or two ago. They illustrated my point so clearly that I am sorry I can not read them to you now. This young man, who was a graduate of some Western college, began by saying that he had always taken for granted that when you entered a philosophic classroom you had to open relations with a universe entirely distinct from the one you left behind you in the street. The two were supposed, he said, to have so little to do with each other, that you could not possibly occupy your mind with them at the same time. The world of concrete personal experiences to which the street belongs is multitudinous beyond imagination, tangled, muddy, painful and perplexed. The world to which your philosophy-professor introduces you is simple, clean and noble. The contradictions of real life are absent from it. Its architecture is classic. Principles of reason trace its outlines, logical necessities cement its parts. Purity and dignity are what it most expresses. It is a kind of marble temple shining on a hill.

In point of fact it is far less an account of this actual world than a clear addition built upon it, a classic sanctuary in which the rationalist fancy may take refuge from the intolerably confused and gothic character which mere facts present. It is no *explanation* of our concrete universe, it is another thing altogether, a substitute for it, a remedy, a way of escape.

Its temperament, if I may use the word temperament here, is utterly alien to the temperament of existence in the concrete. *Refinement* is what characterizes our intellectualist philosophies. They exquisitely satisfy that craving for a refined object of contemplation which is so powerful an appetite of the mind. But I ask you in all seriousness to look abroad on this colossal universe of concrete facts, on their awful bewilderments, their surprises and cruelties, on the wildness which they show, and then to tell me whether 'refined' is the one inevitable descriptive adjective that springs to your lips.

Refinement has its place in things, true enough. But a philosophy that breathes out nothing but refinement will never satisfy the empiricist temper of mind. It will seem rather a monument of artificiality. So we find men of science preferring to turn their backs on metaphysics as on something altogether cloistered and spectral, and practical men shaking philosophy's dust off their feet and following the call of the wild.

Truly there is something a little ghastly in the satisfaction with which a pure but unreal system will fill a rationalist mind. Leibnitz was a rationalist mind, with infinitely more interest in facts than most rationalist minds can show. Yet if you wish for superficiality incarnate, you have only to read that charmingly written 'Théodicée' of his, in which he sought to justify the ways of God to man, and to prove that the world we live in is the best of possible worlds. Let me quote a specimen of what I mean.

Among other obstacles to his optimistic philosophy, it falls to Leibnitz to consider the number of the eternally damned. That it is infinitely greater, in our human case, than that of those saved, he assumes as a premise from the theologians, and then proceeds to argue in this way. Even then, he says:

"The evil will appear as almost nothing in comparison with the good, if we once consider the real magnitude of the City of God. Coelius Secundus Curio has written a little book, 'De Amplitudine Regni Coelestis,' which was reprinted not long ago. But he failed to compass the extent of the kingdom of the heavens. The ancients had small ideas of the works of God. . . . It seemed to them that only our earth had inhabitants, and even the notion of our antipodes gave them pause. The rest of the world for them consisted of some shining globes and a few crystalline spheres. But to-day, whatever be the limits that we may grant or refuse to the Universe we must recognize in it a countless number of globes, as big as ours or bigger, which have just as much right as it has to support rational inhabitants, tho it does not follow that these need all be men. Our earth is only one among the six principal satellites of our sun. As all the fixed stars are suns, one sees how small a place among visible things our earth takes up, since it is only a satellite of one among them. Now all these suns *may* be inhabited by none but happy creatures; and nothing obliges us to believe that the number of damned persons is very great; for *a very few instances and samples suffice for the utility which good draws from evil.* Moreover, since there is no reason to suppose that there are stars everywhere, may there not be a great space beyond the region of the stars? And this immense space, surrounding all this region, . . . may be replete with happiness and glory. . . . What now becomes of the consideration of our Earth and of its denizens? Does it not dwindle to something incomparably less than a physical point, since our Earth is but a point compared with the distance of the fixed stars. Thus the part of the Universe which we know, being almost lost in nothingness compared with that which is unknown to us, but which we are yet obliged to admit; and all the evils that we know lying in this almost-nothing; it follows that the evils may be almost-nothing in comparison with the goods that the Universe contains."

Leibnitz continues elsewhere:

"There is a kind of justice which aims neither at the amendment of the criminal, nor at furnishing an example to others, nor at the reparation of the injury. This justice is founded in pure fitness, which finds a certain satisfaction in the expiation of a wicked deed. The Socinians and Hobbes objected to this punitive justice, which is properly vindictive justice, and which God has reserved for himself at many junctures. . . . . It is always founded in the fitness of things, and satisfies not only the offended party, but all wise lookers-on, even as beautiful music or a fine piece of architecture satisfies a well-constituted mind. It is thus that the torments of the damned continue, even tho they serve no longer to turn any one away from sin, and that the rewards of the blest continue, even tho they confirm no one in good ways. The damned draw to themselves ever new penalties by their continuing sins, and the blest attract ever fresh joys by their unceasing progress in good. Both facts are founded on the principle of fitness, . . . for God has made all things harmonious in perfection as I have already said."

Leibnitz's feeble grasp of reality is too obvious to need comment from me. It is evident that no realistic image of the experience of a damned soul had ever approached the portals of his mind. Nor had it occurred to him that the smaller is the number of 'samples' of the genus 'lost-soul' whom God throws as a sop to the eternal fitness, the more unequitably grounded is the glory of the blest. What he gives us is a cold literary exercise, whose cheerful substance even hell-fire does not warm.

And do not tell me that to show the shallowness of rationalist philosophizing I have had to go back to a shallow wigpated age. The optimism of present-day rationalism sounds just as shallow to the fact-loving mind. The actual universe is a thing wide open, but rationalism makes systems, and systems must be closed. For men in practical life perfection is something far off and still in process of achievement. This for rationalism is but the illusion of the finite and relative: the absolute ground of things is a perfection eternally complete.

I find a fine example of revolt against the airy and shallow optimism of current religious philosophy in a publication of that valiant anarchistic writer Morrison I. Swift. Mr. Swift's anarchism goes a little farther than mine does, but I confess that I sympathize a good deal, and some of you, I know, will sympathize heartily with his dissatisfaction with the idealistic optimisms now in vogue. He begins his pamphlet on 'Human Submission' with a series of city reporter's items from newspapers (suicides, deaths from starvation, and the like) as specimens of our civilized régime. For instance:

"After trudging through the snow from one end of the city to the other in the vain hope of securing employment, and with his wife and six children without food and ordered to leave their home in an upper

east-side tenement-house because of non-payment of rent, John Corcoran, a clerk, to-day ended his life by drinking carbolic acid. Corcoran lost his position three weeks ago through illness, and during the
period of idleness his scanty savings disappeared. Yesterday he obtained work with a gang of city snow-shovelers, but he was too weak
from illness, and was forced to quit after an hour's trial with the
shovel. Then the weary task of looking for employment was again
resumed. Thoroughly discouraged, Corcoran returned to his home last
night to find his wife and children without food and the notice of
dispossession on the door. On the following morning he drank the
poison.

"The records of many more such cases lie before me [Mr. Swift
goes on]; an encyclopedia might easily be filled with their kind. These
few I cite as an interpretation of the Universe. 'We are aware of the
presence of God in his world,' says a writer in a recent English review.
[The very presence of ill in the temporal order is the condition of the
perfection of the eternal order, writes Professor Royce (The World
and the Individual, ii, 385).] 'The Absolute is the richer for every
discord and for all the diversity which it embraces,' says F. H. Bradley
(Appearance and Reality, 204). He means that these slain men
make the universe richer, and that is philosophy. But while Professors
Royce and Bradley and a whole host of guileless thoroughfed thinkers
are unveiling Reality and the Absolute and explaining away evil and
pain, this is the condition of the only beings known to us anywhere in
the universe with a developed consciousness of what the universe is.
What these people experience *is* Reality. It gives us an absolute phase
of the universe. It is the personal experience of those best qualified in
our circle of knowledge to *have* experience, to tell us *what is*. Now
what does *thinking about* the experience of these persons come to,
compared to directly and personally feeling it as they feel it? The
philosophers are dealing in shades, while those who live and feel know
truth. And the mind of mankind—not yet the mind of philosophers
and of the proprietary class—but of the great mass of the silently
thinking men and feeling men, is coming to this view. They are judging the universe as they have hitherto permitted the hierophants of
religion and learning to judge *them*. . . .

"This Cleveland workingman, killing his children and himself
[another of the cited cases] is one of the elemental stupendous facts
of this modern world and of this universe. It cannot be glozed over or
minimized away by all the treatises on God, and Love, and Being,
helplessly existing in their monumental vacuity. This is one of the
simple irreducible elements of this world's life, after millions of years
of opportunity and twenty centuries of Christ. It is in the mental
world what atoms or sub-atoms are in the physical, primary, inde-

structible. And what it blazons to man is the imposture of all philosophy which does not see in such events the consummate factor of all conscious experience. These facts invincibly prove religion a nullity. Man will not give religion two thousand centuries or twenty centuries more to try itself and waste human time. Its time is up; its probation is ended; its own record ends it. Mankind has not æons and eternities to spare for trying out discredited systems." [12]

Such is the reaction of an empiricist mind upon the rationalist bill of fare. It is an absolute 'No, I thank you.' 'Religion,' says Mr. Swift, 'is like a sleep-walker to whom actual things are blank.' And such, tho possibly less tensely charged with feeling, is the verdict of every seriously inquiring amateur in philosophy to-day who turns to the philosophy-professors for the wherewithal to satisfy the fulness of his nature's needs. Empiricist writers give him a materialism, rationalists give him something religious, but to that religion 'actual things are blank.' He becomes thus the judge of us philosophers. Tender or tough, he finds us wanting. None of us may treat his verdicts disdainfully, for after all, his is the typically perfect mind, the mind the sum of whose demands is greatest, the mind whose criticisms and dissatisfactions are fatal in the long run.

It is at this point that my own solution begins to appear. I offer the oddly-named thing pragmatism as a philosophy that can satisfy both kinds of demand. It can remain religious like the rationalisms, but at the same time, like the empiricisms, it can preserve the richest intimacy with facts. I hope I may be able to leave many of you with as favorable an opinion of it as I preserve myself. Yet, as I am near the end of my hour, I will not introduce pragmatism bodily now. I will begin with it on the stroke of the clock next time. I prefer at the present moment to return a little on what I have said.

If any of you here are professional philosophers, and some of you I know to be such, you will doubtless have felt my discourse so far to have been crude in an unpardonable, nay, in an almost incredible degree. Tender-minded and tough-minded, what a barbaric disjunction! And, in general, when philosophy is all compacted of delicate intellectualities and subtleties and scrupulosities, and when every possible sort of combination and transition obtains within its bounds, what a brutal caricature and reduction of highest things to the lowest possible expression is it to represent its field of conflict as a sort of rough-and-tumble fight between two hostile temperaments! What a childishly external view! And again, how stupid it is to treat the abstractness of rationalist systems as a crime, and to damn them because they offer

[12] Morrison I. Swift, *Human Submission*, Part Second, Philadelphia Liberty Press, 1905, pp. 4–10.

themselves as sanctuaries and places of escape, rather than as prolongations of the world of facts. Are not all our theories just remedies and places of escape? And, if philosophy is to be religious, how can she be anything else than a place of escape from the crassness of reality's surface? What better thing can she do than raise us out of our animal senses and show us another and a nobler home for our minds in that great framework of ideal principles subtending all reality, which the intellect divines? How can principles and general views ever be anything but abstract outlines? Was Cologne cathedral built without an architect's plan on paper? Is refinement in itself an abomination? Is concrete rudeness the only thing that's true?

Believe me, I feel the full force of the indictment. The picture I have given is indeed monstrously over-simplified and rude. But like all abstractions, it will prove to have its use. If philosophers can treat the life of the universe abstractly, they must not complain of an abstract treatment of the life of philosophy itself. In point of fact the picture I have given is, however coarse and sketchy, literally true. Temperaments with their cravings and refusals do determine men in their philosophies, and always will. The details of systems may be reasoned out piecemeal, and when the student is working at a system, he may often forget the forest for the single tree. But when the labor is accomplished, the mind always performs its big summarizing act, and the system forthwith stands over against one like a living thing, with that strange simple note of individuality which haunts our memory, like the wraith of the man, when a friend or enemy of ours is dead.

Not only Walt Whitman could write 'who touches this book touches a man.' The books of all the great philosophers are like so many men. Our sense of an essential personal flavor in each one of them, typical but indescribable, is the finest fruit of our own accomplished philosophic education. What the system pretends to be is a picture of the great universe of God. What it is,—and oh so flagrantly!—is the revelation of how intensely odd the personal flavor of some fellow creature is. Once reduced to these terms (and all our philosophies get reduced to them in minds made critical by learning) our commerce with the systems reverts to the informal, to the instinctive human reaction of satisfaction or dislike. We grow as peremptory in our rejection or admission, as when a person presents himself as a candidate for our favor; our verdicts are couched in as simple adjectives of praise or dispraise. We measure the total character of the universe as we feel it, against the flavor of the philosophy proffered us, and one word is enough.

'Statt der lebendigen Natur,' we say, 'da Gott die Menschen schuf hinein,'—that nebulous concoction, that wooden, that straight-laced thing, that crabbed artificiality, that musty schoolroom product, that sick man's dream! Away with it. Away with all of them! Impossible! Impossible!

Our work over the details of his system is indeed what gives us our resultant impression of the philosopher, but it is on the resultant impression itself that we react. Expertness in philosophy is measured by the definiteness of our summarizing reactions, by the immediate perceptive epithet with which the expert hits such complex objects off. But great expertness is not necessary for the epithet to come. Few people have definitely articulated philosophies of their own. But almost every one has his own peculiar sense of a certain total character in the universe, and of the inadequacy fully to match it of the peculiar systems that he knows. They don't just cover *his* world. One will be too dapper, another too pedantic, a third too much of a job-lot of opinions, a fourth too morbid, and a fifth too artificial, or what not. At any rate he and we know off-hand that such philosophies are out of plumb and out of key and out of 'whack,' and have no business to speak up in the universe's name. Plato, Locke, Spinoza, Mill, Caird, Hegel—I prudently avoid names nearer home!—I am sure that to many of you, my hearers, these names are little more than reminders of as many curious personal ways of falling short. It would be an obvious absurdity if such ways of taking the universe were actually true.

We philosophers have to reckon with such feelings on your part. In the last resort, I repeat, it will be by them that all our philosophies shall ultimately be judged. The finally victorious way of looking at things will be the most completely *impressive* way to the normal run of minds.

One word more—namely about philosophies necessarily being abstract outlines. There are outlines and outlines, outlines of buildings that are *fat,* conceived in the cube by their planner, and outlines of buildings invented flat on paper, with the aid of ruler and compass. These remain skinny and emaciated even when set up in stone and mortar, and the outline already suggests that result. An outline in itself is meagre, truly, but it does not necessarily suggest a meagre thing. It is the essential meagreness of *what is suggested* by the usual rationalistic philosophies that moves empiricists to their gesture of rejection. The case of Herbert Spencer's system is much to the point here. Rationalists feel his fearful array of insufficiencies. His dry schoolmaster temperament, the hurdy-gurdy monotony of him, his preference for cheap makeshifts in argument, his lack of education even in mechanical principles, and in general the vagueness of all his fundamental ideas, his whole system wooden, as if knocked together out of cracked hemlock boards—and yet the half of England wants to bury him in Westminster Abbey.

Why? Why does Spencer call out so much reverence in spite of his weakness in rationalistic eyes? Why should so many educated men who feel that weakness, you and I perhaps, wish to see him in the Abbey notwithstanding?

Simply because we feel his heart to be *in the right place* philosophically. His principles may be all skin and bone, but at any rate his books try to mould themselves upon the particular shape of this particular world's carcase. The noise of facts resounds through all his chapters, the citations of fact never cease, he emphasizes facts, turns his face towards their quarter; and that is enough. It means the right *kind* of thing for the empiricist mind.

The pragmatistic philosophy of which I hope to begin talking in my next lecture preserves as cordial a relation with facts, and, unlike Spencer's philosophy, it neither begins nor ends by turning positive religious constructions out of doors—it treats them cordially as well.

I hope I may lead you to find it just the mediating way of thinking that you require.

WHAT PRAGMATISM MEANS*

Some years ago, being with a camping party in the mountains, I returned from a solitary ramble to find every one engaged in a ferocious metaphysical dispute. The *corpus* of the dispute was a squirrel—a live squirrel supposed to be clinging to one side of a tree-trunk; while over against the tree's opposite side a human being was imagined to stand. This human witness tries to get sight of the squirrel by moving rapidly round the tree, but no matter how fast he goes, the squirrel moves as fast in the opposite direction, and always keeps the tree between himself and the man, so that never a glimpse of him is caught. The resultant metaphysical problem now is this: *Does the man go round the squirrel or not?* He goes round the tree, sure enough, and the squirrel is on the tree; but does he go round the squirrel? In the unlimited leisure of the wilderness, discussion had been worn threadbare. Everyone had taken sides, and was obstinate; and the numbers on both sides were even. Each side, when I appeared therefore appealed to me to make it a majority. Mindful of the scholastic adage that whenever you meet a contradiction you must make a distinction, I immediately sought and found one, as follows: "Which party is

* From: Pragm., 43–81.

right," I said, "depends on what you *practically mean* by 'going round' the squirrel. If you mean passing from the north of him to the east, then to the south, then to the west, and then to the north of him again, obviously the man does go round him, for he occupies these successive positions. But if on the contrary you mean being first in front of him, then on the right of him, then behind him, then on his left, and finally in front again, it is quite as obvious that the man fails to go round him, for by the compensating movements the squirrel makes, he keeps his belly turned towards the man all the time, and his back turned away. Make the distinction, and there is no occasion for any farther dispute. You are both right and both wrong according as you conceive the verb 'to go round' in one practical fashion or the other."

Although one or two of the hotter disputants called my speech a shuffling evasion, saying they wanted no quibbling or scholastic hair-splitting, but meant just plain honest English 'round,' the majority seemed to think that the distinction had assuaged the dispute.

I tell this trivial anecdote because it is a peculiarly simple example of what I wish now to speak of as *the pragmatic method*. The pragmatic method is primarily a method of settling metaphysical disputes that otherwise might be interminable. Is the world one or many?—fated or free?—material or spiritual?—here are notions either of which may or may not hold good of the world; and disputes over such notions are unending. The pragmatic method in such cases is to try to interpret each notion by tracing its respective practical consequences. What difference would it practically make to any one if this notion rather than that notion were true? If no practical difference whatever can be traced, then the alternatives mean practically the same thing, and all dispute is idle. Whenever a dispute is serious, we ought to be able to show some practical difference that must follow from one side or the other's being right.

A glance at the history of the idea will show you still better what pragmatism means. The term is derived from the same Greek word πρᾶγμα, meaning action, from which our words 'practice' and 'practical' come. It was first introduced into philosophy by Mr. Charles Peirce in 1878. In an article entitled 'How to Make Our Ideas Clear,' in the 'Popular Science Monthly' for January of that year[13] Mr. Peirce, after pointing out that our beliefs are really rules for action, said that, to develop a thought's meaning, we need only determine what conduct it is fitted to produce: that conduct is for us its sole significance. And the tangible fact at the root of all our thought-distinctions, however subtle, is that there is no one of them so fine as to consist in anything but a possible difference of practice. To attain perfect clearness in our

[13] Translated in the *Revue Philosophique* for January, 1879 (vol. vii).

thoughts of an object, then, we need only consider what conceivable effects of a practical kind the object may involve—what sensations we are to expect from it, and what reactions we must prepare. Our conception of these effects, whether immediate or remote, is then for us the whole of our conception of the object, so far as that conception has positive significance at all.

This is the principle of Peirce, the principle of pragmatism. It lay entirely unnoticed by any one for twenty years, until I, in an address before Professor Howison's philosophical union at the University of California, brought it forward again and made a special application of it to religion. By that date (1898) the times seemed ripe for its reception. The word 'pragmatism' spread, and at present it fairly spots the pages of the philosophic journals. On all hands we find the 'pragmatic movement' spoken of, sometimes with respect, sometimes with contumely, seldom with clear understanding. It is evident that the term applies itself conveniently to a number of tendencies that hitherto have lacked a collective name, and that it has 'come to stay.'

To take in the importance of Peirce's principle, one must get accustomed to applying it to concrete cases. I found a few years ago that Ostwald, the illustrious Leipzig chemist, had been making perfectly distinct use of the principle of pragmatism in his lectures on the philosophy of science, though he had not called it by that name.

"All realities influence our practice," he wrote me, "and that influence is their meaning for us. I am accustomed to put questions to my classes in this way: In what respects would the world be different if this alternative or that were true? If I can find nothing that would become different, then the alternative has no sense."

That is, the rival views mean practically the same thing, and meaning, other than practical, there is for us none. Ostwald in a published lecture gives this example of what he means. Chemists have long wrangled over the inner constitution of certain bodies called 'tautomerous.' Their properties seemed equally consistent with the notion that an instable hydrogen atom oscillates inside of them, or that they are instable mixtures of two bodies. Controversy raged, but never was decided. "It would never have begun," says Ostwald, "if the combatants had asked themselves what particular experimental fact could have been made different by one or the other view being correct. For it would then have appeared that no difference of fact could possibly ensue; and the quarrel was as unreal as if, theorizing in primitive times about the raising of dough by yeast, one party should have invoked a 'brownie,' while another insisted on an 'elf' as the true cause of the phenomenon." [14]

[14] 'Theorie und Praxis,' *Zeitsch. des Oesterreichischen Ingenieur u. Architecten-Vereines*, 1905, Nr. 4 u. 6. I find a still more radical pragmatism

It is astonishing to see how many philosophical disputes collapse into insignificance the moment you subject them to this simple test of tracing a concrete consequence. There can *be* no difference anywhere that does n't *make* a difference elsewhere—no difference in abstract truth that does n't express itself in a difference in concrete fact and in conduct consequent upon that fact, imposed on somebody, somehow, somewhere, and somewhen. The whole function of philosophy ought to be to find out what definite difference it will make to you and me, at definite instants of our life, if this world-formula or that world-formula be the true one.

There is absolutely nothing new in the pragmatic method. Socrates was an adept at it. Aristotle used it methodically. Locke, Berkeley, and Hume made momentous contributions to truth by its means. Shadworth Hodgson keeps insisting that realities are only what they are 'known as.' But these forerunners of pragmatism used it in fragments: they were preluders only. Not until in our time has it generalized itself, become conscious of a universal mission, pretended to a conquering destiny. I believe in that destiny, and I hope I may end by inspiring you with my belief.

Pragmatism represents a perfectly familiar attitude in philosophy, the empiricist attitude, but it represents it, as it seems to me, both in a more radical and in a less objectionable form than it has ever yet assumed. A pragmatist turns his back resolutely and once for all upon a lot of inveterate habits dear to professional philosophers. He turns away from abstraction and insufficiency, from verbal solutions, from bad *a priori* reasons, from fixed principles, closed systems, and pretended absolutes and origins. He turns towards concreteness and adequacy, towards facts, towards action and towards power. That means the empiricist temper regnant and the rationalist temper sincerely given up. It means the open air and possibilities of nature, as against dogma, artificiality, and the pretence of finality in truth.

At the same time it does not stand for any special results. It is a method only. But the general triumph of that method would mean an enormous change in what I called in my last lecture the 'temperament' of philosophy. Teachers of the ultra-rationalistic type would be frozen out, much as the courtier type is frozen out in republics, as the ultramontane type of priest is frozen out in protestant lands. Science and metaphysics would come much nearer together, would in fact work absolutely hand in hand.

---

than Ostwald's in an address by Professor W. S. Franklin: "I think that the sickliest notion of physics, even if a student gets it, is that it is 'the science of masses, molecules, and the ether.' And I think that the healthiest notion, even if a student does not wholly get it, is that physics is the science of the ways of taking hold of bodies and pushing them!" (*Science,* January 2, 1903.)

Metaphysics has usually followed a very primitive kind of quest. You know how men have always hankered after unlawful magic, and you know what a great part in magic *words* have always played. If you have his name, or the formula of incantation that binds him, you can control the spirit, genie, afrite, or whatever the power may be. Solomon knew the names of all the spirits and having their names, he held them subject to his will. So the universe has always appeared to the natural mind as a kind of enigma, of which the key must be sought in the shape of some illuminating or power-bringing word or name. That word names the universe's *principle,* and to possess it is after a fashion to possess the universe itself. 'God,' 'Matter,' 'Reason,' 'the Absolute,' 'Energy,' are so many solving names. You can rest when you have them. You are at the end of your metaphysical quest.

But if you follow the pragmatic method, you cannot look on any such word as closing your quest. You must bring out of each word its practical cash-value, set it at work within the stream of your experience. It appears less as a solution, then, than as a program for more work, and more particularly as an indication of the ways in which existing realities may be *changed.*

Theories thus become instruments, not answers to enigmas, in which we can rest. We don't lie back upon them, we move forward, and, on occasion, make nature over again by their aid. Pragmatism unstiffens all our theories, limbers them up and sets each one at work. Being nothing essentially new, it harmonizes with many ancient philosophic tendencies. It agrees with nominalism for instance, in always appealing to particulars; with utilitarianism in emphasizing practical aspects; with positivism in its disdain for verbal solutions, useless questions and metaphysical abstractions.

All these, you see, are *anti-intellectualist* tendencies. Against rationalism as a pretension and a method pragmatism is fully armed and militant. But, at the outset, at least, it stands for no particular results. It has no dogmas, and no doctrines save its method. As the young Italian pragmatist Papini has well said, it lies in the midst of our theories, like a corridor in a hotel. Innumerable chambers open out of it. In one you may find a man writing an atheistic volume; in the next some one on his knees praying for faith and strength; in a third a chemist investigating a body's properties. In a fourth a system of idealistic metaphysics is being excogitated; in a fifth the impossibility of metaphysics is being shown. But they all own the corridor, and all must pass through it if they want a practicable way of getting into or out of their respective rooms.

No particular results then, so far, but only an attitude of orientation, is what the pragmatic method means. *The attitude of looking away from first things, principles, 'categories,' supposed necessities; and of looking towards last things, fruits, consequences, facts.*

So much for the pragmatic method! You may say that I have been praising it rather than explaining it to you, but I shall presently explain it abundantly enough by showing how it works on some familiar problems. Meanwhile the word pragmatism has come to be used in a still wider sense, as meaning also a certain *theory of truth*. I mean to give a whole lecture to the statement of that theory, after first paving the way, so I can be very brief now. But brevity is hard to follow, so I ask for your redoubled attention for a quarter of an hour. If much remains obscure, I hope to make it clearer in the later lectures.

One of the most successfully cultivated branches of philosophy in our time is what is called inductive logic, the study of the conditions under which our sciences have evolved. Writers on this subject have begun to show a singular unanimity as to what the laws of nature and elements of fact mean, when formulated by mathematicians, physicists and chemists. When the first mathematical, logical, and natural uniformities, the first *laws*, were discovered, men were so carried away by the clearness, beauty and simplification that resulted, that they believed themselves to have deciphered authentically the eternal thoughts of the Almighty. His mind also thundered and reverberated in syllogisms. He also thought in conic sections, squares and roots and ratios, and geometrized like Euclid. He made Kepler's laws for the planets to follow; he made velocity increase proportionally to the time in falling bodies; he made the law of the sines for light to obey when refracted; he established the classes, orders, families and genera of plants and animals, and fixed the distances between them. He thought the archetypes of all things, and devised their variations; and when we rediscover any one of these his wondrous institutions, we seize his mind in its very literal intention.

But as the sciences have developed farther the notion has gained ground that most, perhaps all, of our laws are only approximations. The laws themselves, moreover, have grown so numerous that there is no counting them; and so many rival formulations are proposed in all the branches of science that investigators have become accustomed to the notion that no theory is absolutely a transcript of reality, but that any one of them may from some point of view be useful. Their great use is to summarize old facts and to lead to new ones. They are only a man-made language, a conceptual shorthand, as some one calls them, in which we write our reports of nature; and languages, as is well known, tolerate much choice of expression and many dialects.

Thus human arbitrariness has driven divine necessity from scientific logic. If I mention the names of Sigwart, Mach, Ostwald, Pearson, Milhaud, Poincaré, Duhem, Ruyssen, those of you who are students will easily identify the tendency I speak of, and will think of additional names.

Riding now on the front of this wave of scientific logic Messrs.

Schiller and Dewey appear with their pragmatistic account of what truth everywhere signifies. Everywhere, these teachers say, 'truth' in our ideas and beliefs means the same thing that it means in science. It means, they say, nothing but this, *that ideas (which themselves are but parts of our experience) become true just in so far as they help us to get into satisfactory relation with other parts of our experience,* to summarize them and get about among them by conceptual short-cuts instead of following the interminable succession of particular phenomena. Any idea upon which we can ride, so to speak; any idea that will carry us prosperously from any one part of our experience to any other part, linking things satisfactorily, working securely, simplifying, saving labor; is true for just so much, true in so far forth, true *instrumentally.* This is the 'instrumental' view of truth taught so successfully at Chicago, the view that truth in our ideas means their power to 'work,' promulgated so brilliantly at Oxford.

Messrs. Dewey, Schiller and their allies, in reaching this general conception of all truth, have only followed the example of geologists, biologists and philologists. In the establishment of these other sciences, the successful stroke was always to take some simple process actually observable in operation—as denudation by weather, say, or variation from parental type, or change of dialect by incorporation of new words and pronunciations—and then to generalize it, making it apply to all times, and produce great results by summating its effects through the ages.

The observable process which Schiller and Dewey particularly singled out for generalization is the familiar one by which any individual settles into *new opinions*. The process here is always the same. The individual has a stock of old opinions already, but he meets a new experience that puts them to a strain. Somebody contradicts them; or in a reflective moment he discovers that they contradict each other; or he hears of facts with which they are incompatible; or desires arise in him which they cease to satisfy. The result is an inward trouble to which his mind till then had been a stranger, and from which he seeks to escape by modifying his previous mass of opinions. He saves as much of it as he can, for in this matter of belief we are all extreme conservatives. So he tries to change first this opinion, and then that (for they resist change very variously), until at last some new idea comes up which he can graft upon the ancient stock with a minimum of disturbance of the latter, some idea that mediates between the stock and the new experience and runs them into one another most felicitously and expediently.

This new idea is then adopted as the true one. It preserves the older stock of truths with a minimum of modification, stretching them just enough to make them admit the novelty, but conceiving that in ways as familiar as the case leaves possible. An *outrée* explanation, violating all our preconceptions, would never pass for a true account of a novelty. We should scratch round industriously till we found something less excentric. The most violent revolutions in an individual's beliefs leave most of his old order standing. Time and space, cause and effect, nature and history, and one's own biography remain untouched. New truth is always a go-between, a smoother-over of transitions. It marries old opinion to new fact so as ever to show a minimum of jolt, a maximum of continuity. We hold a theory true just in proportion to its success in solving this 'problem of maxima and minima.' But success in solving this problem is eminently a matter of approximation. We say this theory solves it on the whole more satisfactorily than that theory; but that means more satisfactorily to ourselves, and individuals will emphasize their points of satisfaction differently. To a certain degree, therefore, everything here is plastic.

The point I now urge you to observe particularly is the part played by the older truths. Failure to take account of it is the source of much of the unjust criticism levelled against pragmatism. Their influence is absolutely controlling. Loyalty to them is the first principle—in most cases it is the only principle; for by far the most usual way of handling phenomena so novel that they would make for a serious rearrangement of our preconception is to ignore them altogether, or to abuse those who bear witness for them.

You doubtless wish examples of this process of truth's growth, and the only trouble is their superabundance. The simplest case of new truth is of course the mere numerical addition of new kinds of facts, or of new single facts of old kinds, to our experience—an addition that involves no alteration in the old beliefs. Day follows day, and its contents are simply added. The new contents themselves are not true, they simply *come* and *are*. Truth is *what we say about* them, and when we say that they have come, truth is satisfied by the plain additive formula.

But often the day's contents oblige a rearrangement. If I should now utter piercing shrieks and act like a maniac on this platform, it would make many of you revise your ideas as to the probable worth of my philosophy. 'Radium' came the other day as part of the day's content, and seemed for a moment to contradict our ideas of the whole order of nature, that order having come to be identified with what is called the conservation of energy. The mere sight of radium paying heat away indefinitely out of its own pocket seemed to violate that conservation. What to think? If the radiations from it were nothing but an escape of unsuspected 'potential' energy, pre-existent inside of the atoms, the principle of conservation would be saved. The discovery of 'helium' as the radiation's outcome, opened a way to this belief.

So Ramsay's view is generally held to be true, because, although it extends our old ideas of energy, it causes a minimum of alteration in their nature.

I need not multiply instances. A new opinion counts as 'true' just in proportion as it gratifies the individual's desire to assimilate the novel in his experience to his beliefs in stock. It must both lean on old truth and grasp new fact; and its successes (as I said a moment ago) in doing this, is a matter for the individual's appreciation. When old truth grows, then, by new truth's addition, it is for subjective reasons. We are in the process and obey the reasons. That new idea is truest which performs most felicitously its function of satisfying our double urgency. It makes itself true, gets itself classed as true, by the way it works; grafting itself then upon the ancient body of truth, which thus grows much as a tree grows by the activity of a new layer of cambium.

Now Dewey and Schiller proceed to generalize this observation and to apply it to the most ancient parts of truth. They also once were plastic. They also were called true for human reasons. They also mediated between still earlier truths and what in those days were novel observations. Purely objective truth, truth in whose establishment the function of giving human satisfaction in marrying previous parts of experience with newer parts played no rôle whatever, is nowhere to be found. The reasons why we call things true is the reason why they *are* true, for 'to be true' *means* only to perform this marriage-function.

The trail of the human serpent is thus over everything. Truth independent; truth that we *find* merely; truth no longer malleable to human need; truth incorrigible, in a word; such truth exists indeed superabundantly—or is supposed to exist by rationalistically minded thinkers; but then it means only the dead heart of the living tree, and its being there means only that truth also has its paleontology, and its 'prescription,' and may grow stiff with years of veteran service and petrified in men's regard by sheer antiquity. But how plastic even the oldest truths nevertheless really are has been vividly shown in our day by the transformation of logical and mathematical ideas, a transformation which seems even to be invading physics. The ancient formulas are reinterpreted as special expressions of much wider principles, principles that our ancestors never got a glimpse of in their present shape and formulation.

Mr. Schiller still gives to all this view of truth the name of 'Humanism,' but, for this doctrine too, the name of pragmatism seems fairly to be in the ascendant, so I will treat it under the name of pragmatism in these lectures.

Such then would be the scope of pragmatism—first, a method; and second, a genetic theory of what is meant by truth. And these two things must be our future topics.

What I have said of the theory of truth will, I am sure, have appeared obscure and unsatisfactory to most of you by reason of its brevity. I shall make amends for that hereafter. In a lecture on 'common sense' I shall try to show what I mean by truths grown petrified by antiquity. In another lecture I shall expatiate on the idea that our thoughts become true in proportion as they successfully exert their go-between function. In a third I shall show how hard it is to discriminate subjective from objective factors in Truth's development. You may not follow me wholly in these lectures; and if you do, you may not wholly agree with me. But you will, I know, regard me at least as serious, and treat my effort with respectful consideration.

You will probably be surprised to learn, then, that Messrs. Schiller's and Dewey's theories have suffered a hailstorm of contempt and ridicule. All rationalism has risen against them. In influential quarters Mr. Schiller, in particular, has been treated like an impudent schoolboy who deserves a spanking. I should not mention this, but for the fact that it throws so much sidelight upon that rationalistic temper to which I have opposed the temper of pragmatism. Pragmatism is uncomfortable away from facts. Rationalism is comfortable only in the presence of abstractions. This pragmatist talk about truths in the plural, about their utility and satisfactoriness, about the success with which they 'work,' etc., suggests to the typical intellectualist mind a sort of coarse lame second-rate makeshift article of truth. Such truths are not real truth. Such tests are merely subjective. As against this, objective truth must be something non-utilitarian, haughty, refined, remote, august, exalted. It must be an absolute correspondence of our thoughts with an equally absolute reality. It must be what we *ought* to think unconditionally. The conditioned ways in which we *do* think are so much irrelevance and matter for psychology. Down with psychology, up with logic, in all this question!

See the exquisite contrast of the types of mind! The pragmatist clings to facts and concreteness, observes truth at its work in particular cases, and generalizes. Truth, for him, becomes a class-name for all sorts of definite working-values in experience. For the rationalist it remains a pure abstraction, to the bare name of which we must defer. When the pragmatist undertakes to show in detail just *why* we must defer, the rationalist is unable to recognize the concretes from which his own abstraction is taken. He accuses us of *denying* truth; whereas we have only sought to trace exactly why people follow it and always ought to follow it. Your typical ultra-abstractionist fairly shudders at concreteness: other things equal, he positively prefers the pale and spectral. If the two universes were offered, he would always choose the skinny outline rather than the rich thicket of reality. It is so much purer, clearer, nobler.

I hope that as these lectures go on, the concreteness and closeness to facts of the pragmatism which they advocate may be what approves itself to you as its most satisfactory peculiarity. It only follows here the example of the sister-sciences, interpreting the unobserved by the observed. It brings old and new harmoniously together. It converts the absolutely empty notion of a static relation of 'correspondence' (what that may mean we must ask later) between our minds and reality, into that of a rich and active commerce (that any one may follow in detail and understand) between particular thoughts of ours, and the great universe of other experiences in which they play their parts and have their uses.

But enough of this at present? The justification of what I say must be postponed. I wish now to add a word in further explanation of the claim I made at our last meeting, that pragmatism may be a happy harmonizer of empiricist ways of thinking with the more religious demands of human beings.

Men who are strongly of the fact-loving temperament, you may remember me to have said, are liable to be kept at a distance by the small sympathy with facts which that philosophy from the present-day fashion of idealism offers them. It is far too intellectualistic. Old fashioned theism was bad enough, with its notion of God as an exalted monarchy, made up of a lot of unintelligible or preposterous 'attributes'; but, so long as it held strongly by the argument from design, it kept some touch with concrete realities. Since, however, darwinism has once for all displaced design from the minds of the 'scientific,' theism has lost that foothold; and some kind of an immanent or pantheistic deity working *in* things rather than above them is, if any, the kind recommended to our contemporary imagination. Aspirants to a philosophic religion turn, as a rule, more hopefully nowadays towards idealistic pantheism than towards the older dualistic theism, in spite of the fact that the latter still counts able defenders.

But, as I said in my first lecture, the brand of pantheism offered is hard for them to assimilate if they are lovers of facts, or empirically minded. It is the absolutistic brand, spurning the dust and reared upon pure logic. It keeps no connexion whatever with concreteness. Affirming the Absolute Mind, which is its substitute for God, to be the rational presupposition of all particulars of fact, whatever they may be, it remains supremely indifferent to what the particular facts in our world actually are. Be they what they may, the Absolute will father them. Like the sick lion in Esop's fable, all footprints lead into his den, but *nulla vestigia retrorsum*. You cannot redescend into the world of particulars by the Absolute's aid, or deduce any necessary consequences of detail important for your life from your idea of his nature. He gives you indeed the assurance that all is well with *Him,* and for his eternal way of thinking; but thereupon he leaves you to be finitely saved by your own temporal devices.

Far be it from me to deny the majesty of this conception, or its capacity to yield religious comfort to a most respectable class of minds. But from the human point of view, no one can pretend that it does n't suffer from the faults of remoteness and abstractness. It is eminently a product of what I have ventured to call the rationalistic temper. It disdains empiricism's needs. It substitutes a pallid outline for the real world's richness. It is dapper, it is noble in the bad sense, in the sense in which to be noble is to be inapt for humble service. In this real world of sweat and dirt, it seems to me that when a view of things is 'noble,' that ought to count as a presumption against its truth, and as a philosophic disqualification. The prince of darkness may be a gentleman, as we are told he is, but whatever the God of earth and heaven is, he can surely be no gentleman. His menial services are needed in the dust of our human trials, even more than his dignity is needed in the empyrean.

Now pragmatism, devoted though she be to facts, has no such materialistic bias as ordinary empiricism labors under. Moreover, she has no objection whatever to the realizing of abstractions, so long as you get about among particulars with their aid and they actually carry you somewhere. Interested in no conclusions but those which our minds and our experiences work out together, she has no *a priori* prejudices against theology. *If theological ideas prove to have a value for concrete life, they will be true, for pragmatism, in the sense of being good for so much. For how much more they are true, will depend entirely on their relations to the other truths that also have to be acknowledged.*

What I said just now about the Absolute, of transcendental idealism, is a case in point. First, I called it majestic and said it yielded religious comfort to a class of minds, and then I accused it of remoteness and sterility. But so far as it affords such comfort, it surely is not sterile; it has that amount of value; it performs a concrete function. As a good pragmatist, I myself ought to call the Absolute true 'in so far forth,' then; and I unhesitatingly now do so.

But what does *true in so far forth* mean in this case? To answer, we need only apply the pragmatic method. What do believers in the Absolute mean by saying that their belief affords them comfort? They mean that since, in the Absolute finite evil is 'overruled' already, we may, therefore, whenever we wish, treat the temporal as if it were potentially the eternal, be sure that we can trust its outcome, and, without sin, dismiss our fear and drop the worry of our finite responsibility. In short, they mean that we have a right ever and anon to take a moral holiday, to let the world wag in its own way, feeling that its issues are in better hands than ours and are none of our business.

The universe is a system of which the individual members may relax their anxieties occasionally, in which the don't-care mood is also right for men, and moral holidays in order,—that, if I mistake not, is part, at least, of what the Absolute is 'known-as,' that is the great difference in our particular experiences which his being true makes, for us, that is his cash-value when he is pragmatically interpreted. Farther than that the ordinary lay-reader in philosophy who thinks favorably of absolute idealism does not venture to sharpen his conceptions. He can use the Absolute for so much, and so much is very precious. He is pained at hearing you speak incredulously of the Absolute, therefore, and disregards your criticisms because they deal with aspects of the conception that he fails to follow.

If the Absolute means this, and means no more than this, who can possibly deny the truth of it? To deny it would be to insist that men should never relax, and that holidays are never in order.

I am well aware how odd it must seem to some of you to hear me say that an idea is 'true' so long as to believe it is profitable to our lives. That it is *good,* for as much as it profits, you will gladly admit. If what we do by its aid is good, you will allow the idea itself to be good in so far forth, for we are the better for possessing it. But is it not a strange misuse of the word 'truth,' you will say, to call ideas also 'true' for this reason?

To answer this difficulty fully is impossible at this stage of my account. You touch here upon the very central point of Messrs. Schiller's, Dewey's and my own doctrine of truth, which I can not discuss with detail until my sixth lecture. Let me now say only this, that truth is *one species of good,* and not, as is usually supposed, a category distinct from good, and co-ordinate with it. *The true is the name of whatever proves itself to be good in the way of belief, and good, too, for definite, assignable reasons.* Surely you must admit this, that if there were *no* good for life in true ideas, or if the knowledge of them were positively disadvantageous and false ideas the only useful ones, then the current notion that truth is divine and precious, and its pursuit a duty, could never have grown up or become a dogma. In a world like that, our duty would be to *shun* truth, rather. But in this world, just as certain foods are not only agreeable to our taste, but good for our teeth, our stomach, and our tissues; so certain ideas are not only agreeable to think about, or agreeable as supporting other ideas that we are fond of, but they are also helpful in life's practical struggles. If there be any life that it is really better we should lead, and if there be any idea which, if believed in, would help us to lead that life, then it would be really *better for us* to believe in that idea, *unless, indeed, belief in it incidentally clashed with other greater vital benefits.*

'What would be better for us to believe'! This sounds very like a definition of truth. It comes very near to saying 'what we *ought* to believe': and in *that* definition none of you would find any oddity. Ought we ever not to believe what it is *better for us* to believe? And can we then keep the notion of what is better for us, and what is true for us, permanently apart?

Pragmatism says no, and I fully agree with her. Probably you also agree, so far as the abstract statement goes, but with a suspicion that if we practically did believe everything that made for good in our own personal lives, we should be found indulging all kinds of fancies about this world's affairs, and all kinds of sentimental superstitions about a world hereafter. Your suspicion here is undoubtedly well founded, and it is evident that something happens when you pass from the abstract to the concrete that complicates the situation.

I said just now that what is better for us to believe is true *unless the belief incidentally clashes with some other vital benefit*. Now in real life what vital benefits is any particular belief of ours most liable to clash with? What indeed except the vital benefits yielded by *other beliefs* when these prove incompatible with the first ones? In other words, the greatest enemy of any one of our truths may be the rest of our truths. Truths have once for all this desperate instinct of self-preservation and of desire to extinguish whatever contradicts them. My belief in the Absolute, based on the good it does me, must run the gauntlet of all my other beliefs. Grant that it may be true in giving me a moral holiday. Nevertheless, as I conceive it,—and let me speak now confidentially, as it were, and merely in my own private person, —it clashes with other truths of mine whose benefits I hate to give up on its account. It happens to be associated with a kind of logic of which I am the enemy, I find that it entangles me in metaphysical paradoxes that are inacceptable, etc., etc. But as I have enough trouble in life already without adding the trouble of carrying these intellectual inconsistencies, I personally just give up the Absolute. I just *take* my moral holidays; or else as a professional philosopher, I try to justify them by some other principle.

If I could restrict my notion of the Absolute to its bare holiday-giving value, it would n't clash with my other truths. But we can not easily thus restrict our hypotheses. They carry supernumerary features, and these it is that clash so. My disbelief in the Absolute means then disbelief in those other supernumerary features, for I fully believe in the legitimacy of taking moral holidays.

You see by this what I meant when I called pragmatism a mediator and reconciler and said, borrowing the word from Papini, that she 'unstiffens' our theories. She has in fact no prejudices whatever, no obstructive dogmas, no rigid canons of what shall count as proof. She is completely genial. She will entertain any hypothesis, she will consider any evidence. It follows that in the religious field she is at a great advantage both over positivistic empiricism, with its anti-theological bias, and other religious rationalism, with its exclusive interest in the remote, the noble, the simple, and the abstract in the way of conception.

In short, she widens the field of search for God. Rationalism sticks to logic and the empyrean. Empiricism sticks to the external senses. Pragmatism is willing to take anything, to follow either logic or the senses and to count the humblest and most personal experiences. She will count mystical experiences if they have practical consequences. She will take a God who lives in the very dirt of private fact—if that should seem a likely place to find him.

Her only test of probable truth is what works best in the way of leading us, what fits every part of life best and combines with the collectivity of experience's demands, nothing being omitted. If theological ideas should do this, if the notion of God, in particular, should prove to do it, how could pragmatism possibly deny God's existence? She could see no meaning in treating as 'not true' a notion that was pragmatically so successful. What other kind of truth could there be, for her, than all this agreement with concrete reality?

In my last lecture I shall return again to the relations of pragmatism with religion. But you see already how democratic she is. Her manners are as various and flexible, her resources as rich and endless, and her conclusions as friendly as those of mother nature.

SOME METAPHYSICAL PROBLEMS PRAGMATICALLY CONSIDERED*

I am now to make the pragmatic method more familiar by giving you some illustrations of its application to particular problems. I will begin with what is driest, and the first thing I shall take will be the problem of *substance*. Every one uses the old distinction between substance and attribute, enshrined as it is in the very structure of human language, in the difference between grammatical subject and predicate. Here is a bit of blackboard crayon. Its modes, attributes, properties, accidents, or affections,—use which term you will,—are whiteness, friability, cylindrical shape, insolubility in water, etc., etc. But the bearer of these attributes is so much *chalk,* which thereupon is

* From: Pragm., 85–123.

called the substance in which they inhere. So the attributes of this desk inhere in the substance 'wood,' those of my coat in the substance 'wool,' and so forth. Chalk, wood and wool, show again, in spite of their differences, common properties, and in so far forth they are themselves counted as modes of a still more primal substance, *matter,* the attributes of which are space-occupancy and impenetrability. Similarly our thoughts and feelings are affections or properties of our several *souls,* which are substances, but again not wholly in their own right, for they are modes of the still deeper substance 'spirit.'

Now it was very early seen that all *we know* of the chalk is the whiteness, friability, etc., all *we know* of the wood is the combustibility and fibrous structure. A group of attributes is what each substance here is known-as, they form its sole cash-value for our actual experience. The substance is in every case revealed through *them;* if we were cut off from *them* we should never suspect its existence; and if God should keep sending them to us in an unchanged order, miraculously annihilating at a certain moment the substance that supported them, we never could detect the moment, for our experiences themselves would be unaltered. Nominalists accordingly adopt the opinion that substance is a spurious idea due to our inveterate human trick of turning names into things. Phenomena come in groups—the chalk-group, the wood-group, etc.,—and each group gets its name. The name we then treat as in a way supporting the group of phenomena. The low thermometer to-day, for instance, is supposed to come from something called the 'climate.' Climate is really only the name for a certain group of days, but it is treated as if it lay *behind* the day, and in general we place the name, as if it were a being, behind the facts it is the name of. But the phenomenal properties of things, nominalists say, surely do not really inhere in names, and if not in names then they do not inhere in anything. They *ad*here, or *co*here, rather, *with each other,* and the notion of a substance inaccessible to us, which we think accounts for such cohesion by supporting it, as cement might support pieces of mosaic, must be abandoned. The fact of the bare cohesion itself is all that the notion of the substance signifies. Behind that fact is nothing.

Scholasticism has taken the notion of substance from common sense and made it very technical and articulate. Few things would seem to have fewer pragmatic consequences for us than substances, cut off as we are from every contact with them. Yet in one case scholasticism has proved the importance of the substance-idea by treating it pragmatically. I refer to certain disputes about the mystery of the Eucharist. Substance here would appear to have momentous pragmatic value. Since the accidents of the wafer don't change in the Lord's supper, and yet it has become the very body of Christ, it must be that the change is in the substance solely. The bread-substance must have been withdrawn, and the divine substance substituted miraculously without altering the immediate sensible properties. But tho these don't alter, a tremendous difference has been made, no less a one than this, that we who take the sacrament, now feed upon the very substance of divinity. The substance-notion breaks into life, then, with tremendous effect, if once you allow that substances can separate from their accidents, and exchange these latter.

This is the only pragmatic application of the substance-idea with which I am acquainted; and it is obvious that it will only be treated seriously by those who already believe in the 'real presence' on independent grounds.

Material substance was criticised by Berkeley with such telling effect that his name has reverberated through all subsequent philosophy. Berkeley's treatment of the notion of matter is so well known as to need hardly more than a mention. So far from denying the external world which we know, Berkeley corroborated it. It was the scholastic notion of a material substance unapproachable by us, *behind* the external world, deeper and more real than it, and needed to support it, which Berkeley maintained to be the most effective of all reducers of the external world to unreality. Abolish that substance, he said, believe that God, whom you can understand and approach, sends you the sensible world directly, and you confirm the latter and back it up by his divine authority. Berkeley's criticism of 'matter' was consequently absolutely pragmatistic. Matter is known as our sensations of colour, figure, hardness and the like. They are the cash-value of the term. The difference matter makes to us by truly being is that we then get such sensations; by not being, is that we lack them. These sensations then are its sole meaning. Berkeley does n't deny matter, then; he simply tells us what it consists of. It is a true name for just so much in the way of sensations.

Locke, and later Hume, applied a similar pragmatic criticism to the notion of *spiritual substance.* I will only mention Locke's treatment of our 'personal identity.' He immediately reduces this notion to its pragmatic value in terms of experience. It means, he says, so much 'consciousness,' namely the fact that at one moment of life we remember other moments, and feel them all as parts of one and the same personal history. Rationalism had explained this practical continuity in our life by the unity of our soul-substance. But Locke says: suppose that God should take away the consciousness, should *we* be any the better for having still the soul-principle? Suppose he annexed the same consciousness to different souls, should *we,* as we realize *ourselves,* be any the worse for that fact? In Locke's day the soul was chiefly a thing to be rewarded or punished. See how Locke, discussing it from this point of view, keeps the question pragmatic:

"Suppose," he says, "one to think himself to be the same *soul* that once was Nestor or Thersites. Can he think their actions his own any more than the actions of any other man that ever existed? But let him once find himself *conscious* of any of the actions of Nestor, he then finds himself the same person with Nestor . . . In this personal identity is founded all the right and justice of reward and punishment. It may be reasonable to think, no one shall be made to answer for what he knows nothing of, but shall receive his doom, his consciousness accusing or excusing. Supposing a man punished now for what he had done in another life, whereof he could be made to have no consciousness at all, what difference is there between that punishment and being created miserable?"

Our personal identity, then, consists, for Locke, solely in pragmatically definable particulars. Whether, apart from these verifiable facts, it also inheres in a spiritual principle, is a merely curious speculation. Locke, compromiser that he was, passively tolerated the belief in a substantial soul behind our consciousness. But his successor Hume, and most empirical psychologists after him, have denied the soul, save as the name for verifiable cohesions in our inner life. They redescend into the stream of experience with it, and cash it into so much small-change value in the way of 'ideas' and their peculiar connexions with each other. As I said of Berkeley's matter, the soul is good or 'true' for just *so much,* but no more.

The mention of material substance naturally suggests the doctrine of 'materialism,' but philosophical materialism is not necessarily knit up with belief in 'matter,' as a metaphysical principle. One may deny matter in that sense, as strongly as Berkeley did, one may be a phenomenalist like Huxley, and yet one may still be a materialist in the wider sense, of explaining higher phenomena by lower ones, and leaving the destinies of the world at the mercy of its blinder parts and forces. It is in this wider sense of the word that materialism is opposed to spiritualism or theism. The laws of physical nature are what run things, materialism says. The highest productions of human genius might be ciphered by one who had complete acquaintance with the facts, out of their physiological conditions, regardless whether nature be there only for our minds, as idealists contend, or not. Our minds in any case would have to record the kind of nature it is, and write it down as operating through blind laws of physics. This is the complexion of present-day materialism, which may better be called naturalism. Over against it stands 'theism,' or what in a wide sense may be termed 'spiritualism.' Spiritualism says that mind not only witnesses and records things, but also runs and operates them: the world being thus guided, not by its lower, but by its higher element.

Treated as it often is, this question becomes little more than a conflict between æsthetic preferences. Matter is gross, coarse, crass, muddy; spirit is pure, elevated, noble; and since it is more consonant with the dignity of the universe to give the primacy in it to what appears superior, spirit must be affirmed as the ruling principle. To treat abstract principles as finalities, before which our intellects may come to rest in a state of admiring contemplation, is the great rationalist failing. Spiritualism, as often held, may be simply a state of admiration for one kind, and of dislike for another kind, of abstraction. I remember a worthy spiritualist professor who always referred to materialism as the 'mud-philosophy,' and deemed it thereby refuted.

To such spiritualism as this there is an easy answer, and Mr. Spencer makes it effectively. In some well-written pages at the end of the first volume of his Psychology he shows us that a 'matter' so infinitely subtle, and performing motions as inconceivably quick and fine as those which modern science postulates in her explanations, has no trace of grossness left. He shows that the conception of spirit, as we mortals hitherto have framed it, is itself too gross to cover the exquisite tenuity of nature's facts. Both terms, he says, are but symbols, pointing to that one unknowable reality in which their oppositions cease.

To an abstract objection an abstract rejoinder suffices; and so far as one's opposition to materialism springs from one's disdain of matter as something 'crass,' Mr. Spencer cuts the ground from under one. Matter is indeed infinitely and incredibly refined. To any one who has ever looked on the face of a dead child or parent the mere fact that matter *could* have taken for a time that precious form, ought to make matter sacred ever after. It makes no difference what the *principle* of life may be, material or immaterial, matter at any rate co-operates, lends itself to all life's purposes. That beloved incarnation was among matter's possibilities.

But now, instead of resting in principles, after this stagnant intellectualist fashion, let us apply the pragmatic method to the question. What do we *mean* by matter? What practical difference can it make *now* that the world should be run by matter or by spirit? I think we find that the problem takes with this a rather different character.

And first of all I call your attention to a curious fact. It makes not a single jot of difference so far as the *past* of the world goes, whether we deem it to have been the work of matter or whether we think a divine spirit was its author.

Imagine, in fact, the entire contents of the world to be once for all irrevocably given. Imagine it to end this very moment, and to have no future; and then let a theist and a materialist apply their rival explanations to its history. The theist shows how a God made it; the materialist shows, and we will suppose with equal success, how it resulted from blind physical forces. Then let the pragmatist be asked to choose between their theories. How can he apply his test if a world is already completed? Concepts for him are things to come back into experience with, things to make us look for differences. But by hypothesis there is to be no more experience and no possible differences can now be looked for. Both theories have shown all their consequences and, by the hypothesis we are adopting, these are identical. The pragmatist must consequently say that the two theories, in spite of their different-sounding names, mean exactly the same thing, and that the dispute is purely verbal. [I am supposing, of course, that the theories *have* been equally successful in their explanations of what is.]

For just consider the case sincerely, and say what would be the *worth* of a God if he *were* there, with his work accomplished and his world run down. He would be worth no more than just that world was worth. To that amount of result, with its mixed merits and defects, his creative power could attain but go no farther. And since there is to be no future; since the whole value and meaning of the world has been already paid in and actualized in the feelings that went with it in the passing, and now go with it in the ending; since it draws no supplemental significance (such as our real world draws) from its function of preparing something yet to come; why then, by it we take God's measure, as it were. He is the Being who could once for all do *that;* and for that much we are thankful to him, but for nothing more. But now, on the contrary hypothesis, namely, that the bits of matter following their laws could make that world and do no less, should we not be just as thankful to them? Wherein should we suffer loss, then, if we dropped God as an hypothesis and made the matter alone responsible? Where would any special deadness, or crassness, come in? And how, experience being what is once for all, would God's presence in it make it any more living or richer?

Candidly, it is impossible to give any answer to this question. The actually experienced world is supposed to be the same in its details on either hypothesis, 'the same, for our praise or blame,' as Browning says. It stands there indefeasibly: a gift which can't be taken back. Calling matter the cause of it retracts no single one of the items that have made it up, nor does calling God the cause augment them. They are the God or the atoms, respectively, of just that and no other world. The God, if there, has been doing just what atoms could do—appearing in the character of atoms, so to speak—and earning such gratitude as is due to atoms, and no more. If his presence lends no different turn or issue to the performance, it surely can lend it no increase of dignity. Nor would indignity come to it were he absent, and did the atoms remain the only actors on the stage. When a play is once over, and the curtain down, you really make it no better by claiming an illustrious genius for its author, just as you make it no worse by calling him a common hack.

Thus if no future detail of experience or conduct is to be deduced from our hypothesis, the debate between materialism and theism becomes quite idle and insignificant. Matter and God in that event mean exactly the same thing—the power, namely, neither more nor less, that could make just this completed world—and the wise man is he who in such a case would turn his back on such a supererogatory discussion. Accordingly, most men instinctively, and positivists and scientists deliberately, do turn their backs on philosophical disputes from which nothing in the line of definite future consequences can be seen to follow. The verbal and empty character of philosophy is surely a reproach with which we are but too familiar. If pragmatism be true, it is a perfectly sound reproach unless the theories under fire can be shown to have alternative practical outcomes, however delicate and distant these may be. The common man and the scientist say they discover no such outcomes, and if the metaphysician can discern none either, the others certainly are in the right of it, as against him. His science is then but pompous trifling; and the endowment of a professorship for such a being would be silly.

Accordingly, in every genuine metaphysical debate some practical issue, however conjectural and remote, is involved. To realize this, revert with me to our question, and place yourselves this time in the world we live in, in the world that *has* a future, that is yet uncompleted whilst we speak. In this unfinished world the alternative of 'materialism or theism?' is intensely practical; and it is worth while for us to spend some minutes of our hour in seeing that it is so.

How, indeed, does the program differ for us, according as we consider that the facts of experience up to date are purposeless configurations of blind atoms moving according to eternal laws, or that on the other hand they are due to the providence of God? As far as the past facts go, indeed, there is no difference. Those facts are in, are bagged, are captured; and the good that's in them is gained, be the atoms or be the God their cause. There are accordingly many materialists about us to-day who, ignoring altogether the future and practical aspects of the question, seek to eliminate the odium attaching to the word materialism, and even to eliminate the word itself, by showing that, if matter could give birth to all these gains, why then matter, functionally considered, is just as divine an entity as God, in fact coalesces with God, is what you mean by God. Cease, these persons advise us, to use either of these terms, with their outgrown opposition. Use a term free of the clerical connotations, on the one hand; of the suggestion of grossness, coarseness, ignobility, on the other. Talk of the primal mystery, of the unknowable energy, of the one and only power, instead of saying either God or matter. This is the course to which Mr. Spencer urges us; and if philosophy were purely retrospective, he would thereby proclaim himself an excellent pragmatist.

But philosophy is prospective also, and, after finding what the world has been and done, and yielded, still asks the further question 'what does the world *promise?*' Give us a matter that promises *success,* that is bound by its laws to lead our world ever nearer to perfection, and any rational man will worship that matter as readily as Mr. Spencer worships his own so-called unknowable power. It not only has made for righteousness up to date, but it will make for righteousness forever; and that is all we need. Doing practically all that a God can do, it is equivalent to God, its function is a God's function, and in a world in which a God would be superfluous; from such a world a God could never lawfully be missed. 'Cosmic emotion' would here be the right name for religion.

But *is* the matter by which Mr. Spencer's process of cosmic evolution is carried on any such principle of never-ending perfection as this? Indeed it is not, for the future end of every cosmically evolved thing or system of things is foretold by science to be death tragedy; and Mr. Spencer, in confining himself to the æsthetic and ignoring the practical side of the controversy, has really contributed nothing serious to its relief. But apply now our principle of practical results, and see what a vital significance the question of materialism or theism immediately acquires.

Theism and materialism, so indifferent when taken retrospectively, point, when we take them prospectively, to wholly different outlooks of experience. For, according to the theory of mechanical evolution, the laws of redistribution of matter and motion, though they are certainly to thank for all the good hours which our organisms have ever yielded us and for all the ideals which our minds now frame, are yet fatally certain to undo their work again, and to redissolve everything that they have once evolved. You all know the picture of the last state of the universe, which evolutionary science foresees. I can not state it better than in Mr. Balfour's words: "The energies of our system will decay, the glory of the sun will be dimmed, and the earth, tideless and inert, will no longer tolerate the race which has for a moment disturbed its solitude. Man will go down into the pit, and all his thoughts will perish. The uneasy consciousness which in this obscure corner has for a brief space broken the contented silence of the universe, will be at rest. Matter will know itself no longer. 'Imperishable monuments' and 'immortal deeds,' death itself, and love stronger than death, will be as if they had not been. Nor will anything that is, be better or worse for all that the labor, genius, devotion, and suffering of man have striven through countless ages to effect." [15]

That is the sting of it, that in the vast driftings of the cosmic weather, though many a jeweled shore appears, and many an en-

[15] *The Foundations of Belief,* p. 30.

chanted cloud-bank floats away, long lingering ere it be dissolved—
even as our world now lingers, for our joy—yet when these transient
products are gone, nothing, absolutely *nothing* remains, to represent
those particular qualities, those elements of preciousness which they
may have enshrined. Dead and gone are they, gone utterly from the
very sphere and room of being. Without an echo; without a memory;
without an influence on aught that may come after, to make it care for
similar ideals. This utter final wreck and tragedy is of the essence of
scientific materialism as at present understood. The lower and not the
higher forces are the eternal forces, or the last surviving forces within
the only cycle of evolution which we can definitely see. Mr. Spencer
believes this as much as any one; so why should he argue with us as if
we were making silly æsthetic objections to the 'grossness' of 'matter
and motion,' the principles of his philosophy, when what really dismays us is the disconsolateness of its ulterior practical results?

No, the true objection to materialism is not positive but negative.
It would be farcical at this day to make complaint of it for what it *is,*
for 'grossness.' Grossness is what grossness *does*—we now know *that.*
We make complaint of it, on the contrary, for what it is *not*—not
a permanent warrant for our more ideal interests, not a fulfiller of our
remotest hopes.

The notion of God, on the other hand, however inferior it may be
in clearness to those mathematical notions so current in mechanical
philosophy, has at least this practical superiority over them, that it
guarantees an ideal order that shall be permanently preserved. A
world with a God in it to say the last word, may indeed burn up or
freeze, but we then think of him as still mindful of the old ideals and
sure to bring them elsewhere to fruition; so that, where he is, tragedy
is only provisional and partial, and shipwreck and dissolution not the
absolutely final things. This need of an eternal moral order is one of
the deepest needs of our breast. And those poets, like Dante and
Wordsworth, who live on the conviction of such an order, owe to that
fact the extraordinary tonic and consoling power of their verse. Here
then, in these different emotional and practical appeals, in these adjustments of our concrete attitudes of hope and expectation, and all
the delicate consequences which their differences entail, lie the real
meanings of materialism and spiritualism—not in hair-splitting abstractions about matter's inner essence, or about the metaphysical attributes of God. Materialism means simply the denial that the moral
order is eternal, and the cutting off of ultimate hopes; spiritualism
means the affirmation of an eternal moral order and the letting loose
of hope. Surely here is an issue genuine enough, for any one who feels
it; and, as long as men are men, it will yield matter for a serious philosophic debate.

But possibly some of you may still rally to their defence. Even whilst admitting that spiritualism and materialism make different prophecies of the world's future, you may yourself pooh-pooh the difference as something so infinitely remote as to mean nothing for a sane mind. The essence of a sane mind, you may say, is to take shorter views, and to feel no concern about such chimæras as the latter end of the world. Well, I can only say that if you say this, you do injustice to human nature. Religious melancholy is not disposed of by a simple flourish of the word insanity. The absolute things, the last things, the overlapping things, are the truly philosophic concerns; all superior minds feel seriously about them, and the mind with the shortest views is simply the mind of the more shallow man.

The issues of fact at stake in the debate are of course vaguely enough conceived by us at present. But spiritualistic faith in all its forms deals with a world of *promise,* while materialism's sun sets in a sea of disappointment. Remember what I said of the Absolute: it grants us moral holidays. Any religious view does this. It not only incites our more strenuous moments, but it also takes our joyous, careless, trustful moments, and it justifies them. It paints the grounds of justification vaguely enough, to be sure. The exact features of the saving future facts that our belief in God insures, will have to be ciphered out by the interminable methods of science: we can *study* our God only by studying his Creation. But we can *enjoy* our God, if we have one, in advance of all that labor. I myself believe that the evidence for God lies primarily in inner personal experiences. When they have once given you your God, his name means at least the benefit of the holiday. You remember what I said yesterday about the way in which truths clash and try to 'down' each other. The truth of 'God' has to run the gauntlet of all our other truths. It is on trial by them and they on trial by it. Our *final* opinion about God can be settled only after all the truths have straightened themselves out together. Let us hope that they shall find a *modus vivendi!*

Let me pass to a very cognate philosophic problem, the *question of design in nature.* God's existence has from time immemorial been held to be proved by certain natural facts. Many facts appear as if expressly designed in view of one another. Thus the woodpecker's bill, tongue, feet, tail, etc., fit him wondrously for a world of trees, with grubs hid in their bark to feed upon. The parts of our eye fit the laws of light to perfection, leading its rays to a sharp picture on our retina. Such mutual fitting of things diverse in origin argued design, it was held; and the designer was always treated as a man-loving deity.

The first step in these arguments was to prove that the design *existed.* Nature was ransacked for results obtained through separate things being co-adapted. Our eyes, for instance, originate in intrauterine darkness, and the light originates in the sun, yet see how they fit each other. They are evidently made *for* each other. Vision is the end designed, light and eyes the separate means devised for its attainment.

It is strange, considering how unanimously our ancestors felt the force of this argument, to see how little it counts for since the triumph of the darwinian theory. Darwin opened our minds to the power of chance-happenings to bring forth 'fit' results if only they have time to add themselves together. He showed the enormous waste of nature in producing results that get destroyed because of their unfitness. He also emphasized the number of adaptations which, if designed, would argue an evil rather than a good designer. *Here,* all depends upon the point of view. To the grub under the bark the exquisite fitness of the woodpecker's organism to extract him would certainly argue a diabolical designer.

Theologians have by this time stretched their minds so as to embrace the darwinian facts, and yet to interpret them as still showing divine purpose. It used to be a question of purpose against mechanism, of one *or* the other. It was as if one should say "My shoes are evidently designed to fit my feet, hence it is impossible that they should have been produced by machinery." We know that they are both: they are made by a machinery itself designed to fit the feet with shoes. Theology need only stretch similarly the designs of God. As the aim of a football-team is not merely to get the ball to a certain goal (if that were so, they would simply get up on some dark night and place it there), but to get it there by a fixed *machinery of conditions*—the game's rules and the opposing players; so the aim of God is not merely, let us say, to make men and to save them, but rather to get this done through the sole agency of nature's vast machinery. Without nature's stupendous laws and counter-forces, man's creation and perfection, we might suppose, would be too insipid achievements for God to have proposed them.

This saves the form of the design-argument at the expense of its old easy human content. The designer is no longer the old man-like deity. His designs have grown so vast as to be incomprehensible to us humans. The *what* of them so overwhelms us that to establish the mere *that* of a designer for them becomes of very little consequence in comparison. We can with difficulty comprehend the *character* of a cosmic mind whose purposes are fully revealed by the strange mixture of goods and evils that we find in this actual world's particulars. Or rather we cannot by any possibility comprehend it. The mere word 'design' by itself has no consequences and explains nothing. It is the barrenest of principles. The old question of *whether* there is design is idle. The real question is what *is* the world, whether or not it have a designer—and that can be revealed only by the study of all nature's particulars.

Remember that *no matter what* nature may have produced or may be producing, the means must necessarily have been adequate, must have been *fitted to that production.* The argument from fitness to design would consequently always apply, whatever were the product's character. The recent Mont-Pelée eruption, for example, required all previous history to produce that exact combination of ruined houses, human and animal corpses, sunken ships, volcanic ashes, etc., in just that one hideous configuration of positions. France had to be a nation and colonize Martinique. Our country had to exist and send our ships there. *If* God aimed at just that result, the means by which the centuries bent their influences towards it, showed exquisite intelligence. And so of any state of things whatever, either in nature or in history, which we find actually realized. For the parts of things must always make *some* definite resultant, be it chaotic or harmonious. When we look at what has actually come, the conditions must always appear perfectly designed to ensure it. We can always say, therefore, in any conceivable world, of any conceivable character, that the whole cosmic machinery *may* have been designed to produce it.

Pragmatically, then, the abstract word 'design' is a blank cartridge. It carries no consequences, it does no execution. *What* design? and *what* designer? are the only serious questions, and the study of facts is the only way of getting even approximate answers. Meanwhile, pending the slow answer from facts, any one who insists that there *is* a designer and who is sure he is a divine one, gets a certain pragmatic benefit from the term—the same, in fact, which we saw that the terms God, Spirit, or the Absolute, yield us. 'Design,' worthless tho it be as a mere rationalistic principle set above or behind things for our admiration, becomes, if our faith concretes it into something theistic, a term of *promise.* Returning with it into experience, we gain a more confiding outlook on the future. If not a blind force but a seeing force runs things, we may reasonably expect better issues. This vague confidence in the future is the sole pragmatic meaning at present discernible in the terms design and designer. But if cosmic confidence is right not wrong, better not worse, that is a most important meaning. That much at least of possible 'truth' the terms will then have in them.

Let me take up another well-worn controversy, *the free-will problem.* Most persons who believe in what is called their free-will do so after the rationalistic fashion. It is a principle, a positive faculty or virtue added to man, by which his dignity is enigmatically augmented. He ought to believe it for this reason. Determinists, who deny it, who say that individual men originate nothing, but merely transmit to the future the whole push of the past cosmos of which they are so small an expression, diminish man. He is less admirable, stripped of this creative principle. I imagine that more than half of you share our instinctive belief in free-will, and that admiration of it as a principle of dignity has much to do with your fidelity.

But free-will has also been discussed pragmatically, and, strangely enough, the same pragmatic interpretation has been put upon it by both disputants. You know how large a part questions of *accountability* have played in ethical controversy. To hear some persons, one would suppose that all that ethics aims at is a code of merits and demerits. Thus does the old legal and theological leaven, the interest in crime and sin and punishment abide with us. 'Who's to blame? whom can we punish? whom will God punish?'—these preoccupations hang like a bad dream over man's religious history.

So both free-will and determinism have been inveighed against and called absurd, because each, in the eyes of its enemies, has seemed to prevent the 'imputability' of good or bad deeds to their authors. Queer antinomy this! Free-will means novelty, the grafting on to the past of something not involved therein. If our acts were predetermined, if we merely transmitted the push of the whole past, the free-willists say, how could we be praised or blamed for anything? We should be 'agents' only, not 'principals,' and where then would be our precious imputability and responsibility?

But where would it be if we *had* free-will? rejoin the determinists. If a 'free' act be a sheer novelty, that comes not *from* me, the previous me; but *ex nihilo,* and simply tacks itself on to me, how can *I,* the previous I, be responsible? How can I have any permanent *character* that will stand still long enough for praise or blame to be awarded? The chaplet of my days tumbles into a cast of disconnected beads as soon as the thread of inner necessity is drawn out by the preposterous indeterminist doctrine. Messrs. Fullerton and McTaggart have recently laid about them doughtily with this argument.

It may be good *ad hominem,* but otherwise it is pitiful. For I ask you, quite apart from other reasons, whether any man, woman or child, with a sense for realities, ought not to be ashamed to plead such principles as either dignity or imputability. Instinct and utility between them can safely be trusted to carry on the social business of punishment and praise. If a man does good acts we shall praise him, if he does bad acts we shall punish him,—anyhow, and quite apart from theories as to whether the acts result from what was previous in him or are novelties in a strict sense. To make our human ethics revolve about the question of 'merit' is a piteous unreality—God alone can know our merits, if we have any. The real ground for supposing free-will is indeed pragmatic, but it has nothing to do with this contemptible right to punish which has made such a noise in past discussions of the subject.

Free-will pragmatically means *novelties in the world,* the right to expect that in its deepest elements as well as in its surface phenomena, the future may not identically repeat and imitate the past. That imitation *en masse* is there, who can deny? The general 'uniformity of nature' is presupposed by every lesser law. But nature may be only approximately uniform; and persons in whom knowledge of the world's past has bred pessimism (or doubts as to the world's good character, which become certainties if that character be supposed eternally fixed) may naturally welcome free-will as a *melioristic* doctrine. It holds up improvement as at least possible; whereas determinism assures us that our whole notion of possibility is born of human ignorance, and that necessity and impossibility between them rule the destinies of the world.

Free-will is thus a general cosmological theory of *promise,* just like the Absolute, God, Spirit or Design. Taken abstractly, no one of these terms has any inner content, none of them gives us any picture, and no one of them would retain the least pragmatic value in a world whose character was obviously perfect from the start. Elation at mere existence, pure cosmic emotion and delight, would, it seems to me, quench all interest in those speculations, if the world were nothing but a lubberland of happiness already. Our interest in religious metaphysics arises in the fact that our empirical future feels to us unsafe, and needs some higher guarantee. If the past and present were purely good, who could wish that the future might possibly not resemble them? Who could desire free-will? Who would not say, with Huxley, 'let me be wound up every day like a watch, to go right fatally, and I ask no better freedom.' 'Freedom' in a world already perfect could only mean freedom to *be worse,* and who could be so insane as to wish that? To be necessarily what it is, to be impossibly aught else, would put the last touch of perfection upon optimism's universe. Surely the only *possibility* that one can rationally claim is the possibility that things may be *better*. That possibility, I need hardly say, is one that, as the actual world goes, we have ample grounds for desiderating.

Free-will thus has no meaning unless it be a doctrine of *relief*. As such, it takes its place with other religious doctrines. Between them, they build up the old wastes and repair the former desolations. Our spirit, shut within this courtyard of sense-experience, is always saying to the intellect upon the tower: 'Watchman, tell us of the night, if it aught of promise bear,' and the intellect gives it then these terms of promise.

Other than this practical significance, the words God, free-will, design, etc., have none. Yet dark tho they be in themselves, or intel-lectualistically taken, when we bear them into life's thicket with us the darkness *there* grows light about us. If you stop, in dealing with such words, with their definition, thinking that to be an intellectual finality, where are you? Stupidly staring at a pretentious sham! "Deus est Ens, a se, extra et supra omne genus, necessarium, unum, infinite perfec-tum, simplex, immutabile, immensum, aeternum, intelligens," etc.,— wherein is such a definition really instructive? It means less than nothing, in its pompous robe of adjectives. Pragmatism alone can read a positive meaning into it, and for that she turns her back upon the intellectualist point of view altogether. 'God's in his heaven; all's right with the world!'—*That's* the real heart of your theology, and for that you need no rationalist definitions.

Why should n't all of us, rationalists as well as pragmatists, con-fess this? Pragmatism, so far from keeping her eyes bent on the imme-diate practical foreground, as she is accused of doing, dwells just as much upon the world's remotest perspectives.

See then how all these ultimate questions turn, as it were, upon their hinges; and from looking backwards upon principles, upon an *er-kenntnisstheoretische Ich,* a God, a *Kausalitätsprinzip,* a Design, a Free-will, taken in themselves, as something august and exalted above facts,—see, I say, how pragmatism shifts the emphasis and looks for-ward into facts themselves. The really vital question for us all is, What is this world going to be? What is life eventually to make of itself? The centre of gravity of philosophy must therefore alter its place. The earth of things, long thrown into shadow by the glories of the upper ether, must resume its rights. To shift the emphasis in this way means that philosophic questions will fall to be treated by minds of a less abstractionist type than heretofore, minds more scientific and individ-ualistic in their tone yet not irreligious either. It will be an alteration in 'the seat of authority' that reminds one almost of the protestant reformation. And as, to papal minds, protestantism has often seemed a mere mess of anarchy and confusion, such, no doubt, will pragma-tism often seem to ultra-rationalist minds in philosophy. It will seem so much sheer trash, philosophically. But life wags on, all the same, and compasses its ends, in protestant countries. I venture to think that philosophic protestantism will compass a .not dissimilar prosperity.

THE ONE AND THE MANY*

We saw in the last lecture that the pragmatic method, in its dealings with certain concepts, instead of ending with admiring contemplation, plunges forward into the river of experience with them and prolongs the perspective by their means. Design, free-will, the absolute mind, spirit instead of matter, have for their sole meaning a better promise as to this world's outcome. Be they false or be they true, the meaning of them is this meliorism. I have sometimes thought of the phenomenon called 'total reflexion' in Optics as a good symbol of the relation between abstract ideas and concrete realities, as pragmatism conceives it. Hold a tumbler of water a little above your eyes and look up through the water at its surface—or better still look similarly through the flat wall of an aquarium. You will then see an extraordinarily brilliant reflected image say of a candle-flame, or any other clear object, situated on the opposite side of the vessel. No ray, under these circumstances gets beyond the water's surface: every ray is totally reflected back into the depths again. Now let the water represent the world of sensible facts, and let the air above it represent the world of abstract ideas. Both worlds are real, of course, and interact; but they interact only at their boundary, and the *locus* of everything that lives, and happens to us, so far as full experience goes, is the water. We are like fishes swimming in the sea of sense, bounded above by the superior element, but unable to breathe it pure or penetrate it. We get our oxygen from it, however, we touch it incessantly, now in this part, now in that, and every time we touch it, we turn back into the water with our course re-determined and re-energized. The abstract ideas of which the air consists are indispensable for life, but irrespirable by themselves, as it were, and only active in their re-directing function. All similes are halting, but this one rather takes my fancy. It shows how something, not sufficient for life in itself, may nevertheless be an effective determinant of life elsewhere.

In this present hour I wish to illustrate the pragmatic method by one more application. I wish to turn its light upon the ancient problem of 'the one and the many.' I suspect that in but few of you has this problem occasioned sleepless nights, and I should not be astonished if some of you told me it had never vexed you at all. I myself have come, by long brooding over it, to consider it the most central of all philosophic problems, central because so pregnant. I mean by this that if you know whether a man is a decided monist or a decided

* From: Pragm., 127–162.

pluralist, you perhaps know more about the rest of his opinions than if you give him any other name ending in *ist*. To believe in the one or in the many, that is the classification with the maximum number of consequences. So bear with me for an hour while I try to inspire you with my own interest in this problem.

Philosophy has often been defined as the quest or the vision of the world's unity. Few persons ever challenge this definition, which is true as far as it goes, for philosophy has indeed manifested above all things its interest in unity. But how about the *variety* in things? Is that such an irrelevant matter? If instead of using the term philosophy, we talk in general of our intellect and its needs, we quickly see that unity is only one of them. Acquaintance with the details of fact is always reckoned, along with their reduction to system, as an indispensable mark of mental greatness. Your 'scholarly' mind, of encyclopedic, philological type, your man essentially of *learning,* has never lacked for praise along with your philosopher. What our intellect really aims at is neither variety nor unity taken singly, but *totality*.[16] In this, acquaintance with reality's diversities is as important as understanding their connexion. Curiosity goes *pari passu* with the systematizing passion.

In spite of this obvious fact the unity of things has always been considered more *illustrious,* as it were, than their variety. When a young man first conceives the notion that the whole world forms one great fact, with all its parts moving abreast, as it were, and interlocked, he feels as if he were enjoying a great insight, and looks superciliously on all who still fall short of this sublime conception. Taken thus abstractly as it first comes to one, the monistic insight is so vague as hardly to seem worth defending intellectually. Yet probably every one in this audience in some way cherishes it. A certain abstract monism, a certain emotional response to the character of oneness, as if it were a feature of the world not co-ordinate with its manyness, but vastly more excellent and eminent, is so prevalent in educated circles that we might almost call it a part of philosophic common sense. Of *course* the world is One, we say. How else could it be a world at all? Empiricists as a rule, are as stout monists of this abstract kind as rationalists are.

The difference is that the empiricists are less dazzled. Unity doesn't blind them to everything else, doesn't quench their curiosity for special facts, whereas there is a kind of rationalist who is sure to interpret abstract unity mystically and to forget everything else, to treat it as a principle; to admire and worship it; and thereupon to come to a full stop intellectually.

[16] Compare A. Bellanger: *Les concepts de Cause, et l'activité intentionnelle de l'Esprit.* Paris, Alcan, 1905, p. 79 ff.

'The world is One!'—the formula may become a sort of number-worship. 'Three' and 'seven' have, it is true, been reckoned sacred numbers; but, abstractly taken, why is 'one' more excellent than 'forty-three,' or than 'two million and ten'? In this first vague conviction of the world's unity, there is so little to take hold of that we hardly know what we mean by it.

The only way to get forward with our notion is to treat it pragmatically. Granting the oneness to exist, what facts will be different in consequence? What will the unity be known as? The world is One—yes, but *how* one. What is the practical value of the oneness for *us*.

Asking such questions, we pass from the vague to the definite, from the abstract to the concrete. Many distinct ways in which a oneness predicated of the universe might make a difference, come to view. I will note successively the more obvious of these ways.

1. First, the world is at least *one subject of discourse*. If its many-ness were so irremediable as to permit *no* union whatever of its parts, not even our minds could 'mean' the whole of it at once: they would be like eyes trying to look in opposite directions. But in point of fact we mean to cover the whole of it by our abstract term 'world' or 'universe,' which expressly intends that no part shall be left out. Such unity of discourse carries obviously no farther monistic specifications. A 'chaos,' once so named, has as much unity of discourse as a cosmos. It is an odd fact that many monists consider a great victory scored for their side when pluralists say 'the universe is many.' " 'The Universe'!" they chuckle—"his speech bewrayeth him. He stands confessed of monism out of his own mouth." Well, let things be one in so far forth! You can then fling such a word as universe at the whole collection of them, but what matters it? It still remains to be ascertained whether they are one in any further or more valuable sense.

2. Are they, for example, *continuous*? Can you pass from one to another, keeping always in your one universe without any danger of falling out? In other words, do the parts of our universe *hang together,* instead of being like detached grains of sand?

Even grains of sand hang together through the space in which they are embedded, and if you can in any way move through such space, you can pass continuously from number one of them to number two. Space and time are thus vehicles of continuity by which the world's parts hang together. The practical difference to us, resultant from these forms of union, is immense. Our whole motor life is based upon them.

3. There are innumerable other paths of practical continuity among things. Lines of *influence* can be traced by which they hang together. Following any such line you pass from one thing to another till you may have covered a good part of the universe's extent. Gravity

and heat-conduction are such all-uniting influences, so far as the physical world goes. Electric, luminous and chemical influences follow similar lines of influence. But opaque and inert bodies interrupt the continuity here, so that you have to step round them, or change your mode of progress if you wish to get farther on that day. Practically, you have then lost your universe's unity, *so far as it was constituted by those first lines of influence*.

There are innumerable kinds of connexion that special things have with other special things; and the *ensemble* of any one of these connexions forms one sort of *system* by which things are conjoined. Thus men are conjoined in a vast network of *acquaintanceship*. Brown knows Jones, Jones knows Robinson, etc.; and *by choosing your farther intermediaries rightly* you may carry a message from Jones to the Empress of China, or the Chief of the African Pigmies, or to any one else in the inhabited world. But you are stopped short, as by a nonconductor, when you choose one man wrong in this experiment. What may be called love-systems are grafted on the acquaintance-system. A loves (or hates) B; B loves (or hates) C, etc. But these systems are smaller than the great acquaintance-system that they presuppose.

Human efforts are daily unifying the world more and more in definite systematic ways. We found colonial, postal, consular, commercial systems, all the parts of which obey definite influences that propagate themselves within the system but not to facts outside of it. The result is innumerable little hangings-together of the world's parts within the larger hangings-together, little worlds, not only of discourse but of operation, within the wider universe. Each system exemplifies one type or grade of union, its parts being strung on that peculiar kind of relation, and the same part may figure in many different systems, as a man may hold various offices and belong to several clubs. From this 'systematic' point of view, therefore, the pragmatic value of the world's unity is that all these definite networks actually and practically exist. Some are more enveloping and extensive, some less so; they are superposed upon each other; and between them all they let no individual elementary part of the universe escape. Enormous as is the amount of disconnexion among things (for these systematic influences and conjunctions follow rigidly exclusive paths), everything that exists is influenced in *some* way by something else, if you can only pick the way out rightly. Loosely speaking, and in general, it may be said that all things cohere and adhere to each other *somehow,* and that the universe exists practically in reticulated or concatenated forms which make of it a continuous or 'integrated' affair. Any kind of influence whatever helps to make the world one, so far as you can follow it from next to next. You may then say that 'the world *is* One,'—meaning in these respects, namely, and just so far as they obtain. But just as definitely is it *not* One, so far as they do not obtain; and there is no species of connexion which will not fail, if, instead of choosing conductors for it you choose non-conductors. You are then arrested at your very first step and have to write the world down as a pure *many* from that particular point of view. If our intellect had been as much interested in disjunctive as it is in conjunctive relations, philosophy would have equally successfully celebrated the world's *disunion*.

The great point is to notice that the oneness and the manyness are absolutely co-ordinate here. Neither is primordial or more essential or excellent than the other. Just as with space, whose separating of things seems exactly on a par with its uniting of them, but sometimes one function and sometimes the other is what comes home to us most, so, in our general dealings with the world of influences, we now need conductors and now need non-conductors, and wisdom lies in knowing which is which at the appropriate moment.

4. All these systems of influence or non-influence may be listed under the general problem of the world's *causal unity*. If the minor causal influences among things should converge towards one common causal origin of them in the past, one great first cause for all that is, one might then speak of the absolute causal unity of the world. God's *fiat* on creation's day has figured in traditional philosophy as such an absolute cause and origin. Transcendental Idealism, translating 'creation' into 'thinking' (or 'willing to think') calls the divine act 'eternal' rather than 'first'; but the union of the many here is absolute, just the same—the many would not *be,* save for the One. Against this notion of the unity of origin of all things there has always stood the pluralistic notion of an eternal self-existing many in the shape of atoms or even of spiritual units of some sort. The alternative has doubtless a pragmatic meaning, but perhaps, as far as these lectures go, we had better leave the question of unity of origin unsettled.

5. The most important sort of union that obtains among things, pragmatically speaking, is their *generic unity*. Things exist in kinds, there are many specimens in each kind, and what the 'kind' implies for one specimen, it implies also for every other specimen of that kind. We can easily conceive that every fact in the world might be singular, that is, unlike any other fact and sole of its kind. In such a world of singulars our logic would be useless, for logic works by predicating of the single instance what is true of all its kind. With no two things alike in the world, we should be unable to reason from our past experiences to our future ones. The existence of so much generic unity in things is thus perhaps the most momentous pragmatic specification of what it may mean to say 'the world is One.' *Absolute* generic unity would obtain if there were one *summum genus* under which all things without exception could be eventually subsumed. 'Beings,' 'thinka-

bles,' 'experiences,' would be candidates for this position. Whether the
alternatives expressed by such words have any pragmatic significance
or not, is another question which I prefer to leave unsettled just now.

6. Another specification of what the phrase 'the world is one' may
mean is *unity of purpose*. An enormous number of things in the world
subserve a common purpose. All the man-made systems, administra-
tive, industrial, military, or what not, exist each for its controlling purpose. Every living being pursues its own peculiar purposes. They co-
operate, according to the degree of their development, in collective or
tribal purposes, larger ends thus enveloping lesser ones, until an absolutely single, final and climacteric purpose subserved by all things without exception might conceivably be reached. It is needless to say that
the appearances conflict with such a view. Any resultant, as I said in
my third lecture, *may* have been purposed in advance, but none of the
results we actually know in this world have in point of fact been purposed in advance in all their details. Men and nations start with a
vague notion of being rich, or great, or good. Each step they make
brings unforeseen chances into sight, and shuts out older vistas, and
the specifications of the general purpose have to be daily changed.
What is reached in the end may be better or worse than what was
proposed, but it is always more complex and different.

Our different purposes also are at war with each other. Where one
can't crush the other out, they compromise; and the result is again
different from what anyone distinctly proposed beforehand. Vaguely
and generally, much of what was purposed may be gained; but everything makes strongly for the view that our world is incompletely unified teleologically and is still trying to get its unification better organized.

Whoever claims *absolute* teleological unity, saying that there is
one purpose that every detail of the universe subserves, dogmatizes at
his own risk. Theologians who dogmatize thus find it more and more
impossible, as our acquaintance with the warring interests of the
world's parts grows more concrete, to imagine what the one climacteric purpose may possibly be like. We see indeed that certain evils
minister to ulterior goods, that the bitter makes the cocktail better,
and that a bit of danger or hardship puts us agreeably to our trumps.
We can vaguely generalize this into the doctrine that all the evil in the
universe is but instrumental to its greater perfection. But the scale of
the evil actually in sight defies all human tolerance; and transcendental
idealism, in the pages of a Bradley or a Royce, brings us no farther
than the book of Job did—God's ways are not our ways, so let us put
our hands upon our mouth. A God who can relish such superfluities of
horror is no God for human beings to appeal to. His animal spirits are
too high. In other words the 'Absolute' with his one purpose, is not
the man-like God of common people.

7. *Æsthetic union* among things also obtains, and is very analogous to teleological union. Things tell a story. Their parts hang together so as to work out a climax. They play into each other's hands expressively. Retrospectively, we can see that altho no definite purpose presided over a chain of events, yet the events fell into a dramatic form, with a start, a middle, and a finish. In point of fact all stories end; and here again the point of view of a many is the more natural one to take. The world is full of partial stories that run parallel to one another, beginning and ending at odd times. They mutually interlace and interfere at points, but we can not unify them completely in our minds. In following your life-history, I must temporarily turn my attention from my own. Even a biographer of twins would have to press them alternately upon his reader's attention.

It follows that whoever says that the whole world tells one story utters another of those monistic dogmas that a man believes at his risk. It is easy to see the world's history pluralistically, as a rope of which each fibre tells a separate tale; but to conceive of each cross-section of the rope as an absolutely single fact, and to sum the whole longitudinal series into one being living an undivided life, is harder. We have indeed the analogy of embryology to help us. The microscopist makes a hundred flat cross-sections of a given embryo, and mentally unites them into one solid whole. But the great world's ingredients, so far as they are beings, seem, like the rope's fibres, to be discontinuous, cross-wise, and to cohere only in the longitudinal direction. Followed in that direction they are many. Even the embryologist, when he follows the *development* of his object, has to treat the history of each single organ in turn. *Absolute* æsthetic union is thus another barely abstract ideal. The world appears as something more epic than dramatic.

So far, then, we see how the world is unified by its many systems, kinds, purposes, and dramas. That there is more union in all these ways than openly appears is certainly true. That there *may* be one sovereign purpose, system, kind, and story, is a legitimate hypothesis. All I say here is that it is rash to affirm this dogmatically without better evidence than we possess at present.

8. The *great* monistic *denkmittel* for a hundred years past has been the notion of *the one Knower*. The many exist only as objects for his thought—exist in his dream, as it were; and *as he knows* them, they have one purpose, form one system, tell one tale for him. This notion of an *all enveloping noetic unity* in things is the sublimest achievement of intellectualist philosophy. Those who believe in the Absolute, as the all-knower is termed, usually say that they do so for coercive reasons, which clear thinkers can not evade. The Absolute has far-reaching practical consequences, to some of which I drew attention in my second lecture. Many kinds of difference important to us

would surely follow from its being true. I can not here enter into all the logical proofs of such a Being's existence, farther than to say that none of them seem to me sound. I must therefore treat the notion of an All-Knower simply as an hypothesis, exactly on a par logically with the pluralist notion that there is no point of view, no focus of information extant, from which the entire content of the universe is visible at once. "God's conscience," says Professor Royce,[17] "forms in its wholeness one luminously transparent conscious moment"—this is the type of noetic unity on which rationalism insists. Empiricism on the other hand is satisfied with the type of noetic unity that is humanly familiar. Everything gets known by *some* knower along with something else; but the knowers may in the end be irreducibly many, and the greatest knower of them all may yet not know the whole of everything, or even know what he does know at one single stroke:—he may be liable to forget. Whichever type obtained, the world would still be a universe noetically. Its parts would be conjoined by knowledge, but in the one case the knowledge would be absolutely unified, in the other it would be strung along and overlapped.

The notion of one instantaneous or eternal Knower—either adjective here means the same thing—is, as I said, the great intellectualist achievement of our time. It has practically driven out that conception of 'Substance' which earlier philosophers set such store by, and by which so much unifying work used to be done—universal substance which alone has being in and from itself, and of which all the particulars of experience are but forms to which it gives support. Substance has succumbed to the pragmatic criticisms of the English school. It appears now only as another name for the fact that phenomena as they come are actually grouped and given in coherent forms, the very forms in which we finite knowers experience or think them together. These forms of conjunction are as much parts of the tissue of experience as are the terms which they connect; and it is a great pragmatic achievement for recent idealism to have made the world hang together in these directly representable ways instead of drawing its unity from the 'inherence' of its parts—whatever that may mean—in a unimaginable principle behind the scenes.

'The world is One,' therefore, just so far as we experience it to be concatenated, One by as many definite conjunctions as appear. But then also *not* One by just as many definite *dis*junctions as we find. The oneness and the manyness of it thus obtain in respects which can be separately named. It is neither a universe pure and simple nor a multiverse pure and simple. And its various manners of being One suggest, for their accurate ascertainment, so many distinct programs of scientific work. Thus the pragmatic question 'What is the oneness known

[17] *The Conception of God,* New York, 1897, p. 292.

as? What practical difference will it make?' saves us from all feverish excitement over it as a principle of sublimity and carries us forward into the stream of experience with a cool head. The stream may indeed reveal far more connexion and union than we now suspect, but we are not entitled on pragmatic principles to claim absolute oneness in any respect in advance.

It is so difficult to see definitely what absolute oneness can mean, that probably the majority of you are satisfied with the sober attitude which we have reached. Nevertheless there are possibly some radically monistic souls among you who are not content to leave the one and the many on a par. Union of various grades, union of diverse types, union that stops at non-conductors, union that merely goes from next to next, and means in many cases outer nextness only, and not a more internal bond, union of concatenation, in short; all that sort of thing seems to you a halfway stage of thought. The oneness of things, superior to their manyness, you think must also be more deeply true, must be the more real aspect of the world. The pragmatic view, you are sure, gives us a universe imperfectly rational. The real universe must form an unconditional unit of being, something consolidated, with its parts co-implicated through and through. Only then could we consider our estate completely rational.

There is no doubt whatever that this ultra-monistic way of thinking means a great deal to many minds. "One Life, One Truth, one Love, one Principle, One Good, One God"—I quote from a Christian Science leaflet which the day's mail brings into my hands—beyond doubt such a confession of faith has pragmatically an emotional value, and beyond doubt the word 'one' contributes to the value quite as much as the other words. But if we try to realize *intellectually* what we can possibly *mean* by such a glut of oneness we are thrown right back upon our pragmatistic determinations again. It means either the mere name One, the universe of discourse; or it means the sum total of all the ascertainable particular conjunctions and concatenations; or, finally, it means some one vehicle of conjunction treated as all-inclusive, like one origin, one purpose, or one knower. In point of fact it always means one *knower* to those who take it intellectually to-day. The one knower involves, they think, the other forms of conjunction. His world must have all its parts co-implicated in the one logical-æsthetical-teleological unit-picture which is his eternal dream.

The character of the absolute knower's picture is however so impossible for us to represent clearly, that we may fairly suppose that the authority which absolute monism undoubtedly possesses, and probably always will possess over some persons, draws its strength far less from intellectual than from mystical grounds. To interpret absolute monism worthily, be a mystic. Mystical states of mind in every degree are shown by history, usually tho not always, to make for the monistic view. This is no proper occasion to enter upon the general subject of mysticism, but I will quote one mystical pronouncement to show just what I mean. The paragon of all monistic systems is the Vedânta philosophy of Hindostan, and the paragon of Vedântist missionaries was the late Swami Vivekananda who visited our land some years ago. The method of Vedântism is the mystical method. You do not reason, but after going through a certain discipline *you see,* and having seen, you can report the truth. Vivekananda thus reports the truth in one of his lectures here:

"Where is there any more misery for him who sees this Oneness in the universe, this Oneness of life, Oneness of everything? . . . This separation between man and man, man and woman, man and child, nation from nation, earth from moon, moon from sun, this separation between atom and atom is the cause really of all the misery, and the Vedânta says this separation does not exist, it is not real. It is merely apparent, on the surface. In the heart of things there is unity still. If you go inside you find that unity between man and man, women and children, races and races, high and low, rich and poor, the gods and men: all are One, and animals too, if you go deep enough, and he who has attained to that has no more delusion. . . . Where is there any more delusion for him? What can delude him? He knows the reality of everything, the secret of everything. Where is there any more misery for him? What does he desire? He has traced the reality of everything unto the Lord, that centre, that Unity of everything, and that is Eternal Bliss, Eternal Knowledge, Eternal Existence. Neither death nor disease nor sorrow nor misery nor discontent is There . . . In the Centre, the reality, there is no one to be mourned for, no one to be sorry for. He has penetrated everything, the Pure One, the Formless, the Bodiless, the Stainless, He the Knower, He the great Poet, the Self-Existent, He who is giving to every one what he deserves."

Observe how radical the character of the monism here is. Separation is not simply overcome by the One, it is denied to exist. There is not many. We are not parts of the One; It has no parts; and since in a sense we undeniably *are,* it must be that each of us *is* the One, indivisibly and totally. *An Absolute One, and I that One,*—surely we have here a religion which, emotionally considered, has a high pragmatic value; it imparts a perfect sumptuosity of security. As our Swami says in another place:

"When man has seen himself as One with the infinite Being of the universe, when all separateness has ceased, when all men, all women, all angels, all gods, all animals, all plants, the whole universe has been melted into that oneness, then all fear disappears. Whom to fear? Can I hurt myself? Can I kill myself? Can I injure myself? Do you fear

yourself? Then will all sorrow disappear. What can cause me sorrow?
I am the One Existence of the universe. Then all jealousies will disappear; of whom to be jealous? Of myself? Then all bad feelings disappear. Against whom shall I have this bad feeling? Against myself?
There is none in the universe but me . . . kill out this differentiation,
kill out this superstition that there are many. 'He who, in this world of
many, sees that One; he who, in this mass of insentiency, sees that
One Sentient Being; he who in this world of shadow, catches that
Reality, unto him belongs eternal peace, unto none else, unto none
else.' "

We all have some ear for this monistic music: it elevates and reas-
sures. We all have at least the germ of mysticism in us. And when our
idealists recite their arguments for the Absolute, saying that the slightest union admitted anywhere carries logically absolute Oneness with
it, and that the slightest separation admitted anywhere logically carries disunion remediless and complete, I cannot help suspecting that
the palpable weak places in the intellectual reasonings they use are
protected from their own criticism by a mystical feeling that, logic or
no logic, absolute Oneness must somehow at any cost be true. Oneness overcomes *moral* separateness at any rate. In the passion of love
we have the mystic germ of what might mean a total union of all
sentient life. This mystical germ wakes up in us on hearing the monistic utterances, acknowledges their authority, and assigns to intellectual considerations a secondary place.

I will dwell no longer on these religious and moral aspects of the
question in this lecture. When I come to my final lecture there will be
something more to say.

Leave then out of consideration for the moment the authority
which mystical insights may be conjectured eventually to possess;
treat the problem of the One and the Many in a purely intellectual
way; and we see clearly enough where pragmatism stands. With her
criterion of the practical differences that theories make, we see that she
must equally abjure absolute monism and absolute pluralism. The
world is One just so far as its parts hang together by any definite
connexion. It is many just so far as any definite connexion fails to
obtain. And finally it is growing more and more unified by those systems of connexion at least which human energy keeps framing as time
goes on.

It is possible to imagine alternative universes to the one we know,
in which the most various grades and types of union should be embodied. Thus the lowest grade of universe would be a world of mere
withness, of which the parts were only strung together by the conjunction 'and.' Such a universe is even now the collection of our several
inner lives. The spaces and times of your imagination, the objects and

events of your day-dreams are not only more or less incoherent *inter se,* but are wholly out of definite relation with the similar contents of any one else's mind. Our various reveries now as we sit here compenetrate each other idly without influencing or interfering. They coexist, but in no order and in no receptacle, being the nearest approach to an absolute 'many' that we can conceive. We can not even imagine any reason why they *should* be known all together, and we can imagine even less, if they were known together, how they could be known as one systematic whole.

But add our sensations and bodily actions, and the union mounts to a much higher grade. Our *audita et visa* and our acts fall into those receptacles of time and space in which each event finds its date and place. They form 'things' and are of 'kinds' too, and can be classed. Yet we can imagine a world of things and of kinds in which the causal interactions with which we are so familiar should not exist. Everything there might be inert towards everything else, and refuse to propagate its influence. Or gross mechanical influences might pass, but no chemical action. Such worlds would be far less unified than ours. Again there might be complete physico-chemical interaction, but no minds; or minds, but altogether private ones, with no social life; or social life limited to acquaintance, but no love; or love, but no customs or institutions that should systematize it. No one of these grades of universe would be absolutely irrational or disintegrated, inferior tho it might appear when looked at from the higher grades. For instance, if our minds should ever become 'telepathically' connected, so that we knew immediately, or could under certain conditions know immediately, each what the other was thinking, the world we now live in would appear to the thinkers in that world to have been of an inferior grade.

With the whole of past eternity open for our conjectures to range in, it may be lawful to wonder whether the various kinds of union now realized in the universe that we inhabit may not possibly have been successively evolved after the fashion in which we now see human systems evolving in consequence of human needs. If such an hypothesis were legitimate, total oneness would appear at the end of things rather than at their origin. In other words the notion of the 'Absolute' would have to be replaced by that of the 'Ultimate.' The two notions would have the same content—the maximally unified content of fact, namely—but their time-relations would be positively reversed.[18]

After discussing the unity of the universe in this pragmatic way, you ought to see why I said in my second lecture, borrowing the word from my friend G. Papini, that pragmatism tends to *unstiffen* all our

[18] Compare on the Ultimate, Mr. Schiller's essay "Activity and Substance," in his book entitled *Humanism,* p. 204.

theories. The world's oneness has generally been affirmed abstractly only, and as if any one who questioned it must be an idiot. The temper of monists has been so vehement, as almost at times to be convulsive; and this way of holding a doctrine does not easily go with reasonable discussion and the drawing of distinctions. The theory of the Absolute, in particular, has had to be an article of faith, affirmed dogmatically and exclusively. The One and All, first in the order of being and of knowing, logically necessary itself, and uniting all lesser things in the bonds of mutual necessity, how could it allow of any mitigation of its inner rigidity? The slightest suspicion of pluralism, the minutest wiggle of independence of any one of its parts from the control of the totality would ruin it. Absolute unity brooks no degrees,—as well might you claim absolute purity for a glass of water because it contains but a single little cholera-germ. The independence, however infinitesimal, of a part, however small, would be to the Absolute as fatal as a cholera-germ.

Pluralism on the other hand has no need of this dogmatic rigoristic temper. Provided you grant *some* separation among things, some tremor of independence, some free play of parts on one another, some real novelty or chance, however minute, she is amply satisfied, and will allow you any amount, however great, of real union. How much of union there may be is a question that she thinks can only be decided empirically. The amount may be enormous, colossal; but absolute monism is shattered if, along with all the union, there has to be granted the slightest modicum, the most incipient nascency, or the most residual trace, of a separation that is not 'overcome.'

Pragmatism, pending the final empirical ascertainment of just what the balance of union and disunion among things may be, must obviously range herself upon the pluralistic side. Some day, she admits, even total union, with one knower, one origin, and a universe consolidated in every conceivable way, may turn out to be the most acceptable of all hypotheses. Meanwhile the opposite hypothesis, of a world imperfectly unified still, and perhaps always to remain so, must be sincerely entertained. This latter hypothesis is pluralism's doctrine. Since absolute monism forbids its being even considered seriously, branding it as irrational from the start, it is clear that pragmatism must turn its back on absolute monism, and follow pluralism's more empirical path.

This leaves us with the common-sense world, in which we find things partly joined and partly disjoined. 'Things,' then, and their 'conjunctions'—what do such words mean, pragmatically handled? In my next lecture, I will apply the pragmatic method to the stage of philosophizing known as Common Sense.

PRAGMATISM AND COMMON SENSE*

In the last lecture we turned ourselves from the usual way of talking of the universe's oneness as a principle, sublime in all its blankness, towards a study of the special kinds of union which the universe enfolds. We found many of these to coexist with kinds of separation equally real. 'How far am I verified?' is the question which each kind of union and each kind of separation asks us here, so as good pragmatists we have to turn our face towards experience, towards 'facts.'

Absolute oneness remains, but only as an hypothesis, and that hypothesis is reduced nowadays to that of an omniscient knower who sees all things without exception as forming one single systematic fact. But the knower in question may still be conceived either as an Absolute or as an Ultimate; and over against the hypothesis of him in either form the counter hypothesis that the widest field of knowledge that ever was or will be still contains some ignorance, may be legitimately held. Some bits of information always may escape.

This is the hypothesis of *noetic pluralism,* which monists consider so absurd. Since we are bound to treat it as respectfully as noetic monism, until the facts shall have tipped the beam, we find that our pragmatism, tho originally nothing but a method, has forced us to be friendly to the pluralistic view. It *may* be that some parts of the world are connected so loosely with some other parts as to be strung along by nothing but the copula *and.* They might even come and go without those other parts suffering any internal change. This pluralistic view, of a world of *additive* constitution, is one that pragmatism is unable to rule out from serious consideration. But this view leads one to the farther hypothesis that the actual world, instead of being complete 'eternally,' as the monists assure us, may be eternally incomplete, and at all times subject to addition or liable to loss.

It *is* at any rate incomplete in one respect, and flagrantly so. The very fact that we debate this question shows that *our knowledge* is incomplete at present and subject to addition. In respect of the knowledge it contains the world does genuinely change and grow. Some general remarks on the way in which our knowledge completes itself— when it does complete itself—will lead us very conveniently into our subject for this lecture, which is 'Common Sense.'

To begin with, our knowledge grows *in spots.* The spots may be large or small, but the knowledge never grows all over: some old knowledge always remains what it was. Your knowledge of pragma-

* From: Pragm., 165–194.

tism, let us suppose, is growing now. Later, its growth may involve considerable modification of opinions which you previously held to be true. But such modifications are apt to be gradual. To take the nearest possible example, consider these lectures of mine. What you first gain from them is probably a small amount of new information, a few new definitions, or distinctions, or points of view. But while these special ideas are being added, the rest of your knowledge stands still, and only gradually will you 'line up' your previous opinions with the novelties I am trying to instil, and modify to some slight degree their mass.

You listen to me now, I suppose, with certain prepossessions as to my competency, and these affect your reception of what I say, but were I suddenly to break off lecturing, and to begin to sing 'We won't go home till morning' in a rich baritone voice, not only would that new fact be added to your stock, but it would oblige you to define me differently, and that might alter your opinion of the pragmatic philosophy, and in general bring about a rearrangement of a number of your ideas. Your mind in such processes is strained, and sometimes painfully so, between its older beliefs and the novelties which experience brings along.

Our minds thus grow in spots; and like grease-spots, the spots spread. But we let them spread as little as possible: we keep unaltered as much of our old knowledge, as many of our old prejudices and beliefs, as we can. We patch and tinker more than we renew. The novelty soaks in; it stains the ancient mass; but it is also tinged by what absorbs it. Our past apperceives and co-operates; and in the new equilibrium in which each step forward in the process of learning terminates, it happens relatively seldom that the new fact is added *raw*. More usually it is embedded cooked, as one might say, or stewed down in the sauce of the old.

New truths thus are resultants of new experiences and of old truths combined and mutually modifying one another. And since this is the case in the changes of opinion of to-day, there is no reason to assume that it has not been so at all times. It follows that very ancient modes of thought may have survived through all the later changes in men's opinions. The most primitive ways of thinking may not yet be wholly expunged. Like our five fingers, our ear-bones, our rudimentary caudal appendage, or our other 'vestigial' peculiarities, they may remain as indelible tokens of events in our race-history. Our ancestors may at certain moments have struck into ways of thinking which they might conceivably not have found. But once they did so, and after the fact, the inheritance continues. When you begin a piece of music in a certain key, you must keep the key to the end. You may alter your house *ad libitum,* but the ground-plan of the first architect persists—

you can make great changes, but you can not change a Gothic church into a Doric temple. You may rinse and rinse the bottle, but you can't get the taste of the medicine or whiskey that first filled it wholly out.

My thesis now is this, that *our fundamental ways of thinking about things are discoveries of exceedingly remote ancestors, which have been able to preserve themselves throughout the experience of all subsequent time.* They form one great stage of equilibrium in the human mind's development, the stage of *common sense.* Other stages have grafted themselves upon this stage, but have never succeeded in displacing it. Let us consider this common-sense stage first, as if it might be final.

In practical talk, a man's common sense means his good judgment, his freedom from excentricity, his *gumption,* to use the vernacular word. In philosophy it means something entirely different, it means his use of certain intellectual forms or categories of thought. Were we lobsters, or bees, it might be that our organization would have led to our using quite different modes from these of apprehending our experiences. It *might* be too (we can not dogmatically deny this) that such categories, unimaginable by us to-day, would have proved on the whole as serviceable for handling our experiences mentally as those which we actually use.

If this sounds paradoxical to any one, let him think of analytical geometry. The identical figures which Euclid defined by intrinsic relations were defined by Descartes by the relations of their points to adventitious co-ordinates, the result being an absolutely different and vastly more potent way of handling curves. All our conceptions are what the Germans call *Denkmittel,* means by which we handle facts by thinking them. Experience merely as such doesn't come ticketed and labelled, we have first to discover what it is. Kant speaks of it as being in its first intention a *gewühl der erscheinungen,* a *rhapsodie der wahrnehmungen,* a mere motley which we have to unify by our wits. What we usually do is first to frame some system of concepts mentally classified, serialized, or connected in some intellectual way, and then to use this as a tally by which we 'keep tab' on the impressions that present themselves. When each is referred to some possible place in the conceptual system, it is thereby 'understood.' This notion of parallel 'manifolds' with their elements standing reciprocally in 'one-to-one relations,' is proving so convenient nowadays in mathematics and logic as to supersede more and more the older classificatory conceptions. There are many conceptual systems of this sort; and the sense manifold is also such a system. Find a one-to-one relation for your sense-impressions *anywhere* among the concepts, and in so far forth you rationalize the impressions. But obviously you can rationalize them by using various conceptual systems.

The old common-sense way of rationalizing them is by a set of concepts of which the most important are these:

> Thing;
> The same or different;
> Kinds;
> Minds;
> Bodies;
> One Time;
> One Space;
> Subjects and attributes;
> Causal influences;
> The fancied;
> The real.

We are now so familiar with the order that these notions have woven for us out of the everlasting weather of our perceptions that we find it hard to realize how little of a fixed routine the perceptions follow when taken by themselves. The word weather is a good one to use here. In Boston, for example, the weather has almost no routine, the only law being that if you have had any weather for two days, you will probably but not certainly have another weather on the third. Weather-experience as it thus comes to Boston is discontinuous, and chaotic. In point of temperature, of wind, rain or sunshine, it *may* change three times a day. But the Washington weather-bureau intellectualizes this disorder by making each successive bit of Boston weather *episodic*. It refers it to its place and moment in a continental cyclone, on the history of which the local changes everywhere are strung as beads are strung upon a cord.

Now it seems almost certain that young children and the inferior animals take all their experiences very much as uninstructed Bostonians take their weather. They know no more of time, or space, as world-receptacles, or of permanent subjects and changing predicates, or of causes, or kinds, or thoughts, or things, than our common people know of continental cyclones. A baby's rattle drops out of his hand, but the baby looks not for it. It has 'gone out' for him, as a candle-flame goes out; and it comes back, when you replace it in his hand, as the flame comes back when relit. The idea of its being a 'thing,' whose permanent existence by itself he might interpolate between its successive apparitions has evidently not occurred to him. It is the same with dogs. Out of sight, out of mind, with them. It is pretty evident that they have no *general* tendency to interpolate 'things.' Let me quote here a passage from my colleague G. Santayana's book.

"If a dog, while sniffing about contentedly, sees his master arriving after a long absence . . . the poor brute asks for no reason why his master went, why he has come again, why he should be loved, or why presently while lying at his feet you forget him and begin to grunt and dream of the chase—all that is an utter mystery, utterly unconsidered. Such experience has variety, scenery, and a certain vital rhythm; its story might be told in dithyrambic verse. It moves wholly by inspiration; every event is providential, every act unpremeditated. Absolute freedom and absolute helplessness have met together: you depend wholly on divine favor, yet that unfathomable agency is not distinguishable from your own life. . . . [But] the figures even of that disordered drama have their exits and their entrances; and their cues can be gradually discovered by a being capable of fixing his attention and retaining the order of events. . . . In proportion as such understanding advances, each moment of experience becomes consequential and prophetic of the rest. The calm places in life are filled with power and its spasms with resource. No emotion can overwhelm the mind, for of none is the basis or issue wholly hidden; no event can disconcert it altogether, because it sees beyond. Means can be looked for to escape from the worst predicament; and whereas each moment had been formerly filled with nothing but its own adventures and surprised emotion, each now makes room for the lesson of what went before and surmises what may be the plot of the whole." [19]

Even to-day science and philosophy are still laboriously trying to part fancies from realities in our experience; and in primitive times they made only the most incipient distinctions in this line. Men believed whatever they thought with any liveliness, and they mixed their dreams with their realities inextricably. The categories of 'thought' and 'things' are indispensable here—instead of being realities we now call certain experiences only 'thoughts.' There is not a category, among those enumerated, of which we may not imagine the use to have thus originated historically and only gradually spread.

That one Time which we all believe in and in which each event has its definite date, that one Space in which each thing has its position, these abstract notions unify the world incomparably; but in their finished shape as concepts how different they are from the loose unordered time-and-space experiences of natural men! Everything that happens to us brings its own duration and extension, and both are vaguely surrounded by a marginal 'more' that runs into the duration and extension of the next thing that comes. But we soon lose all our definite bearings; and not only do our children make no distinction between yesterday and the day before yesterday, the whole past being churned up together, but we adults still do so whenever the times are large. It is the same with spaces. On a map I can distinctly see the relation of London, Constantinople, and Pekin to the place where I am; in reality I utterly fail to *feel* the facts which the map symbolizes.

[19] *The Life of Reason: Reason in Common Sense*, 1905, p. 59.

The directions and distances are vague, confused and mixed. Cosmic space and cosmic time, so far from being the intuitions that Kant said they were, are constructions as patently artificial as any that science can show. The great majority of the human race never use these notions, but live in plural times and spaces, interpenetrant and *durcheinander*.

Permanent 'things' again; the 'same' thing and its various 'appearances' and 'alterations'; the different 'kinds' of thing; with the 'kind' used finally as a 'predicate,' of which the thing remains the 'subject'—what a straightening of the tangle of our experience's immediate flux and sensible variety does this list of terms suggest! And it is only the smallest part of his experience's flux that any one actually does straighten out by applying to it these conceptual instruments. Out of them all our lowest ancestors probably used only, and then most vaguely and inaccurately, the notion of 'the same again.' But even then if you had asked them whether the same were a 'thing' that had endured throughout the unseen interval, they would probably have been at a loss, and would have said that they had never asked that question, or considered matters in that light.

Kinds, and sameness of kind—what colossally useful *denkmittel* for finding our way among the many! The manyness might conceivably have been absolute. Experiences might have all been singulars, no one of them occurring twice. In such a world logic would have had no application; for kind and sameness of kind are logic's only instruments. Once we know that whatever is of a kind is also of that kind's kind, we can travel through the universe as if with seven-league boots. Brutes surely never use these abstractions, and civilized men use them in most various amounts.

Causal influence, again! This, if anything, seems to have been an antediluvian conception; for we find primitive men thinking that almost everything is significant and can exert influence of some sort. The search for the more definite influences seems to have started in the question: "Who, or what is to blame?"—for any illness, namely, or disaster, or untoward thing. From this centre the search for causal influences has spread. Hume and 'Science' together have tried to eliminate the whole notion of influence, substituting the entirely different *denkmittel* of 'law.' But law is a comparatively recent invention, and influence reigns supreme in the older realm of common sense.

The 'possible,' as something less than the actual and more than the wholly unreal, is another of these magisterial notions of common sense. Criticise them as you may, they persist; and we fly back to them the moment critical pressure is relaxed. 'Self,' 'body,' in the substantial or metaphysical sense—no one escapes subjection to *those* forms of thought. In practice, the common-sense *denkmittel* are uniformly victorious. Every one, however instructed, still thinks of a 'thing' in the common-sense way, as a permanent unit-subject that 'supports' its attributes interchangeably. No one stably or sincerely uses the more critical notion, of a group of sense-qualities united by a law. With these categories in our hand, we make our plans and plot together, and connect all the remoter parts of experience with what lies before our eyes. Our later and more critical philosophies are mere fads and fancies compared with this natural mother-tongue of thought.

Common sense appears thus as a perfectly definite stage in our understanding of things, a stage that satisfies in an extraordinarily successful way the purposes for which we think. 'Things' do exist, even when we do not see them. Their 'kinds' also exist. Their 'qualities' are what they act by, and are what we act on; and these also exist. These lamps shed their quality of light on every object in this room. We intercept *it* on its way whenever we hold up an opaque screen. It is the very sound that my lips emit that travels into your ears. It is the sensible heat of the fire that migrates into the water in which we boil an egg; and we can change the heat into coolness by dropping in a lump of ice. At this stage of philosophy all non-European men without exception have remained. It suffices for all the necessary practical ends of life; and, among our race even, it is only the highly sophisticated specimens, the minds debauched by learning, as Berkeley calls them, who have ever even suspected common sense of not being absolutely true.

But when we look back, and speculate as to how the common-sense categories may have achieved their wonderful supremacy, no reason appears why it may not have been by a process just like that by which the conceptions due to Democritus, Berkeley, or Darwin, achieved their similar triumphs in more recent times. In other words, they may have been successfully *discovered* by prehistoric geniuses whose names the night of antiquity has covered up; they may have been verified by the immediate facts of experience which they first fitted; and then from fact to fact and from man to man they may have *spread,* until all language rested on them and we are now incapable of thinking naturally in any other terms. Such a view would only follow the rule that has proved elsewhere so fertile, of assuming the vast and remote to conform to the laws of formation that we can observe at work in the small and near.

For all utilitarian practical purposes these conceptions amply suffice; but that they began at special points of discovery and only gradually spread from one thing to another, seems proved by the exceedingly dubious limits of their application to-day. We assume for certain purposes one 'objective' Time that *aequabiliter fluit,* but we don't livingly believe in or realize any such equally-flowing time. 'Space' is a less vague notion; but 'things,' what are they? Is a constellation properly a thing? or an army? or is an *ens rationis* such as space or justice a thing? Is a knife whose handle and blade are changed the 'same'? Is the 'changeling,' whom Locke so seriously discusses, of the human 'kind'? Is 'telepathy' a 'fancy' or a 'fact'? The moment you pass beyond the practical use of these categories (a use usually suggested sufficiently by the circumstances of the special case) to a merely curious or speculative way of thinking, you find it impossible to say within just what limits of fact any one of them shall apply.

The peripatetic philosophy, obeying rationalist propensities, has tried to eternalize the common-sense categories by treating them very technically and articulately. A 'thing' for instance is a being, or *ens*. An *ens* is a subject in which qualities 'inhere.' A subject is a substance. Substances are of kinds, and kinds are definite in number, and discrete. These distinctions are fundamental and eternal. As terms of *discourse* they are indeed magnificently useful, but what they mean, apart from their use in steering our discourse to profitable issues, does not appear. If you ask a scholastic philosopher what a substance may be in itself, apart from its being the support of attributes, he simply says that your intellect knows perfectly what the word means.

But what the intellect knows clearly is only the word itself and its steering function. So it comes about that intellects *sibi permissi*, intellects only curious and idle, have forsaken the common-sense level for what in general terms may be called the 'critical' level of thought. Not merely *such* intellects either—your Humes and Berkeleys and Hegels; but practical observers of facts, your Galileos, Daltons, Faradays, have found it impossible to treat the *naïfs* sense-termini of common sense as ultimately real. As common sense interpolates her constant 'things' between our intermittent sensations, so science *extra*polates her world of 'primary' qualities, her atoms, her ether, her magnetic fields, and the like, beyond the common-sense world. The 'things' are now invisible impalpable things; and the old visible common-sense things are supposed to result from the mixture of these invisibles. Or else the whole *naif* conception of thing gets superseded, and a thing's name is interpreted as denoting only the law or *regel der verbindung* by which certain of our sensations habitually succeed or coexist.

Science and critical philosophy thus burst the bounds of common sense. With science *naif* realism ceases: 'Secondary' qualities become unreal; primary ones alone remain. With critical philosophy, havoc is made of everything. The common-sense categories one and all cease to represent anything in the way of *being;* they are but sublime tricks of human thought, our ways of escaping bewilderment in the midst of sensation's irremediable flow.

But the scientific tendency in critical thought, tho inspired at first by purely intellectual motives, has opened an entirely unexpected range of practical utilities to our astonished view. Galileo gave us accurate clocks and accurate artillery-practice; the chemists flood us with new medicines and dye-stuffs; Ampère and Faraday have endowed us with the New York subway and with Marconi telegrams. The hypothetical things that such men have invented, defined as they have defined them, are showing an extraordinary fertility in consequences verifiable by sense. Our logic can deduce from them a consequence due under certain conditions, we can then bring about the conditions, and presto, the consequence is there before our eyes. The scope of the practical control of nature newly put into our hand by scientific ways of thinking vastly exceeds the scope of the old control grounded on common sense. Its rate of increase accelerates so that no one can trace the limit; one may even fear that the *being* of man may be crushed by his own powers, that his fixed nature as an organism may not prove adequate to stand the strain of the ever increasingly tremendous functions, almost divine creative functions, which his intellect will more and more enable him to wield. He may drown in his wealth like a child in a bath-tub, who has turned on the water and who can not turn it off.

The philosophic stage of criticism, much more thorough in its negations than the scientific stage, so far gives us no new range of practical power. Locke, Hume, Berkeley, Kant, Hegel, have all been utterly sterile, so far as shedding any light on the details of nature goes, and I can think of no invention or discovery that can be directly traced to anything in their peculiar thought, for neither with Berkeley's tar-water nor with Kant's nebular hypothesis had their respective philosophic tenets anything to do. The satisfactions they yield to their disciples are intellectual, not practical; and even then we have to confess that there is a large minus-side to the account.

There are thus at least three well-characterized levels, stages or types of thought about the world we live in, and the notions of one stage have one kind of merit, those of another stage another kind. It is impossible, however, to say that any stage as yet in sight is absolutely more *true* than any other. Common sense is the more *consolidated* stage, because it got its innings first, and made all language into its ally. Whether it or science be the more *august* stage may be left to private judgment. But neither consolidation nor augustness are decisive marks of truth. If common sense were true, why should science have had to brand the secondary qualities, to which our world owes all its living interest, as false, and to invent an invisible world of points and curves, and mathematical equations instead? Why should it have needed to transform causes and activities into laws of 'functional variation'? Vainly did scholasticism, common sense's college-trained younger sister, seek to stereotype the forms the human family had always talked with, to make them definite and fix them for eternity. Substantial forms (in other words our secondary qualities) hardly outlasted the year of our Lord 1600. People were already tired of them then; and Galileo, and Descartes, with his 'new philosophy,' gave them only a little later their *coup de grâce*.

But now if the new kinds of scientific 'thing,' the corpuscular and etheric world, were essentially more 'true,' why should they have excited so much criticism within the body of science itself? Scientific logicians are saying on every hand that these entities and their determinations, however definitely conceived, should not be held for literally real. It is *as if* they existed; but in reality they are like co-ordinates or logarithms, only artificial short-cuts for taking us from one part to another of experience's flux. We can cipher fruitfully with them; they serve us wonderfully; but we must not be their dupes.

There is no *ringing* conclusion possible when we compare these types of thinking, with a view to telling which is the more absolutely true. Their naturalness, their intellectual economy, their fruitfulness for practice, all start up as distinct tests of their veracity, and as a result we get confused. Common sense is *better* for one sphere of life, science for another, philosophic criticism for a third; but whether either be *truer* absolutely, Heaven only knows. Just now, if I understand the matter rightly, we are witnessing a curious reversion to the common sense way of looking at physical nature, in the philosophy of science favored by such men as Mach, Ostwald and Duhem. According to these teachers no hypothesis is truer than any other in the sense of being a more literal copy of reality. They are all but ways of talking on our part, to be compared solely from the point of view of their *use*. The only literally true thing is *reality;* and the only reality we know is, for these logicians, sensible reality, the flux of our sensations and emotions as they pass. 'Energy' is the collective name (according to Ostwald) for the sensations just as they present themselves (the movement, heat, magnetic pull, or light, or whatever it may be) when they are measured in certain ways. So measuring them, we are enabled to describe the correlated changes which they show us, in formulas matchless for their simplicity and fruitfulness for human use. They are sovereign triumphs of economy in thought.

No one can fail to admire the 'energetic' philosophy. But the hypersensible entities, the corpuscles and vibrations, hold their own with most physicists and chemists, in spite of its appeal. It seems too economical to be all-sufficient. Profusion, not economy, may after all be reality's key-note.

I am dealing here with highly technical matters, hardly suitable for popular lecturing and in which my own competence is small. All the better for my conclusion, however, which at this point is this. The whole notion of truth, which naturally and without reflexion we assume to mean the simple duplication by the mind of a ready-made and given reality, proves hard to understand clearly. There is no simple test available for adjudicating offhand between the divers types of thought that claim to possess it. Common sense, common science or corpuscular philosophy, ultra-critical science, or energetics, and critical or idealistic philosophy, all seem insufficiently true in some regard and leave some dissatisfaction. It is evident that the conflict of these so widely differing systems obliges us to overhaul the very idea of truth, for at present we have no definite notion of what the word may mean. I shall face that task in my next lecture, and will add but a few words, in finishing the present one.

There are only two points that I wish you to retain from the present lecture. The first one relates to common sense. We have seen reason to suspect it, to suspect that in spite of their being so venerable, of their being so universally used and built into the very structure of language, its categories may after all be only a collection of extraordinarily successful hypotheses (historically discovered or invented by single men, but gradually communicated, and used by everybody) by which our forefathers have from time immemorial unified and straightened the discontinuity of their immediate experiences, and put themselves into an equilibrium with the surface of nature so satisfactory for ordinary practical purposes that it certainly would have lasted forever, but for the excessive intellectual vivacity of Democritus, Archimedes, Galileo, Berkeley, and of other excentric geniuses whom the example of such men inflamed. Retain, I pray you, this suspicion about common sense.

The other point is this. Ought not the existence of the various types of thinking which we have reviewed, each so splendid for certain purposes, yet all conflicting still, and neither one of them able to support a claim of absolute veracity, to awaken a presumption favorable to the pragmatistic view that all our theories are *instrumental,* are mental modes of *adaptation* to reality, rather than revelations or gnostic answers to some divinely instituted world-engima? I expressed this view as clearly as I could in the second of these lectures. Certainly the restlessness of the actual theoretic situation, the value for some purposes of each thought-level, and the inability of either to expel the others decisively, suggest this pragmatistic view, which I hope that the next lectures may soon make entirely convincing. May there not after all be a possible ambiguity in truth?

PRAGMATISM'S CONCEPTION OF TRUTH*

When Clerk-Maxwell was a child it is written that he had a mania for having everything explained to him, and that when people put him off with vague verbal accounts of any phenomenon he would interrupt them impatiently by saying, 'Yes; but I want you to tell me the *particular go* of it!' Had his question been about truth, only a pragmatist could have told him the particular go of it. I believe that our contemporary pragmatists, especially Messrs. Schiller and Dewey, have given the only tenable account of this subject. It is a very ticklish subject, sending subtle rootlets into all kinds of crannies, and hard to treat in the sketchy way that alone befits. a public lecture. But the Schiller-Dewey view of truth has been so ferociously attacked by rationalistic philosophers, and so abominably misunderstood, that here, if anywhere, is the point where a clear and simple statement should be made.

I fully expect to see the pragmatist view of truth run through the classic stages of a theory's career. First, you know, a new theory is attacked as absurd; then it is admitted to be true, but obvious and insignificant; finally it is seen to be so important that its adversaries claim that they themselves discovered it. Our doctrine of truth is at present in the first of these three stages, with symptoms of the second stage having begun in certain quarters. I wish that this lecture might help it beyond the first stage in the eyes of many of you.

Truth, as any dictionary will tell you, is a property of certain of our ideas. It means their 'agreement,' as falsity means their disagreement, with 'reality.' Pragmatists and intellectualists both accept this definition as a matter of course. They begin to quarrel only after the question is raised as to what may precisely be meant by the term 'agreement,' and what by the term 'reality,' when reality is taken as something for our ideas to agree with.

In answering these questions the pragmatists are more analytic and painstaking, the intellectualists more offhand and irreflective. The popular notion is that a true idea must copy its reality. Like other popular views, this one follows the analogy of the most usual experience. Our true ideas of sensible things do indeed copy them. Shut your eyes and think of yonder clock on the wall, and you get just such a true picture or copy of its dial. But your idea of its 'works' (unless you are a clockmaker) is much less of a copy, yet it passes muster, for it in no way clashes with the reality. Even though it should shrink to

* From: Pragm., 197–236.

the mere word 'works,' that word still serves you truly; and when you speak of the 'time-keeping function' of the clock, or of its spring's 'elasticity,' it is hard to see exactly what your ideas can copy.

You perceive that there is a problem here. Where our ideas cannot copy definitely their object, what does agreement with that object mean? Some idealists seem to say that they are true whenever they are what God means that we ought to think about that object. Others hold the copy-view all through, and speak as if our ideas possessed truth just in proportion as they approach to being copies of the Absolute's eternal way of thinking.

These views, you see, invite pragmatistic discussion. But the great assumption of the intellectualists is that truth means essentially an inert static relation. When you've got your true idea of anything, there's an end of the matter. You're in possession; you *know;* you have fulfilled your thinking destiny. You are where you ought to be mentally; you have obeyed your categorical imperative; and nothing more need follow on that climax of your rational destiny. Epistemologically you are in stable equilibrium.

Pragmatism, on the other hand, asks its usual question. "Grant an idea or belief to be true," it says, "what concrete difference will its being true make in any one's actual life? How will the truth be realized? What experiences will be different from those which would obtain if the belief were false? What, in short, is the truth's cash-value in experiential terms?"

The moment pragmatism asks this question, it sees the answer: *True ideas are those that we can assimilate, validate, corroborate and verify. False ideas are those that we can not.* That is the practical difference it makes to us to have true ideas; that, therefore, is the meaning of truth, for it is all that truth is known-as.

This thesis is what I have to defend. The truth of an idea is not a stagnant property inherent in it. Truth *happens* to an idea. It *becomes* true, is *made* true by events. Its verity *is* in fact an event, a process: the process namely of its verifying itself, its veri-*fication.* Its validity is the process of its valid-*ation.*

But what do the words verification and validation themselves pragmatically mean? They again signify certain practical consequences of the verified and validated idea. It is hard to find any one phrase that characterizes these consequences better than the ordinary agreement-formula—just such consequences being what we have in mind whenever we say that our ideas 'agree' with reality. They lead us, namely, through the acts and other ideas which they instigate, into or up to, or towards, other parts of experience with which we feel all the while—such feeling being among our potentialities—that the original ideas remain in agreement. The connexions and transitions come to us from point to point as being progressive, harmonious, satisfactory. This function of agreeable leading is what we mean by an idea's verification. Such an account is vague and it sounds at first quite trivial, but it has results which it will take the rest of my hour to explain.

Let me begin by reminding you of the fact that the possession of true thoughts means everywhere the possession of invaluable instruments of action; and that our duty to gain truth, so far from being a blank command from out of the blue, or a 'stunt' self-imposed by our intellect, can account for itself by excellent practical reasons.

The importance to human life of having true beliefs about matters of fact is a thing too notorious. We live in a world of realities that can be infinitely useful or infinitely harmful. Ideas that tell us which of them to expect count as the true ideas in all this primary sphere of verification, and the pursuit of such ideas is a primary human duty. The possession of truth, so far from being here an end in itself, is only a preliminary means towards other vital satisfactions. If I am lost in the woods and starved, and find what looks like a cow-path, it is of the utmost importance that I should think of a human habitation at the end of it, for if I do so and follow it, I save myself. The true thought is useful here because the house which is its object is useful. The practical value of true ideas is thus primarily derived from the practical importance of their objects to us. Their objects are, indeed, not important at all times. I may on another occasion have no use for the house; and then my idea of it, however verifiable, will be practically irrelevant, and had better remain latent. Yet since almost any object may some day become temporarily important, the advantage of having a general stock of *extra* truths, of ideas that shall be true of merely possible situations, is obvious. We store such extra truths away in our memories, and with the overflow we fill our books of reference. Whenever such an extra truth becomes practically relevant to one of our emergencies, it passes from cold-storage to do work in the world and our belief in it grows active. You can say of it then either that 'it is useful because it is true' or that 'it is true because it is useful.' Both these phrases mean exactly the same thing, namely that here is an idea that gets fulfilled and can be verified. True is the name for whatever idea starts the verification-process, useful is the name for its completed function in experience. True ideas would never have been singled out as such, would never have acquired a class-name, least of all a name suggesting value, unless they had been useful from the outset in this way.

From this simple cue pragmatism gets her general notion of truth as something essentially bound up with the way in which one moment in our experience may lead us towards other moments which it will be worth while to have been led to. Primarily, and on the common-sense level, the truth of a state of mind means this function of *a leading that is worth while*. When a moment in our experience, of any kind whatever, inspires us with a thought that is true, that means that sooner or later we dip by that thought's guidance into the particulars of experience again and make advantageous connexion with them. This is a vague enough statement, but I beg you to retain it, for it is essential.

Our experience meanwhile is all shot through with regularities. One bit of it can warn us to get ready for another bit, can 'intend' or be 'significant of' that remoter object. The object's advent is the significance's verification. Truth, in these cases, meaning nothing but eventual verification, is manifestly incompatible with waywardness on our part. Woe to him whose beliefs play fast and loose with the order which realities follow in his experience; they will lead him nowhere or else make false connexions.

By 'realities' or 'objects' here, we mean either things of common sense, sensibly present, or else common-sense relations, such as dates, places, distances, kinds, activities. Following our mental image of a house along the cow-path, we actually come to see the house; we get the image's full verification. *Such simply and fully verified leadings are certainly the originals and prototypes of the truth-process*. Experience offers indeed other forms of truth-process, but they are all conceivable as being primary verifications arrested, multiplied or substituted one for another.

Take, for instance, yonder object on the wall. You and I consider it to be a 'clock,' altho no one of us has seen the hidden works that make it one. We let our notion pass for true without attempting to verify. If truths mean verification-process essentially, ought we then to call such unverified truths as this abortive? No, for they form the overwhelmingly large number of the truths we live by. Indirect as well as direct verifications pass muster. Where circumstantial evidence is sufficient, we can go without eye-witnessing. Just as we here assume Japan to exist without ever having been there, because it *works* to do so, everything we know conspiring with the belief, and nothing interfering, so we assume that thing to be a clock. We *use* it as a clock, regulating the length of our lecture by it. The verification of the assumption here means its leading to no frustration or contradiction. Verifi*ability* of wheels and weights and pendulum is as good as verification. For one truth-process completed there are a million in our lives that function in this state of nascency. They turn us *towards* direct verification; lead us into the *surroundings* of the objects they envisage; and then, if everything runs on harmoniously, we are so sure that verification is possible that we omit it, and are usually justified by all that happens.

Truth lives, in fact, for the most part on a credit system. Our thoughts and beliefs 'pass,' so long as nothing challenges them, just as bank-notes pass so long as nobody refuses them. But this all points to direct face-to-face verifications somewhere, without which the fabric of truth collapses like a financial system with no cash-basis whatever. You accept my verification of one thing, I yours of another. We trade on each other's truth. But beliefs verified concretely by *somebody* are the posts of the whole superstructure.

Another great reason—beside economy of time—for waiving complete verification in the usual business of life is that all things exist in kinds and not singly. Our world is found once for all to have that peculiarity. So that when we have once directly verified our ideas about one specimen of a kind, we consider ourselves free to apply them to other specimens without verification. A mind that habitually discerns the kind of thing before it, and acts by the law of the kind immediately, without pausing to verify, will be a 'true' mind in ninety-nine out of a hundred emergencies, proved so by its conduct fitting everything it meets, and getting no refutation.

Indirectly or only potentially verifying processes may thus be true as well as full verification-processes. They work as true processes would work, give us the same advantages, and claim our recognition for the same reasons. All this on the common-sense level of matters of fact, which we are alone considering.

But matters of fact are not our only stock in trade. *Relations among purely mental ideas* form another sphere where true and false beliefs obtain, and here the beliefs are absolute, or unconditional. When they are true they bear the name either of definitions or of principles. It is either a principle or a definition that 1 and 1 make 2, that 2 and 1 make 3, and so on; that white differs less from gray than it does from black; that when the cause begins to act the effect also commences. Such propositions hold of all possible 'ones,' of all conceivable 'whites' and 'grays' and 'causes.' The objects here are mental objects. Their relations are perceptually obvious at a glance, and no sense-verification is necessary. Moreover, once true, always true, of those same mental objects. Truth here has an 'eternal' character. If you can find a concrete thing anywhere that is 'one' or 'white' or 'gray' or an 'effect,' then your principles will everlastingly apply to it. It is but a case of ascertaining the kind, and then applying the law of its kind to the particular object. You are sure to get truth if you can but name the kind rightly, for your mental relations hold good of everything of that kind without exception. If you then, nevertheless, failed to get truth concretely, you would say that you had classed your real objects wrongly.

In this realm of mental relations, truth again is an affair of leading. We relate one abstract idea with another, framing in the end great systems of logical and mathematical truth, under the respective terms of which the sensible facts of experience eventually arrange themselves, so that our eternal truths hold good of realities also. This marriage of fact and theory is endlessly fertile. What we say is here already true in advance of special verification, *if we have subsumed our objects rightly*. Our ready-made ideal framework for all sorts of possible objects follows from the very structure of our thinking. We can no more play fast and loose with these abstract relations than we can do so with our sense-experiences. They coerce us; we must treat them consistently, whether or not we like the results. The rules of addition apply to our debts as rigorously as to our assets. The hundredth decimal of π, the ratio of the circumference to its diameter, is predetermined ideally now, tho no one may have computed it. If we should ever need the figure in our dealings with an actual circle we should need to have it given rightly, calculated by the usual rules; for it is the same kind of truth that those rules elsewhere calculate.

Between the coercions of the sensible order and those of the ideal order, our mind is thus wedged tightly. Our ideas must agree with realities, be such realities concrete or abstract, be they facts or be they principles, under penalty of endless inconsistency and frustration.

So far, intellectualists can raise no protest. They can only say that we have barely touched the skin of the matter.

Realities mean, then, either concrete facts, or abstract kinds of things and relations perceived intuitively between them. They furthermore and thirdly mean, as things that new ideas of ours must no less take account of, the whole body of other truths already in our possession. But what now does 'agreement' with such threefold realities mean?—to use again the definition that is current.

Here it is that pragmatism and intellectualism begin to part company. Primarily, no doubt, to agree means to copy, but we saw that the mere word 'clock' would do instead of a mental picture of its works, and that of many realities our ideas can only be symbols and not copies. 'Past time,' 'power,' 'spontaneity,'—how can our mind copy such realities?

To 'agree' in the widest sense with a reality *can only mean to be guided either straight up to it or into its surroundings, or to be put into such working touch with it as to handle either it or something connected with it better than if we disagreed*. Better either intellectually or practically! And often agreement will only mean the negative fact that nothing contradictory from the quarter of that reality comes to interfere with the way in which our ideas guide us elsewhere. To copy a reality is, indeed, one very important way of agreeing with it, but it is far from being essential. The essential thing is the process of being guided. Any idea that helps us to *deal*, whether practically or intellectually, with either the reality or its belongings, that doesn't entangle our progress in frustrations, that *fits*, in fact, and adapts our life to the reality's whole setting, will agree sufficiently to meet the requirement. It will hold true of that reality.

Thus, *names* are just as 'true' or 'false' as definite mental pictures are. They set up similar verification-processes, and lead to fully equivalent practical results.

All human thinking gets discursified; we exchange ideas; we lend and borrow verifications, get them from one another by means of social intercourse. All truth thus gets verbally built out, stored up, and made available for every one. Hence, we must *talk* consistently just as we must *think* consistently: for both in talk and thought we deal with kinds. Names are arbitrary, but once understood they must be kept to. We mustn't now call Abel 'Cain' or Cain 'Abel.' If we do, we ungear ourselves from the whole book of Genesis, and from all its connexions with the universe of speech and fact down to the present time. We throw ourselves out of whatever truth that entire system of speech and fact may embody.

The overwhelming majority of our true ideas admit of no direct or face-to-face verification—those of past history, for example, as of Cain and Abel. The stream of time can be remounted only verbally, or verified indirectly by the present prolongations or effects of what the past harbored. Yet if they agree with these verbalities and effects, we can know that our ideas of the past are true. *As true as past time itself was,* so true was Julius Cæsar, so true were antediluvian monsters, all in their proper dates and settings. That past time itself was, is guaranteed by its coherence with everything that's present. True as the present *is,* the past *was* also.

Agreement thus turns out to be essentially an affair of leading— leading that is useful because it is into quarters that contain objects that are important. True ideas lead us into useful verbal and conceptual quarters as well as directly up to useful sensible termini. They lead to consistency, stability and flowing human intercourse. They lead away from excentricity and isolation, from foiled and barren thinking. The untrammelled flowing of the leading-process, its general freedom from clash and contradiction, passes for its indirect verification; but all roads lead to Rome, and in the end and eventually, all true processes must lead to the face of directly verifying sensible experiences *somewhere,* which somebody's ideas have copied.

Such is the large loose way in which the pragmatist interprets the word agreement. He treats it altogether practically. He lets it cover any process of conduction from a present idea to a future terminus, provided only it run prosperously. It is only thus that 'scientific' ideas, flying as they do beyond common sense, can be said to agree with their realities. It is, as I have already said, *as if* reality were made of ether, atoms or electrons, but we must n't think so literally. The term 'energy' does n't even pretend to stand for anything 'objective.' It is only a way of measuring the surface of phenomena so as to string their changes on a simple formula.

Yet in the choice of these man-made formulas we can not be capricious with impunity any more than we can be capricious on the common-sense practical level. We must find a theory that will *work;* and that means something extremely difficult; for our theory must mediate between all previous truths and certain new experiences. It must derange common sense and previous belief as little as possible, and it must lead to some sensible terminus or other that can be verified exactly. To 'work' means both these things; and the squeeze is so tight that there is little loose play for any hypothesis. Our theories are wedged and controlled as nothing else is. Yet sometimes alternative theoretic formulas are equally compatible with all the truths we know, and then we choose between them for subjective reasons. We choose the kind of theory to which we are already partial; we follow 'elegance' or 'economy.' Clerk-Maxwell somewhere says it would be 'poor scientific taste' to choose the more complicated of two equally well-evidenced conceptions; and you will all agree with him. Truth in science is what gives us the maximum possible sum of satisfactions, taste included, but consistency both with previous truth and with novel fact is always the most imperious claimant.

I have led you through a very sandy desert. But now, if I may be allowed so vulgar an expression, we begin to taste the milk in the cocoanut. Our rationalist critics here discharge their batteries upon us, and to reply to them will take us out from all this dryness into full sight of a momentous philosophical alternative.

Our account of truth is an account of truths in the plural, of processes of leading, realized *in rebus,* and having only this quality in common, that they *pay.* They pay by guiding us into or towards some part of a system that dips at numerous points into sense-percepts, which we may copy mentally or not, but with which at any rate we are now in the kind of commerce vaguely designated as verification. Truth for us is simply a collective name for verification-processes, just as health, wealth, strength, etc., are names for other processes connected with life, and also pursued because it pays to pursue them. Truth is *made,* just as health, wealth and strength are made, in the course of experience.

Here rationalism is instantaneously up in arms against us. I can imagine a rationalist to talk as follows:

"Truth is not made," he will say; "it absolutely obtains, being a unique relation that does not wait upon any process, but shoots straight over the head of experience, and hits its reality every time. Our belief that yon thing on the wall is a clock is true already, altho no one in the whole history of the world should verify it. The bare quality of standing in that transcendent relation is what makes any thought true that possesses it, whether or not there be verification. You pragmatists put the cart before the horse in making truth's being reside in verification-processes. These are merely signs of its being, merely our lame ways of ascertaining after the fact, which of our ideas already has possessed the wondrous quality. The quality itself is timeless, like all essences and natures. Thoughts partake of it directly, as they partake of falsity or of irrelevancy. It can't be analyzed away into pragmatic consequences."

The whole plausibility of this rationalist tirade is due to the fact to which we have already paid so much attention. In our world, namely, abounding as it does in things of similar kinds and similarly associated, one verification serves for others of its kind, and one great use of knowing things is to be led not so much to them as to their associates, especially to human talk about them. The quality of truth, obtaining *ante rem,* pragmatically means, then, the fact that in such a world innumerable ideas work better by their indirect or possible than by their direct and actual verification. Truth *ante rem* means only verifiability, then; or else it is a case of the stock rationalist trick of treating the *name* of a concrete phenomenal reality as an independent prior entity, and placing it behind the reality as its explanation. Professor Mach quotes somewhere an epigram of Lessing's:

> Sagt Hänschen Schlau zu Vetter Fritz,
> "Wie kommt es, Vetter Fritzen,
> Dass grad' die Reichsten in der Welt,
> Das meiste Geld besitzen?"

Hänschen Schlau here treats the principle 'wealth' as something distinct from the facts denoted by the man's being rich. It antedates them; the facts become only a sort of secondary coincidence with the rich man's essential nature.

In the case of 'wealth' we all see the fallacy. We know that wealth is but a name for concrete processes that certain men's lives play a part in, and not a natural excellence found in Messrs. Rockefeller and Carnegie, but not in the rest of us.

Like wealth, health also lives *in rebus.* It is a name for processes, as digestion, circulation, sleep, etc., that go on happily, tho in this instance we are more inclined to think of it as a principle and to say the man digests and sleeps so well *because* he is so healthy.

With 'strength' we are, I think, more rationalistic still, and decidedly inclined to treat it as an excellence pre-existing in the man and explanatory of the herculean performances of his muscles.

With 'truth' most people go over the border entirely, and treat the rationalistic account as self-evident. But really all these words in *th* are exactly similar. Truth exists *ante rem* just as much and as little as the other things do.

The scholastics, following Aristotle, made much of the distinction between habit and act. Health *in actu* means, among other things, good sleeping and digesting. But a healthy man need not always be sleeping, or always digesting, any more than a wealthy man need be always handling money, or a strong man always lifting weights. All such qualities sink to the status of 'habits' between their times of exercise; and similarly truth becomes a habit of certain of our ideas and beliefs in their intervals of rest from their verifying activities. But those activities are the root of the whole matter, and the condition of there being any habit to exist in the intervals.

'The true,' to put it very briefly, is only the expedient in the way of our thinking, just as 'the right' is only the expedient in the way of our behaving. Expedient in almost any fashion; and expedient in the long run and on the whole of course; for what meets expediently all the experience in sight won't necessarily meet all farther experiences equally satisfactorily. Experience, as we know, has ways of *boiling over,* and making us correct our present formulas.

The 'absolutely' true, meaning what no farther experience will ever alter, is that ideal vanishing-point towards which we imagine that all our temporary truths will some day converge. It runs on all fours with the perfectly wise man, and with the absolutely complete experience; and, if these ideals are ever realized, they will all be realized together. Meanwhile we have to live to-day by what truth we can get to-day, and be ready to-morrow to call it falsehood. Ptolemaic astronomy, euclidean space, aristotelian logic, scholastic metaphysics, were expedient for centuries, but human experience has boiled over those limits, and we now call these things only relatively true, or true within those borders of experience. 'Absolutely' they are false; for we know that those limits were casual, and might have been transcended by past theorists just at they are by present thinkers.

When new experiences lead to retrospective judgments, using the past tense, what these judgments utter *was* true, even tho no past thinker had been led there. We live forwards, a Danish thinker has said, but we understand backwards. The present sheds a backward light on the world's previous processes. They may have been truth-processes for the actors in them. They are not so for one who knows the later revelations of the story.

This regulative notion of a potential better truth to be established later, possibly to be established some day absolutely, and having powers of retroactive legislation, turns its face, like all pragmatist notions, towards concreteness of fact, and towards the future. Like the half-truths, the absolute truth will have to be *made,* made as a relation incidental to the growth of a mass of verification-experience, to which the half-true ideas are all along contributing their quota.

I have already insisted on the fact that truth is made largely out of previous truths. Men's beliefs at any time are so much experience *funded.* But the beliefs are themselves parts of the sum total of the world's experience, and become matter, therefore, for the next day's funding operations. So far as reality means experienceable reality, both it and the truths men gain about it are everlastingly in process of mutation—mutation towards a definite goal, it may be—but still mutation.

Mathematicians can solve problems with two variables. On the Newtonian theory, for instance, acceleration varies with distance, but distance also varies with acceleration. In the realm of truth-processes facts come independently and determine our beliefs provisionally. But these beliefs make us act, and as fast as they do so, they bring into sight or into existence new facts which re-determine the beliefs accordingly. So the whole coil and ball of truth, as it rolls up, is the product of a double influence. Truths emerge from facts; but they dip forward into facts again and add to them; which facts again create or reveal new truth (the word is indifferent) and so on indefinitely. The 'facts' themselves meanwhile are not *true.* They simply *are.* Truth is the function of the beliefs that start and terminate among them.

The case is like a snowball's growth, due as it is to the distribution of the snow on the one hand, and to the successive pushes of the boys on the other, with these factors co-determining each other incessantly.

The most fateful point of difference between being a rationalist and being a pragmatist is now fully in sight. Experience is in mutation, and our psychological ascertainments of truth are in mutation—so much rationalism will allow; but never that either reality itself or truth itself is mutable. Reality stands complete and ready-made from all eternity, rationalism insists, and the agreement of our ideas with it is that unique unanalyzable virtue in them of which she has already told us. As that intrinsic excellence, their truth has nothing to do with our experiences. It adds nothing to the content of experience. It makes no difference to reality itself; it is supervenient, inert, static, a reflexion merely. It doesn't *exist,* it *holds* or *obtains,* it belongs to another dimension from that of either facts or fact-relations, belongs, in short, to the epistemological dimension—and with that big word rationalism closes the discussion.

Thus, just as pragmatism faces forward to the future, so does rationalism here again face backward to a past eternity. True to her inveterate habit, rationalism reverts to 'principles,' and thinks that when an abstraction once is named, we own an oracular solution.

The tremendous pregnancy in the way of consequences for life of this radical difference of outlook will only become apparent in my later lectures. I wish meanwhile to close this lecture by showing that rationalism's sublimity does not save it from inanity.

When, namely, you ask rationalists, instead of accusing pragmatism of desecrating the notion of truth, to define it themselves by saying exactly what *they* understand by it, the only positive attempts I can think of are these two:

1. "Truth is the system of propositions which have an unconditional claim to be recognized as valid." [20]

2. Truth is a name for all those judgments which we find ourselves under obligation to make by a kind of imperative duty.[21]

The first thing that strikes one in such definitions is their unutterable triviality. They are absolutely true, of course, but absolutely insignificant until you handle them pragmatically. What do you mean by 'claim' here, and what do you mean by 'duty'? As summary names for the concrete reasons why thinking in true ways is overwhelmingly expedient and good for mortal men, it is all right to talk of claims on reality's part to be agreed with, and of obligations on our part to agree. We feel both the claims and the obligations, and we feel them for just those reasons.

But the rationalists who talk of claim and obligation *expressly say that they have nothing to do with our practical interests or personal reasons*. Our reasons for agreeing are psychological facts, they say, relative to each thinker, and to the accidents of his life. They are his evidence merely, they are no part of the life of truth itself. That life transacts itself in a purely logical or epistemological, as distinguished from a psychological, dimension, and its claims antedate and exceed all personal motivations whatsoever. Tho neither man nor God should ever ascertain truth, the word would still have to be defined as that which *ought* to be ascertained and recognized.

There never was a more exquisite example of an idea abstracted from the concretes of experience and then used to oppose and negate what it was abstracted from.

Philosophy and common life abound in similar instances. The 'sentimentalist fallacy' is to shed tears over abstract justice and gener-

---

[20] A. E. Taylor, *Philosophical Review*, vol. xiv, p. 288.

[21] H. Rickert, *Der Gegenstand der Erkenntniss*, chapter on 'Die Urtheilsnothwendigkeit.'

osity, beauty, etc., and never to know these qualities when you meet them in the street, because the circumstances make them vulgar. Thus I read in the privately printed biography of an eminently rationalistic mind: "It was strange that with such admiration for beauty in the abstract, my brother had no enthusiasm for fine architecture, for beautiful painting, or for flowers." And in almost the last philosophic work I have read, I find such passages as the following: "Justice is ideal, solely ideal. Reason conceives that it ought to exist, but experience shows that it can not. . . . Truth, which ought to be, can not be. . . . Reason is deformed by experience. As soon as reason enters experience it becomes contrary to reason."

The rationalist's fallacy here is exactly like the sentimentalist's. Both extract a quality from the muddy particulars of experience, and find it so pure when extracted that they contrast it with each and all its muddy instances as an opposite and higher nature. All the while it is *their* nature. It is the nature of truths to be validated, verified. It pays for our ideas to be validated. Our obligation to seek truth is part of our general obligation to do what pays. The payments true ideas bring are the sole why of our duty to follow them. Identical whys exist in the case of wealth and health.

Truth makes no other kind of claim and imposes no other kind of ought than health and wealth do. All these claims are conditional; the concrete benefits we gain are what we mean by calling the pursuit a duty. In the case of truth, untrue beliefs work as perniciously in the long run as true beliefs work beneficially. Talking abstractly, the quality 'true' may thus be said to grow absolutely precious and the quality 'untrue' absolutely damnable: the one may be called good, the other bad, unconditionally. We ought to think the true, we ought to shun the false, imperatively.

But if we treat all this abstraction literally and oppose it to its mother soil in experience, see what a preposterous position we work ourselves into.

We can not take a step forward in our actual thinking. When shall I acknowledge this truth and when that? Shall the acknowledgment be loud?—or silent? If sometimes loud, sometimes silent, which *now?* When may a truth go into cold-storage in the encyclopedia? and when shall it come out for battle? Must I constantly be repeating the truth 'twice two are four' because of its eternal claim on recognition? or is it sometimes irrelevant? Must my thoughts dwell night and day on my personal sins and blemishes, because I truly have them?—or may I sink and ignore them in order to be a decent social unit, and not a mass of morbid melancholy and apology?

It is quite evident that our obligation to acknowledge truth, so far from being unconditional, is tremendously conditioned. Truth with a big T, and in the singular, claims abstractly to be recognized, of course; but concrete truths in the plural need be recognized only when their recognition is expedient. A truth must always be preferred to a falsehood when both relate to the situation; but when neither does, truth is as little of a duty as falsehood. If you ask me what o'clock it is and I tell you that I live at 95 Irving Street, my answer may indeed be true, but you don't see why it is my duty to give it. A false address would be as much to the purpose.

With this admission that there are conditions that limit the application of the abstract imperative, *the pragmatistic treatment of truth sweeps back upon us in its fulness*. Our duty to agree with reality is seen to be grounded in a perfect jungle of concrete expediencies.

When Berkeley had explained what people meant by matter, people thought that he denied matter's existence. When Messrs. Schiller and Dewey now explain what people mean by truth, they are accused of denying *its* existence. These pragmatists destroy all objective standards, critics say, and put foolishness and wisdom on one level. A favorite formula for decribing Mr. Schiller's doctrines and mine is that we are persons who think that by saying whatever you find it pleasant to say and calling it truth you fulfil every pragmatistic requirement.

I leave it to you to judge whether this be not an impudent slander. Pent in, as the pragmatist more than any one else sees himself to be, between the whole body of funded truths squeezed from the past and the coercions of the world of sense about him, who so well as he feels the immense pressure of objective control under which our minds perform their operations? If any one imagines that this law is lax, let him keep its commandment one day, says Emerson. We have heard much of late of the uses of the imagination in science. It is high time to urge the use of a little imagination in philosophy. The unwillingness of some of our critics to read any but the silliest of possible meanings into our statements is as discreditable to their imaginations as anything I know in recent philosophic history. Schiller says the true is that which 'works.' Thereupon he is treated as one who limits verification to the lowest material utilities. Dewey says truth is what gives 'satisfaction.' He is treated as one who believes in calling everything true which, if it were true, would be pleasant.

Our critics certainly need more imagination of realities. I have honestly tried to stretch my own imagination and to read the best possible meaning into the rationalist conception, but I have to confess that it still completely baffles me. The notion of a reality calling on us to 'agree' with it, and that for no reasons, but simply because its claim is 'unconditional' or 'transcendent,' is one that I can make neither head nor tail of. I try to imagine myself as the sole reality in the world, and then to imagine what more I would 'claim' if I were allowed to. If you suggest the possibility of my claiming that a mind should come into being from out of the void inane and stand and *copy* me, I can indeed imagine what the copying might mean, but I can conjure up no motive. What good it would do me to be copied, or what good it would do that mind to copy me, if further consequences are expressly and in principle ruled out as motives for the claim (as they are by our rationalist authorities) I can not fathom. When the Irishman's admirers ran him along to the place of banquet in a sedan with no bottom, he said, "Faith, if it wasn't for the honor of the thing, I might as well have come on foot." So here: but for the honor of the thing, I might as well have remained uncopied. Copying is one genuine mode of knowing (which for some strange reason our contemporary transcendentalists seem to be tumbling over each other to repudiate); but when we get beyond copying, and fall back on unnamed forms of agreeing that are expressly denied to be either copyings or leadings or fittings, or any other processes pragmatically definable, the *what* of the 'agreement' claimed becomes as unintelligible as the why of it. Neither content nor motive can be imagined for it. It is an absolutely meaningless abstraction.[22]

Surely in this field of truth it is the pragmatists and not the rationalists who are the more genuine defenders of the universe's rationality.

A DIALOGUE*

I imagine a residual state of mind on the part of my reader which may still keep him unconvinced, and which it may be my duty to try at least to dispel. I can perhaps be briefer if I put what I have to say in dialogue form. Let then the anti-pragmatist begin:—

Anti-Pragmatist:—You say that the truth of an idea is constituted by its workings. Now suppose a certain state of facts, facts for example of antediluvian planetary history, concerning which the question

[22] I am not forgetting that Professor Rickert long ago gave up the whole notion of truth being founded on agreement with reality. Reality according to him, is whatever agrees with truth, and truth is founded solely on our primal duty. This fantastic flight, together with Mr. Joachim's candid confession of failure in his book *The Nature of Truth,* seems to me to mark the bankruptcy of rationalism when dealing with this subject. Rickert deals with part of the pragmatistic position under the head of what he calls 'Relativismus.' I can not discuss his text here. Suffice it to say that his argumentation in that chapter is so feeble as to seem almost incredible in so generally able a writer.

* From: M.T., 287–298.

may be asked: 'Shall the truth about them ever be known?' And suppose (leaving the hypothesis of an omniscient absolute out of the account) that we assume that the truth is never to be known. I ask you now, brother pragmatist, whether according to you there can be said to be any truth at all about such a state of facts. Is there a truth, or is there not a truth, in cases where at any rate it never comes to be known?

Pragmatist:—Why do you ask me such a question?

Anti-Prag.:—Because I think it puts you in a bad dilemma.

Prag.:—How so?

Anti-Prag.:—Why, because if on the one hand you elect to say that there is a truth, you thereby surrender your whole pragmatist theory. According to that theory, truth requires ideas and workings to constitute it; but in the present instance there is supposed to be no knower, and consequently neither ideas nor workings can exist. What then remains for you to make your truth of?

Prag.:—Do you wish, like so many of my enemies, to force me to make the truth out of the reality itself? I cannot: the truth is something known, thought or said about the reality, and consequently numerically additional to it. But probably your intent is something different; so before I say which horn of your dilemma I choose, I ask you to let me hear what the other horn may be.

Anti-Prag.:—The other horn is this, that if you elect to say that there is *no* truth under the conditions assumed, because there are no ideas or workings, then you fly in the face of common sense. Does n't common sense believe that every state of facts must in the nature of things be truly statable in some kind of a proposition, even tho in point of fact the proposition should never be propounded by a living soul?

Prag.:—Unquestionably common sense believes this, and so do I. There have been innumerable events in the history of our planet of which nobody ever has been or ever will be able to give an account, yet of which it can already be said abstractly that only one sort of possible account can ever be true. The truth about any such event is thus already generically predetermined by the event's nature; and one may accordingly say with a perfectly good conscience that it virtually pre-exists. Common sense is thus right in its instinctive contention.

Anti-Prag.:—Is this then the horn of the dilemma which you stand for? Do you say that there is a truth even in cases where it shall never be known?

Prag.:—Indeed I do, provided you let me hold consistently to my own conception of truth, and do not ask me to abandon it for something which I find impossible to comprehend.—You also believe, do you not, that there is a truth, even in cases where it never shall be known?

Anti-Prag.:—I do indeed believe so.

Prag.:—Pray then inform me in what, according to you, this truth regarding the unknown consists.

Anti-Prag.:—Consists?—pray what do you mean by 'consists'? It consists in nothing but itself, or more properly speaking it has neither consistence nor existence, it obtains, it *holds*.

Prag.:—Well, what relation does it bear to the reality of which it holds?

Anti-Prag.:—How do you mean, 'what relation'? It holds *of* it, of course; it knows it, it represents it.

Prag.:—Who knows it? What represents it?

Anti-Prag.:—The truth does; the truth knows it; or rather not exactly that, but any one knows it who *possesses* the truth. Any true idea of the reality *represents* the truth concerning it.

Prag.:—But I thought that we had agreed that no knower of it, nor any idea representing it was to be supposed.

Anti-Prag.:—Sure enough!

Prag.:—Then I beg you again to tell me in what this truth consists, all by itself, this *tertium quid* intermediate between the facts *per se,* on the one hand, and all knowledge of them, actual or potential, on the other. What is the shape of it in this third estate? Of what stuff, mental, physical, or 'epistemological,' is it built? What metaphysical region of reality does it inhabit?

Anti-Prag.:—What absurd questions! Is n't it enough to say that it *is true* that the facts are so-and-so, and false that they are otherwise?

Prag.:—'It' is true that the facts are so-and-so—I won't yield to the temptation of asking you *what* is true; but I do ask you whether your phrase that 'it is true that' the facts are so-and-so really means anything really additional to the bare *being* so-and-so of the facts themselves.

Anti-Prag.:—It seems to mean more than the bare being of the facts. It is a sort of mental equivalent for them, their epistemological function, their value in noetic terms.

Prag.:—A sort of spiritual double or ghost of them, apparently! If so, may I ask you *where* this truth is found.

Anti-Prag.:—Where? where? There is no 'where'—it simply obtains, absolutely obtains.

Prag.:—Not in any one's mind?

Anti-Prag.:—No, for we agreed that no actual knower of the truth should be assumed.

Prag.:—No actual knower, I agree. But are you sure that no notion of a potential or ideal knower has anything to do with forming this strangely elusive idea of the truth of the facts in your mind?

Anti-Prag.:—Of course if there be a truth concerning the facts, that truth is what the ideal knower would know. To that extent you can't keep the notion of it and the notion of him separate. But it is not him first and then it; it is it first and then him, in my opinion.

Prag.:—But you still leave me terribly puzzled as to the status of this so-called truth, hanging as it does between earth and heaven, between reality and knowledge, grounded in the reality, yet numerically additional to it, and at the same time antecedent to any knower's opinion and entirely independent thereof. Is it as independent of the knower as you suppose? It looks to me terribly dubious, as if it might be only another name for a potential as distinguished from an actual knowledge of the reality. Isn't your truth, after all, simply what any successful knower *would* have to know *in case he existed?* And in a universe where no knowers were even conceivable would any truth about the facts there as something numerically distinguishable from the facts themselves, find a place to exist in? To me such truth would not only be non-existent, it would be unimaginable, inconceivable.

Anti-Prag.:—But I thought you said a while ago that there *is* a truth of past events, even tho no one shall ever know it.

Prag.:—Yes, but you must remember that I also stipulated for permission to define the word in my own fashion. The truth of an event, past, present, or future, is for me only another name for the fact that *if* the event ever *does* get known, the nature of the knowledge is already to some degree predetermined. The truth which precedes actual knowledge of a fact means only what any possible knower of the fact will eventually find himself necessitated to believe about it. He must believe something that will bring him into satisfactory relations with it, that will prove a decent mental substitute for it. What this something may be is of course partly fixed already by the nature of the fact and by the sphere of its associations.

This seems to me all that you can clearly mean when you say that truth pre-exists to knowledge. It is knowledge anticipated, knowledge in the form of possibility merely.

Anti-Prag.:—But what does the knowledge know when it comes? Doesn't it know the *truth?* And, if so, mustn't the truth be distinct from either the fact or the knowledge?

Prag.:—It seems to me that what the knowledge knows is the fact itself, the event, or whatever the reality may be. Where you see three distinct entities in the field, the reality, the knowing, and the truth, I see only two. Moreover, I can see what each of my two entities is *known-as,* but when I ask myself what your third entity, the truth, is known-as, I can find nothing distinct from the reality on the one hand, and the ways in which it may be known on the other. Are you not probably misled by common language, which has found it convenient to introduce a hybrid name, meaning sometimes a kind of knowing and sometimes a reality known, to apply to either of these things interchangeably? And has philosophy anything to gain by perpetuating and consecrating the ambiguity? If you call the object of knowledge 'reality,' and call the manner of its being cognized 'truth,' cognized moreover on particular occasions, and variously, by particular human beings who have their various businesses with it, and if you hold consistently to this nomenclature, it seems to me that you escape all sorts of trouble.

Anti-Prag.:—Do you mean that you think you escape from my dilemma?

Prag.:—Assuredly I escape; for if truth and knowledge are terms correlative and interdependent, as I maintain they are, then wherever knowledge is conceivable truth is conceivable, wherever knowledge is possible truth is possible, wherever knowledge is actual truth is actual. Therefore when you point your first horn at me, I think of truth *actual,* and say it does n't exist. It does n't; for by hypothesis there is no knower, no ideas, no workings. I agree, however, that truth *possible* or *virtual* might exist, for a knower might possibly be brought to birth; and truth *conceivable* certainly exists, for, abstractly taken, there is nothing in the nature of antediluvian events that should make the application of knowledge to them inconceivable. Therefore when you try to impale me on your second horn, I think of the truth in question as a mere abstract possibility, so I say it does exist, and side with common sense.

Do not these distinctions rightly relieve me from embarrassment? And don't you think it might help you to make them yourself?

Anti-Prag..—Never!—so avaunt with your abominable hairsplitting and sophistry! Truth is truth; and never will I degrade it by identifying it with low pragmatic particulars in the way you propose.

Prag.:—Well, my dear antagonist, I hardly hoped to convert an eminent intellectualist and logician like you; so enjoy, as long as you live, your own ineffable conception. Perhaps the rising generation will grow up more accustomed than you are to that concrete and empirical interpretation of terms in which the pragmatic method consists. Perhaps they may then wonder how so harmless and natural an account of truth as mine could have found such difficulty in entering the minds of men far more intelligent than I can ever hope to become, but wedded by education and tradition to the abstractionist manner of thought.

INTERVIEW IN [THE] NEW YORK TIMES, 1907*

It is true that pragmatist writers have laid more stress than any previous philosophers on human action. But nothing could be more ludicrous than to call this their primary interest, or to explain it by their belief that purely theoretical knowledge of reality, and truth as such, are unattainable. Pragmatism's primary interest is in its doctrine of truth. All pragmatist writers make this the centre of their speculations; not one of them is sceptical, not one doubts our ultimate ability to penetrate theoretically into the very core of reality. . . .

Instead of being a practical substitute for philosophy, good for engineers, doctors, sewage experts, and vigorous untaught minds in general to feed upon, pragmatism has proved so over-subtle that even academic critics have failed to catch its question, to say nothing of their misunderstanding of its answer. Whatever propositions or beliefs may, in point of fact, prove true, it says, the truth of them consists in certain definable *relations between them and the reality* of which they make report. . . . Philosophers have generally been satisfied with the word "agreement" here, but pragmatists have seen that this word covers many different concrete possibilities. . . . There are all sorts of ways of having to do with a thing. To know it, we must mean *that* thing, and not another thing; we must be able to portray or copy its inherent nature; and we must know innumerable things *about* it and its relations to other things. To know it rightly, moreover, we must not go astray among all these many ways of knowing it, but select the way that fits in with our momentary interest, be the latter practical or theoretical, and select the way that will work. . . . Thus the first vague notion of "agreement" with reality becomes specified into that of innumerable ways in which our thoughts may *fit* reality, ways in which the mind's activities coöperate on equal terms with the reality in producing the fit resultant truth. . . .

Mind *engenders* truth *upon* reality. . . . Our minds are not here simply to copy a reality that is already complete. They are here to complete it, to add to its importance by their own remodeling of it, to decant its contents over, so to speak, into a more significant shape. In point of fact, the *use* of most of our thinking is to help us to *change* the world. We must for this know definitely *what* we have to change,

---

* From: T.C., II, 478–480. Originally "from W.J.'s mss., the interview, by Edwin Bjorkman, appeared in the *N. Y. Times,* Nov. 3, 1907." [T.C., II, 480]

and thus theoretic truth must at all times come before practical application. But the pragmatist writers have shown that what we here call theoretic truth . . . will be . . . irrelevant unless it fits the . . . purpose in hand. . . . And, moreover, it turns out that the theoretic truth upon which men base their practice today is itself a resultant of previous human practice, based in turn upon still . . . previous truth . . . so that we may think of all truth whatever as containing so much human practice funded. . . . Thus we seem set free to use our theoretical as well as our practical faculties—the practical here in the narrower sense—to get the world into a better shape, and all with a good conscience. The only restriction is that the world resists some lines of attack on our part and opens herself to others, so that we must go on with the grain of her willingness. . . . Hence the *sursum corda* of pragmatism's message. . . .

There never was such confusion. The tower of Babel was monotony in comparison. The fault has lain on both sides. Dewey is obscure; Schiller bumptious and hasty; James's doctrine of radical empiricism, which has nothing to do with pragmatism and sounds idealistic, has been confounded with his pragmatism; pragmatism itself covers two or three distinct theses; the critics . . . opened fire before the pragmatists had got their words out; everyone has spoken at once, and the upshot has made one despair of men's intelligence. But little by little the mud will settle to the bottom. . . . We shall soon find ourselves at home in the pragmatic view and temper, and will then say that it was not worth so much hubbub.

PRAGMATISM AND HUMANISM*

What hardens the heart of every one I approach with the view of truth sketched in my lecture on "Truth" is that typical idol of the tribe, the notion of *the* Truth, conceived as the one answer, determinate and complete, to the one fixed enigma which the world is believed to propound. For popular tradition, it is all the better if the answer be oracular, so as itself to awaken wonder as an enigma of the second order, veiling rather than revealing what its profundities are supposed to contain. All the great single-word answers to the world's riddle, such as God, the One, Reason, Law, Spirit, Matter, Nature, Polarity, the Dialectic Process, the Idea, the Self, the Oversoul, draw the admira-

* From: Pragm., 239–270.

tion that men have lavished on them from this oracular rôle. By amateurs in philosophy and professionals alike, the universe is represented
as a queer sort of petrified sphinx whose appeal to men consists in a
monotonous challenge to his divining powers. *The* Truth: what a perfect idol of the rationalistic mind! I read in an old letter—from a gifted
friend who died too young—these words: "In everything, in science,
art, morals and religion, there *must* be one system that is right and
every other wrong." How characteristic of the enthusiasm of a certain
stage of youth! At twenty-one we rise to such a challenge and expect
to find the system. It never occurs to most of us even later that the
question 'what is *the* truth?' is no real question (being irrelative to all
conditions) and that the whole notion of *the* truth is an abstraction
from the fact of truths in the plural, a mere useful summarizing phrase
like *the* Latin Language or *the* Law.

Common-law judges sometimes talk about the law, and schoolmasters talk about the latin tongue, in a way to make their hearers
think they mean entities pre-existent to the decisions or to the words
and syntax, determining them unequivocally and requiring them to
obey. But the slightest exercise of reflection makes us see that, instead
of being principles of this kind, both law and latin are results. Distinctions between the lawful and the unlawful in conduct, or between the
correct and incorrect in speech, have grown up incidentally among the
interactions of men's experiences in detail; and in no other way do
distinctions between the true and the false in belief ever grow up.
Truth grafts itself on previous truth, modifying it in the process, just
as idiom grafts itself on previous idiom, and law on previous law.
Given previous law and a novel case, and the judge will twist them
into fresh law. Previous idiom; new slang or metaphor or oddity that
hits the public taste;—and presto, a new idiom is made. Previous
truth; fresh facts:—and our mind finds a new truth.

All the while, however, we pretend that the eternal is unrolling,
that the one previous justice, grammar or truth are simply fulgurating
and not being made. But imagine a youth in the courtroom trying
cases with his abstract notion of 'the' law, or a censor of speech let
loose among the theatres with his idea of 'the' mother-tongue, or a
professor setting up to lecture on the actual universe with his rationalistic notion of 'the Truth' with a big T, and what progress do they
make? Truth, law, and language fairly boil away from them at the
least touch of novel fact. These things *make themselves* as we go. Our
rights, wrongs, prohibitions, penalties, words, forms, idioms, beliefs,
are so many new creations that add themselves as fast as history proceeds. Far from being antecedent principles that animate the process,
law, language, truth are but abstract names for its results.

Laws and languages at any rate are thus seen to be man-made

things. Mr. Schiller applies the analogy to beliefs, and proposes the name of 'Humanism' for the doctrine that to an unascertainable extent our truths are man-made products too. Human motives sharpen all our questions, human satisfactions lurk in all our answers, all our formulas have a human twist. This element is so inextricable in the products that Mr. Schiller sometimes seems almost to leave it an open question whether there be anything else. "The world," he says, "is essentially ὕλη, it is what we make it. It is fruitless to define it by what it originally was or by what it is apart from us; it *is* what is made of it. Hence . . . the world *is plastic*." [23] He adds that we can learn the limits of the plasticity only by trying, and that we ought to start as if it were wholly plastic, acting methodically on that assumption, and stopping only when we are decisively rebuked.

This is Mr. Schiller's butt-end-foremost statement of the humanist position, and it has exposed him to severe attack. I mean to defend the humanist position in this lecture, so I will insinuate a few remarks at this point.

Mr. Schiller admits as emphatically as any one the presence of resisting factors in every actual experience of truth-making, of which the new-made special truth must take account, and with which it has perforce to 'agree.' All our truths are beliefs about 'Reality'; and in any particular belief the reality acts as something independent, as a thing *found*, not manufactured. Let me here recall a bit of my last lecture.

'Reality' is in general what truths have to take acount of;[24] and the *first* part of reality from this point of view is the flux of our sensations. Sensations are forced upon us, coming we know not whence. Over their nature, order and quantity we have as good as no control. *They* are neither true nor false; they simply *are*. It is only what we say about them, only the names we give them, our theories of their source and nature and remote relations, that may be true or not.

The *second* part of reality, as something that our beliefs must also obediently take account of is the *relations* that obtain between our sensations or between their copies in our minds. This part falls into two sub-parts: 1) the relations that are mutable and accidental, as those of date and place; and 2) those that are fixed and essential because they are grounded on the inner natures of their terms. Both sorts of relation are matters of immediate perception. Both are 'facts.' But it is the latter kind of fact that forms the more important sub-part of reality for our theories of knowledge. Inner relations namely are 'eternal,' are perceived whenever their sensible terms are compared;

---

[23] *Personal Idealism*, p. 60.
[24] Mr. Taylor in his *Elements of Metaphysics* uses this excellent pragmatic definition.

and of them our thought—mathematical and logical thought so-called —must eternally take account.

The *third* part of reality, additional to these perceptions (tho largely based upon them), is the *previous truths* of which every new inquiry takes account. This third part is a much less obdurately resisting factor: it often ends by giving way. In speaking of these three portions of reality as at all times controlling our belief's formation, I am only reminding you of what we heard in our last hour.

Now however fixed these elements of reality may be, we still have a certain freedom in our dealings with them. Take our sensations. *That* they are is undoubtedly beyond our control; but *which* we attend to, note, and make emphatic in our conclusions depends on our own interests; and, according as we lay the emphasis here or there, quite different formulations of truth result. We read the same facts differently. 'Waterloo,' with the same fixed details, spells a 'victory' for an Englishman; for a Frenchman it spells a 'defeat.' So, for an optimist philosopher the universe spells victory, for a pessimist, defeat.

What we say about reality thus depends on the perspective into which we throw it. The *that* of it is its own; but the *what* depends on the *which;* and the which depends on *us.* Both the sensational and the relational parts of reality are dumb; they say absolutely nothing about themselves. We it is who have to speak for them. This dumbness of sensations has led such intellectualists as T. H. Green and Edward Caird to shove them almost beyond the pale of philosophic recognition, but pragmatists refuse to go so far. A sensation is rather like a client who has given his case to a lawyer and then has passively to listen in the courtroom to whatever account of his affairs, pleasant or unpleasant, the lawyer finds it most expedient to give.

Hence, even in the field of sensation, our minds exert a certain arbitrary choice. By our inclusions and omissions we trace the field's extent; by our emphasis we mark its foreground and its background; by our order we read it in this direction or in that. We receive in short the block of marble, but we carve the statue ourselves.

This applies to the 'eternal' parts of reality as well: we shuffle our perceptions of intrinsic relation and arrange them just as freely. We read them in one serial order or another, class them in this way or in that, treat one or the other as more fundamental, until our beliefs about them form those bodies of truth known as logics, geometrics, or arithmetics, in each and all of which the form and order in which the whole is cast is flagrantly man-made.

Thus, to say nothing of the new *facts* which men add to the matter of reality by the acts of their own lives, they have already impressed their mental forms on that whole third of reality which I have called 'previous truths.' Every hour brings its new percepts, its own facts of sensation and relation, to be truly taken account of; but the whole of our *past* dealings with such facts is already funded in the previous truths. It is therefore only the smallest and recentest fraction of the first two parts of reality that comes to us without the human touch, and that fraction has immediately to become humanized in the sense of being squared, assimilated, or in some way adapted, to the humanized mass already there. As a matter of fact we can hardly take in an impression at all, in the absence of a preconception of what impressions there may possibly be.

When we talk of reality 'independent' of human thinking, then, it seems a thing very hard to find. It reduces to the notion of what is just entering into experience and yet to be named, or else to some imagined aboriginal presence in experience, before any belief about the presence had arisen, before any human conception had been applied. It is what is absolutely dumb and evanescent, the merely ideal limit of our minds. We may glimpse it, but we never grasp it; what we grasp is always some substitute for it which previous human thinking has peptonized and cooked for our consumption. If so vulgar an expression were allowed us, we might say that wherever we find it, it has been already *faked.* This is what Mr. Schiller has in mind when he calls independent reality a mere unresisting ὕλη, which *is* only to be made over by us.

That is Mr. Schiller's belief about the sensible core of reality. We 'encounter' it (in Mr. Bradley's words) but don't possess it. Superficially this sounds like Kant's view; but between categories fulminated before nature began, and categories gradually forming themselves in nature's presence, the whole chasm between rationalism and empiricism yawns. To the genuine 'Kantianer' Schiller will always be to Kant as a satyr to Hyperion.

Other pragmatists may reach more positive beliefs about the sensible core of reality. They may think to get at it in its independent nature, by peeling off the successive man-made wrappings. They make theories that tell us where it comes from and all about it; and *if these theories work satisfactorily they will be true.* The transcendental idealists say there is no core, the finally completed wrapping being reality and truth in one. Scholasticism still teaches that the core is 'matter.' Professor Bergson, Heymans, Strong, and others believe in the core and bravely try to define it. Messrs. Dewey and Schiller treat it as a 'limit.' Which is the truer of all these diverse accounts, or of others comparable with them, unless it be the one that finally proves the most satisfactory? On the one hand there will stand reality, on the other an account of it which it proves impossible to better or to alter. If the impossibility prove permanent, the truth of the account will be absolute. Other content of truth than this I can find nowhere. If the anti-pragmatists have any other meaning, let them for heaven's sake reveal it, let them grant us access to it!

Not *being* reality, but only our belief *about* reality, it will contain human elements, but these will *know* the non-human element, in the only sense in which there can be knowledge of anything. Does the river make its banks, or do the banks make the river? Does a man walk with his right leg or with his left leg more essentially? Just as impossible may it be to separate the real from the human factors in the growth of our cognitive experience.

Let this stand as a first brief indication of the humanistic position. Does it seem paradoxical? If so, I will try to make it plausible by a few illustrations, which will lead to a fuller acquaintance with the subject.

In many familiar objects every one will recognize the human element. We conceive a given reality in this way or in that, to suit our purpose, and the reality passively submits to the conception. You can take the number 27 as the cube of 3, or as the product of 3 and 9, or as 26 *plus* 1, or 100 *minus* 73, or in countless other ways, of which one will be just as true as another. You can take a chess-board as black squares on a white ground, or as white squares on a black ground, and neither conception is a false one.

You can treat the adjoined figure as a star, as two big triangles crossing each other, as a hexagon with legs set up on its angles, as six equal triangles hanging together by their tips, etc. All these treatments

are true treatments—the sensible *that* upon the paper resists no one of them. You can say of a line that it runs east, or you can say that it runs west, and the line *per se* accepts both descriptions without rebelling at the inconsistency.

We carve out groups of stars in the heavens, and call them constellations, and the stars patiently suffer us to do so,—though if they knew what we were doing, some of them might feel much surprised at the partners we had given them. We name the same constellation diversely, as Charles's Wain, the Great Bear, or the Dipper. None of the names will be false, and one will be as true as another, for all are applicable.

In all these cases we humanly make an *addition* to some sensible reality, and that reality tolerates the addition. All the additions 'agree' with the reality; they fit it, while they build it out. No one of them is false. Which may be treated as the *more* true, depends altogether on the human use of it. If the 27 is a number of dollars which I find in a drawer where I had left 28, it is 28 minus 1. If it is the number of inches in a board which I wish to insert as a shelf into a cupboard 26 inches wide, it is 26 plus 1. If I wish to ennoble the heavens by the constellations I see there, 'Charles's Wain' would be more true than 'Dipper.' My friend Frederick Myers was humorously indignant that that prodigious star-group should remind us Americans of nothing but a culinary utensil.

What shall we call a *thing* anyhow? It seems quite arbitrary, for we carve out everything, just as we carve out constellations, to suit our human purposes. For me, this whole 'audience' is one thing, which grows now restless, now attentive. I have no use at present for its individual units, so I don't consider them. So of an 'army,' of a 'nation.' But in your own eyes, ladies and gentlemen, to call you 'audience' is an accidental way of taking you. The permanently real things for you are your individual persons. To an anatomist, again, those persons are but organisms, and the real things are the organs. Not the organs, so much as their constituent cells, say the histologists; not the cells, but their molecules, say in turn the chemists.

We break the flux of sensible reality into things, then, at our will. We create the subjects of our true as well as of our false propositions.

We create the predicates also. Many of the predicates of things express only the relations of the things to us and to our feelings. Such predicates of course are human additions. Cæsar crossed the Rubicon, and was a menace to Rome's freedom. He is also an American schoolroom pest, made into one by the reaction of our schoolboys on his writings. The added predicate is as true of him as the earlier ones.

You see how naturally one comes to the humanistic principle: you can't weed out the human contribution. Our nouns and adjectives are all humanized heirlooms, and in the theories we build them into, the inner order and arrangement is wholly dictated by human considerations, intellectual consistency being one of them. Mathematics and logic themselves are fermenting with human rearrangements; physics, astronomy and biology follow massive cues of preference. We plunge forward into the field of fresh experience with the beliefs our ancestors and we have made already; these determine what we notice; what we notice determines what we do; what we do again determines what we experience; so from one thing to another, altho the stubborn fact remains that there *is* a sensible flux, what is *true of it* seems from first to last to be largely a matter of our own creation.

We build the flux out inevitably. The great question is: does it, with our additions, *rise or fall in value?* Are the additions *worthy* or *unworthy?* Suppose a universe composed of seven stars, and nothing else but three human witnesses and their critic. One witness names the stars 'Great Bear'; one calls them 'Charles's Wain'; one calls them the 'Dipper.' Which human addition has made the best universe of the given stellar material? If Frederic Myers were the critic, he would have no hesitation in 'turning down' the American witness.

Lotze has in several places made a deep suggestion. We naïvely assume, he says, a relation between reality and our minds which may be just the opposite of the true one. Reality, we naturally think, stands ready-made and complete, and our intellects supervene with the one simple duty of describing it as it is already. But may not our descriptions, Lotze asks, be themselves important additions to reality? And may not previous reality itself be there, far less for the purpose of reappearing unaltered in our knowledge, than for the very purpose of stimulating our minds to such additions as shall enhance the universe's total value. *'Die erhöhung des vorgefundenen daseins'* is a phrase used by Professor Eucken somewhere, which reminds one of this suggestion by the great Lotze.

It is identically our pragmatistic conception. In our cognitive as well as in our active life we are creative. We *add,* both to the subject and to the predicate part of reality. The world stands really malleable, waiting to receive its final touches at our hands. Like the kingdom of heaven, it suffers human violence willingly. Man *engenders* truths upon it.

No one can deny that such a rôle would add both to our dignity and to our responsibility as thinkers. To some of us it proves a most inspiring notion. Signore Papini, the leader of Italian pragmatism, grows fairly dithyrambic over the view that it opens of man's divinely-creative functions.

The import of the difference between pragmatism and rationalism is now in sight throughout its whole extent. The essential contrast is that *for rationalism reality is ready-made and complete from all eternity, while for pragmatism it is still in the making, and awaits part of its complexion from the future.* On the one side the universe is absolutely secure, on the other it is still pursuing its adventures.

We have got into rather deep water with this humanistic view, and it is no wonder that misunderstanding gathers round it. It is accused of being a doctrine of caprice. Mr. Bradley, for example, says that a humanist, if he understood his own doctrine, would have to 'hold any end, however perverted, to be rational, if I insist on it personally, and any idea, however mad, to be the truth if only some one is resolved that he will have it so.' The humanist view of 'reality,' as something resisting, yet malleable, which controls our thinking as an energy that must be taken 'account' of incessantly (tho not necessarily merely *copied*) is evidently a difficult one to introduce to novices. The situation reminds me of one that I have personally gone through. I once wrote an essay on our right to believe, which I unluckily called the *Will* to Believe. All the critics, neglecting the essay, pounced upon the title. Psychologically it was impossible, morally it was iniquitous. The 'will to deceive,' the 'will to make believe,' were wittily proposed as substitutes for it.

The alternative between pragmatism and rationalism, in the shape in which we now have it before us, is no longer a question in the theory of knowledge, it concerns the structure of the universe itself.

On the pragmatist side we have only one edition of the universe, unfinished, growing in all sorts of places, especially in the places where thinking beings are at work.

On the rationalist side we have a universe in many editions, one real one, the infinite folio, or *édition de luxe,* eternally complete; and then the various finite editions, full of false readings, distorted and mutilated each in its own way.

So the rival metaphysical hypotheses of pluralism and monism here come back upon us. I will develop their differences during the remainder of our hour.

And first let me say that it is impossible not to see a temperamental difference at work in the choice of sides. The rationalist mind, radically taken, is of a doctrinaire and authoritative complexion: the phrase *'must* be' is ever on its lips. The bellyband of its universe must be tight. A radical pragmatist on the other hand is a happy-go-lucky anarchistic sort of creature. If he had to live in a tub like Diogenes he wouldn't mind at all if the hoops were loose and the staves let in the sun.

Now the idea of this loose universe affects your typical rationalists in much the same way as 'freedom of the press' might affect a veteran official in the Russian bureau of censorship; or as 'simplified spelling' might affect an elderly schoolmistress. It affects him as the swarm of protestant sects affects a papist onlooker. It appears as backboneless and devoid of principle as 'opportunism' in politics appears to an old-fashioned French legitimist, or to a fanatical believer in the divine right of the people.

For pluralistic pragmatism, truth grows up inside of all the finite experiences. They lean on each other, but the whole of them, if such a whole there be, leans on nothing. All 'homes' are in finite experience; finite experience as such is homeless. Nothing outside of the flux secures the issue of it. It can hope salvation only from its own intrinsic promises and potencies.

To rationalists this describes a tramp and vagrant world, adrift in space, with neither elephant nor tortoise to plant the sole of its foot upon. It is a set of stars hurled into heaven without even a centre of gravity to pull against. In other spheres of life it is true that we have got used to living in a state of relative insecurity. The authority of 'the State,' and that of an absolute 'moral law,' have resolved themselves into expediencies, and holy church has resolved itself into 'meeting-houses.' Not so as yet within the philosophic classrooms. A universe with such as *us* contributing to create its truth, a world delivered to *our* opportunisms and our private judgments! Home-rule for Ireland would be a millennium in comparison. We're no more fit for such a part than the Filipinos are 'fit for self-government.' Such a world would not be *respectable* philosophically. It is a trunk without a tag, a dog without a collar in the eyes of most professors of philosophy.

What then would tighten this loose universe, according to the professors?

Something to support the finite many, to tie it to, to unify and anchor it. Something *un*exposed to accident, something eternal and unalterable. The mutable in experience must be founded on immutability. Behind our *de facto* world, our world in act, there must be a *de jure* duplicate fixed and previous, with all that can happen here already there *in posse,* every drop of blood, every smallest item, appointed and provided, stamped and branded, without chance of variation. The negatives that haunt our ideals here below must be themselves negated in the absolutely Real. This alone makes the universe solid. This is the resting deep. We live upon the stormy surface; but with this our anchor holds, for it grapples rocky bottom. This is Wordsworth's 'eternal peace abiding at the heart of endless agitation.' This is Vivekananda's mystic One of which I read to you. This is Reality with the big R, reality that makes the timeless claim, reality to which defeat can't happen. This is what the men of principles, and in general all the men whom I called tender-minded in my first lecture, think themselves obliged to postulate.

And this, exactly this, is what the tough-minded of that lecture find themselves moved to call a piece of perverse abstraction-worship. The tough-minded are the men whose alpha and omega are *facts*. Behind the bare phenomenal facts, as my tough-minded old friend Chauncey Wright, the great Harvard empiricist of my youth, used to say, there is *nothing*. When a rationalist insists that behind the facts there is the *ground* of the facts, the *possibility* of the facts, the tougher empiricists accuse him of taking the mere name and nature of a fact and clapping it behind the fact as a duplicate entity to make it possible. That such sham grounds are often invoked is notorious. At a surgical operation I once heard a bystander ask a doctor why the patient breathed so deeply. 'Because ether is a respiratory stimulant,' the doctor answered. 'Ah!' said the questioner, as if that were a good explanation. But this is like saying that cyanide of potassium kills because it is a 'poison,' or that it is so cold to-night because it is 'winter,' or that we have five fingers because we are 'pentadactyls.' These are but names for the facts, taken from the facts, and then treated as previous and explanatory. The tender-minded notion of an absolute reality is, according to the radically tough-minded, framed on just this pattern. It is but our summarizing name for the whole spread-out and strung-along mass of phenomena, treated as if it were a different entity, both one and previous.

You see how differently people take things. The world we live in exists diffused and distributed, in the form of an indefinitely numerous lot of *eaches,* coherent in all sorts of ways and degrees; and the tough-minded are perfectly willing to keep them at that valuation. They can *stand* that kind of world, their temper being well adapted to its insecurity. Not so the tender-minded party. They must back the world we find ourselves born into by 'another and a better' world in which the eaches form an All and the All a One that logically presupposes, co-implicates, and secures each *each* without exception.

Must we as pragmatists be radically tough-minded? or can we treat the absolute edition of the world as a legitimate hypothesis? It is certainly legitimate, for it is thinkable, whether we take it in its abstract or in its concrete shape.

By taking it abstractly I mean placing it behind our finite life as we place the word 'winter' behind to-night's cold weather. 'Winter' is only the name for a certain number of days which we find generally characterized by cold weather, but it guarantees nothing in that line, for our thermometer to-morrow may soar into the 70's. Nevertheless the word is a useful one to plunge forward with into the stream of our experience. It cuts off certain probabilities and sets up others. You can put away your straw hats; you can unpack your arctics. It is a summary of things to look for. It names a part of nature's habits, and gets you ready for their continuation. It is a definite instrument abstracted from experience, a conceptual reality that you must take account of, and which reflects you totally back into sensible realities. The pragmatist is the last person to deny the reality of such abstractions. They are so much past experience funded.

But taking the absolute edition of the world concretely means a different hypothesis. Rationalists take it concretely and *oppose* it to the world's finite editions. They give it a particular nature. It is perfect, finished. Everything known there is known along with everything else; here, where ignorance reigns, far otherwise. If there is want there, there also is the satisfaction provided. Here all is process; that world is timeless. Possibilities obtain in our world; in the absolute world, where all that is *not* is from eternity impossible, and all that *is* is necessary, the category of possibility has no application. In this world crimes and horrors are regrettable. In that totalized world regret obtains not, for 'the existence of ill in the temporal order is the very condition of the perfection of the eternal order.'

Once more, either hypothesis is legitimate in pragmatist eyes, for either has its uses. Abstractly, or taken like the word winter, as a memorandum of past experience that orients us towards the future, the notion of the absolute world is indispensable. Concretely taken, it is also indispensable, at least to certain minds, for it determines them religiously, being often a thing to change their lives by, and by changing their lives, to change whatever in the outer order depends on them.

We can not therefore methodically join the tough minds in their rejection of the whole notion of a world beyond our finite experience. One misunderstanding of pragmatism is to identify it with positivistic tough-mindedness, to suppose that it scorns every rationalistic notion as so much jabber and gesticulation, that it loves intellectual anarchy as such and prefers a sort of wolf-world absolutely unpent and wild and without a master or a collar to any philosophic classroom product whatsoever. I have said so much in these lectures against the over-tender forms of rationalism, that I am prepared for some misunderstanding here, but I confess that the amount of it that I have found in this very audience surprises me, for I have simultaneously defended rationalistic hypotheses, so far as these re-direct you fruitfully into experience.

For instance I receive this morning this question on a post-card: "Is a pragmatist necessarily a complete materialist and agnostic?" One of my oldest friends, who ought to know me better, writes me a letter that accuses the pragmatism I am recommending of shutting out all wider metaphysical views and condemning us to the most *terre-à-terre* naturalism. Let me read you some extracts from it.

"It seems to me," my friend writes, "that the pragmatic objection to pragmatism lies in the fact that it might accentuate the narrowness of narrow minds.

"Your call to the rejection of the namby-pamby and the wishy-washy is of course inspiring. But altho it is salutary and stimulating to be told that one should be responsible for the immediate issues and bearings of his words and thoughts, I decline to be deprived of the pleasure and profit of dwelling also on remoter bearings and issues, and it is the *tendency* of pragmatism to refuse this privilege.

"In short, it seems to me that the limitations, or rather the dangers, of the pragmatic tendency, are analogous to those which beset the unwary followers of the 'natural sciences.' Chemistry and physics are eminently pragmatic; and many of their devotees, smugly content with the data that their weights and measures furnish, feel an infinite pity and disdain for all students of philosophy and metaphysics whomsoever. And of course everything can be expressed,—after a fashion, and 'theoretically,'—in terms of chemistry and physics, that is, *everything except the vital principle of the whole,* and that, they say, there is no pragmatic use in trying to express; it has no bearings—for *them.* I for my part refuse to be persuaded that we can not look beyond the obvious pluralism of the naturalist and the pragmatist to a logical unity in which they take no interest."

How is such a conception of the pragmatism I am advocating possible, after my first and second lectures? I have all along been offering it expressly as a mediator between tough-mindedness and tender-mindedness. If the notion of a world *ante rem,* whether taken abstractly like the word winter, or concretely as the hypothesis of an Absolute, can be shown to have any consequences whatever for our life, it has a meaning. If the meaning works, it will have *some* truth that ought to be held to through all possible reformulations, for pragmatism.

The absolutistic hypothesis, that perfection is eternal, aboriginal, and most real, has a perfectly definite meaning, and it works religiously. To examine how, will be the subject of my next and final lecture.

PRAGMATISM AND RELIGION*

At the close of the last lecture I reminded you of the first one, in which I had opposed tough-mindedness to tender-mindedness and recommended pragmatism as their mediator. Tough-mindedness positively rejects tender-mindedness's hypothesis of an eternal perfect edition of the universe coexisting with our finite experience.

On pragmatic principles we can not reject any hypothesis if consequences useful to life flow from it. Universal conceptions, as things to take account of, may be as real for pragmatism as particular sensations are. They have, indeed, no meaning and no reality if they have no use. But if they have any use they have that amount of meaning. And the meaning will be true if the use squares well with life's other uses.

Well, the use of the Absolute is proved by the whole course of

* From: Pragm., 273–301.

men's religious history. The eternal arms are then beneath. Remember
Vivekananda's use of the Atman—not indeed a scientific use, for we
can make no particular deductions from it. It is emotional and spiritual altogether.

It is always best to discuss things by the help of concrete examples. Let me read therefore some of those verses entitled 'To You' by
Walt Whitman—'You' of course meaning the reader or hearer of the
poem whosoever he or she may be.

> Whoever you are, now I place my hand upon you that you be
>   my poem;
> I whisper with my lips close to your ear,
> I have loved many men and women and men, but I love none
>   better than you.
>
> O I have been dilatory and dumb;
> I should have made my way to you long ago;
> I should have blabbed nothing but you, I should have chanted
>   nothing but you.
>
> I will leave all and come and make the hymns of you;
> None have understood you, but I understand you;
> None have done justice to you—you have not done justice to
>   yourself;
> None but have found you imperfect—I only find no imper-
>   fection in you.
>
> O I could sing such glories and grandeurs about you;
> You have not known what you are—you have slumbered
>   upon yourself all your life;
> What you have done returns already in mockeries.
>
> But the mockeries are not you;
> Underneath them and within them, I see you lurk;
> I pursue you where none else has pursued you.
> Silence, the desk, the flippant expression, the night, the
>   accustomed routine, if these conceal you from others,
>   or from yourself, they do not conceal you from me;
> The shaved face, the unsteady eye, the impure complexion,
>   if these balk others, they do not balk me;
> The pert apparel, the deformed attitude, drunkenness, greed,
>   premature death, all these I part aside.
>
> There is no endowment in man or woman that is not tallied in
>   you;
> There is no virtue, no beauty, in man or woman, but as good
>   is in you;
> No pluck nor endurance in others, but as good is in you;

No pleasure waiting for others, but an equal pleasure waits
for you.

Whoever you are! claim your own at any hazard!
These shows of the east and west are tame, compared with
you;
These immense meadows—these interminable rivers—you are
immense and interminable as they;
You are he or she who is master or mistress over them,
Master or mistress in your own right over Nature, elements,
pain, passion, dissolution.

The hopples fall from your ankles—you find an unfailing
sufficiency;
Old or young, male or female, rude, low, rejected by the rest
whatever you are promulges itself;
Through birth, life, death, burial, the means are provided,
nothing is scanted;
Through angers, losses, ambition, ignorance, ennui, what you
are picks its way.

Verily a fine and moving poem, in any case, but there are two
ways of taking it, both useful.

One is the monistic way, the mystical way of pure cosmic emotion. The glories and grandeurs, they are yours absolutely, even in the
midst of your defacements. Whatever may happen to you, whatever
you may appear to be, inwardly you are safe. Look back, *lie* back, on
your true principle of being! This is the famous way of quietism, of
indifferentism. Its enemies compare it to a spiritual opium. Yet pragmatism must respect this way, for it has massive historic vindication.

But pragmatism sees another way to be respected also, the pluralistic way of interpreting the poem. The you so glorified, to which the
hymn is sung, may mean your better possibilities phenomenally taken,
or the specific redemptive effects even of your failures, upon yourself
or others. It may mean your loyalty to the possibilities of others
whom you admire and love so that you are willing to accept your own
poor life, for it is that glory's partner. You can at least appreciate, applaud, furnish the audience, of so brave a total world. Forget the low
in yourself, then, think only of the high. Identify your life therewith;
then, through angers, losses, ignorance, ennui, whatever you thus
make yourself, whatever you thus most deeply are, picks its way.

In either way of taking the poem, it encourages fidelity to ourselves. Both ways satisfy; both sanctify the human flux. Both paint the
portrait of the *you* on a gold background. But the background of the
first way is the static One, while in the second way it means possibles
in the plural, genuine possibles, and it has all the restlessness of that
conception.

Noble enough is either way of reading the poem; but plainly the pluralistic way agrees with the pragmatic temper best, for it immediately suggests an infinitely larger number of the details of future experience to our mind. It sets definite activities in us at work. Altho this second way seems prosaic and earth-born in comparison with the first way, yet no one can accuse it of tough-mindedness in any brutal sense of the term. Yet if, as pragmatists, you should positively set up the second way *against* the first way, you would very likely be misunderstood. You would be accused of denying nobler conceptions, and of being an ally of tough-mindedness in the worst sense.

You remember the letter from a member of this audience from which I read some extracts at our previous meeting. Let me read you an additional extract now. It shows a vagueness in realizing the alternatives before us which I think is very widespread.

"I believe," writes my friend and correspondent, "in pluralism; I believe that in our search for truth we leap from one floating cake of ice to another, on an infinite sea, and that by each of our acts we make new truths possible and old ones impossible; I believe that each man is responsible for making the universe better, and that if he does not do this it will be in so far left undone.

"Yet at the same time I am willing to endure that my children should be incurably sick and suffering (as they are not) and I myself stupid and yet with brains enough to see my stupidity, only on one condition, namely, that through the construction, in imagination and by reasoning, of a *rational unity of all things,* I can conceive my acts and my thoughts and my troubles as *supplemented by all the other phenomena of the world, and as forming—when thus supplemented—a scheme which I approve and adopt as my own;* and for my part I refuse to be persuaded that we can not look beyond the obvious pluralism of the naturalist and pragmatist to a logical unity in which they take no interest or stock."

Such a fine expression of personal faith warms the heart of the hearer. But how much does it clear his philosophic head? Does the writer consistently favor the monistic, or the pluralistic, interpretation of the world's poem? His troubles become atoned for *when thus supplemented,* he says, supplemented, that is, by all the remedies that *the other phenomena* may supply. Obviously here the writer faces forward into the particulars of experience, which he interprets in a pluralistic-melioristic way.

But he believes himself to face backward. He speaks of what he calls the rational *unity* of things, when all the while he really means their possible empirical *unification.* He supposes at the same time that the pragmatist, because he criticises rationalism's abstract One, is cut off from the consolation of believing in the saving possibilities of the concrete many. He fails in short to distinguish between taking the world's perfection as a necessary principle, and taking it only as a possible *terminus ad quem.*

I regard the writer of the letter as a genuine pragmatist, but as a pragmatist *sans le savoir.* He appears to me as one of that numerous class of philosophic amateurs whom I spoke of in my first lecture, as wishing to have all the good things going, without being too careful as to how they agree or disagree. 'Rational unity of all things' is so inspiring a formula, that he brandishes it off-hand, and abstractly accuses pluralism of conflicting with it (for the bare names do conflict), altho concretely he means by it just the pragmatistically unified and ameliorated world. Most of us remain in this essential vagueness, and it is well that we should; but in the interest of clearheadedness it is well that some of us should go farther, so I will try now to focus a little more discriminatingly on this particular religious point.

Is then this you of yous, this absolutely real world, this unity that yields the moral inspiration and has the religious value, to be taken monistically or pluralistically? Is it *ante rem* or *in rebus?* Is it a principle or an end, an absolute or an ultimate, a first or a last? Does it make you look forward or lie back? It is certainly worth while not to clump the two things together, for if discriminated, they have decidedly diverse meanings for life.

Please observe that the whole dilemma revolves pragmatically about the notion of the world's possibilities. Intellectually, rationalism invokes its absolute principle of unity, as a ground of possibility for the many facts. Emotionally, it sees it as a container and limiter of possibilities, a guarantee that the upshot shall be good. Taken in this way, the absolute makes all good things certain, and all bad things impossible (in the eternal, namely), and may be said to transmute the entire category of possibility into categories more secure. One sees at this point that the great religious difference lies between the men who insist that the world *must and shall be,* and those who are contented with believing that the world *may be,* saved. The whole clash of rationalistic and empiricist religion is thus over the validity of possibility. It is necessary therefore to begin by focusing upon that word. What may the word 'possible' definitely mean? To unreflecting men it means a sort of third estate of being, less real than existence, more real than non-existence, a twilight realm, a hybrid status, a limbo into which and out of which realities ever and anon are made to pass.

Such a conception is of course too vague and nondescript to satisfy us. Here, as elsewhere, the only way to extract a term's meaning is to use the pragmatic method on it. When you say that a thing is possible, what difference does it make? It makes at least this difference that if any one calls it impossible you can contradict him, if any one calls it actual you can contradict *him,* and if any one calls it necessary you can contradict him too.

But these privileges of contradiction don't amount to much. When you say a thing is possible, does not that make some farther difference in terms of actual fact?

It makes at least this negative difference that if the statement be true, it follows that *there is nothing extant capable of preventing* the possible thing. The absence of real grounds of interference may thus be said to make things *not impossible,* possible therefore in the *bare* or *abstract* sense.

But most possibles are not bare, they are concretely grounded, or well-grounded, as we say. What does this mean pragmatically? It means not only that there are no preventive conditions present, but that some of the conditions of production of the possible thing actually are here. Thus a concretely possible chicken means: (1) that the idea of chicken contains no essential self-contradiction; (2) that no boys, skunks, or other enemies are about; and (3) that at least an actual egg exists. Possible chicken means actual egg—plus actual sitting hen, or incubator, or what not. As the actual conditions approach completeness the chicken becomes a better-and-better-grounded possibility. When the conditions are entirely complete, it ceases to be a possibility, and turns into an actual fact.

Let us apply this notion to the salvation of the world. What does it pragmatically mean to say that this is possible? It means that some of the conditions of the world's deliverance do actually exist. The more of them there are existent, the fewer preventing conditions you can find, the better-grounded is the salvation's possibility, the more *probable* does the fact of the deliverance become.

So much for our preliminary look at possibility.

Now it would contradict the very spirit of life to say that our minds must be indifferent and neutral in questions like that of the world's salvation. Any one who pretends to be neutral writes himself down here as a fool and a sham. We all do wish to minimize the insecurity of the universe; we are and ought to be unhappy when we regard it as exposed to every enemy and open to every life-destroying draft. Nevertheless there are unhappy men who think the salvation of the world impossible. Theirs is the doctrine known as pessimism.

Optimism in turn would be the doctrine that thinks the world's salvation inevitable.

Midway between the two there stands what may be called the doctrine of meliorism, tho it has hitherto figured less as a doctrine than as an attitude in human affairs. Optimism has always been the regnant *doctrine* in European philosophy. Pessimism was only recently introduced by Schopenhauer and counts few systematic defenders as yet. Meliorism treats salvation as neither necessary nor impossible. It treats it as a possibility, which becomes more and more of a probability the more numerous the actual conditions of salvation become.

It is clear that pragmatism must incline towards meliorism. Some conditions of the world's salvation are actually extant, and she can not possibly close her eyes to this fact: and should the residual conditions come, salvation would become an accomplished reality. Naturally the terms I use here are exceedingly summary. You may interpret the word 'salvation' in any way you like, and make it as diffuse and distributive, or as climacteric and integral a phenomenon as you please.

Take, for example, any one of us in this room with the ideals which he cherishes and is willing to live and work for. Every such ideal realized will be one moment in the world's salvation. But these particular ideals are not bare abstract possibilities. They are grounded, they are *live* possibilities, for we are their live champions and pledges, and if the complementary conditions come and add themselves, our ideals will become actual things. What now are the complementary conditions? They are first such a mixture of things as will in the fulness of time give us a chance, a gap that we can spring into, and, finally, *our act*.

Does our act then *create* the world's salvation so far as it makes room for itself, so far as it leaps into the gap? Does it create, not the whole world's salvation of course, but just so much of this as itself covers of the world's extent?

Here I take the bull by the horns, and in spite of the whole crew of rationalists and monists, of whatever brand they be, I ask *why not?* Our acts, our turning-places, where we seem to ourselves to make ourselves and grow, are the parts of the world to which we are closest, the parts of which our knowledge is the most intimate and complete. Why should we not take them at their face-value? Why may they not be the actual turning-places and growing-places which they seem to be, of the world—why not the workshop of being, where we catch fact in the making, so that nowhere may the world grow in any other kind of way than this?

Irrational! we are told. How can new being come in local spots and patches which add themselves or stay away at random, independently of the rest? There must be a reason for our acts, and where in the last resort can any reason be looked for save in the material pressure or the logical compulsion of the total nature of the world? There can be but one real agent of growth, or seeming growth, anywhere, and that agent is the integral world itself. It may grow all-over, if growth there be, but that single parts should grow *per se* is irrational.

But if one talks of rationality—and of reasons for things, and insists that they can't just come in spots, what *kind* of a reason can there ultimately be why anything should come at all? Talk of logic and necessity and categories and the absolute and the contents of the whole philosophical machine-shop as you will, the only *real* reason I can think of why anything should ever come is that *some one wishes it to be here*. It is *demanded,*—demanded, it may be, to give relief to no matter how small a fraction of the world's mass. This is *living reason,* and compared with it material causes and logical necessities are spectral things.

In short the only fully rational world would be the world of wishing-caps, the world of telepathy, where every desire is fulfilled instanter, without having to consider or placate surrounding or intermediate powers. This is the Absolute's own world. He calls upon the phenomenal world to be, and it *is,* exactly as he calls for it, no other condition being required. In our world, the wishes of the individual are only one condition. Other individuals are there with other wishes and they must be propitiated first. So Being grows under all sorts of resistances in this world of the many, and, from compromise to compromise, only gets organized gradually into what may be called secondarily rational shape. We approach the wishing-cap type of organization only in a few departments of life. We want water and we turn a faucet. We want a kodak-picture and we press a button. We want information and we telephone. We want to travel and we buy a ticket. In these and similar cases, we hardly need to do more than the wishing—the world is rationally organized to do the rest.

But this talk of rationality is a parenthesis and a digression. What we were discussing was the idea of a world growing not integrally but piecemeal by the contributions of its several parts. Take the hypothesis seriously and as a live one. Suppose that the world's author put the case to you before creation, saying: "I am going to make a world not certain to be saved, a world the perfection of which shall be conditional merely, the condition being that each several agent does its own 'level best.' I offer you the chance of taking part in such a world. Its safety, you see, is unwarranted. It is a real adventure, with real danger, yet it may win through. It is a social scheme of co-operative work genuinely to be done. Will you join the procession? Will you trust yourself and trust the other agents enough to face the risk?"

Should you in all seriousness, if participation in such a world were proposed to you, feel bound to reject it as not safe enough? Would you say that, rather than be part and parcel of so fundamentally pluralistic and irrational a universe, you preferred to relapse into the slumber of nonentity from which you had been momentarily aroused by the tempter's voice?

Of course if you are normally constituted, you would do nothing of the sort. There is a healthy-minded buoyancy in most of us which such a universe would exactly fit. We would therefore accept the offer

—"Top! und schlag auf schlag!" It would be just like the world we practically live in; and loyalty to our old nurse Nature would forbid us to say no. The world proposed would seem 'rational' to us in the most living way.

Most of us, I say, would therefore welcome the proposition and add our *fiat* to the *fiat* of the creator. Yet perhaps some would not; for there are morbid minds in every human collection, and to them the prospect of a universe with only a fighting chance of safety would probably make no appeal. There are moments of discouragement in us all, when we are sick of self and tired of vainly striving. Our own life breaks down, and we fall into the attitude of the prodigal son. We mistrust the chances of things. We want a universe where we can just give up, fall on our father's neck, and be absorbed into the absolute life as a drop of water melts into the river or the sea.

The peace and rest, the security desiderated at such moments is security against the bewildering accidents of so much finite experience. Nirvana means safety from this everlasting round of adventures of which the world of sense consists. The hindoo and the buddhist, for this is essentially their attitude, are simply afraid, afraid of more experience, afraid of life.

And to men of this complexion, religious monism comes with its consoling words: "All is needed and essential—even you with your sick soul and heart. All are one with God, and with God all is well. The everlasting arms are beneath, whether in the world of finite appearance you seem to fail or to succeed." There can be no doubt that when men are reduced to their last sick extremity absolutism is the only saving scheme. Pluralistic moralism simply makes their teeth chatter, it refrigerates the very heart within their breast.

So we see concretely two types of religion in sharp contrast. Using our old terms of comparison, we may say that the absolutistic scheme appeals to the tender-minded while the pluralistic scheme appeals to the tough. Many persons would refuse to call the pluralistic scheme religious at all. They would call it moralistic, and would apply the word religious to the monistic scheme alone. Religion in the sense of self-surrender, and moralism in the sense of self-sufficingness, have been pitted against each other as incompatibles frequently enough in the history of human thought.

We stand here before the final question of philosophy. I said in my fourth lecture that I believed the monistic-pluralistic alternative to be the deepest and most pregnant question that our minds can frame. Can it be that the disjunction is a final one? that only one side can be true? Are a pluralism and monism genuine incompatibles? So that, if the world were really pluralistically constituted, if it really existed distributively and were made up of a lot of eaches, it could only be saved piecemeal and *de facto* as the result of their behavior, and its epic history in no wise short-circuited by some essential oneness in which the severalness were already 'taken up' beforehand and eternally 'overcome'? If this were so, we should have to choose one philosophy or the other. We could not say 'yes, yes' to both alternatives. There would have to be a 'no' in our relations with the possible. We should confess an ultimate disappointment: we could not remain healthy-minded and sick-minded in one indivisible act.

Of course as human beings we can be healthy minds on one day and sick souls on the next; and as amateur dabblers in philosophy we may perhaps be allowed to call ourselves monistic pluralists, or free-will determinists, or whatever else may occur to us of a reconciling kind. But as philosophers aiming at clearness and consistency, and feeling the pragmatistic need of squaring truth with truth, the question is forced upon us of frankly adopting either the tender or the robus-tious type of thought. In particular *this* query has always come home to me: May not the claims of tender-mindedness go too far? May not the notion of a world already saved *in toto* anyhow, be too saccharine to stand? May not religious optimism be too idyllic? Must *all* be saved? Is *no* price to be paid in the work of salvation? Is the last word sweet? Is all 'yes, yes' in the universe? Does n't the fact of 'no' stand at the very core of life? Does n't the very 'seriousness' that we attribute to life mean that ineluctable noes and losses form a part of it, that there are genuine sacrifices somewhere, and that something permanently drastic and bitter always remains at the bottom of its cup?

I can not speak officially as a pragmatist here; all I can say is that my own pragmatism offers no objection to my taking sides with this more moralistic view, and giving up the claim of total reconciliation. The possibility of this is involved in the pragmatistic willingness to treat pluralism as a serious hypothesis. In the end it is our faith and not our logic that decides such questions, and I deny the right of any pretended logic to veto my own faith. I find myself willing to take the universe to be really dangerous and adventurous, without therefore backing out and crying 'no play.' I am willing to think that the prodi-gal-son attitude, open to us as it is in many vicissitudes, is not the right and final attitude towards the whole of life. I am willing that there should be real losses and real losers, and no total preservation of all that is. I can believe in the ideal as an ultimate, not as an origin, and as an extract, not the whole. When the cup is poured off, the dregs are left behind for ever, but the possibility of what is poured off is sweet enough to accept.

As a matter of fact countless human imaginations live in this mor-alistic and epic kind of a universe, and find its disseminated and strung-along successes sufficient for their rational needs. There is a finely translated epigram in the Greek anthology which admirably expresses this state of mind, this acceptance of loss as unatoned for, even though the lost element might be one's self:

> A shipwrecked sailor, buried on this coast,
>> Bids you set sail.
> Full many a gallant bark, when we were lost,
>> Weathered the gale.

Those puritans who answered 'yes' to the question: Are you willing to be damned for God's glory? were in this objective and magnanimous condition of mind. The way of escape from evil on this system is *not* by getting it 'aufgehoben,' or preserved in the whole as an element essential but 'overcome.' *It is by dropping it out altogether, throwing it overboard and getting beyond it, helping to make a universe that shall forget its very place and name.*

It is then perfectly possible to accept sincerely a drastic kind of a universe from which the element of 'seriousness' is not to be expelled. Whoso does so is, it seems to me, a genuine pragmatist. He is willing to live on a scheme of uncertified possibilities which he trusts; willing to pay with his own person, if need be, for the realization of the ideals which he frames.

What now actually *are* the other forces which he trusts to co-operate with him, in a universe of such a type? They are at least his fellow men, in the stage of being which our actual universe has reached. But are there not superhuman forces also, such as religious men of the pluralistic type we have been considering have always believed in? Their words may have sounded monistic when they said "there is no God but God"; but the original polytheism of mankind has only imperfectly and vaguely sublimated itself into monotheism, and monotheism itself, so far as it was religious and not a scheme of classroom instruction for the metaphysicians, has always viewed God as but one helper, *primus inter pares,* in the midst of all the shapers of the great world's fate.

I fear that my previous lectures, confined as they have been to human and humanistic aspects, may have left the impression on many of you that pragmatism means methodically to leave the superhuman out. I have shown small respect indeed for the Absolute, and I have until this moment spoken of no other superhuman hypothesis but that. But I trust that you see sufficiently that the Absolute has nothing but its superhumanness in common with the theistic God. On pragmatistic principles, if the hypothesis of God works satisfactorily in the widest sense of the word, it is true. Now whatever its residual difficulties may be, experience shows that it certainly does work, and that the problem is to build it out and determine it so that it will combine satisfactorily

with all the other working truths. I can not start upon a whole theology
at the end of this last lecture; but when I tell you that I have written a
book on men's religious experience, which on the whole has been regarded as making for the reality of God, you will perhaps exempt my
own pragmatism from the charge of being an atheistic system. I firmly
disbelieve, myself, that our human experience is the highest form of
experience extant in the universe. I believe rather that we stand in
much the same relation to the whole of the universe as our canine and
feline pets do to the whole of human life. They inhabit our drawing-
rooms and libraries. They take part in scenes of whose significance
they have no inkling. They are merely tangent to curves of history the
beginnings and ends and forms of which pass wholly beyond their ken.
So we are tangent to the wider life of things. But, just as many of the
dog's and cat's ideals coincide with our ideals, and the dogs and cats
have daily living proof of the fact, so we may well believe, on the
proofs that religious experience affords, that higher powers exist and
are at work to save the world on ideal lines similar to our own.

You see that pragmatism can be called religious, if you allow that
religion can be pluralistic or merely melioristic in type. But whether
you will finally put up with that type of religion or not is a question
that only you yourself can decide. Pragmatism has to postpone dogmatic answer, for we do not yet know certainly which type of religion
is going to work best in the long run. The various overbeliefs of men,
their several faith-ventures, are in fact what are needed to bring the
evidence in. You will probably make your own ventures severally. If
radically tough, the hurly-burly of the sensible facts of nature will be
enough for you, and you will need no religion at all. If radically tender, you will take up with the more monistic form of religion: the
pluralistic form, with its reliance on possibilities that are not necessities, will not seem to afford you security enough.

But if you are neither tough nor tender in an extreme and radical
sense, but mixed as most of us are, it may seem to you that the type of
pluralistic and moralistic religion that I have offered is as good a religious synthesis as you are likely to find. Between the two extremes of
crude naturalism on the one hand and transcendental absolutism on
the other, you may find that what I take the liberty of calling the
pragmatistic or melioristic type of theism is exactly what you require.

Historical Judgments

A Pluralistic Universe by William James was originally titled
"The Present Situation in Philosophy." The majority of the
selections which follow are taken from this work. Although
they rarely do justice to the thinkers examined, considerable
light is cast on the major currents of philosophic debate at the
turn of the century. Further, these essays develop essential
themes in the thought of James. The last essay on Emerson,
reveals a quite different type of influence on James.

PHILOSOPHY AND ITS CRITICS*

The progress of society is due to the fact that individuals vary from
the human average in all sorts of directions, and that the originality is
often so attractive or useful that they are recognized by their tribe as
leaders, and become objects of envy or admiration, and setters of new
ideals.

Among the variations, every generation of men produces some
individuals exceptionally preoccupied with theory. Such men find
matter for puzzle and astonishment where no one else does. Their
imagination invents explanations and combines them. They store up
the learning of their time, utter prophecies and warnings, and are regarded as sages. Philosophy, etymologically meaning the love of wisdom, is the work of this class of minds, regarded with an indulgent
relish, if not with admiration, even by those who do not understand
them or believe much in the truth which they proclaim.

Philosophy, thus become a race-heritage, forms in its totality a

* From: S.P.P., 3–28.

monstrously unwieldy mass of learning. So taken, there is no reason why any special science like chemistry, or astronomy, should be excluded from it. By common consent, however, special sciences are today excluded, for reasons presently to be explained; and what remains is manageable enough to be taught under the name of philosophy by one man if his interests be broad enough.

If this were a German textbook I should first give my abstract definition of the topic, thus limited by usage, then proceed to display its *'Begriff, und Eintheilung,'* and its *'Aufgabe und Methode.'* But as such displays are usually unintelligible to beginners, and unnecessary after reading the book, it will conduce to brevity to omit that chapter altogether, useful though it might possibly be to more advanced readers as a summary of what is to follow.

I will tarry a moment, however, over the matter of definition. Limited by the omission of the special sciences, the name of philosophy has come more and more to denote ideas of universal scope exclusively. The principles of explanation that underlie all things without exception, the elements common to gods and men and animals and stones, the first *whence* and the last *whither* of the whole cosmic procession, the conditions of all knowing, and the most general rules of human action—these furnish the problems commonly deemed philosophic *par excellence;* and the philosopher is the man who finds the most to say about them. Philosophy is defined in the usual scholastic textbooks as 'the knowledge of things in general by their ultimate causes, so far as natural reason can attain to such knowledge.' This means that explanation of the universe at large, not description of its details, is what philosophy must aim at; and so it happens that a view of anything is termed philosophic just in proportion as it is broad and connected with other views, and as it uses principles not proximate, or intermediate, but ultimate and all-embracing, to justify itself. Any very sweeping view of the world is a philosophy in this sense, even though it may be a vague one. It is a *Weltanschauung,* an intellectualized attitude towards life. Professor Dewey well describes the constitution of all the philosophies that actually exist, when he says that philosophy expresses a certain attitude, purpose and temper of conjoined intellect and will, rather than a discipline whose boundaries can be neatly marked off.[1]

To know the chief rival attitudes towards life, as the history of human thinking has developed them, and to have heard some of the reasons they can give for themselves, ought to be considered an essential part of liberal education. Philosophy, indeed, in one sense of the term is only a compendious name for the spirit in education which the

[1] Compare the article 'Philosophy' in Baldwin's *Dictionary of Philosophy and Psychology.*

word 'college' stands for in America. Things can be taught in dry dogmatic ways or in a philosophic way. At a technical school a man may grow into a first-rate instrument for doing a certain job, but he may miss all the graciousness of mind suggested by the term liberal culture. He may remain a cad, and not a gentleman, intellectually pinned down to his one narrow subject, literal, unable to suppose anything different from what he has seen, without imagination, atmosphere, or mental perspective.

Philosophy, beginning in wonder, as Plato and Aristotle said, is able to fancy everything different from what it is. It sees the familiar as if it were strange, and the strange as if it were familiar. It can take things up and lay them down again. Its mind is full of air that plays round every subject. It rouses us from our native dogmatic slumber and breaks up our caked prejudices. Historically it has always been a sort of fecundation of four different human interests, science, poetry, religion, and logic, by one another. It has sought by hard reasoning for results emotionally valuable. To have some contact with it, to catch its influence, is thus good for both literary and scientific students. By its poetry it appeals to literary minds; but its logic stiffens them up and remedies their softness. By its logic it appeals to the scientific; but softens them by its other aspects, and saves them from too dry a technicality. Both types of student ought to get from philosophy a livelier spirit, more air, more mental background. 'Hast any philosophy in thee, Shepherd?' —this question of Touchstone's is the one with which men should always meet one another. A man with no philosophy in him is the most inauspicious and unprofitable of all possible social mates.

I say nothing in all this of what may be called the gymnastic use of philosophic study, the purely intellectual power gained by defining the high and abstract concepts of the philosopher, and discriminating between them.

In spite of the advantages thus enumerated, the study of philosophy has systematic enemies, and they were never as numerous as at the present day. The definite conquests of science and the apparent indefiniteness of philosophy's results partly account for this; to say nothing of man's native rudeness of mind, which maliciously enjoys deriding long words and abstractions. 'Scholastic jargon,' 'mediæval dialectics,' are for many people synonyms of the word philosophy. With his obscure and uncertain speculations as to the intimate nature and causes of things, the philosopher is likened to a 'blind man in a dark room looking for a black hat that is not there.' His occupation is described as the art of 'endlessly disputing without coming to any conclusion,' or more contemptuously still as the *'systematische Missbrauch einer eben zu diesem Zwecke erfundenen Terminologie.'*

Only to a very limited degree is this sort of hostility reasonable. I will take up some of the current objections in successive order, since to reply to them will be a convenient way of entering into the interior of our subject.

Objection 1. Whereas the sciences make steady progress and yield applications of matchless utility, philosophy makes no progress and has no practical applications.

Reply. The opposition is unjustly founded, for the sciences are themselves branches of the tree of philosophy. As fast as questions got accurately answered, the answers were called 'scientific,' and what men call 'philosophy' to-day is but the residuum of questions still unanswered. At this very moment we are seeing two sciences, psychology and general biology, drop off from the parent trunk and take independent root as specialties. The more general philosophy cannot as a rule follow the voluminous details of any special science.

A backward glance at the evolution of philosophy will reward us here. The earliest philosophers in every land were encyclopædic sages, lovers of wisdom, sometimes with, and sometimes without a dominantly ethical or religious interest. They were just men curious beyond immediate practical needs, and no particular problems, but rather the problematic generally, was their specialty. China, Persia, Egypt, India, had such wise men, but those of Greece are the only sages who until very recently have influenced the course of western thinking. The earlier Greek philosophy lasted, roughly speaking, for about two hundred and fifty years, say from 600 B.C. onwards. Such men as Thales, Heracleitus, Pythagoras, Parmenides, Anaxagoras, Empedocles, Democritus, were mathematicians, theologians, politicians, astronomers, and physicists. All the learning of their time, such as it was, was at their disposal. Plato and Aristotle continued their tradition, and the great mediæval philosophers only enlarged its field of application. If we turn to Saint Thomas Aquinas's great 'Summa,' written in the thirteenth century, we find opinions expressed about literally everything, from God down to matter, with angels, men, and demons taken in on the way. The relations of almost everything with everything else, of the creator with his creatures, of the knower with the known, of substances with forms, of mind with body, of sin with salvation, come successively up for treatment. A theology, a psychology, a system of duties and morals, are given in fullest detail, while physics and logic are established in their universal principles. The impression made on the reader is of almost superhuman intellectual resources. It is true that Saint Thomas's method of handling the mass of fact, or supposed fact, which he treated, was different from that to which we are accustomed. He deduced and proved everything, either from fixed principles of reason, or from holy Scripture. The properties and changes of bodies, for example, were explained by the two principles of matter and form, as Aristotle had taught. Matter was the quantitative, determinable, passive element; form, the qualitative, unifying, determining, and active principle. All activity was for an end. Things could act on each other only when in contact. The number of species of things was determinate, and their differences discrete, etc., etc.[2]

By the beginning of the seventeenth century, men were tired of the elaborate *a priori* methods of scholasticism. Suarez's treatises availed not to keep them in fashion. But the new philosophy of Descartes, which displaced the scholastic teaching, sweeping over Europe like wildfire, preserved the same encyclopædic character. We think of Descartes nowadays as the metaphysician who said 'Cogito, ergo sum,' separated mind from matter as two contrasted substances, and gave a renovated proof of God's existence. But his contemporaries thought of him much more as we think of Herbert Spencer in our day, as a great cosmic evolutionist, who explained, by 'the redistribution of matter and motion,' and the laws of impact, the rotations of the heavens, the circulation of the blood, the refraction of light, apparatus of vision and of nervous action, the passions of the soul, and the connection of the mind and body.

Descartes died in 1650. With Locke's 'Essay Concerning Human Understanding,' published in 1690, philosophy for the first time turned more exclusively to the problem of knowledge, and became 'critical.' This subjective tendency developed; and although the school of Leibnitz, who was the pattern of a universal sage, still kept up the more universal tradition—Leibnitz's follower Wolff published systematic treatises on everything, physical as well as moral—Hume, who succeeded Locke, woke Kant 'from his dogmatic slumber,' and since Kant's time the word 'philosophy' has come to stand for mental and moral speculations far more than for physical theories. Until a comparatively recent time, philosophy was taught in our colleges under the name of 'mental and moral philosophy,' or 'philosophy of the human mind,' exclusively, to distinguish it from 'natural philosophy.'

But the older tradition is the better as well as the completer one. To know the actual peculiarities of the world we are born into is surely as important as to know what makes worlds anyhow abstractly possible. Yet this latter knowledge has been treated by many since Kant's time as the only knowledge worthy of being called philosophical. Common men feel the question 'What is Nature like?' to be as meritorious as the Kantian question 'How is Nature possible?' So philosophy, in order not to lose human respect, must take some notice of

[2] J. Rickaby's *General Metaphysics* (Longmans, Green and Co.) gives a popular account of the essentials of St. Thomas's philosophy of nature. Thomas J. Harper's *Metaphysics of the School* (Macmillan) goes into minute detail.

the actual constitution of reality. There are signs to-day of a return to the more objective tradition.[3]

Philosophy in the full sense is only *man thinking,* thinking about generalities rather than about particulars. But whether about generalities or particulars, man thinks always by the same methods. He observes, discriminates, generalizes, classifies, looks for causes, traces analogies, and makes hypotheses. Philosophy, taken as something distinct from science or from practical affairs, follows no method peculiar to itself. All our thinking to-day has evolved gradually out of primitive human thought, and the only really important changes that have come over its manner (as distinguished from the matters in which it believes) are a greater hesitancy in asserting its convictions, and the habit of seeking verification[4] for them whenever it can.

It will be instructive to trace very briefly the origins of our present habits of thought.

Auguste Comte, the founder of a philosophy which he called 'positive,'[5] said that human theory on any subject always took three forms in succession. In the theological stage of theorizing, phenomena are explained by spirits producing them; in the metaphysical stage, their essential feature is made into an abstract idea, and this is placed behind them as if it were an explanation; in the positive stage, phenomena are simply described as to their coexistences and successions. Their 'laws' are formulated, but no explanation of their natures or existence is sought after. Thus a *'spiritus rector'* would be a theological,—a 'principle of attraction' a metaphysical,—and a 'law of the squares' would be a positive theory of the planetary movements.

Comte's account is too sharp and definite. Anthropology shows that the earliest attempts at human theorizing mixed the theological and metaphysical together. Common things needed no special explanation, remarkable things alone, odd things, especially deaths, calamities, diseases, called for it. What made things act was the mysterious energy in them, and the more awful they were, the more of this *mana* they possessed. The great thing was to acquire *mana* oneself. 'Sympathetic magic' is the collective name for what seems to have been the primitive philosophy here. You could act on anything by controlling anything else that either was associated with it or resembled it. If you wished to injure an enemy, you should either make an image of him, or get some of his hair or other belongings, or get his name written. Injuring the substitute, you thus made him suffer correspondingly. If you wished the rain to come, you sprinkled the ground, if the wind,

[3] For an excellent defence of it I refer my readers to Paulsen's *Introduction to Philosophy,* translated by Thilly (1895), pp. 19–44.

[4] Compare G. H. Lewes: *Aristotle* (1864), chap. 4.

[5] *Cours de philosophie positive,* 6 volumes, Paris, 1830–1842.

you whistled, etc. If you would have yams grow well in your garden, put a stone there that looks like a yam. Would you cure jaundice, give tumeric, that makes things look yellow; or give poppies for troubles of the head, because their seed vessels form a 'head.' This 'doctrine of signatures' played a great part in early medicine. The various '-mancies' and '-mantics' come in here, in which witchcraft and incipient science are indistinguishably mixed. 'Sympathetic' theorizing persists to the present day. 'Thoughts are things,' for a contemporary school —and on the whole a good school—of practical philosophy. Cultivate the thought of what you desire, affirm it, and it will bring all similar thoughts from elsewhere to reinforce it, so that finally your wish will be fulfilled.[6]

Little by little, more positive ways of considering things began to prevail. Common elements in phenomena began to be singled out and to form the basis of generalizations. But these elements at first had necessarily to be the more dramatic or humanly interesting ones. The hot, the cold, the wet, the dry in things explained their behavior. Some bodies were naturally warm, others cold. Motions were natural or violent. The heavens moved in circles because circular motion was the most perfect. The lever was explained by the greater quantity of perfection embodied in the movement of its longer arm.[7] The sun went south in winter to escape the cold. Precious or beautiful things had exceptional properties. Peacock's flesh resisted putrefaction. The lodestone would drop the iron which it held if the superiorly powerful diamond was brought near, etc.

Such ideas sound to us grotesque, but imagine no tracks made for us by scientific ancestors, and what aspects would we single out from nature to understand things by? Not till the beginning of the seventeenth century did the more insipid kinds of regularity in things abstract men's attention away from the properties originally picked out. Few of us realize how short the career of what we know as 'science' has been. Three hundred and fifty years ago hardly any one believed in the Copernican planetary theory. Optical combinations were not discovered. The circulation of the blood, the weight of air, the conduction of heat, the laws of motion were unknown; the common pump was inexplicable; there were no clocks; no thermometers; no general gravitation; the world was five thousand years old; spirits moved the planets; alchemy, magic, astrology, imposed on every one's belief.

[6] Compare Prentice Mulford and others of the 'new thought' type. For primitive sympathetic magic consult J. Jastrow in *Fact and Fable in Psychology,* the chapter on Analogy; F. B. Jevons: *Introduction to the History of Religion,* chap. iv; J. G. Frazer: *The Golden Bough,* i, 2; R. R. Marett: *The Threshold of Religion, passim;* A. O. Lovejoy: *The Monist,* xvi, 357.

[7] On Greek science, see W. Whewell's *History of the Inductive Sciences,* vol. i, book i; G. H. Lewes, *Aristotle, passim.*

Modern science began only after 1600, with Kepler, Galileo, Descartes, Torricelli, Pascal, Harvey, Newton, Huygens, and Boyle. Five men telling one another in succession the discoveries which their lives had witnessed, could deliver the whole of it into our hands: Harvey might have told Newton, who might have told Voltaire; Voltaire might have told Dalton, who might have told Huxley, who might have told the readers of this book.

The men who began this work of emancipation were philosophers in the original sense of the word, universal sages. Galileo said that he had spent more years on philosophy than months on mathematics. Descartes was a universal philosopher in the fullest sense of the term. But the fertility of the newer conceptions made special departments of truth grow at such a rate that they became too unwieldy with details for the more universal minds to carry them, so the special sciences of mechanics, astronomy, and physics began to drop off from the parent stem.

No one could have foreseen in advance the extraordinary fertility of the more insipid mathematical aspects which these geniuses ferreted out. No one could have dreamed of the control over nature which the search for their concomitant variations would give. 'Laws' describe these variations; and all our present laws of nature have as their model the proportionality of v to t, and of s to t^2 which Galileo first laid bare. Pascal's discovery of the proportionality of altitude to barometric height, Newton's of acceleration to distance, Boyle's of air-volume to pressure, Descartes' of sine to cosine in the refracted ray, were the first fruits of Galileo's discovery. There was no question of agencies, nothing animistic or sympathetic in this new way of taking nature. It was description only, of concomitant variations, after the particular quantities that varied had been successfully abstracted out. The result soon showed itself in a differentiation of human knowledge into two spheres, one called 'Science,' within which the more definite laws apply, the other 'General Philosophy,' in which they do not. The state of mind called positivistic is the result. 'Down with philosophy!' is the cry of innumerable scientific minds. 'Give us measurable facts only, phenomena, without the mind's additions, without entities or principles that pretend to explain.' It is largely from this kind of mind that the objection that philosophy has made no progress, proceeds.

It is obvious enough that if every step forward which philosophy makes, every question to which an accurate answer is found, gets accredited to science the residuum of unanswered problems will alone remain to constitute the domain of philosophy, and will alone bear her name. In point of fact this is just what is happening. Philosophy has become a collective name for questions that have not yet been answered to the satisfaction of all by whom they have been asked. It does not follow, because some of these questions have waited two thousand years for an answer, that no answer will ever be forthcoming. Two thousand years probably measure but one paragraph in that great romance of adventure called the history of the intellect of man. The extraordinary progress of the last three hundred years is due to a rather sudden finding of the way in which a certain order of questions ought to be attacked, questions admitting of mathematical treatment. But to assume therefore, that the only possible philosophy must be mechanical and mathematical, and to disparage all enquiry into the other sorts of question, is to forget the extreme diversity of aspects under which reality undoubtedly exists. To the spiritual questions the proper avenues of philosophic approach will also undoubtedly be found. They have, to some extent, been found already. In some respects, indeed, 'science' has made less progress than 'philosophy'—its most general conceptions would astonish neither Aristotle nor Descartes, could they revisit our earth. The composition of things from elements, their evolution, the conservation of energy, the idea of a universal determinism, would seem to them commonplace enough—the little things, the microscopes, electric lights, telephones, and details of the sciences, would be to them the awe-inspiring things. But if they opened our books on metaphysics, or visited a philosophic lecture room, everything would sound strange. The whole idealistic or 'critical' attitude of our time would be novel, and it would be long before they took it in.[8]

Objection 2. Philosophy is dogmatic, and pretends to settle things by pure reason, whereas the only fruitful mode of getting at truth is to appeal to concrete experience. Science collects, classes, and analyzes facts, and thereby far outstrips philosophy.

Reply. This objection is historically valid. Too many philosophers have aimed at closed systems, established *a priori,* claiming infallibility, and to be accepted or rejected only as totals. The sciences on the other hand, using hypotheses only, but always seeking to verify them by experiment and observation, open a way for indefinite self-correction and increase. At the present day, it is getting more and more difficult for dogmatists claiming finality for their systems, to get a hearing in educated circles. Hypothesis and verification, the watchwords of science, have set the fashion too strongly in academic minds.

Since philosophers are only men thinking about things in the most comprehensive possible way, they can use any method whatsoever freely. Philosophy must, in any case, complete the sciences, and must incorporate their methods. One cannot see why, if such a policy

[8] The reader will find all that I have said, and much more, set forth in an excellent article by James Ward in *Mind,* vol. 15, no. lviii: 'The Progress of Philosophy.'

should appear advisable, philosophy might not end by forswearing all dogmatism whatever, and become as hypothetical in her manners as the most empirical science of them all.

Objection 3. Philosophy is out of touch with real life, for which it substitutes abstractions. The real world is various, tangled, painful. Philosophers have, almost without exception, treated it as noble, simple, and perfect, ignoring the complexity of fact, and indulging in a sort of optimism that exposes their systems to the contempt of common men, and to the satire of such writers as Voltaire and Schopenhauer. The great popular success of Schopenhauer is due to the fact that, first among philosophers, he spoke the concrete truth about the ills of life.

Reply. This objection also is historically valid, but no reason appears why philosophy should keep aloof from reality permanently. Her manners may change as she successfully develops. The thin and noble abstractions may give way to more solid and real constructions, when the materials and methods for making such constructions shall be more and more securely ascertained. In the end philosophers may get into as close contact as realistic novelists with the facts of life.

In conclusion. In its original acceptation, meaning the completest knowledge of the universe, philosophy must include the results of all the sciences, and cannot be contrasted with the latter. It simply aims at making of science what Herbert Spencer calls a 'system of completely unified knowledge.' [9] In the more modern sense, of something contrasted with the sciences, philosophy means 'metaphysics.' The older sense is the more worthy sense, and as the results of the sciences get more available for co-ordination, and the conditions for finding truth in different kinds of question get more methodically defined, we may hope that the term will revert to its original meaning. Science, metaphysics, and religion may then again form a single body of wisdom, and lend each other mutual support.

THE TYPES OF PHILOSOPHIC THINKING*

As these lectures are meant to be public, and so few, I have assumed all very special problems to be excluded, and some topic of general

[9] See the excellent chapter in Spencer's *First Principles,* entitled: 'Philosophy Defined.'
* From: P.U., 3–40.

interest required. Fortunately, our age seems to be growing philosophical again—still in the ashes live the wonted fires. Oxford, long the seed-bed, for the english world, of the idealism inspired by Kant and Hegel, has recently become the nursery of a very different way of thinking. Even non-philosophers have begun to take an interest in a controversy over what is known as pluralism or humanism. It looks a little as if the ancient english empiricism, so long put out of fashion here by nobler sounding germanic formulas, might be repluming itself and getting ready for a stronger flight than ever. It looks as if foundations were being sounded and examined afresh.

Individuality outruns all classification, yet we insist on classifying every one we meet under some general head. As these heads usually suggest prejudicial associations to some hearer or other, the life of philosophy largely consists of resentments at the classing, and complaints of being misunderstood. But there are signs of clearing up, and, on the whole, less acrimony in discussion, for which both Oxford and Harvard are partly to be thanked. As I look back into the sixties, Mill, Bain, and Hamilton were the only official philosophers in Britain. Spencer, Martineau, and Hodgson were just beginning. In France, the pupils of Cousin were delving into history only, and Renouvier alone had an original system. In Germany, the hegelian impetus had spent itself, and, apart from historical scholarship, nothing but the materialistic controversy remained, with such men as Büchner and Ulrici as its champions. Lotze and Fechner were the sole original thinkers, and Fechner was not a professional philosopher at all.

The general impression made was of crude issues and oppositions, of small subtlety and of a widely spread ignorance. Amateurishness was rampant. Samuel Bailey's 'letters on the philosophy of the human mind,' published in 1855, are one of the ablest expressions of english associationism, and a book of real power. Yet hear how he writes of Kant: 'No one, after reading the extracts, etc., can be surprised to hear of a declaration by men of eminent abilities, that, after years of study, they had not succeeded in gathering one clear idea from the speculations of Kant. I should have been almost surprised if they had. In or about 1818, Lord Grenville, when visiting the Lakes of England, observed to Professor Wilson that, after five years' study of Kant's philosophy, he had not gathered from it one clear idea. Wilberforce, about the same time, made the same confession to another friend of my own. "I am endeavoring," exclaims Sir James Mackintosh, in the irritation, evidently, of baffled efforts, "to understand this accursed german philosophy." ' [10]

What Oxford thinker would dare to print such *naïf* and provincial-sounding citations of authority to-day?

[10] Bailey: *op. cit.*, First Series, p. 52.

The torch of learning passes from land to land as the spirit bloweth the flame. The deepening of philosophic consciousness came to us english folk from Germany, as it will probably pass back ere long. Ferrier, J. H. Stirling, and, most of all, T. H. Green are to be thanked. If asked to tell in broad strokes what the main doctrinal change has been, I should call it a change from the crudity of the older english thinking, its ultra-simplicity of mind, both when it was religious and when it was anti-religious, toward a rationalism derived in the first instance from Germany, but relieved from german technicality and shrillness, and content to suggest, and to remain vague, and to be, in the english fashion, devout.

By the time T. H. Green began at Oxford, the generation seemed to feel as if it had fed on the chopped straw of psychology and of associationism long enough, and as if a little vastness, even though it went with vagueness, as of some moist wind from far away, reminding us of our pre-natal sublimity, would be welcome.

Green's great point of attack was the disconnectedness of the reigning english sensationalism. *Relating* was the great intellectual activity for him, and the key to this relating was believed by him to lodge itself at last in what most of you know as Kant's unity of apperception, transformed into a living spirit of the world.

Hence a monism of a devout kind. In some way we must be fallen angels, one with intelligence as such; and a great disdain for empiricism of the sensationalist sort has always characterized this school of thought, which, on the whole, has reigned supreme at Oxford and in the scottish universities until the present day.

But now there are signs of its giving way to a wave of revised empiricism. I confess that I should be glad to see this latest wave prevail; so—the sooner I am frank about it the better—I hope to have my voice counted in its favor as one of the results of this lecture-course.

What do the terms empiricism and rationalism mean? Reduced to their most pregnant difference, *empiricism means the habit of explaining wholes by parts, and rationalism means the habit of explaining parts by wholes*. Rationalism thus preserves affinities with monism, since wholeness goes with union, while empiricism inclines to pluralistic views. No philosophy can ever be anything but a summary sketch, a picture of the world in abridgment, a foreshortened bird's-eye view of the perspective of events. And the first thing to notice is this, that the only material we have at our disposal for making a picture of the whole world is supplied by the various portions of that world of which we have already had experience. We can invent no new forms of conception, applicable to the whole exclusively, and not suggested originally by the parts. All philosophers, accordingly, have conceived of the whole world after the analogy of some particular feature of it which has particularly captivated their attention. Thus, the theists take their cue from manufacture, the pantheists from growth. For one man, the world is like a thought or a grammatical sentence in which a thought is expressed. For such a philosopher, the whole must logically be prior to the parts; for letters would never have been invented without syllables to spell, or syllables without words to utter.

Another man, struck by the disconnectedness and mutual accidentality of so many of the world's details, takes the universe as a whole to have been such a disconnectedness originally, and supposes order to have been superinduced upon it in the second instance, possibly by attrition and the gradual wearing away by internal friction of portions that originally interfered.

Another will conceive the order as only a statistical appearance, and the universe will be for him like a vast grab-bag with black and white balls in it, of which we guess the quantities only probably, by the frequency with which we experience their egress.

For another, again, there is no really inherent order, but it is we who project order into the world by selecting objects and tracing relations so as to gratify our intellectual interests. We *carve out* order by leaving the disorderly parts out; and the world is conceived thus after the analogy of a forest or a block of marble from which parks or statues may be produced by eliminating irrelevant trees or chips of stone.

Some thinkers follow suggestions from human life, and treat the universe as if it were essentially a place in which ideals are realized. Others are more struck by its lower features, and for them, brute necessities express its character better.

All follow one analogy or another; and all the analogies are with some one or other of the universe's subdivisions. Every one is nevertheless prone to claim that his conclusions are the only logical ones, that they are necessities of universal reason, they being all the while, at bottom, accidents more or less of personal vision which had far better be avowed as such; for one man's vision may be much more valuable than another's, and our visions are usually not only our most interesting but our most respectable contributions to the world in which we play our part. What was reason given to men for, said some eighteenth century writer, except to enable them to find reasons for what they want to think and do?—and I think the history of philosophy largely bears him out. 'The aim of knowledge,' says Hegel,[11] 'is to divest the objective world of its strangeness, and to make us more at home in it.' Different men find their minds more at home in very different fragments of the world.

[11] *Smaller Logic,* § 194.

Let me make a few comments, here, on the curious antipathies which these partialities arouse. They are sovereignly unjust, for all the parties are human beings with the same essential interests, and no one of them is the wholly perverse demon which another often imagines him to be. Both are loyal to the world that bears them; neither wishes to spoil it; neither wishes to regard it as an insane incoherence; both want to keep it as a universe of some kind; and their differences are all secondary to this deep agreement. They may be only propensities to emphasize differently. Or one man may care for finality and security more than the other. Or their tastes in language may be different. One may like a universe that lends itself to lofty and exalted characterization. To another this may seem sentimental or rhetorical. One may wish for the right to use a clerical vocabulary, another a technical or professorial one. A certain old farmer of my acquaintance in America was called a rascal by one of his neighbors. He immediately smote the man, saying, 'I won't stand none of your diminutive epithets.' Empiricist minds, putting the parts before the whole, appear to rationalists, who start from the whole, and consequently enjoy magniloquent privileges, to use epithets offensively diminutive. But all such differences are minor matters which ought to be subordinated in view of the fact that, whether we be empiricists or rationalists, we are, ourselves, parts of the universe and share the same one deep concern in its destinies. We crave alike to feel more truly at home with it, and to contribute our mite to its amelioration. It would be pitiful if small æsthetic discords were to keep honest men asunder.

I shall myself have use for the diminutive epithets of empiricism. But if you look behind the words at the spirit, I am sure you will not find it matricidal. I am as good a son as any rationalist among you to our common mother.

What troubles me more than this misapprehension is the genuine abstruseness of many of the matters I shall be obliged to talk about, and the difficulty of making them intelligible at one hearing. But there are two pieces, 'zwei stücke,' as Kant would have said, in every philosophy—the final outlook, belief, or attitude to which it brings us, and the reasonings by which that attitude is reached and mediated. A philosophy, as James Ferrier used to tell us, must indeed be true, but that is the least of its requirements. One may be true without being a philosopher, true by guesswork or by revelation. What distinguishes a philosopher's truth is that it is *reasoned*. Argument, not supposition, must have put it in his possession. Common men find themselves inheriting their beliefs, they know not how. They jump into them with both feet, and stand there. Philosophers must do more; they must first get reason's license for them; and to the professional philosophic mind the operation of procuring the license is usually a thing of much more pith and moment than any particular beliefs to which the license may give the rights of access. Suppose, for example, that a philosopher believes in what is called free-will. That a common man alongside of him should also share that belief, possessing it by a sort of inborn intuition, does not endear the man to the philosopher at all—he may even be ashamed to be associated with such a man. What interests the philosopher is the particular premises on which the free-will he believes in is established, the sense in which it is taken, the objections it eludes, the difficulties it takes account of, in short the whole form and temper and manner and technical apparatus that goes with the belief in question. A philosopher across the way who should use the same technical apparatus, making the same distinctions, etc., but drawing opposite conclusions and denying free-will entirely, would fascinate the first philosopher far more than would the *naïf* co-believer. Their common technical interests would unite them more than their opposite conclusions separate them. Each would feel an essential consanguinity in the other, would think of him, write *at* him, care for his good opinion. The simple-minded believer in free-will would be disregarded by either. Neither as ally nor as opponent would his vote be counted.

In a measure this is doubtless as it should be, but like all professionalism it can go to abusive extremes. The end is after all more than the way, in most things human, and forms and methods may easily frustrate their own purpose. The abuse of technicality is seen in the infrequency with which, in philosophical literature, metaphysical questions are discussed directly and on their own merits. Almost always they are handled as if through a heavy woolen curtain, the veil of previous philosophers' opinions. Alternatives are wrapped in proper names, as if it were indecent for a truth to go naked. The late Professor John Grote of Cambridge has some good remarks about this. 'Thought,' he says, 'is not a professional matter, not something for so-called philosophers only or for professed thinkers. The best philosopher is the man who can think most *simply*. . . . I wish that people would consider that thought—and philosophy is no more than good and methodical thought—is a matter *intimate* to them, a portion of their real selves . . . that they would *value* what they think, and be interested in it. . . . In my own opinion,' he goes on, 'there is something depressing in this weight of learning, with nothing that can come into one's mind but one is told, Oh, that is the opinion of such and such a person long ago. . . . I can conceive of nothing more noxious for students than to get into the habit of saying to themselves about their ordinary philosophic thought, Oh, somebody must have thought it all before.' [12] Yet this is the habit most encouraged at

[12] *Exploratio philosophica,* Part I, 1865, pp. xxxviii, 130.

our seats of learning. You must tie your opinion to Aristotle's or Spinoza's; you must define it by its distance from Kant's; you must refute your rival's view by identifying it with Protagoras's. Thus does all spontaneity of thought, all freshness of conception, get destroyed. Everything you touch is shopworn. The over-technicality and consequent dreariness of the younger disciples at our american universities is appalling. It comes from too much following of german models and manners. Let me fervently express the hope that in this country you will hark back to the more humane english tradition. American students have to regain direct relations with our subject by painful individual effort in later life. Some of us have done so. Some of the younger ones, I fear, never will, so strong are the professional shop-habits already.

In a subject like philosophy it is really fatal to lose connexion with the open air of human nature, and to think in terms of shop-tradition only. In Germany the forms are so professionalized that anybody who has gained a teaching chair and written a book, however distorted and eccentric, has the legal right to figure forever in the history of the subject like a fly in amber. All later comers have the duty of quoting him and measuring their opinions with his opinion. Such are the rules of the professorial game—they think and write from each other and for each other and at each other exclusively. With this exclusion of the open air all true perspective gets lost, extremes and oddities count as much as sanities, and command the same attention; and if by chance any one writes popularly and about results only, with his mind directly focussed on the subject, it is reckoned *oberflächliches zeug* and *ganz unwissenschaftlich*. Professor Paulsen has recently written some feeling lines about this over-professionalism, from the reign of which in Germany his own writings, which sin by being 'literary,' have suffered loss of credit. Philosophy, he says, has long assumed in Germany the character of being an esoteric and occult science. There is a genuine fear of popularity. Simplicity of statement is deemed synonymous with hollowness and shallowness. He recalls an old professor saying to him once: 'Yes, we philosophers, whenever we wish, can go so far that in a couple of sentences we can put ourselves where nobody can follow us.' The professor said this with conscious pride, but he ought to have been ashamed of it. Great as technique is, results are greater. To teach philosophy so that the pupils' interest in technique exceeds that in results is surely a vicious aberration. It is bad form, not good form, in a discipline of such universal human interest. Moreover, technique for technique, does n't David Hume's technique set, after all, the kind of pattern most difficult to follow? Is n't it the most admirable? The english mind, thank heaven, and the french mind, are still kept, by their aversion to crude technique and barbarism, closer to truth's natural probabilities. Their literatures show fewer obvious falsities and monstrosities than that of Germany. Think of the german literature of æsthetics, with the preposterousness of such an unæsthetic personage as Immanuel Kant enthroned in its centre! Think of german books on *religions-philosophie,* with the heart's battles translated into conceptual jargon and made dialectic. The most persistent setter of questions, feeler of objections, insister on satisfactions, is the religious life. Yet all its troubles can be treated with absurdly little technicality. The wonder is that, with their way of working philosophy, individual Germans should preserve any spontaneity of mind at all. That they still manifest freshness and originality in so eminent a degree, proves the indestructible richness of the german cerebral endowment.

Let me repeat once more that a man's vision is the great fact about him. Who cares for Carlyle's reasons, or Schopenhauer's, or Spencer's? A philosophy is the expression of a man's intimate character, and all definitions of the universe are but the deliberately adopted reactions of human characters upon it. In the recent book from which I quoted the words of Professor Paulsen, a book of successive chapters by various living german philosophers,[13] we pass from one idiosyncratic personal atmosphere into another almost as if we were turning over a photograph album.

If we take the whole history of philosophy, the systems reduce themselves to a few main types which, under all the technical verbiage in which the ingenious intellect of man envelops them, are just so many visions, modes of feeling the whole push, and seeing the whole drift of life, forced on one by one's total character and experience, and on the whole *preferred*—there is no other truthful word—as one's best working attitude. Cynical characters take one general attitude, sympathetic characters another. But no general attitude is possible towards the whole as a whole, until the intellect has developed considerable generalizing power and learned to take pleasure in synthetic formulas. The thought of very primitive men has hardly any tincture of philosophy. Nature can have little unity for savages. It is a Walpurgis-nacht procession, a checkered play of light and shadow, a medley of impish and elfish friendly and inimical powers. 'Close to nature' though they live, they are anything but Wordsworthians. If a bit of cosmic emotion ever thrills them, it is likely to be at midnight, when the camp smoke rises straight to the wicked full moon in the zenith, and the forest is all whispering with witchery and danger. The eeriness of the world, the mischief and the manyness, the littleness of the forces, the magical surprises, the unaccountability of every agent,

---

[13] Hinneberg: *Die Kultur der Gegenwart: Systematische Philosophie.* Leipzig: Teubner, 1907.

these surely are the characters most impressive at that stage of culture, these communicate the thrills of curiosity and the earliest intellectual stirrings. Tempests and conflagrations, pestilences and earthquakes, reveal supramundane powers, and instigate religious terror rather than philosophy. Nature, more demonic than divine, is above all things *multifarious*. So many creatures that feed or threaten, that help or crush, so many beings to hate or love, to understand or start at—which is on top and which subordinate? Who can tell? They are coordinate, rather, and to adapt ourselves to them singly, to 'square' the dangerous powers and keep the others friendly, regardless of consistency or unity, is the chief problem. The symbol of nature at this stage, as Paulsen well says, is the sphinx, under whose nourishing breasts the tearing claws are visible.

But in due course of time the intellect awoke, with its passion for generalizing, simplifying, and subordinating, and then began those divergences of conception which all later experience seems rather to have deepened than to have effaced, because objective nature has contributed to both sides impartially, and has let the thinkers emphasize different parts of her, and pile up opposite imaginary supplements.

Perhaps the most interesting opposition is that which results from the clash between what I lately called the sympathetic and the cynical temper. Materialistic and spiritualistic philosophies are the rival types that result: the former defining the world so as to leave man's soul upon it as a sort of outside passenger or alien, while the latter insists that the intimate and human must surround and underlie the brutal. This latter is the spiritual way of thinking.

Now there are two very distinct types or stages in spiritualistic philosophy, and my next purpose in this lecture is to make their contrast evident. Both types attain the sought-for intimacy of view, but the one attains it somewhat less successfully than the other.

The generic term spiritualism, which I began by using merely as the opposite of materialism, thus subdivides into two species, the more intimate one of which is monistic and the less intimate dualistic. The dualistic species is the *theism* that reached its elaboration in the scholastic philosophy, while the monistic species is the *pantheism* spoken of sometimes simply as idealism, and sometimes as 'postkantian' or 'absolute' idealism. Dualistic theism is professed as firmly as ever at all catholic seats of learning, whereas it has of late years tended to disappear at our british and american universities, and to be replaced by a monistic pantheism more or less open or disguised. I have an impression that ever since T. H. Green's time absolute idealism has been decidedly in the ascendent at Oxford. It is in the ascendent at my own university of Harvard.

Absolute idealism attains, I said, to the more intimate point of view; but the statement needs some explanation. So far as theism represents the world as God's world, and God as what Matthew Arnold called a magnified non-natural man, it would seem as if the inner quality of the world remained human, and as if our relations with it might be intimate enough—for what is best in ourselves appears then also outside of ourselves, and we and the universe are of the same spiritual species. So far, so good, then; and one might consequently ask, What more of intimacy do you require? To which the answer is that to be like a thing is not as intimate a relation as to be substantially fused into it, to form one continuous soul and body with it; and that pantheistic idealism, making us entitatively one with God, attains this higher reach of intimacy.

The theistic conception, picturing God and his creation as entities distinct from each other, still leaves the human subject outside of the deepest reality in the universe. God is from eternity complete, it says, and sufficient unto himself; he throws off the world by a free act and as an extraneous substance, and he throws off man as a third substance, extraneous to both the world and himself. Between them, God says 'one,' the world says 'two,' and man says 'three,'—that is the orthodox theistic view. And orthodox theism has been so jealous of God's glory that it has taken pains to exaggerate everything in the notion of him that could make for isolation and separateness. Page upon page in scholastic books go to prove that God is in no sense implicated by his creative act, or involved in his creation. That his relation to the creatures he has made should make any difference to him, carry any consequence, or qualify his being, is repudiated as a pantheistic slur upon his self-sufficingness. I said a moment ago that theism treats us and God as of the same species, but from the orthodox point of view that was a slip of language. God and his creatures are *toto genere* distinct in the scholastic theology, they have absolutely *nothing* in common; nay, it degrades God to attribute to him any generic nature whatever; he can be classed with nothing. There is a sense, then, in which philosophic theism makes us outsiders and keeps us foreigners in relation to God, in which, at any rate, his connexion with us appears as unilateral and not reciprocal. His action can affect us, but he can never be affected by our reaction. Our relation, in short, is not a strictly social relation. Of course in common men's religion the relation is believed to be social, but that is only one of the many differences between religion and theology.

This essential dualism of the theistic view has all sorts of collateral consequences. Man being an outsider and a mere subject to God, not his intimate partner, a character of externality invades the field. God is not heart of our heart and reason of our reason, but our magistrate, rather; and mechanically to obey his commands, however strange they may be, remains our only moral duty. Conceptions of criminal law have in fact played a great part in defining our relations with him. Our relations with speculative truth show the same external- ity. One of our duties is to know truth, and rationalist thinkers have always assumed it to be our sovereign duty. But in scholastic theism we find truth already instituted and established without our help, com- plete apart from our knowing; and the most we can do is to acknowl- edge it passively and adhere to it, altho such adhesion as ours can make no jot of difference to what is adhered to. The situation here again is radically dualistic. It is not as if the world came to know itself, or God came to know himself, partly through us, as pantheistic idealists have maintained, but truth exists *per se* and absolutely, by God's grace and decree, no matter who of us knows it or is ignorant, and it would continue to exist unaltered, even though we finite knowers were all annihilated.

It has to be confessed that this dualism and lack of intimacy has always operated as a drag and handicap on christian thought. Ortho- dox theology has had to wage a steady fight within the schools against the various forms of pantheistic heresy which the mystical experiences of religious persons, on the one hand, and the formal or æsthetic supe- riorities of monism to dualism, on the other, kept producing. God as intimate soul and reason of the universe has always seemed to some people a more worthy conception than God as external creator. So conceived, he appeared to unify the world more perfectly, he made it less finite and mechanical, and in comparison with such a God an external creator seemed more like the product of a childish fancy. I have been told by Hindoos that the great obstacle to the spread of Christianity in their country is the puerility of our dogma of creation. It has not sweep and infinity enough to meet the requirements of even the illiterate natives of India.

Assuredly most members of this audience are ready to side with Hinduism in this matter. Those of us who are sexagenarians have wit- nessed in our own persons one of those gradual mutations of intellec- tual climate, due to innumerable influences, that make the thought of a past generation seem as foreign to its successor as if it were the expression of a different race of men. The theological machinery that spoke so livingly to our ancestors, with its finite age of the world, its creation out of nothing, its juridical morality and eschatology, its rel- ish for rewards and punishments, its treatment of God as an external contriver, an 'intelligent and moral governor,' sounds as odd to most of us as if it were some outlandish savage religion. The vaster vistas which scientific evolutionism has opened, and the rising tide of social democratic ideals, have changed the type of our imagination, and the older monarchical theism is obsolete or obsolescent. The place of the divine in the world must be more organic and intimate. An external creator and his institutions may still be verbally confessed at Church in formulas that linger by their mere inertia, but the life is out of them, we avoid dwelling on them, the sincere heart of us is elsewhere.

I shall leave cynical materialism entirely out of our discussion as not calling for treatment before this present audience, and I shall ignore old-fashioned dualistic theism for the same reason. Our contemporary mind having once for all grasped the possibility of a more intimate *weltanschauung,* the only opinions quite worthy of arresting our attention will fall within the general scope of what may roughly be called the pantheistic field of vision, the vision of God as the indwelling divine rather than the external creator, and of human life as part and parcel of that deep reality.

As we have found that spiritualism in general breaks into a more intimate and a less intimate species, so the more intimate species itself breaks into two subspecies, of which the one is more monistic, the other more pluralistic in form. I say in form, for our vocabulary gets unmanageable if we don't distinguish between form and substance here. The inner life of things must be substantially akin anyhow to the tenderer parts of man's nature in any spiritualistic philosophy. The word 'intimacy' probably covers the essential difference. Materialism holds the foreign in things to be more primary and lasting, it sends us to a lonely corner with our intimacy. The brutal aspects overlap and outwear; refinement has the feebler and more ephemeral hold on reality.

From a pragmatic point of view the difference between living against a background of foreignness and one of intimacy means the difference between a general habit of wariness and one of trust. One might call it a social difference, for after all, the common *socius* of us all is the great universe whose children we are. If materialistic, we must be suspicious of this socius, cautious, tense, on guard. If spiritualistic, we may give way, embrace, and keep no ultimate fear.

The contrast is rough enough, and can be cut across by all sorts of other divisions, drawn from other points of view than that of foreignness and intimacy. We have so many different businesses with nature that no one of them yields us an all-embracing clasp. The philosophic attempt to define nature so that no one's business is left out, so that no ones lies outside the door saying 'Where do *I* come in?' is sure in advance to fail. The most a philosophy can hope for is not to lock out any interest forever. No matter what doors it closes, it must leave other doors open for the interests which it neglects. I have begun by shutting ourselves up to intimacy and foreignness because that makes so generally interesting a contrast, and because it will conveniently introduce a farther contrast to which I wish this hour to lead.

The majority of men are sympathetic. Comparatively few are cynics because they like cynicism, and most of our existing materialists are such because they think the evidence of facts impels them, or because they find the idealists they are in contact with too private and tender-minded; so, rather than join their company, they fly to the opposite extreme. I therefore propose to you to disregard materialists altogether for the present, and to consider the sympathetic party alone.

It is normal, I say, to be sympathetic in the sense in which I use the term. Not to demand intimate relations with the universe, and not to wish them satisfactory, should be accounted signs of something wrong. Accordingly when minds of this type reach the philosophic level, and seek some unification of their vision, they find themselves compelled to correct that aboriginal appearance of things by which savages are not troubled. That sphinx-like presence, with its breasts and claws, that first bald multifariousness, is too discrepant an object for philosophic contemplation. The intimacy and the foreignness cannot be written down as simply coexisting. An order must be made; and in that order the higher side of things must dominate. The philosophy of the absolute agrees with the pluralistic philosophy which I am going to contrast with it in these lectures, in that both identify human substance with the divine substance. But whereas absolutism thinks that the said substance becomes fully divine only in the form of totality, and is not its real self in any form but the *all*-form, the pluralistic view which I prefer to adopt is willing to believe that there may ultimately never be an all-form at all, that the substance of reality may never get totally collected, that some of it may remain outside of the largest combination of it ever made, and that a distributive form of reality, the *each*-form, is logically as acceptable and empirically as probable as the all-form commonly acquiesced in as so obviously the self-evident thing. The contrast between these two forms of a reality which we will agree to suppose substantially spiritual is practically the topic of this course of lectures. You see now what I mean by pantheism's two subspecies. If we give to the monistic subspecies the name of philosophy of the absolute, we may give that of radical empiricism to its pluralistic rival, and it may be well to distinguish them occasionally later by these names.

As a convenient way of entering into the study of their differences, I may refer to a recent article by Professor Jacks of Manchester College. Professor Jacks, in some brilliant pages in the 'Hibbert Journal' for last October, studies the relation between the universe and the philosopher who describes and defines it for us. You may assume two cases, he says. Either what the philosopher tells us is extraneous to the universe he is accounting for, an indifferent parasitic outgrowth, so to speak; or the fact of his philosophizing is itself one of the things taken account of in the philosophy, and self-included in the description. In the former case the philosopher means by the universe everything *except* what his own presence brings; in the latter case his philosophy is itself an intimate part of the universe, and may be a part momentous enough to give a different turn to what the other parts signify. It may be a supreme reaction of the universe upon itself by which it rises to self-comprehension. It may handle itself differently in consequence of this event.

Now both empiricism and absolutism bring the philosopher inside and make man intimate, but the one being pluralistic and the other monistic, they do so in differing ways that need much explanation. Let me then contrast the one with the other way of representing the status of the human thinker.

For monism the world is no collection, but one great all-inclusive fact outside of which is nothing—nothing is its only alternative. When the monism is idealistic, this all-enveloping fact is represented as an absolute mind that makes the partial facts by thinking them, just as we make objects in a dream by dreaming them, or personages in a story by imagining them. To *be*, on this scheme, is, on the part of a finite thing, to be an object for the absolute; and on the part of the absolute it is to be the thinker of that assemblage of objects. If we use the word 'content' here, we see that the absolute and the world have an identical content. The absolute is nothing but the knowledge of those objects; the objects are nothing but what the absolute knows. The world and the all-thinker thus compenetrate and soak each other up without residuum. They are but two names for the same identical material, considered now from the subjective, and now from the objective point of view—gedanke and gedachtes, as we would say if we were Germans. We philosophers naturally form part of the material, on the monistic scheme. The absolute makes us by thinking us, and if we ourselves are enlightened enough to be believers in the absolute, one may then say that our philosophizing is one of the ways in which the absolute is conscious of itself. This is the full pantheistic scheme, the *identitätsphilosophie*, the immanence of God in his creation, a conception sublime from its tremendous unity. And yet that unity is incomplete, as closer examination will show.

The absolute and the world are one fact, I said, when materially considered. Our philosophy, for example, is not numerically distinct from the absolute's own knowledge of itself, not a duplicate and copy of it, it is part of that very knowledge, is numerically identical with as much of it as our thought covers. The absolute just *is* our philosophy, along with everything else that is known, in an act of knowing which (to use the words of my gifted absolutist colleague Royce) forms in its wholeness one luminously transparent conscious moment.

But one as we are in this material sense with the absolute substance, that being only the whole of us, and we only the parts of it, yet in a formal sense something like a pluralism breaks out. When we speak of the absolute we *take* the one universal known material collectively or integrally; when we speak of its objects, of our finite selves, etc., we *take* that same identical material distributively and separately. But what is the use of a thing's *being* only once if it can be *taken* twice over, and if being taken in different ways makes different things true of it? As the absolute takes me, for example, I appear *with* everything else in its field of perfect knowledge. As I take myself, I appear *without* most other things in my field of relative ignorance. And practical differences result from its knowledge and my ignorance. Ignorance breeds mistake, curiosity, misfortune, pain, for me; I suffer those consequences. The absolute knows of those things, of course, for it knows me and my suffering, but it does n't itself suffer. It can't be ignorant, for simultaneous with its knowledge of each question goes its knowledge of each answer. It can't be patient, for it has to wait for nothing, having everything at once in its possession. It can't be surprised; it can't be guilty. No attribute connected with succession can be applied to it, for it is all at once and wholly what it is, 'with the unity of a single instant,' and succession is not of it but in it, for we are continually told that it is 'timeless.'

Things true of the world in its finite aspects, then, are not true of it in its infinite capacity. *Quâ* finite and plural its accounts of itself to itself are different from what its account to itself *quâ* infinite and one must be.

With this radical discrepancy between the absolute and the relative points of view, it seems to me that almost as great a bar to intimacy between the divine and the human breaks out in pantheism as that which we found in monarchical theism, and hoped that pantheism might not show. We humans are incurably rooted in the temporal point of view. The eternal's ways are utterly unlike our ways. 'Let us imitate the All,' said the original prospectus of that admirable Chicago quarterly called the 'Monist.' As if we could, either in thought or conduct! We are invincibly parts, let us talk as we will, and must always apprehend the absolute as if it were a foreign being. If what I mean by this is not wholly clear to you at this point, it ought to grow clearer as my lectures proceed.

MONISTIC IDEALISM*

Let me recall to you the programme which I indicated to you at our last meeting. After agreeing not to consider materialism in any shape, but to place ourselves straightway upon a more spiritualistic platform, I pointed out three kinds of spiritual philosophy between which we are asked to choose. The first way was that of the older dualistic theism, with ourselves represented as a secondary order of substances created by God. We found that this allowed of a degree of intimacy with the creative principle inferior to that implied in the pantheistic belief that we are substantially one with it, and that the divine is therefore the most intimate of all our possessions, heart of our heart, in fact. But we saw that this pantheistic belief could be held in two forms, a monistic form which I called philosophy of the absolute, and a pluralistic form which I called radical empiricism, the former conceiving that the divine exists authentically only when the world is experienced all at once in its absolute totality, whereas radical empiricism allows that the absolute sum-total of things may never be actually experienced or realized in that shape at all, and that a disseminated, distributed, or incompletely unified appearance is the only form that reality may yet have achieved.

I may contrast the monistic and pluralistic forms in question as the 'all-form' and the 'each-form.' At the end of the last hour I animadverted on the fact that the all-form is so radically different from the each-form, which is our human form of experiencing the world, that the philosophy of the absolute, so far as insight and understanding go, leaves us almost as much outside of the divine being as dualistic theism does. I believe that radical empiricism, on the contrary, holding to the each-form, and making of God only one of the eaches, affords the higher degree of intimacy. The general thesis of these lectures I said would be a defence of the pluralistic against the monistic view. Think of the universe as existing solely in the each-form, and you will have on the whole a more reasonable and satisfactory idea of it than if you insist on the all-form being necessary. The rest of my lectures will do little more than make this thesis more concrete, and I hope more persuasive.

It is curious how little countenance radical pluralism has ever had from philosophers. Whether materialistically or spiritualistically minded, philosophers have always aimed at cleaning up the litter with which the world apparently is filled. They have substituted economical

* From: P.U., 43–82.

and orderly conceptions for the first sensible tangle; and whether these were morally elevated or only intellectually neat, they were at any rate always æsthetically pure and definite, and aimed at ascribing to the world something clean and intellectual in the way of inner structure. As compared with all these rationalizing pictures, the pluralistic empiricism which I profess offers but a sorry appearance. It is a turbid, muddled, gothic sort of an affair, without a sweeping outline and with little pictorial nobility. Those of you who are accustomed to the classical constructions of reality may be excused if your first reaction upon it be absolute contempt—a shrug of the shoulders as if such ideas were unworthy of explicit refutation. But one must have lived some time with a system to appreciate its merits. Perhaps a little more familiarity may mitigate your first surprise at such a programme as I offer.

First, one word more than what I said last time about the relative foreignness of the divine principle in the philosophy of the absolute. Those of you who have read the last two chapters of Mr. Bradley's wonderful book, 'Appearance and reality,' will remember what an elaborately foreign aspect *his* absolute is finally made to assume. It is neither intelligence nor will, neither a self nor a collection of selves, neither truthful, good, nor beautiful, as we understand these terms. It is, in short, a metaphysical monster, all that we are permitted to say of it being that whatever it is, it is at any rate *worth* more (worth more to itself, that is) than if any eulogistic adjectives of ours applied to it. It is us, and all other appearances, but none of us *as such,* for in it we are all 'transmuted,' and its own as-suchness is of another denomination altogether.

Spinoza was the first great absolutist, and the impossibility of being intimate with *his* God is universally recognized. *Quatenus infinitus est* he is other than what he is *quatenus humanam mentem constituit*. Spinoza's philosophy has been rightly said to be worked by the word *quatenus*. Conjunctions, prepositions, and adverbs play indeed the vital part in all philosophies; and in contemporary idealism the words 'as' and 'quâ' bear the burden of reconciling metaphysical unity with phenomenal diversity. Quâ absolute the world is one and perfect, quâ relative it is many and faulty, yet it is identically the self-same world—instead of talking of it as many facts, we call it one fact in many aspects.

As absolute, then, or *sub specie eternitatis,* or *quatenus infinitus est* the world repels our sympathy because it has no history. *As such,* the absolute neither acts nor suffers, nor loves nor hates; it has no needs, desires, or aspirations, no failures or successes, friends or enemies, victories or defeats. All such things pertain to the world quâ relative, in which our finite experiences lie, and whose vicissitudes alone have power to arouse our interest. What boots it to tell me that the absolute way is the true way, and to exhort me, as Emerson says, to lift mine eye up to its style, and manners of the sky, if the feat is impossible by definition? I am finite once for all, and all the categories of my sympathy are knit up with the finite world *as such,* and with things that have a history. 'Aus dieser erde quellen meine freuden, und ihre sonne scheinet meinen leiden.' I have neither eyes nor ears nor heart nor mind for anything of an opposite description, and the stagnant felicity of the absolute's own perfection moves me as little as I move it. If we were *readers* only of the cosmic novel, things would be different: we should then share the author's point of view and recognize villains to be as essential as heroes in the plot. But we are not the readers but the very personages of the world-drama. In your own eyes each of you here is its hero, and the villains are your respective friends or enemies. The tale which the absolute reader finds so perfect, we spoil for one another through our several vital identifications with the destinies of the particular personages involved.

The doctrine on which the absolutists lay most stress is the absolute's 'timeless' character. For pluralists, on the other hand, time remains as real as anything, and nothing in the universe is great or static or eternal enough not to have some history. But the world that each of us feels most intimately at home with is that of beings with histories that play into our history, whom we can help in their vicissitudes even as they help us in ours. This satisfaction the absolute denies us; we can neither help nor hinder it, for it stands outside of history. It surely is a merit in a philosophy to make the very life we lead seem real and earnest. Pluralism, in exorcising the absolute, exorcises the great de-realizer of the only life we are at home in, and thus redeems the nature of reality from essential foreignness. Every end, reason, motive, object of desire or aversion, ground of sorrow or joy that we feel is in the world of finite multifariousness, for only in that world does anything really happen, only there do events come to pass.

In one sense this is a far-fetched and rather childish objection, for so much of the history of the finite is as formidably foreign to us as the static absolute can possibly be—in fact that entity derives its own foreignness largely from the bad character of the finite which it simultaneously is—that this sentimental reason for preferring the pluralistic view seems small.[14] I shall return to the subject [later], and meanwhile, with your permission, I will say no more about this objection. The more so as the necessary foreignness of the absolute is cancelled emotionally by its attribute of totality, which is universally

---

[14] The difference is that the bad parts of this finite are eternal and essential for absolutists, whereas pluralists may hope that they will eventually get sloughed off and become as if they had not been.

considered to carry the further attribute of *perfection* in its train. 'Philosophy,' says a recent american philosopher, 'is humanity's hold on totality,' and there is no doubt that most of us find that the bare notion of an absolute all-one is inspiring. 'I yielded myself to the perfect whole,' writes Emerson; and where can you find a more mind-dilating object? A certain loyalty is called forth by the idea; even if not proved actual, it must be believed in somehow. Only an enemy of philosophy can speak lightly of it. Rationalism starts from the idea of such a whole and builds downward. Movement and change are absorbed into its immutability as forms of mere appearance. When you accept this beatific vision of what *is*, in contrast with what *goes on*, you feel as if you had fulfilled an intellectual duty. 'Reality is not in its truest nature a process,' Mr. McTaggart tells us, 'but a stable and timeless state.' [15] 'The true knowledge of God begins,' Hegel writes, 'when we know that things as they immediately are have no truth.' [16] 'The consummation of the infinite aim,' he says elsewhere, 'consists merely in removing the illusion which makes it seem yet unaccomplished. Good and absolute goodness is eternally accomplishing itself in the world: and the result is that it needs not wait upon *us*, but is already . . . accomplished. It is an illusion under which we live. . . . In the course of its process the Idea makes itself that illusion, by setting an antithesis to confront it, and its action consists in getting rid of the illusion which it has created.' [17]

But abstract emotional appeals of any kind sound amateurish in the business that concerns us. Impressionistic philosophizing, like impressionistic watchmaking or land-surveying, is intolerable to experts. Serious discussion of the alternative before us forces me, therefore, to become more technical. The great *claim* of the philosophy of the absolute is that the absolute is no hypothesis, but a presupposition implicated in all thinking, and needing only a little effort of analysis to be seen as a logical necessity. I will therefore take it in this more rigorous character and see whether its claim is in effect so coercive.

It has seemed coercive to an enormous number of contemporaneous thinkers. Professor Henry Jones thus describes the range and influence of it upon the social and political life of the present time:[18] 'For many years adherents of this way of thought have deeply interested the british public by their writings. Almost more important than their writings is the fact that they have occupied philosophical chairs in almost every university in the kingdom. Even the professional critics of idealism are for the most part idealists—after a fashion. And

---

[15] Quoted by W. Wallace: *Lectures and Essays,* Oxford, 1898, p. 560.
[16] *Logic,* tr. Wallace, 1874, p. 181.
[17] *Ibid.,* p. 304.
[18] *Contemporary Review,* December, 1907, vol. 92, p. 618.

when they are not, they are as a rule more occupied with the refutation of idealism than with the construction of a better theory. It follows from their position of academic authority, were it from nothing else, that idealism exercises an influence not easily measured upon the youth of the nation—upon those, that is, who from the educational opportunities they enjoy may naturally be expected to become the leaders of the nation's thought and practice. . . . Difficult as it is to measure the forces . . . it is hardly to be denied that the power exercised by Bentham and the utilitarian school has, for better or for worse, passed into the hands of the idealists. . . . "The Rhine has flowed into the Thames" is the warning note rung out by Mr. Hobhouse. Carlyle introduced it, bringing it as far as Chelsea. Then Jowett and Thomas Hill Green, and William Wallace and Lewis Nettleship, and Arnold Toynbee and David Ritchie—to mention only those teachers whose voices now are silent—guided the waters into those upper reaches known locally as the Isis. John and Edward Caird brought them up the Clyde, Hutchison Stirling up the Firth of Forth. They have passed up the Mersey and up the Severn and Dee and Don. They pollute the bay of St. Andrews and swell the waters of the Cam, and have somehow crept overland into Birmingham. The stream of german idealism has been diffused over the academical world of Great Britain. The disaster is universal.'

Evidently if weight of authority were all, the truth of absolutism would be thus decided. But let us first pass in review the general style of argumentation of that philosophy.

As I read it, its favorite way of meeting pluralism and empiricism is by a *reductio ad absurdum* framed somewhat as follows: You contend, it says to the pluralist, that things, though in some respects connected, are in other respects independent, so that they are not members of one all-inclusive individual fact. Well, your position is absurd on either point. For admit in fact the slightest modicum of independence, and you find (if you will only think accurately) that you have to admit more and more of it, until at last nothing but an absolute chaos, or the proved impossibility of any connexion whatever between the parts of the universe, remains upon your hands. Admit, on the other hand, the most incipient minimum of relation between any two things, and again you can't stop until you see that the absolute unity of all things is implied.

If we take the latter *reductio ad absurdum* first, we find a good example of it in Lotze's well-known proof of monism from the fact of interaction between finite things. Suppose, Lotze says in effect, and for simplicity's sake I have to paraphrase him, for his own words are too long to quote—many distinct beings *a, b, c,* etc., to exist independently of each other: *can a in that case ever act on b?*

What is it to act? Is it not to exert an influence? Does the influence detach itself from *a* and find *b*? If so, it is a third fact, and the problem is not how *a* acts, but how its 'influence' acts on *b*. By another influence perhaps? And how in the end does the chain of influences find *b* rather than *c* unless *b* is somehow prefigured in them already? And when they have found *b,* how do they make *b* respond, if *b* has nothing in common with them? Why don't they go right through *b*? The change in *b* is a *response,* due to *b*'s capacity for taking account of *a*'s influence, and that again seems to prove that *b*'s nature is somehow fitted to *a*'s nature in advance. *A* and *b,* in short, are not really as distinct as we at first supposed them, not separated by a void. Were this so they would be mutually impenetrable, or at least mutually irrelevant. They would form two universes each living by itself, making no difference to each other, taking no account of each other, much as the universe of your day dreams takes no account of mine. They must therefore belong together beforehand, be co-implicated already, their natures must have an inborn mutual reference each to each.

Lotze's own solution runs as follows: The multiple independent things supposed cannot be real in that shape, but all of them, if reciprocal action is to be possible between them, must be regarded as parts of a single real being, M. The pluralism with which our view began has to give place to a monism; and the 'transeunt' interaction, being unintelligible as such, is to be understood as an immanent operation.[19]

The words 'immanent operation' seem here to mean that the single real being M, of which *a* and *b* are members, is the only thing that changes, and that when it changes, it changes inwardly and all over at once. When part *a* in it changes, consequently, part *b* must also change, but without the whole M changing this would not occur.

A pretty argument, but a purely verbal one, as I apprehend it. *Call* your *a* and *b* distinct, they can't interact; *call* them one, they can. For taken abstractly and without qualification the words 'distinct' and 'independent' suggest only disconnection. If this be the only property of your *a* and *b* (and it is the only property your words imply), then of course, since you can't deduce their mutual influence from *it,* you can find no ground of its occurring between them. Your bare word 'separate' contradicting your bare word 'joined,' seems to exclude connexion.

Lotze's remedy for the impossibility thus verbally found is to change the first word. If, instead of calling *a* and *b* independent, we now call them 'interdependent,' 'united,' or 'one,' he says, *these* words do not contradict any sort of mutual influence that may be proposed. If *a* and *b* are 'one,' and the one changes, *a* and *b* of course must coordinately change. What under the old name they could n't do, they now have license to do under the new name.

But I ask you whether giving the name of 'one' to the former 'many' makes us really understand the modus operandi of interaction any better. We have now given verbal permission to the many to change all together, if they can; we have removed a verbal impossibility and substituted a verbal possibility, but the new name, with the possibility it suggests, tells us nothing of the actual process by which real things that are one can and do change at all. In point of fact abstract oneness as such *does n't* change, neither has it parts—any more than abstract independence as such interacts. But then neither abstract oneness nor abstract independence *exists;* only concrete real things exist, which add to these properties the other properties which they possess, to make up what we call their total nature. To construe any one of their abstract names as *making their total nature impossible* is a misuse of the function of naming. The real way of rescue from the abstract consequences of one name is not to fly to an opposite name, equally abstract, but rather to correct the first name by qualifying adjectives that restore some concreteness to the case. Don't take your 'independence' *simpliciter,* as Lotze does, take it *secundum quid.* Only when we know what the process of interaction literally and concretely *consists* in can we tell whether beings independent *in definite respects,* distinct, for example, in origin, separate in place, different in kind, etc., can or cannot interact.

The treating of a name as excluding from the fact named what the name's definition fails positively to include, is what I call 'vicious intellectualism.' Later I shall have more to say about this intellectualism, but that Lotze's argument is tainted by it I hardly think we can deny. As well might you contend (to use an instance from Sigwart) that a person whom you have once called an 'equestrian' is thereby forever made unable to walk on his own feet.

I almost feel as if I should apologize for criticising such subtle arguments in rapid lectures of this kind. The criticisms have to be as abstract as the arguments, and in exposing their unreality, take on such an unreal sound themselves that a hearer not nursed in the intellectualist atmosphere knows not which of them to accuse. But *le vin est versé, il faut le boire,* and I must cite a couple more instances before I stop.

If we are empiricists and go from parts to wholes, we believe that beings may first exist and feed so to speak on their own existence, and then secondarily become known to one another. But philosophers of the absolute tell us that such independence of being from being known would, if once admitted, disintegrate the universe beyond all hope of mending. The argument is one of Professor Royce's proofs that the only alternative we have is to choose the complete disunion of all things or their complete union in the absolute One.

Take, for instance, the proverb 'a cat may look at a king' and adopt the realistic view that the king's being is independent of the cat's witnessing. This assumption, which amounts to saying that it need make no essential difference to the royal object whether the feline subject cognizes him or not, that the cat may look away from him or may even be annihilated, and the king remain unchanged,—this assumption, I say, is considered by my ingenious colleague to lead to the absurd practical consequence that the two beings *can* never later acquire any possible linkages or connexions, but must remain eternally as if in different worlds. For suppose any connexion whatever to ensue, this connexion would simply be a third being additional to the cat and the king, which would itself have to be linked to both by additional links before it could connect them, and so on *ad infinitum,* the argument, you see, being the same as Lotze's about how *a*'s influence does its influencing when it influences *b*.

In Royce's own words, if the king can be without the cat knowing him, then king and cat 'can have no common features, no ties, no true relations; they are separated, each from the other, by absolutely impassable chasms. They can never come to get either ties or community of nature; they are not in the same space, nor in the same time, nor in the same natural or spiritual order.' [20] They form in short two unrelated universes,—which is the *reductio ad absurdum* required.

To escape this preposterous state of things we must accordingly revoke the original hypothesis. The king and the cat are not indifferent to each other in the way supposed. But if not in that way, then in no way, for connexion in that way carries connexion in other ways; so that, pursuing the reverse line of reasoning, we end with the absolute itself as the smallest fact that can exist. Cat and king are co-involved, they are a single fact in two names, they can never have been absent from each other, and they are both equally co-implicated with all the other facts of which the universe consists.

Professor Royce's proof that whoso admits the cat's witnessing the king at all must thereupon admit the the integral absolute, may be briefly put as follows:—

First, to know the king, the cat must intend *that* king, must somehow pass over and lay hold of him individually and specifically. The cat's idea, in short, must transcend the cat's own separate mind and somehow include the king, for were the king utterly outside and independent of the cat, the cat's pure other, the beast's mind could touch the king in no wise. This makes the cat much less distinct from the king than we had at first naïvely supposed. There must be some prior

[20] *The World and the Individual,* vol. i, pp. 131–132.

continuity between them, which continuity Royce interprets idealistically as meaning a higher mind that owns them both as objects, and owning them can also own any relation, such as the supposed witnessing, that may obtain between them. Taken purely pluralistically, neither of them can own any part of a *between,* because, so taken, each is supposed shut up to itself: the fact of a *between* thus commits us to a higher knower.

But the higher knower that knows the two beings we start with proves to be the same knower that knows everything else. For assume any third being, the queen, say, and as the cat knew the king, so let the king know his queen, and let this second knowledge, by the same reasoning, require a higher knower as its presupposition. That knower of the king's knowing must, it is now contended, be the same higher knower that was required for the cat's knowing; for if you suppose otherwise, you have no longer the *same king.* This may not seem immediately obvious, but if you follow the intellectualistic logic employed in all these reasonings, I don't see how you can escape the admission. If it be true that the independent or indifferent cannot be related, for the abstract words 'independent' or 'indifferent' as such imply no relation, then it is just as true that the king known by the cat cannot be the king that knows the queen, for taken merely 'as such,' the abstract term 'what the cat knows' and the abstract term 'what knows the queen' are logically distinct. The king thus logically breaks into two kings, with nothing to connect them, until a higher knower is introduced to recognize them as the self-same king concerned in any previous acts of knowledge which he may have brought about. This he can do because he possesses all the terms as his own objects and can treat them as he will. Add any fourth or fifth term, and you get a like result, and so on, until at last an all-owning knower, otherwise called the absolute, is reached. The co-implicated 'through-and-through' world of monism thus stands proved by irrefutable logic, and all pluralism appears as absurd.

The reasoning is pleasing from its ingenuity, and it is almost a pity that so straight a bridge from abstract logic to concrete fact should not bear our weight. To have the alternative forced upon us of admitting either finite things each cut off from all relation with its environment, or else of accepting the integral absolute with no environment and all relations packed within itself, would be too delicious a simplification. But the purely verbal character of the operation is undisguised. Because the *names* of finite things and their relations are disjoined, it does n't follow that the realities named need a *deus ex machina* from on high to conjoin them. The same things disjoined in one respect *appear* as conjoined in another. Naming the disjunction does n't debar us from also naming the conjunction in a later modifying statement, for the two are absolutely co-ordinate elements in the finite tissue of experience. When at Athens it was found self-contradictory that a boy could be both tall and short (tall namely in respect of a child, short in respect of a man), the absolute had not yet been thought of, but it might just as well have been invoked by Socrates as by Lotze or Royce, as a relief from his peculiar intellectualistic difficulty.

Everywhere we find rationalists using the same kind of reasoning. The primal whole which is their vision must be there not only as a fact but as a logical necessity. It must be the minimum that can exist— either that absolute whole is there, or there is absolutely nothing. The logical proof alleged of the irrationality of supposing otherwise, is that you can deny the whole only in words that implicitly assert it. If you say 'parts,' of *what* are they parts? If you call them a 'many,' that very word unifies them. If you suppose them unrelated in any particular respect, that 'respect' connects them; and so on. In short you fall into hopeless contradiction. You must stay either at one extreme or the other.[21] 'Partly this and partly that,' partly rational, for instance, and partly irrational, is no admissible description of the world. If rationality be in it at all, it must be in it throughout; if irrationality be in it anywhere, that also must pervade it throughout. It must be wholly rational or wholly irrational, pure universe or pure multiverse or nulli-verse; and reduced to this violent alternative, no one's choice ought long to remain doubtful. The individual absolute, with its parts co-implicated through and through, so that there is nothing in any part by which any other part can remain inwardly unaffected, is the only rational supposition. Connexions of an external sort, by which the many became merely continuous instead of being consubstantial, would be an irrational supposition.

Mr. Bradley is the pattern champion of this philosophy *in extremis,* as one might call it, for he shows an intolerance to pluralism so extreme that I fancy few of his readers have been able fully to share it. His reasoning exemplifies everywhere what I call the vice of intellectualism, for abstract terms are used by him as positively excluding all that their definition fails to include. Some Greek sophists could deny that we may say that man is good, for man, they said, means only man, and good means only good, and the word *is* can't be construed to identify such disparate meanings. Mr. Bradley revels in the same type of argument. No adjective can rationally qualify a substantive, he thinks, for if distinct from the substantive, it can't be

[21] A good illustration of this is to be found in a controversy between Mr. Bradley and the present writer, in *Mind* for 1893, Mr. Bradley contending (if I understood him rightly) that 'resemblance' is an illegitimate category, because it admits of degrees, and that the only real relations in comparison are absolute identity and absolute non-comparability.

united with it; and if not distinct, there is only one thing there, and nothing left to unite. Our whole pluralistic procedure in using subjects and predicates as we do is fundamentally irrational, an example of the desperation of our finite intellectual estate, infected and undermined as that is by the separatist discursive forms which are our only categories, but which absolute reality must somehow absorb into its unity and overcome.

Readers of 'Appearance and reality' will remember how Mr. Bradley suffers from a difficulty identical with that to which Lotze and Royce fall a prey—how shall an influence influence? how shall a relation relate? Any conjunctive relation between two phenomenal experiences *a* and *b* must, in the intellectualist philosophy of these authors, be itself a third entity; and as such, instead of bridging the one original chasm, it can only create two smaller chasms, each to be freshly bridged. Instead of hooking *a* to *b*, it needs itself to be hooked by a fresh relation *r'* to *a* and by another *r''* to *b*. These new relations are but two more entities which themselves require to be hitched in turn by four still newer relations—so behold the vertiginous *regressus ad infinitum* in full career.

Since a *regressus ad infinitum* is deemed absurd, the notion that relations come 'between' their terms must be given up. No mere external go-between can logically connect. What occurs must be more intimate. The hooking must be a penetration, a possession. The relation must *involve* the terms, each term must involve *it,* and merging thus their being in it, they must somehow merge their being in each other, tho, as they seem still phenomenally so separate, we can never conceive exactly how it is that they are inwardly one. The absolute, however, must be supposed able to perform the unifying feat in his own inscrutable fashion.

In old times, whenever a philosopher was assailed for some particularly tough absurdity in his system, he was wont to parry the attack by the argument from the divine omnipotence. 'Do you mean to limit God's power?' he would reply: 'do you mean to say that God could not, if he would, do this or that?' This retort was supposed to close the mouths of all objectors of properly decorous mind. The functions of the bradleian absolute are in this particular identical with those of the theistic God. Suppositions treated as too absurd to pass muster in the finite world which we inhabit, the absolute must be able to make good 'somehow' in his ineffable way. First we hear Mr. Bradley convicting things of absurdity; next, calling on the absolute to vouch for them *quand même*. Invoked for no other duty, that duty it must and shall perform.

The strangest discontinuity of our world of appearance with the supposed world of absolute reality is asserted both by Bradley and by

Royce; and both writers, the latter with great ingenuity, seek to soften the violence of the jolt. But it remains violent all the same, and is felt to be so by most readers. Whoever feels the violence strongly sees as on a diagram in just what the peculiarity of all this philosophy of the absolute consists. First, there is a healthy faith that the world must be rational and self-consistent. 'All science, all real knowledge, all experience presuppose,' as Mr. Ritchie writes, 'a coherent universe.' Next, we find a loyal clinging to the rationalist belief that sense-data and their associations are incoherent, and that only in substituting a conceptual order for their order can truth be found. Third, the substituted conceptions are treated intellectualistically, that is as mutually exclusive and discontinuous, so that the first innocent continuity of the flow of sense-experience is shattered for us without any higher conceptual continuity taking its place. Finally, since this broken state of things is intolerable, the absolute *deus ex machina* is called on to mend it in his own way, since we cannot mend it in ours.

Any other picture than this of post-kantian absolutism I am unable to frame. I see the intellectualistic criticism destroying the immediately given coherence of the phenomenal world, but unable to make its own conceptual substitutes cohere, and I see the resort to the absolute for a coherence of a higher type. The situation has dramatic liveliness, but it is inwardly incoherent throughout, and the question inevitably comes up whether a mistake may not somewhere have crept in in the process that has brought it about. May not the remedy lie rather in revising the intellectualist criticism than in first adopting it and then trying to undo its consequences by an arbitrary act of faith in an unintelligible agent. May not the flux of sensible experience itself contain a rationality that has been overlooked, so that the real remedy would consist in harking back to it more intelligently, and not in advancing in the opposite direction away from it and even away beyond the intellectualist criticism that disintegrates it, to the pseudo-rationality of the supposed absolute point of view. I myself believe that this is the real way to keep rationality in the world, and that the traditional rationalism has always been facing in the wrong direction. I hope in the end to make you share, or at any rate respect, this belief, but there is much to talk of before we get to that point.

I employed the word 'violent' just now in describing the dramatic situation in which it pleases the philosophy of the absolute to make its camp. I don't see how any one can help being struck in absolutist writings by that curious tendency to fly to violent extremes of which I have already said a word. The universe must be rational; well and good; but *how* rational? in which sense of that eulogistic but ambiguous word?—this would seem to be the next point to bring up. There are surely degrees in rationality that might be discriminated and described. Things can be consistent or coherent in very diverse ways. But no more in its conception of rationality than in its conception of relations can the monistic mind suffer the notion of more or less. Rationality is one and indivisible: if not rational thus indivisibly, the universe must be completely irrational, and no shadings or mixtures or compromises can obtain. Mr. McTaggart writes, in discussing the notion of a mixture: 'The two principles, of rationality and irrationality, to which the universe is then referred, will have to be absolutely separate and independent. For if there were any common unity to which they should be referred, it would be that unity and not its two manifestations which would be the ultimate explanation . . . and the theory, having thus become monistic,' [22] would resolve itself into the same alternative once more: is the single principle rational through and through or not?

'Can a plurality of reals be possible?' asks Mr. Bradley, and answers, 'No, impossible.' For it would mean a number of beings not dependent on each other, and this independence their plurality would contradict. For to be 'many' is to be related, the word having no meaning unless the units are somehow taken together, and it is impossible to take them in a sort of unreal void, so they must belong to a larger reality, and so carry the essence of the units beyond their proper selves, into a whole which possesses unity and is a larger system.[23] Either absolute independence or absolute mutual dependence—this, then, is the only alternative allowed by these thinkers. Of course 'independence,' if absolute, would be preposterous, so the only conclusion allowable is that, in Ritchie's words, 'every single event is ultimately related to every other, and determined by the whole to which it belongs.' The whole complete block-universe through-and-through, therefore, or no universe at all!

Professor Taylor is so *naïf* in this habit of thinking only in extremes that he charges the pluralists with cutting the ground from under their own feet in not consistently following it themselves. What pluralists say is that a universe really connected loosely, after the pattern of our daily experience, is possible, and that for certain reasons it is the hypothesis to be preferred. What Professor Taylor thinks they naturally must or should say is that any other sort of universe is logically impossible, and that a totality of things interrelated like the world of the monists is not an hypothesis that can be seriously thought out at all.[24] Meanwhile no sensible pluralist ever flies or wants to fly to this dogmatic extreme.

If chance is spoken of as an ingredient of the universe, absolutists

---

[22] *Studies in the Hegelian Dialectic,* p. 184.
[23] *Appearance and Reality,* 1893, pp. 141–142.
[24] Cf. *Elements of Metaphysics,* p. 88.

interpret it to mean that double sevens are as likely to be thrown out of a dice box as double sixes are. If free-will is spoken of, that must mean that an english general is as likely to eat his prisoners to-day as a Maori chief was a hundred years ago. It is as likely—I am using Mr. McTaggart's examples—that a majority of Londoners will burn themselves alive to-morrow as that they will partake of food, as likely that I shall be hanged for brushing my hair as for committing a murder,[25] and so forth, through various suppositions that no indeterminist ever sees real reason to make.

This habit of thinking only in the most violent extremes reminds me of what Mr. Wells says of the current objections to socialism, in his wonderful little book, 'New worlds for old.' The commonest vice of the human mind is its disposition to see everything as yes or no, as black or white, its incapacity for discrimination of intermediate shades. So the critics agree to some hard and fast impossible definition of socialism, and extract absurdities from it as a conjurer gets rabbits from a hat. Socialism abolishes property, abolishes the family, and the rest. The method, Mr. Wells continues, is always the same: It is to assume that whatever the socialist postulates as desirable is wanted without limit of qualification,—for socialist read pluralist and the parallel holds good,—it is to imagine that whatever proposal is made by him is to be carried out by uncontrolled monomaniacs, and so to make a picture of the socialist dream which can be presented to the simple-minded person in doubt—'This is socialism'—or pluralism, as the case may be. 'Surely!—SURELY! you don't want *this!*'

How often have I been replied to, when expressing doubts of the logical necessity of the absolute, of flying to the opposite extreme: 'But surely, SURELY there must be *some* connexion among things!' As if I must necessarily be an uncontrolled monomaniac insanely denying any connexion whatever. The whole question revolves in very truth about the word 'some.' Radical empiricism and pluralism stand out for the legitimacy of the notion of *some:* each part of the world is in some ways connected, in some other ways not connected with its other parts, and the ways can be discriminated, for many of them are obvious, and their differences are obvious to view. Absolutism, on its side, seems to hold that 'some' is a category ruinously infected with self-contradictoriness, and that the only categories inwardly consistent and therefore pertinent to reality are 'all' and 'none.'

The question runs into the still more general one with which Mr. Bradley and later writers of the monistic school have made us abundantly familiar—the question, namely, whether all the relations with other things, possible to a being, are pre-included in its intrinsic nature and enter into its essence, or whether, in respect to some of these

[25] *Some Dogmas of Religion,* p. 184.

relations, it can *be* without reference to them, and, if it ever does enter into them, do so adventitiously and as it were by an after-thought. This is the great question as to whether 'external' relations can exist. They seem to, undoubtedly. My manuscript, for example, is 'on' the desk. The relation of being 'on' does n't seem to implicate or involve in any way the inner meaning of the manuscript or the inner structure of the desk—these objects engage in it only by their outsides, it seems only temporary accident in their respective histories. Moreover, the 'on' fails to appear to our senses as one of those unintelligible 'betweens' that have to be separately hooked on the terms they pretend to connect. All this innocent sense-appearance, however, we are told, cannot pass muster in the eyes of reason. It is a tissue of self-contradiction which only the complete absorption of the desk and the manuscript into the higher unity of a more absolute reality can overcome.

The reasoning by which this conclusion is supported is too subtle and complicated to be properly dealt with in a public lecture, and you will thank me for not inviting you to consider it at all.[26] I feel the more free to pass it by now as I think that the cursory account of the absolutistic attitude which I have already given is sufficient for our present purpose, and that my own verdict on the philosophy of the absolute as 'not proven'—please observe that I go no farther now—need not be backed by argument at every special point. Flanking operations are less costly and in some ways more effective than frontal attacks. Possibly you will yourselves think after hearing my remaining lectures that the alternative of an universe absolutely rational or absolutely irrational is forced and strained, and that a *via media* exists which some of you may agree with me is to be preferred. *Some* rationality certainly does characterize our universe; and, weighing one kind with another, we may deem that the incomplete kinds that appear are on the whole as acceptable as the through-and-through sort of rationality on which the monistic systematizers insist.

All the said systematizers who have written since Hegel have owed their inspiration largely to him. Even when they have found no use for his particular triadic dialectic, they have drawn confidence and courage from his authoritative and conquering tone. I have said nothing about Hegel in this lecture, so I must repair the omission in the next.

[26] For a more detailed criticism of Mr. Bradley's intellectualism, see above, pp. 214–226.

HEGEL AND HIS METHOD*

Directly or indirectly, that strange and powerful genius Hegel has done more to strengthen idealistic pantheism in thoughtful circles than all other influences put together. I must talk a little about him before drawing my final conclusions about the cogency of the arguments for the absolute. In no philosopny is the fact that a philosopher's vision and the technique he uses in proof of it are two different things more palpably evident than in Hegel. The vision in his case was that of a world in which reason holds all things in solution and accounts for all the irrationality that superficially appears by taking it up as a 'moment' into itself. This vision was so intense in Hegel, and the tone of authority with which he spoke from out of the midst of it was so weighty, that the impression he made has never been effaced. Once dilated to the scale of the master's eye, the disciples' sight could not contract to any lesser prospect. The technique which Hegel used to prove his vision was the so-called dialectic method, but here his fortune has been quite contrary. Hardly a recent disciple has felt his particular applications of the method to be satisfactory. Many have let them drop entirely, treating them rather as a sort of provisional stopgap, symbolic of what might some day prove possible of execution, but having no literal cogency or value now. Yet these very same disciples hold to the vision itself as a revelation that can never pass away. The case is curious and worthy of our study.

It is still more curious in that these same disciples, altho they are usually willing to abandon any particular instance of the dialectic method to its critics, are unshakably sure that in some shape the dialectic method is the key to truth. What, then, is the dialectic method? It is itself a part of the hegelian vision or intuition, and a part that finds the strongest echo in empiricism and common sense. Great injustice is done to Hegel by treating him as primarily a reasoner. He is in reality a naïvely observant man, only beset with a perverse preference for the use of technical and logical jargon. He plants himself in the empirical flux of things and gets the impression of what happens. His mind is in very truth *impressionistic;* and his thought, when once you put yourself at the animating centre of it, is the easiest thing in the world to catch the pulse of and to follow.

Any author is easy if you can catch the centre of his vision. From the centre in Hegel come those towering sentences of his that are comparable only to Luther's, as where, speaking of the ontological proof

* From: P.U., 85–129.

of God's existence from the concept of him as the *ens perfectissimum* to which no attribute can be lacking, he says: 'It would be strange if the Notion, the very heart of the mind, or, in a word, the concrete totality we call God, were not rich enough to embrace so poor a category as Being, the very poorest and most abstract of all—for nothing can be more insignificant than Being.' But if Hegel's central thought is easy to catch, his abominable habits of speech make his application of it to details exceedingly difficult to follow. His passion for the slipshod in the way of sentences, his unprincipled playing fast and loose with terms; his dreadful vocabulary, calling what completes a thing its 'negation,' for example; his systematic refusal to let you know whether he is talking logic or physics or psychology, his whole deliberately adopted policy of ambiguity and vagueness, in short: all these things make his present-day readers wish to tear their hair—or his—out in desperation. Like Byron's corsair, he has left a name 'to other times, linked with one virtue and a thousand crimes.'

The virtue was the vision, which was really in two parts. The first part was that reason is all-inclusive, the second was that things are 'dialectic.' Let me say a word about this second part of Hegel's vision.

The impression that any *naïf* person gets who plants himself innocently in the flux of things is that things are off their balance. Whatever equilibriums our finite experiences attain to are but provisional. Martinique volcanoes shatter our wordsworthian equilibrium with nature. Accidents, either moral, mental, or physical, break up the slowly built-up equilibriums men reach in family life and in their civic and professional relations. Intellectual enigmas frustrate our scientific systems, and the ultimate cruelty of the universe upsets our religious attitudes and outlooks. Of no special system of good attained does the universe recognize the value as sacred. Down it tumbles, over it goes, to feed the ravenous appetite for destruction, of the larger system of history in which it stood for a moment as a landing-place and stepping-stone. This dogging of everything by its negative, its fate, its undoing, this perpetual moving on to something future which shall supersede the present, this is the hegelian intuition of the essential provisionality, and consequent unreality, of everything empirical and finite. Take any concrete finite thing and try to hold it fast. You cannot, for so held, it proves not to be concrete at all, but an arbitrary extract or abstract which you have made from the remainder of empirical reality. The rest of things invades and overflows both it and you together, and defeats your rash attempt. Any partial view whatever of the world tears the part out of its relations, leaves out some truth concerning it, is untrue of it, falsifies it. The full truth about anything involves more than that thing. In the end nothing less than the whole of everything can be the truth of anything at all.

Taken so far, and taken in the rough, Hegel is not only harmless, but accurate. There is a dialectic movement in things, if such it please you to call it, one that the whole constitution of concrete life establishes; but it is one that can be described and accounted for in terms of the pluralistic vision of things far more naturally than in the monistic terms to which Hegel finally reduced it. Pluralistic empiricism knows that everything is in an environment, a surrounding world of other things, and that if you leave it to work there it will inevitably meet with friction and opposition from its neighbors. Its rivals and enemies will destroy it unless it can buy them off by compromising some part of its original pretensions.

But Hegel saw this undeniable characteristic of the world we live in in a non-empirical light. Let the *mental idea* of the thing work in your thought all alone, he fancied, and just the same consequences will follow. It will be negated by the opposite ideas that dog it, and can survive only by entering, along with them, into some kind of treaty. This treaty will be an instance of the so-called 'higher synthesis' of everything with its negative; and Hegel's originality lay in transporting the process from the sphere of percepts to that of concepts and treating it as the universal method by which every kind of life, logical, physical, or psychological, is mediated. Not to the sensible facts as such, then, did Hegel point for the secret of what keeps existence going, but rather to the conceptual way of treating them. Concepts were not in his eyes the static self-contained things that previous logicians had supposed, but were germinative, and passed beyond themselves into each other by what he called their immanent dialectic. In ignoring each other as they do, they virtually exclude and deny each other, he thought, and thus in a manner introduce each other. So the dialectic logic, according to him, had to supersede the 'logic of identity' in which, since Aristotle, all Europe had been brought up.

This view of concepts is Hegel's revolutionary performance; but so studiously vague and ambiguous are all his expressions of it that one can hardly tell whether it is the concepts as such, or the sensible experiences and elements conceived, that Hegel really means to work with. The only thing that is certain is that whatever you may say of his procedure, someone will accuse you of misunderstanding it. I make no claim to understanding it, I treat it merely impressionistically.

So treating it, I regret that he should have called it by the name of logic. Clinging as he did to the vision of a really living world, and refusing to be content with a chopped-up intellectualist picture of it, it is a pity that he should have adopted the very word that intellectualism had already pre-empted. But he clung fast to the old rationalist contempt for the immediately given world of sense and all its squalid particulars, and never tolerated the notion that the form of philosophy might be empirical only. His own system had to be a product of eternal reason, so the word 'logic,' with its suggestions of coercive necessity, was the only word he could find natural. He pretended therefore to be using the *a priori* method, and to be working by a scanty equipment of ancient logical terms—position, negation, reflection, universal, particular, individual, and the like. But what he really worked by was his own empirical perceptions, which exceeded and overflowed his miserably insufficient logical categories in every instance of their use.

What he did with the category of negation was his most original stroke. The orthodox opinion is that you can advance logically through the field of concepts only by going from the same to the same. Hegel felt deeply the sterility of this law of conceptual thought; he saw that in a fashion negation also relates things; and he had the brilliant idea of transcending the ordinary logic by treating advance from the different to the different as if it were also a necessity of thought. 'The so-called maxim of identity,' he wrote, 'is supposed to be accepted by the consciousness of every one. But the language which such a law demands, "a planet is a planet, magnetism is magnetism, mind is mind," deserves to be called silliness. No mind either speaks or thinks or forms conceptions in accordance with this law, and no existence of any kind whatever conforms to it. We must never view identity as abstract identity, to the exclusion of all difference. That is the touchstone for distinguishing all bad philosophy from what alone deserves the name of philosophy. If thinking were no more than registering abstract identities, it would be a most superfluous performance. Things and concepts are identical with themselves only in so far as at the same time they involve distinction.' [27]

The distinction that Hegel has in mind here is naturally in the first instance distinction from all other things or concepts. But in his hands this quickly develops into contradiction of them, and finally, reflected back upon itself, into self-contradiction; and the immanent self-contradictoriness of all finite concepts thenceforth becomes the propulsive logical force that moves the world.[28] 'Isolate a thing from all its relations,' says Dr. Edward Caird,[29] expounding Hegel, 'and try to assert it by itself; you find that it has negated itself as well as its relations. The thing in itself is nothing.' Or, to quote Hegel's own words: 'When we suppose an existent A, and another, B, B is at first defined as the other. But A is just as much the other of B. Both are others in the same fashion. . . . "Other" is the other by itself, there-

[27] Hegel, *Smaller Logic*, pp. 184–185.
[28] Cf. Hegel's fine vindication of this function of contradiction in his *Wissenschaft der Logik*, Bk. ii, sec. 1, chap. ii, C, Anmerkung 3.
[29] *Hegel*, in *Blackwood's Philosophical Classics*, p. 162.

fore the other of every other, consequently the other of itself, the simply unlike itself, the self-negator, the self-alterer,' etc.[30] Hegel writes
elsewhere: 'The finite, as implicitly other than what it is, is forced to
surrender its own immediate or natural being, and to turn suddenly
into its opposite. . . . Dialectic is the universal and irresistible power
before which nothing can stay. . . . *Summum jus, summa injuria*—to
drive an abstract right to excess is to commit injustice. . . . Extreme
anarchy and extreme despotism lead to one another. Pride comes before a fall. Too much wit outwits itself. Joy brings tears, melancholy a
sardonic smile.' [31] To which one well might add that most human institutions, by the purely technical and professorial manner in which
they come to be administered, end by becoming obstacles to the very
purposes which their founders had in view.

Once catch well the knack of this scheme of thought and you are
lucky if you ever get away from it. It is all you can see. Let any one
pronounce anything, and your feeling of a contradiction being implied
becomes a habit, almost a motor habit in some persons who symbolize
by a stereotyped gesture the position, sublation, and final reinstatement involved. If you say 'two' or 'many,' your speech bewrayeth you,
for the very name collects them into one. If you express doubt, your
expression contradicts its content, for the doubt itself is not doubted
but affirmed. If you say 'disorder,' what is that but a certain bad kind
of order? if you say 'indetermination,' you are determining just *that*. If
you say 'nothing but the unexpected happens,' the unexpected becomes what you expect. If you say 'all things are relative,' to what is
the all of them itself relative? If you say 'no more,' you have said
more already, by implying a region in which no more is found; to
know a limit as such is consequently already to have got beyond it;
and so forth, throughout as many examples as one cares to cite.

Whatever you posit appears thus as one-sided, and negates its
other, which, being equally one-sided, negates *it;* and, since this situation remains unstable, the two contradictory terms have together, according to Hegel, to engender a higher truth of which they both appear
as indispensable members, mutually mediating aspects of that higher
concept or situation in thought.

Every higher total, however provisional and relative, thus reconciles the contradictions which its parts, abstracted from it, prove implicitly to contain. Rationalism, you remember, is what I called the
way of thinking that methodically subordinates parts to wholes, so
Hegel here is rationalistic through and through. The only whole by
which *all* contradictions are reconciled is for him the absolute whole
of wholes, the all-inclusive reason to which Hegel himself gave the

---

[30] *Wissenschaft der Logik,* Bk. i, sec. 1, chap. ii, B, a.
[31] Wallace's translation of the *Smaller Logic,* p. 128.

name of the absolute Idea, but which I shall continue to call 'the absolute' purely and simply, as I have done hitherto.

Empirical instances of the way in which higher unities reconcile contradictions are innumerable, so here again Hegel's vision, taken merely impressionistically, agrees with countless facts. Somehow life does, out of its total resources, find ways of satisfying opposites at once. This is precisely the paradoxical aspect which much of our civilization presents. Peace we secure by armaments, liberty by laws and constitutions; simplicity and naturalness are the consummate result of artificial breeding and training; health, strength, and wealth are increased only by lavish use, expense, and wear. Our mistrust of mistrust engenders our commercial system of credit; our tolerance of anarchistic and revolutionary utterances is the only way of lessening their danger; our charity has to say no to beggars in order not to defeat its own desires; the true epicurean has to observe great sobriety; the way to certainty lies through radical doubt; virtue signifies not innocence but the knowledge of sin and its overcoming; by obeying nature, we command her, etc. The ethical and the religious life are full of such contradictions held in solution. You hate your enemy?—well, forgive him, and thereby heap coals of fire on his head; to realize yourself, renounce yourself; to save your soul, first lose it; in short, die to live.

From such massive examples one easily generalizes Hegel's vision. Roughly, his 'dialectic' picture is a fair account of a good deal of the world. It sounds paradoxical, but whenever you once place yourself at the point of view of any higher synthesis, you see exactly how it does in a fashion take up opposites into itself. As an example, consider the conflict between our carnivorous appetites and hunting instincts and the sympathy with animals which our refinement is bringing in its train. We have found how to reconcile these opposites most effectively by establishing game-laws and close seasons and by keeping domestic herds. The creatures preserved thus are preserved for the sake of slaughter, truly, but if not preserved for that reason, not one of them would be alive at all. Their will to live and our will to kill them thus harmoniously combine in this peculiar higher synthesis of domestication.

Merely as a reporter of certain empirical aspects of the actual, Hegel, then, is great and true. But he aimed at being something far greater than an empirical reporter, so I must say something about that essential aspect of his thought. Hegel was dominated by the notion of a truth that should prove incontrovertible, binding on every one, and certain, which should be *the* truth, one, indivisible, eternal, objective, and necessary, to which all our particular thinking must lead as to its consummation. This is the dogmatic ideal, the postulate, uncriticised, undoubted, and unchallenged, of all rationalizers in philosophy. '*I have never doubted,'* a recent Oxford writer says, that truth is universal and single and timeless, a single content or significance, one and whole and complete.[32] Advance in thinking, in the hegelian universe, has, in short, to proceed by the apodictic words *must be* rather than by those inferior hypothetic words *may be,* which are all that empiricists can use.

Now Hegel found that his idea of an immanent movement through the field of concepts by way of 'dialectic' negation played most beautifully into the hands of this rationalistic demand for something absolute and *inconcussum* in the way of truth. It is easy to see how. If you affirm anything, for example that A is, and simply leave the matter thus, you leave it at the mercy of any one who may supervene and say 'not A, but B is.' If he does say so, your statement does n't refute him, it simply contradicts him, just as his contradicts you. The only way of making your affirmation about A *self-securing* is by getting it into a form which will by implication negate all possible negations in advance. The mere absence of negation is not enough; it must be present, but present with its fangs drawn. What you posit as A must already have cancelled the alternative or made it innocuous, by having negated it in advance. Double negation is the only form of affirmation that fully plays into the hands of the dogmatic ideal. Simply and innocently affirmative statements are good enough for empiricists, but unfit for rationalist use, lying open as they do to every accidental contradictor, and exposed to every puff of doubt. The *final* truth must be something to which there is no imaginable alternative, because it contains all its possible alternatives inside of itself as moments already taken account of and overcome. Whatever involves its own alternatives as elements of itself is, in a phrase often repeated, its 'own other,' made so by the *methode der absoluten negativität.*

Formally, this scheme of an organism of truth that has already fed as it were on its own liability to death, so that, death once dead for it, there's no more dying then, is the very fulfilment of the rationalistic aspiration. That one and only whole, with all its parts involved in it, negating and making one another impossible if abstracted and taken singly, but necessitating and holding one another in place if the whole of them be taken integrally, is the literal ideal sought after; it is the very diagram and picture of that notion of *the* truth with no outlying alternative, to which nothing can be added, nor from it anything withdrawn, and all variations from which are absurd, which so dominates the human imagination. Once we have taken in the features of this

[32] Joachim, *The Nature of Truth,* Oxford, 1906, pp. 22, 178. The argument in case the belief should be doubted would be the higher synthetic idea: if two truths were possible, the duality of that possibility would itself be the one truth that would unite them.

diagram that so successfully solves the world-old problem, the older ways of proving the necessity of judgments cease to give us satisfaction. Hegel's way we think must be the right way. The true must be essentially the self-reflecting self-contained recurrent, that which secures itself by including its own other and negating it; that makes a spherical system with no loose ends hanging out for foreignness to get a hold upon; that is forever rounded in and closed, not strung along rectilinearly and open at its ends like that universe of simply collective or additive form which Hegel calls the world of the bad infinite, and which is all that empiricism, starting with simply posited single parts and elements, is ever able to attain to.

No one can possibly deny the sublimity of this hegelian conception. It is surely in the grand style, if there be such a thing as a grand style in philosophy. For us, however, it remains, so far, a merely formal and diagrammatic conception; for with the actual content of absolute truth, as Hegel materially tries to set it forth, few disciples have been satisfied, and I do not propose to refer at all to the concreter parts of his philosophy. The main thing now is to grasp the generalized vision, and feel the authority of the abstract scheme of a statement self-secured by involving double negation. Absolutists who make no use of Hegel's own technique are really working by his method. You remember the proofs of the absolute which I instanced in my last lecture, Lotze's and Royce's proofs by *reductio ad absurdum,* to the effect that any smallest connexion rashly supposed in things will logically work out into absolute union, and any minimal disconnexion into absolute disunion,—these are really arguments framed on the hegelian pattern. The truth is that which you implicitly affirm in the very attempt to deny it; it is that from which every variation refutes itself by proving self-contradictory. This is the supreme insight of rationalism, and to-day the best *must-be's* of rationalist argumentation are but so many attempts to communicate it to the hearer.

Thus, you see, my last lecture and this lecture make connexion again and we can consider Hegel and the other absolutists to be supporting the same system. The next point I wish to dwell on is the part played by what I have called vicious intellectualism in this wonderful system's structure.

Rationalism in general thinks it gets the fulness of truth by turning away from sensation to conception, conception obviously giving the more universal and immutable picture. Intellectualism in the vicious sense I have already defined as the habit of assuming that a concept *ex*cludes from any reality conceived by its means everything not included in the concept's definition. I called such intellectualism illegitimate as I found it used in Lotze's, Royce's, and Bradley's proofs of the absolute (which absolute I consequently held to be non-proven by their arguments), and I left off by asserting my own belief that a pluralistic and incompletely integrated universe, describable only by the free use of the word 'some,' is a legitimate hypothesis.

Now Hegel himself, in building up his method of double negation, offers the vividest possible example of this vice of intellectualism. Every idea of a finite thing is of course a concept of *that* thing and not a concept of anything else. But Hegel treats this not being a concept of anything else as if it were *equivalent to the concept of anything else not being,* or in other words as if it were a denial or negation of everything else. Then, as the other things, thus implicitly contradicted by the thing first conceived, also by the same law contradict *it,* the pulse of dialectic commences to beat and the famous triads begin to grind out the cosmos. If any one finds the process here to be a luminous one, he must be left to the illumination, he must remain an undisturbed hegelian. What others feel as the intolerable ambiguity, verbosity, and unscrupulousness of the master's way of deducing things, he will probably ascribe—since divine oracles are notoriously hard to interpret—to the 'difficulty' that habitually accompanies profundity. For my own part, there seems something grotesque and *saugrenu* in the pretension of a style so disobedient to the first rules of sound communication between minds, to be the authentic mother-tongue of reason, and to keep step more accurately than any other style does with the absolute's own ways of thinking. I do not therefore take Hegel's technical apparatus seriously at all. I regard him rather as one of those numerous original seers who can never learn how to articulate. His would-be coercive logic counts for nothing in my eyes; but that does not in the least impugn the philosophic importance of his conception of the absolute, if we take it merely hypothetically as one of the great types of cosmic vision.

Taken thus hypothetically, I wish to discuss it briefly. But before doing so I must call your attention to an odd peculiarity in the hegelian procedure. The peculiarity is one [on which I offer a final judgment, in my lecture on "The Continuity of Experience," above, pp. 292–301], so at present I only note it in passing. Hegel, you remember, considers that the immediate finite data of experience are 'untrue' because they are not their own others. They are negated by what is external to them. The absolute is true because it and it only has no external environment, and has attained to being its own other. (These words sound queer enough, but those of you who know something of Hegel's text will follow them.) Granting his premise that to be true a thing must in some sort be its own other, everything hinges on whether he is right in holding that the several pieces of finite experience themselves cannot be said to be in any wise *their* own others. When conceptually or intellectualistically treated, they of course cannot be their own others. Every abstract concept as such excludes what it does n't include, and if such concepts are adequate substitutes for reality's concrete pulses, the latter must square themselves with intellectualistic logic, and no one of them in any sense can claim to be its own other. If, however, the conceptual treatment of the flow of reality should prove for any good reason to be inadequate and to have a practical rather than a theoretical or speculative value, then an independent empirical look into the constitution of reality's pulses might possibly show that some of them *are* their own others, and indeed are so in the self-same sense in which the absolute is maintained to be so by Hegel. When we come to my [later] lecture, on Professor Bergson, I shall in effect defend this very view, strengthening my thesis by his authority. I am unwilling to say anything more about the point at this time, and what I have just said of it is only a sort of surveyor's note of where our present position lies in the general framework of these lectures.

Let us turn now at last to the great question of fact, *Does the absolute exist or not?* to which all our previous discussion has been preliminary. I may sum up that discussion by saying that whether there really be an absolute or not, no one makes himself absurd or self-contradictory by doubting or denying it. The charges of self-contradiction, where they do not rest on purely verbal reasoning, rest on a vicious intellectualism. I will not recapitulate my criticisms. I will simply ask you to change the *venue,* and to discuss the absolute now as if it were only an open hypothesis. As such, is it more probable or more improbable?

But first of all I must parenthetically ask you to distinguish the notion of the absolute carefully from that of another object with which it is liable to become heedlessly entangled. That other object is the 'God' of common people in their religion, and the creator-God of orthodox christian theology. Only thoroughgoing monists or pantheists believe in the absolute. The God of our popular Christianity is but one member of a pluralistic system. He and we stand outside of each other, just as the devil, the saints, and the angels stand outside of both of us. I can hardly conceive of anything more different from the absolute than the God, say, of David or of Isaiah. *That* God is an essentially finite being *in* the cosmos, not with the cosmos in him, and indeed he has a very local habitation there, and very one-sided local and personal attachments. If it should prove probable that the absolute does not exist, it will not follow in the slightest degree that a God like that of David, Isaiah, or Jesus may not exist, or may not be the most important existence in the universe for us to acknowledge. I pray you, then, not to confound the two ideas as you listen to the criticisms I shall have to proffer. I hold to the finite God, for reasons which I shall touch on in [my lecture on "The Continuity of Experience"]; but I hold that his rival and competitor—I feel almost tempted to say his enemy—the absolute, is not only not forced on us by logic, but that it is an improbable hypothesis.

The great claim made for the absolute is that by supposing it we make the world appear more rational. Any hypothesis that does that will always be accepted as more probably true than an hypothesis that makes the world appear irrational. Men are once for all so made that they prefer a rational world to believe in and to live in. But rationality has at least four dimensions, intellectual, æsthetical, moral, and practical; and to find a world rational to the maximal degree *in all these respects simultaneously* is no easy matter. Intellectually, the world of mechanical materialism is the most rational, for we subject its events to mathematical calculation. But the mechanical world is ugly, as arithmetic is ugly, and it is non-moral. Morally, the theistic world is rational enough, but full of intellectual frustrations. The practical world of affairs, in its turn, so supremely rational to the politician, the military man, or the man of conquering business-faculty that he never would vote to change the type of it, is irrational to moral and artistic temperaments; so that whatever demand for rationality we find satisfied by a philosophic hypothesis, we are liable to find some other demand for rationality unsatisfied by the same hypothesis. The rationality we gain in one coin we thus pay for in another; and the problem accordingly seems at first sight to resolve itself into that of getting a conception which will yield the largest *balance* of rationality rather than one which will yield perfect rationality of every description. In general, it may be said that if a man's conception of the world lets loose any action in him that is easy, or any faculty which he is fond of exercising, he will deem it rational in so far forth, be the faculty that of computing, fighting, lecturing, classifying, framing schematic tabulations, getting the better end of a bargain, patiently waiting and enduring, preaching, joke-making, or what you like. Albeit the absolute is defined as being necessarily an embodiment of objectively perfect rationality, it is fair to its english advocates to say that those who have espoused the hypothesis most concretely and seriously have usually avowed the irrationality to their own minds of certain elements in it.

Probably the weightiest contribution to our feeling of the rationality of the universe which the notion of the absolute brings is the assurance that however disturbed the surface may be, at bottom all is well with the cosmos—central peace abiding at the heart of endless agitation. This conception is rational in many ways, beautiful æsthetically, beautiful intellectually (could we only follow it into detail), and beautiful morally, if the enjoyment of security can be accounted moral.

Practically it is less beautiful; for, as we saw in our last lecture, in representing the deepest reality of the world as static and without a history, it loosens the world's hold upon our sympathies and leaves the soul of it foreign. Nevertheless it does give *peace,* and that kind of rationality is so paramountly demanded by men that to the end of time there will be absolutists, men who choose belief in a static eternal, rather than admit that the finite world of change and striving, even with a God as one of the strivers, is itself eternal. For such minds Professor Royce's words will always be the truest: 'The very presence of ill in the temporal order is the condition of the perfection of the eternal order. . . . We long for the absolute only in so far as in us the absolute also longs, and seeks through our very temporal striving, the peace that is nowhere in time, but only, and yet absolutely, in eternity. Were there no longing in time there would be no peace in eternity. . . . God [*i.e.* the absolute] who here in me aims at what I now temporally miss, not only possesses in the eternal world the goal after which I strive, but comes to possess it even through and because of my sorrow. Through this my tribulation the absolute triumph then is won. . . . In the absolute I am fulfilled. Yet my very fulfilment demands and therefore can transcend this sorrow.' [33] Royce is particularly felicitous in his ability to cite parts of finite experience to which he finds his picture of this absolute experience analogous. But it is hard to portray the absolute at all without rising into what might be called the 'inspired' style of language—I use the word not ironically, but prosaically and descriptively, to designate the only literary form that goes with the kind of emotion that the absolute arouses. One can follow the pathway of reasoning soberly enough,[34] but the picture itself has to be effulgent. This admirable faculty of transcending, whilst inwardly preserving, every contrariety, is the absolute's characteristic form of rationality. We are but syllables in the mouth of the Lord; if the whole sentence is divine, each syllable is absolutely what it should be, in spite of all appearances. In making up the balance for or against absolutism, this emotional value weights heavily the credit side of the account.

The trouble is that we are able to see so little into the positive detail of it, and that if once admitted not to be coercively proven by the intellectualist arguments, it remains only a hypothetic possibility.

On the debit side of the account the absolute, taken seriously, and not as a mere name for our right occasionally to drop the strenuous mood and take a moral holiday, introduces all those tremendous irra-

[33] *The World and the Individual,* vol. ii, pp. 385, 386, 409.

[34] The best *un*inspired argument (again not ironical!) which I know is that in Miss M. W. Calkins's excellent book, *The Persistent Problems of Philosophy,* Macmillan, 1902.

tionalities into the universe which a frankly pluralistic theism escapes, but which have been flung as a reproach at every form of monistic theism or pantheism. It introduces a speculative 'problem of evil' namely, and leaves us wondering why the perfection of the absolute should require just such particular hideous forms of life ás darken the day for our human imaginations. If they were forced on it by something alien, and to 'overcome' them the absolute had still to keep hold of them, we could understand its feeling of triumph, though we, so far as we were ourselves among the elements overcome, could acquiesce but sullenly in the resultant situation, and would never just have chosen it as the most rational one conceivable. But the absolute is represented as a being without environment, upon which nothing alien can be forced, and which has spontaneously chosen from within to give itself the spectacle of all that evil rather than a spectacle with less evil in it.[35] Its perfection is represented as the source of things, and yet the first effect of that perfection is the tremendous imperfection of all finite experience. In whatever sense the word 'rationality' may be taken, it is vain to contend that the impression made on our finite minds by such a way of representing things is altogether rational. Theologians have felt its irrationality acutely, and the 'fall,' the predestination, and the election which the situation involves have given them more trouble than anything else in their attempt to pantheize Christianity. The whole business remains a puzzle, both intellectually and morally.

Grant that the spectacle or world-romance offered to itself by the absolute is in the absolute's eyes perfect. Why would not the world be more perfect by having the affair remain in just those terms, and by not having any finite spectators to come in and add to what was perfect already their innumerable imperfect manners of seeing the same spectacle? Suppose the entire universe to consist of one superb copy of a book, fit for the ideal reader. Is that universe improved or deteriorated by having myriads of garbled and misprinted separate leaves and chapters also created, giving false impressions of the book to whoever looks at them? To say the least, the balance of rationality is not obviously in favor of such added mutilations. So this question becomes urgent: Why, the absolute's own total vision of things being so rational, was it necessary to comminute it into all these coexisting inferior fragmentary visions?

Leibnitz in his theodicy represents God as limited by an antecedent reason in things which makes certain combinations logically incompatible, certain goods impossible. He surveys in advance all the universes he might create, and by an act of what Leibnitz calls his

[35] Cf. Dr. Fuller's excellent article, 'Ethical monism and the problem of evil,' in the *Harvard Journal of Theology*, vol. i, No. 2, April, 1908.

antecedent will he chooses our actual world as the one in which the evil, unhappily necessary anyhow, is at its minimum. It is the best of all the worlds that are possible, therefore, but by no means the most abstractly desirable world. Having made this mental choice, God next proceeds to what Leibnitz calls his act of consequent or decretory will: he says *'Fiat'* and the world selected springs into objective being, with all the finite creatures in it to suffer from its imperfections without sharing in its creator's atoning vision.

Lotze has made some penetrating remarks on this conception of Leibnitz's, and they exactly fall in with what I say of the absolutist conception. The world projected out of the creative mind by the *fiat,* and existing in detachment from its author, is a sphere of being where the parts realize themselves only singly. If the divine value of them is evident only when they are collectively looked at, then, Lotze rightly says, the world surely becomes poorer and not richer for God's utterance of the *fiat.* He might much better have remained contented with his merely antecedent choice of the scheme, without following it up by a creative decree. The scheme *as such* was admirable; it could only lose by being translated into reality.[36] Why, I similarly ask, should the absolute ever have lapsed from the perfection of its own integral experience of things, and refracted itself into all our finite experiences?

It is but fair to recent english absolutists to say that many of them have confessed the imperfect rationality of the absolute from this point of view. Mr. McTaggart, for example, writes: 'Does not our very failure to perceive the perfection of the universe destroy it? . . . In so far as we do not see the perfection of the universe, we are not perfect ourselves. And as we are parts of the universe, that cannot be perfect.' [37]

And Mr. Joachim finds just the same difficulty. Calling the hypothesis of the absolute by the name of the 'coherence theory of truth,' he calls the problem of understanding how the complete coherence of all things in the absolute should involve as a necessary moment in its self-maintenance the self-assertion of the finite minds, a self-assertion which in its extreme form is error,—he calls this problem, I say, an insoluble puzzle. If truth be the universal *fons et origo,* how does error slip in? 'The coherence theory of truth,' he concludes 'may thus be said to suffer shipwreck at the very entrance of the harbor.' [38] Yet in spite of this rather bad form of irrationality, Mr. Joachim stoutly asserts his 'immediate certainty' [39] of the theory shipwrecked, the correctness of which he says he has 'never doubted.' This

---

[36] *Metaphysic,* sec. 79.
[37] *Studies in the Hegelian Dialectic,* secs. 150, 153.
[38] *The Nature of Truth,* 1906, pp. 170–171.
[39] *Ibid.,* p. 179.

candid confession of a fixed attitude of faith in the absolute, which even one's own criticisms and perplexities fail to disturb, seems to me very significant. Not only empiricists, but absolutists also, would all, if they were as candid as this author, confess that the prime thing in their philosophy is their vision of a truth possible, which they then employ their reasoning to convert, as best it can, into a certainty or probability.

I can imagine a believer in the absolute retorting at this point that *he* at any rate is not dealing with mere probabilities, but that the nature of things logically requires the multitudinous erroneous copies, and that therefore the universe cannot be the absolute's book alone. For, he will ask, is not the absolute defined as the total consciousness of everything that is? Must not its field of view consist of parts? And what can the parts of a total consciousness be unless they be fractional consciousnesses? Our finite minds *must* therefore coexist with the absolute mind. We are its constituents, and it cannot live without us.—But if any one of you feels tempted to retort in this wise, let me remind you that you are frankly employing pluralistic weapons, and thereby giving up the absolutist cause. The notion that the absolute is made of constituents on which its being depends is the rankest empiricism. The absolute as such has *objects,* not constituents, and if the objects develop selfhoods upon their own several accounts, those selfhoods must be set down as facts additional to the absolute consciousness, and not as elements implicated in its definition. The absolute is a rationalist conception. Rationalism goes from wholes to parts, and always assumes wholes to be self-sufficing.[40]

My conclusion, so far, then, is this, that altho the hypothesis of the absolute, in yielding a certain kind of religious peace, performs a most important rationalizing function, it nevertheless, from the intellectual point of view, remains decidedly irrational. The *ideally* perfect whole is certainly that whole of which the *parts also are perfect*—if we can depend on logic for anything, we can depend on it for that definition. The absolute is defined as the ideally perfect whole, yet most of its parts, if not all, are admittedly imperfect. Evidently the conception lacks internal consistency, and yields us a problem rather than a solution. It creates a speculative puzzle, the so-called mystery of evil and of error, from which a pluralistic metaphysic is entirely free.

In any pluralistic metaphysic, the problems that evil presents are

---

[40] The psychological analogy that certain finite tracts of consciousness are composed of isolable parts added together, cannot be used by absolutists as proof that such parts are essential elements of all consciousness. Other finite fields of consciousness seem in point of fact not to be similarly resolvable into isolable parts.

practical, not speculative. Not why evil should exist at all, but how we can lessen the actual amount of it, is the sole question we need there consider. 'God,' in the religious life of ordinary men, is the name not of the whole of things, heaven forbid, but only of the ideal tendency in things, believed in as a superhuman person who calls us to co-operate in his purposes, and who furthers ours if they are worthy. He works in an external environment, has limits, and has enemies. When John Mill said that the notion of God's omnipotence must be given up, if God is to be kept as a religious object, he was surely accurately right; yet so prevalent is the lazy monism that idly haunts the region of God's name, that so simple and truthful a saying was generally treated as a paradox: God, it was said, *could* not be finite. I believe that the only God worthy of the name *must* be finite, and I shall return to this point in a later lecture. If the absolute exist in addition—and the hypothesis must, in spite of its irrational features, still be left open—then the absolute is only the wider cosmic whole of which our God is but the most ideal portion, and which in the more usual human sense is hardly to be termed a religious hypothesis at all. 'Cosmic emotion' is the better name for the reaction it may awaken.

Observe that all the irrationalities and puzzles which the absolute gives rise to, and from which the finite God remains free, are due to the fact that the absolute has nothing, absolutely nothing, outside of itself. The finite God whom I contrast with it may conceivably have *almost* nothing outside of himself; he may already have triumphed over and absorbed all but the minutest fraction of the universe; but that fraction, however small, reduces him to the status of a relative being, and in principle the universe is saved from all the irrationalities incidental to absolutism. The only irrationality left would be the irrationality of which pluralism as such is accused, and of this I hope to say a word more later.

I have tired you with so many subtleties in this lecture that I will add only two other counts to my indictment.

First, then, let me remind you that *the absolute is useless for deductive purposes*. It gives us absolute safety if you will, but it is compatible with every relative danger. You cannot enter the phenomenal world with the notion of it in your grasp, and name beforehand any detail which you are likely to meet there. Whatever the details of experience may prove to be, *after the fact of them* the absolute will adopt them. It is an hypothesis that functions retrospectively only, not prospectively. *That,* whatever it may be, will have been in point of fact the sort of world which the absolute was pleased to offer to itself as a spectacle.

Again, the absolute is always represented idealistically, as the all-knower. Thinking this view consistently out leads one to frame an almost ridiculous conception of the absolute mind, owing to the enormous mass of unprofitable information which it would then seem obliged to carry. One of the many *reductiones ad absurdum* of pluralism by which idealism thinks it proves the absolute One is as follows: Let there be many facts; but since on idealist principles facts exist only by being known, the many facts will therefore mean many knowers. But that there are so many knowers is itself a fact, which in turn requires *its* knower, so the one absolute knower has eventually to be brought in. *All* facts lead to him. If it be a fact that this table is not a chair, not a rhinoceros, not a logarithm, not a mile away from the door, not worth five hundred pounds sterling, not a thousand centuries old, the absolute must even now be articulately aware of all these negations. Along with what everything is it must also be conscious of everything which it is not. This infinite atmosphere of explicit negativity—observe that it has to be explicit—around everything seems to us so useless an encumbrance as to make the absolute still more foreign to our sympathy. Furthermore, if it be a fact that certain ideas are silly, the absolute has to have already thought the silly ideas to establish them in silliness. The rubbish in its mind would thus appear easily to outweigh in amount the more desirable material. One would expect it fairly to burst with such an obesity, plethora, and superfœtation of useless information.[41]

I will spare you further objections. The sum of it all is that the absolute is not forced on our belief by logic, that it involves features of irrationality peculiar to itself, and that a thinker to whom it does not come as an 'immediate certainty' (to use Mr. Joachim's words), is in no way bound to treat it as anything but an emotionally rather sublime hypothesis. As such, it might, with all its defects, be, on account of its peace-conferring power and its formal grandeur, more rational than anything else in the field. But meanwhile the strung-along unfinished world in time is its rival: *reality MAY exist in distributive form, in the shape not of an all but of a set of eaches, just as it seems to*—this is the anti-absolutist hypothesis. *Prima facie* there is this in favor of the eaches, that they are at any rate real enough to have made themselves at least *appear* to every one, whereas the absolute has as yet appeared immediately to only a few mystics, and indeed to them very ambiguously. The advocates of the absolute assure

---

[41] Judging by the analogy of the relation which our central consciousness seems to bear to that of our spinal cord, lower ganglia, etc., it would seem natural to suppose that in whatever superhuman mental synthesis there may be, the neglect and elimination of certain contents of which we are conscious on the human level might be as characteristic a feature as is the combination and interweaving of other human contents.

us that any distributive form of being is infected and undermined by self-contradiction. If we are unable to assimilate their arguments, and we have been unable, the only course we can take, it seems to me, is to let the absolute bury the absolute, and to seek reality in more promising directions, even among the details of the finite and the immediately given.

If these words of mine sound in bad taste to some of you, or even sacrilegious, I am sorry. Perhaps the impression may be mitigated by what I have to say in later lectures.

CONCERNING FECHNER*

The prestige of the absolute has rather crumbled in our hands. The logical proofs of it miss fire; the portraits which its best court-painters show of it are featureless and foggy in the extreme; and, apart from the cold comfort of assuring us that with *it* all is well, and that to see that all is well with us also we need only rise to its eternal point of view, it yields us no relief whatever. It introduces, on the contrary, into philosophy and theology certain poisonous difficulties of which but for its intrusion we never should have heard.

But if we drop the absolute out of the world, must we then conclude that the world contains nothing better in the way of consciousness than our consciousness? Is our whole instinctive belief in higher presences, our persistent inner turning towards divine companionship, to count for nothing? Is it but the pathetic illusion of beings with incorrigibly social and imaginative minds?

Such a negative conclusion would, I believe, be desperately hasty, a sort of pouring out of the child with the bath. Logically it is possible to believe in superhuman beings without identifying them with the absolute at all. The treaty of offensive and defensive alliance which certain groups of the christian clergy have recently made with our transcendentalist philosophers seems to me to be based on a well-meaning but baleful mistake. Neither the Jehovah of the old testament nor the heavenly father of the new has anything in common with the absolute except that they are all three greater than man; and if you say that the notion of the absolute is what the gods of Abraham, of David, and of Jesus, after first developing into each other, were inevitably destined to develop into in more reflective and modern minds, I reply

* From: P.U., 133–177.

that although in certain specifically philosophical minds this may have been the case, in minds more properly to be termed religious the development has followed quite another path. The whole history of evangelical Christianity is there to prove it. I propose in these lectures to plead for that other line of development. To set the doctrine of the absolute in its proper framework, so that it shall not fill the whole welkin and exclude all alternative possibilities of higher thought—as it seems to do for many students who approach it with a limited previous acquaintance with philosophy—I will contrast it with a system which, abstractly considered, seems at first to have much in common with absolutism, but which, when taken concretely and temperamentally, really stands at the opposite pole. I refer to the philosophy of Gustav Theodor Fechner, a writer but little known as yet to English readers, but destined, I am persuaded, to wield more and more influence as time goes on.

It is the intense concreteness of Fechner, his fertility of detail, which fills me with an admiration which I should like to make this audience share. Among the philosophic cranks of my acquaintance in the past was a lady all the tenets of whose system I have forgotten except one. Had she been born in the Ionian Archipelago some three thousand years ago, that one doctrine would probably have made her name sure of a place in every university curriculum and examination paper. The world, she said, is composed of only two elements, the Thick, namely, and the Thin. No one can deny the truth of this analysis, as far as it goes (though in the light of our contemporary knowledge of nature it has itself a rather 'thin' sound), and it is nowhere truer than in that part of the world called philosophy. I am sure, for example, that many of you, listening to what poor account I have been able to give of transcendental idealism, have received an impression of its arguments being strangely thin, and of the terms it leaves us with being shiveringly thin wrappings for so thick and burly a world as this. Some of you of course will charge the thinness to my exposition; but thin as that has been, I believe the doctrines reported on to have been thinner. From Green to Haldane the absolute proposed to us to straighten out the confusions of the thicket of experience in which our life is passed remains a pure abstraction which hardly any one tries to make a whit concreter. If we open Green, we get nothing but the transcendental ego of apperception (Kant's name for the fact that to be counted in experience a thing has to be witnessed), blown up into a sort of timeless soap-bubble large enough to mirror the whole universe. Nature, Green keeps insisting, consists only in relations, and these imply the action of a mind that is eternal; a self-distinguishing consciousness which itself escapes from the relations by which it determines other things. Present to whatever is in succession, it is not in succession itself. If we take the Cairds, they tell us little more of the principle of the universe—it is always a return into the identity of the self from the difference of its objects. It separates itself from them and so becomes conscious of them in their separation from one another, while at the same time it binds them together as elements in one higher self-consciousness.

This seems the very quintessence of thinness; and the matter hardly grows thicker when we gather, after enormous amounts of reading, that the great enveloping self in question is absolute reason as such, and that as such it is characterized by the habit of using certain jejune 'categories' with which to perform its eminent relating work. The whole active material of natural fact is tried out, and only the barest intellectualistic formalism remains.

Hegel tried, as we saw, to make the system concreter by making the relations between things 'dialectic,' but if we turn to those who use his name most worshipfully, we find them giving up all the particulars of his attempt, and simply praising his intention—much as in our manner we have praised it ourselves. Mr. Haldane, for example, in his wonderfully clever Gifford lectures, praises Hegel to the skies, but what he tells of him amounts to little more than this, that 'the categories in which the mind arranges its experiences, and gives meaning to them, the universals in which the particulars are grasped in the individual, are a logical chain, in which the first presupposes the last, and the last is its presupposition and its truth.' He hardly tries at all to thicken this thin logical scheme. He says indeed that absolute mind in itself, and absolute mind in its hetereity or otherness, under the distinction which it sets up of itself from itself, have as their real *prius* absolute mind in synthesis; and, this being absolute mind's true nature, its dialectic character must show itself in such concrete forms as Goethe's and Wordsworth's poetry, as well as in religious forms. 'The nature of God, the nature of absolute mind, is to exhibit the triple movement of dialectic, and so the nature of God as presented in religion must be a triplicity, a trinity.' But beyond thus naming Goethe and Wordsworth and establishing the trinity, Mr. Haldane's Hegelianism carries us hardly an inch into the concrete detail of the world we actually inhabit.

Equally thin is Mr. Taylor both in his principles and in their results. Following Mr. Bradley, he starts by assuring us that reality cannot be self-contradictory, but to be related to anything really outside of one's self is to be self-contradictory, so the ultimate reality must be a single all-inclusive systematic whole. Yet all he can say of this whole at the end of his excellently written book is that the notion of it 'can make no addition to our information and can of itself supply no motives for practical endeavor.'

Mr. McTaggart treats us to almost as thin a fare. 'The main practical interest of Hegel's philosophy,' he says, 'is to be found in the abstract certainty which the logic gives us that all reality is rational and righteous, even when we cannot see in the least how it is so. . . . Not that it shows us how the facts around us are good, not that it shows us how we can make them better, but that it proves that they, like other reality, are *sub specie eternitatis,* perfectly good, and *sub specie temporis,* destined to become perfectly good.'

Here again, no detail whatever, only the abstract certainty that whatever the detail may prove to be, it will be good. Common non-dialectical men have already this certainty as a result of the generous vital enthusiasm about the universe with which they are born. The peculiarity of transcendental philosophy is its sovereign contempt for merely vital functions like enthusiasm, and its pretension to turn our simple and immediate trusts and faiths into the form of logically mediated certainties, to question which would be absurd. But the whole basis on which Mr. McTaggart's own certainty so solidly rests, settles down into the one nutshell of an assertion into which he puts Hegel's gospel, namely, that in every bit of experience and thought, however finite, the whole of reality (the absolute idea, as Hegel calls it) is 'implicitly present.'

This indeed is Hegel's *vision,* and Hegel thought that the details of his dialectic proved its truth. But disciples who treat the details of the proof as unsatisfactory and yet cling to the vision, are surely, in spite of their pretension to a more rational consciousness, no better than common men with their enthusiasms or deliberately adopted faiths. We have ourselves seen some of the weakness of the monistic proofs. Mr. McTaggart picks plenty of holes of his own in Hegel's logic, and finally concludes that 'all true philosophy must be mystical, not indeed in its methods but in its final conclusions,' which is as much as to say that the rationalistic methods leave us in the lurch, in spite of all their superiority, and that in the end vision and faith must eke them out. But how abstract and thin is here the vision, to say nothing of the faith! The whole of reality, explicitly absent from our finite experiences, must nevertheless be present in them all implicitly, altho no one of us can ever see how—the bare word 'implicit' here bearing the whole pyramid of the monistic system on its slender point. Mr. Joachim's monistic system of truth rests on an even slenderer point.— '*I have never doubted,*' he says, 'that universal and timeless truth is a single content or significance, one and whole and complete,' and he candidly confesses the failure of rationalistic attempts 'to raise this immediate certainty' to the level of reflective knowledge. There is, in short, no mediation for him between the Truth in capital letters and all the little 'lower-case' truths—and errors—which life presents. The psychological fact that he never has 'doubted' is enough.

The whole monistic pyramid, resting on points as thin as these, seems to me to be a *machtspruch,* a product of will far more than one of reason. Unity is good, therefore things *shall* cohere; they *shall* be one; there *shall* be categories to make them one, no matter what empirical disjunctions may appear. In Hegel's own writings, the *shall-be* temper is ubiquitous and towering; it overrides verbal and logical resistances alike. Hegel's error, as Professor Royce so well says, 'lay not in introducing logic into passion,' as some people charge, 'but in conceiving the logic of passion as the only logic. . . . He is [thus] suggestive,' Royce says, 'but never final. His system as a system has crumbled, but his vital comprehension of our life remains forever.' [42]

That vital comprehension we have already seen. It is that there is a sense in which real things are not merely their own bare selves, but may vaguely be treated as also their own others, and that ordinary logic, since it denies this, must be overcome. Ordinary logic denies this because it substitutes concepts for real things, and concepts *are* their own bare selves and nothing else. What Royce calls Hegel's 'system' was Hegel's attempt to make us believe that he was working by concepts and grinding out a higher style of logic, when in reality sensible experiences, hypotheses, and passion furnished him with all his results.

What I myself may mean by things being their own others, we shall see in a later lecture. It is now time to take our look at Fechner, whose thickness is a refreshing contrast to the thin, abstract, indigent, and threadbare appearance, the starving, school-room aspect, which the speculations of most of our absolutist philosophers present.

There is something really weird and uncanny in the contrast between the abstract pretensions of rationalism and what rationalistic methods concretely can do. If the 'logical prius' of our mind were really the 'implicit presence' of the whole 'concrete universal,' the whole of reason, or reality, or spirit, or the absolute idea, or whatever it may be called, in all our finite thinking, and if this reason worked (for example) by the dialectical method, does n't it seem odd that in the greatest instance of rationalization mankind has known, in 'science,' namely, the dialectical method should never once have been tried? Not a solitary instance of the use of it in science occurs to my mind. Hypotheses, and deductions from these, controlled by sense-observations and analogies with what we know elsewhere, are to be thanked for all of science's results.

Fechner used no methods but these latter ones in arguing for his metaphysical conclusions about reality—but let me first rehearse a few of the facts about his life.

Born in 1801, the son of a poor country pastor in Saxony, he lived from 1817 to 1887, when he died, seventy years therefore, at Leipzig,

[42] *The Spirit of Modern Philosophy,* p. 227.

a typical *gelehrter* of the old-fashioned german stripe. His means were always scanty, so his only extravagances could be in the way of thought, but these were gorgeous ones. He passed his medical examinations at Leipzig University at the age of twenty-one, but decided, instead of becoming a doctor, to devote himself to physical science. It was ten years before he was made professor of physics, although he soon was authorized to lecture. Meanwhile, he had to make both ends meet, and this he did by voluminous literary labors. He translated, for example, the four volumes of Biot's treatise on physics, and the six of Thénard's work on chemistry, and took care of their enlarged editions later. He edited repertories of chemistry and physics, a pharmaceutical journal, and an encyclopædia in eight volumes, of which he wrote about one third. He published physical treatises and experimental investigations of his own, especially in electricity. Electrical measurements, as you know, are the basis of electrical science, and Fechner's measurements in galvanism, performed with the simplest self-made apparatus, are classic to this day. During this time he also published a number of half-philosophical, half-humorous writings, which have gone through several editions, under the name of Dr. Mises, besides poems, literary and artistic essays, and other occasional articles.

But overwork, poverty, and an eye-trouble produced by his observations on after-images in the retina (also a classic piece of investigation) produced in Fechner, then about thirty-eight years old, a terrific attack of nervous prostration with painful hyperæsthesia of all the functions, from which he suffered three years, cut off entirely from active life. Present-day medicine would have classed poor Fechner's malady quickly enough, as partly a habit-neurosis, but its severity was such that in his day it was treated as a visitation incomprehensible in its malignity; and when he suddenly began to get well, both Fechner and others treated the recovery as a sort of divine miracle. This illness, bringing Fechner face to face with inner desperation, made a great crisis in his life. 'Had I not then clung to the faith,' he writes, 'that clinging to faith would somehow or other work its reward, *so hätte ich jene zeit nicht ausgehalten.*' His religious and cosmological faiths saved him—thenceforward one great aim with him was to work out and communicate these faiths to the world. He did so on the largest scale; but he did many other things too ere he died.

A book on the atomic theory, classic also; four elaborate mathematical and experimental volumes on what he called psychophysics—many persons consider Fechner to have practically founded scientific psychology in the first of these books; a volume on organic evolution, and two works on experimental æsthetics, in which again Fechner is considered by some judges to have laid the foundations of a new science, must be included among these other performances. Of the more religious and philosophical works, I shall immediately give a further account.

All Leipzig mourned him when he died, for he was the pattern of the ideal german scholar, as daringly original in his thought as he was homely in his life, a modest, genial, laborious slave to truth and learning, and withal the owner of an admirable literary style of the vernacular sort. The materialistic generation, that in the fifties and sixties called his speculations fantastic, had been replaced by one with greater liberty of imagination, and a Preyer, a Wundt, a Paulsen, and a Lasswitz could now speak of Fechner as their master.

His mind was indeed one of those multitudinously organized crossroads of truth which are occupied only at rare intervals by children of men, and from which nothing is either too far or too near to be seen in due perspective. Patientest observation, exactest mathematics, shrewdest discrimination, humanest feeling, flourished in him on the largest scale, with no apparent detriment to one another. He was in fact a philosopher in the 'great' sense, altho he cared so much less than most philosophers care for abstractions of the 'thin' order. For him the abstract lived in the concrete, and the hidden motive of all he did was to bring what he called the daylight view of the world into ever greater evidence, that daylight view being this, that the whole universe in its different spans and wave-lengths, exclusions and envelopments, is everywhere alive and conscious. It has taken fifty years for his chief book, 'Zend-avesta,' to pass into a second edition (1901). 'One swallow,' he cheerfully writes, 'does not make a summer. But the first swallow would not come unless the summer were coming; and for me that summer means my daylight view some time prevailing.'

The original sin, according to Fechner, of both our popular and our scientific thinking, is our inveterate habit of regarding the spiritual not as the rule but as an exception in the midst of nature. Instead of believing our life to be fed at the breasts of the greater life, our individuality to be sustained by the greater individuality, which must necessarily have more consciousness and more independence than all that it brings forth, we habitually treat whatever lies outside of our life as so much slag and ashes of life only; or if we believe in a Divine Spirit, we fancy him on the one side as bodiless, and nature as soulless on the other. What comfort, or peace, Fechner asks, can come from such a doctrine? The flowers wither at its breath, the stars turn into stone; our own body grows unworthy of our spirit and sinks to a tenement for carnal senses only. The book of nature turns into a volume on mechanics, in which whatever has life is treated as a sort of anomaly; a great chasm of separation yawns between us and all that is higher than ourselves; and God becomes a thin nest of abstractions.

Fechner's great instrument for vivifying the daylight view is analogy; not a rationalistic argument is to be found in all his many pages —only reasonings like those which men continually use in practical life. For example: My house is built by some one, the world too is built by someone. The world is greater than my house, it must be a greater some one who built the world. My body moves by the influence of my feeling and will; the sun, moon, sea, and wind, being themselves more powerful, move by the influence of some more powerful feeling and will. I live now, and change from one day to another; I shall live hereafter, and change still more, etc.

Bain defines genius as the power of seeing analogies. The number that Fechner could perceive was prodigious; but he insisted on the differences as well. Neglect to make allowance for these, he said, is the common fallacy in analogical reasoning. Most of us, for example, reasoning justly that, since all the minds we know are connected with bodies, therefore God's mind should be connected with a body, proceed to suppose that that body must be just an animal body over again, and paint an altogether human picture of God. But all that the analogy comports is *a* body—the particular features of *our* body are adaptations to a habitat so different from God's that if God have a physical body at all, it must be utterly different from ours in structure. Throughout his writings Fechner makes difference and analogy walk abreast, and by his extraordinary power of noticing both, he converts what would ordinarily pass for objections to his conclusions into factors of their support.

The vaster orders of mind go with the vaster orders of body. The entire earth on which we live must have, according to Fechner, its own collective consciousness. So must each sun, moon, and planet; so must the whole solar system have its own wider consciousness, in which the consciousness of our earth plays one part. So has the entire starry system as such its consciousness; and if that starry system be not the sum of all that *is,* materially considered, then that whole system, along with whatever else may be, is the body of that absolutely totalized consciousness of the universe to which men give the name of God.

Speculatively Fechner is thus a monist in his theology; but there is room in his universe for every grade of spiritual being between man and the final all-inclusive God; and in suggesting what the positive content of all this super-humanity may be, he hardly lets his imagination fly beyond simple spirits of the planetary order. The earth-soul he passionately believes in; he treats the earth as our special human guardian angel; we can pray to the earth as men pray to their saints; but I think that in his system, as in so many of the actual historic theologies, the supreme God marks only a sort of limit of enclosure of the worlds above man. He is left thin and abstract in his majesty, men preferring to carry on their personal transactions with the many less remote and abstract messengers and mediators whom the divine order provides.

I shall ask later whether the abstractly monistic turn which Fechner's speculations took was necessitated by logic. I believe it not to have been required. Meanwhile let me lead you a little more into the detail of his thought. Inevitably one does him miserable injustice by summarizing and abridging him. For altho the type of reasoning he employs is almost childlike for simplicity, and his bare conclusions can be written on a single page, the *power* of the man is due altogether to the profuseness of his concrete imagination, to the multitude of the points which he considers successively, to the cumulative effect of his learning, of his thoroughness, and of the ingenuity of his detail, to his admirably homely style, to the sincerity with which his pages glow, and finally to the impression he gives of a man who does n't live at second-hand, but who *see,* who in fact speaks as one having authority, and not as if he were one of the common herd of professorial philosophic scribes.

Abstractly set down, his most important conclusion for my purpose in these lectures is that the constitution of the world is identical throughout. In ourselves, visual consciousness goes with our eyes, tactile consciousness with our skin. But altho neither skin nor eye knows aught of the sensations of the other, they come together and figure in some sort of relation and combination in the more inclusive consciousness which each of us names his *self.* Quite similarly, then, says Fechner, we must suppose that my consciousness of myself and yours of yourself, altho in their immediacy they keep separate and know nothing of each other, are yet known and used together in a higher consciousness, that of the human race, say, into which they enter as constituent parts. Similarly, the whole human and animal kingdoms come together as conditions of a consciousness of still wider scope. This combines in the soul of the earth with the consciousness of the vegetable kingdom, which in turn contributes its share of experience to that of the whole solar system, and so on from synthesis to synthesis and height to height, till an absolutely universal consciousness is reached.

A vast analogical series, in which the basis of the analogy consists of facts directly observable in ourselves.

The supposition of an earth-consciousness meets a strong instinctive prejudice which Fechner ingeniously tries to overcome. Man's mind is the highest consciousness upon the earth, we think—the earth itself being in all ways man's inferior. How should its consciousness, if it have one, be superior to his?

What are the marks of superiority which we are tempted to use here? If we look more carefully into them, Fechner points out that the earth possesses each and all of them more perfectly than we. He considers in detail the points of difference between us, and shows them all to make for the earth's higher rank. I will touch on only a few of these points.

One of them of course is independence of other external beings. External to the earth are only the other heavenly bodies. All the things on which we externally depend for life—air, water, plant and animal food, fellow men, etc.—are included in her as her constituent parts. She is self-sufficing in a million respects in which we are not so. We depend on her for almost everything, she on us for but a small portion of her history. She swings us in her orbit from winter to summer and revolves us from day into night and from night into day.

Complexity in unity is another sign of superiority. The total earth's complexity far exceeds that of any organism, for she includes all our organisms in herself, along with an infinite number of things that our organisms fail to include. Yet how simple and massive are the phases of her own proper life! As the total bearing of any animal is sedate and tranquil compared with the agitation of its blood corpuscles, so is the earth a sedate and tranquil being compared with the animals whom she supports.

To develop from within, instead of being fashioned from without, is also counted as something superior in men's eyes. An egg is a higher style of being than a piece of clay which an external modeler makes into the image of a bird. Well, the earth's history develops from within. It is like that of a wonderful egg which the sun's heat, like that of a mother-hen, has stimulated to its cycles of evolutionary change.

Individuality of type, and difference from other beings of its type, is another mark of rank. The earth differs from every other planet, and as a class planetary beings are extraordinarily distinct from other beings.

Long ago the earth was called an animal; but a planet is a higher class of being than either man or animal; not only quantitatively greater, like a vaster and more awkward whale or elephant, but a being whose enormous size requires an altogether different plan of life. Our animal organization comes from our inferiority. Our need of moving to and fro, of stretching our limbs and bending our bodies, shows only our defect. What are our legs but crutches, by means of which, with restless efforts, we go hunting after the things we have not inside of ourselves. But the earth is no such cripple; why should she who already possesses within herself the things we so painfully pursue, have limbs analogous to ours? Shall she mimic a small part of herself? What need has she of arms, with nothing to reach for? of a neck, with no head to carry? of eyes or nose when she finds her way through space without either, and has the millions of eyes of all her animals to guide their movements on her surface, and all their noses to smell the flowers that grow? For, as we are ourselves a part of the earth, so our organs are her organs. She is, as it were, eye and ear over her whole extent—all that we see and hear in separation she sees and hears at once. She brings forth living beings of countless kinds upon her surface, and their multitudinous conscious relations with each other she takes up into her higher and more general conscious life.

Most of us, considering the theory that the whole terrestrial mass is animated as our bodies are, make the mistake of working the analogy too literally, and allowing for no differences. If the earth be a sentient organism, we say, where are her brain and nerves? What corresponds to her heart and lungs? In other words we expect functions which she already performs through us, to be performed outside of us again, and in just the same way. But we see perfectly well how the earth performs some of these functions in a way unlike our way. If you speak of circulation, what need has she of a heart when the sun keeps all the showers of rain that fall upon her and all the springs and brooks and rivers that irrigate her, going? What need has she of internal lungs, when her whole sensitive surface is in living commerce with the atmosphere that clings to it?

The organ that gives us most trouble is the brain. All the consciousness we directly know seems tied to brains.—Can there be consciousness, we ask, where there is no brain? But our brain, which primarily serves to correlate our muscular reactions with the external objects on which we depend, performs a function which the earth performs in an entirely different way. She has no proper muscles or limbs of her own, and the only objects external to her are the other stars. To these her whole mass reacts by most exquisite alterations in its total gait, and by still more exquisite vibratory responses in its substance. Her ocean reflects the lights of heaven as in a mighty mirror, her atmosphere refracts them like a monstrous lens, the clouds and snow-fields combine them into white, the woods and flowers disperse them into colors. Polarization, interference, absorption, awaken sensibilities in matter of which our senses are too coarse to take any note.

For these cosmic relations of hers, then, she no more needs a special brain than she needs eyes or ears. *Our* brains do indeed unify and correlate innumerable functions. Our eyes know nothing of sound, our ears nothing of light, but, having brains, we can feel sound and light together, and compare them. We account for this by the fibres which in the brain connect the optical with the acoustic centre, but just how these fibres bring together not only the sensations, but the centres, we fail to see. But if fibres are indeed all that is needed to do that trick,

has not the earth pathways, by which you and I are physically continuous, more than enough to do for our two minds what the brain-fibres
do for the sounds and sights in a single mind? Must every higher
means of unification between things be a literal *brain*-fibre, and go by
that name? Cannot the earth-mind know otherwise the contents of
our minds together?

Fechner's imagination, insisting on the differences as well as on
the resemblances, thus tries to make our picture of the whole earth's
life more concrete. He revels in the thought of its perfections. To
carry her precious freight through the hours and seasons what form
could be more excellent than hers—being as it is horse, wheels, and
wagon all in one. Think of her beauty—a shining ball, sky-blue and
sun-lit over one half, the other bathed in starry night, reflecting the
heavens from all her waters, myriads of lights and shadows in the
folds of her mountains and windings of her valleys, she would be a
spectacle of rainbow glory, could one only see her from afar as we see
parts of her from her own mountain-tops. Every quality of landscape
that has a name would then be visible in her at once—all that is delicate or graceful, all that is quiet, or wild, or romantic, or desolate, or
cheerful, or luxuriant, or fresh. That landscape is her face—a peopled
landscape, too, for men's eyes would appear in it like diamonds
among the dewdrops. Green would be the dominant color, but the
blue atmosphere and the clouds would enfold her as a bride is
shrouded in her veil—a veil the vapory transparent folds of which the
earth, through her ministers the winds, never tires of laying and fold-
ing about herself anew.

Every element has its own living denizens. Can the celestial ocean
of ether, whose waves are light, in which the earth herself floats, not
have hers, higher by as much as their element is higher, swimming
without fins, flying without wings, moving, immense and tranquil, as
by a half-spiritual force through the half-spiritual sea which they inhabit, rejoicing in the exchange of luminous influence with one another, following the slightest pull of one another's attraction, and har-
boring, each of them, an inexhaustible inward wealth?

Men have always made fables about angels, dwelling in the light,
needing no earthly food or drink, messengers between ourselves and
God. Here are actually existent beings, dwelling in the light and moving through the sky, needing neither food nor drink, intermediaries
between God and us, obeying his commands. So, if the heavens really
are the home of angels, the heavenly bodies must be those very angels,
for other creatures *there* are none. Yes! the earth is our great common
guardian angel, who watches over all our interests combined.

In a striking page Fechner relates one of his moments of direct
vision of this truth.

'On a certain spring morning I went out to walk. The fields were green, the birds sang, the dew glistened, the smoke was rising, here and there a man appeared; a light as of transfiguration lay on all things. It was only a little bit of the earth; it was only one moment of her existence; and yet as my look embraced her more and more it seemed to me not only so beautiful an idea, but so true and clear a fact, that she is an angel, an angel so rich and fresh and flower-like, and yet going her round in the skies so firmly and so at one with herself, turning her whole living face to Heaven, and carrying me along with her into that Heaven, that I asked myself how the opinions of men could ever have so spun themselves away from life so far as to deem the earth only a dry clod, and to seek for angels above it or about it in the emptiness of the sky,—only to find them nowhere. . . . But such an experience as this passes for fantastic. The earth is a globular body, and what more she may be, one can find in mineralogical cabinets.' [43]

Where there is no vision the people perish. Few professorial philosophers have any vision. Fechner had vision, and that is why one can read him over and over again, and each time bring away a fresh sense of reality.

His earliest book was a vision of what the inner life of plants may be like. He called it 'Nanna.' In the development of animals the nervous system is the central fact. Plants develop centrifugally, spread their organs abroad. For that reason people suppose that they can have no consciousness, for they lack the unity which the central nervous system provides. But the plant's consciousness may be of another type, being connected with other structures. Violins and pianos give out sounds because they have strings. Does it follow that nothing but strings can give out sound? How then about flutes and organ-pipes? Of course their sounds are of a different quality, and so may the consciousness of plants be of a quality correlated exclusively with the kind of organization that they possess. Nutrition, respiration, propagation take place in them without nerves. In us these functions are conscious only in unusual states, normally their consciousness is eclipsed by that which goes with the brain. No such eclipse occurs in plants, and their lower consciousness may therefore be all the more lively. With nothing to do but to drink the light and air with their leaves, to let their cells proliferate, to feel their rootlets draw the sap, is it conceivable that they should not consciously suffer if water, light, and air are suddenly withdrawn? or that when the flowering and fertilization which are the culmination of their life take place, they should not feel their own existence more intensely and enjoy something like what we call pleasure in ourselves? Does the water-lily, rocking in her

[43] Fechner: *Über die Seelenfrage*, 1861, p. 170.

triple bath of water, air, and light, relish in no wise her own beauty? When the plant in our room turns to the light, closes her blossoms in the dark, responds to our watering or pruning by increase of size or change of shape and bloom, who has the right to say she does not feel, or that she plays a purely passive part? Truly plants can foresee nothing, neither the scythe of the mower, nor the hand extended to pluck their flowers. They can neither run away nor cry out. But this only proves how different their modes of feeling life must be from those of animals that live by eyes and ears and locomotive organs, it does not prove that they have no mode of feeling life at all.

How scanty and scattered would sensation be on our globe, if the feeling-life of plants were blotted from existence. Solitary would consciousness move through the woods in the shape of some deer or other quadruped, or fly about the flowers in that of some insect, but can we really suppose that the Nature through which God's breath blows is such a barren wilderness as this?

I have probably by this time said enough to acquaint those of you who have never seen these metaphysical writings of Fechner with their more general characteristics, and I hope that some of you may now feel like reading them yourselves.[44] The special thought of Fechner's with which in these lectures I have most practical concern, is his belief that the more inclusive forms of consciousness are in part *constituted* by the more limited forms. Not that they are the mere sum of the more limited forms. As our mind is not the bare sum of our sights plus our sounds plus our pains, but in adding these terms together also finds relations among them and weaves them into schemes and forms and objects of which no one sense in its separate estate knows anything, so the earth-soul traces relations between the contents of my mind and the contents of yours of which neither of our separate minds is conscious. It has schemes, forms, and objects proportionate to its wider field, which our mental fields are far too narrow to cognize. By ourselves we are simply out of relation with each other, for it we are both of us there, and *different* from each other, which is a positive relation. What we are without knowing, it knows that we are. We are closed against its world, but that world is not closed against us. It is as if the total universe of inner life had a sort of grain or direction, a sort of valvular structure, permitting knowledge to flow in one way only, so that the wider might always have the narrower under observation, but never the narrower the wider.

[44] Fechner's latest summarizing of his views, *Die Tagesansicht gegenüber der Nachtansicht,* Leipzig, 1879, is now, I understand, in process of translation. His *Little Book of Life after Death* exists already in two American versions, one published by Little, Brown & Co., Boston, the other by the Open Court Co., Chicago. [See below, Annotated Bibliography, 1904–2, p. 842.]

Fechner's great analogy here is the relation of the senses to our individual minds. When our eyes are open their sensations enter into our general mental life, which grows incessantly by the addition of what they see. Close the eyes, however, and the visual additions stop, nothing but thoughts and memories of the past visual experiences remain—in combination of course with the enormous stock of other thoughts and memories, and with the data coming in from the senses not yet closed. Our eye-sensations of themselves know nothing of this enormous life into which they fall. Fechner thinks, as any common man would think, that they are taken into it directly when they occur, and form part of it just as they are. They don't stay outside and get represented inside by their copies. It is only the memories and concepts of them that are copies; the sensible perceptions themselves are taken in or walled out in their own proper persons according as the eyes are open or shut.

Fechner likens our individual persons on the earth unto so many sense-organs of the earth's soul. We add to its perceptive life so long as our own life lasts. It absorbs our perceptions, just as they occur, into its larger sphere of knowledge, and combines them with the other data there. When one of us dies, it is as if an eye of the world were closed, for all *perceptive* contributions from that particular quarter cease. But the memories and conceptual relations that have spun themselves round the perceptions of that person remain in the larger earth-life as distinct as ever, and form new relations and grow and develop throughout all the future, in the same way in which our own distinct objects of thought, once stored in memory, form new relations and develop throughout our whole finite life. This is Fechner's theory of immortality, first published in the little 'Büchlein des lebens nach dem tode,' in 1836, and re-edited in greatly improved shape in the last volume of his 'Zend-avesta.'

We rise upon the earth as wavelets rise upon the ocean. We grow out of her soil as leaves grow from a tree. The wavelets catch the sunbeams separately, the leaves stir when the branches do not move. They realize their own events apart, just as in our own consciousness, when anything becomes emphatic, the background fades from observation. Yet the event works back upon the background, as the wavelet works upon the waves, or as the leaf's movements work upon the sap inside the branch. The whole sea and the whole tree are registers of what has happened, and are different for the wave's and the leaf's action having occurred. A grafted twig may modify its stock to the roots:—so our outlived private experiences, impressed on the whole earth-mind as memories, lead the immortal life of ideas there, and become parts of the great system, fully distinguished from one another, just as we ourselves when alive were distinct, realizing themselves no longer isolatedly, but along with one another as so many partial systems, entering thus into new combinations, being affected by the perceptive experiences of those living then, and affecting the living in their turn—altho they are so seldom recognized by living men to do so.

If you imagine that this entrance after the death of the body into a common life of higher type means a merging and loss of our distinct personality, Fechner asks you whether a visual sensation of our own exists in any sense *less for itself* or *less distinctly,* when it enters into our higher relational consciousness and is there distinguished and defined.

—But here I must stop my reporting and send you to his volumes. Thus is the universe alive, according to this philosopher! I think you will admit that he makes it more *thickly* alive than do the other philosophers who, following rationalistic methods solely, gain the same results, but only in the thinnest outlines. Both Fechner and Professor Royce, for example, believe ultimately in one all-inclusive mind. Both believe that we, just as we stand here, are constituent parts of that mind. No other *content* has it than us, with all the other creatures like or unlike us, and the relations which it finds between us. Our eaches, collected into one, are substantively identical with its all, tho the all is perfect while no each is perfect, so that we have to admit that new qualities as well as unperceived relations accrue from the collective form. It is thus superior to the distributive form. But having reached this result, Royce (tho his treatment of the subject on its moral side seems to me infinitely richer and thicker than that of any other contemporary idealistic philosopher) leaves us very much to our own devices. Fechner, on the contrary, tries to trace the superiorities due to the more collective form in as much detail as he can. He marks the various intermediary stages and halting places of collectivity,—as we are to our separate senses, so is the earth to us, so is the solar system to the earth, etc.,—and if, in order to escape an infinitely long summation, he posits a complete God as the all-container and leaves him about as indefinite in feature as the idealists leave their absolute, he yet provides us with a very definite gate of approach to him in the shape of the earth-soul, through which in the nature of things we must first make connexion with all the more enveloping superhuman realms, and with which our more immediate religious commerce at any rate has to be carried on.

Ordinary monistic idealism leaves everything intermediary out. It recognizes only the extremes, as if, after the first rude face of the phenomenal world in all its particularity, nothing but the supreme in all its perfection could be found. First, you and I, just as we are in this room; and the moment we get below that surface, the unutterable absolute itself! Does n't this show a singularly indigent imagination? Is n't this brave universe made on a richer pattern, with room in it for a long hierarchy of beings? Materialistic science makes it infinitely richer in terms, with its molecules, and ether, and electrons, and what not. Absolute idealism, thinking of reality only under intellectual forms, knows not what to do with *bodies* of any grade, and can make no use of any psychophysical analogy or correspondence. The resultant thinness is startling when compared with the thickness and articulation of such a universe as Fechner paints. May not satisfaction with the rationalistic absolute as the alpha and omega, and treatment of it in all its abstraction as an adequate religious object, argue a certain native poverty of mental demand? Things reveal themselves soonest to those who most passionately want them, for our need sharpens our wit. To a mind content with little, the much in the universe may always remain hid.

To be candid, one of my reasons for saying so much about Fechner has been to make the thinness of our current transcendentalism appear more evident by an effect of contrast. Scholasticism ran thick; Hegel himself ran thick; but english and american transcendentalisms run thin. If philosophy is more a matter of passionate vision than of logic,—and I believe it is, logic only finding reasons for the vision afterwards,—must not such thinness come either from the vision being defective in the disciples, or from their passion, matched with Fechner's or with Hegel's own passion, being as moonlight unto sunlight or as water unto wine? [45]

But I have also a much deeper reason for making Fechner a part of my text. His *assumption that conscious experiences freely compound and separate themselves,* the same assumption by which absolutism explains the relation of our minds to the eternal mind, and the same by which empiricism explains the composition of the human mind out of subordinate mental elements, is not one which we ought to let pass without scrutiny. I shall scrutinize it in the next lecture.

[45] Mr. Bradley ought to be to some degree exempted from my attack in these last pages. Compare especially what he says of non-human consciousness in his *Appearance and Reality,* pp. 269–272.

THE COMPOUNDING OF
CONSCIOUSNESS*

In my last lecture I gave a miserably scanty outline of the way of thinking of a philosopher remarkable for the almost unexampled richness of his imagination of details. I owe to Fechner's shade an apology for presenting him in a manner so unfair to the most essential quality of his genius; but the time allotted is too short to say more about the particulars of his work, so I proceed to the programme I suggested at the end of our last hour. I wish to discuss the assumption that states of consciousness, so-called, can separate and combine themselves freely, and keep their own identity unchanged while forming parts of simultaneous fields of experience of wider scope.

Let me first explain just what I mean by this. While you listen to my voice, for example, you are perhaps inattentive to some bodily sensation due to your clothing or your posture. Yet that sensation would seem probably to be there, for in an instant, by a change of attention, you can have it in one field of consciousness with the voice. It seems as if it existed first in a separate form, and then as if, without itself changing, it combined with your other co-existent sensations. It is after this analogy that pantheistic idealism thinks that we exist in the absolute. The absolute, it thinks, makes the world by knowing the whole of it at once in one undivided eternal act.[46] To 'be,' *really* to be, is to be as it knows us to be, along with everything else, namely, and clothed with the fulness of our meaning. Meanwhile we *are* at the same time not only really and as it knows us, but also apparently, for to our separate single selves we appear *without* most other things and unable to declare with any fulness what our own meaning is. Now the classic doctrine of pantheistic idealism, from the Upanishads down to Josiah Royce, is that the finite knowers, in spite of their apparent ignorance, are one with the knower of the all. In the most limited moments of our private experience, the absolute idea, as Dr. McTaggart told us, is implicitly contained. The moments, as Royce says, exist only in relation to it. They are true or erroneous only through its overshadowing presence. Of the larger self that alone eternally is, they are the organic parts. They *are*, only inasmuch as they are implicated in its being.

There is thus in reality but this one self, consciously inclusive of

* From: P.U., 181–221.
[46] Royce: *The Spirit of Modern Philosophy*, p. 379.

all the lesser selves, *logos,* problem-solver, and all-knower; and Royce ingeniously compares the ignorance that in our persons breaks out in the midst of its complete knowledge and isolates me from you and both of us from it, to the inattention into which our finite minds are liable to fall with respect to such implicitly present details as those corporeal sensations to which I made allusion just now. Those sensations stand to our total private minds in the same relation in which our private minds stand to the absolute mind. Privacy means ignorance—I still quote Royce—and ignorance means inattention. We are finite because our wills, as such, are only fragments of the absolute will; because will means interest, and an incomplete will means an incomplete interest; and because incompleteness of interest means inattention to much that a fuller interest would bring us to perceive.[47]

In this account Royce makes by far the manliest of the post-hegelian attempts to read some empirically apprehensible content into the notion of our relation to the absolute mind.

I have to admit, now that I propose to you to scrutinize this assumption rather closely, that trepidation seizes me. The subject is a subtle and abstruse one. It is one thing to delve into subtleties by one's self with pen in hand, or to study out abstruse points in books, but quite another thing to make a popular lecture out of them. Nevertheless I must not flinch from my task here, for I think that this particular point forms perhaps the vital knot of the present philosophic situation, and I imagine that the times are ripe, or almost ripe, for a serious attempt to be made at its untying.

It may perhaps help to lessen the arduousness of the subject if I put the first part of what I have to say in the form of a direct personal confession.

In the year 1890 I published a work on psychology in which it became my duty to discuss the value of a certain explanation of our higher mental states that had come into favor among the more biologically inclined psychologists. Suggested partly by the association of ideas, and partly by the analogy of chemical compounds, this opinion was that complex mental states are resultants of the self-compounding of simpler ones. The Mills had spoken of mental chemistry; Wundt of a 'psychic synthesis,' which might develop properties not contained in the elements; and such writers as Spencer, Taine, Fiske, Barratt, and Clifford had propounded a great evolutionary theory in which, in the absence of souls, selves, or other principles of unity, primordial units of mind-stuff or mind-dust were represented as summing themselves together in successive stages of compounding and re-compounding, and thus engendering our higher and more complex states of mind. The elementary feeling of A, let us say, and the elementary feeling of

[47] *The World and the Individual,* vol. ii, pp. 58–62.

B, when they occur in certain conditions, combine, according to this doctrine, into a feeling of A-plus-B, and this in turn combines with a similarly generated feeling of C-plus-D, until at last the whole alphabet may appear together in one field of awareness, without any other witnessing principle or principles beyond the feelings of the several letters themselves, being supposed to exist. What each of them witnesses separately, 'all' of them are supposed to witness in conjunction. But their distributive knowledge does n't *give rise* to their collective knowledge by any act, it *is* their collective knowledge. The lower forms of consciousness 'taken together' *are* the higher. It, 'taken apart,' consists of nothing and *is* nothing but them. This, at least, is the most obvious way of understanding the doctrine, and is the way I understood it in the chapter in my psychology.

Superficially looked at, this seems just like the combination of H_2 and O into water, but looked at more closely, the analogy halts badly. When a chemist tells us that two atoms of hydrogen and one of oxygen combine themselves of their own accord into the new compound substance 'water,' he knows (if he believes in the mechanical view of nature) that this is only an elliptical statement for a more complex fact. That fact is that when H_2 and O, instead of keeping far apart, get into closer quarters, say into the position H-O-H, they *affect surrounding bodies differently:* they now wet our skin, dissolve sugar, put out fire, etc., which they did n't in their former positions. 'Water' is but *our name* for what acts thus peculiarly. But if the skin, sugar, and fire were absent, no witness would speak of water at all. He would still talk of the H and O distributively, merely noting that they acted now in the new position H-O-H.

In the older psychologies the soul or self took the place of the sugar, fire, or skin. The lower feelings produced *effects on it,* and their apparent compounds were only its reactions. As you tickle a man's face with a feather, and he laughs, so when you tickle his intellectual principle with a retinal feeling, say, and a muscular feeling at once, it laughs responsively by its category of 'space,' but it would be false to treat the space as simply made of those simpler feelings. It is rather a new and unique psychic creation which their combined action on the mind is able to evoke.

I found myself obliged, in discussing the mind-dust theory, to urge this last alternative view. The so-called mental compounds are simple psychic reactions of a higher type. The form itself of them, I said, is something new. We can't say that awareness of the alphabet as such is nothing more than twenty-six awarenesses, each of a separate letter; for those are twenty-six distinct awarenesses, of single letters *without* others, while their so-called sum is one awareness, of every letter *with* its comrades. There is thus something new in the collective consciousness. It knows the same letters, indeed, but it knows them in this novel way. It is safer, I said (for I fought shy of admitting a self or soul or other agent of combination), to treat the consciousness of the alphabet as a twenty-seventh fact, the substitute and not the sum of the twenty-six simpler consciousnesses, and to say that while under certain physiological conditions they alone are produced, other more complex physiological conditions result in its production instead. Do not talk, therefore, I said, of the higher states *consisting* of the simpler, or *being* the same with them; talk rather of their *knowing the same things*. They are different mental facts, but they apprehend, each in its own peculiar way, the same objective A, B, C, and D.

The theory of combination, I was forced to conclude, is thus untenable, being both logically nonsensical and practically unnecessary. Say what you will, twelve thoughts, each of a single word, are not the self-same mental thing as one thought of the whole sentence. The higher thoughts, I insisted, are psychic units, not compounds; but for all that, they may know together as a collective multitude the very same objects which under other conditions are known separately by as many simple thoughts.

For many years I held rigorously to this view,[48] and the reasons for doing so seemed to me during all those years to apply also to the opinion that the absolute mind stands to our minds in the relation of a whole to its parts. If untenable in finite psychology, that opinion ought to be untenable in metaphysics also. The great transcendentalist metaphor has always been, as I lately reminded you, a grammatical sentence. Physically such a sentence is of course composed of clauses, these of words, the words of syllables, and the syllables of letters. We may take each word in, yet not understand the sentence; but if suddenly the meaning of the whole sentence flashes, the sense of each word is taken up into that whole meaning. Just so, according to our transcendentalist teachers, the absolute mind thinks the whole sentence, while we, according to our rank as thinkers, think a clause, a word, a syllable, or a letter. Most of us are, as I said, mere syllables in the mouth of Allah. And as Allah comes first in the order of being, so comes first the entire sentence, the *logos* that forms the eternal absolute thought. Students of language tell us that speech began with men's efforts to make *statements*. The rude synthetic vocal utterances first used for this effect slowly got stereotyped, and then much later got

[48] I hold to it still as the best description of an enormous number of our higher fields of consciousness. They demonstrably do not *contain* the lower states that know the same objects. Of other fields, however this is not so true; so, in the *Psychological Review* for 1895, vol. ii, p. 105 (see especially pp. 119–120), I frankly withdrew, in principle, my former objection to talking of fields of consciousness being made of simpler 'parts,' leaving the facts to decide the question in each special case.

decomposed into grammatical parts. It is not as if men had first invented letters and made syllables of them, then made words of the syllables and sentences of the words;—they actually followed the reverse order. So, the transcendentalists affirm, the complete absolute thought is the pre-condition of our thoughts, and we finite creatures *are* only in so far as it owns us as its verbal fragments.

The metaphor is so beautiful, and applies, moreover, so literally to such a multitude of the minor wholes of experience, that by merely hearing it most of us are convinced that it must apply universally. We see that no smallest raindrop can come into being without a whole shower, no single feather without a whole bird, neck and crop, beak and tail, coming into being simultaneously: so we unhesitatingly lay down the law that no part of anything can be except so far as the whole also is. And then, since everything whatever is part of the whole universe, and since (if we are idealists) nothing, whether part or whole, exists except for a witness, we proceed to the conclusion that the unmitigated absolute as witness of the whole is the one sole ground of being of every partial fact, the fact of our own existence included. We think of ourselves as being only a few of the feathers, so to speak, which help to constitute that absolute bird. Extending the analogy of certain wholes, of which we have familiar experience, to the whole of wholes, we easily become absolute idealists.

But if, instead of yielding to the seductions of our metaphor, be it sentence, shower, or bird, we analyze more carefully the notion suggested by it that we are constituent parts of the absolute's eternal field of consciousness, we find grave difficulties arising. First, the difficulty I found with the mind-dust theory. If the absolute makes us by knowing us, how can we exist otherwise than *as* it knows us? But it knows each of us indivisibly from everything else. Yet if to exist means nothing but to be experienced, as idealism affirms, we surely exist otherwise, for we experience *ourselves* ignorantly and in division. We indeed differ from the absolute not only by defect, but by excess. Our ignorances, for example, bring curiosities and doubts by which it cannot be troubled, for it owns eternally the solution of every problem. Our impotence entails pains, our imperfection sins, which its perfection keeps at a distance. What I said of the alphabet-form and the letters holds good of the absolute experience and our experiences. Their relation, whatever it may be, seems not to be that of identity.

It is impossible to reconcile the peculiarities of our experience with our being only the absolute's mental objects. A God, as distinguished from the absolute, creates things by projecting them beyond himself as so many substances, each endowed with *perseity,* as the scholastics call it. But objects of thought are not things *per se.* They are there only *for* their thinker, and only *as* he thinks them. How, then, can they become severally alive on their own accounts and think themselves quite otherwise than as he thinks them? It is as if the characters in a novel were to get up from the pages, and walk away and transact business of their own outside of the author's story.

A third difficulty is this: The bird-metaphor is physical, but we see on reflection that in the *physical* world there is no real compounding. 'Wholes' are not realities there, parts only are realities. 'Bird' is only our *name* for the physical fact of a certain grouping of organs, just as 'Charles's Wain' is our name for a certain grouping of stars. The 'whole,' be it bird or constellation, is nothing but our vision, nothing but an effect on our sensorium when a lot of things act on it together. It is not realized by any organ or any star, or experienced apart from the consciousness of an onlooker.[49] In the physical world taken by itself there *is* thus no 'all,' there are only the 'eaches'—at least that is the 'scientific' view.

In the mental world, on the contrary, wholes do in point of fact realize themselves *per se*. The meaning of the whole sentence is just as much a real experience as the feeling of each word is; the absolute's experience *is* for itself, as much as yours is for yourself or mine for myself. So the feather-and-bird analogy won't work unless you make the absolute into a distinct sort of mental agent with a vision produced in it *by* our several minds analogous to the 'bird'-vision which the feathers, beak, etc., produce *in* those same minds. The 'whole,' which is *its* experience, would then be its unifying reaction on our experiences, and not those very experiences self-combined. Such a view as this would go with theism, for the theistic God is a separate being; but it would not go with pantheistic idealism, the very essence of which is to insist that we are literally *parts* of God, and he only ourselves in our totality—the word 'ourselves' here standing of course for all the universe's finite facts.

I am dragging you into depths unsuitable, I fear, for a rapid lecture. Such difficulties as these have to be teased out with a needle, so to speak, and lecturers should take only bird's-eye views. The practical upshot of the matter, however, so far as I am concerned, is this, that if I had been lecturing on the absolute a very few years ago, I should unhesitatingly have urged these difficulties, and developed them at still greater length, to show that the hypothesis of the absolute was not only non-coercive from the logical point of view, but self-contradictory as well, its notion that parts and whole are only two names for the same thing not bearing critical scrutiny. If you stick to purely physical terms like stars, there *is* no whole. If you call the whole mental, then the so-called whole, instead of being one fact with

---

[49] I abstract from the consciousness attached to the whole itself, if such consciousness be there.

the parts, appears rather as the integral reaction on those parts of an independent higher witness, such as the theistic God is supposed to be.

So long as this was the state of my own mind, I could accept the notion of self-compounding in the supernal spheres of experience no more easily than in that chapter on mind-dust I had accepted it in the lower spheres. I found myself compelled, therefore, to call the absolute impossible; and the untrammelled freedom with which pantheistic or monistic idealists stepped over the logical barriers which Lotze and others had set down long before I had—I had done little more than quote these previous critics in my chapter—surprised me not a little, and made me, I have to confess, both resentful and envious. Envious because in the bottom of my heart I wanted the same freedom myself, for motives which I shall develop later; and resentful because my absolutist friends seemed to me to be stealing the privilege of blowing both hot and cold. To establish their absolute they used an intellectualist type of logic which they disregarded when employed against it. It seemed to me that they ought at least to have mentioned the objections that had stopped me so completely. I had yielded to them against my 'will to believe,' out of pure logical scrupulosity. They, professing to loathe the will to believe and to follow purest rationality, had simply ignored them. The method was easy, but hardly to be called candid. Fechner indeed was candid enough, for he had never thought of the objections, but later writers, like Royce, who should presumably have heard them, had passed them by in silence. I felt as if these philosophers were granting their will to believe in monism too easy a license. My own conscience would permit me no such license.

So much for the personal confession by which you have allowed me to introduce the subject. Let us now consider it more objectively.

The fundamental difficulty I have found is the number of contradictions which idealistic monists seem to disregard. In the first place they attribute to all existence a mental or experiential character, but I find their simultaneous belief that the higher and the lower in the universe are entitatively identical, incompatible with this character. Incompatible in consequence of the generally accepted doctrine that, whether Berkeley were right or not in saying of material existence that its *esse* is *sentiri,* it is undoubtedly right to say of *mental* existence that its *esse* is *sentiri* or *experiri.* If I feel pain, it is just pain that I feel, however I may have come by the feeling. No one pretends that pain as such only appears like pain, but in itself is different, for to be as a mental experience *is* only to appear to some one.

The idealists in question ought then to do one of two things, but they do neither. They ought either to refute the notion that as mental states appear, so they are; or, still keeping that notion, they ought to admit a distinct agent of unification to do the work of the all-knower, just as our respective souls or selves in popular philosophy do the work of partial knowers. Otherwise it is like a joint-stock company all shareholders and no treasurer or director. If our finite minds formed a billion facts, then its mind, knowing our billion, would make a universe composed of a billion and one facts. But transcendental idealism is quite as unfriendly to active principles called souls as physiological psychology is, Kant having, as it thinks, definitively demolished them. And altho some disciples speak of the transcendental ego of apperception (which they celebrate as Kant's most precious legacy to posterity) as if it were a combining agent, the drift of monistic authority is certainly in the direction of treating it as only an all-witness, whose field of vision we finite witnesses do not cause, but constitute rather. We are the letters, it is the alphabet; we are the features, it is the face; not indeed as if either alphabet or face were something additional to the letters or the features, but rather as if it were only another name for the very letters or features themselves. The all-form assuredly differs from the each-form, but the *matter* is the same in both, and the each-form only an unaccountable appearance.

But this, as you see, contradicts the other idealist principle, of a mental fact being just what it appears to be. If their forms of appearance are so different, the all and the eaches cannot be identical.

The way out (unless, indeed, we are willing to discard the logic of identity altogether) would seem to be frankly to write down the all and the eaches as two distinct orders of witness, each minor witness being aware of its own 'content' solely, while the greater witness knows the minor witnesses, knows their whole content pooled together, knows their relations to one another, and knows of just how much each one of them is ignorant.

The two types of witnessing are here palpably non-identical. We get a pluralism, not a monism, out of them. In my psychology-chapter I had resorted openly to such pluralism, treating each total field of consciousness as a distinct entity, and maintaining that the higher fields merely supersede the lower functionally by knowing more about the same objects.

The monists themselves writhe like worms on the hook to escape pluralistic or at least dualistic language, but they cannot escape it. They speak of the eternal and the temporal 'points of view'; of the universe in its infinite 'aspect' or in its finite 'capacity'; they say that '*quâ* absolute' it is one thing, '*quâ* relative' another; they contrast its 'truth' with its 'appearances'; they distinguish the total from the partial way of 'taking' it, etc.; but they forget that, on idealistic principles, to make such distinctions is tantamount to making different beings, or at any rate that varying points of view, aspects, appearances, ways of taking, and the like, are meaningless phrases unless we suppose outside of the unchanging content of reality a diversity of witnesses who experience or take it variously, the absolute mind being just the witness that takes it most completely.

For consider the matter one moment longer, if you can. Ask what this notion implies, of appearing differently from different points of view. If there be no outside witness, a thing can appear only to itself, the eaches or parts to their several selves temporally, the all or whole to itself eternally. Different 'selves' thus break out inside of what the absolutist insists to be intrinsically one fact. But how can what is *actually* one be *effectively* so many? Put your witnesses anywhere, whether outside or inside of what is witnessed, in the last resort your witnesses must on idealistic principles be distinct, for what is witnessed is different.

I fear that I am expressing myself with terrible obscurity—some of you, I know, are groaning over the logic-chopping. Be a pluralist or be a monist, you say, for heaven's sake, no matter which, so long as you stop arguing. It reminds one of Chesterton's epigram that the only thing that ever drives human beings insane is logic. But whether I be sane or insane, you cannot fail, even tho you be transcendentalists yourselves, to recognize to some degree by my trouble the difficulties that beset monistic idealism. What boots it to call the parts and the whole the same body of experience, when in the same breath you have to say that the all 'as such' means one sort of experience and each part 'as such' means another?

Difficulties, then, so far, but no stable solution as yet, for I have been talking only critically. You will probably be relieved to hear, then, that having rounded this corner, I shall begin to consider what may be the possibilities of getting farther.

To clear the path, I beg you first to note one point. What has so troubled my logical conscience is not so much the absolute by itself as the whole class of suppositions of which it is the supreme example, collective experiences namely, claiming identity with their constituent parts, yet experiencing things quite differently from these latter. If *any* such collective experience can be, then of course, so far as the mere logic of the case goes, the absolute may be. In a previous lecture I have talked against the absolute from other points of view. In this lecture I have meant merely to take it as the example most prominent at Oxford of the thing which has given me such logical perplexity. I don't logically see how a collective experience of any grade whatever can be treated as logically identical with a lot of distributive experiences. They form two different concepts. The absolute happens to be the only collective experience concerning which Oxford idealists have urged the identity, so I took it as my prerogative instance. But Fechner's earth-soul, or any stage of being below or above that, would have served my purpose just as well: the same logical objection applies to these collective experiences as to the absolute.

So much, then, in order that you may not be confused about my strategical objective. The real point to defend against the logic that I have used is the identity of the collective and distributive anyhow, not the particular example of such identity known as the absolute.

So now for the directer question. Shall we say that every complex mental fact is a separate psychic entity succeeding upon a lot of other psychic entities which are erroneously called its parts, and superseding them in function, but not literally being composed of them? This was the course I took in my psychology; and if followed in theology, we should have to deny the absolute as usually conceived, and replace it by the 'God' of theism. We should also have to deny Fechner's 'earth-soul' and all other superhuman collections of experience of every grade, so far at least as these are held to be compounded of our simpler souls in the way which Fechner believed in; and we should have to make all these denials in the name of the incorruptible logic of self-identity, teaching us that to call a thing and its other the same is to commit the crime of self-contradiction.

But if we realize the whole philosophic situation thus produced, we see that it is almost intolerable. Loyal to the logical kind of rationality, it is disloyal to every other kind. It makes the universe discontinuous. These fields of experience that replace each other so punctually, each knowing the same matter, but in ever-widening contexts, from simplest feeling up to absolute knowledge, *can* they have no *being* in common when their cognitive function is so manifestly common? The regular succession of them is on such terms an unintelligible miracle. If you reply that their common *object* is of itself enough to make the many witnesses continuous, the same implacable logic follows you—how *can* one and the same object appear so variously? Its diverse appearances break it into a plurality; and our world of objects then falls into discontinuous pieces quite as much as did our world of subjects. The resultant irrationality is really intolerable.

I said awhile ago that I was envious of Fechner and the other pantheists because I myself wanted the same freedom that I saw them unscrupulously enjoying, of letting mental fields compound themselves and so make the universe more continuous, but that my conscience held me prisoner. In my heart of hearts, however, I knew that my situation was absurd and could be only provisional. That secret of a continuous life which the universe knows by heart and acts on every instant cannot be a contradiction incarnate. If logic says it is one, so much the worse for logic. Logic being the lesser thing, the static incomplete abstraction, must succumb to reality, not reality to logic. Our intelligence cannot wall itself up alive, like a pupa in its chrysalis. It must at any cost keep on speaking terms with the universe that engendered it. Fechner, Royce, and Hegel seem on the truer path. Fechner has never heard of logic's veto, Royce hears the voice but cannily ignores the utterances, Hegel hears them but to spurn them— and all go on their way rejoicing. Shall we alone obey the veto?

Sincerely, and patiently as I could, I struggled with the problem for years, covering hundreds of sheets of paper with notes and memoranda and discussions with myself over the difficulty. How can many consciousnesses be at the same time one consciousness? How can one and the same identical fact experience itself so diversely? The struggle was vain; I found myself in an *impasse*. I saw that I must either forswear that 'psychology without a soul' to which my whole psychological and kantian education had committed me,—I must, in short, bring back distinct spiritual agents to know the mental states, now singly and now in combination, in a word bring back scholasticism and common sense—or else I must squarely confess the solution of the problem impossible, and then either give up my intellectualistic logic, the logic of identity, and adopt some higher (or lower) form of rationality, or, finally, face the fact that life is logically irrational.

Sincerely, this is the actual trilemma that confronts every one of us. Those of you who are scholastic-minded, or simply common-sense minded, will smile at the elaborate groans of my parturient mountain resulting in nothing but this mouse. Accept the spiritual agents, for heaven's sake, you will say, and leave off your ridiculous pedantry. Let but our 'souls' combine our sensations by their intellectual faculties, and let but 'God' replace the pantheistic world-soul, and your wheels will go round again—you will enjoy both life and logic together.

This solution is obvious and I know that many of you will adopt it. It is comfortable, and all our habits of speech support it. Yet it is not for idle or fantastical reasons that the notion of the substantial soul, so freely used by common men and the more popular philosophies, has fallen upon such evil days, and has no prestige in the eyes of critical thinkers. It only shares the fate of other unrepresentable substances and principles. They are without exception all so barren that to sincere inquirers they appear as little more than names masquerading—Wo die begriffe fehlen da stellt ein wort zur rechten zeit sich ein. You see no deeper into the fact that a hundred sensations get compounded or known together by thinking that a 'soul' does the compounding than you see into a man's living eighty years by thinking of him as an octogenarian, or into our having five fingers by calling us pentadactyls. Souls have worn out both themselves and their welcome, that is the plain truth. Philosophy ought to get the manifolds of experience unified on principles less empty. Like the word 'cause,' the word 'soul' is but a theoretic stop-gap—it marks a place and claims it for a future explanation to occupy.

This being our post-humian and post-kantian state of mind, I will ask your permission to leave the soul wholly out of the present discussion and to consider only the residual dilemma. Some day, indeed, souls may get their innings again in philosophy—I am quite ready to admit that possibility—they form a category of thought too natural to the human mind to expire without prolonged resistance. But if the belief in the soul ever does come to life after the many funeral-discourses which humian and kantian criticism have preached over it, I am sure it will be only when some one has found in the term a pragmatic significance that has hitherto eluded observation. When that champion speaks, as he well may speak some day, it will be time to consider souls more seriously.

Let us leave out the soul, then, and confront what I just called the residual dilemma. Can we, on the one hand, give up the logic of identity?—can we, on the other, believe human experience to be fundamentally irrational? Neither is easy, yet it would seem that we must do one or the other.

Few philosophers have had the frankness fairly to admit the necessity of choosing between the 'horns' offered. Reality must be rational, they have said, and since the ordinary intellectualist logic is the only usual test of rationality, reality and logic must agree 'somehow.' Hegel was the first non-mystical writer to face the dilemma squarely and throw away the ordinary logic, saving a pseudo-rationality for the universe by inventing the higher logic of the 'dialectic process.' Bradley holds to the intellectualist logic, and by dint of it convicts the human universe of being irrationality incarnate. But what must be and can be, is, he says; there must and can be relief from *that* irrationality; and the absolute must already have got the relief in secret ways of its own, impossible for us to guess at. *We* of course get no relief, so Bradley's is a rather ascetic doctrine. Royce and Taylor accept similar solutions, only they emphasize the irrationality of our finite universe less than Bradley does; and Royce in particular, being unusually 'thick' for an idealist, tries to bring the absolute's secret forms of relief more sympathetically home to our imagination.

Well, what must we do in this tragic predicament? For my own part, I have finally found myself compelled to *give up the logic,* fairly, squarely, and irrevocably. It has an imperishable use in human life, but that use is not to make us theoretically acquainted with the essential nature of reality—just what it is I can perhaps suggest to you a little later. Reality, life, experience, concreteness, immediacy, use what word you will, exceeds our logic, overflows and surrounds it. If you like to employ words eulogistically, as most men do, and so encourage confusion, you may say that reality obeys a higher logic, or enjoys a higher rationality. But I think that even eulogistic words should be used rather to distinguish than to commingle meanings, so I prefer bluntly to call reality if not irrational then at least non-rational in its constitution,—and by reality here I mean reality where things *happen,* all temporal reality without exception. I myself find no good warrant for even suspecting the existence of any reality of a higher denomination than that distributed and strung-along and flowing sort of reality which we finite beings swim in. That is the sort of reality given us, and that is the sort with which logic is so incommensurable. If there be any higher sort of reality—the 'absolute,' for example— that sort, by the confession of those who believe in it, is still less amenable to ordinary logic; it transcends logic and is therefore still less rational in the intellectualist sense, so it cannot help us to save our logic as an adequate definer and confiner of existence.

These sayings will sound queer and dark, probably they will sound quite wild or childish in the absence of explanatory comment. Only the persuasion that I soon can explain them, if not satisfactorily to all of you, at least intelligibly, emboldens me to state them thus baldly as a sort of programme. Please take them as a thesis, therefore, to be defended by later pleading.

I told you that I had long and sincerely wrestled with the dilemma. I have now to confess (and this will probably re-animate your interest) that I should not now be emancipated, not now subordinate logic with so very light a heart, or throw it out of the deeper regions of philosophy to take its rightful and respectable place in the world of simple human practice, if I had not been influenced by a comparatively young and very original french writer, Professor Henri Bergson. Reading his works is what has made be bold. If I had not read Bergson, I should probably still be blackening endless pages of paper privately, in the hope of making ends meet that were never meant to meet, and trying to discover some mode of conceiving the behavior of reality which should leave no discrepancy between it and the accepted laws of the logic of identity. It is certain, at any rate, that without the confidence which being able to lean on Bergson's authority gives me I should never have ventured to urge these particular views of mine upon this ultra-critical audience.

I must therefore, in order to make my own views more intelligible, give some preliminary account of the bergsonian philosophy. But here, as in Fechner's case, I must confine myself only to the features that are essential to the present purpose, and not entangle you in collateral details, however interesting otherwise. For our present purpose, then, the essential contribution of Bergson to philosophy is his criticism of intellectualism. In my opinion he has killed intellectualism definitively and without hope of recovery. I don't see how it can ever revive again in its ancient platonizing rôle of claiming to be the most authentic, intimate, and exhaustive definer of the nature of reality. Others, as Kant for example, have denied intellectualism's pretensions to define reality *an sich* or in its absolute capacity; but Kant still leaves it laying down laws—and laws from which there is no appeal— to all our human experience; while what Bergson denies is that its methods give any adequate account of this human experience in its very finiteness. Just how Bergson accomplishes all this I must try to tell in my imperfect way in the next lecture; but since I have already used the words 'logic,' 'logic of identity,' 'intellectualistic logic,' and 'intellectualism' so often, and sometimes used them as if they required no particular explanation, it will be wise at this point to say at greater length than heretofore in what sense I take these terms when I claim that Bergson has refuted their pretension to decide what reality can or cannot be. Just what I mean by intellectualism is therefore what I shall try to give a fuller idea of during the remainder of this present hour.

In recent controversies some participants have shown resentment at being classed as intellectualists. I mean to use the word disparagingly, but shall be sorry if it works offence. Intellectualism has its source in the faculty which gives us our chief superiority to the brutes, our power, namely, of translating the crude flux of our merely feeling-experience into a conceptual order. An immediate experience, as yet unnamed or classed, is a mere *that* that we undergo, a thing that asks, '*What* am I?' When we name and class it, we say for the first time what it is, and all these whats are abstract names or concepts. Each concept means a particular *kind* of thing, and as things seem once for all to have been created in kinds, a far more efficient handling of a given bit of experience begins as soon as we have classed the various parts of it. Once classed, a thing can be treated by the law of its class, and the advantages are endless. Both theoretically and practically this power of framing abstract concepts is one of the sublimest of our human prerogatives. We come back into the concrete from our journey into these abstractions, with an increase both of vision and of power. It is no wonder that earlier thinkers, forgetting that concepts are only man-made extracts from the temporal flux, should have ended by treating them as a superior type of being, bright, changeless, true, divine, and utterly opposed in nature to the turbid, restless lower world. The latter then appears as but their corruption and falsification.

Intellectualism in the vicious sense began when Socrates and Plato taught that what a thing really is, is told us by its *definition*. Ever since Socrates we have been taught that reality consists of essences, not of appearances, and that the essences of things are known whenever we know their definitions. So first we identify the thing with a concept and then we identify the concept with a definition, and only then, inasmuch as the thing *is* whatever the definition expresses, are we sure of apprehending the real essence of it or the full truth about it.

So far no harm is done. The misuse of concepts begins with the habit of employing them privately as well as positively, using them not merely to assign properties to things, but to deny the very properties with which the things sensibly present themselves. Logic can extract all its possible consequences from any definition, and the logician who is *unerbittlich consequent* is often tempted, when he cannot extract a certain property from a definition, to deny that the concrete object to which the definition applies can possibly possess that property. The definition that fails to yield it must exclude or negate it. This is Hegel's regular method of establishing his system.

It is but the old story, of a useful practice first becoming a method, then a habit, and finally a tyranny that defeats the end it was used for. Concepts, first employed to make things intelligible, are clung to even when they make them unintelligible. Thus it comes that when once you have conceived things as 'independent,' you must proceed to deny the possibility of any connexion whatever among them, because the notion of connexion is not contained in the definition of independence. For a like reason you must deny any possible forms or modes of unity among things which you have begun by defining as a 'many.' We have cast a glance at Hegel's and Bradley's use of this sort of reasoning, and you will remember Sigwart's epigram that according to it a horseman can never in his life go on foot, or a photographer ever do anything but photograph.

The classic extreme in this direction is the denial of the possibility of change, and the consequent branding of the world of change as unreal, by certain philosophers. The definition of A is changeless, so is the definition of B. The one definition cannot change into the other, so the notion that a concrete thing A should change into another concrete thing B is made out to be contrary to reason. In Mr. Bradley's difficulty in seeing how sugar can be sweet intellectualism outstrips itself and becomes openly a sort of verbalism. Sugar is just sugar and sweet is just sweet; neither is the other; nor can the word 'is' ever be understood to join any subject to its predicate rationally. Nothing 'between' things can connect them, for 'between' is just that third thing, 'between,' and would need itself to be connected to the first and second things by two still finer betweens, and so on ad infinitum.

The particular intellectualistic difficulty that had held my own thought so long in a vise was, as we have seen at such tedious length, the impossibility of understanding how 'your' experience and 'mine,' which 'as such' are defined as not conscious of each other, can nevertheless at the same time be members of a world-experience defined expressly as having all its parts co-conscious, or known together. The definitions are contradictory, so the things defined can in no way be united. You see how unintelligible intellectualism here seems to make the world of our most accomplished philosophers. Neither as they use it nor as we use it does it do anything but make nature look irrational and seem impossible.

In my next lecture, using Bergson as my principal topic, I shall enter into more concrete details and try, by giving up intellectualism frankly, to make, if not the world, at least my own general thesis, less unintelligible.

BERGSON AND HIS CRITIQUE
OF INTELLECTUALISM*

I gave you a very stiff lecture last time, and I fear that this one can be little less so. The best way of entering into it will be to begin immediately with Bergson's philosophy, since I told you that that was what had led me personally to renounce the intellectualistic method and the current notion that logic is an adequate measure of what can or cannot be.

Professor Henri Bergson is a young man, comparatively, as influential philosophers go, having been born at Paris in 1859. His career has been the perfectly routine one of a successful french professor. Entering the école normale supérieure at the age of twenty-two, he spent the next seventeen years teaching at *lycées,* provincial or parisian, until his fortieth year, when he was made professor at the said école normale. Since 1900 he has been professor at the Collège de France, and member of the Institute since 1900.

So far as the outward facts go, Bergson's career has then been commonplace to the utmost. Neither one of Taine's famous principles of explanation of great men, *the race, the environment, or the moment,* no, nor all three together, will explain that peculiar way of looking at things that constitutes his mental individuality. Originality in men dates from nothing previous, other things date from it, rather. I have

* From: P.U., 225–273.

to confess that Bergson's originality is so profuse that many of his ideas baffle me entirely. I doubt whether any one understands him all over, so to speak; and I am sure that he would himself be the first to see that this must be, and to confess that things which he himself has not yet thought out clearly, had yet to be mentioned and have a tentative place assigned them in his philosophy. Many of us are profusely original, in that no man can understand us—violently peculiar ways of looking at things are no great rarity. The rarity is when great peculiarity of vision is allied with great lucidity and unusual command of all the classic expository apparatus. Bergson's resources in the way of erudition are remarkable, and in the way of expression they are simply phenomenal. This is why in France, where *l'art de bien dire* counts for so much and is so sure of appreciation, he has immediately taken so eminent a place in public esteem. Old-fashioned professors, whom his ideas quite fail to satisfy, nevertheless speak of his talent almost with bated breath, while the youngsters flock to him as to a master.

If anything can make hard things easy to follow, it is a style like Bergson's. A 'straightforward' style, an american reviewer lately called it; failing to see that such straightforwardness means a flexibility of verbal resource that follows the thought without a crease or wrinkle, as elastic silk underclothing follows the movements of one's body. The lucidity of Bergson's way of putting things is what all readers are first struck by. It seduces you and bribes you in advance to become his disciple. It is a miracle, and he a real magician.

M. Bergson, if I am rightly informed, came into philosophy through the gateway of mathematics. The old antinomies of the infinite were, I imagine, the irritant that first woke his faculties from their dogmatic slumber. You all remember Zeno's famous paradox, or sophism, as many of our logic books still call it, of Achilles and the tortoise. Give that reptile ever so small an advance and the swift runner Achilles can never overtake him, much less get ahead of him; for if space and time are infinitely divisible (as our intellects tell us they must be), by the time Achilles reaches the tortoise's starting-point, the tortoise has already got ahead of *that* starting-point, and so on *ad infinitum*, the interval between the pursuer and the pursued growing endlessly minuter, but never becoming wholly obliterated. The common way of showing up the sophism here is by pointing out the ambiguity of the expression 'never can overtake.' What the word 'never' falsely suggests, it is said, is an infinite duration of time; what it really means is the inexhaustible number of the steps of which the overtaking must consist. But if these steps are infinitely short, a finite time will suffice for them; and in point of fact they do rapidly converge, whatever be the original interval or the contrasted speeds, toward infinitesimal shortness. This proportionality of the shortness of the times to that of the spaces required frees us, it is claimed, from the sophism which the word 'never' suggests.

But this criticism misses Zeno's point entirely. Zeno would have been perfectly willing to grant that if the tortoise can be overtaken at all, he can be overtaken in (say) twenty seconds, but he would still have insisted that he can't be overtaken at all. Leave Achilles and the tortoise out of the account altogether, he would have said—they complicate the case unnecessarily. Take any single process of change whatever, take the twenty seconds themselves elapsing. If time be infinitely divisible, and it must be so on intellectualist principles, they simply cannot elapse, their end cannot be reached; for no matter how much of them has already elapsed, before the remainder, however minute, can have wholly elapsed, the earlier half of it must first have elapsed. And this ever re-arising need of making the earlier half elapse *first* leaves time with always something to do *before* the last thing is done, so that the last thing never gets done. Expressed in bare numbers, it is like the convergent series ½ plus ¼ plus ⅛ . . . , of which the limit is one. But this limit, simply because it is a limit, stands outside the series, the value of which approaches it indefinitely but never touches it. If in the natural world there were no other way of getting things save by such successive addition of their logically involved fractions, no complete units or whole things would ever come into being, for the fractions' sum would always leave a remainder. But in point of fact nature does n't make eggs by making first half an egg, then a quarter, then an eighth, etc., and adding them together. She either makes a whole egg at once or none at all, and so of all her other units. It is only in the sphere of change, then, where one phase of a thing must needs come into being before another phase can come that Zeno's paradox gives trouble.

And it gives trouble then only if the succession of steps of change be infinitely divisible. If a bottle had to be emptied by an infinite number of successive decrements, it is mathematically impossible that the emptying should ever positively terminate. In point of fact, however, bottles and coffee-pots empty themselves by a finite number of decrements, each of definite amount. Either a whole drop emerges or nothing emerges from the spout. If all change went thus drop-wise, so to speak, if real time sprouted or grew by units of duration of determinate amount, just as our perceptions of it grow by pulses, there would be no zenonian paradoxes or kantian antinomies to trouble us. All our sensible experiences, as we get them immediately, do thus change by discrete pulses of perception, each of which keeps us saying 'more, more, more,' or 'less, less, less,' as the definite increments or diminutions make themselves felt. The discreteness is still more obvious when, instead of old things changing, they cease, or when altogether new things come. Fechner's term of the 'threshold,' which has played such a part in the psychology of perception, is only one way of naming the quantitative discreteness in the change of all our sensible experiences. They come to us in drops. Time itself comes in drops.

Our ideal decomposition of the drops which are all that we feel into still finer fractions is but an incident in that great transformation of the perceptual order into a conceptual order of which I spoke in my last lecture. It is made in the interest of our rationalizing intellect solely. The times directly *felt* in the experiences of living subjects have originally no common measure. Let a lump of sugar melt in a glass, to use one of M. Bergson's instances. We feel the time to be long while waiting for the process to end, but who knows how long or how short it feels to the sugar? All *felt* times coexist and overlap or compenetrate each other thus vaguely, but the artifice of plotting them on a common scale helps us to reduce their aboriginal confusion, and it helps us still more to plot, against the same scale, the successive possible steps into which nature's various changes may be resolved, either sensibly or conceivably. We thus straighten out the aboriginal privacy and vagueness, and can date things publicly, as it were, and by each other. The notion of one objective and 'evenly flowing' time, cut into numbered instants, applies itself as a common measure to all the steps and phases, no matter how many, into which we cut the processes of nature. They are now definitely contemporary, or later or earlier one than another, and we can handle them mathematically, as we say, and far better, practically as well as theoretically, for having thus correlated them one to one with each other on the common schematic or conceptual time-scale.

Motion, to take a good example, is originally a turbid sensation, of which the native shape is perhaps best preserved in the phenomenon of vertigo. In vertigo we feel that movement *is,* and is more or less violent or rapid, more or less in this direction or that, more or less alarming or sickening. But a man subject to vertigo may gradually learn to co-ordinate his felt motion with his real position and that of other things, and intellectualize it enough to succeed at last in walking without staggering. The mathematical mind similarly organizes motion in its way, putting it into a logical definition: motion is now conceived as 'the occupancy of serially successive points of space at serially successive instants of time.' With such a definition we escape wholly from the turbid privacy of sense. But do we not also escape from sense-reality altogether? Whatever motion really may be, it surely is not static; but the definition we have gained is of the absolutely static. It gives a set of one-to-one relations between space-points and time-points, which relations themselves are as fixed as the points are. It gives *positions* assignable ad infinitum, but how the body gets from one position to another it omits to mention. The body gets there by moving, of course; but the conceived positions, however numerously multiplied, contain no element of movement, so Zeno, using nothing but them in his discussion, has no alternative but to say that our intellect repudiates motion as a non-reality. Intellectualism here does what I said it does—it makes experience less instead of more intelligible.

We of course need a stable scheme of concepts, stably related with one another, to lay hold of our experiences and to co-ordinate them withal. When an experience comes with sufficient saliency to stand out, we keep the thought of it for future use, and store it in our conceptual system. What does not of itself stand out, we learn to *cut* out; so the system grows completer, and new reality, as it comes, gets named after and conceptually strung upon this or that element of it which we have already established. The immutability of such an abstract system is its great practical merit; the same identical terms and relations in it can always be recovered and referred to—change itself is just such an unalterable concept. But all these abstract concepts are but as flowers gathered, they are only moments dipped out from the stream of time, snap-shots taken, as by a kinetoscopic camera, at a life that in its original coming is continuous. Useful as they are as samples of the garden, or to re-enter the stream with, or to insert in our revolving lantern, they have no value but these practical values. You cannot explain by them what makes any single phenomenon be or go—you merely dot out the path of appearances which it traverses. For you cannot make continuous being out of discontinuities, and your concepts are discontinuous. The stages into which you analyze a change are *states,* the change itself goes on between them. It lies along their intervals, inhabits what your definition fails to gather up, and thus eludes conceptual explanation altogether.

'When the mathematician,' Bergson writes,* 'calculates the state of a system at the end of a time *t,* nothing need prevent him from supposing that betweenwhiles the universe vanishes, in order suddenly to appear again at the due moment in the new configuration. It is only the *t*-th moment that counts—that which flows throughout the intervals, namely real time, plays no part in his calculation. . . . In short, the world on which the mathematician operates is a world which dies and is born anew at every instant, like the world which Descartes thought of when he spoke of a continued creation.' To know adequately what really *happens* we ought, Bergson insists, to see into the intervals, but the mathematician sees only their extremities. He fixes only a few results, he dots a curve and then interpolates, he substitutes a tracing for a reality.

* *Creative Evolution* (New York, Modern Library, 1944), p. 26. [J. J. McD.]

This being so undeniably the case, the history of the way in which philosophy has dealt with it is curious. The ruling tradition in philosophy has always been the platonic and aristotelian belief that fixity is a nobler and worthier thing than change. Reality must be one and unalterable. Concepts, being themselves fixities, agree best with this fixed nature of truth, so that for any knowledge of ours to be quite true it must be knowledge by universal concepts rather than by particular experiences, for these notoriously are mutable and corruptible. This is the tradition known as rationalism in philosophy, and what I have called intellectualism is only the extreme application of it. In spite of sceptics and empiricists, in spite of Protagoras, Hume, and James Mill, rationalism has never been seriously questioned, for its sharpest critics have always had a tender place in their hearts for it, and have obeyed some of its mandates. They have not been consistent; they have played fast and loose with the enemy; and Bergson alone has been radical.

To show what I mean by this, let me contrast his procedure with that of some of the transcendentalist philosophers whom I have lately mentioned. Coming after Kant, these pique themselves on being 'critical,' on building in fact upon Kant's 'critique' of pure reason. What that critique professed to establish was this, that concepts do not apprehend reality, but only such appearances as our senses feed out to them. They give immutable intellectual forms to these appearances, it is true, but the reality *an sich* from which in ultimate resort the sense-appearances have to come remains forever unintelligible to our intellect. Take motion, for example. Sensibly, motion comes in drops, waves, or pulses; either some actual amount of it, or none, being apprehended. This amount is the datum or *gabe* which reality feeds out to our intellectual faculty; but our intellect makes of it a task or *aufgabe*—this pun is one of the most memorable of Kant's formulas —and insists that in every pulse of it an infinite number of successive minor pulses shall be ascertainable. These minor pulses *we* can indeed *go on* to ascertain or to compute indefinitely if we have patience; but it would contradict the definition of an infinite number to suppose the endless series of them to have actually counted *themselves* out piecemeal. Zeno made this manifest; so the infinity which our intellect requires of the sense-datum is thus a future and potential rather than a past and actual infinity of structure. The datum after it has made itself must be decompos*able* ad infinitum by our conception, but of the steps by which that structure actually got composed we know nothing. Our intellect casts, in short, no ray of light on the processes by which experiences *get made*.

Kant's monistic successors have in general found the data of immediate experience even more self-contradictory, when intellectually treated, than Kant did. Not only the character of infinity involved in the relation of various empirical data to their 'conditions,' but the very notion that empirical things should be related to one another at all, has seemed to them, when the intellectualistic fit was upon them, full of paradox and contradiction. We saw in a former lecture numerous instances of this from Hegel, Bradley, Royce, and others. We saw also where the solution of such an intolerable state of things was sought for by these authors. Whereas Kant had placed it outside of and *before* our experience, in the *dinge an sich* which are the causes of the latter, his monistic successors all look for it either *after* experience, as its absolute completion, or else consider it to be even now implicit within experience as its ideal signification. Kant and his successors look, in short, in diametrically opposite directions. Do not be misled by Kant's admission of theism into his system. His God is the ordinary dualistic God of Christianity, to whom his philosophy simply opens the door; he has nothing whatsoever in common with the 'absolute spirit' set up by his successors. So far as this absolute spirit is logically derived from Kant, it is not from his God, but from entirely different elements of his philosophy. First from his notion that an unconditioned totality of the conditions of any experience must be assignable; and then from his other notion that the presence of some witness, or ego of apperception, is the most universal of all the conditions in question. The post-kantians make of the witness-condition what is called a concrete universal, an individualized all-witness or world-self, which shall imply in its rational constitution each and all of the other conditions put together, and therefore necessitate each and all of the conditioned experiences.

Abridgments like this of other men's opinions are very unsatisfactory, they always work injustice; but in this case those of you who are familiar with the literature will see immediately what I have in mind; and to the others, if there be any here, it will suffice to say that what I am trying so pedantically to point out is only the fact that monistic idealists after Kant have invariably sought relief from the supposed contradictions of our world of sense by looking forward toward an *ens rationis* conceived as its integration or logical completion, while he looked backward toward non-rational *dinge an sich* conceived as its cause. Pluralistic empiricists, on the other hand, have remained in the world of sense, either naïvely and because they overlooked the intellectualistic contradictions, or because, not able to ignore them, they thought they could refute them by a superior use of the same intellectualistic logic. Thus it is that John Mill pretends to refute the Achilles-tortoise fallacy.

The important point to notice here is the intellectualist logic. Both sides treat it as authoritative, but they do so capriciously: the absolutists smashing the world of sense by its means, the empiricists smashing the absolute—for the absolute, they say, is the quintessence of all logical contradictions. Neither side attains consistency. The Hegelians have to invoke a higher logic to supersede the purely destructive efforts of their first logic. The empiricists use their logic against the absolute, but refuse to use it against finite experience. Each party uses it or drops it to suit the vision it has faith in, but neither impugns in principle its general theoretic authority.

Bergson alone challenges its theoretic authority in principle. He alone denies that mere conceptual logic can tell us what is impossible or possible in the world of being or fact; and he does so for reasons which at the same time that they rule logic out from lordship over the whole of life, establish a vast and definite sphere of influence where its sovereignty is indisputable. Bergson's own text, felicitous as it is, is too intricate for quotation, so I must use my own inferior words in explaining what I mean by saying this.

In the first place, logic, giving primarily the relations between concepts as such, and the relations between natural facts only secondarily or so far as the facts have been already identified with concepts and defined by them, must of course stand or fall with the conceptual method. But the conceptual method is a transformation which the flux of life undergoes at our hands in the interests of practice essentially and only subordinately in the interests of theory. We live forward, we understand backward, said a danish writer; and to understand life by concepts is to arrest its movement, cutting it up into bits as if with scissors, and immobilizing these in our logical herbarium where, comparing them as dried specimens, we can ascertain which of them statically includes or excludes which other. This treatment supposes life to have already accomplished itself, for the concepts, being so many views taken after the fact, are retrospective and post mortem. Nevertheless we can draw conclusions from them and project them into the future. We cannot learn from them how life made itself go, or how it will make itself go; but, on the supposition that its ways of making itself go are unchanging, we can calculate what positions of imagined arrest it will exhibit hereafter under given conditions. We can compute, for instance, at what point Achilles will be, and where the tortoise will be, at the end of the twentieth minute. Achilles may then be at a point far ahead; but the full detail of how he will have managed practically to get there our logic never gives us—we have seen, indeed, that it finds that its results contradict the facts of nature. The computations which the other sciences make differ in no respect from those of mathematics. The concepts used are all of them dots through which, by interpolation or extrapolation, curves are drawn, while along the curves other dots are found as consequences. The latest refinements of logic dispense with the curves altogether, and deal solely with the dots and their correspondences each to each in various series. The authors of these recent improvements tell us expressly that their aim is to abolish the last vestiges of intuition, *videlicet* of concrete reality, from the field of reasoning, which then will operate literally on mental dots or bare abstract units of discourse, and on the ways in which they may be strung in naked series.

This is all very esoteric, and my own understanding of it is most likely misunderstanding. So I speak here only by way of brief reminder to those who know. For the rest of us it is enough to recognize this fact, that altho by means of concepts cut out from the sensible flux of the past, we can re-descend upon the future flux and, making another cut, say what particular thing is likely to be found there; and that altho in this sense concepts give us knowledge, and may be said to have some theoretic value (especially when the particular thing foretold is one in which we take no present practical interest); yet in the deeper sense of giving *insight* they have no theoretic value, for they quite fail to connect us with the inner life of the flux, or with the causes that govern its direction. Instead of being interpreters of reality, concepts negate the inwardness of reality altogether. They make the whole notion of a causal influence between finite things incomprehensible. No real activities and indeed no real connexions of any kind can obtain if we follow the conceptual logic; for to be distinguishable, according to what I call intellectualism, is to be incapable of connexion. The work begun by Zeno, and continued by Hume, Kant, Herbart, Hegel, and Bradley, does not stop till sensible reality lies entirely disintegrated at the feet of 'reason.'

Of the 'absolute' reality which reason proposes to substitute for sensible reality I shall have more to say presently. Meanwhile you see what Professor Bergson means by insisting that the function of the intellect is practical rather than theoretical. Sensible reality is too concrete to be entirely manageable—look at the narrow range of it which is all that any animal, living in it exclusively as he does, is able to compass. To get from one point in it to another we have to plough or wade through the whole intolerable interval. No detail is spared us; it is as bad as the barbed-wire complications at Port Arthur, and we grow old and die in the process. But with our faculty of abstracting and fixing concepts we are there in a second, almost as if we controlled a fourth dimension, skipping the intermediaries as by a divine winged power, and getting at the exact point we require without entanglement with any context. What we do in fact is to *harness up* reality in our conceptual systems in order to drive it the better. This process is practical because all the termini to which we drive are *particular* termini, even when they are facts of the mental order. But the

sciences in which the conceptual method chiefly celebrates its triumphs are those of space and matter, where the transformations of
external things are dealt with. To deal with moral facts conceptually,
we have first to transform them, substitute brain-diagrams or physical
metaphors, treat ideas as atoms, interests as mechanical forces, our
conscious 'selves' as 'streams' and the like. Paradoxical effect! as
Bergson well remarks, if our intellectual life were not practical but
destined to reveal the inner natures. One would then suppose that it
would find itself most at home in the domain of its own intellectual
realities. But it is precisely there that it finds itself at the end of its
tether. We know the inner movements of our spirit only perceptually.
We feel them live in us, but can give no distinct account of their elements, nor definitely predict their future; while things that lie along
the world of space, things of the sort that we literally *handle,* are what
our intellects cope with most successfully. Does not this confirm us in
the view that the original and still surviving function of our intellectual life is to guide us in the practical adaptation of our expectancies
and activities?

One can easily get into a verbal mess at this point, and my own
experience with 'pragmatism' makes me shrink from the dangers that
lie in the word 'practical,' and far rather than stand out against you
for that word, I am quite willing to part company with Professor
Bergson, and to ascribe a primarily theoretical function to our intellect, provided you on your part then agree to discriminate 'theoretic'
or scientific knowledge from the deeper 'speculative' knowledge aspired to by most philosophers, and concede that theoretic knowledge,
which is knowledge *about* things, as distinguished from living or sympathetic acquaintance with them, touches only the outer surface of
reality.[50] The surface which theoretic knowledge taken in this sense

[50] For a more explicit vindication of the notion of activity, see above, pp.
277–291, where I try to defend its recognition as a definite form of immediate
experience against its rationalistic critics.

I subjoin here a few remarks destined to disarm some possible critics of
Professor Bergson, who, to defend himself against misunderstandings of his
meaning, ought to amplify and more fully explain his statement that concepts
have a practical but not a theoretical use. Understood in one way, the thesis
sounds indefensible, for by concepts we certainly increase our knowledge about
things, and that seems a theoretical achievement, whatever practical achievements may follow in its train. Indeed, M. Bergson might seem to be easily
refutable out of his own mouth. His philosophy pretends, if anything, to give
a better insight into truth than rationalistic philosophies give: yet what is it in
itself if not a conceptual system? Does its author not reason by concepts exclusively in his very attempt to show that they can give no insight?

To this particular objection, at any rate, it is easy to reply. In using concepts
of his own to discredit the theoretic claims of concepts generally, Bergson does
not contradict, but on the contrary emphatically illustrates his own view of

covers may indeed be enormous in extent; it may dot the whole diameter of space and time with its conceptual creations; but it does not
penetrate a millimeter into the solid dimension. That inner dimension

their practical rôle, for they serve in his hands only to 'orient' us, to show us
to what quarter we must *practically turn* if we wish to gain that completer
insight into reality which he denies that they can give. He directs our hopes
away from them and towards the despised sensible flux. *What he reaches by
their means is thus only a new practical attitude.* He but restores, against
the vetoes of intellectualist philosophy, our naturally cordial relations with
sensible experience and common sense. This service is surely only practical;
but it is a service for which we may be almost immeasurably grateful. To trust
our senses again with a good philosophic conscience!—who ever conferred on
us so valuable a freedom before?

By making certain distinctions and additions it seems easy to meet the other
counts of the indictment. Concepts are realities of a new order, with particular
relations between them. These relations are just as much directly perceived,
when we compare our various concepts, as the distance between two sense-
objects is perceived when we look at it. Conception is an operation which gives
us material for new acts of perception, then; and when the results of these are
written down, we get those bodies of 'mental truth' (as Locke called it) known
as mathematics, logic, and *a priori* metaphysics. To know all this truth is a
theoretic achievement, indeed, but it is a narrow one; for the relations between conceptual objects as such are only the static ones of bare comparison,
as difference or sameness, congruity or contradiction, inclusion or exclusion.
Nothing *happens* in the realm of concepts; relations there are 'eternal' only.
The theoretic gain fails so far, therefore, to touch even the outer hem of the
real world, the world of causal and dynamic relations, of activity and history.
To gain insight into all that moving life, Bergson is right in turning us away
from conception and towards perception.

By combining concepts with percepts, *we can draw maps of the distribution*
of other percepts in distant space and time. To know this distribution is of
course a theoretic achievement, but the achievement is extremely limited, it
cannot be effected without percepts, and even then what it yields is only static
relations. From maps we learn positions only, and the position of a thing is
but the slightest kind of truth about it; but, being indispensable for forming
our plans of action, the conceptual map-making has the enormous practical
importance on which Bergson so rightly insists.

But concepts, it will be said, do not only give us eternal truths of comparison
and maps of the positions of things, they bring new *values* into life. In their
mapping function they stand to perception in general in the same relation in
which sight and hearing stand to touch—Spencer calls these higher senses only
organs of anticipatory touch. But our eyes and ears also open to us worlds of
independent glory: music and decorative art result, and an incredible enhance-
ment of life's value follows. Even so does the conceptual world bring new
ranges of value and of motivation to our life. Its maps not only serve us
practically, but the mere mental possession of such vast pictures is of itself
an inspiring good. New interests and incitements, and feelings of power, sublimity, and admiration are aroused.

Abstractness *per se* seems to have a touch of ideality. ROYCE'S 'loyalty to
loyalty' is an excellent example. 'Causes,' as anti-slavery, democracy, liberty,
etc., dwindle when realized in their sordid particulars. The veritable 'cash-value'
of the idea seems to cleave to it only in the abstract status. Truth at large, as

of reality is occupied by the *activities* that keep it going, but the intellect, speaking through Hume, Kant & Co., finds itself obliged to deny, and persists in denying, that activities have any intelligible existence. What exists for *thought,* we are told, is at most the results that we illusorily ascribe to such activities, strung along the surfaces of space and time by *regeln der verknüpfung,* laws of nature which state only coexistences and successions.

ROYCE contends, in his *Philosophy of Loyalty,* appears another thing altogether from the true particulars in which it is best to believe. It transcends in value all those 'expediencies,' and is something to live for, whether expedient or inexpedient. Truth with a big T is a 'momentous issue'; truths in detail are 'poor scraps,' mere 'crumbling successes.' (*Op. cit.,* Lecture VII, especially § v.)

Is, now, such bringing into existence of a new *value* to be regarded as a theoretic achievement? The question is a nice one, for altho a value is in one sense an objective quality perceived, the essence of that quality is its relation to the will, and consists in its being a dynamogenic spur that makes our action different. So far as their value-creating function goes, it would thus appear that concepts connect themselves more with our active than with our theoretic life, so here again Bergson's formulation seems unobjectionable. Persons who have certain concepts are animated otherwise, pursue their own vital careers differently. It does n't necessarily follow that they understand other vital careers more intimately.

Again it may be said that we combine old concepts into new ones, conceiving thus such realities as the ether, God, souls, or what not, of which our sensible life alone would leave us altogether ignorant. This surely is an increase of our knowledge, and may well be called a theoretical achievement. Yet here again Bergson's criticisms hold good. Much as conception may tell us *about* such invisible objects, it sheds no ray of light into their interior. The completer, indeed, our definitions of ether-waves, atoms, Gods, or souls become, the less instead of the more intelligible do they appear to us. The learned in such things are consequently beginning more and more to ascribe a solely instrumental value to our concepts of them. Ether and molecules may be like co-ordinates and averages, only so many crutches by the help of which we practically perform the operation of getting about among our sensible experiences.

We see from these considerations how easily the question of whether the function of concepts is theoretical or practical may grow into a logomachy. It may be better from this point of view to refuse to recognize the alternative as a sharp one. The sole thing that is certain in the midst of it all is that Bergson is absolutely right in contending that the whole life of activity and change is inwardly impenetrable to conceptual treatment, and that it opens itself only to sympathetic apprehension at the hands of immediate feeling. All the *whats* as well as the *thats* of reality, relational as well as terminal, are in the end contents of immediate concrete perception. Yet the remoter unperceived *arrangements,* temporal, spatial, and logical, of these contents, are also something that we need to know as well for the pleasure of the knowing as for the practical help. We may call this need of arrangement a theoretic need or a practical need, according as we choose to lay the emphasis; but Bergson is accurately right when he limits conceptual knowledge to arrangement, and when he insists that arrangement is the mere skirt and skin of the whole of what we ought to know.

Thought deals thus solely with surfaces. It can name the thickness of reality, but it cannot fathom it, and its insufficiency here is essential and permanent, not temporary.

The only way in which to apprehend reality's thickness is either to experience it directly by being a part of reality one's self, or to evoke it in imagination by sympathetically divining some one else's inner life. But what we thus immediately experience or concretely divine is very limited in duration, whereas abstractly we are able to conceive eternities. Could we feel a million years concretely as we now feel a passing minute, we should have very little employment for our conceptual faculty. We should know the whole period fully at every moment of its passage, whereas we must now construct it laboriously by means of concepts which we project. Direct acquaintance and conceptual knowledge are thus complementary of each other; each remedies the other's defects. If what we care most about be the synoptic treatment of phenomena, the vision of the far and the gathering of the scattered like, we must follow the conceptual method. But if, as metaphysicians, we are more curious about the inner nature of reality or about what really makes it go, we must turn our backs upon our winged concepts altogether, and bury ourselves in the thickness of those passing moments over the surface of which they fly, and on particular points of which they occasionally rest and perch.

Professor Bergson thus inverts the traditional platonic doctrine absolutely. Instead of intellectual knowledge being the profounder, he calls it the more superficial. Instead of being the only adequate knowledge, it is grossly inadequate, and its only superiority is the practical one of enabling us to make short cuts through experience and thereby to save time. The one thing it cannot do is to reveal the nature of things—which last remark, if not clear already, will become clearer as I proceed. Dive back into the flux itself then, Bergson tells us, if you wish to *know* reality, that flux which Platonism, in its strange belief that only the immutable is excellent, has always spurned; turn your face toward sensation, that flesh-bound thing which rationalism has always loaded with abuse.—This, you see, is exactly the opposite remedy from that of looking forward into the absolute, which our idealistic contemporaries prescribe. It violates our mental habits, being a kind of passive and receptive listening quite contrary to that effort to react noisily and verbally on everything, which is our usual intellectual pose.

What, then, are the peculiar features in the perceptual flux which the conceptual translation so fatally leaves out?

The essence of life is its continuously changing character; but our concepts are all discontinuous and fixed, and the only mode of making them coincide with life is by arbitrarily supposing positions of arrest therein. With such arrests our concepts may be made congruent. But these concepts are not *parts* of reality, not real positions taken by it, but *suppositions* rather, notes taken by ourselves, and you can no more dip up the substance of reality with them than you can dip up water with a net, however finely meshed.

When we conceptualize, we cut out and fix, and exclude everything but what we have fixed. A concept means a *that-and-no-other*. Conceptually, time excludes space; motion and rest exclude each other; approach excludes contact; presence excludes absence; unity excludes plurality; independence excludes relativity; 'mine' excludes 'yours'; this connexion excludes that connexion—and so on indefinitely; whereas in the real concrete sensible flux of life experiences compenetrate each other so that it is not easy to know just what is excluded and what not. Past and future, for example, conceptually separated by the cut to which we give the name of present, and defined as being the opposite sides of that cut, are to some extent, however brief, co-present with each other throughout experience. The literally present moment is a purely verbal supposition, not a position; the only present ever realized concretely being the 'passing moment' in which the dying rearward of time and its dawning future forever mix their lights. Say 'now' and it *was* even while you say it.

It is just intellectualism's attempt to substitute static cuts for units of experienced duration that makes real motion so unintelligible. The conception of the first half of the interval between Achilles and the tortoise excludes that of the last half, and the mathematical necessity of traversing it separately before the last half is traversed stands permanently in the way of the last half ever being traversed. Meanwhile the living Achilles (who, for the purposes of this discussion, is only the abstract name of one phenomenon of impetus, just as the tortoise is of another) asks no leave of logic. The velocity of his acts is an indivisible nature in them like the expansive tension in a spring compressed. We define it conceptually as $\frac{s}{t}$, but the s and t are only artificial cuts made after the fact, and indeed most artificial when we treat them in both runners as the same tracts of 'objective' space and time, for the experienced spaces and times in which the tortoise inwardly lives are probably as different as his velocity from the same things in Achilles. The impetus of Achilles is one concrete fact, and carries space, time, and conquest over the inferior creature's motion indivisibly in it. He perceives nothing, while running, of the mathematician's homogeneous time and space, of the infinitely numerous succession of cuts in both, or of their order. End and beginning come for him in the one onrush, and all that he actually experiences is that, in the midst of a certain intense effort of his own, the rival is in point of fact outstripped.

We are so inveterately wedded to the conceptual decomposition of life that I know that this will seem to you like putting muddiest confusion in place of clearest thought, and relapsing into a molluscoid state of mind. Yet I ask you whether the absolute superiority of our higher thought is so very clear, if all that it can find is impossibility in tasks which sense ·experience so easily performs.

What makes you call real life confusion is that it presents, as if they were dissolved in one another, a lot of differents which conception breaks life's flow by keeping apart. But *are* not differents actually dissolved in one another? Has n't every bit of experience its quality, its duration, its extension, its intensity, its urgency, its clearness, and many aspects besides, no one of which can exist in the isolation in which our verbalized logic keeps it? They exist only *durcheinander*. Reality always is, in M. Bergson's phrase, an endosmosis or conflux of the same with the different: they compenetrate and telescope. For conceptual logic, the same is nothing but the same, and all sames with a third thing are the same with each other. Not so in concrete experience. Two spots on our skin, each of which feels the same as a third spot when touched along with it, are felt as different from each other. Two tones, neither distinguishable from a third tone, are perfectly distinct from each other. The whole process of life is due to life's violation of our logical axioms. Take its continuity as an example. Terms like A and C appear to be connected by intermediaries, by B for example. Intellectualism calls this absurd, for 'B-connected-with-A' is, 'as such,' a different term from 'B-connected-with-C.' But real life laughs at logic's veto. Imagine a heavy log which takes two men to carry it. First A and B take it. Then C takes hold and A drops off; then D takes hold and B drops off, so that C and D now bear it; and so on. The log meanwhile never drops, and keeps its sameness throughout the journey. Even so it is with all our experiences. Their changes are not complete annihilations followed by complete creations of something absolutely novel. There is partial decay and partial growth, and all the while a nucleus of relative constancy from which what decays drops off, and which takes into itself whatever is grafted on, until at length something wholly different has taken its place. In such a process we are as sure, in spite of intellectualist logic with its 'as suches,' that it *is* the same nucleus which is able now to make connexion with what goes and again with what comes, as we are sure that the same point can lie on diverse lines that intersect there. Without being one throughout, such a universe is continuous. Its members interdigitate with their next neighbors in manifold directions, and there are no clean cuts between them anywhere.

The great clash of intellectualist logic with sensible experience is where the experience is that of influence exerted. Intellectualism denies [as seen above in the lecture on "Monistic Idealism"] that finite

things can act on one another, for all things, once translated into concepts, remain shut up to themselves. To act on anything means to get
into it somehow; but that would mean to get out of one's self and be
one's other, which is self-contradictory, etc. Meanwhile each of us
actually *is* his own other to that extent, livingly knowing how to perform the trick which logic tells us can't be done. My thoughts animate
and actuate this very body which you see and hear, and thereby influence your thoughts. The dynamic current somehow does get from me
to you, however numerous the intermediary conductors may have to
be. Distinctions may be insulators in logic as much as they like, but in
life distinct things can and do commune together every moment.

The conflict of the two ways of knowing is best summed up in the
intellectualist doctrine that 'the same cannot exist in many relations.'
This follows of course from the concepts of the two relations being so
distinct that 'what-is-in-the-one' means 'as such' something distinct
from what 'what-is-in-the-other' means. It is like Mill's ironical saying, that we should not think of Newton as both an Englishman and a
mathematician, because an Englishman as such is not a mathematician and a mathematician as such is not an Englishman. But the real
Newton was somehow both things at once; and throughout the whole
finite universe each real thing proves to be many differents without
undergoing the necessity of breaking into disconnected editions of itself.

These few indications will perhaps suffice to put you at the bergsonian point of view. The immediate experience of life solves the
problems which so baffle our conceptual intelligence: How can what
is manifold be one? how can things get out of themselves? how be
their own others? how be both distinct and connected? how can they
act on one another? how be for others and yet for themselves? how be
absent and present at once? The intellect asks these questions much as
we might ask how anything can both separate and unite things, or how
sounds can grow more alike by continuing to grow more different. If
you already know space sensibly, you can answer the former question
by pointing to any interval in it, long or short; if you know the musical
scale, you can answer the latter by sounding an octave; but then you
must first have the sensible knowledge of these realities. Similarly
Bergson answers the intellectualist conundrums by pointing back to
our various finite sensational experiences and saying, 'Lo, even thus;
even so are these other problems solved livingly.'

When you have broken the reality into concepts you never can
reconstruct it in its wholeness. Out of no amount of discreteness can
you manufacture the concrete. But place yourself at a bound, or
d'emblée, as M. Bergson says, inside of the living, moving, active
thickness of the real, and all the abstractions and distinctions are
given into your hand: you can now make the intellectualist substitu-

tions to your heart's content. Install yourself in phenomenal movement, for example, and velocity, succession, dates, positions, and
innumerable other things are given you in the bargain. But with only
an abstract succession of dates and positions you can never patch up
movement itself. It slips through their intervals and is lost.

So it is with every concrete thing, however complicated. Our intellectual handling of it is a retrospective patchwork, a post-mortem dis-
section, and can follow any order we find most expedient. We can
make the thing seem self-contradictory whenever we wish to. But
place yourself at the point of view of the thing's interior *doing,* and all
these back-looking and conflicting conceptions lie harmoniously in
your hand. Get at the expanding centre of a human character, the *élan
vital* of a man, as Bergson calls it, by living sympathy, and at a stroke
you see how it makes those who see it from without interpret it in
such diverse ways. It is something that breaks into both honesty and
dishonesty, courage and cowardice, stupidity and insight, at the touch
of varying circumstances, and you feel exactly why and how it does
this, and never seek to identify it stably with any of these single abstractions. Only your intellectualist does that,—and you now also feel
why *he* must do it to the end.

Place yourself similarly at the centre of a man's philosophic vision
and you understand at once all the different things it makes him write
or say. But keep outside, use your post-mortem method, try to build
the philosophy up out of the single phrases, taking first one and then
another and seeking to make them fit, and of course you fail. You
crawl over the thing like a myopic ant over a building, tumbling into
every microscopic crack or fissure, finding nothing but inconsistencies,
and never suspecting that a centre exists. I hope that some of the
philosophers in this audience may occasionally have had something
different from this intellectualist type of criticism applied to their own
works!

What really *exists* is not things made but things in the making.
Once made, they are dead, and an infinite number of alternative conceptual decompositions can be used in defining them. But put yourself
in the making by a stroke of intuitive sympathy with the thing and, the
whole range of possible decompositions coming at once into your possession, you are no longer troubled with the question which of them is
the more absolutely true. Reality *falls* in passing into conceptual analysis; it *mounts* in living its own undivided life—it buds and bour-
geons, changes and creates. Once adopt the movement of this life in
any given instance and you know what Bergson calls the *devenir réel*
by which the thing evolves and grows. Philosophy should seek this
kind of living understanding of the movement of reality, not follow
science in vainly patching together fragments of its dead results.

Thus much of M. Bergson's philosophy is sufficient for my purpose in these lectures, so here I will stop, leaving unnoticed all its other constituent features, original and interesting tho they be. You may say, and doubtless some of you now are saying inwardly, that his remanding us to sensation in this wise is only a regress, a return to that ultra-crude empiricism which your own idealists since Green have buried ten times over. I confess that it is indeed a return to empiricism, but I think that the return in such accomplished shape only proves the latter's immortal truth. What won't stay buried must have some genuine life. *Am anfang war die tat;* fact is a *first;* to which all our conceptual handling comes as an inadequate second, never its full equivalent. When I read recent transcendentalist literature—I must partly except my colleague Royce!—I get nothing but a sort of marking of time, champing of jaws, pawing of the ground, and resettling into the same attitude, like a weary horse in a stall with an empty manger. It is but turning over the same few threadbare categories, bringing the same objections, and urging the same answers and solutions, with never a new fact or a new horizon coming into sight. But open Bergson, and new horizons loom on every page you read. It is like the breath of the morning and the song of birds. It tells of reality itself, instead of merely reiterating what dusty-minded professors have written about what other previous professors have thought. Nothing in Bergson is shop-worn or at second hand.

That he gives us no closed-in system will of course be fatal to him in intellectualist eyes. He only evokes and invites; but he first annuls the intellectualist veto, so that we now join step with reality with a philosophical conscience never quite set free before. As a french disciple of his well expresses it: 'Bergson claims of us first of all a certain inner catastrophe, and not every one is capable of such a logical revolution. But those who have once found themselves flexible enough for the execution of such a psychological change of front, discover somehow that they can never return again to their ancient attitude of mind. They are now Bergsonians . . . and possess the principal thoughts of the master all at once. They have understood in the fashion in which one loves, they have caught the whole melody and can thereafter admire at their leisure the originality, the fecundity, and the imaginative genius with which its author develops, transposes, and varies in a thousand ways by the orchestration of his style and dialectic, the original theme.[51]

This, scant as it is, is all I have to say about Bergson on this occasion—I hope it may send some of you to his original text. I must now turn back to the point where I found it advisable to appeal to his ideas. You remember my own intellectualist difficulties in the last lecture, about how a lot of separate consciousnesses can at the same time

[51] Gaston Rageot, *Revue Philosophique,* vol. lxiv, p. 85 (July, 1907).

be one collective thing. How, I asked, can one and the same identical content of experience, of which on idealist principles the *esse* is to be felt, be felt so diversely if itself be the only feeler? The usual way of escape by 'quatenus' or 'as such' won't help us here if we are radical intellectualists, I said, for appearance-together is as such *not* appearance-apart, the world *quâ* many is not the world *quâ* one, as absolutism claims. If we hold to Hume's maxim, which later intellectualism uses so well, that whatever things are distinguished are as separate as if there were no manner of connexion between them, there seemed no way out of the difficulty save by stepping outside of experience altogether and invoking different spiritual agents, selves or souls, to realize the diversity required. But this rescue by 'scholastic entities' I was unwilling to accept any more than pantheistic idealists accept it.

Yet, to quote Fechner's phrase again, 'nichts wirkliches kann unmöglich sein,' the actual cannot be impossible, and what *is* actual at every moment of our lives is the sort of thing which I now proceed to remind you of. You can hear the vibration of an electric contact-maker, smell the ozone, see the sparks, and feel the thrill, co-consciously as it were or in one field of experience. But you can also isolate any one of these sensations by shutting out the rest. If you close your eyes, hold your nose, and remove your hand, you can get the sensation of sound alone, but it seems still the same sensation that it was; and if you restore the action of the other organs, the sound coalesces with the feeling, the sight, and the smell sensations again. Now the natural way of talking of all this[52] is to say that certain sensations are experienced, now singly, and now together with other sensations, in a common conscious field. Fluctuations of attention give analogous results. We let a sensation in or keep it out by changing our attention; and similarly we let an item of memory in or drop it out. [Please don't raise the question here of how these changes *come to pass*. The immediate condition is probably cerebral in every instance, but it would be irrelevant now to consider it, for now we are thinking only of results, and I repeat that the natural way of thinking of them is that which intellectualist criticism finds so absurd.]

The absurdity charged is that the self-same should function so differently, now with and now without something else. But this it sensibly seems to do. This very desk which I strike with my hand strikes in turn your eyes. It functions at once as a physical object in the outer world and as a mental object in our sundry mental worlds. The very body of mine that *my* thought actuates is the body whose gestures are *your* visual object and to which you give my name. The very log which

---

[52] I have myself talked in other ways as plausibly as I could, in my *Psychology*, and talked truly (as I believe) in certain selected cases; but for other cases the natural way invincibly comes back.

John helped to carry is the log now borne by James. The very girl you love is simultaneously entangled elsewhere. The very place behind me is in front of you. Look where you will, you gather only examples of the same amid the different, and of different relations existing as it were in solution in the same thing. *Quâ* this an experience is not the same as it is *quâ* that, truly enough; but the *quâs* are conceptual shots of ours at its post-mortem remains, and in its sensational immediacy everything is all at once whatever different things it is at once at all. It is before C and after A, far from you and near to me, without this associate and with that one, active and passive, physical and mental, a whole of parts and part of a higher whole, all simultaneously and without interference or need of doubling-up its being, so long as we keep to what I call the 'immediate' point of view, the point of view in which we follow our sensational life's continuity, and to which all living language conforms. It is only when you try—to continue using the hegelian vocabulary—to 'mediate' the immediate, or to substitute concepts for sensational life, that intellectualism celebrates its triumph and the immanent-self-contradictoriness of all this smooth-running finite experience gets proved.

Of the oddity of inventing as a remedy for the inconveniences resulting from this situation a supernumerary conceptual object called an absolute, into which you pack the self-same contradictions unreduced, I will say something in the next lecture. The absolute is said to perform its feats by taking up its other into itself. But that is exactly what is done when every individual morsel of the sensational stream takes up the adjacent morsels by coalescing with them. This is just what we mean by the stream's sensible continuity. No element *there* cuts itself off from any other element, as concepts cut themselves from concepts. No part *there* is so small as not to be a place of conflux. No part there is not really *next* its neighbors; which means that there is literally nothing between; which means again that no part goes exactly so far and no farther; that no part absolutely excludes another, but that they compenetrate and are cohesive; that if you tear out one, its roots bring out more with them; that whatever is real is telescoped and diffused into other reals; that, in short, every minutest thing is already its hegelian 'own other,' in the fullest sense of the term.

Of course this *sounds* self-contradictory, but as the immediate facts don't sound at all, but simply *are,* until we conceptualize and name them vocally, the contradiction results only from the conceptual or discursive form being substituted for the real form. But if, as Bergson shows, that form is superimposed for practical ends only, in order to let us jump about over life instead of wading through it; and if it cannot even pretend to reveal anything of what life's inner nature is or ought to be; why then we can turn a deaf ear to its accusations. The resolve to turn the deaf ear is the inner crisis or 'catastrophe' of which M. Bergson's disciple whom I lately quoted spoke. We are so subject to the philosophic tradition which treats *logos* or discursive thought generally as the sole avenue to truth, that to fall back on raw unverbalized life as more of a revealer, and to think of concepts as the merely practical things which Bergson calls them, comes very hard. It is putting off our proud maturity of mind and becoming again as foolish little children in the eyes of reason. But difficult as such a revolution is, there is no other way, I believe, to the possession of reality.

ADDRESS AT THE EMERSON
CENTENARY IN CONCORD*

The pathos of death is this, that when the days of one's life are ended, those days that were so crowded with business and felt so heavy in their passing, what remains of one in memory should usually be so slight a thing. The phantom of an attitude, the echo of a certain mode of thought, a few pages of print, some invention, or some victory we gained in a brief critical hour, are all that can survive the best of us. It is as if the whole of a man's significance had now shrunk into the phantom of an attitude, into a mere musical note or phrase suggestive of his singularity—happy are those whose singularity gives a note so clear as to be victorious over the inevitable pity of such a diminution and abridgment.

An ideal wraith like this, of Emerson's personality, hovers over all Concord to-day, taking, in the minds of those of you who were his neighbors and intimates a somewhat fuller shape, remaining more abstract in the younger generation, but bringing home to all of us the notion of a spirit indescribably precious. The form that so lately moved upon these streets and country roads, or awaited in these fields and woods the beloved Muse's visits, is now dust; but the soul's note, the spiritual voice, rises strong and clear above the uproar of the times, and seems securely destined to exert an ennobling influence over future generations.

What gave a flavor so matchless to Emerson's individuality was, even more than his rich mental gifts, their singularly harmonious

* From: M.S., 19–34. An Address delivered at the Centenary of the Birth of Ralph Waldo Emerson in Concord, May 25, 1903, and printed in the published proceedings of that meeting.

combination. Rarely has a man so accurately known the limits of his genius or so unfailingly kept within them. "Stand by your order," he used to say to youthful students; and perhaps the paramount impression one gets of his life is of his loyalty to his own personal type and mission. The type was that of what he liked to call the scholar, the perceiver of pure truth; and the mission was that of the reporter in worthy form of each perception. The day is good, he said, in which we have the most perceptions. There are times when the cawing of a crow, a weed, a snowflake, or a farmer planting in his field become symbols to the intellect of truths equal to those which the most majestic phenomena can open. Let me mind my own charge, then, walk alone, consult the sky, the field and forest, sedulously waiting every morning for the news concerning the structure of the universe which the good Spirit will give me.

This was the first half of Emerson, but only half; for genius, as he said, is insatiate for expression, and truth has to be clad in the right verbal garment. The form of the garment was so vital with Emerson that it is impossible to separate it from the matter. They form a chemical combination—thoughts which would be trivial expressed otherwise, are important through the nouns and verbs to which he married them. The style is the man, it has been said; the man Emerson's mission culminated in his style, and if we must define him in one word, we have to call him Artist. He was an artist whose medium was verbal and who wrought in spiritual material.

This duty of spiritual seeing and reporting determined the whole tenor of his life. It was to shield this duty from invasion and distraction that he dwelt in the country, that he consistently declined to entangle himself with associations or to encumber himself with functions which, however he might believe in them, he felt were duties for other men and not for him. Even the care of his garden, "with its stoopings and fingerings in a few yards of space," he found "narrowing and poisoning," and took to long free walks and saunterings instead, without apology. "Causes" innumerable sought to enlist him as their "worker"—all got his smile and word of sympathy, but none entrapped him into service. The struggle against slavery itself, deeply as it appealed to him, found him firm: "God must govern his own world, and knows his way out of this pit without my desertion of my post, which has none to guard it but me. I have quite other slaves to face than those Negroes, to wit, imprisoned thoughts far back in the brain of man, and which have no watchman or lover or defender but me." This in reply to the possible questions of his own conscience. To hot-blooded moralists with more objective ideas of duty, such a fidelity to the limits of his genius must often have made him seem provokingly remote and unavailable; but we, who can see things in more liberal

perspective, must unqualifiably approve the results. The faultless tact
with which he kept his safe limits while he so dauntlessly asserted
himself within them, is an example fitted to give heart to other theorists and artists the world over.

The insight and creed from which Emerson's life followed can be
best summed up in his own verses:

> So nigh is grandeur to our dust,
> So near is God to man!

Through the individual fact there ever shone for him the effulgence of
the Universal Reason. The great Cosmic Intellect terminates and
houses itself in mortal men and passing hours. Each of us is an angle
of its eternal vision, and the only way to be true to our Maker is to be
loyal to ourselves. "O rich and various Man!" he cries, "thou palace
of sight and sound, carrying in thy senses the morning and the night
and the unfathomable galaxy; in thy brain the geometry of the city of
God; in thy heart the bower of love and the realms of right and
wrong."

If the individual open thus directly into the Absolute, it follows
that there is something in each and all of us, even the lowliest, that
ought not to consent to borrowing traditions and living at second
hand. "If John was perfect, why are you and I alive?" Emerson
writes; "As long as any man exists there is some need of him; let him
fight for his own." This faith that in a life at first hand there is something sacred is perhaps the most characteristic note in Emerson's writings. The hottest side of him is this non-conformist persuasion, and if
his temper could ever verge on common irascibility, it would be by
reason of the passionate character of his feelings on this point. The
world is still new and untried. In seeing freshly, and not in hearing of
what others saw, shall a man find what truth is. "Each one of us can
bask in the great morning which rises out of the Eastern Sea, and be
himself one of the children of the light." "Trust thyself, every heart
vibrates to that iron string. There is a time in each man's education
when he must arrive at the conviction that imitation is suicide; when
he must take himself for better or worse as his portion; and know that
though the wide universe is full of good, no kernel of nourishing corn
can come to him but through his toil bestowed on that plot of ground
which it was given him to till."

The matchless eloquence with which Emerson proclaimed the
sovereignty of the living individual electrified and emancipated his
generation, and this bugle-blast will doubtless be regarded by future
critics as the soul of his message. The present man is the aboriginal
reality, the Institution is derivative, and the past man is irrelevant and
obliterate for present issues. "If anyone would lay an axe to your tree

with a text from 1 John, v, 7, or a sentence from Saint Paul, say to
him," Emerson wrote, " 'My tree is Yggdrasil, the tree of life.' Let
him know by your security that your conviction is clear and sufficient,
and, if he were Paul himself, that you also are here and with your
Creator." "Cleave ever to God," he insisted, "against the name of
God;" —and so, in spite of the intensely religious character of his
total thought, when he began his career it seemed to many of his
brethren in the clerical profession that he was little more than an icon-
oclast and desecrator.

Emerson's belief that the individual must in reason be adequate to
the vocation for which the Spirit of the world has called him into
being, is the source of those sublime pages, hearteners and sustainers
of our youth, in which he urges his hearers to be incorruptibly true to
their own private conscience. Nothing can harm the man who rests in
his appointed place and character. Such a man is invulnerable; he
balances the universe, balances it as much by keeping small when he
is small, as by being great and spreading when he is great. "I love and
honor Epaminondas," said Emerson, "but I do not wish to be Epaminondas. I hold it more just to love the world of this hour than the
world of his hour. Nor can you, if I am true, excite me to the least
uneasiness by saying, 'He acted and thou sittest still.' I see action to
be good when the need is, and sitting still to be also good. Epaminondas, if he was the man I take him for, would have sat still with joy and
peace, if his lot had been mine. Heaven is large, and affords space for
all modes of love and fortitude." "The fact that I am here certainly
shows me that the Soul has need of an organ here, and shall I not
assume the post?"

The vanity of all superserviceableness and pretence was never
more happily set forth than by Emerson in the many passages in
which he develops this aspect of his philosophy. Character infallibly
proclaims itself. "Hide your thoughts!—hide the sun and moon. They
publish themselves to the universe. They will speak through you
though you were dumb. They will flow out of your actions, your manners and your face. . . . Don't say things: What you are stands over
you the while and thunders so that I cannot say what you say to the
contrary. . . . What a man *is* engraves itself upon him in letters of
light. Concealment avails him nothing, boasting nothing. There is confession in the glances of our eyes; in our smiles; in salutations; and the
grasp of hands. His sin bedaubs him, mars all his good impression.
Men know not why they do not trust him, but they do not trust him.
His vice glasses the eye, casts lines of mean expression in the cheek,
pinches the nose, sets the mark of the beast upon the back of the head,
and writes, O fool! fool! on the forehead of a king. If you would not
be known to do a thing, never do it; a man may play the fool in the

drifts of a desert, but every grain of sand shall seem to see.—How can a man be concealed? How can he be concealed?"

On the other hand, never was a sincere word or a sincere thought utterly lost. "Never a magnanimity fell to the ground but there is some heart to greet and accept it unexpectedly. . . . The hero fears not that if he withstood the avowal of a just and brave act, it will go unwitnessed and unloved. One knows it,—himself,—and is pledged by it to sweetness of peace and to nobleness of aim, which will prove in the end a better proclamation than the relating of the incident."

The same indefeasible right to be exactly what one is, provided one only be authentic, spreads itself, in Emerson's way of thinking, from persons to things and to times and places. No date, no position is insignificant, if the life that fills it out be only genuine:—

"In solitude, in a remote village, the ardent youth loiters and mourns. With inflamed eye, in this sleeping wilderness, he has read the story of the Emperor, Charles the Fifth, until his fancy has brought home to the surrounding woods the faint roar of cannonades in the Milanese, and marches in Germany. He is curious concerning that man's day. What filled it? The crowded orders, the stern decisions, the foreign despatches, the Castilian etiquette? The soul answers—Behold his day here! In the sighing of these woods, in the quiet of these gray fields, in the cool breeze that sings out of these northern mountains; in the workmen, the boys, the maidens you meet, —in the hopes of the morning, the *ennui* of noon, and sauntering of the afternoon; in the disquieting comparisons; in the regrets at want of vigor; in the great idea and the puny execution,—behold Charles the Fifth's day; another, yet the same; behold Chatham's, Hampden's, Bayard's, Alfred's, Scipio's, Pericles's day,—day of all that are born of women. The difference of circumstance is merely costume. I am tasting the self-same life,—its sweetness, its greatness, its pain, which I so admire in other men. Do not foolishly ask of the inscrutable, obliterated past what it cannot tell,—the details of that nature, of that day, called Byron or Burke;—but ask it of the enveloping Now. . . . Be lord of a day, and you can put up your history books."

"The deep to-day which all men scorn" receives thus from Emerson superb revindication. "Other world! there is no other world." All God's life opens into the individual particular, and here and now, or nowhere, is reality. "The present hour is the decisive hour, and every day is doomsday."

Such a conviction that Divinity is everywhere may easily make of one an optimist of the sentimental type that refuses to speak ill of anything. Emerson's drastic perception of differences kept him at the opposite pole from this weakness. After you have seen men a few times, he could say, you find most of them as alike as their barns and

pantries, and soon as musty and as dreary. Never was such a fastidious lover of significance and distinction, and never an eye so keen for
their discovery. His optimism had nothing in common with that indiscriminate hurrahing for the Universe with which Walt Whitman has
made us familiar. For Emerson, the individual fact and moment were
indeed suffused with absolute radiance, but it was upon a condition
that saved the situation—they must be worthy specimens,—sincere,
authentic, archetypal; they must have made connection with what he
calls the Moral Sentiment, they must in some way act as symbolic
mouthpieces of the Universe's meaning. To know just which thing
does act in this way, and which thing fails to make the true connection, is the secret (somewhat incommunicable, it must be confessed)
of seership, and doubtless we must not expect of the seer too rigorous
a consistency. Emerson himself was a real seer. He could perceive the
full squalor of the individual fact, but he could also see the transfiguration. He might easily have found himself saying of some present-day
agitator against our Philippine conquest what he said of this or that
reformer of his own time. He might have called him, as a private
person, a tedious bore and canter. But he would infallibly have added
what he then added: "It is strange and horrible to say this, for I feel
that under him and his partiality and exclusiveness is the earth and the
sea, and all that in them is, and the axis round which the Universe
revolves passes through his body where he stands."

Be it how it may, then, this is Emerson's revelation:—The point
of any pen can be an epitome of reality; the commonest person's act,
if genuinely actuated, can lay hold on eternity. This vision is the head-
spring of all his outpourings; and it is for this truth, given to no previous literary artist to express in such penetratingly persuasive tones,
that posterity will reckon him a prophet, and, perhaps neglecting other
pages, piously turn to those that convey this message. His life was one
long conversation with the invisible divine, expressing itself through
individuals and particulars:—"So nigh is grandeur to our dust, so
near is God to man!"

I spoke of how shrunken the wraith, how thin the echo, of men is
after they are departed. Emerson's wraith comes to me now as if it
were but the very voice of this victorious argument. His words to this
effect are certain to be quoted and extracted more and more as time
goes on, and to take their place among the Scriptures of humanity.
" 'Gainst death and all oblivious enmity, shall you pace forth," beloved Master. As long as our English language lasts men's hearts will
be cheered and their souls strengthened and liberated by the noble and
musical pages with which you have enriched it.

— vi —

Ethical and Religious
Dimensions of
Radical Empiricism

It is most misleading to separate James's doctrine of the "Will
to Believe" and his fascination for psychic phenomena, from
the overall texture of a radically empirical world. When considered within the context of the previously described radical
empiricism, the following essays take on new life and meaning.

THE DILEMMA OF DETERMINISM* [1]

A common opinion prevails that the juice has ages ago been pressed
out of the free-will controversy, and that no new champion can do
more than warm up stale arguments which every one has heard. This
is a radical mistake. I know of no subject less worn out, or in which
inventive genius has a better chance of breaking open new ground,—
not, perhaps, of forcing a conclusion or of coercing assent, but of
deepening our sense of what the issue between the two parties really
is, of what the ideas of fate and of free-will imply. At our very side
almost, in the past few years, we have seen falling in rapid succession
from the press works that present the alternative in entirely novel
lights. Not to speak of the English disciples of Hegel, such as Green
and Bradley; not to speak of Hinton and Hodgson, nor of Hazard

* From: W.B., 145–183.
[1] An Address to the Harvard Divinity Students, published in the *Unitarian
Review* for September, 1884.

here,—we see in the writings of Renouvier, Fouillée, and Delbœuf [2] how completely changed and refreshed is the form of all the old disputes. I cannot pretend to vie in originality with any of the masters I have named, and my ambition limits itself to just one little point. If I can make two of the necessarily implied corollaries of determinism clearer to you than they have been made before, I shall have made it possible for you to decide for or against that doctrine with a better understanding of what you are about. And if you prefer not to decide at all, but to remain doubters, you will at least see more plainly what the subject of your hesitation is. I thus disclaim openly on the threshold all pretension to prove to you that the freedom of the will is true. The most I hope is to induce some of you to follow my own example in assuming it true, and acting as if it were true. If it be true, it seems to me that this is involved in the strict logic of the case. Its truth ought not to be forced willy-nilly down our indifferent throats. It ought to be freely espoused by men who can equally well turn their backs upon it. In other words, our first act of freedom, if we are free, ought in all inward propriety to be to affirm that we are free. This should exclude, it seems to me, from the free-will side of the question all hope of a coercive demonstration,—a demonstration which I, for one, am perfectly contented to go without.

With thus much understood at the outset, we can advance. But not without one more point understood as well. The arguments I am about to urge all proceed on two suppositions: first, when we make theories about the world and discuss them with one another, we do so in order to attain a conception of things which shall give us subjective satisfaction; and, second, if there be two conceptions, and the one seems to us, on the whole, more rational than the other, we are entitled to suppose that the more rational one is the truer of the two. I hope that you are all willing to make these suppositions with me; for I am afraid that if there be any of you here who are not, they will find little edification in the rest of what I have to say. I cannot stop to argue the point; but I myself believe that all the magnificent achievements of mathematical and physical science—our doctrines of evolution, of uniformity of law, and the rest—proceed from our indomitable desire to cast the world into a more rational shape in our minds than the shape into which it is thrown there by the crude order of our experience. The world has shown itself, to a great extent, plastic to this demand of ours for rationality. How much farther it will show itself plastic no one can say. Our only means of finding out is to try; and I, for one, feel as free to try conceptions of moral as of mechanical or of logical rationality. If a certain formula for expressing the nature of the world violates my moral demand, I shall feel as free to

[2] And I may now say Charles S. Peirce,—see the *Monist*, for 1892–93.

throw it overboard, or at least to doubt it, as if it disappointed my demand for uniformity of sequence, for example; the one demand being, so far as I can see, quite as subjective and emotional as the other is. The principle of causality, for example,—what is it but a postulate, an empty name covering simply a demand that the sequence of events shall some day manifest a deeper kind of belonging of one thing with another than the mere arbitrary juxtaposition which now phenomenally appears? It is as much an altar to an unknown god as the one that Saint Paul found at Athens. All our scientific and philosophic ideals are altars to unknown gods. Uniformity is as much so as is free-will. If this be admitted, we can debate on even terms. But if any one pretends that while freedom and variety are, in the first instance, subjective demands, necessity and uniformity are something altogether different, I do not see how we can debate at all.[3]

To begin, then, I must suppose you acquainted with all the usual arguments on the subject. I cannot stop to take up the old proofs from causation, from statistics, from the certainty with which we can foretell one another's conduct, from the fixity of character, and all the rest. But there are two *words* which usually encumber these classical arguments, and which we must immediately dispose of if we are to make any progress. One is the eulogistic word *freedom,* and the other is the opprobrious word *chance.* The word 'chance' I wish to keep, but

[3] "The whole history of popular beliefs about Nature refutes the notion that the thought of a universal physical order can possibly have arisen from the purely passive reception and association of particular perceptions. Indubitable as it is that men infer from known cases to unknown, it is equally certain that this procedure, if restricted to the phenomenal materials that spontaneously offer themselves, would never have led to the belief in a general uniformity, but only to the belief that law and lawlessness rule the world in motley alternation. From the point of view of strict experience, nothing exists but the sum of particular perceptions, with their coincidences on the one hand, their contradictions on the other.

"That there is more order in the world than appears at first sight is not discovered *till the order is looked for.* The first impulse to look for it proceeds from practical needs: where ends must be attained, we must know trustworthy means which infallibly possess a property, or produce a result. But the practical need is only the first occasion for our reflection on the conditions of true knowledge; and even were there no such need, motives would still be present for carrying us beyond the stage of mere association. For not with an equal interest, or rather with an equal lack of interest, does man contemplate those natural processes in which a thing is linked with its former mate, and those in which it is linked to something else. *The former processes harmonize with the conditions of his own thinking:* the latter do not. In the former, his *concepts, general judgments,* and *inferences* apply to reality: in the latter, they have no such application. And thus the intellectual satisfaction which at first comes to him without reflection, at last excites in him the conscious wish to find realized throughout the entire phenomenal world those rational continuities, uniformities, and necessities which are the fundamental element and guiding principle of his own thought." (Sigwart, *Logik,* bd. 2, s. 382.)

I wish to get rid of the word 'freedom.' Its eulogistic associations have so far overshadowed all the rest of its meaning that both parties claim the sole right to use it, and determinists to-day insist that they alone are freedom's champions. Old-fashioned determinism was what we may call *hard* determinism. It did not shrink from such words as fatality, bondage of the will, necessitation, and the like. Nowadays, we have a *soft* determinism which abhors harsh words, and, repudiating fatality, necessity, and even predetermination, says that its real name is freedom; for freedom is only necessity understood, and bondage to the highest is identical with true freedom. Even a writer as little used to making capital out of soft words as Mr. Hodgson hesitates not to call himself a 'free-will determinist.'

Now, all this is a quagmire of evasion under which the real issue of fact has been entirely smothered. Freedom in all these senses presents simply no problem at all. No matter what the soft determinist mean by it,—whether he mean the acting without external constraint; whether he mean the acting rightly, or whether he mean the acquiescing in the law of the whole,—who cannot answer him that sometimes we are free and sometimes we are not? But there *is* a problem, an issue of fact and not of words, an issue of the most momentous importance, which is often decided without discussion in one sentence,—nay, in one clause of a sentence,—by those very writers who spin out whole chapters in their efforts to show what 'true' freedom is; and that is the question of determinism, about which we are to talk to-night.

Fortunately, no ambiguities hang about this word or about its opposite, indeterminism. Both designate an outward way in which things may happen, and their cold and mathematical sound has no sentimental associations that can bribe our partiality either way in advance. Now, evidence of an external kind to decide between determinism and indeterminism is, as I intimated a while back, strictly impossible to find. Let us look at the difference between them and see for ourselves. What does determinism profess?

It professes that those parts of the universe already laid down absolutely appoint and decree what the other parts shall be. The future has no ambiguous possibilities hidden in its womb: the part we call the present is compatible with only one totality. Any other future complement than the one fixed from eternity is impossible. The whole is in each and every part, and welds it with the rest into an absolute unity, an iron block, in which there can be no equivocation or shadow of turning.

> With earth's first clay they did the last man knead,
> And there of the last harvest sowed the seed.
> And the first morning of creation wrote
> What the last dawn of reckoning shall read.

Indeterminism, on the contrary, says that the parts have a certain amount of loose play on one another, so that the laying down of one of them does not necessarily determine what the others shall be. It admits that possibilities may be in excess of actualities, and that things not yet revealed to our knowledge may really in themselves be ambiguous. Of two alternative futures which we conceive, both may now be really possible; and the one become impossible only at the very moment when the other excludes it by becoming real itself. Indeterminism thus denies the world to be one unbending unit of fact. It says there is a certain ultimate pluralism in it; and, so saying, it corroborates our ordinary unsophisticated view of things. To that view, actualities seem to float in a wider sea of possibilities from out of which they are chosen; and, *somewhere,* indeterminism says, such possibilities exist, and form a part of truth.

Determinism, on the contrary, says they exist *nowhere,* and that necessity on the one hand and impossibility on the other are the sole categories of the real. Possibilities that fail to get realized are, for determinism, pure illusions: they never were possibilities at all. There is nothing inchoate, it says, about this universe of ours, all that was or is or shall be actual in it having been from eternity virtually there. The cloud of alternatives our minds escort this mass of actuality withal is a cloud of sheer deceptions, to which 'impossibilities' is the only name that rightfully belongs.

The issue, it will be seen, is a perfectly sharp one, which no eulogistic terminology can smear over or wipe out. The truth *must* lie with one side or the other, and its lying with one side makes the other false.

The question relates solely to the existence of possibilities, in the strict sense of the term, as things that may, but need not, be. Both sides admit that a volition, for instance, has occurred. The indeterminists say another volition might have occurred in its place: the determinists swear that nothing could possibly have occurred in its place. Now, can science be called in to tell us which of these two point-blank contradicters of each other is right? Science professes to draw no conclusions but such as are based on matters of fact, things that have actually happened; but how can any amount of assurance that something actually happened give us the least grain of information as to whether another thing might or might not have happened in its place? Only facts can be proved by other facts. With things that are possibilities and not facts, facts have no concern. If we have no other evidence than the evidence of existing facts, the possibility-question must remain a mystery never to be cleared up.

And the truth is that facts practically have hardly anything to do with making us either determinists or indeterminists. Sure enough, we make a flourish of quoting facts this way or that; and if we are determinists, we talk about the infallibility with which we can predict one another's conduct; while if we are indeterminists, we lay great stress on the fact that it is just because we cannot foretell one another's conduct, either in war or statecraft or in any of the great and small intrigues and businesses of men, that life is so intensely anxious and hazardous a game. But who does not see the wretched insufficiency of this so-called objective testimony on both sides? What fills up the gaps in our minds is something not objective, not external. What divides us into possibility men and anti-possibility men is different faiths or postulates,—postulates of rationality. To this man the world seems more rational with possibilities in it,—to that man more rational with possibilities excluded; and talk as we will about having to yield to evidence, what makes us monists or pluralists, determinists or indeterminists, is at bottom always some sentiment like this.

The stronghold of the deterministic sentiment is the antipathy to the idea of chance. As soon as we begin to talk indeterminism to our friends, we find a number of them shaking their heads. This notion of alternative possibility, they say, this admission that any one of several things may come to pass, is, after all, only a roundabout name for chance; and chance is something the notion of which no sane mind can for an instant tolerate in the world. What is it, they ask, but barefaced crazy unreason, the negation of intelligibility and law? And if the slightest particle of it exist anywhere, what is to prevent the whole fabric from falling together, the stars from going out, and chaos from recommencing her topsy-turvy reign?

Remarks of this sort about chance will put an end to discussion as quickly as anything one can find. I have already told you that 'chance' was a word I wished to keep and use. Let us then examine exactly what it means, and see whether it ought to be such a terrible bugbear to us. I fancy that squeezing the thistle boldly will rob it of its sting.

The sting of the word 'chance' seems to lie in the assumption that it means something positive, and that if anything happens by chance, it must needs be something of an intrinsically irrational and preposterous sort. Now, chance means nothing of the kind. It is a purely negative and relative term,[4] giving us no information about that of which it is predicated, except that it happens to be disconnected with something else,—not controlled, secured, or necessitated by other things in advance of its own actual presence. As this point is the most subtle one of the whole lecture, and at the same time the point on

---

[4] Speaking technically, it is a word with a positive denotation, but a connotation that is negative. Other things must be silent about *what* it is: it alone can decide that point at the moment in which it reveals itself.

which all the rest hinges, I beg you to pay particular attention to it. What I say is that it tells us nothing about what a thing may be in itself to call it 'chance.' It may be a bad thing, it may be a good thing. It may be lucidity, transparency, fitness incarnate, matching the whole system of other things, when it has once befallen, in an unimaginably perfect way. All you mean by calling it 'chance' is that this is not guaranteed, that it may also fall out otherwise. For the system of other things has no positive hold on the chance-thing. Its origin is in a certain fashion negative: it escapes, and says, Hands off! coming, when it comes, as a free gift, or not at all.

This negativeness, however, and this opacity of the chance-thing when thus considered *ab extra,* or from the point of view of previous things or distant things, do not preclude its having any amount of positiveness and luminosity from within, and at its own place and moment. All that its chance-character asserts about it is that there is something in it really of its own, something that is not the unconditional property of the whole. If the whole wants this property, the whole must wait till it can get it, if it be a matter of chance. That the universe may actually be a sort of joint-stock society of this sort, in which the sharers have both limited liabilities and limited powers, is of course a simple and conceivable notion.

Nevertheless, many persons talk as if the minutest dose of disconnectedness of one part with another, the smallest modicum of independence, the faintest tremor of ambiguity about the future, for example, would ruin everything, and turn this goodly universe into a sort of insane sand-heap or nulliverse, no universe at all. Since future human volitions are as a matter of fact the only ambiguous things we are tempted to believe in, let us stop for a moment to make ourselves sure whether their independent and accidental character need be fraught with such direful consequences to the universe as these.

What is meant by saying that my choice of which way to walk home after the lecture is ambiguous and matter of chance as far as the present moment is concerned? It means that both Divinity Avenue and Oxford Street are called; but that only one, and that one *either* one, shall be chosen. Now, I ask you seriously to suppose that this ambiguity of my choice is real; and then to make the impossible hypothesis that the choice is made twice over, and each time falls on a different street. In other words, imagine that I first walk through Divinity Avenue, and then imagine that the powers governing the universe annihilate ten minutes of time with all that it contained, and set me back at the door of this hall just as I was before the choice was made. Imagine then that, everything else being the same, I now make a different choice and traverse Oxford Street. You, as passive spectators, look on and see the two alternative universes,—one of them with me walking through Divinity Avenue in it, the other with the same me walking through Oxford Street. Now, if you are determinists you believe one of these universes to have been from eternity impossible: you believe it to have been impossible because of the intrinsic irrationality or accidentality somewhere involved in it. But looking outwardly at these universes, can you say which is the impossible and accidental one, and which the rational and necessary one? I doubt if the most ironclad determinist among you could have the slightest glimmer of light on this point. In other words, either universe *after the fact* and once there would, to our means of observation and understanding, appear just as rational as the other. There would be absolutely no criterion by which we might judge one necessary and the other matter of chance. Suppose now we relieve the gods of their hypothetical task and assume my choice, once made, to be made forever. I go through Divinity Avenue for good and all. If, as good determinists, you now begin to affirm, what all good determinists punctually do affirm, that in the nature of things I *could n't* have gone through Oxford Street,—had I done so it would have been chance, irrationality, insanity, a horrid gap in nature,—I simply call your attention to this, that your affirmation is what the Germans call a *Machtspruch,* a mere conception fulminated as a dogma and based on no insight into details. Before my choice, either street seemed as natural to you as to me. Had I happened to take Oxford Street, Divinity Avenue would have figured in your philosophy as the gap in nature; and you would have so proclaimed it with the best deterministic conscience in the world.

But what a hollow outcry, then, is this against a chance which, if it were present to us, we could by no character whatever distinguish from a rational necessity! I have taken the most trivial of examples, but no possible example could lead to any different result. For what are the alternatives which, in point of fact, offer themselves to human volition? What are those futures that now seem matters of chance? Are they not one and all like the Divinity Avenue and Oxford Street of our example? Are they not all of them *kinds* of things already here and based in the existing frame of nature? Is any one ever tempted to produce an *absolute* accident, something utterly irrelevant to the rest of the world? Do not all the motives that assail us, all the futures that offer themselves to our choice, spring equally from the soil of the past; and would not either one of them, whether realized through chance or through necessity, the moment it was realized, seem to us to fit that past, and in the completest and most continuous manner to interdigitate with the phenomena already there? [5]

[5] A favorite argument against free-will is that if it be true, a man's murderer may as probably be his best friend as his worst enemy, a mother be as likely to strangle as to suckle her first-born, and all of us be as ready to jump from

The more one thinks of the matter, the more one wonders that so empty and gratuitous a hubbub as this outcry against chance should have found so great an echo in the hearts of men. It is a word which tells us absolutely nothing about what chances, or about the *modus operandi* of the chancing; and the use of it as a war-cry shows only a temper of intellectual absolutism, a demand that the world shall be a solid block, subject to one control,—which temper, which demand, the world may not be bound to gratify at all. In every outwardly verifiable and practical respect, a world in which the alternatives that now actually distract *your* choice were decided by pure chance would be by *me* absolutely undistinguished from the world in which I now live. I am, therefore, entirely willing to call it, so far as your choices go, a world of chance for me. To *yourselves,* it is true, those very acts of choice, which to me are so blind, opaque, and external, are the opposites of this, for you are within them and effect them. To you they appear as decisions; and decisions, for him who makes them, are altogether peculiar psychic facts. Self-luminous and self-justifying at the living moment at which they occur, they appeal to no outside moment to put its stamp upon them or make them continuous with the rest of nature. Themselves it is rather who seem to make nature continuous; and in their strange and intense function of granting consent to one possibility and withholding it from another, to transform an equivocal and double future into an inalterable and simple past.

But with the psychology of the matter we have no concern this evening. The quarrel which determinism has with chance fortunately has nothing to do with this or that psychological detail. It is a quarrel altogether metaphysical. Determinism denies the ambiguity of future volitions, because it affirms that nothing future can be ambiguous. But we have said enough to meet the issue. Indeterminate future volitions *do* mean chance. Let us not fear to shout it from the house-tops if need be; for we now know that the idea of chance is, at bottom, exactly the same thing as the idea of gift,—the one simply being a disparaging, and the other a eulogistic, name for anything on which we have no effective *claim.* And whether the world be the better or the worse for having either chances or gifts in it will depend altogether on *what* these uncertain and unclaimable things turn out to be.

· · ·

fourth-story windows as to go out of front doors, etc. Users of this argument should properly be excluded from debate till they learn what the real question is. 'Free-will' does not say that everything that is physically conceivable is also morally possible. It merely says that of alternatives that really *tempt* our will more than one is really possible. Of course, the alternatives that do thus tempt our will are vastly fewer than the physical possibilities we can coldly fancy. Persons really tempted often do murder their best friends, mothers do strangle their first-born, people do jump out of fourth-story windows, etc.

And this at last brings us within sight of our subject. We have seen what determinism means: we have seen that indeterminism is rightly described as meaning chance; and we have seen that chance, the very name of which we are urged to shrink from as from a metaphysical pestilence, means only the negative fact that no part of the world, however big, can claim to control absolutely the destinies of the whole. But although, in discussing the word 'chance,' I may at moments have seemed to be arguing for its real existence, I have not meant to do so yet. We have not yet ascertained whether this be a world of chance or no; at most, we have agreed that it seems so. And I now repeat what I said at the outset, that, from any strict theoretical point of view, the question is insoluble. To deepen our theoretic sense of the *difference* between a world with chances in it and a deterministic world is the most I can hope to do; and this I may now at last begin upon, after all our tedious clearing of the way.

I wish first of all to show you just what the notion that this is a deterministic world implies. The implications I call your attention to are all bound up with the fact that it is a world in which we constantly have to make what I shall, with your permission, call judgments of regret. Hardly an hour passes in which we do not wish that something might be otherwise; and happy indeed are those of us whose hearts have never echoed the wish of Omar Khayam—

> That we might clasp, ere closed, the book of fate,
>   And make the writer on a fairer leaf
> Inscribe our names, or quite obliterate.
>
> Ah! Love, could you and I with fate conspire
> To mend this sorry scheme of things entire,
>   Would we not shatter it to bits, and then
> Remould it nearer to the heart's desire?

Now, it is undeniable that most of these regrets are foolish, and quite on a par in point of philosophic value with the criticisms on the universe of that friend of our infancy, the hero of the fable The Atheist and the Acorn,—

> Fool! had that bough a pumpkin bore,
> Thy whimsies would have worked no more, etc.

Even from the point of view of our own ends, we should probably make a botch of remodelling the universe. How much more then from the point of view of ends we cannot see! Wise men therefore regret as little as they can. But still some regrets are pretty obstinate and hard to stifle,—regrets for acts of wanton cruelty or treachery, for example, whether performed by others or by ourselves. Hardly any one can remain *entirely* optimistic after reading the confession of the murderer at Brockton the other day: how, to get rid of the wife whose continued existence bored him, he inveigled her into a desert spot, shot her four times, and then, as she lay on the ground and said to him, "You did n't do it on purpose, did you, dear?" replied, "No, I did n't do it on purpose," as he raised a rock and smashed her skull. Such an occurrence, with the mild sentence and self-satisfaction of the prisoner, is a field for a crop of regrets, which one need not take up in detail. We feel that, although a perfect mechanical fit to the rest of the universe, it is a bad moral fit, and that something else would really have been better in its place.

But for the deterministic philosophy the murder, the sentence, and the prisoner's optimism were all necessary from eternity; and nothing else for a moment had a ghost of a chance of being put into their place. To admit such a chance, the determinists tell us, would be to make a suicide of reason; so we must steel our hearts against the thought. And here our plot thickens, for we see the first of those difficult implications of determinism and monism which it is my purpose to make you feel. If this Brockton murder was called for by the rest of the universe, if it had to come at its preappointed hour, and if nothing else would have been consistent with the sense of the whole, what are we to think of the universe? Are we stubbornly to stick to our judgment of regret, and say, though it *could n't* be, yet it *would* have been a better universe with something different from this Brockton murder in it? That, of course, seems the natural and spontaneous thing for us to do; and yet it is nothing short of deliberately espousing a kind of pessimism. The judgment of regret calls the murder bad. Calling a thing bad means, if it mean anything at all, that the thing ought not to be, that something else ought to be in its stead. Determinism, in denying that anything else can be in its stead, virtually defines the universe as a place in which what ought to be is impossible,—in other words, as an organism whose constitution is afflicted with an incurable taint, an irremediable flaw. The pessimism of a Schopenhauer says no more than this,—that the murder is a symptom; and that it is a vicious symptom because it belongs to a vicious whole, which can express its nature no otherwise than by bringing forth just such a symptom as that at this particular spot. Regret for the murder must transform itself, if we are determinists and wise, into a larger regret. It is absurd to regret the murder alone. Other things being what they are, *it* could not be different. What we should regret is that whole frame of things of which the murder is one member. I see no escape whatever from this pessimistic conclusion, if, being determinists, our judgment of regret is to be allowed to stand at all.

The only deterministic escape from pessimism is everywhere to abandon the judgment of regret. That this can be done, history shows to be not impossible. The devil, *quoad existentiam,* may be good. That is, although he be a *principle* of evil, yet the universe, with such a principle in it, may practically be a better universe than it could have been without. On every hand, in a small way, we find that a certain amount of evil is a condition by which a higher form of good is bought. There is nothing to prevent anybody from generalizing this view, and trusting that if we could but see things in the largest of all ways, even such matters as this Brockton murder would appear to be paid for by the uses that follow in their train. An optimism *quand même,* a systematic and infatuated optimism like that ridiculed by Voltaire in his Candide, is one of the possible ideal ways in which a man may train himself to look on life. Bereft of dogmatic hardness and lit up with the expression of a tender and pathetic hope, such an optimism has been the grace of some of the most religious characters that ever lived.

> Throb thine with Nature's throbbing breast,
> And all is clear from east to west.

Even cruelty and treachery may be among the absolutely blessed fruits of time, and to quarrel with any of their details may be blasphemy. The only real blasphemy, in short, may be that pessimistic temper of the soul which lets it give way to such things as regrets, remorse, and grief.

Thus, our deterministic pessimism may become a deterministic optimism at the price of extinguishing our judgments of regret.

But does not this immediately bring us into a curious logical predicament? Our determinism leads us to call our judgments of regret wrong, because they are pessimistic in implying that what is impossible yet ought to be. But how then about the judgments of regret themselves? If they are wrong, other judgments, judgments of approval presumably, ought to be in their place. But as they are necessitated, nothing else *can* be in their place; and the universe is just what it was before,—namely, a place in which what ought to be appears impossible. We have got one foot out of the pessimistic bog, but the other one sinks all the deeper. We have rescued our actions from the bonds of evil, but our judgments are now held fast. When murders and treacheries cease to be sins, regrets are theoretic absurdities and errors. The theoretic and the active life thus play a kind of seesaw with each other on the ground of evil. The rise of either sends the other down. Murder and treachery cannot be good without regret being bad: regret cannot be good without treachery and murder being bad. Both, however, are supposed to have been foredoomed; so something must be fatally unreasonable, absurd, and wrong in the world. It must be a place of which either sin or error forms a necessary part. From this dilemma there seems at first sight no escape. Are we then so soon to fall back into the pessimism from which we thought we had emerged? And is there no possible way by which we may, with good intellectual consciences, call the cruelties and the treacheries, the reluctances and the regrets, *all* good together?

Certainly there is such a way, and you are probably most of you ready to formulate it yourselves. But, before doing so, remark how inevitably the question of determinism and indeterminism slides us into the question of optimism and pessimism, or, as our fathers called it, 'the question of evil.' The theological form of all these disputes is the simplest and the deepest, the form from which there is the least escape,—not because, as some have sarcastically said, remorse and regret are clung to with a morbid fondness by the theologians as spiritual luxuries, but because they are existing facts of the world, and as such must be taken into account in the deterministic interpretation of all that is fated to be. If they are fated to be error, does not the bat's wing of irrationality still cast its shadow over the world?

The refuge from the quandary lies, as I said, not far off. The necessary acts we erroneously regret may be good, and yet our error in so regretting them may be also good, on one simple condition; and that condition is this: The world must not be regarded as a machine whose final purpose is the making real of any outward good, but rather as a contrivance for deepening the theoretic consciousness of what goodness and evil in their intrinsic natures are. Not the doing either of good or of evil is what nature cares for, but the knowing of them. Life is one long eating of the fruit of the tree of *knowledge*. I am in the habit, in thinking to myself, of calling this point of view the *gnostical* point of view. According to it, the world is neither an optimism nor a pessimism, but a *gnosticism*. But as this term may perhaps lead to some misunderstandings, I will use it as little as possible here, and speak rather of *subjectivism,* and the *subjectivistic* point of view.

Subjectivism has three great branches,—we may call them scientificism, sentimentalism, and sensualism, respectively. They all agree essentially about the universe, in deeming that what happens there is subsidiary to what we think or feel about it. Crime justifies its criminality by awakening our intelligence of that criminality, and eventually our remorses and regrets; and the error included in remorses and regrets, the error of supposing that the past could have been different, justifies itself by its use. Its use is to quicken our sense of *what* the irretrievably lost is. When we think of it as that which might have been ('the saddest words of tongue or pen'), the quality of its worth speaks to us with a wilder sweetness; and, conversely, the dissatisfaction wherewith we think of what seems to have driven it from its natural place gives us the severer pang. Admirable artifice of nature! we might be tempted to exclaim,—deceiving us in order the better to enlighten us, and leaving nothing undone to accentuate to our consciousness the yawning distance of those opposite poles of good and evil between which creation swings.

We have thus clearly revealed to our view what may be called the dilemma of determinism, so far as determinism pretends to think things out at all. A merely mechanical determinism, it is true, rather rejoices in not thinking them out. It is very sure that the universe must satisfy its postulate of a physical continuity and coherence, but it smiles at any one who comes forward with a postulate of moral coherence as well. I may suppose, however, that the number of purely mechanical or hard determinists among you this evening is small. The determinism to whose seductions you are most exposed is what I have called soft determinism,—the determinism which allows considerations of good and bad to mingle with those of cause and effect in deciding what sort of a universe this may rationally be held to be. The dilemma of this determinism is one whose left horn is pessimism and whose right horn is subjectivism. In other words, if determinism is to escape pessimism, it must leave off looking at the goods and ills of life in a simple objective way, and regard them as materials, indifferent in themselves, for the production of consciousness, scientific and ethical, in us.

To escape pessimism is, as we all know, no easy task. Your own studies have sufficiently shown you the almost desperate difficulty of making the notion that there is a single principle of things, and that principle absolute perfection, rhyme together with our daily vision of the facts of life. If perfection be the principle, how comes there any imperfection here? If God be good, how came he to create—or, if he did not create, how comes he to permit—the devil? The evil facts must be explained as seeming: the devil must be whitewashed, the universe must be disinfected, if neither God's goodness nor his unity and power are to remain impugned. And of all the various ways of operating the disinfection, and making bad seem less bad, the way of subjectivism appears by far the best.[6]

For, after all, is there not something rather absurd in our ordinary

[6] To a reader who says he is satisfied with a pessimism, and has no objection to thinking the whole bad, I have no more to say: he makes fewer demands on the world than I, who, making them, wish to look a little further before I give up all hope of having them satisfied. If, however, all he means is that the badness of some parts does not prevent his acceptance of a universe whose *other* parts give him satisfaction, I welcome him as an ally. He has abandoned the notion of the *Whole,* which is the essence of deterministic monism, and views things as a pluralism, just as I do in this paper.

notion of external things being good or bad in themselves? Can murders and treacheries, considered as mere outward happenings, or motions of matter, be bad without any one to feel their badness? And could paradise properly be good in the absence of a sentient principle by which the goodness was perceived? Outward goods and evils seem practically indistinguishable except in so far as they result in getting moral judgments made about them. But then the moral judgments seem the main thing, and the outward facts mere perishing instruments for their production. This is subjectivism. Every one must at some time have wondered at that strange paradox of our moral nature, that, though the pursuit of outward good is the breath of its nostrils, the attainment of outward good would seem to be in suffocation and death. Why does the painting of any paradise or utopia, in heaven or on earth, awaken such yawnings for nirvana and escape? The white-robed harp-playing heaven of our sabbath-schools and the ladylike tea-table elysium represented in Mr. Spencer's Data of Ethics, as the final consummation of progress, are exactly on a par in this respect—lubberlands, pure and simple, one and all.[7] We look upon them from this delicious mess of insanities and realities, strivings and deadnesses, hopes and fears, agonies and exultations, which forms our present state, and *tedium vitæ* is the only sentiment they awaken in our breasts. To our crepuscular natures, born for the conflict, the Rembrandtesque moral chiaroscuro, the shifting struggle of the sunbeam in the gloom, such pictures of light upon light are vacuous and expressionless, and neither to be enjoyed nor understood. If *this* be the whole fruit of the victory, we say; if the generations of mankind suffered and laid down their lives; if prophets confessed and martyrs sang in the fire, and all the sacred tears were shed for no other end than that a race of creatures of such unexampled insipidity should succeed, and protract *in saecula saeculorum* their contented and inoffensive lives,—why, at such a rate, better lose than win the battle, or at all events better ring down the curtain before the last act of the play, so that a business that began so importantly may be saved from so singularly flat a winding-up.

All this is what I should instantly say, were I called on to plead for gnosticism; and its real friends, of whom you will presently perceive I am not one, would say without difficulty a great deal more. Regarded as a stable finality, every outward good becomes a mere weariness to the flesh. It must be menaced, be occasionally lost, for its goodness to be fully felt as such. Nay, more than occasionally lost. No one knows the worth of innocence till he knows it is gone forever, and that money cannot buy it back. Not the saint, but the sinner that repenteth,

[7] Compare Sir James Stephen's *Essays by a Barrister,* London, 1862, pp. 138, 318.

is he to whom the full length and breadth, and height and depth, of life's meaning is revealed. Not the absence of vice, but vice there, and virtue holding her by the throat, seems the ideal human state. And there seems no reason to suppose it not a permanent human state. There is a deep truth in what the school of Schopenhauer insists on,— the illusoriness of the notion of moral progress. The more brutal forms of evil that go are replaced by others more subtle and more poisonous. Our moral horizon moves with us as we move, and never do we draw nearer to the far-off line where the black waves and the azure meet. The final purpose of our creation seems most plausibly to be the greatest possible enrichment of our ethical consciousness, through the intensest play of contrasts and the widest diversity of characters. This of course obliges some of us to be vessels of wrath, while it calls others to be vessels of honor. But the subjectivist point of view reduces all these outward distinctions to a common denominator. The wretch languishing in the felon's cell may be drinking draughts of the wine of truth that will never pass the lips of the so-called favorite of fortune. And the peculiar consciousness of each of them is an indispensable note in the great ethical concert which the centuries as they roll are grinding out of the living heart of man.

So much for subjectivism! If the dilemma of determinism be to choose between it and pessimism, I see little room for hesitation from the strictly theoretical point of view. Subjectivism seems the more rational scheme. And the world may, possibly, for aught I know, be nothing else. When the healthy love of life is on one, and all its forms and its appetites seem so unutterably real; when the most brutal and the most spiritual things are lit by the same sun, and each is an integral part of the total richness,—why, then it seems a grudging and sickly way of meeting so robust a universe to shrink from any of its facts and wish them not to be. Rather take the strictly dramatic point of view, and treat the whole thing as a great unending romance which the spirit of the universe, striving to realize its own content, is eternally thinking out and representing to itself.[8]

No one, I hope, will accuse me, after I have said all this, of underrating the reasons in favor of subjectivism. And now that I proceed to say why those reasons, strong as they are, fail to convince my own mind, I trust the presumption may be that my objections are stronger still.

I frankly confess that they are of a practical order. If we practically take up subjectivism in a sincere and radical manner and follow

[8] Cet univers est un spectacle que Dieu se donne à lui-même. Servons les intentions du grand chorège en contribuant à rendre le spectacle aussi brillant, aussi varié que possible.—RENAN.

its consequences, we meet with some that make us pause. Let a subjectivism begin in never so severe and intellectual a way, it is forced by the law of its nature to develop another side of itself and end with the corruptest curiosity. Once dismiss the notion that certain duties are good in themselves, and that we are here to do them, no matter how we feel about them; once consecrate the opposite notion that our performances and our violations of duty are for a common purpose, the attainment of subjective knowledge and feeling, and that the deepening of these is the chief end of our lives,—and at what point on the downward slope are we to stop? In theology, subjectivism develops as its 'left wing' antinomianism. In literature, its left wing is romanticism. And in practical life it is either a nerveless sentimentality or a sensualism without bounds.

Everywhere it fosters the fatalistic mood of mind. It makes those who are already too inert more passive still; it renders wholly reckless those whose energy is already in excess. All through history we find how subjectivism, as soon as it has a free career, exhausts itself in every sort of spiritual, moral, and practical license. Its optimism turns to an ethical indifference, which infallibly brings dissolution in its train. It is perfectly safe to say now that if the Hegelian gnosticism, which has begun to show itself here and in Great Britain, were to become a popular philosophy, as it once was in Germany, it would certainly develop its left wing here as there, and produce a reaction of disgust. Already I have heard a graduate of this very school express in the pulpit his willingness to sin like David, if only he might repent like David. You may tell me he was only sowing his wild, or rather his tame, oats; and perhaps he was. But the point is that in the subjectivistic or gnostical philosophy oat sowing, wild or tame, becomes a systematic necessity and the chief function of life. After the pure and classic truths, the exciting and rancid ones must be experienced; and if the stupid virtues of the philistine herd do not then come in and save society from the influence of the children of light, a sort of inward putrefaction becomes its inevitable doom.

Look at the last runnings of the romantic school, as we see them in that strange contemporary Parisian literature, with which we of the less clever countries are so often driven to rinse out our minds after they have become clogged with the dulness and heaviness of our native pursuits. The romantic school began with the worship of subjective sensibility and the revolt against legality of which Rousseau was the first great prophet: and through various fluxes and refluxes, right wings and left wings, it stands to-day with two men of genius, M. Renan and M. Zola, as its principal exponents,—one speaking with its masculine, and the other with what might be called its feminine, voice. I prefer not to think now of less noble members of the school, and the

Renan I have in mind is of course the Renan of latest dates. As I have used the term gnostic, both he and Zola are gnostics of the most pronounced sort. Both are athirst for the facts of life, and both think the facts of human sensibility to be of all facts the most worthy of attention. Both agree, moreover, that sensibility seems to be there for no higher purpose,—certainly not, as the Philistines say, for the sake of bringing mere outward rights to pass and frustrating outward wrongs. One dwells on the sensibilities for their energy, the other for their sweetness; one speaks with a voice of bronze, the other with that of an Æolian harp; one ruggedly ignores the distinction of good and evil, the other plays the coquette between the craven unmanliness of his Philosophic Dialogues and the butterfly optimism of his Souvenirs de Jeunesse. But under the pages of both there sounds incessantly the hoarse bass of *vanitas vanitatum, omnia vanitas,* which the reader may hear, whenever he will, between the lines. No writer of this French romantic school has a word of rescue from the hour of satiety with the things of life,—the hour in which we say, "I take no pleasure in them,"—or from the hour of terror at the world's vast meaningless grinding, if perchance such hours should come. For terror and satiety are facts of sensibility like any others; and at their own hour they reign in their own right. The heart of the romantic utterances, whether poetical, critical, or historical, is this inward remedilessness, what Carlyle calls this far-off whimpering of wail and woe. And from this romantic state of mind there is absolutely no possible *theoretic* escape. Whether, like Renan, we look upon life in a more refined way, as a romance of the spirit; or whether, like the friends of M. Zola, we pique ourselves on our 'scientific' and 'analytic' character, and prefer to be cynical, and call the world a 'roman expérimental' on an infinite scale,—in either case the world appears to us potentially as what the same Carlyle once called it, a vast, gloomy, solitary Golgotha and mill of death.

The only escape is by the practical way. And since I have mentioned the nowadays much-reviled name of Carlyle, let me mention it once more, and say it is the way of his teaching. No matter for Carlyle's life, no matter for a great deal of his writing. What was the most important thing he said to us? He said: "Hang your sensibilities! Stop your snivelling complaints, and your equally snivelling raptures! Leave off your general emotional tomfoolery, and get to WORK like men!" But this means a complete rupture with the subjectivist philosophy of things. It says conduct, and not sensibility, is the ultimate fact for our recognition. With the vision of certain works to be done, of certain outward changes to be wrought or resisted, it says our intellectual horizon terminates. No matter how we succeed in doing these outward duties, whether gladly and spontaneously, or heavily and unwillingly, do them we somehow must; for the leaving of them undone is perdition. No matter how we feel; if we are only faithful in the outward act and refuse to do wrong, the world will in so far be safe, and we quit of our debt toward it. Take, then, the yoke upon our shoulders; bend our neck beneath the heavy legality of its weight; regard something else than our feeling as our limit, our master, and our law; be willing to live and die in its service,—and, at a stroke, we have passed from the subjective into the objective philosophy of things, much as one awakens from some feverish dream, full of bad lights and noises, to find one's self bathed in the sacred coolness and quiet of the air of the night.

But what is the essence of this philosophy of objective conduct, so old-fashioned and finite, but so chaste and sane and strong, when compared with its romantic rival? It is the recognition of limits, foreign and opaque to our understanding. It is the willingness, after bringing about some external good, to feel at peace; for our responsibility ends with the performance of that duty, and the burden of the rest we may lay on higher powers.[9]

> Look to thyself, O Universe,
> Thou art better and not worse,

we may say in that philosophy, the moment we have done our stroke of conduct, however small. For in the view of that philosophy the universe belongs to a plurality of semi-independent forces, each one of which may help or hinder, and be helped or hindered by, the operations of the rest.

But this brings us right back, after such a long détour, to the question of indeterminism and to the conclusion of all I came here to say to-night. For the only consistent way of representing a pluralism and a world whose parts may affect one another through their conduct being either good or bad is the indeterministic way. What interest, zest, or excitement can there be in achieving the right way, unless we are enabled to feel that the wrong way is also a possible and a natural way,—nay, more, a menacing and an imminent way? And what sense can there be in condemning ourselves for taking the wrong way, unless we need have done nothing of the sort, unless the right way was open to us as well? I cannot understand the willingness to act, no matter how we feel, without the belief that acts are really good and bad. I cannot understand the belief that an act is bad, without regret at its happening. I cannot understand regret without the admission of real, genuine possibilities in the world. Only *then* is it other than a mockery to feel, after we have failed to do our best, that an irreparable

---

[9] The burden, for example, of seeing to it that the *end* of all our righteousness be some positive universal gain.

opportunity is gone from the universe, the loss of which it must forever after mourn.

If you insist that this is all superstition, that possibility is in the eye of science and reason impossibility, and that if I act badly it is that the universe was foredoomed to suffer this defect, you fall right back into the dilemma, the labyrinth, of pessimism and subjectivism, from out of whose toils we have just wound our way.

Now, we are of course free to fall back, if we please. For my own part, though, whatever difficulties may beset the philosophy of objective right and wrong, and the indeterminism it seems to imply, determinism, with its alternative of pessimism or romanticism, contains difficulties that are greater still. But you will remember that I expressly repudiated awhile ago the pretension to offer any arguments which could be coercive in a so-called scientific fashion in this matter. And I consequently find myself, at the end of this long talk, obliged to state my conclusions in an altogether personal way. This personal method of appeal seems to be among the very conditions of the problem; and the most any one can do is to confess as candidly as he can the grounds for the faith that is in him, and leave his example to work on others as it may.

Let me, then, without circumlocution say just this. The world is enigmatical enough in all conscience, whatever theory we may take up toward it. The indeterminism I defend, the free-will theory of popular sense based on the judgment of regret, represents that world as vulnerable, and liable to be injured by certain of its parts if they act wrong. And it represents their acting wrong as a matter of possibility or accident, neither inevitable nor yet to be infallibly warded off. In all this, it is a theory devoid either of transparency or of stability. It gives us a pluralistic, restless universe, in which no single point of view can ever take in the whole scene; and to a mind possessed of the love of unity at any cost, it will, no doubt, remain forever inacceptable. A friend with such a mind once told me that the thought of my universe made him sick, like the sight of the horrible motion of a mass of maggots in their carrion bed.

But while I freely admit that the pluralism and the restlessness are repugnant and irrational in a certain way, I find that every alternative to them is irrational in a deeper way. The indeterminism with its maggots, if you please to speak so about it, offends only the native absolutism of my intellect,—an absolutism which, after all, perhaps, deserves to be snubbed and kept in check. But the determinism with its necessary carrion, to continue the figure of speech, and with no possible maggots to eat the latter up, violates my sense of moral reality through and through. When, for example, I imagine such carrion as the Brockton murder, I cannot conceive it as an act by which the universe, as a whole, logically and necessarily expresses its nature without shrinking from complicity with such a whole. And I deliberately refuse to keep on terms of loyalty with the universe by saying blankly that the murder, since it does flow from the nature of the whole, is not carrion. There are *some* instinctive reactions which I, for one, will not tamper with. The only remaining alternative, the attitude of gnostical romanticism, wrenches my personal instincts in quite as violent a way. It falsifies the simple objectivity of their deliverance. It makes the goose-flesh the murder excites in me a sufficient reason for the perpetration of the crime. It transforms life from a tragic reality into an insincere melodramatic exhibition, as foul or as tawdry as any one's diseased curiosity pleases to carry it out. And with its consecration of the 'roman naturaliste' state of mind, and its enthronement of the baser crew of Parisian *littérateurs* among the eternally indispensable organs by which the infinite spirit of things attains to that subjective illumination which is the task of its life, it leaves me in presence of a sort of subjective carrion considerably more noisome than the objective carrion I called it in to take away.

No! better a thousand times, than such systematic corruption of our moral sanity, the plainest pessimism, so that it be straightforward; but better far than that the world of chance. Make as great an uproar about chance as you please, I know that chance means pluralism and nothing more. If some of the members of the pluralism are bad, the philosophy of pluralism, whatever broad views it may deny me, permits me, at least, to turn to the other members with a clean breast of affection and an unsophisticated moral sense. And if I still wish to think of the world as a totality, it lets me feel that a world with a *chance* in it of being altogether good, even if the chance never come to pass, is better than a world with no such chance at all. That 'chance' whose very notion I am exhorted and conjured to banish from my view of the future as the suicide of reason concerning it, that 'chance' is—what? Just this,—the chance that in moral respects the future may be other and better than the past has been. This is the only chance we have any motive for supposing to exist. Shame, rather, on its repudiation and its denial! For its presence is the vital air which lets the world live, the salt which keeps it sweet.

And here I might legitimately stop, having expressed all I care to see admitted by others to-night. But I know that if I do stop here, misapprehensions will remain in the minds of some of you, and keep all I have said from having its effect; so I judge it best to add a few more words.

In the first place, in spite of all my explanations, the word 'chance' will still be giving trouble. Though you may yourselves be adverse to the deterministic doctrine, you wish a pleasanter word than 'chance' to name the opposite doctrine by; and you very likely consider my preference for such a word a perverse sort of a partiality on my part. It certainly *is* a bad word to make converts with; and you wish I had not thrust it so butt-foremost at you,—you wish to use a milder term.

Well, I admit there may be just a dash of perversity in its choice. The spectacle of the mere word-grabbing game played by the soft determinists has perhaps driven me too violently the other way; and, rather than be found wrangling with them for the good words, I am willing to take the first bad one which comes along, provided it be unequivocal. The question is of things, not of eulogistic names for them; and the best word is the one that enables men to know the quickest whether they disagree or not about the things. But the word 'chance,' with its singular negativity, is just the word for this purpose. Whoever uses it instead of 'freedom,' squarely and resolutely gives up all pretence to control the things he says are free. For *him,* he confesses that they are no better than mere chance would be. It is a word of *impotence,* and is therefore the only sincere word we can use, if, in granting freedom to certain things, we grant it honestly, and really risk the game. "Who chooses me must give and forfeit all he hath." Any other word permits of quibbling, and lets us, after the fashion of the soft determinists, make a pretence of restoring the caged bird to liberty with one hand, while with the other we anxiously tie a string to its leg to make sure it does not get beyond our sight.

But now you will bring up your final doubt. Does not the admission of such an unguaranteed chance or freedom preclude utterly the notion of a Providence governing the world? Does it not leave the fate of the universe at the mercy of the chance-possibilities, and so far insecure? Does it not, in short, deny the craving of our nature for an ultimate peace behind all tempests, for a blue zenith above all clouds?

To this my answer must be very brief. The belief in free-will is not in the least incompatible with the belief in Providence, provided you do not restrict the Providence to fulminating nothing but *fatal* decrees. If you allow him to provide possibilities as well as actualities to the universe, and to carry on his own thinking in those two categories just as we do ours, chances may be there, uncontrolled even by him, and the course of the universe be really ambiguous; and yet the end of all things may be just what he intended it to be from all eternity.

An analogy will make the meaning of this clear. Suppose two men before a chessboard,—the one a novice, the other an expert player of the game. The expert intends to beat. But he cannot foresee exactly what any one actual move of his adversary may be. He knows, however, all the *possible* moves of the latter; and he knows in advance how to meet each of them by a move of his own which leads in the direction of victory. And the victory infallibly arrives, after no matter how devious a course, in the one predestined form of check-mate to the novice's king.

Let now the novice stand for us finite free agents, and the expert for the infinite mind in which the universe lies. Suppose the latter to be thinking out his universe before he actually creates it. Suppose him to say, I will lead things to a certain end, but I will not *now*[10] decide on all the steps thereto. At various points, ambiguous possibilities shall be left open, *either* of which, at a given instant, may become actual. But whichever branch of these bifurcations become real, I know what I shall do at the *next* bifurcation to keep things from drifting away from the final result I intend.[11]

The creator's plan of the universe would thus be left blank as to many of its actual details, but all possibilities would be marked down. The realization of some of these would be left absolutely to chance; that is, would only be determined when the moment of realization came. Other possibilities would be *contingently* determined; that is, their decision would have to wait till it was seen how the matters of absolute chance fell out. But the rest of the plan, including its final upshot, would be rigorously determined once for all. So the creator himself would not need to know *all* the details of actuality until they

[10] This of course leaves the creative mind subject to the law of time. And to any one who insists on the timelessness of that mind I have no reply to make. A mind to whom all time is simultaneously present must see all things under the form of actuality, or under some form to us unknown. If he thinks certain moments as ambiguous in their content while future, he must simultaneously know how the ambiguity will have been decided when they are past. So that none of his mental judgments can possibly be called hypothetical, and his world is one from which chance is excluded. Is not, however, the timeless mind rather a gratuitous fiction? And is not the notion of eternity being given at a stroke to omniscience only just another way of whacking upon us the block-universe, and of denying that possibilities exist?—just the point to be proved. To say that time is an illusory appearance is only a roundabout manner of saying there is no real plurality, and that the frame of things is an absolute unit. Admit plurality, and time may be its form.

[11] And this of course means 'miraculous' interposition, but not necessarily of the gross sort our fathers took such delight in representing, and which has so lost its magic for us. Emerson quotes some Eastern sage as saying that if evil were really done under the sun, the sky would incontinently shrivel to a snakeskin and cast it out in spasms. But, says Emerson, the spasms of Nature are years and centuries; and it will tax man's patience to wait so long. We may think of the reserved possibilities God keeps in his own hand, under as invisible and molecular and slowly self-summating a form as we please. We may think of them as counteracting human agencies which he inspires *ad hoc*. In short, signs and wonders and convulsions of the earth and sky are not the only neutralizers of obstruction to a god's plans of which it is possible to think.

came; and at any time his own view of the world would be a view partly of facts and partly of possibilities, exactly as ours is now. Of one thing, however, he might be certain; and that is that his world was safe, and that no matter how much it might zigzag he could surely bring it home at last.

Now, it is entirely immaterial, in this scheme, whether the creator leave the absolute chance-possibilities to be decided by himself, each when its proper moment arrives, or whether, on the contrary, he alienate this power from himself, and leave the decision out and out to finite creatures such as we men are. The great point is that the possibilities are really *here*. Whether it be we who solve them, or he working through us, at those soul-trying moments when fate's scales seem to quiver, and good snatches the victory from evil or shrinks nerveless from the fight, is of small account, so long as we admit that the issue is decided nowhere else than *here* and *now*. *That* is what gives the palpitating reality to our moral life and makes it tingle, as Mr. Mallock says, with so strange and elaborate an excitement. This reality, this excitement, are what the determinisms, hard and soft alike, suppress by their denial that *anything* is decided here and now, and their dogma that all things were foredoomed and settled long ago. If it be so, may you and I then have been foredoomed to the error of continuing to believe in liberty.[12] It is fortunate for the winding up of controversy that in every discussion with determinism this *argumentum ad hominem* can be its adversary's last word.

THE MORAL PHILOSOPHER AND THE MORAL LIFE* [13]

The main purpose of this paper is to show that there is no such thing possible as an ethical philosophy dogmatically made up in advance. We all help to determine the content of ethical philosophy so far as we

[12] As long as languages contain a future perfect tense, determinists, following the bent of laziness or passion, the lines of least resistance, can reply in that tense, saying, "It will have been fated," to the still small voice which urges an opposite course; and thus excuse themselves from effort in a quite unanswerable way.

* From: W.B., 184–215.

[13] An Address to the Yale Philosophical Club, published in the *International Journal of Ethics,* April, 1891.

contribute to the race's moral life. In other words, there can be no final truth in ethics any more than in physics, until the last man has had his experience and said his say. In the one case as in the other, however, the hypotheses which we now make while waiting, and the acts to which they prompt us, are among the indispensable conditions which determine what that 'say' shall be.

First of all, what is the position of him who seeks an ethical philosophy? To begin with, he must be distinguished from all those who are satisfied to be ethical sceptics. He *will* not be a sceptic; therefore so far from ethical scepticism being one possible fruit of ethical philosophizing, it can only be regarded as that residual alternative to all philosophy which from the outset menaces every would-be philosopher who may give up the quest discouraged, and renounce his original aim. That aim is to find an account of the moral relations that obtain among things, which will weave them into the unity of a stable system, and make of the world what one may call a genuine universe from the ethical point of view. So far as the world resists reduction to the form of unity, so far as ethical propositions seem unstable, so far does the philosopher fail of his ideal. The subject-matter of his study is the ideals he finds existing in the world; the purpose which guides him is this ideal of his own, of getting them into a certain form. This ideal is thus a factor in ethical philosophy whose legitimate presence must never be overlooked; it is a positive contribution which the philosopher himself necessarily makes to the problem. But it is his only positive contribution. At the outset of his inquiry he ought to have no other ideals. Were he interested peculiarly in the triumph of any one kind of good, he would *pro tanto* cease to be a judicial investigator, and become an advocate for some limited element of the case.

There are three questions in ethics which must be kept apart. Let them be called respectively the *psychological* question, the *metaphysical* question, and the *casuistic* question. The psychological question asks after the historical *origin* of our moral ideas and judgments; the metaphysical question asks what the very *meaning* of the words 'good,' 'ill,' and 'obligation' are; the casuistic question asks what is the *measure* of the various goods and ills which men recognize, so that the philosopher may settle the true order of human obligations.

I

The psychological question is for most disputants the only question. When your ordinary doctor of divinity has proved to his own satisfac-

tion that an altogether unique faculty called 'conscience' must be postulated to tell us what is right and what is wrong, or when your
popular-science enthusiast has proclaimed that 'apriorism' is an ex-
ploded superstition, and that our moral judgments have gradually resulted from the teaching of the environment, each of these persons
thinks that ethics is settled and nothing more is to be said. The familiar pair of names, Intuitionist and Evolutionist, so commonly used
now to connote all possible differences in ethical opinion, really refer
to the psychological question alone. The discussion of this question
hinges so much upon particular details that it is impossible to enter
upon it at all within the limits of this paper. I will therefore only
express dogmatically my own belief, which is this,—that the Ben-
thams, the Mills, and the Bains have done a lasting service in taking
so many of our human ideals and showing how they must have arisen
from the association with acts of simple bodily pleasures and reliefs
from pain. Association with many remote pleasures will unquestionably make a thing significant of goodness in our minds; and the more
vaguely the goodness is conceived of, the more mysterious will its
source appear to be. But it is surely impossible to explain all our sentiments and preferences in this simple way. The more minutely psychology studies human nature, the more clearly it finds there traces of
secondary affections, relating the impressions of the environment with
one another and with our impulses in quite different ways from those
mere associations of coexistence and succession which are practically
all that pure empiricism can admit. Take the love of drunkenness;
take bashfulness, the terror of high places, the tendency to seasickness, to faint at the sight of blood, the susceptibility to musical
sounds; take the emotion of the comical, the passion for poetry, for
mathematics, or for metaphysics,—no one of these things can be
wholly explained by either association or utility. They *go with* other
things that can be so explained, no doubt; and some of them are prophetic of future utilities, since there is nothing in us for which some
use may not be found. But their origin is in incidental complications
to our cerebral structure, a structure whose original features arose
with no reference to the perception of such discords and harmonies as
these.

Well, a vast number of our moral perceptions also are certainly
of this secondary and brain-born kind. They deal with directly felt
fitnesses between things, and often fly in the teeth of all the prepossessions of habit and presumptions of utility. The moment you get
beyond the coarser and more commonplace moral maxims, the Dec-
alogues and Poor Richard's Almanacs, you fall into schemes and
positions which to the eye of common-sense are fantastic and over-
strained. The sense for abstract justice which some persons have is as

excentric a variation, from the natural-history point of view, as is the passion for music or for the higher philosophical consistencies which consumes the soul of others. The feeling of the inward dignity of certain spiritual attitudes, as peace, serenity, simplicity, veracity; and of the essential vulgarity of others, as querulousness, anxiety, egoistic fussiness, etc.,—are quite inexplicable except by an innate preference of the more ideal attitude for its own pure sake. The nobler thing *tastes* better, and that is all that we can say. 'Experience' of consequences may truly teach us what things are *wicked,* but what have consequences to do with what is *mean* and *vulgar?* If a man has shot his wife's paramour, by reason of what subtile repugnancy in things is it that we are so disgusted when we hear that the wife and the husband have made it up and are living comfortably together again? Or if the hypothesis were offered us of a world in which Messrs. Fourier's and Bellamy's and Morris's utopias should all be outdone, and millions kept permanently happy on the one simple condition that a certain lost soul on the far-off edge of things should lead a life of lonely torture, what except a specifical and independent sort of emotion can it be which would make us immediately feel, even though an impulse arose within us to clutch at the happiness so offered, how hideous a thing would be its enjoyment when deliberately accepted as the fruit of such a bargain? To what, once more, but subtile brain-born feelings of discord can be due all these recent protests against the entire race-tradition of retributive justice?—I refer to Tolstoï with his ideas of non-resistance, to Mr. Bellamy with his substitution of oblivion for repentance (in his novel of Dr. Heidenhain's Process), to M. Guyau with his radical condemnation of the punitive ideal. All these subtileties of the moral sensibility go as much beyond what can be ciphered out from the 'laws of association' as the delicacies of sentiment possible between a pair of young lovers go beyond such precepts of the 'etiquette to be observed during engagement' as are printed in manuals of social form.

No! Purely inward forces are certainly at work here. All the higher, more penetrating ideals are revolutionary. They present themselves far less in the guise of effects of past experience than in that of probable causes of future experience, factors to which the environment and the lessons it has so far taught us must learn to bend.

This is all I can say of the psychological question now. In the last chapter of a recent work[14] I have sought to prove in a general way the existence, in our thought, of relations which do not merely repeat the couplings of experience. Our ideals have certainly many sources. They are not all explicable as signifying corporeal pleasures to be gained,

[14] *The Principles of Psychology,* New York, H. Holt & Co., 1890. [Cf. above, pp. 74–133.]

and pains to be escaped. And for having so constantly perceived this psychological fact, we must applaud the intuitionist school. Whether or not such applause must be extended to that school's other characteristics will appear as we take up the following questions.

The next one in order is the metaphysical question, of what we mean by the words 'obligation,' 'good,' and 'ill.'

II

First of all, it appears that such words can have no application or relevancy in a world in which no sentient life exists. Imagine an absolutely material world, containing only physical and chemical facts, and existing from eternity without a God, without even an interested spectator: would there be any sense in saying of that world that one of its states is better than another? Or if there were two such worlds possible, would there be any rhyme or reason in calling one good and the other bad,—good or bad positively, I mean, and apart from the fact that one might relate itself better than the other to the philosopher's private interests? But we must leave these private interests out of the account, for the philosopher is a mental fact, and we are asking whether goods and evils and obligations exist in physical facts *per se*. Surely there is no *status* for good and evil to exist in, in a purely insentient world. How can one physical fact, considered simply as a physical fact, be 'better' than another? Betterness is not a physical relation. In its mere material capacity, a thing can no more be good or bad than it can be pleasant or painful. Good for what? Good for the production of another physical fact, do you say? But what in a purely physical universe demands the production of that other fact? Physical facts simply *are* or are *not;* and neither when present or absent, can they be supposed to make demands. If they do, they can only do so by having desires; and then they have ceased to be purely physical facts, and have become facts of conscious sensibility. Goodness, badness, and obligation must be *realized* somewhere in order really to exist; and the first step in ethical philosophy is to see that no merely inorganic 'nature of things' can realize them. Neither moral relations nor the moral law can swing *in vacuo*. Their only habitat can be a mind which feels them; and no world composed of merely physical facts can possibly be a world to which ethical propositions apply.

The moment one sentient being, however, is made a part of the universe, there is a chance for goods and evils really to exist. Moral relations now have their *status,* in that being's consciousness. So far as he feels anything to be good, he *makes* it good. It *is* good, for him; and being good for him, is absolutely good, for he is the sole creator of values in that universe, and outside of his opinion things have no moral character at all.

In such a universe as that it would of course be absurd to raise the question of whether the solitary thinker's judgments of good and ill are true or not. Truth supposes a standard outside of the thinker to which he must conform; but here the thinker is a sort of divinity, subject to no higher judge. Let us call the supposed universe which he inhabits a *moral solitude*. In such a moral solitude it is clear that there can be no outward obligation, and that the only trouble the god-like thinker is liable to have will be over the consistency of his own several ideals with one another. Some of these will no doubt be more pungent and appealing than the rest, their goodness will have a profounder, more penetrating taste; they will return to haunt him with more obstinate regrets if violated. So the thinker will have to order his life with them as its chief determinants, or else remain inwardly discordant and unhappy. Into whatever equilibrium he may settle, though, and however he may straighten out his system, it will be a right system; for beyond the facts of his own subjectivity there is nothing moral in the world.

If now we introduce a second thinker with his likes and dislikes into the universe, the ethical situation becomes much more complex, and several possibilities are immediately seen to obtain.

One of these is that the thinkers may ignore each other's attitude about good and evil altogether, and each continue to indulge his own preferences, indifferent to what the other may feel or do. In such a case we have a world with twice as much of the ethical quality in it as our moral solitude, only it is without ethical unity. The same object is good or bad there, according as you measure it by the view which this one or that one of the thinkers takes. Nor can you find any possible ground in such a world for saying that one thinker's opinion is more correct than the other's, or that either has the truer moral sense. Such a world, in short, is not a moral universe but a moral dualism. Not only is there no single point of view within it from which the values of things can be unequivocally judged, but there is not even a demand for such a point of view, since the two thinkers are supposed to be indifferent to each other's thoughts and acts. Multiply the thinkers into a pluralism, and we find realized for us in the ethical sphere something like that world which the antique sceptics conceived of,— in which individual minds are the measures of all things, and in which no one 'objective' truth, but only a multitude of 'subjective' opinions, can be found.

But this is the kind of world with which the philosopher, so long as he holds to the hope of a philosophy, will not put up. Among the various ideals represented, there must be, he thinks, some which have the more truth or authority; and to these the others *ought* to yield, so that system and subordination may reign. Here in the word 'ought' the notion of *obligation* comes emphatically into view, and the next thing in order must be to make its meaning clear.

Since the outcome of the discussion so far has been to show us that nothing can be good or right except so far as some consciousness feels it to be good or thinks it to be right, we perceive on the very threshold that the real superiority and authority which are postulated by the philosopher to reside in some of the opinions, and the really inferior character which he supposes must belong to others, cannot be explained by any abstract moral 'nature of things' existing antecedently to the concrete thinkers themselves with their ideals. Like the positive attributes good and bad, the comparative ones better and worse must be *realized* in order to be real. If one ideal judgment be objectively better than another, that betterness must be made flesh by being lodged concretely in some one's actual perception. It cannot float in the atmosphere, for it is not a sort of meteorological phenomenon, like the aurora borealis or the zodiacal light. Its *esse* is *percipi*, like the *esse* of the ideals themselves between which it obtains. The philosopher, therefore, who seeks to know which ideal ought to have supreme weight and which one ought to be subordinated, must trace the *ought* itself to the *de facto* constitution of some existing consciousness, behind which, as one of the data of the universe, he as a purely ethical philosopher is unable to go. This consciousness must make the one ideal right by feeling it to be right, the other wrong by feeling it to be wrong. But now what particular consciousness in the universe *can* enjoy this prerogative of obliging others to conform to a rule which it lays down?

If one of the thinkers were obviously divine, while all the rest were human, there would probably be no practical dispute about the matter. The divine thought would be the model, to which the others should conform. But still the theoretic question would remain, What is the ground of the obligation, even here?

In our first essays at answering this question, there is an inevitable tendency to slip into an assumption which ordinary men follow when they are disputing with one another about questions of good and bad. They imagine an abstract moral order in which the objective truth resides; and each tries to prove that this pre-existing order is more accurately reflected in his own ideas than in those of his adversary. It is because one disputant is backed by this overarching abstract order that we think the other should submit. Even so, when it is a question no longer of two finite thinkers, but of God and ourselves,—we follow our usual habit, and imagine a sort of *de jure* relation, which antedates and overarches the mere facts, and would make it right that we should conform our thoughts to God's thoughts, even though he made no claim to that effect, and though we preferred *de facto* to go on thinking for ourselves.

But the moment we take a steady look at the question, *we see not only that without a claim actually made by some concrete person there can be no obligation, but that there is some obligation wherever there is a claim.* Claim and obligation are, in fact, coextensive terms; they cover each other exactly. Our ordinary attitude of regarding ourselves as subject to an overarching system of moral relations, true 'in themselves,' is therefore either an out-and-out superstition, or else it must be treated as a merely provisional abstraction from that real Thinker in whose actual demand upon us to think as he does our obligation must be ultimately based. In a theistic-ethical philosophy that thinker in question is, of course, the Deity to whom the existence of the universe is due.

I know well how hard it is for those who are accustomed to what I have called the superstitious view, to realize that every *de facto* claim creates in so far forth an obligation. We inveterately think that something which we call the 'validity' of the claim is what gives to it its obligatory character, and that this validity is something outside of the claim's mere existence as a matter of fact. It rains down upon the claim, we think, from some sublime dimension of being, which the moral law inhabits, much as upon the steel of the compass-needle the influence of the Pole rains down from out of the starry heavens. But again, how can such an inorganic abstract character of imperativeness, additional to the imperativeness which is in the concrete claim itself, *exist?* Take any demand, however slight, which any creature, however weak, may make. Ought it not, for its own sole sake, to be satisfied? If not, prove why not. The only possible kind of proof you could adduce would be the exhibition of another creature who should make a demand that ran the other way. The only possible reason there can be why any phenomenon ought to exist is that such a phenomenon actually is desired. Any desire is imperative to the extent of its amount; it *makes* itself valid by the fact that it exists at all. Some desires, truly enough, are small desires; they are put forward by insignificant persons, and we customarily make light of the obligations which they bring. But the fact that such personal demands as these impose small obligations does not keep the largest obligations from being personal demands.

If we must talk impersonally, to be sure we can say that 'the universe' requires, exacts, or makes obligatory such or such an action, whenever it expresses itself through the desires of such or such a creature. But it is better not to talk about the universe in this personified way, unless we believe in a universal or divine consciousness which actually exists. If there be such a consciousness, then its demands carry the most of obligation simply because they are the greatest in amount. But it is even then not *abstractly* right that we should respect them. It is only *concretely* right,—or right after the fact, and by virtue of the fact, that they are actually made. Suppose we do not respect them, as seems largely to be the case in this queer world. That ought not to be, we say; that is wrong. But in that way is this fact of wrongness made more acceptable or intelligible when we imagine it to consist rather in the laceration of an *à priori* ideal order than in the disappointment of a living personal God? Do we, perhaps, think that we cover God and protect him and make his impotence over us less ultimate, when we back him up with this *à priori* blanket from which he may draw some warmth of further appeal? But the only force of appeal to *us,* which either a living God or an abstract ideal order can wield, is found in the 'everlasting ruby vaults' of our own human hearts, as they happen to beat responsive and not irresponsive to the claim. So far as they do feel it when made by a living consciousness, it is life answering to life. A claim thus livingly acknowledged is acknowledged with a solidity and fulness which no thought of an 'ideal' backing can render more complete; while if, on the other hand, the heart's response is withheld, the stubborn phenomenon is there of an impotence in the claims which the universe embodies, which no talk about an eternal nature of things can gloze over or dispel. An ineffective *à priori* order is as impotent a thing as an ineffective God; and in the eye of philosophy, it is as hard a thing to explain.

We may now consider that what we distinguished as the metaphysical question in ethical philosophy is sufficiently answered, and that we have learned what the words 'good,' 'bad,' and 'obligation' severally mean. They mean no absolute natures, independent of personal support. They are objects of feeling and desire, which have no foothold or anchorage in Being, apart from the existence of actually living minds.

Wherever such minds exist, with judgments of good and ill, and demands upon one another, there is an ethical world in its essential features. Were all other things, gods and men and starry heavens, blotted out from this universe, and were there left but one rock with two loving souls upon it, that rock would have as thoroughly moral a constitution as any possible world which the eternities and immensities could harbor. It would be a tragic constitution, because the rock's inhabitants would die. But while they lived, there would be real good things and real bad things in the universe; there would be obligations, claims, and expectations; obediences, refusals, and disappointments;

compunctions and longings for harmony to come again, and inward peace of conscience when it was restored; there would, in short, be a moral life, whose active energy would have no limit but the intensity of interest in each other with which the hero and heroine might be endowed.

We, on this terrestrial globe, so far as the visible facts go, are just like the inhabitants of such a rock. Whether a God exist, or whether no God exist, in yon blue heaven above us bent, we form at any rate an ethical republic here below. And the first reflection which this leads to is that ethics have as genuine and real a foothold in a universe where the highest consciousness is human, as in a universe where there is a God as well. 'The religion of humanity' affords a basis for ethics as well as theism does. Whether the purely human system can gratify the philosopher's demand as well as the other is a different question, which we ourselves must answer ere we close.

III

The last fundamental question in Ethics was, it will be remembered, the *casuistic* question. Here we are, in a world where the existence of a divine thinker has been and perhaps always will be doubted by some of the lookers-on, and where, in spite of the presence of a large number of ideals in which human beings agree, there are a mass of others about which no general consensus obtains. It is hardly necessary to present a literary picture of this, for the facts are too well known. The wars of the flesh and the spirit in each man, the concupiscences of different individuals pursuing the same unshareable material or social prizes, the ideals which contrast so according to races, circumstances, temperaments, philosophical beliefs, etc.,—all form a maze of apparently inextricable confusion with no obvious Ariadne's thread to lead one out. Yet the philosopher, just because he is a philosopher, adds his own peculiar ideal to the confusion (with which if he were willing to be a sceptic he would be passably content), and insists that over all these individual opinions there is a *system of truth* which he can discover if he only takes sufficient pains.

We stand ourselves at present in the place of that philosopher, and must not fail to realize all the features that the situation comports. In the first place we will not be sceptics; we hold to it that there is a truth to be ascertained. But in the second place we have just gained the insight that that truth cannot be a self-proclaiming set of laws, or an abstract 'moral reason,' but can only exist in act, or in the shape of an opinion held by some thinker really to be found. There is, however, no visible thinker invested with authority. Shall we then simply proclaim our own ideals as the lawgiving ones? No; for if we are true philosophers we must throw our own spontaneous ideals, even the dearest, impartially in with that total mass of ideals which are fairly to be judged. But how then can we as philosophers ever find a test; how avoid complete moral scepticism on the one hand, and on the other escape bringing a wayward personal standard of our own along with us, on which we simply pin faith?

The dilemma is a hard one, nor does it grow a bit more easy as we revolve it in our minds. The entire undertaking of the philosopher obliges him to seek an impartial test. That test, however, must be incarnated in the demand of some actually existent person; and how can he pick out the person save by an act in which his own sympathies and prepossessions are implied?

One method indeed presents itself, and has as a matter of history been taken by the more serious ethical schools. If the heap of things demanded proved on inspection less chaotic than at first they seemed, if they furnished their own relative test and measure, then the casuistic problem would be solved. If it were found that all goods *quâ* goods contained a common essence, then the amount of this essence involved in any one good would show its rank in the scale of goodness, and order could be quickly made; for this essence would be *the* good upon which all thinkers were agreed, the relatively objective and universal good that the philosopher seeks. Even his own private ideals would be measured by their share of it, and find their rightful place among the rest.

Various essences of good have thus been found and proposed as bases of the ethical system. Thus, to be a mean between two extremes; to be recognized by a special intuitive faculty; to make the agent happy for the moment; to make others as well as him happy in the long run; to add to his perfection or dignity; to harm no one; to follow from reason or flow from universal law; to be in accordance with the will of God; to promote the survival of the human species on this planet,—are so many tests, each of which has been maintained by somebody to constitute the essence of all good things or actions so far as they are good.

No one of the measures that have been actually proposed has, however, given general satisfaction. Some are obviously not universally present in all cases,—*e.g.*, the character of harming no one, or that of following a universal law; for the best course is often cruel; and many acts are reckoned good on the sole condition that they be exceptions, and serve not as examples of a universal law. Other characters, such as following the will of God, are unascertainable and vague. Others again, like survival, are quite indeterminate in their consequences, and leave us in the lurch where we most need their help: a philosopher of the Sioux Nation, for example, will be certain to use the survival-criterion in a very different way from ourselves. The best, on the whole, of these marks and measures of goodness seems to be the capacity to bring happiness. But in order not to break down fatally, this test must be taken to cover innumerable acts and impulses that never *aim* at happiness; so that, after all, in seeking for a universal principle we inevitably are carried onward to the *most* universal principle,—that *the essence of good is simply to satisfy demand*. The demand may be for anything under the sun. There is really no more ground for supposing that all our demands can be accounted for by one universal underlying kind of motive than there is ground for supposing that all physical phenomena are cases of a single law. The elementary forces in ethics are probably as plural as those of physics are. The various ideals have no common character apart from the fact that they are ideals. No single abstract principle can be so used as to yield to the philosopher anything like a scientifically accurate and genuinely useful casuistic scale.

A look at another peculiarity of the ethical universe, as we find it, will still further show us the philosopher's perplexities. As a purely theoretic problem, namely, the casuistic question would hardly ever come up at all. If the ethical philosopher were only asking after the best *imaginable* system of goods he would indeed have an easy task; for all demands as such are *primâ facie* respectable, and the best simply imaginary world would be one in which *every* demand was gratified as soon as made. Such a world would, however, have to have a physical constitution entirely different from that of the one which we inhabit. It would need not only a space, but a time, 'of *n*-dimensions,' to include all the acts and experiences incompatible with one another here below, which would then go on in conjunction,—such as spending our money, yet growing rich; taking our holiday, yet getting ahead with our work; shooting and fishing, yet doing no hurt to the beasts; gaining no end of experience, yet keeping our youthful freshness of heart; and the like. There can be no question that such a system of things, however brought about, would be the absolutely ideal system; and that if a philosopher could create universes *à priori,* and provide all the mechanical conditions, that is the sort of universe which he should unhesitatingly create.

But this world of ours is made on an entirely different pattern, and the casuistic question here is most tragically practical. The actually possible in this world is vastly narrower than all that is demanded; and there is always a *pinch* between the ideal and the actual which can only be got through by leaving part of the ideal behind. There is

hardly a good which we can imagine except as competing for the possession of the same bit of space and time with some other imagined
good. Every end of desire that presents itself appears exclusive of
some other end of desire. Shall a man drink and smoke, *or* keep his
nerves in condition?—he cannot do both. Shall he follow his fancy for
Amelia, *or* for Henrietta?—both cannot be the choice of his heart.
Shall he have the dear old Republican party, *or* a spirit of unsophisti-
cation in public affairs?—he cannot have both, etc. So that the ethical
philosopher's demand for the right scale of subordination in ideals is
the fruit of an altogether practical need. Some part of the ideal must
be butchered, and he needs to know which part. It is a tragic situation,
and no mere speculative conundrum, with which he has to deal.

Now *we* are blinded to the real difficulty of the philosopher's task
by the fact that we are born into a society whose ideals are largely
ordered already. If we follow the ideal which is conventionally highest, the others which we butcher either die and do not return to haunt
us; or if they come back and accuse us of murder, everyone ap-
plauds us for turning to them a deaf ear. In other words, our environment encourages us not to be philosophers but partisans. The
philosopher, however, cannot, so long as he clings to his own ideal of
objectivity, rule out any ideal from being heard. He is confident, and
rightly confident, that the simple taking counsel of his own intuitive
preferences would be certain to end in a mutilation of the fulness of
the truth. The poet Heine is said to have written 'Bunsen' in the place
of 'Gott' in his copy of that author's work entitled "God in History,"
so as to make it read 'Bunsen in der Geschichte.' Now, with no disrespect to the good and learned Baron, is it not safe to say that any
single philosopher, however wide his sympathies, must be just such a
Bunsen in der Geschichte of the moral world, so soon as he attempts
to put his own ideas of order into that howling mob of desires, each
struggling to get breathing-room for the ideal to which it clings? The
very best of men must not only be insensible, but be ludicrously and
peculiarly insensible, to many goods. As a militant, fighting free-
handed that the goods to which he *is* sensible may not be submerged
and lost from out of life, the philosopher, like every other human
being, is in a natural position. But think of Zeno and of Epicurus, think
of Calvin and of Paley, think of Kant and Schopenhauer, of Herbert
Spencer and John Henry Newman, no longer as one-sided champions
of special ideals, but as schoolmasters deciding what all must think,—
and what more grotesque topic could a satirist wish for on which to
exercise his pen? The fabled attempt of Mrs. Partington to arrest the
rising tide of the North Atlantic with her broom was a reasonable
spectacle compared with their effort to substitute the content of their
clean-shaven systems for that exuberant mass of goods with which all

human nature is in travail, and groaning to bring to the light of day. Think, furthermore, of such individual moralists, no longer as mere schoolmasters, but as pontiffs armed with the temporal power, and having authority in every concrete case of conflict to order which good shall be butchered and which shall be suffered to survive,—and the notion really turns one pale. All one's slumbering revolutionary instincts waken at the thought of any single moralist wielding such powers of life and death. Better chaos forever than an order based on any closet-philosopher's rule, even though he were the most enlightened possible member of his tribe. No! if the philosopher is to keep his judicial position, he must never become one of the parties to the fray.

What can he do, then, it will now be asked, except to fall back on scepticism and give up the notion of being a philosopher at all?

But do we not already see a perfectly definite path of escape which is open to him just because he is a philosopher, and not the champion of one particular ideal? Since everything which is demanded is by that fact a good, must not the guiding principle for ethical philosophy (since all demands conjointly cannot be satisfied in this poor world) be simply to satisfy at all times *as many demands as we can?* That act must be the best act, accordingly, which makes for the *best whole,* in the sense of awakening the least sum of dissatisfactions. In the casuistic scale, therefore, those ideals must be written highest which *prevail at the least cost,* or by whose realization the least possible number of other ideals are destroyed. Since victory and defeat there must be, the victory to be philosophically prayed for is that of the more inclusive side,—of the side which even in the hour of triumph will to some degree do justice to the ideals in which the vanquished party's interests lay. The course of history is nothing but the story of men's struggles from generation to generation to find the more and more inclusive order. *Invent some manner* of realizing your own ideals which will also satisfy the alien demands,—that and that only is the path of peace! Following this path, society has shaken itself into one sort of relative equilibrium after another by a series of social discoveries quite analogous to those of science. Polyandry and polygamy and slavery, private warfare and liberty to kill, judicial torture and arbitrary royal power have slowly succumbed to actually aroused complaints; and though some one's ideals are unquestionably the worse off for each improvement, yet a vastly greater total number of them find shelter in our civilized society than in the older savage ways. So far then, and up to date, the casuistic scale is made for the philosopher already far better than he can ever make it for himself. An experiment of the most searching kind has proved that the laws and usages of land are what yield the maximum of satisfaction to the thinkers taken all together. The presumption in cases of conflict must always be in favor of the conventionally recognized good. The philosopher must be a conservative, and in the construction of his casuistic scale must put the things most in accordance with the customs of the community on top.

And yet if he be a true philosopher he must see that there is nothing final in any actually given equilibrium of human ideals, but that, as our present laws and customs have fought and conquered other past ones, so they will in their turn be overthrown by any newly discovered order which will hush up the complaints that they still give rise to, without producing others louder still. "Rules are made for man, not man for rules,"—that one sentence is enough to immortalize Green's Prolegomena to Ethics. And although a man always risks much when he breaks away from established rules and strives to realize a larger ideal whole than they permit, yet the philosopher must allow that it is at all times open to any one to make the experiment, provided he fear not to stake his life and character upon the throw. The pinch is always here. Pent in under every system of moral rules are innumerable persons whom it weighs upon, and goods which it represses; and these are always rumbling and grumbling in the background, and ready for any issue by which they may get free. See the abuses which the institution of private property covers, so that even today it is shamelessly asserted among us that one of the prime functions of the national government is to help the adroiter citizens to grow rich. See the unnamed and unnamable sorrows which the tyranny, on the whole so beneficent, of the marriage-institution brings to so many, both of the married and the unwed. See the wholesale loss of opportunity under our *régime* of so-called equality and industrialism, with the drummer and the counter-jumper in the saddle, for so many faculties and graces which could flourish in the feudal world. See our kindliness for the humble and the outcast, how it wars with that stern weeding-out which until now has been the condition of every perfection in the breed. See everywhere the struggle and the squeeze; and everlastingly the problem how to make them less. The anarchists, nihilists, and free-lovers; the free-silverites, socialists, and single-tax men; the free-traders and civil-service reformers; the prohibitionists and anti-vivisectionists; the radical darwinians with their idea of the suppression of the weak,—these and all the conservative sentiments of society arrayed against them, are simply deciding through actual experiment by what sort of conduct the maximum amount of good can be gained and kept in this world. These experiments are to be judged, not *à priori,* but by actually finding, after the fact of their making, how much more outcry or how much appeasement comes about. What closet-solutions can possibly anticipate the result of trials made on such a scale? Or what can any superficial theorist's judgment be worth, in a world where every one of hundreds of ideals has its special champion already provided in the shape of some genius expressly born to feel it, and to fight to death in its behalf? The pure philosopher can only follow the windings of the spectacle, confident that the line of least resistance will always be towards the richer and the more inclusive arrangement, and that by one tack after another some approach to the kingdom of heaven is incessantly made.

IV

All this amounts to saying that, so far as the casuistic question goes, ethical science is just like physical science, and instead of being deducible all at once from abstract principles, must simply bide its time, and be ready to revise its conclusions from day to day. The presumption of course, in both sciences, always is that the vulgarly accepted opinions are true, and the right casuistic order that which public opinion believes in; and surely it would be folly quite as great, in most of us, to strike out independently and to aim at originality in ethics as in physics. Every now and then, however, some one is born with the right to be original, and his revolutionary thought or action may bear prosperous fruit. He may replace old 'laws of nature' by better ones; he may, by breaking old moral rules in a certain place, bring in a total condition of things more ideal than would have followed had the rules been kept.

On the whole, then, we must conclude that no philosophy of ethics is possible in the old-fashioned absolute sense of the term. Everywhere the ethical philosopher must wait on facts. The thinkers who create the ideals come he knows not whence, their sensibilities are evolved he knows not how; and the question as to which of two conflicting ideals will give the best universe then and there, can be answered by him only through the aid of the experience of other men. I said some time ago, in treating of the 'first' question, that the intuitional moralists deserve credit for keeping most clearly to the psychological facts. They do much to spoil this merit on the whole, however, by mixing with it that dogmatic temper which, by absolute distinctions and unconditional 'thou shalt nots,' changes a growing, elastic, and continuous life into a superstitious system of relics and dead bones. In point of fact, there are no absolute evils, and there are no non-moral goods; and the *highest* ethical life—however few may be called to bear its burdens—consists at all times in the breaking of rules which have grown too narrow for the actual case. There is but one unconditional commandment, which is that we should seek incessantly, with fear and trembling, so to vote and to act as to bring about the very largest total universe of good which we can see. Abstract rules indeed can help; but they help the less in proportion as our intuitions are more piercing, and our vocation is the stronger for the moral life. For every real dilemma is in literal strictness a unique situation; and the exact combination of ideals realized and ideals disappointed which each decision creates is always a universe without a precedent, and for which no adequate previous rule exists. The philosopher, then, *quâ* philosopher, is no better able to determine the best universe in the concrete emergency than other men. He sees, indeed, somewhat better than most men what the question always is,—not a question of this good or that good simply taken, but of the two total universes with which these goods respectively belong. He knows that he must vote always for the richer universe, for the good which seems most organizable, most fit to enter into complex combinations, most apt to be a member of a more inclusive whole. But which particular universe this is he cannot know for certain in advance; he only knows that if he makes a bad mistake the cries of the wounded will soon inform him of the fact. In all this the philosopher is just like the rest of us non-philosophers, so far as we are just and sympathetic instinctively, and so far as we are open to the voice of complaint. His function is in fact indistinguishable from that of the best kind of statesman at the present day. His books upon ethics, therefore, so far as they truly touch the moral life, must more and more ally themselves with a literature which is confessedly tentative and suggestive rather than dogmatic,— I mean with novels and dramas of the deeper sort, with sermons, with books on statecraft and philanthropy and social and economical reform. Treated in this way ethical treatises may be voluminous and luminous as well; but they never can be *final,* except in their abstractest and vaguest features; and they must more and more abandon the old-fashioned, clear-cut, and would-be 'scientific' form.

V

The chief of all the reasons why concrete ethics cannot be final is that they have to wait on metaphysical and theological beliefs. I said some time back that real ethical relations existed in a purely human world. They would exist even in what we called a moral solitude if the thinker had various ideals which took hold of him in turn. His self of one day would make demands on his self of another; and some of the demands might be urgent and tyrannical, while others were gentle and easily put aside. We call the tyrannical demands *imperatives.* If we ignore these we do not hear the last of it. The good which we have wounded returns to plague us with interminable crops of consequential damages, compunctions, and regrets. Obligation can thus exist inside a single thinker's consciousness; and perfect peace can abide with him only so far as he lives according to some sort of a casuistic scale which keeps his more imperative goods on top. It is the nature of these goods to be cruel to their rivals. Nothing shall avail when weighed in the balance against them. They call out all the mercilessness in our disposition, and do not easily forgive us if we are so softhearted as to shrink from sacrifice in their behalf.

The deepest difference, practically, in the moral life of man is the difference between the easy-going and the strenuous mood. When in the easy-going mood the shrinking from present ill is our ruling consideration. The strenuous mood, on the contrary, makes us quite indifferent to present ill, if only the greater ideal be attained. The capacity for the strenuous mood probably lies slumbering in every man, but it has more difficulty in some than in others in waking up. It needs the wilder passions to arouse it, the big fears, loves, and indignations; or else the deeply penetrating appeal of some one of the higher fidelities, like justice, truth, or freedom. Strong relief is a necessity of its vision; and a world where all the mountains are brought down and all the valleys are exalted is no congenial place for its habitation. This is why in a solitary thinker this mood might slumber on forever without waking. His various ideals, known to him to be mere preferences of his own, are too nearly of the same denominational value: he can play fast or loose with them at will. This too is why, in a merely human world without a God, the appeal to our moral energy falls short of its maximal stimulating power. Life, to be sure, is even in such a world a genuinely ethical symphony; but it is played in the compass of a couple of poor octaves, and the infinite scale of values fails to open up. Many of us, indeed,—like Sir James Stephen in those eloquent 'Essays by a Barrister,'—would openly laugh at the very idea of the strenuous mood being awakened in us by those claims of remote posterity which constitute the last appeal of the religion of humanity. We do not love these men of the future keenly enough; and we love them perhaps the less the more we hear of their evolutionized perfection, their high average longevity and education, their freedom from war and crime, their relative immunity from pain and zymotic disease, and all their other negative superiorities. This is all too finite, we say; we see too well the vacuum beyond. It lacks the note of infinitude and mystery, and may all be dealt with in the don't-care mood. No need of agonizing ourselves or making others agonize for these good creatures just at present.

When, however, we believe that a God is there, and that he is one of the claimants, the infinite perspective opens out. The scale of the symphony is incalculably prolonged. The more imperative ideals now begin to speak with an altogether new objectivity and significance, and to utter the penetrating, shattering, tragically challenging note of appeal. They ring out like the call of Victor Hugo's alpine eagle, "qui parle au précipice et que le gouffre entend," and the strenuous mood awakens at the sound. It saith among the trumpets, ha, ha! it smelleth the battle afar off, the thunder of the captains and the shouting. Its blood is up; and cruelty to the lesser claims, so far from being a deterrent element, does but add to the stern joy with which it leaps to answer to the greater. All through history, in the periodical conflicts of puritanism with the don't-care temper, we see the antagonism of the strenuous and genial moods, and the contrast between the ethics of infinite and mysterious obligation from on high, and those of prudence and the satisfaction of merely finite need.

The capacity of the strenuous mood lies so deep down among our natural human possibilities that even if there were no metaphysical or traditional grounds for believing in a God, men would postulate one simply as a pretext for living hard, and getting out of the game of existence its keenest possibilities of zest. Our attitude towards concrete evils is entirely different in a world where we believe there are none but finite demanders, from what it is in one where we joyously face tragedy for an infinite demander's sake. Every sort of energy and endurance, of courage and capacity for handling life's evils, is set free in those who have religious faith. For this reason the strenuous type of character will on the battle-field of human history always outwear the easy-going type, and religion will drive irreligion to the wall.

It would seem, too,—and this is my final conclusion,—that the stable and systematic moral universe for which the ethical philosopher asks is fully possible only in a world where there is a divine thinker with all-enveloping demands. If such a thinker existed, his way of subordinating the demands to one another would be the finally valid casuistic scale; his claims would be the most appealing; his ideal universe would be the most inclusive realizable whole. If he now exist, then actualized in his thought already must be that ethical philosophy which we seek as the pattern which our own must evermore approach.[15] In the interests of our own ideal of systematically unified moral truth, therefore, we, as would-be philosophers, must postulate a divine thinker, and pray for the victory of the religious cause. Meanwhile, exactly what the thought of the infinite thinker may be is hidden from us even were we sure of his existence; so that our postula-

[15] All this is set forth with great freshness and force in the work of my colleague, Professor Josiah Royce: *The Religious Aspect of Philosophy.* Boston, 1885.

tion of him after all serves only to let loose in us the strenuous mood. But this is what it does in all men, even those who have no interest in philosophy. The ethical philosopher, therefore, whenever he ventures to say which course of action is the best, is on no essentially different level from the common man. "See, I have set before thee this day life and good, and death and evil; therefore, choose life that thou and thy seed may live,"—when this challenge comes to us, it is simply our total character and personal genius that are on trial; and if we invoke any so-called philosophy, our choice and use of that also are but revelations of our personal aptitude or incapacity for moral life. From this unsparing practical ordeal no professor's lectures and no array of books can save us. The solving word, for the learned and the unlearned man alike, lies in the last resort in the dumb willingnesses and unwillingnesses of their interior characters, and nowhere else. It is not in heaven, neither is it beyond the sea; but the word is very nigh unto thee, in thy mouth and in thy heart, that thou mayest do it.

ON A CERTAIN BLINDNESS
IN HUMAN BEINGS*

Our judgments concerning the worth of things, big or little, depend on the *feelings* the things arouse in us. Where we judge a thing to be precious in consequence of the *idea* we frame of it, this is only because the idea is itself associated already with a feeling. If we were radically feelingless, and if ideas were the only things our mind could entertain, we should lose all our likes and dislikes at a stroke, and be unable to point to any one situation or experience in life more valuable or significant than any other.

Now the blindness in human beings, of which this discourse will treat, is the blindness with which we all are afflicted in regard to the feelings of creatures and people different from ourselves.

We are practical beings, each of us with limited functions and duties to perform. Each is bound to feel intensely the importance of his own duties and the significance of the situations that call these forth. But this feeling is in each of us a vital secret, for sympathy with which we vainly look to others. The others are too much absorbed in their own vital secrets to take an interest in ours. Hence the stupidity

* From: T.T., 229–264.

and injustice of our opinions, so far as they deal with the significance of alien lives. Hence the falsity of our judgments, so far as they presume to decide in an absolute way on the value of other persons' conditions or ideals.

Take our dogs and ourselves, connected as we are by a tie more intimate than most ties in this world; and yet, outside of that tie of friendly fondness, how insensible, each of us, to all that makes life significant for the other!—we to the rapture of bones under hedges, or smells of trees and lamp-posts, they to the delights of literature and art. As you sit reading the most moving romance you ever fell upon, what sort of a judge is your fox-terrier of your behavior? With all his good will toward you, the nature of your conduct is absolutely excluded from his comprehension. To sit there like a senseless statue, when you might be taking him to walk and throwing sticks for him to catch! What queer disease is this that comes over you every day, of holding things and staring at them like that for hours together, paralyzed of motion and vacant of all conscious life? The African savages came nearer the truth; but they, too, missed it, when they gathered wonderingly round one of our American travellers who, in the interior, had just come into possession of a stray copy of the New York *Commercial Advertiser,* and was devouring it column by column. When he got through, they offered him a high price for the mysterious object; and, being asked for what they wanted it, they said: "For an eye medicine,"—that being the only reason they could conceive of for the protracted bath which he had given his eyes upon its surface.

The spectator's judgment is sure to miss the root of the matter, and to possess no truth. The subject judged knows a part of the world of reality which the judging spectator fails to see, knows more while the spectator knows less; and, wherever there is conflict of opinion and difference of vision, we are bound to believe that the truer side is the side that feels the more, and not the side that feels the less.

Let me take a personal example of the kind that befalls each one of us daily:—

Some years ago, while journeying in the mountains of North Carolina, I passed by a large number of 'coves,' as they call them there, or heads of small valleys between the hills, which had been newly cleared and planted. The impression on my mind was one of unmitigated squalor. The settler had in every case cut down the more manageable trees, and left their charred stumps standing. The larger trees he had girdled and killed, in order that their foliage should not cast a shade. He had then built a log cabin, plastering its chinks with clay, and had set up a tall zigzag rail fence around the scene of his havoc, to keep the pigs and cattle out. Finally, he had irregularly planted the intervals between the stumps and trees with Indian corn, which grew among the chips; and there he dwelt with his wife and babes—an axe, a gun, a few utensils, and some pigs and chickens feeding in the woods, being the sum total of his possessions.

The forest had been destroyed; and what had 'improved' it out of existence was hideous, a sort of ulcer, without a single element of artificial grace to make up for the loss of Nature's beauty. Ugly, indeed, seemed the life of the squatter, scudding, as the sailors say, under bare poles, beginning again away back where our first ancestors started, and by hardly a single item the better off for all the achievements of the intervening generations.

Talk about going back to nature! I said to myself, oppressed by the dreariness, as I drove by. Talk of a country life for one's old age and for one's children! Never thus, with nothing but the bare ground and one's bare hands to fight the battle! Never, without the best spoils of culture woven in! The beauties and commodities gained by the centuries are sacred. They are our heritage and birthright. No modern person ought to be willing to live a day in such a state of rudimentariness and denudation.

Then I said to the mountaineer who was driving me, "What sort of people are they who have to make these new clearings?" "All of us," he replied. "Why, we ain't happy here, únless we are getting one of these coves under cultivation." I instantly felt that I had been losing the whole inward significance of the situation. Because to me the clearings spoke of naught but denudation, I thought that to those whose sturdy arms and obedient axes had made them they could tell no other story. But, when *they* looked on the hideous stumps, what they thought of was personal victory. The chips, the girdled trees, and the vile split rails spoke of honest sweat, persistent toil and final reward. The cabin was a warrant of safety for self and wife and babes. In short, the clearing, which to me was a mere ugly picture on the retina, was to them a symbol redolent with moral memories and sang a very pæan of duty, struggle, and success.

I had been as blind to the peculiar ideality of their conditions as they certainly would also have been to the ideality of mine, had they had a peep at my strange indoor academic ways of life at Cambridge.

Wherever a process of life communicates an eagerness to him who lives it, there the life becomes genuinely significant. Sometimes the eagerness is more knit up with the motor activities, sometimes with the perceptions, sometimes with the imagination, sometimes with reflective thought. But, wherever it is found, there is the zest, the tingle, the excitement of reality; and there *is* 'importance' in the only real and positive sense in which importance ever anywhere can be.

Robert Louis Stevenson has illustrated this by a case, drawn from the sphere of the imagination, in an essay which I really think deserves to become immortal, both for the truth of its matter and the excellence of its form.

"Toward the end of September," Stevenson writes, "when schooltime was drawing near, and the nights were already black, we would begin to sally from our respective villas, each equipped with a tin bull's-eye lantern. The thing was so well known that it had worn a rut in the commerce of Great Britain; and the grocers, about the due time, began to garnish their windows with our particular brand of luminary. We wore them buckled to the waist upon a cricket belt, and over them, such was the rigor of the game, a buttoned top-coat. They smelled noisomely of blistered tin. They never burned aright, though they would always burn our fingers. Their use was naught, the pleasure of them merely fanciful, and yet a boy with a bull's-eye under his top-coat asked for nothing more. The fishermen used lanterns about their boats, and it was from them, I suppose, that we had got the hint; but theirs were not bull's-eyes, nor did we ever play at being fishermen. The police carried them at their belts, and we had plainly copied them in that; yet we did not pretend to be policemen. Burglars, indeed, we may have had some haunting thought of; and we had certainly an eye to past ages when lanterns were more common, and to certain story-books in which we had found them to figure very largely. But take it for all in all, the pleasure of the thing was substantive; and to be a boy with a bull's-eye under his top-coat was good enough for us.

"When two of these asses met, there would be an anxious 'Have you got your lantern?' and a gratified 'Yes!' That was the shibboleth, and very needful, too; for, as it was the rule to keep our glory contained, none could recognize a lantern-bearer unless (like the polecat) by the smell. Four or five would sometimes climb into the belly of a ten-man lugger, with nothing but the thwarts above them,—for the cabin was usually locked,—or chose out some hollow of the links where the wind might whistle overhead. Then the coats would be unbuttoned, and the bull's-eyes discovered; and in the chequering glimmer, under the huge, windy hall of the night, and cheered by a rich steam of toasting tinware, these fortunate young gentlemen would crouch together in the cold sand of the links, or on the scaly bilges of the fishing-boat, and delight them with inappropriate talk. Woe is me that I cannot give some specimens! . . . But the talk was but a condiment, and these gatherings themselves only accidents in the career of the lantern-bearer. The essence of this bliss was to walk by yourself in the black night, the slide shut, the top-coat buttoned, not a ray escaping, whether to conduct your footsteps or to make your glory public,—a mere pillar of darkness in the dark; and all the while, deep down in the privacy of your fool's heart, to know you had a bull's-eye at your belt, and to exult and sing over the knowledge.

"It is said that a poet has died young in the breast of the most stolid. It may be contended rather that a (somewhat minor) bard in almost every case survives, and is the spice of life to his possessor. Justice is not done to the versatility and the unplumbed childishness of man's imagination. His life from without may seem but a rude mound of mud: there will be some golden chamber at the heart of it, in which he dwells delighted; and for as dark as his pathway seems to the observer, he will have some kind of bull's-eye at his belt.

. . . "There is one fable that touches very near the quick of life, —the fable of the monk who passed into the woods, heard a bird break into song, hearkened for a trill or two, and found himself at his return a stranger at his convent gates; for he had been absent fifty years, and of all his comrades there survived but one to recognize him. It is not only in the woods that this enchanter carols, though perhaps he is native there. He sings in the most doleful places. The miser hears him and chuckles, and his days are moments. With no more apparatus than an evil-smelling lantern, I have evoked him on the naked links. All life that is not merely mechanical is spun out of two strands,—seeking for that bird and hearing him. And it is just this that makes life so hard to value, and the delight of each so incommunicable. And it is just a knowledge of this, and a remembrance of those fortunate hours in which the bird *has* sung to *us,* that fills us with such wonder when we turn to the pages of the realist. There, to be sure, we find a picture of life in so far as it consists of mud and of old iron, cheap desires and cheap fears, that which we are ashamed to remember and that which we are careless whether we forget; but of the note of that time-devouring nightingale we hear no news.

. . . "Say that we came [in such a realistic romance] on some such business as that of my lantern-bearers on the links, and described the boys as very cold, spat upon by flurries of rain, and drearily surrounded, all of which they were; and their talk as silly and indecent, which it certainly was. To the eye of the observer they *are* wet and cold and drearily surrounded; but ask themselves, and they are in the heaven of a recondite pleasure, the ground of which is an ill-smelling lantern.

"For, to repeat, the ground of a man's joy is often hard to hit. It may hinge at times upon a mere accessory, like the lantern; it may reside in the mysterious inwards of psychology. . . . It has so little bond with externals . . . that it may even touch them not, and the man's true life, for which he consents to live, lie together in the field of fancy. . . . In such a case the poetry runs underground. The observer (poor soul, with his documents!) is all abroad. For to look at the man is but to court deception. We shall see the trunk from which he draws his nourishment; but he himself is above and abroad in the green dome of foliage, hummed through by winds and nested in by nightingales. And the true realism were that of the poets, to climb after him like a squirrel, and catch some glimpse of the heaven in which he lives. And the true realism, always and everywhere, is that of the poets: to find out where joy resides, and give it a voice far beyond singing.

"For to miss the joy is to miss all. In the joy of the actors lies the sense of any action. That is the explanation, that the excuse. To one who has not the secret of the lanterns the scene upon the links is meaningless. And hence the haunting and truly spectral unreality of realistic books. . . . In each we miss the personal poetry, the enchanted atmosphere, that rainbow work of fancy that clothes what is naked and seems to ennoble what is base; in each, life falls dead like dough, instead of soaring away like a balloon into the colors of the sunset; each is true, each inconceivable; for no man lives in the external truth among salts and acids, but in the warm, phantasmagoric chamber of his brain, with the painted windows and the storied wall." [16]

These paragraphs are the best thing I know in all Stevenson. "To miss the joy is to miss all." Indeed, it is. Yet we are but finite, and each one of us has some single specialized vocation of his own. And it seems as if energy in the service of its particular duties might be got only by hardening the heart toward everything unlike them. Our deadness toward all but one particular kind of joy would thus be the price we inevitably have to pay for being practical creatures. Only in some pitiful dreamer, some philosopher, poet, or romancer, or when the common practical man becomes a lover, does the hard externality give way, and a gleam of insight into the ejective world, as Clifford called it, the vast world of inner life beyond us, so different from that of outer seeming, illuminate our mind. Then the whole scheme of our customary values gets confounded, then our self is riven and its narrow interests fly to pieces, then a new centre and a new perspective must be found.

The change is well described by my colleague, Josiah Royce:—

"What, then, is our neighbor? Thou hast regarded his thought, his feeling, as somehow different from thine. Thou hast said, 'A pain in him is not like a pain in me, but something far easier to bear.' He seems to thee a little less living than thou; his life is dim, it is cold, it is a pale fire beside thy own burning desires. . . . So, dimly and by instinct hast thou lived with thy neighbor, and hast known him not,

---

[16] 'The Lantern-bearers,' in the volume entitled *Across the Plains*. Abridged in the quotation.

being blind. Thou hast made [of him] a thing, no Self at all. Have done with this illusion, and simply try to learn the truth. Pain is pain, joy is joy, everywhere, even as in thee. In all the songs of the forest birds; in all the cries of the wounded and dying, struggling in the captor's power; in the boundless sea where the myriads of water-creatures strive and die; amid all the countless hordes of savage men; in all sickness and sorrow; in all exultation and hope, everywhere, from the lowest to the noblest, the same conscious, burning, wilful life is found, endlessly manifold as the forms of the living creatures, unquenchable as the fires of the sun, real as these impulses that even now throb in thine own little selfish heart. Lift up thy eyes, behold that life, and then turn away, and forget it as thou canst; but, if thou hast *known* that, thou hast begun to know thy duty." [17]

This higher vision of an inner significance in what, until then, we had realized only in the dead external way, often comes over a person suddenly; and, when it does so, it makes an epoch in his history. As Emerson says, there is a depth in those moments that constrains us to ascribe more reality to them than to all other experiences. The passion of love will shake one like an explosion, or some act will awaken a remorseful compunction that hangs like a cloud over all one's later day.

This mystic sense of hidden meaning starts upon us often from non-human natural things. I take this passage from 'Obermann,' a French novel that had some vogue in its day: "Paris, March 7.—It was dark and rather cold. I was gloomy, and walked because I had nothing to do. I passed by some flowers placed breast-high upon a wall. A jonquil in bloom was there. It is the strongest expression of desire: it was the first perfume of the year. I felt all the happiness destined for man. This unutterable harmony of souls, the phantom of the ideal world, arose in me complete. I never felt anything so great or so instantaneous. I know not what shape, what analogy, what secret of relation it was that made me see in this flower a limitless beauty. . . . I shall never enclose in a conception this power, this immensity that nothing will express; this form that nothing will contain; this ideal of a better world which one feels, but which it would seem that nature has not made." [18]

Wordsworth and Shelley are similarly full of this sense of a limitless significance in natural things. In Wordsworth it was a somewhat austere and moral significance,—a 'lonely cheer.'

> To every natural form, rock, fruit, or flower,
> Even the loose stones that cover the highway,

[17] *The Religious Aspect of Philosophy,* pp. 157–162 (abridged).
[18] De Sénancour: *Obermann,* Lettre XXX.

> I gave a moral life: I saw them feel
> Or linked them to some feeling: the great mass
> Lay bedded in some quickening soul, and all
> That I beheld respired with inward meaning.[19]

"Authentic tidings of invisible things!" Just what this hidden presence in nature was, which Wordsworth so rapturously felt, and in the light of which he lived, tramping the hills for days together, the poet never could explain logically or in articulate conceptions. Yet to the reader who may himself have had gleaming moments of a similar sort the verses in which Wordsworth simply proclaims the fact of them come with a heart-satisfying authority:—

> Magnificent
> The morning rose, in memorable pomp,
> Glorious as ere I had beheld. In front
> The sea lay laughing at a distance; near
> The solid mountains shone, bright as the clouds,
> Grain-tinctured, drenched in empyrean light;
> And in the meadows and the lower grounds
> Was all the sweetness of a common dawn,—
> Dews, vapors, and the melody of birds,
> And laborers going forth to till the fields.
>
> Ah! need I say, dear Friend, that to the brim
> My heart was full; I made no vows, but vows
> Were then made for me; bond unknown to me
> Was given, that I should be, else sinning greatly,
> A dedicated Spirit. On I walked,
> In thankful blessedness, which yet survives.[20]

As Wordsworth walked, filled with his strange inner joy, responsive thus to the secret life of nature round about him, his rural neighbors, tightly and narrowly intent upon their own affairs, their crops and lambs and fences, must have thought him a very insignificant and foolish personage. It surely never occurred to any one of them to wonder what was going on inside of *him* or what it might be worth. And yet that inner life of his carried the burden of a significance that has fed the souls of others, and fills them to this day with inner joy.

Richard Jefferies has written a remarkable autobiographic document entitled The Story of my Heart. It tells, in many pages, of the rapture with which in youth the sense of the life of nature filled him. On a certain hill-top he says:—

"I was utterly alone with the sun and the earth. Lying down on the grass, I spoke in my soul to the earth, the sun, the air, and the distant

[19] *The Prelude*, Book III.
[20] *The Prelude*, Book IV.

sea, far beyond sight. . . . With all the intensity of feeling which exalted me, all the intense communion I held with the earth, the sun and sky, the stars hidden by the light, with the ocean,—in no manner can the thrilling depth of these feelings be written,—with these I prayed as if they were the keys of an instrument. . . . The great sun, burning with light, the strong earth,—dear earth,—the warm sky, the pure air, the thought of ocean, the inexpressible beauty of all filled me with a rapture, an ecstasy, an inflatus. With this inflatus, too, I prayed. . . . The prayer, this soul-emotion, was in itself, not for an object: it was a passion. I hid my face in the grass. I was wholly prostrated, I lost myself in the wrestle, I was rapt and carried away. . . . Had any shepherd accidentally seen me lying on the turf, he would only have thought I was resting a few minutes. I made no outward show. Who could have imagined the whirlwind of passion that was going on in me as I reclined there!" [21]

Surely, a worthless hour of life, when measured by the usual standards of commercial value. Yet in what other *kind* of value can the preciousness of any hour, made precious by any standard, consist, if it consist not in feelings of excited significance like these, engendered in some one, by what the hour contains?

Yet so blind and dead does the clamor of our own practical interests make us to all other things, that it seems almost as if it were necessary to become worthless as a practical being, if one is to hope to attain to any breadth of insight into the impersonal world of worths as such, to have any perception of life's meaning on a large objective scale. Only your mystic, your dreamer, or your insolvent tramp or loafer, can afford so sympathetic an occupation, an occupation which will change the usual standards of human value in the twinkling of an eye, giving to foolishness a place ahead of power, and laying low in a minute the distinctions which it takes a hard-working conventional man a lifetime to build up. You may be a prophet, at this rate; but you cannot be a worldly success.

Walt Whitman, for instance, is accounted by many of us a contemporary prophet. He abolishes the usual human distinctions, brings all conventionalisms into solution, and loves and celebrates hardly any human attributes save those elementary ones common to all members of the race. For this he becomes a sort of ideal tramp, a rider on omnibus-tops and ferry-boats, and, considered either practically or academically, a worthless, unproductive being. His verses are but ejaculations—things mostly without subject or verb, a succession of interjections on an immense scale. He felt the human crowd as rapturously as Wordsworth felt the mountains, felt it as an overpoweringly significant presence, simply to absorb one's mind in which

[21] *Op. cit.,* Boston, Roberts, 1883, pp. 5,6.

should be business sufficient and worthy to fill the days of a serious man. As he crosses Brooklyn ferry, this is what he feels:—

Flood-tide below me! I watch you, face to face;

Clouds of the west! sun there half an hour high! I see you also face to face.

Crowds of men and women attired in the usual costumes! how curious you are to me!

On the ferry-boats, the hundreds and hundreds that cross, returning home, are more curious to me than you suppose;

And you that shall cross from shore to shore years hence, are more to me, and more in my meditations, than you might suppose.

Others will enter the gates of the ferry, and cross from shore to shore;

Others will watch the run of the flood-tide;

Others will see the shipping of Manhattan north and west, and the heights of Brooklyn to the south and east;

Others will see the islands large and small;

Fifty years hence, others will see them as they cross, the sun half an hour high.

A hundred years hence, or ever so many hundred years hence, others will see them,

Will enjoy the sunset, the pouring in of the flood-tide, the falling back to the sea of the ebb-tide.

It avails not, neither time or place—distance avails not.

Just as you feel when you look on the river and sky, so I felt;

Just as any of you is one of a living crowd, I was one of a crowd;

Just as you are refresh'd by the gladness of the river and the bright flow, I was refresh'd;

Just as you stand and lean on the rail, yet hurry with the swift current, I stood, yet was hurried;

Just as you look on the numberless masts of ships, and the thick-stemmed pipes of steamboats, I looked.

I too many and many a time cross'd the river, the sun half an hour high;

I watched the Twelfth-month sea-gulls—I saw them high in the air, with motionless wings, oscillating their bodies,

I saw how the glistening yellow lit up parts of their bodies, and left the rest in strong shadow,

I saw the slow-wheeling circles, and the gradual edging toward the south.

Saw the white sails of schooners and sloops, saw the ships at anchor,

The sailors at work in the rigging, or out astride the spars;
The scallop-edged waves in the twilight, the ladled cups,
    the frolicsome crests and glistening;
The stretch afar growing dimmer and dimmer, the gray
    walls of the granite store-houses by the docks;
On the neighboring shores, the fires from the foundry
    chimneys burning high . . . . into the night,
Casting their flicker of black . . . . into the clefts of
    streets.
These, and all else, were to me the same as they are to
    you.[22]

And so on, through the rest of a divinely beautiful poem. And, if you wish to see what this hoary loafer considered the most worthy way of profiting by life's heaven-sent opportunities, read the delicious volume of his letters to a young car-conductor who had become his friend:—

"NEW YORK, Oct. 9, 1868.

"Dear Pete,—It is splendid here this forenoon—bright and cool. I was out early taking a short walk by the river only two squares from where I live. . . . Shall I tell you about [my life] just to fill up? I generally spend the forenoon in my room writing, etc., then take a bath fix up and go out about twelve and loafe somewhere or call on someone down town or on business, or perhaps if it is very pleasant and I feel like it ride a trip with some driver friend on Broadway from 23rd Street to Bowling Green, three miles each way. (Every day I find I have plenty to do, every hour is occupied with something.) You know it is a never ending amusement and study and recreation for me to ride a couple of hours on a pleasant afternoon on a Broadway stage in this way. You see everything as you pass, a sort of living, endless panorama—shops and splendid buildings and great windows: on the broad sidewalks crowds of women richly dressed continually passing, altogether different, superior in style and looks from any to be seen anywhere else—in fact a perfect stream of people—men too dressed in high style, and plenty of foreigners—and then in the streets the thick crowd of carriages, stages, carts, hotel and private coaches, and in fact all sorts of vehicles and many first class teams, mile after mile, and the splendor of such a great street and so many tall, ornamental, noble buildings many of them of white marble, and the gayety and motion on every side: you will not wonder how much attraction all this is on a fine day, to a great loafer like me, who enjoys so much seeing the busy world move by him, and exhibiting itself for his

[22] *Crossing Brooklyn Ferry* (abridged).

amusement, while he takes it easy and just looks on and observes." [23]

Truly a futile way of passing the time, some of you may say, and not altogether creditable to a grown-up man. And yet, from the deepest point of view, who knows the more of truth, and who knows the less,—Whitman on his omnibus-top, full of the inner joy with which the spectacle inspires him, or you, full of the disdain which the futility of his occupation excites?

When your ordinary Brooklynite or New Yorker, leading a life replete with too much luxury, or tired and careworn about his personal affairs, crosses the ferry or goes up Broadway, *his* fancy does not thus 'soar away into the colors of the sunset' as did Whitman's, nor does he inwardly realize at all the indisputable fact that this world never did anywhere or at any time contain more of essential divinity, or of eternal meaning, than is embodied in the fields of vision over which his eyes so carelessly pass. There is life; and there, a step away, is death. There is the only kind of beauty there ever was. There is the old human struggle and its fruits together. There is the text and the sermon, the real and the ideal in one. But to the jaded and unquickened eye it is all dead and common, pure vulgarism, flatness, and disgust. "Hech! it is a sad sight!" says Carlyle, walking at night with some one who appeals to him to note the splendor of the stars. And that very repetition of the scene to new generations of men *in secula seculorum,* that eternal recurrence of the common order, which so fills a Whitman with mystic satisfaction, is to a Schopenhauer, with the emotional anæsthesia, the feeling of 'awful inner emptiness' from out of which he views it all, the chief ingredient of the tedium it instils. What is life on the largest scale, he asks, but the same recurrent inanities, the same dog barking, the same fly buzzing, forevermore? Yet of the kind of fibre of which such inanities consist is the material woven of all the excitements, joys, and meanings that ever were, or ever shall be, in this world.

To be rapt with satisfied attention, like Whitman, to the mere spectacle of the world's presence, is one way, and the most fundamental way, of confessing one's sense of its unfathomable significance and importance. But how can one attain to the feeling of the vital significance of an experience, if one have it not to begin with? There is no receipt which one can follow. Being a secret and a mystery, it often comes in mysteriously unexpected ways. It blossoms sometimes from out of the very grave wherein we imagined that our happiness was buried. Benvenuto Cellini, after a life all in the outer sunshine, made of adventures and artistic excitements, suddenly finds himself cast into a dungeon in the Castle of San Angelo. The place is horrible. Rats and wet

[23] *Calamus,* Boston, 1897, pp. 41, 42.

and mould possess it. His leg is broken and his teeth fall out, apparently with scurvy. But his thoughts turn to God as they have never turned before. He gets a Bible, which he reads during the one hour in the twenty-four in which a wandering ray of daylight penetrates his cavern. He has religious visions. He sings psalms to himself, and composes hymns. And thinking, on the last day of July, of the festivities customary on the morrow in Rome, he says to himself: "All these past years I celebrated this holiday with the vanities of the world: from this year henceforward I will do it with the divinity of God. And then I said to myself, 'Oh, how much more happy I am for this present life of mine than for all those things remembered!' " [24]

But the great understander of these mysterious ebbs and flows is Tolstoï. They throb all through his novels. In his 'War and Peace,' the hero, Peter, is supposed to be the richest man in the Russian empire. During the French invasion he is taken prisoner, and dragged through much of the retreat. Cold, vermin, hunger, and every form of misery assail him, the result being a revelation to him of the real scale of life's values. "Here only, and for the first time, he appreciated, because he was deprived of it, the happiness of eating when he was hungry, of drinking when he was thirsty, of sleeping when he was sleepy, and of talking when he felt the desire to exchange some words. . . . Later in life he always recurred with joy to this month of captivity, and never failed to speak with enthusiasm of the powerful and ineffaceable sensations, and especially of the moral calm which he had experienced at this epoch. When at daybreak, on the morrow of his imprisonment, he saw [I abridge here Tolstoï's description] the mountains with their wooded slopes disappearing in the grayish mist; when he felt the cool breeze caress him; when he saw the light drive away the vapors, and the sun rise majestically behind the clouds and cupolas, and the crosses, the dew, the distance, the river, sparkle in the splendid, cheerful rays,—his heart overflowed with emotion. This emotion kept continually with him, and increased a hundred-fold as the difficulties of his situation grew graver. . . . He learnt that man is meant for happiness, and that this happiness is in him, in the satisfaction of the daily needs of existence, and that unhappiness is the fatal result, not of our need, but of our abundance. . . . When calm reigned in the camp, and the embers paled, and little by little went out, the full moon had reached the zenith. The woods and the fields roundabout lay clearly visible; and, beyond the inundation of light which filled them, the view plunged into the limitless horizon. Then Peter cast his eyes upon the firmament, filled at that hour with myriads of stars. 'All that is mine,' he thought. 'All that is in me, is me! And

[24] *Vita,* lib. 2, chap. iv.

that is what they think they have taken prisoner! That is what they have shut up in a cabin!' So he smiled, and turned in to sleep among his comrades." [25]

The occasion and the experience, then, are nothing. It all depends on the capacity of the soul to be grasped, to have its life-currents absorbed by what is given. "Crossing a bare common," says Emerson, "in snow puddles, at twilight, under a clouded sky, without having in my thoughts any occurrence of special good fortune, I have enjoyed a perfect exhilaration. I am glad to the brink of fear."

Life is always worth living, if one have such responsive sensibilities. But we of the highly educated classes (so called) have most of us got far, far away from Nature. We are trained to seek the choice, the rare, the exquisite exclusively, and to overlook the common. We are stuffed with abstract conceptions, and glib with verbalities and verbosities; and in the culture of these higher functions the peculiar sources of joy connected with our simpler functions often dry up, and we grow stone-blind and insensible to life's more elementary and general goods and joys.

The remedy under such conditions is to descend to a more profound and primitive level. To be imprisoned or shipwrecked or forced into the army would permanently show the good of life to many an over-educated pessimist. Living in the open air and on the ground, the lop-sided beam of the balance slowly rises to the level line; and the over-sensibilities and insensibilities even themselves out. The good of all the artificial schemes and fevers fades and pales; and that of seeing, smelling, tasting, sleeping, and daring and doing with one's body, grows and grows. The savages and children of nature, to whom we deem ourselves so much superior, certainly are alive where we are often dead, along these lines; and, could they write as glibly as we do, they would read us impressive lectures on our impatience for improvement and on our blindness to the fundamental static goods of life. "Ah! my brother," said a chieftain to his white guest, "thou wilt never know the happiness of both thinking of nothing and doing nothing. This, next to sleep, is the most enchanting of all things. Thus we were before our birth, and thus we shall be after death. Thy people, . . . when they have finished reaping one field, they begin to plough another; and, if the day were not enough, I have seen them plough by moonlight. What is their life to ours,—the life that is as naught to them? Blind that they are, they lose it all! But we live in the present." [26]

The intense interest that life can assume when brought down to

[25] *La Guerre et la Paix,* Paris, 1884, vol. iii. pp. 268, 275, 316.
[26] Quoted by Lotze, *Microcosmus,* English translation, vol. ll. p. 240.

the non-thinking level, the level of pure sensorial perception, has been beautifully described by a man who *can* write,—Mr. W. H. Hudson, in his volume, "Idle Days in Patagonia."

"I spent the greater part of one winter," says this admirable author, "at a point on the Rio Negro, seventy or eighty miles from the sea.

. . . "It was my custom to go out every morning on horseback with my gun, and, followed by one dog, to ride away from the valley; and no sooner would I climb the terrace, and plunge into the gray, universal thicket, than I would find myself as completely alone as if five hundred instead of only five miles separated me from the valley and river. So wild and solitary and remote seemed that gray waste, stretching away into infinitude, a waste untrodden by man, and where the wild animals are so few that they have made no discoverable path in the wilderness of thorns. . . . Not once nor twice nor thrice, but day after day I returned to this solitude, going to it in the morning as if to attend a festival, and leaving it only when hunger and thirst and the westering sun compelled me. And yet I had no object in going,— no motive which could be put into words; for, although I carried a gun, there was nothing to shoot,—the shooting was all left behind in the valley. . . . Sometimes I would pass a whole day without seeing one mammal, and perhaps not more than a dozen birds of any size. The weather at that time was cheerless, generally with a gray film of cloud spread over the sky, and a bleak wind, often cold enough to make my bridle-hand quite numb. . . . At a slow pace, which would have seemed intolerable under other circumstances, I would ride about for hours together at a stretch. On arriving at a hill, I would slowly ride to its summit, and stand there to survey the prospect. On every side it stretched away in great undulations, wild and irregular. How gray it all was! Hardly less so near at hand than on the haze-wrapped horizon where the hills were dim and the outline obscured by distance. Descending from my outlook, I would take up my aimless wanderings again, and visit other elevations to gaze on the same landscape from another point; and so on for hours. And at noon I would dismount, and sit or lie on my folded poncho for an hour or longer. One day in these rambles I discovered a small grove composed of twenty or thirty trees, growing at a convenient distance apart, that had evidently been resorted to by a herd of deer or other wild animals. This grove was on a hill differing in shape from other hills in its neighborhood; and, after a time, I made a point of finding and using it as a resting-place every day at noon. I did not ask myself why I made choice of that one spot, sometimes going out of my way to sit there, instead of sitting down under any one of the milllions of trees and bushes on any other hillside. I thought nothing about it, but acted unconsciously. Only afterward it seemed to me that, after having rested there once, each time I wished to rest again, the wish came associated with the image of that particular clump of trees, with polished stems and clean bed of sand beneath; and in a short time I formed a habit of returning, animal like, to repose at that same spot.

"It was, perhaps, a mistake to say that I would sit down and rest, since I was never tired; and yet, without being tired, that noon-day pause, during which I sat for an hour without moving, was strangely grateful. All day there would be no sound, not even the rustling of a leaf. One day, while *listening* to the silence, it occurred to my mind to wonder what the effect would be if I were to shout aloud. This seemed at the time a horrible suggestion, which almost made me shudder. But during those solitary days it was a rare thing for any thought to cross my mind. In the state of mind I was in, thought had become impossible. My state was one of *suspense* and *watchfulness;* yet I had no expectation of meeting an adventure, and felt as free from apprehension as I feel now while sitting in a room in London. The state seemed familiar rather than strange, and accompanied by a strong feeling of elation; and I did not know that something had come between me and my intellect until I returned to my former self,—to thinking, and the old insipid existence [again].

"I had undoubtedly *gone back;* and that state of intense watchfulness or alertness, rather, with suspension of the higher intellectual faculties, represented the mental state of the pure savage. He thinks little, reasons little, having a surer guide in his [mere sensory perceptions]. He is in perfect harmony with nature, and is nearly on a level, mentally, with the wild animals he preys on, and which in their turn sometimes prey on him." [27]

For the spectator, such hours as Mr. Hudson writes of form a mere tale of emptiness, in which nothing happens, nothing is gained, and there is nothing to describe. They are meaningless and vacant tracts of time. To him who feels their inner secret, they tingle with an importance that unutterably vouches for itself. I am sorry for the boy or girl, or man or woman, who has never been touched by the spell of this mysterious sensorial life, with its irrationality, if so you like to call it, but its vigilance and its supreme felicity. The holidays of life are its most vitally significant portions, because they are, or at least should be, covered with just this kind of magically irresponsible spell.

And now what is the result of all these considerations and quotations? It is negative in one sense, but positive in another. It absolutely forbids us to be forward in pronouncing on the meaninglessness of forms of existence other than our own; and it commands us to toler-

[27] *Op. cit.,* pp. 210–222 (abridged).

ate, respect, and indulge those whom we see harmlessly interested and happy in their own ways, however unintelligible these may be to us. Hands off: neither the whole of truth nor the whole of good is revealed to any single observer, although each observer gains a partial superiority of insight from the peculiar position in which he stands. Even prisons and sick-rooms have their special revelations. It is enough to ask of each of us that he should be faithful to his own opportunities and make the most of his own blessings, without presuming to regulate the rest of the vast field.

WHAT MAKES A LIFE SIGNIFICANT*

In my previous talk, 'On a Certain Blindness,' I tried to make you feel how soaked and shot-through life is with values and meanings which we fail to realize because of our external and insensible point of view. The meanings are there for the others, but they are not there for us. There lies more than a mere interest of curious speculation in understanding this. It has the most tremendous practical importance. I wish that I could convince you of it as I feel it myself. It is the basis of all our tolerance, social, religious, and political. The forgetting of it lies at the root of every stupid and sanguinary mistake that rulers over subject-peoples make. The first thing to learn in intercourse with others is non-interference with their own peculiar ways of being happy, provided those ways do not assume to interfere by violence with ours. No one has insight into all the ideals. No one should presume to judge them off-hand. The pretension to dogmatize about them in each other is the root of most human injustices and cruelties, and the trait in human character most likely to make the angels weep.

Every Jack sees in his own particular Jill charms and perfections to the enchantment of which we stolid onlookers are stone-cold. And which has the superior view of the absolute truth, he or we? Which has the more vital insight into the nature of Jill's existence, as a fact? Is he in excess, being in this matter a maniac? or are we in defect, being victims of a pathological anæsthesia as regards Jill's magical importance? Surely the latter; surely to Jack are the profounder truths revealed; surely poor Jill's palpitating little life-throbs *are* among the wonders of creation, *are* worthy of this sympathetic interest; and it is to our shame that the rest of us cannot feel like Jack. For Jack realizes Jill concretely, and we do not. He struggles toward a union with her

* From: T.T., 265–301.

inner life, divining her feelings, anticipating her desires, understanding her limits as manfully as he can, and yet inadequately, too; for he is also afflicted with some blindness, even here. Whilst we, dead clods that we are, do not even seek after these things, but are contented that that portion of eternal fact named Jill should be for us as if it were not. Jill, who knows her inner life, knows that Jack's way of taking it—so importantly—is the true and serious way; and she responds to the truth in him by taking him truly and seriously, too. May the ancient blindness never wrap its clouds about either of them again! Where would any of *us* be, were there no one willing to know us as we really are or ready to repay us for *our* insight by making recognizant return? We ought, all of us, to realize each other in this intense, pathetic, and important way.

If you say that this is absurd, and that we cannot be in love with everyone at once, I merely point out to you that, as a matter of fact, certain persons do exist with an enormous capacity for friendship and for taking delight in other people's lives; and that such persons know more of truth than if their hearts were not so big. The vice of ordinary Jack and Jill affection is not its intensity, but its exclusions and its jealousies. Leave those out, and you see that the ideal I am holding up before you, however impracticable to-day, yet contains nothing intrinsically absurd.

We have unquestionably a great cloud-bank of ancestral blindness weighing down upon us, only transiently riven here and there by fitful revelations of the truth. It is vain to hope for this state of things to alter much. Our inner secrets must remain for the most part impenetrable by others, for beings as essentially practical as we are are necessarily short of sight. But, if we cannot gain much positive insight into one another, cannot we at least use our sense of our own blindness to make us more cautious in going over the dark places? Cannot we escape some of those hideous ancestral intolerances and cruelties, and positive reversals of the truth?

For the remainder of this hour I invite you to seek with me some principle to make our tolerance less chaotic. And, as I began my previous lecture by a personal reminiscence, I am going to ask your indulgence for a similar bit of egotism now.

A few summers ago I spent a happy week at the famous Assembly Grounds on the borders of Chautauqua Lake. The moment one treads that sacred enclosure, one feels one's self in an atmosphere of success. Sobriety and industry, intelligence and goodness, orderliness and ideality, prosperity and cheerfulness, pervade the air. It is a serious and studious picnic on a gigantic scale. Here you have a town of many thousands of inhabitants, beautifully laid out in the forest and drained, and equipped with means for satisfying all the necessary lower and most of the superfluous higher wants of man. You have a first-class college in full blast. You have magnificent music—a chorus of seven hundred voices, with possibly the most perfect open-air auditorium in the world. You have every sort of athletic exercise from sailing, rowing, swimming, bicycling, to the ball-field and the more artificial doings which the gymnasium affords. You have kindergartens and model secondary schools. You have general religious services and special club-houses for the several sects. You have perpetually running soda-water fountains, and daily popular lectures by distinguished men. You have the best of company, and yet no effort. You have no zymotic diseases, no poverty, no drunkenness, no crime, no police. You have culture, you have kindness, you have cheapness, you have equality, you have the best fruits of what mankind has fought and bled and striven for under the name of civilization for centuries. You have, in short, a foretaste of what human society might be, were it all in the light, with no suffering and no dark corners.

I went in curiosity for a day. I stayed for a week, held spell-bound by the charm and ease of everything, by the middle-class paradise, without a sin, without a victim, without a blot, without a tear.

And yet what was my own astonishment, on emerging into the dark and wicked world again, to catch myself quite unexpectedly and involuntarily saying: "Ouf! what a relief! Now for something primordial and savage, even though it were as bad as an Armenian massacre, to set the balance straight again. This order is too tame, this culture too second-rate, this goodness too uninspiring. This human drama without a villain or a pang; this community so refined that ice-cream soda-water is the utmost offering it can make to the brute animal in man; this city simmering in the tepid lakeside sun; this atrocious harmlessness of all things,—I cannot abide with them. Let me take my chances again in the big outside worldly wilderness with all its sins and sufferings. There are the heights and depths, the precipices and the steep ideals, the gleams of the awful and the infinite; and there is more hope and help a thousand times than in this dead level and quintessence of every mediocrity."

Such was the sudden right-about-face performed for me by my lawless fancy! There had been spread before me the realization—on a small, sample scale of course—of all the ideals for which our civilization has been striving: security, intelligence, humanity, and order; and here was the instinctive hostile reaction, not of the natural man, but of a so-called cultivated man upon such a Utopia. There seemed thus to be a self-contradiction and paradox somewhere, which I, as a professor drawing a full salary, was in duty bound to unravel and explain, if I could.

So I meditated. And, first of all, I asked myself what the thing was that was so lacking in this Sabbatical city, and the lack of which kept one forever falling short of the higher sort of contentment. And I soon recognized that it was the element that gives to the wicked outer world all its moral style, expressiveness and picturesqueness,—the element of precipitousness, so to call it, of strength and strenuousness, intensity and danger. What excites and interests the looker-on at life, what the romances and the statues celebrate and the grim civic monuments remind us of, is the everlasting battle of the powers of light with those of darkness; with heroism, reduced to its bare chance, yet ever and anon snatching victory from the jaws of death. But in this unspeakable Chautauqua there was no potentiality of death in sight anywhere, and no point of the compass visible from which danger might possibly appear. The ideal was so completely victorious already that no sign of any previous battle remained, the place just resting on its oars. But what our human emotions seem to require is the sight of the struggle going on. The moment the fruits are being merely eaten, things become ignoble. Sweat and effort, human nature strained to its uttermost and on the rack, yet getting through alive, and then turning its back on its success to pursue another more rare and arduous still— this is the sort of thing the presence of which inspires us, and the reality of which it seems to be the function of all the higher forms of literature and fine art to bring home to us and suggest. At Chautauqua there were no racks, even in the place's historical museum; and no sweat, except possibly the gentle moisture on the brow of some lecturer, or on the sides of some player in the ball-field.

Such absence of human nature *in extremis* anywhere seemed, then, a sufficient explanation for Chautauqua's flatness and lack of zest.

But was not this a paradox well calculated to fill one with dismay? It looks indeed, thought I, as if the romantic idealists with their pessimism about our civilization were, after all, quite right. An irremediable flatness is coming over the world. Bourgeoisie and mediocrity, church sociables and teachers' conventions, are taking the place of the old heights and depths and romantic chiaroscuro. And, to get human life in its wild intensity, we must in future turn more and more away from the actual, and forget it, if we can, in the romancer's or the poet's pages. The whole world, delightful and sinful as it may still appear for a moment to one just escaped from the Chautauquan enclosure, is nevertheless obeying more and more just those ideals that are sure to make of it in the end a mere Chautauqua Assembly on an enormous scale. *Was in Gesang soll leben muss im Leben untergehn.* Even now, in our own country, correctness, fairness, and compromise for every small advantage are crowding out all other qualities. The higher heroisms and the old rare flavors are passing out of life.[28]

[28] This address was composed before the Cuban and Philippine wars. Such outbursts of the passion of mastery are, however, only episodes in a social proc-

With these thoughts in my mind, I was speeding with the train toward Buffalo, when, near that city, the sight of a workman doing something on the dizzy edge of a sky-scaling iron construction brought me to my senses very suddenly. And now I perceived, by a flash of insight, that I had been steeping myself in pure ancestral blindness, and looking at life with the eyes of a remote spectator. Wishing for heroism and the spectacle of human nature on the rack, I had never noticed the great fields of heroism lying round about me, I had failed to see it present and alive. I could only think of it as dead and embalmed, labelled and costumed, as it is in the pages of romance. And yet there it was before me in the daily lives of the laboring classes. Not in clanging fights and desperate marches only is heroism to be looked for, but on every railway bridge and fire-proof building that is going up to-day. On freight-trains, on the decks of vessels, in cattle-yards and mines, on lumber-rafts, among the firemen and the policemen, the demand for courage is incessant; and the supply never fails. There, every day of the year somewhere, is human nature *in extremis* for you. And wherever a scythe, an axe, a pick, or a shovel is wielded, you have it sweating and aching and with its powers of patient endurance racked to the utmost under the length of hours of the strain.

As I awoke to all this unidealized heroic life around me, the scales seemed to fall from my eyes; and a wave of sympathy greater than anything I had ever before felt with the common life of common men began to fill my soul. It began to seem as if virtue with horny hands and dirty skin were the only virtue genuine and vital enough to take account of. Every other virtue poses; none is absolutely unconscious and simple, and unexpectant of decoration or recognition, like this. These are our soldiers, thought I, these our sustainers, these the very parents of our life.

Many years ago, when in Vienna, I had had a similar feeling of awe and reverence in looking at the peasant-women, in from the country on their business at the market for the day. Old hags many of them were, dried and brown and wrinkled, kerchiefed and short-petti-coated, with thick wool stockings on their bony shanks, stumping through the glittering thoroughfares, looking neither to the right nor the left, bent on duty, envying nothing, humble-hearted, remote;—and yet at bottom, when you came to think of it, bearing the whole fabric of the splendors and corruptions of that city on their laborious backs. For where would any of it have been without their unremitting, unrewarded labor in the fields? And so with us: not to our generals

---

ess which in the long run seems everywhere tending toward the Chautauquan ideals.

and poets, I thought, but to the Italian and Hungarian laborers in the Subway, rather, ought the monuments of gratitude and reverence of a city like Boston to be reared.

If any of you have been readers of Tolstoï, you will see that I passed into a vein of feeling similar to his, with its abhorrence of all that conventionally passes for distinguished, and its exclusive deification of the bravery, patience, kindliness, and dumbness of the unconscious natural man.

Where now is *our* Tolstoï, I said, to bring the truth of all this home to our American bosoms, fill us with a better insight, and wean us away from that spurious literary romanticism on which our wretched culture—as it calls itself—is fed? Divinity lies all about us, and culture is too hide-bound to even suspect the fact. Could a Howells or a Kipling be enlisted in this mission? or are they still too deep in the ancestral blindness, and not humane enough for the inner joy and meaning of the laborer's existence to be really revealed? Must we wait for some one born and bred and living as a laborer himself, but who, by grace of Heaven, shall also find a literary voice?

And there I rested on that day, with a sense of widening of vision, and with what it is surely fair to call an increase of religious insight into life. In God's eyes the differences of social position, of intellect, of culture, of cleanliness, of dress, which different men exhibit, and all the other rarities and exceptions on which they so fantastically pin their pride, must be so small as practically quite to vanish; and all that should remain is the common fact that here we are, a countless multitude of vessels of life, each of us pent in to peculiar difficulties, with which we must severally struggle by using whatever of fortitude and goodness we can summon up. The exercise of the courage, patience, and kindness, must be the significant portion of the whole business; and the distinctions of position can only be a manner of diversifying the phenomenal surface upon which these underground virtues may manifest their effects. At this rate, the deepest human life is every-- where, is eternal. And, if any human attributes exist only in particular individuals, they must belong to the mere trapping and decoration of the surface-show.

Thus are men's lives levelled up as well as levelled down,—levelled up in their common inner meaning, levelled down in their outer gloriousness and show. Yet always, we must confess, this levelling insight tends to be obscured again; and always the ancestral blindness returns and wraps us up, so that we end once more by thinking that creation can be for no other purpose than to develop remarkable situations and conventional distinctions and merits. And then always some new leveller in the shape of a religious prophet has to arise—the

Buddha, the Christ, or some Saint Francis, some Rousseau or Tolstoï
—to redispel our blindness. Yet, little by little, there comes one
stable gain; for the world does get more humane, and the religion of
democracy tends toward permanent increase.

This, as I said, became for a time my conviction, and gave me
great content. I have put the matter into the form of a personal reminiscence, so that I might lead you into it more directly and completely,
and so save time. But now I am going to discuss the rest of it with you
in a more impersonal way.

Tolstoï's levelling philosophy began long before he had the crisis
of melancholy commemorated in that wonderful document of his entitled 'My Confession,' which led the way to his more specifically religious works. In his masterpiece 'War and Peace,'—assuredly the
greatest of human novels,—the rôle of the spiritual hero is given to a
poor little soldier named Karataïeff, so helpful, so cheerful, and so
devout that, in spite of his ignorance and filthiness, the sight of him
opens the heavens, which have been closed, to the mind of the principal character of the book; and his example evidently is meant by Tolstoï to let God into the world again for the reader. Poor little
Karataïeff is taken prisoner by the French; and, when too exhausted
by hardship and fever to march, is shot as other prisoners were in the
famous retreat from Moscow. The last view one gets of him is his little
figure leaning against a white birch-tree, and uncomplainingly await-
ing the end.

"The more," writes Tolstoï in the work 'My Confession,' "the
more I examined the life of these laboring folks, the more persuaded I
became that they veritably have faith, and get from it alone the sense
and the possibility of life. . . . Contrariwise to those of our own
class, who protest against destiny and grow indignant at its rigor,
these people receive maladies and misfortunes without revolt, without
opposition, and with a firm and tranquil confidence that all had to be
like that, could not be otherwise, and that it is all right so. . . . The
more we live by our intellect, the less we understand the meaning of
life. We see only a cruel jest in suffering and death, whereas these
people live, suffer, and draw near to death with tranquillity, and of-
tener than not with joy. . . . There are enormous multitudes of them
happy with the most perfect happiness, although deprived of what for
us is the sole good of life. Those who understand life's meaning, and
know how to live and die thus, are to be counted not by twos, threes,
tens, but by hundreds, thousands, millions. They labor quietly, endure
privations and pains, live and die, and throughout everything see the
good without seeing the vanity. I had to love these people. The more I
entered into their life, the more I loved them; and the more it became
possible for me to live, too. It came about not only that the life of our

society, of the learned and of the rich, disgusted me—more than that, it lost all semblance of meaning in my eyes. All our actions, our deliberations, our sciences, our arts, all appeared to me with a new significance. I understood that these things might be charming pastimes, but that one need seek in them no depth, whereas the life of the hardworking populace, of that multitude of human beings who really contribute to existence, appeared to me in its true light. I understood that there veritably is life, that the meaning which life there receives is the truth; and I accepted it." [29]

In a similar way does Stevenson appeal to our piety toward the elemental virtue of mankind.

"What a wonderful thing," he writes,[30] "is this Man! How surprising are his attributes! Poor soul, here for so little, cast among so many hardships, savagely surrounded, savagely descended, irremediably condemmed to prey upon his fellow-lives,—who should have blamed him, had be been of a piece with his destiny and a being merely barbarous? . . . [Yet] it matters not where we look, under what climate we observe him, in what stage of society, in what depth of ignorance, burdened with what erroneous morality; in ships at sea, a man inured to hardship and vile pleasures, his brightest hope a fiddle in a tavern, and a bedizened trull who sells herself to rob him, and he, for all that, simple, innocent, cheerful, kindly like a child, constant to toil, brave to drown, for others; . . . in the slums of cities, moving among indifferent millions to mechanical employments, without hope of change in the future, with scarce a pleasure in the present, and yet true to his virtues, honest up to his lights, kind to his neighbors, tempted perhaps in vain by the bright gin-palace, . . . often repaying the world's scorn with service, often standing firm upon a scruple; . . . everywhere some virtue cherished or affected, everywhere some decency of thought and courage, everywhere the ensign of man's ineffectual goodness,—ah! if I could show you this! If I could show you these men and women all the world over, in every stage of history, under every abuse of error, under every circumstance of failure, without hope, without help, without thanks, still obscurely fighting the lost fight of virtue, still clinging to some rag of honor, the poor jewel of their souls."

All this is as true as it is splendid, and terribly do we need our Tolstoïs and Stevensons to keep our sense for it alive. Yet you remember the Irishman who, when asked, "Is not one man as good as another?" replied, "Yes; and a great deal better, too!" Similarly (it seems to me) does Tolstoï overcorrect our social prejudices, when he

[29] *My Confession*, X. (condensed).
[30] *Across the Plains:* "Pulvis et Umbra" (abridged).

makes his love of the peasant so exclusive, and hardens his heart toward the educated man as absolutely as he does. Grant that at Chautauqua there was little moral effort, little sweat or muscular strain in view. Still, deep down in the souls of the participants we may be sure that something of the sort was hid, some inner stress, some vital virtue not found wanting when required. And, after all, the question recurs, and forces itself upon us: Is it so certain that the surroundings and circumstances of the virtue do make so little difference in the importance of the result? Is the functional utility, the worth to the universe of a certain definite amount of courage, kindliness, and patience, no greater if the possessor of these virtues is in an educated situation, working out far-reaching tasks, than if he be an illiterate nobody, hewing wood and drawing water, just to keep himself alive? Tolstoï's philosophy, deeply enlightening though it certainly is, remains a false abstraction. It savors too much of that Oriental pessimism and nihilism of his, which declares the whole phenomenal world and its facts and their distinctions to be a cunning fraud.

A mere bare fraud is just what our Western common sense will never believe the phenomenal world to be. It admits fully that the inner joys and virtues are the *essential* part of life's business, but it is sure that *some* positive part is also played by the adjuncts of the show. If it is idiotic in romanticism to recognize the heroic only when it sees it labelled and dressed-up in books, it is really just as idiotic to see it only in the dirty boots and sweaty shirt of some one in the fields. It is with us really under every disguise: at Chautauqua; here in your college; in the stock-yards and on the freight-trains; and in the czar of Russia's court. But, instinctively, we make a combination of two things in judging the total significance of a human being. We feel it to be some sort of a product (if such a product only could be calculated) of his inner virtue *and* his outer place,—neither singly taken, but both conjoined. If the outer differences had no meaning for life, why indeed should all this immense variety of them exist? They *must* be significant elements of the world as well.

Just test Tolstoï's deification of the mere manual laborer by the facts. This is what Mr. Walter Wyckoff, after working as an unskilled laborer in the demolition of some buildings at West Point, writes of the spiritual condition of the class of men to which he temporarily chose to belong:—

"The salient features of our condition are plain enough. We are grown men, and are without a trade. In the labor-market we stand ready to sell to the highest bidder our mere muscular strength for so many hours each day. We are thus in the lowest grade of labor. And, selling our muscular strength in the open market for what it will bring, we sell it under peculiar conditions. It is all the capital that we have. We have no reserve means of subsistence, and cannot, therefore, stand off for a 'reserve price.' We sell under the necessity of satisfying imminent hunger. Broadly speaking, we must sell our labor or starve; and, as hunger is a matter of a few hours, and we have no other way of meeting this need, we must sell at once for what the market offers for our labor.

"Our employer is buying labor in a dear market, and he will certainly get from us as much work as he can at the price. The gang-boss is secured for this purpose, and thoroughly does he know his business. He has sole command of us. He never saw us before, and he will discharge us all when the débris is cleared away. In the mean time he must get from us, if he can, the utmost of physical labor which we, individually and collectively, are capable of. If he should drive some of us to exhaustion, and we should not be able to continue at work, he would not be the loser; for the market would soon supply him with others to take our places.

"We are ignorant men, but so much we clearly see,—that we have sold our labor where we could sell it dearest, and our employer has bought it where he could buy it cheapest. He has paid high, and he must get all the labor that he can; and, by a strong instinct which possesses us, we shall part with as little as we can. From work like ours there seems to us to have been eliminated every element which constitutes the nobility of labor. We feel no personal pride in its progress, and no community of interest with our employer. There is none of the joy of responsibility, none of the sense of achievement, only the dull monotony of grinding toil, with the longing for the signal to quit work, and for our wages at the end.

"And being what we are, the dregs of the labor-market, and having no certainty of permanent employment, and no organization among ourselves, we must expect to work under the watchful eye of a gang-boss, and be driven, like the wage-slaves that we are, through our tasks.

"All this is to tell us, in effect, that our lives are hard, barren, hopeless lives."

And such hard, barren, hopeless lives, surely, are not lives in which one ought to be willing permanently to remain. And why is this so? Is it because they are so dirty? Well, Nansen grew a great deal dirtier on his polar expedition; and we think none the worse of his life for that. Is it the insensibility? Our soldiers have to grow vastly more insensible, and we extol them to the skies. Is it the poverty? Poverty has been reckoned the crowning beauty of many a heroic career. Is it the slavery to a task, the loss of finer pleasures? Such slavery and loss are of the very essence of the higher fortitude, and are always counted to its credit,—read the records of missionary devotion all over the world. It is not any one of these things, then, taken by itself,—no, nor all of them together,—that make such a life undesirable. A man might in truth live like an unskilled laborer, and do the work of one, and yet count as one of the noblest of God's creatures. Quite possibly there were some such persons in the gang that our author describes; but the current of their souls ran underground; and he was too steeped in the ancestral blindness to discern it.

If there *were* any such morally exceptional individuals, however, what made them different from the rest? It can only have been this,— that their souls worked and endured in obedience to some inner *ideal,* while their comrades were not actuated by anything worthy of that name. These ideals of other lives are among those secrets that we can almost never penetrate, although something about the man may often tell us when they are there. In Mr. Wyckoff's own case we know exactly what the self-imposed ideal was. Partly he had stumped himself, as the boys say, to carry through a strenuous achievement; but mainly he wished to enlarge his sympathetic insight into fellow-lives. For this his sweat and toil acquire a certain heroic significance, and make us accord to him exceptional esteem. But it is easy to imagine his fellows with various other ideals. To say nothing of wives and babies, one may have been a convert of the Salvation Army, and had a nightingale singing of expiation and forgiveness in his heart all the while he labored. Or there might have been an apostle like Tolstoï himself, or his compatriot Bondareff, in the gang, voluntarily embracing labor as their religious mission. Class-loyalty was undoubtedly an ideal with many. And who knows how much of that higher manliness of poverty, of which Phillips Brooks has spoken so penetratingly, was or was not present in that gang?

"A rugged, barren land," says Phillips Brooks, "is poverty to live in,—a land where I am thankful very often if I can get a berry or a root to eat. But living in it really, letting it bear witness to me of itself, not dishonoring it all the time by judging it after the standard of the other lands, gradually there come out its qualities. Behold! no land like this barren and naked land of poverty could show the moral geology of the world. See how the hard ribs . . . stand out strong and solid. No life like poverty could so get one to the heart of things and make men know their meaning, could so let us feel life and the world with all the soft cushions stripped off and thrown away. . . . Poverty makes men come very near each other, and recognize each other's human hearts; and poverty, highest and best of all, demands and cries out for faith in God. . . . I know how superficial and unfeeling, how like mere mockery, words in praise of poverty may seem. . . . But I am sure that the poor man's dignity and freedom, his self-respect and energy, depend upon his cordial knowledge that his poverty is a true region and kind of life, with its own chances of character, its own springs of happiness and revelations of God. Let him resist the characterlessness which often goes with being poor. Let him insist on respecting the condition where he lives. Let him learn to love it, so that by and by, [if] he grows rich, he shall go out of the low door of the old familiar poverty with a true pang of regret, and with a true honor for the narrow home in which he has lived so long." [31]

The barrenness and ignobleness of the more usual laborer's life consist in the fact that it is moved by no such ideal inner springs. The backache, the long hours, the danger, are patiently endured—for what? To gain a quid of tobacco, a glass of beer, a cup of coffee, a meal, and a bed, and to begin again the next day and shirk as much as one can. This really is why we raise no monument to the laborers in the Subway, even though they be our conscripts, and even though after a fashion our city is indeed based upon their patient hearts and enduring backs and shoulders. And this is why we do raise monuments to our soldiers, whose outward conditions were even brutaller still. The soldiers are supposed to have followed an ideal, and the laborers are supposed to have followed none.

You see, my friends, how the plot 'now thickens; and how strangely the complexities of this wonderful human nature of ours begin to develop under our hands. We have seen the blindness and deadness to each other which are our natural inheritance; and, in spite of them, we have been led to acknowledge an inner meaning which passeth show, and which may be present in the lives of others where we least descry it. And now we are led to say that such inner meaning can be *complete* and *valid for us also,* only when the inner joy, courage, and endurance are joined with an ideal.

But what, exactly, do we mean by an ideal? Can we give no definite account of such a word?

To a certain extent we can. An ideal, for instance, must be something intellectually conceived, something of which we are not unconscious, if we have it; and it must carry with it that sort of outlook, uplift, and brightness that go with all intellectual facts. Secondly, there must be *novelty* in an ideal,—novelty at least for him whom the ideal grasps. Sodden routine is incompatible with ideality, although what is sodden routine for one person may be ideal novelty for another. This shows that there is nothing absolutely ideal: ideals are relative to the lives that entertain them. To keep out of the gutter is for us here no part of consciousness at all, yet for many of our brethren it is the most legitimately engrossing of ideals.

[31] *Sermons,* 5th Series, New York, 1893, pp. 166, 167.

Now, taken nakedly, abstractly, and immediately, you see that mere ideals are the cheapest things in life. Everybody has them in some shape or other, personal or general, sound or mistaken, low or high; and the most worthless sentimentalists and dreamers, drunkards, shirks and verse-makers, who never show a grain of effort, courage, or endurance, possibly have them on the most copious scale. Education, enlarging as it does our horizon and perspective, is a means of multiplying our ideals, of bringing new ones into view. And your college professor, with a starched shirt and spectacles, would, if a stock of ideals were all alone by itself enough to render a life significant, be the most absolutely and deeply significant of men. Tolstoï would be completely blind in despising him for a prig, a pedant and a parody; and all our new insight into the divinity of muscular labor would be altogether off the track of truth.

But such consequences as this, you instinctively feel, are erroneous. The more ideals a man has, the more contemptible, on the whole, do you continue to deem him, if the matter ends there for him, and if none of the laboring man's virtues are called into action on his part,—no courage shown, no privations undergone, no dirt or scars contracted in the attempt to get them realized. It is quite obvious that something more than the mere possession of ideals is required to make a life significant in any sense that claims the spectator's admiration. Inner joy, to be sure, it may *have,* with its ideals; but that is its own private sentimental matter. To extort from us, outsiders as we are, with our own ideals to look after, the tribute of our grudging recognition, it must back its ideal visions with what the laborers have, the sterner stuff of manly virtue; it must multiply their sentimental surface by the dimension of the active will, if we are to have *depth,* if we are to have anything cubical and solid in the way of character.

The significance of a human life for communicable and publicly recognizable purposes is thus the offspring of a marriage of two different parents, either of whom alone is barren. The ideals taken by themselves give no reality, the virtues by themselves no novelty. And let the orientalists and pessimists say what they will, the thing of deepest —or, at any rate, of comparatively deepest—significance in life does seem to be its character of *progress,* or that strange union of reality with ideal novelty which it continues from one moment to another to present. To recognize ideal novelty is the task of what we call intelligence. Not every one's intelligence can tell which novelties are ideal. For many the ideal thing will always seem to cling still to the older more familiar good. In this case character, though not significant totally, may be still significant pathetically. So, if we are to choose which is the more essential factor of human character, the fighting virtue or the intellectual breadth, we must side with Tolstoï, and choose that simple faithfulness to his light or darkness which any common un-intellectual man can show.

But, with all this beating and tacking on my part, I fear you take me to be reaching a confused result. I seem to be just taking things up and dropping them again. First I took up Chautauqua, and dropped that; then Tolstoï and the heroism of common toil, and dropped them; finally, I took up ideals, and seem now almost dropping those. But please observe in what sense it is that I drop them. It is when they pretend *singly* to redeem life from insignificance. Culture and refinement all alone are not enough to do so. Ideal aspirations are not enough, when uncombined with pluck and will. But neither are pluck and will, dogged endurance and insensibility to danger enough, when taken all alone. There must be some sort of fusion, some chemical combination among these principles, for a life objectively and thoroughly significant to result.

Of course, this is a somewhat vague conclusion. But in a question of significance, of worth, like this, conclusions can never be precise. The answer of appreciation, of sentiment, is always a more or a less, a balance struck by sympathy, insight, and good will. But it is an answer, all the same, a real conclusion. And, in the course of getting it, it seems to me that our eyes have been opened to many important things. Some of you are, perhaps, more livingly aware than you were an hour ago of the depths of worth that lie around you, hid in alien lives. And, when you ask how much sympathy you ought to bestow, although the amount is, truly enough, a matter of ideal on your own part, yet in this notion of the combination of ideals with active virtues you have a rough standard for shaping your decision. In any case, your imagination is extended. You divine in the world about you matter for a little more humility on your own part, and tolerance, reverence, and love for others; and you gain a certain inner joyfulness at the increased importance of our common life. Such joyfulness is a religious inspiration and an element of spiritual health, and worth more than large amounts of that sort of technical and accurate information which we professors are supposed to be able to impart.

To show the sort of thing I mean by these words, I will just make one brief practical illustration, and then close.

We are suffering to-day in America from what is called the labor-question; and, when you go out into the world, you will each and all of you be caught up in its perplexities. I use the brief term labor-question to cover all sorts of anarchistic discontents and socialistic projects, and the conservative resistances which they provoke. So far as this conflict is unhealthy and regrettable,—and I think it is so only to a limited extent,—the unhealthiness consists solely in the fact that one-half of our fellow-countrymen remain entirely blind to the internal significance of the lives of the other half. They miss the joys and sorrows, they fail to feel the moral virtue, and they do not guess the presence of the intellectual ideals. They are at cross-purposes all along the line, regarding each other as they might regard a set of dangerously gesticulating automata, or, if they seek to get at the inner motivation, making the most horrible mistakes. Often all that the poor man can think of in the rich man is a cowardly greediness for safety, luxury, and effeminacy, and a boundless affectation. What he is, is not a human being, but a pocket-book, a bank-account. And a similar greediness, turned by disappointment into envy, is all that many rich men can see in the state of mind of the dissatisfied poor. And, if the rich man begins to do the sentimental act over the poor man, what senseless blunders does he make, pitying him for just those very duties and those very immunities which, rightly taken, are the condition of his most abiding and characteristic joys! Each, in short, ignores the fact that happiness and unhappiness and significance are a vital mystery; each pins them absolutely on some ridiculous feature of the external situation; and everybody remains outside of everybody else's sight.

Society has, with all this, undoubtedly got to pass toward some newer and better equilibrium, and the distribution of wealth has doubtless slowly got to change: such changes have always happened, and will happen to the end of time. But if, after all that I have said, any of you expect that they will make any *genuine vital difference* on a large scale, to the lives of our descendants, you will have missed the significance of my entire lecture. The solid meaning of life is always the same eternal thing,—the marriage, namely, of some unhabitual ideal, however special, with some fidelity, courage, and endurance; with some man's or woman's pains.—And, whatever or wherever life may be, there will always be the chance for that marriage to take place.

Fitz-James Stephen wrote many years ago words to this effect more eloquent than any I can speak: "The 'Great Eastern,' or some of her successors," he said, "will perhaps defy the roll of the Atlantic, and cross the seas without allowing their passengers to feel that they have left the firm land. The voyage from the cradle to the grave may come to be performed with similar facility. Progress and science may perhaps enable untold millions to live and die without a care, without a pang, without an anxiety. They will have a pleasant passage and plenty of brilliant conversation. They will wonder that men ever believed at all in clanging fights and blazing towns and sinking ships and praying hands; and, when they come to the end of their course, they will go their way, and the place thereof will know them no more. But it seems unlikely that they will have such a knowledge of the great ocean on which they sail, with its storms and wrecks, its currents and icebergs, its huge waves and mighty winds, as those who battled with it for years together in the little craft, which, if they had few other merits, brought those who navigated them full into the presence of time and eternity, their maker and themselves, and forced them to have some definite view of their relations to them and to each other." [32]

In this solid and tridimensional sense, so to call it, those philosophers are right who contend that the world is a standing thing, with no progress, no real history. The changing conditions of history touch only the surface of the show. The altered equilibriums and redistributions only diversify our opportunities and open chances to us for new ideals. But, with each new ideal that comes into life, the chance for a life based on some old ideal will vanish; and he would needs be a presumptuous calculator who should with confidence say that the total sum of significances is positively and absolutely greater at any one epoch than at any other of the world.

I am speaking broadly, I know, and omitting to consider certain qualifications in which I myself believe. But one can only make one point in one lecture, and I shall be well content if I have brought my point home to you this evening in even a slight degree. *There are compensations:* and no outward changes of condition in life can keep the nightingale of its eternal meaning from singing in all sorts of different men's hearts. That is the main fact to remember. If we could not only admit it with our lips, but really and truly believe it, how our convulsive insistencies, how our antipathies and dreads of each other, would soften down! If the poor and the rich could look at each other in this way, *sub specie æternitatis,* how gentle would grow their disputes! what tolerance and good humor, what willingness to live and let live, would come into the world!

THE MORAL EQUIVALENT OF WAR* [33]

The war against war is going to be no holiday excursion or camping party. The military feelings are too deeply grounded to abdicate their

[32] *Essays by a Barrister,* London, 1862, p. 318.

* From: M.S., 267–296.

[33] Written for and first published by the Association for International Conciliation (Leaflet No. 27) and also published in *McClure's Magazine,* August, 1910, and *The Popular Science Monthly,* October, 1910.

place among our ideals until better substitutes are offered than the glory and shame that come to nations as well as to individuals from the ups and downs of politics and the vicissitudes of trade. There is something highly paradoxical in the modern man's relation to war. Ask all our millions, north and south, whether they would vote now (were such a thing possible) to have our war for the Union expunged from history, and the record of a peaceful transition to the present time substituted for that of its marches and battles, and probably hardly a handful of eccentrics would say yes. Those ancestors, those efforts, those memories and legends, are the most ideal part of what we now own together, a sacred spiritual possession worth more than all the blood poured out. Yet ask those same people whether they would be willing in cold blood to start another civil war now to gain another similar possession, and not one man or woman would vote for the proposition. In modern eyes, precious though wars may be, they must not be waged solely for the sake of the ideal harvest. Only when forced upon one, only when an enemy's injustice leaves us no alternative, is a war now thought permissible.

It was not thus in ancient times. The earlier men were hunting men, and to hunt a neighboring tribe, kill the males, loot the village and possess the females, was the most profitable, as well as the most exciting, way of living. Thus were the more martial tribes selected, and in chiefs and peoples a pure pugnacity and love of glory came to mingle with the more fundamental appetite for plunder.

Modern war is so expensive that we feel trade to be a better avenue to plunder; but modern man inherits all the innate pugnacity and all the love of glory of his ancestors. Showing war's irrationality and horror is of no effect upon him. The horrors make the fascination. War is the *strong* life; it is life *in extremis;* war-taxes are the only ones men never hesitate to pay, as the budgets of all nations show us.

History is a bath of blood. The Iliad is one long recital of how Diomedes and Ajax, Sarpedon and Hector *killed*. No detail of the wounds they made is spared us, and the Greek mind fed upon the story. Greek history is a panorama of jingoism and imperialism—war for war's sake, all the citizens being warriors. It is horrible reading, because of the irrationality of it all—save for the purpose of making "history"—and the history is that of the utter ruin of a civilization in intellectual respects perhaps the highest the earth has ever seen.

Those wars were purely piratical. Pride, gold, women, slaves, excitement, were their only motives. In the Peloponnesian war for example, the Athenians ask the inhabitants of Melos (the island where the "Venus of Milo" was found), hitherto neutral, to own their lordship. The envoys meet, and hold a debate which Thucydides gives in full, and which, for sweet reasonableness of form, would have satisfied Matthew Arnold. "The powerful exact what they can," said the

Athenians, "and the weak grant what they must." When the Meleans say that sooner than be slaves they will appeal to the gods, the Athenians reply: "Of the gods we believe and of men we know that, by a law of their nature, wherever they can rule they will. This law was not made by us, and we are not the first to have acted upon it; we did but inherit it, and we know that you and all mankind, if you were as strong as we are, would do as we do. So much for the gods; we have told you why we expect to stand as high in their good opinion as you." Well, the Meleans still refused, and their town was taken. "The Athenians," Thucydides quietly says, "thereupon put to death all who were of military age and made slaves of the women and children. They then colonized the island, sending thither five hundred settlers of their own."

Alexander's career was piracy pure and simple, nothing but an orgy of power and plunder, made romantic by the character of the hero. There was no rational principle in it, and the moment he died his generals and governors attacked one another. The cruelty of those times is incredible. When Rome finally conquered Greece, Paulus Æmilius was told by the Roman Senate to reward his soldiers for their toil by "giving" them the old kingdom of Epirus. They sacked seventy cities and carried off a hundred and fifty thousand inhabitants as slaves. How many they killed I know not; but in Etolia they killed all the senators, five hundred and fifty in number. Brutus was "the noblest Roman of them all," but to reanimate his soldiers on the eve of Philippi he similarly promises to give them the cities of Sparta and Thessalonica to ravage, if they win the fight.

Such was the gory nurse that trained societies to cohesiveness. We inherit the warlike type; and for most of the capacities of heroism that the human race is full of we have to thank this cruel history. Dead men tell no tales, and if there were any tribes of other type than this they have left no survivors. Our ancestors have bred pugnacity into our bone and marrow, and thousands of years of peace won't breed it out of us. The popular imagination fairly fattens on the thought of wars. Let public opinion once reach a certain fighting pitch, and no ruler can withstand it. In the Boer war both governments began with bluff but could n't stay there, the military tension was too much for them. In 1898 our people had read the word "war" in letters three inches high for three months in every newspaper. The pliant politician McKinley was swept away by their eagerness, and our squalid war with Spain became a necessity.

At the present day, civilized opinion is a curious mental mixture. The military instincts and ideals are as strong as ever, but are confronted by reflective criticisms which sorely curb their ancient freedom. Innumerable writers are showing up the bestial side of military service. Pure loot and mastery seem no longer morally avowable motives, and pretexts must be found for attributing them solely to the enemy. England and we, our army and navy authorities repeat without ceasing, arm solely for "peace," Germany and Japan it is who are bent on loot and glory. "Peace" in military mouths to-day is a synonym for "war expected." The word has become a pure provocative, and no government wishing peace sincerely should allow it ever to be printed in a newspaper. Every up-to-date dictionary should say that "peace" and "war" mean the same thing, now *in posse,* now *in actu.* It may even reasonably be said that the intensely sharp competitive *preparation* for war by the nations *is the real war,* permanent, unceasing; and that the battles are only a sort of public verification of the mastery gained during the "peace" interval.

It is plain that on this subject civilized man has developed a sort of double personality. If we take European nations, no legitimate interest of any one of them would seem to justify the tremendous destructions which a war to compass it would necessarily entail. It would seem as though common sense and reason ought to find a way to reach agreement in every conflict of honest interests. I myself think it our bounden duty to believe in such international rationality as possible. But, as things stand, I see how desperately hard it is to bring the peace-party and the war-party together, and I believe that the difficulty is due to certain deficiencies in the program of pacificism which set the militarist imagination strongly, and to a certain extent justifiably, against it. In the whole discussion both sides are on imaginative and sentimental ground. It is but one utopia against another, and everything one says must be abstract and hypothetical. Subject to this criticism and caution, I will try to characterize in abstract strokes the opposite imaginative forces, and point out what to my own very fallible mind seems the best utopian hypothesis, the most promising line of conciliation.

In my remarks, pacificist though I am, I will refuse to speak of the bestial side of the war-*régime* (already done justice to by many writers) and consider only the higher aspects of militaristic sentiment. Patriotism no one thinks discreditable; nor does any one deny that war is the romance of history. But inordinate ambitions are the soul of every patriotism, and the possibility of violent death the soul of all romance. The militarily patriotic and romantic-minded everywhere, and especially the professional military class, refuse to admit for a moment that war may be a transitory phenomenon in social evolution. The notion of a sheep's paradise like that revolts, they say, our higher imagination. Where then would be the steeps of life? If war had ever stopped, we should have to re-invent it, on this view, to redeem life from flat degeneration.

Reflective apologists for war at the present day all take it religiously. It is a sort of sacrament. Its profits are to the vanquished as well as to the victor; and quite apart from any question of profit, it is an absolute good, we are told, for it is human nature at its highest dynamic. Its "horrors" are a cheap price to pay for rescue from the only alternative supposed, of a world of clerks and teachers, of co-education and zo-ophily, of "consumer's leagues" and "associated charities," of industrialism unlimited, and femininism unabashed. No scorn, no hardness, no valor any more! Fie upon such a cattleyard of a planet!

So far as the central essence of this feeling goes, no healthy minded person, it seems to me, can help to some degree partaking of it. Militarism is the great preserver of our ideals of hardihood, and human life with no use for hardihood would be contemptible. Without risks or prizes for the darer, history would be insipid indeed; and there is a type of military character which every one feels that the race should never cease to breed, for every one is sensitive to its superiority. The duty is incumbent on mankind, of keeping military characters in stock—of keeping them, if not for use, then as ends in themselves and as pure pieces of perfection,—so that Roosevelt's weaklings and mollycoddles may not end by making everything else disappear from the face of nature.

This natural sort of feeling forms, I think, the innermost soul of army-writings. Without any exception known to me, militarist authors take a highly mystical view of their subject, and regard war as a biological or sociological necessity, uncontrolled by ordinary psychological checks and motives. When the time of development is ripe the war must come, reason or no reason, for the justifications pleaded are invariably fictitious. War is, in short, a permanent human *obligation*. General Homer Lea, in his recent book "The Valor of Ignorance," plants himself squarely on this ground. Readiness for war is for him the essence of nationality, and ability in it the supreme measure of the health of nations.

Nations, General Lea says, are never stationary—they must necessarily expand or shrink, according to their vitality or decrepitude. Japan now is culminating; and by the fatal law in question it is impossible that her statesmen should not long since have entered, with extraordinary foresight, upon a vast policy of conquest—the game in which the first moves were her wars with China and Russia and her treaty with England, and of which the final objective is the capture of the Philippines, the Hawaiian Islands, Alaska, and the whole of our Coast west of the Sierra Passes. This will give Japan what her ineluctable vocation as a state absolutely forces her to claim, the possession of the entire Pacific Ocean; and to oppose these deep designs we

Americans have, according to our author, nothing but our conceit, our ignorance, our commercialism, our corruption, and our feminism. General Lea makes a minute technical comparison of the military strength which we at present could oppose to the strength of Japan, and concludes that the islands, Alaska, Oregon, and Southern California, would fall almost without resistance, that San Francisco must surrender in a fortnight to a Japanese investment, that in three or four months the war would be over, and our republic, unable to regain what it had heedlessly neglected to protect sufficiently, would then "disintegrate," until perhaps some Cæsar should arise to weld us again into a nation.

A dismal forecast indeed! Yet not unplausible, if the mentality of Japan's statesmen be of the Cæsarian type of which history shows so many examples, and which is all that General Lea seems able to imagine. But there is no reason to think that women can no longer be the mothers of Napoleonic or Alexandrian characters; and if these come in Japan and find their opportunity, just such surprises as "The Valor of Ignorance" paints may lurk in ambush for us. Ignorant as we still are of the innermost recesses of Japanese mentality, we may be foolhardy to disregard such possibilities.

Other militarists are more complex and more moral in their considerations. The "Philosophie des Krieges," by S. R. Steinmetz is a good example. War, according to this author, is an ordeal instituted by God, who weighs the nations in its balance. It is the essential form of the State, and the only function in which peoples can employ all their powers at once and convergently. No victory is possible save as the resultant of a totality of virtues, no defeat for which some vice or weakness is not responsible. Fidelity, cohesiveness, tenacity, heroism, conscience, education, inventiveness, economy, wealth, physical health and vigor—there is n't a moral or intellectual point of superiority that does n't tell, when God holds his assizes and hurls the peoples upon one another. *Die Weltgeschichte ist das Weltgericht;* and Dr. Steinmetz does not believe that in the long run chance and luck play any part in apportioning the issues.

The virtues that prevail, it must be noted, are virtues anyhow, superiorities that count in peaceful as well as in military competition; but the strain on them, being infinitely intenser in the latter case, makes war infinitely more searching as a trial. No ordeal is comparable to its winnowings. Its dread hammer is the welder of men into cohesive states, and nowhere but in such states can human nature adequately develop its capacity. The only alternative is "degeneration."

Dr. Steinmetz is a conscientious thinker, and his book, short as it is, takes much into account. Its upshot can, it seems to me, be summed up in Simon Patten's word, that mankind was nursed in pain and fear, and that the transition to a "pleasure-economy" may be fatal to a being wielding no powers of defence against its disintegrative influences. If we speak of the *fear of emancipation from the fear-régime,* we put the whole situation into a single phrase; fear regarding ourselves now taking the place of the ancient fear of the enemy.

Turn the fear over as I will in my mind, it all seems to lead back to two unwillingnesses of the imagination, one æsthetic, and the other moral; unwillingness, first to envisage a future in which army-life, with its many elements of charm, shall be forever impossible, and in which the destinies of peoples shall nevermore be decided quickly, thrillingly, and tragically, by force, but only gradually and insipidly by "evolution"; and, secondly, unwillingness to see the supreme theatre of human strenuousness closed, and the splendid military aptitudes of men doomed to keep always in a state of latency and never show themselves in action. These insistent unwillingnesses, no less than other æsthetic and ethical insistencies, have, it seems to me, to be listened to and respected. One cannot meet them effectively by mere counter-insistency on war's expensiveness and horror. The horror makes the thrill; and when the question is of getting the extremest and supremest out of human nature, talk of expense sounds ignominious. The weakness of so much merely negative criticism is evident—pacificism makes no converts from the military party. The military party denies neither the bestiality nor the horror, nor the expense; it only says that these things tell but half the story. It only says that war is *worth* them; that, taking human nature as a whole, its wars are its best protection against its weaker and more cowardly self, and that mankind cannot *afford* to adopt a peace-economy.

Pacificists ought to enter more deeply into the æsthetical and ethical point of view of their opponents. Do that first in any controversy, says J. J. Chapman, *then move the point,* and your opponent will follow. So long as anti-militarists propose no substitute for war's disciplinary function, no *moral equivalent* of war, analogous, as one might say, to the mechanical equivalent of heat, so long they fail to realize the full inwardness of the situation. And as a rule they do fail. The duties, penalties, and sanctions pictured in the utopias they paint are all too weak and tame to touch the military-minded. Tolstoï's pacificism is the only exception to this rule, for it is profoundly pessimistic as regards all this world's values, and makes the fear of the Lord furnish the moral spur provided elsewhere by the fear of the enemy. But our socialistic peace-advocates all believe absolutely in this world's values; and instead of the fear of the Lord and the fear of the enemy, the only fear they reckon with is the fear of poverty if one be lazy. This weakness pervades all the socialistic literature with which I am acquainted. Even in Lowes Dickinson's exquisite dialogue,[34] high wages and short hours are the only forces invoked for overcoming man's distaste for repulsive kinds of labor. Meanwhile men at large still live as they always have lived, under a pain-and-fear economy—for those of us who live in an ease-economy are but an island in the stormy ocean—and the whole atmosphere of present-day utopian literature tastes mawkish and dishwatery to people who still keep a sense for life's more bitter flavors. It suggests, in truth, ubiquitous inferiority.

Inferiority is always with us, and merciless scorn of it is the keynote of the military temper. "Dogs, would you live forever?" shouted Frederick the Great. "Yes," say our utopians, "let us live forever, and raise our level gradually." The best thing about our "inferiors" to-day is that they are as tough as nails, and physically and morally almost as insensitive. Utopianism would see them soft and squeamish, while militarism would keep their callousness, but transfigure it into a meritorious characteristic, needed by "the service," and redeemed by that from the suspicion of inferiority. All the qualities of a man acquire dignity when he knows that the service of the collectivity that owns him needs them. If proud of the collectivity, his own pride rises in proportion. No collectivity is like an army for nourishing such pride; but it has to be confessed that the only sentiment which the image of pacific cosmopolitan industrialism is capable of arousing in countless worthy breasts is shame at the idea of belonging to *such* a collectivity. It is obvious that the United States of America as they exist to-day impress a mind like General Lea's as so much human blubber. Where is the sharpness and precipitousness, the contempt for life, whether one's own, or another's? Where is the savage "yes" and "no," the unconditional duty? Where is the conscription? Where is the blood-tax? Where is anything that one feels honored by belonging to?

Having said thus much in preparation, I will now confess my own utopia. I devoutly believe in the reign of peace and in the gradual advent of some sort of a socialistic equilibrium. The fatalistic view of the war-function is to me nonsense, for I know that war-making is due to definite motives and subject to prudential checks and reasonable criticisms, just like any other form of enterprise. And when whole nations are the armies, and the science of destruction vies in intellectual refinement with the sciences of production, I see that war becomes absurd and impossible from its own monstrosity. Extravagant ambitions will have to be replaced by reasonable claims, and nations must make common cause against them. I see no reason why all this should not apply to yellow as well as to white countries, and I look

[34] "Justice and Liberty," N.Y., 1909.

forward to a future when acts of war shall be formally outlawed as between civilized peoples.

All these beliefs of mine put me squarely into the anti-militarist party. But I do not believe that peace either ought to be or will be permanent on this globe, unless the states pacifically organized preserve some of the old elements of army-discipline. A permanently successful peace-economy cannot be a simple pleasure-economy. In the more or less socialistic future towards which mankind seems drifting we must still subject ourselves collectively to those severities which answer to our real position upon this only partly hospitable globe. We must make new energies and hardihoods continue the manliness to which the military mind so faithfully clings. Martial virtues must be the enduring cement; intrepidity, contempt of softness, surrender of private interest, obedience to command, must still remain the rock upon which states are built—unless, indeed, we wish for dangerous reactions against commonwealths fit only for contempt, and liable to invite attack whenever a centre of crystallization for military-minded enterprise gets formed anywhere in their neighborhood.

The war-party is assuredly right in affirming and reaffirming that the martial virtues, although originally gained by the race through war, are absolute and permanent human goods. Patriotic pride and ambition in their military form are, after all, only specifications of a more general competitive passion. They are its first form, but that is no reason for supposing them to be its last form. Men now are proud of belonging to a conquering nation, and without a murmur they lay down their persons and their wealth, if by so doing they may fend off subjection. But who can be sure that *other aspects of one's country* may not, with time and education and suggestion enough, come to be regarded with similarly effective feelings of pride and shame? Why should men not some day feel that it is worth a blood-tax to belong to a collectivity superior in *any* ideal respect? Why should they not blush with indignant shame if the community that owns them is vile in any way whatsoever? Individuals, daily more numerous, now feel this civic passion. It is only a question of blowing on the spark till the whole population gets incandescent, and on the ruins of the old morals of military honor, a stable system of morals of civic honor builds itself up. What the whole community comes to believe in grasps the individual as in a vise. The war-function has grasped us so far; but constructive interests may some day seem no less imperative, and impose on the individual a hardly lighter burden.

Let me illustrate my idea more concretely. There is nothing to make one indignant in the mere fact that life is hard, that men should toil and suffer pain. The planetary conditions once for all are such, and we can stand it. But that so many men, by mere accidents of birth and opportunity, should have a life of *nothing else* but toil and pain and hardness and inferiority imposed upon them, should have *no* vacation, while others natively no more deserving never get any taste of this campaigning life at all,—*this* is capable of arousing indignation in reflective minds. It may end by seeming shameful to all of us that some of us have nothing but campaigning, and others nothing but unmanly ease. If now—and this is my idea—there were, instead of military conscription a conscription of the whole youthful population to form for a certain number of years a part of the army enlisted against *Nature,* the injustice would tend to be evened out, and numerous other goods to the commonwealth would follow. The military ideals of hardihood and discipline would be wrought into the growing fibre of the people; no one would remain blind as the luxurious classes now are blind, to man's relations to the globe he lives on, and to the permanently sour and hard foundations of his higher life. To coal and iron mines, to freight trains, to fishing fleets in December, to dishwashing, clothes-washing, and window-washing, to road-building and tunnel-making, to foundries and stoke-holes, and to the frames of skyscrapers, would our gilded youths be drafted off, according to their choice, to get the childishness knocked out of them, and to come back into society with healthier sympathies and soberer ideas. They would have paid their blood-tax, done their own part in the immemorial human warfare against nature; they would tread the earth more proudly, the women would value them more highly, they would be better fathers and teachers of the following generation.

Such a conscription, with the state of public opinion that would have required it, and the many moral fruits it would bear, would preserve in the midst of a pacific civilization the manly virtues which the military party is so afraid of seeing disappear in peace. We should get toughness without callousness, authority with as little criminal cruelty as possible, and painful work done cheerily because the duty is temporary, and threatens not, as now, to degrade the whole remainder of one's life. I spoke of the "moral equivalent" of war. So far, war has been the only force that can discipline a whole community, and until an equivalent discipline is organized, I believe that war must have its way. But I have no serious doubt that the ordinary prides and shames of social man, once developed to a certain intensity, are capable of organizing such a moral equivalent as I have sketched, or some other just as effective for preserving manliness of type. It is but a question of time, of skilful propagandism, and of opinion-making men seizing historic opportunities.

The martial type of character can be bred without war. Strenuous honor and disinterestedness abound elsewhere. Priests and medical men are in a fashion educated to it, and we should all feel some degree of it imperative if we were conscious of our work as an obligatory service to the state. We should be *owned,* as soldiers are by the army, and our pride would rise accordingly. We could be poor, then, without humiliation, as army officers now are. The only thing needed henceforward is to inflame the civic temper as past history has inflamed the military temper. H. G. Wells, as usual, sees the centre of the situation. "In many ways," he says, "military organization is the most peaceful of activities. When the contemporary man steps from the street, of clamorous insincere advertisement, push, adulteration, underselling and intermittent employment into the barrack-yard, he steps on to a higher social plane, into an atmosphere of service and cooperation and of infinitely more honorable emulations. Here at least men are not flung out of employment to degenerate because there is no immediate work for them to do. They are fed and drilled and trained for better services. Here at least a man is supposed to win promotion by self-forgetfulness and not by self-seeking. And beside the feeble and irregular endowment of research by commercialism, its little short-sighted snatches at profit by innovation and scientific economy, see how remarkable is the steady and rapid development of method and appliances in naval and military affairs! Nothing is more striking than to compare the progress of civil conveniences which has been left almost entirely to the trader, to the progress in military apparatus during the last few decades. The house-appliances of to-day for example, are little better than they were fifty years ago. A house of to-day is still almost as ill-ventilated, badly heated by wasteful fires, clumsily arranged and furnished as the house of 1858. Houses a couple of hundred years old are still satisfactory places of residence, so little have our standards risen. But the rifle or battleship of fifty years ago was beyond all comparison inferior to those we possess; in power, in speed, in covenience alike. No one has a use now for such superannuated things." [35]

Wells adds[36] that he thinks that the conceptions of order and discipline, the tradition of service and devotion, of physical fitness, unstinted exertion, and universal responsibility, which universal military duty is now teaching European nations, will remain a permanent acquisition, when the last ammunition has been used in the fireworks that celebrate the final peace. I believe as he does. It would be simply preposterous if the only force that could work ideals of honor and standards of efficiency into English or American natures should be the fear of being killed by the Germans or the Japanese. Great indeed is Fear; but it is not, as our military enthusiasts believe and try to make us believe, the only stimulus known for awakening the higher ranges

[35] "First and Last Things," 1908, p. 215.
[36] "First and Last Things," 1908, p. 226.

of men's spiritual energy. The amount of alteration in public opinion which my utopia postulates is vastly less than the difference between the mentality of those black warriors who pursued Stanley's party on the Congo with their cannibal war-cry of "Meat! Meat!" and that of the "general-staff" of any civilized nation. History has seen the latter interval bridged over: the former one can be bridged over much more easily.

THE ENERGIES OF MEN* 37

Everyone knows what it is to start a piece of work, either intellectual or muscular, feeling stale—or *oold,* as an Adirondack guide once put it to me. And everybody knows what it is to "warm up" to his job. The process of warming up gets particularly striking in the phenomenon known as "second wind." On usual occasions we make a practice of stopping an occupation as soon as we meet the first effective layer (so to call it) of fatigue. We have then walked, played, or worked "enough," so we desist. That amount of fatigue is an efficacious obstruction on this side of which our usual life is cast. But if an unusual necessity forces us to press onward, a surprising thing occurs. The fatigue gets worse up to a certain critical point, when gradually or suddenly it passes away, and we are fresher than before. We have evidently tapped a level of new energy, masked until then by the fatigue-obstacle usually obeyed. There may be layer after layer of this experience. A third and a fourth "wind" may supervene. Mental activity shows the phenomenon as well as physical, and in exceptional cases we may find, beyond the very extremity of fatigue-distress, amounts of ease and power that we never dreamed ourselves to own, —sources of strength habitually not taxed at all, because habitually we never push through the obstruction, never pass those early critical points.

For many years I have mused on the phenomenon of second wind,

---

* From: M.S., 229–264.

37 This was the title originally given to the Presidential Address delivered before the American Philosophical Association at Columbia University, December 28, 1906, and published as there delivered in the *Philosophical Review* for January, 1907. The address was later published, after slight alteration, in the *American Magazine* for October, 1907, under the title "The Powers of Men." The more popular form is here reprinted under the title which the author himself preferred.

trying to find a physiological theory. It is evident that our organism has stored-up reserves of energy that are ordinarily not called upon, but that may be called upon: deeper and deeper strata of combustible or explosible material, discontinuously arranged, but ready for use by anyone who probes so deep, and repairing themselves by rest as well as do the superficial strata. Most of us continue living unnecessarily near our surface. Our energy-budget is like our nutritive budget. Physiologists say that a man is in "nutritive equilibrium" when day after day he neither gains nor loses weight. But the odd thing is that this condition may obtain on astonishingly different amounts of food. Take a man in nutritive equilibrium, and systematically increase or lessen his rations. In the first case he will begin to gain weight, in the second case to lose it. The change will be greatest on the first day, less on the second, less still on the third; and so on, till he has gained all that he will gain, or lost all that he will lose, on that altered diet. He is now in nutritive equilibrium again, but with a new weight; and this neither lessens nor increases because his various combustion-processes have adjusted themselves to the changed dietary. He gets rid, in one way or another, of just as much N, C, H, etc., as he takes in *per diem*.

Just so one can be in what I might call "efficiency-equilibrium" (neither gaining nor losing power when once the equilibrium is reached) on astonishingly different quantities of work, no matter in what direction the work may be measured. It may be physical work, intellectual work, moral work, or spiritual work.

Of course there are limits: the trees don't grow into the sky. But the plain fact remains that men the world over possess amounts of resource which only very exceptional individuals push to their extremes of use. But the very same individual, pushing his energies to their extreme, may in a vast number of cases keep the pace up day after day, and find no "reaction" of a bad sort, so long as decent hygienic conditions are preserved. His more active rate of energizing does not wreck him; for the organism adapts itself, and as the rate of waste augments, augments correspondingly the rate of repair.

I say the *rate* and not the *time* of repair. The busiest man needs no more hours of rest than the idler. Some years ago Professor Patrick, of the Iowa State University, kept three young men awake for four days and nights. When his observations on them were finished, the subjects were permitted to sleep themselves out. All awoke from this sleep completely refreshed, but the one who took longest to restore himself from his long vigil only slept one-third more time than was regular with him.

If my reader will put together these two conceptions, first, that few men live at their maximum of energy, and second, that anyone may be in vital equilibrium at very different rates of energizing, he will find, I think, that a very pretty practical problem of national economy, as well as of individual ethics, opens upon his view. In rough terms, we may say that a man who energizes below his normal maximum fails by just so much to profit by his chance at life; and that a nation filled with such men is inferior to a nation run at higher pressure. The problem is, then, how can men be trained up to their most useful pitch of energy? And how can nations make such training most accessible to all their sons and daughters. This, after all, is only the general problem of education, formulated in slightly different terms.

"Rough" terms, I said just now, because the words "energy" and "maximum" may easily suggest only *quantity* to the reader's mind, whereas in measuring the human energies of which I speak, qualities as well as quantities have to be taken into account. Everyone feels that his total *power* rises when he passes to a higher *qualitative* level of life.

Writing is higher than walking, thinking is higher than writing, deciding higher than thinking, deciding "no" higher than deciding "yes" —at least the man who passes from one of these activities to another will usually say that each later one involves a greater element of *inner work* than the earlier ones, even though the total heat given out or the foot-pounds expended by the organism, may be less. Just how to conceive this inner work physiologically is as yet impossible, but psychologically we all know what the word means. We need a particular spur or effort to start us upon inner work; it tires us to sustain it; and when long sustained, we know how easily we lapse. When I speak of "energizing," and its rates and levels and sources, I mean therefore our inner as well as our outer work.

Let no one think, then, that our problem of individual and national economy is solely that of the maximum of pounds raisable against gravity, the maximum of locomotion, or of agitation of any sort, that human beings can accomplish. That might signify little more than hurrying and jumping about in inco-ordinated ways; whereas inner work, though it so often reinforces outer work, quite as often means its arrest. To relax, to say to ourselves (with the "new thoughters") "Peace! be still!" is sometimes a great achievement of inner work. When I speak of human energizing in general, the reader must therefore understand that sum-total of activities, some outer and some inner, some muscular, some emotional, some moral, some spiritual, of whose waxing and waning in himself he is at all times so well aware. How to keep it at an appreciable maximum? How not to let the level lapse? That is the great problem. But the work of men and women is of innumerable kinds, each kind being, as we say, carried on by a particular faculty; so the great problem splits into two sub-problems, thus:

(1). What are the limits of human faculty in various directions?

(2). By what diversity of means, in the differing types of human beings, may the faculties be stimulated to their best results?

Read in one way, these two questions sound both trivial and familiar: there is a sense in which we have all asked them ever since we were born. Yet *as a methodical programme of scientific inquiry,* I doubt whether they have ever been seriously taken up. If answered fully, almost the whole of mental science and of the science of conduct would find a place under them. I propose, in what follows, to press them on the reader's attention in an informal way.

The first point to agree upon in this enterprise is that *as a rule men habitually use only a small part of the powers which they actually possess and which they might use under appropriate conditions.*

Every one is familiar with the phenomenon of feeling more or less alive on different days. Every one knows on any given day that there are energies slumbering in him which the incitements of that day do not call forth, but which he might display if these were greater. Most of us feel as if a sort of cloud weighed upon us, keeping us below our highest notch of clearness in discernment, sureness in reasoning, or firmness in deciding. Compared with what we ought to be, we are only half awake. Our fires are damped, our drafts are checked. We are making use of only a small part of our possible mental and physical resources. In some persons this sense of being cut off from their rightful resources is extreme, and we then get the formidable neurasthenic and psychasthenic conditions, with life grown into one tissue of impossibilities, that so many medical books describe.

Stating the thing broadly, the human individual thus lives usually far within his limits; he possesses powers of various sorts which he habitually fails to use. He energizes below his *maximum,* and he behaves below his *optimum.* In elementary faculty, in co-ordination, in power of *inhibition* and control, in every conceivable way, his life is contracted like the field of vision of an hysteric subject—but with less excuse, for the poor hysteric is diseased, while in the rest of us it is only an inveterate *habit*—the habit of inferiority to our full self—that is bad.

Admit so much, then, and admit also that the charge of being inferior to their full self is far truer of some men than of others; then the practical question ensues: *to what do the better men owe their escape? and, in the fluctuations which all men feel in their own degree of energizing, to what are the improvements due, when they occur?*

In general terms the answer is plain:

Either some unusual stimulus fills them with emotional excitement, or some unusual idea of necessity induces them to make an extra effort of will. *Excitements, ideas, and efforts,* in a word, are what carry us over the dam.

In those "hyperesthetic" conditions which chronic invalidism so often brings in its train, the dam has changed its normal place. The slightest functional exercise gives a distress which the patient yields to and stops. In such cases of "habit-neurosis" a new range of power often comes in consequence of the "bullying-treatment," of efforts which the doctor obliges the patient, much against his will, to make. First comes the very extremity of distress, then follows unexpected relief. There seems no doubt that *we are each and all of us to some extent victims of habit-neurosis*. We have to admit the wider potential range and the habitually narrow actual use. We live subject to arrest by degrees of fatigue which we have come only from habit to obey. Most of us may learn to push the barrier farther off, and to live in perfect comfort on much higher levels of power.

Country people and city people, as a class, illustrate this difference. The rapid rate of life, the number of decisions in an hour, the many things to keep account of, in a busy city man's or woman's life, seem monstrous to a country brother. He does n't see how we live at all. A day in New York or Chicago fills him with terror. The danger and noise make it appear like a permanent earthquake. But *settle* him there, and in a year or two he will have caught the pulse-beat. He will vibrate to the city's rhythms; and if he only succeeds in his avocation, whatever that may be, he will find a joy in all the hurry and the tension, he will keep the pace as well as any of us, and get as much out of himself in any week as he ever did in ten weeks in the country.

The stimuli of those who successfully respond and undergo the transformation here, are duty, the example of others, and crowd-pressure and contagion. The transformation, moreover, is a chronic one: the new level of energy becomes permanent. The duties of new offices of trust are constantly producing this effect on the human beings appointed to them. The physiologists call a stimulus "dynamogenic" when it increases the muscular contractions of men to whom it is applied; but appeals can be dynamogenic morally as well as muscularly. We are witnessing here in America to-day the dynamogenic effect of a very exalted political office upon the energies of an individual who had already manifested a healthy amount of energy before the office came.

Humbler examples show perhaps still better what chronic effects duty's appeal may produce in chosen individuals. John Stuart Mill somewhere says that women excel men in the power of keeping up sustained moral excitement. Every case of illness nursed by wife or mother is a proof of this; and where can one find greater examples of sustained endurance than in those thousands of poor homes, where the woman successfully holds the family together and keeps it going by taking all the thought and doing all the work—nursing, teaching, cooking, washing, sewing, scrubbing, saving, helping neighbors, "choring" outside—where does the catalogue end? If she does a bit of scolding now and then who can blame her? But often she does just the reverse; keeping the children clean and the man good tempered, and soothing and smoothing the whole neighborhood into finer shape.

Eighty years ago a certain Montyon left to the Académie Française a sum of money to be given in small prizes, to the best examples of "virtue" of the year. The academy's committees, with great good sense, have shown a partiality to virtues simple and chronic, rather than to her spasmodic and dramatic flights; and the exemplary housewives reported on have been wonderful and admirable enough. In Paul Bourget's report for this year we find numerous cases, of which this is a type; Jeanne Chaix, eldest of six children; mother insane, father chronically ill. Jeanne, with no money but her wages at a pasteboard-box factory, directs the household, brings up the children, and successfully maintains the family of eight, which thus subsists, morally as well as materially, by the sole force of her valiant will. In some of these French cases charity to outsiders is added to the inner family burden; or helpless relatives, young or old, are adopted, as if the strength were inexhaustible and ample for every appeal. Details are too long to quote here; but human nature, responding to the call of duty, appears nowhere sublimer than in the person of these humble heroines of family life.

Turning from more chronic to acuter proofs of human nature's reserves of power, we find that the stimuli that carry us over the usually effective dam are most often the classic emotional ones, love, anger, crowd-contagion or despair. Despair lames most people, but it wakes others fully up. Every siege or shipwreck or polar expedition brings out some hero who keeps the whole company in heart. Last year there was a terrible colliery explosion at Courrières in France. Two hundred corpses, if I remember rightly, were exhumed. After twenty days of excavation, the rescuers heard a voice. *"Me voici,"* said the first man unearthed. He proved to be a collier named Nemy, who had taken command of thirteen others in the darkness, disciplined them and cheered them, and brought them out alive. Hardly any of them could see or speak or walk when brought into the day. Five days later, a different type of vital endurance was unexpectedly unburied in the person of one Berton who, isolated from any but dead companions, had been able to sleep away most of his time.

A new position of responsibility will usually show a man to be a far stronger creature than was supposed. Cromwell's and Grant's careers are the stock examples of how war will wake a man up. I owe to Professor C. E. Norton, my colleague, the permission to print part of a private letter from Colonel Baird-Smith written shortly after the six weeks' siege of Delhi, in 1857, for the victorious issue of which the excellent officer was chiefly to be thanked. He writes as follows:

". . . My poor wife had some reason to think that war and disease between them had left very little of a husband to take under nursing when she got him again. An attack of camp-scurvy had filled my mouth with sores, shaken every joint in my body, and covered me all over with sores and livid spots, so that I was marvellously unlovely to look upon. A smart knock on the ankle-joint from the splinter of a shell that burst in my face, in itself a mere *bagatelle* of a wound, had been of necessity neglected under the pressing and incessant calls upon me, and had grown worse and worse till the whole foot below the ankle became a black mass and seemed to threaten mortification. I insisted, however, on being allowed to use it till the place was taken, mortification or no; and though the pain was sometimes horrible, I carried my point and kept up to the last. On the day after the assault I had an unlucky fall on some bad ground, and it was an open question for a day or two whether I had n't broken my arm at the elbow. Fortunately it turned out to be only a severe sprain, but I am still conscious of the wrench it gave me. To crown the whole pleasant catalogue, I was worn to a shadow by a constant diarrhœa, and consumed as much opium as would have done credit to my father-in-law [Thomas De Quincey]. However, thank God, I have a good share of Tapleyism in me and come out strong under difficulties. I think I may confidently say that no man ever saw me out of heart, or ever heard one croaking word from me even when our prospects were gloomiest. We were sadly scourged by the cholera, and it was almost appalling to me to find that out of twenty-seven officers present, I could only muster fifteen for the operations of the attack. However, it was done, and after it was done came the collapse. Don't be horrified when I tell you that for the whole of the actual siege, and in truth for some little time before, I almost lived on brandy. Appetite for food I had none, but I forced myself to eat just sufficient to sustain life, and I had an incessant craving for brandy as the strongest stimulant I could get. Strange to say, I was quite unconscious of its affecting me in the slightest degree. *The excitement of the work was so great that no lesser one seemed to have any chance against it, and I certainly never found my intellect clearer or my nerves stronger in my life.* It was only my wretched body that was weak, and the moment the real work was done by our becoming complete masters of Delhi, I broke down without delay and discovered that if I wished to live I must continue no longer the system that had kept me up until the crisis was passed. With it passed away as if in a moment all desire to stimulate, and a perfect loathing of my late staff of life took possession of me."

Such experiences show how profound is the alteration in the manner in which, under excitement, our organism will sometimes perform its physiological work. The processes of repair become different when the reserves have to be used, and for weeks and months the deeper use may go on.

Morbid cases, here as elsewhere, lay the normal machinery bare. In the first number of Dr. Morton Prince's *Journal of Abnormal Psychology,* Dr. Janet has discussed five cases of morbid impulse, with an explanation that is precious for my present point of view. One is a girl who eats, eats, eats, all day. Another walks, walks, walks, and gets her food from an automobile that escorts her. Another is a dipsomaniac. A fourth pulls out her hair. A fifth wounds her flesh and burns her skin. Hitherto such freaks of impulse have received Greek names (as bulimia, dromomania, etc.) and been scientifically disposed of as "episodic syndromata of hereditary degeneration." But it turns out that Janet's cases are all what he calls psychasthenics, or victims of a chronic sense of weakness, torpor, lethargy, fatigue, insufficiency, impossibility, unreality and powerlessness of will; and that in each and all of them the particular activity pursued, deleterious though it be, has the temporary result of raising the sense of vitality and making the patient feel alive again. These things reanimate: they would reanimate *us,* but it happens that in each patient the particular freak-activity chosen is the only thing that does reanimate; and therein lies the morbid state. The way to treat such persons is to discover to them more usual and useful ways of throwing their stores of vital energy into gear.

Colonel Baird-Smith, needing to draw on altogether extraordinary stores of energy, found that brandy and opium were ways of throwing them into gear.

Such cases are humanly typical. We are all to some degree oppressed, unfree. We don't come to our own. It is there, but we don't get at it. The threshold must be made to shift. Then many of us find that an eccentric activity—a "spree," say—relieves. There is no doubt that to some men sprees and excesses of almost any kind are medicinal, temporarily at any rate, in spite of what the moralists and doctors say.

But when the normal tasks and stimulations of life don't put a man's deeper levels of energy on tap, and he requires distinctly deleterious excitements, his constitution verges on the abnormal. The normal opener of deeper and deeper levels of energy is the will. The difficulty is to use it, to make the effort which the word volition implies. But if we *do* make it (or if a god, though he were only the god Chance, makes it through us), it will act dynamogenically on us for a month. It is notorious that a single successful effort of moral volition, such as saying "no" to some habitual temptation, or performing some courageous act, will launch a man on a higher level of energy for days and weeks, will give him a new range of power. "In the act of uncorking the whiskey bottle which I had brought home to get drunk upon," said a man to me, "I suddenly found myself running out into the garden, where I smashed it on the ground. I felt so happy and uplifted after this act, that for two months I was n't tempted to touch a drop."

The emotions and excitements due to usual situations are the usual inciters of the will. But these act discontinuously; and in the intervals the shallower levels of life tend to close in and shut us off. Accordingly the best practical knowers of the human soul have invented the thing known as methodical ascetic discipline to keep the deeper levels constantly in reach. Beginning with easy tasks, passing to harder ones, and exercising day by day, it is, I believe, admitted that disciples of asceticism can reach very high levels of freedom and power of will.

Ignatius Loyola's spiritual exercises must have produced this result in innumerable devotees. But the most venerable ascetic system, and the one whose results have the most voluminous experimental corroboration is undoubtedly the Yoga system in Hindustan. From time immemorial, by Hatha Yoga, Raja Yoga, Karma Yoga, or whatever code of practice it might be, Hindu aspirants to perfection have trained themselves, month in and out, for years. The result claimed, and certainly in many cases accorded by impartial judges, is strength of character, personal power, unshakability of soul. In an article in the *Philosophical Review*,[38] from which I am largely copying here, I have quoted at great length the experience with "Hatha Yoga" of a very gifted European friend of mine who, by persistently carrying out for several months its methods of fasting from food and sleep, its exercises in breathing and thought-concentration, and its fantastic posture-gymnastics, seems to have succeeded in waking up deeper and deeper levels of will and moral and intellectual power in himself, and to have escaped from a decidedly menacing brain-condition of the "circular" type, from which he had suffered for years.

Judging by my friend's letters, of which the last I have is written fourteen months after the Yoga training began, there can be no doubt of his relative regeneration. He has undergone material trials with indifference, travelled third-class on Mediterranean steamers, and fourth-class on African trains, living with the poorest Arabs and sharing their unaccustomed food, all with equanimity. His devotion to certain interests has been put to heavy strain, and nothing is more remarkable to me than the changed moral tone with which he reports the situation. A profound modification has unquestionably occurred

[38] "The Energies of Men." *Philosophical Review,* vol. xvi, No. 1, January, 1907. [Cf. above, note 37. J. J. McD.]

in the running of his mental machinery. The gearing has changed, and his will is available otherwise than it was.

My friend is a man of very peculiar temperament. Few of us would have had the will to start upon the Yoga training, which, once started, seemed to conjure the further will-power needed out of itself. And not all of those who could launch themselves would have reached the same results. The Hindus themselves admit that in some men the results may come without call or bell. My friend writes to me: "You are quite right in thinking that religious crises, love-crises, indignation-crises may awaken in a very short time powers similar to those reached by years of patient Yoga-practice."

Probably most medical men would treat this individual's case as one of what it is fashionable now to call by the name of "self-suggestion," or "expectant attention"—as if those phrases were explanatory, or meant more than the fact that certain men can be influenced, while others cannot be influenced, by certain sorts of *ideas*. This leads me to say a word about ideas considered as dynamogenic agents, or stimuli for unlocking what would otherwise be unused reservoirs of individual power.

One thing that ideas do is to contradict other ideas and keep us from believing them. An idea that thus negates a first idea may itself in turn be negated by a third idea, and the first idea may thus regain its natural influence over our belief and determine our behavior. Our philosophic and religious development proceeds thus by credulities, negations, and the negating of negations.

But whether for arousing or for stopping belief, ideas may fail to be efficacious, just as a wire at one time alive with electricity, may at another time be dead. Here our insight into causes fails us, and we can only note results in general terms. In general, whether a given idea shall be a live idea depends more on the person into whose mind it is injected than on the idea itself. Which is the suggestive idea for this person, and which for that one? Mr. Fletcher's disciples regenerate them selves by the idea (and the fact) that they are chewing, and re-chewing, and super-chewing their food. Dr. Dewey's pupils regenerate themselves by going without their breakfast—a fact, but also an ascetic idea. Not every one can use *these* ideas with the same success.

But apart from such individually varying susceptibilities, there are common lines along which men simply as men tend to be inflammable by ideas. As certain objects naturally awaken love, anger, or cupidity, so certain ideas naturally awaken the energies of loyalty, courage, endurance, or devotion. When these ideas are effective in an individual's life, their effect is often very great indeed. They may transfigure it, unlocking innumerable powers which, but for the idea, would never have come into play. "Fatherland," "the Flag," "the Union," "Holy

Church," "the Monroe Doctrine," "Truth," "Science," "Liberty," Garibaldi's phrase, "Rome or Death," etc., are so many examples of energy-releasing ideas. The social nature of such phrases is an essential factor of their dynamic power. They are forces of detent in situations in which no other force produces equivalent effects, and each is a force of detent only in a specific group of men.

The memory that an oath or vow has been made will nerve one to abstinences and efforts otherwise impossible; witness the "pledge" in the history of the temperance movement. A mere promise to his sweetheart will clean up a youth's life all over—at any rate for a time. For such effects an educated susceptibility is required. The idea of one's "honor," for example, unlocks energy only in those of us who have had the education of a "gentleman," so called.

That delightful being, Prince Pueckler-Muskau, writes to his wife from England that he has invented "a sort of artificial resolution respecting things that are difficult of performance. My device," he continues, "is this: *I give my word of honor most solemnly to myself* to do or to leave undone this or that. I am of course extremely cautious in the use of this expedient, but when once the word is given, even though I afterwards think I have been precipitate or mistaken, I hold it to be perfectly irrevocable, whatever inconveniences I foresee likely to result. If I were capable of breaking my word after such mature consideration, I should lose all respect for myself,—and what man of sense would not prefer death to such an alternative? . . . When the mysterious formula is pronounced, no alteration in my own view, nothing short of physical impossibilities, must, for the welfare of my soul, alter my will. . . . I find something very satisfactory in the thought that man has the power of framing such props and weapons out of the most trivial materials, indeed out of nothing, merely by the force of his will, which thereby truly deserves the name of omnipotent." [39]

Conversions, whether they be political, scientific, philosophic, or religious, form another way in which bound energies are let loose. They unify us, and put a stop to ancient mental interferences. The result is freedom, and often a great enlargement of power. A belief that thus settles upon an individual always acts as a challenge to his will. But, for the particular challenge to operate, he must be the right challeng*ee.* In religious conversions we have so fine an adjustment that the idea may be in the mind of the challengee for years before it exerts effects; and why it should do so then is often so far from obvious that the event is taken for a miracle of grace, and not a natural occurrence. Whatever it is, it may be a highwater mark of energy, in

[39] "Tour in England, Ireland, and France," Philadelphia, 1833, p. 435.

which "noes," once impossible, are easy, and in which a new range of "yeses" gains the right of way.

We are just now witnessing a very copious unlocking of energies by ideas in the persons of those converts to "New Thought," "Christian Science," "Metaphysical Healing," or other forms of spiritual philosophy, who are so numerous among us to-day. The ideas here are healthy-minded and optimistic; and it is quite obvious that a wave of religious activity, analogous in some respects to the spread of early Christianity, Buddhism, and Mohammedanism, is passing over our American world. The common feature of these optimistic faiths is that they all tend to the suppression of what Mr. Horace Fletcher calls "fearthought." Fearthought he defines as the "self-suggestion of inferiority"; so that one may say that these systems all operate by the suggestion of power. And the power, small or great, comes in various shapes to the individual,—power, as he will tell you, not to "mind" things that used to vex him, power to concentrate his mind, good cheer, good temper—in short, to put it mildly, a firmer, more elastic moral tone.

The most genuinely saintly person I have ever known is a friend of mine now suffering from cancer of the breast—I hope that she may pardon my citing her here as an example of what ideas can do. Her ideas have kept her a practically well woman for months after she should have given up and gone to bed. They have annulled all pain and weakness and given her a cheerful active life, unusually beneficent to others to whom she has afforded help. Her doctors, acquiescing in results they could not understand, have had the good sense to let her go her own way.

How far the mind-cure movement is destined to extend its influence, or what intellectual modifications it may yet undergo, no one can foretell. It is essentially a religious movement, and to academically nurtured minds its utterances are tasteless and often grotesque enough. It also incurs the natural enmity of medical politicians, and of the whole trades-union wing of that profession. But no unprejudiced observer can fail to recognize its importance as a social phenomenon to-day, and the higher medical minds are already trying to interpret it fairly, and make its power available for their own therapeutic ends.

Dr. Thomas Hyslop, of the great West Riding Asylum in England, said last year to the British Medical Association that the best sleep-producing agent which his practice had revealed to him, was *prayer*. I say this, he added (I am sorry here that I must quote from memory), purely as a medical man. The exercise of prayer, in those who habitually exert it, must be regarded by us doctors as the most adequate and normal of all the pacifiers of the mind and calmers of the nerves.

But in few of us are functions not tied up by the exercise of other functions. Relatively few medical men and scientific men, I fancy, can pray. Few can carry on any living commerce with "God." Yet many of us are well aware of how much freer and abler our lives would be, were such important forms of energizing not sealed up by the critical atmosphere in which we have been reared. There are in every one potential forms of activity that actually are shunted out from use. Part of the imperfect vitality under which we labor can thus be easily explained. One part of our mind dams up—even *damns* up!—the other parts.

Conscience makes cowards of us all. Social conventions prevent us from telling the truth after the fashion of the heroes and heroines of Bernard Shaw. We all know persons who are models of excellence, but who belong to the extreme philistine type of mind. So deadly is their intellectual respectability that we can't converse about certain subjects at all, can't let our minds play over them, can't even mention them in their presence. I have numbered among my dearest friends persons thus inhibited intellectually, with whom I would gladly have been able to talk freely about certain interests of mine, certain authors, say, as Bernard Shaw, Chesterton, Edward Carpenter, H. G. Wells, but it would n't do, it made them too uncomfortable, they would n't play, I had to be silent. An intellect thus tied down by literality and decorum makes on one the same sort of an impression that an able-bodied man would who should habituate himself to do his work with only one of his fingers, locking up the rest of his organism and leaving it unused.

I trust that by this time I have said enough to convince the reader both of the truth and of the importance of my thesis. The two questions, first, that of the possible extent of our powers; and, second, that of the various avenues of approach to them, the various keys for unlocking them in diverse individuals, dominate the whole problem of individual and national education. We need a topography of the limits of human power, similar to the chart which oculists use of the field of human vision. We need also a study of the various types of human being with reference to the different ways in which their energy-reserves may be appealed to and set loose. Biographies and individual experiences of every kind may be drawn upon for evidence here.[40]

[40] "This would be an absolutely concrete study . . . The limits of power must be limits that have been realized in actual persons, and the various ways of unlocking the reserves of power must have been exemplified in individual lives . . . So here is a program of concrete individual psychology . . . It is replete with interesting facts, and points to practical issues superior in importance to anything we know." *From the address as originally delivered before the Philosophical Association;* See xvi. *Philosophical Review,* 1, 19.

WILL*

VOLUNTARY ACTS

Desire, wish, will, are states of mind which everyone knows, and which no definition can make plainer. We desire to feel, to have, to do, all sorts of things which at the moment are not felt, had, or done. If with the desire there goes a sense that attainment is not possible, we simply *wish;* but if we believe that the end is in our power, we *will* that the desired feeling, having, or doing shall be real; and real it presently becomes, either immediately upon the willing or after certain preliminaries have been fulfilled.

The only ends which follow *immediately* upon our willing seem to be movements of our own bodies. Whatever *feelings* and *havings* we may will to get come in as results of preliminary movements which we make for the purpose. This fact is too familiar to need illustration; so that we may start with the proposition that the only *direct* outward effects of our will are bodily movements. The mechanism of production of these voluntary movements is what befalls us to study now.

They are secondary performances. The movements we have studied hitherto have been automatic and reflex, and (on the first occasion of their performance, at any rate) unforeseen by the agent. The movements to the study of which we now address ourselves, being desired and intended beforehand, are of course done with full prevision of what they are to be. It follows from this that *voluntary movements must be secondary, not primary, functions of our organism.* This is the first point to understand in the psychology of Volition. Reflex, instinctive, and emotional movements are all primary performances. The nerve-centres are so organized that certain stimuli pull the trigger of certain explosive parts; and a creature going through one of these explosions for the first time undergoes an entirely novel experience. The other day I was standing at a railroad station with a little child, when an express-train went thundering by. The child, who was near the edge of the platform, started, winked, had his breathing convulsed, turned pale, burst out crying, and ran frantically towards me and hid his face. I have no doubt that this youngster was almost as much astonished by his own behavior as he was by the train, and more than I was, who stood by. Of course if such a reaction has many times occurred we learn what to expect of ourselves, and can then foresee our conduct, even though it remain as involuntary and uncontrollable

* From: P.B.C., 415–460.

as it was before. But if, in voluntary action properly so called, the act must be foreseen, it follows that no creature not endowed with prophetic power can perform an act voluntarily for the first time. Well, we are no more endowed with prophetic vision of what movements lie in our power than we are endowed with prophetic vision of what sensations we are capable of receiving. As we must wait for the sensations to be given us, so we must wait for the movements to be performed involuntarily, before we can frame ideas of what either of these things are. We learn all our possibilities by the way of experience. When a particular movement, having once occurred in a random, reflex, or involuntary way, has left an image of itself in the memory, then the movement can be desired again, and deliberately willed. But it is impossible to see how it could be willed before.

A supply of ideas of the various movements that are possible, left in the memory by experiences of their involuntary performance, is thus the first prerequisite of the voluntary life.

TWO KINDS OF IDEAS OF MOVEMENT

Now these ideas may be either *resident* or *remote*. That is, they may be of the movement as it feels, when taking place, in the moving parts; or they may be of the movement as it feels in some other part of the body which it affects (strokes, presses, scratches, etc.), or as it sounds, or as it looks. The resident sensations in the parts that move have been called *kinæsthetic* feelings, the memories of them are kinæsthetic ideas. It is by these kinæsthetic sensations that we are made conscious of *passive movements*—movements communicated to our limbs by others. If you lie with closed eyes, and another person noiselessly places your arm or leg in an arbitrarily chosen attitude, you receive a feeling of what attitude it is, and can reproduce it yourself in the arm or leg of the opposite side. Similarly a man waked suddenly from sleep in the dark is aware of how he finds himself lying. At least this is what happens in normal cases. But when the feelings of passive movement as well as all the other feelings of a limb are lost, we get such results as are given in the following account by Prof. A. Strümpell of his wonderful anæsthetic boy, whose only sources of feeling were the right eye and the left ear:[41]

> Passive movements could be imprinted on all the extremities to the greatest extent, without attracting the patient's notice. Only in violent forced hyperextension of the joints, especially of the knees, there arose a dull vague feeling of strain, but this was seldom precisely localized.

[41] *Deutsches Archiv. f. Klin. Medicin,* xxii. 321.

We have often, after bandaging the eyes of the patient, carried him about the room, laid him on a table, given to his arms and legs the most fantastic and apparently the most inconvenient attitudes without his having a suspicion of it. The expression of astonishment in his . face, when all at once the removal of the handkerchief revealed his situation, is indescribable in words. Only when his head was made to hang away down he immediately spoke of dizziness, but could not assign its ground. Later he sometimes inferred from the sounds connected with the manipulation that something special was being done with him. . . . He had no feelings of muscular fatigue. If, with his eyes shut, we told him to raise his arm and to keep it up, he did so without trouble. After one or two minutes, however, the arm began to tremble and sink without his being aware of it. He asserted still his ability to keep it up. . . . Passively holding still his fingers did not affect him. He thought constantly that he opened and shut his hand, whereas it was really fixed.

No third kind of idea is called for. We need, then, when we perform a movement, either a kinæsthetic or a remote idea of which special movement it is to be. In addition to this it has often been supposed that we need an *idea of the amount of innervation* required for the muscular contraction. The discharge from the motor centre into the motor nerve is supposed to give a sensation *sui generis,* opposed to all our other sensations. These accompany incoming currents, whilst that, it is said, accompanies an outgoing current, and no movement is supposed to be totally defined in our mind, unless an anticipation of this feeling enter into our idea. The movement's degree of strength, and the effort required to perform it, are supposed to be specially revealed by the feeling of innervation. Many authors deny that this feeling exists, and the proofs given of its existence are certainly insufficient.

The various degrees of "effort" actually felt in making the same movement against different resistances are all accounted for by the incoming feelings from our chest, jaws, abdomen, and other parts sympathetically contracted whenever the effort is great. There is no need of a consciousness of the amount of outgoing current required. If anything be obvious to introspection, it is that the degree of strength put forth is completely revealed to us by incoming feelings from the muscles themselves and their insertions, from the vicinity of the joints, and from the general fixation of the larynx, chest, face, and body. When a certain degree of energy of contraction rather than another is thought of by us, this complex aggregate of afferent feelings, forming the material of our thought, renders absolutely precise and distinctive our mental image of the exact strength of movement to be made, and the exact amount of resistance to be overcome.

Let the reader try to direct his will towards a particular movement, and then notice what *constituted* the direction of the will. Was it anything over and above the notion of the different feelings to which the movement when effected would give rise? If we abstract from these feelings, will any sign, principle, or means of orientation be left by which the will may innervate the proper muscles with the right intensity, and not go astray into the wrong ones? Strip off these images anticipative of the results of the motion, and so far from leaving us with a complete assortment of directions into which our will may launch itself, you leave our consciousness in an absolute and total vacuum. If I will to write *Peter* rather than *Paul,* it is the thought of certain digital sensations, of certain alphabetic sounds, of certain appearances on the paper, and of no others, which immediately precedes the notion of my pen. If I will to utter the word *Paul* rather than *Peter,* it is the thought of my voice falling on my ear, and of certain muscular feelings in my tongue, lips, and larynx, which guide the utterance. All these are incoming feelings, and between the thought of them, by which the act is mentally specified with all possible completeness, and the act itself, there is no room for any third order of mental phenomenon.

There is indeed the *fiat,* the element of consent, or resolve that the act shall ensue. This, doubtless, to the reader's mind, as to my own, constitutes the essence of the voluntariness of the act. This *fiat* will be treated of in detail farther on. It may be entirely neglected here, for it is a constant co-efficient, affecting all voluntary actions alike, and incapable of serving to distinguish them. No one will pretend that its quality varies according as the right arm, for example, or the left is used.

An anticipatory image, then, of the sensorial consequences of a movement, plus (on certain occasions) the fiat that these consequences shall become actual, is the only psychic state which introspection lets us discern as the forerunner of our voluntary acts. There is no coercive evidence of any feeling attached to the efferent discharge.

The entire content and material of our consciousness—consciousness of movement, as of all things else—seems thus to be of peripheral origin, and to come to us in the first instance through the peripheral nerves.

THE MOTOR-CUE

Let us call the last idea which in the mind precedes the motor discharge the "motor-cue." Now do "resident" images form the only motor-cue, or will "remote" ones equally suffice?

There can be no doubt whatever that the cue may be an image either of the resident or of the remote kind. Although, at the outset of our learning a movement, it would seem that the resident feelings must come strongly before consciousness, later this need not be the case. The rule, in fact, would seem to be that they tend to lapse more and more from consciousness, and that the more practised we become in a movement, the more "remote" do the ideas become which form its mental cue. What we are *interested* in is what sticks in our consciousness; everything else we get rid of as quickly as we can. Our resident feelings of movement have no substantive interest for us at all, as a rule. What interest us are the ends which the movement is to attain. Such an end is generally a remote sensation, an impression which the movement produces on the eye or ear, or sometimes on the skin, nose, or palate. Now let the idea of such an end associate itself definitely with the right discharge, and the thought of the innervation's *resident* effects will become as great an encumbrance as we have already concluded that the feeling of the innervation itself is. This mind does not need it; the end alone is enough.

The idea of the end, then, tends more and more to make itself all-sufficient. Or, at any rate, if the kinæsthetic ideas are called up at all, they are so swamped in the vivid kinæsthetic feelings by which they are immediately overtaken that we have no time to be aware of their separate existence. As I write, I have no anticipation, as a thing distinct from my sensation, of either the look or the digital feel of the letters which flow from my pen. The words chime on my mental *ear,* as it were, before I write them, but not on my mental eye or hand. This comes from the rapidity with which the movements follow on their mental cue. An end consented to as soon as conceived innervates directly the centre of the first movement of the chain which leads to its accomplishment, and then the whole chain rattles off *quasi*-reflexly, as was described [in my chapter on "Habit"].

The reader will certainly recognize this to be true in all fluent and unhesitating voluntary acts. The only special fiat there is at the outset of the performance. A man says to himself, "I must change my clothes," and involuntarily he has taken off his coat, and his fingers are at work in their accustomed manner on his waistcoat-buttons, etc.; or we say, "I must go downstairs," and ere we know it we have risen, walked, and turned the handle of the door; all through the idea of an end coupled with a series of guiding sensations which successively arise. It would seem indeed that we fail of accuracy and certainty in our attainment of the end whenever we are preoccupied with the way in which the movement will feel. We walk a beam the better the less we think of the position of our feet upon it. We pitch or catch, we shoot or chop the better the less tactile and muscular (the less resident), and the more exclusively optical (the more remote), our consciousness is. Keep your *eye* on the place aimed at, and your hand will fetch it; think of your hand, and you will very likely miss your aim. Dr. Southard found that he could touch a spot, with a pencil-point more accurately with a visual than with a tactile mental cue. In the former case he looked at a small object and closed his eyes before trying to touch it. In the latter case he *placed* it with closed eyes, and then after removing his hand tried to touch it again. The average error with touch (when the results were most favorable) was 17.13 mm. With sight it was only 12.37 mm.—All these are plain results of introspection and observation. By what neural machinery they are made possible we do not know.

In [the chapter on "Imagination"] we saw how enormously individuals differ in respect to their mental imagery. In the type of imagination called *tactile* by the French authors, it is probable that the kinæsthetic ideas are more prominent than in my account. We must not expect too great a uniformity in individual accounts, nor wrangle overmuch as to which one "truly" represents the process.

I trust that I have now made clear what that "idea of a movement" is which must precede it in order that it be voluntary. It is not the thought of the innervation which the movement requires. It is the anticipation of the movement's sensible effects, resident or remote, and sometimes very remote indeed. Such anticipations, to say the least, determine *what* our movements shall be. I have spoken all along as if they also might determine *that* they shall be. This, no doubt, has disconcerted many readers, for it certainly seems as if a special fiat, or consent to the movement, were required in addition to the mere conception of it, in many cases of volition; and this fiat I have altogether left out of my account. This leads us to the next point in our discussion.

IDEO-MOTOR ACTION

The question is this: *Is the bare idea of a movement's sensible effects its sufficient motor-cue, or must there be an additional mental antecedent, in the shape of a fiat, decision, consent, volitional mandate, or other synonymous phenomenon of consciousness, before the movement can follow?*

I answer: Sometimes the bare idea is sufficient, but sometimes an additional conscious element, in the shape of a fiat, mandate, or express consent, has to intervene and precede the movement. The cases without a fiat constitute the more fundamental, because the more simple, variety. The others involve a special complication, which must be fully discussed at the proper time. For the present let us turn to *ideo-*

motor action, as it has been termed, or the sequence of movement upon the mere thought of it, without a special fiat, as the type of the process of volition.

Wherever a movement *unhesitatingly and immediately* follows upon the idea of it, we have ideo-motor action. We are then aware of nothing between the conception and the execution. All sorts of neuro-muscular processes come between, of course, but we know absolutely nothing of them. We think the act, and it is done; and that is all that introspection tells us of the matter. Dr. Carpenter, who first used, I believe, the name of ideo-motor action, placed it, if I mistake not, among the curiosities of our mental life. The truth is that it is no curiosity, but simply the normal process stripped of disguise. Whilst talking I become conscious of a pin on the floor, or of some dust on my sleeve. Without interrupting the conversation I brush away the dust or pick up the pin. I make no express resolve, but the mere perception of the object and the fleeting notion of the act seem of themselves to bring the latter about. Similarly, I sit at table after dinner and find myself from time to time taking nuts or raisins out of the dish and eating them. My dinner properly is over, and in the heat of the conversation I am hardly aware of what I do; but the perception of the fruit, and the fleeting notion that I may eat it, seem fatally to bring the act about. There is certainly no express fiat here; any more than there is in all those habitual goings and comings and rearrangements of ourselves which fill every hour of the day, and which incoming sensations instigate so immediately that it is often difficult to decide whether not to call them reflex rather than voluntary acts. As Lotze says:

> We see in writing or piano-playing a great number of very complicated movements following quickly one upon the other, the instigative representations of which remained scarcely a second in consciousness, certainly not long enough to awaken any other volition than the general one of resigning one's self without reserve to the passing over of representation into action. All the acts of our daily life happen in this wise: Our standing up, walking, talking, all this never demands a distinct impulse of the will, but is adequately brought about by the pure flux of thought.[42]

In all this the determining condition of the unhesitating and resistless sequence of the act seems to be *the absence of any conflicting notion in the mind.* Either there is nothing else at all in the mind, or what is there does not conflict. We know what it is to get out of bed on a freezing morning in a room without a fire, and how the very vital principle within us protests against the ordeal. Probably most persons

[42] *Medicinische Psychologie,* p. 293.

have lain on certain mornings for an hour at a time unable to brace themselves to the resolve. We think how late we shall be, how the duties of the day will suffer; we say, "I *must* get up, this is ignominious," etc.; but still the warm couch feels too delicious, the cold outside too cruel, and resolution faints away and postpones itself again and again just as it seemed on the verge of bursting the resistance and passing over into the decisive act. Now how do we *ever* get up under such circumstances? If I may generalize from my own experience, we more often than not get up without any struggle or decision at all. We suddenly find that we *have* got up. A fortunate lapse of consciousness occurs; we forget both the warmth and the cold; we fall into some revery connected with the day's life, in the course of which the idea flashes across us, "Hollo! I must lie here no longer"—an idea which at that lucky instant awakens no contradictory or paralyzing suggestions, and consequently produces immediately its appropriate motor effects. It was our acute consciousness of both the warmth and the cold during the period of struggle, which paralyzed our activity then and kept our idea of rising in the condition of *wish* and not of *will*. The moment these inhibitory ideas ceased, the original idea exerted its effects.

This case seems to me to contain in miniature form the data for an entire psychology of volition. It was in fact through meditating on the phenomenon in my own person that I first became convinced of the truth of the doctrine which these pages present, and which I need here illustrate by no farther examples. The reason why that doctrine is not a self-evident truth is that we have so many ideas which *do not* result in action. But it will be seen that in every such case, without exception, that is because other ideas simultaneously present rob them of their impulsive power. But even here, and when a movement is inhibited from *completely* taking place by contrary ideas, it will *incipiently* take place. To quote Lotze once more:

> The spectator accompanies the throwing of a billiard-ball, or the thrust of the swordsman, with slight movements of his arm; the untaught narrator tells his story with many gesticulations; the reader while absorbed in the perusal of a battle-scene feels a slight tension run through his muscular system, keeping time as it were with the actions he is reading of. These results become the more marked the more we are absorbed in thinking of the movements which suggest them; they grow fainter exactly in proportion as a complex consciousness, under the dominion of a crowd of other representations, withstands the passing over of mental contemplation into outward action.

The "willing-game," the exhibitions of so-called "mind-reading," or more properly muscle-reading, which have lately grown so fashionable, are based on this incipient obedience of muscular contraction to idea, even when the deliberate intention is that no contraction shall occur.

We may then lay it down for certain that *every representation of a movement awakens in some degree the actual movement which is its object; and awakens it in a maximum degree whenever it is not kept from so doing by an antagonistic representation present simultaneously to the mind.*

The express fiat, or act of mental consent to the movement, comes in when the neutralization of the antagonistic and inhibitory idea is required. But that there is no express fiat needed when the conditions are simple, the reader ought now to be convinced. Lest, however, he should still share the common prejudice that voluntary action without "exertion of will-power" is Hamlet with the prince's part left out, I will make a few farther remarks. The first point to start from, in understanding voluntary action and the possible occurrence of it with no fiat or express resolve, is the fact that consciousness is *in its very nature impulsive.* We do not first have a sensation or thought, and then have to *add* something dynamic to it to get a movement. Every pulse of feeling which we have is the correlate of some neural activity that is already on its way to instigate a movement. Our sensations and thoughts are but cross-sections, as it were, of currents whose essential consequence is notion, and which have no sooner run in at one nerve than they are ready to run out by another. The popular notion that consciousness is not essentially a forerunner of activity, but that the latter must result from some superadded "will-force," is a very natural inference from those special cases in which we think of an act for an indefinite length of time without the action taking place. These cases, however, are not the norm; they are cases of inhibition by antagonistic thoughts. When the blocking is released we feel as if an inward spring were let loose, and this is the additional impulse or *fiat* upon which the act effectively succeeds. We shall study anon the blocking and its release. Our higher thought is full of it. But where there is no blocking, there is naturally no hiatus between the thought-process and the motor discharge. *Movement is the natural immediate effect of the process of feeling, irrespective of what the quality of the feeling may be. It is so in reflex action, it is so in emotional expression, it is so in the voluntary life.* Ideo-motor action is thus no paradox, to be softened or explained away. It obeys the type of all conscious action, and from it one must start to explain the sort of action in which a special fiat is involved.

It may be remarked in passing, that the inhibition of a movement no more involves an express effort or command than its execution does. Either of them *may* require it. But in all simple and ordinary cases, just as the bare presence of one idea prompts a movement, so the bare presence of another idea will prevent its taking place. Try to feel as if you were crooking your finger, whilst keeping it straight. In a minute it will fairly tingle with the imaginary change of position; yet it will not sensibly move, because *its not really moving* is also a part of what you have in mind. Drop *this* idea, think purely and simply of the movement, and nothing else, and, presto! it takes place with no effort at all.

A waking man's behavior is thus at all times the resultant of two opposing neural forces. With unimaginable fineness some currents among the cells and fibres of his brain are playing on his motor nerves, whilst other currents, as unimaginably fine, are playing on the first currents, damming or helping them, altering their direction or their speed. The upshot of it all is, that whilst the currents must always end by being drained off through *some* motor nerves, they are drained off sometimes through one set and sometimes through another; and sometimes they keep each other in equilibrium so long that a superficial observer may think they are not drained off at all. Such an observer must remember, however, that from the physiological point of view a gesture, an expression of the brow, or an expulsion of the breath are movements as much as an act of locomotion is. A king's breath slays as well as an assassin's blow; and the outpouring of those currents which the magic imponderable streaming of our ideas accompanies need not always be of an explosive or otherwise physically conspicuous kind.

ACTION AFTER DELIBERATION

We are now in a position to describe *what happens in deliberate action,* or when the mind has many objects before it, related to each other in antagonistic or in favorable ways. One of these objects of its thought may be an act. By itself this would prompt a movement; some of the additional objects or considerations, however, block the motor discharge, whilst others, on the contrary, solicit it to take place. The result is that peculiar feeling of inward unrest known as *indecision.* Fortunately it is too familiar to need description, for to describe it would be impossible. As long as it lasts, with the various objects before the attention, we are said to *deliberate;* and when finally the original suggestion either prevails and makes the movement take place, or gets definitively quenched by its antagonists, we are said to *decide,* or to *utter our voluntary fiat,* in favor of one or the other course. The reinforcing and inhibiting objects meanwhile are termed the *reasons* or *motives* by which the decision is brought about.

The process of deliberation contains endless degrees of complication. At every moment of it our consciousness is of an extremely complex thing, namely, the whole set of motives and their conflict. Of this complicated object, the totality of which is realized more or less dimly all the while by consciousness, certain parts stand out more or less sharply at one moment in the foreground, and at another moment other parts, in consequence of the oscillations of our attention, and of the "associative" flow of our ideas. But no matter how sharp the foreground-reasons may be, or how imminently close to bursting through the dam and carrying the motor consequences their own way, the background, however dimly felt, is always there as a fringe; and its presence (so long as the indecision actually lasts) serves as an effective check upon the irrevocable discharge. The deliberation may last for weeks or months, occupying at intervals the mind. The motives which yesterday seemed full of urgency and blood and life to-day feel strangely weak and pale and dead. But as little to-day as to-morrow is the question finally resolved. Something tells us that all this is provisional; that the weakened reasons will wax strong again, and the stronger weaken; that equilibrium is unreached; that testing our reasons, not obeying them, is still the order of the day, and that we must wait awhile, patiently or impatiently, until our mind is made up "for good and all." This inclining first to one, then to another future, both of which we represent as possible, resembles the oscillations to and fro of a material body within the limits of its elasticity. There is inward strain, but no outward rupture. And this condition, plainly enough, is susceptible of indefinite continuance, as well in the physical mass as in the mind. If the elasticity give way, however, if the dam ever do break, and the currents burst the crust, vacillation is over and decision is irrevocably there.

The decision may come in either of many modes. I will try briefly to sketch the most characteristic types of it, merely warning the reader that this is only an introspective account of symptoms and phenomena, and that all questions of causal agency, whether neural or spiritual, are relegated to a later page.

FIVE CHIEF TYPES OF DECISIONS

Turning now to the form of the decision itself, we may distinguish five chief types. *The first may be called the reasonable type.* It is that of those cases in which the arguments for and against a given course seem gradually and almost insensibly to settle themselves in the mind and to end by leaving a clear balance in favor of one alternative, which alternative we then adopt without effort or constraint. Until this rational balancing of the books is consummated we have a calm feeling that the evidence is not yet all in, and this keeps action in suspense. But some day we wake with the sense that we see the matter rightly, that no new light will be thrown on it by farther delay, and that it had better be settled *now*. In this easy transition from doubt to assurance we seem to ourselves almost passive; the "reasons" which decide us appearing to flow in from the nature of things, and to owe nothing to our will. We have, however, a perfect sense of being *free,* in that we are devoid of any feeling of coercion. The conclusive reason for the decision in these cases usually is the discovery that we can refer the case to a *class* upon which we are accustomed to act unhesitatingly in a certain stereotyped way. It may be said in general that a great part of every deliberation consists in the turning over of all the possible modes of *conceiving* the doing or not doing of the act in point. The moment we hit upon a conception which lets us apply some principle of action which is a fixed and stable part of our Ego, our state of doubt is at an end. Persons of authority, who have to make many decisions in the day, carry with them a set of heads of classification, each bearing its volitional consequence, and under these they seek as far as possible to range each new emergency as it occurs. It is where the emergency belongs to a species without precedent, to which consequently no cut-and-dried maxim will apply, that we feel most at a loss, and are distressed at the indeterminateness of our task. As soon, however, as we see our way to a familiar classification, we are at ease again. *In action as in reasoning, then, the great thing is the quest of the right conception.* The concrete dilemmas do not come to us with labels gummed upon their backs. We may name them by many names. The wise man is he who succeeds in finding the name which suits the needs of the particular occasion best. A "reasonable" character is one who has a store of stable and worthy ends, and who does not decide about an action till he has calmly ascertained whether it be ministerial or detrimental to any one of these.

In the next two types of decision, the final fiat occurs before the evidence is all "in." It often happens that no paramount and authoritative reason for either course will come. Either seems a good, and there is no umpire to decide which should yield its place to the other. We grow tired of long hesitation and inconclusiveness, and the hour may come when we feel that even a bad decision is better than no decision at all. Under these conditions it will often happen that some accidental circumstance, supervening at a particular movement upon our mental weariness, will upset the balance in the direction of one of the alternatives, to which then we feel ourselves committed, although an opposite accident at the same time might have produced the opposite result.

In the *second type* our feeling is to a great extent that of letting ourselves drift with a certain indifferent acquiescence in a direction accidentally determined *from without,* with the conviction that, after all, we might as well stand by this course as by the other, and that things are in any event sure to turn out sufficiently right.

In the third type the determination seems equally accidental, but it comes from within, and not from without. It often happens, when the absence of imperative principle is perplexing and suspense distracting, that we find ourselves acting, as it were, automatically, and as if by a spontaneous discharge of our nerves, in the direction of one of the horns of the dilemma. But so exciting is this sense of motion after our intolerable pent-up state that we eagerly throw ourselves into it. "Forward now!" we inwardly cry, "though the heavens fall." This reckless and exultant espousal of an energy so little premeditated by us that we feel rather like passive spectators cheering on the display of some extraneous force than like voluntary agents is a type of decision too abrupt and tumultuous to occur often in humdrum and cool-blooded natures. But it is probably frequent in persons of strong emotional endowment and unstable or vacillating character. And in men of the world-shaking type, the Napoleons, Luthers, etc., in whom tenacious passion combines with ebullient activity, when by any chance the passion's outlet has been dammed by scruples or apprehensions, the resolution is probably often of this catastrophic kind. The flood breaks quite unexpectedly through the dam. That it should so often do so is quite sufficient to account for the tendency of these characters to a fatalistic mood of mind. And the fatalistic mood itself is sure to reinforce the strength of the energy just started on its exciting path of discharge.

There is *a fourth form* of decision, which often ends deliberation as suddenly as the third form does. It comes when, in consequence of some outer experience or some inexplicable inward change, *we suddenly pass from the easy and careless to the sober and strenuous mood,* or possibly the other way. The whole scale of values of our motives and impulses then undergoes a change like that which a change of the observer's level produces on a view. The most sobering possible agents are objects of grief and fear. When one of these affects us, all "light fantastic" notions lose their motive power, all solemn ones find theirs multiplied many-fold. The consequence is an instant abandonment of the more trivial projects with which we had been dallying, and an instant practical acceptance of the more grim and earnest alternative which till then could not extort our mind's consent. All those "changes of heart," "awakenings of conscience," etc., which make new men of so many of us may be classed under this head. The character abruptly rises to another "level," and deliberation comes to an immediate end.

In the *fifth and final type* of decision, the feeling that the evidence is all in, and that reason has balanced the books, may be either present or absent. But in either case we feel, in deciding, as if we ourselves by our own wilful act inclined the beam: in the former case by adding our living effort to the weight of the logical reason which, taken alone, seems powerless to make the act discharge; in the latter by a kind of creative contribution of something instead of a reason which does a reason's work. The slow dead heave of the will that is felt in these instances makes of them a class altogether different subjectively from all the four preceding classes. What the heave of the will betokens metaphysically, what the effort might lead us to infer about a will-power distinct from motives, are not matters that concern us yet. Subjectively and phenomenally, the *feeling of effort,* absent from the former decisions, accompanies these. Whether it be the dreary resignation for the sake of austere and naked duty of all sorts of rich mundane delights; or whether it be the heavy resolve that of two mutually exclusive trains of future fact, both sweet and good and with no strictly objective or imperative principle of choice between them, one shall forevermore become impossible, while the other shall become reality; it is a desolate and acrid sort of act, an entrance into a lonesome moral wilderness. If examined closely, its chief difference from the former cases appears to be that in those cases the mind at the moment of deciding on the triumphant alternative dropped the other one wholly or nearly out of sight, whereas here both alternatives are steadily held in view, and in the very act of murdering the vanquished possibility the chooser realizes how much in that instant he is making himself lose. It is deliberately driving a thorn into one's flesh; and the sense of *inward effort* with which the act is accompanied is an element which sets this fifth type of decision in strong contrast with the previous four varieties, and makes of it an altogether peculiar sort of mental phenomenon. The immense majority of human decisions are decisions without effort. In comparatively few of them, in most people, does effort accompany the final act. We are, I think, misled into supposing that effort is more frequent than it is by the fact that *during deliberation* we so often have a feeling of how great an effort it would take to make a decision *now.* Later, after the decision has made itself with ease, we recollect this and erroneously suppose the effort also to have been made then.

The existence of the effort as a phenomenal fact in our consciousness cannot of course be doubted or denied. Its significance, on the other hand, is a matter about which the gravest difference of opinion prevails. Questions as momentous as that of the very existence of spiritual causality, as vast as that of universal predestination or free-will, depend on its interpretation. It therefore becomes essential that we study with some care the conditions under which the feeling of volitional effort is found.

THE FEELING OF EFFORT

When I said, awhile back, that *consciousness* (or the neural process which goes with it) *is in its very nature impulsive,* I should have added the proviso that *it must be sufficiently intense.* Now there are remarkable differences in the power of different sorts of consciousness to excite movement. The intensity of some feelings is practically apt to be below the discharging point, whilst that of others is apt to be above it. By practically apt, I mean apt under ordinary circumstances. These circumstances may be habitual inhibitions, like that comfortable feeling of the *dolce far niente* which gives to each and all of us a certain dose of laziness only to be overcome by the acuteness of the impulsive spur; or they may consist in the native inertia, or internal resistance, of the motor centres themselves, making explosion impossible until a certain inward tension has been reached and overpassed. These conditions may vary from one person to another, and in the same person from time to time. The neural inertia may wax or wane, and the habitual inhibitions dwindle or augment. The intensity of particular thought-processes and stimulations may also change independently, and particular paths of association grow more pervious or less so. There thus result great possibilities of alteration in the actual impulsive efficacy of particular motives compared with others. It is where the normally less efficacious motive becomes more efficacious, and the normally more efficacious one less so, that actions ordinarily effortless, or abstinences ordinarily easy, either become impossible, or are effected (if at all) by the expenditure of effort. A little more description will make it plainer what these cases are.

HEALTHINESS OF WILL

There is a certain normal ratio in the impulsive power of different mental objects, which characterizes what may be called ordinary healthiness of will, and which is departed from only at exceptional times or by exceptional individuals. The states of mind which normally possess the most impulsive quality are either those which represent objects of passion, appetite, or emotion—objects of instinctive reaction, in short; or they are feelings or ideas of pleasure or of pain; or ideas which for any reason we have grown accustomed to obey, so that the habit of reacting on them is ingrained; or finally, in comparison with ideas of remoter objects, they are ideas of objects present or near in space and time. Compared with these various objects, all far-off considerations, all highly abstract conceptions, unaccustomed reasons, and motives foreign to the instinctive history of the race, have little or no impulsive power. They prevail, when they ever do prevail, *with effort; and the normal,* as distinguished from the pathological, *sphere of effort is thus found wherever non-instinctive motives to behavior must be reinforced so as to rule the day.*

Healthiness of will moreover requires a certain amount of complication in the process which precedes the fiat or the act. Each stimulus or idea, at the same time that it wakens its own impulse, must also arouse other ideas along with *their* characteristic impulses, and action must finally follow, neither too slowly nor too rapidly, as the resultant of all the forces thus engaged. Even when the decision is pretty prompt, the normal thing is thus a sort of preliminary survey of the field and a vision of which course is best before the fiat comes. And where the will is healthy, *the vision must be right* (i.e., the motives must be on the whole in a normal or not too unusual ratio to each other), *and the action must obey the vision's lead.*

UNHEALTHINESS OF WILL

Unhealthiness of will may thus come about in many ways. The action may follow the stimulus or idea too rapidly, leaving no time for the arousal of restraining associates—*we then have a precipitate will.* Or, although the associates may come, the ratio which the impulsive and inhibitive forces normally bear to each other may be distorted, and we then have *a will which is perverse.* The perversity, in turn, may be due to either of many causes—too much intensity, or too little, here; too much or too little inertia there; or elsewhere too much or too little inhibitory power. *If we compare the outward symptoms of perversity together, they fall into two groups,* in one of which normal actions are impossible, and in the other abnormal ones are irrepressible. Briefly, *we may call them respectively the obstructed and the explosive will.*

It must be kept in mind, however, that since the resultant action is always due to the *ratio* between the obstructive and the explosive forces which are present, we never can tell by the mere outward symptoms to what *elementary* cause the perversion of a man's will may be due, whether to an increase of one component or a diminution of the other. One may grow explosive as readily by losing the usual brakes as by getting up more of the impulsive steam; and one may find things impossible as well through the enfeeblement of the original desire as through the advent of new lions in the path. As Dr. Clouston says, "the driver may be so weak that he cannot control well-broken horses, or the horses may be so hard-mouthed that no driver can pull them up."

THE EXPLOSIVE WILL

1) *From defective inhibition.* There is a normal type of character, for example, in which impulses seem to discharge so promptly into movements that inhibitions get no time to arise. There are the "dare-devil" and "mercurial" temperaments, overflowing with animation and fizzling with talk, which are so common in the Slavic and Celtic races, and with which the cold-blooded and long-headed English character forms so marked a contrast. Simian these people seem to us, whilst we seem to them reptilian. It is quite impossible to judge, as between an obstructed and an explosive individual, which has the greater sum of vital energy. An explosive Italian with good perception and intellect will cut a figure as a perfectly tremendous fellow, on an inward capital that could be tucked away inside of an obstructed Yankee and hardly let you know that it was there. He will be the king of his company, sing the songs and make the speeches, lead the parties, carry out the practical jokes, kiss the girls, fight the men, and, if need be, lead the forlorn hopes and enterprises, so that an onlooker would think he has more life in his little finger than can exist in the whole body of a correct judicious fellow. But the judicious fellow all the while may have all these possibilities and more besides, ready to break out in the same or even a more violent way, if only the brakes were taken off. It is the absence of scruples, of consequences, of considerations, the extraordinary simplification of each moment's mental outlook, that gives to the explosive individual such motor energy and ease; it need not be the greater intensity of any of his passions, motives, or thoughts. As mental evolution goes on, the complexity of human consciousness grows ever greater, and with it the multiplication of the inhibitions to which every impulse is exposed. How much freedom of discourse we English folk lose because we feel obliged always to speak the truth! This predominance of inhibition has a bad as well as a good side; and if a man's impulses are in the main orderly as well as prompt, if he has courage to accept their consequences, and intellect to lead them to a successful end, he is all the better for his hair-trigger organization, and for not being "sicklied o'er with the pale cast of thought." Many of the most successful military and revolutionary characters in history have belonged to this simple but quick-witted impulsive type. Problems come much harder to reflective and inhibitive minds. They can, it is true, solve much vaster problems; and they can avoid many a mistake to which the men of impulse are exposed. But when the latter do

not make mistakes, or when they are always able to retrieve them, theirs is one of the most engaging and indispensable of human types.

In infancy, and in certain conditions of exhaustion, as well as in peculiar pathological states, the inhibitory power may fail to arrest the explosions of the impulsive discharge. We have then an explosive temperament temporarily realized in an individual who at other times may be of a relatively obstructed type. In other persons, again, hysterics, epileptics, criminals of the neurotic class called *dégénérés* by French authors, there is such a native feebleness in the mental machinery that before the inhibitory ideas can arise the impulsive ones have already discharged into act. In persons healthy-willed by nature bad habits can bring about this condition, especially in relation to particular sorts of impulse. Ask half the common drunkards you know why it is that they fall so often a prey to temptation, and they will say that most of the time they cannot tell. It is a sort of vertigo with them. Their nervous centres have become a sluice-way pathologically unlocked by every passing conception of a bottle and a glass. They do not thirst for the beverage; the taste of it may even appear repugnant; and they perfectly foresee the morrow's remorse. But when they think of the liquor or see it, they find themselves preparing to drink, and do not stop themselves: and more than this they cannot say. Similarly a man may lead a life of incessant love-making or sexual indulgence, though what spurs him thereto seems to be trivial suggestions and notions of possibility rather than any real solid strength of passion or desire. Such characters are too flimsy even to be bad in any deep sense of the word. The paths of natural (or it may be unnatural) impulse are so pervious in them that the slightest rise in the level of innervation produces an overflow. It is the condition recognized in pathology as "irritable weakness." The phase known as nascency or latency is so short in the excitement of the neural tissues that there is no opportunity for strain or tension to accumulate within them; and the consequence is that with all the agitation and activity, the amount of real feeling engaged may be very small. The hysterical temperament is the playground *par excellence* of this unstable equilibrium. One of these subjects will be filled with what seems the most genuine and settled aversion to a certain line of conduct, and the very next *instant* follow the stirring of temptation and plunge in it up to the neck.

2) *From exaggerated impulsion.* Disorderly and impulsive conduct may, on the other hand, come about where the neural tissues preserve their proper inward tone, and where the inhibitory power is normal or even unusually great. In such cases *the strength of the impulsive idea is preternaturally exalted,* and what would be for most people the passing suggestion of a possibility becomes a gnawing, craving urgency to act. Works on insanity are full of examples of these morbid

insistent ideas, in obstinately struggling against which the unfortunate victim's soul often sweats with agony ere at last it gets swept away.

The craving for drink in real dipsomaniacs, or for opium or chloral in those subjugated, is of a strength of which normal persons can form no conception. "Were a keg of rum in one corner of a room and were a cannon constantly discharging balls between me and it, I could not refrain from passing before that cannon in order to get the rum"; "If a bottle of brandy stood at one hand and the pit of hell yawned at the other, and I were convinced that I should be pushed in as sure as I took one glass, I could not refrain." Such statements abound in dipsomaniacs' mouths. Dr. Mussey of Cincinnati relates this case:

> A few years ago a tippler was put into an almshouse in this State. Within a few days he had devised various expedients to procure rum, but failed. At length, however, he hit upon one which was successful. He went into the wood-yard of the establishment, placed one hand upon the block, and with an axe in the other struck it off at a single blow. With the stump raised and streaming he ran into the house and cried, "Get some rum! get some rum! My hand is off!" In the confusion and bustle of the occasion a bowl of rum was brought, into which he plunged the bleeding member of his body, then raising the bowl to his mouth, drank freely, and exultingly exclaimed, "Now I am satisfied." Dr. J. E. Turner tells of a man who, while under treatment for inebriety, during four weeks secretly drank the alcohol from six jars containing morbid specimens. On asking him why he had committed this loathsome act, he replied: "Sir, it is as impossible for me to control this diseased appetite as it is for me to control the pulsations of my heart."

Often the insistent idea is of a trivial sort, but it may wear the patient's life out. His hands feel dirty, they must be washed. He *knows* they are not dirty; yet to get rid of the teasing idea he washes them. The idea, however, returns in a moment, and the unfortunate victim, who is not in the least deluded *intellectually*, will end by spending the whole day at the wash-stand. Or his clothes are not "rightly" put on; and to banish the thought he takes them off and puts them on again, till his toilet consumes two or three hours of time. Most people have the potentiality of this disease. To few has it not happened to conceive, after getting into bed, that they may have forgotten to lock the front door, or to turn out the entry gas. And few of us have not on some occasion got up to repeat the performance, less because we believed in the reality of its omission than because only so could we banish the worrying doubt and get to sleep.

THE OBSTRUCTED WILL

In striking contrast with the cases in which inhibition is insufficient or impulsion in excess are those in which impulsion is insufficient or inhibition in excess. We all know the condition described [in the chapter on "Attention"], in which the mind for a few moments seems to lose its focusing power and to be unable to rally its attention to any determinate thing. At such times we sit blankly staring and do nothing. The objects of consciousness fail to touch the quick or break the skin. They are there, but do not reach the level of effectiveness. This state of non-efficacious presence is the normal condition of *some* objects, in all of us. Great fatigue or exhaustion may make it the condition of almost all objects; and an apathy resembling that then brought about is recognized in asylums under the name of *abulia* as a symptom of mental disease. The healthy state of the will requires, as aforesaid, both that vision should be right, and that action should obey its lead. But in the morbid condition in question the vision may be wholly unaffected, and the intellect clear, and yet the act either fails to follow or follows in some other way.

"Video meliora proboque, deteriora sequor" is the classic expression of this latter condition of mind. The moral tragedy of human life comes almost wholly from the fact that the link is ruptured which normally should hold between vision of the truth and action, and that this pungent sense of effective reality will not attach to certain ideas. Men do not differ so much in their mere feelings and conceptions. Their notions of possibility and their ideals are not as far apart as might be argued from their differing fates. No class of them have better sentiments or feel more constantly the difference between the higher and the lower path in life than the hopeless failures, the sentimentalists, the drunkards, the schemers, the "deadbeats," whose life is one long contradiction between knowledge and action, and who, with full command of theory, never get to holding their limp characters erect. No one eats of the fruit of the tree of knowledge as they do; as far as moral insight goes, in comparison with them, the orderly and prosperous philistines whom they scandalize are sucking babes. And yet their moral knowledge, always there grumbling and rumbling in the background,—discerning, commenting, protesting, longing, half resolving,—never wholly resolves, never gets its voice out of the minor into the major key, or its speech out of the subjunctive into the imperative mood, never breaks the spell, never takes the helm into its hands. In such characters as Rousseau and Restif it would seem as if the lower motives had all the impulsive efficacy in their hands. Like

trains with the right of way, they retain exclusive possession of the track. The more ideal motives exist alongside of them in profusion, but they never get switched on, and the man's conduct is no more influenced by them than an express train is influenced by a wayfarer standing by the roadside and calling to be taken aboard. They are an inert accompaniment to the end of time; and the consciousness of inward hollowness that accrues from habitually seeing the better only to do the worse, is one of the saddest feelings one can bear with him through this vale of tears.

Effort feels like an original force. We now see at one view when it is that effort complicates volition. It does so whenever a rarer and more ideal impulse is called upon to neutralize others of a more instinctive and habitual kind; it does so whenever strongly explosive tendencies are checked, or strongly obstructive conditions overcome. The *âme bien née,* the child of the sunshine, at whose birth the fairies made their gifts, does not need much of it in his life. The hero and the neurotic subject, on the other hand, do. Now our spontaneous way of conceiving the effort, under all these circumstances, is as an active force adding its strength to that of the motives which ultimately prevail. When outer forces impinge upon a body, we say that the resultant motion is in the line of least resistance, or of greatest traction. But it is a curious fact that our spontaneous language never speaks of volition with effort in this way. Of course if we proceed *a priori* and define the line of least resistance as the line that is followed, the physical law must also hold good in the mental sphere. But we *feel,* in all hard cases of volition, as if the line taken, when the rarer and more ideal motives prevail, were the line of greater resistance, and as if the line of coarser motivation were the more pervious and easy one, even at the very moment when we refuse to follow it. He who under the surgeon's knife represses cries of pain, or he who exposes himself to social obloquy for duty's sake, feels as if he were following the line of greatest temporary resistance. He speaks of conquering and overcoming his impulses and temptations.

But the sluggard, the drunkard, the coward, never talk of their conduct in that way, or say they resist their energy, overcome their sobriety, conquer their courage, and so forth. If in general we class all springs of action as propensities on the one hand and ideals on the other, the sensualist never says of his behavior that it results from a victory over his ideals, but the moralist always speaks of his as a victory over his propensities. The sensualist uses terms of inactivity, says he forgets his ideals, is deaf to duty, and so forth; which terms seem to imply that the ideal motives *per se* can be annulled without energy or effort, and that the strongest mere traction lies in the line of the propensities. The ideal impulse appears, in comparison with this, a still small voice which must be artificially reinforced to prevail. Effort is what reinforces it, making things seem as if, while the force of propensity were essentially a fixed quantity, the ideal force might be of various amount. But what determines the amount of the effort when, by its aid, an ideal motive becomes victorious over a great sensual resistance? The very greatness of the resistance itself. If the sensual propensity is small, the effort is small. The latter is *made great* by the presence of a great antagonist to overcome. And if a brief definition of ideal or moral action were required, none could be given which would better fit the appearances than this: *It is action in the line of the greatest resistance.*

The facts may be most briefly symbolized thus, P standing for the propensity, I for the ideal impulse, and E for the effort:

$$I \ per \ se < P$$
$$I + E > P$$

In other words, if E adds itself to I, P immediately offers the least resistance, and motion occurs in spite of it.

But the E does not seem to form an integral part of the I. It appears adventitious and indeterminate in advance. We can make more or less as we please, and *if* we make enough we can convert the greatest mental resistance into the least. Such, at least, is the impression which the facts spontaneously produce upon us. But we will not discuss the truth of this impression at present; let us rather continue our descriptive detail.

PLEASURE AND PAIN AS SPRINGS OF ACTION

Objects and thoughts of objects start our action, but the pleasures and pains which action brings modify its course and regulate it; and later the thoughts of the pleasures and the pains acquire themselves impulsive and inhibitive power. Not that the thought of a pleasure need be itself a pleasure, usually it is the reverse—*nessun maggior dolore*—as Dante says—and not that the thought of pain need be a pain, for, as Homer says, "griefs are often afterwards an entertainment." But as present pleasures are tremendous reinforcers, and present pains tremendous inhibitors of whatever action leads to them, so the thoughts of pleasures and pains take rank amongst the thoughts which have most impulsive and inhibitive power. The precise relation which these thoughts hold to other thoughts is thus a matter demanding some attention.

· · ·

If a movement feels agreeable, we repeat and repeat it as long as the pleasure lasts. If it hurts us, our muscular contractions at the instant stop. So complete is the inhibition in this latter case that it is almost impossible for a man to cut or mutilate himself slowly and deliberately—his hand invincibly refusing to bring on the pain. And there are many pleasures which, when once we have begun to taste them, make it all but obligatory to keep up the activity to which they are due. So widespread and searching is this influence of pleasures and pains upon our movements that a premature philosophy has decided that these are our only spurs to action, and that wherever they seem to be absent, it is only because they are so far on among the "remoter" images that prompt the action that they are overlooked.

This is a great mistake, however. Important as is the influence of pleasures and pains upon our movements, they are far from being our only stimuli. With the manifestations of instinct and emotional expression, for example, they have absolutely nothing to do. Who smiles for the pleasure of the smiling, or frowns for the pleasure of the frown? Who blushes to escape the discomfort of not blushing? Or who in anger, grief, or fear is actuated to the movements which he makes by the pleasures which they yield? In all these cases the movements are discharged fatally by the *vis a tergo* which the stimulus exerts upon a nervous system framed to respond in just that way. The objects of our rage, love, or terror, the occasions of our tears and smiles, whether they be present to our senses, or whether they be merely represented in idea, have this peculiar sort of impulsive power. The *impulsive quality* of mental states is an attribute behind which we cannot go. Some states of mind have more of it than others, some have it in this direction and some in that. Feelings of pleasure and pain have it, and perceptions and imaginations of fact have it, but neither have it exclusively or peculiarly. It is of the essence of all consciousness (or of the neural process which underlies it) to instigate movement of some sort. That with one creature and object it should be of one sort, with others of another sort, is a problem for evolutionary history to explain. However the actual impulsions may have arisen, they must now be described as they exist; and those persons obey a curiously narrow teleological superstition who think themselves bound to interpret them in every instance as effects of the secret solicitancy of pleasure and repugnancy of pain. If the thought of pleasure can impel to action, surely other thoughts may. Experience only can decide which thoughts do. The chapters on Instinct and Emotion have shown us that their name is legion; and with this verdict we ought to remain contented, and not seek an illusory simplification at the cost of half the facts.

If in these our *first* acts pleasures and pains bear no part, as little do they bear in our last acts, or those artificially acquired perform-ances which have become habitual. All the daily routine of life, our dressing and undressing, the coming and going from our work or car-rying through of its various operations, is utterly without mental refer-ence to pleasure and pain, except under rarely realized conditions. It is ideo-motor action. As I do not breathe for the pleasure of the breathing, but simply find that I *am* breathing, so I do not write for the pleasure of the writing, but simply because I have once begun, and being in a state of intellectual excitement which keeps venting itself in that way, find that I *am* writing still. Who will pretend that when he idly fingers his knife-handle at the table, it is for the sake of any pleas-ure which it gives him, or pain which he thereby avoids? We do all these things because at the moment we cannot help it; our nervous systems are so shaped that they overflow in just that way; and for many of our idle or purely "nervous" and fidgety performances we can assign absolutely no *reason* at all.

Or what shall be said of a shy and unsociable man who receives point-blank an invitation to a small party? The thing is to him an abomination; but your presence exerts a compulsion on him, he can think of no excuse, and so says yes, cursing himself the while for what he does. He is unusually *sui compos* who does not every week of his life fall into some such blundering act as this. Such instances of *vol-untas invita* show not only that our acts cannot all be conceived as effects of represented pleasure, but they cannot even be classed as cases of represented *good*. The class "goods" contains many more generally influential motives to action than the class "pleasants." But almost as little as under the form of pleasures do our acts invariably appear to us under the form of *goods*. All diseased impulses and path-ological fixed ideas are instances to the contrary. It is the very badness of the act that gives it then its vertiginous fascination. Remove the prohibition, and the attraction stops. In my university days a student threw himself from an upper entry window of one of the college build-ings and was nearly killed. Another student, a friend of my own, had to pass the window daily in coming and going from his room, and experi-enced a dreadful temptation to imitate the deed. Being a Catholic, he told his director, who said, "All right! if you must, you must," and added, "Go ahead and do it," thereby instantly quenching his desire. This director knew how to minister to a mind diseased. But we need not go to minds diseased for examples of the occasional tempting-power of simple badness and unpleasantness as such. Every one who has a wound or hurt anywhere, a sore tooth, e.g., will ever and anon press it just to bring out the pain. If we are near a new sort of stink, we must sniff it again just to verify once more how bad it is. This very day I have been repeating over and over to myself a verbal jingle whose mawkish silliness was the secret of its haunting power. I loathed yet could not banish it.

What holds attention determines action. If one must have a single name for the condition upon which the impulsive and inhibitive quality of objects depends, one had better call it their *interest.* "The interesting" is a title which covers not only the pleasant and the painful, but also the morbidly fascinating, the tediously haunting, and even the simply habitual, inasmuch as the attention usually travels on habitual lines, and what-we-attend-to and what-interests-us are synonymous terms. It seems as if we ought to look for the secret of an idea's impulsiveness, not in any peculiar relations which it may have with paths of motor discharge,—for *all* ideas have relations with some such paths,—but rather in a preliminary phenomenon, the *urgency, namely, with which it is able to compel attention and dominate in consciousness.* Let it once so dominate, let no other ideas succeed in displacing it, and whatever motor effects belong to it by nature will inevitably occur —its impulsion, in short, will be given to boot, and will manifest itself as a matter of course. This is what we have seen in instinct, in emotion, in common ideo-motor action, in hypnotic suggestion, in morbid impulsion, and in *voluntas invita,*—the impelling idea is simply the one which possesses the attention. It is the same where pleasure and pain are the motor spurs—they drive other thoughts from consciousness at the same time that they instigate their own characteristic "volitional" effects. And this is also what happens at the moment of the *fiat,* in all the five types of "decision" which we have described. In short, one does not see any case in which the steadfast occupancy of consciousness does not appear to be the prime condition of impulsive power. It is still more obviously the prime condition of inhibitive power. What checks our impulses is the mere thinking of reasons to the contrary—it is their bare presence to the mind which gives the veto, and makes acts, otherwise seductive, impossible to perform. If we could only *forget* our scruples, our doubts, our fears, what exultant energy we should for a while display!

Will is a relation between the mind and its "ideas." In closing in, therefore, after all these preliminaries, upon the more *intimate* nature of the volitional process, we find ourselves driven more and more exclusively to consider the conditions which make ideas prevail in the mind. With the prevalence, once there as a fact, of the motive idea, the *psychology* of volition properly stops. The movements which ensue are exclusively physiological phenomena, following according to physiological laws upon the neural events to which the idea corresponds. The *willing* terminates with the prevalence of the idea; and whether the act then follows or not is a matter quite immaterial, so far as the willing itself goes. I will to write, and the act follows. I will to sneeze, and it does not. I will that the distant table slide over the floor towards me; it also does not. My willing representation can no more instigate my sneezing-centre than it can instigate the table to activity. But in both cases it is as true and good willing as it was when I willed. to write. In a word, volition is a psychic or moral fact pure and simple, and is absolutely completed when the stable state of the idea is there. The supervention of motion is a supernumerary phenomenon depending on executive ganglia whose function lies outside the mind. If the ganglia work duly, the act occurs perfectly. If they work, but work wrongly, we have St. Vitus's dance, locomotor ataxy, motor aphasia, or minor degrees of awkwardness. If they don't work at all, the act fails altogether, and we say the man is paralyzed. He may make a tremendous effort, and contract the other muscles of the body, but the paralyzed limb fails to move. In all these cases, however, the volition considered as a psychic process is intact.

Volitional effort is effort of attention. We thus find that *we reach the heart of our inquiry into volition when we ask by what process it is that the thought of any given action comes to prevail stably in the mind.* Where thoughts prevail without effort, we have sufficiently studied in the several chapters on Sensation, Association, and Attention, the laws of their advent before consciousness and of their stay. We shall not go over that ground again, for we know that interest and association are the words, let their worth be what it may, on which our explanations must perforce rely. Where, on the other hand, the prevalence of the thought is accompanied by the phenomena of effort, the case is much less clear. Already in the chapter on Attention we postponed the final consideration of voluntary attention with effort to a later place. We have now brought things to a point at which we see that attention with effort is all that any case of volition implies. *The essential achievement of the will, in short, when it is most "voluntary," is to attend to a difficult object and hold it fast before the mind.* The so-doing *is* the *fiat;* and it is a mere physiological incident that when the object is thus attended to, immediate motor consequences should ensue.

Effort of attention is thus the essential phenomenon of will.[43]

---

[43] This *volitional* effort pure and simple must be carefully distinguished from the *muscular* effort with which it is usually confounded. The latter consists of all those peripheral feelings to which a muscular "exertion" may give rise. These feelings, whenever they are massive and the body is not "fresh," are rather disagreeable, especially when accompanied by stopped breath, congested head, bruised skin of fingers, toes, or shoulders, and strained joints. And it is only *as thus disagreeable* that the mind must make its *volitional* effort in stably representing their reality and consequently bringing it about. That they happen to be made real by muscular activity is a purely accidental circumstance. There are instances where the fiat demands great volitional effort though the muscular

Every reader must know by his own experience that this is so, for every reader must have felt some fiery passion's grasp. What constitutes the difficulty for a man laboring under an unwise passion of acting as if the passion were wise? Certainly there is no physical difficulty. It is as easy physically to avoid a fight as to begin one, to pocket one's money as to squander it on one's cupidities, to walk away from as towards a coquette's door. The difficulty is mental: it is that of getting the idea of the wise action to stay before our mind at all. When any strong emotional state whatever is upon us, the tendency is for no images but such as are congruous with it to come up. If others by chance offer themselves, they are instantly smothered and crowded out. If we be joyous, we cannot keep thinking of those uncertainties and risks of failure which abound upon our path; if lugubrious, we cannot think of new triumphs, travels, loves, and joys; nor if vengeful, of our oppressor's community of nature with ourselves. The cooling advice which we get from others when the fever-fit is on us is the most jarring and exasperating thing in life. Reply we cannot, so we get angry; for by a sort of self-preserving instinct which our passion has, it feels that these chill objects, if they once but gain a lodgment, will work and work until they have frozen the very vital spark from out of all our mood and brought our airy castles in ruin to the ground. Such is the inevitable effect of reasonable ideas over others—*if they can once get a quiet hearing;* and passion's cue accordingly is always and everywhere to prevent their still small voice from being heard at all. "Let me not think of that! Don't speak to me of that!" This is the sudden cry of all those who in a passion perceive some sobering considerations about to check them in mid-career. There is something so icy in this cold-water bath, something which seems so hostile to the movement of our life, so purely negative, in Reason, when she lays her corpse-like finger on our heart and says, "Halt! give up! leave off! go back! sit down!" that it is no wonder that to most men the steadying influence seems, for the time being, a very minister of death.

The strong-willed man, however, is the man who hears the still small voice unflinchingly, and who, when the death-bringing consideration comes, looks at its face, consents to its presence, clings to it, affirms it, and holds it fast, in spite of the host of exciting mental images which rise in revolt against it and would expel it from the mind. Sustained in this way by a resolute effort of attention, the difficult object erelong begins to call up its own congeners and associates

---

exertion be insignificant, e.g. the getting out of bed and bathing one's self on a cold morning. Again, a soldier standing still to be fired at expects disagreeable sensations from his muscular passivity. The action of his will, in sustaining the expectation, is identical with that required for a painful muscular effort. What is hard for both is *facing an idea as real.*

and ends by changing the disposition of the man's consciousness altogether. And with his consciousness his action changes, for the new object, once stably in possession of the field of his thoughts, infallibly produces its own motor effects. The difficulty lies in the gaining possession of that field. Though the spontaneous drift of thought is all the other way, the attention must be kept strained on that one object until at last it *grows,* so as to maintain itself before the mind with ease. This strain of the attention is the fundamental act of will. And the will's work is in most cases practically ended when the bare presence to our thought of the naturally unwelcome object has been secured. For the mysterious tie between the thought and the motor centres next comes into play, and, in a way which we cannot even guess at, the obedience of the bodily organs follows as a matter of course.

In all this one sees how the immediate point of application of the volitional effort lies exclusively in the mental world. The whole drama is a mental drama. The whole difficulty is a mental difficulty, a difficulty with an ideal object of our thought. It is, in one word, an *idea* to which our will applies itself, an idea which if we let it go would slip away, but which we will not let go. *Consent to the idea's undivided presence, this is effort's sole achievement.* Its only function is to get this feeling of consent into the mind. And for this there is but one way. The idea to be consented to must be kept from flickering and going out. It must be held steadily before the mind until it *fills* the mind. Such filling of the mind by an idea, with its congruous associates, *is* consent to the idea and to the fact which the idea represents. If the idea be that, or include that, of a bodily movement of our own, then we call the consent thus laboriously gained a motor volition. For Nature here "backs" us instantaneously and follows up our inward willingness by outward changes on her own part. She does this in no other instance. Pity she should not have been more generous, nor made a world whose other parts were as immediately subject to our will!

On page 694, in describing the "reasonable type" of decision, it was said that it usually came when the right conception of the case was found. Where, however, the right conception is an anti-impulsive one, the whole intellectual ingenuity of the man usually goes to work to crowd it out of sight, and to find for the emergency names by the help of which the dispositions of the moment may sound sanctified, and sloth or passion may reign unchecked. How many excuses does the drunkard find when each new temptation comes! It is a new brand of liquor which the interests of intellectual culture in such matters oblige him to test; moreover it is poured out and it is sin to waste it; also others are drinking and it would be churlishness to refuse. Or it is but to enable him to sleep, or just to get through this job of work;

or it isn't drinking, it is because he feels so cold; or it is Christmas day; or it is a means of stimulating him to make a more powerful resolution in favor of abstinence than any he has hitherto made; or it is just this once, and once doesn't count, etc., etc., *ad libitum*—it is, in fact, anything you like except *being a drunkard*. *That* is the conception that will not stay before the poor soul's attention. But if he once gets able to pick out that way of conceiving, from all the other possible ways of conceiving the various opportunities which occur, if through thick and thin he holds to it that this is being a drunkard and is nothing else, he is not likely to remain one long. The effort by which he succeeds in keeping the right *name* unwaveringly present to his mind proves to be his saving moral act.

Everywhere, then, the function of the effort is the same: to keep affirming and adopting a thought which, if left to itself, would slip away. It may be cold and flat when the spontaneous mental drift is towards excitement, or great and arduous when the spontaneous drift is towards repose. In the one case the effort has to inhibit an explosive, in the other to arouse an obstructed will. The exhausted sailor on a wreck has a will which is obstructed. One of his ideas is that of his sore hands, of the nameless exhaustion of his whole frame which the act of farther pumping involves, and of the deliciousness of sinking into sleep. The other is that of the hungry sea ingulfing him. "Rather the aching toil!" he says; and it becomes reality then, in spite of the inhibiting influence of the relatively luxurious sensations which he gets from lying still. Often again it may be the thought of sleep and what leads to it which is the hard one to keep before the mind. If a patient afflicted with insomnia can only control the whirling chase of his ideas so far as to think of *nothing at all* (which can be done), or so far as to imagine one letter after another of a verse of Scripture or poetry spelt slowly and monotonously out, it is almost certain that here, too, specific bodily effects will follow, and that sleep will come. The trouble is to keep the mind upon a train of objects naturally so insipid. *To sustain a representation, to think,* is, in short, the only moral act, for the impulsive and the obstructed, for sane and lunatics alike. Most maniacs know their thoughts to be crazy, but find them too pressing to be withstood. Compared with them the sane truths are so deadly sober, so cadaverous, that the lunatic cannot bear to look them in the face and say, "Let these alone be my reality!" But with sufficient effort, as Dr. Wigan says,

> Such a man can for a time *wind himself up*, as it were, and determine that the notions of the disordered brain shall not be manifested. Many instances are on record similar to that told by Pinel, where an inmate of the Bicêtre, having stood a long cross-examination, and given every mark of restored reason, signed his name to the paper

authorizing his discharge "Jesus Christ," and then went off into all the
vagaries connected with that delusion. In the phraseology of the gentleman whose case is related in an early part of this [Wigan's] work
he had "held himself tight" during the examination in order to attain
his object; this once accomplished he "let himself down" again, and,
if even *conscious* of his delusion, could not control it. I have observed
with such persons that it requires a considerable time to wind themselves up to the pitch of complete self-control, that the effort is a painful tension of the mind. . . . When thrown off their guard by any
accidental remark or worn out by the length of the examination, they
let themselves go, and cannot gather themselves up again without
preparation.

To sum it all up in a word, *the terminus of the psychological process in volition, the point to which the will is directly applied, is always
an idea.* There are at all times *some* ideas from which we shy away
like frightened horses the moment we get a glimpse of their forbidding
profile upon the threshold of our thought. *The only resistance which
our will can possibly experience is the resistance which such an idea
offers to being attended to at all.* To attend to it is the volitional act,
and the only inward volitional act which we ever perform.

THE QUESTION OF "FREE WILL"

As was remarked on p. 704, in the experience of effort we feel as if we
might make more or less than we actually at any moment are making.
The effort appears, in other words, not as a fixed reaction on our
part which the object that resists us necessarily calls forth, but as what
the mathematicians call an "independent variable" amongst the fixed
data of the case, our motives, character, etc. If it be really so, if the
amount of our effort is not a determinate function of those other data,
then, in common parlance, *our wills are free.* If, on the contrary, the
amount of effort be a fixed function, so that whatever object at any
time fills our consciousness was from eternity bound to fill it then and
there, and compel from us the exact effort, neither more nor less,
which we bestow upon it—then our wills are not free, and all our acts
are foreordained. *The question of fact in the free-will controversy is
thus extremely simple. It relates solely to the amount of effort of attention which we can at any time put forth.* Are the duration and intensity of this effort fixed functions of the object, or are they not? Now,
as I just said, it *seems* as if we might exert more or less in any given
case. When a man has let his thoughts go for days and weeks until at
last they culminate in some particularly dirty or cowardly or cruel act,
it is hard to persuade him, in the midst of his remorse, that he might

not have reined them in; hard to make him believe that this whole goodly universe (which his act so jars upon) required and exacted it of him at that fatal moment, and from eternity made aught else impossible. But, on the other hand, there is the certainty that all his *effortless* volitions are resultants of interests and associations whose strength and sequence are mechanically determined by the structure of that physical mass, his brain; and the general continuity of things and the monistic conception of the world may lead one irresistibly to postulate that a little fact like effort can form no real exception to the overwhelming reign of deterministic law. Even in effortless volition we have the consciousness of the alternative being also possible. This is surely a delusion here; why is it not a delusion everywhere?

The fact is that the question of free-will is insoluble on strictly psychologic grounds. After a certain amount of effort of attention has been given to an idea, it is manifestly impossible to tell whether either more or less of it *might* have been given or not. To tell that, we should have to ascend to the antecedents of the effort, and defining them with mathematical exactitude, prove, by laws of which we have not at present even an inkling, that the only amount of sequent effort which could *possibly* comport with them was the precise amount that actually came. Such measurements, whether of psychic or of neural quantities, and such deductive reasonings as this method of proof implies, will surely be forever beyond human reach. No serious psychologist or physiologist will venture even to suggest a notion of how they might be practically made. Had one no motives drawn from elsewhere to make one partial to either solution, one might easily leave the matter undecided. But a psychologist cannot be expected to be thus impartial, having a great motive in favor of determinism. He wants to build a *Science;* and a Science is a system of fixed relations. Wherever there are independent variables, there Science stops. So far, then, as our volitions may be independent variables, a scientific psychology must ignore that fact, and treat of them only so far as they are fixed functions. In other words, she must deal with the *general laws* of volition exclusively; with the impulsive and inhibitory character of ideas; with the nature of their appeals to the attention; with the conditions under which effort may arise, etc.; but not with the precise amounts of effort, for these, if our wills be free, are impossible to compute. She thus abstracts from free-will, without necessarily denying its existence. Practically, however, such abstraction is not distinguished from rejection; and most actual psychologists have no hesitation in denying that free-will exists.

For ourselves, we can hand the free-will controversy over to metaphysics. Psychology will surely never grow refined enough to discover, in the case of any individual's decision, a discrepancy between her scientific calculations and the fact. Her prevision will never foretell, whether the effort be completely predestinate or not, the way in which each individual emergency is resolved. Psychology will be psychology, and Science science, as much as ever (as much and no more) in this world, whether free-will be true in it or not.

We can thus ignore the free-will question in psychology. As was said on p. 711, the operation of free effort; if it existed, could only be to hold some one ideal object, or part of an object, a little longer or a little more intensely before the mind. Amongst the alternatives which present themselves as *genuine possibles,* it would thus make one effective. And although such quickening of one idea might be morally and historically momentous, yet, if considered *dynamically,* it would be an operation amongst those physiological infinitesimals which an actual science must forever neglect.

ETHICAL IMPORTANCE OF THE PHENOMENON OF EFFORT

But whilst eliminating the question about the amount of our effort as one which psychology will never have a practical call to decide, I must say one word about the extraordinarily intimate and important character which the phenomenon of effort assumes in our own eyes as individual men. Of course we measure ourselves by many standards. Our strength and our intelligence, our wealth and even our good luck, are things which warm our heart and make us feel ourselves a match for life. But deeper than all such things, and able to suffice unto itself without them, is the sense of the amount of effort which we can put forth. Those are, after all, but effects, products, and reflections of the outer world within. But the effort seems to belong to an altogether different realm, as if it were the substantive thing which we *are,* and those were but externals which we *carry.* If the "searching of our heart and reins" be the purpose of this human drama, then what is sought seems to be what effort we can make. He who can make none is but a shadow; he who can make much is a hero. The huge world that girdles us about puts all sorts of questions to us, and tests us in all sorts of ways. Some of the tests we meet by actions that are easy, and some of the questions we answer in articulately formulated words. But the deepest question that is ever asked admits of no reply but the dumb turning of the will and tightening of our heart-strings as we say, *"Yes, I will even have it so!"* When a dreadful object is presented, or when life as a whole turns up its dark abysses to our view, then the worthless ones among us lose their hold on the situation altogether, and either escape from its difficulties by averting their attention, or if they cannot do that, collapse into yielding masses of plaintiveness and fear. The effort required for facing and consenting to such objects is beyond their power to make. But the heroic mind does differently. To it, too, the objects are sinister and dreadful, unwelcome, incompatible with wished-for things. But it can face them if necessary, without for that losing its hold upon the rest of life. The world thus finds in the heroic man its worthy match and mate; and the effort which he is able to put forth to hold himself erect and keep his heart unshaken is the direct measure of his worth and function in the game of human life. He can *stand* this Universe. He can meet it and keep up his faith in it in presence of those same features which lay his weaker brethren low. He can still find a zest in it, not by "ostrich-like forgetfulness," but by pure inward willingness to face it with these deterrent objects there. And hereby he makes himself one of the masters and the lords of life. He must be counted with henceforth; he forms a part of human destiny. Neither in the theoretic nor in the practical sphere do we care for, or go for help to, those who have no head for risks, or sense for living on the perilous edge. Our religious life lies more, our practical life lies less, than it used to, on the perilous edge. But just as our courage is so often a reflex of another's courage, so our faith is apt to be a faith in some one else's faith. We draw new life from the heroic example. The prophet has drunk more deeply than anyone of the cup of bitterness, but his countenance is so unshaken and he speaks such mighty words of cheer that his will becomes our will, and our life is kindled at his own.

Thus not only our morality but our religion, so far as the latter is deliberate, depend on the effort which we can make. *"Will you or won't you have it so?"* is the most probing question we are ever asked; we are asked it every hour of the day, and about the largest as well as the smallest, the most theoretical as well as the most practical, things. We answer by *consents or non-consents* and not by words. What wonder that these dumb responses should seem our deepest organs of communication with the nature of things! What wonder if the effort demanded by them be the measure of our worth as men! What wonder if the amount which we accord of it were the one strictly underived and original contribution which we make to the world!

THE WILL TO BELIEVE* 44

In the recently published Life by Leslie Stephen of his brother, Fitz-James, there is an account of a school to which the latter went when he was a boy. The teacher, a certain Mr. Guest, used to converse with his pupils in this wise: "Gurney, what is the difference between justification and sanctification?—Stephen, prove the omnipotence of God!" etc. In the midst of our Harvard freethinking and indifference we are prone to imagine that here at your good old orthodox College conversation continues to be somewhat upon this order; and to show you that we at Harvard have not lost all interest in these vital subjects, I have brought with me to-night something like a sermon on justification by faith to read to you,—I mean an essay in justification *of* faith, a defence of our right to adopt a believing attitude in religious matters, in spite of the fact that our merely logical intellect may not have been coerced. 'The Will to Believe,' accordingly, is the title of my paper.

I have long defended to my own students the lawfulness of voluntarily adopted faith; but as soon as they have got well imbued with the logical spirit, they have as a rule refused to admit my contention to be lawful philosophically, even though in point of fact they were personally all the time chock-full of some faith or other themselves. I am all the while, however, so profoundly convinced that my own position is correct, that your invitation has seemed to me a good occasion to make my statements more clear. Perhaps your minds will be more open than those with which I have hitherto had to deal. I will be as little technical as I can, though I must begin by setting up some technical distinctions that will help us in the end.

1

Let us give the name of *hypothesis* to anything that may be proposed to our belief; and just as the electricians speak of live and dead wires, let us speak of any hypothesis as either *live* or *dead*. A live hypothesis is one which appeals as a real possibility to him to whom it is proposed. If I ask you to believe in the Mahdi, the notion makes no

* From: W.B., 1–31.

44 An address to the Philosophical Clubs of Yale and Brown Universities. Published in the *New World*, June, 1896.

electric connection with your nature,—it refuses to scintillate with any credibility at all. As an hypothesis it is completely dead. To an Arab, however (even if he be not one of the Mahdi's followers), the hypothesis is among the mind's possibilities: it is alive. This shows that deadness and liveness in an hypothesis are not intrinsic properties, but relations to the individual thinker. They are measured by his willingness to act. The maximum of liveness in an hypothesis means willingness to act irrevocably. Practically, that means belief; but there is some believing tendency wherever there is willingness to act at all.

Next, let us call the decision between two hypotheses an *option.* Options may be of several kinds. They may be—1, *living* or *dead;* 2, *forced or avoidable;* 3, *momentous* or *trivial;* and for our purposes we may call an option a *genuine* option when it is of the forced, living, and momentous kind.

1. A living option is one in which both hypotheses are live ones. If I say to you: "Be a theosophist or be a Mohammedan," it is probably a dead option, because for you neither hypothesis is likely to be alive. But if I say: "Be an agnostic or be a Christian," it is otherwise: trained as you are, each hypothesis makes some appeal, however small, to your belief.

2. Next, if I say to you: "Choose between going out with your umbrella or without it," I do not offer you a genuine option, for it is not forced. You can easily avoid it by not going out at all. Similarly, if I say, "Either love me or hate me," "Either call my theory true or call it false," your option is avoidable. You may remain indifferent to me, neither loving nor hating, and you may decline to offer any judgment as to my theory. But if I say, "Either accept this truth or go without it," I put on you a forced option, for there is no standing place outside of the alternative. Every dilemma based on a complete logical disjunction, with no possibility of not choosing, is an option of this forced kind.

3. Finally, if I were Dr. Nansen and proposed to you to join my North Pole expedition, your option would be momentous; for this would probably be your only similar opportunity, and your choice now would either exclude you from the North Pole sort of immortality altogether or put at least the chance of it into your hands. He who refuses to embrace a unique opportunity loses the prize as surely as if he tried and failed. *Per contra,* the option is trivial when the opportunity is not unique, when the stake is insignificant, or when the decision is reversible if it later prove unwise. Such trivial options abound in the scientific life. A chemist finds an hypothesis live enough to spend a year in its verification: he believes in it to that extent. But if his experiments prove inconclusive either way, he is quit for his loss of time, no vital harm being done.

It will facilitate our discussion if we keep all these distinctions well in mind.

II

The next matter to consider is the actual psychology of human opinion. When we look at certain facts, it seems as if our passional and volitional nature lay at the root of all our convictions. When we look at others, it seems as if they could do nothing when the intellect had once said its say. Let us take the latter facts up first.

Does it not seem preposterous on the very face of it to talk of our opinions being modifiable at will? Can our will either help or hinder our intellect in its perceptions of truth? Can we, by just willing it, believe that Abraham Lincoln's existence is a myth, and that the portraits of him in McClure's Magazine are all of some one else? Can we, by any effort of our will, or by any strength of wish that it were true, believe ourselves well and about when we are roaring with rheumatism in bed, or feel certain that the sum of the two one-dollar bills in our pocket must be a hundred dollars? We can *say* any of these things, but we are absolutely impotent to believe them; and of just such things is the whole fabric of the truths that we do believe in made up,—matters of fact, immediate or remote, as Hume said, and relations between ideas, which are either there or not there for us if we see them so, and which if not there cannot be put there by any action of our own.

In Pascal's Thoughts there is a celebrated passage known in literature as Pascal's wager. In it he tries to force us into Christianity by reasoning as if our concern with truth resembled our concern with the stakes in a game of chance. Translated freely his words are these: You must either believe or not believe that God is—which will you do? Your human reason cannot say. A game is going on between you and the nature of things which at the day of judgment will bring out either heads or tails. Weigh what your gains and your losses would be if you should stake all you have on heads, or God's existence: if you win in such case, you gain eternal beatitude; if you lose, you lose nothing at all. If there were an infinity of chances, and only one for God in this wager, still you ought to stake your all on God; for though you surely risk a finite loss by this procedure, any finite loss is reasonable, even a certain one is reasonable, if there is but the possibility of infinite gain. Go, then, and take holy water, and have masses said; belief will come and stupefy your scruples,—*Cela vous fera croire et vous abêtira.* Why should you not? At bottom, what have you to lose?

You probably feel that when religious faith expresses itself thus, in the language of the gaming-table, it is put to its last trumps. Surely Pascal's own personal belief in masses and holy water had far other springs; and this celebrated page of his is but an argument for others, a last desperate snatch at a weapon against the hardness of the unbelieving heart. We feel that a faith in masses and holy water adopted wilfully after such a mechanical calculation would lack the inner soul of faith's reality; and if we were ourselves in the place of the Deity, we should probably take particular pleasure in cutting off believers of this pattern from their infinite reward. It is evident that unless there be some pre-existing tendency to believe in masses and holy water, the option offered to the will by Pascal is not a living option. Certainly no Turk ever took to masses and holy water on its account; and even to us Protestants these means of salvation seem such foregone impossibilities that Pascal's logic, invoked for them specifically, leaves us unmoved. As well might the Mahdi write to us, saying, "I am the Expected One whom God has created in his effulgence. You shall be infinitely happy if you confess me; otherwise you shall be cut off from the light of the sun. Weigh, then, your infinite gain if I am genuine against your finite sacrifice if I am not!" His logic would be that of Pascal; but he would vainly use it on us, for the hypothesis he offers us is dead. No tendency to act on it exists in us to any degree.

The talk of believing by our volition seems, then, from one point of view, simply silly. From another point of view it is worse than silly, it is vile. When one turns to the magnificent edifice of the physical sciences, and sees how it was reared; what thousands of disinterested moral lives of men lie buried in its mere foundations; what patience and postponement, what choking down of preference, what submission to the icy laws of outer fact are wrought into its very stones and mortar; how absolutely impersonal it stands in its vast augustness,— then how besotted and contemptible seems every little sentimentalist who comes blowing his voluntary smoke-wreaths, and pretending to decide things from out of his private dream! Can we wonder if those bred in the rugged and manly school of science should feel like spewing such subjectivism out of their mouths? The whole system of loyalties which grow up in the schools of science go dead against its toleration; so that it is only natural that those who have caught the scientific fever should pass over to the opposite extreme, and write sometimes as if the incorruptibly truthful intellect ought positively to prefer bitterness and unacceptableness to the heart in its cup.

> It fortifies my soul to know
> That, though I perish, Truth is so—

sings Clough, while Huxley exclaims: "My only consolation lies in the reflection that, however bad our posterity may become, so far as they hold by the plain rule of not pretending to believe what they have no reason to believe, because it may be to their advantage so to pretend [the word 'pretend' is surely here redundant], they will not have reached the lowest depth of immorality." And that delicious *enfant terrible* Clifford writes: "Belief is desecrated when given to unproved and unquestioned statements for the solace and private pleasure of the believer. . . . Whoso would deserve well of his fellows in this matter will guard the purity of his belief with a very fanaticism of jealous care, lest at any time it should rest on an unworthy object, and catch a stain which can never be wiped away. . . . If [a] belief has been accepted on insufficient evidence [even though the belief be true, as Clifford on the same page explains] the pleasure is a stolen one. . . . It is sinful because it is stolen in defiance of our duty to mankind. That duty is to guard ourselves from such beliefs as from a pestilence which may shortly master our own body and then spread to the rest of the town. . . . It is wrong always, everywhere, and for every one, to believe anything upon insufficient evidence."

III

All this strikes one as healthy, even when expressed, as by Clifford, with somewhat too much of robustious pathos in the voice. Free-will and simple wishing do seem, in the matter of our credences, to be only fifth wheels to the coach. Yet if any one should thereupon assume that intellectual insight is what remains after wish and will and sentimental preference have taken wing, or that pure reason is what then settles our opinions, he would fly quite as directly in the teeth of the facts.

It is only our already dead hypotheses that our willing nature is unable to bring to life again. But what has made them dead for us is for the most part a previous action of our willing nature of an antagonistic kind. When I say 'willing nature,' I do not mean only such deliberate volitions as may have set up habits of belief that we cannot now escape from,—I mean all such factors of belief as fear and hope, prejudice and passion, imitation and partisanship, the circumpressure of our caste and set. As a matter of fact we find ourselves believing, we hardly know how or why. Mr. Balfour gives the name of 'authority' to all those influences, born of the intellectual climate, that make hypotheses possible or impossible for us, alive or dead. Here in this room, we all of us believe in molecules and the conservation of energy, in democracy and necessary progress, in Protestant Christianity and the duty of fighting for 'the doctrine of the immortal Monroe,' all for no reasons worthy of the name. We see into these matters with no more inner clearness, and probably with much less, than any disbeliever in them might possess. His unconventionality would probably have some grounds to show for its conclusions; but for us, not insight, but the *prestige* of the opinions, is what makes the spark shoot from them and light up our sleeping magazines of faith. Our reason is quite satisfied, in nine hundred and ninety-nine cases out of every thousand of us, if it can find a few arguments that will do to recite in case our credulity is criticised by someone else. Our faith is faith in some one else's faith, and in the greatest matters this is most the case. Our belief in truth itself, for instance, that there is a truth, and that our minds and it are made for each other,—what is it but a passionate affirmation of desire, in which our social system backs us up? We want to have a truth; we want to believe that our experiments and studies and discussions must put us in a continually better and better position towards it; and on this line we agree to fight out our thinking lives. But if a pyrrhonistic sceptic asks us *how we know* all this, can our logic find a reply? No! certainly it cannot. It is just one volition against another,—we willing to go in for life upon a trust or assumption which he, for his part, does not care to make.[45]

As a rule we disbelieve all facts and theories for which we have no use. Clifford's cosmic emotions find no use for Christian feelings. Huxley belabors the bishops because there is no use for sacerdotalism in his scheme of life. Newman, on the contrary, goes over to Romanism, and finds all sorts of reasons good for staying there, because a priestly system is for him an organic need and delight. Why do so few 'scientists' even look at the evidence for telepathy, so called? Because they think, as a leading biologist, now dead, once said to me, that even if such a thing were true, scientists ought to band together to keep it suppressed and concealed. It would undo the uniformity of Nature and all sorts of other things without which scientists cannot carry on their pursuits. But if this very man had been shown something which as a scientist he might *do* with telepathy, he might not only have examined the evidence, but even have found it good enough. This very law which the logicians would impose upon us—if I may give the name of logicians to those who would rule out our willing nature here—is based on nothing but their own natural wish to exclude all elements for which they, in their professional quality of logicians, can find no use.

Evidently, then, our non-intellectual nature does influence our convictions. There are passional tendencies and volitions which run before and others which come after belief, and it is only the latter that are too late for the fair; and they are not too late when the previous passional work has been already in their own direction. Pascal's argument, instead of being powerless, then seems a regular clincher, and is

<hr>

[45] Compare the admirable page 310 in S. H. Hodgson's *Time and Space*, London, 1865.

the last stroke needed to make our faith in masses and holy water complete. The state of things is evidently far from simple; and pure insight and logic, whatever they might do ideally, are not the only things that really do produce our creeds.

IV

Our next duty, having recognized this mixed-up state of affairs, is to ask whether it be simply reprehensible and pathological, or whether, on the contrary, we must treat it as a normal element in making up our minds. The thesis I defend is, briefly stated, this: *Our passional nature not only lawfully may, but must, decide an option between propositions, whenever it is a genuine option that cannot by its nature be decided on intellectual grounds; for to say, under such circumstances, "Do not decide, but leave the question open," is itself a passional decision,—just like deciding yes or no,—and is attended with the same risk of losing the truth.* The thesis thus abstractly expressed will, I trust, soon become quite clear. But I must first indulge in a bit more of preliminary work.

V

It will be observed that for the purposes of this discussion we are on 'dogmatic' ground,—ground, I mean, which leaves systematic philosophical scepticism altogether out of account. The postulate that there is truth, and that it is the destiny of our minds to attain it, we are deliberately resolving to make, though the sceptic will not make it. We part company with him, therefore, absolutely, at this point. But the faith that truth exists, and that our minds can find it, may be held in two ways. We may talk of the *empiricist* way and of the *absolutist* way of believing in truth. The absolutists in this matter say that we not only can attain to knowing truth, but we can *know when* we have attained to knowing it; while the empiricists think that although we may attain it, we cannot infallibly know when. To *know* is one thing, and to know for certain *that* we know is another. One may hold to the first being possible without the second; hence the empiricists and the absolutists, although neither of them is a sceptic in the usual philosophic sense of the term, show very different degrees of dogmatism in their lives.

If we look at the history of opinons, we see that the empiricist tendency has largely prevailed in science, while in philosophy the absolutist tendency has had everything its own way. The characteristic

sort of happiness, indeed, which philosophies yield has mainly consisted in the conviction felt by each successive school or system that
by it bottom-certitude had been attained. "Other philosophies are collections of opinions, mostly false; *my* philosophy gives standing-
ground forever,"—who does not recognize in this the key-note of
every system worthy of the name? A system, to be a system at all,
must come as a *closed* system, reversible in this or that detail, perchance, but in its essential features never!

Scholastic orthodoxy, to which one must always go when one
wishes to find perfectly clear statement, has beautifully elaborated this
absolutist conviction in a doctrine which it calls that of 'objective evidence.' If, for example, I am unable to doubt that I now exist before
you, that two is less than three, or that if all men are mortal then I am
mortal too, it is because these things illumine my intellect irresistibly.
The final ground of this objective evidence possessed by certain propositions is the *adæquatio intellectûs nostri cum rê.* The certitude it
brings involves an *aptitudinem ad extorquendum certum assensum* on
the part of the truth envisaged, and on the side of the subject a *qui-
etem in cognitione,* when once the object is mentally received, that
leaves no possibility of doubt behind; and in the whole transaction
nothing operates but the *entitas ipsa* of the object and the *entitas ipsa*
of the mind. We slouchy modern thinkers dislike to talk in Latin,—indeed, we dislike to talk in set terms at all; but at bottom our own state
of mind is very much like this whenever we uncritically abandon ourselves: You believe in objective evidence, and I do. Of some things we
feel that we are certain: we know, and we know that we do know.
There is something that gives a click inside of us, a bell that strikes
twelve, when the hands of our mental clock have swept the dial and
meet over the meridian hour. The greatest empiricists among us are
only empiricists on reflection: when left to their instincts, they dogmatize like infallible popes. When the Cliffords tell us how sinful it is to
be Christians on such 'insufficient evidence,' insufficiency is really the
last thing they have in mind. For them the evidence is absolutely sufficient, only it makes the other way. They believe so completely in an
anti-christian order of the universe that there is no living option:
Christianity is a dead hypothesis from the start.

VI

But now, since we are all such absolutists by instinct, what in our
quality of students of philosophy ought we to do about the fact? Shall
we espouse and indorse it? Or shall we treat it as a weakness of our
nature from which we must free ourselves, if we can?

I sincerely believe that the latter course is the only one we can follow as reflective men. Objective evidence and certitude are doubt-less very fine ideals to play with, but where on this moonlit and dream-visited planet are they found? I am, therefore, myself a com-plete empiricist so far as my theory of human knowledge goes. I live, to be sure, by the practical faith that we must go on experiencing and thinking over our experience, for only thus can our opinions grow more true; but to hold any one of them—I absolutely do not care which—as if it never could be reinterpretable or corrigible, I believe to be a tremendously mistaken attitude, and I think that the whole history of philosophy will bear me out. There is but one indefectibly certain truth, and that is the truth that pyrrhonistic scepticism itself leaves standing,—the truth that the present phenomenon of con-sciousness exists. That, however, is the bare starting-point of knowl-edge, the mere admission of a stuff to be philosophized about. The various philosophies are but so many attempts at expressing what this stuff really is. And if we repair to our libraries what disagreement do we discover! Where is a certainly true answer found? Apart from abstract propositions of comparison (such as two and two are the same as four), propositions which tell us nothing by themselves about concrete reality, we find no proposition ever regarded by any one as evidently certain that has not either been called a falsehood, or at least had its truth sincerely questioned by some one else. The tran-scending of the axioms of geometry, not in play but in earnest, by certain of our contemporaries (as Zöllner and Charles H. Hinton), and the rejection of the whole Aristotelian logic by the Hegelians, are striking instances in point.

No concrete test of what is really true has ever been agreed upon. Some make the criterion external to the moment of perception, put-ting it either in revelation, the *consensus gentium,* the instincts of the heart, or the systematized experience of the race. Others make the perceptive moment its own test,—Descartes, for instance, with his clear and distinct ideas guaranteed by the veracity of God; Reid with his 'common-sense'; and Kant with his forms of synthetic judgment *a priori.* The inconceivability of the oppositite; the capacity to be verified by sense; the possession of complete organic unity or self-relation, realized when a thing is its own other,—are standards which, in turn, have been used. The much lauded objective evidence is never triumph-antly there; it is a mere aspiration or *Grenzbegriff,* marking the infi-nitely remote ideal of our thinking life. To claim that certain truths now possess it, is simply to say that when you think them true and they *are* true, then their evidence is objective, otherwise it is not. But practically one's conviction that the evidence one goes by is of the real objective brand, is only one more subjective opinion added to the lot.

For what a contradictory array of opinions have objective evidence and absolute certitude been claimed! The world is rational through and through,—its existence is an ultimate brute fact; there is a personal God,—a personal God is inconceivable; there is an extra-mental physical world immediately known,—the mind can only know its own ideas; a moral imperative exists,—obligation is only the resultant of desires; a permanent spiritual principle is in every one,—there are only shifting states of mind; there is an endless chain of causes,—there is an absolute first cause; an eternal necessity,—a freedom; a purpose,—no purpose; a primal One,—a primal Many; a universal continuity,—an essential discontinuity in things; an infinity,—no infinity. There is this,—there is that; there is indeed nothing which some one has not thought absolutely true, while his neighbor deemed it absolutely false; and not an absolutist among them seems ever to have considered that the trouble may all the time be essential, and that the intellect, even with truth directly in its grasp, may have no infallible signal for knowing whether it be truth or no. When, indeed, one remembers that the most striking practical application to life of the doctrine of objective certitude has been the conscientious labors of the Holy Office of the Inquisition, one feels less tempted than ever to lend the doctrine a respectful ear.

But please observe, now, that when as empiricists we give up the doctrine of objective certitude, we do not thereby give up the quest or hope of truth itself. We still pin our faith on its existence, and still believe that we gain an ever better position towards it by systematically continuing to roll up experiences and think. Our great difference from the scholastic lies in the way we face. The strength of his system lies in the principles, the origin, the *terminus a quo* of his thought; for us the strength is in the outcome, the upshot, the *terminus ad quem*. Not where it comes from but what it leads to is to decide. It matters not to an empiricist from what quarter an hypothesis may come to him: he may have acquired it by fair means or by foul; passion may have whispered or accident suggested it; but if the total drift of thinking continues to confirm it, that is what he means by its being true.

VII

One more point, small but important, and our preliminaries are done. There are two ways of looking at our duty in the matter of opinion,— ways entirely different, and yet ways about whose difference the theory of knowledge seems hitherto to have shown very little concern. *We must know the truth;* and *we must avoid error,*—these are our first and great commandments as would-be knowers; but they are not two ways of stating an identical commandment, they are two separable laws. Although it may indeed happen that when we believe the truth *A,* we escape as an incidental consequence from believing the falsehood *B,* it hardly ever happens that by merely disbelieving *B* we necessarily believe *A.* We may in escaping *B* fall into believing other falsehoods, *C* or *D,* just as bad as *B;* or we may escape *B* by not believing anything at all, not even *A.*

Believe truth! Shun error!—these, we see, are two materially different laws; and by choosing between them we may end by coloring differently our whole intellectual life. We may regard the chase for truth as paramount, and the avoidance of error as secondary; or we may, on the other hand, treat the avoidance of error as more imperative, and let truth take its chance. Clifford, in the instructive passage which I have quoted, exhorts us to the latter course. Believe nothing, he tells us, keep your mind in suspense forever, rather than by closing it on insufficient evidence incur the awful risk of believing lies. You, on the other hand, may think that the risk of being in error is a very small matter when compared with the blessings of real knowledge, and be ready to be duped many times in your investigation rather than postpone indefinitely the chance of guessing true. I myself find it impossible to go with Clifford. We must remember that these feelings of our duty about either truth or error are in any case only expressions of our passional life. Biologically considered, our minds are as ready to grind out falsehood as veracity, and he who says, "Better go without belief forever than believe a lie!" merely shows his own preponderant private horror of becoming a dupe. He may be critical of many of his desires and fears, but this fear he slavishly obeys. He cannot imagine any one questioning its binding force. For my own part, I have also a horror of being duped; but I can believe that worse things than being duped may happen to a man in this world: so Clifford's exhortation has to my ears a thoroughly fantastic sound. It is like a general informing his soldiers that it is better to keep out of battle forever than to risk a single wound. Not so are victories either over enemies or over nature gained. Our errors are surely not such awfully solemn things. In a world where we are so certain to incur them in spite of all our caution, a certain lightness of heart seems healthier than this excessive nervousness on their behalf. At any rate, it seems the fittest thing for the empiricist philosopher.

VIII

And now, after all this introduction, let us go straight at our question. I have said, and now repeat it, that not only as a matter of fact do we find our passional nature influencing us in our opinions, but that there are some options between opinions in which this influence must be regarded both as an inevitable and as a lawful determinant of our choice.

I fear hear that some of you my hearers will begin to scent danger, and lend an inhospitable ear. Two first steps of passion you have indeed had to admit as necessary,—we must think so as to avoid dupery, and we must think so as to gain truth; but the surest path to those ideal consummations, you will probably consider, is from now onwards to take no further passional step.

Well, of course, I agree as far as the facts will allow. Wherever the option between losing truth and gaining it is not momentous, we can throw the chance of *gaining truth* away, and at any rate save ourselves from any chance of *believing falsehood,* by not making up our minds at all till objective evidence has come. In scientific questions, this is almost always the case; and even in human affairs in general, the need of acting is seldom so urgent that a false belief to act on is better than no belief at all. Law courts, indeed, have to decide on the best evidence attainable for the moment, because a judge's duty is to make law as well as to ascertain it, and (as a learned judge once said to me) few cases are worth spending much time over: the great thing is to have them decided on *any* acceptable principle, and got out of the way. But in our dealings with objective nature we obviously are recorders, not makers, of the truth; and decisions for the mere sake of deciding promptly and getting on to the next business would be wholly out of place. Throughout the breadth of physical nature facts are what they are quite independently of us, and seldom is there any such hurry about them that the risks of being duped by believing a premature theory need be faced. The questions here are always trivial options, the hypotheses are hardly living (at any rate not living for us spectators), the choice between believing truth or falsehood is seldom forced. The attitude of sceptical balance is therefore the absolutely wise one if we would escape mistakes. What difference, indeed, does it make to most of us whether we have or have not a theory of the Röntgen rays, whether we believe or not in mind-stuff, or have a conviction about the causality of conscious states? It makes no difference. Such options are not forced on us. On every account it is better not to make them, but still keep weighing reasons *pro et contra* with an indifferent hand.

I speak, of course, here of the purely judging mind. For purposes of discovery such indifference is to be less highly recommended, and science would be far less advanced than she is if the passionate desires of individuals to get their own faiths confirmed had been kept out of the game. See for example the sagacity which Spencer and Weismann now display. On the other hand, if you want an absolute duffer in an investigation, you must, after all, take the man who has no interest whatever in its results: he is the warranted incapable, the positive fool. The most useful investigator, because the most sensitive observer, is always he whose eager interest in one side of the question is balanced by an equally keen nervousness lest he become deceived.[46] Science has organized this nervousness into a regular *technique,* her so-called method of verification; and she has fallen so deeply in love with the method that one may even say she has ceased to care for truth by itself at all. It is only truth as technically verified that interests her. The truth of truths might come in merely affirmative form, and she would decline to touch it. Such truth as that, she might repeat with Clifford, would be stolen in defiance of her duty to mankind. Human passions, however, are stronger than technical rules. "Le cœur a ses raisons," as Pascal says, "que la raison ne connaît pas"; and however indifferent to all but the bare rules of the game the umpire, the abstract intellect, may be, the concrete players who furnish him the materials to judge of are usually, each one of them, in love with some pet 'live hypothesis' of his own. Let us agree, however, that wherever there is no forced option, the dispassionately judicial intellect with no pet hypothesis, saving us, as it does, from dupery at any rate, ought to be our ideal.

The question next arises: Are there not somewhere forced options in our speculative questions, and can we (as men who may be interested at least as much in positively gaining truth as in merely escaping dupery) always wait with impunity till the coercive evidence shall have arrived? It seems *a priori* improbable that the truth should be so nicely adjusted to our needs and powers as that. In the great boardinghouse of nature, the cakes and the butter and the syrup seldom come out so even and leave the plates so clean. Indeed, we should view them with scientific suspicion if they did.

IX

Moral questions immediately present themselves as questions whose solution cannot wait for sensible proof. A moral question is a question not of what sensibly exists, but of what is good, or would be good if it

---

[46] Compare Wilfrid Ward's Essay, "The Wish to Believe," in his *Witnesses to the Unseen,* Macmillan & Co., 1893.

did exist. Science can tell us what exists; but to compare the *worths*, both of what exists and of what does not exist, we must consult not science, but what Pascal calls our heart. Science herself consults her heart when she lays it down that the infinite ascertainment of fact and correction of false belief are the supreme goods for man. Challenge the statement, and science can only repeat it oracularly, or else prove it by showing that such ascertainment and correction bring man all sorts of other goods which man's heart in turn declares. The question of having moral beliefs at all or not having them is decided by our will. Are our moral preferences true or false, or are they only odd biological phenomena, making things good or bad for *us*, but in themselves indifferent? How can your pure intellect decide? If your heart does not *want* a world of moral reality, your head will assuredly never make you believe in one. Mephistophelian scepticism, indeed, will satisfy the head's play-instincts much better than any rigorous idealism can. Some men (even at the student age) are so naturally cool-hearted that the moralistic hypothesis never has for them any pungent life, and in their supercilious presence the hot young moralist always feels strangely ill at ease. The appearance of knowingness is on their side, of *naïveté* and gullibility on his. Yet, in the inarticulate heart of him, he clings to it that he is not a dupe, and that there is a realm in which (as Emerson says) all their wit and intellectual superiority is no better than the cunning of a fox. Moral scepticism can no more be refuted or proved by logic than intellectual scepticism can. When we stick to it that there *is* truth (be it of either kind), we do so with our whole nature, and resolve to stand or fall by the results. The sceptic with his whole nature adopts the doubting attitude; but which of us is the wiser, Omniscience only knows.

Turn now from these wide questions of good to a certain class of questions of fact, questions concerning personal relations, states of mind between one man and another. *Do you like me or not?*—for example. Whether you do or not depends, in countless instances, on whether I meet you half-way, am willing to assume that you must like me, and show you trust and expectation. The previous faith on my part in your liking's existence is in such cases what makes your liking come. But if I stand aloof, and refuse to budge an inch until I have objective evidence, until you shall have done something apt, as the absolutists say, *ad extorquendum assensum meum,* ten to one your liking never comes. How many women's hearts are vanquished by the mere sanguine insistence of some man that they *must* love him! he will not consent to the hypothesis that they cannot. The desire for a certain kind of truth here brings about that special truth's existence; and so it is in innumerable cases of other sorts. Who gains promotions, boons, appointments, but the man in whose life they are seen to play the part of live hypotheses, who discounts them, sacrifices other things for their sake before they have come, and takes risks for them in advance? His faith acts on the powers above him as a claim, and creates its own verification.

A social organism of any sort whatever, large or small, is what it is because each member proceeds to his own duty with a trust that the other members will simultaneously do theirs. Wherever a desired result is achieved by the co-operation of many independent persons, its existence as a fact is a pure consequence of the precursive faith in one another of those immediately concerned. A government, an army, a commercial system, a ship, a college, an athletic team, all exist on this condition, without which not only is nothing achieved, but nothing is even attempted. A whole train of passengers (individually brave enough) will be looted by a few highwaymen, simply because the latter can count on one another, while each passenger fears that if he makes a movement of resistance, he will be shot before any one else backs him up. If we believed that the whole car-full would rise at once with us, we should each severally rise, and train-robbing would never even be attempted. There are, then, cases where a fact cannot come at all unless a preliminary faith exists in its coming. *And where faith in a fact can help create the fact,* that would be an insane logic which should say that faith running ahead of scientific evidence is the 'lowest kind of immorality' into which a thinking being can fall. Yet such is the logic by which our scientific absolutists pretend to regulate our lives!

X

In truths dependent on our personal action, then, faith based on desire is certainly a lawful and possibly an indispensable thing.

But now, it will be said, these are all childish human cases, and have nothing to do with great cosmical matters, like the question of religious faith. Let us then pass on to that. Religions differ so much in their accidents that in discussing the religious question we must make it very generic and broad. What then do we now mean by the religious hypothesis? Science says things are; morality says some things are better than other things; and religion says essentially two things.

First, she says that the best things are the more eternal things, the overlapping things, the things in the universe that throw the last stone, so to speak, and say the final word. "Perfection is eternal,"—this phrase of Charles Secrétan seems a good way of putting this first affirmation of religion, an affirmation which obviously cannot yet be verified scientifically at all.

The second affirmation of religion is that we are better off even now if we believe her first affirmation to be true.

Now, let us consider what the logical elements of this situation are *in case the religious hypothesis in both its branches be really true.* (Of course, we must admit that possibility at the outset. If we are to discuss the question at all, it must involve a living option. If for any of you religion be a hypothesis that cannot, by any living possibility be true, then you need go no farther. I speak to the 'saving remnant' alone.) So proceeding, we see, first, that religion offers itself as a *momentous* option. We are supposed to gain, even now, by our belief, and to lose by our non-belief, a certain vital good. Secondly, religion is a *forced* option, so far as that good goes. We cannot escape the issue by remaining sceptical and waiting for more light, because, although we do avoid error in that way *if religion be untrue,* we lose the good, *if it be true,* just as certainly as if we positively chose to disbelieve. It is as if a man should hesitate indefinitely to ask a certain woman to marry him because he was not perfectly sure that she would prove an angel after he brought her home. Would he not cut himself off from that particular angel-possibility as decisively as if he went and married some one else? Scepticism, then, is not avoidance of option; it is option of a certain particular kind of risk. *Better risk loss of truth than chance of error,*—that is your faith-vetoer's exact position. He is actively playing his stake as much as the believer is; he is backing the field against the religious hypothesis, just as the believer is backing the religious hypothesis against the field. To preach scepticism to us as a duty until 'sufficient evidence' for religion be found, is tantamount therefore to telling us, when in presence of the religious hypothesis, that to yield to our fear of its being error is wiser and better than to yield to our hope that it may be true. It is not intellect against all passions, then; it is only intellect with one passion laying down its law. And by what, forsooth, is the supreme wisdom of this passion warranted? Dupery for dupery, what proof is there that dupery through hope is so much worse than dupery through fear? I, for one, can see no proof; and I simply refuse obedience to the scientist's command to imitate his kind of option, in a case where my own stake is important enough to give me the right to choose my own form of risk. If religion be true and the evidence for it be still insufficient, I do not wish, by putting your extinguisher upon my nature (which feels to me as if it had after all some business in this matter), to forfeit my sole chance in life of getting upon the winning side,—that chance depending, of course, on my willingness to run the risk of acting as if my passional need of taking the world religiously might be prophetic and right.

All this is on the supposition that it really may be prophetic and right, and that, even to us who are discussing the matter, religion is a live hypothesis which may be true. Now, to most of us religion comes in a still further way that makes a veto on our active faith even more illogical. The more perfect and more eternal aspect of the universe is represented in our religions as having personal form. The universe is no longer a mere *It* to us, but a *Thou,* if we are religious; and any relation that may be possible from person to person might be possible here. For instance, although in one sense we are passive portions of the universe, in another we show a curious autonomy, as if we were small active centres on our own account. We feel, too, as if the appeal of religion to us were made to our own active good-will, as if evidence might be forever withheld from us unless we met the hypothesis half-way. To take a trivial illustration: just as a man who in a company of gentlemen made no advances, asked a warrant for every concession, and believed no one's word without proof, would cut himself off by such churlishness from all the social rewards that a more trusting spirit would earn,—so here, one who should shut himself up in snarling logicality and try to make the gods extort his recognition willy-nilly, or not get it at all, might cut himself off forever from his only opportunity of making the gods' acquaintance. This feeling, forced on us we know not whence, that by obstinately believing that there are gods (although not to do so would be so easy both for our logic and our life) we are doing the universe the deepest service we can, seems part of the living essence of the religious hypothesis. If the hypothesis *were* true in all its parts, including this one, then pure intellectualism, with its veto on our making willing advances, would be an absurdity; and some participation of our sympathetic nature would be logically required. I, therefore, for one, cannot see my way to accepting the agnostic rules for truth-seeking, or wilfully agree to keep my willing nature out of the game. I cannot do so for this plain reason, that *a rule of thinking which would absolutely prevent me from acknowledging certain kinds of truth if those kinds of truth were really there, would be an irrational rule.* That for me is the long and short of the formal logic of the situation, no matter what the kinds of truth might materially be.

I confess I do not see how this logic can be escaped. But sad experience makes me fear that some of you may still shrink from radically saying with me, *in abstracto,* that we have the right to believe at our own risk any hypothesis that is live enough to tempt our will. I suspect, however, that if this is so, it is because you have got away from the abstract logical point of view altogether, and are thinking (perhaps without realizing it) of some particular religious hypothesis which for you is dead. The freedom to 'believe what we will' you apply to the case of some patent superstition; and the faith you think of is the faith defined by the schoolboy when he said, "Faith is when you believe something that you know ain't true." I can only repeat that this is misapprehension. *In concreto,* the freedom to believe can only cover living options which the intellect of the individual cannot by itself resolve; and living options never seem absurdities to him who has them to consider. When I look at the religious question as it really puts itself to concrete men, and when I think of all the possibilities which both practically and theoretically it involves, then this command that we shall put a stopper on our heart, instincts, and courage, and *wait*—acting of course meanwhile more or less as if religion were *not* true[47]—till doomsday, or till such time as our intellect and senses working together may have raked in evidence enough,—this command, I say, seems to me the queerest idol ever manufactured in the philosophic cave. Were we scholastic absolutists, there might be more excuse. If we had an infallible intellect with its objective certitudes, we might feel ourselves disloyal to such a perfect organ of knowledge in not trusting to it exclusively, in not waiting for its releasing word. But if we are empiricists, if we believe that no bell in us tolls to let us know for certain when truth is in our grasp, then it seems a piece of idle fantasticality to preach so solemnly our duty of waiting for the bell. Indeed we *may* wait if we will,—I hope you do not think that I am denying that,—but if we do so, we do so at our peril as much as if we believed. In either case we *act,* taking our life in our hands. No one of us ought to issue vetoes to the other, nor should we bandy words of abuse. We ought, on the contrary, delicately and profoundly to respect one another's mental freedom: then only shall we bring about the intellectual republic; then only shall we have that spirit of inner tolerance without which all our outer tolerance is soulless, and which is empiricism's glory; then only shall we live and let live, in speculative as well as in practical things.

I began by a reference to Fitz-James Stephen; let me end by a quotation from him. "What do you think of yourself? What do you think of the world? . . . These are questions with which all must deal as it seems good to them. They are riddles of the Sphinx, and in some

[47] Since belief is measured by action, he who forbids us to believe religion to be true, necessarily also forbids us to act as we should if we did believe it to be true. The whole defence of religious faith hinges upon action. If the action required or inspired by the religious hypothesis is in no way different from that dictated by the naturalistic hypothesis, then religious faith is a pure superfluity, better pruned away, and controversy about its legitimacy is a piece of idle trifling, unworthy of serious minds. I myself believe, of course, that the religious hypothesis gives to the world an expression which specifically determines our reactions, and makes them in a large part unlike what they might be on a purely naturalistic scheme of belief.

way or other we must deal with them. . . . In all important transactions of life we have to take a leap in the dark. . . . If we decide to leave the riddles unanswered, that is a choice; if we waver in our answer, that, too, is a choice: but whatever choice we make, we make it at our peril. If a man chooses to turn his back altogether on God and the future, no one can prevent him; no one can show beyond reasonable doubt that he is mistaken. If a man thinks otherwise and acts as he thinks, I do not see that any one can prove that *he* is mistaken. Each must act as he thinks best; and if he is wrong, so much the worse for him. We stand on a mountain pass in the midst of whirling snow and blinding mist, through which we get glimpses now and then of paths which may be deceptive. If we stand still we shall be frozen to death. If we take the wrong road we shall be dashed to pieces. We do not certainly know whether there is any right one. What must we do? 'Be strong and of a good courage.' Act for the best, hope for the best, and take what comes. . . . If death ends all, we cannot meet death better." [48]

FAITH AND THE RIGHT TO BELIEVE* [49]

'Intellectualism' is the belief that our mind comes upon a world complete in itself, and has the duty of ascertaining its contents; but has no power of re-determining its character, for that is already given.

Among intellectualists two parties may be distinguished. Rationalizing intellectualists lay stress on deductive and 'dialectic' arguments, making large use of abstract concepts and pure logic (Hegel, Bradley, Taylor, Royce). Empiricist intellectualists are more 'scientific,' and think that the character of the world must be sought in our sensible experiences, and found in hypotheses based exclusively thereon (Clifford, Pearson).

Both sides insist that in our conclusions personal preferences should play no part, and that no argument from what *ought to be* to what *is,* is valid. 'Faith,' being the greeting of our whole nature to a kind of world conceived as well adapted to that nature, is forbidden,

---

[48] *Liberty, Equality, Fraternity,* p. 353, 2d edition. London, 1874.

* From: S.P.P., 221–231.

[49] [The following pages, part of a syllabus printed for the use of students in an introductory course in philosophy, were found with the MS. of this book, with the words, 'To be printed as part of the Introduction to Philosophy,' noted thereon in the author's handwriting. ED.]

until purely intellectual *evidence* that such *is* the actual world has come in. Even if evidence should eventually prove a faith true, the truth, says Clifford, would have been 'stolen,' if assumed and acted on too soon.

Refusal to believe anything concerning which 'evidence' has not yet come in, would thus be the rule of intellectualism. Obviously it postulates certain conditions, which for aught we can see need not necessarily apply to all the dealings of our minds with the Universe to which they belong.

1. It postulates that *to escape error* is our paramount duty. Faith *may* grasp truth; but also it *may* not. By resisting it always, we are sure of escaping error; and if by the same act we renounce our chance at truth, that loss is the lesser evil, and should be incurred.

2. It postulates that in every respect the universe is finished in advance of our dealings with it;

That the knowledge of what it thus is, is best gained by a passively receptive mind, with no native sense of probability, or good-will towards any special result;

That 'evidence' not only needs no good-will for its reception; but is able, if patiently waited for, to neutralize ill-will;

Finally, that our beliefs and our acts based thereupon, although they are parts of the world, and although the world without them is unfinished, are yet such mere externalities as not to alter in any way the significance of the rest of the world when they are added to it.

In our dealings with many details of fact these postulates work well. Such details exist in advance of our opinion; truth concerning them is often of no pressing importance; and by believing nothing, we escape error while we wait. But even here we often *cannot* wait but must act, somehow; so we act on the most *probable* hypothesis, trusting that the event may prove us wise. Moreover, not to act on one belief, is often equivalent to acting as if the opposite belief were true, so inaction would not always be as 'passive' as the intellectualists assume. It is one attitude of will.

Again, Philosophy and Religion have to interpret the total character of the world, and it is by no means clear that here the intellectualist postulates obtain. It may be true all the while (even though the evidence be still imperfect) that, as Paulsen says, 'the natural order is at bottom a moral order.' It may be true that work is still doing in the world-process, and that in that work we are called to bear our share. The character of the world's results may in part depend upon our acts. Our acts may depend on our religion,—on our not-resisting our faith-tendencies, or on our sustaining them in spite of 'evidence' being incomplete. These faith-tendencies in turn are but expressions of our good-will towards certain forms of result.

Such faith-tendencies are extremely active psychological forces, constantly outstripping evidence. The following steps may be called the 'faith-ladder':

1. There is nothing absurd in a certain view of the world being true, nothing self-contradictory;
2. It *might* have been true under certain conditions;
3. It *may* be true, even now;
4. It is *fit* to be true;
5. It *ought* to be true;
6. It *must* be true;
7. It *shall* be true, at any rate true for *me*.

Obviously this is no intellectual chain of inferences, like the *sorites* of the logic-books. Yet it is a slope of good-will on which in the larger questions of life men habitually live.

Intellectualism's proclamation that our good-will, our 'will to believe,' is a pure disturber of truth, is itself an act of faith of the most arbitrary kind. It implies the will to insist on a universe of intellectualist constitution, and the willingness to stand in the way of a pluralistic universe's success, such success requiring the good-will and active faith, theoretical as well as practical, of all concerned, to make it 'come true.'

Intellectualism thus contradicts itself. It is a sufficient objection to it, that if a 'pluralistically' organized, or 'co-operative' universe or the 'melioristic' universe above, were really here, the veto of intellectualism on letting our good-will ever have any vote would debar us from ever admitting that universe to be true.

Faith thus remains as one of the inalienable birthrights of our mind. Of course it must remain a practical, and not a dogmatic attitude. It must go with toleration of other faiths, with the search for the most probable, and with the full consciousness of responsibilities and risks.

It may be regarded as a formative factor in the universe, if we be integral parts thereof, and co-determinants, by our behavior, of what its total character may be.

HOW WE ACT ON PROBABILITIES

In most emergencies we have to act on probability, and incur the risk of error.

'Probability' and 'possibility' are terms applied to things of the conditions of whose coming we are (to some degree at least) ignorant.

If we are entirely ignorant of the conditions that make a thing come, we call it a 'bare' possibility. If we know that some of the conditions already exist, it is for us in so far forth a 'grounded' possibility. It is in that case *probable* just in proportion as the said conditions are numerous, and few hindering conditions are in sight.

When the conditions are so numerous and confused that we can hardly follow them, we treat a thing as probable in proportion to the *frequency* with which things of that *kind* occur. Such frequency being a fraction, the probability is expressed by a fraction. Thus, if one death in 10,000 is by suicide, the antecedent probability of my death being a suicide is 1–10,000th. If one house in 5000 burns down annually, the probability that my house will burn is 1–5000th, etc.

Statistics show that in most kinds of thing the frequency is pretty regular. Insurance companies bank on this regularity, undertaking to pay (say) 5000 dollars to each man whose house burns, provided he and the other house-owners each pay enough to give the company that sum, plus something more for profits and expenses.

The company, hedging on the large number of cases it deals with, and working by the long run, need run no risk of loss by the single fires.

The individual householder deals with his own single case exclusively. The probability of his house burning is only 1–5000, but if that lot befall he will lose everything. He has no 'long run' to go by, if his house takes fire, and he can't hedge as the company does, by taxing his more fortunate neighbors. But in this particular kind of risk, the company helps him out. It translates his one chance in 5000 of a big loss, into a certain loss 5000 times smaller, and the bargain is a fair one on both sides. It is clearly better for the man to lose *certainly,* but *fractionally,* than to trust to his 4999 chances of no loss, and then have the improbable chance befall.

But for most of our emergencies there is no insurance company at hand, and fractional solutions are impossible. Seldom can we *act* fractionally. If the probability that a friend is waiting for you in Boston is 1–2, how should you act on that probability? By going as far as the bridge? Better stay at home! Or if the probability is 1–2 that your partner is a villain, how should you act on that probability? By treating him as a villain one day, and confiding your money and your secrets to him the next? That would be the worst of all solutions. In all such cases we must act wholly for one *or* the other horn of the dilemma. We must go in for the more probable alternative as if the other one did not exist, and suffer the full penalty if the event belie our faith.

Now the metaphysical and religious alternatives are largely of this kind. We have but this one life in which to take up our attitude towards them, no insurance company is there to cover us, and if we are wrong, our error, even though it be not as great as the old hell-fire theology pretended, may yet be momentous. In such questions as that of the *character* of the world, of life being moral in its essential meaning, of our playing a vital part therein, etc., it would seem as if a certain *wholeness* in our faith were necessary. To calculate the probabilities and act fractionally, and treat life one day as a farce, and another day as a very serious business, would be to make the worst possible mess of it. Inaction also often counts as action. In many issues the inertia of one member will impede the success of the whole as much as his opposition will. To refuse, *e.g.*, to testify against villainy, is practically to help it to prevail.[50]

THE PLURALISTIC OR MELIORISTIC UNIVERSE

Finally, if the 'melioristic' universe were *really* here, it would require the active good-will of all of us, in the way of belief as well as of our other activities, to bring it to a prosperous issue.

The melioristic universe is conceived after a *social* analogy, as a pluralism of independent powers. It will succeed just in proportion as more of these work for its success. If none work, it will fail. If each does his best, it will not fail. Its destiny thus hangs on an *if,* or on a lot of *ifs*—which amounts to saying (in the technical language of logic) that, the world being as yet unfinished, its total character can be expressed only by *hypothetical* and not by *categorical* propositions.

(Empiricism, believing in possibilities, is willing to formulate its universe in hypothetical propositions. Rationalism, believing only in impossibilities and necessities, insists on the contrary on their being categorical.)

As individual members of a pluralistic universe, we must recognize that, even though we do *our* best, the other factors also will have a voice in the result. If they refuse to conspire, our good-will and labor may be thrown away. No insurance company can here cover us or save us from the risks we run in being part of such a world.

We *must* take one of four attitudes in regard to the other powers: either

1. Follow intellectualist advice: wait for evidence; and while waiting, do nothing; or

2. *Mistrust* the other powers and, sure that the universe will fail, *let* it fail; or

3. *Trust* them; and at any rate do *our* best, in spite of the *if;* or, finally,

4. *Flounder,* spending one day in one attitude, another day in another.

[50] Cf. Wm. James: *The Will to Believe*, pp. 333–345 and pp. 717–735, above.

This 4th way is no systematic solution. The 2d way spells faith in failure. The 1st way may in practice be indistinguishable from the 2d way. The 3d way seems the only wise way.

'If we do *our* best, *and* the other powers do *their* best, the world will be perfected'—this proposition expresses no actual fact, but only the complexion of a fact thought of as eventually possible. As it stands, *no* conclusion can be positively deduced from it. *A conclusion would require another premise of fact, which only we can supply. The original proposition* per se *has no pragmatic value whatsoever, apart from its power to challenge our will to produce the premise of fact required.* Then indeed the perfected world emerges as a logical conclusion.

We can *create* the conclusion, then. We can and we may, as it were, jump with both feet off the ground into or towards a world of which we trust the other parts to meet our jump—and *only so* can the *making* of a perfected world of the pluralistic pattern ever take place. Only through our precursive trust in it can it come into being.

There is no inconsistency anywhere in this, and no 'vicious circle' unless a circle of poles holding themselves upright by leaning on one another, or a circle of dancers revolving by holding each other's hands, be 'vicious.'

The faith circle is so congruous with human nature that the only explanation of the veto that intellectualists pass upon it must be sought in the offensive character *to them* of the faiths of certain concrete persons.

Such possibilities of offense have, however, to be put up with on empiricist principles. The long run of experience may weed out the more foolish faiths. Those who held them will then have failed; but without the wiser faiths of the others the world could never be perfected.

(Compare G. Lowes Dickinson: "Religion, a Criticism and a Forecast," N.Y. 1905, Introduction; and chaps. iii, iv.)

[EXPERIENCE AND RELIGION: A COMMENT*]

[In preparing the *Varieties*], the problem I have set myself is a hard one: *first,* to defend (against all the prejudices of my "class") "experi-

* From: L.W.J., II, 127. [To Miss Frances R. Morse.]

ence" against "philosophy" as being the real backbone of the world's religious life—I mean prayer, guidance, and all that sort of thing immediately and privately felt, as against high and noble general views of our destiny and the world's meaning; and *second,* to make the hearer or reader believe, what I myself invincibly do believe, that, although all the special manifestations of religion may have been absurd (I mean its creeds and theories), yet the life of it as a whole is mankind's most important function. A task well-nigh impossible, I fear, and in which I shall fail; but to attempt it is *my* religious act.

CIRCUMSCRIPTION OF THE
[RELIGIOUS] TOPIC*

Most books on the philosophy of religion try to begin with a precise definition of what its essence consists of. Some of these would-be definitions may possibly come before us in later portions of this course, and I shall not be pedantic enough to enumerate any of them to you now. Meanwhile the very fact that they are so many and so different from one another is enough to prove that the word 'religion' cannot stand for any single principle or essence, but is rather a collective name. The theorizing mind tends always to the over-simplification of its materials. This is the root of all that absolutism and one-sided dogmatism by which both philosophy and religion have been infested. Let us not fall immediately into a one-sided view of our subject, but let us rather admit freely at the outset that we may very likely find no one essence, but many characters which may alternately be equally important in religion. If we should inquire for the essence of 'government,' for example, one man might tell us it was authority, another submission, another police, another an army, another an assembly, another a system of laws; yet all the while it would be true that no concrete government can exist without all these things, one of which is more important at one moment and others at another. The man who knows governments most completely is he who troubles himself least about a definition which shall give their essence. Enjoying an intimate acquaintance with all their particularities in turn, he would naturally regard an abstract conception in which these were unified as a thing

* From: V.R.E., 26–52.

more misleading then enlightening. And why may not religion be a conception equally complex? [51]

Consider also the 'religious sentiment' which we see referred to in so many books, as if it were a single sort of mental entity.

In the psychologies and in the philosophies of religion, we find the authors attempting to specify just what entity it is. One man allies it to the feeling of dependence; one makes it a derivative from fear; others connect it with the sexual life; others still identify it with the feeling of the infinite; and so on. Such different ways of conceiving it ought of themselves to arouse doubt as to whether it possibly can be one specific thing; and the moment we are willing to treat the term 'religious sentiment' as a collective name for the many sentiments which religious objects may arouse in alternation, we see that it probably contains nothing whatever of a psychologically specific nature. There is religious fear, religious love, religious awe, religious joy, and so forth. But religious love is only man's natural emotion of love directed to a religious object; religious fear is only the ordinary fear of commerce, so to speak, the common quaking of the human breast, in so far as the notion of divine retribution may arouse it; religious awe is the same organic thrill which we feel in a forest at twilight, or in a mountain gorge; only this time it comes over us at the thought of our supernatural relations; and similarly of all the various sentiments which may be called into play in the lives of religious persons. As concrete states of mind, made up of a feeling *plus* a specific sort of object, religious emotions of course are psychic entities distinguishable from other concrete emotions; but there is no ground for assuming a simple abstract 'religious emotion' to exist as a distinct elementary mental affection by itself, present in every religious experience without exception.

As there thus seems to be no one elementary religious emotion, but only a common storehouse of emotions upon which religious objects may draw, so there might conceivably also prove to be no one specific and essential kind of religious object, and no one specific and essential kind of religious act.

The field of religion being as wide as this, it is manifestly impossible that I should pretend to cover it. My lectures must be limited to a fraction of the subject. And, although it would indeed be foolish to set up an abstract definition of religion's essence, and then proceed to defend that definition against all comers, yet this need not prevent me

[51] I can do no better here than refer my readers to the extended and admirable remarks on the futility of all these definitions of religion, in an article by Professor Leuba, published in the *Monist* for January, 1901, after my own text was written.

from taking my own narrow view of what religion shall consist in *for the purpose of these lectures,* or, out of the many meanings of the word, from choosing the one meaning in which I wish to interest you particularly, and proclaiming arbitrarily that when I say 'religion' I mean *that.* This, in fact, is what I must do, and I will now preliminarily seek to mark out the field I choose.

One way to mark it out easily is to say what aspects of the subject we leave out. At the outset we are struck by one great partition which divides the religious field. On the one side of it lies institutional, on the other personal religion. As M. P. Sabatier says, one branch of religion keeps the divinity, another keeps man most in view. Worship and sacrifice, procedures for working on the dispositions of the deity, theology and ceremony and ecclesiastical organization, are the essentials of religion in the institutional branch. Were we to limit our view to it, we should have to define religion as an external art, the art of winning the favor of the gods. In the more personal branch of religion it is on the contrary the inner dispositions of man himself which form the centre of interest, his conscience, his deserts, his helplessness, his incompleteness. And although the favor of the God, as forfeited or gained, is still an essential feature of the story, and theology plays a vital part therein, yet the acts to which this sort of religion prompts are personal not ritual acts, the individual transacts the business by himself alone, and the ecclesiastical organization, with its priests and sacraments and other go-betweens, sinks to an altogether secondary place. The relation goes direct from heart to heart, from soul to soul, between man and his maker.

Now in these lectures I propose to ignore the institutional branch entirely, to say nothing of the ecclesiastical organization, to consider as little as possible the systematic theology and the ideas about the gods themselves, and to confine myself as far as I can to personal religion pure and simple. To some of you personal religion, thus nakedly considered, will no doubt seem too incomplete a thing to wear the general name. "It is a part of religion," you will say, "but only its unorganized rudiment; if we are to name it by itself, we had better call it man's conscience or morality than his religion. The name 'religion' should be reserved for the fully organized system of feeling, thought, and institution, for the Church, in short, of which this personal religion so called, is but a fractional element."

But if you say this, it will only show the more plainly how much the question of definition tends to become a dispute about names. Rather than prolong such a dispute, I am willing to accept almost any name for the personal religion of which I propose to treat. Call it conscience or morality, if you yourselves prefer, and not religion— under either name it will be equally worthy of our study. As for myself, I think it will prove to contain some elements which morality pure and simple does not contain, and these elements I shall soon seek to point out; so I will myself continue to apply the word 'religion' to it; and in the last lecture of all, I will bring in the theologies and the ecclesiasticisms, and say something of its relation to them.

In one sense at least the personal religion will prove itself more fundamental than either theology or ecclesiasticism. Churches, when once established, live at second-hand upon tradition; but the *founders* of every church owed their power originally to the fact of their direct personal communion with the divine. Not only the superhuman founders, the Christ, the Buddha, Mahomet, but all the originators of Christian sects have been in this case;—so personal religion should still seem the primordial thing, even to those who continue to esteem it incomplete.

There are, it is true, other things in religion chronologically more primordial than personal devoutness in the moral sense. Fetishism and magic seem to have preceded inward piety historically—at least our records of inward piety do not reach back so far. And if fetishism and magic be regarded as stages of religion, one may say that personal religion in the inward sense and the genuinely spiritual ecclesiasticisms which it founds are phenomena of secondary or even tertiary order. But, quite apart from the fact that many anthropologists—for instance, Jevons and Frazer—expressly oppose 'religion' and 'magic' to each other, it is certain that the whole system of thought which leads to magic, fetishism, and the lower superstitions may just as well be called primitive science as called primitive religion. The question thus becomes a verbal one again; and our knowledge of all these early stages of thought and feeling is in any case so conjectural and imperfect that farther discussion would not be worth while.

Religion, therefore, as I now ask you arbitrarily to take it, shall mean for us *the feelings, acts, and experiences of individual men in their solitude, so far as they apprehend themselves to stand in relation to whatever they may consider the divine.* Since the relation may be either moral, physical, or ritual, it is evident that out of religion in the sense in which we take it, theologies, philosophies, and ecclesiastical organizations may secondarily grow. In these lectures, however, as I have already said, the immediate personal experiences will amply fill our time, and we shall hardly consider theology or ecclesiasticism at all.

We escape much controversial matter by this arbitrary definition of our field. But, still, a chance of controversy comes up over the word 'divine,' if we take it in the definition in too narrow a sense. There are systems of thought which the world usually calls religious, and yet which do not positively assume a God. Buddhism is in this case. Popularly, of course, the Buddha himself stands in place of a God; but in strictness the Buddhistic system is atheistic. Modern transcendental idealism, Emersonianism, for instance, also seems to let God evaporate into abstract Ideality. Not a deity *in concreto,* not a superhuman person, but the immanent divinity in things, the essentially spiritual structure of the universe, is the object of the transcendentalist cult. In that address to the graduating class at Divinity College in 1838 which made Emerson famous, the frank expression of this worship of mere abstract laws was what made the scandal of the performance.

"These laws," said the speaker, "execute themselves. They are out of time, out of space, and not subject to circumstance: Thus, in the soul of man there is a justice whose retributions are instant and entire. He who does a good deed is instantly ennobled. He who does a mean deed is by the action itself contracted. He who puts off impurity thereby puts on purity. If a man is at heart just, then in so far is he God; the safety of God, the immortality of God, the majesty of God, do enter into that man with justice. If a man dissemble, deceive, he deceives himself, and goes out of acquaintance with his own being. Character is always known. Thefts never enrich; alms never impoverish; murder will speak out of stone walls. The least admixture of a lie—for example, the taint of vanity, any attempt to make a good impression, a favorable appearance—will instantly vitiate the effect. But speak the truth, and all things alive or brute are vouchers, and the very roots of the grass underground there do seem to stir and move to bear your witness. For all things proceed out of the same spirit, which is differently named love, justice, temperance, in its different applications, just as the ocean receives different names on the several shores which it washes. In so far as he roves from these ends, a man bereaves himself of power, of auxiliaries. His being shrinks . . . he becomes less and less, a mote, a point, until absolute badness is absolute death. The perception of this law awakens in the mind a sentiment which we call the religious sentiment, and which makes our highest happiness. Wonderful is its power to charm and to command. It is a mountain air. It is the embalmer of the world. It makes the sky and the hills sublime, and the silent song of the stars is it. It is the beatitude of man. It makes him illimitable. When he says 'I ought'; when love warns him; when he chooses, warned from on high, the good and great deed; then, deep melodies wander through his soul from supreme wisdom. Then he can worship, and be enlarged by his worship; for he can never go behind this sentiment. All the expressions of this sentiment are sacred and permanent in proportion to their purity. [They] affect us more than all other compositions. The sentences of the olden time, which ejaculate this piety, are still fresh and fragrant. And the unique impression of Jesus upon mankind, whose name is not so much written as ploughed into the history of this world, is proof of the subtle virtue of this infusion." [52]

[52] *Miscellanies,* 1868, p. 120 (abridged).

. . .

Such is the Emersonian religion. The universe has a divine soul of order, which soul is moral, being also the soul within the soul of man. But whether this soul of the universe be a mere quality like the eye's brilliancy or the skin's softness, or whether it be a self-conscious life like the eye's seeing or the skin's feeling, is a decision that never unmistakably appears in Emerson's pages. It quivers on the boundary of these things, sometimes leaning one way, sometimes the other, to suit the literary rather than the philosophic need. Whatever it is, though, it is active. As much as if it were a God, we can trust it to protect all ideal interests and keep the world's balance straight. The sentences in which Emerson, to the very end, gave utterance to this faith are as fine as anything in literature: "If you love and serve men, you cannot by any hiding or stratagem escape the remuneration. Secret retributions are always restoring the level, when disturbed, of the divine justice. It is impossible to tilt the beam. All the tyrants and proprietors and monopolists of the world in vain set their shoulders to heave the bar. Settles forevermore the ponderous equator to its line, and man and mote, and star and sun, must range to it, or be pulverized by the recoil." [53]

Now it would be too absurd to say that the inner experiences that underlie such expressions of faith as this and impel the writer to their utterance are quite unworthy to be called religious experiences. The sort of appeal that Emersonian optimism, on the one hand, and Buddhistic pessimism, on the other, make to the individual and the sort of response which he makes to them in his life are in fact indistinguishable from, and in many respects identical with, the best Christian appeal and response. We must therefore, from the experiential point of view, call these godless or quasi-godless creeds 'religions'; and accordingly, when in our definition of religion we speak of the individual's relation to 'what he considers the divine,' we must interpret the term 'divine' very broadly, as denoting any object that is god*like,* whether it be a concrete deity or not.

But the term 'godlike,' if thus treated as a floating general quality, becomes exceedingly vague, for many gods have flourished in religious history, and their attributes have been discrepant enough. What then is that essentially godlike quality—be it embodied in a concrete deity or not—our relation to which determines our character as religious men? It will repay us to seek some answer to this question before we proceed farther.

For one thing, gods are conceived to be first things in the way of being and power. They overarch and envelop, and from them there is

[53] *Lectures and Biographical Sketches,* 1868, p. 186.

no escape. What relates to them is the first and last word in the way of truth. Whatever then were most primal and enveloping and deeply true might at this rate be treated as godlike, and a man's religion might thus be identified with his attitude, whatever it might be, towards what he felt to be the primal truth.

Such a definition as this would in a way be defensible. Religion, whatever it is, is a man's total reaction upon life, so why not say that any total reaction upon life is a religion? Total reactions are different from casual reactions, and total attitudes are different from usual or professional attitudes. To get at them you must go behind the foreground of existence and reach down to that curious sense of the whole residual cosmos as an everlasting presence, intimate or alien, terrible or amusing, lovable or odious, which in some degree every one possesses. This sense of the world's presence, appealing as it does to our peculiar individual temperament, makes us either strenuous or careless, devout or blasphemous, gloomy or exultant, about life at large; and our reaction, involuntary and inarticulate and often half unconscious as it is, is the completest of all our answers to the question, "What is the character of this universe in which we dwell?" It expresses our individual sense of it in the most definite way. Why then not call these reactions our religion, no matter what specific character they may have? Non-religious as some of these reactions may be, in one sense of the word 'religious,' they yet belong to *the general sphere of the religious life,* and so should generically be classed as religious reactions. "He believes in No-God, and he worships him," said a colleague of mind of a student who was manifesting a fine atheistic ardor; and the more fervent opponents of Christian doctrine have often enough shown a temper which, psychologically considered, is indistinguishable from religious zeal.

But so very broad a use of the word 'religion' would be inconvenient, however defensible it might remain on logical grounds. There are trifling, sneering attitudes even towards the whole of life; and in some men these attitudes are final and systematic. It would strain the ordinary use of language too much to call such attitudes religious, even though, from the point of view of an unbiased critical philosophy, they might conceivably be perfectly reasonable ways of looking upon life. Voltaire, for example, writes thus to a friend, at the age of seventy-three: "As for myself," he says, "weak as I am, I carry on the war to the last moment, I get a hundred pike-thrusts, I return two hundred, and I laugh. I see near my door Geneva on fire with quarrels over nothing, and I laugh again; and, thank God, I can look upon the world as a farce even when it becomes as tragic as it sometimes does. All comes out even at the end of the day, and all comes out still more even when all the days are over."

Much as we may admire such a robust old gamecock spirit in a valetudinarian, to call it a religious spirit would be odd. Yet it is for the moment Voltaire's reaction on the whole of life. *Je m'en fiche* is the vulgar French equivalent for our English ejaculation 'Who cares?' And the happy term *je m'en fichisme* recently has been invented to designate the systematic determination not to take anything in life too solemnly. 'All is vanity' is the relieving word in all difficult crises for this mode of thought, which that exquisite literary genius Renan took pleasure, in his later days of sweet decay, in putting into coquettishly sacrilegious forms which remain to us as excellent expressions of the 'all is vanity' state of mind. Take the following passage, for example, —we must hold to duty, even against the evidence, Renan says,—but he then goes on:—

> There are many chances that the world may be nothing but a fairy pantomime of which no God has care. We must therefore arrange ourselves so that on neither hypothesis we shall be completely wrong. We must listen to the superior voices, but in such a way that if the second hypothesis were true we should not have been too completely duped. If in effect the world be not a serious thing, it is the dogmatic people who will be the shallow ones, and the worldly minded whom the theologians now call frivolous will be those who are really wise.
>
> *In utrumque paratus,* then. Be ready for anything—that perhaps is wisdom. Give ourselves up, according to the hour, to confidence, to scepticism, to optimism, to irony, and we may be sure that at certain moments at least we shall be with the truth. . . . Good-humor is a philosophic state of mind; it seems to say to Nature that we take her no more seriously than she takes us. I maintain that one should always talk of philosophy with a smile. We owe it to the Eternal to be virtuous; but we have the right to add to this tribute our irony as a sort of personal reprisal. In this way we return to the right quarter jest for jest; we play the trick that has been played on us. Saint Augustine's phrase: *Lord, if we are deceived, it is by thee!* remains a fine one, well suited to our modern feeling. Only we wish the Eternal to know that if we accept the fraud, we accept it knowingly and willingly. We are resigned in advance to losing the interest on our investments of virtue, but we wish not to appear ridiculous by having counted on them too securely.[54]

Surely all the usual associations of the word 'religion' would have to be stripped away if such a systematic *parti pris* of irony were also to be denoted by the name. For common men 'religion,' whatever more special meanings it may have, signifies always a *serious* state of mind. If any one phrase could gather its universal message, that phrase would be, 'All is *not* vanity in this Universe, whatever the appearances may suggest.' If it can stop anything, religion as commonly

[54] *Feuilles détachées*, pp. 394–398 (abridged).

apprehended can stop just such chaffing talk as Renan's. It favors gravity, not pertness; it says 'hush' to all vain chatter and smart wit.

But if hostile to light irony, religion is equally hostile to heavy grumbling and complaint. The world appears tragic enough in some religions, but the tragedy is realized as purging, and a way of deliverance is held to exist. We shall see enough of the religious melancholy in a future lecture; but melancholy, according to our ordinary use of language, forfeits all title to be called religious when, in Marcus Aurelius's racy words, the sufferer simply lies kicking and screaming after the fashion of a sacrificed pig. The mood of a Schopenhauer or a Nietzsche,—and in a less degree one may sometimes say the same of our own sad Carlyle,—though often an ennobling sadness, is almost as often only peevishness running away with the bit between its teeth. The sallies of the two German authors remind one, half the time, of the sick shriekings of two dying rats. They lack the purgatorial note which religious sadness gives forth.

There must be something solemn, serious, and tender about any attitude which we denominate religious. If glad, it must not grin or snicker; if sad, it must not scream or curse. It is precisely as being *solemn* experiences that I wish to interest you in religious experiences. So I propose—arbitrarily again, if you please—to narrow our definition once more by saying that the word 'divine,' as employed therein, shall mean for us not merely the primal and enveloping and real, for that meaning if taken without restriction might well prove too broad. The divine shall mean for us only such a primal reality as the individual feels impelled to respond to solemnly and gravely, and neither by a curse nor a jest.

But solemnity, and gravity, and all such emotional attributes, admit of various shades; and, do what we will with our defining, the truth must at last be confronted that we are dealing with a field of experience where there is not a single conception that can be sharply drawn. The pretension, under such conditions, to be rigorously 'scientific' or 'exact' in our terms would only stamp us as lacking in understanding of our task. Things are more or less divine, states of mind are more or less religious, reactions are more or less total, but the boundaries are always misty, and it is everywhere a question of amount and degree. Nevertheless, at their extreme of development, there can never be any question as to what experiences are religious. The divinity of the object and the solemnity of the reaction are too well marked for doubt. Hesitation as to whether a state of mind is 'religious,' or 'irreligious,' or 'moral,' or 'philosophical,' is only likely to arise when the state of mind is weakly characterized, but in that case it will be hardly worthy of our study at all. With states that can only by courtesy be called religious we need have nothing to do, our only profitable business being with what nobody can possibly feel tempted to call anything else. I said in my former lecture that we learn most about a thing when we view it under a microscope, as it were, or in its most exaggerated form. This is as true of religious phenomena as of any other kind of fact. The only cases likely to be profitable enough to repay our attention will therefore be cases where the religious spirit is unmistakable and extreme. Its fainter manifestations we may tranquilly pass by. Here, for example, is the total reaction upon life of Frederick Locker Lampson, whose autobiography, entitled 'Confidences,' proves him to have been a most amiable man.

> I am so far resigned to my lot that I feel small pain at the thought of having to part from what has been called the pleasant habit of existence, the sweet fable of life. I would not care to live my wasted life over again, and so to prolong my span. Strange to say, I have but little wish to be younger. I submit with a chill at my heart. I humbly submit because it is the Divine Will, and my appointed destiny. I dread the increase of infirmities that will make me a burden to those around me, those dear to me. No! let me slip away as quietly and comfortably as I can. Let the end come, if peace come with it.
>
> I do not know that there is a great deal to be said for this world, or our sojourn here upon it; but it has pleased God so to place us, and it must please me also. I ask you, what is human life? Is not it a maimed happiness—care and weariness, weariness and care, with the baseless expectation, the strange cozenage of a brighter to-morrow? At best it is but a froward child, that must be played with and humored, to keep it quiet till it falls asleep, and then the care is over.[55]

This is a complex, a tender, a submissive, and a graceful state of mind. For myself, I should have no objection to calling it on the whole a religious state of mind, although I dare say that to many of you it may seem too listless and half-hearted to merit so good a name. But what matters it in the end whether we call such a state of mind religious or not? It is too insignificant for our instruction in any case; and its very possessor wrote it down in terms which he would not have used unless he had been thinking of more energetically religious moods in others, with which he found himself unable to compete. It is with these more energetic states that our sole business lies, and we can perfectly well afford to let the minor notes and the uncertain border go.

It was the extremer cases that I had in mind a little while ago when I said that personal religion, even without theology or ritual, would prove to embody some elements that morality pure and simple does not contain. You may remember that I promised shortly to point

[55] Op. cit., pp. 313 and 314.

out what those elements were. In a general way I can now say what I had in mind.

"I accept the universe" is reported to have been a favorite utterance of our New England transcendentalist, Margaret Fuller; and when some one repeated this phrase to Thomas Carlyle, his sardonic comment is said to have been: "Gad! she'd better!" At bottom the whole concern of both morality and religion is with the manner of our acceptance of the universe. Do we accept it only in part and grudgingly, or heartily and altogether? Shall our protests against certain things in it be radical and unforgiving, or shall we think that, even with evil, there are ways of living that must lead to good? If we accept the whole, shall we do so as if stunned into submission,—as Carlyle would have us—"Gad! we'd better!"—or shall we do so with enthusiastic assent? Morality pure and simple accepts the law of the whole which it finds reigning, so far as to acknowledge and obey it, but it may obey it with the heaviest and coldest heart, and never cease to feel it as a yoke. But for religion, in its strong and fully developed manifestations, the service of the highest never is felt as a yoke. Dull submission is left far behind, and a mood of welcome, which may fill any place on the scale between cheerful serenity and enthusiastic gladness, has taken its place.

It makes a tremendous emotional and practical difference to one whether one accept the universe in the drab discolored way of stoic resignation to necessity, or with the passionate happiness of Christian saints. The difference is as great as that between passivity and activity, as that between the defensive and the aggressive mood. Gradual as are the steps by which an individual may grow from one state into the other, many as are the intermediate stages which different individuals represent, yet when you place the typical extremes beside each other for comparison, you feel that two discontinuous psychological universes confront you, and that in passing from one to the other a 'critical point' has been overcome.

If we compare stoic with Christian ejaculations we see much more than a difference of doctrine; rather is it a difference of emotional mood that parts them. When Marcus Aurelius reflects on the eternal reason that has ordered things, there is a frosty chill about his words which you rarely find in a Jewish, and never in a Christian piece of religious writing. The universe is 'accepted' by all these writers; but how devoid of passion or exultation the spirit of the Roman Emperor is! Compare his fine sentence: "If gods care not for me or my children, here is a reason for it," with Job's cry: "Though he slay me, yet will I trust in him!" and you immediately see the difference I mean. The *anima mundi,* to whose disposal of his own personal destiny the Stoic consents, is there to be respected and submitted to, but the Christian God is there to be loved; and the difference of emotional atmosphere is like that between an arctic climate and the tropics, though the outcome in the way of accepting actual conditions uncomplainingly may seem in abstract terms to be much the same.

"It is a man's duty," says Marcus Aurelius, "to comfort himself and wait for the natural dissolution, and not to be vexed, but to find refreshment solely in these thoughts—first that nothing will happen to me which is not conformable to the nature of the universe; and secondly that I need do nothing contrary to the God and deity within me; for there is no man who can compel me to transgress.[56] He is an abscess on the universe who withdraws and separates himself from the reason of our common nature, through being displeased with the things which happen. For the same nature produces these, and has produced thee too. And so accept everything which happens, even if it seem disagreeable, because it leads to this, the health of the universe and to the prosperity and felicity of Zeus. For he would not have brought on any man what he has brought, if it were not useful for the whole. The integrity of the whole is mutilated if thou cuttest off anything. And thou dost cut off, as far as it is in thy power, when thou art dissatisfied, and in a manner triest to put anything out of the way." [57]

Compare now this mood with that of the old Christian author of the Theologia Germanica:—

Where men are enlightened with the true light, they renounce all desire and choice, and commit and commend themselves and all things to the eternal Goodness, so that every enlightened man could say: "I would fain be to the Eternal Goodness what his own hand is to a man." Such men are in a state of freedom, because they have lost the fear of pain or hell, and the hope of reward or heaven, and are living in pure submission to the eternal Goodness, in the perfect freedom of fervent love. When a man truly perceiveth and considereth himself, who and what he is, and findeth himself utterly vile and wicked and unworthy, he falleth into such a deep abasement that it seemeth to him reasonable that all creatures in heaven and earth should rise up against him. And therefore he will not and dare not desire any consolation and release; but he is willing to be unconsoled and unreleased; and he doth not grieve over his sufferings, for they are right in his eyes, and he hath nothing to say against them. This is what is meant by true repentance for sin; and he who in this present time entereth into this hell, none may console him. Now God hath not forsaken a man in this hell, but He is laying his hand upon him, that the man may not desire nor regard anything but the eternal Good only. And then, when the man neither careth for nor desireth anything but the eternal

[56] Book V., ch. x. (abridged).
[57] Book V., ch. ix. (abridged).

Good alone, and seeketh not himself nor his own things, but the honour of God only, he is made a partaker of all manner of joy, bliss, peace, rest, and consolation, and so the man is henceforth in the kingdom of heaven. This hell and this heaven are two good safe ways for a man, and happy is he who truly findeth them.[58]

How much more active and positive the impulse of the Christian writer to accept his place in the universe is! Marcus Aurelius agrees *to* the scheme—the German theologian agrees *with* it. He literally *abounds* in agreement, he runs out to embrace the divine decrees.

Occasionally, it is true, the Stoic rises to something like a Christian warmth of sentiment, as in the often quoted passage of Marcus Aurelius:—

Everything harmonizes with me which is harmonious to thee, O Universe. Nothing for me is too early nor too late, which is in due time for thee. Everything is fruit to me which thy seasons bring, O Nature: from thee are all things, in thee are all things, to thee all things return. The poet says, Dear City of Cecrops; and wilt thou not say, Dear City of Zeus? [59]

But compare even as devout a passage as this with a genuine Christian outpouring, and it seems a little cold. Turn, for instance, to the Imitation of Christ:—

Lord, thou knowest what is best; let this or that be according as thou wilt. Give what thou wilt, so much as thou wilt, when thou wilt. Do with me as thou knowest best, and as shall be most to thine honour. Place me where thou wilt, and freely work thy will with me in all things. . . . When could it be evil when thou wert near? I had rather be poor for thy sake than rich without thee. I choose rather to be a pilgrim upon the earth with thee, than without thee to possess heaven. Where thou art, there is heaven; and where thou art not, behold there death and hell.[60]

It is a good rule in physiology, when we are studying the meaning of an organ, to ask after its most peculiar and characteristic sort of performance, and to seek its office in that one of its functions which no other organ can possibly exert. Surely the same maxim holds good in our present quest. The essense of religious experiences, the thing by which we finally must judge them, must be that element or quality in them which we can meet nowhere else. And such a quality will be of

[58] Chaps. x., xi. (abridged): Winkworth's translation.
[59] *Book IV.*, § 23.
[60] Benham's translation: *Book III.*, chaps. xv., lix. Compare Mary Moody Emerson: "Let me be a blot on this fair world, the obscurest, the loneliest sufferer, with one proviso,—that I know it is His agency. I will love Him though He shed frost and darkness on every way of mine." R. W. EMERSON: *Lectures and Biographical Sketches*, p. 188.

course most prominent and easy to notice in those religious experiences which are most one-sided, exaggerated, and intense.

Now when we compare these intenser experiences with the experiences of tamer minds, so cool and reasonable that we are tempted to call them philosophical rather than religious, we find a character that is perfectly distinct. That character, it seems to me, should be regarded as the practically important *differentia* of religion for our purpose; and just what it is can easily be brought out by comparing the mind of an abstractly conceived Christian with that of a moralist similarly conceived.

A life is manly, stoical, moral, or philosophical, we say, in proportion as it is less swayed by paltry personal considerations and more by objective ends that call for energy, even though that energy bring personal loss and pain. This is the good side of war, in so far as it calls for 'volunteers.' And for morality life is a war, and the service of the highest is a sort of cosmic patriotism which also calls for volunteers. Even a sick man, unable to be militant outwardly, can carry on the moral welfare. He can willfully turn his attention away from his own future, whether in this world or the next. He can train himself to indifference to his present drawbacks and immerse himself in whatever objective interests still remain accessible. He can follow public news, and sympathize with other people's affairs. He can cultivate cheerful manners, and be silent about his miseries. He can contemplate whatever ideal aspects of existence his philosophy is able to present to him, and practice whatever duties, such as patience, resignation, trust, his ethical system requires. Such a man lives on his loftiest, largest plane. He is a high-hearted freeman and no pining slave. And yet he lacks something which the Christian *par excellence,* the mystic and ascetic saint, for example, has in abundant measure, and which makes of him a human being of an altogether different denomination.

The Christian also spurns the pinched and mumping sick-room attitude, and the lives of saints are full of a kind of callousness to diseased conditions of body which probably no other human records show. But whereas the merely moralistic spurning takes an effort of volition, the Christian spurning is the result of the excitement of a higher kind of emotion, in the presence of which no exertion of volition is required. The moralist must hold his breath and keep his muscles tense; and so long as this athletic attitude is possible all goes well—morality suffices. But the athletic attitude tends ever to break down, and it inevitably does break down even in the most stalwart when the organism begins to decay, or when morbid fears invade the mind. To suggest personal will and effort to one all sicklied o'er with the sense of irremediable impotence is to suggest the most impossible of things. What he craves is to be consoled in his very powerlessness, to feel that the spirit of the universe recognizes and secures him, all decaying and failing as he is. Well, we are all such helpless failures in the last resort. The sanest and best of us are of one clay with lunatics and prison inmates, and death finally runs the robustest of us down. And whenever we feel this, such a sense of the vanity and provisionality of our voluntary career comes over us that all our morality appears but as a plaster hiding a sore it can never cure, and all our well-doing as the hollowest substitute for that well-*being* that our lives ought to be grounded in, but, alas! are not.

And here religion comes to our rescue and takes our fate into her hands. There is a state of mind, known to religious men, but to no others, in which the will to assert ourselves and hold our own has been displaced by a willingness to close our mouths and be as nothing in the floods and waterspouts of God. In this state of mind, what we most dreaded has become the habitation of our safety, and the hour of our moral death has turned into our spiritual birthday. The time for tension in our soul is over, and that of happy relaxation, of calm deep breathing, of an eternal present, with no discordant future to be anxious about, has arrived. Fear is not held in abeyance as it is by mere morality, it is positively expunged and washed away.

We shall see abundant examples of this happy state of mind in later lectures of this course. We shall see how infinitely passionate a thing religion at its highest flights can be. Like love, like wrath, like hope, ambition, jealousy, like every other instinctive eagerness and impulse, it adds to life an enchantment which is not rationally or logically deducible from anything else. This enchantment, coming as a gift when it does come,—a gift of our organism, the physiologists will tell us, a gift of God's grace, the theologians say,—is either there or not there for us, and there are persons who can no more become possessed by it than they can fall in love with a given woman by mere word of command. Religious feeling is thus an absolute addition to the Subject's range of life. It gives him a new sphere of power. When the outward battle is lost, and the outer world disowns him, it redeems and vivifies an interior world which otherwise would be an empty waste.

If religion is to mean anything definite for us, it seems to me that we ought to take it as meaning this added dimension of emotion, this enthusiastic temper of espousal, in regions where morality strictly so called can at best but bow its head and acquiesce. It ought to mean nothing short of this new reach of freedom for us, with the struggle over, the keynote of the universe sounding in our ears, and everlasting possession spread before our eyes.[61]

[61] Once more, there are plenty of men, constitutionally sombre men, in whose religious life this rapturousness is lacking. They are religious in the wider sense;

This sort of happiness in the absolute and everlasting is what we find nowhere but in religion. It is parted off from all mere animal happiness, all mere enjoyment of the present, by that element of solemnity of which I have already made so much account. Solemnity is a hard thing to define abstractly, but certain of its marks are patent enough. A solemn state of mind is never crude or simple—it seems to contain a certain measure of its own opposite in solution. A solemn joy preserves a sort of bitter in its sweetness; a solemn sorrow is one to which we intimately consent. But there are writers who, realizing that happiness of a supreme sort is the prerogative of religion, forget this complication, and call all happiness, as such, religious. Mr. Havelock Ellis, for example, identifies religion with the entire field of the soul's liberation from oppressive moods.

> "The simplest functions of physiological life," he writes, "may be its ministers. Every one who is at all acquainted with the Persian mystics knows how wine may be regarded as an instrument of religion. Indeed, in all countries and in all ages, some form of physical enlargement—singing, dancing, drinking, sexual excitement—has been intimately associated with worship. Even the momentary expansion of the soul in laughter is, to however slight an extent, a religious exercise. . . . Whenever an impulse from the world strikes against the organism, and the resultant is not discomfort or pain, not even the muscular contraction of strenuous manhood, but a joyous expansion or aspiration of the whole soul—there is religion. It is the infinite for which we hunger, and we ride gladly on every little wave that promises to bear us towards it." [62]

But such a straight identification of religion with any and every form of happiness leaves the essential peculiarity of religious happiness out. The more commonplace happinesses which we get are 'reliefs,' occasioned by our momentary escapes from evils either experienced or threatened. But in its most characteristic embodiments, religious happiness is no mere feeling of escape. It cares no longer to escape. It consents to the evil outwardly as a form of sacrifice—inwardly it knows it to be permanently overcome. If you ask *how* religion thus falls on the thorns and faces death, and in the very act annuls annihilation, I cannot explain the matter, for it is religion's secret, and to understand it you must yourself have been a religious man of the extremer type. In our future examples, even of the simplest and healthiest-minded type of religious consciousness, we shall find this complex sacrificial constitution, in which a higher happiness holds

---

yet in this acutest of all senses they are not so, and it is religion in the acutest sense that I wish, without disputing about words, to study first, so as to get at its typical *differentia*.

[62] *The New Spirit,* p. 232.

a lower unhappiness in check. In the Louvre there is a picture, by Guido Reni, of St. Michael with his foot on Satan's neck. The richness of the picture is in large part due to the fiend's figure being there. The richness of its allegorical meaning also is due to his being there—that is, the world is all the richer for having a devil in it, *so long as we keep our foot upon his neck*. In the religious consciousness, that is just the position in which the fiend, the negative or tragic principle, is found; and for that very reason the religious consciousness is so rich from the emotional point of view.[63] We shall see how in certain men and women it takes on a monstrously ascetic form. There are saints who have literally fed on the negative principle, on humiliation and privation, and the thought of suffering and death,—their souls growing in happiness just in proportion as their outward state grew more intolerable. No other emotion than religious emotion can bring a man to this peculiar pass. And it is for that reason that when we ask our question about the value of religion for human life, I think we ought to look for the answer among these violenter examples rather than among those of a more moderate hue.

Having the phenomenon of our study in its acutest possible form to start with, we can shade down as much as we please later. And if in these cases, repulsive as they are to our ordinary worldly way of judging, we find ourselves compelled to acknowledge religion's value and treat it with respect, it will have proved in some way its value for life at large. By subtracting and toning down extravagances we may thereupon proceed to trace the boundaries of its legitimate sway.

To be sure, it makes our task difficult to have to deal so much with eccentricities and extremes. "How *can* religion on the whole be the most important of all human functions," you may ask, "if every several manifestation of it in turn have to be corrected and sobered down and pruned away?" Such a thesis seems a paradox impossible to sustain reasonably,—yet I believe that something like it will have to be our final contention. That personal attitude which the individual finds himself impelled to take up towards what he apprehends to be the divine—and you will remember that this was our definition—will prove to be both a helpless and a sacrificial attitude. That is, we shall have to confess to at least some amount of dependence on sheer mercy, and to practice some amount of renunciation, great or small, to save our souls alive. The constitution of the world we live in requires it:—

> Entbehren sollst du! sollst entbehren!
> Das ist der ewige Gesang

[63] I owe this allegorical illustration to my lamented colleague and friend, Charles Carroll Everett.

Der jedem an die Ohren klingt,
Den, unser ganzes Leben lang
Uns heiser jede Stunde singt.

For when all is said and done, we are in the end absolutely dependent on the universe; and into sacrifices and surrenders of some sort, deliberately looked at and accepted, we are drawn and pressed as into our only permanent positions of repose. Now in those states of mind which fall short of religion, the surrender is submitted to as an imposition of necessity, and the sacrifice is undergone at the very best without complaint. In the religious life, on the contrary, surrender and sacrifice are positively espoused: even unnecessary givings-up are added in order that the happiness may increase. *Religion thus makes easy and felicitous what in any case is necessary;* and if it be the only agency that can accomplish this result, its vital importance as a human faculty stands vindicated beyond dispute. It becomes an essential organ of our life, performing a function which no other portion of our nature can so successfully fulfill. From the merely biological point of view, so to call it, this is a conclusion to which, so far as I can now see, we shall inevitably be led, and led moreover by following the purely empirical method of demonstration which I sketched to you in the first lecture. Of the farther office of religion as a metaphysical revelation I will say nothing now.

But to foreshadow the terminus of one's investigations is one thing, and to arrive there safely is another. Abandoning [for now] the extreme generalities which have engrossed us hitherto, I propose that we begin our actual journey by addressing ourselves directly to the concrete facts.

CONCLUSIONS [to *The Varieties of Religious Experience*]*

The material of our study of human nature is now spread before us; and in this parting hour, set free from the duty of description, we can draw our theoretical and practical conclusions. In my first lecture [on Neurology], defending the empirical method, I foretold that whatever conclusions we might come to could be reached by spiritual judgments only, appreciations of the significance for life of religion, taken 'on the

* From: V.R.E., 485–519.

whole.' Our conclusions cannot be as sharp as dogmatic conclusions would be, but I will formulate them, when the time comes, as sharply as I can.

Summing up in the broadest possible way the characteristics of the religious life, as we have found them, it includes the following beliefs:—

1. That the visible world is part of a more spiritual universe from which it draws its chief significance;

2. That union or harmonious relation with that higher universe is our true end;

3. That prayer or inner communion with the spirit thereof—be that spirit 'God' or 'law'—is a process wherein work is really done, and spiritual energy flows in and produces effects, psychological or material, within the phenomenal world.

Religion includes also the following psychological characteristics:—

4. A new zest which adds itself like a gift to life, and takes the form either of lyrical enchantment or of appeal to earnestness and heroism.

5. An assurance of safety and a temper of peace, and, in relation to others, a preponderance of loving affections.

In illustrating these characteristics by documents, we have been literally bathed in sentiment. In re-reading my manuscript, I am almost appalled at the amount of emotionality which I find in it. After so much of this, we can afford to be dryer and less sympathetic in the rest of the work that lies before us.

The sentimentality of many of my documents is a consequence of the fact that I sought them among the extravagances of the subject. If any of you are enemies of what our ancestors used to brand as enthusiasm, and are, nevertheless, still listening to me now, you have probably felt my selection to have been sometimes almost perverse, and have wished I might have stuck to soberer examples. I reply that I took these extremer examples as yielding the profounder information. To learn the secrets of any science, we go to expert specialists, even though they may be eccentric persons, and not to commonplace pupils. We combine what they tell us with the rest of our wisdom, and form our final judgment independently. Even so with religion. We who have pursued such radical expressions of it may now be sure that we know its secrets as authentically as any one can know them who learns them from another; and we have next to answer, each of us for himself, the practical question: what are the dangers in this element of life? and in what proportion may it need to be restrained by other elements, to give the proper balance?

·   ·   ·

But this question suggests another one which I will answer immediately and get it out of the way, for it has more than once already vexed us. Ought it to be assumed that in all men the mixture of religion with other elements should be identical? Ought it, indeed, to be assumed that the lives of all men should show identical religious elements? In other words, is the existence of so many religious types and sects and creeds regrettable?

To those questions I answer 'No' emphatically. And my reason is that I do not see how it is possible that creatures in such different positions and with such different powers as human individuals are, should have exactly the same functions and the same duties. No two of us have identical difficulties, nor should we be expected to work out identical solutions. Each, from his peculiar angle of observation, takes in a certain sphere of fact and trouble, which each must deal with in a unique manner. One of us must soften himself, another must harden himself; one must yield a point, another must stand firm,—in order the better to defend the position assigned him. If an Emerson were forced to be a Wesley, or a Moody forced to be a Whitman, the total human consciousness of the divine would suffer. The divine can mean no single quality, it must mean a group of qualities, by being champions of which in alternation, different men may all find worthy missions. Each attitude being a syllable in human nature's total message, it takes the whole of us to spell the meaning out completely. So a 'god of battles' must be allowed to be the god for one kind of person, a god of peace and heaven and home, the god for another. We must frankly recognize the fact that we live in partial systems, and that parts are not interchangeable in the spiritual life. If we are peevish and jealous, destruction of the self must be an element of our religion; why need it be one if we are good and sympathetic from the outset? If we are sick souls, we require a religion of deliverance; but why think so much of deliverance, if we are healthy-minded? [64] Unquestionably, some men

[64] From this point of view, the contrasts between the healthy and the morbid mind, and between the once-born and the twice-born types, of which I spoke in earlier lectures, cease to be the radical antagonisms which many think them. The twice-born look down upon the rectilinear consciousness of life of the once-born as being 'mere morality,' and not properly religion. "Dr. Channing," an orthodox minister is reported to have said, "is excluded from the highest form of religious life by the extraordinary rectitude of his character." It is indeed true that the outlook upon life of the twice-born—holding as it does more of the element of evil in solution—is the wider and completer. The 'heroic' or 'solemn' way in which life comes to them is a 'higher synthesis' into which healthy-mindedness and morbidness both enter and combine. Evil is not evaded, but sublated in the higher religious cheer of these persons [see above, pp. 755–758]. But the final consciousness which each type reaches of union with the divine has the same practical significance for the individual; and individuals may well be allowed to get to it by the channels which lie most open to their several tem-

have the completer experience and the higher vocation, here just as in the social world; but for each man to stay in his own experience, whate'er it be, and for others to tolerate him there, is surely best.

But, you may now ask, would not this one-sidedness be cured if we should all espouse the science of religions as our own religion? In answering this question I must open again the general relations of the theoretic to the active life.

Knowledge about a thing is not the thing itself. You remember what Al-Ghazzali told us in the Lecture on Mysticism,—that to understand the causes of drunkenness, as a physician understands them, is not to be drunk. A science might come to understand everything about the causes and elements of religion, and might even decide which elements were qualified, by their general harmony with other branches of knowledge, to be considered true; and yet the best man at this science might be the man who found it hardest to be personally devout. *Tout savoir c'est tout pardonner.* The name of Renan would doubtless occur to many persons as an example of the way in which breadth of knowledge may make one only a dilettante in possibilities, and blunt the acuteness of one's living faith.[65] If religion be a function by which either God's cause or man's cause is to be really advanced, then he who lives the life of it, however narrowly, is a better servant than he who merely knows about it, however much. Knowledge about life is one thing; effective occupation of a place in life, with its dynamic currents passing through your being, is another.

For this reason, the science of religions may not be an equivalent for living religion; and if we turn to the inner difficulties of such a science, we see that a point comes when she must drop the purely theoretic attitude, and either let her knots remain uncut, or have them cut by active faith. To see this, suppose that we have our science of religions constituted as a matter of fact. Suppose that she has assimilated all the necessary historical material and distilled out of it as its essence the same conclusions which I myself a few moments ago pronounced. Suppose that she agrees that religion, wherever it is an active thing, involves a belief in ideal presences, and a belief that in our prayerful communion with them, work is done, and something real comes to pass. She has now to exert her critical activity, and to decide

---

peraments. In the cases which were quoted in Lecture IV, of the mind-cure form of healthy-mindedness, we found abundant examples of regenerative process. The severity of the crisis in this process is a matter of degree. How long one shall continue to drink the consciousness of evil, and when one shall begin to short-circuit and get rid of it, are also matters of amount and degree, so that in many instances it is quite arbitrary whether we class the individual as a once-born or a twice-born subject.

[65] Compare, e.g., the quotation from Renan on p. 748, above.

how far, in the light of other sciences and in that of general philosophy, such beliefs can be considered *true*.

Dogmatically to decide this is an impossible task. Not only are the other sciences and the philosophy still far from being completed, but in their present state we find them full of conflicts. The sciences of nature know nothing of spiritual presences, and on the whole hold no practical commerce whatever with the idealistic conceptions towards which general philosophy inclines. The scientist, so-called, is, during his scientific hours at least, so materialistic that one may well say that on the whole the influence of science goes against the notion that religion should be recognized at all. And this antipathy to religion finds an echo within the very science of religions itself. The cultivator of this science has to become acquainted with so many groveling and horrible superstitions that a presumption easily arises in his mind that any belief that is religious probably is false. In the 'prayerful communion' of savages with such mumbo-jumbos of deities as they acknowledge, it is hard for us to see what genuine spiritual work—even though it were work relative only to their dark savage obligations— can possibly be done.

The consequence is that the conclusions of the science of religions are as likely to be adverse as they are to be favorable to the claim that the essence of religion is true. There is a notion in the air about us that religion is probably only an anachronism, a case of 'survival,' an atavistic relapse into a mode of thought which humanity in its more enlightened examples has outgrown; and this notion our religious anthropologists at present do little to counteract.

This view is so widespread at the present day that I must consider it with some explicitness before I pass to my own conclusions. Let me call it the 'Survival theory,' for brevity's sake.

The pivot round which the religious life, as we have traced it, revolves, is the interest of the individual in his private personal destiny. Religion, in short, is a monumental chapter in the history of human egotism. The gods believed in—whether by crude savages or by men disciplined intellectually—agree with each other in recognizing personal calls. Religious thought is carried on in terms of personality, this being, in the world of religion, the one fundamental fact. Today, quite as much as at any previous age, the religious individual tells you that the divine meets him on the basis of his personal concerns.

Science, on the other hand, has ended by utterly repudiating the personal point of view. She catalogues her elements and records her laws indifferent as to what purpose may be shown forth by them, and constructs her theories quite careless of their bearing on human anxieties and fates. Though the scientist may individually nourish a religion, and be a theist in his irresponsible hours, the days are over when it could be said that for Science herself the heavens declare the glory of God and the firmament showeth his handiwork. Our solar system, with its harmonies, is seen now as but one passing case of a certain sort of moving equilibrium in the heavens, realized by a local accident in an appalling wilderness of worlds where no life can exist. In a span of time which as a cosmic interval will count but as an hour, it will have ceased to be. The Darwinian notion of chance production, and subsequent destruction, speedy or deferred, applies to the largest as well as to the smallest facts. It is impossible, in the present temper of the scientific imagination, to find in the driftings of the cosmic atoms, whether they work on the universal or on the particular scale, any-thing but a kind of aimless weather, doing and undoing, achieving no proper history, and leaving no result. Nature has no one distinguisha-ble ultimate tendency with which it is possible to feel a sympathy. In the vast rhythm of her processes, as the scientific mind now follows them, she appears to cancel herself. The books of natural theology which satisfied the intellects of our grandfathers seem to us quite gro-tesque,[66] representing, as they did, a God who conformed the largest

[66] How was it ever conceivable, we ask, that a man like Christian Wolff, in whose dry-as-dust head all the learning of the early eighteenth century was con-centrated, should have preserved such a baby-like faith in the personal and hu-man character of Nature as to expound her operations as he did in his work on the uses of natural things? This, for example, is the account he gives of the sun and its utility:—

"We see that God has created the sun to keep the changeable conditions on the earth in such an order that living creatures, men and beasts, may inhabit its surface. Since men are the most reasonable of creatures, and able to infer God's invisible being from the contemplation of the world, the sun in so far forth con-tributes to the primary purpose of creation: without it the race of man could not be preserved or continued. . . . The sun makes daylight, not only on our earth, but also on the other planets; and daylight is of the utmost utility to us; for by its means we can commodiously carry on those occupations which in the night-time would either be quite impossible, or at any rate impossible without our going to the expense of artificial light. The beasts of the field can find food by day which they would not be able to find at night. Moreover we owe it to the sunlight that we are able to see everything that is on the earth's surface, not only near by, but also at a distance, and to recognize both near and far things accord-ing to their species, which again is of manifold use to us not only in the business necessary to human life, and when we are traveling, but also for the scientific knowledge of Nature, which knowledge for the most part depends on observa-tions made with the help of sight, and, without the sunshine, would have been impossible. If any one would rightly impress on his mind the great advantages which he derives from the sun, let him imagine himself living through only one month, and see how it would be with all his undertakings, if it were not day but night. He would then be sufficiently convinced out of his own experience, es-pecially if he had much work to carry on in the street or in the fields. . . . From the sun we learn to recognize when it is midday, and by knowing this point of time exactly, we can set our clocks right, on which account astronomy owes much to the sun. . . . By help of the sun one can find the meridian. . . .

things of nature to the paltriest of our private wants. The God whom science recognizes must be a God of universal laws exclusively, a God who does a wholesale, not a retail business. He cannot accommodate

---

But the meridian is the basis of our sun-dials, and generally speaking, we should have no sun-dials if we had no sun." *Vernünftige Gedanken von den Absichten der natürlichen Dinge,* 1782, pp. 74–84.

Or read the account of God's beneficence in the institution of "the great variety throughout the world of men's faces, voices, and handwriting," given in Derham's *Physico-theology,* a book that had much vogue in the eighteenth century. "Had Man's body," says Dr. Derham, "been made according to any of the Atheistical Schemes, or any other Method than that of the infinite Lord of the World, this wise Variety would never have been: but Men's Faces would have been cast in the same, or not a very different Mould, their Organs of Speech would have sounded the same or not so great a Variety of Notes; and the same Structure of Muscles and Nerves would have given the Hand the same Direction in Writing. And in this Case, what Confusion, what Disturbance, what Mischiefs would the world eternally have lain under! No Security could have been to our persons; no Certainty, no Enjoyment of our Possessions; no Justice between Man and Man; no Distinction between Good and Bad, between Friends and Foes, between Father and Child, Husband and Wife, Male or Female; but all would have been turned topsy-turvy, by being exposed to the Malice of the Envious and ill-Natured, to the Fraud and Violence of Knaves and Robbers, to the Forgeries of the crafty Cheat, to the Lusts of the Effeminate and Debauched, and what not! Our Courts of Justice can abundantly testify the dire Effects of Mistaking Men's Faces, of counterfeiting their Hands, and forging Writings. But now as the infinitely wise Creator and Ruler hath ordered the Matter, every man's Face can distinguish him in the Light, and his Voice in the Dark; his Hand-writing can speak for him though absent, and be his Witness, and secure his Contracts in future Generations. A manifest as well as admirable Indication of the divine Superintendence and Management."

A God so careful as to make provision even for the unmistakable signing of bank checks and deeds was a deity truly after the heart of eighteenth century Anglicanism.

I subjoin, omitting the capitals, Derham's *Vindication of God by the Institution of Hills and Valleys,* and Wolff's altogether culinary account of the institution of *Water:*—

"The uses," says Wolff, "which water serves in human life are plain to see and need not be described at length. Water is a universal drink of man and beasts. Even though men have made themselves drinks that are artificial, they could not do this without water. Beer is brewed of water and malt, and it is the water in it which quenches thirst. Wine is prepared from grapes, which could never have grown without the help of water; and the same is true of those drinks which in England and other places they produce from fruit. . . . Therefore since God so planned the world that men and beasts should live upon it and find there everything required for their necessity and convenience, he also made water as one means whereby to make the earth into so excellent a dwelling. And this is all the more manifest when we consider the advantages which we obtain from this same water for the cleaning of our household utensils, of our clothing, and of other matters. . . . When one goes into a grinding-mill one sees that the grindstone must always be kept wet and then one will get a still greater idea of the use of water."

Of the hills and valleys, Derham, after praising their beauty, discourses as

his processes to the convenience of individuals. The bubbles on the foam which coats a stormy sea are floating episodes, made and unmade by the forces of the wind and water. Our private selves are like those bubbles,—epiphenomena, as Clifford, I believe, ingeniously called them; their destinies weigh nothing and determine nothing in the world's irremediable currents of events.

You see how natural it is, from this point of view, to treat religion as a mere survival, for religion does in fact perpetuate the traditions of the most primeval thought. To coerce the spiritual powers, or to square them and get them on our side, was, during enormous tracts of time, the one great object in our dealings with the natural world. For our ancestors, dreams, hallucinations, revelations, and cock-and-bull stories were inextricably mixed with facts. Up to a comparatively recent date such distinctions as those between what has been verified and what is only conjectured, between the impersonal and the personal aspects of existence, were hardly suspected or conceived. Whatever you imagined in a lively manner, whatever you thought fit to be true, you affirmed confidently; and whatever you affirmed, your com-

---

follows: "Some constitutions are indeed of so happy a strength, and so confirmed an health, as to be indifferent to almost any place or temperature of the air. But then others are so weakly and feeble, as not to be able to bear one, but can live comfortably in another place. With some the more subtle and finer air of the hills doth best agree, who are languishing and dying in the feculent and grosser air of great towns, or even the warmer and vaporous air of the valleys and waters. But contrariwise, others languish on the hills, and grow lusty and strong in the warmer air of the valleys.

"So that this opportunity of shifting our abode from the hills to the vales, is an admirable easement, refreshment, and great benefit to the valetudinarian, feeble part of mankind; affording those an easy and comfortable life, who would otherwise live miserably, languish, and pine away.

"To this salutary conformation of the earth we may add another great convenience of the hills, and that is affording commodious places for habitation, serving (as an eminent author wordeth it) as screens to keep off the cold and nipping blasts of the northern and easterly winds, and reflecting the benign and cherishing sunbeams, and so rendering our habitations both more comfortable and more cheerly in winter.

"Lastly, it is to the hills that the fountains owe their rise and the rivers their conveyance, and consequently those vast masses and lofty piles are not, as they are charged, such rude and useless excrescences of our ill-formed globe; but the admirable tools of nature, contrived and ordered by the infinite Creator, to do one of its most useful works. For, was the surface of the earth even and level, and the middle parts of its islands and continents not mountainous and high as now it is, it is most certain there could be no descent for the rivers, no conveyance for the waters; but, instead of gliding along those gentle declivities which the higher lands now afford them quite down to the sea, they would stagnate and perhaps stink, and also drown large tracts of land.

"[Thus] the hills and vales, though to a peevish and weary traveler they may seem incommodious and troublesome, yet are a noble work of the great Creator, and wisely appointed by him for the good of our sublunary world."

rades believed. Truth was what had not yet been contradicted, most things were taken into the mind from the point of view of their human suggestiveness, and the attention confined itself exclusively to the æsthetic and dramatic aspects of events.[67]

[67] Until the seventeenth century this mode of thought prevailed. One need only recall the dramatic treatment even of mechanical questions by Aristotle, as, for example, his explanation of the power of the lever to make a small weight raise a larger one. This is due, according to Aristotle, to the generally miraculous character of the circle and of all circular movement. The circle is both convex and concave; it is made by a fixed point and a moving line, which contradict each other; and whatever moves in a circle moves in opposite directions. Nevertheless, movement in a circle is the most 'natural' movement; and the long arm of the lever, moving, as it does, in the larger circle, has the greater amount of this natural motion, and consequently requires the lesser force. Or recall the explanation by Herodotus of the position of the sun in winter: It moves to the south because of the cold which drives it into the warm parts of the heavens over Libya. Or listen to Saint Augustine's speculations: "Who gave to chaff such power to freeze that it preserves snow buried under it, and such power to warm that it ripens green fruit? Who can explain the strange properties of fire itself, which blackens all that it burns, though itself bright, and which, though of the most beautiful colors, discolors almost all that it touches and feeds upon, and turns blazing fuel into grimy cinders? . . . Then what wonderful properties do we find in charcoal, which is so brittle that a light tap breaks it, and a slight pressure pulverizes it, and yet is so strong that no moisture rots it, nor any time causes it to decay." *City of God,* book xxi. ch. iv.

Such aspects of things as these, their naturalness and unnaturalness, the sympathies and antipathies of their superficial qualities, their eccentricities, their brightness and strength and destructiveness, were inevitably the ways in which they originally fastened our attention.

If you open early medical books, you will find sympathetic magic invoked on every page. Take, for example, the famous vulnerary ointment attributed to Paracelsus. For this there were a variety of receipts, including usually human fat, the fat of either a bull, a wild boar, or a bear; powdered earthworms, the *usnia,* or mossy growth on the weathered skull of a hanged criminal, and other materials equally unpleasant—the whole prepared under the planet Venus if possible, but never under Mars or Saturn. Then, if a splinter of wood, dipped in the patient's blood, or the bloodstained weapon that wounded him, be immersed in this ointment, the wound itself being tightly bound up, the latter infallibly gets well,—I quote now Van Helmont's account,—for the blood on the weapon or splinter, containing in it the spirit of the wounded man, is roused to active excitement by the contact of the ointment, whence there results to it a full commission or power to cure its cousin-german, the blood in the patient's body. This it does by sucking out the dolorous and exotic impression from the wounded part. But to do this it has to implore the aid of the bull's fat, and other portions of the unguent. The reason why bull's fat is so powerful is that the bull at the time of slaughter is full of secret reluctancy and vindictive murmurs, and therefore dies with a higher flame of revenge about him than any other animal. And thus we have made it out, says this author, that the admirable efficacy of the ointment ought to be imputed, not to any auxiliary concurrence of Satan, but simply to the energy of the *posthumous character of Revenge* remaining firmly impressed upon the blood and concreted fat in the unguent. J. B. VAN HELMONT: *A Ternary of Paradoxes,* translated by WALTER CHARLETON, London, 1650.—I much abridge the original in my citations.

How indeed could it be otherwise? The extraordinary value, for explanation and prevision, of those mathematical and mechanical modes of conception which science uses, was a result that could not possibly have been expected in advance. Weight, movement, velocity, direction, position, what thin, pallid, uninteresting ideas! How could the richer animistic aspects of Nature, the peculiarities and oddities that make phenomena picturesquely striking or expressive, fail to have been first singled out and followed by philosophy as the more promising avenue to the knowledge of Nature's life? Well, it is still in these richer animistic and dramatic aspects that religion delights to dwell. It is the terror and beauty of phenomena, the 'promise' of the dawn and of the rainbow, the 'voice' of the thunder, the 'gentleness' of the summer rain, the 'sublimity' of the stars, and not the physical laws which these things follow, by which the religious mind still continues to be most impressed; and just as of yore, the devout man tells you that in the solitude of his room or of the fields he still feels the divine presence, that inflowings of help come in reply to his prayers, and that sacrifices to this unseen reality fill him with security and peace.

Pure anachronism! says the survival-theory;—anachronism for which deanthropomorphization of the imagination is the remedy re-

---

The author goes on to prove by the analogy of many other natural facts that this sympathetic action between things at a distance is the true rationale of the case. "If," he says, "the heart of a horse, slain by a witch, taken out of the yet reeking carcase, be impaled upon an arrow and roasted, immediately the whole witch becomes tormented with the insufferable pains and cruelty of the fire, which could by no means happen unless there preceded a conjunction of the spirit of the witch with the spirit of the horse. In the reeking and yet panting heart, the spirit of the witch is kept captive, and the retreat of it prevented by the arrow transfixed. Similarly hath not many a murdered carcase at the coroner's inquest suffered a fresh hæmorrhage or cruentation at the presence of the assassin?—the blood being, as in a furious fit of anger, enraged and agitated by the impress of revenge conceived against the murderer, at the instant of the soul's compulsive exile from the body. So, if you have dropsy, gout, or jaundice, by including some of your warm blood in the shell and white of an egg, which, exposed to a gentle heat, and mixed with a bait of flesh, you shall give to a hungry dog or hog, the disease shall instantly pass from you into the animal, and leave you entirely. And similarly again, if you burn some of the milk either of a cow or a woman, the gland from which it issued will dry up. A gentleman at Brussels had his nose mowed off in a combat, but the celebrated surgeon Tagliacozzus digged a new nose for him out of the skin of the arm of a porter at Bologna. About thirteen months after his return to his own country, the engrafted nose grew cold, putrefied, and in a few days dropped off, and it was then discovered that the porter had expired, near about the same punctilio of time. There are still at Brussels eye-witnesses of this occurrence," says Van Helmont; and adds, "I pray what is there in this of superstition or of exalted imagination?"

Modern mind-cure literature—the works of Prentice Mulford, for example—is full of sympathetic magic.

quired. The less we mix the private with the cosmic, the more we dwell in universal and impersonal terms, the truer heirs of Science we become.

In spite of the appeal which this impersonality of the scientific attitude makes to a certain magnanimity of temper, I believe it to be shallow, and I can now state my reason in comparatively few words. That reason is that, so long as we deal with the cosmic and the general, we deal only with the symbols of reality, but *as soon as we deal with private and personal phenomena as such, we deal with realities in the completest sense of the term*. I think I can easily make clear what I mean by these words.

The world of our experience consists at all times of two parts, an objective and a subjective part, of which the former may be incalculably more extensive than the latter, and yet the latter can never be omitted or suppressed. The objective part is the sum total of what so ever at any given time we may be thinking of, the subjective part is the inner 'state' in which the thinking comes to pass. What we think of may be enormous,—the cosmic times and spaces, for example,—whereas the inner state may be the most fugitive and paltry activity of mind. Yet the cosmic objects, so far as the experience yields them, are but ideal pictures of something whose existence we do not inwardly possess but only point at outwardly, while the inner state is our very experience itself; its reality and that of our experience are one. A conscious field *plus* its object as felt or thought of *plus* an attitude towards the object *plus* the sense of a self to whom the attitude belongs—such a concrete bit of personal experience may be a small bit, but it is a solid bit as long as it lasts; not hollow, not a mere abstract element of experience, such as the 'object' is when taken all alone. It is a *full* fact, even though it be an insignificant fact; it is of the *kind* to which all realities whatsoever must belong; the motor currents of the world run through the like of it; it is on the line connecting real events with real events. That unsharable feeling which each one of us has of the pinch of his individual destiny as he privately feels it rolling out on fortune's wheel may be disparaged for its egotism, may be sneered at as unscientific, but it is the one thing that fills up the measure of our concrete actuality, and any would-be existent that should lack such a feeling, or its analogue, would be a piece of reality only half made up.[68]

If this be true, it is absurd for science to say that the egotistic elements of experience should be suppressed. The axis of reality runs

[68] Compare Lotze's doctrine that the only meaning we can attach to the notion of a thing as it is 'in itself' is by conceiving it as it is *for* itself; i.e., as a piece of full experience with a private sense of 'pinch' or inner activity of some sort going with it.

solely through the egotistic places,—they are strung upon it like so many beads. To describe the world with all the various feelings of the individual pinch of destiny, all the various spiritual attitudes, left out from the description—they being as describable as anything else— would be something like offering a printed bill of fare as the equivalent for a solid meal. Religion makes no such blunder. The individual's religion may be egotistic, and those private realities which it keeps in touch with may be narrow enough; but at any rate it always remains infinitely less hollow and abstract, as far as it goes, than a science which prides itself on taking no account of anything private at all.

A bill of fare with one real raisin on it instead of the word 'raisin,' with one real egg instead of the word 'egg,' might be an inadequate meal, but it would at least be a commencement of reality. The contention of the survival-theory that we ought to stick to non-personal elements exclusively seems like saying that we ought to be satisfied forever with reading the naked bill of fare. I think, therefore, that however particular questions connected with our individual destinies may be answered, it is only by acknowledging them as genuine questions, and living in the sphere of thought which they open up, that we become profound. But to live thus is to be religious; so I unhesitatingly repudiate the survival-theory of religion, as being founded on an egregious mistake. It does not follow, because our ancestors made so many errors of fact and mixed them with their religion, that we should therefore leave off being religious at all.[69] By being religious we estab-

[69] Even the errors of fact may possibly turn out not to be as wholesale as the scientist assumes. We saw previously how the religious conception of the universe seems to many mind-curers 'verified' from day to day by their experience of fact. 'Experience of fact' is a field with so many things in it that the sectarian scientist, methodically declining, as he does, to recognize such 'facts' as mind-curers and others like them experience, otherwise than by such rude heads of classification as 'bosh,' 'rot,' 'folly,' certainly leaves out a mass of raw fact which, save for the industrious interest of the religious in the more personal aspects of reality, would never have succeeded in getting itself recorded at all. We know this to be true already in certain cases; it may, therefore, be true in others as well. Miraculous healings have always been part of the supernaturalist stock in trade, and have always been dismissed by the scientist as figments of the imagination. But the scientist's tardy education in the facts of hypnotism has recently given him an apperceiving mass for phenomena of this order, and he consequently now allows that the healings may exist, provided you expressly call them effects of 'suggestion.' Even the stigmata of the cross on Saint Francis's hands and feet may on these terms not be a fable. Similarly, the time-honored phenomenon of diabolical possession is on the point of being admitted by the scientist as a fact, now that he has the name of 'hystero-demonopathy' by which to apperceive it. No one can foresee just how far this legitimation of occultist phenomena under newly found scientist titles may proceed—even 'prophecy,' even 'levitation,' might creep into the pale.

Thus the divorce between scientist facts and religious facts may not necessarily be as eternal as it at first sight seems, nor the personalism and romanti-

lish ourselves in possession of ultimate reality at the only points at which reality is given us to guard. Our responsible concern is with our private destiny, after all.

You see now why I have been so individualistic throughout these lectures, and why I have seemed so bent on rehabilitating the element of feeling in religion and subordinating its intellectual part. Individuality is founded in feeling; and the recesses of feeling, the darker, blinder strata of character, are the only places in the world in which we catch real fact in the making, and directly perceive how events happen, and how work is actually done.[70] Compared with this world of living individualized feelings, the world of generalized objects which the intellect contemplates is without solidity or life. As in stereoscopic or kinetoscopic pictures seen outside the instrument, the third dimension, the movement, the vital element, are not there. We get a beautiful picture of an express train supposed to be moving, but where in the picture, as I have heard a friend say, is the energy or the fifty miles an hour? [71]

---

cism of the world, as they appeared to primitive thinking, be matters so irrevocably outgrown. The final human opinion may, in short, in some manner now impossible to foresee, revert to the more personal style, just as any path of progress may follow a spiral rather than a straight line. If this were so, the rigorously impersonal view of science might one day appear as having been a temporarily useful eccentricity rather than the definitively triumphant position which the sectarian scientist at present so confidently announces it to be.

[70] Hume's criticism has banished causation from the world of physical objects, and 'Science' is absolutely satisfied to define cause in terms of concomitant change—read Mach, Pearson, Ostwald. The 'original' of the notion of causation is in our inner personal experience, and only there can causes in the old-fashioned sense be directly observed and described.

[71] When I read in a religious paper words like these: "Perhaps the best thing we can say of God is that he is *the Inevitable Inference*," I recognize the tendency to let religion evaporate in intellectual terms. Would martyrs have sung in the flames for a mere inference, however inevitable it might be? Original religious men, like Saint Francis, Luther, Behmen, have usually been enemies of the intellect's pretension to meddle with religious things. Yet the intellect, everywhere invasive, shows everywhere its shallowing effect. See how the ancient spirit of Methodism evaporates under those wonderfully able rationalistic booklets (which every one should read) of a philosopher like Professor Bowne (The Christian Revelation, The Christian Life, The Atonement: Cincinnati and New York, 1898, 1899, 1900). See the positively expulsive purpose of philosophy properly so called:—

"Religion," writes M. Vacherot (*La Religion,* Paris, 1869, pp. 313, 436, et passim), "answers to a transient state or condition, not to a permanent determination of human nature, being merely an expression of that stage of the human mind which is dominated by the imagination. . . . Christianity has but a single possible final heir to its estate, and that is scientific philosophy."

In a still more radical vein, Professor Ribot (*Psychologie des Sentiments,* p. 310) describes the evaporation of religion. He sums it up in a single formula —the ever-growing predominance of the rational intellectual element, with the

Let us agree, then, that Religion, occupying herself with personal destinies and keeping thus in contact with the only absolute realities which we know, must necessarily play an eternal part in human history. The next thing to decide is what she reveals about those destinies, or whether indeed she reveals anything distinct enough to be considered a general message to mankind. We have done as you see, with our preliminaries, and our final summing up can now begin.

I am well aware that after all the palpitating documents which I have quoted, and all the perspectives of emotion-inspiring institution and belief that my previous lectures have opened, the dry analysis to which I now advance may appear to many of you like an anti-climax, a tapering-off and flattening out of the subject, instead of a crescendo of interest and result. I said awhile ago that the religious attitude of Protestants appears poverty-stricken to the Catholic imagination. Still more poverty-stricken, I fear, may my final summing up of the subject appear at first to some of you. On which account I pray you now to bear this point in mind, that in the present part of it I am expressly trying to reduce religion to its lowest admissible terms, to that minimum, free from individualistic excrescences, which all religions contain as their nucleus, and on which it may be hoped that all religious persons may agree. That established, we should have a result which might be small, but would at least be solid; and on it and round it the ruddier additional beliefs on which the different individuals make their venture might be grafted, and flourish as richly as you please. I shall add my own over-belief (which will be, I confess, of a somewhat pallid kind, as befits a critical philosopher), and you will, I hope, also add your over-beliefs, and we shall soon be in the varied world of concrete religious constructions once more. For the moment, let me dryly pursue the analytic part of the task.

Both thought and feeling are determinants of conduct, and the same conduct may be determined either by feeling or by thought. When we survey the whole field of religion, we find a great variety in

gradual fading out of the emotional element, this latter tending to enter into the group of purely intellectual sentiments. "Of religious sentiment properly so called, nothing survives at last save a vague respect for the unknowable *x* which is a last relic of the fear, and a certain attraction towards the ideal, which is a relic of the love, that characterized the earlier periods of religious growth. To state this more simply, *religion tends to turn into religious philosophy.*—These are psychologically entirely different things, the one being a theoretic construction of ratiocination, whereas the other is the living work of a group of persons, or of a great inspired leader, calling into play the entire thinking and feeling organism of man."

I find the same failure to recognize that the stronghold of religion lies in individuality in attempts like those of Professor Baldwin (*Mental Development, Social and Ethical Interpretations,* ch. x.) and Mr. H. R. Marshall (*Instinct and Reason,* chaps. viii. to xii.) to make it a purely 'conservative social force.'

the thoughts that have prevailed there; but the feelings on the one hand and the conduct on the other are almost always the same, for Stoic, Christian, and Buddhist saints are practically indistinguishable in their lives. The theories which Religion generates, being thus variable, are secondary; and if you wish to grasp her essence, you must look to the feelings and the conduct as being the more constant elements. It is between these two elements that the short circuit exists on which she carries on her principle business while the ideas and symbols and other institutions form loop-lines which may be perfections and improvements, and may even some day all be united into one harmonious system, but which are not to be regarded as organs with an indispensable function, necessary at all times for religious life to go on. This seems to me the first conclusion which we are entitled to draw from the phenomena we have passed in review.

The next step is to characterize the feelings. To what psychological order do they belong?

The resultant outcome of them is in any case what Kant calls a 'sthenic' affection, an excitement of the cheerful, expansive, 'dynamogenic' order which, like any tonic, freshens our vital powers. In almost every lecture, but especially in the lectures on Conversion and on Saintliness, we have seen how this emotion overcomes temperamental melancholy and imparts endurance to the Subject, or a zest, or a meaning, or an enchantment and glory to the common objects of life.[72] The name of 'faith-state,' by which Professor Leuba designates it, is a good one.[73] It is a biological as well as a psychological condition, and Tolstoy is absolutely accurate in classing faith among the forces *by which men live*.[74] The total absence of it, anhedonia,[75] means collapse.

The faith-state may hold a very minimum of intellectual content. We saw examples of this in those sudden raptures of the divine presence, or in such mystical seizures as Dr. Bucke described.[76] It may be a mere vague enthusiasm, half spiritual, half vital, a courage, and a feeling that great and wondrous things are in the air.[77]

[72] Cf. V.R.E., *Lectures IX–XV* [J. J. McD.].
[73] *American Journal of Psychology*, vii. 345.
[74] Cf. V.R.E., *Lectures VIII* [J. J. McD.].
[75] Cf. V.R.E., *Lectures VI–VII* [J. J. McD.].
[76] Cf. V.R.E., *Lectures XVI–XVII* [J. J. McD.].
[77] Example: Henri Perreyve writes to Gratry: "I do not know how to deal with the happiness which you aroused in me this morning. It overwhelms me; I want to *do* something, yet I can do nothing and am fit for nothing. . . . I would fain do *great things*." Again, after an inspiring interview, he writes: "I went homewards, intoxicated with joy, hope, and strength. I wanted to feed upon my happiness in solitude, far from all men. It was late; but, unheeding that, I took a mountain path and went on like a madman, looking at the heavens, regardless of earth. Suddenly an instinct made me draw hastily back—I was on the very edge of a precipice, one step more and I must have fallen. I took

When, however, a positive intellectual content is associated with a faith-state, it gets invincibly stamped in upon belief,[78] and this explains the passionate loyalty of religious persons everywhere to the minutest details of their so widely differing creeds. Taking creeds and faith-state together, as forming 'religions,' and treating these as purely subjective phenomena, without regard to the question of their 'truth,' we are obliged, on account of their extraordinary influence upon action and endurance, to class them amongst the most important biological functions of mankind. Their stimulant and anæsthetic effect is so great that Professor Leuba, in a recent article,[79] goes so far as to say that so long as men can *use* their God, they care very little who he is, or even whether he is at all. "The truth of the matter can be put," says Leuba, "in this way: *God is not known, he is not understood; he is used*—sometimes as meat-purveyor, sometimes as moral support, sometimes as friend, sometimes as an object of love. If he proves himself useful, the religious consciousness asks for no more than that. Does God really exist? How does he exist? What is he? are so many irrelevant questions. Not God, but life, more life, a larger, richer, more satisfying life, is, in the last analysis, the end of religion. The love of life, at any and every level of development, is the religious impulse." [80]

---

fright and gave up my nocturnal promenade." A. GRATRY: *Henri Perreyve*, London, 1872, pp. 92, 89.

This primacy, in the faith-state, of vague expansive impulse over direction is well expressed in Walt Whitman's lines (*Leaves of Grass*, 1872, p. 190):—

> O to confront night, storms, hunger, ridicule, accidents, rebuffs, as the trees and animals do. . . .
> Dear Camerado! I confess I have urged you onward with me, and still urge you, without the least idea what is our destination,
> Or whether we shall be victorious, or utterly quell'd and defeated.

This readiness for great things, and this sense that the world by its importance, wonderfulness, etc., is apt for their production, would seem to be the undifferentiated germ of all the higher faiths. Trust in our own dreams of ambition, or in our country's expansive destinies, and faith in the providence of God, all have their source in that onrush of our sanguine impulses, and in that sense of the exceedingness of the possible over the real.

[78] Compare LEUBA: Loc. cit., pp. 346–349.

[79] The Contents of Religious Consciousness, in *The Monist*, xi. 536, July, 1901.

[80] Loc. cit., pp. 571, 572, abridged. See, also, this writer's extraordinarily true criticism of the notion that religion primarily seeks to solve the intellectual mystery of the world. Compare what W. BENDER says (in his *Wesen der Religion*, Bonn, 1888, pp. 85, 38): "Not the question about God, and not the inquiry into the origin and purpose of the world is religion, but the question about Man. All religious views of life are anthropocentric." "Religion is that activity of the human impulse towards self-preservation by means of which Man seeks to carry

At this purely subjective rating, therefore, Religion must be considered vindicated in a certain way from the attacks of her critics. It would seem that she cannot be a mere anachronism and survival, but must exert a permanent function, whether she be with or without intellectual content, and whether, if she have any, it be true or false.

We must next pass beyond the point of view of merely subjective utility, and make inquiry into the intellectual content itself.

First, is there, under all the discrepancies of the creeds, a common nucleus to which they bear their testimony unanimously?

And second, ought we to consider the testimony true?

I will take up the first question first, and answer it immediately in the affirmative. The warring gods and formulas of the various religions do indeed cancel each other, but there is a certain uniform deliverance in which religions all appear to meet. It consists of two parts:—

1. An uneasiness; and
2. Its solution.

1. The uneasiness, reduced to its simplest terms, is a sense that there is *something wrong about us* as we naturally stand.

2. The solution is a sense that *we are saved from the wrongness* by making proper connection with the higher powers.

In those more developed minds which alone we are studying, the wrongness takes a moral character, and the salvation takes a mystical tinge. I think we shall keep well within the limits of what is common to all such minds if we formulate the essence of their religious experience in terms like these:—

The individual, so far as he suffers from his wrongness and criticises it, is to that extent consciously beyond it, and in at least possible touch with something higher, if anything higher exist. Along with the wrong part there is thus a better part of him, even though it may be but a most helpless germ. With which part he should identify his real being is by no means obvious at this stage; but when stage 2 (the stage of solution or salvation) arrives,[81] the man identifies his real being with the germinal higher part of himself; and does so in the following way. *He becomes conscious that this higher part is conterminous and continuous with a* MORE *of the same quality, which is operative in the universe outside of him, and which he can keep in working touch*

---

his essential vital purposes through against the adverse pressure of the world by raising himself freely towards the world's ordering and governing powers when the limits of his own strength are reached." The whole book is little more than a development of these words.

[81] Remember that for some men it arrives suddenly, for others gradually, whilst others again practically enjoy it all their life.

with, and in a fashion get on board of and save himself when all his lower being has gone to pieces in the wreck.

It seems to me that all the phenomena are accurately describable in these very simple general terms.[82] They allow for the divided self and the struggle; they involve the change of personal centre and the surrender of the lower self; they express the appearance of exteriority of the helping power and yet account for our sense of union with it;[83] and they fully justify our feelings of security and joy. There is probably no autobiographic document, among all those which I have quoted, to which the description will not well apply. One need only add such specific details as will adapt it to various theologies and various personal temperaments, and one will then have the various experiences reconstructed in their individual forms.

So far, however, as this analysis goes, the experiences are only psychological phenomena. They possess, it is true, enormous biological worth. Spiritual strength really increases in the subject when he has them, a new life opens for him, and they seem to him a place of conflux where the forces of two universes meet; and yet this may be nothing but his subjective way of feeling things, a mood of his own fancy, in spite of the effects produced. I now turn to my second question: What is the objective 'truth' of their content? [84]

The part of the content concerning which the question of truth most pertinently arises is that 'MORE of the same quality' with which our own higher self appears in the experience to come into harmonious working relation. Is such a 'more' merely our own notion, or does it really exist? If so, in what shape does it exist? Does it act, as well as exist? And in what form should we conceive of that 'union' with it of which religious geniuses are so convinced?

It is in answering these questions that the various theologies perform their theoretic work, and that their divergencies most come to light. They all agree that the 'more' really exists; though some of them hold it to exist in the shape of a personal god or gods, while others are satisfied to conceive it as a stream of ideal tendency embedded in the eternal structure of the world. They all agree, moreover, that it acts as

---

[82] The practical difficulties are: 1, to 'realize the reality' of one's higher part; 2, to identify one's self with it exclusively; and 3, to identify it with all the rest of ideal being.

[83] "When mystical activity is at its height, we find consciousness possessed by the sense of a being at once *excessive* and *identical* with the self: great enough to be God; interior enough to be *me*. The 'objectivity' of it ought in that case to be called *excessivity,* rather, or exceedingness." RÉCÉJAC: *Essai sur les fondements de la conscience mystique,* 1897, p. 46.

[84] The word 'truth' is here taken to mean something additional to bare value for life, although the natural propensity of man is to believe that whatever has great value for life is thereby certified as true.

well as exists, and that something really is effected for the better when you throw your life into its hands. It is when they treat of the experience of 'union' with it that their speculative differences appear most clearly. Over this point pantheism and theism, nature⁺ and second birth, works and grace and karma, immortality and reincarnation, rationalism and mysticism, carry on inveterate disputes.

At the end of my lecture on Philosophy [V.R.E., *Lecture* XVIII], I held out the notion that an impartial science of religions might sift out from the midst of their discrepancies a common body of doctrine which she might also formulate in terms to which physical science need not object. This, I said, she might adopt as her own reconciling hypothesis, and recommend it for general belief. I also said that in my last lecture I should have to try my own hand at framing such an hypothesis.

The time has now come for this attempt. Who says 'hypothesis' renounces the ambition to be coercive in his arguments. The most I can do is, accordingly, to offer something that may fit the facts so easily that your scientific logic will find no plausible pretext for vetoing your impulse to welcome it as true.

The 'more,' as we called it, and the meaning of our 'union' with it, form the nucleus of our inquiry. Into what definite description can these words be translated, and for what definite facts do they stand? It would never do for us to place ourselves offhand at the position of a particular theology, the Christian theology, for example, and proceed immediately to define the 'more' as Jehovah, and the 'union' as his imputation to us of the righteousness of Christ. That would be unfair to other religions, and, from our present standpoint at least, would be an over-belief.

We must begin by using less particularized terms; and, since one of the duties of the science of religions is to keep religion in connection with the rest of science, we shall do well to seek first of all a way of describing the 'more,' which psychologists may also recognize as real. The *subconscious self* is nowadays a well-accredited psychological entity; and I believe that in it we have exactly the mediating term required. Apart from all religious considerations, there is actually and literally more life in our total soul than we are at any time aware of. The exploration of the transmarginal field has hardly yet been seriously undertaken, but what Mr. Myers said in 1892 in his essay on the Subliminal Consciousness[85] is as true as when it was first written:

---

[85] *Proceedings of the Society for Psychical Research,* vol. vii. p. 305. For a full statement of Mr. Myers's views, I may refer to his posthumous work, 'Human Personality in the Light of Recent Research,' which is already announced by Messrs. Longmans, Green & Co. as being in press. Mr. Myers for the first time proposed as a general psychological problem the exploration of the sub-

"Each of us is in reality an abiding psychical entity far more extensive than he knows—an individuality which can never express itself completely through any corporeal manifestation. The Self manifests through the organism; but there is always some part of the Self unmanifested; and always, as it seems, some power of organic expression in abeyance or reserve." Much of the content of this larger background against which our conscious being stands out in relief is insignificant. Imperfect memories, silly jingles, inhibitive timidities, 'dissolutive' phenomena of various sorts, as Myers calls them, enter into it for a large part. But in it many of the performances of genius seem also to have their origin; and in our study of conversion, of mystical experiences, and of prayer, we have seen how striking a part invasions from this region play in the religious life.

Let me then propose, as an hypothesis, that whatever it may be on its *farther* side, the 'more' with which in religious experience we feel ourselves connected is on its *hither* side the subconscious continuation of our conscious life. Starting thus with a recognized psychological fact as our basis, we seem to preserve a contact with 'science' which the ordinary theologian lacks. At the same time the theologian's contention that the religious man is moved by an external power is vindicated, for it is one of the peculiarities of invasions from the subconscious region to take on objective appearances, and to suggest to the Subject an external control. In the religious life the control is felt as 'higher'; but since on our hypothesis it is primarily the higher faculties of our own hidden mind which are controlling, the sense of union with the power beyond us is a sense of something, not merely apparently, but literally true.

This doorway into the subject seems to me the best one for a science of religions, for it mediates between a number of different points of view. Yet it is only a doorway, and difficulties present themselves as soon as we step through it, and ask how far our transmarginal consciousness carries us if we follow it on its remoter side. Here the over-beliefs begin: here mysticism and the conversion-rapture and Vedantism and transcendental idealism bring in their monistic interpretations[86] and tell us that the finite self rejoins the absolute self, for it was always one with God and identical with the soul of the world.[87]

liminal region of consciousness throughout its whole extent, and made the first methodical steps in its topography by treating as a natural series a mass of subliminal facts hitherto considered only as curious isolated facts, and subjecting them to a systematized nomenclature. How important this exploration will prove, future work upon the path which Myers has opened can alone show. Compare my paper: 'Frederic Myers's Services to Psychology,' in the said *Proceedings*, part xlii., May, 1901.

[86] Cf. V.R.E., *Lectures XVI–XVII* [J. J. McD.].

[87] One more expression of this belief, to increase the reader's familiarity with the notion of it:—

Here the prophets of all the different religions come with their visions, voices, raptures, and other openings, supposed by each to authenticate his own peculiar faith.

Those of us who are not personally favored with such specific revelations must stand outside of them altogether and, for the present at least, decide that, since they corroborate incompatible theological doctrines, they neutralize one another and leave no fixed result. If we follow any one of them, or if we follow philosophical theory and embrace monistic pantheism on non-mystical grounds, we do so in the exercise of our individual freedom, and build out our religion in the way most congruous with our personal susceptibilities. Among these susceptibilities intellectual ones play a decisive part. Although the religious question is primarily a question of life, of living or not living in the higher union which opens itself to us as a gift, yet the spiritual excitement in which the gift appears a real one will often fail to be aroused in an individual until certain particular intellectual beliefs or ideas which, as we say, come home to him, are touched.[88] These ideas

---

"If this room is full of darkness for thousands of years, and you come in and begin to weep and wail, 'Oh, the darkness,' will the darkness vanish? Bring the light in, strike a match, and light comes in a moment. So what good will it do you to think all your lives, 'Oh, I have done evil, I have made many mistakes'? It requires no ghost to tell us that. Bring in the light, and the evil goes in a moment. Strengthen the real nature, build up yourselves, the effulgent, the resplendent, the ever pure, call that up in every one whom you see. I wish that every one of us had come to such a state that even when we see the vilest of human beings we can see the God within, and instead of condemning, say, 'Rise, thou effulgent One, rise thou who art always pure, rise thou birthless and deathless, rise almighty, and manifest your nature.' . . . This is the highest prayer that the Advaita teaches. This is the one prayer: remembering our nature." . . . "Why does man go out to look for a God? . . . It is your own heart beating, and you did not know, you were mistaking it for something external. He, nearest of the near, my own self, the reality of my own life, my body and my soul.—I am Thee and Thou art Me. That is your own nature. Assert it, manifest it. Not to become pure, you are pure already. You are not to be perfect, you are that already. Every good thought which you think or act upon is simply tearing the veil, as it were, and the purity, the Infinity, the God behind, manifests itself—the eternal Subject of everything, the eternal Witness in this universe, your own Self. Knowledge is, as it were, a lower step, a degradation. We are It already; how to know It?" SWAMI VIVEKANANDA: *Addresses, No. XII., Practical Vedanta*, part iv. pp. 172, 174, London, 1897; and *Lectures, The Real and the Apparent Man*, p. 24, abridged.

[88] For instance, here is a case where a person exposed from her birth to Christian ideas had to wait till they came to her clad in spiritistic formulas before the saving experience set in:—

"For myself I can say that spiritualism has saved me. It was revealed to me at a critical moment of my life, and without it I don't know what I should have done. It has taught me to detach myself from worldly things and to place my hope in things to come. Through it I have learned to see in all men, even in those most criminal, even in those from whom I have most suffered, undevel-

will thus be essential to that individual's religion;—which is as much as to say that over-beliefs in various directions are absolutely indispensable, and that we should treat them with tenderness and tolerance so long as they are not intolerant themselves. As I have elsewhere written, the most interesting and valuable things about a man are usually his over-beliefs.

Disregarding the over-beliefs, and confining ourselves to what is common and generic, we have in *the fact that the conscious person is continuous with a wider self through which saving experiences come,*[89] a positive content of religious experience which, it seems to me, *is literally and objectively true as far as it goes.* If I now proceed to state my own hypothesis about the farther limits of this extension of our personality, I shall be offering my own over-belief—though I know it will appear a sorry under-belief to some of you—for which I can only bespeak the same indulgence which in a converse case I should accord to yours.

The further limits of our being plunge, it seems to me, into an altogether other dimension of existence from the sensible and merely 'understandable' world. Name it the mystical region, or the supernatural region, whichever you choose. So far as our ideal impulses originate in this region (and most of them do originate in it, for we find them possessing us in a way for which we cannot articulately account), we belong to it in a more intimate sense than that in which we belong to the visible world, for we belong in the most intimate sense wherever our ideals belong. Yet the unseen region in question is not merely ideal, for it produces effects in this world. When we commune with it, work is actually done upon our finite personality, for we are turned into new men, and consequences in the way of conduct follow in the natural world upon our regenerative change.[90] But that which

---

oped brothers to whom I owed assistance, love, and forgiveness. I have learned that I must lose my temper over nothing, despise no one, and pray for all. Most of all I have learned to pray! And although I have still much to learn in this domain, prayer ever brings me more strength, consolation, and comfort. I feel more than ever that I have only made a few steps on the long road of progress; but I look at its length without dismay, for I have confidence that the day will come when all my efforts shall be rewarded. So Spiritualism has a great place in my life, indeed it holds the first place there." Flournoy Collection.

[89] "The influence of the Holy Spirit, exquisitely called the Comforter, is a matter of actual experience, as solid a reality as that of electro-magnetism." W. C. BROWNELL, *Scribner's Magazine,* vol. xxx. p. 112.

[90] That the transaction of opening ourselves, otherwise called prayer, is a perfectly definite one for certain persons, appears abundantly in the preceding lectures. I append another concrete example to reinforce the impression on the reader's mind:—

"Man can learn to transcend these limitations [of finite thought] and draw

produces effects within another reality must be termed a reality itself, so I feel as if we had no philosophic excuse for calling the unseen or mystical world unreal.

God is the natural appellation, for us Christians at least, for the supreme reality, so I will call this higher part of the universe by the name of God.[91] We and God have business with each other; and in opening ourselves to his influence our deepest destiny is fulfilled. The universe, at those parts of it which our personal being constitutes, takes a turn genuinely for the worse or for the better in proportion as each one of us fulfills or evades God's demands. As far as this goes I probably have you with me, for I only translate into schematic language what I may call the instinctive belief of mankind: God is real since he produces real effects.

The real effects in question, so far as I have as yet admitted them, are exerted on the personal centres of energy of the various subjects, but the spontaneous faith of most of the subjects is that they embrace a wider sphere than this. Most religious men believe (or 'know,' if they be mystical) that not only they themselves, but the whole universe of beings to whom the God is present, are secure in his parental hands. There is a sense, a dimension, they are sure, in which we are *all* saved, in spite of the gates of hell and all adverse terrestrial appearances. God's existence is the guarantee of an ideal order that shall be permanently preserved. This world may indeed, as science assures us, some day burn up or freeze; but if it is part of his order, the old ideals are sure to be brought elsewhere to fruition, so that where God is, tragedy is only provisional and partial, and shipwreck and dissolution are not the absolutely final things. Only when this farther step of faith concerning God is taken, and remote objective consequences are predicted, does religion, as it seems to me, get wholly free from the

---

power and wisdom at will. . . . The divine presence is known through experience. The turning to a higher plane is a distinct act of consciousness. It is not a vague, twilight or semi-conscious experience. It is not an ecstasy; it is not a trance. It is not super-consciousness in the Vedantic sense. It is not due to self-hypnotization. It is a perfectly calm, sane, sound, rational, common-sense shifting of consciousness from the phenomena of sense-perception to the phenomena of seership, from the thought of self to a distinctively higher realm. . . . For example, if the lower self be nervous, anxious, tense, one can in a few moments compel it to be calm. This is not done by a word simply. Again I say, it is not hypnotism. It is by the exercise of power. One feels the spirit of peace as definitely as heat is perceived on a hot summer day. The power can be as surely used as the sun's rays can be focused and made to do work, to set fire to wood." *The Higher Law,* vol. iv. pp. 4, 6, Boston, August, 1901.

[91] Transcendentalists are fond of the term 'Over-soul,' but as a rule they use it in an intellectualist sense, as meaning only a medium of communion. 'God' is a causal agent as well as a medium of communion, and that is the aspect which I wish to emphasize.

first immediate subjective experience, and bring a *real hypothesis* into play. A good hypothesis in science must have other properties than those of the phenomenon it is immediately invoked to explain, other-wise it is not prolific enough. God, meaning only what enters into the religious man's experience of union, falls short of being an hypothesis of this more useful order. He needs to enter into wider cosmic rela-tions in order to justify the subject's absolute confidence and peace.

That the God with whom, starting from the hither side of our own extra-marginal self, we come at its remoter margin into commerce should be the absolute world-ruler, is of course a very considerable over-belief. Over-belief as it is, though, it is an article of almost every one's religion. Most of us pretend in some way to prop it upon our philosophy, but the philosophy itself is really propped upon this faith. What is this but to say that Religion, in her fullest exercise of func-tion, is not a mere illumination of facts already elsewhere given, not a mere passion, like love, which views things in a rosier light. It is in-deed that, as we have seen abundantly. But it is something more, namely, a postulator of new *facts* as well. The world interpreted reli-giously is not the materialistic world over again, with an altered ex-pression; it must have, over and above the altered expression, *a natural constitution* different at some point from that which a materialistic world would have. It must be such that different events can be ex-pected in it, different conduct must be required.

This thoroughly 'pragmatic' view of religion has usually been taken as a matter of course by common men. They have interpolated divine miracles into the field of nature, they have built a heaven out beyond the grave. It is only transcendentalist metaphysicians who think that, without adding any concrete details to Nature, or subtract-ing any, but by simply calling it the expression of absolute spirit, you make it more divine just as it stands. I believe the pragmatic way of taking religion to be the deeper way. It gives it body as well as soul, it makes it claim, as everything real must claim, some characteristic realm of fact as its very own. What the more characteristically divine facts are, apart from the actual inflow of energy in the faith-state and the prayer-state, I know not. But the over-belief on which I am ready to make my personal venture is that they exist. The whole drift of my education goes to persuade me that the world of our present con-sciousness is only one out of many worlds of consciousness that exist, and that those other worlds must contain experiences which have a meaning for our life also; and that although in the main their ex-periences and those of this world keep discrete, yet the two become continuous at certain points, and higher energies filter in. By being faithful in my poor measure to this over-belief, I seem to myself to keep more sane and true. I *can,* of course, put myself into the sectarian scientist's attitude, and imagine vividly that the world of sensations and of scientific laws and objects may be all. But whenever I do this, I hear that inward monitor of which W. K. Clifford once wrote, whispering the word 'bosh!' Humbug is humbug, even though it bear the scientific name, and the total expression of human experience, as I view it objectively, invincibly urges me beyond the narrow 'scientific' bounds. Assuredly, the real world is of a different temperament,—more intricately built than physical science allows. So my objective and my subjective conscience both hold me to the over-belief which I express. Who knows whether the faithfulness of individuals here below to their own poor over-beliefs may not actually help God in turn to be more effectively faithful to his own greater tasks?

POSTSCRIPT [to *The Varieties of Religious Experience*]*

In writing my concluding lecture I had to aim so much at simplification that I fear that my general philosophic position received so scant a statement as hardly to be intelligible to some of my readers. I therefore add this epilogue, which must also be so brief as possibly to remedy but little the defect. In a later work I may be enabled to state my position more amply and consequently more clearly.

Originality cannot be expected in a field like this, where all the attitudes and tempers that are possible have been exhibited in literature long ago, and where any new writer can immediately be classed under a familiar head. If one should make a division of all thinkers into naturalists and supernaturalists, I should undoubtedly have to go, along with most philosophers, into the supernaturalist branch. But there is a crasser and a more refined supernaturalism, and it is to the refined division that most philosophers at the present day belong. If not regular transcendental idealists, they at least obey the Kantian direction enough to bar out ideal entities from interfering causally in the course of phenomenal events. Refined supernaturalism is universalistic supernaturalism; for the 'crasser' variety 'piecemeal' supernaturalism would perhaps be the better name. It went with that older theology which to-day is supposed to reign only among uneducated people, or to be found among the few belated professors of the dualisms which Kant is thought to have displaced. It admits miracles and

* From: V.R.E., 520–527.

providential leadings, and finds no intellectual difficulty in mixing the ideal and the real worlds together by interpolating influences from the ideal region among the forces that causally determine the real world's details. In this the refined supernaturalists think that it muddles disparate dimensions of existence. For them the world of the ideal has no efficient causality, and never bursts into the world of phenomena at particular points. The ideal world, for them, is not a world of facts, but only of the meaning of facts; it is a point of view for judging facts. It appertains to a different '-ology,' and inhabits a different dimension of being altogether from that in which existential propositions obtain. It cannot get down upon the flat level of experience and interpolate itself piecemeal between distinct portions of nature, as those who believe, for example, in divine aid coming in response to prayer, are bound to think it must.

Notwithstanding my own inability to accept either popular Christianity or scholastic theism, I suppose that my belief that in communion with the Ideal new force comes into the world, and new departures are made here below, subjects me to being classed among the supernaturalists of the piecemeal or crasser type. Universalistic supernaturalism surrenders, it seems to me, too easily to naturalism. It takes the facts of physical science at their face-value, and leaves the laws of life just as naturalism finds them, with no hope of remedy, in case their fruits are bad. It confines itself to sentiments about life as a whole, sentiments which may be admiring and adoring, but which need not be so, as the existence of systematic pessimism proves. In this universalistic way of taking the ideal world, the essence of practical religion seems to me to evaporate. Both instinctively and for logical reasons, I find it hard to believe that principles can exist which make no difference in facts.[92] But all facts are particular facts, and the whole interest of the question of God's existence seems to me to lie in the consequences for particulars which that existence may be expected to entail. That no concrete particular of experience should alter its complexion in consequence of a God being there seems to me an incredible proposition,

[92] Transcendental idealism, of course, insists that its ideal world makes *this* difference, that facts *exist*. We owe it to the Absolute that we have a world of fact at all. 'A world' of fact!—that exactly is the trouble. An entire world is the smallest unit with which the Absolute can work, whereas to our finite minds work for the better ought to be done within this world, setting in at single points. Our difficulties and our ideals are all piecemeal affairs, but the Absolute can do no piecework for us; so that all the interests which our poor souls compass raise their heads too late. We should have spoken earlier, prayed for another world absolutely, before this world was born. It is strange, I have heard a friend say, to see this blind corner into which Christian thought has worked itself at last, with its God who can raise no particular weight whatever, who can help us with no private burden, and who is on the side of our enemies as much as he is on our own. Odd evolution from the God of David's psalms!

and yet it is the thesis to which (implicitly at any rate) refined super-naturalism seems to cling. It is only with experience *en bloc,* it says, that the Absolute maintains relations. It condescends to no transactions of detail.

I am ignorant of Buddhism and speak under correction, and merely in order the better to describe my general point of view; but as I apprehend the Buddhistic doctrine of Karma, I agree in principle with that. All supernaturalists admit that facts are under the judgment of higher law; but for Buddhism as I interpret it, and for religion generally so far as it remains unweakened by transcendentalistic metaphysics, the word 'judgment' here means no such bare academic verdict or platonic appreciation as it means in Vedantic or modern absolutist systems; it carries, on the contrary, *execution* with it, is *in rebus* as well as *post rem,* and operates 'causally' as partial factor in the total fact. The universe becomes a gnosticism[93] pure and simple on any other terms. But this view that judgment and execution go together is that of the crasser supernaturalist way of thinking, so the present volume must on the whole be classed with the other expressions of that creed.

I state the matter thus bluntly, because the current of thought in academic circles runs against me, and I feel like a man who must set his back against an open door quickly if he does not wish to see it closed and locked. In spite of its being so shocking to the reigning intellectual tastes, I believe that a candid consideration of piecemeal supernaturalism and a complete discussion of all its metaphysical bearings will show it to be the hypothesis by which the largest number of legitimate requirements are met. That of course would be a program for other books than this; what I now say sufficiently indicates to the philosophic reader the place where I belong.

If asked just where the differences in fact which are due to God's existence come in, I should have to say that in general I have no hypothesis to offer beyond what the phenomenon of 'prayerful communion,' especially when certain kinds of incursion from the subconscious region take part in it, immediately suggests. The appearance is that in this phenomenon something ideal, which in one sense is part of ourselves and in another sense is not ourselves, actually exerts in influence, raises our centre of personal energy, and produces regenerative effects unattainable in other ways. If, then, there be a wider world of being than that of our every-day consciousness, if in it there be forces whose effects on us are intermittent, if one facilitating condition of the effects be the openness of the 'subliminal' door, we have the elements of a theory to which the phenomena of religious life lend

[93] See my *Will to Believe and other Essays* in *Popular Philosophy,* 1897. [Cf. above, p. 599.]

plausibility. I am so impressed by the importance of these phenomena that I adopt the hypothesis which they so naturally suggest. At these places at least, I say, it would seem as though transmundane energies, God, if you will, produced immediate effects within the natural world to which the rest of our experience belongs.

The difference in natural 'fact' which most of us would assign as the first difference which the existence of a God ought to make would, I imagine, be personal immortality. Religion, in fact, for the great majority of our own race *means* immortality, and nothing else. God is the producer of immortality; and whoever has doubts of immortality is written down as an atheist without farther trial. I have said nothing in my lectures about immortality or the belief therein, for to me it seems a secondary point. If our ideals are only cared for in 'eternity,' I do not see why we might not be willing to resign their care to other hands than ours. Yet I sympathize with the urgent impulse to be present ourselves, and in the conflict of impulses, both of them so vague yet both of them noble, I know not how to decide. It seems to me that it is eminently a case for facts to testify. Facts, I think, are yet lacking to prove 'spirit-return,' though I have the highest respect for the patient labors of Messrs. Myers, Hodgson, and Hyslop, and am somewhat impressed by their favorable conclusions. I consequently leave the matter open, with this brief word to save the reader from a possible perplexity as to why immortality got no mention in the body of this book.

The ideal power with which we feel ourselves in connection, the 'God' of ordinary men, is, both by ordinary men and by philosophers, endowed with certain of those metaphysical attributes which in the lecture on philosophy I treated with such disrespect. He is assumed as a matter of course to be 'one and only' and to be 'infinite'; and the notion of many finite gods is one which hardly any one thinks it worth while to consider, and still less to uphold. Nevertheless, in the interests of intellectual clearness, I feel bound to say that religious experience, as we have studied it, cannot be cited as unequivocally supporting the infinitist belief. The only thing that it unequivocally testifies to is that we can experience union with *something* larger than ourselves and in that union find our greatest peace. Philosophy, with its passion for unity, and mysticism with its mono-ideistic bent, both 'pass to the limit' and identify the something with a unique God who is the all-inclusive soul of the world. Popular opinion, respectful to their authority, follows the example which they set.

Meanwhile the practical needs and experiences of religion seem to me sufficiently met by the belief that beyond each man and in a fashion continuous with him there exists a larger power which is friendly to him and to his ideals. All that the facts require is that the power should be both other and larger than our conscious selves. Anything larger will do, if only it be large enough to trust for the next step. It need not be infinite, it need not be solitary. It might conceivably even be only a larger and more godlike self, of which the present self would then be but the mutilated expression, and the universe might conceivably be a collection of such selves, of different degrees of inclusiveness, with no absolute unity realized in it at all.[94] Thus would a sort of polytheism return upon us—a polytheism which I do not on this occasion defend, for my only aim at present is to keep the testimony of religious experience clearly within its proper bounds.

Upholders of the monistic view will say to such a polytheism (which, by the way, has always been the real religion of common people, and is so still to-day) that unless there be one all-inclusive God, our guarantee of security is left imperfect. In the Absolute, and in the Absolute only, *all* is saved. If there be different gods, each caring for his part, some portion of some of us might not be covered with divine protection, and our religious consolation would thus fail to be complete. It goes back to what was said [before], about the possibility of there being portions of the universe that may irretrievably be lost. Common sense is less sweeping in its demands than philosophy or mysticism have been wont to be, and can suffer the notion of this world being partly saved and partly lost. The ordinary moralistic state of mind makes the salvation of the world conditional upon the success with which each unit does its part. Partial and conditional salvation is in fact a most familiar notion when taken in the abstract, the only difficulty being to determine the details. Some men are even disinterested enough to be willing to be in the unsaved remnant as far as their persons go, if only they can be persuaded that their cause will prevail —all of us are willing, whenever our activity-excitement rises sufficiently high. I think, in fact, that a final philosophy of religion will have to consider the pluralistic hypothesis more seriously than it has hitherto been willing to consider it. For practical life at any rate, the *chance* of salvation is enough. No fact in human nature is more characteristic than its willingness to live on a chance. The existence of the chance makes the difference, as Edmund Gurney says, between a life of which the keynote is resignation and a life of which the keynote is hope.[95] But all these statements are unsatisfactory from their brevity, and I can only say that I hope to return to the same questions in another book.

[94] Such a notion is suggested in my *Ingersoll Lectures On Human Immortality,* Boston and London, 1899.
[95] *Tertium Quid,* 1887, p. 99. See also pp. 148, 149.

[PSYCHIC PHENOMENA: A COMMENT]*

I don't know whether you have heard of the London "Society for Psychical Research," which is seriously and laboriously investigating all sorts of "supernatural" matters, clairvoyance, apparitions, etc. I don't know what you think of such work; but I think that the present condition of opinion regarding it is scandalous, there being a mass of testimony, or apparent testimony, about such things, at which the only men capable of a critical judgment—men of scientific education—will not even look. We have founded a similar society here within the year, —some of us thought that the publications of the London society deserved at least to be treated as if worthy of experimental disproof,— and although work advances very slowly owing to the small amount of disposable time on the part of the members, who are all very busy men, we have already stumbled on some rather inexplicable facts out of which something may come. It is a field in which the sources of deception are extremely numerous. But I believe there is no source of deception in the investigation of nature which can compare with a fixed belief that certain kinds of phenomenon are *impossible*.

FINAL IMPRESSIONS OF A
PSYCHICAL RESEARCHER*[96]

The late Professor Henry Sidgwick was celebrated for the rare mixture of ardor and critical judgment which his character exhibited. The liberal heart which he possessed had to work with an intellect which acted destructively on almost every particular object of belief that was offered to its acceptance. A quarter of a century ago, scandalized by

* From: L.W.J., I, 248. [To Carl Stumpf.]
* From: M.S., 173–206.
[96] Published under the title "Confidences of a Psychical Researcher" in the *American Magazine*, October, 1909. For a more complete and less popular statement of some theories suggested in this article see the last pages of a "Report on Mrs. Piper's Hodgson-Control" in *Proceedings of the [Eng.] Society for Psychical Research*, 1909, 470; also printed in *Proc. of Am. Soc. for Psychical Research* for the same year.

the chaotic state of opinion regarding the phenomena now called by the rather ridiculous name of "psychic"—phenomena, of which the supply reported seems inexhaustible, but which scientifically trained minds mostly refuse to look at—he established, along with Professor Barrett, Frederic Myers and Edmund Gurney, the Society for Psychical Research. These men hoped that if the material were treated rigorously, and, as far as possible, experimentally, objective truth would be elicited, and the subject rescued from sentimentalism on the one side and dogmatizing ignorance on the other. Like all founders, Sidgwick hoped for a certain promptitude of result; and I heard him say, the year before his death, that if anyone had told him at the outset that after twenty years he would be in the same identical state of doubt and balance that he started with, he would have deemed the prophecy incredible. It appeared impossible that that amount of handling evidence should bring so little finality of decision.

My own experience has been similar to Sidgwick's. For twenty-five years I have been in touch with the literature of psychical research, and have had acquaintance with numerous "researchers." I have also spent a good many hours (though far fewer than I ought to have spent) in witnessing (or trying to witness) phenomena. Yet I am theoretically no "further" than I was at the beginning; and I confess that at times I have been tempted to believe that the Creator has eternally intended this department of nature to remain *baffling,* to prompt our curiosities and hopes and suspicions all in equal measure, so that, although ghosts and clairvoyances, and raps and messages from spirits, are always seeming to exist and can never be fully explained away, they also can never be susceptible of full corroboration.

The peculiarity of the case is just that there are so many sources of possible deception in most of the observations that the whole lot of them *may* be worthless, and yet that in comparatively few cases can aught more fatal than this vague general possibility of error be pleaded against the record. Science meanwhile needs something more than bare possibilities to build upon; so your genuinely scientific inquirer—I don't mean your ignoramus "scientist"—has to remain unsatisfied. It is hard to believe, however, that the Creator has really put any big array of phenomena into the world merely to defy and mock our scientific tendencies; so my deeper belief is that we psychical researchers have been too precipitate with our hopes, and that we must expect to mark progress not by quarter-centuries, but by half-centuries or whole centuries.

I am strengthened in this belief by my impression that just at this moment a faint but distinct step forward is being taken by competent opinion in these matters. "Physical phenomena" (movements of matter without contact, lights, hands and faces "materialized," etc.) have been one of the most baffling regions of the general field (or perhaps one of the least baffling *prima facie,* so certain and great has been the part played by fraud in their production); yet even here the balance of testimony seems slowly to be inclining towards admitting the super-naturalist view. Eusapia Paladino, the Neapolitan medium, has been under observation for twenty years or more. Schiaparelli, the astrono-mer, and Lombroso were the first scientific men to be converted by her performances. Since then innumberable men of scientific standing have seen her, including many "psychic" experts. Every one agrees that she cheats in the most barefaced manner whenever she gets an opportunity. The Cambridge experts, with the Sidgwicks and Richard Hodgson at their head, rejected her *in toto* on that account. Yet her credit has steadily risen, and now her last converts are the eminent psychiatrist, Morselli, the eminent physiologist, Botazzi, and our own psychical researcher, Carrington, whose book on "The Physical Phe-nomena of Spiritualism" (*against* them rather!) makes his conquest strategically important. If Mr. Podmore, hitherto the prosecuting at-torney of the S. P. R., so far as physical phenomena are concerned becomes converted also, we may indeed sit up and look around us. Getting a good health bill from "Science," Eusapia will then throw retrospective credit on Home and Stainton Moses, Florence Cook (Prof. Crookes' medium), and all similar wonder-workers. The bal-ance of *presumptions* will be changed in favor of genuineness being possible at least, in all reports of this particularly crass and low type of supernatural phenomena.

Not long after Darwin's "Origin of Species" appeared I was study-ing with that excellent anatomist and man, Jeffries Wyman, at Har-vard. He was a convert, yet so far a half-hesitating one, to Darwin's views; but I heard him make a remark that applies well to the subject I now write about. When, he said, a theory gets propounded over and over again, coming up afresh after each time orthodox criticism has buried it, and each time seeming solider and harder to abolish, you may be sure that there is truth in it. Oken and Lamarck and Chambers had been triumphantly despatched and buried, but here was Darwin making the very same heresy seem only more plausible. How often has "Science" killed off all spook philosophy, and laid ghosts and raps and "telepathy" away underground as so much popular delusion. Yet never before were these things offered us so voluminously, and never in such authentic-seeming shape or with such good credentials. The tide seems steadily to be rising, in spite of all the expedients of scien-tific orthodoxy. It is hard not to suspect that here may be something different from a mere chapter in human gullibility. It may be a genu-ine realm of natural phenomena.

Falsus in uno, falsus in omnibus, once a cheat, always a cheat, such has been the motto of the English psychical researchers in dealing with mediums. I am disposed to think that, as a matter of policy, it has been wise. Tactically, it is far better to believe much too little than a little too much; and the exceptional credit attaching to the row of volumes of the S. P. R.'s Proceedings, is due to the fixed intention of the editors to proceed very slowly. Better a little belief tied fast, better a small investment *salted down,* than a mass of comparative insecurity.

But, however wise as a policy the S. P. R.'s maxim may have been, as a test of truth, I believe it to be almost irrelevant. In most things human the accusation of deliberate fraud and falsehood is grossly superficial. Man's character is too sophistically mixed for the alternative of "honest or dishonest" to be a sharp one. Scientific men themselves will cheat—at public lectures—rather than let experiments obey their well-known tendency towards failure. I have heard of a lecturer on physics, who had taken over the apparatus of the previous incumbent, consulting him about a certain machine intended to show that, however the peripheral parts of it might be agitated, its centre of gravity remained immovable. "It *will* wobble," he complained. "Well," said the predecessor, apologetically, "to tell the truth, whenever *I* used that machine I found it advisable to *drive a nail* through the centre of gravity." I once saw a distinguished physiologist, now dead, cheat most shamelessly at a public lecture, at the expense of a poor rabbit, and all for the sake of being able to make a cheap joke about its being an "American rabbit"—for no other, he said, could survive such a wound as he pretended to have given it.

To compare small men with great, I have myself cheated shamelessly. In the early days of the Sanders Theater at Harvard, I once had charge of a heart on the physiology of which Professor Newell Martin was giving a popular lecture. This heart, which belonged to a turtle, supported an index-straw which threw a moving shadow, greatly enlarged, upon the screen, while the heart pulsated. When certain nerves were stimulated, the lecturer said, the heart would act in certain ways which he described. But the poor heart was too far gone and, although it stopped duly when the nerve of arrest was excited, that was the final end of its life's tether. Presiding over the performance, I was terrified at the fiasco, and found myself suddenly acting like one of those military geniuses who on the field of battle convert disaster into victory. There was no time for deliberation; so, with my forefinger under a part of the straw that cast no shadow, I found myself impulsively and automatically imitating the rhythmical movements which my colleague had prophesied the heart would undergo. I kept the experiment from failing; and not only saved my colleague (and the turtle) from a humiliation that but for my presence of mind would have been their lot, but I established in the audience the true view of the subject. The lecturer was stating this; and the misconduct of one half-dead specimen of heart ought not to destroy the impression of his words. "There is no worse lie than a truth misunderstood," is a maxim which I have heard ascribed to a former venerated President of Harvard. The heart's failure would have been misunderstood by the audience and given the lie to the lecturer. It was hard enough to make them understand the subject anyhow; so that even now as I write in cool blood I am tempted to think that I acted quite correctly. I was acting for the *larger* truth, at any rate, however automatically; and my sense of this was probably what prevented the more pedantic and literal part of my conscience from checking the action of my sympathetic finger. To this day the memory of that critical emergency has made me feel charitable towards all mediums who make phenomena come in one way when they won't come easily in another. On the principles of the S. P. R., my conduct on that one occasion ought to discredit everything I ever do, everything, for example, I may write in this article,—a manifestly unjust conclusion.

Fraud, conscious or unconscious, seems ubiquitous throughout the range of physical phenomena of spiritism, and false pretence, prevarication and fishing for clues are ubiquitous in the mental manifestations of mediums. If it be not everywhere fraud simulating reality, one is tempted to say, then the reality (if any reality there be) has the bad luck of being fated everywhere to simulate fraud. The suggestion of humbug seldom stops, and mixes itself with the best manifestations. Mrs. Piper's control, "Rector," is a most impressive personage, who discerns in an extraordinary degree his sitter's inner needs, and is capable of giving elevated counsel to fastidious and critical minds. Yet in many respects he is an arrant humbug—such he seems to me at least—pretending to a knowledge and power to which he has no title, nonplussed by contradiction, yielding to suggestion, and covering his tracks with plausible excuses. Now the non-"researching" mind looks upon such phenomena simply according to their face-pretension and never thinks of asking what they may signify below the surface. Since they profess for the most part to be revealers of spirit life, it is either as being absolutely that, or as being absolute frauds, that they are judged. The result is an inconceivably shallow state of public opinion on the subject. One set of persons, emotionally touched at hearing the names of their loved ones given, and consoled by assurances that they are "happy," accept the revelation, and consider spiritualism "beautiful." More hard-headed subjects, disgusted by the revelation's contemptible contents, outraged by the fraud, and prejudiced beforehand against all "spirits," high or low, avert their minds from what they call such "rot" or "bosh" entirely. Thus do two opposite sentimentalisms divide opinion between them! A good expression of the "scientific" state of mind occurs in Huxley's "Life and Letters":

"I regret," he writes, "that I am unable to accept the invitation of the Committee of the Dialectical Society. . . . I take no interest in the subject. The only case of 'Spiritualism' I have ever had the opportunity of examining into for myself was as gross an imposture as ever came under my notice. But supposing these phenomena to be genuine— they do not interest me. If anybody would endow me with the faculty of listening to the chatter of old women and curates in the nearest provincial town, I should decline the privilege, having better things to do. And if the folk in the spiritual world do not talk more wisely and sensibly than their friends report them to do, I put them in the same category. The only good that I can see in the demonstration of the 'Truth of Spiritualism' is to furnish an additional argument against suicide. Better live a crossing-sweeper, than die and be made to talk twaddle by a 'medium' hired at a guinea a *Seance*." [97]

Obviously the mind of the excellent Huxley has here but two whole-souled categories, namely revelation or imposture, to apperceive the case by. Sentimental reasons bar revelation out, for the messages, he thinks, are not romantic enough for that; fraud exists anyhow; therefore the whole thing is nothing but imposture. The odd point is that so few of those who talk in this way realize that they and the spiritists are using the same major premise and differing only in the minor. The major premise is: "Any spirit-revelation must be romantic." The minor of the spiritist is: "This *is* romantic"; that of the Huxleyan is: "this is dingy twaddle"—whence their opposite conclusions!

Meanwhile the first thing that anyone learns who attends seriously to these phenomena is that their causation is far too complex for our feelings about what is or is not romantic enough to be spiritual to throw any light upon it. The causal factors must be carefully distinguished and traced through series, from their simplest to their strongest forms, before we can begin to understand the various resultants in which they issue. Myers and Gurney began this work, the one by his serial study of the various sorts of "automatism," sensory and motor, the other by his experimental proofs that a split-off consciousness may abide after a post-hypnotic suggestion has been given. Here we have subjective factors; but are not transsubjective or objective forces also at work? Veridical messages, apparitions, movements without contact, seem *prima facie* to be such. It was a good stroke on Gurney's part to construct a theory of apparitions which brought the subjective and the objective factors into harmonious co-operation. I doubt whether this telepathic theory of Gurney's will hold along the whole

[97] T. H. Huxley, "Life and Letters," I, 240.

line of apparitions to which he applied it, but it is unquestionable that some theory of that mixed type is required for the explanation of all mediumistic phenomena; and that when all the psychological factors and elements involved have been told off—and they are many—the question still forces itself upon us: Are these all, or are there indications of any residual forces acting on the subject from beyond, or of any "metapsychic" faculty (to use Richet's useful term), exerted by him? This is the problem that requires real expertness, and this is where the simple sentimentalisms of the spiritist and scientist leave us in the lurch completely.

"Psychics" form indeed a special branch of education, in which experts are only gradually becoming developed. The phenomena are as massive and wide-spread as is anything in Nature, and the study of them is as tedious, repellent and undignified. To reject it for its unromantic character is like rejecting bacteriology because *penicillium glaucum* grows on horse-dung and *bacterium termo* lives in putrefaction. Scientific men have long ago ceased to think of the dignity of the materials they work in. When imposture has been checked off as far as possible, when chance coincidence has been allowed for, when opportunities for normal knowledge on the part of the subject have been noted, and skill in "fishing" and following clues unwittingly furnished by the voice or face of bystanders have been counted in, those who have the fullest acquaintance with the phenomena admit that in good mediums *there is a residuum of knowledge displayed* that can only be called supernormal: the medium taps some source of information not open to ordinary people. Myers used the word "telepathy" to indicate that the sitter's own thoughts or feelings may be thus directly tapped. Mrs. Sidgwick has suggested that if living minds can be thus tapped telepathically, so possibly may the minds of spirits be similarly tapped—if spirits there be. On this view we should have one distinct theory of the performances of a typical test-medium. They would be all originally due to an odd *tendency to personate,* found in her dream life as it expresses itself in trance. [Most of us reveal such a tendency whenever we handle a "ouija-board" or a "planchet," or let ourselves write automatically with a pencil.] The result is a "control," who purports to be speaking; and all the resources of the automatist, including his or her trance-faculty of telepathy, are called into play in building this fictitious personage out plausibly. On such a view of the control, the medium's *will to personate* runs the whole show; and if spirits be involved in it at all, they are passive beings, stray bits of whose memory she is able to seize and use for her purposes, without the spirit being any more aware of it than the sitter is aware of it when his own mind is similarly tapped.

This is one possible way of interpreting a certain type of psychical phenomenon. It uses psychological as well as "spiritual" factors, and quite obviously it throws open for us far more questions than it answers, questions about our subconscious constitution and its curious tendency to humbug, about the telepathic faculty, and about the possibility of an existent spirit-world.

I do not instance this theory to defend it, but simply to show what complicated hypotheses one is inevitably led to consider, the moment one looks at the facts in their complexity and turns one's back on the *naïve* alternative of "revelation or imposture," which is as far as either spiritist thought or ordinary scientist thought goes. The phenomena are endlessly complex in their factors, and they are so little understood as yet that off-hand judgments, whether of "spirits" or of "bosh" are the one as silly as the other. When we complicate the subject still farther by considering what connection such things as rappings, apparitions, poltergeists, spirit-photographs, and materializations may have with it, the bosh end of the scale gets heavily loaded, it is true, but your genuine inquirer still is loath to give up. He lets the data collect, and bides his time. He belives that "bosh" is no more an ultimate element in Nature, or a really explanatory category in human life than "dirt" is in chemistry. Every kind of "bosh" has its own factors and laws; and patient study will bring them definitely to light.

The only way to rescue the "pure bosh" view of the matter is one which has sometimes appealed to my own fancy, but which I imagine few readers will seriously adopt. If, namely, one takes the theory of evolution radically, one ought to apply it not only to the rock-strata, the animals and the plants, but to the stars, to the chemical elements, and to the laws of nature. There must have been a far-off antiquity, one is then tempted to suppose, when things were really chaotic. Little by little, out of all the haphazard possibilities of that time, a few connected things and habits arose, and the rudiments of regular performance began. Every variation in the way of law and order added itself to this nucleus, which inevitably grew more considerable as history went on; while the aberrant and inconstant variations, not being similarly preserved, disappeared from being, wandered off as unrelated vagrants, or else remained so imperfectly connected with the part of the world that had grown regular as only to manifest their existence by occasional lawless intrusions, like those which "psychic" phenomena now make into our scientifically organized world. On such a view, these phenomena ought to remain "pure bosh" forever, that is, they ought to be forever intractable to intellectual methods, because they should not yet be organized enough in themselves to follow any laws. Wisps and shreds of the original chaos, they would be connected enough with the cosmos to affect its periphery every now and then, as by a momentary whiff or touch or gleam, but not enough ever to be followed up and hunted down and bagged. Their relation to the cosmos would be tangential solely.

Looked at dramatically, most occult phenomena make just this sort of impression. They are inwardly as incoherent as they are outwardly wayward and fitful. If they express anything, it is pure "bosh," pure discontinuity, accident, and disturbance, with no law apparent but to interrupt, and no purpose but to baffle. They seem like stray vestiges of that primordial irrationality, from which all our rationalities have been evolved.

To settle dogmatically into this bosh-view would save labor, but it would go against too many intellectual prepossessions to be adopted save as a last resort of despair. Your psychical researcher therefore bates no jot of hope, and has faith that when we get out data numerous enough, some sort of rational treatment of them will succeed.

When I hear good people say (as they often say, not without show of reason), that dabbling in such phenomena reduces us to a sort of jelly, disintegrates the critical faculties, liquifies the character, and makes of one a *gobe-mouche* generally, I console myself by thinking of my friends Frederic Myers and Richard Hodgson. These men lived exclusively for psychical research, and it converted both to spiritism. Hodgson would have been a man among men anywhere; but I doubt whether under any other baptism he would have been that happy, sober and righteous form of energy which his face proclaimed him in his later years, when heart and head alike were wholly satisfied by his occupation. Myers' character also grew stronger in every particular for his devotion to the same inquiries. Brought up on literature and sentiment, something of a courtier, passionate, disdainful, and impatient naturally, he was made over again from the day when he took up psychical research seriously. He became learned in sicence, circumspect, democratic in sympathy, endlessly patient, and above all, happy. The fortitude of his last hours touched the heroic, so completely were the atrocious sufferings of his body cast into insignificance by his interest in the cause he lived for. When a man's pursuit gradually makes his face shine and grow handsome, you may be sure it is a worthy one. Both Hodgson and Myers kept growing ever handsomer and stronger-looking.

Such personal examples will convert no one, and of course they ought not to. Nor do I seek at all in this article to convert any one to my belief that psychical research is an important branch of science. To do that, I should have to quote evidence; and those for whom the volumes of S.P.R. "Proceedings" already published count for nothing would remain in their dogmatic slumber, though one rose from the dead. No, not to convert readers, but simply to *put my own state of mind upon record publicly* is the purpose of my present writing. Some one said to me a short time ago, that after my twenty-five years of dabbling in "Psychics," it would be rather shameful were I unable to state any definite conclusions whatever as a consequence. I had to agree; so I now proceed to take up the challenge and express such convictions as have been engendered in me by that length of experience, be the same true or false ones. I may be dooming myself to the pit in the eyes of better-judging posterity; I may be raising myself to honor; I am willing to take the risk, for what I shall write is *my* truth, as I now see it.

I began this article by confessing myself baffled. I *am* baffled, as to spirit-return, and as to many other special problems. I am also constantly baffled as to what to think of this or that particular story, for the sources of error in any one observation are seldom fully knowable. But weak sticks make strong faggots; and when the stories fall into consistent sorts that point each in a definite direction, one gets a sense of being in presence of genuinely natural types of phenomena. As to there being such real natural types of phenomena ignored by orthodox science, I am not baffled at all, for I am fully convinced of it. One cannot get demonstrative proof here. One has to follow one's personal sense, which, of course, is liable to err, of the dramatic probabilities of nature. Our critics here obey their sense of dramatic probability as much as we do. Take "raps" for example, and the whole business of objects moving without contact. "Nature," thinks the scientific man, is not so unutterably silly. The cabinet, the darkness, the tying, suggest a sort of human rat-hole life exclusively and "swindling" is for him the dramatically sufficient explanation. It probably is, in an indefinite majority of instances; yet it is to me dramatically improbable that the swindling should not have accreted round some originally genuine nucleus. If we look at human imposture as a historic phenomenon, we find it always imitative. One swindler imitates a previous swindler, but the first swindler of that kind imitated some one who was honest. You can no more create an absolutely new trick than you can create a new word without any previous basis.—You don't know how to go about it. Try, reader, youself, to invent an unprecedented kind of "physical phenomenon of spiritualism." When I try, I find myself mentally turning over the regular medium-stock, and thinking how I might improve some item. This being the dramatically probable human way, I think differently of the whole type, taken collectively, from the way in which I may think of the single instance. I find myself believing that there is "something in" these never ending reports of physical phenomena, although I have n't yet the least positive notion of the something. It becomes to my mind simply a very worthy problem for investigation.

Either I or the scientist is of course a fool, with our opposite views of probability here; and I only wish he might feel the liability, as cordially as I do, to pertain to both of us.

I fear I look on Nature generally with more charitable eyes than his, though perhaps he would pause if he realized as I do, how vast the fraudulency is which inconsistency he must attribute to her. Nature is brutal enough, Heaven knows; but no one yet has held her non-human side to be *dishonest,* and even in the human sphere deliberate deceit is far rarer than the "classic" intellect, with its few and rigid categories, was ready to acknowledge. There is a hazy penumbra in us all where lying and delusion meet, where passion rules beliefs as well as conduct, and where the term "scoundrel" does not clear up everything to the depths as it did for our forefathers. The first automatic writing I ever saw was forty years ago. I unhesitatingly thought of it as deceit, although it contained vague elements of supernormal knowledge. Since then I have come to see in automatic writing one example of a department of human activity as vast as it is enigmatic. Every sort of person is liable to it, or to something equivalent to it; and whoever encourages it in himself finds himself personating someone else, either signing what he writes by fictitious name, or spelling out, by ouija-board or table-tips, messages from the departed. Our subconscious region seems, as a rule, to be dominated either by a crazy "will to make-believe," or by some curious external force impelling us to personation. The first difference between the psychical researcher and the inexpert person is that the former realizes the commonness and typicality of the phenomenon here, while the latter, less informed, thinks it so rare as to be unworthy of attention. *I wish to go on record for the commonness.*

The next thing I wish to go on record for is *the presence,* in the midst of all the humbug, *of really supernormal knowledge.* By this I mean knowledge that cannot be traced to the ordinary sources of information—the senses namely, of the automatist. In really strong mediums this knowledge seems to be abundant, though it is usually spotty, capricious and unconnected. Really strong mediums are rarities; but when one starts with them and works downwards into less brilliant regions of the automatic life, one tends to interpret many slight but odd coincidences with truth as possibly rudimentary forms of this kind of knowledge.

What is one to think of this queer chapter in human nature? It is odd enough on any view. If all it means is a preposterous and inferior monkey-like tendency to forge messages, systematically embedded in the soul of all of us, it is weird; and weirder still that it should then own all this supernormal information. If on the other hand the supernormal information be the key to the phenomenon, it ought to be superior; and then how ought we to account for the "wicked partner," and for the undeniable mendacity and inferiority of so much of the performance? We are thrown, for our conclusions, upon our instinctive sense of the dramatic probabilities of nature. My own dramatic sense tends instinctively to picture the situation as an interaction between slumbering faculties in the automatist's mind and a cosmic environment of *other consciousness* of some sort which is able to work upon them. If there were in the universe a lot of diffuse soul-stuff, unable of itself to get into consistent personal form, or to take permanent possession of an organism, yet always craving to do so, it might get its head into the air, parasitically, so to speak, by profiting by weak spots in the armor of human minds, and slipping in and stirring up there the sleeping tendency to personate. It would induce habits in the subconscious region of the mind it used thus, and would seek above all things to prolong its social opportunities by making itself agreeable and plausible. It would drag stray scraps of truth with it from the wider environment, but would betray its mental inferiority by knowing little how to weave them into any important or significant story.

This, I say, is the dramatic view which my mind spontaneously takes, and it has the advantage of falling into line with ancient human traditions. The views of others are just as dramatic, *for the phenomenon is actuated by will of some sort anyhow,* and wills give rise to dramas. The spiritist view, as held by Messrs. Hyslop and Hodgson, sees a "will to communicate," struggling through inconceivable layers of obstruction in the conditions. I have heard Hodgson liken the difficulties to those of two persons who on earth should have only dead-drunk servants to use as their messengers. The scientist, for his part, sees a "will to deceive," watching its chance in all of us, and able (possibly?) to use "telepathy" in its service.

Which kind of will, and how many kinds of will are most inherently probable? Who can say with certainty? The only certainty is that the phenomena are enormously complex, especially if one includes in them such intellectual flights of mediumship as Swedenborg's, and if one tries in any way to work the physical phenomena in. That is why I personally am as yet neither a convinced believer in parasitic demons, nor a spiritist, nor a scientist, but still remain a psychical researcher waiting for more facts before concluding.

Out of my experience, such as it is (and it is limited enough) one fixed conclusion dogmatically emerges, and that is this, that we with our lives are like islands in the sea, or like trees in the forest. The maple and the pine may whisper to each other with their leaves, and Conanicut and Newport hear each other's foghorns. But the trees also commingle their roots in the darkness underground, and the islands also hang together through the ocean's bottom. Just so there is a continuum of cosmic consciousness, against which our individuality builds but accidental fences, and into which our several minds plunge as into a mother-sea or reservoir. Our "normal" consciousness is circumscribed for adaptation to our external earthly environment, but the fence is weak in spots, and fitful influences from beyond leak in, showing the otherwise unverifiable common connection. Not only psychic research, but metaphysical philosophy, and speculative biology are led in their own ways to look with favor on some such "panpsychic" view of the universe as this. Assuming this common reservoir of consciousnes to exist, this bank upon which we all draw, and in which so many of earth's memories must in some way be stored, or mediums would not get at them as they do, the question is, What is its own structure? What is its inner topography? This question, first squarely formulated by Myers, deserves to be called "Myers' problem" by scientific men hereafter. What are the conditions of individuation or insulation in this mother-sea? To what tracts, to what active systems functioning separately in it, do personalities correspond? Are individual "spirits" constituted there? How numerous, and of how many hierarchic orders may these then be? How permanent? How transient? And how confluent with one another may they become?

What again, are the relations between the cosmic consciousness and matter? Are there subtler forms of matter which upon occasion may enter into functional connection with the individuations in the psychic sea, and then, and then only, show themselves?—So that our ordinary human experience, on its material as well as on its mental side, would appear to be only an extract from the larger psychophysical world?

Vast, indeed, and difficult is the inquirer's prospect here, and the most significant data for his purpose will probably be just these dingy little mediumistic facts which the Huxleyan minds of our time find so unworthy of their attention. But when was not the science of the future stirred to its conquering activities by the little rebellious exceptions to the science of the present? Hardly, as yet, has the surface of the facts called "psychic" begun to be scratched for scientific purposes. It is through following these facts, I am persuaded, that the greatest scientific conquests of the coming generation will be achieved. *Kühn ist das Mühen, herrlich der Lohn!*

[AN OVERVIEW]*

[In previous essays] I referred to the existence of religious experiences of a specific nature. I must now explain just what I mean by such a claim. Briefly, the facts I have in mind may all be described as experiences of an unexpected life succeeding upon death. By this I don't mean immortality, or the death of the body. I mean the death-like termination of certain mental processes within the individual's experience, processes that run to failure, and in some individuals, at least, eventuate in despair. Just as romantic love seems a comparatively recent literary invention, so these experiences of a life that supervenes upon despair seem to have played no great part in official theology till Luther's time; and possibly the best way to indicate their character will be to point to a certain contrast between the inner life of ourselves and of the ancient Greeks and Romans.

Mr. Chesterton, I think, says somewhere, that the Greeks and Romans, in all that concerned their moral life, were an extraordinarily solemn set of folks. The Athenians thought that the very gods must admire the rectitude of Phocion and Aristides; and those gentlemen themselves were apparently of much the same opinion. Cato's veracity was so impeccable that the extremest incredulity a Roman could express of anything was to say, 'I would not believe it even if Cato had told me.' Good was good, and bad was bad, for these people. Hypocrisy, which church-Christianity brought in, hardly existed; the naturalistic system held firm; its values showed no hollowness and brooked no irony. The individual, if virtuous enough, could meet all possible requirements. The pagan pride had never crumbled. Luther was the first moralist who broke with any effectiveness through the crust of all this naturalistic self-sufficiency, thinking (and possibly he was right) that Saint Paul had done it already. Religious experience of the lutheran type brings all our naturalistic standards to bankruptcy. You are strong only by being weak, it shows. You cannot live on pride or self-sufficingness. There is a light in which all the naturally founded and currently accepted distinctions, excellences, and safeguards of our characters appear as utter childishness. Sincerely to give up one's conceit or hope of being good in one's own right is the only door to the universe's deeper reaches.

These deeper reaches are familiar to evangelical Christianity and to what is nowadays becoming known as 'mind-cure' religion or 'new thought.' The phenomenon is that of new ranges of life succeeding on

* From: P.U., 303–331.

our most despairing moments. There are resources in us that naturalism with its literal and legal virtues never recks of, possibilities that take our breath away, of another kind of happiness and power, based on giving up our own will and letting something higher work for us, and these seem to show a world wider than either physics or philistine ethics can imagine. Here is a world in which all is well, in *spite* of certain forms of death, indeed *because* of certain forms of death— death of hope, death of strength, death of responsibility, of fear and worry, competency and desert, death of everything that paganism, naturalism, and legalism pin their faith on and tie their trust to.

Reason, operating on our other experiences, even our psychological experiences, would never have inferred these specifically religious experiences in advance of their actual coming. She could not suspect their existence, for they are discontinuous with the 'natural' experiences they succeed upon and invert their values. But as they actually come and are given, creation widens to the view of their recipients. They suggest that our natural experience, our strictly moralistic and prudential experience, may be only a fragment of real human experience. They soften nature's outlines and open out the strangest possibilities and perspectives.

This is why it seems to me that the logical understanding, working in abstraction from such specifically religious experiences, will always omit something, and fail to reach completely adequate conclusions. Death and failure, it will always say, *are* death and failure simply, and can nevermore be one with life; so religious experience, peculiarly so called, needs, in my opinion, to be carefully considered and interpreted by every one who aspires to reason out a more complete philosophy.

The sort of belief that religious experience of this type naturally engenders in those who have it is fully in accord with Fechner's theories. To quote words which I used elsewhere, the believer finds that the tenderer parts of his personal life are continuous with a *more* of the same quality which is operative in the universe outside of him and which he can keep in working touch with, and in a fashion get on board of and save himself, when all his lower being has gone to pieces in the wreck. In a word, the believer is continuous, to his own consciousness, at any rate, with a wider self from which saving experiences flow in. Those who have such experiences distinctly enough and often enough to live in the light of them remain quite unmoved by criticism, from whatever quarter it may come, be it academic or scientific, or be it merely the voice of logical common sense. They have had their vision and they *know*—that is enough—that we inhabit an invisible spiritual environment from which help comes, our soul being mysteriously one with a larger soul whose instruments we are.

One may therefore plead, I think, that Fechner's ideas are not without direct empirical verification. There is at any rate one side of life which would be easily explicable if those ideas were true, but of which there appears no clear explanation so long as we assume either with naturalism that human consciousness is the highest conciousness there is, or with dualistic theism that there is a higher mind in the cosmos, but that it is discontinuous with our own. It has always been a matter of surprise with me that philosophers of the absolute should have shown so little interest in this department of life, and so seldom put its phenomena in evidence, even when it seemed obvious that personal experience of some kind must have made their confidence in their own vision so strong. The logician's bias has always been too much with them. They have preferred the thinner to the thicker method, dialectical abstraction being so much more dignified and academic than the confused and unwholesome facts of personal biography.

In spite of rationalism's disdain for the particular, the personal, and the unwholesome, the drift of all the evidence we have seems to me to sweep us very strongly towards the belief in some form of superhuman life with which we may, unknown to ourselves, be coconscious. We may be in the universe as dogs and cats are in our libraries, seeing the books and hearing the conversation, but having no inkling of the meaning of it all. The intellectualist objections to this fall away when the authority of intellectualist logic is undermined by criticism, and then the positive empirical evidence remains. The analogies with ordinary psychology and with the facts of pathology, with those of psychical research, so called, and with those of religious experience, establish, when taken together, a decidedly *formidable* probability in favor of a general view of the world almost identical with Fechner's. The outlines of the superhuman consciousness thus made probable must remain, however, very vague, and the number of functionally distinct 'selves' it comports and carries has to be left entirely problematic. It may be polytheistically or it may be monotheistically conceived of. Fechner, with his distinct earth-soul functioning as our guardian angel, seems to me clearly polytheistic; but the word 'polytheism' usually gives offence, so perhaps it is better not to use it. Only one thing is certain, and that is the result of our criticism of the absolute: the only way to escape from the paradoxes and perplexities that a consistently thought-out monistic universe suffers from as from a species of auto-intoxication—the mystery of the 'fall' namely, of reality lapsing into appearance, truth into error, perfection into imperfection; of evil, in short; the mystery of universal determinism, of the block-universe eternal and without a history, etc;—the only way of escape, I say, from all this is to be frankly pluralistic and assume that the superhuman consciousness, however vast it may be, has itself an

external environment, and consequently is finite. Present day monism
carefully repudiates complicity with spinozistic monism. In that, it explains, the many get dissolved in the one and lost, whereas in the
improved idealistic form they get preserved in all their manyness as
the one's eternal object. The absolute itself is thus represented by
absolutists as having a pluralistic object. But if even the absolute has
to have a pluralistic vision, why should we ourselves hesitate to be
pluralists on our own sole account? Why should we envelop our many
with the 'one' that brings so much poison in its train?

The line of least resistance, then, as it seems to me, both in theology and in philosophy, is to accept, along with the superhuman consciousness, the notion that it is not all-embracing, the notion, in other
words, that there is a God, but that he is finite, either in power or in
knowledge, or in both at once. These, I need hardly tell you, are the
terms in which common men have usually carried on their active commerce with God; and the monistic perfections that make the notion of
him so paradoxical practically and morally are the colder addition of
remote professorial minds operating *in distans* upon conceptual substitutes for him alone.

Why cannot 'experience' and 'reason' meet on this common
ground? Why cannot they compromise? May not the godlessness usually but needlessly associated with the philosophy of immediate
experience give way to a theism now seen to follow directly from that
experience more widely taken? and may not rationalism, satisfied with
seeing her *a priori* proofs of God so effectively replaced by empirical
evidence, abate something of her absolutist claims? Let God but have
the least infinitesimal *other* of any kind beside him, and empiricism
and rationalism might strike hands in a lasting treaty of peace. Both
might then leave abstract thinness behind them, and seek together, as
scientific men seek, by using all the analogies and data within reach,
to build up the most probable approximate idea of what the divine
consciousness concretely may be like. I venture to beg the younger
Oxford idealists to consider seriously this alternative. Few men are as
qualified by their intellectual gifts to reap the harvests that seem certain to any one who, like Fechner and Bergson, will leave the thinner
for the thicker path.

Compromise and mediation are inseparable from the pluralistic
philosophy. Only monistic dogmatism can say of any of its hypotheses,
'It is either that or nothing; take it or leave it just as it stands.' The
type of monism prevalent at Oxford has kept this steep and brittle
attitude, partly through the proverbial academic preference for thin
and elegant logical solutions, partly from a mistaken notion that the
only solidly grounded basis for religion was along those lines. If Oxford men could be ignorant of anything, it might almost seem that they

had remained ignorant of the great empirical movement towards a pluralistic panpsychic view of the universe, into which our own generation
has been drawn, and which threatens to short-circuit their methods entirely and become their religious rival unless they are willing to make
themselves its allies. Yet, wedded as they seem to be to the logical
machinery and technical apparatus of absolutism, I cannot but believe that their fidelity to the religious ideal in general is deeper still.
Especially do I find it hard to believe that the more clerical adherents
of the school would hold so fast to its particular machinery if only
they could be made to think that religion could be secured in some
other way. Let empiricism once become associated with religion, as
hitherto, through some strange misunderstanding, it has been associated with irreligion, and I believe that a new era of religion as well
as of philosophy will be ready to begin. That great awakening of
a new popular interest in philosophy, which is so striking a phenomenon at the present day in all countries, is undoubtedly due in
part to religious demands. As the authority of past tradition tends
more and more to crumble, men naturally turn a wistful ear to the
authority of reason or to the evidence of present fact. They will assuredly not be disappointed if they open their minds to what the thicker
and more radical empiricism has to say. I fully believe that such an
empiricism is a more natural ally than dialectics ever were, or can be,
of the religious life. It is true that superstitions and wild-growing over-
beliefs of all sorts will undoubtedly begin to abound if the notion of
higher consciousnesses enveloping ours, of fechnerian earth-souls and
the like, grows orthodox and fashionable; still more will they super-
abound if science ever puts her approving stamp on the phenomena of
which Frederic Myers so earnestly advocated the scientific recognition, the phenomena of psychic research so-called—and I myself
firmly believe that most of these phenomena are rooted in reality. But
ought one seriously to allow such a timid consideration as that to
deter one from following the evident path of greatest religious promise? Since when, in this mixed world, was any good thing given us in
purest outline and isolation? One of the chief characteristics of life is
life's redundancy. The sole condition of our having anything, no matter what, is that we should have so much of it, that we are fortunate if
we do not grow sick of the sight and sound of it altogether. Everything
is smothered in the litter that is fated to accompany it. Without too
much you cannot have enough, of anything. Lots of inferior books, lots
of bad statues, lots of dull speeches, of tenth-rate men and women, as
a condition of the few precious specimens in either kind being realized!
The gold-dust comes to birth with the quartz-sand all around it, and
this is as much a condition of religion as of any other excellent possession. There must be extrication; there must be competition for sur-

vival; but the clay matrix and the noble gem must first come into being unsifted. Once extricated, the gem can be examined separately, conceptualized, defined, and insulated. But this process of extrication cannot be short-circuited—or if it is, you get the thin inferior abstractions which we have seen, either the hollow unreal god of scholastic theology, or the unintelligible pantheistic monster, instead of the more living divine reality with which it appears certain that empirical methods tend to connect men in imagination.

Arrived at this point, I ask you to go back to my first lecture [above, pp. 482–496] and remember, if you can, what I quoted there from your own Professor Jacks—what he said about the philosopher himself being taken up into the universe which he is accounting for. This is the fechnerian as well as the hegelian view, and thus our end rejoins harmoniously our beginning. Philosophies are intimate parts of the universe, they express something of its own thought of itself. A philosophy may indeed be a most momentous reaction of the universe upon itself. It may, as I said, possess and handle itself differently in consequence of us philosophers, with our theories, being here; it may trust itself or mistrust itself the more, and, by doing the one or the other, deserve more the trust or the mistrust. What mistrusts itself deserves mistrust.

This is the philosophy of humanism in the widest sense. Our philosophies swell the current of being, add their character to it. They are part of all that we have met, of all that makes us be. As a French philosopher says, 'Nous sommes du réel dans le réel.' Our thoughts determine our acts, and our acts redetermine the previous nature of the world.

Thus does foreignness get banished from our world, and far more so when we take the system of it pluralistically than when we take it monistically. We are indeed internal parts of God and not external creations, on any possible reading of the panpsychic system. Yet because God is not the absolute, but is himself a part when the system is conceived pluralistically, his functions can be taken as not wholly dissimilar to those of the other smaller parts,—as similar to our functions consequently.

Having an environment, being in time, and working out a history just like ourselves, he escapes from the foreignness from all that is human, of the static timeless perfect absolute.

Remember that one of our troubles with that was its essential foreignness and monstrosity—there really is no other word for it than that. Its having the all-inclusive form gave to it an essentially heterogeneous *nature* from ourselves. And this great difference between absolutism and pluralism demands no difference in the universe's material content—it follows from a difference in the form alone. The all-form or monistic form makes the foreignness result, the each-form or pluralistic form leaves the intimacy undisturbed.

No matter what the content of the universe may be, if you only allow that it is *many* everywhere and always, that *nothing* real escapes from having an environment; so far from defeating its rationality, as the absolutists so unanimously pretend, you leave it in possession of the maximum amount of rationality practically attainable by our minds. Your relations with it, intellectual, emotional, and active, remain fluent and congruous with your own nature's chief demands.

It would be a pity if the word 'rationality' were allowed to give us trouble here. It is one of those eulogistic words that both sides claim —for almost no one is willing to advertise his philosophy as a system of irrationality. But like most of the words which people used eulogistically, the word 'rational' carries too many meanings. The most objective one is that of the older logic—the connexion between two things is rational when you can infer one from the other, mortal from Socrates, *e.g.;* and you can do that only when they have a quality in common. But this kind of rationality is just that logic of identity which all disciples of Hegel find insufficient. They supersede it by the higher rationality of negation and contradiction and make the notion vague again. Then you get the æsthetic or teleologic kinds of rationality, saying that whatever fits in any way, whatever is beautiful or good, whatever is purposive or gratifies desire, is rational in so far forth. Then again, according to Hegel, whatever is 'real' is rational. I myself said awhile ago that whatever lets loose any action which we are fond of exerting seems rational. It would be better to give up the word 'rational' altogether than to get into a merely verbal fight about who has the best right to keep it.

Perhaps the words 'foreignness' and 'intimacy,' which I put forward in my first lecture, express the contrast I insist on better than the words 'rationality' and 'irrationality'—let us stick to them, then. I now say that the notion of the 'one' breeds foreignness and that of the 'many' intimacy, for reasons which I have urged at only too great length, and with which, whether they convince you or not, I may suppose that you are now well acquainted. But what at bottom is meant by calling the universe many or by calling it one?

Pragmatically interpreted, pluralism or the doctrine that it is many means only that the sundry parts of reality *may be externally related*. Everything you can think of, however vast or inclusive, has on the pluralistic view a genuinely 'external' environment of some sort or amount. Things are 'with' one another in many ways, but nothing includes everything, or dominates over everything. The word 'and' trails along after every sentence. Something always escapes. 'Ever not quite' has to be said of the best attempts made anywhere in the universe at attaining all-inclusiveness. The pluralistic world is thus more like a federal republic than like an empire or a kingdom. However much may be collected, however much may report itself as present at any effective centre of consciousness or action, something else is self-governed and absent and unreduced to unity.

Monism, on the other hand, insists that when you come down to reality as such, to the reality of realities, everything is present to *everything* else in one vast instantaneous co-implicated completeness —nothing can in *any* sense, functional or substantial, be really absent from anything else, all things interpenetrate and telescope together in the great total conflux.

For pluralism, all that we are required to admit as the constitution of reality is what we ourselves find empirically realized in every minimum of finite life. Briefly it is this, that nothing real is absolutely simple, that every smallest bit of experience is a *multum in parvo* plurally related, that each relation is one aspect, character, or function, way of its being taken, or way of its taking something else; and that a bit of reality when actively engaged in one of these relations is not *by that very fact* engaged in all the other relations simultaneously. The relations are not *all* what the French call *solidaires* with one another. Without losing its identity a thing can either take up or drop another thing, like the log I spoke of, which by taking up new carriers and dropping old ones can travel anywhere with a light escort.

For monism, on the contrary, everything, whether we realize it or not, drags the whole universe along with itself and drops nothing. The log starts and arrives with all its carriers supporting it. If a thing were once disconnected, it could never be connected again, according to monism. The pragmatic difference between the two systems is thus a definite one. It is just thus, that if *a* is once out of sight of *b* or out of touch with it, or more briefly, 'out' of it at all, then, according to monism, it must always remain so, they can never get together; whereas pluralism admits that on another occasion they may work together, or in some way be connected again. Monism allows for no such things as 'other occasions' in reality—in *real* or absolute reality, that is.

The difference I try to describe amounts, you see, to nothing more than the difference between what I formerly called the each-form and the all-form of reality. Pluralism lets things really exist in the each-form or distributively. Monism thinks that the all-form or collective-unit form is the only form that is rational. The all-form allows of no taking up and dropping of connexions, for in the all the parts are essentially and eternally co-implicated. In the each-form, on the contrary, a thing may be connected by intermediary things, with a thing with which it has no immediate or essential connexion. It is thus at all times in many possible connexions which are not necessarily actualized at the moment. They depend on which actual path of intermediation it may functionally strike into: the word 'or' names a genuine reality. Thus, as I speak here, I may look ahead *or* to the right *or* to the left, and in either case the intervening space and air and ether enable me to see the faces of a different portion of this audience. My being here is independent of any one set of these faces.

If the each-form be the eternal form of reality no less than it is the form of temporal appearance, we still have a coherent world, and not an incarnate incoherence, as is charged by so many absolutists. Our 'multiverse' still makes a 'universe'; for every part, tho it may not be in actual or immediate connexion, is nevertheless in some possible or mediated connexion, with every other part however remote, through the fact that each part hangs together with its very next neighbors in inextricable interfusion. The type of union, it is true, is different here from the monistic type of *all-einheit*. It is not a universal co-implication, or integration of all things *durcheinander*. It is what I call the strung-along type, the type of continuity, contiguity, or concatenation. If you prefer greek words, you may call it the synechistic type. At all events, you see that it forms a definitely conceivable alternative to the through-and-through unity of all things at once, which is the type opposed to it by monism. You see also that it stands or falls with the notion I have taken such pains to defend, of the through-and-through union of adjacent minima of experience, of the confluence of every passing moment of concretely felt experience with its immediately next neighbors. The recognition of this fact of coalescence of next with next in concrete experience, so that all the insulating cuts we make there are artificial products of the conceptualizing faculty, is what distinguishes the empiricism which I call 'radical,' from the bugaboo empiricism of the traditional rationalist critics, which (rightly or wrongly) is accused of chopping up experience into atomistic sensations, incapable of union with one another until a purely intellectual principle has swooped down upon them from on high and folded them in its own conjunctive categories.

Here, then, you have the plain alternative, and the full mystery of the difference between pluralism and monism, as clearly as I can set it forth on this occasion. It packs up into a nutshell:—Is the manyness in oneness that indubitably characterizes the world we inhabit, a property only of the absolute whole of things, so that you must postulate that one-enormous-whole indivisibly as the *prius* of there being any many at all—in other words, start with the rationalistic block-universe, entire, unmitigated, and complete?—or can the finite elements have their own aboriginal forms of manyness in oneness, and where they have no immediate oneness still be continued into one another by intermediary terms—each one of these terms being one with its next neighbors, and yet the total 'oneness' never getting absolutely complete?

The alternative is definite. It seems to me, moreover, that the two horns of it make pragmatically different ethical appeals—at least they *may* do so, to certain individuals. But if you consider the pluralistic horn to be intrinsically irrational, self-contradictory, and absurd, I can now say no more in its defence. Having done what I could in my earlier lectures to break the edge of the intellectualistic *reductiones ad absurdum*, I must leave the issue in your hands. Whatever I may say, each of you will be sure to take pluralism or leave it, just as your own sense of rationality moves and inclines. The only thing I emphatically insist upon is that it is a fully co-ordinate hypothesis with monism. This world *may,* in the last resort, be a block-universe; but on the other hand it *may* be a universe only strung-along, not rounded in and closed. Reality *may* exist distributively just as it sensibly seems to, after all. On that possibility I do insist.

One's general vision of the probable usually decides such alternatives. They illustrate what I once wrote of as the 'will to believe.' In some of my lectures at Harvard I have spoken of what I call the 'faith-ladder,' as something quite different from the *sorites* of the logic-books, yet seeming to have an analogous form. I think you will quickly recognize in yourselves, as I describe it, the mental process to which I give this name.

A conception of the world arises in you somehow, no matter how. Is it true or not? you ask.

It *might* be true somewhere, you say, for it is not self-contradictory.

It *may* be true, you continue, even here and now.

It is *fit* to be true, it would be *well if it were true,* it *ought* to be true, you presently feel.

It *must* be true, something persuasive in you whispers next; and then—as a final result—

It shall be *held for true,* you decide; it *shall be* as if true, for *you.*

And your acting thus may in certain special cases be a means of making it securely true in the end.

Not one step in this process is logical, yet it is the way in which monists and pluralists alike espouse and hold fast to their visions. It is life exceeding logic, it is the practical reason for which the theoretic reason finds arguments after the conclusion is once there. In just this way do some of us hold to the unfinished pluralistic universe; in just this way do others hold to the timeless universe eternally complete.

Meanwhile the incompleteness of the pluralistic universe, thus assumed and held to as the most probable hypothesis, is also represented by the pluralistic philosophy as being self-reparative through us, as getting its disconnections remedied in part by our behavior. 'We use what we are and have, to know; and what we know, to be and have still more.' [98] Thus do philosophy and reality, theory and action, work in the same circle indefinitely.

I have now finished these poor lectures, and as you look back on them, they doubtless seem rambling and inconclusive enough. My only hope is that they may possibly have proved suggestive; and if indeed they have been suggestive of one point of method, I am almost willing to let all other suggestions go. That point is that *it is high time for the basis of discussion in these questions to be broadened and thickened up.* It is for that that I have brought in Fechner and Bergson, and descriptive psychology and religious experiences, and have ventured even to hint at psychical research and other wild beasts of the philosophic desert. Owing possibly to the fact that Plato and Aristotle, with their intellectualism, are the basis of philosophic study here, the Oxford brand of transcendentalism seems to me to have confined itself too exclusively to thin logical considerations, that would hold good in all conceivable worlds, worlds of an empirical constitution entirely different from ours. It is as if the actual peculiarities of the world that is were entirely irrelevant to the content of truth. But they cannot be irrelevant; and the philosophy of the future must imitate the sciences in taking them more and more elaborately into account. I urge some of the younger members of this learned audience to lay this hint to heart. If you can do so effectively, making still more concrete advances upon the path which Fechner and Bergson have so enticingly opened up, if you can gather philosophic conclusions of any kind, monistic or pluralistic, from the *particulars of life,* I will say, as I now do say, with the cheerfullest of hearts, 'Ring out, ring out my mournful rhymes, but ring the fuller minstrel in.'

[98] Blondel: *Annales de Philosophie Chrétienne.* June, 1906, p. 241.

vii

Annotated Bibliography of the Writings of William James

PREFATORY NOTE

"A List of the Published Writings of William James" was prepared by Henry James, Jr. and Edwin B. Holt, and published in the *Journal of Philosophy, Psychology, and Scientific Methods,* 1911, *18,* 157–165. That list furnished the nucleus of the present completer bibliography. It is probable that there are still omissions, and I shall be grateful for additions as well as for corrections. Translations are appearing from time to time in a variety of languages. It is obvious that there is no way of obtaining a complete or final list of these, but I have thought it best to refer to those of which I have a record.

Titles will be referred to in the notes by their date and serial number; thus *"1897–3"* refers to the third title under the date 1897.

Reviews cited without comment are as a rule merely summaries of the texts reviewed.

I hope that the notes which I have appended to most of the titles, together with the alphabetical index, will help the reader to find his way among the writings of William James. In view of the fact that much of James's most important thought appeared in the form of essays and reviews, often under a title which gave no clue to the contents, some such guide as this is indispensable to an adequate knowledge of his contributions to philosophy and psychology.

RALPH BARTON PERRY.

Cambridge, Mass.
April 22, 1920.

Addenda and corrections to this bibliography have been provided by Mr. Ralph Barton Perry III, who worked from material obtained from Ralph Barton Perry. The version of Mr. Perry III, took the bibliography to 1950, and can be found in the Houghton Library at Harvard University. The references to what is by now the numerous translations of James's writings, have for the most part been deleted. Some slight further corrections and additional material to 1975 have been integrated by the present editor. (J.J.McD.)

1867

1. Review (unsigned) of A German-American Novel (Grimm). *Nation*, Nov. 28, 1867, *5*, 432–433.

   Review of Herman Grimm's *Unüberwindliche Mächte*.

1868

1. Review (unsigned) on Moral Medication. *Nation*, July 16, 1868, *7*, 50–52.

   Review of A. A. Liébault's *Du Sommeil et des États analogues, considérés surtout au point de vue de l'action du Moral sur le Physique*. Manifests interest in scientific method in abnormal psychology.

2. Review (unsigned) of Ch. Darwin's *The Variation of Animals and Plants under Domestication*. *Atlantic Monthly*, 1868, *22*, 122–124.

   Shows rigorous scientific temper; suspects Darwin of placing too much reliance on "ingenious reasoning."

3. Review (unsigned) of Claude Bernard's *Rapport sur le Progrès et la Marche de la Physiologie générale en France*. *North Amer. Rev.*, 1868, *107*, 322–328.

   Discussion of the extravagant claims of physiology, then just beginning its career as an independent science; and of the difficulties of the medical student who is called upon to master a considerable amount of science of which the applications are not developed.

4. Review (unsigned) of Ch. Darwin's *The Variation of Animals and Plants under Domestication*. *North Amer. Rev.*, 1868, *107*, 362–368.

   Calls attention to the complicatedness of the phenomena which Darwin has brought together, and the absence of any law of their origin, unless it be the law of caprice.

* The weekly of that name published in New York.

5. Review (unsigned) of E. Feydeau's *La Comtesse de Chalis.* "The Manners of the Day" in Paris. *Nation*, 1868, *6*, 73–74.

1869

1. Review (unsigned) of E. Sargent's *Planchette: or the Despair of Science. Boston Daily Advertiser*, March 10, 1869.

   Urges the vigorous scientific study of a few test cases of alleged spiritistic phenomena.
   Partly reprinted in *1920–2*. Complete *1960–1*.

2. Review (unsigned) of H. Bushnell's *Woman Suffrage* and J. S. Mill's *Subjection of Women. North American Review*, 1869, *109*, 556–565.

1872

1. Review (unsigned) of H. Taine's *On Intelligence. Nation*, 1872, *15*, 139–141.

   Mainly expository; shows James's early philosophical interests.

2. Review (unsigned) of John Morley's *Voltaire. Atlantic Monthly*, 1872, *30*, 624–625.

   Estimates of Morley, Mill, Tyndall, Spencer, and Huxley.
   Quoted in *1920–1*.

1873

1. Review (unsigned) of I. Ray's *Contributions to Mental Pathology. Atlantic Monthly*, 1873, *31*, 748–750.

2. Vacations (unsigned). *Nation*, 1873, *17*, 90–91.

   Comments on American over-strenuousness, and the need for leisure and recreation.

3. A paragraph under *Notes* in which attention is called to *La Critique Philosophique. Nation*, Feb. 6, 1873, *16*, 94.

1874

1. Review (unsigned) of Recent Work on Mental Hygiene (D. A. Gorton, H. Maudsley, W. B. Carpenter). *Nation*, 1874, *19*, 43.

2. Notice (unsigned) of J. B. Pettigrew's *Physiology of the Circulation in Plants, in the Lower Animals, and in Man. Nation*, 1874, *19*, 63.

3. Notice (unsigned) of J. Hinton's *Physiology for Practical Use. Nation*, 1874, *19*, 190.

4. Review (unsigned) of the *Fifth Annual Report of the State Board of Health of Massachusetts. Atlantic Monthly*, 1874, *34*, 234.

   Contains statement of author's learning-to-skate-in-summer theory, apropos of half-time schooling.

5. Review (unsigned) of H. Maudsley's *Responsibility in Mental Disease. Atlantic Monthly,* 1874, *34,* 364–365.

   Notable advance in style; anti-positivistic. Opposes undue leniency in dealing with insane; their punishment a matter of public policy.

6. Review (unsigned) of W. B. Carpenter's *Principles of Mental Physiology. Atlantic Monthly,* 1874, *34,* 495.

7. Professor Jeffries Wyman (unsigned). *Harvard Advocate,* 1874, *18,* 8–9.

   Characteristic tribute to one who greatly influenced him in early years. Reprinted in part, *1920–1, I,* 48–49.

8. Review (unsigned) of B. P. Blood's *Anæsthetic Revelation. Atlantic Monthly,* 1874, *34,* 627–629.

   Indicative of his liberal personal sympathies, and of his early interest in mystical experience.
   Referred to in *1879–7,* 345. *Cf.* also *1897–3* (Preface) and *1910–5.*

9. The Mood of Science and the Mood of Faith. Letter to the Editor, signed "Ignoramus." *Nation,* Dec. 31, 1874, *19,* 437.

   Criticises the speculative scientist for invoking the authority of science when dealing with ultimate problems.

1875

1. Review (unsigned) of W. S. Jevons's *The Principles of Science. Atlantic Monthly,* April, 1875, *35,* 500–501.

   Shows early leanings towards J. S. Mill and the empirical school.

2. Review (unsigned) of G. H. Lewes's *Problems of Life and Mind. Atlantic Monthly,* Sept., 1875, *36,* 361–363.

   Earliest statement of the central features of his philosophy. Scepticism the only theoretically unassailable position; but truth is to be gained rather by taking a risk, staking one's person on a belief.
   Reprinted in *1920–2.*

3. Vivisection (unsigned). *Nation,* Feb. 25, 1875, *20,* 128–129.

   Plea for vivisection, while admitting its abuses.

4. Review (unsigned) of *The Unseen Universe. Nation,* 1875, *20,* 366–367.

   Contains reference to the "subjective method." Notable in style.

5. Note (unsigned) on Professors Wundt and Hitzig. *Nation,* 1875, *20,* 377–378.

   Appointment of W. Wundt and E. Hitzig at Zürich hailed as marking a new era.

6. Notice (unsigned) of F. Papillon's *Nature and Life*. *Nation*, 1875, *20*, 429.

   Contains a characterization of French philosophical style.

7. Notice (unsigned) of N. Morgan's *The Skull and Brain*. *Nation*, 1875, *21*, 185.

   Criticism of phrenology.

8. Chauncey Wright (unsigned). *Nation*, 1875, *21*, 194.

   Characterization of a friend to whose inspiring "intellectual companionship in old times" James acknowledges his indebtedness in the Preface to the *Principles* (*1890–4*, I, vii). From Wright he borrowed the expression cosmical "weather" to describe the waywardness of nature (*1897–3*, 52). Wright embodied the uncompromisingly positivistic attitude of mind; against which James reacted, but not without retaining much of its empiricism and pluralism. There are points of resemblance between Wright and C. S. Peirce, whom James names as the author of pragmatism. Wright's *Philosophical Discussions* have been collected and edited with a biography, by C. E. Norton, New York, 1877. Wright died in Cambridge, September 12, 1875, *æt.* 45.
   Reprinted in *1920–2*.

9. "Moment." Note (unsigned) on the German word. *Nation*, 1875, *21*, 214.

10. Review (unsigned) on German Pessimism. *Nation*, 1875, *21*, 233–234.

    Review of E. Pfleiderer's pamphlet, *Der moderne Pessimismus*, dealing with Schopenhauer and Hartmann. Comment on the self-consciousness and self-justification that characterize the German. As between pessimism and optimism, it is a matter of *choice;* and the goodness of things may be hypothetical, depending on our choice and coöperation.
    Reprinted in *1920–2*.

11. Notice (unsigned) of H. S. Williams's *Descriptive Anatomy of Typical Animals*. *Nation*, 1875, *21*, 252.

12. Notice (unsigned) of A. Wynter's *Border-Lands of Insanity and other allied Papers*. *Nation*, 1875, *21*, 330.

13. Letter to Editor, with reply by Editor. *The Neo-Pagans*, (letter dated Oct. 29, 1875), *Nation*, Dec. 2, 1875, *21*, 355.

14. Notice (unsigned) of Wilhelm Wundt's *Grundzüge der Physiologischen Psychologie*. *North American Review*, 1875, *121*, pp. 195–201, July.

1876

1. Notice (unsigned) of F. von Holzendorf's *Die Psychologie des Mordes*. *Nation*, 1876, *22*, 16.

2. Note (unsigned) on C. Letourneau's *La Biologie*. *Nation*, 1876, *22*, 98.

3. Note (unsigned) on the *Revue Philosophique*. *Nation*, March 2, 1876, *22*, 147.

Comment on contemporary thought. Recommends that philosophy and science be pursued together, and that philosophers study physiological psychology.

4. Note (unsigned) on P. Topinard's *Anthropologie*. *Nation*, 1876, *22*, 180.

Observes greater regard for facts among the French as result of the war.

5. Review (unsigned) of Bain and Renouvier. *Nation*, June 8, 1876, *22*, 367–369.

Preference of Renouvier to Bain as exponent of positivism, because Renouvier gives attention to the laws and relations that group phenomena together, and because he defends the doctrine of freedom of the will, as being in the last analysis a doctrine to be *chosen*. First record of James's regard for Renouvier, who exerted a strong and lasting influence on him. Reprinted in *1920–2*.

6. Note (unsigned) on Vivisection. *Nation*, 1876, *22*, 415.

Same view as *1875–3*.

7. Review (unsigned) of Renan's *Dialogues*. *Nation*, Aug. 3, 1876, *23*, 78–79.

Vigorous criticism of Renan's "foppishness," and "dandified despair," as contrasted with the courageous and *helpful* man who will always be reckoned the best man.
Partly reprinted in *1920–2*.

8. The Teaching of Philosophy in our Colleges (unsigned). *Nation*, Sept. 21, 1876, *23*, 178–179.

Contains interesting account of the shortcomings and difficulties of philosophical teaching in the 70's, with special reference to religious restraints and to new developments at Harvard.
Partly reprinted in *1920–1*.

9. Notice (unsigned) of W. von Bezold's *Theory of Color in its Relation to Art and Industry*. *Nation*, 1876, *23*, 289.

1877

1. Review (unsigned) on The Mind and the Brain (D. Ferrier, H. Maudsley, J. Luys). *Nation*, 1877, *24*, 355–356.

Criticism of Maudsley's *"odium anti-theologicum."* General remarks on introspection, and relation of psychology to physiology. On Luys, *cf. 1879–7*, 323.

2. Review (unsigned) of G. Allen's *Physiological Æsthetics*. *Nation*, 1877, *25*, 185–186.

> Criticism of Spencerian methods; urges need of intensive research in field of psychology.

3. Review (unsigned) of G. H. Lewes's *Physical Basis of Mind*. *Nation*, 1877, *25*, 290.

> Criticism of Lewes's redundancy of method.
> Partly reprinted in *1920–2*.

1878

1. Remarks on Spencer's *Definition of Mind as Correspondence*. *Jour. of Speculative Phil.*, Jan. 1878, *12*, 1–18.

> This important essay develops the thesis that the central fact in mind is interest or preference. It is scarcely too much to say that this is the germinal idea of James's psychology, epistemology, and philosophy of religion. He referred to this essay when in speaking of "the reflex theory of mind" he said: "I am not sure that all physiologists see that it commits them to regarding the mind as an essentially teleological mechanism. I mean by this that the conceiving or theorizing faculty—the mind's middle department—functions *exclusively for the sake of ends* that do not exist at all in the world of impressions we receive by way of our senses, but are set by our emotional and practical subjectivity altogether" (*Reflex Action and Theism, 1897–3*, 117).
> Reprinted in *1920–2*.

2. Quelques Considérations sur la méthode subjective. *Critique Philosophique*, Jan. 24, 1878, 6me année, *2*, 407–413.

> A communication to the editors of the *Critique Philosophique*, and dated November 20, 1877. It was thus written before the publication in 1878 of the earliest psychological articles. It contains a brief preliminary statement of parts of *1882–2*, and indicates that the author had worked out the *practical* motives of belief before the theoretical. See notes under *1879–7* and *1882–2*. The highly appreciative note appended to the present article by the editor (Renouvier) suggests that James was known abroad as a philosopher before he was known as a psychologist.
> Reprinted in *1920–2*.

3. Review (unsigned) of R. L. Dugdale's *The Jukes: a Study in Crime, Pauperism, Disease and Heredity. Atlantic Monthly*, 1878, *41*, 405.

4. Brute and Human Intellect. *Jour. of Speculative Phil.*, July 1878, *12*, 236–276.

> Pages 237–241 contain first statement of author's theory of association, differing from treatment in *1880–1* and *1890–4* in placing less emphasis on neural conditions. Pages 241–247 contain the earliest statement of the general principles of reasoning, differing from *1890–4*, II, 325–340, in its slight emphasis on the factor of subjective interest and on the relations to formal logic.
> Otherwise this article is reprinted almost verbatim in *1890–4*, I, 506–507

(Discrimination); II, 325–326, 340–344, 345–369 (Reasoning). It is referred to in *1879–5*, 12, 20.

The article was expounded and criticised by C. Renouvier in a series of articles entitled "De la caractéristique intellectuelle de l'homme," *Critique Philosophique*, 1879, 8me année, *1*, 369–376, 394–397; *2*, 17–26, 41–48.

1879

1. Review (unsigned) of Herbert Spencer's *Data of Ethics. Nation*, 1879, *29*, 178–179.

   Contains criticism of Spencer on ground that he fails to provide for the factor of personal bias, which will determine what one shall struggle for, and what shall therefore prevail in the evolutionary process.
   Partly reprinted in *1920–2*.

2. Notice (unsigned) of A. J. Balfour's *Defense of Philosophic Doubt. Nation*, 1879, *29*, 280.

3. Review (unsigned) of W. K. Clifford's *Lectures and Essays. Nation*, 1879, *29*, 312–313.

   A characterization and criticism of Clifford, exemplifying James's chivalrous admiration for every heroic spirit, however differing in opinion from himself. Shows the causes of Clifford's failure, and the defects in his evolutionary principles. Clifford's views on "The Ethics of Belief" most perfectly embodied that rigorous positivism to which James opposed his "Will-to-Believe" doctrine. See references to Clifford in *1897–3, passim*.
   Reprinted in *1920–2*.

4. Notice (unsigned) of H. Calderwood's *Relations of Mind and Brain. Nation*, 1879, *29*, 410.

   Comment on psychology new and old; affirms importance of physiological psychology.

5. Are we Automata? *Mind*, 1879, *4*, 1–22.

   General defense of the efficacy of consciousness and its essentially selective or interested character, against the theory of automatism. Closely related to *1878–1*. The topic is treated more fully here than in Chapter V of *1890–4*.
   Parts reprinted in *1890–4*, I, 134–135, 139–140, 142–144 (The Automaton Theory); and 284–289 (The Stream of Thought).

6. The Spatial Quale. *Jour. of Speculative Phil.*, 1879, *13*, 64–87.

   The earliest statement of the nativistic theory of space-perception afterwards developed more fully in *1887–2*. Quoted in *1890–4*, II, 169. Referred to in *1890–4*, Preface, and II, 282, as a briefer and substantially identical statement which the reader might advantageously substitute for Chapter XX.

7. The Sentiment of Rationality. *Mind*, 1879, *4*, 317–346.

   A note at the end of this article states that it is designed to be the first chapter of a psychological work on motives of philosophizing. The pres-

ent article deals with the theoretic motives; *1882–2*, with the practical. Contains copious references to other philosophers and psychologists. Statement of the instrumentalist doctrine of knowledge (p. 318) quoted in *1890–4*, II, 335–336, note. About one-fifth of this essay was combined with *1882–2*, and reprinted in *1897–3*, afterwards in *1905–11* and *1917–1*. This new article bears the name of "The Sentiment of Rationality," but is not to be confused with the original article. The latter is reprinted entire in *1920–2*.
Translated into French, with note of tribute by C. Renouvier, *Critique Philosophique*, 1879, 8me année, *2*, 72–89, 113–118, 129–138.

8. Review of *Modern Chromatics with Applications to Art and Industry*. Ogden N. Rood, N.Y. Appleton and Co. *Nation*, 1879, *29*, 260.

1880

1. The Association of Ideas. *Popular Sci. Monthly*, 1880, *16*, 577–593.

   Pages 577–581 contain orientation of author's view in relation to Associationism and Hegelianism. Remainder of article reprinted almost verbatim in *1890–4*, I, 554–582 (Association).

2. Great Men, Great Thoughts and the Environment. *Atlantic Monthly*, Oct. 1880, *46*, 441–459.

   Address delivered before the Harvard Natural History Society. This constitutes James's contribution to the philosophy of history. Insists on the importance of the examples, initiatives, and decisions of individuals in bringing about historical events. Criticises the school of Spencer, in particular Grant Allen.
   Reprinted in *1897–3*, and in *1917–1*, under the title of "Great Men and their Environment."
   Translated into French, *Critique Philosophique*, 1881, 9me année, *2*, 396–400, 407–415; 1881, 10me année, *1*, 1–14.

3. The Feeling of Effort. *Anniversary Memoirs of the Boston Society of Natural History*. Boston, 1880. Pp. 32.

   The author's earliest discussion of the will, including "the feeling of innervation," ideo-motor action, and the psychology of free-will. Last pages contain useful summary of author's position.
   About seven pages are reprinted in *1890–4*, II, 498–511. Otherwise Chapter VI of *1890–4* (the chapter on Will) is a rewriting rather than a reprinting of the present article. Summary by Editor in *Mind*, 1880, *5*, 582. Fragments incorporated in *1888–1*. The whole reprinted in *1920–2*. Translated into French, *Critique Philosophique*, 1880, 9me année, *2*, 123–128, 129–135, 145–148, 200–208, 220–224, 225–231, 289–291.

4. Review (unsigned) of T. L. Lindsay's *Mind in the Lower Animals*. *Nation*, 1880, *30*, 270–271.

   Contains earliest statements regarding instinct, and an account of acquisitiveness afterwards reprinted in *1890–4*, II, 423–424.

5. Notice (unsigned) of M. Guthrie's *On Mr. Spencer's Formula of Evolution*. *Nation*, 1880, *30*, 392.

Deprecates a purely negative criticism of Spencer's generalization, which generalization he thinks must appeal strongly to the popular mind until superseded by a better one.

6. Notice (unsigned) of J. E. Walter's *Perception of Space and Matter.* *Nation*, 1880, *31*, 119.

Contains interesting paragraph comparing English and American style.

7. Review (unsigned) on The Brain as a Mental Organ (H. C. Bastian). *Nation*, 1880, *31*, 224–225.

Discusses insentiency of efferent nerve currents, attributing the view to Bastian.

8. Letter on Sensibility of Articular Surfaces. *Boston Med. and Surg. Jour.*, 1880, *102*, 94.

Request for observations.

9. Review on Experimental and Critical Contribution to the Physiology of the Semicircular Canals (Spamer). *Amer. Jour. of Otology*, 1880, *2*, 341–343.

Critical notice of experiments conducted by K. Spamer, and reported in *Pflüger's Archiv, 21*, 479. Alludes to experiments of the reviewer tending to invalidate Breuer's theories regarding the semicircular canals.

10. *Le sentiment de l'effort.* Paris, Bureau de la critique philosophique, littéraire, politique, scientifique, 1880, *4*, Vol. 2, 123–135, (145)–148, 200–208, (289)–291.

1881

1. Notice (unsigned) of J. Le Conte's *Sight: An Exposition of the Principles of Monocular and Binocular Vision. Nation*, 1881, *32*, 190–191.

Contains statement of James's adherence to the nativistic view of space-perception.

2. Notes on the Sense of Dizziness in Deaf-Mutes. *Harvard University Bulletin*, 1881, *2*, 173.

Brief summary of results afterwards published in *1882–3*.

3. Reflex Action and Theism. *Unitarian Rev.*, 1881, *16*, 389–416.

Address delivered before Unitarian Ministers' Institute at Princeton, Mass., October 4, 1881. Note at opening states that this essay, *1879–7*, and *1882–2*, are fragments of "a larger essay on 'The Sentiment of Rationality.' " The present article maintains that theism is rational in the sense of furnishing adequate stimuli to man's practical nature.
Reprinted with slight changes in *1897–3*.
Translated into French, *Critique Philosophique*, 1881, 10me année, *2*, 385–391, 401–410; 1882, 11me année, *1*, 5–13.

4. William James on Temperance. *Independent,* June 23, 1881.

> Synopsis of address delivered before students of Harvard College and stating that the evidence of physiology and of general experience supported total abstinence.

1882

1. On Some Hegelisms. *Mind,* April 1882, *7,* 186–208.

> A general attack on the Hegelian logic, with an appended note in which the Hegelian identification of opposites is compared with the experience of nitrous-oxide-gas-intoxication. (*Cf. 1898–1.*)
> Reprinted in *1897–3.*

2. Rationality, Activity and Faith. *Princeton Rev.,* July 1882, *2,* 58–86.

> Written in 1879 as sequel to *1879–7,* the latter dealing with the theoretical, the former with the practical, motives of rationality. (See explanatory opening paragraph in present essay, and note appended to opening of *1881–3.*)
> Combined with selections from *1879–7,* and reprinted under title of "The Sentiment of Rationality" in *1897–3* and in *1917–1.* Pages 64–69 were also quoted in *1890–4,* II, 312–315.
> Translated into French, *Critique Philosophique,* 1882, 11me année, *2,* 129–140, 161–166.

3. The Sense of Dizziness in Deaf-Mutes. *Amer. Jour. of Otology,* 1882, *4,* 239–254.

> Observations on 519 cases of deaf-mutes, of whom 186 were reported insusceptible to dizziness. A line of investigation that might be pursued further (*cf. 1881–2* and *1887–7*). This article is referred to briefly in *1890–4,* II, 89, note.
> Reprinted in *1920–2.*

4. The Philosophical System of Antonio Rosmini-Serbati. *Nation,* 1882, *35,* 313.

> Contains classification of philosophies into sensationalistic and rationalistic.

1884

1. On Some Omissions of Introspective Psychology. *Mind,* 1884, *9,* 1–26.

> Earliest statement of many of James's characteristic doctrines, such as his critique of introspection, his provision for feelings of relation, his critique of associationism, and the views regarding the unity of consciousness which later gave him so much difficulty (*cf.* note to *1895–4,* below). Fragments of this essay are scattered through *1890–4,* Chapter VII (Methods and Snares of Psychology), Chapter IX (Stream of Thought), Chapter X (Consciousness of Self), Chapter XII (Conception).

2. What is an Emotion? *Mind*, April 1884, *9*, 188–205.

James's original statement of the famous "James-Lange" theory of the Emotions, written before James was acquainted with Lange's views, which were published in 1885 (*cf. 1890–4*, II, 449).
Most of this article was reprinted in scattered paragraphs in *1890–4*, Chapter XXV, where the treatment was, however, reorganized and greatly amplified. Reprinted in full in *1920–2*.

3. Absolutism and Empiricism. *Mind*, 1884, *9*, 281–286.

Contends that absolutism like empiricism should admit that it is a hypothesis, which appeals to both our logical and our emotional faculties. Written with special reference to J. S. Haldane's "Life and Mechanism," *Mind*, 1884, *9*, 27–47.
Reprinted in *1912–1*.

4. The Dilemma of Determinism. *Unitarian Rev.*, 1884, *22*, 193–224.

A lecture delivered to the Harvard Divinity School, March 13, 1884. Defense of indeterminism with special reference to the problem of evil.
Reprinted in *1897–3* (omitting introductory paragraph).
Translated into French, *Critique Philosophique*, 1884, 14me année, *2*, 273–280, 305–312; 1885, 13me année, *2*, 353–362.

5. *The Literary Remains of the Late Henry James.* Edited with an Introduction, by William James. Boston: Houghton Mifflin, 1884, 12mo, pp. 471.

The Introduction, pages 1–119, presents many of the editor's characteristic views, such as the antithesis between monism and pluralism, healthy-mindedness and the sick soul, religion and moralism, and the appeal to practice for the decision between them. It contains in germ the principles elaborated in *1902–1*.
Reprinted almost complete in *1947–1*.

6. Letter to *Pall Mall Budget* on Seasickness, Oct. 3, 1884. (Written Cambridge, Sept. 11). Cf. *1887–7*.

1885

1. On the Function of Cognition. *Mind*, 1885, *10*, 27–44.

Read before the Aristotelian Society, December 1, 1884. The most important of James's early articles as respects the special problems of epistemology. Distinguishes between knowledge by acquaintance and knowledge-about; discusses meaning, objective reference, correspondence, truth, and error. This article was reprinted almost verbatim in *1909–8*. On relation of the views here expressed to the author's later pragmatism, *cf. ibid.*, 41–42, note.

2. Review (unsigned) of J. Royce's *The Religious Aspect of Philosophy*. *Atlantic Monthly*, 1885, *55*, 840–843.

Throws interesting light on the development of James's theory of knowledge. In this review he is inclined to accept Royce's solution of the problem of thought's reference to reality. See *1885–1*, and *1909–8*, 22, note.
Reprinted in *1920–2*.

3. Letter to the Editors. *Daily Crimson*, June 8, 1885.

   Advocates student government, with special reference to the matter of celebrations.

4. Experiments in Memory. Review of H. Ebbinghaus's *Ueber das Gedächtnis. Science*, 1885, *6*, 198–199.

   Summary and appreciation of Ebbinghaus's "heroic" experimentation.

5. Review of Th. Lipps's *Psychologische Studien. Science*, 1885, *6*, 308–310.

   Favorable review of the author's method and of his nativistic tendencies in the matter of space-perception.

1886

1. (and G. M. Carnochan) Report of the Committee on Hypnotism. *Proc. of the Amer. Soc. for Psychical Research*, 1886, *1*, 95–102.

   Study of mental functions in hypnosis; sensation, apperception, discrimination, recognition.
   Pages 96–97 reprinted in *1890–4*, II, 607–608; pages 98–100 in *ibid.*, II, 351 (note). Page 95 cited in *ibid.*, I, 208, and II, 490.

2. Report of the Committee on Mediumistic Phenomena. *Proc. of the Amer. Soc. for Psychical Research*, 1886, *1*, 102–106.

   First account of Mrs. Piper and of the author's attitude towards mediumistic phenomena. Several paragraphs quoted in *1890–3*, 652–654.

3. The Perception of Time. *Jour. of Speculative Phil.*, 1886, *20*, 374–407.

   Reprinted almost *verbatim* in *1890–4*, I, Chapter XV (Perception of Time).

4. Letter to the Editors. *Daily Crimson*, June 2, 1886.

5. Letter to the Editors. *Daily Crimson*, June 4, 1886.

   In this letter and the above the writer urges students to take steps to preserve order in the college yard, and deprecates the students' lack of moral courage and of effective public opinion.

6. Review of Rosmini's *Psychology. Science*, 1886, *8*, 130.

   Rosmini a giant, but a "dead giant."

1887

1. Review of E. Gurney's, F. W. H. Myers's, and F. Podmore's *Phantasms of the Living. Science*, 1887, *9*, 18–20.

   Mainly summary, but contains interesting concluding paragraph predicting that the verdict of posterity will be favorable to the authors.

2. Review (unsigned) of G. T. Ladd's *Physiological Psychology. Nation*, 1887, *44*, 473.

Contains anticipation of pragmatic method as applied to the soul-theory; also statement of cognitive character of sensation.

3. Review (unsigned) of H. T. Finck's *Romantic Love and Personal Beauty. Nation*, 1887, *45*, 237–238.

Criticises confusion between feelings and ideas about them; also the author's loose generalizations of Darwinism.

4. The Perception of Space. *Mind*, 1887, *12*, 1–30, 183–211, 321–353, 516–548.

Reprinted with considerable revision in *1890–4*, II, Chapter XX (Perception of Space). Changes are mainly in style and arrangement.

5. The Laws of Habit. *Popular Sci. Monthly*, 1887, *30*, 433–451.

Reprinted in *1890–4*, I, Chapter IV (Habit).

6. What is an Instinct? *Scribner's Mag.*, 1887, *1*, 355–365.

Reprinted, almost verbatim, in *1890–4*, II, 383–402, where it is combined with *1887–8* to form the chapter on Instinct.

7. A Suggestion for the Prevention of Seasickness. Letter to the Editor. *Boston Med. and Surg. Jour.*, 1887, *116*, 490–491. Cf. *1884–6*.

Written May 12, 1887. Referring to *1883–3*, the writer suggests prevention of seasickness by counter-irritation of the skin in the neighborhood of the ears, on the hypothesis that the source of seasickness is in the semicircular canals. James's priority in this field does not appear to have been fully recognized. *Cf.* J. Byrne: *The Physiology of the Semicircular Canals and their Relation to Seasickness*, 478–485, 487.

8. Some Human Instincts. *Popular Sci. Monthly*, 1887, *31*, 160–170, 666–681.

Contains introductory paragraphs summarizing *1887–6;* the rest is reprinted with some amplification in *1890–4*, II, 403–441, where it is combined with *1887–6*, to form the chapter on Instinct.

9. Reaction-Time in the Hypnotic Trance. *Proc. of the Amer. Soc. for Psychical Research*, 1887, *1*, 246–248.

Shows that hypnotic trance has no constant effect on reaction-time. Cited in *1890–4*, I, 97.

10. The Consciousness of Lost Limbs. *Proc. of the Amer. Soc. for Psychical Research*, 1887, *1*, 249–258.

Summary of report from 154 cases. Results bearing on subjects of sensation, perception, and will referred to briefly in *1890–4*, II, 105, 516. *Cf.* also *ibid.*, II, 38–39.
Reprinted in *1920–2*.

11. *The Foundations of Ethics*. By John Edward Maude. Edited, with a Preface, by William James. New York: Holt, 1887, 12mo, pp. 1–9.

Preface devoted to an account of the author.

12. Review (unsigned) of J. G. Schurman's *Ethical Import of Darwinism.*
Nation, 1887, *45*, 376.

1888

1. What the Will Effects. *Scribner's Mag.*, 1888, *3*, 240–250.

A brief and popular version of the theories (omitting "feeling of innervation") developed in *1890–4*, II, Chapter XXVI, only a small amount
(pp. 242–243, 245–246) being there reprinted. Present article contains al-
lusions to and characterizations of "the new psychology," especially in
opening paragraphs, page 240.
Translated into French, *Critique Philosophique*, 1888, nouv. série, 4me
année, *1*, 401–420.

2. Réponse de M. W. James aux Remarques de M. Renouvier sur sa
théorie de la volonté. *Critique Philosophique*, 1888, nouv. série, 4me
année, *2*, 401–404.

James's "What the Will Effects" (1888) was translated into French in
the *Critique Philosophique*, 1888, *1*, 401–420. The same periodical, 1888,
2, 117–126, contains "Quelques remarques sur la théorie de la volonté de
M. W. James," by Renouvier. The present communication contains James's
reply. It contains a brief elucidation of the author's theory of the will, and
a statement regarding his indebtedness to Lotze and to Renouvier.
Reprinted in *1920–2*.

3. Review of A. Seth's *Hegelianism and Personality. Nation*, 1888, *46*,
246.

Brief survey of Anglo-American philosophy from the time of Mill and
Bain. Estimate of the "Anglo-Hegelian" movement.

4. Letter to the Editors. *Daily Crimson*, January 25, 1888.

Advocates "effective moral opinion," and the honor system at examinations.

5. Professor von Gizycki and Determinism. *Open Court*, 1888, *2*, 889.

Reply to G. von Gizycki's criticisms in *Open Court*, 1887, *1*, 729, 758, of
James's definition of determinism (*1884–4*). Argues that a "One and All"
that necessitates evil is morally irrational.

6. Letter to the Editors. *Daily Crimson*, February 3, 1888.

Signed "A Professor." Continues discussion begun in *1888–4*, of formation of student organization to introduce honor system at examinations.

7. Review of E. Gurney's *Tertium Quid. Nation*, 1888, *46*, 349.

8. Note on E. Gurney's death. *Nation*, July 19, 1888, *47*, 53.

1889

1. The Psychological Theory of Extension. *Mind*, 1889, *14*, 107–109.

A succinct restatement of the nativistic position as regards space perception, written in reply to a criticism by George Croom Robertson, in *Mind*,

1888, *13*, 418–424, of James's articles on "The Perception of Space," published in 1887. The present paper is part of a general discussion provoked by Robertson's criticism, a discussion in which James Ward, among others, participated.

Reprinted in *1920–2*.

2. Note to *Second Report on Experimental Psychology*. *Proc. of the Amer. Soc. for Psychical Research*, 1889, *1*, 317–319.

Denies C. S. Minot's contention that "diagram-habits" invalidate results reported by the English Society for Psychical Research on diagram-drawing in demonstrations of thought-transferences.

3. Notes on Automatic Writing. *Proc. of the Amer. Soc. for Psychical Research*, 1889, *1*, 548–564.

Description of scattered cases, one of which is reprinted in *1890–4*, I, 394–396. Evidence adduced here for anæsthesia in arm and hand of automatic writer forms basis for statement in *1890–4*, I, 398.

4. The Psychology of Belief. *Mind*, 1889, *14*, 321–352. A note of the article was suppressed in *1890–4*.

Reprinted almost verbatim, but with additions, in *1890–4*, II, Chapter XXI (The Perception of Reality).

5. Report on the Congress of Physiological Psychology at Paris. *Mind*, 1889, *14*, 614–615.

Congress held in Paris, August 5–10, 1889, James being present. Notes interest in psychical research.

6. Edmond Scherer. *Nation*, 1889, *48*, 280–281.

Written on the occasion of the death of Scherer, who is favorably compared with Renan and Taine. James's authorship of this article cannot be absolutely verified, but there is no reasonable doubt of it.

1890

1. The Hidden Self. *Scribner's Mag.*, 1890, *7*, 361–373.

Pages 361–362 reprinted in *1897–3*, 299–303, where it is combined with *1892–1* and *1896–1* under the title of "What Psychical Research has Accomplished"; pages 364–367 reprinted in *1890–4*, I, Chapter X, 385–388. The balance of this essay consists of a popular account of the work of the French school of abnormal psychology, especially that of Janet and Binet.

2. The Importance of Individuals. *Open Court*, 1890, *4*, 2437–2440.

Sequel to *1880–2;* and written as a rejoinder to a reply by Grant Allen in *Atlantic Monthly*, 1881, *47*, 371–381.

Reprinted in *1897–3*.

3. A Record of Observations of Certain Phenomena of Trance. Part III. *Proc. of the (Eng.) Soc. for Psychical Research*, 1890, *6*, 651–659.

A review of the author's experience with Mrs. Piper since his first acquaintance with her in 1885. Testifies to his belief in her honesty, and her possession in trances of knowledge which she cannot have had in her waking state; but has no explanation to offer.

4. The Principles of Psychology. New York: Holt, 1890, 2 vols., 8vo, pp. xii + 689, vi + 704.

Preface formulates the author's "positivistic" method. In Preface to *1892–2*, page v, the author says of *1890–4*, "With a single exception all the chapters were written for the book; and then by an afterthought some of them were sent to magazines, because the completion of the whole work seemed so distant." Contains the following chapters, reprinted as indicated: Vol. I, I, the Scope of Psychology; II, The Functions of the Brain; III, On Some General Conditions of Brain-Activity; IV, Habit, *1887–5;* V, The Automaton Theory, parts (pp. 134–135, 139–140, 142–144) from *1879–1;* VI, The Mind-Stuff Theory; VII, The Methods and Snares of Psychology, part (pp. 190–191) from *1884–1;* VIII, The Relations of Minds to Other Things; IX, The Stream of Thought, parts (pp. 232, 234–235, 243–246, 250–256, 275–276) from *1884–1,* and (pp. 284–289) from *1879–1;* X, The Consciousness of Self, parts (pp. 385–388) from *1890–1,* and (pp. 394–396) from *1889–3;* XI, Attention; XII, Conception, part (pp. 477–479, note) from *1884–1;* XIII, Discrimination and Comparison, part (pp. 506–507) from *1878–4;* XIV, Association, part (pp. 554–583) from *1880–1;* XV, The Perception of Time, *1886–3;* XVI, Memory; Vol. II, XVII, Sensation (pp. 13–27 written by E. B. Delabarre); XVIII, Imagination; XIX, The Perception of "Things"; XX, The Perception of Space, *1887–4,* and note (p. 169) from *1879–2;* XXI, The Perception of Reality, *1889–4,* and (pp. 312–315) from *1882–2;* XXII, Reasoning, parts (pp. 325–326, 340–369) from *1878–4,* (pp. 335–336, note) from *1879–7,* (p. 351, note) from *1886–1;* XXIII, The Production of Movement; XXIV, Instinct, *1887–6* and *1887–8;* XXV, The Emotions, part (pp. 449–453, 456–459, 462–463, 467–468, 470–473) from *1884–2;* XXVI, Will, parts (pp. 496–511, 523, 525–526, 548–549, 562, 566) from *1880–3,* and (pp. 524–525, 562–574) from *1888–1;* XXVII, Hypnotism, part (pp. 607–608) from *1886–1;* XXVIII, Necessary Truths and the Effects of Experience, part (pp. 634–635, note) from *1881–1.*
Chapter IV partly reprinted in *1915–1.* Chapter XXVI partly reprinted in *1917–1.* Book reprinted 1893, 1899, 1908, 1927, 1950.

5. Psychology at Harvard University. *Amer. Jour. of Psychol.,* 1890, *3,* 278.

Account of courses in psychology offered at Harvard in year 1889–90.

6. Letter to the Editor. *Amer. Jour. of Psychol.,* 1890, *3,* 292.

Asks coöperation in census of hallucinations projected by Congress of Physiological Psychology. *Cf. 1889–5.*

7. The Origin of Right-handedness. Letter to the Editor. *Science,* 1890, *16,* 275.

Reply to J. M. Baldwin's claim that right-handedness is acquired through feelings of innervation. James regards it as instinctive or semi-reflexive.

8. "Assistance Wanted for Psychological Statistics," letter to the editor of *Open Court,* 4, May 22, 1890. Asks for information on hallucinations for census committee of the "Society for Psychical Research."

1891

1. The Proposed Shortening of the College Course. *Harvard Monthly,* 1891, *11,* 127–137.

   Defense of three-year A.B. at Harvard on ground that it will improve the tone of the college and relate it more closely to American life; contains impressions of Harvard, comparison of American with European methods, etc.

2. The Moral Philosopher and the Moral Life. *Internat. Jour. of Ethics,* 1891, *1,* 330–354.

   Published as read before the Philosophical Club of Yale University, February 9, 1891. This address was originally delivered before the students' Philosophical Club at Harvard, and at that time bore the title "The Essentials of an Ethical Universe," referring to the assumptions that must be made in order to obtain one common moral world for all moral subjects. Reprinted in *1897–3.*

3. Letter on Abbott against Royce. *Nation,* 1891, *53,* 389–390.

   Written November 15, 1891. Defense of Royce in controversy with Dr. Francis Ellingwood Abbott regarding former's criticisms in *International Journal of Ethics,* 1891, *1,* 98–113.

4. A Charming North Carolina Resort. Letter to the Editor. *New York Evening Post,* September 3, 1891.

   An account of Linville, N.C., written from that place on August 31, 1891.

1892

1. What Psychical Research Has Accomplished. *Forum,* 1892, *13,* 727–742.

   A brief history of the British Society for Psychical Research. Most of it is reprinted in *1897–3,* 303–317, 320–323, where it is combined with *1890–1,* and *1896–1.*

2. Psychology (Briefer Course). New York: Holt, 1892, 12mo, pp. xiii + 478.

   Abridgment of *1890–4.* "About two-fifths of the volume is either new or rewritten, the rest is 'scissors and paste'" (Preface, p. iii). Contains the following chapters, abridged from *1890–4* as indicated: I, Introductory; II, Sensation in General; III, Sight; IV, Hearing; V, Touch, the Temperature Sense, the Muscular Sense, and Pain; VI, Sensations of Motion; VII, The Structure of the Brain; VIII, The Functions of the Brain, *1890–4,* Chapter II; IX, Some General Conditions of Neural Activity, *1890–4,* Chapter III; X, Habit, *1890–4,* Chapter IV; XI, The Stream of Consciousness, *1890–4,* Chapter IX; XII, The Self, *1890–4,* Chapter X; XIII, Attention, *1890–4,* Chapter XI; XIV, Conception, *1890–4,* Chapter XII; XV, Discrimination, *1890–4,* Chapter XIII; XVI, Association, *1890–4,* Chapter XIV; XVII, The Sense of Time, *1890–4,* Chapter XV; XVIII, Memory, *1890–4,* Chapter XVI; XIX, Imagination, *1890–4,* Chapter

XVIII; XX, Perception, *1890–4*, Chapter XIX; XXI, The Perception of Space, *1890–4*, Chapter XX; XXII, Reasoning, *1890–4*, Chapter XXII; XXIII, Consciousness and Movement, *1890–4*, Chapter XXIII; XXIV, Emotion, *1890–4*, Chapter XXV; XXV, Instinct, *1890–4*, Chapter XXIV; XXVI, Will, *1890–4*, Chapter XXVI; Epilogue, Psychology and Philosophy. Preface contains important statements regarding arrangement of topics in psychology, and regarding the composition of *1890–4*.

Chapter X partly reprinted in *1917–1*. Book reprinted 1893, 1900, 1905, 1907, 1908, 1909, 1910, 1913, 1914, 1915, 1923, 1925. Republished (66 diagrams) with foreword by Ralph Barton Perry, by World Publishing Co., Cleveland and New York, 1948.

Reprinted in abridged edition, 1961 (Harper Torchbooks); complete, 1962 (Collier Books); complete, 1963 (Premier).

3. Review (unsigned) of J. Sully's *Human Mind. Nation*, 1892, *55*, 285–286.

4. A Plea for Psychology as a "Natural Science." *Phil. Rev.*, 1892, *1*, 146–153.

Occasioned by an article entitled "Psychology as So-called 'Natural Science,'" by G. T. Ladd, *Phil. Rev.*, 1892, *1*, 24–53. In this reply James briefly sets forth his "program" for a scientific psychology, and the relation to that program of his own *Principles*. He contends that psychology should make the necessary assumptions, regard "mental states" as its data, and explain their order in terms of their physiological, organic, and physical conditions. In this way he hopes to make psychology useful in education, medicine, religion, and other activities involving "the control of states of mind."
Reprinted in *1920–2*.

5. Thought before Language: A Deaf-Mute's Recollections. *Phil. Rev.*, 1892, *1*, 613–624.

The greater part of this article consists of the narrative of T. H. d'Estrella, a deaf-mute, throwing light on the development of ideas without means of communication, the naïve moral and cosmological speculation of an isolated mind. Also contains confirmation of the trustworthiness of the deaf-mute, M. Ballard, cited in *1890–4*, I, 266.

6. Review of H. Schmidkunz's *Psychologie der Suggestion. Phil. Rev.*, 1892, *1*, 306–309.

7. Review of F. Courmont's *Le Cervelet et ses Fonctions. Phil. Rev.*, 1892, *1*, 319–322.

8. Review of F. Pillon's *L'Année Philosophique. Phil. Rev.*, 1892, *1*, 649–652.

9. The Steel-Wire-Binding Nuisance. Letter to the Editor. *Nation*, 1892, *55*, 374.

Written in Florence, October 27, 1892, apropos of the appearance of the *Phil. Rev.* with wire instead of stitched binding. Cf. also New York *Evening Post*, Nov. 17, 1892.

1893

1. The Original Datum of Space Consciousness. *Mind,* 1893, n.s. *2,* 363–365.

    An elucidation of the nativistic doctrine of "local signs," in reply to E. Ford's "The Original Datum of Space-Consciousness," *Mind,* 1893, n.s. *2,* 217–218.
    Reprinted in *1920–2.*

2*a.* Mr. Bradley on Immediate Resemblance. *Mind,* 1893, n.s. *2,* 208–210.

    Written in reply to F. H. Bradley's "On Professor James' Doctrine of Simple Resemblance," *Mind,* 1893, n.s. *2,* 83–88. James defends the simple and irreducible character of the relation of resemblance. This and the following discussion are referred to in *1909–5,* 335, note; where Bradley is cited as an illustration of the "philosophy *in extremis,*" which will not admit of degrees of resemblance, but only of "absolute identity" or absolute non-comparability.
    Reprinted in *1920–2.*

2*b.* Immediate Resemblance. *Mind,* 1893, n.s. *2,* 509–510.

    Written in reply to Bradley's "Professor James on Simple Resemblance," *Mind,* 1893, n.s. *2,* 366–369, in which Bradley defends the conception of identity-in-difference. In the present reply James contends that this differs only in name from his "resemblance."
    Reprinted in *1920–2.*

3. Review of C. Renouvier's *Principes de la Nature. Phil. Rev.,* 1893, *2,* 212–218.

    Brief account of Renouvier's general position, with antithesis between Renouvier and Hegel.

4. The Galileo Festival at Padua. *Nation,* 1893, *56,* 8–9.

    Written in Florence, December 12, 1892. Description of Padua and of the celebration of the three hundredth anniversary of the installation of Galileo as Professor of Mathematics at the Paduan University. Comments on the sameness of human nature in different times and places.

5. Review of A. D. Waller's *Sense of Effort. Phil. Rev.,* 1893, *2,* 69–73.

6. Letter on death of G. C. Robertson. *Phil. Rev.,* 1893, *2,* 255.

    Characteristic personal tribute.

7. Review of C. Féré's *La Pathologie des Emotions. Phil. Rev.,* 1893, *2,* 333–336.

8. Review of L. Luciani's *Il Cervelletto. Phil. Rev.,* 1893, *2,* 475–477.

9. Review of L. Arréat's *Psychologie du Peintre. Phil. Rev.,* 1893, *2,* 590–594.

    Contains James's views on the psychology of the painter.

10. Review of M. Fouillée's *La Psychologie des Idées-forces. Phil. Rev.,* 1893, *2,* 716–720.

    Contains interesting remarks on determinism.

11. Notice of F. Pillon's *L'Année Philosophique. Phil. Rev.,* 1893, *2,* 629–630.

12. Notice of E. Schrader's *Die Bewusste Beziehung zwischen Vorstellungen. Phil. Rev.,* 1893, *2,* 746–747.

13. Review of F. W. H. Myers's *Science and a Future Life. Nation,* 1893, *57,* 176–177.

14. Letter in reply to J. Ward on Psychical Research, *Mind 2,* 1893, p. 144.

1894

1. Professor Wundt and Feelings of Innervation. *Psychol. Rev.,* 1894, *1,* 70–73.

    Regarding Wundt's abandonment of "feelings of innervation," and the failure of that psychologist to acknowledge his change of view and to give credit to other writers.

2. The Physical Basis of Emotion. *Psychol. Rev.,* 1894, *1,* 516–529.

    A reply by James to the criticisms of the James-Lange theory of the emotions, and particularly to the criticisms of Wundt, Lehmann, and Irons. There is also reference to the supporting evidence derived from certain cases of "generalized anæsthesia."
    Reprinted in *1920–2.*

3. Letter on the Medical Registration Act. *Boston Transcript,* March 24, 1894.

    Written March 17, 1894. Expresses dislike of paternalistic regulation, and shows a sympathetic interest in mental therapy. See note in *1920–1.*

4. Review (unsigned) of H. R. Marshall's *Pain, Pleasure, and Æsthetics. Nation,* 1894, *59,* 49–51.

5. Letter on the Medical Advertisement Abomination. *Nation,* 1894, *58,* 84–85.

    Written January 22, 1894. Style characteristic.

6. Review of T. Flournoy's *Des Phénomènes de Synopsie. Phil. Rev.,* 1894, *3,* 88–92.

    Last paragraph contains remarks on individual differences of mentality.

7. Notice of H. Bernheim's *Psychical Nature of Hysterical Unilateral Amblyopia,* etc. *Psychol. Rev.,* 1894, *1,* 93–94.

8. Notice of A. Lalande's *Des Paramnésies. Psychol. Rev.,* 1894, *1,* 94–95.

9. Notice of P. Janet's *État Mental des Hystériques,* and *L'Amnésie Continue. Psychol. Rev.,* 1894, *1,* 195–199.

    Résumé and brief estimate of Janet's work.

10. Notice of J. Breuer's and S. Freud's *Ueber den Psychischen Mechanismus Hysterischer Phänomene. Psychol. Rev.,* 1894, *1,* 199.

11. Notice of L. E. Whipple's *Philosophy of Mental Healing. Psychol. Rev.,* 1894, *1,* 199–200.

12. Notice of J. M. Baldwin's *Internal Speech and Song. Psychol. Rev.,* 1894, *1,* 209–210.

13. Review of G. T. Ladd's *Psychology: Descriptive and Explanatory. Psychol. Rev.,* 1894, *1,* 286–293.

    Contains a sympathetic exposition of the text, followed by a general criticism of its method in illustrating the purely descriptive type of psychology. This part of the review may be read as a sequel to *1892–4,* above. Reprinted in *1920–2.*

14. Notice of P. Janet's *Histoire d'une Idée Fixe. Psychol. Rev.,* 1894, *1,* 315–316.

15. Notice of R. O. Mason's *Duplex Personality. Psychol. Rev.,* 1894, *1,* 316.

16. Notice of B. Bourdon's *La Reconnaissance des Phénomènes Nouveaux. Psychol. Rev.,* 1894, *1,* 317.

17. Notice of J. Le Lorrain's *A Propos de la Paramnésie. Psychol. Rev.,* 1894, *1,* 317.

18. Notice of *Annales des Sciences Psychiques. Psychol. Rev.,* 1894, *1,* 317–318.

19. Notice of A. Godfernaux's *Le Sentiment et la Pensée et leurs Principaux Aspects Physiologiques. Psychol. Rev.,* 1894, *1,* 624–627.

20. Notice of W. Bateson's *Materials for the Study of Variation. Psychol. Rev.,* 1894, *1,* 627–630.

21. Notice of A. Lang's *Cock-Lane and Common Sense,* and of C. du Prel's *Die Entdeckung der Seele durch die Geheimwissenschaften. Psychol. Rev.,* 1894, *1,* 630–632.

    Characterization of Andrew Lang in opening paragraph.

22. Letter on the Medical Registration Bill. *Boston Evening Transcript,* Mar. 24, 1894, and also April 2, 1894. Same published in *Banner of Light,* Mar. 19, 1894.

    Approves a bill limiting use of title of physician.

1895

1. Notice of E. Parrish's *Ueber die Trugwahrnehmung*. *Psychol. Rev.*, 1895, *2*, 65–67.

   Discusses census of hallucinations; *cf. 1895–3*.

2. Notice of F. Podmore's *Apparitions and Thought Transference*. *Psychol. Rev.*, 1895, *2*, 67–69.

3. Review of Report on the Census of Hallucinations (H. Sidgwick, A. Johnson, etc.). *Psychol. Rev.*, 1895, *2*, 69–75.

   Careful assessment by James of the results; believes them to be indecisive though creating favorable presumption.

4. The Knowing of Things Together. *Psychol. Rev.*, 1895, *2*, 105–124.

   The Presidential Address as delivered before the American Psychological Association at Princeton, in December, 1894. This article presents the problem of the unity of consciousness, and the several theories proposed for its solution in place of associationism. The author announces his abandonment of the view maintained throughout the *Principles* that each state of consciousness is an indecomposable unity (*cf. 1890–4*, I, 177, 278, etc.). The sequel is to be found in *The Pluralistic Universe* (1909), pp. 190, 205–212, 338 (note). It was on this issue that James finally broke with "logic," and adopted Bergsonism (*ibid.*, 212, 214).
   Pages 107–110, dealing with the difference between representative and immediate knowledge, were reprinted in *1909–8*, 43–50, under title of "The Tigers in India"; the whole is reprinted in *1920–2*.

5. Notice of J. Dallemagne's *Dégénérés et Déséquilibrés*. *Psychol. Rev.*, 1895, *2*, 287–288.

6. Notice of C. Lombroso's *Entartung und Genie*. *Psychol. Rev.*, 1895, *2*, 288–289.

7. Notice of M. Nordau's *Degeneration*. *Psychol. Rev.*, 1895, *2*, 289–290.

8. Review of W. Hirsch's *Genie und Entartung*. *Psychol. Rev.*, 1895, *2*, 290–294.

   A general judgment by James on "the genius controversy," the service rendered by "Moreau, Lombroso & Co."
   Reprinted in part in *1920–2*.

9. Notice of G. Sergi's *Dolore e Piacere*. *Psychol. Rev.*, 1895, *2*, 601–604.

10. A Correction. (Note on Hallucination Census.) *Psychol. Rev.*, 1895, *2*, 174.

11. Is Life Worth Living? *Internat. Jour. of Ethics*, 1895, *6*, 1–24.

> Address before Harvard Y.M.C.A. Argues that life is worth living if one believes that it is, and makes it so.
> Reprinted in *1896–5* and in *1897–3*.
> New editions 1904, 1914.

12. Experimental Psychology in America. *Science*, 1895, n.s. *2*, 626.

> Letter to the editor, taking exception to editorial statements made in the *Amer. Jour. of Psychol.*, 1895, *7*, 3–4, regarding the origin of experimental psychology in America.

13. Preface to F. Thilly's translation of *Introduction to Philosophy*, by Friedrich Paulsen. New York: Holt, 1895, pp. iii–vii.

> Sympathetic exposition of Paulsen with praise of his "anti-absolutism."

14. Letter to Hon. Samuel W. McCall. *Congressional Record*, December 28, 1895, *28*, Part I, 399.

> Protest against administration's policy in the Venezuelan crisis.

15. Art. on "Person and Personality." *Johnsons' Universal Cyclopedia*, D. Appleton and Co., 1895, *6*, 538–540.

16. "Telepathy," *Ibid.*, 1895, *8*, 45–47.

1896

1. Address of the President before the Society for Psychical Research. *Proc. of the (Eng.) Soc. for Psychical Research*, 1896, *12*, 2–10.

> Also in *Science*, 1896, n.s. *3*, 881–888.
> Pages 5–6, 8–10 (about one-half in all), in which the author discusses the evidential values of psychical research, reprinted in *1897–3*, 317–320, 323–327, under title of "What Psychical Research Has Accomplished." *Cf. 1890–1* and *1892–1*. The balance of the present address is devoted to a summary of the work of the Society to date.

2. The Will to Believe. *New World*, 1896, *5*, 327–347.

> Address before Philosophical Clubs of Yale and Brown Universities. Maintains the following thesis: "Our passional nature not only lawfully may, but must, decide an option between propositions, whenever it is a genuine option that cannot by its nature be decided on intellectual grounds." Contains preliminary note acknowledging obligations to Renouvier.
> Reprinted in *1897–3* and in *1917–1*.

3. Psychical Research. *Psychol. Rev.*, 1896, *3*, 649–652.

> Discussion of the question of evidence in psychical research. Contains extract from James's report of American census of hallucinations.

4. A Case of Psychic Automatism, including "Speaking with Tongues." *Proc. of the (Eng.) Soc. for Psychical Research*, 1896, *12*, 277–279.

Narrative of Albert Le Baron (pseudonym) communicated by James with preface and explanatory letters.

5. Is Life Worth Living? Philadelphia: S. B. Weston, 1896, 18mo, pp. 63.

    Reprint of *1895–11*.

6. Notice of F. F. C. Hansen's and A. Lehmann's *Ueber Unwillkürliches Flüstern*. *Psychol. Rev.*, 1896, *3*, 98–99.

7. Notice of G. B. Ermacora's *Telepathic Dreams Experimentally Induced*. *Psychol. Rev.*, 1896, *3*, 99–100.

8. Notice of T. Lipps's *Review of A. Lehmann on "Die Hauptgesetze des Menschlichen Gefühlslebens."* *Psychol. Rev.*, 1896, *3*, 113.

    Summary of Lipps's criticism of the James-Lange theory of the emotions.

9. Notice of E. Morselli's *Manuale della Semejotica delle Malattie Mentali*. *Psychol. Rev.*, 1896, *3*, 679–681.

    Critical comment by James.

10. Notice of S. de Sanctis's *I Sogni*, etc. *Psychol. Rev.*, 1896, *3*, 681–682.

11. Notice of A. H. Pierce's *Subliminal Self*, F. Podmore's *Reply*, F. von Schrenk-Notzing's *Ueber Spaltung der Persönlichkeit*, and S. Landmann's *Die Mehrheit Geistiger Persönlichkeiten*. *Psychol. Rev.*, 1896, *3*, 682–684.

    Criticised as making no empirical contributions to the subject.

12. Letter to the Editor. *Harvard Crimson*, January 9, 1896.

    Opposes administration's Venezuelan policy, replies to letter from Roosevelt, and urges students to express their opinions.

13. Review of B. Berenson's *Florentine Painters of the Renaissance. Science*, 1896, n.s. *4*, 318.

    Brief discussion of the psychological differentia of good art.

1897

1. Louis Agassiz. *Science*, 1897, n.s. *5*, 285–289.

    Also in *Harvard Graduates' Magazine*, 1897, *5*, 532–536, printed for the University, Cambridge, Mass., 1897, pp. 12. Also Anonymously in *Amer. Naturalist*, 1898, *32*, 147–157.
    Words spoken at the reception given to the American Society of Naturalists by the President and Fellows of Harvard College, December 30, 1896. Estimate of Agassiz's character and influence, with personal recollections.
    Reprinted in *1911–2*.

2. Robert Gould Shaw. *The Monument to Robert Gould Shaw*. Boston: Houghton Mifflin, 1897, pp. 71–87.

Also in *Exercises at the Dedication of the Monument to Colonel Robert Gould Shaw*. Boston: Municipal Printing Office, 1897, *11*, 35–53, and in *Harvard Graduates' Magazine*, 1897, *6*, 28–37.

Oration, delivered at the unveiling of the monument to Robert Gould Shaw, on May 31, 1897. Interpretations of the Civil War and of the qualities of heroism.

Reprinted in *1911–2*.

3. The Will to Believe, and Other Essays in Popular Philosophy. New York and London: Longmans, Green & Co., 1897, 8vo, pp. xvii–332.

Contains following essays, reprinted as indicated: The Will to Believe, *1896–2*, reprinted also in *1917–1*; Is Life Worth Living? *1895–11*; The Sentiment of Rationality, *1879–7* and *1882–2*, reprinted also in *1905–11* and *1917–1*; Reflex Action and Theism, *1881–3*; The Dilemma of Determinism, *1884–4*; The Moral Philosopher and the Moral Life, *1891–2*; Great Men and their Environment, *1880–2*, reprinted also in *1917–1*; The Importance of Individuals, *1890–2*; On Some Hegelisms, *1882–1*; What Psychical Research Has Accomplished, *1890–1*, *1892–1*, and *1896–1*. Preface contains general statement of "Radical Empiricism" and pluralism. Reprinted in 1898, 1899, 1905, 1912 (New Imp.), 1921, 1927, 1931, 1937. In 1956, with the second edition of "Human Immortality."

4. Notice of J. G. Schurman's *Agnosticism and Religion. Psychol. Rev.*, 1897, *4*, 192.

5. Notice of C. Wernicke's *Grundriss der Psychiatrie. Psychol. Rev.*, 1897, *4*, 225–227.

Contains paragraph of general comment on psychology of hallucination, dissociation, "subconscious ideas," etc.

6. Notice of G. LeBon's *The Crowd. Psychol. Rev.*, 1897, *4*, 313–316.

Emphasizes the book's importance, but deprecates its misanthropy and lack of social philosophy.

7. Review (unsigned) of G. Santayana's *Sense of Beauty. Nation*, 1897, *65*, 75.

8. Notice of H. Sidgwick's *Involuntary Whispering*, etc. *Psychol. Rev.*, 1897, *4*, 654–655.

Review of Sidgwick's reply to criticism of Hansen and Lehmann, noticed in *1896–6*. Cf. also *1898–4*, *1899–4a*, and *1899–4b*.

9. Notice of E. Morselli's *I Fenomeni Telepatici e le Allucinazioni Veridiche. Psychol. Rev.*, 1897, *4*, 655–657.

Discusses question of evidence in psychical research.

10. Notice of E. Parrish's *Zum Kritik des Telepathischen Beweismaterials* and *Hallucinations and Illusions. Psychol. Rev.*, 1897, *4*, 657–658.

Discussion of Parrish's criticisms of the Sidgwick report, *1895–3*.

11. Notice of S. de Sanctis's *Le Studie dell' Attenzione Conativa. Psychol. Rev.*, 1897, *4*, 659.

12. Notice of S. de Sanctis's *Collezionismo e Impulsi Collezionistici.* *Psychol. Rev.*, 1897, *4*, 659.

1898

1. Consciousness under Nitrous Oxide. *Psychol. Rev.*, 1898, *5*, 194–196.

   Narrative of an English correspondent, suggested by *1897–3*, 294–298, and communicated by James.

2. Mrs. Piper "the Medium." *Science*, 1898, n.s. *7*, 640–641.

   Letter to the Editor; sequel to *1896–3*.

3. Philosophical Conceptions and Practical Results. *University of California Chronicle*, 1898, pp. 24.

   An address delivered before the Philosophical Union of the University of California on August 26, 1898. It marks the beginning of the pragmatic movement. Nine years later, speaking of the pragmatist principle which he attributed to Charles Peirce, James wrote:
   "It lay entirely unnoticed by any one for twenty years, until I, in an address before Professor Howison's philosophical union at the University of California, brought it forward again and made a special application of it to religion. By that date (1898) the times seemed ripe for its reception. The word 'pragmatism' spread, and at present it fairly spots the pages of the philosophical journals" (*1907–11*, 47).
   Reprinted with slight verbal revision and with omission of the first three pages and concluding paragraph, in *1904–13*. Afterwards most of page 6 was used in *1902–1*, 444; and pages 9–15 were reprinted with further slight revisions in *1907–11*, 97–108. The whole reprinted in *1920–2*.

4. Lehmann and Hansen "on the Telepathic Problem." *Science*, 1898, n.s. *8*, 956.

   Letter to the Editor, written December 23, replying to E. B. Titchener's claims that Lehmann's work on unconscious whispering is unfavorable to the telepathic hypothesis. *Cf. 1897–8* and *1899–4*.

5. Human Immortality: Two Supposed Objections to the Doctrine. Boston and New York: Houghton Mifflin, 1898, 12mo, pp. 70. (Also London: Constable & Co., Dent & Sons.)

   The Ingersoll Lecture delivered at Harvard University in 1897, together with explanatory notes by the author. Replies to the objections that thought is a function of the brain; and that universal human immortality would be too promiscuous.
   New edition in 1899; *cf. 1899–11*.
   Reprinted, 1900, 1922, 1956.

6. Introduction to *The Psychology of Suggestion*, by Boris Sidis. New York: Appleton, 1898, pp. vii–386.

   Brief sketch of the subject of abnormal psychology.

7. Review of R. Hodgson's *A Further Record of Observations of Certain Phenomena of Trance. Psychol. Rev.*, 1898, *5*, 420–424.

Contains examination of the alternative hypotheses fitting the Piper case. This together with *1909–6* gives James's mature view of mediumistic phenomena in comparatively technical form. Hodgson's report is in *Proc. of the (Eng.) Soc. for Psychical Research,* 1898, *13,* 284–583.
Partly reprinted in *1920–2; cf.* note, page 438.

8. "Brute and Human Intellect." *The Journal of Speculative Philosophy,* 1898, *12,* (236)–276.

9. Report of William James' speech before the Committee on Public Health on Medical Registration Bill. *Boston Evening Transcript,* Mar. 2, 1898. (Not complete: "Prof. Wm. James . . . in part said.") Mar. 12, 1898, report of the above speech, *Banner of Light,* (in full).

1899

1. Talks to Teachers on Psychology. *Atlantic Monthly,* 1899, *83,* 155–162, 320–329, 510–517, 617–626.

   Reprinted in *1899–7,* with additions. See note under that title.

2. Letter on the Philippine Tangle. *Boston Evening Transcript,* March 1, 1899.

   Written February 26, 1899. Reprinted in *Cambridge Anti-Imperialist Broadside,* May 17, 1899. Strong statement of anti-imperialistic opinions. Comment on evil effects of arousing the war-spirit. *Cf. 1903–7.*

3. The Gospel of Relaxation. *Scribner's Mag.,* 1899, *25,* 499–507.

   An application of the James-Lange theory of the emotions to mental hygiene and American life.
   Reprinted with slight verbal revisions in *1899–7* and in *1917–1.*

4a. Lehmann and Hansen on Telepathy. *Science,* 1898, n.s. *9,* 654–655.

   Letter to the Editor, written April 20, 1899. Continues *1898–4.* Quotes personal letter from Lehmann.

4b. Telepathy Once More. *Science,* 1899, n.s. *9,* 752–753.

   Letter to the Editor. Continues *1898–4 and 1899–4a.*

5. Preface to E. D. Starbuck's *Psychology of Religion.* London: W. Scott, 1899, pp. v–x.

   General remarks on the methods and the importance of the psychology of religion.

6. Controversy with Professor Titchener, on Messrs. Lehmann and Hansen's *Experiments in Unconscious Whispering. Jour. of the (Eng.) Soc. for Psychical Research,* 1899, *9,* 113–120.

   Reprint of *1898–4, 1899–4a,* and *1899–4b,* with comments by the Editor.

7. Talks to Teachers on Psychology: and to Students on Some of Life's Ideals. New York: Holt, 1899, 8vo, pp. xi–301. (Also London: Longmans, Green & Co.)

Talks to Teachers on Psychology constitutes about two-thirds of the volume. It grew out of public lectures to teachers, given in Cambridge in 1892, and afterwards given at various teachers' institutes and summer schools. It contains the following lectures, reprinted where indicated: I, Psychology and the Teaching Art; II, The Stream of Consciousness; III, The Child as a Behaving Organism; IV, Education and Behavior; V, The Necessity of Reactions; VI, Native and Acquired Reactions; VII, What the Native Reactions Are; VIII, The Laws of Habit, parts (pp. 66–71, 75–76) from *1890–4*, Chapter IV; IX, The Association of Ideas; X, Interest; XI, Attention; XII, Memory, parts (pp. 123, 125–126) from *1890–4*, Chapter XVI; XIII, The Acquisition of Ideas; XIV, Apperception; XV, The Will. Of the above lectures, Nos. I–VII, X, XI, XV, were also published in *1899–1*.

The last third of the volume consists of addresses written for delivery at several women's colleges, and contains: I, The Gospel of Relaxation, *1899–3*, reprinted also in *1917–1*; II, On a Certain Blindness in Human Beings (the Preface emphasizes the democratic and individualistic bearings of this essay), reprinted in *1912–2* and in *1917–1*; III, What Makes a Life Significant, reprinted in *1912–2*. Reprinted in 1899, 1900, 1901, 1905, 1906, 1907, 1908, 1909, 1912, 1916, 1920, 1921, 1923, 1939, 1958, 1962.

8. Letter on Philippine Question. *Boston Evening Transcript*, March 4, 1899.

Written March 2, 1899. Replying to editorial comment on *1899–2*, states that American Philippine policy lacks psychological insight.

9. Letter on Governor Roosevelt's Oration. *Boston Evening Transcript*, April 15, 1899.

Written April 12, 1899. Accuses Governor Roosevelt and his party of dealing abstractly and emotionally with Philippine question. Refers to Roosevelt's speeches of April 11, 1899, in Chicago and Ann Arbor, on "The Strenuous Life." Published also in the *Conservative*, May 1899.

10. Letter on the Philippines. *New York Evening Post*, March 10, 1899.

Written March 8, 1899. Remarks upon the failure of America's alleged benevolence.

11. Human Immortality: Two Supposed Objections to the Doctrine. Boston and New York: Houghton Mifflin, 1899.

New edition of *1898–5*, with Preface containing replies to criticisms.

12. Preface to W. Lutoslawski's *The World of Souls*, George Allen and Unwin Ltd., London, 1924, 5–8.

1900

1. Letter to the Editor, with translation of extracts from the diary of a French naval officer. *Springfield Daily Republican*, June 4, 1900.

Letter criticises American Philippine policy. Diary of French naval officer deals with events at Manila in spring and summer of 1898; six columns translated from *Revue de Paris*, October 15, November 15, 1899.

2. Letter to the Editor, with translation of extracts from Professor F. Blumentritt's book on the Philippines. *Springfield Daily Republican*, July 2, 1900.

> Short letter accompanying translation of last eleven pages of the above book, containing an account of the American occupation of the Philippines and a sympathetic account of the Filipinos' aspiration for freedom.

3. The International Psychical Institute. Letter to the Editor. *Science*, 1900, n.s. *12*, 376.

> Written from Nauheim, August 24, 1900, to state that the publication of his name as American representative on the Council of Organization of the "Institut Psychique International" was unauthorized.

1901

1. Frederic Myers's Services to Psychology. *Proc. of the (Eng.) Soc. for Psychical Research*, 1901, *17*, 13–23.

> Published also in *Popular Sci. Monthly*, 1901, *59*, 380–389.
> Written for the Society for Psychical Research shortly after Myers's death. Praises the genuinely naturalistic and empirical nature of his work and predicts his permanent fame.
> Reprinted in *1911–2*. Reprinted in *1960–1*.

2. Translation of "A Soldier's Observations of the Customs and Ways of 'The Little Brown People.'" Signed Sergeant of Volunteers on Philippine Americanization. *Springfield Daily Republican*, Feb. 22, 1901.

1902

1. The Varieties of Religious Experience: A Study in Human Nature. New York and London: Longmans, Green & Co., 1902, 8vo, pp. xii–534.

> The Gifford Lectures on Natural Religion delivered at Edinburgh in 1901–02. Originally designed as the psychological part of a more comprehensive treatise on religion: *cf.* Preface, p. v.
> The volume contains the following lectures: I, Religion and Neurology; II, Circumscription of the Topic; III, The Reality of the Unseen; IV, V, The Religion of Healthy-mindedness; VI, VII, The Sick Soul; VIII, The Divided Self, and the Process of Its Unification; IX, X, Conversion; XI, XII, XIII, Saintliness; XIV, XV, The Value of Saintliness; XVI, XVII, Mysticism; XVIII, Philosophy; XIX, Other Characteristics; XX, Conclusions; Postscript. Lecture XX and Postscript reprinted in *1917–1*, under the title of "The Positive Content of Religious Experience."
> Reprinted in 1903, 1909, 1915, 1916, 1922, 1925, 1928, 1929, 1935, 1936, 1955, 1958, 1961, 1963.

2. Pragmatic and Pragmatism. Contribution to *Dictionary of Philosophy and Psychology*, edited by J. M. Baldwin, Vol. II, 321. New York and London: Macmillan, 1902.

> Brief definition of the pragmatic method.

3. "Experience." Article in Baldwin's *Dictionary of Philosophy and Psychology*, 1902.

1903

1. The Ph.D. Octopus. *Harvard Monthly*, 1903, *36*, 1–9.

   Deplores the growing emphasis on the doctor's degree as tending to the formation of artificial standards and as un-American.
   Reprinted in *1911–2*.

2. Address at the Centenary of Ralph Waldo Emerson. Printed at the Riverside Press for the Social Circle in Concord, June, 1903, pp. 67–77.

   Address delivered at the centenary of the birth of Emerson, in Concord, May 25, 1903, and containing a summary of Emerson's teaching.
   Reprinted in *1911–2*.

3. Review of F. W. H. Myers's *Human Personality and Its Survival of Bodily Death*. *Proc. of the* (*Eng.*) *Soc. for Psychical Research*, 1903, *18*, 22–33.

   Exposition and criticism of Myers's comprehensive hypothesis to explain subliminal phenomena.

4. Review of Sturt's *Personal Idealism*. *Mind*, 1903, n.s. *12*, 93–97.

   The book reviewed consists of philosophical essays by eight members of the University of Oxford, G. F. Stout, F. C. S. Schiller, W. R. Boyce Gibson, G. E. Underhill, R. R. Marett, H. Sturt, F. W. Bussell, and Hastings Rashdall. The reviewer summarizes the tendency of the book and relates it to other movements in modern thought.
   Partly reprinted in *1920–2*.

5. The True Harvard. *Harvard Graduates' Magazine*, 1903, *12*, 5–8.

   Speech made at Harvard Commencement Dinner, June 24, 1903. Praise of Harvard's individualism and tolerance.
   Reprinted in *1911–2*.

6. Remarks on the Dedication of the Germanic Museum. Cambridge, Mass., November 10, 1903. *Harvard Illustrated Magazine*, 1903, *5*, 48–50.

   Also in *Harvard Bulletin*, 1903, 6–7. Emphasizes importance of "background," "contact with the general probabilities of things, in an age of specialization"; characterizes the Germanic spirit of individualism in art.

7. Address on Philippine Question. Published in report of its Fifth Annual Meeting by the New England Anti-Imperialist League, 1903, pp. 21–26.

   Published also in the *New York Evening Post*, December 3, 1903. Delivered before New England Anti-Imperialist League, November 30, 1903. Expresses the view that America has permanently abandoned its traditional policy and joined the circle of militant international powers. American liberals must now join the general cosmopolitan party of protest, "the party of conscience and intelligence."

8. Herbert Spencer Dead. *New York Evening Post,* December 8, 1903.

> Also published anonymously in an abbreviated form under title of "Herbert Spencer" in the *Nation,* 1903, *77,* 460–461; also in *Critic,* January, 1904. A less carefully matured estimate of Spencer than *1904–8;* but contains fuller treatment of the Ethics, Sociology, and Psychology, with a more systematic exposition of Spencer's achievements.

9. Letter to *Springfield Daily Republican* on Lynching, July 23, 1903. Reprinted under the title, "Can Lynching Be Stopped?" in *Literary Digest,* Aug. 8, 1903.

10. "Reminiscences of Thomas Davidson," Oct. 21, 1903, published in *Memorials of Thomas Davidson,* ed. by William Knight, 1907.

11. "Epidemic of Lynching." The Boston *Journal,* July 29, 1903.

12. Review of Frederic W. H. Myers's *Human Personality and Its Survival of Bodily Death.* Two vols. Longmans Green & Co., London, New York, Bombay, 1903 in *Proceedings of the Society For Psychical Research* (London) Vol. XVIII, Part XLVI, June 1903.

1904

1. Laura Bridgman. *Atlantic Monthly,* 1904, *93,* 95–98.

> Comparison of Laura Bridgman and Helen Keller. Written as a review of a book by Maud Howe and Florence Howe Hall, entitled *"Laura Bridgman, Dr. Howe's Famous Pupil, and what He taught Her."*
> Reprinted with omissions in *1920–2.*

2. Introduction to M. C. Wadsworth's Translation of G. T. Fechner's *Little Book of Life after Death.* Boston: Little, Brown & Co., 1904, pp. vii–xix.

> Written June 21, 1904. Exposition and appreciation of Fechner.

3. The Chicago School. *Psychol. Bull.,* 1904, *1,* 1–5.

> Appreciative acknowledgment of the importance of the work of J. Dewey and his students.
> Reprinted in *1920–2.*

4. A Case of Automatic Drawing. *Popular Sci. Monthly,* 1904, *64,* 195–201.

> Illustrated report of automatic drawing of C. H. P., including the latter's own narrative.

5. Review (unsigned) of F. C. S. Schiller's *Humanism. Nation,* 1904, *78,* 175–176.

> Summary of European variation of pragmatism, and of the difficulties in the humanistic philosophy.
> Reprinted in *1920–2.*

6. Letter on Secretary Taft. *Boston Transcript,* May 2, 1904.

   Written May 1, 1904. Reprinted in *New York Evening Post,* May 5, 1904. Argues that Secretary Taft is a biased judge as to whether the promise of independence to the Filipinos should be inserted in the party platforms at the presidential election.

7. Francis Boott. *Harvard Monthly,* 1904, *38,* 125–128.

   Also published anonymously in *Nation,* 1904, *78,* 192–193.
   An address delivered at the service held in Appleton Chapel, Harvard, Sunday, May 8, 1904, in memory of Francis Boott, the musical composer and critic.
   Reprinted in *1911–2.*

8. Herbert Spencer. *Atlantic Monthly,* 1904, *94,* 99–108.

   A characterization of Spencer's personality together with a survey and estimate of his work.
   Reprinted under title of "Herbert Spencer's Autobiography," in *1911–2.*

9. Does "Consciousness" Exist? *Jour. of Phil., Psychol., and Sci. Methods,* 1904, *1,* 477–491.

   The opening paper of the series defining the position known as "radical empiricism." See note under *1912–1.* In this essay the traditional substantive view of consciousness is rejected in favor of the view that consciousness is a relation.
   Reprinted in *1912–1.*

10. A World of Pure Experience. *Jour. of Phil., Psychol., and Sci. Methods,* 1904, *1,* 533–543, 561–570.

    Radical empiricism as applied to theory of knowledge.
    Extract reprinted in *1909–8,* under title "The Relation between Knower and Known." The whole reprinted in *1912–1.*

11. Humanism and Truth. *Mind,* 1904, n.s. *13,* 457–475.

    A discussion of the relation between "the pragmatic method" of the author and the philosophical generalization of pragmatism, known as "humanism." Discussion of relations with Dewey and Schiller, and reply to Bradley, Taylor, and other critics.
    Reprinted in *1909–8,* with slight revisions and additions from *1905–5;* also in *1917–1.*

12. Remarks at Peace Banquet. *Official Report of the Thirteenth Universal Peace Congress,* Boston: Peace Congress Committee, 1904, pp. 266–269.

    Also in *Atlantic Monthly,* 1904, *94,* 845–847. Describes the strong human appeal of war. "We must go in for preventive medicine, not radical cure."
    Reprinted in *1911–2.*

13. The Pragmatic Method. *Jour. of Phil., Psychol., and Sci. Methods,* 1904, *1,* 673–687.

Reprinted with slight verbal revisions from *1898–3*, omitting introductory pages and concluding paragraph. Later partly reprinted in *1907–11*, 97–108.

14. Letter on Philippine Independence. *New York Evening Post*, May 21, 1904.

Written May 19, 1904, continuing *1904–6*, and replying to a letter of J. A. LeRoy, *New York Evening Post*, May 17, 1904.

15. "Catholicisme et Protestantisme," article in *Revue des Revues* on the reunion of Catholic and Protestant Churches, *52* (1904), 37.

16. "Prof. Wm. James on War," and (in same col.) Letter to *Boston Evening Transcript*, Oct. 10, 1904.

17. Letter to J. G. Piddington, *Proceedings of English Society for Psychical Research*, 18 (Jan. 1904), 106.

18. Prefatory "Note" to Henry James, Sr., "Emerson," *Atlantic*, XCIV (1904), 740.

1905

1. The Experience of Activity. *Psychol. Rev.*, Jan. 19, 1905, *12*, 1–17.

Presidential address before American Psychological Association, 1904. An application of the methods of pragmatism and radical empiricism to the topic of activity, including the issue between mechanism and teleology.
Reprinted in *1912–1*, and with omissions in *1909–5*. Quoted in *1911–1*, 212.

2. The Thing and Its Relations. *Jour. of Phil., Psychol., and Sci. Methods*, Jan. 19, 1905, *2*, 29–41.

Development of the doctrine of radical empiricism. Detailed criticism of Bradley's views on relation.
Reprinted in *1909–5*, and in *1912–1*.

3. The Essence of Humanism. *Jour. of Phil., Psychol., and Sci. Methods*, June 8, 1905, *2*, 113–118.

An account of the fundamentals of the pragmatist-radical-empiricist view of the world.
Reprinted in *1909–8*.

4. How Two Minds Can Know One Thing. *Jour. of Phil., Psychol., and Sci. Methods*, Mar. 30, 1905, *2*, 176–181.

A special application of radical empiricism.
Reprinted in *1912–1*.

5. Humanism and Truth Once More. *Mind*, April 1905, n.s. *14*, 190–198.

Reply to a criticism of *1904–11*, by H. W. B. Joseph in *Mind*, 1905, n.s. *14*, 28–41.
Reprinted in *1912–1*; parts reprinted in *1909–8*, 54–57, 97–100.

6. Is Radical Empiricism Solipsistic? *Jour. of Phil., Psychol., and Sci. Methods*, April 27, 1905, *2*, 235–238.

   Reply to a criticism of radical empiricism by B. H. Bode in *Jour. of Phil., Psychol., and Sci. Methods*, 1905, *2*, 128–133.
   Reprinted in *1912–1*.

7. The Place of Affectional Facts in a World of Pure Experience. *Jour. of Phil., Psychol., and Sci. Methods*, May 25, 1905, *2*, 281–287.

   Application of radical empiricism to the case of feeling.
   Reprinted in *1912–1*.

8. A Knight-Errant of the Intellectual Life: Thomas Davidson. *McClure's Magazine*, 1905, *25*, 3–11.

   Written five years after Davidson's death, as tribute to a robust individualism James greatly admired and in memory of days of companionship at Glenmore in the Adirondack Mountains.
   Reprinted in *1911–2*.

9. La Notion de Conscience. *Archives de Psychol.*, 1905, *5*, 1–12.

   A communication made (in French) at the Fifth International Congress of Psychology, in Rome, April 30, 1905. It is a condensed statement of the view presented in *1904–9*, *1904–10*, and *1905–7*.
   Reprinted in *1912–1*.
   Translated into Italian, *Leonardo*, 1905, *3*, 77–82.

10. Introduction to *The Elements of Psychology*, by Edward L. Thorndike. New York: A. G. Seiler, 1905, pp. v–vii.

    Praise of the concrete, realistic, non-pedantic method in psychology.

11. The Sentiment of Rationality. New York and London: Longmans, Green & Co., 1905, pp. xiv, 110.

    Reprinted from *1897–3*, including Preface of that volume and essay with above title. Printed for the use of students and privately circulated.

1906

1. Stanford's Ideal Destiny. *Leland Stanford Junior University Publications, Trustees' Series*, 1906, *14*, 5–8.

   Also in *Science*, 1906, n.s. *23*, 801–804. Address at Stanford University on Founders' Day, 1906. Emphasizes the importance of the great teacher or the genius as the source of intellectual and spiritual life.
   Reprinted in *1911–2*.

2. On Some Mental Effects of the Earthquake. *Youth's Companion*, 1906, *80*, 283–284.

The author was at Leland Stanford when the great San Francisco earth-quake of April 18, 1906, occurred. He succeeded in reaching San Francisco that morning and spent the day there.
Reprinted in *1911–2*.

3. G. Papini and the Pragmatist Movement in Italy. *Jour. of Phil., Psychol., and Sci. Methods*, 1906, *3*, 337–341.

An appreciative recognition of the recent work of a group of young Italian philosophers, with references to the latent possibilities of pragmatism, especially in the sphere of religion.
Reprinted in *1920–2*.

4. The Mad Absolute. *Jour. of Phil., Psychol., and Sci. Methods*, 1906, *3*, 656–657.

Reply to an article in *Jour. of Phil., Psychol., and Sci. Methods*, 1906, *3*, 575–577, by W. C. Gore, entitled "The Mad Absolute of a Pluralist." Urges a more empirical treatment of the question of a "world consciousness."
Reprinted in *1920–2*.

5. Mr. Pitkin's Refutation of "Radical Empiricism." *Jour. of Phil., Psychol., and Sci. Methods*, 1906, *3*, 712.

Reply to an article in *Jour. of Phil., Psychol., and Sci. Methods*, 1906, *3*, 645–650, by W. B. Pitkin, entitled "A Problem of Evidence in Radical Empiricism." Limits reality to experience only by a "methodological postulate."
Reprinted in *1912–1*.

6. Preface to *The Problems of Philosophy*, by Harald Höffding, translated by G. M. Fisher. New York: Macmillan, 1906, pp. v–xiv.

Describes the antithesis between rationalism and empiricism, and characterizes present book as "empiricist matter presented in a rationalist's manner"; contains brief estimates of Höffding's philosophy of religion.

1907

1. The Energies of Men. *Phil. Rev.*, Jan. 1907, *16*, 1–20.

Also in *Science*, 1907, n.s. *25*, 321–332. Presidential Address before the American Philosophical Association in 1906. This article deals with the human reserves brought into play in emergencies.
Largely reprinted in *1907–2*, but contains considerable matter not reprinted, such as opening pages distinguishing the "analytical" and "clinical" methods in psychology (1–3), references to Fechner (4), and Papini (19), extracts from Lutoslawski's letters on the Hatha Yoga (10–14), remarks on mental work (18), and suggestions for future psychological procedure (19–20).
New ed. in 1917 by Moffat, Yard and Co., N.Y.; also in 1926, by Dodd, Mead and Co., New York.

2. The Powers of Men. *American Mag.*, October, 1907, 57–65.

Popular version of *1907–1*, with considerable omission and some amplification. Reprinted in *1908–6* under the title of "The Energies of Men"; also in *1911–2* and in *1917–1*.

3. A Reply to Mr. Pitkin. *Jour. of Phil., Psychol., and Sci. Methods*, Feb. 14, 1907, *4*, 105–106.

   Amplification of *1906–5*, in reply to an article in *Jour. of Phil., Psychol., and Sci. Methods*, 1907, *4*, 44–45, by W. B. Pitkin, entitled "In Reply to Professor James."
   Reprinted in *1912–1*, appended to *1906–5*.

4. Pragmatism's Conception of Truth. *Jour. of Phil., Psychol., and Sci. Methods*, Mar. 14, 1907, *4*, 141–155.

   An account of truth as "expedient thinking"; with discussion of "agreement with reality," verification, etc.
   Reprinted in *1907–11*.

5. A Defense of Pragmatism. *Popular Sci. Monthly*, Mar.–April 1907, *70*, 193–206, 351–364.

   General discussion of pragmatism, its origins and relation to other philosophies.
   Reprinted in *1907–11*, under titles of "The Present Dilemma in Philosophy," and "What Pragmatism Means," the latter being reprinted also in *1917–1*.

6. (and John E. Russell) Controversy about Truth. *Jour. of Phil., Psychol., and Sci. Methods*, May 23, 1907, *4*, 289–296.

   A series of letters in which the issue between pragmatism and intellectualism is defined and sharpened.
   Reprinted in *1920–2*.

7. A Word More about Truth. *Jour. of Phil., Psychol., and Sci. Methods*, July 18, 1907, *4*, 396–406.

   Emphasizes importance of intermediaries between the idea and its object.
   Reprinted in *1909–8*.

8. Professor Pratt on Truth. *Jour. of Phil., Psychol., and Sci. Methods*, Aug. 15, 1907, *4*, 464–467.

   Written in reply to J. B. Pratt's "Truth and its Verification," *Jour. of Phil., Psychol., and Sci. Methods*, 1907, *4*, 320–324.
   Reprinted in *1909–8*.

9. The Absolute and the Strenuous Life. *Jour. of Phil., Psychol., and Sci. Methods*, Sept. 26, 1907, *4*, 546–548.

   Written in reply to W. A. Brown's "Pragmatic Value of the Absolute," *Jour. of Phil., Psychol., and Sci. Methods*, 1907, *4*, 459–464.
   Reprinted in *1909–8*.

10. A Case of Clairvoyance. *Proc. of the Amer. Soc. for Psychical Research*, Jan. 1907, *1*, part 2, 221–236.

The evidence in the Lebanon (N.H.) case of the discovery of a body through the alleged clairvoyant powers of a Mrs. Titus; evidence declared to be favorable to the hypothesis of supernormal powers.

11. Pragmatism: A New Name for Some Old Ways of Thinking. New York and London: Longmans, Green & Co., 1907, 8vo, pp. xiii–309.

Lectures delivered at the Lowell Institute in Boston in 1906, and at Columbia University in 1907. Preface distinguishes between "pragmatism" and "radical empiricism," and contains references to other writers illustrating the pragmatist tendency. Contains the following lectures, reprinted as indicated: I, The Present Dilemma in Philosophy, *1907–5;* II, What Pragmatism Means, *1907–5* (reprinted also in *1917–1*); III, Some Metaphysical Problems Pragmatically Considered, *1904–13* (in part); IV, The One and the Many; V, Pragmatism and Common Sense; VI, Pragmatism's Conception of Truth, *1907–4;* VII, Pragmatism and Humanism; VIII, Pragmatism and Religion.
Reprinted in 1908, 1909, 1910, 1912, 1914, 1916, 1922, 1925, 1928, cf. 1943–2.

12. Interview of William James by Edwin Bjorkman, *The New York Times,* Nov. 3, 1907.

1908

1. The Pragmatist Account of Truth and Its Misunderstanders. *Phil. Rev.,* Jan. 1908, *17,* 1–17.

An attempt to deal comprehensively with misunderstandings that have stood in the way of the acceptance of pragmatism.
Reprinted in *1909–8.*

2. The Social Value of the College Bred. *McClure's Magazine,* 1908, *30,* 419–422.

Address delivered at a meeting of the Association of American Alumnæ at Radcliffe College, November 7, 1907. The value of a college education is held to consist in the ability to know a good man when one sees him.
Reprinted in *1911–2.*

3. "Truth" *versus* "Truthfulness." *Jour. of Phil., Psychol., and Sci. Methods,* Mar. 26, 1908, *5,* 179–181.

Application of pragmatic theory of truth to the case of a past event.
Reprinted in *1909–8,* under the title of "The Existence of Julius Cæsar," and with last two paragraphs omitted.

4. The Meaning of the Word Truth. Privately printed, 1908, pp. 4.

Remarks at the Cornell Meeting of the American Philosophical Association in 1907.
Reprinted in *1909–8.*
Published in *Mind,* July 1908, *17,* 455.

5. Pluralism and Religion. *Hibbert Jour.,* 1908, *6,* 721–728.

Advocates the application of empiricism to religion, in place of the traditional rationalism.

Published also in *1909–5*, 303–316, under "Conclusions," with difference of emphasis in concluding sentence.

6. The Energies of Men. (Religion and Medicine Series.) New York: Moffat, Yard & Co., 1908, *3*, 7–38.

   1907–2 reprinted under the title of *1907–1*.

7. Hegel and His Method. *Hibbert Jour.*, 1908, *7*, 63–75.

   Dismisses Hegel's intellectualistic method, but regards his system as a "significant" hypothesis.
   Published also in *1909–5*, 85–109, with slight verbal differences and some additions.

8. Review of Marcel Hébert's *Le Pragmatisme et ses Diverses Formes Anglo-Américaines. Jour. of Phil., Psychol., and Sci. Methods*, 1908, *5*, 689–694.

   Restatement by the reviewer of the pragmatic theory of truth, and comparison of his own view with that of Schiller.
   Reprinted in *1909–8*, under the title of "Professor Hébert on Pragmatism."

9. "Two English Critics." *Albany Review*, Jan. 1908 reprinted in *1909–8*.

1909

1. The Doctrine of the Earth-Soul and of Beings Intermediate between Man and God. An Account of the Philosophy of G. T. Fechner. *Hibbert Jour.*, 1909, *7*, 278–294.

   A sympathetic exposition of Fechner as an example of "passionate vision," and calling special attention to this author's "assumption that conscious experiences freely compound and separate themselves."
   Published also, with slight verbal differences, in *1909–5*, 145–176, under the title of "Concerning Fechner."

2. Physical Phenomena at a Private Circle. *Jour. of the Amer. Soc. for Psychical Research*, 1909, *3*, 109–113.

   Account of table-tipping and like phenomena witnessed at a private circle of spiritualists in a New England town.

3. The Philosophy of Bergson. *Hibbert Jour.*, 1909, *7*, 562–577.

   Exposition of the philosophy which had led James "to renounce the intellectualistic method and the current notion that logic is an adequate measure of what can or cannot be."
   Published also, considerably abridged and with numerous verbal differences in *1909–5*, 225–267, under the title of "Bergson and his Critique of Intellectualism."

4. On a Very Prevalent Abuse of Abstraction. *Popular Sci. Monthly*, 1909, *74*, 485–493.

   Criticism of "vicious intellectualism" or the privative use of concepts; defense against charge of relativism brought by Rickert and Münsterberg.

Reprinted in *1909–8*, under the title of "Abstractionism and 'Relativismus.'"

5. A Pluralistic Universe. Hibbert Lectures at Manchester College on the Present Situation in Philosophy. New York and London: Longmans, Green & Co., 1909, 8vo, pp. vi–405.

Lectures given at Manchester College, Oxford, in 1908–09. Contains the following lectures, elsewhere published as indicated: I, The Types of Philosophic Thinking; II, Monistic Idealism; III, Hegel and his Method, *1908–7;* IV, Concerning Fechner, *1909–1;* V, The Compounding of Consciousness; VI, Bergson and his Critique of Intellectualism, *1909–3;* VII, The Continuity of Experience; VIII, Conclusions, *1908–5.* Also: Appendix A, The Thing and Its Relations, *1905–2* (also reprinted in *1912–1*); Appendix B, The Experience of Activity, *1905–1* (also reprinted in *1912–1*); Appendix C, On the Notion of Reality as Changing.
Translated into French, under the title of "Philosophie de l'Expérience," Le Brun and Paris, Paris, 1910, Flammarion. This change of title was made with the author's approval.

6. Report on Mrs. Piper's Hodgson-Control. *Proc. of the (Eng.) Soc. for Psychical Research,* 1909, *23,* 1–121. Also in *Proc. of the Amer. Soc. for Psychical Research,* 1909, *3,* 470–589.

Report of sittings with Mrs. Piper, in which alleged messages from the late Richard Hodgson are recorded and tested. The conclusions embody mature opinions on mediumistic phenomena, given in technical form. Various psychological and metaphysical alternatives are considered.
The conclusions are reprinted in *1920–2.*

7. The Confidences of a "Psychical Researcher." *American Mag.,* October, 1909, 580–589.

A popular statement of the author's latest opinion of mediumistic phenomena.
Reprinted in *1911–2,* under the title of "Final Impressions of a Psychical Researcher." Reprinted in *1960–1.*

8. The Meaning of Truth: A Sequel to "Pragmatism." New York and London: Longmans, Green & Co., Dec. 3, 1909, 8vo, pp. xvii–298.

Preface contains important review of the subject of pragmatism, with definition of "radical empiricism," and statement of James's relation to Schiller and Dewey. The volume contains the following articles, reprinted as indicated, with slight verbal revision: I, The Function of Cognition, *1885–1;* II, The Tigers in India, extract from *1895–4;* III, Humanism and Truth, *1904–11* with additions from *1905–5* (reprinted also in *1917–1*); IV, The Relation between Knower and Known, extract from *1904–10;* V, The Essence of Humanism, *1905–3;* VI, A Word More about Truth, *1907–7;* VII, Professor Pratt on Truth, *1907–8;* VIII, The Pragmatist Account of Truth and Its Misunderstanders, *1908–1;* IX, The Meaning of the Word Truth, *1908–4;* X, The Existence of Julius Cæsar, *1908–3;* XI, The Absolute and the Strenuous Life, *1907–9;* XII, Professor Hébert on Pragmatism, *1908–8;* XIII, Abstractionism and "Relativism," *1909–4;* XIV, Two English Critics (B. Russell and R. Hawtrey); XV, A Dialogue. Reprinted 1911, 1914, 1919, 1927, 1932, partially in *1943–2.*

9. Letters on Vivisection. *New York Evening Post,* May 22, 1909.

> Also in *Boston Evening Transcript,* May 24, 1909. Two letters addressed to the Secretary of the Vivisection Reform Society, defending vivisection, opposing government regulation, but advocating establishment of rules by the vivisectors themselves.

10. Letter to Tausch. *The Monist,* Jan. 1909, *19,* 156.

11. "A Possible Case of Projections of the Double." *Journal of the American Society for Psychical Research.* April 1909, II, No. 4. Reprinted *1960–1.*

1910

1. Bradley or Bergson? *Jour. of Phil., Psychol., and Sci. Methods,* 1910, *7,* 29–33.

> Discussion of the philosophy of F. H. Bradley as set forth in the latter's "Coherence and Contradiction." *Mind,* 1909, n.s. *18,* 489–508.
> Reprinted in *1920–2.*

2. A Suggestion about Mysticism. *Jour. of Phil., Psychol., and Sci. Methods,* 1910, *7,* 85–92.

> Suggests explanation of the mystical experience in terms of the subliminal consciousness.
> Reprinted in *1920–2.*

3. The Moral Equivalent of War. *Internat. Conciliation,* Feb. 1910, No. 27.

> Also in *McClure's Mag.,* 1910, *35,* 463–468, and *Popular Sci. Monthly,* 1910, *77,* 400–412. If war is to be eliminated, there must be some other way of securing discipline and the other martial virtues. Suggests conscription of youth for manual labor.
> Reprinted in *1911–2.*

4. A Great French Philosopher at Harvard. *Nation,* 1910, *90,* 312–314.

> Comment on the professorial exchange, and on E. Boutroux as an anti-scholastic philosopher of immediate experience.

5. A Pluralistic Mystic. *Hibbert Jour.,* 1910, *8,* 739–759.

> Account of the philosophy of Benjamin Paul Blood. This article was written during the early summer of 1910 and its pages are the last which the author wrote for publication.
> Reprinted in *1911–2.*

6. "A Correction," a letter to the editor of the *Journal of Philosophy,* 1910, 7, 183–184. Consisting of a defense against a biting critique by Prof. W. P. Montague on James's "Pluralistic Universe." Reprinted in *1920–1,* Vol. II, 212–215.

1911

1. Some Problems of Philosophy. A Beginning of an Introduction to Philosophy. New York and London: Longmans, Green & Co., 1911, 8vo, pp. xii + 237.*

   This volume was designed by the author as an introductory text-book in philosophy. It was prepared for the press by H. M. Kallen from an unfinished manuscript, and edited with a Prefatory Note by Henry James, Jr. Contains the following chapters: I, Philosophy and Its Critics; II, The Problems of Metaphysics; III, The Problem of Being; IV, V, VI, Percept and Concept; VII, VIII, The One and the Many; IX, The Problem of Novelty; X, XI, Novelty and the Infinite; XII, XIII, Novelty and Causation; Appendix, Faith and the Right to Believe.
   Chapter I reprinted in *1917–1*. Reprinted 1916, 1919, 1921, 1924, 1928, 1931, 1940, 1948.

2. Memories and Studies. New York and London: Longmans, Green & Co., 1911, 8vo, pp. 411.

   Edited, with Prefatory Note, by Henry James, Jr., in accordance with intention formed by Professor James before his death. Contains the following articles, reprinted as indicated: I, Louis Agassiz, *1897–1;* II, Address at the Emerson Centenary in Concord, *1903–2;* III, Robert Gould Shaw, *1897–2;* IV, Francis Boott, *1904–7;* V, Thomas Davidson: A Knight-Errant of the Intellectual Life, *1905–8;* VI, Herbert Spencer's Autobiography, *1903–8;* VII, Frederic Myers' Services to Psychology, *1901–1;* VIII, Final Impressions of a Psychical Researcher, *1909–7;* IX, On Some Mental Effects of the Earthquake, *1906–2;* X, The Energies of Men, *1907–2* (reprinted also in *1908–6* and *1917–1*); XI, The Moral Equivalent of War, *1910–3;* XII, Remarks at the Peace Banquet, *1904–12;* XIII, The Social Value of the College-Bred, *1908–2;* XIV, The Ph.D. Octopus, *1903–1;* The True Harvard, *1903–5;* Stanford's Ideal Destiny, *1906–1;* XV, A Pluralistic Mystic, *1910–5*.
   Reprinted 1912, 1917.

3. Letter on Determinism. Appended to "The Trilemma of Determinism," by Alfred C. Lane, *Western Jour. of Education,* 1911, *4,* 168.

   Written in the fall of 1907. Emphasizes the unalterability of past events.

4. "The Religious Philosophy of Wm. James," A reply to an inquiry by James Bisset Pratt in the *Hibbert Journal,* Oct. 1911.

5. "On Vital Reserves"; "The Energies of Man"; "The Gospel of Relaxation": by Wm. James: New York, H. Holt, 1911.

1912

1. Essays in Radical Empiricism. New York and London: Longmans, Green & Co., 1912, 8vo, pp. xiii + 282.

---

* William James died on August 26, 1910. This and the following titles have been published posthumously.

Edited, with a Preface, by Ralph Barton Perry. The title and the contents of this volume were virtually selected by the author himself several years before his death. It was his aim to present systematically the outlines of the doctrine of "Radical Empiricism" which he regarded as of not less importance than "Pragmatism." Contains the following articles, reprinted as indicated: I, Does Consciousness Exist? *1904–9;* II, A World of Pure Experience, *1904–10;* III, The Thing and Its Relations, *1905–2* (also reprinted in *1909–5*); IV, How Two Minds Can Know One Thing, *1905–4;* V, The Place of Affectional Facts in a World of Pure Experience, *1905–7;* VI, The Experience of Activity, *1905–1* (also reprinted in *1909–5*); VII, The Essence of Humanism, *1905–3;* VIII, La Notion de Conscience, *1905–9;* IX, Is Radical Empiricism Solipsistic? *1905–6;* X, Mr. Pitkin's Refutation of "Radical Empiricism," *1906–5* and *1907–3;* XI, Humanism and Truth Once More, *1905–5* (parts also reprinted in *1905–5* under title of "Humanism and Truth"); XII, Absolutism and Empiricism, *1884–3.* New impression 1922, 1938.

2. On Some of Life's Ideals. New York: Holt, 1912, pp. 94.

Contains "On a Certain Blindness in Human Beings" and "What Makes a Life Significant," reprinted from *1899–7.*

1914

1. "The Pragmatic Test" by M. T. MacMillan (Mrs. Wade MacMillan) *Harper's Weekly,* April 18, 1914 (incl. letters from W.J. to Mrs. MacMillan).

1915

1. Habit. New York and Boston: Houghton Mifflin, 1915, 225–244.

Reprinting of pp. 120–127 of *1890–4,* Vol. I, together with addresses by H. L. Higginson and L. B. R. Briggs.

1917

1. Selected Papers on Philosophy. Everyman's Library: London, Dent & Co., New York, E. P. Dutton, 1917, pp. xvii + 273.

Edited, with an Introduction, by C. M. Bakewell. Contains the following articles, reprinted as indicated: I, On a Certain Blindness in Human Beings, *1899–7;* II, The Gospel of Relaxation, *1899–7;* III, The Energies of Men, *1911–2;* IV, Habit, *1892–2;* V, The Will, *1890–4;* VI, Philosophy and Its Critics, *1911–1;* VII, The Will to Believe, *1897–3;* VIII, The Sentiment of Rationality, *1897–3;* IX, Great Men and Their Environment, *1897–3;* X, What Pragmatism Means, *1907–11;* XI, Humanism and Truth, *1909–8;* XII, The Positive Content of Religious Experience, *1902–1.* Reprinted 1924, 1927, 1929, 1947.

1920

1. Letters of William James. Boston: Atlantic Monthly Press. London: Longmans, Green & Co., 1920. 2 vols. 8vo, pp. xxii + 348, pp. xvi + 382.

Edited, with a Biographical Introduction and Notes, by his son, Henry James, and illustrated with photographs and reproductions of drawings and manuscripts. Also Limited Edition, containing additional reproductions of manuscripts and drawings. Reprinted 1926.

2. Collected Essays and Reviews. New York and London: Longmans, Green & Co., 1920, 8vo, pp. x, 515.

Edited, with a Preface and notes, by Ralph Barton Perry. Contains the following articles, reprinted as indicated: Sargent's *Planchette, 1869–1;* Lewes's *Problems of Life and Mind, 1875–2;* German Pessimism, *1875–10;* Chauncey Wright, *1875–8;* Bain and Renouvier, *1876–5;* Renan's *Dialogues, 1876–7;* Lewes's *Physical Basis of Mind, 1877–3;* Spencer's Definition of Mind, *1878–1;* Quelques Considérations sur la Méthode Subjective, *1878–2;* The Sentiment of Rationality, *1879–7;* Clifford's *Lectures and Essays, 1879–3;* Spencer's *Data of Ethics, 1879–1;* The Feeling of Effort, *1880–3;* The Sense of Dizziness in Deaf-Mutes, *1882–5;* What is an Emotion? *1884–2;* Royce's *Religious Aspect of Philosophy, 1885–2;* The Consciousness of Lost Limbs, *1887–10;* Réponse aux Remarques de M. Renouvier, *1888–2;* The Psychological Theory of Extension, *1889–1;* Plea for Psychology as a Natural Science, *1892–3;* The Original Datum of Space Consciousness, *1893–1;* Mr. Bradley on Immediate Resemblance, *1893–2a;* Immediate Resemblance, *1893–2b;* Ladd's *Psychology, 1894–13;* The Physical Basis of Emotion, *1894–2;* The Knowing of Things Together, *1895–4;* Degeneration and Genius, *1895–8;* Philosophical Conceptions and Practical Results, *1898–3;* Hodgson's *Observations of Trance, 1898–7;* Personal Idealism, *1903–4;* The Chicago School, *1904–3;* Humanism, *1904–5;* Laura Bridgman, *1904–1;* G. Papini and the Pragmatist Movement in Italy, *1906–3;* The Mad Absolute, *1906–4;* Controversy about Truth, *1907–6;* Report on Mrs. Piper's Hodgson-Control, *1909–6;* Bradley or Bergson? *1910–1;* A Suggestion about Mysticism, *1910–2.*

1922

1. "G. Papini et le mouvement pragmatiste in Italie." Introduction to *Le Crépuscule des Philosophers de Papini,* trans. by Mele F. Bertrand, pp. v–viii, Paris: Chiron, 1922. Trans. of *1906–3.*

2. *The Emotions* by Carl George Lange and William James, Baltimore, Williams and Wilkins Co., 1922. A new trans. of Lange's "Ueber Gemüthsbewegungen" made by Miss Ustar from Kurella's German version; together with a reprinting of James's *What is Emotion* and his chapter on "The Emotions" from the *Principles of Psychology* (*1890–4*).

3. *The One Way,* by Jane Revere Burke, New York, E. P. Dutton, 1922. Alleged spirit messages received from Wm. James. See *1936–1, 1931–1, 1934–1.*

1924

1. Preface to *The World of Souls,* by W. Lutoslawski, London, 1924.

2. *Wm. James; extraits de sa correspondance,* trans. by F. Delattre and M. Le Breton with Preface by H. Bergson. Paris, Payot, 1924. Partial trans. of *1920–1.*

3. *Études et réflexions d'un psychiste,* trans. by E. Durandeaud, Paris, Payot, 1924. Trans. of 12 articles relating to psychical research, most of which had not been reprinted in book form in English. Cf. *1960–1.*

4. "Reason and Faith," *Journal of Philosophy,* 24, 1924, 197. Lecture before the Unitarian Club of San Francisco, Feb. 5, 1906.

1925

1. *The Philosophy of William James.* Selected, with an Introduction, by Horace M. Kallen, New York, Modern Library, 1925.

1929

1. "Wm. James and his Wife" by Elizabeth Glendower Evans, *Atlantic Monthly,* 144, 1929, 374–87. A brief character sketch of the life of Wm. James and his wife, containing interesting letters from both to a relatively intimate friend, Eliz. G. Evans.

1931

1. *Let us In,* by Jane Revere Burke, N.Y., Dutton, Reprinted 1933. Alleged spirit messages received from W.J., cf. *1922–3, 1934–1, 1936–1.*

1934

1. *The Bundle of Life* by J. R. Burke, N.Y., Dutton, Third of a series printed by Dutton, of communications believed to have come from W.J. Cf. *1922–3, 1931–1, 1936–1.*

1935

1. *The Thought and Character of William James,* 2 vols. Boston, Little, Brown and Co. Contains some five hundred letters by William James not found in the earlier edition of the *Letters of William James.*

1936

1. *Messages on Healing* by J. R. Burke, privately printed. Alleged spirit messages from W.J. Cf. *1922–3, 1931–1, 1934–1.*

1942

1. *As William James Said,* selected and edited by Elizabeth Perkins Aldrich. With a number of hitherto unpublished drawings. New York, The Vanguard Press.

1943

1. *Essays on Faith and Morals,* ed. by Ralph Barton Perry, New York, Longmans Green and Co. Reprinted in 1947. Translated into German, 1948. Reprinted 1962.

2. *Pragmatism,* ed. by Ralph Barton Perry. Contains *1907–11* plus pp. v–xx and 1–101 of *The Meaning of Truth.* Reprinted 1955, 1963.

3. *Essays in Radical Empiricism and A Pluralistic Universe,* ed. by Ralph Barton Perry. New York, Longmans Green and Co. Contains first eight essays of *1912–1* and all of *1909–5.* Appendices A and B of *1909–5* are printed as Essays III and VI in the *Radical Empiricism* section.

1947

1. *The James Family* by F. O. Matthiessen, New York, Alfred A. Knopf. This includes selections from the writings of Henry James, Sr., William Henry and Alice James. With the exception of a few paragraphs, this book has a complete reprinting of William James's detailed "Introduction" to *The Literary Remains of the Late Henry James.*

1948

1. *Essays in Pragmatism,* ed. with an introduction by Alburey Castell. New York, Hafner Publishing Co., Inc. Contains "The Sentiment of Rationality," "The Dilemma of Determinism," "The Moral Philosopher and the Moral Life," "The Will to Believe," "Conclusions on Varieties of Religious Experience," "What Pragmatism Means," "Pragmatism's Conception of Truth." Reprinted 1949, 1951, 1952, 1954, 1955, 1957, 1959, 1960, 1961, 1962, 1964.

2. *The Thought and Character of William James*—Briefer version; ed. by Ralph Barton Perry, Boston, Harvard University Press. Reprinted 1954. Contains three previously unpublished letters from William James to Edgar B. Van Winkle.

1950

1. *William James—A Selection From His Writing on Psychology,* ed. with an "Introduction" by Margaret Knight, Baltimore, Penguin Books.

1957

1. *William James—Philosopher and Man.* (Quotations and References in 652 books.) Compiled by Charles H. Compton, with a foreword by Lucien Price. New York, The Scarecrow Press.

1960

1. *William James on Psychical Research.* Compiled and edited by Gardner Murphy, M.D. and Robert O. Ballou, New York, The Viking Press. Contains "Review of 'Planchette' "; "What Psychical Research Has Accomplished"; "On Mediumship"; "Letter from F. W. H. Myers"; "Letter to F. W. H. Myers"; "Address by the President"; "Extracts from Letters and a Lecture"; "A Case of Clairvoyance"; "Psychical Phenomena at a Private Circle"; "A Possible Case of Projection of the Double"; "Report of the Committee on Mediumistic Phenomena"; "Letters"; "Certain Phenomena of Trance"; "Letters"; "Report on Mrs. Piper's Hodgson-Control"; "Frederic Myers's Service to Psychology"; "Review of 'Human Personality and Its Survival of Bodily Death' "; "The Final Impressions of a Psychical Researcher."

1961

1. *The Selected Letters of William James.* Ed. with an "Introduction" by Elizabeth Hardwick, New York, Farrar, Straus and Cudahy. Some new letters not found in *1920–1, 1935–1* or *1948–2.*

1963

1. *Pragmatism and Other Essays,* ed. by Joseph L. Blau, New York, Washington Square Press. Contains *1943–2* plus "The Will to Believe," "The Moral Philosopher and the Moral Life," "The Gospel of Relaxation," "On a Certain Blindness in Human Beings," "What Makes a Life Significant," "The Moral Equivalent of War."

2. *The Varieties of Religious Experience.* (Enlarged edition with Appendices.) Ed. with an "Introduction" by Joseph Ratner. Contains *1902–1* plus following selections, frequently excerpted: "The Pratt Questionnaire"; "Letters Concerning the 'Varieties' "; "Christianity Monotheism Polytheism"; "The Human Soul"; "Cosmic Souls: Concerning Fechner"; "Human Immortality"; "Psychical Research"; "A Suggestion about Mysticism"; "Faith: Its Place, Functions and Rights"; "Pragmatistic or Melioristic Religion."

1966

1. "Ten unpublished letters from William James, 1842–1910, to Francis Herbert Bradley, 1846–1924," with Introduction and Notes by J. C. Kenna, *Mind,* Vol. XXXV, No. 299. (July 1966) 309–331.

2. *The Letters of William James and Theodore Flournoy,* ed. by Robert C. Le Clair, Madison, Milwaukee and London, University of Wisconsin Press, 1966. Approximately 70 letters and postcards from James and 54 from Flournoy.

1967

1. *William James* by Gay Wilson Allen, New York, The Viking Press. Contains manuscript sources, a genealogical table, illustrations, and photographs. A detailed biography which utilizes, for the first time, letters and diaries of William James's wife Alice. Published after the Introduction to the present volume was written, this book, enjoying full access to the James family papers, makes an important contribution to our understanding of the total life situation in which the thought of William James matured. (Cf. above, pp. xviii–xxvi.)

2. *Introduction to William James,* edited and with an introduction by Andrew J. Reck, Bloomington, Indiana University Press.

1969

1. *The Moral Philosophy of William James,* edited and with an introduction by John K. Roth, New York, Thomas Y. Crowell Company.

1971

1. *A William James Reader,* edited and with an introduction by Gay Wilson Allen, Boston, Houghton, Mifflin Company.

2. *William James: The Essential Writings,* edited and with an introduction by Bruce Wilshire, New York, Harper Torchbooks.

3. *The Moral Equivalent of War and Other Essays and Selections from Some Problems in Philosophy,* edited and with an introduction by John K. Roth, New York, Harper Torchbooks.

4. *Essays in Radical Empiricism* and *A Pluralistic Universe,* a reprint of 1912–1 and 1909–5 with a new introduction by Richard J. Bernstein, New York, E. P. Dutton and Co.

1975–

1. *The Works of William James,* Cambridge, Harvard University Press. (A sealed, critical edition of *The Works of William James.* General editor, Frederick H. Burkhardt; textual editor, Fredson Bowers. Published thus far: *Pragmatism,* introduction by H. S. Thayer (1975); *The Meaning of Truth,* introduction by H. S. Thayer (1975); *Essays in Radical Empiricism,* introduction by John J. McDermott; *A Pluralistic Universe,* introduction by Richard J. Bernstein (1977).